HOCKEY REGISTER

1984-85 EDITION

Editor/Hockey Register
LARRY WIGGE

Compiled by
FRANK POLNASZEK

Contributing Editors/Hockey Register
CRAIG CARTER
BARRY SIEGEL
DAVE SLOAN

President-Chief Executive Officer
RICHARD WATERS

Editor
DICK KAEGEL

Director of Books and Periodicals
RON SMITH

Published by

The Sporting News

1212 North Lindbergh Boulevard
P.O. Box 56 — St. Louis, MO 63166

Copyright © 1984
The Sporting News Publishing Company
a Times Mirror company

IMPORTANT NOTICE

ISBN 0-89204-166-8   ISSN 0090-2292

Table of Contents

Players included are those who played in at least one National Hockey League game in 1983-84 and selected invitees to training camps.

▰▰▰▰

ON THE COVER: Washington's Rod Langway won the Norris Trophy as the league's best defenseman for the second consecutive season in 1983-84.

—Photograph by Richard Pilling

EXPLANATIONS OF AWARDS

National Hockey League

HART MEMORIAL TROPHY (or Hart Trophy)—Most Valuable Player.

LADY BYNG MEMORIAL TROPHY (or Lady Byng Trophy)—Awarded to player exhibiting best type of sportsmanship and gentlemanly conduct combined with a high standard of playing ability.

CALDER MEMORIAL TROPHY (or Calder Trophy)—Rookie-of-the-Year.

WILLIAM JENNINGS TROPHY —Awarded to leading goaltender(s) based on goals against average. Must appear in minimum of 25 games to be eligible.

ART ROSS TROPHY—Leading scorer.

JAMES NORRIS MEMORIAL TROPHY—Outstanding defenseman.

CONN SMYTHE TROPHY—Most Valuable Player during Stanley Cup Playoffs.

BILL MASTERTON MEMORIAL TROPHY—Awarded to player who best exemplifies qualities of perseverance, sportsmanship and dedication to hockey.

LESTER PATRICK TROPHY—For outstanding service to hockey in the United States.

VEZINA MEMORIAL TROPHY (or Vezina Trophy)—Top goaltender.

American Hockey League

HARRY "HAP" HOLMES MEMORIAL TROPHY—Leading goaltender.

LES CUNNINGHAM AWARD (or Plaque)—Most Valuable Player.

DUDLEY "RED" GARRETT MEMORIAL TROPHY (or Award)—Rookie-of-the-Year.

EDDIE SHORE PLAQUE—Outstanding defenseman.

JOHN G. SOLLENBERGER TROPHY—Leading scorer (since 1955-56).

CARL LISCOMBE TROPHY—Leading scorer (prior to 1955-56).

Western Hockey League

FRED J. HUME AWARD—Most Gentlemanly Player.

LEADER CUP—Most Valuable Player.

HAL LAYCOE CUP—Outstanding defenseman.

GUYLE FIELDER CUP—Leading scorer.

International Hockey League

LEO P. LAMOUREUX MEMORIAL TROPHY—Leading scorer (since 1960-61).

GEORGE H. WILKENSON TROPHY—Leading scorer (1946-47 thru 1959-60).

GOVERNORS' TROPHY—Outstanding defenseman.

GARY LONGMAN MEMORIAL TROPHY—Rookie-of-the-Year.

JAMES NORRIS MEMORIAL TROPHY—Leading goaltender(s) based on goals against. (Formerly awarded to goaltender on first All-Star team.)

JAMES GATSCHENE MEMORIAL TROPHY—Most Valuable Player.

Other Leagues

BOB GASSOFF TROPHY—Central Hockey League's most improved defenseman (new in 1977-78).

TOMMY IVAN TROPHY—Most Valuable Player in Central Hockey League.

TERRY SAWCHUK AWARD—Leading goaltender in CHL.

EDDIE POWERS MEMORIAL TROPHY—Leading scorer in Jr. "A" OHA.

DAVE PINKNEY TROPHY—Leading goaltender in Jr. "A" OHA.

MAX KAMINSKY MEMORIAL TROPHY—Best defenseman in Jr. "A" OHA.

RED TILSON MEMORIAL TROPHY—Most Valuable Player in Jr. "A" OHA.

EXPLANATION OF ABBREVIATIONS

A—Assists.
AHL—American Hockey League.
AJHL—Alberta Junior Hockey League.
ASHL—Alberta Senior Hockey League.
Avg.—Goals against per game average.
BCHL—British Columbia Hockey League.
CAHL—Central Alberta Hockey League.
CCHA—Central Collegiate Hockey Association.
Cent. OHA—Central Ontario Hockey Association.
CHL—California Hockey League or Central Hockey League.
CMJHL—Canadian Major Junior Hockey League.
CPHL—Central Pro Hockey League.
EHL—Eastern Hockey League.
EPHL—Eastern Pro Hockey League.
G—Goals scored.
Games—Games played.
Goals—Goals against.
IHL—International Hockey League.
MJHL—Manitoba Junior Hockey League or Midwest Junior Hockey League.
NAHL—North American Hockey League.
NEHL—Northeastern Hockey League.
NHL—National Hockey League.
NOHA—Northern Ontario Hockey Association.
NSHL—North Shore (New Brunswick) Hockey League.
NYMJHA—New York Metropolitan Junior Hockey Association.
OHA—Ontario Hockey Association.
OMJHL—Ontario Major Junior Hockey League.
OPHL—Ontario Provincial Hockey League.
Pen.—Minutes in penalties.
PHL—Prairie Hockey League.
Pts.—Points.
QHL—Quebec Hockey League.
QJHL—Quebec Junior Hockey League.
SHL—Southern Hockey League.
SJHL—Saskatchewan Junior Hockey League.
SOJHL—Southern Ontario Junior Hockey League.
TBJHL—Thunder Bay Junior Hockey League.
USHL—United States Hockey League.
WCHA—Western Collegiate Hockey Association.
WCHL—Western Canada Hockey League (Juniors).
WCJHL—Western Canada Junior League.
WHA—World Hockey Association.
WHL—Western Hockey League.
WHL—Western Hockey League (Junior "A" League since 1978-79).
WIHL—Western International Hockey League.
WOJHL—Western Ontario Junior Hockey League.
*—Indicates either led or was tied for league lead.
  Footnotes (a) indicates player was member of first all-star team.
  Footnotes (b) indicates player was member of second all-star team.
Scoring totals (goals plus assists) do not always balance in certain leagues due to un-balanced schedules and scoring system.
Junior "A" Ontario Hockey Association also includes Metro League and OHA Major Junior.
Quebec Junior Hockey League also includes Montreal Metro League and OJHL Major.

FORWARDS AND DEFENSEMEN

(a)—First team all-star selection.   (b)—Second team.   * Denotes league leader.

ALLAN ACTON

Left wing . . . 5'11" . . . 190 lbs. . . . Born, Unity, Sask., August 28, 1965 . . . Shoots left . . . Also plays center.

Year	Team	League	Games	G.	A.	Pts.	Pen.
1981-82—Battleford Barons		SJHL	53	15	21	36	173
1982-83—Saskatoon Blades (c)		WHL	56	5	13	18	41
1983-84—Saskatoon Blades		WHL	14	3	3	6	19
1983-84—Regina Pats (d)		WHL	54	7	11	18	56

(c)—June, 1983—Drafted by Hartford Whalers in NHL entry draft. Thirteenth Whalers pick, 204th overall, 11th round.

(d)—June, 1984—Released by Hartford Whalers.

KEITH EDWARD ACTON

Center . . . 5'10" . . . 167 lbs. . . . Born, Newmarket, Ont., April 15, 1958 . . . Shoots left . . . (April 20, 1984)—Injured left wrist in playoff game at St. Louis.

Year	Team	League	Games	G.	A.	Pts.	Pen.
1974-75—Wexford Raiders		OPJHL	43	23	29	52	46
1975-76—Peterborough Petes		Jr."A"OHA	35	9	17	26	30
1976-77—Peterborough Petes		Jr."A"OHA	65	52	69	121	93
1977-78—Peterborough Petes (c)		Jr."A"OHA	68	42	86	128	52
1978-79—Nova Scotia Voyageurs		AHL	79	15	26	41	22
1979-80—Nova Scotia Voyageurs (b)		AHL	75	45	53	98	38
1979-80—Montreal Canadiens		NHL	2	0	1	1	0
1980-81—Montreal Canadiens		NHL	61	15	24	39	74
1981-82—Montreal Canadiens		NHL	78	36	52	88	88
1982-83—Montreal Canadiens		NHL	78	24	26	50	63
1983-84—Montreal Canadiens (d)		NHL	9	3	7	10	4
1983-84—Minnesota North Stars		NHL	62	17	38	55	60
NHL TOTALS			300	95	148	243	289

(c)—Drafted from Peterborough Petes by Montreal Canadiens in sixth round of 1978 amateur draft.

(d)—October, 1983—Traded with Mark Napier and third round 1984 draft pick (Kenneth Hodge) by Montreal Canadiens to Minnesota North Stars for Bobby Smith.

RUSSELL NORM ADAM

Center . . . 5'10"   185 lbs. . . . Born, Windsor, Ont., May 5, 1961 . . . Shoots left . . . Also plays left wing.

Year	Team	League	Games	G.	A.	Pts.	Pen.
1977-78—Windsor Spitfires		OMJHL	3	1	2	3	0
1978-79—Kitchener Rangers		OMJHL	63	20	17	37	37
1979-80—Kitchener Rangers (c)		OMJHL	54	37	34	71	143
1980-81—Kitchener Rangers		OHL	64	37	50	87	215
1981-82—New Brunswick Hawks		AHL	52	11	21	32	50
1982-83—Toronto Maple Leafs		NHL	8	1	2	3	11
1982-83—St. Catharines Saints		AHL	64	19	17	36	119
1983-84—St. Catharines Saints		AHL	70	32	24	56	76
NHL TOTALS			8	1	2	3	11

(c)—June, 1980—Drafted as underage junior by Toronto Maple Leafs in 1980 NHL entry draft. Seventh Maple Leafs pick, 137th overall, seventh round.

GREG ADAMS

Center . . . 6'4" . . . 185 lbs. . . . Born, Nelson, B.C., August 1, 1963 . . . Shoots left.

Year	Team	League	Games	G.	A.	Pts.	Pen.
1982-83—Northern Arizona Univ.		NCAA	29	14	21	35	46
1983-84—Northern Arizona Univ. (c)		NCAA	47	40	50	90	16

(c)—June, 1984—Signed by New Jersey Devils as a free agent.

GREGORY CHARLES ADAMS

Left Wing . . . 6'1" . . . 190 lbs. . . . Born, Duncan, B. C., May 31, 1960 . . . Shoots left.

Year	Team	League	Games	G.	A.	Pts.	Pen.
1977-78—Nanaimo		BCJHL	62	53	60	113	150
1978-79—Victoria Cougars		WHL	71	23	31	54	151
1979-80—Victoria Cougars (c)		WHL	71	62	48	110	212

Year Team	League	Games	G.	A.	Pts.	Pen.
1980-81—Philadelphia Flyers	NHL	6	3	0	3	8
1980-81—Maine Mariners	AHL	71	19	20	39	158
1981-82—Maine Mariners	AHL	45	16	21	37	241
1981-82—Philadelphia Flyers (d)	NHL	33	4	15	19	105
1982-83—Hartford Whalers	NHL	79	10	13	23	216
1983-84—Washington Capitals (e)	NHL	57	2	6	8	133
NHL TOTALS		175	19	34	53	462

(c)—August, 1980—Signed by Philadelphia Flyers as a free agent.
(d)—August, 1982—Traded by Philadelphia Flyers with Ken Linseman and Flyers' No. 1 draft choice (David A. Jensen) in 1983 to Hartford Whalers for Mark Howe. Hartford and Philadelphia will also swap third-round choices in '83 draft.
(e)—October, 1983—Traded by Hartford Whalers to Washington Capitals for Torrie Robertson.

PAUL ADEY

Right wing . . . 5'9" . . . 173 lbs. . . . Born, Montreal, Que., August 28, 1963 . . . Shoots right.

Year Team	League	Games	G.	A.	Pts.	Pen.
1981-82—Hull Olympics	QMJHL	54	17	24	41	0
1982-83—Hull Olympics	QHL	70	58	104	162	14
1983-84—Shawinigan Cataracts	QHL	56	37	52	89	78
1983-84—Toledo Goaldiggers	IHL	2	0	0	0	0

ROBERT BRUCE AFFLECK
(Known by middle name.)

Defense . . . 6' . . . 200 lbs. . . . Born, Salmon Arm, B.C., May 5, 1954 . . . Shoots left . . . Attended Denver University . . . Broke right shoulder in auto accident, April 1, 1975.

Year Team	League	Games	G.	A.	Pts.	Pen.
1970-71—Penticton Broncos (a)	Jr."A"BCHL	....	23	46	69	49
1971-72—Penticton Broncos (a)	Jr."A"BCHL	....	31	69	100	...
1972-73—Denver University (a)	WCHA	39	6	19	25	30
1973-74—Denver University (b-c)	WCHA	38	8	23	31	42
1974-75—Springfield Kings	AHL	8	1	3	4	12
1974-75—Salt Lake Golden Eagles (d)	CHL	35	0	14	14	28
1974-75—St. Louis Blues	NHL	13	0	2	2	4
1975-76—St. Louis Blues	NHL	80	4	26	30	20
1976-77—St. Louis Blues	NHL	80	5	20	24	24
1977-78—St. Louis Blues	NHL	75	4	14	18	26
1978-79—Salt Lake Golden Eagles	CHL	48	8	31	39	30
1978-79—St. Louis Blues	NHL	26	1	3	4	12
1979-80—Vancouver Canucks	NHL	5	0	1	1	0
1979-80—Dallas Black Hawks (a-e-f)	CHL	72	10	53	63	39
1980-81—Indianapolis Checkers (a-g-h)	CHL	77	8	50	58	41
1981-82—Indianapolis Checkers (i)	CHL	16	5	17	22	4
1982-83—Played in Europe		....	...	....	....	....
1982-83—Indianapolis Checkers (j-k)	CHL	8	2	12	14	0
1983-84—Indianapolis Checkers (a-l)	CHL	54	13	40	53	18
1983-84—New York Islanders	NHL	1	0	0	0	0
NHL TOTALS		280	14	66	80	86

(c)—Drafted from Denver University by California Golden Seals in second round of 1974 amateur draft.
(d)—Traded to St. Louis Blues by California Seals for Frank Spring and cash, January, 1975.
(e)—February, 1980—Traded by St. Louis Blues to Vancouver Canucks for future considerations. At close of season Vancouver returned Affleck to St. Louis.
(f)—Won Bobby Orr Trophy (CHL Most Valuable Defenseman).
(g)—September, 1980—Signed by New York Islanders as a free agent.
(h)—Winner of Bobby Orr Trophy (Most Valuable CHL Defenseman).
(i)—Co-leader in CHL playoffs with 17 assists (with Kelly Kisio).
(j)—Led CHL Playoffs with 18 assists.
(k)—Winner of Max McNab Trophy (CHL Playoff MVP).
(l)—Won Tommy Ivan Award (CHL MVP).

JIM AGNEW

Defense . . . 6'1" . . . 179 lbs. . . . Born, Deloraine, Man., March 21, 1966 . . . Shoots left.

Year Team	League	Games	G.	A.	Pts.	Pen.
1982-83—Brandon Wheat Kings	WHL	14	1	1	2	9
1983-84—Brandon Wheat Kings (c)	WHL	71	6	17	23	107

(c)—June, 1984—Drafted as underage junior by Vancouver Canucks in NHL entry draft. Tenth Canucks pick, 157th overall, eighth round.

CLIFF ALBRECHT

Defense . . . 6' . . . 185 lbs. . . . Born, Toronto, Ont., May 24, 1963 . . . Shoots right.

Year	Team	League	Games	G.	A.	Pts.	Pen.
1982-83—Princeton University (c)		ECAC	24	4	10	14	52
1983-84—Princeton University		ECAC	23	9	9	18	62

(c)—June, 1983—Drafted by Toronto Maple Leafs in NHL entry draft. Seventh Maple Leafs pick, 168th overall, ninth round.

JAMES ALDRED

Defense . . . 6'1" . . . 185 lbs. . . . Born, Toronto, Ont., April 28, 1963 . . . Shoots left.

Year	Team	League	Games	G.	A.	Pts.	Pen.
1979-80—Kingston Canadians		OMJHL	16	0	1	1	9
1980-81—Kingston Canadians (c)		OHL	67	20	28	48	140
1981-82—Kingston Canadians		OHL	10	2	4	6	18
1981-82—Sault Ste. Marie Greyhounds		OHL	43	16	15	31	179
1982-83—Sault Ste. Marie Greyhounds		OHL	63	22	22	44	176
1983-84—Rochester Americans		AHL	64	10	9	19	57

(c)—June, 1981—Drafted as underage junior by Buffalo Sabres in NHL entry draft. Third Sabres pick, 59th overall, third round.

BOB ALEXANDER

Defense . . . 5'10" . . . 170 lbs. . . . Born, St. Paul, Minn., October 31, 1964 . . . Shoots left.

Year	Team	League	Games	G.	A.	Pts.	Pen.
1982-83—Rosemont H.S. (c)		Minn.	23	14	20	34	0
1983-84—University of Minnesota		WCHA	3	0	2	2	2

(c)—June, 1983—Drafted by New York Rangers in 1983 NHL entry draft. Seventh Rangers pick, 113th overall, sixth round.

TOM ALLEN

Defense . . . 6'2" . . . 180 lbs. . . . Born, London, Ont., May 3, 1966 . . . Shoots left.

Year	Team	League	Games	G.	A.	Pts.	Pen.
1982-83—London City Midgets		....	59	33	64	97	135
1983-84—Kingston Canadians		OHL	26	0	4	4	18
1983-84—Kingston Canadians (c)		OHL	50	1	7	8	30

(c)—June, 1984—Drafted as underage junior by Philadelphia Flyers in NHL entry draft. Eighth Flyers pick, 142nd overall, seventh round.

DAVE BRYAN ALLISON

Defense and Right Wing . . . 6'1" . . . 198 lbs. . . . Born, Ft. Francis, Ontario, April 14, 1959 . . . Shoots right . . . Injured right shoulder in 1976-77 . . . Slipped vertabra in back in 1977-78 . . . Brother of Mike Allison.

Year	Team	League	Games	G.	A.	Pts.	Pen.
1976-77—Cornwall Royals		QMJHL	63	2	11	13	180
1977-78—Cornwall Royals		QMJHL	60	9	29	38	302
1978-79—Cornwall Royals		QMJHL	66	7	31	38	*407
1979-80—Nova Scotia Voyageurs		AHL	49	1	12	13	119
1980-81—Nova Scotia Voyageurs		AHL	70	5	12	17	298
1981-82—Nova Scotia Voyageurs (c)		AHL	78	8	25	33	332
1982-83—Nova Scotia Voyageurs		AHL	70	3	22	25	180
1983-84—Montreal Canadiens		NHL	3	0	0	0	12
1983-84—Nova Scotia Voyageurs		AHL	53	2	18	20	155
NHL TOTALS			3	0	0	0	12

(c)—Led AHL Playoffs with 84 penalty minutes.

MICHAEL EARNEST ALLISON

Center . . . 6' . . . 202 lbs. . . . Born, Ft. Francis, Ont., March 28, 1961 . . . Shoots right . . . Brother of Dave Allison . . . (January 13, 1981)—Strained ligaments in right knee . . . (October 25, 1981)—Bruised kneecap . . . (January 20, 1982)—Sprained medial collatoral ligament in right knee vs. NY Islanders requiring surgery . . . (November 20, 1982) Strained ligaments in right knee at Toronto . . . (October, 1983)—Sprained left knee.

Year	Team	League	Games	G.	A.	Pts.	Pen.
1977-78—New Westminster Bruins		WCHL	5	0	1	1	2
1977-78—Kenora Thistles		MJHL	47	30	36	66	70
1978-79—Sudbury Wolves		OMJHL	59	24	32	56	41
1979-80—Sudbury Wolves (c)		OMJHL	67	24	71	95	74
1980-81—New York Rangers		NHL	75	26	38	64	83

Year	Team	League	Games	G.	A.	Pts.	Pen.
1981-82—Springfield Indians	AHL	2	0	0	0	0
1981-82—New York Rangers	NHL	48	7	15	22	74
1982-83—Tulsa Oilers	CHL	6	2	2	4	2
1982-83—New York Rangers	NHL	39	11	9	20	37
1983-84—New York Rangers	NHL	45	8	12	20	64
NHL TOTALS			207	52	74	126	258

(c)—June, 1980—Drafted as underage junior by New York Rangers in NHL entry draft. Second Rangers pick, 35th overall, second round.

RAYMOND PETER ALLISON

Right Wing . . . 5'9" . . . 190 lbs. . . . Born, Cranbrook, B.C., March 4, 1959 . . . Shoots right . . . (February 17, 1983) Injured hip vs. Edmonton . . . (December 30, 1983)—Broke right ankle in game at N.Y. Rangers.

Year	Team	League	Games	G.	A.	Pts.	Pen.
1974-75—Brandon Wheat Kings	WCHL	2	0	0	0	0
1975-76—Brandon Travellers	MJHL	31	22	21	43	158
1975-76—Brandon Wheat Kings	WCHL	36	9	17	26	50
1976-77—Brandon Wheat Kings	WCHL	71	45	92	137	198
1977-78—Brandon Wheat Kings (b)	WCHL	71	74	86	160	254
1978-79—Brandon Wheat Kings (a-c)	WHL	62	60	93	153	191
1979-80—Hartford Whalers	NHL	64	16	12	28	13
1979-80—Springfield Indians	AHL	13	6	9	15	18
1980-81—Binghamton Whalers	AHL	74	31	39	70	81
1980-81—Hartford Whalers (d)	NHL	6	1	0	1	0
1981-82—Maine Mariners	AHL	26	15	13	28	75
1981-82—Philadelphia Flyers	NHL	51	17	37	54	104
1982-83—Philadelphia Flyers	NHL	67	21	30	51	57
1983-84—Philadelphia Flyers	NHL	37	8	13	21	47
NHL TOTALS			225	63	92	155	221

(c)—August, 1979—Drafted by Hartford Whalers in NHL entry draft. First Hartford pick, 18th overall, first round.

(d)—July, 1981—Traded with Fred Arthur, first and third round 1982 draft picks by the Hartford Whalers to Philadelphia Flyers for Rick MacLeish, Don Gillen, Blake Wesley, first, second and third round 1982 draft picks.

PAUL AMES

Defense . . . 6' . . . 165 lbs. . . . Born, Woburn, Mass., March 12, 1965 . . . Shoots right.

Year	Team	League	Games	G.	A.	Pts.	Pen.
1982-83—Billerica H.S. (c)	Mass.	16	9	26	35	....
1983-84—University of Lowell	ECAC	31	1	13	14	16

(c)—June, 1983—Drafted by Pittsburgh Penguins in NHL entry draft. Sixth Penguins pick, 123rd overall, seventh round.

GLENN CHRIS ANDERSON

Right Wing . . . 5'11" . . . 175 lbs. . . . Born, Vancouver, B.C., October 2, 1960 . . . Shoots left . . . Attended Denver University . . . Played on Canadian Olympic Team in 1980. . . . (November, 1980)—Knee surgery to remove bone chips . . . (Spring, 1982)—Nose surgery to correct breathing problem caused during a December 1, 1981 altercation with Mark Hunter of Montreal. . . . Also plays left wing.

Year	Team	League	Games	G.	A.	Pts.	Pen.
1977-78—New Westminster Bruins	WHL	1	0	1	1	2
1978-79—Seattle Breakers	WHL	2	0	1	1	0
1978-79—Denver University (c)	WCHA	40	26	29	55	58
1979-80—Canadian Olympic Team	Int'l	49	21	21	42	46
1979-80—Seattle Breakers	WHL	7	5	5	10	4
1980-81—Edmonton Oilers	NHL	58	30	23	53	24
1981-82—Edmonton Oilers	NHL	80	38	67	105	71
1982-83—Edmonton Oilers	NHL	72	48	56	104	70
1983-84—Edmonton Oilers	NHL	80	54	45	99	65
NHL TOTALS			290	170	191	361	230

(c)—August, 1979—Drafted by Edmonton Oilers in NHL entry draft. Third Oilers pick, 69th overall, fourth round.

JOHN MURRAY ANDERSON

Left Wing . . . 5'11" . . . 180 lbs. . . . Born, Toronto, Ont., March 28, 1957 . . . Shoots left . . . Missed part of 1975-76 season with shoulder separation . . . (December, 1981)—Elbow injury.

Year	Team	League	Games	G.	A.	Pts.	Pen.
1973-74—Toronto Marlboros		Jr. "A" OHA	38	22	22	44	6
1974-75—Toronto Marlboros		Jr. "A" OHA	70	49	64	113	31
1975-76—Toronto Marlboros		Jr. "A" OHA	39	26	25	51	19
1976-77—Toronto Marlboros (a-c)		Jr. "A" OHA	64	57	62	119	42
1977-78—Dallas Black Hawks (b-d)		CHL	52	22	23	45	6
1977-78—Toronto Maple Leafs		NHL	17	1	2	3	2
1978-79—Toronto Maple Leafs		NHL	71	15	11	26	10
1979-80—Toronto Maple Leafs		NHL	74	25	28	53	22
1980-81—Toronto Maple Leafs		NHL	75	17	26	43	31
1981-82—Toronto Maple Leafs		NHL	69	31	26	57	306
1982-83—Toronto Maple Leafs		NHL	80	31	49	80	24
1983-84—Toronto Maple Leafs		NHL	73	37	31	68	22
NHL TOTALS			459	157	173	330	141

(c)—Drafted from Toronto Marlboros by Toronto Maple Leafs in first round of 1977 amateur draft.
(d)—Led in goals (11) and points (19) during playoffs.

MIKE ANDERSON

Center . . . 6'1" . . . 180 lbs. . . . Born, St. Paul, Minn., May 2, 1964 . . . Shoots left . . . Also plays left wing.

Year	Team	League	Games	G.	A.	Pts.	Pen.
1981-82—North St. Paul H.S. (c)		Minn. H.S.	24	19	31	50	18
1982-83—Univ. of Minnesota		WCHA	38	8	11	19	19
1983-84—Univ. of Minnesota		WCHA	23	1	7	8	4

(c)—June, 1982—Drafted as underage player by Buffalo Sabres in NHL entry draft. Fourth Sabres pick, 26th overall, second round.

PERRY LYNN ANDERSON

Left Wing . . . 6' . . . 210 lbs. . . . Born, Barrie, Ont., October 14, 1961 . . . Shoots left. . . . (March, 1984)—Broke bone in foot.

Year	Team	League	Games	G.	A.	Pts.	Pen.
1978-79—Kingston Canadians		OMJHL	60	6	13	19	85
1979-80—Kingston Canadians (c)		OMJHL	63	17	16	33	52
1980-81—Kingston Canadians		OHL	38	9	13	22	118
1980-81—Brantford Alexanders		OHL	31	8	27	35	43
1981-82—Salt Lake Golden Eagles (b)		CHL	71	32	32	64	117
1981-82—St. Louis Blues		NHL	5	1	2	3	0
1982-83—Salt Lake Golden Eagles		CHL	57	23	19	42	140
1982-83—St. Louis Blues		NHL	18	5	2	7	14
1983-84—Montana Magic		CHL	8	7	3	10	34
1983-84—St. Louis Blues		NHL	50	7	5	12	195
NHL TOTALS			73	13	9	22	209

(c)—June, 1980—Drafted by St. Louis Blues as an underage junior in NHL entry draft. Fifth Blues pick, 117th overall, sixth round.

RUSSELL VINCENT ANDERSON

Defense . . . 6'3" . . . 210 lbs. . . . Born, Minneapolis, Minn., February 12, 1955 . . . Shoots left . . . Attended University of Minnesota . . . (November, 1980)—Compound fracture of ring finger of right hand. He broke the same finger twice more before the end of the season . . . (February, 1982)—Separated shoulder.

Year	Team	League	Games	G.	A.	Pts.	Pen.
1974-75—University of Minnesota (c)		WCHA	30	2	7	9	56
1975-76—University of Minnesota		WCHA	28	0	5	5	81
1976-77—Hershey Bears		AHL	11	0	4	4	35
1976-77—Pittsburgh Penguins		NHL	66	2	11	13	81
1977-78—Pittsburgh Penguins		NHL	74	2	16	18	150
1978-79—Pittsburgh Penguins		NHL	72	3	13	16	93
1979-80—Pittsburgh Penguins		NHL	76	5	22	27	150
1980-81—Pittsburgh Penguins		NHL	34	3	14	17	112
1981-82—Pittsburgh Penguins (d)		NHL	31	0	1	1	98
1981-82—Hartford Whalers		NHL	25	1	3	4	85
1982-83—Hartford Whalers (e)		NHL	57	0	6	6	171
1983-84—Los Angeles Kings		NHL	70	5	12	17	126
NHL TOTALS			505	21	98	119	1066

(c)—Drafted from University of Minnesota by Pittsburgh Penguins in second round of 1975 amateur draft.
(d)—December, 1981—Traded with 1983 eighth-round pick in NHL entry draft by Pittsburgh Penguins to Hartford Whalers for Rick MacLeish.
(e)—September, 1983—Signed by Los Angeles Kings as a free agent.

BO MIKAEL ANDERSSON

Center . . . 5'9" . . . 183 lbs. . . . Born, Malmo, Sweden, May 10, 1966 . . . Shoots left.

Year	Team	League	Games	G.	A.	Pts.	Pen.
1983-84—Vastra Frolunda (c)		Sweden	12	0	2	2	6

(c)—June, 1984—Drafted by Buffalo Sabres in NHL entry draft. Sabres first pick, 18th overall, first round.

KENT-ERIK ANDERSSON

Right and Left Wing . . . 6'2" . . . 185 lbs. . . . Born, Orebro, Sweden, May 24, 1951 . . . Shoots right . . . Missed final part of 1978-79 season with broken arm . . . (January, 1984)—Fractured ribs.

Year	Team	League	Games	G.	A.	Pts.	Pen.
1976-77—Farjestads (c)		Sweden	80	17	17	34	....
1977-78—Minnesota North Stars		NHL	73	15	18	33	4
1978-79—Minnesota North Stars		NHL	41	9	4	13	4
1979-80—Oklahoma City Stars		CHL	3	0	2	2	2
1979-80—Minnesota North Stars		NHL	61	9	10	19	8
1980-81—Minnesota North Stars		NHL	77	17	24	41	22
1981-82—Minnesota North Stars (d)		NHL	70	9	12	21	18
1982-83—New York Rangers		NHL	71	8	20	28	14
1983-84—New York Rangers		NHL	63	5	15	20	8
NHL TOTALS			456	72	103	175	78

(c)—Signed by Minnesota North Stars, August, 1977.

(d)—October, 1982—Traded with Mark Johnson by Minnesota North Stars to Hartford Whalers for 1984 fifth-round pick in NHL entry draft and future considerations (Jordy Douglas). Andersson was subsequently traded to New York Rangers for Ed Hospodar.

PETER ANDERSSON

Defense . . . 6'2" . . . 195 lbs. . . . Born, Federalve, Sweden, March 2, 1962 . . . Shoots left . . . Played with Swedish National Junior team and Swedish National team . . . (September 25, 1983)—Injured knee in pre-season game vs. Pittsburgh and missed first three months of season.

Year	Team	League	Games	G.	A.	Pts.	Pen.
1979-80—Timra IF (c)		Sweden Jr.	....	...	....	....	....
1980-81—Timra IF		Sweden Jr.	....	...	....	....	....
1980-81—Bjorkloven IF Umea		Sweden	31	1	2	3	16
1981-82—Bjorkloven IF Umea		Sweden	33	7	7	14	36
1982-83—Bjorkloven IF Umea		Sweden	34	8	16	24	30
1983-84—Washington Capitals		NHL	42	3	7	10	20
NHL TOTALS			42	3	7	10	20

(c)—June, 1980—Drafted by the Washington Capitals in NHL entry draft. Eighth Capitals pick, 173rd overall, ninth round.

JIM ANDONOFF

Right Wing . . . 6'2" . . . 205 lbs. . . . Born, Grosse Point, Mich., August 7, 1965 . . . Shoots right.

Year	Team	League	Games	G.	A.	Pts.	Pen.
1981-82—Detroit Compuware		Midget	78	75	115	190	77
1982-83—Belleville Bulls (c)		OHL	69	17	24	41	36
1983-84—Belleville Bulls		OHL	68	7	24	31	55

(c)—June, 1983—Drafted by New York Rangers in NHL entry draft. Sixth Rangers pick, 93rd overall, fifth round.

DAVID ANDREYCHUK

Center . . . 6'4" . . . 198 lbs. . . . Born, Hamilton, Ont., September 29, 1963 . . . Shoots right . . . (March, 1983)—Sprained knee . . . Played with Team Canada in 1982-83 World Junior Championship.

Year	Team	League	Games	G.	A.	Pts.	Pen.
1980-81—Oshawa Generals		OHL	67	22	22	44	80
1981-82—Oshawa Generals (c)		OHL	67	58	43	101	71
1982-83—Oshawa Generals		OHL	14	8	24	32	6
1982-83—Buffalo Sabres		NHL	43	14	23	37	16
1983-84—Buffalo Sabres		NHL	78	38	42	80	42
NHL TOTALS			121	52	65	117	58

(c)—June, 1982—Drafted as underage junior by Buffalo Sabres in NHL entry draft. Third Sabres pick, 16th overall, first round.

DARRELL ANHOLT

Defense . . . 6'1" . . . 230 lbs. . . . Born, Hardisty, Alta., November 23, 1962 . . . Shoots left.

Year	Team	League	Games	G.	A.	Pts.	Pen.
1979-80—Red Deer Rustlers		AJHL	50	2	14	16	147
1980-81—Calgary Wranglers (c)		WHL	72	5	23	28	286
1981-82—Calgary Wranglers		WHL	64	10	29	39	294
1982-83—Springfield Indians		AHL	80	2	18	20	109
1983-84—Chicago Black Hawks		NHL	1	0	0	0	0
1983-84—Springfield Indians		AHL	80	13	21	34	142
NHL TOTALS			1	0	0	0	0

(c)—June, 1981—Drafted as underage junior by Chicago Black Hawks in NHL entry draft. Third Black Hawks pick, 54th overall, third round.

MICHAEL ANTONOVICH

Center and Left Wing . . . 5'6" . . . 155 lbs. . . . Born, Calumet, Minn., October 18, 1951 . . . Shoots left . . . Attended University of Minnesota . . . Missed part of 1971-72 season with damaged ligaments in right knee requiring surgery and part of 1973-74 season with broken right wrist . . . Missed parts of 1979-80 season with broken jaw and sciatic nerve in lower back. . . . (December, 1982)—Broken wrist.

Year	Team	League	Games	G.	A.	Pts.	Pen.
1969-70—University of Minnesota		WCHA	32	23	20	43	60
1970-71—University of Minnesota (c)		WCHA	32	14	16	32	20
1971-72—University of Minnesota (d)		WCHA	13	8	2	10	19
1972-73—Minnesota Fighting Saints		WHA	75	20	19	39	46
1973-74—Minnesota Fighting Saints		WHA	68	21	29	50	4
1974-75—Minnesota Fighting Saints		WHA	67	24	26	50	20
1975-76—Minnesota Fighting Saints		WHA	57	25	21	46	18
1975-76—Minnesota North Stars (e-f)		NHL	12	0	2	2	8
1976-77—Minnesota Fighting Saints (g)		WHA	42	27	21	48	28
1976-77—Edmonton Oilers (h)		WHA	7	1	1	2	0
1976-77—New England Whalers		WHA	26	12	9	21	10
1977-78—New England Whalers		WHA	75	32	35	67	32
1978-79—Springfield Indians		AHL	7	2	3	5	2
1978-79—New England Whalers (i)		WHA	69	20	27	47	35
1979-80—Hartford Whalers		NHL	5	0	1	1	2
1979-80—Springfield Indians (j)		AHL	24	14	6	20	35
1980-81—Tulsa Oilers (k)		CHL	60	28	32	60	36
1981-82—Minnesota North Stars (l)		NHL	2	0	0	0	0
1981-82—Nashville South Stars (b)		CHL	80	29	77	106	76
1982-83—Wichita Wind		CHL	10	8	12	20	0
1982-83—New Jersey Devils		NHL	30	7	7	14	11
1983-84—Maine Mariners		AHL	25	17	13	30	8
1983-84—New Jersey Devils		NHL	38	3	5	8	16
NHL TOTALS			87	10	15	25	37
WHA TOTALS			486	182	188	370	193

(c)—Drafted from University of Minnesota by Minnesota North Stars in ninth round of 1971 amateur draft.

(d)—Selected by Minnesota Fighting Saints in WHA Player Selection draft, February, 1972.

(e)—Signed by Minnesota North Stars following demise of Minnesota Fighting Saints, March, 1976.

(f)—WHA rights traded to Minnesota Fighting Saints by Calgary Cowboys with Jack Carlson and Butch Deadmarsh for Jim Harrison, August, 1976.

(g)—Sold to Edmonton Oilers by Minnesota Fighting Saints, January, 1977.

(h)—Traded to New England Whalers by Edmonton Oilers with Bill Butters for Brett Callighen and Ron Busniuk, February, 1977.

(i)—Led in goals (10) and points (17) during playoffs.

(j)—June, 1980—Signed with HC Lugano (Switzerland).

(k)—November, 1980—Signed by Tulsa Oilers as a free agent after returning from Switzerland.

(l)—September, 1981—Signed by Minnesota North Stars as free agent.

HARRY ARMSTRONG

Defense . . . 6'2" . . . 195 lbs. . . . Born, Anchorage, Alaska, January 30, 1965 . . . Shoots right.

Year	Team	League	Games	G.	A.	Pts.	Pen.
1982-83—Dubuque (c)		USHL	63	1	6	7	34
1983-84—U. of Illinois-Chicago		CCHA	25	4	11	15	21

(c)—June, 1983—Drafted by Winnipeg Jets in NHL entry draft. Sixth Jets pick, 89th overall, fifth round.

SCOTT ARNIEL

Left Wing . . . 6'1" . . . 170 lbs. . . . Born, Kingston, Ont., September 17, 1962 . . . Shoots left . . . Also plays center.

Year	Team	League	Games	G.	A.	Pts.	Pen.
1979-80—Cornwall Royals		QMJHL	61	22	28	50	51
1980-81—Cornwall Royals (c)		QMJHL	68	52	71	123	102
1981-82—Cornwall Royals		OHL	24	18	26	44	43
1981-82—Winnipeg Jets		NHL	17	1	8	9	14
1982-83—Winnipeg Jets		NHL	75	13	5	18	46
1983-84—Winnipeg Jets		NHL	80	21	35	56	68
NHL TOTALS			172	35	48	83	128

(c)—June, 1981—Drafted as underage junior by Winnipeg Jets in NHL entry draft. Second Jets pick, 22nd overall, second round.

BRENT KENNETH ASHTON

Center . . . 6'1" . . . 200 lbs. . . . Born, Saskatoon, Sask., May 18, 1960 . . . Shoots left . . . Missed part of 1979-80 season with knee ligament injury . . . Also plays Left Wing.

Year	Team	League	Games	G.	A.	Pts.	Pen.
1975-76—Saskatoon Blades		WCHL	11	3	4	7	11
1976-77—Saskatoon Blades		WCHL	54	26	25	51	84
1977-78—Saskatoon Blades		WCHL	46	38	28	66	47
1978-79—Saskatoon Blades (c)		WHL	62	64	55	119	80
1979-80—Vancouver Canucks		NHL	47	5	14	19	11
1980-81—Vancouver Canucks (d-e)		NHL	77	18	11	29	57
1981-82—Colorado Rockies		NHL	80	24	36	60	26
1982-83—New Jersey Devils		NHL	76	14	19	33	47
1983-84—Minnesota North Stars (f)		NHL	68	7	10	17	54
NHL TOTALS			348	68	90	158	195

(c)—August, 1979—Drafted by Vancouver Canucks as underage junior in NHL entry draft. Second Canucks pick, 26th overall, second round.

(d)—July, 1981—Traded with a fourth-round draft pick in 1982 by Vancouver to Winnipeg Jets as compensation for Canucks signing of Ivan Hlinka, a Czechoslovakian player drafted by Winnipeg in a special draft on May 28, 1981.

(e)—July, 1981—Traded with a third-round 1982 draft pick (Dave Kasper) by Winnipeg Jets to Colorado Rockies for Lucien DeBlois.

(f)—October, 1983—Traded by New Jersey Devils to Minnesota North Stars for Dave Lewis.

BOB ATTWELL

Right Wing . . . 6' . . . 194 lbs. . . . Born, Spokane, Wash., December 26, 1959 . . . Shoots right . . . Son of Ron Attwell (NHL 1967-68, AHL 1954-70), Nephew of Bill McCreary, Sr. (NHL 1965-71) and Keith McCreary (NHL 1967-75) and cousin of Bill McCreary, Jr.

Year	Team	League	Games	G.	A.	Pts.	Pen.
1976-77—Peterborough Petes		OMJHL	64	18	25	43	10
1977-78—Peterborough Petes		OMJHL	68	23	43	66	32
1978-79—Peterborough Petes (c)		OMJHL	68	32	61	93	39
1979-80—Colorado Rockies		NHL	7	1	1	2	0
1979-80—Fort Worth Texans		CHL	74	26	35	61	18
1980-81—Colorado Rockies		NHL	15	0	4	4	0
1980-81—Fort Worth Texans		CHL	60	13	18	31	30
1981-82—Fort Worth Texans		CHL	79	31	36	67	66
1982-83—Moncton Alpines		AHL	74	14	19	33	31
1983-84—Fort Wayne Komets		IHL	70	25	35	60	22
NHL TOTALS			22	1	5	6	0

(c)—August, 1979—Drafted by Colorado Rockies in NHL entry draft. Third Colorado pick, 106th overall, sixth round.

NORMAND AUBIN

Center . . . 6' . . . 185 lbs. . . . Born, St. Leonard, Que., July 26, 1960 . . . Shoots left . . . Led QMJHL with 91 goals in 1979-80 . . . (November, 1981)—Pulled groin . . . (February 9, 1983)—Played goal during a 6-3 loss at Adirondack (AHL). Regular goalie (Vince Tremblay) pulled a hamstring, and backup goalie was serving a suspension (Bob Parent).

Year	Team	League	Games	G.	A.	Pts.	Pen.
1976-77—Sorel Black Hawks		QJHL	50	25	26	51	32
1977-78—Verdun Maple Leafs		QJHL	71	62	73	135	107
1978-79—Verdun Maple Leafs (a-c)		QJHL	70	80	69	149	84
1979-80—Sorel Black Hawks		QMJHL	21	41	29	70	28
1979-80—Sherbrooke Beavers		QMJHL	42	50	60	110	38
1980-81—New Brunswick Hawks		AHL	79	43	46	89	99
1981-82—Cincinnati Tigers		CHL	31	15	17	32	36
1981-82—Toronto Maple Leafs		NHL	43	14	12	26	22
1982-83—St. Catharines Saints		AHL	49	31	26	57	40

Year	Team	League	Games	G.	A.	Pts.	Pen.
1982-83—Toronto Maple Leafs		NHL	26	4	1	5	8
1983-84—St. Catharines Saints		AHL	80	47	47	94	63
NHL TOTALS			69	18	13	31	30

(c)—August, 1979—Drafted by Toronto Maple Leafs in NHL entry draft. Second Maple Leafs pick, 51st overall, third round.

PIERRE AUBRY

Center . . . 5'10" . . . 170 lbs. . . . Born, Cap-de-la-Madeleine, Que., April 15, 1960 . . . Shoots left . . . Also plays left wing.

Year	Team	League	Games	G.	A.	Pts.	Pen.
1977-78—Quebec Remparts		QMJHL	32	18	19	37	19
1977-78—Trois-Rivieres Draveurs		QMJHL	41	20	25	45	34
1978-79—Quebec Remparts		QMJHL	7	2	3	5	5
1978-79—Trois-Rivieres Draveurs		QMJHL	67	53	45	98	97
1979-80—Trois-Rivieres Draveurs		QMJHL	72	85	62	147	82
1980-81—Quebec Nordiques (c)		NHL	1	0	0	0	0
1980-81—Erie Blades (a)		EHL	71	*66	*68	*134	99
1980-81—Rochester Americans		AHL	1	0	0	0	0
1981-82—Fredericton Express		AHL	11	6	5	11	10
1981-82—Quebec Nordiques		NHL	62	10	13	23	27
1982-83—Quebec Nordiques		NHL	77	7	9	16	48
1983-84—Fredericton Express		AHL	12	4	5	9	4
1983-84—Quebec Nordiques (d)		NHL	23	1	1	2	17
1983-84—Detroit Red Wings		NHL	14	4	1	5	8
NHL TOTALS			177	22	24	46	100

(c)—September, 1980—Signed by Quebec Nordiques as a free agent.
(d)—February, 1984—Sold by Quebec Nordiques to Detroit Red Wings.

JERRY AUGUST

Defense . . . 5'10" . . . 192 lbs. . . . Born, Sommerville, Mass., November 21, 1960 . . . Shoots right.

Year	Team	League	Games	G.	A.	Pts.	Pen.
1979-80—Boston University		ECAC	27	2	13	15	40
1980-81—Boston University		ECAC	29	3	12	15	62
1981-82—Boston University		ECAC	28	3	13	16	70
1982-83—Boston University		ECAC	27	3	23	26	18
1983-84—Peoria Prancers		IHL	71	12	22	34	56

SHAWN PATRICK BABCOCK

Right Wing . . . 5'10" . . . 195 lbs. . . . Born, Wallaceburg, Ont., July 24, 1962 . . . Shoots right.

Year	Team	League	Games	G.	A.	Pts.	Pen.
1979-80—Windsor Spitfires (c)		OMJHL	51	12	13	25	241
1980-81—Windsor Spitfires		OHL	36	8	12	20	180
1980-81—Kingston Canadians		OHL	26	2	6	8	144
1981-82—Kingston Canadians		OHL	56	17	18	35	273
1981-82—Wichita Wind (d)		CHL	..	..	..	..	....
1982-83—Moncton Alpines		AHL	38	0	3	3	135
1982-83—Sherbrooke Jets		AHL	9	3	2	5	14
1983-84—Moncton Alpines		AHL	48	2	8	10	163

(c)—June, 1980—Drafted as underage junior by Edmonton Oilers in NHL entry draft. Second Oilers pick, 48th overall, third round.
(d)—No regular-season record. Played in two playoff games only.

DAVID MICHAEL BABYCH

Defense . . . 6'2" . . . 215 lbs. . . . Born, Edmonton, Alta., May 23, 1961 . . . Shoots left . . . Brother of Wayne Babych . . . First member of Winnipeg Jets to be voted to mid-season All-Star game (1983) starting team . . . (March, 1984)—Separated shoulder.

Year	Team	League	Games	G.	A.	Pts.	Pen.
1977-78—Portland Winter Hawks		WCHL	6	1	3	4	4
1977-78—Ft. Sask. Traders (a-c-d)		AJHL	56	31	69	100	37
1978-79—Portland Winter Hawks		WHL	67	20	59	79	63
1979-80—Portland Winter Hawks (a-e-f)		WHL	50	22	60	82	71
1980-81—Winnipeg Jets		NHL	69	6	38	44	90
1981-82—Winnipeg Jets		NHL	79	19	49	68	92
1982-83—Winnipeg Jets		NHL	79	13	61	74	56
1983-84—Winnipeg Jets		NHL	66	18	39	57	62
NHL TOTALS			293	56	187	243	300

(c)—Named winner of AJHL Rookie of the Year Trophy.
(d)—Named winner of AJHL Top Defenseman Trophy.
(e)—Named winner of WHL Top Defenseman Trophy.
(f)—June, 1980—Drafted as underage junior by Winnipeg Jets in NHL entry draft. First Jets pick, second overall, first round.

WAYNE JOSEPH BABYCH

Right Wing ... 5'11" ... 191 lbs.... Born, Edmonton, Alta., June 6, 1958 ... Shoots right ... Missed part of 1978-79 season with a broken left ankle and parts of 1979-80 season with right shoulder and knee injuries ... Brother of Dave Babych ... (September, 1981)— Missed first 12 games of season with training camp shoulder injury. Continued to aggra- vate injury and underwent shoulder manipulation in January, 1982 ... (January 1, 1983)— Broken nose and cracked cheekbone in fight with Behn Wilson in game vs. Philadelphia.

Year	Team	League	Games	G.	A.	Pts.	Pen.
1973-74—Edmonton Mets		AJHL	56	20	18	38	68
1973-74—Edmonton Oil Kings		WCHL	1	0	1	1	0
1974-75—Edmonton Oil Kings		WCHL	68	19	17	36	157
1975-76—Edmonton Oil Kings		WCHL	61	32	46	78	98
1976-77—Portland Winter Hawks (a)		WCHL	71	50	62	112	76
1977-78—Portland Winter Hawks (a-c)		WCHL	68	50	71	121	218
1978-79—St. Louis Blues		NHL	67	27	36	63	75
1979-80—St. Louis Blues		NHL	59	26	35	61	49
1980-81—St. Louis Blues		NHL	78	54	42	96	93
1981-82—St. Louis Blues		NHL	51	19	25	44	51
1982-83—St. Louis Blues		NHL	71	16	23	39	62
1983-84—St. Louis Blues		NHL	70	13	29	42	52
NHL TOTALS			396	155	190	345	382

(c)—Drafted from Portland Winter Hawks by St. Louis Blues in first round of 1978 amateur draft.

MIKE BACKMAN

Right Wing ... 5'10" ... 175 lbs.... Born, Halifax, N. S., January 2, 1955 ... Shoots right ... (January, 1981)—Broken hand.

Year	Team	League	Games	G.	A.	Pts.	Pen.
1974-75—Mont. Red, White and Blue (c)		QMJHL	38	13	20	33	85
1975-76—St. Mary's University		AUAA	....	...	....	....	....
1976-77—St. Mary's University		AUAA	....	...	....	....	....
1977-78—St. Mary's University		AUAA	....	...	....	....	....
1978-79—Toledo Goaldiggers (d)		IHL	66	25	38	63	171
1978-79—New Haven Nighthawks		AHL	6	2	1	3	0
1979-80—New Haven Nighthawks		AHL	74	18	28	46	156
1980-81—New Haven Nighthawks		AHL	62	27	27	54	224
1981-82—Springfield Indians		AHL	74	24	27	51	147
1981-82—New York Rangers		NHL	3	0	2	2	4
1982-83—New York Rangers		NHL	7	1	3	4	6
1982-83—Tulsa Oilers (a)		CHL	71	29	47	76	170
1983-84—Tulsa Oilers		CHL	50	12	28	40	103
1983-84—New York Rangers		NHL	8	0	1	1	8
NHL TOTALS			18	1	6	7	18

(c)—May, 1975—Drafted by Quebec Nordiques in WHA amateur draft. Seventh Nordiques pick, 100th overall, seventh round.
(d)—September, 1979—Signed by New York Rangers as a free agent.

RENE BADEAU

Defense ... 6'0" ... 190 lbs.... Born, Trois-Rivieres, Que., January 31, 1964 ... Shoots left.

Year	Team	League	Games	G.	A.	Pts.	Pen.
1981-82—Quebec Remparts (c)		QMJHL	49	5	18	23	232
1982-83—Quebec Remparts		QHL	13	1	3	4	63
1982-83—Trois-Rivieres Draveurs		QHL	46	4	30	34	205
1982-83—Springfield Indians		AHL	4	0	0	0	4
1983-84—Laval Voisins		QHL	64	13	40	53	279

(c)—June, 1982—Drafted as underage junior by Chicago Black Hawks in NHL entry draft. Second Black Hawks pick, 28th overall, second round.

REID BAILEY

Defense ... 6'2" ... 195 lbs.... Born, Toronto, Ont., May 28, 1956 ... Shoots left.

Year	Team	League	Games	G.	A.	Pts.	Pen.
1975-76—S. Ste. Marie Greyhounds		Jr."A"OHA	9	0	2	2	47
1975-76—Kitchener Rangers		Jr."A"OHA	24	0	15	15	80

Year	Team	League	Games	G.	A.	Pts.	Pen.
1975-76—Cornwall Royals		QJHL	26	1	8	9	32
1976-77—Port Huron Flags		IHL	72	3	14	17	148
1977-78—Port Huron Flags		IHL	72	3	28	31	162
1978-79—Maine Mariners (c)		AHL	56	6	8	14	127
1979-80—Maine Mariners		AHL	75	0	12	12	155
1980-81—Maine Mariners		AHL	59	6	29	35	155
1980-81—Philadelphia Flyers		NHL	17	1	3	4	55
1981-82—Maine Mariners		AHL	54	4	26	30	55
1981-82—Philadelphia Flyers		NHL	10	0	0	0	23
1982-83—Moncton Alpines (d-e)		AHL	21	0	9	9	22
1982-83—St. Catharines Saints		AHL	34	0	14	14	62
1982-83—Toronto Maple Leafs		NHL	1	0	0	0	2
1983-84—St. Catharines Saints		AHL	25	0	8	8	73
1983-84—Binghamton Whalers (f)		AHL	33	2	11	13	95
1983-84—Hartford Whalers		NHL	12	0	0	0	25
NHL TOTALS			40	1	3	4	105

(c)—November, 1978—Signed by Philadelphia Flyers as a free agent.
(d)—September, 1982—Signed by Edmonton Oilers as a free agent.
(e)—January, 1983—Traded by Edmonton Oilers to Toronto Maple Leafs for Serge Boisvert.
(f)—December, 1983—Signed by Hartford Whalers as a free agent.

JOEL BAILLARGEON

Left Wing . . . 6'1" . . . 205 lbs. . . . Born, Charlesbourg, Que., October 6, 1964 . . . Shoots left.

Year	Team	League	Games	G.	A.	Pts.	Pen.
1981-82—Trois-Rivieres Draveurs		QMJHL	26	1	3	4	47
1982-83—Trois-Rivieres		QHL	29	4	5	9	197
1982-83—Hull Olympics (c)		QHL	25	15	7	22	76
1983-84—Chicoutimi Sagueneens		QHL	60	48	35	83	184
1983-84—Sherbrooke Jets		AHL	8	0	0	0	26

(c)—June, 1983—Drafted as underage junior by Winnipeg Jets in NHL entry draft. Seventh Jets pick, 109th overall, sixth round.

WILLIAM ROBERT BAKER

Defense . . . 6'1" . . . 195 lbs. . . . Born, Grand Rapids, Minn., November 29, 1956 . . . Shoots left . . . Member of 1980 U.S. Gold Medal Winning Olympic Team . . . (November 22, 1980)—Broken nose . . . Set records at University of Minnesota in 1978-79 for most assists (42) and points (54) by a defenseman.

Year	Team	League	Games	G.	A.	Pts.	Pen.
1975-76—University of Minnesota (c)		WCHA	44	8	15	23	28
1976-77—University of Minnesota		WCHA	28	0	8	8	42
1977-78—University of Minnesota (a)		WCHA	38	10	23	33	24
1978-79—University of Minnesota (a-d)		WCHA	44	12	42	54	38
1979-80—U.S. Olympic Team		Int'l	60	5	25	30	74
1979-80—Nova Scotia Voyageurs		AHL	12	4	8	12	5
1980-81—Nova Scotia Voyageurs		AHL	18	5	12	17	42
1980-81—Montreal Canadiens (e)		NHL	11	0	0	0	32
1980-81—Colorado Rockies		NHL	13	0	3	3	12
1981-82—Ft. Worth Texans		CHL	10	3	12	15	20
1981-82—Colorado Rockies (f)		NHL	14	0	3	3	17
1981-82—St. Louis Blues (g)		NHL	35	3	5	8	50
1982-83—New York Rangers		NHL	70	4	14	18	64
1983-84—Tulsa Oilers		CHL	59	11	22	33	47
NHL TOTALS			143	7	25	32	175

(c)—May, 1976—Drafted by Montreal Canadiens in NHL amateur draft. Fifth Canadiens pick, 54th overall, third round.
(d)—All-America Team (West).
(e)—March, 1981—Traded with fourth-round 1984 draft pick by Montreal Canadiens to Colorado Rockies for third-round 1983 draft pick and fourth-round 1984 draft pick.
(f)—December, 1981—Traded by Colorado Rockies to St. Louis Blues for Joe Micheletti and Dick Lamby.
(g)—Claimed by New York Rangers in 1982 NHL waiver draft.

DOUGLAS MICHAEL BARAN

Defense . . . 6'1" . . . 185 lbs. . . . Born, Winnipeg, Man., October 14, 1962 . . . Shoots left.

Year	Team	League	Games	G.	A.	Pts.	Pen.
1979-80—Sorel Black Hawks		QMJHL	69	3	20	23	91
1980-81—Sorel Black Hawks		QMJHL	72	13	43	56	179
1981-82—Sherbrooke Beavers (c)		QMJHL	18	3	11	14	27

Year	Team	League	Games	G.	A.	Pts.	Pen.
1981-82—Laval Voisins (d)		QMJHL	44	7	38	45	75
1982-83—Peoria Prancers (e)		IHL	36	8	12	20	34
1982-83—Tulsa Oilers		CHL	22	2	5	7	23
1983-84—Tulsa Oilers		CHL	51	5	7	12	24

(c)—August, 1981—Selected by Sherbrooke Beavers in dispersal draft of players from defunct Sorel Black Hawks.

(d)—November, 1981—Traded by Sherbrooke Beavers to Laval Voisins for Michael Morrissette.

(e)—October, 1982—Signed by New York Rangers as a free agent.

DON BARBER

Left Wing . . . 6'1" . . . 205 lbs. . . . Born, Victoria, B.C., December 2, 1964 . . . Shoots left.

Year	Team	League	Games	G.	A.	Pts.	Pen.
1982-83—Kelowna Buckaroos (c)		BCJHL	35	26	31	57	54
1983-84—St. Albert Saints		AJHL	53	42	38	80	74

(c)—June, 1983—Drafted as underage junior by Edmonton Oilers in NHL entry draft. Fifth Oilers pick, 120th overall, sixth round.

WILLIAM CHARLES BARBER

Left Wing . . . 6' . . . 195 lbs. . . . Born, Callender, Ont., July 11, 1952 . . . Shoots left . . . Played center prior to 1972-73 season . . . Brother of Danny Barber . . . (March, 1977)—Tore Anterior cruciate ligament in right knee . . . (December 4, 1982)—Partial tear of medial collateral ligament in right knee during game at Pittsburgh . . . (October, 1983)—Pinched nerve in shoulder . . . (January 15, 1984)—Broke jaw in game vs. Chicago. Lost 15 lbs. by end of season due to liquid diet . . . (April, 1984)—Surgery to reconstruct right knee. Expected to miss much, if not all, of 1984-85 season.

Year	Team	League	Games	G.	A.	Pts.	Pen.
1968-69—North Bay Trappers	Jr."A" NOHA		....	...	....	....	....
1969-70—Kitchener Rangers	Jr."A" OHA		54	37	49	86	42
1970-71—Kitchener Rangers	Jr."A" OHA		61	46	59	105	129
1971-72—Kitchener Rangers (c-d)	Jr."A" OHA		62	44	63	107	89
1972-73—Richmond Robins		AHL	11	9	5	14	4
1972-73—Philadelphia Flyers (e)		NHL	69	30	34	64	46
1973-74—Philadelphia Flyers		NHL	75	34	35	69	54
1974-75—Philadelphia Flyers		NHL	79	34	37	71	66
1975-76—Philadelphia Flyers (a)		NHL	80	50	62	112	104
1976-77—Philadelphia Flyers		NHL	73	20	35	55	62
1977-78—Philadelphia Flyers		NHL	80	41	31	72	34
1978-79—Philadelphia Flyers (b)		NHL	79	34	46	80	22
1979-80—Philadelphia Flyers (f)		NHL	79	40	32	72	17
1980-81—Philadelphia Flyers (b)		NHL	80	43	42	85	69
1981-82—Philadelphia Flyers		NHL	80	45	44	89	85
1982-83—Philadelphia Flyers		NHL	66	27	33	60	28
1983-84—Philadelphia Flyers		NHL	63	22	32	54	36
NHL TOTALS			903	420	463	883	623

(c)—Selected by New York Raiders in WHA Player Selection Draft, February, 1972.

(d)—Drafted from Kitchener Rangers by Philadelphia Flyers in first round of 1972 amateur draft.

(e)—Named Rookie-of-the-Year in West Division poll of players by THE SPORTING NEWS.

(f)—Co-leader (with Bryan Trottier) with 12 goals in playoffs.

BLAIR BARNES

Right Wing . . . 5'11" . . . 190 lbs. . . . Born, Windsor, Ont., September 21, 1960 . . . Shoots right.

Year	Team	League	Games	G.	A.	Pts.	Pen.
1977-78—Windsor Spitfires		OMJHL	65	22	26	48	163
1978-79—Windsor Spitfires (c)		OMJHL	67	42	76	118	195
1979-80—Windsor Spitfires		OMJHL	66	63	67	130	98
1980-81—Wichita Wind		CHL	30	10	14	24	49
1981-82—Wichita Wind (d)		CHL	80	28	34	62	99
1982-83—Los Angeles Kings		NHL	1	0	0	0	0
1982-83—New Haven Nighthawks		AHL	72	29	34	63	80
1983-84—Nova Scotia Voyaguers		AHL	80	31	32	63	91
NHL TOTALS			1	0	0	0	0

(c)—August, 1979—Drafted as underage junior by Edmonton Oilers in NHL entry draft. Sixth Oilers pick, 126 overall, sixth round.

(d)—June, 1982—Traded by Edmonton Oilers to Los Angeles Kings for Paul Mulvey.

NORMAND BARON

Left Wing . . . 6' . . . 205 lbs. . . . Born, Verdun, Que., December 15, 1957 . . . Shoots left . . . Mr. Montreal and Mr. Quebec in 1981 bodybuilding competition.

Year	Team	League	Games	G.	A.	Pts.	Pen.
1983-84—Nova Scotia Voyageurs (c)		AHL	68	11	11	22	275
1983-84—Montreal Canadiens		NHL	4	0	0	0	12
NHL TOTALS			4	0	0	0	12

(c)—October, 1983—Signed by Montreal Canadiens as a free agent.

DAVID BARR

Center . . . 6'1" . . . 185 lbs. . . . Born, Edmonton, Alta., November 30, 1960 . . . Shoots right . . . Also plays Right Wing.

Year	Team	League	Games	G.	A.	Pts.	Pen.
1977-78—Pincher Creek		AJHL	60	16	32	48	53
1978-79—Edmonton Oil Kings		WHL	72	16	19	35	61
1979-80—Lethbridge Broncos		WHL	60	16	38	54	47
1980-81—Lethbridge Broncos		WHL	72	26	62	88	106
1981-82—Erie Blades		AHL	76	18	48	66	29
1981-82—Boston Bruins (c)		NHL	2	0	0	0	0
1982-83—Baltimore Skipjacks		AHL	72	27	51	78	67
1982-83—Boston Bruins		NHL	10	1	1	2	7
1983-84—New York Rangers (d)		NHL	6	0	0	0	2
1983-84—Tulsa Oilers		CHL	50	28	37	65	24
1983-84—St. Louis Blues (e)		NHL	1	0	0	0	0
NHL TOTALS			19	1	1	2	9

(c)—September, 1981—Signed by Boston Bruins as a free agent.

(d)—October, 1983—Traded by Boston Bruins to New York Rangers for Dave Silk.

(e)—March, 1984—Traded with third-round 1984 draft pick (Alan Perry) and cash by New York Rangers to St. Louis Blues for Larry Patey and NHL rights to Bob Brooke.

FREDERICK WILLIAM BARRETT

Defense . . . 5'11" . . . 195 lbs. . . . Born, Ottawa, Ont., January 26, 1950 . . . Shoots left . . . Missed most of 1965-66 season with split kneecap, most of 1966-67 season with chipped ankle bone, final weeks of 1970-71 season with broken left thigh bone and part of 1971-72 season with shoulder separation . . . Missed start of 1972-73 season with broken hand (suffered during training camp) and part of season with ankle injury . . . Missed final month of 1973-74 season with broken jaw, part of 1974-75 season with broken right hand and part of 1978-79 season with calcium deposits in left thigh . . . (May, 1980)—Broke hand vs. Philadelphia in Stanley Cup Semifinals . . . Brother of John Barrett . . . (December 20, 1982)—Injured back in game at Winnipeg.

Year	Team	League	Games	G.	A.	Pts.	Pen.
1965-66—Ottawa Capitals		Cent.Jr.OHA	....	...	....	....	....
1966-67—Toronto Marlboros		Jr."A" OHA	2	0	0	0	2
1967-68—Toronto Marlboros		Jr."A" OHA	51	5	8	13	98
1968-69—Toronto Marlboros		Jr."A" OHA	52	3	17	20	113
1969-70—Toronto Marlboros (c)		Jr."A" OHA	48	8	20	28	146
1970-71—Minnesota North Stars		NHL	57	0	13	13	75
1971-72—Cleveland Barons		AHL	51	2	27	29	91
1972-73—Minnesota North Stars		NHL	46	2	4	6	21
1973-74—Minnesota North Stars		NHL	40	0	7	7	12
1974-75—Minnesota North Stars		NHL	62	3	18	21	82
1975-76—Minnesota North Stars		NHL	79	2	9	11	66
1976-77—Minnesota North Stars		NHL	60	1	8	9	46
1977-78—Minnesota North Stars		NHL	79	0	15	15	59
1978-79—Minnesota North Stars		NHL	45	1	9	10	48
1979-80—Minnesota North Stars		NHL	80	8	14	22	71
1980-81—Minnesota North Stars		NHL	62	4	8	12	72
1981-82—Minnesota North Stars		NHL	69	1	15	16	89
1982-83—Minnesota North Stars		NHL	51	1	3	4	22
1983-84—Los Angeles Kings (d-e)		NHL	15	2	0	2	8
NHL TOTALS			745	25	123	148	671

(c)—Drafted from Toronto Marlboros by Minnesota North Stars in second round of 1970 amateur draft.

(d)—October, 1983—Traded by Minnesota North Stars to Los Angeles Kings for Dave Lewis.

(e)—August, 1984—Released by Los Angeles Kings.

JOHN DAVID BARRETT

Defense . . . 6'1" . . . 210 lbs. . . . Born, Ottawa, Ont., July 1, 1958 . . . Shoots left . . . (December 16, 1980)—Separated left shoulder vs. Edmonton . . . Brother of Fred Barrett.

Year—Team	League	Games	G.	A.	Pts.	Pen.
1976-77—Windsor Spitfires	OMJHL	63	7	17	24	168
1977-78—Windsor Spitfires (c)	OMJHL	67	8	18	26	133
1978-79—Milwaukee Admirals	IHL	42	8	13	21	117
1978-79—Kalamazoo Wings	IHL	31	1	12	13	54
1979-80—Kalamazoo Wings	IHL	52	8	33	41	63
1979-80—Adirondack Red Wings	AHL	28	0	4	4	59
1980-81—Adirondack Red Wings	AHL	21	4	11	15	63
1980-81—Detroit Red Wings	NHL	56	3	10	13	60
1981-82—Detroit Red Wings	NHL	69	1	12	13	93
1982-83—Detroit Red Wings	NHL	79	4	10	14	74
1983-84—Detroit Red Wings	NHL	78	2	8	10	78
NHL TOTALS		282	10	40	50	305

(c)—June, 1978—Drafted by Detroit Red Wings in NHL amateur draft. Tenth Red Wings pick, 129th overall, eighth round.

FRANCIS LEONARD (FRANK) BATHE

Defense . . . 6'1" . . . 195 lbs. . . . Born, Oshawa, Ont., September 27, 1954 . . . Shoots left . . . (December, 1981)—Herniated disc in back requiring surgery . . . (December 18, 1982)— Pulled hip muscle in game vs. N.Y. Islanders . . . (March 5, 1983)—Sprained knee in game at Washington . . . (October, 1983)—Herniated disc . . . (November, 1983)—Back surgery.

Year—Team	League	Games	G.	A.	Pts.	Pen.
1972-73—Windsor Spitfires	SOJHL	59	10	25	35	232
1973-74—Windsor Spitfires	SOJHL	58	19	34	53	306
1974-75—Virginia Wings	AHL	50	7	11	18	146
1974-75—Detroit Red Wings	NHL	19	0	3	3	31
1975-76—New Haven Nighthawks	AHL	7	0	1	1	24
1975-76—Kalamazoo Wings (c)	IHL	14	0	5	5	46
1975-76—Port Huron Flags	IHL	43	2	3	5	148
1975-76—Detroit Red Wings	NHL	7	0	1	1	9
1976-77—Port Huron Flags	IHL	71	7	30	37	250
1977-78—Maine Mariners (d)	AHL	78	4	11	15	159
1977-78—Philadelphia Flyers	NHL	1	0	0	0	0
1978-79—Maine Mariners	AHL	26	3	3	6	106
1978-79—Philadelphia Flyers	NHL	21	1	3	4	76
1979-80—Philadelphia Flyers	NHL	47	0	7	7	111
1980-81—Philadelphia Flyers	NHL	44	0	3	3	175
1981-82—Philadelphia Flyers	NHL	28	1	3	4	68
1982-83—Philadelphia Flyers	NHL	57	1	8	9	72
1983-84—Maine Mariners	AHL	4	1	0	1	2
NHL TOTALS		224	3	28	31	542

(c)—Traded to Port Huron Flags by Kalamazoo Wings for Henry Lehvonen, December, 1975.
(d)—October, 1977—Signed by Philadelphia Flyers as a free agent.

PAUL GORDON BAXTER

Defense . . . 5'11" . . . 200 lbs. . . . Born, Winnipeg, Man., October 25, 1955 . . . Shoots right . . . Missed most of 1974-75 season with knee injury requiring surgery . . . (November, 1980)— Surgery for cut wrist tendons . . . (February, 1984)—Sprained right knee.

Year—Team	League	Games	G.	A.	Pts.	Pen.
1972-73—Winnipeg Monarchs	MJHL	44	9	22	31	*359
1973-74—Winnipeg Clubs (c)	WCHL	63	10	30	40	384
1974-75—Cape Codders	NAHL	2	1	0	1	11
1974-75—Cleveland Crusaders (d)	WHA	5	0	0	0	37
1975-76—Syracuse Blazers	NAHL	3	1	2	3	9
1975-76—Cleveland Crusaders	WHA	67	3	7	10	201
1976-77—Maine Nordiques	NAHL	6	1	4	5	52
1976-77—Quebec Nordiques	WHA	66	6	17	23	244
1977-78—Quebec Nordiques	WHA	76	6	29	35	240
1978-79—Quebec Nordiques (e)	WHA	76	10	36	46	240
1979-80—Quebec Nordiques (f)	NHL	61	7	13	20	145
1980-81—Pittsburgh Penguins	NHL	51	5	14	19	204
1981-82—Pittsburgh Penguins	NHL	76	9	34	43	*409
1982-83—Pittsburgh Penguins (g)	NHL	75	11	21	32	238
1983-84—Calgary Flames (h)	NHL	74	7	20	27	182
WHA TOTALS		290	25	89	114	962
NHL TOTALS		337	39	102	141	1178

(c)—Selected by Cleveland Crusaders in World Hockey Association amateur player draft, May, 1974.
(d)—Drafted from Cleveland Crusaders (WHA) by Pittsburgh Penguins in third round of 1975 amateur draft.

(e)—June, 1979—Selected by Pittsburgh Penguins in NHL reclaim draft, but remained with Quebec Nordiques as a priority selection for the expansion draft.
(f)—August, 1980—Signed by Pittsburgh Penguins as free agent with Quebec Nordiques receiving Kim Clackson as compensation.
(g)—August, 1983—Released by Pittsburgh Penguins.
(h)—September, 1983—Signed by Calgary Flames as a free agent.

SANDY JAMES BEADLE

Left Wing . . . 6'2" . . . 185 lbs. . . . Born, Regina, Sask., July 12, 1960 . . . Shoots left.

Year	Team	League	Games	G.	A.	Pts.	Pen.
1978-79—Regina Blues	SJHL	52	41	57	98	25
1978-79—Regina Pats	WCHL	2	1	1	2	0
1979-80—Northeastern Univ. (c)	ECAC	23	11	16	27	6
1980-81—Northeastern Univ. (a-d)	ECAC	26	29	30	59	26
1980-81—Winnipeg Jets (e)	NHL	6	1	0	1	2
1980-81—Tulsa Oilers (f)	CHL	....	....	....	....	....
1981-82—Tulsa Oilers	CHL	54	12	21	33	34
1982-83—Sherbrooke Jets	AHL	9	2	3	5	0
1982-83—Fort Wayne Komets	IHL	13	3	10	13	11
1983-84—Sherbrooke Jets	AHL	70	2	5	7	8
NHL TOTALS		6	1	0	1	2

(c)—June, 1980—Drafted by Winnipeg Jets in NHL entry draft. Eighth Jets pick, 149th overall, eighth round.
(d)—Named to All-America Team (East).
(e)—March, 1981—Signed by Winnipeg Jets.
(f)—No regular season games, played in six playoff games.

YVES BEAUDOIN

Defense . . . 5'11" . . . 180 lbs. . . . Born, Pointe Aux Trombles, Que., January 7, 1965 . . . Shoots right.

Year	Team	League	Games	G.	A.	Pts.	Pen.
1981-82—Hull Olympics	QMJHL	50	2	18	20	39
1982-83—Hull Olympics	QHL	6	1	2	3	9
1982-83—Shawinigan Cataracts (c)	QHL	56	11	23	34	51
1983-84—Shawinigan Cataracts	QHL	68	14	43	57	93

(c)—June, 1983—Drafted as underage junior by Washington Capitals in NHL entry draft. Sixth Capitals pick, 195th overall, tenth round.

BARRY DAVID BECK

Defense . . . 6'3" . . . 216 lbs. . . . Born, N. Vancouver, B.C., June 3, 1957 . . . Shoots left . . . Missed part of 1976-77 season with pneumonia . . . Set NHL record for goals by a rookie defenseman with 22 in 1977-78 . . . Missed part of 1978-79 season with knee injury . . . (October 3, 1980)—Broke middle finger on right hand in exhibition game vs. Islanders at New Haven . . . (October, 1981)—Served three-game league suspension . . . (December, 1981)—Served six-game league suspension . . . Set New York Rangers record for penalty minutes in a single season in 1980-81 . . . (January, 1983)—Strained neck muscles . . . (February, 1984)—Sprained right wrist.

Year	Team	League	Games	G.	A.	Pts.	Pen.
1973-74—Langley	Jr. "A" BCHL	63	8	28	36	329
1973-74—Kamloops Chiefs	WCHL	1	0	0	0	0
1974-75—New Westminster Bruins	WCHL	58	9	33	42	162
1975-76—N. Westminster Bruins (a)	WCHL	68	19	80	99	325
1976-77—N. Westminster Bruins (a-c-d)	WCHL	61	16	46	62	167
1977-78—Colorado Rockies	NHL	75	22	38	60	89
1978-79—Colorado Rockies	NHL	63	14	28	42	91
1979-80—Colorado Rockies (e)	NHL	10	1	5	6	8
1979-80—New York Rangers	NHL	61	14	45	59	98
1980-81—New York Rangers	NHL	75	11	23	34	231
1981-82—New York Rangers	NHL	60	9	29	38	111
1982-83—New York Rangers	NHL	66	12	22	34	112
1983-84—New York Rangers	NHL	72	9	27	36	132
NHL TOTALS		482	92	217	309	872

(c)—Won Most Valuable Player and Outstanding Defenseman awards.
(d)—Drafted from New Westminster Bruins by Colorado Rockies in first round of 1977 amateur draft.
(e)—November, 1979—Traded by Colorado Rockies to New York Rangers for Mike McEwen, Lucien DeBlois, Pat Hickey, Dean Turner and future consideration (Bobby Crawford).

BRAD BECK

Defense . . . 5'11" . . . 185 lbs. . . . Born, Vancouver, B.C., February 10, 1964 . . . Shoots right.

Year	Team	League	Games	G.	A.	Pts.	Pen.
1980-81—Penticton Knights		BCJHL	....	10	24	34	....
1981-82—Penticton Knights (c)		BCJHL	52	13	32	45	116
1982-83—Michigan State Univ.		CCHA	42	5	15	20	40
1983-84—Michigan State Univ.		CCHA	42	2	7	9	67

(c)—June, 1982—Drafted as underage player by Chicago Black Hawks in NHL entry draft. Fifth Black Hawks pick, 91st overall, fifth round.

RUSS BECKER

Defense . . . 6'3" . . . 200 lbs. . . . Born, Iowa City, Iowa, December 20, 1965 . . . Shoots left.

Year	Team	League	Games	G.	A.	Pts.	Pen.
1983-84—Virginia H.S. (c)		Minn. H.S.	21	4	11	15	22

(c)—June, 1984—Drafted by N.Y. Islanders in NHL entry draft. 12th Islanders pick, 228th overall, 11th round.

EDDY JOSEPH BEERS

Left Wing . . . 6'2" . . . 195 lbs. . . . Born, Merritt, B.C., October 12, 1959 . . . Shoots left . . . 1981-82 WCHA scoring leader with 49 points in 26 WCHA games (30g, 19a) . . . (March 16, 1983)—Concussion and twisted neck after collision with Bill Hajt in game at Buffalo . . . (February, 1984)—Sprained ankle.

Year	Team	League	Games	G.	A.	Pts.	Pen.
1978-79—University of Denver		WCHA	17	7	5	12	23
1979-80—University of Denver		WCHA	36	13	20	33	24
1980-81—University of Denver		WCHA	39	24	15	39	63
1981-82—University of Denver (a-c)		WCHA	42	50	34	84	59
1981-82—Calgary Flames		NHL	5	1	1	2	21
1982-83—Colorado Flames		CHL	29	12	17	29	52
1982-83—Calgary Flames		NHL	41	11	15	26	21
1983-84—Calgary Flames		NHL	73	36	39	75	88
NHL TOTALS			119	48	55	103	130

(c)—March, 1982—Signed by Calgary Flames as a free agent.

JOHN BEKKERS

Center . . . 6'2" . . . 195 lbs. . . . Born, Halifax, N.S., May 18, 1965 . . . Shoots left.

Year	Team	League	Games	G.	A.	Pts.	Pen.
1982-83—Regina Pats (c)		WHL	70	18	24	42	43
1983-84—Regina Pats		WHL	32	8	1	9	25
1983-84—Portland Winter Hawks		WHL	22	21	14	35	17

(c)—June, 1983—Drafted by Calgary Flames as underage junior in NHL entry draft. Fourth Flames pick, 66th overall, fourth round.

ROGER BELANGER

Right Wing and Center . . . 6' . . . 192 lbs. . . . Born, St. Catharines, Ont., December 1, 1965 . . . Shoots right.

Year	Team	League	Games	G.	A.	Pts.	Pen.
1981-82—London Midgets		Ont. Midget	25	20	21	41	..
1982-83—London Knights		OHL	68	17	14	31	53
1983-84—Kingston Canadians (c)		OHL	67	44	46	90	66

(c)—June, 1984—Drafted by Pittsburgh Penguins in NHL entry draft. Third Penguins pick, 16th overall, first round.

BRUCE BELL

Defense . . . 5'11" . . . 195 lbs. . . . Born, Toronto, Ont., February 15, 1965 . . . Shoots left.

Year	Team	League	Games	G.	A.	Pts.	Pen.
1981-82—Sault Ste. Marie Greyhounds		OHL	67	11	18	29	63
1982-83—Sault Ste. Marie Greyhounds		OHL	5	0	2	2	2
1982-83—Windsor Spitfires (c)		OHL	61	10	35	45	39
1983-84—Brantford Alexanders		OHL	63	7	41	48	55

(c)—June, 1983—Drafted as underage junior by Quebec Nordiques in NHL entry draft. Second Nordiques pick, 52nd overall, third round.

NEIL BELLAND

Defense . . . 5'11" . . . 175 lbs. . . . Born, Parry Sound, Ont., April 3, 1961 . . . Shoots left . . . (February, 1983)—Shoulder separation.

Year	Team	League	Games	G.	A.	Pts.	Pen.
1977-78—North Bay Trappers		OMJHL	49	25	35	60	24
1978-79—Kingston Canadians		OMJHL	64	8	41	49	14
1979-80—Kingston Canadians		OMJHL	54	7	44	51	44
1980-81—Kingston Canadians (c)		OHL	53	28	54	82	45
1981-82—Dallas Black Hawks		CHL	27	2	20	22	18
1981-82—Vancouver Canucks		NHL	28	3	6	9	16
1982-83—Vancouver Canucks		NHL	14	2	4	6	4
1982-83—Fredericton Express		AHL	46	4	17	21	12
1983-84—Vancouver Canucks		NHL	44	7	13	20	24
1983-84—Fredericton Express		AHL	17	3	15	18	2
NHL TOTALS			86	12	23	35	44

(c)—October, 1980—Signed by Vancouver Canucks as a free agent.

BRIAN BELLOWS

Right Wing . . . 6' . . . 196 lbs. . . . Born, St. Catharines, Ont., September 1, 1964 . . . Shoots right . . . Also plays center . . . (November, 1981)—Separated shoulder in game at Niagara Falls. Coached two games while recovering to become the youngest coach in OHL history (17) . . . (January, 1984)—Became youngest team captain in Minnesota North Stars history.

Year	Team	League	Games	G.	A.	Pts.	Pen.
1980-81—Kitchener Rangers		OHL	66	49	67	116	23
1981-82—Kitchener Rangers (a-c)		OHL	47	45	52	97	23
1982-83—Minnesota North Stars		NHL	78	35	30	65	27
1983-84—Minnesota North Stars		NHL	78	41	42	83	66
NHL TOTALS			156	76	72	148	93

(c)—June, 1982—Drafted as underage junior by Minnesota North Stars in NHL entry draft. First North Stars pick, second overall, first round.

BRIAN BENNING

Defense . . . 6' . . . 175 lbs. . . . Born, Edmonton, Alta., June 10, 1966 . . . Shoots left . . . Brother of Jim Benning . . . (December, 1983)—Cracked bone in his right wrist.

Year	Team	League	Games	G.	A.	Pts.	Pen.
1983-84—Portland Winter Hawks (c)		WHL	38	6	41	47	108

(c)—June, 1984—Drafted as underage junior by St. Louis Blues in NHL entry draft. First Blues pick, 26th overall, second round.

JAMES BENNING

Defense . . . 6' . . . 183 lbs. . . . Born, Edmonton, Alta., April 29, 1963 . . . Shoots left . . . Brother of Brian Benning.

Year	Team	League	Games	G.	A.	Pts.	Pen.
1978-79—Ft. Saskatchewan Traders		AJHL	45	14	57	71	10
1979-80—Portland Winter Hawks		WHL	71	11	60	71	42
1980-81—Portland Winter Hawks (a-c-d)		WHL	72	28	*111	139	61
1981-82—Toronto Maple Leafs		NHL	74	7	24	31	46
1982-83—Toronto Maple Leafs		NHL	74	5	17	22	47
1983-84—Toronto Maple Leafs		NHL	79	12	39	51	66
NHL TOTALS			227	24	80	104	159

(c)—Winner of WHL Top Defenseman Trophy.

(d)—June, 1981—Drafted as underage junior by Toronto Maple Leafs in NHL entry draft. First Toronto pick, sixth overall, first round.

GUY BENOIT

Center . . . 5'10" . . . 190 lbs. . . . Born, Ste. Hyacinthe, Que., June 18, 1965 . . . Shoots left . . . (January, 1982)—Strained ligaments in left knee.

Year	Team	League	Games	G.	A.	Pts.	Pen.
1981-82—Richelieu AAA		Que. Midget	40	47	57	104	14
1982-83—Shawinigan Cataracts (c)		QHL	61	42	63	105	10
1983-84—Drummondville Voltigeurs		QHL	61	26	56	82	25

(c)—June, 1983—Drafted as underage junior by Los Angeles Kings in NHL entry draft. Second Kings pick, 67th overall, fourth round.

PERRY BEREZAN

Center . . . 6'1" . . . 180 lbs. . . . Born, Edmonton, Alta., December 25, 1964 . . . Shoots right.

Year	Team	League	Games	G.	A.	Pts.	Pen.
1981-82—St. Albert Saints		AJHL	47	16	36	52	47

Year	Team	League	Games	G.	A.	Pts.	Pen.
1982-83—St. Albert Saints (c)		AJHL	57	37	40	77	110
1983-84—Univ. of North Dakota		WCHA	44	28	24	52	29

(c)—June, 1983—Drafted as underage junior by Calgary Flames in NHL entry draft. Third Flames pick, 55th overall, third round.

TODD BERGEN

Center . . . 6'3" . . . 185 lbs. . . . Born, Prince Albert, Sask., July 11, 1963 . . . Shoots left.

Year	Team	League	Games	G.	A.	Pts.	Pen.
1981-82—Prince Albert Raiders (c)		SJHL	59	30	62	92	35
1982-83—Prince Albert Raiders		WHL	70	34	47	81	17
1983-84—Prince Albert Raiders		WHL	43	57	39	96	15
1983-84—Springfield Indians		AHL	1	0	0	0	0

(c)—June, 1982—Drafted as underage player by Philadelphia Flyers in NHL entry draft. Fifth Flyers pick, 98th overall, fifth round.

JEAN-GUY BERGERON

Defense . . . 5'11" . . . 195 lbs. . . . Born, Montreal, Que., April 14, 1965 . . . Shoots right.

Year	Team	League	Games	G.	A.	Pts.	Pen.
1982-83—Shawinigan Cataracts (c)		QHL	66	1	16	17	59
1983-84—St. Jean Beavers		QHL	71	9	34	43	126

(c)—June, 1983—Drafted as an underage junior by Montreal Canadiens in NHL entry draft. Fourteenth Canadiens pick, 238th overall, 12th round.

MARC BERGEVIN

Defense . . . 6' . . . 185 lbs. . . . Born, Montreal, Que., August 11, 1965 . . . Shoots left.

Year	Team	League	Games	G.	A.	Pts.	Pen.
1982-83—Chicoutimi Sagueneens (c)		QHL	64	3	27	30	113
1983-84—Chicoutimi Sagueneens		QHL	70	10	35	45	125
1983-84—Springfield Indians		AHL	7	0	1	1	2

(c)—June, 1983—Drafted as underage junior by Chicago Black Hawks in NHL entry draft. Third Black Hawks pick, 59th overall, third round.

BOB BERGLOFF

Defense . . . 6'1" . . . 185 lbs. . . . Born, Dickinson, North Dakota, July 26, 1958 . . . Shoots right.

Year	Team	League	Games	G.	A.	Pts.	Pen.
1979-80—University of Minnesota (c)		WCHA	40	9	22	31	54
1980-81—University of Minnesota		WCHA	45	2	16	18	89
1981-82—Nashville South Stars		CHL	74	2	20	22	111
1981-82—Toledo Goaldiggers		IHL	3	1	1	2	11
1982-83—Birmingham South Stars		CHL	78	6	20	26	156
1982-83—Minnesota North Stars		NHL	2	0	0	0	5
1983-84—Salt Lake Golden Eagles		CHL	44	4	17	21	78
NHL TOTALS			2	0	0	0	5

(c)—June, 1978—Drafted by Minnesota North Stars in NHL amateur draft. Sixth North Stars pick, 87th overall, sixth round.

BO BERGLUND

Right Wing . . . 5'10" . . . 175 lbs. . . . Born, Sjalevad, Sweden, April 6, 1955 . . . Shoots left . . . Member of 1980 Swedish Olympic Team (Bronze Medal).

Year	Team	League	Games	G.	A.	Pts.	Pen.
1976-77—MoDo AIK		Sweden	33	17	20	37	30
1977-78—			..	..	..	..	..
1978-79—Djurgardens IF		Sweden	36	23	18	41	46
1979-80—Djurgardens IF		Sweden	36	21	16	37	50
1979-80—Olympics		Sweden	7	1	3	4	4
1980-81—Djurgardens IF		Sweden	31	13	9	22	64
1981.82—Djurgardens IF		Sweden	34	20	17	37	58
1982-83—Djurgardens IF (c)		Sweden	32	19	13	32	..
1983-84—Quebec Nordiques		NHL	75	16	27	43	20
NHL TOTALS			75	16	27	43	20

(c)—June, 1983—Drafted by Quebec Nordiques in NHL entry draft. 11th Nordiques pick, 232nd overall, 12th round.

TIMOTHY BERGLUND

Center ... 6'3" ... 180 lbs. ... Born, Crookston, Minn., January 11, 1965 ... Shoots right.

Year	Team	League	Games	G.	A.	Pts.	Pen.
1982-83	Lincoln High School (c)	Minn. H.S.	20	26	22	48	....
1983-84	Univ. of Minnesota	WCHA	24	4	11	15	4

(c)—June, 1983—Drafted by Washington Capitals as underage junior in NHL entry draft. First Capitals pick, 75th overall, fourth round.

BRAD BERRY

Defense ... 6'2" ... 190 lbs. ... Born, Barshaw, Alta., April 1, 1965 ... Shoots left.

Year	Team	League	Games	G.	A.	Pts.	Pen.
1982-83	St. Albert Junior Saints (c)	AJHL	55	9	33	42	97
1983-84	Univ. of North Dakota	WCHA	32	2	7	9	8

(c)—June, 1983—Drafted as underage junior by Winnipeg Jets in NHL entry draft. Third Jets pick, 29th overall, second round.

FRED BERRY

Center ... 5'10" ... 170 lbs. ... Born, Stoney Plain, Alta., March 26, 1956 ... Shoots left.

Year	Team	League	Games	G.	A.	Pts.	Pen.
1973-74	Merritt Luckies	Jr. "A" BCHL	60	60	76	136	91
1974-75	Victoria Cougars	WCHL	1	0	1	1	0
1974-75	New Westminster Bruins	WCHL	69	32	43	75	120
1975-76	New Westminster Bruins (c)	WCHL	72	59	87	146	164
1976-77	Kalamazoo Wings	IHL	66	17	42	59	146
1976-77	Detroit Red Wings	NHL	3	0	0	0	0
1977-78	Kansas City Red Wings	CHL	65	11	14	25	79
1978-79	Kalamazoo Wings (d)	IHL	19	7	11	18	43
1978-79	Toledo Goaldiggers	IHL	49	27	43	70	91
1979-80	Toledo Goaldiggers	IHL	33	11	29	40	33
1979-80	Milwaukee Admirals	IHL	26	9	22	31	29
1979-80	Hampton Aces	EHL	6	3	4	7	4
1980-81	Milwaukee Admirals	IHL	72	35	71	106	73
1981-82	Milwaukee Admirals (b)	IHL	76	47	65	112	114
1982-83	Milwaukee Admirals	IHL	71	47	74	121	57
1983-84	Milwaukee Admirals	IHL	82	38	58	96	50
NHL TOTALS			3	0	0	0	0

(c)—Drafted from New Westminster Bruins by Detroit Red Wings in third round of 1976 amateur draft.

(d)—December, 1978—Traded with Alan Stoneman and Dean Willers by Kalamazoo Wings to Toledo Goaldiggers for Peter Crawford and Randy Mohns.

KEN E. BERRY

Left Wing ... 5'9" ... 165 lbs. ... Born, Barnaby, B.C., June 21, 1960 ... Shoots left ... Member of 1980 Canadian Olympic Team.

Year	Team	League	Games	G.	A.	Pts.	Pen.
1977-78	New Westminster Bruins	WCHL	5	0	0	0	0
1978-79	Denver University	WCHA	39	17	20	37	52
1979-80	Canadian Olympic Team (c)	Int'l	46	19	19	38	38
1979-80	Olympics		6	4	1	5	8
1980-81	Denver University (a-d)	WCHA	40	22	34	56	84
1980-81	Wichita Wind (e)	CHL	9	7	6	13	13
1981-82	Edmonton Oilers	NHL	15	2	3	5	9
1981-82	Wichita Wind	CHL	58	28	29	57	70
1982-83	Moncton Alpines	AHL	76	24	26	50	80
1983-84	Moncton Alpines	AHL	53	18	20	38	75
1983-84	Edmonton Oilers	NHL	13	2	3	5	10
NHL TOTALS			28	4	6	10	19

(c)—June, 1980—Drafted by Vancouver Canucks in NHL entry draft. Fifth Canucks pick, 112th overall, sixth round.

(d)—March, 1981—NHL rights traded with Garry Lariviere by Vancouver Canucks to Edmonton Oilers for Blair MacDonald.

(e)—March, 1981—Signed by Edmonton Oilers.

BRIAN BERTUZZI

Center ... 5'11" ... 175 lbs. ... Born, Vancouver, B.C., January 24, 1966 ... Shoots left.

Year	Team	League	Games	G.	A.	Pts.	Pen.
1983-84	Kamloops Junior Oilers (c)	WHL	69	29	21	50	99

(c)—June, 1984—Drafted as underage junior by Vancouver Canucks in NHL entry draft. Fifth Canucks pick, 73rd overall, fourth round.

JEFF BEUKEBOOM

Defense . . . 6'4" . . . 210 lbs. . . . Born, Ajax, Ont., March 28, 1965 . . . Shoots right . . . Brother of John Beukeboom and Brian Beukeboom. Nephew of Ed Kea (Atlanta/St. Louis, '73-'83) . . . First non-goalie to be drafted in first round not to have scored a goal in season prior to being drafted.

Year	Team	League	Games	G.	A.	Pts.	Pen.
1981-82—Newmarket		OPJHL	49	5	30	35	218
1982-83—Sault Ste. Marie Greyhounds (c)		OHL	70	0	25	25	143
1983-84—Sault Ste. Marie Greyhounds		OHL	61	6	30	36	178

(c)—June, 1983—Drafted as underage junior by Edmonton Oilers in NHL entry draft. First Oilers pick, 19th overall, first round.

JOHN BEUKEBOOM

Right Wing and Defense . . . 6'2" . . . 195 lbs. . . . Born, Ajax, Ont., January 1, 1961 . . . Shoots left . . . (February, 1981)—Bruised knee . . . Brother of Jeff Beukeboom and Brian Beukeboom. Nephew of Ed Kea (Atlanta/St. Louis, '73-'83).

Year	Team	League	Games	G.	A.	Pts.	Pen.
1978-79—Peterborough Petes		OMJHL	65	3	15	18	132
1979-80—Peterborough Petes (c)		OMJHL	61	12	23	35	115
1980-81—Peterborough Petes		OHL	58	11	35	46	189
1981-82—Adirondack Red Wings		AHL	59	2	10	12	123
1982-83—Adirondack Red Wings		AHL	72	3	14	17	157
1983-84—Adirondack Red Wings		AHL	16	2	2	4	66
1983-84—Montana Magic		CHL	59	6	26	32	166

(c)—June, 1980—Drafted as underage junior by Detroit Red Wings in NHL entry draft. Sixth Red Wings pick, 151st overall, eighth round.

RICHARD TODD BIDNER
(Known by middle name.)

Left Wing . . . 6'2" . . . 205 lbs. . . . Born, Petrolia, Ont., July 5, 1961 . . . Shoots left . . . (November, 1981)—Broken leg.

Year	Team	League	Games	G.	A.	Pts.	Pen.
1977-78—Petrolia Jr. B (c)		OPJHL	44	10	33	43	50
1978-79—Toronto Marlboros		OMJHL	64	10	12	22	64
1979-80—Toronto Marlboros (d)		OMJHL	68	22	26	48	69
1980-81—Toronto Marlboros		OHL	67	34	43	77	124
1980-81—Hershey Bears		AHL	1	0	0	0	0
1981-82—Washington Capitals (e)		NHL	12	2	1	3	7
1981-82—Hershey Bears		AHL	30	6	12	18	28
1981-82—Wichita Wind		CHL	15	2	9	11	17
1982-83—Moncton Alpines		AHL	59	15	12	27	64
1983-84—Moncton Alpines		AHL	60	17	16	33	75
NHL TOTALS			12	2	1	3	7

(c)—Fourth Toronto Marlboros pick in 1978 OMJHL Midget Draft.

(d)—June, 1980—Drafted as underage junior by Washington Capitals in NHL entry draft. Fifth Capitals pick, 110th overall, sixth round.

(e)—March, 1982—Traded by Washington Capitals to Edmonton Oilers for Doug Hicks.

DON BIGGS

Center . . . 5'8" . . . 180 lbs. . . . Born, Mississauga, Ont., April 7, 1965 . . . Shoots right . . . (April, 1982)—Injured knee ligaments.

Year	Team	League	Games	G.	A.	Pts.	Pen.
1981-82—Mississauga Reds		MTHL	54	49	67	116	125
1982-83—Oshawa Generals (c)		OHL	70	22	53	75	145
1983-84—Oshawa Generals		OHL	58	31	60	91	149

(c)—June, 1983—Drafted as underage junior by Minnesota North Stars in NHL entry draft. Ninth North Stars pick, 156th overall, eighth round.

SCOT BIRNIE

Right Wing . . . 6'1" . . . 190 lbs. . . . Born, Kingston, Ont., May 1, 1965 . . . Shoots right.

Year	Team	League	Games	G.	A.	Pts.	Pen.
1981-82—Brockville Braves		OPJHL	46	10	22	32	145
1982-83—Cornwall Royals (c)		OHL	63	15	13	28	87
1983-84—Cornwall Royals		OHL	5	2	1	3	12
1983-84—North Bay Centennials		OHL	59	10	24	34	108

(c)—June, 1983—Drafted as underage junior by Chicago Black Hawks in NHL entry draft. Eighth Black Hawks pick, 139th overall, seventh round.

ALLEN BISHOP

Defense . . . 6'2" . . . 205 lbs. . . . Born, Sudbury, Ont., March 19, 1964 . . . Shoots left . . . (January, 1980)—Fractured left shoulder.

Year	Team	League	Games	G.	A.	Pts.	Pen.
1980-81—Onaping Falls (c)	NOHL	36	22	41	63	..
1981-82—Niagara Falls Flyers (d)	OHL	57	6	22	28	78
1982-83—North Bay Centennials	OHL	63	7	30	37	116
1983-84—North Bay Centennials	OHL	14	0	8	8	8
1983-84—Kingston Canadians	OHL	48	8	34	42	103

        (c)—Selected by Niagara Falls Flyers in 1981 OHL Priority Draft. Third Flyers pick, 48th overall, fourth round.
        (d)—June, 1982—Drafted as underage junior by Buffalo Sabres in NHL entry draft. Eleventh Sabres pick, 142nd overall, seventh round.

WAYNE HAROLD BISHOP

Defense . . . 6'1" . . . 190 lbs. . . . Born, Toronto, Ont., October 12, 1960 . . . Shoots right.

Year	Team	League	Games	G.	A.	Pts.	Pen.
1977-78—London Knights	OMJHL	65	3	8	11	27
1978-79—London Knights	OMJHL	66	7	20	27	67
1979-80—London Knights	OMJHL	66	2	21	23	91
1980-81—Ft. Worth Texans (c)	CHL	75	3	11	14	62
1981-82—Ft. Worth Texans	CHL	75	3	10	13	58
1982-83—Ft. Wayne Komets	IHL	81	5	16	21	162
1983-84—Ft. Wayne Komets	IHL	79	3	19	22	130

        (c)—October, 1980—Signed by Colorado Rockies as free agent.

JAMES F. BISSETT

Center . . . 5'9" . . . 175 lbs. . . . Born, Seattle, Wash., August 15, 1959 . . . Shoots left.

Year	Team	League	Games	G.	A.	Pts.	Pen.
1980-81—Michigan Tech	WCHA	41	7	9	16	49
1981-82—Michigan Tech	CCHA	31	3	14	17	34
1982-83—Michigan Tech	CCHA	37	27	28	55	54
1983-84—Toledo Goaldiggers (c)	IHL	79	37	49	86	73

        (c)—Shared IHL playoff point lead with Jeff Pyle, Lawrie Nisker and Kevin Conway with 15 points; and shared IHL playoff assist lead with Lawrie Nisker and Kevin Conway with 10 assists.

KIRT BJORK

Center . . . 5'9" . . . 170 lbs. . . . Born, Ann Arbor, Mich., March 5, 1961 . . . Shoots left . . . Also plays left wing.

Year	Team	League	Games	G.	A.	Pts.	Pen.
1979-80—Notre Dame University	WCHA	35	6	13	19	22
1980-81—Notre Dame University	WCHA	36	19	16	35	38
1981-82—Notre Dame University	CCHA	35	22	22	44	26
1982-83—Notre Dame University (b-c)	CCHA	35	29	34	63	26
1983-84—Adirondack Red Wings	AHL	7	1	3	4	4

        (c)—Named to All-America Team (West).

JOHN BJORKMAN

Center . . . 6'1" . . . 180 lbs. . . . Born, Dover, N.H., July 14, 1964 . . . Shoots left.

Year	Team	League	Games	G.	A.	Pts.	Pen.
1982-83—Warroad H.S. (c)	Minn. H.S.	22	30	18	48	....
1983-84—Univ. of Michigan	CCHA	36	9	12	21	33

        (c)—June, 1983—Drafted by New York Islanders in NHL entry draft. Thirteenth Islanders pick, 217th overall, 11th round.

SCOTT BJUGSTAD

Center . . . 6'1" . . . 185 lbs. . . . Born St. Paul, Minn., June 2, 1981 . . . Shoots left . . . 1979 graduate of Minnesota Irondale High School where he was All-Conference for three years and All-State as a senior . . . Named prep All-America in Soccer . . . Member of 1984 U.S. Olympic Team.

Year	Team	League	Games	G.	A.	Pts.	Pen.
1979-80—University of Minnesota	WCHA	18	2	2	4	2
1980-81—University of Minnesota (c)	WCHA	35	12	13	25	34
1981-82—University of Minnesota	WCHA	36	29	14	43	24
1982-83—University of Minnesota	WCHA	44	43	48	91	30
1983-84—U.S. National Team	Int'l	54	31	20	51	28
1983-84—U.S. Olympic Team	Int'l	6	3	2	5	6

Year	Team	League	Games	G.	A.	Pts.	Pen.
1983-84—Minnesota North Stars		NHL	5	0	0	0	2
1983-84—Salt Lake Golden Eagles		CHL	15	10	8	18	6
NHL TOTALS			5	0	0	0	2

(c)—June, 1981—Drafted by Minnesota North Stars in NHL entry draft. Thirteenth North Stars pick, 181st overall, ninth round.

MICHAEL WALTER BLAISDELL

Right Wing . . . 6'1" . . . 196 lbs. . . . Born, Moose Jaw, Sask., January 18, 1960 . . . Shoots right.

Year	Team	League	Games	G.	A.	Pts.	Pen.
1977-78—Regina Pats		WCHL	6	5	5	10	2
1977-78—Regina Blues		SJHL	60	70	46	116	43
1978-79—University of Wisconsin		WCHA	20	7	1	8	15
1979-80—Regina Pats (b-c)		WHL	63	71	38	109	62
1980-81—Adirondack Red Wings		AHL	41	10	4	14	8
1980-81—Detroit Red Wings		NHL	32	3	6	9	10
1981-82—Detroit Red Wings		NHL	80	23	32	55	48
1982-83—Detroit Red Wings (d)		NHL	80	18	23	41	22
1983-84—Tulsa Oilers		CHL	32	10	8	18	23
1983-84—New York Rangers		NHL	36	5	6	11	31
NHL TOTALS			228	49	67	116	111

(c)—June, 1980—Drafted by Detroit Red Wings in NHL entry draft. First Red Wings pick, 11th overall, first round.

(d)—June, 1983—Traded with Mark Osborne and Willie Huber by Detroit Red Wings to New York Rangers for Ron Duguay, Eddie Johnstone and Eddie Mio.

TIMO BLOMQVIST

Defense . . . 6' . . . 198 lbs. . . . Born, Helsinki, Finland, January 23, 1961 . . . Shoots right . . . (September, 1981)—Broken jaw during exhibition series in Finland . . . (October, 1983)— Ankle injury.

Year	Team	League	Games	G.	A.	Pts.	Pen.
1978-79—Jokerit Helsinki		Finland	36	4	2	6	35
1979-80—Jokerit Helsinki		Finland	32	3	1	4	52
1980-81—Kiekkoreipas Lahti (c)		Finland	30	6	7	13	14
1981-82—Hershey Bears		AHL	13	0	8	8	13
1981-82—Washington Capitals		NHL	44	1	11	12	62
1982-83—Hershey Bears		AHL	8	2	7	9	16
1982-83—Washington Capitals		NHL	61	1	17	18	67
1983-84—Washington Capitals		NHL	65	1	19	20	84
NHL TOTALS			170	3	47	50	213

(c)—June, 1980—Drafted by Washington Capitals in NHL entry draft. Fourth Capitals pick, 89th overall, fifth round.

JOHN BLUM

Defense . . . 6'3" . . . 205 lbs. . . . Born, Minneapolis, Minn., October 8, 1959 . . . Shoots right.

Year	Team	League	Games	G.	A.	Pts.	Pen.
1980-81—University of Michigan		WCHA	....	8	32	40	....
1981-82—Wichita Wind (c)		CHL	79	8	33	41	247
1982-83—Moncton Alpines		AHL	76	10	30	40	219
1982-83—Edmonton Oilers		NHL	5	0	3	3	24
1983-84—Moncton Alpines		AHL	57	3	22	25	202
1983-84—Edmonton Oilers (d)		NHL	4	0	1	1	2
1983-84—Boston Bruins		NHL	12	1	1	2	30
NHL TOTALS			21	1	5	6	56

(c)—May, 1981—Signed by Edmonton Oilers as a free agent.

(d)—March, 1983—Traded by Edmonton Oilers to Boston Bruins for Larry Melnyk.

STEVEN BLYTH

Defense . . . 6'3" . . . 200 lbs. . . . Born, Calgary, Alta., July 16, 1960 . . . Shoots left.

Year	Team	League	Games	G.	A.	Pts.	Pen.
1982-83—Springfield Indians (c)		AHL	73	2	12	14	152
1983-84—Springfield Indians		AHL	77	4	20	24	112

(c)—October, 1983—Signed by Chicago Black Hawks as a free agent.

DOUG BODGER

Defense ... 6'2" ... 200 lbs. ... Born, Chemainus, B.C., June 18, 1966 ... Shoots left.

Year	Team	League	Games	G.	A.	Pts.	Pen.
1982-83—Kamloops Junior Oilers (b)		WHL	72	26	66	92	98
1983-84—Kamloops Junior Oilers (a-c)		WHL	70	21	77	98	90

(c)—June, 1984—Drafted as underage junior by Pittsburgh Penguins in NHL entry draft. Second Penguins pick, ninth overall, first round.

DWAYNE BOETTGER

Defense ... 6'1" ... 190 lbs. ... Born, Brampton, Ont., February 6, 1963 ... Shoots left.

Year	Team	League	Games	G.	A.	Pts.	Pen.
1980-81—Markham Tier II		OPJHL	26	3	5	8	61
1981-82—Toronto Marlboros (c)		OHL	66	4	21	25	138
1982-83—Toronto Marlboros		OHL	68	3	15	18	120
1983-84—Moncton Alpines		AHL	75	1	18	19	160

(c)—June, 1982—Drafted as underage junior by Edmonton Oilers in NHL entry draft. Fifth Oilers pick, 104th overall, fifth round.

FRED BOIMISTRUCK

Defense ... 5'11" ... 190 lbs. ... Born, Sudbury, Ont., January 14, 1962 ... Shoots right.

Year	Team	League	Games	G.	A.	Pts.	Pen.
1979-80—Cornwall Royals (c)		QMJHL	70	12	34	46	99
1980-81—Cornwall Royals (a-d)		QMJHL	68	22	48	70	158
1981-82—Toronto Maple Leafs		NHL	57	2	11	13	32
1982-83—St. Catharines Saints		AHL	50	6	23	29	32
1982-83—Toronto Maple Leafs		NHL	26	2	3	5	13
1983-84—St. Catharines Saints		AHL	80	2	28	30	68
NHL TOTALS			83	4	14	18	45

(c)—June, 1980—Drafted as underage junior by Toronto Maple Leafs in NHL entry draft. Third Maple Leafs pick, 43rd overall, third round.
(d)—Winner of Emile "Butch" Bouchard Trophy (Top QMJHL Defenseman).

SERGE BOISVERT

Center ... 5'9" ... 175 lbs. ... Born, Drummondville, Que., June 1, 1959 ... Shoots right ... Also plays right wing.

Year	Team	League	Games	G.	A.	Pts.	Pen.
1977-78—Sherbrooke Beavers		QMJHL	55	17	33	50	19
1978-79—Sherbrooke Beavers		QMJHL	72	50	72	122	45
1979-80—Sherbrooke Beavers		QMJHL	69	52	72	124	47
1979-80—New Brunswick Hawks (c)		AHL	..	..	..	..	..
1980-81—New Brunswick Hawks		AHL	60	19	27	46	31
1981-82—		...	..	..	..	..	..
1982-83—Toronto Maple Leafs (d)		NHL	17	0	2	2	4
1982-83—St. Catharines Saints		AHL	19	10	9	19	2
1982-83—Moncton Alpines		AHL	29	6	12	18	7
1983-84—Moncton Alpines		AHL	66	15	13	28	34
NHL TOTALS			17	0	2	2	4

(c)—No regular season record. Scored four goals in seven playoff games.
(d)—January, 1983—Traded by Toronto Maple Leafs to Edmonton Oilers for Reid Bailey.

MICHAEL JOHN BOLAND

Defense ... 6' ... 190 lbs. ... Born, London, Ont., October 29, 1954 ... Shoots right.

Year	Team	League	Games	G.	A.	Pts.	Pen.
1972-73—Sault Ste. Marie Greyhounds		OMJHL	55	4	15	19	139
1973-74—S. Ste. Marie Greyhounds (c)		OMJHL	67	11	39	50	200
1974-75—Port Huron Flags		IHL	71	2	12	14	172
1975-76—Port Huron Flags		IHL	75	8	16	24	208
1976-77—Port Huron Flags		IHL	66	7	37	44	306
1977-78—Port Huron Flags (d)		IHL	2	0	0	0	4
1977-78—Fort Wayne Komets		IHL	74	7	39	46	228
1978-79—Hershey Bears		AHL	46	3	17	20	86
1978-79—Buffalo Sabres (e)		NHL	22	1	2	3	29
1979-80—Rochester Americans		AHL	80	4	28	32	178
1980-81—Rochester Americans		AHL	5	0	1	1	8
1980-81—Salt Lake Golden Eagles (f)		CHL	69	5	21	26	188
1981-82—Salt Lake Golden Eagles		CHL	64	1	13	14	161

Year	Team	League	Games	G.	A.	Pts.	Pen.
1982-83—Hershey Bears		AHL	57	0	11	11	68
1983-84—Fort Wayne Komets		IHL	81	8	49	57	161
NHL TOTALS			22	1	2	3	29

(c)—Drafted by Kansas City Scouts in 1974 amateur draft. Seventh Scout pick, 110th overall, seventh round.

(d)—October, 1977—Traded by Port Huron Flags to Fort Wayne Komets for Dave Faulkner.

(e)—September, 1978—Signed by Buffalo Sabres as a free agent.

(f)—Led CHL Playoffs with 70 penalty minutes.

IVAN BOLDIREV

Center . . . 6'1" . . . 195 lbs. . . . Born, Zranjanin, Yugoslavia, August 15, 1949 . . . Shoots left . . . Missed part of 1972-73 season with torn knee ligaments. . . (December, 1980)—Fractured cheekbone.

Year	Team	League	Games	G.	A.	Pts.	Pen.
1966-67—Sault Greyhounds	Jr. "A" NOHA	40	26	42	68	35
1967-68—Oshawa Generals	Jr. "A" OHA	50	18	26	44	76
1968-69—Oshawa Generals (c)	Jr. "A" OHA	54	25	34	59	101
1969-70—Oklahoma City Blazers	CHL	65	18	49	67	114
1970-71—Oklahoma City Blazers (b)	CHL	68	19	52	71	98
1970-71—Boston Bruins	NHL	2	0	0	0	0
1971-72—Boston Bruins (d)	NHL	11	0	2	2	6
1971-72—California Golden Seals	NHL	57	16	23	39	54
1972-73—California Golden Seals	NHL	56	11	23	34	58
1973-74—California Golden Seals (e)	NHL	78	25	31	56	22
1974-75—Chicago Black Hawks	NHL	80	24	43	67	54
1975-76—Chicago Black Hawks	NHL	78	28	34	62	33
1976-77—Chicago Black Hawks	NHL	80	24	38	62	40
1977-78—Chicago Black Hawks	NHL	80	35	45	80	34
1978-79—Chicago Black Hawks (f)	NHL	66	29	35	64	25
1978-79—Atlanta Flames	NHL	13	6	8	14	6
1979-80—Atlanta Flames (g)	NHL	52	16	24	40	20
1979-80—Vancouver Canucks	NHL	27	16	11	27	14
1980-81—Vancouver Canucks	NHL	72	26	33	59	34
1981-82—Vancouver Canucks	NHL	78	33	40	73	45
1982-83—Vancouver Canucks (h)	NHL	39	5	20	25	12
1982-83—Detroit Red Wings	NHL	33	13	17	30	14
1983-84—Detroit Red Wings	NHL	75	35	48	83	20
NHL TOTALS		977	342	475	817	491

(c)—Drafted from Oshawa Generals by Boston Bruins in first round of 1969 amateur draft.

(d)—Traded to California Golden Seals by Boston Bruins for Chris Oddleifson and player to be named (Richard Leduc), November, 1971.

(e)—Traded to Chicago Black Hawks by California Golden Seals for Len Frig and Mike Christie, May, 1974.

(f)—March, 1979—Traded with Phil Russell and Darcy Rota to Atlanta Flames by Chicago Black Hawks for Tom Lysiak, Harold Phillipoff, Pat Ribble, Greg Fox and Miles Zaharko.

(g)—February, 1980—Traded with Darcy Rota by Atlanta Flames to Vancouver Canucks for Don Lever and Brad Smith.

(h)—January, 1983—Traded by Vancouver Canucks to Detroit Red Wings for Mark Kirton.

DANIEL GEORGE BOLDUC

Right Wing . . . 5'9" . . . 180 lbs. . . . Born, Waterville, Maine, April 6, 1953 . . . Shoots left . . . Attended Harvard University . . . Member of U.S.A. Olympic Team in 1976 . . . Missed part of 1972-73 season with knee injury.

Year	Team	League	Games	G.	A.	Pts.	Pen.
1972-73—Harvard University (freshmen)		13	15	17	32	17
1973-74—Harvard University	ECAC	29	15	9	24	24
1974-75—Harvard University	ECAC	29	13	11	24	18
1975-76—U.S. National Team	Int'l	60	41	31	72	54
1975-76—U.S. Olympic Team	Int'l	6	2	0	2	6
1975-76—New England Whalers	WHA	14	2	5	7	14
1976-77—Rhode Island Reds	AHL	44	11	22	33	23
1976-77—New England Whalers	WHA	33	8	3	11	15
1977-78—Springfield Indians	AHL	35	14	9	23	35
1977-78—New England Whalers	WHA	41	5	5	10	22
1978-79—Detroit Red Wings	NHL	56	16	13	29	14
1978-79—Kansas City Red Wings	CHL	23	21	11	32	11
1979-80—Detroit Red Wings	NHL	44	6	5	11	19
1979-80—Adirondack Red Wings	AHL	13	1	3	4	4

Year	Team	League	Games	G.	A.	Pts.	Pen.
1980-81—Adirondack Red Wings		AHL	77	23	25	48	58
1981-82—Nova Scotia Voyageurs (c)		AHL	74	39	40	79	60
1982-83—Colorado Flames (b-d)		CHL	79	27	45	72	39
1983-84—Calgary Flames		NHL	2	0	1	1	0
1983-84—Colorado Flames		CHL	60	37	17	54	34
WHA TOTALS			88	15	13	28	51
NHL TOTALS			102	22	19	41	33

(c)—October, 1981—Signed by Montreal Canadiens as free agent and assigned to Nova Scotia.
(d)—September, 1982—Signed by Calgary Flames as a free agent.

MICHEL BOLDUC

Defense . . . 6'2" . . . 210 lbs. . . . Born, Ange-Gardien, Que., March 13, 1961 . . . Shoots left.

Year	Team	League	Games	G.	A.	Pts.	Pen.
1977-78—Hull Festivals		QMJHL	60	1	5	6	36
1978-79—Hull Olympics		QMJHL	6	0	1	1	5
1978-79—Chicoutimi Sagueneens		QMJHL	66	1	23	24	142
1979-80—Chicoutimi Sagueneens (c)		QMJHL	65	3	29	32	219
1980-81—Chicoutimi Sagueneens		QMJHL	67	11	35	46	244
1981-82—Quebec Nordiques		NHL	3	0	0	0	0
1981-82—Fredericton Express		AHL	69	4	9	13	130
1982-83—Fredericton Express		AHL	68	4	18	22	165
1982-83—Quebec Nordiques		NHL	7	0	0	0	6
1983-84—Fredericton Express		AHL	70	2	15	17	96
NHL TOTALS			10	0	0	0	6

(c)—June, 1980—Drafted as underage junior by Quebec Nordiques in NHL entry draft. Sixth Nordiques pick, 150th overall, eighth round.

DAN BONAR

Center . . . 5'9" . . . 175 lbs. . . . Born, Deloraine, Man., September 23, 1956 . . . Shoots right . . . (October 12, 1982)—Dislocated left elbow in game at Winnipeg, missed 30 games.

Year	Team	League	Games	G.	A.	Pts.	Pen.
1973-74—Portage Terriers		MJHL	48	39	41	80	81
1974-75—Brandon Wheat Kings		WCHL	70	43	41	84	62
1975-76—Brandon Wheat Kings		WCHL	69	44	59	103	49
1976-77—Brandon Wheat Kings		WCHL	72	75	50	125	70
1977-78—Fort Wayne Komets (a-c-d)		IHL	79	47	61	108	43
1978-79—Springfield Indians (e)		AHL	80	33	39	72	30
1979-80—Binghamton Dusters		AHL	64	29	32	61	91
1980-81—Los Angeles Kings		NHL	71	11	15	26	57
1981-82—Los Angeles Kings		NHL	79	13	23	36	111
1982-83—New Haven Nighthawks		AHL	22	10	13	23	29
1982-83—Los Angeles Kings		NHL	20	1	1	2	40
1983-84—New Haven Nighthawks (f)		AHL	35	9	14	23	27
1983-84—Nova Scotia Voyageurs		AHL	44	14	23	37	75
NHL TOTALS			170	25	39	64	208

(c)—Won Garry F. Longman Memorial Trophy (rookie-of-the-year).
(d)—Won James Gatschene Memorial Trophy (Most Valuable Player).
(e)—August, 1978—Signed by Los Angeles Kings as free agent.
(f)—December, 1983—Traded by Los Angeles Kings to Montreal Canadiens for John Goodwin.

GRAEME BONAR

Right Wing . . . 6'3" . . . 205 lbs. . . . Born, Toronto, Ont., January 21, 1966 . . . Shoots right.

Year	Team	League	Games	G.	A.	Pts.	Pen.
1981-82—Henry Carr H.S.		MTJHL	35	27	24	51	32
1982-83—Windsor Spitfires		OHL	70	14	26	40	78
1983-84—Windsor Spitfires		OHL	21	5	9	14	37
1983-84—Sault Ste. Marie Greyhounds (c)		OHL	44	10	30	40	43

(c)—June, 1984—Drafted as underage junior by Montreal Canadiens in NHL entry draft. Fifth Canadiens pick, 54th overall, third round.

LUCIANO BORSATO

Center . . . 5'10" . . . 165 lbs. . . . Born, Richmond Hill, Ont., January 7, 1966 . . . Shoots right.

Year	Team	League	Games	G.	A.	Pts.	Pen.
1983-84—Bramalea Blues (c)		MTJHL	37	20	36	56	59

(c)—June, 1984—Drafted as underage junior by Winnipeg Jets in NHL entry draft. Seventh Jets pick, 135th overall, seventh round.

LAURIE JOSEPH BOSCHMAN

Center ... 6' ... 185 lbs. ... Born, Major, Sask., June 4, 1960 ... Shoots left ... (December 7, 1980)—Finger tendon injury ... (January, 1981)—Mononucleous ... (December 7, 1983)—Dislocated shoulder in game at New Jersey.

Year	Team	League	Games	G.	A.	Pts.	Pen.
1976-77	Brandon	MJHL	47	17	40	57	139
1976-77	Brandon Wheat Kings	WCHL	3	0	1	1	0
1977-78	Brandon Wheat Kings	WCHL	72	42	57	99	227
1978-79	Brandon Wheat Kings (a-c)	WCHL	65	66	83	149	215
1979-80	Toronto Maple Leafs	NHL	80	16	32	48	78
1980-81	New Brunswick Hawks	AHL	4	4	1	5	47
1980-81	Toronto Maple Leafs	NHL	53	14	19	33	178
1981-82	Toronto Maple Leafs (d)	NHL	54	9	19	28	150
1981-82	Edmonton Oilers	NHL	11	2	3	5	37
1982-83	Edmonton Oilers (e)	NHL	62	8	12	20	183
1982-83	Winnipeg Jets	NHL	12	3	5	8	33
1983-84	Winnipeg Jets	NHL	61	28	46	74	234
	NHL TOTALS		333	80	136	216	893

(c)—August, 1979—Drafted by Toronto Maple Leafs in NHL entry draft. First Toronto pick, ninth overall, first round.

(d)—March, 1982—Traded by Toronto Maple Leafs to Edmonton Oilers for Walt Poddubny and Phil Drouillard.

(e)—March, 1983—Traded by Edmonton Oilers to Winnipeg Jets for Willy Lindstrom.

MICHEL (MIKE) BOSSY

Right Wing ... 6' ... 186 lbs. ... Born, Montreal, Que., January 22, 1957 ... Shoots right ... Set NHL record for goals in season by a rookie—53 in 1977-78 ... Set NHL record for fastest 100 goals (129 games) ... Tied NHL record with goals in 10 straight games 1977-78 (Since broken by Charlie Simmer)... Tied NHL record of Rocket Richard for fastest 50 goals (in 50 games) 1980-81 (Since broken by Wayne Gretzky) ... Set record for most goals in regular season plus playoffs (85) 1980-81 (Since broken by Wayne Gretzky) ... Set record for most points in a playoff year (35) 1981 (Since broken by Wayne Gretzky) ... Set record for most hat tricks in one season (9) 1980-81 (Since broken by Wayne Gretzky) ... Set NHL record for fastest 250 goals (315 games) ... Set record for most goals (69) by a right wing 1978-79 ... Set record for most assists by a right wing (83) 1981-82 ... Set record for most points by a right wing (147) 1981-82 ... Injured left knee during 1983 Playoffs ... (October, 1983)—Pulled hip muscle ... (January 28, 1984)—Sprained right knee in collision with Dwight Foster during third period of game vs. Detroit ... First NHL player to have seven consecutive 50-goal seasons.

Year	Team	League	Games	G.	A.	Pts.	Pen.
1972-73	Laval National	QJHL	4	1	2	3	0
1973-74	Laval National	QJHL	68	70	48	118	45
1974-75	Laval National (a)	QJHL	67	*84	65	149	42
1975-76	Laval National (b)	QJHL	64	79	57	136	25
1976-77	Laval National (b-c-d)	QJHL	61	75	51	126	12
1977-78	New York Islanders (b-e)	NHL	73	53	38	91	6
1978-79	New York Islanders (b)	NHL	80	*69	57	126	25
1979-80	New York Islanders	NHL	75	51	41	92	12
1980-81	New York Islanders (a-f)	NHL	79	*68	51	119	32
1981-82	New York Islanders (a-g-h)	NHL	80	64	83	147	22
1982-83	New York Islanders (a-h-i)	NHL	79	60	58	118	20
1983-84	New York Islanders (a-i)	NHL	67	51	67	118	8
	NHL TOTALS		533	416	395	811	125

(c)—Most Gentlemanly Player Award winner.

(d)—Drafted from Laval National by New York Islanders in first round of 1977 amateur draft.

(e)—Won Calder Memorial Trophy and named THE SPORTING NEWS NHL Rookie of the Year.

(f)—Tied with Steve Payne (Minn.) for playoff lead in goals (17), tied Bryan Trottier (NYI) for playoff lead in assists (18) and led 1981 playoffs with 35 points.

(g)—Won Conn Smythe Trophy (Most Valuable Player in Stanley Cup Playoffs).

(h)—Led Stanley Cup Playoffs with 17 goals.

(i)—Won Lady Byng Trophy (Combination of Sportsmanship and Quality play).

MARK BOTELL

Defense ... 6'4" ... 220 lbs. ... Born, Scarborough, Ont., August 27, 1961 ... Shoots left.

Year	Team	League	Games	G.	A.	Pts.	Pen.
1978-79	Niagara Falls Flyers	OMJHL	55	2	8	10	122
1979-80	Niagara Falls Flyers	OMJHL	20	2	5	7	11
1979-80	Windsor Spitfires	OMJHL	2	0	0	0	2
1979-80	Brantford Alexanders (c)	OMJHL	15	2	3	5	24

Year	Team	League	Games	G.	A.	Pts.	Pen.
1980-81—Brantford Alexanders		OHL	58	11	20	31	143
1980-81—Maine Mariners		AHL	2	0	1	1	0
1981-82—Maine Mariners		AHL	42	3	14	17	41
1981-82—Philadelphia Flyers		NHL	32	4	10	14	31
1982-83—Maine Mariners		AHL	30	1	4	5	26
1982-83—Toledo Goaldiggers		IHL	24	6	14	20	43
1983-84—Montana Magic		CHL	2	0	0	0	2
1983-84—Toledo Goaldiggers		IHL	78	16	27	43	164
NHL TOTALS			32	4	10	14	31

(c)—June, 1980—Drafted as underage junior by Philadelphia Flyers in NHL entry draft. Eighth Flyers pick, 168th overall, eighth round.

TIM BOTHWELL

Defense . . . 6'3" . . . 195 lbs. . . . Born, Vancouver, B.C., May 6, 1955 . . . Shoots left . . . Attended Brown University . . . Missed part of 1974-75 season with broken ankle . . . Missed part of 1978-79 season with fractured cheekbone that required surgery . . . (October, 1981)—Badly strained stomach muscles . . . (March 1, 1983)—Cut tendons in left hand in game vs. Los Angeles . . . (January, 1984)—Injured ligament in right knee during CHL game.

Year	Team	League	Games	G.	A.	Pts.	Pen.
1973-74—Burlington Mohawks		....	..		..		..	..
1974-75—Brown University JV		ECAC	9	6	9	15	14
1975-76—Brown University		ECAC	29	12	22	34	30
1976-77—Brown University (a)		ECAC	27	7	27	34	40
1977-78—Brown University (a-c)		ECAC	29	9	26	35	48
1978-79—New York Rangers		NHL	1	0	0	0	2
1978-79—New Haven Nighthawks		AHL	66	15	33	48	44
1979-80—New Haven Nighthawks		AHL	22	6	7	13	25
1979-80—New York Rangers		NHL	45	4	6	10	20
1980-81—New Haven Nighthawks		AHL	73	10	53	63	98
1980-81—New York Rangers		NHL	3	0	1	1	0
1981-82—Springfield Indians		AHL	10	0	4	4	7
1981-82—New York Rangers (d)		NHL	13	0	3	3	10
1982-83—St. Louis Blues		NHL	61	4	11	15	34
1983-84—Montana Magic		CHL	4	0	3	3	0
1983-84—St. Louis Blues		NHL	62	2	13	15	65
NHL TOTALS			185	10	34	44	131

(c)—Signed by New York Rangers, May, 1978.
(d)—October, 1982—Claimed by St. Louis Blues in NHL waiver draft.

BRUCE ALLAN BOUDREAU

Center . . . 5'10" . . . 170 lbs. . . . Born, Toronto, Ont., January 9, 1955 . . . Shoots left . . . Set OMJHL record with 165 pts. in '74-75 (Broken in '75-76 by Mike Kaszycki's 170 pts.) . . . Set OMJHL record with 68 goals in '74-75 (Broken in '77-78 by Bobby Smith's 69) . . . (1983-84)—Assistant coach at St. Catharines.

Year	Team	League	Games	G.	A.	Pts.	Pen.
1972-73—Toronto Marlboros		Jr."A"OHA	61	38	49	87	22
1973-74—Toronto Marlboros (b-c)		Jr."A"OHA	53	46	67	113	51
1974-75—Toronto Marlboros (d-e)		Jr."A"OHA	69	*68	97	*165	52
1975-76—Johnstown Jets		NAHL	34	25	35	60	14
1975-76—Minnesota Fighting Saints (f)		WHA	30	3	6	9	4
1976-77—Dallas Black Hawks		CHL	58	*37	34	71	40
1976-77—Toronto Maple Leafs		NHL	15	2	5	7	4
1977-78—Dallas Black Hawks		CHL	22	13	9	22	11
1977-78—Toronto Maple Leafs		NHL	40	11	18	29	12
1978-79—Toronto Maple Leafs		NHL	26	4	3	7	2
1978-79—New Brunswick Hawks		AHL	49	20	38	58	22
1979-80—Toronto Maple Leafs		NHL	2	0	0	0	2
1979-80—New Brunswick Hawks		AHL	75	36	54	90	47
1980-81—New Brunswick Hawks		AHL	40	17	41	58	22
1980-81—Toronto Maple Leafs		NHL	39	10	14	24	18
1981-82—Cincinnati Tigers (b)		AHL	65	42	61	103	42
1981-82—Toronto Maple Leafs		NHL	12	0	2	2	6
1982-83—St. Catharines Saints		AHL	80	50	72	122	65
1982-83—Toronto Maple Leafs (g)		NHL	..	..	..	..	..
1983-84—St. Catharines Saints		AHL	80	47	62	109	44
NHL TOTALS			134	27	42	69	44
WHA TOTALS			30	3	6	9	4

(c)—Selected by Minnesota Fighting Saints in World Hockey Association amateur player draft, May, 1974.
(d)—Won Eddie Powers Memorial Trophy (leading scorer).
(e)—Drafted from Toronto Marlboros by Toronto Maple Leafs in third round of 1975 amateur draft.
(f)—Signed by Toronto Maple Leafs, August, 1976.
(g)—Played four playoff games (1 goal), none in regular season.

MARTIN BOULIANE

Center . . . 5'10" . . . 175 lbs. . . . Born, Amqui, Que., April 9, 1965 . . . Shoots right.

Year	Team	League	Games	G.	A.	Pts.	Pen.
1981-82—Ste. Foy Midget	Que. Midget	44	48	45	93	14
1982-83—Granby Bisons (c)	QHL	70	39	64	103	10
1983-84—Granby Bisons	QHL	62	41	41	82	6

(c)—June, 1983—Drafted as underage junior by Washington Capitals in 1983 NHL entry draft. Second Capitals pick, 95th overall, fifth round.

ALLEN BOURBEAU

Center . . . 5'9" . . . 170 lbs. . . . Born, Worcester, Mass., May 17, 1965 . . . Shoots right.

Year	Team	League	Games	G.	A.	Pts.	Pen.
1982-83—Acton Boxboro H.S. (c)	Mass. H.S.	22	62	40	102	..
1983-84—Harvard University	ECAC	..	..	..	..	..

(c)—June, 1983—Drafted as underage player by Philadelphia Flyers in 1983 NHL entry draft. Third Flyers pick, 81st overall, fourth round.

DAN BOURBONNAIS

Left Wing . . . 5'10" . . . 185 lbs. . . . Born, Winnipeg, Man., March 6, 1962 . . . Shoots left.

Year	Team	League	Games	G.	A.	Pts.	Pen.
1978-79—Pincher Creek	AJHL	60	17	41	58	36
1978-79—Calgary Wranglers	WHL	2	0	2	2	0
1979-80—Calgary Wranglers	WHL	66	14	29	43	41
1980-81—Calgary Wranglers (c)	WHL	72	41	62	103	34
1981-82—Hartford Whalers	NHL	24	3	9	12	11
1981-82—Calgary Wranglers	WHL	50	27	32	59	175
1982-83—Binghamton Whalers	AHL	75	31	33	64	24
1983-84—Binghamton Whalers	AHL	38	16	32	48	40
1983-84—Hartford Whalers	NHL	35	0	16	16	0
NHL TOTALS		59	3	25	28	11

(c)—June, 1981—Drafted as underage junior by Hartford Whalers in 1981 NHL entry draft. Fifth Whalers pick, 103rd overall, fifth round.

CHARLES BOURGEOIS

Defense . . . 6'4" . . . 205 lbs. . . . Born, Moncton, N.B., November 11, 1959 . . . Shoots right.

Year	Team	League	Games	G.	A.	Pts.	Pen.
1980-81—University of Moncton (a-c-d)	AUAA	24	8	23	31	..
1981-82—Oklahoma City Stars	CHL	13	2	2	4	17
1981-82—Calgary Flames	NHL	54	2	13	15	112
1982-83—Calgary Flames	NHL	15	2	3	5	21
1982-83—Colorado Flames	CHL	51	10	18	28	128
1983-84—Colorado Flames (a)	CHL	54	12	32	44	133
1983-84—Calgary Flames	NHL	17	1	3	4	35
NHL TOTALS		86	5	19	24	168

(c)—Named to All Canada Team (East).
(d)—April, 1981—Signed by Calgary Flames as free agent.

GLEN ROBERT (BOB) BOURNE

Center and Left Wing . . . 6'3" . . . 195 lbs. . . . Born, Kindersley, Sask., June 21, 1954 . . . Shoots left . . . Signed a contract with Houston Astros at Covington, Va. Batted .257 . . . (October 17, 1981)—Pulled muscles in upper thigh . . . (October 8, 1983)—Scored first overtime goal in NHL since November 10, 1942 when Lynn Patrick scored in a N.Y. Rangers' 5-3 OT win vs. Chicago. Bourne's goal beat Washington Capitals, 7-6, at the Capital Centre at 2:01 of overtime.

Year	Team	League	Games	G.	A.	Pts.	Pen.
1971-72—Saskatoon Blades	WCHL	63	28	32	60	36
1972-73—Saskatoon Blades	WCHL	66	40	53	93	74
1973-74—Saskatoon Blades (c-d)	WCHL	63	29	42	71	41
1974-75—New York Islanders	NHL	77	16	23	39	12

Year	Team	League	Games	G.	A.	Pts.	Pen.
1975-76—Fort Worth Texans (b)	CHL	62	29	44	73	80
1975-76—New York Islanders	NHL	14	2	3	5	13
1976-77—New York Islanders	NHL	75	16	19	35	30
1977-78—New York Islanders	NHL	80	30	33	63	31
1978-79—New York Islanders	NHL	80	30	31	61	48
1979-80—New York Islanders	NHL	73	15	25	40	52
1980-81—New York Islanders	NHL	78	35	41	76	62
1981-82—New York Islanders	NHL	76	27	26	53	77
1982-83—New York Islanders	NHL	77	20	42	62	55
1983-84—New York Islanders	NHL	78	22	34	56	75
NHL TOTALS		708	213	277	490	455

(c)—Drafted from Saskatoon Blades by Kansas City Scouts in third round of 1974 amateur draft.
(d)—NHL rights traded to New York Islanders by Kansas City Scouts for NHL rights to Larry Hornung and a player to be named later, September, 1974. (New York sent Bart Crashley to Kansas City to complete deal, September, 1974).

PHILLIPPE RICHARD BOURQUE

Defense . . . 6' . . . 180 lbs. . . . Born, Chelmsford, Mass., June 8, 1962 . . . Shoots left.

Year	Team	League	Games	G.	A.	Pts.	Pen.
1980-81—Kingston Canadians	OHL	47	4	4	8	46
1981-82—Kingston Canadians	OHL	67	11	40	51	111
1982-83—Baltimore Skipjacks	AHL	65	1	15	16	93
1983-84—Baltimore Skipjacks	AHL	58	5	17	22	96
1983-84—Pittsburgh Penguins	NHL	5	0	1	1	12
NHL TOTALS		5	0	1	1	12

RAYMOND JEAN BOURQUE

Defense . . . 5'11" . . . 197 lbs. . . . Born, Montreal, Que., December 28, 1960 . . . Shoots left . . . Set record for most points by a rookie defenseman 1979-80 (65 pts) (Broken by Larry Murphy of L.A. Kings in '80-81 with 76 pts.) . . . (November 11, 1980)—Broken jaw . . . Brother of Richard Bourque (203rd NHL '81 draft pick) . . . (October, 1981)—Injured left shoulder . . . (April 21, 1982)—Broke left wrist vs. Quebec in playoffs. During the summer he refractured the wrist and his left forearm . . . (October, 1982)—Broken bone over left eye when hit by puck during preseason game against Montreal.

Year	Team	League	Games	G.	A.	Pts.	Pen.
1976-77—Sorel Black Hawks	QMJHL	69	12	36	48	61
1977-78—Verdun Black Hawks (a)	QMJHL	72	22	57	79	90
1978-79—Verdun Black Hawks (a-c)	QMJHL	63	22	71	93	44
1979-80—Boston Bruins (a-d-e)	NHL	80	17	48	65	73
1980-81—Boston Bruins (b)	NHL	67	27	29	56	96
1981-82—Boston Bruins (a)	NHL	65	17	49	66	51
1982-83—Boston Bruins (b)	NHL	65	22	51	73	20
1983-84—Boston Bruins (a)	NHL	78	31	65	96	57
NHL TOTALS		355	114	242	356	297

(c)—August, 1979—Drafted by Boston Bruins in 1979 entry draft. First Bruins pick, eighth overall, first round.
(d)—Selected NHL Rookie of the Year in poll of players by THE SPORTING NEWS.
(e)—Won Calder Memorial Trophy (Top NHL Rookie).

PATRICK MICHAEL BOUTETTE

Center and Left Wing . . . 5'8" . . . 175 lbs. . . . Born, Windsor, Ont., March 1, 1952 . . . Shoots left . . . Attended University of Minnesota-Duluth.

Year	Team	League	Games	G.	A.	Pts.	Pen.
1969-70—London Knights	Jr."A"OHA	53	11	17	28	87
1970-71—U. of Minnesota-Duluth	WCHA	33	18	13	31	86
1971-72—U. of Minnesota-Duluth (c)	WCHA	34	17	20	37	71
1972-73—U. of Minnesota-Duluth (b-d)	WCHA	34	18	45	63	91
1973-74—Oklahoma City Blazers	CHL	70	17	34	51	118
1974-75—Oklahoma City Blazers	CHL	77	26	42	68	163
1975-76—Toronto Maple Leafs	NHL	77	10	22	32	140
1976-77—Toronto Maple Leafs	NHL	80	18	18	36	107
1977-78—Toronto Maple Leafs	NHL	80	17	19	36	120
1978-79—Toronto Maple Leafs	NHL	80	14	19	33	136
1979-80—Toronto Maple Leafs (e)	NHL	32	0	4	4	17
1979-80—Hartford Whalers	NHL	47	13	31	44	75
1980-81—Hartford Whalers (f)	NHL	80	28	52	80	160
1981-82—Pittsburgh Penguins	NHL	80	23	51	74	230

— 33 —

Year	Team	League	Games	G.	A.	Pts.	Pen.
1982-83—Pittsburgh Penguins		NHL	80	27	29	56	152
1983-84—Pittsburgh Penguins		NHL	73	14	26	40	142
NHL TOTALS			709	164	271	435	1279

(c)—Drafted from University of Minnesota-Duluth by Toronto Maple Leafs in ninth round of 1972 amateur draft.

(d)—Named to first team (Western) All-America.

(e)—December, 1979—Traded by Toronto Maple Leafs to Hartford Whalers for Bob Stephenson.

(f)—July, 1981—Acquired by Pittsburgh Penguins with Kevin McClelland as compensation from the Hartford Whalers for signing of free agent Greg Millen. Decision required by NHL Arbitrator Judge Joseph Kane when Hartford and Pittsburgh were unable to agree on compensation following the Whalers signing of Millen.

PAUL ANDRE BOUTILIER

Defense . . . 5'11" . . . 188 lbs. . . . Born, Sydney, N.S., May 3, 1963 . . . Shoots left.

Year	Team	League	Games	G.	A.	Pts.	Pen.
1980-81—Sherbrooke Beavers (c)		QMJHL	72	10	29	39	95
1981-82—Sherbrooke Beavers		QMJHL	57	20	60	80	62
1981-82—New York Islanders		NHL	1	0	0	0	0
1982-83—St. Jean Beavers (d)		QHL	22	5	14	19	30
1982-83—New York Islanders		NHL	29	4	5	9	24
1983-84—Indianapolis Checkers		CHL	50	6	17	23	56
1983-84—New York Islanders		NHL	28	0	11	11	36
NHL TOTALS			58	4	16	20	60

(c)—June, 1981—Drafted as underage junior by New York Islanders in 1981 NHL entry draft. Islanders first pick, 21st overall, first round.

(d)—January, 1983—QHL rights traded by St. Jean Beavers to Shawinigan Cataracts for Yves Lapointe.

RANDY KEITH JOSEPH BOYD

Defense . . .5'11" . . . 192 lbs. . . . Born, Coniston, Ont., January 23, 1962 . . . Shoots left.

Year	Team	League	Games	G.	A.	Pts.	Pen.
1979-80—Ottawa 67's (c)		OMJHL	65	3	21	24	148
1980-81—Ottawa 67's (a-d)		OHL	64	11	43	54	225
1981-82—Ottawa 67's		OHL	26	9	29	38	51
1981-82—Pittsburgh Penguins		NHL	23	0	2	2	49
1982-83—Baltimore Skipjacks		AHL	21	5	10	15	43
1982-83—Pittsburgh Penguins		NHL	56	4	14	18	71
1983-84—Pittsburgh Penguins		NHL	5	0	1	1	6
1983-84—Baltimore Skipjacks		AHL	20	6	13	19	69
1983-84—Chicago Black Hawks (e)		NHL	23	0	4	4	16
1983-84—Springfield Indians		AHL	27	2	11	13	48
NHL TOTALS			107	4	21	25	142

(c)—June, 1980—Drafted by Pittsburgh Penguins as underage junior in 1980 NHL entry draft. Second Penguins pick, 51st overall, third round.

(d)—Won Max Kaminsky Trophy (Top OHL Defenseman).

(e)—December, 1983—Traded by Pittsburgh Penguins to Chicago Black Hawks for Greg Fox.

STEVEN MICHAEL BOZEK

Left Wing . . . 5'11" . . . 170 lbs. . . . Born, Kelowna, B. C., November 26, 1960 . . . Shoots left . . . Set Los Angeles club record for most goals by a rookie in 1981-82 . . . (January 20, 1983)—Sprained left knee in game vs. Hartford.

Year	Team	League	Games	G.	A.	Pts.	Pen.
1978-79—Northern Michigan Univ.		CCHA	33	12	12	24	21
1979-80—Northern Michigan Univ. (a-c)		CCHA	41	42	47	89	32
1980-81—Northern Michigan Univ. (a-d)		CCHA	44	*35	*55	*90	46
1981-82—Los Angeles Kings		NHL	71	33	23	56	68
1982-83—Los Angeles Kings (e)		NHL	53	13	13	26	14
1983-84—Calgary Flames		NHL	46	10	10	20	16
NHL TOTALS			170	56	46	102	98

(c)—June, 1980—Drafted by Los Angeles Kings in 1980 NHL entry draft. Fifth Kings pick, 52nd overall, third round.

(d)—Selected to All-America (West) team.

(e)—June, 1983—Traded by Los Angeles Kings to Calgary Flames for Kevin LaVallee and Carl Mokosak.

BRIAN BRADLEY

Center . . . 5'9" . . . 165 lbs. . . . Born, Kitchener, Ont., January 21, 1965 . . . Shoots right.

Year	Team	League	Games	G.	A.	Pts.	Pen.
1981-82—London Knights		OHL	62	34	44	78	34
1982-83—London Knights (c)		OHL	67	37	82	119	37
1983-84—London Knights		OHL	49	40	60	100	24

(c)—June, 1983—Drafted by Calgary Flames as underage junior in 1983 NHL entry draft. Second Flames pick, 51st overall, third round.

DAN BRENNAN

Left Wing . . . 6'3" . . . 210 lbs. . . . Born, Dawson Creek, B.C., October 1, 1962 . . . Shoots left.

Year	Team	League	Games	G.	A.	Pts.	Pen.
1980-81—Univ. of North Dakota (c)		WCHA	37	3	9	12	66
1981-82—Univ. of North Dakota		WCHA	42	10	17	27	78
1982-83—Univ. of North Dakota		WCHA	31	9	11	20	60
1983-84—Univ. of North Dakota		WCHA	45	28	37	65	36
1983-84—Los Angeles Kings		NHL	2	0	0	0	0
NHL TOTALS			2	0	0	0	0

(c)—June, 1981—Drafted by Los Angeles Kings in 1981 NHL entry draft. Seventh Kings pick, 165th overall, eighth round.

RENE BRETON

Center . . . 5'11" . . . 190 lbs. . . . Born, Princeville, Que., January 10, 1964 . . . Shoots left.

Year	Team	League	Games	G.	A.	Pts.	Pen.
1980-81—Cantons L'est		Que. Midget 'AAA'	47	18	28	46	10
1981-82—Granby Bisons (c)		QMJHL	64	17	19	36	13
1982-83—Granby Bisons		QHL	59	38	48	86	21
1983-84—Granby Bisons		QHL	59	23	47	70	23

(c)—June, 1982—Drafted as underage junior by New York Islanders in 1982 NHL entry draft. Fifth Islanders pick, 103th overall, fifth round.

ANDY BRICKLEY

Left Wing . . . 5'11" . . . 185 lbs. . . . Born, Melrose, Mass., August 9, 1961 . . . Shoots left. . . . (December, 1983)—Strained ankle.

Year	Team	League	Games	G.	A.	Pts.	Pen.
1979-80—University of New Hampshire (c)		ECAC	27	15	17	32	8
1980-81—University of New Hampshire		ECAC	31	27	25	52	16
1981-82—University of New Hampshire (d)		ECAC	35	26	27	53	6
1982-83—Philadelphia Flyers		NHL	3	1	1	2	0
1982-83—Maine Mariners (b)		AHL	76	29	54	83	10
1983-84—Springfield Indians		AHL	7	1	5	6	2
1983-84—Pittsburgh Penguins (e)		NHL	50	18	20	38	9
1983-84—Baltimore Skipjacks		AHL	4	0	5	5	2
NHL TOTALS			53	19	21	40	9

(c)—June, 1980—Drafted by Philadelphia Flyers in 1980 NHL entry draft. Tenth Flyers pick, 210th overall, tenth round.

(d)—Named to All-American Team (East).

(e)—October, 1983—Traded with Ron Flockhart, Mark Taylor and first-round 1984 draft pick (Roger Belanger) by Philadelphia Flyers to Pittsburgh Penguins for Rich Sutter and second (Greg Smyth) and third round (David McLay) 1984 draft picks.

MELVIN JOHN BRIDGMAN

Center . . . 6' . . . 185 lbs. . . . Born, Trenton, Ont., April 28, 1955 . . . Shoots left.

Year	Team	League	Games	G.	A.	Pts.	Pen.
1971-72—Nanaimo Clippers		Jr."A" BCHL	....	...	....	....	....
1971-72—Victoria Cougars		WCHL	4	0	0	0	0
1972-73—Nanaimo Clippers		Jr."A" BCHL	49	37	50	87	13
1972-73—Victoria Cougars		WCHL	4	1	1	2	0
1973-74—Victoria Cougars		WCHL	62	26	39	65	149
1974-75—Victoria Cougars (a-c)		WCHL	66	66	91	*157	175
1975-76—Philadelphia Flyers		NHL	80	23	27	50	86
1976-77—Philadelphia Flyers		NHL	70	19	38	57	120
1977-78—Philadelphia Flyers		NHL	76	16	32	48	203
1978-79—Philadelphia Flyers		NHL	76	24	35	59	184
1979-80—Philadelphia Flyers		NHL	74	16	31	47	136
1980-81—Philadelphia Flyers		NHL	77	14	37	51	195
1981-82—Philadelphia Flyers (d)		NHL	9	7	5	12	47
1981-82—Calgary Flames		NHL	63	26	49	75	94

Year	Team	League	Games	G.	A.	Pts.	Pen.
1982-83—Calgary Flames (e)		NHL	79	19	31	50	103
1983-84—New Jersey Devils		NHL	79	23	38	61	121
NHL TOTALS			683	187	323	510	1289

(c)—Drafted from Victoria Cougars by Philadelphia Flyers in first round of 1975 amateur draft (Flyers obtained draft choice from Washington Capitals for Bill Clement and Don McLean, June, 1975).

(d)—November, 1981—Traded by Philadelphia Flyers to Calgary Flames for Brad Marsh.

(e)—July, 1983—Traded by Calgary Flames with Phil Russell to New Jersey Devils for Steve Tambellini and Joel Quenneville.

MICHEL BRISEBOIS

Left Wing . . . 5'11" . . . 201 lbs. . . . Born, Montreal, Que., January 27, 1960 . . . Shoots left.

Year	Team	League	Games	G.	A.	Pts.	Pen.
1976-77—Sherbrooke Beavers		QMJHL	61	6	7	13	40
1977-78—Sherbrooke Beavers		QMJHL	4	1	2	3	0
1977-78—Chicoutimi Sagueneens		QMJHL	58	25	34	59	25
1978-79—Chicoutimi Sagueneens		QMJHL	21	18	14	32	15
1978-79—Hull Olympiques		QMJHL	51	36	28	64	49
1979-80—Hull Olympiques (c)		QMJHL	70	57	45	102	96
1980-81—Saginaw Gears		IHL	79	42	25	67	30
1981-82—New Haven Nighthawks		AHL	44	10	14	24	23
1981-82—Saginaw Gears		IHL	35	19	18	37	7
1982-83—Carolina Thunderbirds		ACHL	57	43	33	76	106
1983-84—Pinebridge/Carolina		ACHL	72	40	33	73	45

(c)—August, 1980—Signed by Los Angeles Kings as a free agent.

GREG BRITZ

Right Wing . . . 6' . . . 190 lbs. . . . Born, Palos Verdes, Calif., March 1, 1961 . . . Shoots right.

Year	Team	League	Games	G.	A.	Pts.	Pen.
1979-80—Harvard University		ECAC	26	8	5	13	17
1980-81—Harvard University		ECAC	17	3	4	7	10
1981-82—Harvard University		ECAC	24	11	13	24	12
1982-83—Harvard University		ECAC	33	16	23	39	18
1983-84—St. Catharines Saints (c)		AHL	44	23	16	39	25
1983-84—Toronto Maple Leafs		NHL	6	0	0	0	2
NHL TOTALS			6	0	0	0	2

(c)—October, 1983—Signed by Toronto Maple Leafs as a free agent.

LEE BRODEUR

Right Wing . . . 6'1" . . . 180 lbs. . . . Born, Grafton, N. Dak., February 14, 1966 . . . Shoots right.

Year	Team	League	Games	G.	A.	Pts.	Pen.
1983-84—Grafton H.S. (c)		No.Dak.H.S.	23	40	36	76	42

(c)—June, 1984—Drafted by Montreal Canadiens in 1984 NHL entry draft. Sixth Canadiens pick, 65th overall, fourth round.

ROBERT W. BROOKE

Right Wing . . . 6'2" . . . 185 lbs. . . . Born, Melrose, Mass., December 18, 1960 . . . Shoots right . . . Holds Yale career records for goals (42), assists (113) and points (155) . . . Also plays defense . . . Played shortstop on Yale baseball team . . . Member of 1984 U.S. Olympic Team.

Year	Team	League	Games	G.	A.	Pts.	Pen.
1979-80—Yale University (c)		ECAC	24	7	22	29	38
1980-81—Yale University		ECAC	27	12	30	42	59
1981-82—Yale University		ECAC	25	12	30	42	60
1982-83—Yale University (a-d)		ECAC	27	11	31	42	50
1983-84—U.S. National Team		Int'l	54	7	18	25	75
1983-84—U.S. Olympic Team		Int'l	6	1	2	3	10
1983-84—New York Rangers (e)		NHL	9	1	2	3	4
NHL TOTALS			9	1	2	3	4

(c)—June, 1980—Drafted by St. Louis Blues in 1980 NHL entry draft. Third Blues pick, 75th overall, fourth round.

(d)—Named to All-America Team (East).

(e)—March, 1984—Traded with Larry Patey by St. Louis Blues to New York Rangers for Dave Barr, a third round (Alan Perry) 1984 draft pick and cash.

AARON BROTEN

Center . . . 5'10" . . . 168 lbs. . . . Born, Roseau, Minn., November 14, 1960 . . . Shoots left . . . Brother of Neal Broten and Paul Broten . . . Also plays left wing.

Year	Team	League	Games	G.	A.	Pts.	Pen.
1979-80	University of Minnesota (c-d)	WCHA	41	25	47	72	8
1980-81	University of Minnesota(b-e-f)	WCHA	45	*47	*59	*106	24
1980-81	Colorado Rockies	NHL	2	0	0	0	0
1981-82	Ft. Worth Texans	CHL	19	15	21	36	11
1981-82	Colorado Rockies	NHL	58	15	24	39	6
1982-83	Wichita Wind	CHL	4	0	4	4	0
1982-83	New Jersey Devils	NHL	73	16	39	55	28
1983-84	New Jersey Devils	NHL	80	13	23	36	36
NHL TOTALS			213	44	86	130	70

(c)—Named top WCHA Rookie.
(d)—June, 1980—Drafted by Colorado Rockies in 1980 NHL entry draft. Fifth Rockies pick, 106th overall, sixth round.
(e)—WCHA Scoring Leader.
(f)—March, 1981—Signed by Colorado Rockies.

NEAL LaMOY BROTEN

Center . . . 5'9" . . . 160 lbs. . . . Born, Roseau, Minn., November 29, 1959 . . . Shoots left . . . Brother of Aaron Broten and Paul Broten . . . Scored game winning goal to give University of Minnesota 1979 NCAA Championship over North Dakota. Member of 1980 U.S. Olympic Gold Medal Team . . . (December 26, 1981)—Ankle fracture . . . Set NHL record for most points by American-born player (97), 1981-82 . . . Set NHL record for most goals by an American-born player (38), 1981-82 (broken by Joe Mullen in 1983-84). . . . Set NHL record for most assists by American-born player (59), 1981-82.

Year	Team	League	Games	G.	A.	Pts.	Pen.
1978-79	University of Minnesota (c-d)	WCHA	40	21	50	71	18
1979-80	U. S. Olympic Team	Int'l	62	27	31	58	22
1980-81	University of Minnesota (a-e-f-g)	WCHA	36	17	54	71	56
1980-81	Minnesota North Stars (h)	NHL	3	2	0	2	12
1981-82	Minnesota North Stars	NHL	73	38	60	98	42
1982-83	Minnesota North Stars	NHL	79	32	45	77	43
1983-84	Minnesota North Stars	NHL	76	28	61	89	43
NHL TOTALS			231	100	166	266	140

(c)—Named top WCHA Rookie player.
(d)—August, 1979—Drafted by Minnesota North Stars in 1979 NHL entry draft. Third North Stars pick, 42nd overall, second round.
(e)—Named to All-America Team (West).
(f)—Named to All-NCAA Tournament team.
(g)—First winner of Hobey Baker Memorial Trophy (Top U. S. College Hockey Player).
(h)—March, 1981—Signed by Minnesota North Stars.

PAUL BROTEN

Center . . . 5'11" . . . 155 lbs. . . . Born, Roseau, Minn., October 27, 1965 . . . Shoots right . . . Brother of Aaron and Neal Broten.

Year	Team	League	Games	G.	A.	Pts.	Pen.
1983-84	Roseau H.S. (c)	Minn. H.S.	26	26	29	55	4

(c)—June, 1984—Drafted by New York Rangers in 1984 NHL entry draft. Third Rangers pick, 77th overall, fourth round.

ALLISTER BROWN

Defense . . . 6' . . . 185 lbs. . . . Born, Cornwall, Ont., November 12, 1965 . . . Shoots right.

Year	Team	League	Games	G.	A.	Pts.	Pen.
1983-84	Univ. of New Hampshire (c)	ECAC	36	1	7	8	12

(c)—June, 1984—Drafted by New York Islanders in 1984 NHL entry draft, 13th Islanders pick, 249th overall, 12th round.

DAVID BROWN

Right Wing . . . 6'5" . . . 205 lbs. . . . Born, Saskatoon, Sask., October 12, 1962 . . . Shoots right.

Year	Team	League	Games	G.	A.	Pts.	Pen.
1980-81	Spokane Flyers	WHL	9	2	2	4	21
1981-82	Saskatoon Blades (c)	WHL	62	11	33	44	344
1982-83	Maine Mariners (d)	AHL	71	8	6	14	*418
1982-83	Philadelphia Flyers	NHL	2	0	0	0	5
1983-84	Philadelphia Flyers	NHL	19	1	5	6	98
1983-84	Springfield Indians	AHL	59	17	14	31	150
NHL TOTALS			21	1	5	6	103

(c)—June, 1982—Drafted by Philadelphia Flyers in 1982 NHL entry draft. Seventh Flyers pick, 140th overall, seventh round.
(d)—Led AHL Playoffs with 107 penalty minutes.

JEFF BROWN

Defense . . . 6'1" . . . 185 lbs. . . . Born, Ottawa, Ont., April 30, 1966 . . . Shoots right.

Year	Team	League	Games	G.	A.	Pts.	Pen.
1981-82—Hawkesbury Tier II		Ont. Jr.	49	12	47	59	72
1982-83—Sudbury Wolves		OHL	65	9	37	46	39
1983-84—Sudbury Wolves (c)		OHL	68	17	60	77	39

(c)—June, 1984—Drafted as underage junior by Quebec Nordiques in 1984 NHL entry draft. Second Nordiques pick, 36th overall, second round.

KEITH JEFFREY BROWN

Defense . . . 6'1" . . . 192 lbs. . . . Born, Corner Brook, Nfld., May 6, 1960 . . . Shoots right . . . (December 23, 1981)—Torn ligaments in right knee . . . (January 26, 1983)—Separated right shoulder in game vs. Vancouver.

Year	Team	League	Games	G.	A.	Pts.	Pen.
1976-77—Ft. Saskatchewan Traders		AJHL	59	14	61	75	14
1976-77—Portland Winter Hawks		WCHL	2	0	0	0	0
1977-78—Portland Winter Hawks (b-c)		WCHL	72	11	53	64	51
1978-79—Portland Winter Hawks (a-d-e)		WHL	70	11	85	96	75
1979-80—Chicago Black Hawks		NHL	76	2	18	20	27
1980-81—Chicago Black Hawks		NHL	80	9	34	43	80
1981-82—Chicago Black Hawks		NHL	33	4	20	24	26
1982-83—Chicago Black Hawks		NHL	50	4	27	31	20
1983-84—Chicago Black Hawks		NHL	74	10	25	35	94
NHL TOTALS			313	29	124	153	247

(c)—Shared WCHL Top Rookie with John Ogrodnick.
(d)—Named outstanding WHL defenseman.
(e)—August, 1979—Drafted as underage junior by Chicago Black Hawks in 1979 NHL entry draft. First Black Hawks pick, seventh overall, first round.

JEFFREY PAUL BROWNSCHIDLE

Defense . . . 6'2" . . . 205 lbs. . . . Born, East Amherst, N. Y., March 1, 1959 . . . Shoots right . . . Brother of Jack Brownschidle.

Year	Team	League	Games	G.	A.	Pts.	Pen.
1977-78—University of Notre Dame		WCHA	35	6	10	16	30
1978-79—University of Notre Dame		WCHA	32	5	15	20	40
1979-80—University of Notre Dame		WCHA	39	14	37	51	50
1980-81—University of Notre Dame (c)		WCHA	36	4	28	32	56
1981-82—Binghamton Whalers		AHL	52	4	23	27	24
1981-82—Hartford Whalers		NHL	3	0	1	1	2
1982-83—Hartford Whalers		NHL	4	0	0	0	0
1982-83—Binghamton Whalers		AHL	64	9	18	27	52
1983-84—Binghamton Whalers (d)		AHL	30	2	7	9	50
1983-84—Salt Lake Golden Eagles		CHL	11	1	7	8	12
NHL TOTALS			7	0	1	1	2

(c)—May, 1981—Signed by Hartford Whalers as a free agent.
(d)—July, 1984—Released by Hartford Whalers.

JOHN J. (Jack) BROWNSCHIDLE, JR.

Defense . . . 6'2" . . . 195 lbs. . . . Born, Buffalo, N.Y., October 2, 1955 . . . Shoots left . . . Attended University of Notre Dame . . . Brother of Jeff Brownschidle.

Year	Team	League	Games	G.	A.	Pts.	Pen.
1972-73—Niagara Falls Flyers		SOJHL	32	9	19	28	20
1973-74—University of Notre Dame		WCHA	36	2	7	9	24
1973-74—U.S. National Team			18	2	3	5	....
1974-75—University of Notre Dame (c)		WCHA	38	4	12	16	24
1975-76—University of Notre Dame (d)		WCHA	38	12	24	36	24
1976-77—University of Notre Dame (d)		WCHA	38	13	35	48	30
1977-78—Salt Lake City Golden Eagles		CHL	25	4	12	16	0
1977-78—St. Louis Blues		NHL	40	2	15	17	23
1978-79—St. Louis Blues		NHL	64	10	24	34	14
1978-79—Salt Lake Golden Eagles		CHL	11	0	10	10	0
1979-80—St. Louis Blues		NHL	77	12	32	44	8
1980-81—St. Louis Blues		NHL	71	5	23	28	12

Year	Team	League	Games	G.	A.	Pts.	Pen.
1981-82—St. Louis Blues		NHL	80	5	33	38	26
1982-83—St. Louis Blues		NHL	72	1	22	23	30
1983-84—St. Louis Blues (e)		NHL	51	1	7	8	19
1983-84—Hartford Whalers		NHL	13	2	2	4	10
NHL TOTALS			468	38	158	196	142

(c)—Drafted from University of Notre Dame by St. Louis Blues in sixth round of 1975 amateur draft.
(d)—Selected First Team (West) All America.
(e)—March, 1984—Claimed by Hartford Whalers on waivers from St. Louis Blues for the waiver price of $12,500.

JEFFREY BRUBAKER

Defense . . . 6'2" . . . 205 lbs. . . . Born, Hagerstown, Maryland, February 24, 1958 . . . Shoots left . . . Attended Michigan State University . . . Also plays Left Wing . . . Missed parts of 1979-80 season with dislocated shoulder and a sprained knee . . . (October, 1980)—Shoulder injury.

Year	Team	League	Games	G.	A.	Pts.	Pen.
1974-75—St. Paul Vulcans		MWJHL	57	13	14	27	130
1975-76—St. Paul Vulcans		MWJHL	47	6	34	40	152
1976-77—Michigan State University		WCHA	18	0	3	3	30
1976-77—Peterborough Petes		Jr."A" OHA	26	0	5	5	143
1977-78—Peterborough Petes (c-d)		Jr."A" OHA	68	20	24	44	307
1978-79—New England Whalers		WHA	12	0	0	0	19
1978-79—Rochester Americans		AHL	57	4	10	14	253
1979-80—Hartford Whalers		NHL	3	0	1	1	2
1979-80—Springfield Indians		AHL	50	12	13	25	165
1980-81—Binghamton Whalers		AHL	38	18	11	29	138
1980-81—Hartford Whalers		NHL	43	5	3	8	93
1981-82—Montreal Canadiens (e)		NHL	3	0	1	1	32
1981-82—Nova Scotia Voyageurs		AHL	60	28	12	40	256
1982-83—Nova Scotia Voyageurs		AHL	78	31	27	58	183
1983-84—Calgary Flames (f)		NHL	4	0	0	0	19
1983-84—Colorado Flames		CHL	57	16	19	35	218
WHA TOTALS			12	0	0	0	19
NHL TOTALS			53	5	5	10	146

(c)—Selected by New England Whalers in World Hockey Association amateur players' draft and signed by Whalers, June, 1978.
(d)—Drafted from Peterborough Petes by Boston Bruins in sixth round of 1978 amateur draft.
(e)—October, 1981—Selected by Montreal Canadiens in 1981 NHL waiver draft.
(f)—October, 1983—Selected by Calgary Flames in 1983 NHL waiver draft.

DAVE BRUCE

Right Wing . . . 5'11" . . . 170 lbs. . . . Born, Thunder Bay, Ont., October 7, 1964 . . . Shoots right . . . Also plays center.

Year	Team	League	Games	G.	A.	Pts.	Pen.
1981-82—Thunder Bay Kings		Tier II	35	27	31	58	74
1982-83—Kitchener Rangers (c)		OHL	67	36	35	71	199
1983-84—Kitchener Rangers		OHL	62	52	40	92	203

(c)—June, 1983—Drafted as underage junior by Vancouver Canucks in 1983 NHL entry draft. Second Canucks pick, 30th overall, second round.

JAMES MURRAY BRUMWELL
(Known by middle name)

Defense . . . 6'1" . . . 190 lbs. . . . Born, Calgary, Alta., March 31, 1960 . . . Shoots left . . . (February, 1979)—Mononucleosis . . . (January, 1982)—Back injury.

Year	Team	League	Games	G.	A.	Pts.	Pen.
1977-78—Calgary Canucks		AJHL	59	4	40	44	79
1977-78—Calgary Wranglers		WCHL	1	0	0	0	2
1977-78—Saskatoon Blades		WCHL	1	0	2	2	0
1978-79—Billings Bighorns		WHL	61	11	32	43	62
1979-80—Billings Bighorns		WHL	67	18	54	72	50
1980-81—Minnesota North Stars (c)		NHL	1	0	0	0	0
1980-81—Oklahoma City Stars		CHL	79	12	43	55	79
1981-82—Nashville South Stars		CHL	55	4	21	25	66
1981-82—Minnesota North Stars (d)		NHL	21	0	3	3	18
1982-83—Wichita Wind		CHL	11	4	1	5	4
1982-83—New Jersey Devils		NHL	59	5	14	19	34

Year	Team	League	Games	G.	A.	Pts.	Pen.
1983-84—Maine Mariners		AHL	34	4	25	29	16
1983-84—New Jersey Devils		NHL	42	7	13	20	14
NHL TOTALS			123	12	30	42	66

(c)—September, 1980—Signed by Minnesota North Stars as a free agent.
(d)—Claimed by New Jersey Devils in 1982 NHL waiver draft.

BOB BRYDEN

Left Wing . . . 6'3" . . . 205 lbs. . . . Born, Toronto, Ont., April 5, 1963 . . . Shoots left.

Year	Team	League	Games	G.	A.	Pts.	Pen.
1982-83—Henry Carr H.S. (c)		Toronto H.S.	32	28	39	67	65
1983-84—Western Michigan Univ.		CCHA	36	17	12	29	60

(c)—June, 1983—Drafted by Montreal Canadiens in 1983 NHL entry draft. Tenth Canadiens pick, 158th overall, eighth round.

SCOTT BRYDGES

Defense . . . 6'1" . . . 185 lbs. . . . Born, Chicago, Ill., July 11, 1964 . . . Shoots right . . . Also plays right wing.

Year	Team	League	Games	G.	A.	Pts.	Pen.
1981-82—St. Paul Mariner H.S.(c)		Minn. H.S.	28	14	24	38	54
1982-83—Oshawa Generals		OHL	56	1	7	8	55
1983-84—Oshawa Generals		OHL	51	8	17	25	71

(c)—June, 1982—Drafted as underage player by New Jersey Devils in 1982 NHL entry draft. Fifth Devils pick, 85th overall, fifth round.

JIRI BUBLA

Defense . . . 5'11" . . . 197 lbs. . . . Born, Usti nad Labem, Czechoslovakia, January 27, 1950 . . . Shoots right . . . (November, 1981)—Broken ankle . . . (December, 1983)—Broken foot.

Year	Team	League	Games	G.	A.	Pts.	Pen.
1980-81—Sparta Praha (c)		Czech.	....	8	20	28	....
1981-82—Vancouver Canucks		NHL	23	1	1	2	16
1982-83—Vancouver Canucks		NHL	72	2	28	30	59
1983-84—Vancouver Canucks		NHL	62	6	33	39	43
NHL TOTALS			157	9	62	71	118

(c)—May, 1981—Drafted by Colorado Rockies in special draft of Czechoslovakian veterans. Colorado subsequently received a fourth-round draft choice and Bret Ashton from Vancouver via Winnipeg as compensation for Vancouver's signing of Bubla.

DAVID BUCKLEY

Defense . . . 6'4" . . . 195 lbs. . . . Born, Newton, Mass., January 27, 1966 . . . Shoots left.

Year	Team	League	Games	G.	A.	Pts.	Pen.
1983-84—Trinity Pawling Prep (c)		N.Y. H.S.	20	10	17	27	0

(c)—June, 1984—Drafted by Toronto Maple Leafs in 1984 NHL entry draft. Ninth Maple Leafs pick. 192nd overall, tenth round.

MICHAEL BRIAN BULLARD

Center . . . 5'10" . . . 183 lbs. . . . Born, Ottawa, Ont., March 10, 1961 . . . Shoots left . . . (February 21, 1982)—Scored winning goal with 4:29 to play to stop New York Islanders 15-game win streak in 4-3 win at Pittsburgh . . . (October, 1982)—Missed first 20 games of the season with mononucleosis . . . (1981-82)—Set Pittsburgh club record for goals in a rookie season (36).

Year	Team	League	Games	G.	A.	Pts.	Pen.
1978-79—Brantford Alexanders		OMJHL	66	43	56	99	66
1979-80—Brantford Alexanders (b-c)		OMJHL	66	66	84	150	86
1980-81—Brantford Alexanders		OHL	42	47	60	107	55
1980-81—Pittsburgh Penguins		NHL	15	1	2	3	19
1981-82—Pittsburgh Penguins		NHL	75	36	27	63	91
1982-83—Pittsburgh Penguins		NHL	57	22	22	44	60
1983-84—Pittsburgh Penguins		NHL	76	51	41	92	57
NHL TOTALS			223	110	92	202	227

(c)—June, 1980—Drafted as underage junior by Pittsburgh Penguins in 1980 NHL entry draft. First Penguins pick, ninth overall, first round.

EDWARD H. (Ted) BULLEY

Left Wing . . . 6'1" . . . 192 lbs. . . . Born, Windsor, Ont., March 25, 1955 . . . Shoots left.

Year	Team	League	Games	G.	A.	Pts.	Pen.
1973-74—Hull Festivals		QJHL	67	28	37	65	116
1974-75—Hull Festivals (c)		QJHL	70	48	61	109	124
1975-76—Flint Generals		IHL	38	15	13	28	123
1975-76—Dallas Black Hawks		CHL	2	0	0	0	0
1976-77—Dallas Black Hawks		CHL	2	2	2	4	10
1976-77—Flint Generals		IHL	70	46	46	92	122
1976-77—Chicago Black Hawks		NHL	2	0	0	0	0
1977-78—Chicago Black Hawks		NHL	79	23	28	51	141
1978-79—Chicago Black Hawks		NHL	75	27	23	50	153
1979-80—Chicago Black Hawks		NHL	66	14	17	31	136
1980-81—Chicago Black Hawks		NHL	68	18	16	34	95
1981-82—Chicago Black Hawks (d)		NHL	59	12	18	30	120
1982-83—Washington Capitals (e)		NHL	39	4	9	13	47
1983-84—Pittsburgh Penguins (f)		NHL	26	3	2	5	12
1983-84—Baltimore Skipjacks		AHL	49	16	19	35	82
NHL TOTALS			414	101	113	214	704

(c)—Drafted from Hull Festivals by Chicago Black Hawks in seventh round of 1975 amateur draft.
(d)—September, 1982—Traded with Dave Hutchison by Chicago Black Hawks to Washington Capitals for sixth round draft pick (Jari Torkki) in 1983 and fifth round pick in 1984.
(e)—June, 1983—Released by Washington Capitals.
(f)—August, 1983—Signed by Pittsburgh Penguins as a free agent.

TIM BURGESS

Defense . . . 5'11" . . . 185 lbs. . . . Born, Ottawa, Ont., January 25, 1965 . . . Shoots left.

Year	Team	League	Games	G	A	Pts	Pen
1981-82—Sudbury North Stars		Ont. Midget	78	35	66	101	38
1982-83—Oshawa Generals (c)		OHL	62	1	16	17	23
1983-84—Oshawa Generals		OHL	11	1	4	5	7
1983-84—Windsor Spitfires		OHL	25	2	2	4	18

(c)—June, 1983—Drafted by Los Angeles Kings as underage junior in 1983 NHL entry draft. Seventh Kings pick, 127th overall, seventh round.

GARY BURNS

Left Wing . . . 6'1" . . . 190 lbs. . . . Born, Cambridge, Mass., January 16, 1955 . . . Shoots left . . . Attended University of New Hampshire.

Year	Team	League	Games	O.	A.	Pts.	Pen.
1974-75—University of New Hampshire		ECAC	31	17	15	32	42
1975-76—University of New Hampshire		ECAC	....	6	12	18	....
1976-77—University of New Hampshire		ECAC	38	9	6	15	24
1977-78—University of New Hampshire		ECAC	29	9	19	28	55
1978-79—Rochester Americans		AHL	79	16	30	46	99
1979-80—Binghamton Dusters		AHL	79	30	29	59	105
1980-81—New Haven Nighthawks (c)		AHL	69	25	29	54	137
1980-81—New York Rangers		NHL	11	2	2	4	18
1981-82—Springfield Indians		AHL	78	27	39	66	71
1981-82—New York Rangers (d)		NHL	....	...	....	....	....
1982-83—Tulsa Oilers		CHL	80	21	33	54	61
1983-84—Tulsa Oilers		CHL	68	28	30	58	95
NHL TOTALS			11	2	2	4	18

(c)—September, 1980—Signed by New York Rangers as a free agent.
(d)—No regular-season record. Played in four playoff games.

SHAWN BURR

Center . . . 6'1" . . . 180 lbs. . . . Born, Sarnia, Ont., July 1, 1966 . . . Shoots left.

Year	Team	League	Games	G.	A.	Pts.	Pen.
1982-83—Sarnia Midgets		OPHL	52	50	85	135	125
1983-84—Kitchener Rangers (c-d)		OHL	68	41	44	85	50

(c)—June, 1984—Drafted as underage junior by Detroit Red Wings in 1984 NHL entry draft. First Red Wings pick, seventh overall, first round.
(d)—Won Emms Family Award (Top OHL Rookie).

NELSON KEITH BURTON

Left Wing . . . 6'1" . . . 205 lbs. . . . Born, Sydney, N.S., November 6, 1957 . . . Shoots left . . .

Missed part of 1977-78 season with elbow surgery . . . Missed part of 1978-79 season with fractured jaw that required surgery.

Year	Team	League	Games	G.	A.	Pts.	Pen.
1974-75—Hull Festivals		QJHL	67	20	19	39	333
1975-76—Quebec Remparts		QJHL	71	26	25	51	322
1976-77—Quebec Remparts (c)		QJHL	67	22	28	50	398
1977-78—Hershey Bears		AHL	57	4	7	11	*323
1977-78—Washington Capitals		NHL	5	1	0	1	8
1978 79 Washington Capitals (d)		NHL	3	0	0	0	13
1978-79—Hershey Bears		AHL	51	6	19	25	204
1979-80—Syracuse Blazers		AHL	2	0	1	1	0
1979-80—Nova Scotia Voyageurs		AHL	70	3	10	13	190
1980-81—Erie Blades		EHL	68	20	24	44	*385
1981-82—Nashville South Stars (e)		CHL	49	1	4	5	128
1982-83—Baltimore Skipjacks		AHL	60	3	8	11	71
1983-84—Erie Golden Blades		ACHL	65	10	12	22	156
NHL TOTALS			8	1	0	1	21

(c)—Drafted from Quebec Remparts by Washington Capitals in fourth round of 1977 amateur draft.
(d)—June, 1979—Traded by Washington Capitals to Quebec Nordiques for Dave Parro.
(e)—September, 1981—Traded by Quebec Nordiques to Minnesota North Stars for Dan Chicoine.

ROD DALE BUSKAS

Defense . . . 6'2" . . . 195 lbs. . . . Born, Wetaskiwin, Alta., January 7, 1961 . . . Shoots right.

Year	Team	League	Games	G.	A.	Pts.	Pen.
1978-79—Red Deer Rustlers		AJHL	37	13	22	35	63
1978-79—Billings Bighorns		WHL	1	0	0	0	0
1978-79—Medicine Hat Tigers		WHL	35	1	12	13	60
1979-80—Medicine Hat Tigers		WHL	72	7	40	47	284
1980-81—Medicine Hat Tigers (c)		WHL	72	14	46	60	164
1981-82—Erie Blades		AHL	69	1	18	19	78
1982-83—Muskegon Mohawks		IHL	1	0	0	0	9
1982-83—Baltimore Skipjacks		AHL	31	2	8	10	45
1982-83—Pittsburgh Penguins		NHL	41	2	2	4	102
1983-84—Baltimore Skipjacks		AHL	33	2	12	14	100
1983-84—Pittsburgh Penguins		NHL	47	2	4	6	60
NHL TOTALS			88	4	6	10	162

(c)—June, 1981—Drafted by Pittsburgh Penguins in 1981 NHL entry draft. Fifth Penguins pick, 112th overall, sixth round.

MICHAEL BUSNIUK

Right Wing . . . 6'3" . . . 200 lbs. . . . Born, Thunder Bay, Ont., December 13, 1951 . . . Shoots right . . . Attended Denver University . . . Brother of Ron Busniuk . . . Also plays Defense.

Year	Team	League	Games	G.	A.	Pts.	Pen.
1970-71—Denver University (c)		WCHA	36	1	10	11	46
1971-72—Denver University		WCHA	38	1	19	20	77
1972-73—Denver University		WCHA	39	20	17	37	70
1973-74—Denver University		WCHA	....	...	....	....	....
1974-75—Nova Scotia Voyageurs		AHL	69	15	17	32	94
1975-76—Beauce Jaros		NAHL	65	14	52	66	179
1976-77—Nova Scotia Voyageurs		AHL	80	1	15	16	160
1977-78—Maine Mariners (d)		AHL	75	5	15	20	72
1978-79—Maine Mariners		AHL	79	10	35	45	215
1979-80—Maine Mariners		AHL	3	2	1	3	7
1979-80—Philadelphia Flyers		NHL	71	2	18	20	93
1980-81—Philadelphia Flyers		NHL	72	1	5	6	204
1981-82—Maine Mariners		AHL	78	12	26	38	203
1982-83—Maine Mariners (e)		AHL	11	0	5	5	14
1983-84—Maine Mariners (f)		AHL	2	0	1	1	2
NHL TOTALS			143	3	23	26	297

(c)—Drafted from Denver University by Montreal Canadiens in fifth round of 1971 amateur draft.
(d)—July, 1977—Signed by Philadelphia Flyers as free agent.
(e)—March, 1983—Signed by Maine Mariners as a free agent after completing season in Italy.
(f)—Led AHL Playoffs with 105 penalty minutes.

GARTH BUTCHER

Defense . . . 6' . . . 194 lbs. . . . Born, Regina, Sask., January 8, 1963 . . . Shoots right.

Year	Team	League	Games	G.	A.	Pts.	Pen.
1978-79—Regina Canadians		AMHL	22	4	22	26	72
1979-80—Regina Tier II		SJHL	51	15	31	46	236

Year	Team	League	Games	G.	A.	Pts.	Pen.
1979-80—Regina Pats		WHI	13	0	4	4	20
1980-81—Regina Pats (a-c)		WHL	69	9	77	86	230
1981-82—Regina Pats (a)		WHL	65	24	68	92	318
1981-82—Vancouver Canucks		NHL	5	0	0	0	9
1982-83—Kamloops Junior Oilers		WHL	5	4	2	6	4
1982-83—Vancouver Canucks		NHL	55	1	13	14	104
1983-84—Fredericton Express		AHL	25	4	13	17	43
1983-84—Vancouver Canucks		NHL	28	2	0	2	34
NHL TOTALS			88	3	13	16	147

(c)—June, 1981—Drafted as underage junior by Vancouver Canucks in 1981 NHL entry draft. First Canucks pick, 10th overall, first round.

CRAIG BUTZ

Defense . . . 6' . . . 200 lbs. . . . Born, Swift Current, Sask., March 2, 1965 . . . Shoots left . . . Led WHL with 273 penalty minutes in 1983-84.

Year	Team	League	Games	G.	A.	Pts.	Pen.
1981-82—Red Deer Rustlers		AJHL	56	3	10	13	245
1982-83—Kelowna Wings (c)		WHL	71	5	20	25	*307
1983-84—Kelowna Wings		WHL	20	3	7	10	59
1983-84—Portland Winter Hawks		WHL	54	2	10	12	214

(c)—June, 1983—Drafted as underage junior by Detroit Red Wings in 1983 NHL entry draft. Ninth Red Wings pick, 146th overall, eighth round.

LYNDON BYERS

Right Wing . . . 6'2" . . . 195 lbs. . . . Born, Nipawin, Sask., February 29, 1964 . . . Shoots right . . . (April 1981)—Broken right wrist.

Year	Team	League	Games	G.	A.	Pts.	Pen.
1980-81—Notre Dame Hounds (b)		SCMHL	37	35	42	77	106
1981-82—Regina Pats (c-d)		WHL	57	18	25	43	169
1982-83—Regina Pats		WHL	70	32	38	70	153
1983-84—Regina Pats		WHL	58	32	57	89	154
1983-84—Boston Bruins		NHL	10	2	4	6	32
NHL TOTALS			10	2	4	6	32

(c)—September, 1981—Traded by Saskatoon Blades to Regina Pats for Todd Strueby.
(d)—June, 1982—Drafted as underage junior by Boston Bruins in 1982 NHL entry draft. Third Bruins pick, 39th overall, second round.

ERIC CALDER

Defense . . . 6'1" . . . 184 lbs. . . . Born, Kitchener, Ont., June 26, 1963 . . . Shoots right.

Year	Team	League	Games	G.	A.	Pts.	Pen.
1979-80—Waterloo Jr. 'B'		....	42	13	36	49	33
1980-81—Cornwall Royals (c)		QMJHL	66	9	34	43	39
1981-82—Washington Capitals		NHL	1	0	0	0	0
1981-82—Cornwall Royals		OHL	65	12	36	48	95
1982-83—Cornwall Royals		OHL	66	5	30	35	72
1982-83—Washington Capitals		NHL	1	0	0	0	0
1983-84—Hershey Bears		AHL	68	2	6	8	50
1983-84—Fort Wayne Komets		IHL	3	0	2	2	0
NHL TOTALS			2	0	0	0	0

(c)—June, 1981—Drafted as underage junior by Washington Capitals in 1981 NHL entry draft. Second Capitals pick, 45th overall, third round.

JOHN (JOCK) CALLANDER

Center . . . 6'1" . . . 170 lbs. . . . Born, Regina, Sask., April 23, 1961 . . . Shoots right . . . Brother of Drew Callander.

Year	Team	League	Games	G.	A.	Pts.	Pen.
1978-79—Regina Pats		WHL	19	3	2	5	0
1978-79—Regina Blues		SJHL	42	44	42	86	24
1979-80—Regina Pats		WHL	39	9	11	20	25
1980-81—Regina Pats		WHL	72	67	86	153	37
1981-82—Regina Pats (c-d)		WHL	71	79	111	*190	59
1982-83—Salt Lake Golden Eagles		CHL	68	20	27	47	26
1983-84—Montana Magic		CHL	72	27	32	59	69
1983-84—Toledo Goaldiggers		IHL	2	0	0	0	0

(c)—Won Bob Brownridge Memorial Trophy (WHL scoring leader).
(d)—Led WHL playoffs with 26 assists.

ANTHONY BERT (Tony) CAMAZZOLA

Defense . . . 6'2" . . . 205 lbs. . . . Born, Burnaby, B.C., September 11, 1962 . . . Shoots left . . . Brother of Jim Camazzola.

Year	Team	League	Games	G.	A.	Pts.	Pen.
1979-80	Brandon Wheat Kings (c)	WHL	7	0	2	2	21
1980-81	Brandon Wheat Kings	WHL	69	4	20	24	144
1981-82	Brandon Wheat Kings	WHL	64	6	23	29	210
1981-82	Washington Capitals	NHL	3	0	0	0	4
1982-83	Hershey Bears	AHL	52	3	8	11	106
1983-84	Hershey Bears	AHL	63	6	10	16	138
	NHL TOTALS		3	0	0	0	4

(c)—June, 1980—Drafted as underage junior by Washington Capitals in 1980 NHL entry draft. Ninth Capitals pick, 195th overall, 10th round.

JIM CAMAZZOLA

Left Wing . . . 5'11" . . . 190 lbs. . . . Born, Burnaby, B.C., January 5, 1964 . . . Shoots left . . . Brother of Tony Camazzola.

Year	Team	League	Games	G.	A.	Pts.	Pen.
1982-83	Kamloops Junior Oilers (c)	WHL	66	57	58	115	54
1983-84	Seattle Breakers	WHL	3	1	1	2	0
1983-84	Kamloops Junior Oilers	WHL	29	26	24	50	25
1983-84	Chicago Black Hawks	NHL	1	0	0	0	0
	NHL TOTALS		1	0	0	0	0

(c)—June, 1982—Drafted as underage junior by Chicago Black Hawks in 1982 NHL entry draft. Tenth Black Hawks pick, 196th overall, 10th round.

DAVID WILLIAM CAMERON

Center . . . 6' . . . 185 lbs. . . . Born, Charlottetown, P.E.I., July 29, 1958 . . . Shoots left . . . (October 8, 1982)—Strained right knee in game vs. N.Y. Islanders . . . (January, 1984)— Elbow injury.

Year	Team	League	Games	G.	A.	Pts.	Pen.
1978-79	University of P.E.I (c)	AUAA	....	...	....	....	....
1979-80	Fort Wayne Komets	IHL	6	3	6	9	9
1979-80	Indianapolis Checkers	CHL	70	15	21	36	101
1980-81	Indianapolis Checkers (b)	CHL	78	40	30	70	156
1981-82	Colorado Rockies (d)	NHL	66	11	12	23	103
1981-82	Ft. Worth Texans	CHL	2	0	0	0	0
1982-83	Wichita Wind	CHL	25	6	9	15	40
1982-83	New Jersey Devils	NHL	35	5	4	9	50
1983-84	New Jersey Devils	NHL	67	9	12	21	85
	NHL TOTALS		168	25	28	53	238

(c)—June, 1978—Drafted by New York Islanders in 1978 NHL amateur draft. Seventh Islanders pick, 135th overall, eighth round.

(d)—October, 1981—Traded with Bob Lorimer by New York Islanders to Colorado Rockies for 1983 first round pick (Pat LaFontaine).

RANDY CAMERON

Defense . . . 6'3" . . . 200 lbs. . . . Born, Thunder Bay, Ont., January 2, 1964 . . . Shoots left.

Year	Team	League	Games	G.	A.	Pts.	Pen.
1981-82	Winnipeg Warriors (c)	WHL	68	3	6	9	197
1982-83	Winnipeg Warriors	WHL	70	0	10	10	191
1983-84	Winnipeg Warriors	WHL	26	1	2	3	88
1983-84	Brandon Wheat Kings (d)	WHL	35	0	6	6	67

(c)—June, 1982—Drafted as underage junior by Hartford Whalers in 1982 NHL entry draft. Eleventh Whalers pick, 235th overall, 12th round.

(d)—June, 1984—Released by Hartford Whalers.

BILLY CAMPBELL

Defense . . . 6' . . . 173 lbs. . . . Born, Montreal, Que., March 20, 1964 . . . Shoots right.

Year	Team	League	Games	G.	A.	Pts.	Pen.
1980-81	Montreal Juniors (c)	QMJHL	72	20	48	68	28
1981-82	Montreal Juniors (b-d)	QMJHL	64	21	41	62	30
1982-83	Verdun Juniors	QHL	67	35	64	99	34
1983-84	Verdun Juniors (e)	QHL	65	24	66	90	59

(c)—First winner of Raymond Lagace Trophy (Top Rookie QMJHL Defenseman).

(d)—June, 1982—Drafted as underage junior by Philadelphia Flyers in 1982 NHL entry draft. Third Flyers pick, 47th overall, third round.
(e)—Won Emile "Butch" Bouchard Trophy (Top Defenseman).

COLIN JOHN CAMPBELL

Defense . . . 5'9" . . . 190 lbs. . . . Born, London, Ont., January 28, 1953 . . . Shoots left . . . Missed part of 1975-76 season with elbow surgery . . . (December 10, 1980)—Broken wrist . . . Holds single season penalty minute record for Edmonton (196) . . . (November, 1982) —Rib injury . . . (November 10, 1983)—Injured ribs in game vs. Toronto.

Year	Team	League	Games	G.	A.	Pts.	Pen.
1970-71—Peterborough TPTs		Jr."A"OHA	59	5	18	23	160
1971-72—Peterborough TPTs		Jr."A"OHA	50	2	23	25	158
1972-73—Peterborough TPTs (c-d)		Jr."A"OHA	60	7	40	47	189
1973-74—Vancouver Blazers		WHA	78	3	20	23	191
1974-75—Hershey Bears		AHL	15	1	3	4	55
1974-75—Pittsburgh Penguins		NHL	59	4	15	19	172
1975-76—Pittsburgh Penguins (e)		NHL	64	7	10	17	105
1976-77—Oklahoma City Blazers (f)		CHL	7	1	2	3	9
1976-77—Colorado Rockies (g)		NHL	54	3	8	11	67
1977-78—Pittsburgh Penguins		NHL	55	1	9	10	103
1978-79—Pittsburgh Penguins (h)		NHL	65	2	18	20	137
1979-80—Edmonton Oilers		NHL	72	2	11	13	196
1980-81—Vancouver Canucks (i)		NHL	42	1	8	9	75
1981-82—Vancouver Canucks (j)		NHL	47	0	8	8	131
1982-83—Detroit Red Wings		NHL	53	1	7	8	74
1983-84—Detroit Red Wings		NHL	68	3	4	7	108
WHA TOTALS			78	3	20	23	191
NHL TOTALS			579	24	98	122	1168

(c)—Drafted from Peterborough TPTs by Pittsburgh Penguins in second round of 1973 amateur draft.
(d)—Selected by Vancouver Blazers in WHA amateur draft, May, 1973.
(e)—Traded to Colorado Rockies by Pittsburgh Penguins with Michel Plasse and Simon Nolet as compensation for Pittsburgh signing free agent Denis Herron, August, 1976.
(f)—Loaned to Oklahoma City Blazers by Colorado Rockies, January, 1977.
(g)—Returned to Pittsburgh Penguins by Colorado Rockies for "future considerations," May, 1977.
(h)—June, 1979—Selected by Edmonton Oilers in NHL expansion draft.
(i)—October, 1980—Selected by Vancouver in 1980 NHL waiver draft.
(j)—July, 1982—Signed by Detroit Red Wings as a free agent.

WADE CAMPBELL

Defense . . . 6'4"   220 lbs. . . . Born, Peace River, Alta., February 1, 1061 . . . Shoots right.

Year	Team	League	Games	G.	A.	Pts.	Pen.
1980-81—University of Alberta		CWJAA	24	3	15	18	46
1981-82—University of Alberta (c)		CWJAA	24	6	12	18	....
1982-83—Sherbrooke Jets		AHL	18	4	2	6	23
1982-83—Winnipeg Jets		NHL	42	1	2	3	50
1983-84—Winnipeg Jets		NHL	79	7	14	21	147
NHL TOTALS			121	8	16	24	197

(c)—September, 1982—Signed by Winnipeg Jets as a free agent.

JACK CAPUANO

Defense . . . 6'2" . . . 210 lbs. . . . Born, Cranston, R.I., July 7, 1966 . . . Shoots left.

Year	Team	League	Games	G.	A.	Pts.	Pen.
1983-84—Kent Prep (c)		Conn. H.S.	25	10	8	18	20

(c)—June, 1984—Drafted by Toronto Maple Leafs in 1984 NHL entry draft. Fourth Maple Leafs pick, 88th overall, fifth round.

GUY CARBONNEAU

Center . . . 5'10" . . . 165 lbs. . . . Born, Sept Iles, Que., March 18, 1960 . . . Shoots right.

Year	Team	League	Games	G.	A.	Pts.	Pen.
1976-77—Chicoutimi Sagueneens		QMJHL	59	9	20	29	8
1977-78—Chicoutimi Sagueneens		QMJHL	70	28	55	83	60
1978-79—Chicoutimi Sagueneens (c)		QMJHL	72	62	79	141	47
1979-80—Chicoutimi Saguennens (b)		QMJHL	72	72	110	182	66
1979-80—Nova Scotia Voyageurs (d)		AHL	....	...	....	....	....
1980-81—Montreal Canadiens		NHL	2	0	1	1	0
1980-81—Nova Scotia Voyageurs		AHL	78	35	53	88	87
1981-82—Nova Scotia Voyageurs		AHL	77	27	67	94	124

Year	Team	League	Games	G.	A.	Pts.	Pen.
1982-83—Montreal Canadiens		NHL	77	18	29	47	68
1983-84—Montreal Canadiens		NHL	78	24	30	54	75
NHL TOTALS			157	42	60	102	143

(c)—August, 1979—Drafted by Montreal Canadiens as underage junior in 1979 NHL entry draft. Fourth Canadiens pick, 44th overall, third round.

(d)—No regular season appearance, played in one playoff game.

TERRY CARKNER

Defense . . . 6'3" . . . 200 lbs. . . . Born, Smith Falls, Ont., March 7, 1966 . . . Shoots left.

Year	Team	League	Games	G.	A.	Pts.	Pen.
1982-83—Brockville Braves		COJHL	47	8	32	40	94
1983-84—Peterborough Petes (c)		OHL	66	4	21	25	91

(c)—June, 1984—Drafted as underage junior by New York Rangers in 1984 NHL entry draft. First Rangers pick, 14th overall, first round.

TODD CARLILE

Defense . . . 5'11" . . . 185 lbs. . . . Born, St. Paul, Minn., January 22, 1964 . . . Shoots right . . . (June, 1980)—Partial separation of shoulder.

Year	Team	League	Games	G.	A.	Pts.	Pen.
1981-82—North St. Paul H.S. (c)		Minn. H.S.	22	8	18	26	32
1982-83—University of Michigan		CCHA	36	5	14	19	67
1983-84—University of Michigan		CCHA	33	11	20	31	70

(c)—June, 1982—Drafted as underage player by Minnesota North Stars in 1982 NHL entry draft. Sixth North Stars pick, 122nd overall, sixth round.

JACK CARLSON

Left Wing . . . 6'3" . . . 205 lbs. . . . Born, Virginia, Minn., August 23, 1954 . . . Shoots left . . . Brother of Jeff and Steve Carlson . . . Also plays Right Wing . . . (April 4, 1979)—Injured back in game at Chicago that required spinal fusion surgery. He missed all of 1979-80 season and returned to action November 7, 1980 . . . (November 26, 1980)—Pulled muscle in lower back . . . (September, 1982)—Injured shoulder in fight with Jim Pavese of St. Louis during a preseason game . . . (Summer/83)—Shoulder surgery.

Year	Team	League	Games	G.	A.	Pts.	Pen.
1973-74—Marquette Rangers (a-c-d)		USHL	42	42	29	71	159
1974-75—Johnstown Jets		NAHL	50	27	22	49	246
1974-75—Minnesota Fighting Saints		WHA	32	5	5	10	85
1975-76—Minnesota Fighting Saints		WHA	58	8	10	18	189
1975-76—Edmonton Oilers (e-f)		WHA	10	1	1	2	31
1976-77—Minnesota Fighting Saints (g)		WHA	36	4	3	7	55
1976-77—New England Whalers (h)		WHA	35	7	5	12	81
1977-78—New England Whalers		WHA	67	9	20	29	192
1978-79—New England Whalers (i)		WHA	34	2	7	9	61
1978-79—Minnesota North Stars		NHL	16	3	0	3	40
1979-80—Did Not Play		NHL					
1980-81—Minnesota North Stars		NHL	43	7	2	9	108
1981-82—Minnesota North Stars (j)		NHL	57	8	4	12	103
1982-83—St. Louis Blues		NHL	54	6	1	7	58
1983-84—St. Louis Blues (k)		NHL	58	6	8	14	85
WHA TOTALS			272	36	51	87	694
NHL TOTALS			228	30	15	45	394

(c)—Won Most Valuable Player Award.

(d)—Drafted from Marquette Rangers by Detroit Red Wings in seventh round of 1974 amateur draft.

(e)—Signed by Edmonton Oilers as free agent following demise of Minnesota Fighting Saints, March, 1976.

(f)—Drafted from Edmonton Oilers by Calgary Cowboys in intra-league draft, June, 1976.

(g)—Sold to Edmonton Oilers by Minnesota Fighting Saints, January, 1977.

(h)—Traded to New England Whalers by Edmonton Oilers with Dave Dryden, Steve Carlson, Dave Keon and John McKenzie for Danny Arndt, WHA rights to Dave Debol and cash, January, 1977.

(i)—February, 1979—Traded by New England Whalers to Minnesota North Stars for future considerations.

(j)—Claimed by St. Louis Blues in 1982 NHL waiver draft.

(k)—July, 1984—Released by St. Louis Blues.

KENT CARLSON

Defense . . . 6'3" . . . 200 lbs. . . . Born, Concord, N.H., January 11, 1962 . . . Shoots left.

Year	Team	League	Games	G.	A.	Pts.	Pen.
1981-82—St. Lawrence University (c)		ECAC	28	8	14	22	24

Year	Team	League	Games	G.	A.	Pts.	Pen.
1982-83—St. Lawrence University		ECAC	36	10	23	33	56
1983-84—Montreal Canadiens		NHL	65	3	7	10	73
NHL TOTALS			65	3	7	10	73

(c)—June, 1982—Drafted by Montreal Canadiens in 1982 NHL entry draft. Third Canadiens pick, 32nd overall, second round.

STEVE CARLSON

Center . . . 6'3" . . . 180 lbs. . . . Born, Virginia, Minn., August 26, 1955 . . . Shoots left . . . Brother of Jack and Jeff Carlson . . . Missed part of 1975-76 season with broken right hand . . . (October, 1980)—Lower back problems . . . (December, 1982)—Separated shoulder.

Year	Team	League	Games	G.	A.	Pts.	Pen.
1973-74—Marquette Rangers (a)		USHL	42	34	45	79	77
1974-75—Johnstown Jets		NAHL	70	30	58	88	84
1975-76—Johnstown Jets		NAHL	40	22	24	46	55
1975-76—Minnesota Fighting Saints (c-d)		WHA	10	0	1	1	23
1976-77—Minnesota Fighting Saints (e-f)		WHA	21	5	8	13	8
1976-77—New England Whalers		WHA	31	4	9	13	40
1977-78—Springfield Indians		AHL	37	21	15	36	46
1977-78—New England Whalers		WHA	38	6	7	13	11
1978-79—Edmonton Oilers (g-h)		WHA	73	18	22	40	50
1979-80—Los Angeles Kings		NHL	52	9	12	21	23
1980-81—Springfield Indians		AHL	32	10	14	24	44
1980-81—Houston Apollos		CHL	27	13	21	34	29
1981-82—Nashville South Stars (i)		CHL	59	23	39	62	63
1982-83—Birmingham South Stars		CHL	69	25	42	67	73
1983-84—Baltimore Skipjacks (j)		AHL	63	9	30	39	70
WHA TOTALS			173	33	47	80	132
NHL TOTALS			52	9	12	21	23

(c)—Signed by New England Whalers following demise of Minnesota Fighting Saints, March, 1976.

(d)—Drafted from New England Whalers by Cleveland Crusaders in intra-league draft, June, 1976. (Later rejoined Minnesota Fighting Saints.)

(e)—Sold to Edmonton Oilers by Minnesota Fighting Saints, January, 1977.

(f)—Traded to New England Whalers by Edmonton Oilers with Dave Dryden, Jack Carlson, Dave Keon and John McKenzie for Danny Arndt, WHA rights to Dave Debol and cash, January, 1977.

(g)—January, 1979—NHL rights traded by Detroit Red Wings to Los Angeles Kings for NHL rights to Steve Short.

(h)—June, 1979—Selected by Los Angeles Kings in NHL reclaim draft.

(i)—December, 1981—Signed by Minnesota North Stars as a free agent and assigned to Nashville South Stars.

(j)—August, 1983—Signed by Pittsburgh Penguins as a free agent.

RANDY ROBERT CARLYLE

Defense . . . 5'10" . . . 198 lbs. . . . Born, Sudbury, Ont., April 19, 1956 . . . Shoots left. . . . Missed part of 1978-79 season with broken ankle . . . (October, 1982)—Injured back . . . (January, 1983)—Injured knee . . . (March, 1984)—Knee injury.

Year	Team	League	Games	G.	A.	Pts.	Pen.
1973-74—Sudbury Wolves		Jr."A" OHA	12	0	8	8	21
1974-75—Sudbury Wolves		Jr."A" OHA	67	17	47	64	118
1975-76—Sudbury Wolves (b-c)		Jr."A" OHA	60	15	64	79	126
1976-77—Dallas Black Hawks		CHL	26	2	7	9	63
1976-77—Toronto Maple Leafs		NHL	45	0	5	5	51
1977-78—Dallas Black Hawks		CHL	21	3	14	17	31
1977-78—Toronto Maple Leafs (d)		NHL	49	2	11	13	31
1978-79—Pittsburgh Penguins		NHL	70	13	34	47	78
1979-80—Pittsburgh Penguins		NHL	67	8	28	36	45
1980-81—Pittsburgh Penguins (a-e)		NHL	76	16	67	83	136
1981-82—Pittsburgh Penguins		NHL	73	11	64	75	131
1982-83—Pittsburgh Penguins		NHL	61	15	41	56	110
1983-84—Pittsburgh Penguins (f)		NHL	50	3	23	26	82
1983-84—Winnipeg Jets		NHL	5	0	3	3	2
NHL TOTALS			496	68	276	344	666

(c)—Drafted from Sudbury Wolves by Toronto Maple Leafs in second round of 1976 amateur draft.

(d)—Traded to Pittsburgh Penguins by Toronto Maple Leafs with George Ferguson for Dave Burrows, June, 1978.

(e)—Won James Norris Memorial Trophy (Top NHL Defenseman).

(f)—March, 1984—Traded by Pittsburgh Penguins to Winnipeg Jets for first round 1984 draft pick (Doug Bodger) and player to be named after the 1983-84 season (Moe Mantha).

ROBERT CARPENTER

Center . . . 6' . . . 190 lbs. . . . Born, Beverly, Mass., July 13, 1963 . . . Shoots left . . . First to play in NHL directly from U.S. high school hockey.

Year	Team	League	Games	G.	A.	Pts.	Pen.
1979-80—St. Johns Prep. H.S. (a)		Mass. H.S.	....	28	37	65	....
1980-81—St. Johns Prep. H.S. (a-c)		Mass. H.S.	....	14	24	38	....
1981-82—Washington Capitals		NHL	80	32	35	67	69
1982-83—Washington Capitals		NHL	80	32	37	69	64
1983-84—Washington Capitals		NHL	80	28	40	68	51
NHL TOTALS			240	92	112	204	184

(c)—June, 1981—Drafted as underage junior by Washington Capitals in 1981 NHL entry draft. First Capitals pick, third overall, first round.

JEROME CARRIER

Defense . . . 5'10" . . . 155 lbs. . . . Born, Beaumont, Que., June 10, 1965 . . . Shoots left . . . (November, 1982)—Stretched shoulder ligaments.

Year	Team	League	Games	G.	A.	Pts.	Pen.
1982-83—Verdun Juniors (c)		QHL	58	8	26	34	40
1983-84—Verdun Juniors		QHL	69	14	38	52	42

(c)—June, 1983—Drafted as underage junior by Philadelphia Flyers in 1983 NHL entry draft. Fourth Flyers pick, 101st overall, fifth round.

WILLIAM ALLAN (BILLY) CARROLL

Center . . . 5'10" . . . 191 lbs . . . Born, Toronto, Ont., January 19, 1959 . . . Shoots left . . . (1978-79)—Mononucleosis.

Year	Team	League	Games	G.	A.	Pts.	Pen.
1976-77—London Knights		OMJHL	64	18	31	49	37
1977-78—London Knights		OMJHL	68	37	36	73	42
1978-79—London Knight (b-c)		OMJHL	63	35	50	85	38
1979-80—Indianapolis Checkers		CHL	49	9	17	26	19
1980-81—Indianapolis Racers		CHL	59	27	37	64	67
1980-81—New York Islanders		NHL	18	4	4	8	6
1981-82—New York Islanders		NHL	72	9	20	29	32
1982-83—New York Islanders		NHL	71	1	11	12	24
1983-84—New York Islanders		NHL	39	5	2	7	12
NHL TOTALS			200	19	37	56	74

(c)—August, 1979—Drafted by New York Islanders in 1979 NHL entry draft. Third Islanders pick, 38th overall, second round.

LINDSAY WARREN CARSON

Center . . . 6'2" . . . 190 lbs. . . . Born, Oxbow, Sask., November 21, 1960 . . . Shoots left . . . Also plays left wing . . . (October 15, 1983)—Broke left arm when checked by Bob Nystrom in game vs. N.Y. Islanders.

Year	Team	League	Games	G.	A.	Pts.	Pen.
1977-78—Saskatoon Blades		WCHL	62	23	55	78	124
1978-79—Saskatoon Blades		WHL	37	21	29	50	55
1978-79—Billings Bighorns (c)		WHL	40	13	22	35	50
1979-80—Billings Bighorns		WHL	70	42	66	108	101
1980-81—Maine Mariners		AHL	79	11	25	36	84
1981-82—Maine Mariners		AHL	54	20	31	51	92
1981-82—Philadelphia Flyers		NHL	18	0	1	1	32
1982-83—Philadelphia Flyers		NHL	78	18	19	37	68
1983-84—Springfield Indians		AHL	5	2	4	6	5
1983-84—Philadelphia Flyers		NHL	16	1	3	4	10
NHL TOTALS			112	19	23	42	110

(c)—August, 1979—Drafted as underage junior by Philadelphia Flyers in 1979 NHL entry draft. Fourth Flyers pick, 56th overall, third round.

RON CARTER

Right Wing . . . 6'1" . . . 205 lbs. . . . Born, Chateauguay, Que., March 14, 1958 . . . Shoots left.

Year	Team	League	Games	G.	A.	Pts.	Pen.
1975-76—Sherbrooke Beavers		QJHL	65	34	36	70	12
1976-77—Sherbrooke Beavers		QJHL	72	77	50	127	18
1977-78—Sherbrooke Beavers (a-c-d)		QJHL	71	*88	86	*174	28
1978-79—Dallas Black Hawks		CHL	54	22	16	38	8
1978-79—Springfield Indians		AHL	1	0	0	0	0

Year	Team	League	Games	G.	A.	Pts.	Pen.
1979-80—Houston Apollos	CHL	76	40	30	70	17
1979-80—Edmonton Oilers (e)	NHL	2	0	0	0	0
1980-81—Rochester Americans	AHL	38	31	19	50	8
1980-81—Erie Blades	EHL	38	23	21	44	6
1981-82—Rochester Americans (f)	AHL	12	6	4	10	0
1981-82—Flint Generals	IHL	49	29	23	52	2
1982-83—Nashville South Stars (b)	ACHL	58	47	49	96	21
1983-84—Virginia Lancers	ACHL	62	51	59	110	20
NHL TOTALS		2	0	0	0	0

(c)—Drafted from Sherbrooke Beavers by Montreal Canadiens in second round of 1978 amateur draft.
(d)—Selected by Edmonton Oilers in World Hockey Association amateur players' draft, June, 1978. Signed multi-year contract with Oilers, July, 1978.
(e)—July, 1980—Acquired on waivers by Buffalo Sabres from Edmonton Oilers.
(f)—December, 1981—Released by Rochester Americans.

BRUCE CASSIDY

Defense . . . 5'11" . . . 175 lbs. . . . Born, Ottawa, Ont., May 20, 1965 . . . Shoots left.

Year	Team	League	Games	G.	A.	Pts.	Pen.
1981-82—Hawkesbury Hawks	COJHL	37	13	30	43	32
1982-83—Ottawa 67's (c-d)	OHL	70	25	86	111	33
1983-84—Ottawa 67's (b)	OHL	67	27	68	95	58
1983-84—Chicago Black Hawks	NHL	1	0	0	0	0
NHL TOTALS		1	0	0	0	0

(c)—Won Emms Family Award (OHL Rookie-of-the-Year).
(d)—June, 1983—Drafted as underage junior by Chicago Black Hawks in 1983 NHL entry draft. First Black Hawks pick, 18th overall, first round.

RORY LOUIS CAVA

Defense . . . 6'5" . . . 220 lbs. . . . Born, Thunder Bay, Ont., February 12, 1960 . . . Shoots right.

Year	Team	League	Games	G.	A.	Pts.	Pen.
1977-78—Ottawa 67's	OMJHL	66	1	8	9	110
1978-79—Ottawa 67's	OMJHL	67	6	18	24	138
1979-80—Ottawa 67's	OMJHL	53	4	19	23	179
1980-81—Fort Wayne Komets (c)	IHL	69	2	20	22	139
1980-81—Dallas Black Hawks	CHL	1	0	0	0	4
1981-82—Dallas Black Hawks	CHL	66	4	27	31	184
1982-83—Carolina Thunderbirds (a-d)	ACHL	63	23	*60	83	151
1983-84—Adirondack Red Wings	AHL	75	2	19	21	160

(c) September, 1980—Signed by Vancouver Canucks as a free agent.
(d)—Named ACHL MVP.

GINO CAVALLINI

Left Wing . . . 6'2" . . . 215 lbs. . . . Born, Toronto, Ont., November 24, 1962 . . . Shoots left.

Year	Team	League	Games	G.	A.	Pts.	Pen.
1981-82—Toronto St. Mikes	OJHL	37	27	56	83	..
1982-83—Bowling Green Univ.	CCHA	40	8	16	24	52
1983-84—Bowling Green Univ. (c)	CCHA	43	25	23	48	16

(c)—July, 1984—Signed by Calgary Flames as a free agent.

PAUL CAVALLINI

Defense . . . 6'2" . . . 202 lbs. . . . Born, Toronto, Ont., October 13, 1965 . . . Shoots left.

Year	Team	League	Games	G.	A.	Pts.	Pen.
1983-84—Henry Carr H.S. (c)	MTHL	54	20	41	61	190

(c)—June, 1984—Drafted as underage junior by Washington Capitals in 1984 NHL entry draft. Ninth Capitals pick, 205th overall, 10th round.

FRANTISEK CERNIK

Left Wing . . . 5'9" . . . 185 lbs. . . . Born, Novy Jicin, Czechoslovakia, June 3, 1953 . . . Shoots left . . . Member of Czechoslovakian National Team in 1976, 77, 78, 79, 80, 81 and 82.

Year	Team	League	Games	G.	A.	Pts.	Pen.
1976-77—Jihlava Dukla	Czech.	..	30	13	43	..
1977-78—Jihlava Dukla	Czech.	..	..	..	..	..
1978-79—Ostrava Vitkovice VZKG	Czech.	..	24	15	39	..
1979-80—Ostrava Vitkovice VZKG	Czech.	..	16	12	28	..
1980-81—Ostrava Vitkovice VZKG	Czech.	43	25	26	51	..

Year	Team	League	Games	G.	A.	Pts.	Pen.
1981-82—Ostrava Vitkovice VZKG		Czech.	41	28	23	51	50
1982-83—Ostrava Vitkovice VZKG		Czech.	..	..	..	..	..
1983-84—Ostrava Vitkovice VZKG (c)		Czech.	44	25	23	48	..

(c)—July, 1984—Signed by Detroit Red Wings after Detroit had purchased Cernik's NHL rights from Quebec Nordiques.

JOHN DAVID CHABOT
(Given Name: John Kahlbaitche)
Center . . . 6'1" . . . 185 lbs. . . . Born Summerside, P.E.I., May 18, 1962 . . . Shoots left.

Year	Team	League	Games	G.	A.	Pts.	Pen.
1979-80—Hull Olympics (c)		QMJHL	68	26	57	83	28
1980-81—Hull Olympics		QMJHL	70	27	62	89	24
1980-81—Nova Scotia Voyageurs		AHL	1	0	0	0	0
1981-82—Sherbrooke Beavers (a-d-e)		QMJHL	62	34	*109	143	40
1982-83—Nova Scotia Voyageurs		AHL	76	16	73	89	19
1983-84—Montreal Canadiens		NHL	56	18	25	43	13
NHL TOTALS			56	18	25	43	13

(c)—June, 1980—Drafted as underage junior by Montreal Canadiens in 1980 NHL entry draft. Third Canadiens pick, 40th overall, second round.

(d)—September 1981—Traded by Hull Olympics to Sherbrooke Beavers for Tim Cranston and Rousell MacKenzie.

(e)—Won Michel Briere Trophy (regular season QMJHL MVP).

MILAN CHALUPA
Defense . . . 5'10" . . . 183 lbs., Born, Oudolen, Czechoslovakia, July 4, 1953. . . . Shoots right.

Year	Team	League	Games	G.	A.	Pts.	Pen.
1983-84—Dukla Jihlava (c)		Czech.	39	3	11	14	..

(c)—June, 1984—Drafted by Detroit Red Wings in NHL entry draft. Third Red Wings pick, 49th overall, third round.

CRAIG CHANNELL
Defense . . . 5'11" . . . 195 lbs. . . . Born, Moncton, N.B., April 24, 1962 . . . Shoots left.

Year	Team	League	Games	G.	A.	Pts.	Pen.
1979-80—Seattle Breakers		WHL	70	3	21	24	191
1980-81—Seattle Breakers		WHL	71	9	66	75	181
1981-82—Seattle Breakers (c)		WHL	71	9	79	88	244
1982-83—Sherbrooke Jets		AHL	65	0	15	15	109
1983-84—Sherbrooke Jets		AHL	80	5	18	23	112

(c)—September, 1982—Signed by Winnipeg Jets as a free agent.

WALLY CHAPMAN
Center . . . 6' . . . 190 lbs. . . . Born, Ft. Leonard Wood, Mo., July 6, 1964 . . . Shoots left.

Year	Team	League	Games	G.	A.	Pts.	Pen.
1981-82—Edina H.S. (c)		Minn. H.S.	26	27	11	38	14
1982-83—University of Minnesota		WCHA	20	3	6	9	18
1983-84—University of Minnesota		WCHA	30	10	6	16	20

(c)—June, 1982—Drafted by Minnesota North Stars as underage player in 1982 NHL entry draft. Second North Stars pick, 59th overall, third round.

TODD CHARLESWORTH
Defense . . . 6'1" . . . 185 lbs. . . . Born, Calgary, Alta., March 22, 1965 . . . Shoots left.

Year	Team	League	Games	G.	A.	Pts.	Pen.
1981-82—Gloucester Rangers		COJHL	50	13	24	37	67
1982-83—Oshawa Generals (c)		OHL	70	6	23	29	55
1983-84—Oshawa Generals		OHL	57	11	35	46	54
1983-84—Pittsburgh Penguins		NHL	10	0	0	0	8
NHL TOTALS			10	0	0	0	8

(c)—June, 1983—Drafted as underage junior by Pittsburgh Penguins in 1983 NHL entry draft. Second Penguins pick, 22nd overall, second round.

DAVE CHARTIER
Defense . . . 6' . . . 175 lbs. . . . Born, Saskatoon, Sask., March 16, 1964 . . . Shoots right.

Year	Team	League	Games	G.	A.	Pts.	Pen.
1980-81—Saskatoon Blazers		Midget	20	18	20	38	104
1981-82—Saskatoon Blades (c)		WHL	65	8	13	21	157

Year	Team	League	Games	G.	A.	Pts.	Pen.
1982-83—Saskatoon Blades		WHL	59	9	39	48	104
1983-84—Saskatoon Blades		WHL	59	9	21	30	136

(c)—June, 1982—Drafted as underage junior by Los Angeles in 1982 NHL entry draft. Ninth Kings pick, 174th overall, ninth round.

DAVE CHARTIER

Center ... 5'9" ... 170 lbs. ... Born, St. Lazare, Man., February 15, 1961 ... Shoots right ... (October, 1982)—Broken Finger.

Year	Team	League	Games	G.	A.	Pts.	Pen.
1977-78—Brandon Travellers		SJHL	47	30	22	52	98
1977-78—Brandon Wheat Kings		WCHL	2	1	0	1	0
1978-79—Brandon Wheat Kings		WHL	48	14	12	26	83
1979-80—Brandon Wheat Kings (c)		WHL	69	39	29	68	285
1980-81—Brandon Wheat Kings		WHL	69	64	60	124	295
1980-81—Winnipeg Jets		NHL	1	0	0	0	0
1980-81—Tulsa Oilers		CHL	1	1	0	1	4
1981-82—Tulsa Oilers		CHL	74	18	17	35	126
1982-83—Sherbrooke Jets		AHL	48	9	10	19	87
1983-84—Sherbrooke Jets		AHL	43	13	14	27	59
NHL TOTALS			1	0	0	0	0

(c)—June, 1980—Drafted as an underage junior by Winnipeg Jets in 1980 NHL entry draft. Tenth Jets pick, 191st overall, 10th round.

ANDRE CHARTRAIN

Center ... 5'8" ... 175 lbs. ... Born, Beaconsfield, Que., March 24, 1962 ... Shoots right ... (January, 1983)—Injured wrist.

Year	Team	League	Games	G	A	Pts	Pen.
1979-80—Sorel Black Hawks		QMJHL	64	21	17	38	40
1980-81—Sorel Black Hawks		QMJHL	72	35	73	108	98
1981-82—Quebec Remparts (c-d)		QMJHL	46	26	30	56	36
1981-82—Fredericton Express		AHL	9	1	1	2	4
1982-83—Fredericton Express		AHL	29	7	4	11	7
1982-83—Erie Golden Blades		ACHL	1	0	2	2	0
1983-84—Fredericton Express		AHL	5	0	0	0	2
1983-84—Erie Golden Blades		ACHL	20	9	19	28	16

(c)—August, 1981—Acquired by Quebec Remparts in dispersal draft of players from defunct Sorel Black Hawks.

(d)—October, 1981—Signed by Quebec Nordiques as a free agent.

RAYMOND RICHARD (RICK) CHARTRAW

Defense ... 6'2" ... 205 lbs. ... Born, Caracas, Venezuela, July 13, 1954 ... Shoots right ... Raised in Erie, Pa. ... Has also played Right Wing ... (October, 1982)—Sprained right wrist.

Year	Team	League	Games	G.	A.	Pts.	Pen.
1972-73—Kitchener Rangers		Jr. "A" OHA	59	10	22	32	102
1973-74—Kitchener Rangers (b-c)		Jr. "A" OHA	70	17	44	61	150
1974-75—Nova Scotia Voyageurs (a)		AHL	58	7	20	27	148
1974-75—Montreal Canadiens		NHL	12	0	0	0	6
1975-76—Nova Scotia Voyageurs		AHL	33	12	24	36	49
1975-76—Montreal Canadiens		NHL	16	1	3	4	25
1976-77—Montreal Canadiens		NHL	43	3	4	7	59
1977-78—Montreal Canadiens		NHL	68	4	12	16	64
1978-79—Montreal Canadiens		NHL	62	5	11	16	29
1979-80—Montreal Canadiens		NHL	66	5	7	12	35
1980-81—Montreal Canadiens (d)		NHL	14	0	0	0	4
1980-81—Los Angeles Kings		NHL	21	1	6	7	28
1981-82—New Haven Nighthawks		AHL	33	3	9	12	39
1981-82—Los Angeles Kings		NHL	33	2	8	10	56
1982-83—Los Angeles Kings (e)		NHL	31	3	5	8	31
1982-83—New York Rangers		NHL	26	2	2	4	37
1983-84—Tulsa Oilers		CHL	28	1	4	5	25
1983-84—New York Rangers (f)		NHL	4	0	0	0	4
1983-84—Edmonton Oilers		NHL	24	2	6	8	21
NHL TOTALS			420	28	64	92	399

(c)—Drafted from Kitchener Rangers by Montreal Canadiens in first round of 1974 amateur draft.

(d)—February, 1981—Traded by Montreal Canadiens to Los Angeles Kings for future considerations.

(e)—January, 1983—Claimed on waivers by the New York Rangers from Los Angeles Kings.

(f)—January, 1984—Traded by New York Rangers to Edmonton Oilers for future considerations.

LANDIS CHAULK

Left Wing . . . 6'1" . . . 200 lbs. . . . Born, Swift Current, Sask., May 17, 1966 . . . Shoots left.

Year	Team	League	Games	G.	A.	Pts.	Pen.
1983-84	Calgary Wranglers (c)	WHL	72	21	28	49	123

(c)—June, 1984—Drafted as underage junior by Vancouver Canucks in 1984 NHL entry draft. Third Canucks pick, 55th overall, third round.

CHRIS CHELIOS

Defense . . . 6'1" . . . 187 lbs. . . . Born, Chicago, Ill., January 25, 1962 . . . Shoots right. . . . Member of 1984 U.S. Olympic Team.

Year	Team	League	Games	G.	A.	Pts.	Pen.
1979-80	Moose Jaw Canucks	SJHL	53	12	31	43	118
1980-81	Moose Jaw Canucks (c)	SJHL	54	23	64	87	175
1981-82	University of Wisconsin	WCHA	43	6	43	49	50
1982-83	University of Wisconsin (b)	WCHA	45	16	32	48	62
1983-84	U.S. National Team	Int'l.	60	14	35	49	58
1983-84	U.S. Olympic Team	Int'l.	6	0	4	4	8
1983-84	Montreal Canadiens	NHL	12	0	2	2	12
	NHL TOTALS		12	0	2	2	12

(c)—June, 1981—Drafted as underage junior by Montreal Canadiens in 1981 NHL entry draft. Fifth Canadiens pick, 40th overall, second round.

RICHARD CHERNOMAZ

Right Wing . . . 5'10" . . . 175 lbs. . . . Born, Selkirk, Man., September 1, 1963 . . . Shoots right . . . Missed parts of 1981-82 season with recurring pain caused by separated shoulder . . . (January, 1983)—Injured knee ligaments.

Year	Team	League	Games	G.	A.	Pts.	Pen.
1979-80	Saskatoon	SJHL	51	33	37	70	75
1979-80	Saskatoon Blades	WHL	25	9	10	19	33
1980-81	Victoria Cougars (c)	WHL	72	49	64	113	92
1981-82	Victoria Cougars	WHL	49	36	62	98	69
1981-82	Colorado Rockies	NHL	2	0	0	0	0
1982-83	Victoria Cougars (a)	WHL	64	71	53	124	113
1983-84	Maine Mariners	AHL	69	17	29	46	39
1983-84	New Jersey Devils	NHL	7	2	1	3	2
	NHL TOTALS		9	2	1	3	2

(c)—June, 1981—Drafted as underage junior by Colorado Rockies in 1981 NHL entry draft. Third Rockies pick, 26th overall, second round.

MARC CHORNEY

Defense . . . 6' . . . 196 lbs. . . . Born, Sudbury, Ont., November 8, 1959 . . . Shoots left.

Year	Team	League	Games	G.	A.	Pts.	Pen.
1977-78	University of North Dakota	WCHA	38	1	8	9	54
1978-79	Univ. of North Dakota (c)	WCHA	31	5	11	16	70
1979-80	Univ. of North Dakota (b-d)	WCHA	39	7	38	45	54
1980-81	Univ. of North Dakota (a-e)	WCHA	35	8	34	42	72
1980-81	Pittsburgh Penguins	NHL	8	1	6	7	14
1981-82	Erie Blades	AHL	6	1	3	4	4
1981-82	Pittsburgh Penguins	NHL	60	1	6	7	63
1982-83	Pittsburgh Penguins	NHL	67	3	5	8	66
1983-84	Pittsburgh Penguins (f)	NHL	4	0	1	1	8
1983-84	Los Angeles Kings (g)	NHL	71	3	9	12	58
	NHL TOTALS		210	8	27	35	209

(c)—August, 1979—Drafted by Pittsburgh Penguins in 1979 NHL entry draft. Sixth Penguins pick, 115th overall, sixth round.

(d)—Named to NCAA Tournament All-Star team.

(e)—Named to All-America team (West).

(f)—October, 1983—Traded by Pittsburgh Penguins to Los Angeles Kings for future considerations.

(g)—July, 1984—Signed by Washington Capitals as a free agent.

GUY CHOUINARD

Center . . . 5'11" . . . 175 lbs. . . . Born, Quebec City, Que., October 20, 1956 . . . Shoots right . . . (November 26, 1980)—Dislocated shoulder during practice session which required surgery . . . Brother of Jean Chouinard . . . (October 28, 1981)—Severe groin pull at Minnesota.

Year	Team	League	Games	G.	A.	Pts.	Pen.
1972-73—Quebec Remparts		QJHL	59	43	86	129	11
1973-74—Quebec Remparts (c)		QJHL	62	75	85	160	22
1974-75—Omaha Knights (d)		CHL	70	28	40	68	6
1974-75—Atlanta Flames		NHL	5	0	0	0	2
1975-76—Nova Scotia Voyageurs (b-e)		AHL	70	40	40	80	14
1975-76—Atlanta Flames		NHL	4	0	2	2	2
1976-77—Atlanta Flames		NHL	80	17	33	50	8
1977-78—Atlanta Flames		NHL	73	28	30	58	8
1978-79—Atlanta Flames		NHL	80	50	57	107	14
1979-80—Atlanta Flames		NHL	76	31	46	77	22
1980-81—Calgary Flames		NHL	52	31	52	83	24
1981-82—Calgary Flames		NHL	64	23	57	80	12
1982-83—Calgary Flames		NHL	80	13	59	72	18
1983-84—St. Louis Blues (f-g)		NHL	64	12	34	46	10
NHL TOTALS			578	205	370	575	120

(c)—Drafted from Quebec Remparts by Atlanta Flames in second round of 1974 amateur draft.
(d)—CHL Rookie of the Year.
(e)—Led in assists (9) and points (15) during playoffs.
(f)—September, 1983—Traded by Calgary Flames to St. Louis Blues for future considerations.
(g)—July, 1984—Released by St. Louis Blues.

RON CHOULES

Left Wing . . . 6'1" . . . 205 lbs. . . . Born, Montreal, Que., July 11, 1963 . . . Shoots left . . . Brother of Greg Choules.

Year	Team	League	Games	G.	A.	Pts.	Pen.
1980-81—Hull Olympics		QMJHL	57	7	7	14	167
1981-82—Hull Olympics		QMJHL	47	10	14	24	140
1982-83—Hull Olympics		QHL	77	25	34	59	162
1982-83—Trois-Rivieres (c-d)		QHL	31	28	26	54	127
1983-84—Quebec Remparts		QHL	37	24	31	55	145
1983-84—St. Catharines Saints		AHL	14	1	1	2	26

(c)—December, 1982—Traded with Michel Boucher and Alain Raymond by Hull Olympics to Trois-Rivievers Draveurs for Joel Baillargeon and Patrick Emond.
(d)—June, 1983—Drafted by Toronto Maple Leafs in 1983 NHL entry draft. Eleventh Maple Leafs pick, 228th overall, 12th round.

BLAINE CHREST

Center . . . 5'11" . . . 175 lbs. . . . Born, Gainsborough, Sask., January 10, 1966 . . . Shoots left.

Year	Team	League	Games	G.	A.	Pts.	Pen.
1982-83—Estevan Bruins		SJHL	45	19	28	47	30
1982-83—Brandon Wheat Kings		WHL	4	1	0	1	5
1983-84—Estevan		SJHL	66	50	53	103	12
1983-84—Portland Winter Hawks (c)		WHL	12	5	4	9	2

(c)—June, 1984—Drafted as underage junior by Vancouver Canucks in 1984 NHL entry draft. Eighth Canucks pick, 136th overall, seventh round.

MATHEW CHRISTENSEN

Center . . . 6'1" . . . 185 lbs. . . . Born, Aurora, Minn., June 6, 1964 . . . Shoots left.

Year	Team	League	Games	G.	A.	Pts.	Pen.
1981-82—Aurora-Hoyt Lakes H.S. (c)		Minn. H.S.	23	26	37	63	8
1982-83—Univ. of Minnesota-Duluth		WCHA	45	6	16	22	10
1983-84—Univ. of Minnesota-Duluth		WCHA	42	24	39	63	16

(c)—June, 1982—Drafted as underage player by St. Louis Blues in 1982 NHL entry draft. Sixth Blues pick, 176th overall, ninth round.

DAVE CHRISTIAN

Center . . . 5'11" . . . 170 lbs. . . . Born, Warroad, Minn., May 12, 1959 . . . Shoots right . . . Member of 1978 U.S. National Junior Team and 1980 U.S. Olympic Gold Medal Team . . . Son of Bill Christian ('60 & '64 Olympic Teams), Nephew of Roger Christian ('60 & '64 Olympic Teams) and nephew of Gordon Christian ('56 Olympic Team) . . . His Father (Bill) and Uncle (Roger) own the Christian Brothers Hockey Stick Company . . . Also plays right wing . . . Brother of Edward Christian (Winnipeg '80 draft pick) . . . (December, 1982)— Torn shoulder muscles, missed 25 games.

Year	Team	League	Games	G.	A.	Pts.	Pen.
1977-78—University of North Dakota		WCHA	38	8	16	24	14
1978-79—University of North Dakota (c)		WCHA	40	22	24	46	22
1979-80—U.S. Olympic Team		Int'l	*66	10	28	38	32

Year	Team	League	Games	G.	A.	Pts.	Pen.
1979-80—Winnipeg Jets		NHL	15	8	10	18	2
1980-81—Winnipeg Jets		NHL	80	28	43	71	22
1981-82—Winnipeg Jets		NHL	80	25	51	76	28
1982-83—Winnipeg Jets (d)		NHL	55	18	26	44	23
1983-84—Washington Capitals		NHL	80	29	52	81	28
NHL TOTALS			310	108	182	290	103

(c)—August, 1979—Drafted by Winnipeg Jets in 1979 NHL entry draft. Second Jets pick, 40th overall, second round.

(d)—June, 1983—Traded by Winnipeg Jets to Washington Capitals for first round draft pick in 1983 (Jets drafted Bob Dollas).

STEVE CHRISTOFF

Left Wing . . . 6'1" . . . 180 lbs. . . . Born, Springfield, Ill., January 23, 1958 . . . Shoots right . . . Member of 1979 U.S. National Team and 1980 U.S. Olympic Gold Medal Team . . . Set NHL record for most goals in the playoffs (8) by a rookie in 1980 (Broken by Dino Ciccarelli in 1981 with 14) . . . (October, 1980)—Broke collarbone and missed 20 games during preseason game vs. Edmonton . . . (April, 1982)—Surgery to repair injured shoulder . . . (October, 1982)—Cut forearm and missed first ten days of season . . . (December, 1982)—Pin installed in April surgery came loose causing shoulder to stiffen and required further surgery . . . Also plays right wing and center.

Year	Team	League	Games	G.	A.	Pts.	Pen.
1976-77—University of Minnesota		WCHA	38	7	9	16	20
1977-78—University of Minnesota (b-c)		WCHA	38	32	34	66	18
1978-79—University of Minnesota (b)		WCHA	43	38	39	77	50
1979-80—U.S. Olympic Team		Int'l	64	37	27	64	28
1979-80—Minnesota North Stars (d)		NHL	20	8	7	15	19
1980-81—Minnesota North Stars		NHL	56	26	13	39	58
1980-81—Oklahoma City Stars		CHL	3	1	0	1	0
1981-82—Minnesota North Stars (e)		NHL	69	26	29	55	14
1982-83—Calgary Flames (f)		NHL	45	9	8	17	4
1983-84—Los Angeles Kings		NHL	58	8	7	15	13
NHL TOTALS			248	77	64	141	108

(c)—June, 1978—Drafted by Minnesota North Stars in 1978 NHL amateur draft. Third North Stars pick, 24th overall, second round.

(d)—Scored eight goals in Stanley Cup playoffs, more than any first year player in NHL history.

(e)—June, 1982—Traded by Minnesota North Stars with Bill Nyrop and second-round draft pick in 1982 (Calgary drafted Dave Reierson) to Calgary Flames for Willi Plett and fourth-round draft pick (Minnesota drafted Dusan Pasek) in 1982.

(f)—June, 1983—Traded by Calgary Flames with second-round draft pick in 1985 to Minnesota North Stars for Murray Eaves and Keith Hanson.

JEFF CHYCHRUN

Defense . . . 6'4" . . . 190 lbs. . . . Born, Lasalle, Que., May 3, 1966 . . . Shoots right.

Year	Team	League	Games	G.	A.	Pts.	Pen.
1983-84—Kingston Canadians (c)		OHL	63	1	13	14	137

(c)—June, 1984—Drafted as underage junior by Philadelphia Flyers in 1984 NHL entry draft. Second Flyers pick, 37th overall, second round.

RON CHYZOWSKI

Center . . . 5'10" . . . 165 lbs. . . . Born, Edmonton, Alta., August 14, 1965 . . . Shoots right.

Year	Team	League	Games	G.	A.	Pts.	Pen.
1982-83—St. Albert Saints (c)		AJHL	59	34	43	77	38
1983-84—Northern Michigan University		CCHA	40	16	10	26	12

(c)—June, 1983—Drafted by Hartford Whalers in 1983 NHL entry draft. Sixth Whalers pick, 72nd overall, fourth round.

DINO CICCARELLI

Right Wing . . . 5'11" . . . 185 lbs. . . . Born, Sarnia, Ontario, February 8, 1960 . . . Shoots right . . . (Spring, 1978)—Fractured midshaft of right femur that required the insertion of 16 inch metal rod in leg . . . Set NHL Playoff record for most goals as a rookie (14) in 1981 . . . First Minnesota player to score 50 goals in a season.

Year	Team	League	Games	G.	A.	Pts.	Pen.
1976-77—London Knights		OMJHL	66	39	43	82	45
1977-78—London Knights (b)		OMJHL	68	72	70	142	49
1978-79—London Knights (c)		OMJHL	30	8	11	19	25
1979-80—London Knights		OMJHL	62	50	53	103	72
1979-80—Oklahoma City Stars		CHL	6	3	2	5	0

Year	Team	League	Games	G.	A.	Pts.	Pen.
1980-81—Oklahoma City Stars		CHL	48	32	25	57	45
1980-81—Minnesota North Stars		NHL	32	18	12	30	29
1981-82—Minnesota North Stars		NHL	76	55	51	106	138
1982-83—Minnesota North Stars		NHL	77	37	38	75	94
1983-84—Minnesota North Stars		NHL	79	38	33	71	58
NHL TOTALS			264	148	134	282	319

(c)—September, 1979—Signed by Minnesota North Stars as free agent.

CARMINE CIRELLA

Left Wing and Center . . . 6'4" . . . 215 lbs. . . . Born, Hamilton, Ont., January 16, 1960 . . . Shoots left . . . Brother of Joe Cirella.

Year	Team	League	Games	G.	A.	Pts.	Pen.
1977-78—Hamilton Fincups		OMJHL	1	0	0	0	0
1978-79—Peterborough Petes (c)		OMJHL	60	14	18	32	119
1979-80—Peterborough Petes		OMJHL	62	24	40	64	118
1980-81—Adirondack Red Wings		AHL	73	9	14	23	161
1981-82—Adirondack Red Wings		AHL	78	6	22	28	31
1982-83—Adirondack Red Wings		AHL	80	6	21	27	99
1983-84—Maine Mariners (d)		AHL	24	1	7	8	55

(c)—August, 1979—Drafted as underage junior by Detroit Red Wings in 1979 NHL entry draft. Sixth Red Wings pick, 108th overall, sixth round.

(d)—October, 1983—Signed by Maine Mariners as a free agent.

JOE CIRELLA

Defense . . . 6'2" . . . 205 lbs. . . . Born, Hamilton, Ont., May 9, 1963 . . . Shoots right . . . Brother of Carmine Cirella.

Year	Team	League	Games	G.	A.	Pts.	Pen.
1979-80—Hamilton Major Midgets		....	21	5	26	31	....
1980-81—Oshawa Generals (c)		OHL	56	5	31	36	220
1981-82—Oshawa Generals		OHL	3	0	1	1	10
1981-82—Colorado Rockies		NHL	65	7	12	19	52
1982-83—Oshawa Generals (a)		OHL	56	13	55	68	110
1982-83—New Jersey Devils		NHL	2	0	1	1	4
1983-84—New Jersey Devils		NHL	79	11	33	44	137
NHL TOTALS			146	18	46	64	193

(c)—June, 1981—Drafted as underage junior by Colorado Rockies in 1981 NHL entry draft. First Rockies pick, fifth overall, first round.

DEAN CLARK

Defense . . . 6' . . . 180 lbs. . . . Born, Edmonton, Alta., January 16, 1964 . . . Shoots left.

Year	Team	League	Games	G.	A.	Pts.	Pen.
1981-82—St. Albert Saints (c)		AJHL	59	21	32	53	257
1982-83—Kamloops Junior Oilers		WHL	39	17	24	41	63
1983-84—Kamloops Junior Oilers		WHL	54	18	28	46	64
1983-84—Edmonton Oilers		NHL	1	0	0	0	0
NHL TOTALS			1	0	0	0	0

(c)—June, 1982—Drafted as underage junior by Edmonton Oilers in 1982 NHL entry draft. Eighth Oilers pick, 167th overall, eighth round.

DOUG CLARKE

Defense . . . 6' . . . 190 lbs. . . . Born, Toronto, Ont., February 29, 1964 . . . Shoots left.

Year	Team	League	Games	G.	A.	Pts.	Pen.
1983-84—Colorado College (c)		WCHA	35	6	26	32	70

(c)—June, 1984—Drafted by Vancouver Canucks in 1984 NHL entry draft. 12th Canucks pick, 219th overall, 11th round.

MICHAEL CLARKE

Center . . . 5'11" . . . 178 lbs. . . . Born, Didsbury, Alta., August 12, 1953 . . . Shoots left . . . Has also played Defense.

Year	Team	League	Games	G.	A.	Pts.	Pen.
1970-71—Ponoka Stampeders		AJHL	41	5	13	18	62
1971-72—Lethbridge Sugar Kings		AJHL	23	13	22	35	16
1971-72—Calgary Centennials		WCHL	38	0	6	6	8
1972-73—Calgary Centennials (c)		WCHL	68	21	38	59	25
1973-74—Richmond Robins		AHL	73	17	30	47	23

Year	Team	League	Games	G.	A.	Pts.	Pen.
1974-75—Richmond Robins		AHL	11	1	3	4	6
1974-75—Philadelphia Firebirds		NAHL	56	23	29	52	63
1975-76—Springfield Indians		AHL	7	0	3	3	13
1975-76—Flint Generals		IHL	63	39	34	73	16
1976-77—Flint Generals (b)		IHL	78	43	65	108	40
1977-78—Flint Generals		IHL	79	33	45	78	44
1978-79—Flint Generals		IHL	80	44	46	90	31
1979-80—Adirondack Red Wings		AHL	12	3	2	5	2
1979-80—Richmond Rifles (b)		EHL	61	44	34	78	25
1980-81—New Haven Nighthawks		AHL	23	1	3	4	32
1980-81—Richmond Rifles		EHL	52	31	16	47	38
1981-82—Flint Generals		IHL	42	16	15	31	12
1981-82—Fort Wayne Komets		IHL	32	12	30	42	14
1982-83—Fort Wayne Komets		IHL	76	35	37	72	11
1983-84—Fort Wayne Komets (d)		IHL	19	5	8	13	10
1983-84—Kalamazoo Wings		IHL	39	11	15	26	20

(c)—Drafted from Calgary Centennials by Philadelphia Flyers in third round of 1973 amateur draft.
(d)—January, 1984—Traded by Fort Wayne Komets to Kalamazoo Wings for Dan Poliziani.

ROBERT EARLE CLARKE

Center . . . 5'10" . . . 176 lbs. . . . Born, Flin Flon, Man., August 13, 1949 . . . Shoots left . . . Set WCHL records for assists (Broken by Bruce Eakin, 1981-82) and points in a season in 1967-68 (broken by Bernie Federko in 1975-76) . . . Missed part of 1977-78 season with fractured thumb. . . . (January 9, 1982)—Broke bone in left foot at N.Y. Islanders.

Year	Team	League	Games	G.	A.	Pts.	Pen.
1967-68—Flin Flon Bombers		WCJHL	59	51	*117	*168	148
1968-69—Flin Flon Bombers (a-c)		WCHL	58	51	*86	*137	123
1969-70—Philadelphia Flyers (d)		NHL	76	15	31	46	68
1970-71—Philadelphia Flyers		NHL	77	27	36	63	78
1971-72—Philadelphia Flyers (e)		NHL	78	35	46	81	87
1972-73—Philadelphia Flyers (b-f-g)		NHL	78	37	67	104	80
1973-74—Philadelphia Flyers (b)		NHL	77	35	52	87	113
1974-75—Philadelphia Flyers (a-f-h-i)		NHL	80	27	*89	116	125
1975-76—Philadelphia Flyers (a-f-j-k)		NHL	76	30	*89	119	136
1976-77—Philadelphia Flyers		NHL	80	27	63	90	71
1977-78—Philadelphia Flyers		NHL	71	21	68	89	83
1978-79—Philadelphia Flyers		NHL	80	16	57	73	68
1979-80—Philadelphia Flyers		NHL	76	12	57	69	65
1980-81—Philadelphia Flyers (l)		NHL	80	19	46	65	140
1981-82—Philadelphia Flyers		NHL	62	17	46	63	154
1982-83—Philadelphia Flyers (m)		NHL	80	23	62	85	115
1983-84—Philadelphia Flyers (n)		NHL	73	17	43	60	70
NHL TOTALS			1144	358	852	1210	1453

(c)—Drafted from Flin Flon Bombers by Philadelphia Flyers in second round of 1969 amateur draft.
(d)—Named Rookie-of-the-Year in West Division in poll of players by THE SPORTING NEWS.
(e)—Won Bill Masterton Memorial Trophy.
(f)—Won Hart Memorial Trophy (MVP).
(g)—Selected Most Valuable Player in West Division in poll of players by THE SPORTING NEWS.
(h)—Selected Most Valuable Player in Clarence Campbell Conference in poll of players by THE SPORTING NEWS.
(i)—Tied for lead in assists (12) during playoffs.
(j)—Tied for lead in assists (14) during playoffs.
(k)—Selected Most Valuable Player in NHL in poll of players by THE SPORTING NEWS.
(l)—Named a co-winner of 1981 Lester Patrick Award (With Ed Snider and Fred Shero).
(m)—Won Frank Selke Trophy (Best Defensive Forward).
(n)—June, 1984—Announced retirement as a player to become General Manager of the Philadelphia Flyers.

WILLIAM CLAVITER

Left Wing . . . 6'1" . . . 175 lbs. . . . Born, Virginia, Minn., March 24, 1965 . . . Shoots left.

Year	Team	League	Games	G.	A.	Pts.	Pen.
1982-83—Virginia H.S. (c)		Minn. H.S.	18	18	20	38	...
1983-84—Univ. of North Dakota		WCHA	18	2	5	7	4

(c)—June, 1983—Drafted by Calgary Flames in 1983 NHL entry draft. Sixth Flames pick, 77th overall, fourth round.

SEAN CLEMENT

Defense . . . 6'2" . . . 185 lbs. . . . Born, Winnipeg, Man., February 26, 1966 . . . Shoots left.

Year	Team	League	Games	G.	A.	Pts.	Pen.
1983-84—Brockville Braves (c)		COJHL	52	13	41	54	135

(c)—June, 1984—Drafted as underage junior by Winnipeg Jets in 1984 NHL entry draft. Third Jets pick, 72nd overall, fourth round.

REAL (BUDDY) CLOUTIER

Right Wing . . . 5'10" . . . 185 lbs. . . . Born, St. Emile, Que., July 30, 1956 . . . Shoots left . . . Also plays Left Wing . . . Tied WHA record with five goals in game (October 26, 1976 vs. Phoenix Roadrunners) . . . (August, 1980)—Broken ankle suffered in Charity Softball Game. . . . (December, 1981)—Bruised ankle . . . (January, 1983)—Sprained thumb.

Year	Team	League	Games	G.	A.	Pts.	Pen.
1972-73—Quebec Remparts		QJHL	57	39	60	99	15
1973-74—Quebec Remparts (b-c)		QJHL	69	93	123	216	40
1974-75—Quebec Nordiques		WHA	63	26	27	53	36
1975-76—Quebec Nordiques (b-d)		WHA	80	60	54	114	27
1976-77—Quebec Nordiques (b-e-f)		WHA	76	66	75	*141	39
1977-78—Quebec Nordiques (a)		WHA	73	56	73	129	19
1978-79—Quebec Nordiques (a-f)		WHA	77	*75	54	*129	48
1979-80—Quebec Nordiques		NHL	67	42	47	89	12
1980-81—Quebec Nordiques		NHL	34	15	16	31	18
1981-82—Quebec Nordiques		NHL	67	37	60	97	34
1982-83—Quebec Nordiques (g)		NHL	68	28	39	67	30
1983-84—Buffalo Sabres		NHL	77	24	36	60	25
WHA TOTALS			369	283	283	566	169
NHL TOTALS			313	146	198	344	119

(c)—Selected by Quebec Nordiques in WHA amateur player draft, May, 1974.
(d)—Drafted from Quebec Nordiques by Chicago Black Hawks in first round of 1976 amateur draft.
(e)—Tied for lead in goals (14) during playoffs.
(f)—Won Bill Hunter Trophy (leading scorer in WHA).
(g)—June, 1983—Traded by Quebec Nordiques with first round draft pick in 1983 (Buffalo drafted Adam Creighton) to Buffalo Sabres for Tony McKegney, Andre Savard, Jean-Francois Sauve and Sabres third-round 1983 draft pick (Quebec drafted Iiro Jarvi).

REJEAN CLOUTIER

Defense . . . 6'1" . . . 185 lbs. . . . Born, Windsor, Que., February 15, 1960 . . . Shoots left.

Year	Team	League	Games	G.	A.	Pts.	Pen.
1977-78—Sherbrooke Beavers		QMJHL	23	8	11	19	59
1978-79—Sherbrooke Beavers		QMJHL	70	6	31	37	93
1979-80—Detroit Red Wings		NHL	3	0	1	1	0
1979-80—Sherbrooke Beavers		QMJHL	65	11	57	68	163
1980-81—Adirondack Red Wings		AHL	76	7	30	37	193
1981-82—Adirondack Red Wings		AHL	64	11	27	38	140
1981-82—Detroit Red Wings		NHL	2	0	1	1	2
1982-83—Adirondack Red Wings (b)		AHL	80	13	44	57	137
1983-84—Adirondack Red Wings		AHL	77	9	30	39	218
NHL TOTALS			5	0	2	2	2

GLEN MACLEOD COCHRANE

Defense . . . 6'3" . . . 205 lbs. . . . Born, Cranbrook, B. C., January 29, 1958 . . . Shoots left . . . (March, 1984)—Knee surgery.

Year	Team	League	Games	G.	A.	Pts.	Pen.
1974-75—The Pass Red Devils		AJHL	16	1	4	5	61
1975-76—The Pass Red Devils		AJHL	60	17	42	59	210
1975-76—Calgary Centennials		WCHL	3	0	0	0	0
1976-77—Calgary Centennials		WCHL	35	1	5	6	105
1976-77—Victoria Cougars		WCHL	36	1	7	8	60
1977-78—Victoria Cougars (c)		WCHL	72	7	40	47	311
1978-79—Philadelphia Flyers		NHL	1	0	0	0	0
1978-79—Maine Mariners		AHL	76	1	22	23	320
1979-80—Maine Mariners		AHL	77	1	11	12	269
1980-81—Maine Mariners		AHL	38	4	13	17	201
1980-81—Philadelphia Flyers		NHL	31	1	8	9	219
1981-82—Philadelphia Flyers		NHL	63	6	12	18	329
1982-83—Philadelphia Flyers		NHL	77	2	22	24	237
1983-84—Philadelphia Flyers		NHL	67	7	16	23	225
NHL TOTALS			239	16	58	74	1010

(c)—Drafted from Victoria Cougars by Philadelphia Flyers in third round of 1978 amateur draft.

PAUL DOUGLAS COFFEY

Defense . . . 6'1" . . . 185 lbs. . . . Born, Weston, Ont., June 1, 1961 . . . Shoots left . . . Also plays left wing . . . Became only third defenseman in NHL history to have a 100-point season (Potvin & Orr) with 126 points in 1983-84.

Year	Team	League	Games	G.	A.	Pts.	Pen.
1977-78—Kingston Canadians		OHL	8	2	2	4	11
1977-78—North York Rangers		MTHL	50	14	33	47	64
1978-79—Sault Ste. Marie Greyhounds		OPJHL	68	17	72	89	99
1979-80—Sault Ste. Marie Grehhounds		OPJHL	23	10	21	31	63
1979-80—Kitchener Rangers (b-c)		OPJHL	52	19	52	71	130
1980-81—Edmonton Oilers		NHL	74	9	23	32	130
1981-82—Edmonton Oilers (b)		NHL	80	29	60	89	106
1982-83—Edmonton Oilers (b)		NHL	80	29	67	96	87
1983-84—Edmonton Oilers (b)		NHL	80	40	86	126	104
NHL TOTALS			314	107	236	343	427

(c)—June, 1980—Drafted by Edmonton Oilers in NHL entry draft. First Oilers pick, sixth overall, first round.

PAT CONACHER

Center . . . 5'8" . . . 188 lbs. . . . Born, Edmonton, Alta., May 1, 1959 . . . Shoots left . . . (September 21, 1980)—Fractured left ankle in rookie scrimmage vs. Washington that required surgery . . . (November, 1982)—Injured shoulder.

Year	Team	League	Games	G.	A.	Pts.	Pen.
1977-78—Billings Bighorns		WCHL	72	31	44	75	105
1978-79—Billings Bighorns		WHL	39	25	37	62	50
1978-79—Saskatoon Blades (c)		WHL	33	15	32	47	37
1979-80—New York Rangers		NHL	17	0	5	5	4
1979-80—New Haven Nighthawks		AHL	53	11	14	25	43
1980-81—Did not play							
1981-82—Springfield Indians		AHL	77	23	22	45	38
1981-82—Springfield Indians		AHL	77	23	22	45	38
1982-83—Tulsa Oilers		CHL	63	29	28	57	44
1982-83—New York Rangers		NHL	5	0	1	1	4
1983-84—Moncton Alpines		AHL	28	7	16	23	30
1983-84—Edmonton Oilers		NHL	45	2	8	10	31
NHL TOTALS			67	2	14	16	39

(c)—August, 1979—Drafted by New York Rangers in 1979 NHL entry draft. Third Rangers' pick, 76th overall, fourth round.

CAMERON DUNCAN (CAM) CONNOR

Left Wing . . . 6'2" . . . 200 lbs. . . . Born, Winnipeg, Man., August 10, 1954 . . . Shoots left . . . Missed part of 1974-75 season with broken left leg . . . Missed part of 1977-78 season with fractured left hand requiring surgery.

Year	Team	League	Games	G.	A.	Pts.	Pen.
1971-72—Winnipeg Jets		WCHL	5	0	4	4	4
1971-72—St. Boniface Saints		MJHL	32	4	10	14	97
1972-73—St. Boniface Saints		MJHL	29	11	8	19	161
1972-73—Winnipeg Jets		WCHL	14	3	1	4	35
1973-74—Flin Flon Bombers (c-d-e)		WCHL	65	47	44	91	376
1974-75—Phoenix Roadrunners		WHA	57	9	19	28	168
1975-76—Phoenix Roadrunners		WHA	73	18	21	39	295
1976-77—Houston Aeros (f)		WHA	76	35	32	67	224
1977-78—Houston Aeros (g)		WHA	68	21	16	37	217
1978-79—Montreal Canadiens (h)		NHL	23	1	3	4	39
1979-80—Edmonton Oilers (i)		NHL	38	7	13	20	136
1979-80—New York Rangers		NHL	12	0	3	3	37
1980-81—New York Rangers		NHL	15	1	3	4	44
1980-81—New Haven Nighthawks		AHL	61	33	28	61	243
1981-82—Springfield Indians		AHL	78	17	34	51	195
1981-82—New York Rangers (j)		NHL	....	...	....	....	....
1982-83—Tulsa Oilers		CHL	3	2	2	4	0
1982-83—New York Rangers		NHL	1	0	0	0	0
1983-84—Tulsa Oilers		CHL	64	18	32	50	218
WHA TOTALS			274	83	88	171	904
NHL TOTALS			89	9	22	31	256

(c)—Selected by Phoenix Roadrunners in World Hockey Association amateur player draft, May, 1974.

(d)—Drafted from Flin Flon Bombers by Montreal Canadiens in first round of 1974 amateur draft.

(e)—Won WCHL rookie-of-the-year award.

(f)—Traded to Houston Aeros by Phoenix Roadrunners for Bob Liddington, October, 1976.

(g)—Sold to Winnipeg Jets with Houston Aeros' franchise, July, 1978. (Subsequently gained free agency and signed with Montreal Canadiens. October. 1978.)

(h)—June, 1979—Selected by Edmonton Oilers in NHL expansion draft.

(i)—March, 1980—Traded with a third round entry draft pick by Edmonton Oilers to New York Rangers for Don Murdoch.

(j)—Played in four playoff games.

JEFF CORNELIUS

Defense . . . 6'1" . . . 185 lbs. . . . Born, Kingston, Ont., February 28, 1966 . . . Shoots left.

Year	Team	League	Games	G.	A.	Pts.	Pen.
1982-83	Kingston Canadians	OHL	5	0	1	1	5
1983-84	Toronto Marlboros (c)	OHL	64	2	14	16	117

(c)—June, 1984—Drafted as underage junior by Boston Bruins in 1984 NHL entry draft. Third Bruins pick, 61st overall, third round.

MIKE JOSEPH CORRIGAN

Right Wing . . . 6'2" . . . 200 lbs. . . . Born, Timmons, Ont., May 6, 1961 . . . Shoots right.

Year	Team	League	Games	G.	A.	Pts.	Pen.
1977-78	Sudbury Wolves	OMJHL	2	0	0	0	5
1978-79	Cornwall Royals	QMJHL	71	30	36	66	231
1979-80	Cornwall Royals (c)	QMJHL	71	30	41	71	186
1980-81	Sudbury Wolves	OHL	55	24	31	55	205
1981-82	Kalamazoo Wings	IHL	56	25	19	44	164
1981-82	Adirondack Red Wings	AHL	24	2	2	4	46
1982-83	Adirondack Red Wings	AHL	72	13	15	28	107
1983-84	Adirondack Red Wings	AHL	4	1	0	1	0
1983-84	Kalamazoo Wings	IHL	68	17	23	40	128

(c)—June, 1980—Drafted as underage junior by Detroit Red Wings in 1980 NHL entry draft. Third Red Wings pick, 88th overall, fifth round.

SHAYNE CORSON

Center . . . 6' . . . 175 lbs. . . . Born, Barrie, Ont., August 13, 1966 . . . Shoots left.

Year	Team	League	Games	G.	A.	Pts.	Pen.
1982-83	Barrie Flyers	COJHL	23	13	29	42	87
1983-84	Brantford Alexanders (c)	OHL	66	25	46	71	165

(c)—June, 1984—Drafted as underage junior by Montreal Canadiens in 1984 NHL entry draft. Second Canadiens pick, 8th overall, first round.

RICHARD COSTELLO

Center . . . 6' . . . 170 lbs. . . . Born, Natick, Mass., June, 27, 1963 . . . Shoots right . . . Member of 1984 U.S. Olympic Team.

Year	Team	League	Games	G.	A.	Pts.	Pen.
1979-80	Natick High School	Mass.H.S.	18	26	32	58	....
1980-81	Natick High School (a-c)	Mass.H.S.	....	30	36	66	....
1981-82	Providence College (d)	ECAC	32	11	16	27	39
1982-83	Providence College	ECAC	43	19	26	45	60
1983-84	U.S. National Team	Int'l.	38	7	19	26	31
1983-84	St. Catharines Saints	AHL	20	0	0	0	12
1983-84	Toronto Maple Leafs	NHL	10	2	1	3	2
NHL TOTALS			10	2	1	3	2

(c)—June, 1981—Drafted as underage junior by Philadelphia Flyers in 1981 NHL entry draft. Second Flyers pick, 37th overall, second round.

(d)—January, 1982—NHL rights traded with second-round 1982 entry draft pick (Peter Ihnacak) by Philadelphia Flyers to Toronto Maple Leafs for Darryl Sittler and future considerations.

DARREN COTA

Right Wing . . . 5'11" . . . 195 lbs. . . . Born, McLellan, Alta., April 7, 1966 . . . Shoots right.

Year	Team	League	Games	G.	A.	Pts.	Pen.
1982-83	Kelowna Wings	WHL	49	5	13	18	141
1983-84	Kelowna Wings (c)	WHL	66	30	31	61	152

(c)—June, 1984—Drafted as underage junior by Quebec Nordiques in 1984 NHL entry draft. Fifth Nordiques pick, 120th overall, sixth round.

ALAIN COTE

Left Wing . . . 5'10" . . . 203 lbs. . . . Born, Matane, Que., May 3, 1957 . . . Shoots left . . . Brother-in-law of Luc Dufour.

Year	Team	League	Games	G.	A.	Pts.	Pen.
1974-75—Chicoutimi Sagueneens		QJHL	57	15	29	44	43
1975-76—Chicoutimi Sagueneens		QJHL	72	35	49	84	93
1976-77—Chicoutimi Sagueneens (c-d)		QJHL	56	42	45	87	86
1977-78—Hampton Gulls		AHL	36	15	17	32	38
1977-78—Quebec Nordiques		WHA	27	3	5	8	8
1978-79—Quebec Nordiques (e)		WHA	79	14	13	27	23
1979-80—Quebec Nordiques		NHL	41	5	11	16	13
1979-80—Syracuse Firebirds		AHL	6	0	5	5	9
1980-81—Rochester Americans		AHL	23	1	6	7	14
1980-81—Quebec Nordiques		NHL	51	8	18	26	64
1981-82—Quebec Nordiques		NHL	79	15	16	31	82
1982-83—Quebec Nordiques		NHL	79	12	28	40	45
1983-84—Quebec Nordiques		NHL	77	19	24	43	41
WHA TOTALS			106	17	18	35	31
NHL TOTALS			327	59	97	156	245

(c)—Drafted from Chicoutimi Sagueneens by Montreal Canadiens in third round of 1977 amateur draft.
(d)—Selected by Quebec Nordiques in World Hockey Association amateur players' draft, May, 1977.
(e)—June, 1979—Selected by Montreal Canadiens in NHL reclaim draft. Selected by Quebec Nordiques in NHL expansion draft.

ANDRE COTE

Right Wing . . . 6'1" . . . 180 lbs. . . . Born, Baie Comeau, Que., June 19, 1961 . . . Shoots left.

Year	Team	League	Games	G.	A.	Pts.	Pen.
1978-79—Sherbrooke Beavers		QMJHL	71	29	42	71	8
1979-80—Sherbrooke Beavers		QMJHL	22	13	28	41	7
1979-80—Sorel Black Hawks		QMJHL	39	21	25	46	14
1980-81—Sorel Black Hawks (c)		QMJHL	37	36	32	68	2
1980-81—Quebec Remparts (d)		QMJHL	35	30	31	61	10
1981-82—Fredericton Express		AHL	66	18	16	34	6
1982-83—Fredericton Express		AHL	73	18	21	39	11
1983-84—Fredericton Express		AHL	34	6	12	18	4
1983-84—Milwaukee Admirals		IHL	13	2	7	9	2
1983-84—Peoria Prancers		IHL	11	2	5	7	2

(c)—December, 1980—Traded by Sorel Black Hawks to Quebec Remparts for Jean Marc Lanthier, Jr.
(d)—June, 1981—Drafted by Quebec Nordiques in 1981 NHL entry draft. Sixth Nordiques pick, 158th overall, eighth round.

MICHEL COTE

Right Wing . . . 5'10" . . . 175 lbs. . . . Born, Sherbrooke, Que., August 11, 1961 . . . Shoots right.

Year	Team	League	Games	G.	A.	Pts.	Pen.
1978-79—Shawinigan Cataracts		QMJHL	32	15	23	38	155
1979-80—Shawinigan Cataracts		QMJHL	59	25	33	58	246
1980-81—Shawinigan Cataracts		QMJHL	71	38	39	77	171
1981-82—Shawinigan Cataracts		QMJHL	31	13	11	24	81
1981-82—Fredericton Express (c)		AHL	41	8	7	15	37
1982-83—Sherbrooke Jets		AHL	43	5	8	13	68
1982-83—Erie Golden Blades		ACHL	17	19	17	36	35
1983-84—Erie Golden Blades (a)		ACHL	63	54	67	121	150

(c)—January, 1982—Signed by Fredericton Express as free agent.

RAYMOND COTE

Center . . . 5'11" . . . 165 lbs. . . . Born, Pincher Creek, Alberta, May 31, 1961 . . . Shoots right.

Year	Team	League	Games	G.	A.	Pts.	Pen.
1977-78—Pincher Creek Panthers		AJHL	59	13	34	47	12
1978-79—Calgary Chinooks		AJHL	53	17	30	47	35
1978-79—Calgary Wranglers		WHL	7	2	1	3	0
1979-80—Calgary Wranglers		WHL	72	33	34	67	43
1980-81—Calgary Wranglers		WHL	70	36	52	88	73
1981-82—Wichita Wind (c)		CHL	80	20	34	54	83
1982-83—Moncton Alpines		AHL	80	28	63	91	35
1982-83—Edmonton Oilers (d)		NHL	..	..	..	..	..
1983-84—Edmonton Oilers		NHL	13	0	0	0	2
1983-84—Moncton Alpines		AHL	66	26	36	62	99
NHL TOTALS			13	0	0	0	2

(c)—October, 1981—Signed by Edmonton Oilers as a free agent.
(d)—No regular season record. Played in 14 playoff games.

SYLVAIN COTE

Defense ... 6' ... 170 lbs. ... Born, Quebec City, Que., January 19, 1966 ... Shoots right.

Year	Team	League	Games	G.	A.	Pts.	Pen.
1982-83	Quebec Remparts	QHL	66	10	24	34	50
1983-84	Quebec Remparts (c)	QHL	66	15	50	65	89

(c)—June, 1984—Drafted as underage junior by Hartford Whalers in 1984 NHL entry draft. First Whalers pick, 11th overall, first round.

TIM COULIS

Left Wing ... 6' ... 199 lbs. ... Born, Kenora, Ont., February 24, 1958 ... Shoots left ... Missed entire 1978-79 season with a broken bone in left wrist ... Also plays right wing ... Suspended for all of 1982-83 season by Central Hockey League after slugging official during 1982 CHL playoffs.

Year	Team	League	Games	G.	A.	Pts.	Pen.
1975-76	Sault Ste. Marie Greyhounds	OMJHL	37	15	18	33	226
1976-77	Sault Ste. Marie Greyhounds (c)	OMJHL	27	13	20	33	114
1976-77	St. Catharines Fincups	OMJHL	28	10	22	32	136
1977-78	Hamilton Fincups (d)	OMJHL	46	27	25	52	203
1978-79	Did not play						
1979-80	Hershey Bears	AHL	47	6	12	18	138
1979-80	Washington Capitals (e)	NHL	19	1	2	3	27
1980-81	Dallas Black Hawks	CHL	63	16	15	31	149
1981-82	Dallas Black Hawks (f)	CHL	68	20	32	52	209
1982-83	Did not play						
1983-84	Minnesota North Stars (g)	NHL	2	0	0	0	4
1983-84	Salt Lake Golden Eagles	CHL	63	25	35	60	225
	NHL TOTALS		21	1	2	3	31

(c)—January, 1977—Traded by Sault Ste. Marie Greyhounds to St. Catharines Fincups for Mark Locken.

(d)—June, 1978—Drafted by Washington Capitals in 1978 NHL amateur draft. Second Capitals pick, 18th overall, first round.

(e)—June, 1980—Traded with Robert Picard and second round (Bob McGill) 1980 draft pick by Washington Capitals to Toronto Maple Leafs for Mike Palmateer and third round (Torrie Robertson) 1980 draft pick.

(f)—October, 1981—Signed by Vancouver Canucks as a free agent.

(g)—July, 1983—Signed by Minnesota North Stars as a free agent.

NEAL COULTIER

Right Wing ... 6'2" ... 190 lbs. ... Born, Toronto, Ont., January 2, 1963 ... Shoots right.

Year	Team	League	Games	G.	A.	Pts.	Pen.
1979-80	Oakridge Midgets	...	60	35	30	65	150
1980-81	Toronto Marlboros (c)	OHL	18	4	3	7	22
1981-82	Toronto Marlboros	OHL	62	14	16	30	79
1982-83	Toronto Marlboros	OHL	59	13	37	50	60
1982-83	Indianapolis Checkers	CHL	3	0	1	1	0
1983-84	Toledo Goaldiggers	IHL	5	1	3	4	0
1983-84	Indianapolis Checkers	CHL	58	7	10	17	25

(c)—June, 1981—Drafted as underage junior by New York Islanders in 1981 NHL entry draft. Fourth Islanders pick, 63rd overall, third round.

YVES COURTEAU

Right Wing ... 5'11" ... 183 lbs. ... Born, Montreal, Que., April 25, 1964 ... Shoots left.

Year	Team	League	Games	G.	A.	Pts.	Pen.
1980-81	Laval Voisins	QMJHL	70	24	39	63	80
1981-82	Laval Voisins (c)	QMJHL	64	30	38	68	15
1982-83	Laval Voisins (d)	QHL	68	44	78	122	52
1983-84	Laval Voisins	QHL	62	45	75	120	52

(c)—June, 1982—Drafted as underage junior by Detroit Red Wings in 1982 NHL entry draft. Second Red Wings pick, 23rd overall, second round.

(d)—December, 1982—NHL rights traded by Detroit Red Wings to Calgary Flames for Bobby Francis.

GEOFF COURTNALL

Left Wing ... 6' ... 165 lbs. ... Born, Victoria, B.C., August 18, 1962 ... Shoots left.

Year	Team	League	Games	G.	A.	Pts.	Pen.
1980-81	Victoria Cougars	WHL	11	3	5	8	6
1981-82	Victoria Cougars	WHL	72	35	57	92	100
1983-84	Victoria Cougars	WHL	71	41	73	114	186

Year	Team	League	Games	G.	A.	Pts.	Pen.
1983-84—Hershey Bears (c)	AHL	74	14	12	26	51
1983-84—Boston Bruins	NHL	5	0	0	0	0
NHL TOTALS		5	0	0	0	0

(c)—September, 1983—Signed by Boston Bruins as a free agent.

RUSS COURTNALL

Center . . . 5'10" . . . 175 lbs. . . . Born, Victoria, B.C., June 3, 1965 . . . Shoots right . . . Member of 1984 Canadian Olympic Team.

Year	Team	League	Games	G.	A.	Pts.	Pen.
1982-83—Victoria Cougars (c)	WHL	60	36	61	97	33
1983-84—Victoria Cougars	WHL	32	29	37	66	63
1983-84—Canadian Olympic Team	Int'l	16	4	7	11	10
1983-84—Toronto Maple Leafs	NHL	14	3	9	12	6
NHL TOTALS		14	3	9	12	6

(c)—June, 1983—Drafted by Toronto Maple Leafs as underage junior in NHL entry draft. First Maple Leafs pick, seventh overall, first round.

GRANT COUTURE

Defense . . . 5'11" . . . 180 lbs. . . . Born, Edmonton, Alta., June 25, 1964 . . . Shoots right . . . (September, 1982)—Sprained leg during Pittsburgh training camp.

Year	Team	League	Games	G.	A.	Pts.	Pen.
1981-82—Lethbridge Broncos (c)	WHL	71	5	33	38	103
1982-83—Lethbridge Broncos (d)	WHL	55	7	20	27	142
1983-84—Lethbridge Broncos	WHL	70	9	23	32	149

(c)—June, 1982—Drafted as underage junior by Pittsburgh Penguins in 1982 NHL entry draft. Fifth Penguins pick, 136th overall, seventh round.

(d)—Led WHL Playoffs with 60 penalty minutes in 20 games.

DAVID COWAN

Left Wing . . . 5'10" . . . 180 lbs. . . . Born, Minneapolis, Minn., July 23, 1965 . . . Shoots left.

Year	Team	League	Games	G.	A.	Pts.	Pen.
1982-83—Mpls. Washburn H.S. (c)	Minn. H.S.	23	35	30	65	....
1983-84—University of Minnesota-Duluth	WCHA	12	1	2	3	8

(c)—June, 1983—Drafted by Washington Capitals in 1983 NHL entry draft. Fifth Capitals pick, 175th overall, ninth round.

CRAIG COXE

Center . . . 6'4" . . . 185 lbs. . . . Born, Chula Vista, Calif., January 21, 1964 . . . Shoots left.

Year	Team	League	Games	G.	A.	Pts.	Pen.
1980-81—Los Angeles Midgets	Calif.	..	..	..	..	..
1981-82—St. Albert Saints (c)	AJHL	51	17	48	65	212
1982-83—Belleville Bulls	OHL	64	14	27	41	102
1983-84—Belleville Bulls	OHL	45	17	28	45	90

(c)—June, 1982—Drafted as underage junior by Detroit Red Wings in 1982 NHL entry draft. Fourth Red Wings pick, 66th overall, fourth round.

VITO CRAMAROSSA

Right Wing . . . 6' . . . 195 lbs. . . . Born, Toronto, Ont., March 9, 1966 . . . Shoots right.

Year	Team	League	Games	G.	A.	Pts.	Pen.
1982-83—Don Mills Midgets	COJHL	36	21	47	68	118
1983-84—Toronto Marlboros (c)	OHL	66	18	40	58	63

(c)—June, 1984—Drafted as underage junior by Washington Capitals in 1984 NHL entry draft. Fifth Capitals pick, 122nd overall, sixth round.

MURRAY CRAVEN

Center . . . 6'2" . . . 175 lbs. . . . Born, Medicine Hat, Alta., July 20, 1964 . . . Shoots left . . . Also plays left wing . . . (January 15, 1983)—Injured left knee cartilage in game vs. Toronto.

Year	Team	League	Games	G.	A.	Pts.	Pen.
1980-81—Medicine Hat Tigers	WHL	69	5	10	15	18
1981-82—Medicine Hat Tigers (c)	WHL	72	35	46	81	49
1982-83—Medicine Hat Tigers	WHL	28	17	29	46	35
1982-83—Detroit Red Wings	NHL	31	4	7	11	6
1983-84—Medicine Hat Tigers	WHL	48	38	56	94	53
1983-84—Detroit Red Wings	NHL	15	0	4	4	6
NHL TOTALS		46	4	11	15	12

BOB CRAWFORD

Right Wing . . . 5'11" . . . 177 lbs. . . . Born, Belleville, Ont., April 6, 1959 . . . Shoots right . . . Brother of Peter and Marc Crawford . . . Son of Floyd Crawford (Member of Belleville MacFarlands, 1959 Canadian World Cup Winners).

Year	Team	League	Games	G.	A.	Pts.	Pen.
1976-77—Cornwall Royals		QMJHL	71	36	34	70	39
1977-78—Cornwall Royals		QMJHL	69	54	67	121	29
1978-79—Cornwall Royals (c)		QMJHL	65	62	70	132	45
1979-80—St. Louis Blues		NHL	8	1	0	1	2
1979-80—Salt Lake Golden Eagles		CHL	67	30	21	51	32
1980-81—Salt Lake Golden Eagles		CHL	79	35	26	61	27
1981-82—Salt Lake Golden Eagles (a)		CHL	74	54	45	99	43
1981-82—St. Louis Blues		NHL	3	0	1	1	0
1982-83—Salt Lake Golden Eagles		CHL	25	15	23	38	2
1982-83—St. Louis Blues		NHL	27	5	9	14	2
1983-84—Hartford Whalers (d)		NHL	80	36	25	61	32
NHL TOTALS			118	42	35	77	36

(c)—August, 1979—Drafted by St. Louis Blues in 1979 NHL entry draft. Second Blues pick, 65th overall, fourth round.

(d)—October, 1983—Selected by Hartford Whalers in 1983 NHL waiver draft.

MARC JOSEPH JOHN CRAWFORD

Left Wing . . . 5'11" . . . 181 lbs. . . . Born, Belleville, Ont., February 13, 1961 . . . Shoots left . . . Son of Floyd Crawford (Member of Belleville MacFarlands, 1959 Canadian World Cup Winners) . . . Brother of Peter and Bob Crawford.

Year	Team	League	Games	G.	A.	Pts.	Pen.
1978-79—Cornwall Royals		QMJHL	70	28	41	69	206
1979-80—Cornwall Royals (c)		QMJHL	54	27	36	63	127
1980-81—Cornwall Royals		QMJHL	63	42	57	99	242
1981-82—Dallas Black Hawks		CHL	34	13	21	34	71
1981-82—Vancouver Canucks		NHL	40	4	8	12	29
1982-83—Fredericton Express		AHL	30	15	9	24	59
1982-83—Vancouver Canucks		NHL	41	4	5	9	28
1983-84—Vancouver Canucks		NHL	19	0	1	1	9
1983-84—Fredericton Express		AHL	56	9	22	31	96
NHL TOTALS			100	8	14	22	66

(c)—June, 1980—Drafted as underage junior by Vancouver Canucks in 1980 NHL entry draft. Third Canucks pick, 70th overall, fourth round.

WAYNE KENNETH CRAWFORD

Center and Right Wing . . . 5'11" . . . 180 lbs. . . . Born, Toronto, Ont., April 18, 1961 . . . Shoots left.

Year	Team	League	Games	G.	A.	Pts.	Pen.
1978-79—Niagara Falls Flyers		OMJHL	64	25	41	66	74
1979-80—Niagara Falls Flyers		OMJHL	2	0	0	0	0
1979-80—Toronto Marlboros (c)		OMJHL	64	48	66	114	18
1980-81—Toronto Marlboros		OHL	65	44	58	102	101
1981-82—Adirondack Red Wings		AHL	65	14	26	40	42
1982-83—Adirondack Red Wings		AHL	69	18	31	49	16
1983-84—Adirondack Red Wings		AHL	67	28	25	53	97

(c)—June, 1980—Drafted as underage junior by Detroit Red Wings in 1980 NHL entry draft. Fourth Red Wings pick, 109th overall, sixth round.

ADAM CREIGHTON

Center . . . 6'5" . . . 21) lbs. . . . Born, Burlington, Ont., June 2, 1965 . . . Shoots left . . . Son of Dave Creighton (NHL, '50s-'60s).

Year	Team	League	Games	G.	A.	Pts.	Pen.
1981-82—Ottawa 67's		OHL	60	14	27	42	73
1982-83—Ottawa 67's (c)		OHL	68	44	46	90	88
1983-84—Ottawa 67's		OHL	56	42	49	91	79
1983-84—Buffalo Sabres		NHL	7	2	2	4	4
NHL TOTALS			7	2	2	4	4

(c)—June, 1983—Drafted as underage junior by Buffalo Sabres in 1983 NHL entry draft. Third Sabres pick, 11th overall, first round.

MIKE CROMBEEN

Right Wing . . . 5'10" . . . 190 lbs. . . . Born, Sarnia, Ont., April 16, 1957 . . . Shoots right . . . Brother of Pat and Brian (1980 Canadian Olympic Team) Crombeen . . . (February 23, 1984)—Fractured right wrist vs. Buffalo.

Year	Team	League	Games	G.	A.	Pts.	Pen.
1973-74—Kingston Canadians		Jr."A"OHA	69	19	29	48	59
1974-75—Kingston Canadians		Jr."A"OHA	69	56	58	114	50
1975-76—Kingston Canadians (b)		Jr."A"OHA	57	43	39	82	65
1976-77—Kingston Canadians (b-c)		Jr."A"OHA	49	42	36	78	49
1977-78—Salt Lake City Golden Eagles		CHL	12	4	4	8	4
1977-78—Binghamton Dusters		AHL	13	1	2	3	4
1977-78—Cleveland Barons (d)		NHL	48	3	4	7	13
1978-79—St. Louis Blues		NHL	37	3	8	11	34
1978-79—Salt Lake Golden Eagles		CHL	30	6	9	15	48
1979-80—St. Louis Blues		NHL	71	10	12	22	20
1980-81—St. Louis Blues		NHL	66	9	14	23	58
1981-82—St. Louis Blues		NHL	71	19	8	27	32
1982-83—St. Louis Blues		NHL	80	6	11	17	20
1983-84—Hartford Whalers (e)		NHL	56	1	4	5	25
NHL TOTALS			429	51	61	112	202

(c)—Drafted from Kingston Canadians by Cleveland Barons in first round of 1977 amateur draft.
(d)—Selected by St. Louis Blues in dispersal draft of Cleveland Barons, June, 1978.
(e)—October, 1983—Selected by Hartford Whalers in 1983 NHL waiver draft.

TOM CRONIN

Defense . . . 6' . . . 195 lbs. . . . Born, Melrose, Mass., September 9, 1960 . . . Shoots right.

Year	Team	League	Games	G.	A.	Pts.	Pen.
1982-83—Lowell University (c)		ECAC-II	26	3	13	16	37
1983-84—Binghamton Whalers		AHL	75	2	12	14	90

(c)—September, 1983—Signed by Hartford Whalers as a free agent.

DOUG CROSSMAN

Defense . . . 6'2" . . . 190 lbs. . . . Born, Peterborough, Ont., June 30, 1960 . . . Shoots left . . . (February, 1983)—Injured thumb.

Year	Team	League	Games	G.	A.	Pts.	Pen.
1976-77—London Knights		OMJHL	1	0	0	0	0
1977-78—Ottawa 67's		OMJHL	65	4	17	21	17
1978-79—Ottawa 67's (c)		OMJHL	67	12	51	63	63
1979-80—Ottawa 67's (a)		OMJHL	66	20	96	116	48
1980-81—Chicago Black Hawks		NHL	9	0	2	2	2
1980-81—New Brunswick Hawks		AHL	70	13	43	56	90
1981-82—Chicago Black Hawks		NHL	70	12	28	40	24
1982-83—Chicago Black Hawks (d)		NHL	80	13	40	53	46
1983-84—Philadelphia Flyers		NHL	78	7	28	35	63
NHL TOTALS			237	32	98	130	135

(c)—August, 1979—Drafted by Chicago Black Hawks as underage junior in 1979 NHL entry draft. Sixth Black Hawks pick, 112th overall, sixth round.
(d)—June, 1983—Traded by Chicago Black Hawks with second-round draft pick (Scott Mellanby) in 1984 to Philadelphia Flyers for Behn Wilson.

JEFF CROSSMAN

Center . . . 6' . . . 200 lbs. . . . Born, Detroit, Mich., December 3, 1964 . . . Shoots left.

Year	Team	League	Games	G.	A.	Pts.	Pen.
1982-83—Western Michigan Univ.		CCHA	30	3	2	5	43
1983-84—Western Michigan Univ. (c)		CCHA	39	9	12	21	91

(c)—June, 1984—Drafted by Los Angeles Kings in 1984 NHL entry draft. 10th Kings pick. 191st overall. 10th round.

BRUCE CROWDER

Right Wing . . . 6' . . . 180 lbs. . . . Born, Essex, Ont., March 25, 1957 . . . Shoots right . . . Brother of Keith Crowder . . . Also plays Left Wing . . . (December, 1983)—Bruised knee.

Year	Team	League	Games	G.	A.	Pts.	Pen.
1977-78—Univ. of New Hampshire (c)		ECAC	30	10	35	45	58
1978-79—Univ. of New Hampshire		ECAC	35	22	30	52	34
1979-80—Maine Mariners		AHL	49	16	11	27	23
1980-81—Maine Mariners (d)		AHL	68	25	19	44	94

Year	Team	League	Games	G.	A.	Pts.	Pen.
1981-82—Erie Blades		AHL	15	6	6	12	6
1981-82—Boston Bruins (e)		NHL	63	16	11	27	31
1982-83—Boston Bruins		NHL	80	21	19	40	58
1983-84—Boston Bruins		NHL	74	6	14	20	44
NHL TOTALS			217	43	44	87	133

(c)—June, 1977—Drafted by the Philadelphia Flyers in 1977 NHL amateur draft. Fourteenth Flyers pick, 153rd overall, ninth round.

(d)—Led AHL playoff with 11 goals.

(e)—June, 1981—Signed by Boston Bruins as a free agent.

KEITH SCOTT CROWDER

Right Wing . . . 6' . . . 190 lbs. . . . Born, Windsor, Ont., January 6, 1959 . . . Shoots right . . . Also plays Center . . . Brother of Bruce Crowder . . . (February, 1978)—Broken ankle . . . Set Bruins team record for most penalty minutes by a rookie (172) in 1980-81 . . . (December, 1983)—Sprained right knee, missed 16 games.

Year	Team	League	Games	G.	A.	Pts.	Pen.
1976-77—Peterborough Petes		Jr.''A''OHA	58	13	19	32	99
1977-78—Peterborough Petes (c)		Jr.''A''OHA	58	30	30	60	139
1978-79—Birmingham Bulls (d)		WHA	5	1	0	1	17
1978-79—Peterborough Petes (e)		OMJHL	43	25	41	66	76
1979-80—Binghamton Dusters		AHL	13	4	0	4	15
1979-80—Grand Rapids Owls		IHL	20	10	13	23	22
1980-81—Springfield Indians		AHL	26	12	18	30	34
1980-81—Boston Bruins		NHL	47	13	12	25	172
1981-82—Boston Bruins		NHL	71	23	21	44	101
1982-83—Boston Bruins		NHL	74	35	39	74	105
1983-84—Boston Bruins		NHL	63	24	28	52	128
WHA TOTALS			5	1	0	1	17
NHL TOTALS			255	95	100	195	506

(c)—Signed by Birmingham Bulls (WHA) as underage player, July, 1978.

(d)—November, 1978—Returned to Peterborough to play final year of junior eligibility.

(e)—August, 1979—Drafted by Boston Bruins in entry draft: fourth Boston pick, 57th overall, third round.

PAUL CROWLEY

Left Wing . . . 5'9" . . . 182 lbs. . . . Born, Montreal, Quebec, December 26, 1955 . . . Shoots right . . . (December, 1977)—Missed six games with shoulder separation. Starts the 1984-85 season with 447 consecutive AHL games played since December 29, 1978, the longest current streak in the AHL. The all-time record is 548 (Billy Dea, Buffalo).

Year	Team	League	Games	G.	A.	Pts.	Pen.
1973-74—Sudbury Wolves		OMJHL	67	17	21	38	92
1974-75—Sudbury Wolves (c)		OMJHL	68	29	45	74	110
1975-76—Toronto Toros		WHA	4	0	0	0	0
1975-76—Buffalo Norseman		NAHL	72	26	34	60	138
1976-77—Charlotte Checkers		SHL	50	19	26	45	73
1976-77—Mohawk Valley Comets		NAHL	4	1	2	3	2
1977-78—Hershey Bears (d)		AHL	74	13	23	36	57
1978-79—Binghamton Dusters		AHL	75	27	20	47	77
1979-80—Rochester Americans		AHL	80	24	37	61	171
1980-81—Rochester Americans (e)		AHL	80	24	19	43	144
1981-82—Binghamton Whalers		AHL	80	28	28	56	135
1982-83—Binghamton Whalers		AHL	80	23	28	51	97
1983-84—Binghamton Whalers		AHL	80	14	14	28	90
WHA TOTALS			4	0	0	0	0

(c)—June, 1975—Drafted by Toronto Maple Leafs in NHL amateur draft. Tenth Maple Leafs' pick, 166th overall, 10th round.

(d)—October, 1977—Signed by Buffalo Sabres as a free agent.

(e)—July, 1981—Signed by Binghamton Whalers as a free agent.

JIM CULHANE

Defense . . . 6' . . . 190 lbs. . . . Born, Halleybury, Ont., August 8, 1960 . . . Shoots left.

Year	Team	League	Games	G.	A.	Pts.	Pen.
1983-84—Western Michigan Univ. (c)		CCHA	42	1	14	15	88

(c)—June, 1984—Drafted by Hartford Whalers in 1984 NHL entry draft. Sixth Whalers pick, 214th overall, 11th round.

RANDY WILLIAM CUNNEYWORTH

Center and Left Wing . . . 6' . . . 180 lbs. . . . Born, Etobicoke, Ont., May 10, 1961 . . . Shoots left.

Year	Team	League	Games	G.	A.	Pts.	Pen.
1979-80—Ottawa 67's (c)		OMJHL	63	16	25	41	145
1980-81—Ottawa 67's		OHL	67	54	74	128	240
1980-81—Rochester Americans		AHL	1	0	1	1	2
1980-81—Buffalo Sabres		NHL	1	0	0	0	2
1981-82—Rochester Americans		AHL	57	12	15	27	86
1981-82—Buffalo Sabres		NHL	20	2	4	6	47
1982-83—Rochester Americans		AHL	78	23	33	56	111
1983-84—Rochester Americans		AHL	54	18	17	35	85
NHL TOTALS			21	2	4	6	49

(c)—June, 1980—Drafted as underage junior by Buffalo Sabres in 1980 NHL entry draft. Ninth Sabres pick, 167th overall, eighth round.

MARK CUPOLO

Left Wing . . . 6' . . . 180 lbs. . . . Born, Niagara Falls, Ont., November 17, 1965 . . . Shoots left.

Year	Team	League	Games	G.	A.	Pts.	Pen.
1982-83—Guelph Platers		OHL	8	0	0	0	7
1983-84—Guelph Platers (c)		OHL	60	28	13	41	61

(c)—June, 1984—Drafted by St. Louis Blues in 1984 NHL entry draft. Thirteenth Blues pick, 217th overall, 11th round.

BRIAN CURRAN

Defense . . . 6'4" . . . 200 lbs. . . . Born, Toronto, Ont., November 5, 1963 . . . Shoots left . . . (November, 1981)—Appendectomy . . . (September, 1982)—Broken ankle.

Year	Team	League	Games	G.	A.	Pts.	Pen.
1980-81—Portland Winter Hawks		WHL	51	2	16	18	132
1981-82—Portland Winter Hawks (c)		WHL	59	2	28	30	275
1982-83—Portland Winter Hawks		WHL	56	1	30	31	187
1983-84—Hershey Bears		AHL	23	0	2	2	94
1983-84—Boston Bruins		NHL	16	1	1	2	57
NHL TOTALS			16	1	1	2	57

(c)—June, 1982—Drafted as underage junior by Boston Bruins in 1982 NHL entry draft. Second Bruins pick, 22nd overall, second round.

GLEN CURRIE

Center . . . 6'1" . . . 175 lbs. . . . Born, Lachine, Que., July 18, 1958 . . . Shoots left . . . Nephew of Jim Peters (NHL player in late '40s and early '50s).

Year	Team	League	Games	G.	A.	Pts.	Pen.
1975-76—Laval National		QJHL	72	15	54	69	20
1976-77—Laval National		QJHL	72	28	51	79	42
1977-78—Laval National (b-c)		QJHL	72	63	82	145	29
1978-79—Port Huron Flags		IHL	69	27	36	63	43
1979-80—Hershey Bears		AHL	45	17	26	43	16
1979-80—Washington Capitals		NHL	32	2	0	2	2
1980-81—Washington Capitals		NHL	40	5	13	18	16
1980-81—Hershey Bears		AHL	35	18	21	39	10
1981-82—Hershey Bears		AHL	31	12	12	24	6
1981-82—Washington Capitals		NHL	43	7	7	14	14
1982-83—Hershey Bears		AHL	12	5	11	16	6
1982-83—Washington Capitals		NHL	68	11	28	39	20
1983-84—Washington Capitals		NHL	80	12	24	36	20
NHL TOTALS			263	37	72	109	72

(c)—Drafted from Laval National by Washington Capitals in third round of 1978 amateur draft.

TONY CURRIE

Right Wing . . . 5'11" . . . 166 lbs. . . . Born, Sidney, N. S., November 12, 1957 . . . Shoots right . . . (February, 1984)—Fractured toe.

Year	Team	League	Games	G.	A.	Pts.	Pen.
1973-74—Edmonton Mets		AJHL	29	20	16	36	35
1973-74—Edmonton Oil Kings		WCHL	22	0	1	1	2
1974-75—Spruce Grove Mets		AJHL	35	36	44	80	73
1974-75—Edmonton Oil Kings		WCHL	39	28	17	45	12
1975-76—Edmonton Oil Kings		WCHL	71	41	40	81	56
1976-77—Portland Winter Hawks (c)		WCHL	72	73	52	125	50

Year	Team	League	Games	G.	A.	Pts.	Pen.
1977-78—S. L. City Golden Eagles (a)	CHL	53	33	17	50	17
1977-78—St. Louis Blues	NHL	22	4	5	9	4
1978-79—St. Louis Blues	NHL	36	4	15	19	0
1978-79—Salt Lake Golden Eagles	CHL	28	22	12	34	6
1979-80—Salt Lake Golden Eagles	CHL	33	24	23	47	17
1979-80—St. Louis Blues	NHL	40	19	14	33	4
1980-81—St. Louis Blues	NHL	61	23	32	55	38
1981-82—St. Louis Blues (d)	NHL	48	18	22	40	17
1981-82—Vancouver Canucks	NHL	12	5	3	8	2
1982-83—Vancouver Canucks	NHL	8	1	1	2	0
1982-83—Fredericton Express (a)	AHL	68	47	48	95	16
1983-84—Fredericton Express	AHL	12	6	11	17	16
1983-84—Vancouver Canucks (e)	NHL	18	3	3	6	2
1983-84—Hartford Whalers	NHL	32	12	16	28	4
NHL TOTALS		277	89	111	200	71

(c)—Drafted from Portland Winter Hawks by St. Louis Blues in fourth round of 1977 amateur draft.
(d)—March, 1982—Traded with Rick Heinz, Jim Nill and a fourth-round 1982 draft pick (Shawn Kilroy) by St. Louis Blues to Vancouver Canucks for Glen Hanlon.
(e)—January, 1984—Released by Vancouver Canucks and signed by Hartford Whalers as a free agent.

ANTHONY GLENN CURTALE

Defense . . . 6' . . . 190 lbs. . . . Born, Detroit, Mich., January 29, 1962 . . . Shoots left.

Year	Team	League	Games	G.	A.	Pts.	Pen.
1979-80—Brantford Alexanders (c)	OMJHL	59	10	35	45	227
1980-81—Brantford Alexanders	OHL	59	14	71	85	141
1980-81—Calgary Flames	NHL	2	0	0	0	0
1981-82—Brantford Alexanders	OHL	36	17	32	49	118
1981-82—Oklahoma City Stars (d)	CHL	..	..			....
1982-83—Colorado Flames	CHL	74	7	22	29	61
1983-84—Peoria Prancers	IHL	2	0	0	0	2
1983-84—Colorado Flames	CHL	54	3	20	23	80
NHL TOTALS		2	0	0	0	0

(c)—June, 1980—Drafted by Calgary Flames as an underage junior in 1980 NHL entry draft. Second Flames pick, 31st overall, second round.
(d)—No regular-season record. Appeared in four playoff games.

JOEL CURTIS

Left Wing . . . 6'1" . . . 185 lbs. . . . Born, Montreal, Que., January 13, 1966 . . . Shoots left.

Year	Team	League	Games	G.	A.	Pts.	Pen.
1982-83—New Market Tier II	COJHL	48	15	18	33	47
1983-84—Oshawa Generals (c)	OHL	67	8	12	20	68

(c)—June, 1984—Drafted as underage junior by Edmonton Oilers in 1984 NHL entry draft. Ninth Oilers pick, 209th overall, 10th round.

DENIS CYR

Right Wing . . . 5'11" . . . 186 lbs. . . . Born, Verdun, Que., February 4, 1961 . . . Shoots left . . . (January, 1982)—Dislocated shoulder . . . (January 15, 1983)—Broke nose in game at Philadelphia.

Year	Team	League	Games	G.	A.	Pts.	Pen.
1977-78—Montreal Red White & Blue	QMJHL	72	46	55	101	25
1978-79—Montreal Juniors (b)	QMJHL	72	70	56	126	61
1979-80—Montreal Juniors (c)	QMJHL	70	70	76	146	61
1980-81—Calgary Flames	NHL	10	1	4	5	0
1980-81—Montreal Juniors	QMJHL	57	50	40	90	53
1981-82—Oklahoma City Stars	CHL	14	10	4	14	16
1981-82—Calgary Flames	NHL	45	12	10	22	13
1982-83—Calgary Flames (d)	NHL	11	1	1	2	0
1982-83—Chicago Black Hawks	NHL	41	7	8	15	2
1983-84—Springfield Indians	AHL	17	4	13	17	11
1983-84—Chicago Black Hawks (e-f)	NHL	46	12	13	25	19
NHL TOTALS		153	33	36	69	34

(c)—June, 1980—Drafted as underage junior by Calgary Flames in 1980 NHL entry draft. First Flames pick, 13th overall, first round.
(d)—November, 1982—Traded by Calgary Flames to Chicago Black Hawks for NHL rights to Carey Wilson.
(e)—June, 1984—Released by Chicago Black Hawks.
(f)—August, 1984—Signed by St. Louis Blues as a free agent.

PAUL CYR

Left Wing . . . 5'10" . . . 180 lbs. . . . Born, Port Alberni, B.C., October 31, 1963 . . . Shoots left . . . (December 16, 1982)—Injured thumb while playing for Team Canada at World Junior Championships . . . (March 6, 1984)—Broken knuckle in finger during game at Montreal.

Year	Team	League	Games	G.	A.	Pts.	Pen.
1979-80—Nanaimo		BCJHL	60	28	52	80	202
1980-81—Victoria Cougars		WHL	64	36	22	58	85
1981-82—Victoria Cougars (b-c)		WHL	58	52	56	108	167
1982-83—Victoria Cougars		WHL	20	21	22	43	61
1982-83—Buffalo Sabres		NHL	36	15	12	27	59
1983-84—Buffalo Sabres		NHL	71	16	27	43	52
NHL TOTALS			107	31	39	70	111

(c)—June, 1982—Drafted as underage junior by Buffalo Sabres in 1982 NHL entry draft. Second Sabres pick, ninth overall, first round.

DEAN DACHYSHYN

Left Wing . . . 6'1" . . . 195 lbs. . . . Born, West Bank, B.C., May 4, 1959 . . . Shoots left.

Year	Team	League	Games	G.	A.	Pts.	Pen.
1979-80—University of North Dakota		WCHA	40	12	8	20	88
1980-81—University of North Dakota		WCHA	35	8	13	21	91
1981-82—University of North Dakota		WCHA	30	6	13	19	82
1982-83—University of North Dakota		WCHA	20	5	1	6	28
1983-84—Moncton Alpines (c)		AHL	74	9	7	16	92

(c)—October, 1983—Signed by Edmonton Oilers as a free agent.

ROLAND ALAIN DAIGLE
(Known by middle name)

Right Wing . . . 5'10" . . . 180 lbs. . . . Born, Cap-de-la-Madelein, Que., August 24, 1954 . . . Shoots right.

Year	Team	League	Games	G.	A.	Pts.	Pen.
1971-72—Three Rivers Dukes		QJHL	60	30	31	61	161
1972-73—Three Rivers Dukes		QJHL	61	42	32	74	97
1973-74—Three Rivers Dukes (c)		QJHL	67	80	68	148	72
1974-75—Chicago Black Hawks		NHL	52	5	4	9	6
1975-76—Chicago Black Hawks		NHL	71	15	9	24	15
1976-77—Chicago Black Hawks		NHL	73	12	8	20	11
1977-78—Chicago Black Hawks		NHL	53	6	6	12	13
1978-79—Chicago Black Hawks		NHL	74	11	14	25	55
1979-80—Chicago Black Hawks		NHL	66	7	9	16	20
1980-81—New Brunswick Hawks (d)		AHL	15	5	5	10	14
1981-82—Out of hockey.							
1982-83—Sherbrooke Jets		AHL	43	11	22	33	18'
1983-84—Sherbrooke Jets		AHL	79	22	26	48	24
NHL TOTALS			389	56	50	160	120

(c)—May, 1974—Drafted by Chicago Black Hawks in 1974 NHL amateur draft. Second Black Hawks pick, 34th overall, second round.

(d)—October, 1981—Released by Washington Capitals.

JEAN-JACQUES DAIGNEAULT

Defense . . . 5'11" . . . 180 lbs. . . . Born, Montreal, Que., October 12, 1965 . . . Shoots left . . . (March, 1984)—Knee surgery.

Year	Team	League	Games	G.	A.	Pts.	Pen.
1981-82—Laval Voisins		QMJHL	64	4	25	29	41
1982-83—Longueuil Chevaliers (a)		QHL	70	26	58	84	58
1983-84—Canadian Olympic Team		Int'l	62	6	15	21	40
1983-84—Longueuil Chevaliers (c)		QHL	10	2	11	13	6

(c)—June, 1984—Drafted as underage junior by Vancouver Canucks in 1984 NHL entry draft. First Canucks pick, 10th overall, first round.

MARTY DALLMAN

Center . . . 5'10" . . . 183 lbs. . . . Born, Niagara Falls, Ont., February 15, 1963 . . . Shoots right.

Year	Team	League	Games	G.	A.	Pts.	Pen.
1979-80—Niagara Falls Canucks		OPJHL	40	39	43	82	....
1980-81—R.P.I. (c)		ECAC	22	8	10	18	6
1981-82—R.P.I.		ECAC	28	22	18	40	27
1982-83—R.P.I.		ECAC	29	21	29	50	42
1983-84—R.P.I.		ECAC	38	30	24	54	32

(c)—June, 1981—Drafted as underage junior by Los Angeles Kings in 1981 NHL entry draft. Third Kings pick, 81st overall, fourth round.

KENNETH DANEYKO

Defense . . . 6'1" . . . 195 lbs. . . . Born, Windsor, Ont., April 17, 1964 . . . Shoots left. . . . (November 2, 1983)—Broke right fibula in game at Hartford.

Year	Team	League	Games	G.	A.	Pts.	Pen.
1980-81—Spokane Flyers		WHL	62	6	13	19	140
1981-82—Spokane Flyers		WHL	26	1	11	12	147
1981-82—Seattle Breakers (c-d)		WHL	38	1	22	23	151
1982-83—Seattle Breakers		WHL	69	17	43	60	150
1983-84—Kamloops Junior Oilers		WHL	19	6	28	34	52
1983-84—New Jersey Devils		NHL	11	1	4	5	17
NHL TOTALS			11	1	4	5	17

(c)—December, 1981—Drafted by Seattle Breakers in WHL Dispersal draft of players from Spokane Flyers.

(d)—June, 1982—Drafted as underage junior by New Jersey Devils in 1982 entry draft. Second Devils pick, 18th overall, first round.

DAN ARMAND DAOUST

Center . . . 5'11" . . . 160 lbs. . . . Born, Kirkland Lake, Ont., February 29, 1960 . . . Shoots left.

Year	Team	League	Games	G.	A.	Pts.	Pen.
1977-78—Cornwall Royals		QMJHL	68	24	44	68	74
1978-79—Cornwall Royals		QMJHL	72	42	55	97	85
1979-80—Cornwall Royals (c)		QMJHL	70	40	62	102	82
1980-81—Nova Scotia Voyageurs (a)		AHL	80	38	60	98	106
1981-82—Nova Scotia Voyageurs		AHL	61	25	40	65	75
1982-83—Montreal Canadiens (d)		NHL	4	0	1	1	4
1982-83—Toronto Maple Leafs		NHL	48	18	33	51	31
1983-84—Toronto Maple Leafs		NHL	78	18	56	74	88
NHL TOTALS			130	36	90	126	123

(c)—September, 1980—Signed by Montreal Canadiens as a free agent.

(d)—December, 1982—Traded by Montreal Canadiens with Gaston Gingras to Toronto Maple Leafs for future draft considerations.

NEAL DAVEY

Defense . . . 6'2" . . . 205 lbs. . . . Born, Edmonton, Alta., December 29, 1965 . . . Shoots right.

Year	Team	League	Games	G.	A.	Pts.	Pen.
1983-84—Michigan State Univ. (c)		CCHA	33	1	5	6	50

(c)—June, 1984—Drafted by New Jersey Devils in 1984 NHL entry draft. Third Devils pick, 44th overall, third round.

MALCOLM STERLING DAVIS

Right Wing . . . 5'11" . . . 180 lbs. . . . Born, Lockeport, Nova Scotia, October 10, 1956 . . . Shoots right . . . Attended University of Alberta.

Year	Team	League	Games	G.	A.	Pts.	Pen.
1978-79—Kansas City Red Wings (a)		CHL	71	42	24	66	29
1978-79—Detroit Red Wings		NHL	6	0	0	0	0
1979-80—Adirondack Red Wings		AHL	79	34	31	65	45
1980-81—Detroit Red Wings		NHL	5	2	0	2	0
1980-81—Adirondack Red Wings		AHL	58	23	12	35	48
1981-82—Rochester Americans		AHL	75	32	33	65	14
1982-83—Rochester Americans		AHL	57	43	32	75	15
1982-83—Buffalo Sabres		NHL	24	8	12	20	0
1983-84—Buffalo Sabres (c)		NHL	11	2	1	3	4
1983-84—Rochester Americans (a-d)		AHL	71	*55	48	103	53
NHL TOTALS			46	12	13	25	4

(c)—October, 1981—Signed by Buffalo Sabres as a free agent.

(d)—Co-Winner of Les Cunningham Plaque (AHL MVP) with Garry Lariviere.

LEONARD JAMES DAWES

Defense . . . 6'3" . . . 190 lbs. . . . Born, Nanaimo, B.C., April 11, 1962 . . . Shoots right . . . (March, 1980)—Surgery to remove tumor on ball of right foot.

Year	Team	League	Games	G.	A.	Pts.	Pen.
1978-79—Nanaimo		BCJHL	49	21	51	72	30
1978-79—Victoria Cougars		WHL	8	2	1	3	4
1979-80—Victoria Cougars (c)		WHL	67	7	19	26	48

Year	Team	League	Games	G.	A.	Pts.	Pen.
1980-81—Victoria Cougars (b)		WHL	67	14	49	63	66
1981-82—Victoria Cougars		WHL	35	5	26	31	53
1982-83—Springfield Indians		AHL	30	0	3	3	36
1983-84—Springfield Indians		AHL	13	1	4	5	2

(c)—June, 1980—Drafted as underage junior by Chicago Black Hawks in 1980 NHL entry draft. Fifth Black Hawks pick, 36th overall, second round.

LUCIEN DeBLOIS

Right Wing . . . 5'11" . . . 200 lbs. . . . Born, Joliette, Que., June 21, 1957 . . . Shoots right . . . (November, 1980)—Groin pull.

Year	Team	League	Games	G.	A.	Pts.	Pen.
1973-74—Sorel Black Hawks		QJHL	56	30	35	65	53
1974-75—Sorel Black Hawks		QJHL	72	46	53	99	62
1975-76—Sorel Black Hawks (a)		QJHL	70	56	55	111	112
1976-77—Sorel Black Hawks (a-c-d)		QJHL	72	56	78	134	131
1977-78—New York Rangers		NHL	71	22	8	30	27
1978-79—New York Rangers		NHL	62	11	17	28	26
1978-79—New Haven Nighthawks		AHL	7	4	6	10	6
1979-80—New York Rangers (e)		NHL	6	3	1	4	7
1979-80—Colorado Rockies		NHL	70	24	19	43	36
1980-81—Colorado Rockies (f)		NHL	74	26	16	42	78
1981-82—Winnipeg Jets		NHL	65	25	27	52	87
1982-83—Winnipeg Jets		NHL	79	27	27	54	69
1983-84—Winnipeg Jets (g)		NHL	80	34	45	79	50
NHL TOTALS			507	172	160	332	380

(c)—Won Most Valuable Player Award.
(d)—Drafted from Sorel Black Hawks by New York Rangers in first round of 1977 amateur draft.
(e)—November, 1979—Traded with Mike McEwen, Pat Hickey, Dean Turner and future considerations (Bobby Sheehan and Bobby Crawford) by New York Rangers to Colorado Rockies for Barry Beck.
(f)—July, 1981—Traded by Colorado Rockies to Winnipeg Jets for Brent Ashton and a third-round 1982 draft pick (Dave Kasper).
(g)—June, 1984—Traded by Winnipeg Jets to Montreal Canadiens for Perry Turnbull.

SHANNON DEEGAN

Center . . . 6'2" . . . 190 lbs. . . . Born, Montreal, Que., March 19, 1963 . . . Shoots left.

Year	Team	League	Games	G.	A.	Pts.	Pen.
1983-84—Univ. of Vermont (c)		ECAC	28	5	5	10	14

(c)—June, 1984—Drafted by Los Angeles Kings in 1984 NHL entry draft. Eighth Kings pick, 150th overall, eighth round.

DEAN DeFAZIO

Left Wing . . . 5'11" . . . 183 lbs. . . . Born, Ottawa, Ont., April 16, 1963 . . . Shoots left.

Year	Team	League	Games	G.	A.	Pts.	Pen.
1979-80—Ottawa Senators (c)		OPJHL	47	27	25	52	80
1980-81—Brantford Alexanders (d)		OHL	60	6	13	19	104
1981-82—Brantford Alexanders (e)		OHL	10	2	6	8	30
1981-82—Sudbury Wolves		OHL	50	21	32	53	81
1982-83—Oshawa Generals (f)		OHL	52	22	23	45	108
1983-84—Pittsburgh Penguins		NHL	22	0	2	2	28
1983-84—Baltimore Skipjacks		AHL	46	18	13	31	114
NHL TOTALS			22	0	2	2	28

(c)—June, 1980—Drafted by Brantford Alexanders in OHL player draft. First Brantford pick, fifth overall, first round.
(d)—June, 1981—Drafted as underage junior by Pittsburgh Penguins in 1981 NHL entry draft. Eighth Penguins pick, 175th overall, ninth round.
(e)—October, 1981—Traded with Tom DellaMaestra by Brantford Alexanders to Sudbury Wolves for Dan Zavarise and Gary Corbiere.
(f)—October, 1982—Traded by Sudbury Wolves to Oshawa Generals for Ali Butorac, Jim Uens and future considerations.

DALE DEGRAY

Defense . . . 5'10" . . . 190 lbs. . . . Born, Oshawa, Ont., September 3, 1963 . . . Shoots right.

Year	Team	League	Games	G.	A.	Pts.	Pen.
1979-80—Oshawa Legionaires		Metro Jr.B	42	14	14	28	34
1979-80—Oshawa Generals		OMJHL	1	0	0	0	2
1980-81—Oshawa Generals (c)		OHL	61	11	10	21	93
1981-82—Oshawa Generals		OHL	66	11	22	33	162

Year	Team	League	Games	G.	A.	Pts.	Pen.
1982-83—Oshawa Generals		OHL	69	20	30	50	149
1983-84—Colorado Flames		CHL	67	16	14	30	67

(c)—June, 1981—Drafted as underage junior by Calgary Flames in 1981 NHL entry draft. Seventh Flames pick, 162nd overall, eighth round.

GARY DEGRIO

Left Wing . . . 5'11" . . . 180 lbs. . . . Born, Duluth, Minn., February 16, 1960 . . . Shoots left . . . Also plays right wing.

Year	Team	League	Games	G.	A.	Pts.	Pen.
1978-79—Univ. of Minnesota/Duluth		WCHA	34	2	8	10	6
1979-80—Univ. of Minnesota/Duluth		WCHA	33	14	5	19	2
1980-81—Univ. of Minnesota/Duluth		WCHA	38	25	8	33	24
1981-82—Univ. of Minnesota/Duluth		WCHA	40	18	17	35	18
1982-83—Tulsa Oilers (c)		CHL	77	18	21	39	25
1983-84—Tulsa Oilers		CHL	65	10	19	29	24

(c)—April, 1982—Signed by New York Rangers as a free agent.

JOHN DEL COL

Left Wing . . . 5'10" . . . 190 lbs. . . . Born, St. Catharines, Ont., May 1, 1965 . . . Shoots left.

Year	Team	League	Games	G.	A.	Pts.	Pen.
1982-83—Toronto Marlboros		OHL	5	2	0	2	0
1984-85—Toronto Marlboros (c)		OHL	67	22	24	46	94

(c)—June, 1984—Drafted as underage junior by Pittsburgh Penguins in 1984 NHL entry draft. Seventh Penguins pick, 169th overall, ninth round.

GRANT DELCOURT

Right Wing . . . 5'11" . . . 180 lbs . . . Born, Prince George, B.C., August 10, 1966 . . . Shoots right.

Year	Team	League	Games	G.	A.	Pts.	Pen.
1983-84—Kelowna Wings (c)		WHL	72	22	53	75	55

(c)—June, 1984—Drafted as underage junior by Buffalo Sabres in 1984 NHL entry draft. Tenth Sabres pick, 226th overall, 11th round.

GILBERT DELORME

Defense . . . 5'11" . . . 205 lbs. . . . Born, Boucherville, Que., November 25, 1962 . . . Shoots right . . . (January 3, 1982)—Dislocated left shoulder in game at Buffalo.

Year	Team	League	Games	G.	A.	Pts.	Pen.
1978-79—Chicoutimi Sagueneens		QMJHL	72	13	47	60	53
1979-80—Chicoutimi Sagueneens		QMJHL	71	25	86	111	68
1980-81—Chicoutimi Sagueneens (b-c)		QMJHL	70	27	79	106	77
1981-82—Montreal Canadiens		NHL	60	3	8	11	55
1982-83—Montreal Canadiens		NHL	78	12	21	33	89
1983-84—Montreal Canadiens (d)		NHL	27	2	7	9	8
1983-84—St. Louis Blues		NHL	44	0	5	5	41
NHL TOTALS			209	17	41	58	193

(c)—June, 1981—Drafted as underage junior by Montreal Canadiens in 1981 NHL entry draft. Second Canadiens pick, 18th overall, first round.

(d)—December, 1983—Traded with Doug Wickenheiser and Greg Paslawski by Montreal Canadiens to St. Louis Blues for Perry Turnbull.

RONALD ELMER DELORME

Right Wing . . . 6'3" . . . 182 lbs. . . . Born, North Battleford, Sask., September 3, 1955 . . . Shoots right. . . . (March, 1980)—Knee injury . . . (January 3, 1981)—Separated shoulder . . . (October 14, 1982)—Strained knee ligaments in game at Boston.

Year	Team	League	Games	G.	A.	Pts.	Pen.
1972-73—Prince Albert Mintos		SJHL	....	...	....	....	....
1973-74—Swift Current Broncos		WCHL	59	19	15	34	96
1974-75—Lethbridge Broncos (c-d)		WCHL	69	30	57	87	144
1975-76—Lethbridge Broncos		WCHL	26	8	12	20	87
1975-76—Tucson Mavericks		CHL	18	2	5	7	18
1975-76—Denver Spurs		WHA	22	1	3	4	28
1976-77—Baltimore Clippers		SHL	25	4	6	10	4
1976-77—Tulsa Oilers		CHL	6	1	2	3	0
1976-77—Colorado Rockies (e)		NHL	29	6	4	10	23
1977-78—Colorado Rockies		NHL	68	10	11	21	47
1978-79—Colorado Rockies		NHL	77	20	8	28	68

Year	Team	League	Games	G.	A.	Pts.	Pen.
1979-80—Colorado Rockies		NHL	75	19	24	43	76
1980-81—Colorado Rockies		NHL	65	11	16	27	70
1981-82—Vancouver Canucks (f)		NHL	59	9	8	17	177
1982-83—Vancouver Canucks		NHL	56	5	8	13	87
1983-84—Vancouver Canucks		NHL	64	2	2	4	68
NHL TOTALS			493	82	81	163	616
WHA TOTALS			22	1	3	4	28

(c)—Drafted from Lethbridge Broncos by Kansas City Scouts in fourth round of 1975 amateur draft.
(d)—Selected by Denver Spurs in World Hockey Association amateur player draft, June, 1975.
(e)—Signed by Colorado Rockies, September, 1977.
(f)—October, 1981—Selected by Vancouver in 1981 NHL waiver draft.

ERIC DEMERS

Left Wing . . . 6'3" . . . 180 lbs. . . . Born, Montreal, Que., March 1, 1966 . . . Shoots left.

Year	Team	League	Games	G.	A.	Pts.	Pen.
1983-84—Shawinigan Cataracts (c)		QHL	65	5	13	18	153

(c)—June, 1984—Drafted as an underage junior by Montreal Canadiens in 1984 NHL entry draft, 11th Canadiens pick, 179th overall, ninth round.

DALE DERKATCH

Center . . . 5'6" . . . 140 lbs. . . . Born, Preeceville, Sask., October 17, 1964 . . . Shoots left . . . Tied WHL record (set by Brian Propp) for most assists in a rookie season, and set a record for most points in a rookie WHL season . . . Set WHL record for most consecutive 60-goal seasons (3), most points in a playoff season (53 in '83-84) and most assists in a playoff season (41 in '83-84).

Year	Team	League	Games	G.	A.	Pts.	Pen.
1980-81—Notre Dame Hounds		SAHA	20	35	35	70	33
1981-82—Regina Pats (c)		WHL	71	62	80	142	92
1982-83—Regina Pats (a-d-e)		WHL	67	*84	95	*179	62
1983-84—Regina Pats (f)		WHL	62	72	87	159	92

(c)—Won Stuart 'Butch' Paul Memorial Trophy (Top WHL Rookie).
(d)—Won Bob Brownridge Memorial Trophy (Top WHL Scorer).
(e)—June, 1983—Drafted as underage junior by Edmonton Oilers in 1983 NHL entry draft. Sixth Oilers pick, 140th overall, seventh round.
(f)—Set WHL playoff records for assists with 41 and points with 53.

DOUG DERKSON

Center . . . 5'11" . . . 173 lbs. . . . Born, Saskatoon, Sask., June 5, 1958 . . . Shoots right.

Year	Team	League	Games	G.	A.	Pts.	Pen.
1975-76—Chilliwack Bruins		Jr. "A" BCHL	70	35	35	70	58
1976-77—New Westminster Bruins		WCHL	72	20	40	60	35
1977-78—New Westminster Bruins (c)		WCHL	70	38	35	73	63
1978-79—Kalamazoo Wings		IHL	66	26	48	74	20
1979-80—Adirondack Red Wings		AHL	8	0	0	0	0
1979-80—Kalamazoo Wings		IHL	59	23	43	66	41
1980-81—Kalamazoo Wings		IHL	75	26	43	69	34
1981-82—Kalamazoo Wings		IHL	81	25	48	73	47
1982-83—Kalamazoo Wings		IHL	82	27	44	71	46
1983-84—Milwaukee Admirals		IHL	9	1	2	3	6

(c)—Drafted from New Westminster Bruins by Detroit Red Wings in third round of 1978 amateur draft.

PETER DERKSON

Left Wing . . . 5'11" . . . 180 lbs. . . . Born, Altona, Man., July 19, 1964 . . . Shoots left . . . (October, 1981)—Kidney infection.

Year	Team	League	Games	G.	A.	Pts.	Pen.
1980-81—Portland Winter Hawks		WHL	72	22	25	47	24
1981-82—Portland Winter Hawks (c)		WHL	63	13	18	31	96
1982-83—Saskatoon Blades (d)		WHL	71	28	78	106	97
1983-84—Winnipeg Warriors		WHL	34	9	21	30	40

(c)—June, 1982—Drafted as underage junior by Pittsburgh Penguins in 1982 NHL entry draft. Sixth Penguins pick, 157th overall, eighth round.
(d)—July, 1983—Traded with Ian Spencer by Saskatoon Blades to Winnipeg Warriors for Grant Jennings.

WILLIAM ANTHONY DERLAGO

Center . . . 5'10" . . . 194 lbs. . . . Born, Birtle, Man., August 25, 1958 . . . Shoots left . . . Missed part of 1977-78 season with knee injury . . . Set WCHL record for goals in season with 96 in

1976-77 . . . **Missed most of the 1978-79 season with severed knee ligaments that required surgery . . . (December, 1981)—Bruised ankle . . . (November 22, 1982)—Tore knee ligaments during team practice.**

Year	Team	League	Games	G.	A.	Pts.	Pen.
1974-75—Brandon Travellers		MJHL	....	...	....	....	....
1974-75—Brandon Wheat Kings		WCHL	17	0	4	4	2
1975-76—Brandon Wheat Kings		WCHL	68	49	54	103	43
1976-77—Brandon Wheat Kings (a-c)		WCHL	72	*96	82	*178	63
1977-78—Brandon Wheat Kings (b)		WCHL	52	89	63	152	105
1978-79—Vancouver Canucks (d)		NHL	9	4	4	8	2
1978-79—Dallas Black Hawks		CHL	11	5	8	13	9
1979-80—Vancouver Canucks (e)		NHL	54	11	15	26	27
1979-80—Toronto Maple Leafs		NHL	23	5	12	17	13
1980-81—Toronto Maple Leafs		NHL	80	35	39	74	26
1981-82—Toronto Maple Leafs		NHL	75	34	50	84	42
1982-83—Toronto Maple Leafs		NHL	58	13	24	37	27
1983-84—Toronto Maple Leafs		NHL	79	40	20	60	50
NHL TOTALS			378	142	164	306	187

(c)—Led in goals (14), assists (16) and points (30) during playoffs.
(d)—Drafted from Brandon Wheat Kings by Vancouver Canucks in first round of 1978 amateur draft.
(e)—February, 1980—Traded with Rick Vaive by Vancouver Canucks to Toronto Maple Leafs for Jerry Butler and Dave Williams.

FRANCO DESANTIS

Defense . . . 6' . . . 190 lbs. . . . Born, Montreal, Que., September 5, 1966 . . . Shoots left.

Year	Team	League	Games	G.	A.	Pts.	Pen.
1983-84—Verdun Juniors (c)		QHL	69	9	26	35	76

(c)—June, 1984—Drafted as underage junior by New York Islanders in 1984 NHL entry draft. Ninth Islanders pick. 167th overall, eighth round.

JOHN DEVEREAUX

Center . . . 6' . . . 174 lbs. . . . Born, Scituate, Mass., June 8, 1965 . . . Shoots right.

Year	Team	League	Games	G.	A.	Pts.	Pen.
1983-84—Scituate H.S. (c)		Mass. H.S.	20	41	34	75	..

(c)—June, 1984—Drafted by Hartford Whalers in 1984 NHL entry draft. Fourth Whalers pick, 173rd overall, ninth round.

KEVIN DEVINE

Left Wing . . . 5'7" . . . 170 lbs. . . . Born, Toronto, Ont., December 9, 1954 . . . Shoots left.

Year	Team	League	Games	G.	A.	Pts.	Pen.
1971-72—Toronto Marlboros		OMJHL	55	5	12	17	86
1972-73—Toronto Marlboros		OMJHL	58	30	40	70	150
1973-74—Toronto Marlboros (c)		OMJHL	67	40	29	69	218
1974-75—Syracuse Blazers		NAHL	27	11	12	23	23
1974-75—San Diego Mariners		WHA	46	4	10	14	48
1975-76—San Diego Mariners		WHA	80	21	28	49	102
1976-77—San Diego Mariners (d-e)		WHA	81	30	20	50	114
1977-78—Indianapolis Racers		WHA	76	19	23	42	141
1978-79—Quebec Nordiques		WHA	5	0	0	0	6
1978-79—San Diego Hawks (a-f)		PHL	58	36	36	72	119
1979-80—Indianapolis Checkers (g)		CHL	79	27	26	53	171
1980-81—Indianapolis Checkers (h)		CHL	80	28	26	54	153
1981-82—Indianapolis Checkers		CHL	80	24	27	51	199
1982-83—New York Islanders		NHL	2	0	1	1	8
1982-83—Indianapolis Checkers		CHL	78	21	27	48	245
1983-84—Indianapolis Checkers		CHL	71	23	30	53	201
WHA TOTALS			288	74	81	155	411
NHL TOTALS			290	74	82	156	419

(c)—May, 1974—Drafted by NHL and WHA in their respective amateur drafts. NHL Toronto Maple Leafs picked Devine eighth, 121st overall, second round. WHA San Diego Mariners picked Devine second, 21st overall, in the second round.
(d)—August, 1977—Sold to Edmonton Oilers in WHA dispersal of players from defunct teams.
(e)—September, 1977—Traded with Barry Wilkins, Rusty Patenaude and Claude St. Sauveur by Edmonton Oilers to Indianapolis Racers for Blair MacDonald, Mike Zuke and Dave Inkpen.
(f)—Named 'Most Inspirational Player' by Pacific Hockey League.
(g)—September, 1979—Signed as a free agent by New York Islanders and assigned to Indianapolis (CHL).
(h)—Winner of CHL Ironman Award.

JOHN DeVOE

Right Wing . . . 6'2" . . . 190 lbs. . . . Born, Minneapolis, Minn., November 1, 1963 . . . Shoots right . . . Son of Don DeVoe (Basketball coach, University of Tennessee).

Year	Team	League	Games	G.	A.	Pts.	Pen.
1981-82—Edina H.S. (c)		Minn. H.S.	36	22	15	37	24
1982-83—University of Notre Dame		CCHA	34	7	8	15	52
1983-84—Providence College		ECAC	28	14	6	20	18

(c)—June, 1982—Drafted as underage player by Montreal Canadiens in 1982 NHL entry draft. Seventh Canadiens pick, 69th overall, fourth round.

GERALD DIDUCK

Defense . . . 6'2" . . . 195 lbs. . . . Born, Edmonton, Alta., April 6, 1965 . . . Shoots right.

Year	Team	League	Games	G.	A.	Pts.	Pen.
1981-82—Lethbridge Broncos		WHL	71	1	15	16	81
1982-83—Lethbridge Broncos (c)		WHL	67	8	16	24	151
1983-84—Lethbridge Broncos		WHL	65	10	24	34	133

(c)—June, 1983—Drafted as underage junior by New York Islanders in 1983 NHL entry draft. Second Islanders pick, 16th overall, first round.

DON ARMOND DIETRICH

Defense . . . 6'2" . . . 205 lbs. . . . Born, Deloraine, Man., April 5, 1961 . . . Shoots left.

Year	Team	League	Games	G.	A.	Pts.	Pen.
1978-79—Brandon Wheat Kings		WHL	69	6	37	43	29
1979-80—Brandon Wheat Kings (c)		WHL	63	15	45	60	56
1980-81—Brandon Wheat Kings		WHL	72	16	64	80	84
1981-82—New Brunswick Hawks		AHL	62	1	5	6	14
1982-83—Springfield Indians		AHL	76	6	26	32	26
1983-84—Springfield Indians		AHL	50	14	21	35	14
1983-84—Chicago Black Hawks (d)		NHL	17	0	5	5	0
NHL TOTALS			17	0	5	5	0

(c)—June, 1980—Drafted as an underage junior by Chicago Black Hawks in 1980 NHL entry draft. Fourteenth Black Hawks pick, 183rd overall, ninth round.

(d)—July, 1984—Traded by Chicago Black Hawks to New Jersey Devils with Rich Preston as payment for not taking Ed Olczyk in 1984 draft.

RALPH DIFIORE

Defense . . . 6'1" . . . 180 lbs. . . . Born, Montreal, Que., April 20, 1966 . . . Shoots left.

Year	Team	League	Games	G.	A.	Pts.	Pen.
1983-84—Shawinigan Cataracts (c)		QHL	65	6	22	28	38

(c)—June, 1984—Drafted as underage junior by Chicago Black Hawks in 1984 entry draft. Ninth Black Hawks pick, 174th overall, ninth round.

GORDON DINEEN

Defense . . . 5'11" . . . 180 lbs. . . . Born, Toronto, Ont., September 21, 1962 . . . Shoots right . . . Brother of Shawn, Peter and Kevin Dineen and son of Bill Dineen (Detroit and Chicago, mid-1950s).

Year	Team	League	Games	G.	A.	Pts.	Pen.
1979-80—St. Michaels Junior 'B'		....	42	15	35	50	103
1980-81—Sault Ste. Marie Greyhounds (c)		OHL	68	4	26	30	158
1981-82—Sault Ste. Marie Greyhounds		OHL	68	9	45	54	185
1982-83—Indianapolis Racers (a-d-e)		CHL	73	10	47	57	78
1982-83—New York Islanders		NHL	2	0	0	0	4
1983-84—Indianapolis Checkers		IHL	26	4	13	17	63
1983-84—New York Islanders		NHL	43	1	11	12	32
NHL TOTALS			45	1	11	12	36

(c)—June, 1981—Drafted as underage junior by New York Islanders in 1981 NHL entry draft. Second Islanders pick, 42nd overall, second round.

(d)—Won Bobby Orr Trophy (Most Valuable CHL Defenseman).

(e)—Won Bob Gassoff Award (Most Improved CHL Defenseman).

KEVIN DINEEN

Defense . . . 5'10" . . . 180 lbs. . . . Born, Toronto, Ont., October 28, 1963 . . . Shoots right . . . Also plays wing . . . Brother of Shawn, Peter and Gordon Dineen and son of Bill Dineen (Detroit and Chicago, mid-1950s.) . . . Set University of Denver penalty-minute record (105) as a freshman . . . Member of 1984 U.S. Olympic Team.

Year	Team	League	Games	G.	A.	Pts.	Pen.
1980-81—St. Michaels Jr. B	MTJHL	40	15	28	43	167
1981-82—University of Denver (c)	WCHA	38	12	22	34	105
1982-83—University of Denver	WCHA	36	16	13	29	108
1983-84—U.S. Olympic Team	Int'l.					

(c)—June, 1982—Drafted as underage player by Hartford Whalers in 1982 NHL entry draft. Third Whalers pick, 56th overall, third round.

PETER DINEEN

Defense ... 5'11" ... 181 lbs. ... Born, Kingston, Ont., November 19, 1960 ... Shoots right ... Brother of Shawn, Gordon and Kevin Dineen and son of Bill Dineen (Detroit and Chicago, mid-1950s) ... (October, 1980)—Broken ankle.

Year	Team	League	Games	G.	A.	Pts.	Pen.
1977-78—Seattle Breakers	WCHL	2	0	0	0	0
1978-79—Kingston Canadians	OMJHL	60	7	14	21	70
1979-80—Kingston Canadians (c)	OMJHL	32	4	10	14	54
1980-81—Maine Mariners	AHL	41	6	7	13	100
1981-82—Maine Mariners	AHL	71	6	14	20	156
1982-83—Maine Mariners (d)	AHL	2	0	0	0	0
1982-83—Moncton Alpines	AHL	59	0	10	10	76
1983-84—Moncton Alpines	AHL	63	0	10	10	120
1983-84—Hershey Bears	AHL	12	0	1	1	32

(c)—June, 1980—Drafted by Philadelphia Flyers in 1980 NHL entry draft. Ninth Flyers pick, 189th overall, ninth round.

(d)—October, 1982—Traded by Philadelphia Flyers to Edmonton Oilers for Bob Hoffmeyer.

SHAWN DINEEN

Defense ... 5'11" ... 188 lbs. ... Born, Detroit, Mich., March 1, 1958 ... Shoots left ... Also plays left wing ... Brother of Peter, Gordon and Kevin Dineen and son of Bill Dineen (Detroit and Chicago, mid-1950s).

Year	Team	League	Games	G.	A.	Pts.	Pen.
1979-80—University of Denver	WCHA	27	4	16	20	60
1980-81—University of Denver	WCHA	38	3	15	18	72
1981-82—Nashville South Stars (c)	CHL	29	1	2	3	60
1981-82—Toledo Goaldiggers (d)	IHL	44	3	19	22	56
1982-83—Tulsa Oilers	CHL	71	6	16	22	163
1983-84—New Haven Nighthawks	AHL	8	0	1	1	4
1983-84—Moncton Alpines	AHL	43	0	11	11	116

(c)—June, 1981—Signed by Minnesota North Stars as a free agent.

(d)—September, 1982—Traded by Minnesota North Stars to New York Rangers for Dan McCarthy.

MARCEL ELPHEGE DIONNE

Center ... 5'8" ... 185 lbs. ... Born, Drummondville, Que., August 3, 1951 ... Shoots right ... Missed part of 1970-71 season with broken collarbone ... Set NHL record for points in rookie season in 1971-72 (broken by Bryan Trottier in 1975-76) ... Established record for shorthanded goals (10) in single season, 1974-75 (broken by Wayne Gretzky in 1983-84) ... Missed part of 1977-78 season with shoulder separations ... (January 7, 1981)—Collected 1,000th NHL point in 740th NHL game, the fastest by any player in history (record broken by Guy Lafleur, 720th game) ... (January 11, 1984)—Sprained left ankle in game vs. Washington ... (February 14, 1984)—Aggravated ankle injury in game at New Jersey.

Year	Team	League	Games	G.	A.	Pts.	Pen.
1967-68—Drummondville Rangers	QJHL	....	...	....	....	....
1968-69—St. Cath. Black Hawks	Jr."A"OHA	48	37	63	100	38
1969-70—St. Cath. B. Hawks (b-c)	Jr."A"OHA	54	*55	*77	*132	46
1970-71—St. Cath. B. Hawks (a-c-d)	Jr."A"OHA	46	62	81	*143	20
1971-72—Detroit Red Wings	NHL	78	28	49	77	14
1972-73—Detroit Red Wings	NHL	77	40	50	90	21
1973-74—Detroit Red Wings	NHL	74	24	54	78	10
1974-75—Detroit Red Wings (e-f)	NHL	80	47	74	121	14
1975-76—Los Angeles Kings	NHL	80	40	54	94	38
1976-77—Los Angeles Kings (a-f)	NHL	80	53	69	122	12
1977-78—Los Angeles Kings	NHL	70	36	43	79	37
1978-79—Los Angeles Kings (b)	NHL	80	59	71	130	30
1979-80—Los Angeles Kings (a-g-h)	NHL	80	53	84	*137	32
1980-81—Los Angeles Kings (b)	NHL	80	58	77	135	70
1981-82—Los Angeles Kings	NHL	78	50	67	117	50
1982-83—Los Angeles Kings	NHL	80	56	51	107	22
1983-84—Los Angeles Kings	NHL	66	39	53	92	28
NHL TOTALS		1003	583	796	1379	378

(d)—Drafted from St. Catharines Black Hawks by Detroit Red Wings in first round of 1971 amateur draft.

(e)—Signed by Los Angeles Kings as "free agent" after playing out option. Kings sent Terry Harper, Dan Maloney and second-round 1976 draft choice to Red Wings as compensation. L.A. received Bart Crashley from Detroit as part of deal, June, 1975.

(f)—Won Lady Byng Memorial Trophy.

(g)—Won Art Ross Trophy.

(h)—Selected NHL Player of the Year by THE SPORTING NEWS in poll of players.

ROBERT DIRK

Defense . . . 6'4" . . . 210 lbs. . . . Born, Regina, Sask., August 20, 1966 . . . Shoots left.

Year	Team	League	Games	G.	A.	Pts.	Pen.
1982-83—Kelowna Bucks		BCJHL	40	8	23	31	87
1982-83—Regina Pats		WHL	1	0	0	0	0
1983-84—Regina Pats (c)		WHL	62	2	10	12	64

(c)—June, 1984—Drafted as underage junior by St. Louis Blues in 1984 NHL entry draft. Fourth Blues pick, 53rd overall, third round.

BRIAN DOBBIN

Right Wing . . . 5'11" . . . 195 lbs. . . . Born, Petrolia, Ont., August 18, 1966 . . . Shoots right.

Year	Team	League	Games	G.	A.	Pts.	Pen.
1981-82—Mooretown Flags Jr. C		GLOHA	38	31	24	55	50
1982-83—Kingston Canadians		OHL	69	16	39	55	35
1983-84—London Knights (c)		OHL	70	30	40	70	70

(c)—June, 1984—Drafted as underage junior by Philadelphia Flyers in 1984 NHL entry draft. Sixth Flyers pick, 100th overall, fifth round.

JIM HEROLD DOBSON

Right Wing and Center . . . 6'1" . . . 194 lbs. . . . Born, Winnipeg, Man., February 29, 1960 . . . Shoots right.

Year	Team	League	Games	G.	A.	Pts.	Pen.
1977-78—New Westminster Bruins		WCHL	12	4	2	6	121
1978-79—Portland Winter Hawks (c)		WHL	71	38	39	77	143
1979-80—Portland Winter Hawks (a)		WHL	72	66	68	134	181
1979-80—Minnesota North Stars		NHL	1	0	0	0	0
1980-81—Oklahoma City Stars		CHL	35	23	16	39	46
1980-81—Minnesota North Stars		NHL	1	0	0	0	0
1981-82—Nashville South Stars		CHL	29	19	13	32	29
1981-82—Minnesota North Stars (d)		NHL	6	0	0	0	4
1981-82—Colorado Rockies		NHL	3	0	0	0	2
1981-82—Ft. Worth Texans		CHL	34	15	12	27	65
1982-83—Birmingham South Stars		CHL	80	36	37	73	100
1983-84—Quebec Nordiques		NHL	1	0	0	0	0
1983-84—Fredericton Express		AHL	75	33	44	77	74
NHL TOTALS			12	0	0	0	6

(c)—August, 1979—Drafted as underage junior by Minnesota North Stars in 1979 NHL entry draft. Fifth North Stars pick, 90th overall, fifth round.

(d)—December, 1981—Traded with Kevin Maxwell by Minnesota North Stars to Colorado Rockies for cash.

BOBBY DOLLAS

Defense . . . 6'2" . . . 220 lbs. . . . Born, Montreal, Que., January 31, 1965 . . . Shoots left.

Year	Team	League	Games	G.	A.	Pts.	Pen.
1981-82—Lac St. Louis AAA		Que. Midget	44	9	31	40	138
1982-83—Laval Voisins (b-c-d)		QHL	63	16	45	61	144
1983-84—Laval Voisins		QHL	54	12	33	45	80
1983-84—Winnipeg Jets		NHL	1	0	0	0	0
NHL TOTALS			1	0	0	0	0

(c)—Won Raymond Lagace Trophy (Top rookie defenseman).

(d)—June, 1983—Drafted as underage junior by Winnipeg Jets in 1983 NHL entry draft. Second Jets pick, 14th overall, first round.

CLARK DONATELLI

Left Wing . . . 5'10" . . . 190 lbs. . . . Born, Providence, R.I., November 22, 1965 . . . Shoots left.

Year	Team	League	Games	G.	A.	Pts.	Pen.
1983-84—Stratford Collitons Jr. B (c)		MWOHA	38	41	49	90	46

(c)—June, 1984—Drafted by New York Rangers in 1984 NHL entry draft. Fourth Rangers pick, 98th overall, fifth round.

DAVID DONNELLY

Left Wing . . . 5'11" . . . 185 lbs. . . . Born, Edmonton, Alta., February 2, 1963 . . . Shoots left . . . Member of 1984 Canadian Olympic Team.

Year	Team	League	Games	G.	A.	Pts.	Pen.
1979-80—St. Albert Saints		AJHL	59	27	33	60	146
1980-81—St. Albert Saints (c)		AJHL	53	39	55	94	243
1981-82—University of North Dakota (d)		WCHA	38	10	15	25	38
1982-83—University of North Dakota		WCHA	34	18	16	34	106
1983-84—Canadian Olympic Team		Int'l	64	17	13	30	52
1983-84—Boston Bruins		NHL	16	3	4	7	2
NHL TOTALS			16	3	4	7	2

(c)—June, 1981—Drafted as underage junior by Minnesota North Stars in 1981 NHL entry draft. Second North Stars pick, 27th overall, second round.

(d)—June, 1982—NHL rights traded by Minnesota North Stars along with Brad Palmer to Boston Bruins for future considerations (Boston passed over Brian Bellows in 1982 entry draft).

GORDON DONNELLY

Defense . . . 6'2" . . . 202 lbs. . . . Born, Montreal, Que., April 5, 1962 . . . Shoots right.

Year	Team	League	Games	G.	A.	Pts.	Pen.
1978-79—Laval Nationals		QMJHL	71	1	14	15	79
1979-80—Laval Nationals		QMJHL	44	5	10	15	47
1979-80—Chicoutimi Sagueneens		QMJHL	24	1	5	6	64
1980-81—Sherbrooke Beavers (c)		QMJHL	67	15	23	38	252
1981-82—Sherbrooke Beavers (d)		QMJHL	60	8	41	49	250
1982-83—Salt Lake Golden Eagles (e)		CHL	67	3	12	13	222
1983-84—Fredericton Express		AHL	30	2	3	5	146
1983-84—Quebec Nordiques		NHL	38	0	5	5	60
NHL TOTALS			38	0	5	5	60

(c)—June, 1981—Drafted by St. Louis Blues in 1981 NHL entry draft. Third Blues pick, 62nd overall, third round.

(d)—Led QMJHL Playoffs with 106 penalty minutes.

(e)—August, 1983—Sent by St. Louis Blues along with Claude Julien to Quebec Nordiques as compensation for St. Louis signing coach Jacques Demers.

ANDRE HECTOR DORE

Defense . . . 6'2" . . . 200 lbs. . . . Born, Montreal, Que., February 11, 1958 . . . Shoots right.

Year	Team	League	Games	G.	A.	Pts.	Pen.
1975-76—Hull Festivals		QJHL	59	4	11	15	67
1976-77—Hull Olympics		QJHL	72	9	42	51	178
1977-78—Hull Olympics		QJHL	15	3	9	12	22
1977-78—Trois-Rivieres Draveurs		QJHL	27	2	14	16	61
1977-78—Quebec Remparts (c)		QJHL	32	6	17	23	51
1978-79—New York Rangers		NHL	2	0	0	0	0
1978-79—New Haven Nighthawks		AHL	71	6	23	29	134
1979-80—New Haven Nighthawks		AHL	63	9	21	30	99
1979-80—New York Rangers		NHL	2	0	0	0	0
1980-81—New York Rangers		NHL	15	1	3	4	15
1980-81—New Haven Nighthawks		AHL	58	8	41	49	105
1981-82—Springfield Indians		AHL	23	3	8	11	20
1981-82—New York Rangers		NHL	56	4	16	20	64
1982-83—New York Rangers (d)		NHL	39	3	12	15	39
1982-83—St. Louis Blues		NHL	38	2	15	17	25
1983-84—St. Louis Blues (e)		NHL	55	3	12	15	58
1983-84—Quebec Nordiques		NHL	25	1	16	17	25
NHL TOTALS			232	14	74	88	226

(c)—Drafted from Quebec Remparts by New York Rangers in fourth round of 1978 amateur draft.

(d)—January, 1983—Traded by New York Rangers to St. Louis Blues for Vaclav Nedomansky and Glen Hanlon.

(e)—February, 1984—Traded by St. Louis Blues to Quebec Nordiques for Dave Pichette.

JORDY PAUL DOUGLAS

Left Wing . . . 6' . . . 199 lbs. . . . Born, Winnipeg, Man., January 20, 1958 . . . Shoots left . . . (February 18, 1981)—Broken bone in left foot . . . (November 11, 1981)—Separated left shoulder that required surgery, out for 16 weeks . . . Also plays center.

Year	Team	League	Games	G.	A.	Pts.	Pen.
1975-76—Flin Flon Bombers		WCHL	72	12	22	34	48
1976-77—Flin Flon Bombers		WCHL	59	40	23	63	71
1977-78—Flin Flon Bombers (c-d)		WCHL	71	60	56	116	131
1978-79—Springfield Indians		AHL	26	7	9	16	21
1978-79—New England Whalers (e)		WHA	51	6	10	16	15
1979-80—Hartford Whalers		NHL	77	33	24	57	39
1980-81—Hartford Whalers		NHL	55	13	9	22	29
1981-82—Binghamton Whalers		AHL	2	0	0	0	0
1981-82—Hartford Whalers (f)		NHL	30	10	7	17	44
1982-83—Minnesota North Stars		NHL	68	13	14	27	30
1983-84—Minnesota North Stars (g)		NHL	14	3	4	7	10
1983-84—Winnipeg Jets		NHL	17	4	2	6	8
WHA TOTALS			51	6	10	16	15
NHL TOTALS			261	76	60	136	160

(c)—Drafted from Flin Flon Bombers by Toronto Maple Leafs in fifth round of 1978 amateur draft.

(d)—Selected by New England Whalers in World Hockey Association amateur players' draft, June, 1978.

(e)—June, 1979—Selected by Toronto Maple Leafs in NHL reclaim draft, but remained with Hartford Whalers as a priority selection for the expansion draft.

(f)—October, 1982—Traded by Hartford Whalers to Minnesota North Stars as a future consideration to complete earlier trade. Mark Johnson and Kent-Erik Andersson were traded from Minnesota North Stars to Hartford Whalers for a 1984 fourth-round pick in NHL entry draft and future considerations.

(g)—January, 1984—Traded by Minnesota North Stars to Winnipeg Jets for Tim Trimper.

PETER DOURIS

Center . . . 6' . . . 195 lbs. . . . Born, Toronto, Ont., February 19, 1966 . . . Shoots right.

Year	Team	League	Games	G.	A.	Pts.	Pen.
1983-84—Univ. of New Hampshire (c)		ECAC	38	19	15	34	14

(c)—June, 1984—Drafted by Winnipeg Jets in 1984 NHL entry draft. First Jets pick, 30th overall, second round.

RON DREGER

Left Wing . . . 6' . . . 190 lbs. . . . Born, St. Boniface, Man., January 19, 1964 . . . Shoots left.

Year	Team	League	Games	G.	A.	Pts.	Pen.
1981-82—Saskatoon Blades (c)		WHL	59	18	15	33	41
1982-83—Saskatoon Blades		WHL	66	27	22	49	65
1983-84—Saskatoon Blades		WHL	71	29	37	66	56

(c)—June, 1982—Drafted as underage junior by Toronto Maple Leafs in 1982 NHL entry draft. Eighth Maple Leafs pick, 108th overall, sixth round.

STEVE DRISCOLL

Left Wing . . . 5'9" . . . 175 lbs. . . . Born, Montreal, Que., June 7, 1964 . . . Shoots left.

Year	Team	League	Games	G.	A.	Pts.	Pen.
1980-81—Belleville Bulls		OPJHL	37	4	16	20	107
1981-82—Cornwall Royals (c)		OHL	65	24	50	74	28
1982-83—Cornwall Royals (b)		OHL	64	49	77	126	34
1983-84—Cornwall Royals		OHL	63	38	51	89	13
1983-84—Fredericton Express		AHL	2	0	0	0	0

(c)—June, 1982—Drafted as underage junior by Vancouver Canucks in 1982 NHL entry draft. Ninth Canucks pick, 221st overall, 11th round.

BRUCE DRIVER

Defense . . . 6' . . . 174 lbs. . . . Born, Toronto, Ont., April 29, 1962 . . . Shoots left . . . Member of 1984 Canadian Olympic Team.

Year	Team	League	Games	G.	A.	Pts.	Pen.
1979-80—Royal York Royals		OPJHL	43	13	57	70	102
1980-81—University of Wisconsin (c)		WCHA	42	5	15	20	42
1981-82—University of Wisconsin (a-d)		WCHA	46	7	37	44	84
1982-83—University of Wisconsin (b)		WCHA	39	16	34	50	50
1983-84—Canadian Olympic Team		Int'l	61	11	17	28	44
1983-84—Maine Mariners		AHL	12	2	6	8	15
1983-84—New Jersey Devils		NHL	4	0	2	2	0
NHL TOTALS			4	0	2	2	0

(c)—June, 1981—Drafted as underage junior by Colorado Rockies in 1981 NHL entry draft. Sixth Rockies pick, 108th overall, sixth round.

(d)—Named to All-America Team (West).

GAETAN DUCHESNE

Left Wing . . . 5'11" . . . 195 lbs. . . . Born, Quebec City, Que., July 11, 1962 . . . Shoots left . . . (December 30, 1981)—Bruised right ankle in game at Pittsburgh.

Year	Team	League	Games	G.	A.	Pts.	Pen.
1979-80—Quebec Remparts		QJHL	46	9	28	37	22
1980-81—Quebec Remparts (c)		QJHL	72	27	45	72	63
1981-82—Washington Capitals		NHL	74	9	14	23	46
1982-83—Hershey Bears		AHL	1	1	0	1	0
1982-83—Washington Capitals		NHL	77	18	19	37	52
1983-84—Washington Capitals		NHL	79	17	19	36	29
NHL TOTALS			230	44	52	96	127

(c)—June, 1981—Drafted by Washington Capitals in 1981 NHL entry draft. Eighth Capitals pick, 152nd overall, eighth round.

TOBY DUCOLON

Left Wing . . . 6' . . . 195 lbs. . . . Born, St. Albans, Vt., June 18, 1966 . . . Shoots right.

Year	Team	League	Games	G.	A.	Pts.	Pen.
1983-84—Bellows Free Academy (c)		Ver. H.S.	22	38	26	64	36

(c)—June, 1984—Drafted by St. Louis Blues in 1984 NHL entry draft. Third Blues pick, 50th overall, third round.

LUC DUFOUR

Left Wing . . . 6' . . . 180 lbs. . . . Born, Chicoutimi, Que., February 13, 1963 . . . Shoots left . . . Brother-in-law of Alain Cote . . . (November, 1982)—Fractured finger on right hand.

Year	Team	League	Games	G.	A.	Pts.	Pen.
1980-81—Chicoutimi Sagueneens (c)		QMJHL	69	43	53	96	89
1981-82—Chicoutimi Sagueneens (a)		QMJHL	62	55	60	115	94
1982-83—Boston Bruins		NHL	73	14	11	25	107
1983-84—Boston Bruins		NHL	41	6	4	10	47
1983-84—Hershey Bears		AHL	37	9	19	28	51
NHL TOTALS			114	20	15	35	154

(c)—June, 1981—Drafted as underage junior by Boston Bruins in 1981 NHL entry draft. Second Bruins pick, 35th overall, second round.

RON DUGUAY

Center . . . 6'2" . . . 210 lbs. . . . Born, Sudbury, Ont., July 6, 1957 . . . Shoots right . . . Missed part of 1977-78 season with strained groin . . . (October 30, 1980)—Lacerated tendons in right leg . . . Also plays right wing . . . (January, 1982)—Separated left shoulder . . . (February, 1983)—Pulled stomach muscle.

Year	Team	League	Games	G.	A.	Pts.	Pen.
1973-74—Sudbury Wolves		Jr."A"OHA	59	20	20	40	73
1974-75—Sudbury Wolves		Jr."A"OHA	64	26	52	78	43
1975-76—Sudbury Wolves		Jr."A"OHA	61	42	92	134	101
1976-77—Sudbury Wolves (c)		Jr."A"OHA	61	43	66	109	109
1977-78—New York Rangers		NHL	71	20	20	40	43
1978-79—New York Rangers		NHL	79	27	36	63	35
1979-80—New York Rangers		NHL	73	28	22	50	37
1980-81—New York Rangers		NHL	50	17	21	38	83
1981-82—New York Rangers		NHL	72	40	36	76	82
1982-83—New York Rangers (d)		NHL	72	19	25	44	58
1983-84—Detroit Red Wings		NHL	80	33	47	80	34
NHL TOTALS			497	184	207	391	372

(c)—Drafted from Sudbury Wolves by New York Rangers in first round of 1977 amateur draft.

(d)—June, 1983—Traded with Eddie Johnstone and Ed Mio by New York Rangers to Detroit Red Wings for Mark Osborne, Mike Blaisdell and Willie Huber.

BLAKE ROBERT DUNLOP

Center . . . 5'10" . . . 170 lbs. . . . Born, Hamilton, Ont., April 4, 1953 . . . Shoots right . . . Missed part of 1974-75 season with pulled hamstring muscle and part of 1975-76 season with knee injury . . . Also plays right wing . . . (October, 1982)—Inflammation of iris of eye.

Year	Team	League	Games	G.	A.	Pts.	Pen.
1969-70—Ottawa 67's		Jr."A"OHA	45	17	15	32	10
1970-71—Ottawa 67's		Jr."A"OHA	62	44	46	90	39
1971-72—Ottawa 67's		Jr."A"OHA	62	32	52	84	41
1972-73—Ottawa 67's (b-c-d)		Jr."A"OHA	62	60	*99	*159	50

Year	Team	League	Games	G.	A.	Pts.	Pen.
1973-74—New Haven Nighthawks		AHL	59	37	41	78	25
1973-74—Minnesota North Stars		NHL	12	0	0	0	2
1974-75—Minnesota North Stars		NHL	52	9	18	27	8
1975-76—New Haven Nighthawks		AHL	10	2	10	12	8
1975-76—Minnesota North Stars		NHL	33	9	11	20	8
1976-77—New Haven Nighthawks		AHL	76	33	*60	93	16
1976-77—Minnesota North Stars		NHL	3	0	1	1	0
1977-78—Maine Mariners (a-f)		AHL	62	29	53	82	24
1977-78—Philadelphia Flyers (e)		NHL	3	0	1	1	0
1978-79—Maine Mariners		AHL	12	9	6	15	6
1978-79—Philadelphia Flyers (g)		NHL	66	20	28	48	16
1979-80—St. Louis Blues		NHL	72	18	27	45	28
1980-81—St. Louis Blues (h)		NHL	80	20	67	87	40
1981-82—St. Louis Blues		NHL	77	25	53	78	32
1982-83—St. Louis Blues		NHL	78	22	44	66	14
1983-84—St. Louis Blues (i)		NHL	17	1	10	11	4
1983-84—Detroit Red Wings		NHL	57	6	14	20	20
NHL TOTALS			550	130	274	404	172

(c)—Won Eddie Powers Memorial Trophy (Leading Scorer).
(d)—Drafted from Ottawa 67's by Minnesota North Stars in second round of 1973 amateur draft.
(e)—Traded to Philadelphia Flyers by Minnesota North Stars with third round draft choice for Harvey Bennett, October, 1977.
(f)—Won Les Cunningham Plaque (MVP) and Fred Hunt Memorial Award (AHL Coaches' MVP).
(g)—June, 1979—Traded with Rick LaPointe by Philadelphia Flyers to St. Louis Blues for Phil Myre.
(h)—Winner of Bill Masterton Memorial Trophy.
(i)—December, 1983—Signed by Detroit Red Wings as a free agent after being released by St. Louis Blues.

RICHARD DUNN

Defense . . . 6' . . . 192 lbs. . . . Born, Canton, Mass., May 12, 1957 . . . Shoots left . . . (December, 1981)—Shoulder injury.

Year	Team	League	Games	G.	A.	Pts.	Pen.
1975-76—Kingston Canadians		Jr."A"OHA	61	7	18	25	62
1976-77—Windsor Spitfires (c)		Jr."A"OHA	65	5	21	26	98
1977-78—Hershey Bears		AHL	54	7	22	29	17
1977-78—Buffalo Sabres		NHL	25	0	3	3	16
1978-79—Buffalo Sabres		NHL	24	0	3	3	14
1978-79—Hershey Bears		AHL	34	5	18	23	10
1979-80—Buffalo Sabres		NHL	80	7	31	38	61
1980-81—Buffalo Sabres		NHL	79	7	42	49	34
1981-82—Buffalo Sabres (d)		NHL	72	7	19	26	73
1982-83—Calgary Flames (e)		NHL	80	3	11	14	47
1983-84—Hartford Whalers		NHL	63	5	20	25	30
NHL TOTALS			423	29	129	158	273

(c)—September, 1977—Signed by Buffalo Sabres as free agent.
(d)—June, 1982—Traded by Buffalo Sabres with goaltender Don Edwards and a second-round choice in 1982 NHL entry draft to Calgary Flames for Calgary's first and second round draft choices in 1982 and their second round pick in 1983 plus the option to switch first-round picks in '83.
(e)—July, 1983—Traded by Calgary Flames with Joel Quenneville to Hartford Whalers for Mickey Volcan.

CHRISTIAN DuPERRON

Defense . . . 6'1" . . . 185 lbs. . . . Born, Montreal, Que., January 29, 1965 . . . Shoots right . . . Also plays right wing.

Year	Team	League	Games	G.	A.	Pts.	Pen.
1982-83—Bourassa AAA		Que. Midget	31	4	2	6	63
1982-83—Chicoutimi Sagueneens (c)		QHL	60	1	5	6	20
1983-84—Chicoutimi Sagueneens (d)		QHL	62	3	13	16	115

(c)—June, 1983—Drafted as underage junior by Hartford Whalers in 1983 NHL entry draft. Whalers ninth pick, 143rd overall, eighth round.
(d)—June, 1984—Released by Hartford Whalers.

JEROME DUPONT

Defense . . . 6'3" . . . 190 lbs. . . . Born, Ottawa, Ont., February 21, 1962 . . . Shoots left.

Year	Team	League	Games	G.	A.	Pts.	Pen.
1978-79—Toronto Marlboros		OMJHL	68	5	21	26	49
1979-80—Toronto Marlboros (c)		OMJHL	67	7	37	44	88

Year	Team	League	Games	G.	A.	Pts.	Pen.
1980-81—Toronto Marlboros		OHI	67	6	38	44	116
1981-82—Toronto Marlboros		OHL	7	0	8	8	18
1981-82—Chicago Black Hawks		NHL	34	0	4	4	51
1982-83—Chicago Black Hawks		NHL	1	0	0	0	0
1982-83—Springfield Indians		AHL	78	12	22	34	114
1983-84—Springfield Indians		AHL	12	2	3	5	65
1983-84—Chicago Black Hawks		NHL	36	2	2	4	116
NHL TOTALS			71	2	6	8	167

(c)—June, 1980—Drafted as underage junior by Chicago Black Hawks in 1980 NHL entry draft. Second Black Hawks pick, 15th overall, first round.

NORMAND DUPONT

Left Wing . . . 5'10" . . . 185 lbs. . . . Born, Montreal, Que., February 5, 1957 . . . Shoots left . . . Missed part of 1978-79 season with broken ankle.

Year	Team	League	Games	G.	A.	Pts.	Pen.
1973-74—Montreal Red, White and Blue		QJHL	70	55	70	125	4
1974-75—Montreal Red, White and Blue		QJHL	72	*84	74	*158	13
1975-76—Montreal Juniors (b-c)		QJHL	70	69	63	132	8
1976-77—Montreal Juniors (b-d)		QJHL	71	70	83	153	52
1977-78—Nova Scotia Voyageurs (e)		AHL	81	31	29	60	21
1978-79—Nova Scotia Voyageurs (f)		AHL	48	27	31	58	10
1979-80—Montreal Canadiens (g)		NHL	35	1	3	4	4
1980-81—Winnipeg Jets		NHL	80	27	26	53	8
1981-82—Winnipeg Jets		NHL	62	13	25	38	22
1982-83—Sherbrooke Jets		AHL	3	2	1	3	2
1982-83—Winnipeg Jets (h)		NHL	39	7	16	23	6
1983-84—Binghamton Whalers		AHL	27	15	24	39	6
1983-84—Hartford Whalers		NHI	40	7	15	22	12
NHL TOTALS			256	55	85	140	52

(c)—Won Most Gentlemanly Player award.

(d)—Drafted from Montreal Juniors by Montreal Canadiens in first round of 1977 amateur draft.

(e)—Won Dudley "Red" Garrett Memorial Trophy (AHL rookie of the year).

(f)—Tied for lead in goals (7) during playoffs.

(g)—September, 1980—Traded by Montreal Canadiens to Winnipeg Jets for second round 1982 entry draft pick (David Maley).

(h)—July, 1983—Traded by Winnipeg Jets to Hartford Whalers for future considerations.

BRIAN DURAND

Center . . . 6'2" . . . 190 lbs. . . . Born, Duluth, Minn., August 5, 1965 . . . Shoots right.

Year	Team	League	Games	G.	A.	Pts.	Pen.
1982-83—Cloquet H.S. (c)		Minn. H.S.	23	34	33	67	....
1983-84—University of Minnesota/Duluth		WCHA	24	2	5	7	4

(c)—June, 1983—Drafted by Minnesota North Stars in 1983 NHL entry draft. Fifth North Stars pick, 76th overall, fourth round.

HAROLD DUVALL

Left Wing . . . 5'11" . . . 185 lbs. . . . Born, Ogdenburg, N.Y. April 21, 1964 . . . Shoots left.

Year	Team	League	Games	G.	A.	Pts.	Pen.
1982-83—Belmont Hills H.S. (c)		Mass. H.S.	20	25	18	43	....
1983-84—Colgate University		ECAC	26	1	9	10	37

(c)—June, 1983—Drafted by Philadelphia Flyers in 1983 NHL entry draft. Eleventh Flyers pick, 241st overall, 12th round.

MIROSLAV DVORAK

Defense . . . 5'10" . . . 200 lbs. . . . Born, Hluboka Nad Vitavou, Czechoslovakia, October 11, 1951 . . . Shoots left.

Year	Team	League	Games	G.	A.	Pts.	Pen.
1980-81—Motor Ceske Budejoivice		Czech.	44	8	27	35	....
1981-82—Motor Ceske Budejoivice (c)		Czech.	....	6	20	26	....
1982-83—Philadelphia Flyers		NHL	80	4	33	37	20
1983-84—Philadelphia Flyers		NHL	66	4	27	31	27
NHL TOTALS			146	8	60	68	47

(c)—June, 1982—Drafted by Philadelphia Flyers in 1982 NHL entry draft. Second Flyers pick, 46th overall, third round.

STEVE DYKSTRA

Defense ... 6'2" ... 190 lbs. ... Born, Edmonton, Alta., February 3, 1962 ... Shoots left.

Year	Team	League	Games	G.	A.	Pts.	Pen.
1981-82—Seattle Flyers		WHL	57	8	26	34	139
1982-83—Rochester Americans (c)		AHL	70	2	16	18	100
1983-84—Rochester Americans		AHL	64	3	19	22	141

(c)—October, 1982—Signed by Buffalo Sabres as a free agent.

JOHN DZIKOWSKI

Left Wing ... 6'3" ... 190 lbs. ... Born, Portage La Prairie, Man., January 28, 1966 ... Shoots left.

Year	Team	League	Games	G.	A.	Pts.	Pen.
1983-84—Brandon Wheat Kings (c)		WHL	47	12	11	23	99

(c)—June, 1984—Drafted as underage junior by Philadelphia Flyers in 1984 entry draft. Seventh Flyers pick, 121st overall, sixth round.

CARY EADES

Right Wing ... 6'2" ... 195 lbs. ... Born, Burnaby, B.C., October 20, 1961 ... Shoots right ... Attended North Dakota University.

Year	Team	League	Games	G.	A.	Pts.	Pen.
1978-79—North Dakota University		WCHA	42	27	23	50	66
1979-80—North Dakota University		WCHA	30	16	12	28	50
1980-81—North Dakota University		WCHA	31	21	21	42	60
1981-82—North Dakota University		WCHA	41	21	23	44	52
1981-82—Salt Lake Golden Eagles (c)		CHL	1	1	0	1	0
1982-83—Salt Lake Golden Eagles		CHL	59	13	23	36	57
1983-84—Montana Magic		CHL	34	10	12	22	60

(c)—August, 1982—Signed by St. Louis Blues as a free agent.

MICHAEL EAGLES

Center ... 5'10" ... 180 lbs. ... Born, Susex, N.B., March 7, 1963 ... Shoots left.

Year	Team	League	Games	G.	A.	Pts.	Pen.
1979-80—Melville		SJHL	55	46	30	76	77
1980-81—Kitchener Rangers (c)		OHL	56	11	27	38	64
1981-82—Kitchener Rangers		OHL	62	26	40	66	148
1982-83—Kitchener Rangers		OHL	58	26	36	62	133
1982-83—Quebec Nordiques		NHL	2	0	0	0	2
1983-84—Fredericton Express		AHL	68	13	29	42	85
NHL TOTALS			2	0	0	0	2

(c)—June, 1981—Drafted as underage junior by Quebec Nordiques in 1981 NHL entry draft. Fifth Nordiques pick, 116th overall, sixth round.

BRUCE EAKIN

Center ... 5'11" ... 185 lbs. ... Born, Winnipeg, Man., September 28, 1962 ... Shoots left ... Set WHL record for regular season assists (125), 1981-82.

Year	Team	League	Games	G.	A.	Pts.	Pen.
1979-80—St. James Canadians		MJHL	48	42	62	104	76
1980-81—Saskatoon Blades (c)		WHL	52	18	46	64	54
1981-82—Saskatoon Blades (a)		WHL	66	42	*125	167	120
1981-82—Calgary Flames		NHL	1	0	0	0	0
1981-82—Oklahoma City Stars		CHL	1	0	3	3	0
1982-83—Colorado Flames		CHL	73	24	46	70	45
1983-84—Colorado Flames (b)		CHL	67	33	69	102	18
1983-84—Calgary Flames		NHL	7	2	1	3	4
NHL TOTALS			8	2	1	3	4

(c)—June, 1981—Drafted by Calgary Flames in 1981 NHL entry draft. Ninth Flames pick, 204th overall, 10th round.

JEFF EATOUGH

Right Wing ... 5'9" ... 168 lbs. ... Born, Cornwall, Ont., June 2, 1963 ... Shoots right.

Year	Team	League	Games	G.	A.	Pts.	Pen.
1979-80—Niagara Falls Flyers		OHL	6	0	1	1	4
1980-81—Cornwall Royals (c)		QMJHL	68	30	42	72	142
1981-82—Cornwall Royals		OHL	66	53	37	90	180
1981-82—Buffalo Sabres		NHL	1	0	0	0	0

Year	Team	League	Games	G.	A.	Pts.	Pen.
1982-83—Cornwall Royals (d)		OHL	9	5	3	8	18
1982-83—North Bay Centennials		OHL	50	25	24	49	73
1983-84—Rochester Americans		AHL	24	1	5	6	5
1983-84—Flint Generals		IHL	5	4	1	5	6
NHL TOTALS			1	0	0	0	0

(c)—June, 1981—Drafted as underage junior by Buffalo Sabres in 1981 NHL entry draft. Fifth Sabres pick, 80th overall, fourth round.

(d)—October, 1982—Traded by Cornwall Royals to North Bay Centennials for Tom Thornbury.

MICHAEL GORDON EAVES

Center . . . 5'10" . . . 180 lbs. . . . Born, Denver, Colo., June 10, 1956 . . . Shoots right . . . Attended University of Wisconsin . . . Holds school records for points in season and career . . . (October, 1980)—Knee injury . . . (February 12, 1981)—Hip injury . . . (February 23, 1981)—Suffered concussion, one of three concussions of the season . . . Brother of Murray Eaves . . . (October, 1981)—Back Spasms . . . (December 26, 1981)—Injured ribs when checked by Gerry Hart of St. Louis . . . (January, 1984)—Broken foot.

Year	Team	League	Games	G.	A.	Pts.	Pen.
1973-74—Nepean Raiders	Cent. "A" Jr. OHA		....	54	48	*102	....
1974-75—University of Wisconsin		WCHA	38	17	37	54	12
1975-76—University of Wisconsin (c)		WCHA	34	18	25	43	22
1975-76—U. S. National Team			....	...	....	....	....
1976-77—University of Wisconsin (b-d)		WCHA	45	28	53	81	18
1977-78—University of Wisconsin (a-d)		WCHA	43	31	58	89	16
1978-79—Minnesota North Stars		NHL	3	0	0	0	0
1978-79—Oklahoma City Stars (b-e)		CHL	68	26	61	87	21
1979-80—Oklahoma City Stars		CHL	12	9	8	17	2
1979-80—Minnesota North Stars		NHL	56	18	28	46	11
1980-81—Minnesota North Stars		NHL	48	10	24	34	18
1981-82—Minnesota North Stars		NHL	25	11	10	21	0
1982-83—Minnesota North Stars (f)		NHL	75	16	16	32	21
1983-84—Calgary Flames		NHL	61	14	36	50	20
NHL TOTALS			268	69	114	183	70

(c)—Drafted from University of Wisconsin by St. Louis Blues in seventh round of 1976 amateur draft.

(d)—Named to first-team (Western) All-America.

(e)—Won Ken McKenzie Trophy (CHL top rookie).

(f)—June, 1983—Traded by Minnesota North Stars with Keith Hanson to Calgary Flames for Steve Christoff and a second round pick in the 1983 NHL entry draft (Frantisek Musil).

MURRAY EAVES

Center . . . 5'10" . . . 185 lbs. . . . Born, Calgary, Alta., May 10, 1960 . . . Shoots right . . . Attended University of Michigan . . . Brother of Mike Eaves.

Year	Team	League	Games	G.	A.	Pts.	Pen.
1977-78—Windsor Spitfires		OMJHL	3	0	0	0	0
1978-79—University of Michigan		WCHA	23	12	22	34	14
1979-80—University of Michigan (a-c)		WCHA	33	36	49	85	34
1980-81—Winnipeg Jets		NHL	12	1	2	3	5
1980-81—Tulsa Oilers		CHL	59	24	34	58	59
1981-82—Tulsa Oilers		CHL	68	30	49	79	33
1981-82—Winnipeg Jets		NHL	2	0	0	0	0
1982-83—Winnipeg Jets		NHL	26	2	7	9	2
1982-83—Sherbrooke Jets		AHL	40	25	34	59	16
1983-84—Winnipeg Jets		NHL	2	0	0	0	0
1983-84—Sherbrooke Jets (a)		AHL	78	47	68	115	40
NHL TOTALS			42	3	9	12	7

(c)—June, 1980—Drafted by Winnipeg Jets in 1980 NHL entry draft. Third Jets pick, 44th overall, third round.

JAMES FRANK EGERTON

Right Wing . . . 6' . . . 180 lbs. . . . Born, Toronto, Ont., April 15, 1961 . . . Shoots right . . . (September, 1979)—Broken hand . . . (October, 1979)—Separated shoulder . . . Played one game in 1980-81 season with London as a goaltender (allowed 12 goals in 60 minutes).

Year	Team	League	Games	G.	A.	Pts.	Pen.
1977-78—Toronto Nats		MTHL	44	50	57	107	94
1978-79—London Knights		OMJHL	63	30	43	73	86
1979-80—London Knights		OMJHL	53	35	36	71	117
1980-81—London Knights		OMJHL	65	43	53	96	175
1980-81—Muskegon Mohawks		IHL	2	0	4	4	4

Year	Team	League	Games	G.	A.	Pts.	Pen.
1981-82—Muskegon Mohawks		IHL	50	34	27	61	34
1982-83—Muskegon Mohawks (b)		IHL	79	56	50	106	79
1983-84—Muskegon Mohawks		IHL	12	2	8	10	15

KELLY ELCOMBE

Defense . . . 5'11" . . . 195 lbs. . . . Born, Winnipeg, Man., March 14, 1960 . . . Shoots right.

Year	Team	League	Games	G.	A.	Pts.	Pen.
1978-79—Brandon Wheat Kings		WHL	45	3	15	18	145
1979-80—Brandon Wheat Kings		WHL	65	9	35	44	221
1980-81—Dallas Black Hawks (c)		CHL	16	3	1	4	31
1980-81—Fort Wayne Komets		IHL	58	12	38	50	214
1981-82—Dallas Black Hawks		CHL	64	10	31	41	179
1982-83—Fredericton Express (d)		AHL	62	2	24	26	157
1983-84—Sherbrooke Jets		AHL	32	10	24	34	26

(c)—October, 1980—Signed by Vancouver Canucks as a free agent.
(d)—August, 1983—Signed by Winnipeg Jets as a free agent.

DAVE ELLETT

Defense . . . 6'1" . . . 200 lbs. . . . Born, Cleveland, O., March 30, 1964 . . . Shoots left . . . Son of Dave Ellett Sr., who played for Cleveland Barons in AHL.

Year	Team	League	Games	G.	A.	Pts.	Pen.
1981-82—Ottawa Senators		CJOHL	50	9	35	44	..
1982-83—Bowling Green Univ. (c)		CCHA	40	4	13	17	34
1983-84—Bowling Green Univ.		CCHA	43	15	39	54	9

(c)—June, 1982—Drafted as underage player by Winnipeg Jets in NHL entry draft. Third Jets pick, 75th overall, fourth round.

KARI ELORANTA

Defense . . . 6'2" . . . 200 lbs. . . . Born, Lahti, Finland, February 29, 1956 . . . Shoots left.

Year	Team	League	Games	G.	A.	Pts.	Pen.
1979-80—Leksand		Sweden	36	3	11	14	32
1980-81—Leksand		Sweden	36	4	13	17	35
1981-82—Oklahoma City Stars		CHL	39	3	27	30	31
1981-82—Calgary Flames (c-d)		NHL	19	0	5	5	14
1981-82—St. Louis Blues		NHL	12	1	7	8	6
1982-83—Calgary Flames		NHL	80	4	40	44	43
1983-84—Calgary Flames		NHL	78	5	34	39	44
NHL TOTALS			189	10	86	96	107

(c)—September, 1981—Signed by Calgary Flames as a free agent.
(d)—March, 1982—Traded by Calgary Flames to St. Louis Blues for future considerations. Returned to Calgary, June, 1982.

PATRICK EMOND

Center . . . 6' . . . 175 lbs. . . . Born, Quebec City, Que., January 31, 1965 . . . Shoots left.

Year	Team	League	Games	G.	A.	Pts.	Pen.
1981-82—Trois-Rivieres Draveurs		QMJHL	64	26	32	58	24
1982-83—Trois-Rivieres Draveurs		QHL	37	25	37	62	24
1982-83—Hull Olympics (c)		QHL	32	19	32	51	16
1983-84—Chicoutimi Sagueneens		QHL	68	33	65	98	24

(c)—June, 1983—Drafted as underage junior by Pittsburgh Penguins in 1983 NHL entry draft. Fifth Penguins pick, 103rd overall, sixth round.

BRIAN PAUL ENGBLOM

Defense . . . 6'2" . . . 200 lbs. . . . Born Winnipeg, Man., January 27, 1955 . . . Shoots left . . . Attended University of Wisconsin . . . (March, 1983)—Eye injury.

Year	Team	League	Games	G.	A.	Pts.	Pen.
1973-74—University of Wisconsin		WCHA	36	10	21	31	54
1974-75—University of Wisconsin (c-g)		WCHA	38	13	23	36	58
1975-76—Nova Scotia Voyageurs		AHL	73	4	34	38	79
1976-77—Nova Scotia Voyageurs (a-d)		AHL	80	8	42	50	89
1976-77—Montreal Canadiens (e)		NHL	....	...	....	....	....
1977-78—Nova Scotia Voyageurs		AHL	7	1	5	6	4
1977-78—Montreal Canadiens		NHL	28	1	2	3	23
1978-79—Montreal Canadiens		NHL	62	3	11	14	60
1979-80—Montreal Canadiens		NHL	70	3	20	23	43
1980-81—Montreal Canadiens		NHL	80	3	25	28	96

Year	Team	League	Games	G.	A.	Pts.	Pen.
1981-82—Montreal Canadiens (h-f)		NHL	76	4	29	33	76
1982-83—Washington Capitals		NHL	68	11	28	39	20
1983-84—Washington Capitals (h)		NHL	6	0	1	1	8
1983-84—Los Angeles Kings		NHL	74	2	27	29	59
NHL TOTALS			464	27	143	170	385

(c)—Drafted from University of Wisconsin by Montreal Canadiens in second round of 1975 amateur draft.
(d)—Won Eddie Shore Plaque (outstanding defenseman in AHL).
(e)—No league record. Appeared in 2 playoff games.
(f)—September, 1982—Traded by Montreal Canadiens with Rod Langway, Doug Jarvis and Craig Laughlin to Washington Capitals for Ryan Walter and Rick Green.
(g)—Named to All-American team (West).
(h)—October, 1983—Traded with Ken Houston by Washington Capitals to Los Angeles Kings for Larry Murphy.

JOHN ENGLISH

Defense . . . 6'2" . . . 185 lbs. . . . Born, Toronto, Ont., May 3, 1966 . . . Shoots right.

Year	Team	League	Games	G.	A.	Pts.	Pen.
1982-83—St. Michaels Jr.		..	34	2	10	12	92
1983-84—Sault Ste. Marie Greyhounds (c)		OHL	64	6	11	17	144

(c)—June, 1984—Drafted as underage junior by Los Angeles Kings in 1984 NHL entry draft. Third Kings pick, 48th overall, third round.

BRYAN (Butsy) ERICKSON

Right Wing . . . 5'9" . . . 170 lbs. . . . Born, Roseau, Minn., March 7, 1960 . . . Shoots right . . . (January, 1983)—Fractured wrist.

Year	Team	League	Games	G.	A.	Pts.	Pen.
1979-80—University of Minnesota		WCHA	23	10	15	25	14
1980-81—University of Minnesota		WCHA	44	39	47	86	30
1981-82—University of Minnesota (b)		WCHA	35	25	20	45	20'
1982-83—University of Minnesota (a-c)		WCHA	42	35	47	82	30
1982-83—Hershey Bears		AHL	1	0	1	1	0
1983-84—Hershey Bears		AHL	31	16	12	28	11
1983-84—Washington Capitals		NHL	45	12	17	29	16
NHL TOTALS			45	12	17	29	16

(c)—April, 1983—Signed by Washington Capitals as a free agent.

THOMAS ERIKSSON

Defense . . . 6'2" . . . 182 lbs. . . . Born, Stockholm, Sweden, October 16, 1959 . . . Shoots left . . . Member of Swedish Nationals in 1979 and 1980 and Swedish Olympic Team in 1980.

Year	Team	League	Games	G.	A.	Pts.	Pen.
1975-76—Norsborgs IF (jr.)		Stockholm	....	...	....	....	....
1976-77—			....	...	....	....	....
1977-78—Djurgardens IF		Swed. Elite	25	6	4	10	30
1978-79—Djurgardens IF (c)		Swed. Elite	35	6	13	19	70
1979-80—Djurgardens IF		Swed. Elite	36	12	11	23	63
1979-80—Swedish Olympic Team		Int'l	7	2	0	2	10
1980-81—Maine Mariners		AHL	54	11	20	31	75
1980-81—Philadelphia Flyers		NHL	24	1	10	11	14
1981-82—Philadelphia Flyers		NHL	1	0	0	0	4
1981-82—Djurgardens IF		Swed. Elite	27	7	5	12	48
1982-83—Djurgardens IF		Swed. Elite	32	12	9	21	51
1983-84—Philadelphia Flyers		NHL	68	11	33	44	37
NHL TOTALS			93	12	43	55	55

(c)—August, 1979—Drafted by Philadelphia Flyers in 1979 NHL entry draft. Sixth Flyers pick, 98th overall, fifth round.

JAN ERIXON

Right Wing . . . 6' . . . 190 lbs. . . . Born, Skelleftea, Sweden, July 8, 1962 . . . Shoots left.

Year	Team	League	Games	G.	A.	Pts.	Pen.
1979-80—Skelleftea AIK		Sweden	32	9	3	12	22
1980-81—Skelleftea AIK (c)		Sweden	32	6	6	12	4
1981-82—Skelleftea AIK		Sweden	30	7	7	14	26
1982-83—Skelleftea AIK		Sweden	36	10	18	28	..
1983-84—New York Rangers		NHL	75	5	25	30	16
NHL TOTALS			75	5	25	30	16

(c)—June, 1981—Drafted by New York Rangers in 1981 NHL entry draft. Second Rangers pick, 30th overall, second round.

BOB ERREY

Left Wing . . . 5'10" . . . 185 lbs. . . . Born, Montreal, Que., September 21, 1964 . . . Shoots left.

Year	Team	League	Games	G.	A.	Pts.	Pen.
1981-82—Peterborough Petes		OHL	68	29	31	60	39
1982-83—Peterborough Petes (a-c)		OHL	67	53	47	100	74
1983-84—Pittsburgh Penguins		NHL	65	9	13	22	29
NHL TOTALS			65	9	13	22	29

(c)—June, 1983—Drafted as underage junior by Pittsburgh Penguins in 1983 NHL entry draft. Penguins first pick, 15th overall, first round.

PAT ETHIER

Defense . . . 6'1" . . . 195 lbs. . . . Born, March 17, 1961 . . . Shoots right.

Year	Team	League	Games	G.	A.	Pts.	Pen.
1979-80—University of Wisconsin		WCHA	27	4	3	7	24
1980-81—University of Wisconsin		WCHA	37	1	17	18	92
1981-82—University of Wisconsin		WCHA	44	7	34	41	61
1982-83—University of Wisconsin		WCHA	47	7	20	27	88
1983-84—Carolina Thunderbirds		ACHL	68	19	27	46	67

DARYL THOMAS EVANS

Left Wing . . . 5'9" . . . 180 lbs. . . . Born, Toronto, Ont., January 12, 1961 . . . Shoots left . . . (1981-82)—Broken wrist while playing for New Haven Nighthawks.

Year	Team	League	Games	G.	A.	Pts.	Pen.
1977-78—Senaca Nats		OHA Jr. B	40	25	35	60	50
1978-79—Niagara Falls Flyers		OMJHL	65	38	26	64	110
1979-80—Niagara Falls Flyers (c)		OMJHL	63	43	52	95	47
1980-81—Niagara Falls Flyers (d)		OHL	5	3	4	7	11
1980-81—Brantford Alexanders (a)		OHL	58	58	54	112	50
1980-81—Saginaw Gears		IHL	3	3	2	5	0
1981-82—New Haven Nighthawks		AHL	41	14	14	28	10
1981-82—Los Angeles Kings		NHL	14	2	6	8	2
1982-83—Los Angeles Kings		NHL	80	18	22	40	21
1983-84—New Haven Nighthawks (b)		AHL	69	51	35	86	14
1983-84—Los Angeles Kings		NHL	4	0	1	1	0
NHL TOTALS			98	20	29	49	23

(c)—June, 1980—Drafted as underage junior by Los Angeles Kings in 1980 NHL entry draft. Eleventh Kings pick, 178th overall, ninth round.

(d)—October, 1980—Traded by Niagara Falls Flyers to Brantford Alexanders for Vinci Sebek.

JOHN PAUL EVANS
(Known by middle name.)

Center . . . 5'9" . . . 180 lbs. . . . Born, Toronto, Ont., May 2, 1954 . . . Shoots left . . . Missed final weeks of 1974-75 season with knee injury . . . (December, 1982)—Stretched knee ligaments.

Year	Team	League	Games	G.	A.	Pts.	Pen.
1970-71—North York Rangers		Jr."B" OHA	..	..	..	..	....
1971-72—Kitchener Rangers		Jr."A" OHA	57	30	38	68	10
1972-73—Kitchener Rangers		Jr."A" OHA	63	29	47	76	22
1973-74—Kitchener Rangers (c)		Jr."A" OHA	69	52	60	112	45
1974-75—Saginaw Gears		IHL	60	21	35	56	42
1975-76—Saginaw Gears		IHL	78	32	53	85	65
1976-77—Saginaw Gears (a-d)		IHL	78	50	62	112	53
1977-78—Springfield Indians (e)		AHL	8	4	6	10	6
1977-78—Maine Mariners		AHL	66	26	35	61	28
1978-79—Philadelphia Flyers		NHL	44	6	5	11	12
1978-79—Maine Mariners (f)		AHL	32	16	24	40	36
1979-80—Maine Mariners		AHL	80	21	56	77	66
1980-81—Philadelphia Flyers		NHL	1	0	0	0	2
1980-81—Maine Mariners (b)		AHL	78	28	52	80	49
1981-82—Maine Mariners		AHL	79	33	57	90	42
1982-83—Philadelphia Flyers		NHL	58	8	20	28	20
1983-84—Maine Mariners		AHL	76	23	36	59	65
1983-84—Birmingham Bulls		ACHL	1	0	0	0	0
NHL TOTALS			103	14	25	39	34

(c)—Drafted from Kitchener Rangers by Los Angeles Kings in fifth round of 1974 amateur draft.
(d)—Led in points (21) during playoffs.
(e)—Sent to Philadelphia Flyers by Los Angeles Kings to complete earlier deal for Steve Short, November, 1977.
(f)—Led in assists (13) and tied for lead in points (17) during playoffs.

SHAWN EVANS

Defense . . . 6'3" . . . 195 lbs. . . . Born, Kingston, Ont., September 7, 1965 . . . Shoots left . . . Cousin of Dennis Kearns (Vancouver, 1970s).

Year	Team	League	Games	G.	A.	Pts.	Pen.
1981-82—Kitchener Rangers MW Jr. B		OHA	21	9	13	22	55
1982-83—Peterborough Petes (c)		OHL	58	7	41	48	116
1983-84—Peterborough Petes (b)		OHL	67	21	88	109	116

(c)—June, 1983—Drafted by New Jersey Devils as underage junior in 1983 NHL entry draft. Second Devils pick, 24th overall, second round.

DEAN EVASON

Center . . . 5'10" . . . 175 lbs. . . . Born, Flin Flon, Man., August 22, 1964 . . . Shoots left.

Year	Team	League	Games	G.	A.	Pts.	Pen.
1980-81—Spokane Flyers		WHL	3	1	1	2	0
1981-82—Kamloops Junior Oilers (c-d)		WHL	70	29	69	98	112
1982-83—Kamloops Junior Oilers		WHL	70	71	93	164	102
1983-84—Kamloops Junior Oilers (a-e)		WHL	57	49	88	137	89
1983-84—Washington Capitals		NHL	2	0	0	0	2
NHL TOTALS			2	0	0	0	2

(c)—December, 1981—Drafted by Kamloops Junior Oilers in WHL disperal draft of players of Spokane Flyers.
(d)—June, 1982—Drafted as underage junior by Washington Capitals in 1982 NHL entry draft. Third Capitals pick, 89th overall, fifth round.
(e)—Shared WHL playoff scoring with Taylor Hall, each had 21 goals.

GREG EVTUSHEVSKI

Right Wing . . . 5'10" . . . 185 lbs. . . . Born, St. Paul, Alta., May 4, 1965 . . . Shoots right.

Year	Team	League	Games	G.	A.	Pts.	Pen.
1982-83—Kamloops Junior Oilers (c)		WHL	70	32	49	81	245
1983-84—Kamloops Junior Oilers		WHL	64	27	43	70	176

(c)—June, 1983—Drafted as underage junior by New Jersey Devils in 1983 NHL entry draft. Fifth Devils pick, 125th overall, seventh round.

TODD EWEN

Right Wing . . . 6'2" . . . 185 lbs. . . . Born, Saskatoon, Sask., March 26, 1966 . . . Shoots right.

Year	Team	League	Games	G.	A.	Pts.	Pen.
1982-83—Vernon Lakers		BCJHL	42	20	23	53	195
1982-83—Kamloops Junior Oilers		WHL	3	0	0	0	2
1983-84—New Westminster Bruins (c)		WHL	68	11	13	24	176

(c)—June, 1984—Drafted as underage junior by Edmonton Oilers in 1984 NHL entry draft. Eighth Oilers pick, 168th overall, eighth round.

DAVID ALLAN FARRISH

Defense . . . 6'1" . . . 195 lbs. . . . Born, Wingham, Ont., August 1, 1956 . . . Shoots left . . . Sprained ankle (March, 1980) . . . (November 1980)—Groin injury . . . (November, 1983)—Neok injury.

Year	Team	League	Games	G.	A.	Pts.	Pen.
1973-74—Sudbury Wolves		Jr."A" OHA	58	11	20	31	205
1974-75—Sudbury Wolves		Jr."A" OHA	60	20	44	64	258
1975-76—Sudbury Wolves (a-c)		Jr."A" OHA	66	27	48	75	155
1976-77—New York Rangers		NHL	80	2	17	19	102
1977-78—New Haven Nighthawks		AHL	10	0	3	3	4
1977-78—New York Rangers		NHL	66	3	5	8	62
1978-79—New York Rangers (d)		NHL	71	1	19	20	61
1979-80—Syracuse Firebirds		AHL	14	4	10	14	17
1979-80—Quebec Nordiques (e)		NHL	4	0	0	0	0
1979-80—New Brunswick Hawks		AHL	20	3	1	4	22
1979-80—Toronto Maple Leafs		NHL	20	1	8	9	30
1980-81—Toronto Maple Leafs		NHL	74	2	18	20	90
1981-82—New Brunswick Hawks (a-f)		AHL	67	13	24	37	80
1982-83—St. Catharines Saints		AHL	14	2	12	14	18

Year	Team	League	Games	G.	A.	Pts.	Pen.
1982-83—Toronto Maple Leafs		NHL	56	4	24	28	38
1983-84—St. Catharines Saints		AHL	4	0	2	2	6
1983-84—Toronto Maple Leafs		NHL	59	4	19	23	57
NHL TOTALS			430	17	110	127	440

(c)—Drafted from Sudbury Wolves by New York Rangers in second round of 1976 amateur draft.
(d)—June, 1979—Selected by Quebec Nordiques in NHL expansion draft.
(e)—December, 1979—Traded by Quebec Nordiques to Toronto Maple Leafs for Reg Thomas.
(f)—Winner of Eddie Shore Plaque (Outstanding AHL Defenseman).

TED FAUSS

Defense ... 6'2" ... 218 lbs. ... Born, Clinton, N.Y., June 30, 1961 ... Shoots left.

Year	Team	League	Games	G.	A.	Pts.	Pen.
1979-80—Clarkson College		ECAC	34	2	4	6	36
1980-81—Clarkson College		ECAC	37	0	5	5	56
1981-82—Clarkson College		ECAC	35	3	6	9	79
1982-83—Clarkson College		ECAC	25	4	6	10	60
1982-83—Nova Scotia Voyageurs (c)		AHL	5	0	1	1	11
1983-84—Nova Scotia Voyageurs		AHL	71	4	11	15	123

(c)—March, 1983—Signed by Montreal Canadiens as a free agent.

DAVE ALLAN FEAMSTER

Defense ... 5'11" ... 180 lbs. ... Born, Detroit, Mich., September 10, 1958 ... Shoots left ... (December, 1980)—Knee injury.

Year	Team	League	Games	G.	A.	Pts.	Pen.
1976-77—Colorado College		WCHA	37	9	28	37	96
1977-78—Colorado College (c)		WCHA	39	8	34	42	92
1978-79—Colorado College (b)		WCHA	31	10	37	47	78
1979-80—Colorado College (a-d)		WCHA	37	17	33	50	135
1980-81—Dallas Black Hawks (e)		CHL	77	12	33	45	117
1981-82—New Brunswick Hawks		AHL	42	6	30	36	69
1981-82—Chicago Black Hawks		NHL	29	0	2	2	29
1982-83—Chicago Black Hawks		NHL	78	6	12	18	69
1983-84—Chicago Black Hawks		NHL	46	6	7	13	42
NHL TOTALS			153	12	21	33	140

(c)—June, 1978—Drafted by Chicago Black Hawks in 1978 amateur draft. Sixth Black Hawks pick, 96th overall, sixth round.
(d)—Named to All-American Team (West).
(e)—Winner of Bob Gassoff Award (Most improved CHL defenseman).

BERNARD ALLAN FEDERKO

Center ... 6' ... 185 lbs. ... Born, Foam Lake, Sask., May 12, 1956 ... Shoots left ... Brother of Ken Federko (Salt Lake—CHL 1980-82) ... Missed final games of 1978-79 season with broken right wrist ... (December 29, 1981)—Tore rib cartilage in game vs. Hartford.

Year	Team	League	Games	G.	A.	Pts.	Pen.
1973-74—Saskatoon Blades		WCHL	68	22	28	50	19
1974-75—Saskatoon Blades (c)		WCHL	66	39	68	107	30
1975-76—Saskatoon Blades (a-d-e-f)		WCHL	72	72	*115	*187	108
1976-77—Kansas City Blues (b-g)		CHL	42	30	39	69	41
1976-77—St. Louis Blues		NHL	31	14	9	23	15
1977-78—St. Louis Blues		NHL	72	17	24	41	27
1978-79—St. Louis Blues		NHL	74	31	64	95	14
1979-80—St. Louis Blues		NHL	79	38	56	94	24
1980-81—St. Louis Blues		NHL	78	31	73	104	47
1981-82—St. Louis Blues		NHL	74	30	62	92	70
1982-83—St. Louis Blues		NHL	75	24	60	84	24
1983-84—St. Louis Blues		NHL	79	41	66	107	43
NHL TOTALS			562	226	414	640	264

(c)—Led in goals (15) during playoffs.
(d)—Named Most Valuable Player in WCHL.
(e)—Drafted from Saskatoon Blades by St. Louis Blues in first round of 1976 amateur draft.
(f)—Led in assists (27) and points (45) during playoffs.
(g)—CHL Rookie-of-the-Year.

TONY FELTRIN

Defense ... 6'1" ... 185 lbs. ... Born, Ladysmith, B. C., December 6, 1961 ... Shoots left ... (October 18, 1980)—Injured ligaments in right knee.

Year	Team	League	Games	G.	A.	Pts.	Pen.
1977-78—Nanaimo		BCJHL	63	2	13	15	65
1970-79—Victoria Cougars		WHL	47	2	11	13	119
1979-80—Victoria Cougars (c)		WHL	71	6	25	31	138
1980-81—Victoria Cougars		WHL	43	4	25	29	81
1980-81—Pittsburgh Penguins		NHL	2	0	0	0	0
1981-82—Erie Blades		AHL	72	4	15	19	117
1981-82—Pittsburgh Penguins		NHL	4	0	0	0	4
1982-83—Baltimore Skipjacks		AHL	31	2	3	5	34
1982-83—Pittsburgh Penguins		NHL	32	3	3	6	40
1983-84—Baltimore Skipjacks		AHL	4	0	0	0	2
1983-84—Salt Lake Golden Eagles		CHL	65	8	22	30	94
NHL TOTALS			38	3	3	6	44

(c)—June, 1980—Drafted by Pittsburgh Penguins as underage junior in 1980 NHL entry draft. Third Penguins pick, 72nd overall, fourth round.

PAUL FENTON

Center . . . 5'11" . . . 180 lbs. . . . Born, Springfield, Mass., December 22, 1959 . . . Shoots left.

Year	Team	League	Games	G.	A.	Pts.	Pen.
1979-80—Boston University		ECAC	28	12	21	33	18
1980-81—Boston University		ECAC	7	4	4	8	0
1981-82—Boston University		ECAC	28	20	13	33	28
1982-83—Peoria Prancers (b-c)		IHL	82	60	51	111	53
1982-83—Colorado Flames		CHL	1	0	1	1	0
1983-84—Binghamton Whalers (d)		AHL	78	41	24	65	67

(c)—Won Ken McKenzie Trophy (Top U.S. born IHL Rookie)
(d)—October, 1983—Signed by Hartford Whalers as a free agent.

DAVE ALAN FENYVES

Defense . . . 5'10" . . . 188 lbs. . . . Born, Dunnville, Ont., April 29, 1960 . . . Shoots left . . . (October, 1977)—Separated shoulder.

Year	Team	League	Games	G.	A.	Pts.	Pen.
1977-78—Peterborough Petes		OMJHL	59	3	12	15	36
1978-79—Peterborough Petes		OMJHL	66	2	23	25	122
1979-80—Peterborough Petes (c)		OMJHL	66	9	36	45	92
1980-81—Rochester Americans		AHL	77	6	16	22	146
1981-82—Rochester Americans		AHL	73	3	14	17	68
1982-83—Rochester Americans		AHL	51	2	19	21	45
1982-83—Buffalo Sabres		NHL	24	0	8	8	14
1983-84—Buffalo Sabres		NHL	10	0	4	4	9
1983-84—Rochester Americans		AHL	70	3	16	19	55
NHL TOTALS			34	0	12	12	23

(c)—October, 1979—Signed by Buffalo Sabres as a free agent.

TOM JOSEPH FERGUS

Center . . . 6' . . . 176 lbs. . . . Born, Chicago, Ill., June 16, 1962 . . . Shoots left . . . (January 20, 1982)—Tore ligaments in left knee in game at Pittsburgh . . . (February, 1984)—Damaged knee ligaments.

Year	Team	League	Games	G.	A.	Pts.	Pen.
1979-80—Peterborough Petes (c)		OMJHL	63	8	6	14	14
1980-81—Peterborough Petes		OMJHL	63	43	45	88	33
1981-82—Boston Bruins		NHL	61	15	24	39	12
1982-83—Boston Bruins		NHL	80	28	35	63	39
1983-84—Boston Bruins		NHL	69	25	36	61	12
NHL TOTALS			210	68	95	163	63

(c)—June, 1980—Drafted as underage junior by Boston Bruins in 1980 NHL entry draft. Second Bruins pick, 60th overall, third round.

GEORGE STEPHEN FERGUSON

Center . . . 6' . . . 190 lbs. . . . Born, Trenton, Ont., August 22, 1952 . . . Shoots right . . . Missed part of 1973-74 season with shoulder separation and part of 1976-77 season with torn knee ligaments . . . Also plays Left Wing or Right Wing.

Year	Team	League	Games	G.	A.	Pts.	Pen.
1969-70—Oshawa Generals		Jr. "A" OHA	49	19	21	40	20
1970-71—Oshawa Generals		Jr. "A" OHA	8	2	0	2	19
1970-71—Toronto Marlboros		Jr. "A" OHA	53	12	15	27	83
1971-72—Toronto Marlboros (c-d)		Jr. "A" OHA	62	36	56	92	104

Year	Team	League	Games	G.	A.	Pts.	Pen.
1972-73—Toronto Maple Leafs		NHL	72	10	13	23	34
1973-74—Oklahoma City Blazers		CHL	35	16	33	49	21
1973-74—Toronto Maple Leafs		NHL	16	0	4	4	4
1974-75—Toronto Maple Leafs		NHL	69	19	30	49	61
1975-76—Toronto Maple Leafs		NHL	79	12	32	44	76
1976-77—Toronto Maple Leafs		NHL	50	9	15	24	24
1977-78—Toronto Maple Leafs (e)		NHL	73	7	16	23	37
1978-79—Pittsburgh Penguins		NHL	80	21	29	50	37
1979-80—Pittsburgh Penguins		NHL	73	21	28	49	36
1980-81—Pittsburgh Penguins		NHL	79	25	18	43	42
1981-82—Pittsburgh Penguins		NHL	71	22	31	53	45
1982-83—Pittsburgh Penguins (f)		NHL	7	0	0	0	2
1982-83—Minnesota North Stars		NHL	65	8	12	20	14
1983-84—Minnesota North Stars		NHL	63	6	10	16	19
NHL TOTALS			797	160	238	398	431

(c)—Selected by Miami Screaming Eagles in World Hockey Association player selection draft, February, 1972.

(d)—Drafted from Toronto Marlboros by Toronto Maple Leafs in first round of 1972 amateur draft.

(e)—Traded to Pittsburgh Penguins by Toronto Maple Leafs with Randy Carlyle for Dave Burrows, June, 1978.

(f)—October, 1982—Traded with first round 1983 draft pick (Minnesota drafted Brian Lawton) by Pittsburgh Penguins to Minnesota North Stars for Ron Meighan, Anders Hakansson and North Stars first round pick in 1983 (Pittsburgh drafted Bob Errey).

IAN FERGUSON

Defense . . . 6'2" . . . 175 lbs. . . . Born, Winnipeg, Man., June 24, 1966 . . . Shoots left.

Year	Team	League	Games	G.	A.	Pts.	Pen.
1983-84—Oshawa Generals (c)		OHL	65	2	7	9	30

(c)—June, 1984—Drafted as underage junior by New Jersey Devils in 1984 NHL entry draft. Seventh Devils pick, 128th overall, seventh round.

MARK FERNER

Defense . . . 6' . . . 170 lbs. . . . Born, Regina, Sask., September 5, 1965 . . . Shoots left.

Year	Team	League	Games	G.	A.	Pts.	Pen.
1982-83—Kamloops Junior Oilers (c)		WHL	69	6	15	21	81
1983-84—Kamloops Junior Oilers		WHL	72	9	30	39	162

(c)—June, 1983—Drafted as underage junior by Buffalo Sabres in 1983 NHL entry draft. Twelfth Sabres pick, 194th overall, 10th round.

RAY FERRARO

Center . . . 5'10" . . . 180 lbs. . . . Born, Trail, B.C., August 23, 1964 . . . Shoots left . . . (1983-84) Set WHL record for most goals in a season (108), most power-play goals (43) and most three-goal games (15).

Year	Team	League	Games	G.	A.	Pts.	Pen.
1981-82—Penticton (c)		BCJHL	48	65	70	135	50
1982-83—Portland Winter Hawks		WHL	50	41	49	90	39
1983-84—Brandon Wheat Kings (a-d-e-f)		WHL	72	*108	84	*192	84

(c)—June, 1982—Drafted as underage junior by Hartford Whalers in 1982 NHL entry draft. Fifth Whalers pick, 88th overall, fifth round.

(d)—Named WHL's Most Valuable Player.

(e)—Won Bob Brownridge Memorial Trophy (Top WHL Scorer).

(f)—WHL's Molson Player of the Year.

MICHAEL EDWARD FIDLER

Left Wing . . . 5'11" . . . 190 lbs. . . . Born, Charleston, Mass., August 19, 1956 . . . Shoots left . . . Attended Boston University . . . Missed part of 1976-77 season with broken leg . . . Brother of Mark and Joe Fidler . . . Missed most of 1979-80 season with shoulder surgery . . . Also missed part of '79-80 season with broken bone near his knee . . . (October, 1980)—Dislocated shoulder during training camp . . . (October, 1981)—Recurring shoulder problems diagnosed as damaged rotator cuff in left shoulder.

Year	Team	League	Games	G.	A.	Pts.	Pen.
1974-75—Boston University		ECAC	31	24	24	48	12
1975-76—Boston University (c)		ECAC	29	22	24	46	78
1976-77—Salt Lake City Golden Eagles		CHL	10	12	6	18	0
1976-77—Cleveland Barons		NHL	46	17	16	33	17

Year	Team	League	Games	G.	A.	Pts.	Pen.
1977-78—Cleveland Barons		NHL	78	23	28	51	38
1978-79—Minnesota North Stars		NHL	59	23	26	49	42
1978-79—Oklahoma City Stars		CHL	8	6	4	10	7
1979-80—Minnesota North Stars		NHL	24	5	4	9	13
1980-81—Minnesota North Stars (d)		NHL	20	5	12	17	6
1980-81—Hartford Whalers		NHL	38	9	9	18	4
1981-82—Hartford Whalers (e)		NHL	2	0	1	1	0
1981-82—Erie Blades		AHL	5	1	2	3	0
1981-82—Oklahoma City Stars		CHL	6	3	5	8	0
1982-83—Springfield Indians		AHL	30	10	17	27	38
1982-83—Chicago Black Hawks (f-g)		NHL	4	2	1	3	4
1982-83—U.S. National Team		Int'l	8	10	10	20	8
1983-84—New Haven Nighthawks		AHL	16	6	7	13	6
NHL TOTALS			271	84	97	181	124

(c)—Drafted from Boston University by California Seals in third round of 1976 amateur draft.
(d)—December, 1980—Traded by Minnesota North Stars to Hartford Whalers for Gordie Roberts.
(e)—December, 1981—Released by Hartford Whalers and signed by Boston Bruins as a free agent.
(f)—January, 1983—Released by Chicago Black Hawks.
(g)—January, 1983—Signed by Weiner EV (Austria Elite) as a free agent.

STEVEN FINN

Defense . . . 6' . . . 190 lbs. . . . Born, Laval, Que., August 20, 1966 . . . Shoots left.

Year	Team	League	Games	G.	A.	Pts.	Pen.
1982-83—Laval Voisins		QHL	69	7	30	37	108
1983-84—Laval Voisins (c)		QHL	68	7	39	46	159

(c)—June, 1984—Drafted as underage junior by Quebec Nordiques in 1984 NHL entry draft. Third Nordiques pick, 57th overall, third round.

RON FISCHER

Defense . . . 6'2" . . . 195 lbs. . . . Born, Merritt, B.C., April 12, 1959 . . . Shoots right . . . (February, 1983)—Tore knee cartilage.

Year	Team	League	Games	G.	A.	Pts.	Pen.
1980-81—University of Alberta		CCWC	24	7	22	29	53
1980-81—Rochester Americans (c)		AHL	4	0	0	0	0
1981-82—Rochester Americans		AHL	61	6	20	26	122
1981-82—Buffalo Sabres		NHL	15	0	7	7	6
1982-83—Rochester Americans		AHL	40	2	19	21	56
1982-83—Buffalo Sabres		NHL	3	0	0	0	0
1983-84—Rochester Americans		AHL	80	10	32	42	94
NHL TOTALS			18	0	7	7	6

(c)—March, 1981—Signed by Buffalo Sabres as a free agent.

BRUCE FISHBACK

Center . . . 6'1" . . . 185 lbs. . . . Born, White Bear Lake, Minn., January 19, 1965 . . . Shoots right.

Year	Team	League	Games	G.	A.	Pts.	Pen.
1982-83—St. Paul Mariner H.S. (c)		Minn. H.S.	23	12	16	28	...
1983-84—Univ. of Minnesota-Duluth		WCHA	13	2	2	4	4

(c)—June, 1983—Drafted by Los Angeles Kings in 1983 NHL entry draft. Ninth Kings pick, 167th overall, ninth round.

ROSS FITZPATRICK

Left Wing . . . 6'1" . . . 190 lbs. . . . Born, Penticton, B.C., October 7, 1960 . . . Shoots left . . . (December, 1982)—Broke hand in game vs. Hershey (AHL).

Year	Team	League	Games	G.	A.	Pts.	Pen.
1979-80—Univ. of Western Mich. (c)		CCHA	34	26	33	59	22
1980-81—Univ. of Western Mich. (a)		CCHA	36	28	43	71	22
1981-82—Univ. of Western Mich.		CCHA	33	30	28	58	34
1982-83—Maine Mariners		AHL	66	29	28	57	32
1982-83—Philadelphia Flyers		NHL	1	0	0	0	0
1983-84—Springfield Indians		AHL	45	33	30	63	28
1983-84—Philadelphia Flyers		NHL	12	4	2	6	0
NHL TOTALS			13	4	2	6	0

(c)—June, 1980—Drafted by Philadelphia Flyers in 1980 NHL entry draft. Seventh Flyers pick, 147th overall, seventh round.

PAUL FITZSIMMONS

Defense . . . 6'2" . . . 200 lbs. . . . Born, August 25, 1963 . . . Shoots right.

Year	Team	League	Games	G.	A.	Pts.	Pen.
1982-83—Northeastern Univ. (c)		ECAC	27	1	2	3	24
1983-84—Northeastern University		ECAC	24	2	3	5	56

(c)—June, 1983—Drafted by Boston Bruins in 1983 NHL entry draft. Tenth Bruins pick, 202nd overall, 10th round.

MIKE FLANAGAN

Defense . . . 6'4" . . . 210 lbs. . . . Born, Boston, Mass., April 27, 1965 . . . Shoots left.

Year	Team	League	Games	G.	A.	Pts.	Pen.
1982-83—Acton-Boxboro H.S. (c)		Mass. H.S.	23	17	31	48	...
1983-84—Providence College		ECAC	19	1	0	1	2

(c)—June, 1983—Drafted by Edmonton Oilers in 1983 NHL entry draft. Third Oilers pick, 60th overall, third round.

PATRICK FLATLEY

Right Wing . . . 6'3" . . . 200 lbs. . . . Born, Toronto, Ont., October 3, 1963 . . . Shoots right . . . Member of 1984 Canadian Olympic hockey team.

Year	Team	League	Games	G.	A.	Pts.	Pen.
1980-81—Henry Carr H.S.		Ont. Tier II	42	30	61	91	122
1981-82—University of Wisconsin (c)		WCHA	33	17	20	37	65
1982-83—University of Wisconsin (a-d)		WCHA	43	25	44	69	76
1983-84—Canadian Olympic Team		Int'l	57	33	17	50	136
1983-84—New York Islanders		NHL	16	2	7	9	6
NHL TOTALS			16	2	7	9	6

(c)—June, 1982—Drafted as underage player by New York Islanders in 1982 NHL entry draft. First Islanders pick, 21st overall, first round.

(d)—Named to All-America Team (West).

JOHN PATRICK FLESCH

Left Wing . . . 6'2" . . . 195 lbs. . . . Born, Sudbury, Ont., July 15, 1953 . . . Shoots left . . . Attended Lake Superior State College . . . Played defense prior to 1972-73 . . . Missed part of 1974-75 season with torn knee ligaments.

Year	Team	League	Games	G.	A.	Pts.	Pen.
1971-72—Sudbury Wolves		Jr. "A" NOHA	....	17	24	41	182
1972-73—Lake Superior St. College (c)		CCHA	29	28	32	60	108
1973-74—Omaha Knights (d)		CHL	69	27	27	54	98
1974-75—Minnesota North Stars		NHL	57	8	15	23	47
1975-76—New Haven Nighthawks		AHL	31	11	10	21	95
1975-76—Minnesota North Stars		NHL	33	3	2	5	47
1976-77—Columbus Owls		IHL	74	34	39	73	210
1977-78—Grand Rapids Owls		IHL	43	11	19	30	106
1977-78—Pittsburgh Penguins		NHL	29	7	5	12	19
1978-79—Grand Rapids Owls		IHL	67	26	56	82	149
1979-80—Colorado Rockies (e)		NHL	5	0	1	1	4
1979-80—Grand Rapid Owls		IHL	76	39	54	93	66
1980-81—Milwaukee Admirals		IHL	70	27	44	71	70
1981-82—Milwaukee Admirals (a)		IHL	82	39	54	93	45
1982-83—Milwaukee Admirals		IHL	51	24	31	55	56
1983-84—Milwaukee Admirals		IHL	81	43	44	87	27
NHL TOTALS			124	18	23	41	117

(c)—Drafted from Lake Superior State College by Atlanta Flames in fifth round of 1973 amateur draft.

(d)—Traded to Minnesota North Stars by Atlanta Flames with Don Martineau for Buster Harvey and Jerry Byers, May, 1974.

(e)—January, 1980—Acquired from Pittsburgh Penguins by Colorado Rockies.

STEVEN FLETCHER

Defense . . . 6'2" . . . 180 lbs. . . . Born, Montreal, Que., March 31, 1962 . . . Shoots left.

Year	Team	League	Games	G.	A.	Pts.	Pen.
1979-80—Hull Olympics (c)		QMJHL	61	2	14	16	183
1980-81—Hull Olympics		QMJHL	66	4	13	17	231
1981-82—Hull Olympics		QMJHL	60	4	20	24	230
1982-83—Fort Wayne Komets		IHL	34	1	9	10	115
1982-83—Sherbrooke Jets		AHL	36	0	1	1	119
1983-84—Sherbrooke Jets		AHL	77	3	7	10	208

(c)—June, 1980—Drafted as underage junior by Calgary Flames in 1980 NHL entry draft. Eleventh Flames pick, 202nd overall, 10th round.

ROBERT WALTER (ROB) FLOCKHART

Left Wing . . . 6' . . . 185 lbs. . . . Born, Smithers, B.C., February 6, 1956 . . . Shoots left . . . Missed part of 1974-75 season with knee surgery and part of 1976-77 season with shoulder separation . . . Brother of Ron Flockhart . . . Also plays right wing.

Year	Team	League	Games	G.	A.	Pts.	Pen.
1972-73—The Pass Red Devils		AJHL	50	35	45	80	82
1973-74—Kamloops Chiefs		WCHL	67	13	16	29	49
1974-75—Kamloops Chiefs		WCHL	36	19	20	39	52
1975-76—Kamloops Chiefs (c)		WCHL	72	51	47	98	91
1976-77—Tulsa Oilers		CHL	65	22	32	54	70
1976-77—Vancouver Canucks		NHL	5	0	0	0	0
1977-78—Tulsa Oilers		CHL	43	17	11	28	55
1977-78—Vancouver Canucks		NHL	24	0	1	1	12
1978-79—Vancouver Canucks		NHL	14	1	1	2	0
1978-79—Dallas Black Hawks (d)		CHL	44	18	27	45	46
1979-80—Minnesota North Stars (e)		NHL	10	1	3	4	2
1979-80—Oklahoma City Stars (a)		CHL	67	31	40	71	51
1980-81—Minnesota North Stars		NHL	2	0	0	0	0
1980-81—Oklahoma City Stars		CHL	75	33	42	75	89
1981-82—Nashville South Stars		CHL	79	27	30	57	98
1982-83—Springfield Indians (f)		AHL	74	22	34	56	55
1983-84—Toledo Goaldiggers		IHL	54	33	20	53	33
NHL TOTALS			55	2	5	7	14

(c)—Drafted from Kamloops Chiefs by Vancouver Canucks in third round of 1976 amateur draft.
(d)—Led in penalty minutes (34) during playoffs.
(e)—October, 1979—Signed by Minnesota North Stars as a free agent.
(f)—October, 1982—Signed by Chicago Black Hawks as a free agent.

RON FLOCKHART

Center . . . 5'11" . . . 185 lbs. . . . Born, Smithers, B.C., October 10, 1960 . . . Shoots left . . . Brother of Rob Flockhart . . . (January, 1984)—Missed games due to atopic dermitis (body rash).

Year	Team	League	Games	G.	A.	Pts.	Pen.
1978-79—Revelstoke		BCJHL	61	47	41	88	54
1979-80—Regina Pats		WHL	65	54	76	130	63
1980-81—Philadelphia Flyers (c)		NHL	14	3	7	10	11
1980-81—Maine Mariners		AHL	59	33	33	66	76
1981-82—Philadelphia Flyers		NHL	72	33	39	72	44
1982-83—Philadelphia Flyers		NHL	73	29	31	60	49
1983-84—Philadelphia Flyers (d)		NHL	8	0	3	3	4
1983-84—Pittsburgh Penguins		NHL	68	27	18	45	40
NHL TOTALS			235	92	98	190	148

(c)—September, 1980—Signed by Philadelphia Flyers as a free agent.
(d)—October, 1983—Traded with Mark Taylor, Andy Brickley and first (Roger Belanger) and third (traded to Vancouver) round 1984 draft picks by Philadelphia Flyers to Pittsburgh Penguins for Rich Sutter and second (Greg Smyth) and third (David McLay) round 1984 draft picks.

LARRY FLOYD

Center . . . 5'8" . . . 180 lbs. . . . Born, Peterborough, Ont., May 1, 1961 . . . Shoots left.

Year	Team	League	Games	G.	A.	Pts.	Pen.
1979-80—Peterborough Petes		OMJHL	66	21	37	58	54
1980-81—Peterborough Petes		OHL	44	26	37	63	43
1981-82—Peterborough Petes		OHL	39	32	37	69	26
1981-82—Rochester Americans		AHL	1	0	2	2	0
1982-83—New Jersey Devils (c)		NHL	5	1	0	1	2
1982-83—Wichita Wind (d)		CHL	75	40	43	83	16
1983-84—New Jersey Devils		NHL	7	1	3	4	7
1983-84—Maine Mariners		AHL	69	37	49	86	40
NHL TOTALS			12	2	3	5	9

(c)—September, 1982—Signed by New Jersey Devils as a free agent.
(d)—Won Ken McKenzie Trophy (Top CHL Rookie).

LEE JOSEPH FOGOLIN

Defense . . . 6' . . . 200 lbs. . . . Born, Chicago, Ill., February 7, 1955 . . . Shoots right . . . Son of former NHL Defenseman Lee Fogolin . . . Missed part of 1974-75 season with injury to left eye and part for surgery for removal of bone chips from wrist . . . (December, 1982)—Hospitalized with severe case of influenza.

Year	Team	League	Games	G.	A.	Pts.	Pen.
1972-73—Oshawa Generals (c)	Jr. "A" OHA	55	5	21	26	132
1973-74—Oshawa Generals (d)	Jr. "A" OHA	47	7	19	26	108
1974-75—Buffalo Sabres	NHL	50	2	2	4	59
1975-76—Hershey Bears	AHL	20	1	8	9	61
1975-76—Buffalo Sabres	NHL	58	0	9	9	64
1976-77—Buffalo Sabres	NHL	71	3	15	18	100
1977-78—Buffalo Sabres	NHL	76	0	23	23	98
1978-79—Buffalo Sabres (e)	NHL	74	3	19	22	103
1979-80—Edmonton Oilers	NHL	80	5	10	15	104
1980-81—Edmonton Oilers	NHL	80	13	17	30	139
1981-82—Edmonton Oilers	NHL	80	4	25	29	154
1982-83—Edmonton Oilers	NHL	72	0	18	18	92
1983-84—Edmonton Oilers	NHL	80	5	16	21	125
NHL TOTALS			721	35	154	189	1036

(c)—Traded to Oshawa Generals by Hamilton Red Wings for Dennis Higgins, Doug Ferguson and Oshawa's No. 1 draft choice in 1973 midget draft.

(d)—Drafted from Oshawa Generals by Buffalo Sabres in first round of 1974 amateur draft.

(e)—June, 1979—Selected by Edmonton Oilers in NHL expansion draft.

MIKE ANTHONY FOLIGNO

Right Wing ... 6'2" ... 190 lbs. ... Born, Sudbury, Ont., January 29, 1959 ... Shoots right ... (December 27, 1980)—Set Detroit record for most penalty minutes in one game (37 vs. Philadelphia) ... (October 31, 1982)—Injured tailbone in game vs. Montreal ... (February 12, 1983)—Injured shoulder in game at Calgary.

Year	Team	League	Games	G.	A.	Pts.	Pen.
1975-76—Sudbury Wolves	OMJHL	57	22	14	36	45
1976-77—Sudbury Wolves	OMJHL	66	31	44	75	62
1977-78—Sudbury Wolves	OMJHL	67	47	39	86	112
1978-79—Sudbury Wolves (a-c-d-e-f)	OMJHL	68	65	85	*150	98
1979-80—Detroit Red Wings	NHL	80	36	35	71	109
1980-81—Detroit Red Wings	NHL	80	28	35	63	210
1981-82—Detroit Red Wings (g)	NHL	26	13	13	26	28
1981-82—Buffalo Sabres	NHL	56	20	31	51	149
1982-83—Buffalo Sabres	NHL	66	22	25	47	135
1983-84—Buffalo Sabres	NHL	70	32	31	63	151
NHL TOTALS			378	151	170	321	782

(c)—Won Red Tilson Memorial Trophy (OMJHL-MVP).

(d)—Won Eddie Powers Memorial Trophy (OMJHL leading scorer).

(e)—Won Jim Mahon Memorial Trophy (OMJHL top scoring right wing).

(f)—August, 1979—Drafted by Detroit Red Wings in 1979 NHL entry draft. First Red Wings pick, third overall, first round.

(g)—December, 1981—Traded with Dale McCourt, Brent Peterson and future considerations by Detroit Red Wings to Buffalo Sabres for Bob Sauve, Jim Schoenfeld and Derek Smith.

MIKE FORBES

Defense ... 6'2" ... 195 lbs. ... Born, Brampton, Ont., September 20, 1957 ... Shoots right ... Missed part of 1977-78 season with badly sprained right ankle ... (January, 1983)—Pulled rib muscle.

Year	Team	League	Games	G.	A.	Pts.	Pen.
1974-75—Kingston Canadians	Jr."A"OHA	64	0	10	10	98
1975-76—Kingston Canadians	Jr."A"OHA	48	4	13	17	117
1976-77—St. Catharines Fincups (c)	Jr."A"OHA	61	12	41	53	134
1977-78—Rochester Americans	AHL	32	3	12	15	65
1977-78—Boston Bruins	NHL	32	0	4	4	15
1978-79—Rochester Americans (d)	AHL	75	4	20	24	97
1979-80—Houston Apollos	CHL	55	5	30	35	63
1979-80—Edmonton Oilers	NHL	2	0	0	0	0
1980-81—Wichita Wind	CHL	79	4	44	48	129
1981-82—Wichita Wind	CHL	49	4	28	32	94
1981-82—Edmonton Oilers	NHL	16	1	7	8	26
1982-83—Wichita Wind (b)	CHL	75	15	46	61	73
1983-84—Montana Magic	CHL	76	13	38	51	83
NHL TOTALS			50	1	11	12	41

(c)—Drafted from St. Catharines Fincups by Boston Bruins in third round of 1977 amateur draft.

(d)—June, 1979—Selected by Edmonton Oilers in NHL expansion draft.

BILL FORDY

Left Wing . . . 6' . . . 180 lbs. . . . Born, Oshawa, Ont., February 11, 1965 . . . Shoots left.

Year	Team	League	Games	G.	A.	Pts.	Pen.
1982-83—Guelph Platers (c)		OHL	68	12	22	34	26
1983-84—Guelph Platers (d)		OHL	53	3	15	18	25

    (c)—June, 1983—Drafted as underage junior by Hartford Whalers in 1983 NHL entry draft. Eleventh Whalers pick, 164th overall, ninth round.

    (d)—June, 1984—Released by Hartford Whalers.

DWIGHT ALEXANDER FOSTER

Center . . . 5'11" . . . 190 lbs. . . . Born, Toronto, Ont., April 2, 1957 . . . Shoots right . . . Missed most of 1977-78 season with torn cartilage in left knee requiring surgery . . . Arthroscopic surgery to right knee (October 20, 1979) . . . (October 10, 1981)—Separated shoulder vs. N.Y. Islanders . . . (October 27, 1982)—Tore ligaments in right ankle during CHL game with Wichita . . . (March, 1984)—Shoulder injury.

Year	Team	League	Games	G.	A.	Pts.	Pen.
1973-74—Kitchener Rangers		Jr."A"OHA	67	23	32	55	61
1974-75—Kitchener Rangers		Jr."A"OHA	70	39	51	90	88
1975-76—Kitchener Rangers		Jr."A"OHA	61	36	58	94	110
1976-77—Kitchener Rangers (c-d)		Jr."A"OHA	64	60	*83	*143	88
1977-78—Rochester Americans		AHL	3	0	3	3	2
1977-78—Boston Bruins		NHL	14	2	1	3	6
1978-79—Boston Bruins		NHL	44	11	13	24	14
1978-79—Rochester Americans		AHL	22	11	18	29	8
1979-80—Binghamton Dusters		AHL	7	1	3	4	2
1979-80—Boston Bruins		NHL	57	10	28	38	42
1980-81—Boston Bruins (e)		NHL	77	24	28	52	62
1981-82—Colorado Rockies (f)		NHL	70	12	19	31	41
1982-83—Wichita Wind		CHL	2	0	1	1	2
1982-83—New Jersey Devils (g)		NHL	4	0	0	0	2
1982-83—Detroit Red Wings		NHL	58	17	22	39	58
1983-84—Detroit Red Wings		NHL	52	9	12	21	50
NHL TOTALS			376	85	123	208	375

    (c)—Won Eddie Powers Memorial Trophy (leading scorer).

    (d)—Drafted from Kitchener Rangers by Boston Bruins in first round of 1977 amateur draft.

    (e)—July, 1981—Traded by Boston Bruins to Colorado Rockies for Rockies second round 1982 draft pick. Boston also had the option of switching places with Colorado in the first round of the 1982 NHL Entry Draft.

    (f)—June, 1982—Boston exercised option of changing places with Colorado (then New Jersey) and drafted Gord Kluzak in the first round, and Brian Curran in the second. New Jersey drafted Ken Daneyko in the first round.

    (g)—October, 1982—Sold by New Jersey Devils to Detroit Red Wings for $1.00.

NICHOLAS EVLAMPIOS FOTIU

Left Wing . . . 6'2" . . . 200 lbs. . . . Born, Staten Island, N.Y., May 25, 1952 . . . Shoots left . . . Missed entire 1972-73 season with knee injury and part of 1975-76 season with severed tendons in right hand . . . (March, 1981)—Given 8-game suspension by NHL for going into stands at Detroit during a 7-3 loss on February 19, 1981 . . . (January 31, 1982)—Slight shoulder separation in game vs. Los Angeles Kings . . . First New York City-born player to play with N.Y. Rangers . . . (November, 1983)—Bruised left instep . . . (January, 1984)— Bruised ribs . . . (March 20, 1984)—Confrontation with fan at Madison Square Garden cost $500 and three-game suspension.

Year	Team	League	Games	G.	A.	Pts.	Pen.
1971-72—New Hyde Park Arrows		N.Y. MJHA	32	6	17	23	135
1972-73—Did not play							
1973-74—Cape Cod Cubs (c)		NAHL	72	12	24	36	*371
1974-75—Cape Codders		NAHL	5	2	1	3	13
1974-75—New England Whalers		WHA	61	2	2	4	144
1975-76—Cape Codders		NAHL	6	2	1	3	15
1975-76—New England Whalers (d)		WHA	49	3	2	5	94
1976-77—New York Rangers		NHL	70	4	8	12	174
1977-78—New Haven Nighthawks		AHL	5	1	1	2	9
1977-78—New York Rangers		NHL	59	2	7	9	105
1978-79—New York Rangers (e)		NHL	71	3	5	8	190
1979-80—Hartford Whalers		NHL	74	10	8	18	107
1980-81—Hartford Whalers (f)		NHL	42	4	3	7	79
1980-81—New York Rangers		NHL	27	5	6	11	91
1981-82—New York Rangers		NHL	70	8	10	18	151

Year	Team	League	Games	G.	A.	Pts.	Pen.
1982-83—New York Rangers		NHL	72	8	13	21	90
1983-84—New York Rangers		NHL	40	7	6	13	115
WHA TOTALS			110	6	15	21	279
NHL TOTALS			525	51	66	117	1102

(c)—Tied for lead in penalty minutes (80) during playoffs.
(d)—Signed by New York Rangers, June, 1976.
(e)—June, 1979—Selected by Hartford Whalers in NHL expansion draft.
(f) January, 1981—Traded by Hartford Whalers to New York Rangers for New York's fifth-round draft pick in 1981 (Bill McGuire).

GUY FOURNIER

Center . . . 6' . . . 180 lbs. . . . Born, Portneuf, Que., January 30, 1962 . . . Shoots left . . . (September, 1981)—Injured knee at Winnipeg Jet training camp.

Year	Team	League	Games	G.	A.	Pts.	Pen.
1979-80—Shawinigan Cataracts (c)		QMJHL	70	47	32	79	31
1980-81—Shawinigan Cataracts		QMJHL	68	56	62	118	64
1981-82—Shawinigan Cataracts		QMJHL	48	31	47	78	62
1982-83—Sherbrooke Jets		AHL	79	16	29	45	35
1983-84—Sherbrooke Jets		AHL	80	25	28	53	30

(c)—June, 1980—Drafted as underage junior by Winnipeg Jets in 1980 NHL entry draft. Fourth Jets pick, 65th overall, fourth round.

GREGORY BRENT FOX

Defense . . . 6'2" . . . 190 lbs. . . . Born, Port McNeil, B. C., August 12, 1953 . . . Shoots left . . . Attended University of Michigan.

Year	Team	League	Games	G.	A.	Pts.	Pen.
1972-73—University of Michigan (c)		WCHL	30	2	15	17	68
1973-74—University of Michigan		WCHL	32	0	11	11	64
1974-75—University of Michigan		WCHL	36	0	19	19	80
1975-76—University of Michigan		WCHL	39	1	21	22	99
1976-77—Nova Scotia Voyageurs		AHL	56	2	14	16	110
1976-77—Tulsa Oilers		CHL	10	1	7	8	6
1977-78—Nova Scotia Voyageurs		AHL	51	2	10	12	124
1977-78—Atlanta Flames		NHL	16	1	2	3	25
1978-79—Atlanta Flames (d)		NHL	64	0	12	12	70
1978-79—Chicago Black Hawks		NHL	14	0	5	5	16
1979-80—Chicago Black Hawks		NHL	71	4	11	15	73
1980-81—Chicago Black Hawks		NHL	75	3	16	19	112
1981-82—Chicago Black Hawks		NHL	79	2	19	21	137
1982-83—Chicago Black Hawks		NHL	76	0	13	13	81
1983-84—Chicago Black Hawks (e)		NHL	24	0	5	5	31
1983-84—Pittsburgh Penguins		NHL	49	2	5	7	66
NHL TOTALS			468	12	88	100	611

(c)—Drafted from University of Michigan by Atlanta Flames in 11th round of 1973 amateur draft.
(d)—March, 1979—Traded with Tom Lysiak, Harold Phillipoff, Pat Ribble and Miles Zaharko to Chicago Black Hawks by Atlanta Flames for Ivan Boldirev, Phil Russell and Darcy Rota.
(e)—December, 1983—Traded by Chicago Black Hawks to Pittsburgh Penguins for Randy Boyd.

JAMES CHARLES FOX

Right Wing . . . 5'8" . . . 183 lbs. . . . Born, Coniston, Ont., May 18, 1960 . . . Shoots right.

Year	Team	League	Games	G.	A.	Pts.	Pen.
1975-76—North Bay Trappers		OPJHL	44	30	45	75	16
1976-77—North Bay Trappers (c)		OPJHL	38	44	*108	*108	4
1977-78—Ottawa 67's		OMJHL	59	44	83	127	12
1978-79—Ottawa 67's		OMJHL	53	37	66	103	4
1979-80—Ottawa 67's (d-e-f-g)		OMJHL	52	65	*101	*166	30
1980-81—Los Angeles Kings		NHL	71	18	25	43	8
1981-82—Los Angeles Kings		NHL	77	30	38	68	23
1982-83—Los Angeles Kings		NHL	77	28	40	68	8
1983-84—Los Angeles Kings		NHL	80	30	42	72	26
NHL TOTALS			305	106	145	251	65

(c)—Led OPJHL Playoffs in points (38) and assists (25) in 19 games, and was co-leader (with teammate Jim Omiciolli) in goals (13).
(d)—Won Eddie Powers Memorial Trophy (OMJHL Leading Scorer).
(e)—Won Albert (Red) Tilson Memorial Trophy (OMJHL—MVP).
(f)—Won Jim Mahon Memorial Trophy (Top Scoring OMJHL Right Wing).
(g)—June, 1980—Drafted by Los Angeles Kings in 1980 NHL entry draft. Second Kings pick, 10th overall, first round.

LOU FRANCESCHETTI

Left Wing . . . 6' . . . 190 lbs. . . . Born, Toronto, Ont., March 28, 1958 . . . Shoots left.

Year	Team	League	Games	G.	A.	Pts.	Pen.
1975-76	St. Catharines Black Hawks	OMJHL	1	0	0	0	0
1976-77	Niagara Falls Flyers	OMJHL	61	23	30	53	80
1977-78	Niagara Falls Flyers (c)	OMJHL	62	40	50	90	46
1978-79	Saginaw Gears	IHL	2	1	1	2	0
1978-79	Port Huron Flags	IHL	76	45	58	103	131
1979-80	Port Huron Flags	IHL	15	3	8	11	31
1979-80	Hershey Bears	AHL	65	27	29	56	58
1980-81	Hershey Bears	AHL	79	32	36	68	173
1981-82	Washington Capitals	NHL	30	2	10	12	23
1981-82	Hershey Bears	AHL	50	22	33	55	89
1982-83	Hershey Bears	AHL	80	31	44	75	176
1983-84	Washington Capitals	NHL	2	0	0	0	0
1983-84	Hershey Bears	AHL	73	26	34	60	130
	NHL TOTALS		32	2	10	12	23

(c)—June, 1978—Drafted by the Washington Capitals in the 1978 NHL amateur draft. Seventh Capitals pick, 71st overall, fifth round.

BOBBY FRANCIS

Center . . . 5'9" . . . 175 lbs. . . . Born, North Battleford, Sask., December 5, 1958 . . . Shoots right . . . Son of Emile Francis (Hartford Whalers President and G.M.) . . . (January, 1981)—Injured knee.

Year	Team	League	Games	G.	A.	Pts.	Pen.
1978-79	University of New Hampshire	ECAC	35	20	46	66	44
1979-80	University of New Hampshire	ECAC	28	19	23	42	30
1980-81	Muskegon Mohawks (c)	IHL	27	16	17	33	33
1980-81	Birmingham Bulls	CHL	18	6	21	27	20
1981-82	Oklahoma City Stars (a-d-e-f)	CHL	80	48	66	*114	76
1982-83	Adirondack Red Wings	AHL	17	3	8	11	0
1982-83	Detroit Red Wings (g)	NHL	14	2	0	2	0
1982-83	Colorado Flames	CHL	26	20	16	36	24
1983-84	Colorado Flames	CHL	68	32	50	82	53
	NHL TOTALS		14	2	0	2	0

(c)—October, 1980—Signed by Calgary Flames as a free agent.
(d)—Winner of Phil Esposito Trophy (Leading CHL scorer).
(e)—Winner of Tom Ivan Trophy (CHL MVP).
(f)—Winner of Ken McKenzie Trophy (Top CHL Rookie).
(g)—November, 1982—Traded by Calgary Flames to Detroit Red Wings for Yves Courteau.

RONALD FRANCIS

Center . . . 6'1" . . . 170 lbs. . . . Born, Sault Ste. Marie, Ont. . . . Shoots left . . . Cousin of Mike Liut . . . (January 27, 1982)—Out of lineup for three weeks with eye injury . . . (November 30, 1983)—Strained ligaments in right knee vs. Vancouver.

Year	Team	League	Games	G.	A.	Pts.	Pen.
1979-80	Sault Ste. Marie Legion	OMHL	45	57	92	149	....
1980-81	Sault Ste. Marie Greyhounds (c)	OHL	64	26	43	69	33
1981-82	Sault Ste. Marie Greyhounds	OHL	25	18	30	48	46
1981-82	Hartford Whalers	NHL	59	25	43	68	51
1982-83	Hartford Whalers	NHL	79	31	59	90	60
1983-84	Hartford Whalers	NHL	72	23	60	83	45
	NHL TOTALS		210	79	162	241	156

(c)—June, 1981—Drafted as underage junior by Hartford Whalers in 1981 NHL entry draft. First Whalers pick, fourth overall, first round.

TODD FRANCIS

Right Wing . . . 6'3" . . . 215 lbs. . . . Born, Kitchener, Ont., August 1, 1965 . . . Shoots right.

Year	Team	League	Games	G.	A.	Pts.	Pen.
1981-82	Waterloo Siskins MW Jr.B	OHA	39	19	21	40	196
1982-83	Brantford Alexanders (c)	OHL	64	12	10	22	94
1983-84	Brantford Alexanders	OHL	55	13	33	46	109

(c)—June, 1983—Drafted as underage junior by Montreal Canadiens in 1983 NHL entry draft. Fourth Canadiens pick, 35th overall, second round.

JEFF FRANK

Right Wing . . . 6'1" . . . 200 lbs. . . . Born, Seattle, Wash., July 11, 1965 . . . Shoots right . . . Son of Bill Frank (Former CFL player).

Year	Team	League	Games	G.	A.	Pts.	Pen.
1981-82—Sherwood Park Midget		Alberta Midg.	36	27	27	54	99
1982-83—Regina Pats (c)		WHL	68	7	16	23	35
1983-84—Kelowna Wings		WHL	1	1	1	2	5
1983-84—Winnipeg Warriors		WHL	29	10	10	20	23

(c)—June, 1983—Drafted as underage junior by Detroit Red Wings in 1983 NHL entry draft. Twelfth Red Wings pick, 206th overall, 11th round.

ARTHUR WELDON (JAY) FRASER

Left Wing . . . 6'2" . . . 195 lbs. . . . Born, Ottawa, Ont., October 26, 1961 . . . Shoots left.

Year	Team	League	Games	G.	A.	Pts.	Pen.
1977-78—So. Ottawa Canadians		OMHL	30	20	10	30	....
1978-79—Brantford Alexanders		OMJHL	17	1	3	4	48
1978-79—Ottawa 67's		OMJHL	32	8	2	10	114
1979-80—Ottawa 67's (c)		OMJHL	64	30	20	50	115
1980-81—Ottawa 67's		OMJHL	55	17	23	40	204
1981-82—Toledo Goaldiggers		IHL	19	14	8	22	8
1981-82—Maine Mariners		AHL	44	5	5	10	116
1982-83—Carolina Thunderbirds		ACHL	68	28	37	65	118
1983-84—Carolina Thunderbirds		ACHL	29	16	29	45	85

(c)—June, 1980—Drafted as underage junior by Philadelphia Flyers in 1980 NHL entry draft. Second Flyers pick, 42nd overall, second round.

CURT FRASER

Left Wing . . . 6' . . . 190 lbs. . . . Born, Cincinnati, Ohio, January 12, 1958 . . . Shoots left . . . (November, 1983)—Torn knee ligaments.

Year	Team	League	Games	G.	A.	Pts.	Pen.
1973-74—Kelowna Buckaroos		Jr."A"BCHL	52	32	32	64	85
1974-75—Victoria Cougars		WCHL	68	17	32	49	105
1975-76—Victoria Cougars		WCHL	71	43	64	107	167
1976-77—Victoria Cougars		WCHL	60	34	41	75	82
1977-78—Victoria Cougars (c)		WCHL	66	48	44	92	256
1978-79—Vancouver Canucks		NHL	78	16	19	35	116
1979-80—Vancouver Canucks		NHL	78	17	25	42	143
1980-81—Vancouver Canucks		NHL	77	25	24	49	118
1981-82—Vancouver Canucks		NHL	79	28	39	67	175
1982-83—Vancouver Canucks (d)		NHL	36	6	7	13	99
1982-83—Chicago Black Hawks		NHL	38	6	13	19	77
1983-84—Chicago Black Hawks		NHL	29	5	12	17	26
NHL TOTALS			415	103	139	242	754

(c)—Drafted from Victoria Cougars by Vancouver Canucks in second round of 1978 amateur draft.
(d)—January, 1983—Traded by Vancouver Canucks to Chicago Black Hawks for Tony Tanti.

WILLIAM DANNY FRAWLEY
(Known by middle name.)

Right Wing . . . 6' . . . 165 lbs. . . . Born, Sturgeon Falls, Ont., June 2, 1962 . . . Shoots right.

Year	Team	League	Games	G.	A.	Pts.	Pen.
1979-80—Sudbury Wolves (c)		OHL	63	21	26	47	67
1980-81—Cornwall Royals		QMJHL	28	10	14	24	76
1981-82—Cornwall Royals		OHL	64	27	50	77	239
1982-83—Springfield Indians		AHL	80	30	27	57	107
1983-84—Chicago Black Hawks		NHL	3	0	0	0	0
1983-84—Springfield Indians		AHL	69	22	34	56	137
NHL TOTALS			3	0	0	0	0

(c)—June, 1980—Drafted as underage junior by Chicago Black Hawks in 1980 NHL entry draft. Fifteenth Black Hawks pick, 204th overall, 10th round.

MARCEL HENRY FRERE

Left Wing . . . 6' . . . 180 lbs. . . . Born, Trochu, Alta., January 18, 1962 . . . Shoots left.

Year	Team	League	Games	G.	A.	Pts.	Pen.
1978-79—Red Deer Rustlers		AJHL	58	6	2	8	77
1978-79—Billings Bighorns		WHL	1	1	0	1	0

Year	Team	League	Games	G.	A.	Pts.	Pen.
1979-80—Billings Bighorns (c)		WHL	72	22	29	51	126
1980-81—Billings Bighorns		WHL	65	31	22	53	263
1981-82—Billings Bighorns		WHL	67	22	43	65	249
1982-83—Springfield Indians		AHL	80	10	12	22	69
1983-84—Springfield Indians		AHL	1	0	0	0	10
1983-84—Peoria Prancers		IHL	34	5	11	16	97

(c)—June, 1980—Drafted as underage junior by Chicago Black Hawks in 1980 entry draft. Seventh Black Hawks pick, 58th overall, third round.

DAN FRIDGEN

Left Wing . . . 5'11" . . . 180 lbs. . . . Born, Arnprior, Ont., May 18, 1959 . . . Shoots left . . . (February, 1983)—Separated shoulder.

Year	Team	League	Games	G.	A.	Pts.	Pen.
1979-80—Colgate University		ECAC	25	19	18	37	74
1980-81—Colgate University (b)		ECAC	33	*37	31	*68	*164
1981-82—Colgate University (c)		ECAC	29	*38	17	55	95
1981-82—Hartford Whalers		NHL	2	0	1	1	0
1982-83—Hartford Whalers		NHL	11	2	2	4	2
1982-83—Binghamton Whalers		AHL	48	22	16	38	24
1983-84—Binghamton Whalers		AHL	77	23	27	50	61

(c)—April, 1982—Signed by Hartford Whalers as a free agent.

RON FRIEST

Right Wing . . . 6' . . . 185 lbs. . . . Born, Windsor, Ont., November 4, 1958 . . . Shoots left . . . (February, 1983)—Back Injury . . . Missed 1983-84 season while recovering from back surgery.

Year	Team	League	Games	G.	A.	Pts.	Pen.
1976-77—Niagara Falls Flyers		OMJHL	5	1	0	1	2
1976-77—Windsor Spitfires		OMJHL	57	19	18	37	50
1977-78—Windsor Spitfires		OMJHL	67	11	20	31	197
1978-79—Oklahoma City Stars		CHL	2	0	4	4	0
1978-79—Flint Generals		IHL	54	21	18	39	141
1979-80—Oklahoma City Stars		CHL	11	3	3	6	39
1979-80—Baltimore Clippers		EHL	48	35	40	75	162
1980-81—Minnesota North Stars (c)		NHL	4	1	0	1	10
1980-81—Oklahoma City Stars		CHL	71	25	20	45	170
1981-82—Nashville South Stars		CHL	60	32	31	63	199
1981-82—Minnesota North Stars		NHL	10	0	0	0	31
1982-83—Minnesota North Stars		NHL	50	6	7	13	150
1983-84—Did not play.							
NHL TOTALS			64	7	7	14	191

(c)—June, 1980—Signed by Minnesota North Stars as a free agent.

MIROSLAV OPAVA FRYCER

Right Wing . . . 6' . . . 200 lbs. . . . Born, Ostrava, Czech., September 27, 1959 . . . Shoots left . . . (December 26, 1982)—Strained stomach muscles during team practice . . . Member of Czechoslovakian National team in 1979, 1980 and 1981 . . . (January, 1984)—Knee injury . . . (February 25, 1984)—Injured shoulder at Edmonton . . . (March 8, 1984)—Torn knee ligaments during game vs. New Jersey.

Year	Team	League	Games	G.	A.	Pts.	Pen.
1977-78—VZKG Ostrava		Czech. Jr.	....	...	....	....	....
1978-79—Tj Vitkovice (b)		Czech.	44	22	12	34	....
1979-80—Tj Vitkovice		Czech.	44	31	15	46	....
1980-81—Tj Vitkovice		Czech.	34	33	24	57	....
1981-82—Fredericton Express (c)		AHL	11	9	5	14	16
1981-82—Quebec Nordiques		NHL	49	20	17	37	47
1981-82—Toronto Maple Leafs (d)		NHL	10	4	6	10	31
1982-83—Toronto Maple Leafs		NHL	67	25	30	55	90
1983-84—Toronto Maple Leafs		NHL	47	10	16	26	55
NHL TOTALS			173	59	69	128	223

(c)—April, 1980—Signed by Quebec Nordiques as a free agent.
(d)—March, 1982—Traded with seventh round 1982 draft pick (Toronto drafted Jeff Triano) by Quebec Nordiques to Toronto Maple Leafs for Wilf Paiement.

ROBERT BRIAN (ROBBIE) FTOREK

Center and Left Wing . . . 5'8" . . . 160 lbs. . . . Born, Needham, Mass., January 2, 1952 . . . Shoots left . . . Was member of 1972 USA Olympic Team . . . Missed final month of 1972-73 season with broken leg . . . Attended St. Mary's University . . . Missed part of 1979-80 season with torn knee ligaments . . . (September, 1981)—Stretched ligaments in left knee during Canada Cup Tourney . . . (February 17, 1982)—Sprained right ankle when skate caught in rut in Pittsburgh.

Year	Team	League	Games	G.	A.	Pts.	Pen.
1970-71—Halifax Atlantics		MJHL	....	...	....	....	....
1971-72—USA Olympic Team			....	...	....	....	....
1972-73—Virginia Wings		AHL	55	17	42	59	36
1972-73—Detroit Red Wings		NHL	3	0	0	0	0
1973-74—Virginia Wings		AHL	65	24	42	66	37
1973-74—Detroit Red Wings (c)		NHL	12	2	5	7	4
1974-75—Tulsa Oilers		CHL	11	6	10	16	14
1974-75—Phoenix Roadrunners		WHA	53	31	37	68	29
1975-76—Phoenix Roadrunners (b)		WHA	80	41	72	113	109
1976-77—Phoenix Roadrunners (a-e-f-g)		WHA	80	46	71	117	86
1977-78—Cincinnati Stingers (b)		WHA	80	59	50	109	54
1978-79—Cincinnati Stingers (a-d-g)		WHA	80	39	*77	116	87
1979-80—Quebec Nordiques		NHL	52	18	33	51	28
1980-81—Quebec Nordiques		NHL	78	24	49	73	104
1981-82—Quebec Nordiques (h)		NHL	19	1	8	9	4
1981-82—New York Rangers		NHL	30	8	24	32	24
1982-83—New York Rangers		NHL	61	12	19	31	41
1983-84—New York Rangers		NHL	31	3	2	5	22
1983-84—Tulsa Oilers		CHL	25	11	11	22	10
NHL TOTALS			286	68	140	208	227
WHA TOTALS			373	216	307	523	365

(c)—Signed by Phoenix Roadrunners (WHA), June, 1974.
(d)—Named THE SPORTING NEWS' WHA Player of the Year.
(e)—Named Most Valuable Player in WHA.
(f)—Sold to Cincinnati Stingers by Phoenix Roadrunners, April, 1977.
(g)—June, 1979—Claimed by Quebec Nordiques in WHA dispersal draft.
(h)—December, 1981—Traded by Quebec Nordiques with eighth round 1982 entry draft pick (Brian Glynn) to New York Rangers for Jere Gillis and Dean Talafous. Talafous retired from hockey rather than go to Quebec and the NHL awarded Pat Hickey to the Nordiques as compensation in March, 1982.

MARK FUSCO

Defense . . . 5'9" . . . 175 lbs. . . . Born, Woburn, Mass, March 12, 1961 . . . Shoots right . . . Member of 1984 U.S. Olympic Team . . . Brother of Scott Fusco.

Year	Team	League	Games	G.	A.	Pts.	Pen.
1979-80—Harvard University (c-d-e-f)		ECAC	26	13	16	29	20
1980-81—Harvard University (a-g)		ECAC	23	7	13	20	28
1981-82—Harvard University (b-g)		ECAC	30	11	29	40	46
1982-83—Harvard University (a-g-h)		ECAC	33	13	33	46	30
1983-84—U.S. National Team		Int'l	50	4	24	28	20
1983-84—U.S. Olympic Team		Int'l	6	0	3	3	6
1983-84—Hartford Whalers (i)		NHL	17	0	4	4	2
NHL TOTALS			17	0	4	4	2

(c)—Ivy League First Team All-Star.
(d)—Named to All-New England Team. (Second Team).
(e)—Named Ivy League Rookie-of-the-Year.
(f)—Named ECAC Rookie-of-the-Year.
(g)—Named to All-America Team (East).
(h)—Won Hobey Baker Award (Top NCAA Hockey Player).
(i)—February, 1984—Signed by Hartford Whalers as a free agent.

JOSEPH (JODY) GAGE

Right Wing . . . 5'11" . . . 182 lbs. . . . Born, Toronto, Ont., November 29, 1959 . . . Shoots right.

Year	Team	League	Games	G.	A.	Pts.	Pen.
1976-77—St. Catharines Black Hawks		OMJHL	47	13	20	33	2
1977-78—Hamilton Fincups		OMJHL	32	15	18	33	19
1977-78—Kitchener Rangers		OMJHL	36	17	27	44	21
1978-79—Kitchener Rangers (c)		OMJHL	59	46	43	89	40
1979-80—Adirondack Red Wings		AHL	63	25	21	46	15
1979-80—Kalamazoo Wings		IHL	14	17	12	29	0

Year	Team	League	Games	G.	A.	Pts.	Pen.
1980-81—Detroit Red Wings		NHL	16	2	2	4	22
1980-81—Adirondack Red Wings		AHL	59	17	31	48	44
1981-82—Adirondack Red Wings		AHL	47	21	20	41	21
1981-82—Detroit Red Wings		NHL	31	9	10	19	2
1982-83—Adirondack Red Wings		AHL	65	23	30	53	33
1983-84—Detroit Red Wings		NHL	3	0	0	0	0
1983-84—Adirondack Red Wings		AHL	73	40	32	72	32
NHL TOTALS			50	11	12	23	24

(c)—August, 1979—Drafted by Detroit Red Wings in entry draft. Second Detroit pick, 46th overall, third round.

PAUL GAGNE

Left Wing . . . 5'10" . . . 178 lbs. . . . Born, Iroquois Falls, Ont., February 6, 1962 . . . Shoots left . . . (December 18, 1980)—Tore knee ligaments . . . (October, 1981)—Fractured cheekbone . . . (January 2, 1982)—Shoulder separation vs. Detroit.

Year	Team	League	Games	G.	A.	Pts.	Pen.
1978-79—Windsor Spitfires		OMJHL	67	24	18	42	64
1979-80—Windsor Spitfires (b-c)		OMJHL	65	48	53	101	67
1980-81—Colorado Rockies		NHL	61	25	16	41	12
1981-82—Colorado Rockies		NHL	59	10	12	22	17
1982-83—Wichita Wind		CHL	16	1	9	10	9
1982-83—New Jersey Devils		NHL	53	14	15	29	13
1983-84—New Jersey Devils		NHL	66	14	18	32	33
NHL TOTALS			239	63	61	124	75

(c)—June, 1980—Drafted by Colorado Rockies in 1980 NHL entry draft as an underage junior. First Rockies pick, 19th overall, first round.

REMI GAGNE

Right Wing . . . 5'11" . . . 190 lbs. . . . Born, Gagnon, Que., January 24, 1962 . . . Shoots right.

Year	Team	League	Games	G.	A.	Pts.	Pen.
1978-79—Chicoutimi Sagueneens		QMJHL	72	15	15	30	120
1979-80—Chicoutimi Sagueneens (c)		QMJHL	70	24	40	64	191
1980-81—Chicoutimi Sagueneens (d)		QMJHL	72	23	58	81	2
1981-82—Trois-Rivieres Draveurs (e)		QMJHL	50	22	34	56	151
1982-83—Nova Scotia Voyageurs		AHL	7	1	1	2	9
1982-83—Flint Generals		IHL	66	30	36	66	159
1983-84—Nova Scotia Voyageurs		AHL	74	7	18	25	178

(c)—June, 1980—Drafted as underage junior by Montreal Canadiens in 1980 NHL entry draft. Seventh Canadiens pick, 103rd overall, fifth round.

(d)—November, 1980—Traded by Chicoutimi Sagueneens to Sorel Black Hawks for Andre Mercier. Mercier left Chicoutimi after arriving and Gagne was returned to Sagueneens.

(e)—August, 1981—Acquired by Trois-Rivieres Draveurs in QMJHL dispersal draft of players from defunct Sorel Black Hawks.

DAVE GAGNER

Center . . . 5'10" . . . 185 lbs. . . . Born, Chatham, Ont., December 11, 1964 . . . Shoots left . . . Member of 1984 Canadian Olympic Team.

Year	Team	League	Games	G.	A.	Pts.	Pen.
1981-82—Brantford Alexanders		OHL	68	30	46	76	31
1982-83—Brantford Alexanders (b-c)		OHL	70	55	66	121	57
1983-84—Canadian Olympic Team		Int'l	50	19	18	37	26
1983-84—Brantford Alexanders		OHL	12	7	13	20	4

(c)—June, 1983—Drafted as underage junior by New York Rangers in 1983 NHL entry draft. First Rangers pick, 12th overall, first round.

ROBERT MICHAEL GAINEY

Left Wing . . . 6'2" . . . 195 lbs. . . . Born, Peterborough, Ont., December 13, 1953 . . . Shoots left . . . Missed part of 1977-78 season with shoulder separation.

Year	Team	League	Games	G.	A.	Pts.	Pen.
1970-71—Peterborough TPTs		Jr."A" OHA	4	0	0	0	0
1971-72—Peterborough TPTs		Jr."A" OHA	4	2	1	3	33
1972-73—Peterborough TPTs (c)		Jr."A" OHA	52	22	21	43	99

Year	Team	League	Games	G.	A.	Pts.	Pen.
1973-74—Nova Scotia Voyageurs		AHL	6	2	5	7	4
1973-74—Montreal Canadiens		NHL	66	3	7	10	34
1974-75—Montreal Canadiens		NHL	80	17	20	37	49
1975-76—Montreal Canadiens		NHL	78	15	13	28	57
1976-77—Montreal Canadiens		NHL	80	14	19	33	41
1977-78—Montreal Canadiens (d)		NHL	66	15	16	31	57
1978-79—Montreal Canadiens (d-e)		NHL	79	20	18	38	44
1979-80—Montreal Canadiens (d)		NHL	64	14	19	33	32
1980-81—Montreal Canadiens (d)		NHL	78	23	24	47	36
1981-82—Montreal Canadiens		NHL	79	21	24	45	24
1982-83—Montreal Canadiens		NHL	80	12	18	30	43
1983-84—Montreal Canadiens		NHL	77	17	22	39	41
NHL TOTALS			827	171	200	371	458

(c)—Drafted from Peterborough TPTs by Montreal Canadiens in first round of 1973 amateur draft.
(d)—Won Frank J. Selke Trophy (best defensive forward).
(e)—Won Conn Smythe Trophy (MVP-NHL Playoffs).

RICK GAL

Center . . . 6'1" . . . 195 lbs. . . . Born, Lethbridge, Alta., September 29, 1963 . . . Shoots left.

Year	Team	League	Games	G.	A.	Pts.	Pen.
1979-80—Lethbridge Broncos		WHL	3	0	0	0	2
1980-81—Lethbridge Broncos		WHL	68	17	24	41	4
1981-82—Lethbridge Broncos (c)		WHL	72	40	52	92	25
1982-83—Lethbridge Broncos		WHL	72	26	37	63	14
1983-84—Lethbridge Broncos		WHL	72	40	49	89	16

(c)—June, 1982—Drafted as underage junior by Philadelphia Flyers in 1982 NHL entry draft. Eleventh Flyers pick, 224th overall, 11th round.

MICHEL GALARNEAU

Center . . . 6'1" . . . 172 lbs. . . . Born, Montreal, Que., March 1, 1961 . . . Shoots right . . . (March 5, 1983)—Hairline fracture of left ankle in game at Quebec.

Year	Team	League	Games	G.	A.	Pts.	Pen.
1977-78—Hull Olympiques		QMJHL	3	1	0	1	0
1978-79—Hull Olympiques		QMJHL	67	22	37	59	70
1979-80—Hull Olympiques (c)		QMJHL	72	39	64	103	49
1980-81—Hull Olympiques		QMJHL	30	9	21	30	48
1980-81—Hartford Whalers		NHL	30	2	6	8	9
1980-81—Binghamton Whalers		AHL	9	1	0	1	4
1981-82—Binghamton Whalers		AHL	64	15	17	32	52
1981-82—Hartford Whalers		NHL	10	0	0	0	4
1982-83—Binghamton Whalers		AHL	25	4	6	10	20
1982-83—Hartford Whalers		NHL	38	5	4	9	21
1983-84—Binghamton Whalers		AHL	4	1	0	1	0
1983-84—Fredericton Express		AHL	2	0	0	0	0
1983-84—Montana Magic (d)		CHL	66	18	22	40	44
NHL TOTALS			78	7	10	17	34

(c)—June, 1980—Drafted as underage junior by Hartford Whalers in 1980 NHL entry draft. Second Whalers pick, 29th overall, second round.
(d)—July, 1984—Released by Hartford Whalers.

BERNARD GALLANT

Left Wing . . . 5'10" . . . 176 lbs. . . . Born, Montreal, Que., February 13, 1960 . . . Shoots left . . . Also plays Center and Right Wing.

Year	Team	League	Games	G.	A.	Pts.	Pen.
1978-79—Montreal Juniors		QMJHL	11	1	2	3	2
1978-79—Trois-Rivieres Draveurs		QMJHL	44	23	62	85	38
1979-80—Laval Voisins		QMJHL	17	4	8	12	25
1979-80—Sherbrooke Beavers		QMJHL	50	28	52	80	82
1980-81—Rochester Americans (c)		AHL	69	8	18	26	64
1981-82—Flint Generals		IHL	75	31	29	60	95
1982-83—Rochester Americans		AHL	3	0	0	0	0
1982-83—Flint Generals		IHL	80	27	54	81	19
1983-84—Flint Generals (a)		IHL	81	50	53	103	22

(c)—August, 1980—Signed by Buffalo Sabres as a free agent.

GERARD GALLANT

Left Wing . . . 5'11" . . . 164 lbs. . . . Born, Summerside, P.E.I., September 2, 1963 . . . Shoots left . . . Also plays center.

Year	Team	League	Games	G.	A.	Pts.	Pen.
1979-80—Summerside		PEIHA	45	60	55	115	90
1980-81—Sherbrooke Beavers (c)		QMJHL	68	41	60	101	220
1981-82—Sherbrooke Beavers		QMJHL	58	34	58	92	260
1982-83—St. Jean Beavers		QHL	33	28	25	53	139
1982-83—Verdun Juniors		QHL	29	26	49	75	105
1983-84—Adirondack Red Wings		AHL	77	31	33	64	195

(c)—June, 1981—Drafted as underage junior by Detroit Red Wings in 1981 NHL entry draft. Fourth Red Wings pick, 107th overall, sixth round.

GARRY GALLEY

Defense . . . 5'11" . . . 190 lbs. . . . Born, Ottawa, Ont., April 16, 1963 . . . Shoots left.

Year	Team	League	Games	G.	A.	Pts.	Pen.
1981-82—Bowling Green Univ.		CCHA	42	3	36	39	48
1982-83—Bowling Green Univ. (a-c)		CCHA	40	17	29	46	40
1983-84—Bowling Green Univ.		CCHA	44	15	52	67	61

(c)—June, 1983—Drafted by Los Angeles Kings in 1983 NHL entry draft. Fourth Kings pick, 100th overall, fifth round.

PERRY GANCHAR

Right Wing . . . 5'9" . . . 175 lbs. . . . Born, Saskatoon, Sask., October 28, 1963 . . . Shoots right.

Year	Team	League	Games	G.	A.	Pts.	Pen.
1977-78—Saskatoon Blades		WHL	4	2	0	2	2
1978-79—Saskatoon		SJHL	50	21	33	54	72
1978-79—Saskatoon Blades		WHL	14	5	3	8	15
1979-80—Saskatoon Blades		WHL	70	41	24	65	116
1980-81—Saskatoon Blades		WHL	68	36	20	56	195
1981-82—Saskatoon Blades (c)		WHL	53	38	52	90	82
1982-83—Saskatoon Blades		WHL	68	68	48	116	105
1982-83—Salt Lake Golden Eagles (d)		CHL	..	..	..	..	..
1983-84—Montana Magic		CHL	59	23	22	45	77
1983-84—St. Louis Blues		NHL	1	0	0	0	0
NHL TOTALS			1	0	0	0	0

(c)—June, 1982—Drafted as underage junior by St. Louis Blues in 1982 NHL entry draft. Third Blues pick, 113th overall, sixth round.

(d)—Appeared in one playoff game with one assist.

DARREN GANI

Defense . . . 6' . . . 180 lbs. . . . Born, Perth, Australia, November 2, 1965 . . . Shoots left.

Year	Team	League	Games	G.	A.	Pts.	Pen.
1982-83—Belleville Bulls		OHL	63	1	21	22	22
1983-84—Belleville Bulls (c)		OHL	67	16	40	56	22

(c)—June, 1984—Drafted as underage junior by Edmonton Oilers in 1984 NHL entry draft. 11th Oilers pick, 250th overall, 12th round. Last player chosen in 1984 draft.

DAVID GANS

Center . . . 5'11" . . . 170 lbs. . . . Born, Brantford, Ont., June 6, 1964 . . . Shoots right.

Year	Team	League	Games	G.	A.	Pts.	Pen.
1980-81—Blue Haven Penguins		Brantford Jr. 'B'	36	46	45	91	146
1981-82—Oshawa Generals (c)		OHL	66	22	51	73	112
1982-83—Oshawa Generals (d)		OHL	64	41	64	105	90
1982-83—Los Angeles Kings		NHL	3	0	0	0	0
1983-84—Oshawa Generals		OHL	62	56	76	132	89
NHL TOTALS			3	0	0	0	0

(c)—June, 1982—Drafted as underage junior by Los Angeles Kings in 1982 NHL entry draft. Second Kings pick, 64th overall, fourth round.

(d)—Led OHL Playoffs with 24 assists, and tied teammate John MacLean for playoff lead with 38 points.

PAUL MALONE GARDNER

Center . . . 5'11" . . . 193 lbs. . . . Born, Fort Erie, Ont., March 5, 1956 . . . Shoots left . . . Son of former NHL forward Cal Gardner and brother of Dave Gardner . . . Missed part of 1977-78 season with fractured vertebra . . . Missed part of 1978-79 season with knee surgery . . . (January 13, 1982)—Suffered broken jaw when punched by Jimmy Mann at Winnipeg . . . (December, 1983)—Broke both heels while falling off ladder in mishap at home.

Year	Team	League	Games	G.	A.	Pts.	Pen.
1973-74—Toronto St. Michael's		Jr."B"OHA	....	...	....	....	....
1974-75—Oshawa Generals		Jr."A"OHA	64	27	36	63	54
1975-76—Oshawa Generals (c)		Jr."A"OHA	65	69	75	144	75
1976-77—Rhode Island Reds		AHL	14	10	4	14	12
1976-77—Colorado Rockies		NHL	60	30	29	59	25
1977-78—Colorado Rockies		NHL	46	30	22	52	29
1978-79—Colorado Rockies (d)		NHL	64	23	26	49	32
1978-79—Toronto Maple Leafs		NHL	11	7	2	9	0
1979-80—New Brunswick Hawks		AHL	20	11	16	27	14
1979-80—Toronto Maple Leafs		NHL	45	11	13	24	10
1980-81—Springfield Indians (e)		AHL	14	9	12	21	6
1980-81—Pittsburgh Penguins		NHL	62	34	40	74	59
1981-82—Pittsburgh Penguins		NHL	59	36	33	69	28
1982-83—Pittsburgh Penguins		NHL	70	28	27	55	12
1983-84—Baltimore Skipjacks		AHL	54	32	49	81	14
1983-84—Pittsburgh Penguins (f)		NHL	16	0	5	5	6
NHL TOTALS			433	199	197	396	*201

(c)—Drafted from Oshawa Generals by Kansas City Scouts in first round of 1976 amateur draft.
(d)—March, 1979—Traded by Colorado Rockies to Toronto Maple Leafs for Don Ashby and Trevor Johansen.
(e)—November, 1980—Traded by Toronto Maple Leafs with Dave Burrows to Pittsburgh Penguins for Paul Marshall and Kim Davis.
(f)—July, 1984—Signed by Washington Capitals as a free agent.

WILLIAM SCOTT GARDNER

Center . . . 5'10" . . . 170 lbs. . . . Born, Toronto, Ont., March 19, 1960 . . . Shoots left.

Year	Team	League	Games	G.	A.	Pts.	Pen.
1976-77—Peterborough Petes		OMJHL	1	0	0	0	0
1977-78—Peterborough Petes		OMJHL	65	23	32	55	10
1978-79—Peterborough Petes (c)		OMJHL	68	33	71	104	19
1979-80—Peterborough Petes		OMJHL	59	43	63	106	17
1980-81—New Brunswick Hawks		AHL	48	19	29	48	12
1980-81—Chicago Black Hawks		NHL	1	0	0	0	0
1981-82—Chicago Black Hawks		NHL	69	8	15	23	20
1982-83—Chicago Black Hawks		NHL	77	15	25	40	12
1983-84—Chicago Black Hawks		NHL	79	27	21	48	12
NHL TOTALS			226	50	61	111	44

(c)—August, 1979—Drafted by Chicago Black Hawks as underage junior in entry draft. Third Chicago pick, 49th overall, third round.

DANIEL MIRL GARE

Right Wing . . . 5'10" . . . 176 lbs. . . . Born, Nelson, B. C., May 14, 1954 . . . Shoots right . . . Also plays Center . . . Son of Ernie Gare (Former hockey coach at B.C. Notre Dame University) . . . Set WCHL record by scoring goals in 13 consecutive games during 1973-74 season . . . Missed most of 1976-77 season with cracked vertebrae in back . . . (December, 1981)—Eye injury . . . (November, 1983)—Bruised sternum. Came back in December to play wearing a special 'flak-jacket.'

Year	Team	League	Games	G.	A.	Pts.	Pen.
1971-72—Calgary Centennials		WCHL	56	10	17	27	15
1972-73—Calgary Centennials		WCHL	65	45	43	88	107
1973-74—Calgary Centennials (a-c)		WCHL	65	68	59	127	238
1974-75—Buffalo Sabres		NHL	78	31	31	62	75
1975-76—Buffalo Sabres		NHL	79	50	23	73	129
1976-77—Buffalo Sabres		NHL	35	11	15	26	73
1977-78—Buffalo Sabres		NHL	69	39	38	77	95
1978-79—Buffalo Sabres		NHL	71	27	40	67	90
1979-80—Buffalo Sabres		NHL	76	*56	33	89	90
1980-81—Buffalo Sabres		NHL	73	46	39	85	109
1981-82—Buffalo Sabres (d)		NHL	22	7	14	21	25
1981-82—Detroit Red Wings		NHL	36	13	9	22	74

Year	Team	League	Games	G.	A.	Pts.	Pen.
1982-83—Detroit Red Wings		NHL	79	26	35	61	107
1983-84—Detroit Red Wings		NHL	63	13	13	26	147
NHL TOTALS			681	319	290	609	1014

(c)—Drafted from Calgary Centennials by Buffalo Sabres in second round of 1974 amateur draft.
(d)—December, 1981—Traded with Bob Sauve, Jim Schoenfeld and Derek Smith by Buffalo Sabres to Detroit Red Wings for Dale McCourt, Mike Foligno, Brent Peterson and future considerations.

MICHAEL ALFRED GARTNER

Right Wing . . . 6' . . . 180 lbs. . . . Born, Ottawa, Ont., October 29, 1959 . . . Shoots right . . . (February, 1983)—Eye Injury.

Year	Team	League	Games	G.	A.	Pts.	Pen.
1975-76—St. Cath. Black Hawks		Jr."A"OHA	3	1	3	4	0
1976-77—Niagara Falls Flyers		Jr."A"OHA	62	33	42	75	125
1977-78—Niagara Falls Flyers (a-c)		Jr."A"OHA	64	41	49	90	56
1978-79—Cincinnati Stingers (d)		WHA	78	27	25	52	123
1979-80—Washington Capitals		NHL	77	36	32	68	66
1980-81—Washington Capitals		NHL	80	48	46	94	100
1981-82—Washington Capitals		NHL	80	35	45	80	121
1982-83—Washington Capitals		NHL	73	38	38	76	54
1983-84—Washington Capitals		NHL	80	40	45	85	90
WHA TOTALS			78	27	25	52	123
NHL TOTALS			390	197	206	403	431

(c)—Signed by Cincinnati Stingers (WHA) as underage junior, August, 1978.
(d)—August, 1979—Drafted by Washington Capitals in 1979 entry draft. First Capitals pick, fourth overall, first round.

JAMES GASSEAU

Defense . . . 6'2" . . . 200 lbs. . . . Born, Carleton, Que., May 4, 1966 . . . Shoots right.

Year	Team	League	Games	G.	A.	Pts.	Pen.
1983-84—Drummondville Voltigeurs (c)		QHL	68	6	25	31	72

(c)—June, 1984—Drafted as underage junior by Buffalo Sabres in 1984 NHL entry draft. Sixth Sabres pick, 123rd overall, sixth round.

STEVE GATZOS

Right Wing . . . 5'11" . . . 185 lbs. . . . Born, Toronto, Ont., June 22, 1961 . . . Shoots right . . . (December, 1982)—Ankle injury.

Year	Team	League	Games	G.	A.	Pts.	Pen.
1978-79—Sault Ste. Marie Greyhounds		OMJHL	36	3	9	12	21
1979-80—Sault Ste. Marie Greyhounds		OMJHL	64	36	38	74	64
1980-81—Sault Ste. Marie Greyhounds (c)		OHL	68	78	50	128	114
1981-82—Erie Blades		AHL	54	18	19	37	67
1981-82—Pittsburgh Penguins		NHL	16	6	8	14	14
1982-83—Pittsburgh Penguins		NHL	44	6	7	13	52
1982-83—Baltimore Skipjacks		AHL	12	5	4	9	22
1983-84—Baltimore Skipjacks		AHL	48	14	19	33	43
1983-84—Pittsburgh Penguins		NHL	23	3	3	6	15
NHL TOTALS			83	15	18	33	81

(c)—June, 1981—Drafted by Pittsburgh Penguins in 1981 NHL entry draft. First Penguins pick, 28th overall, second round.

JEAN-MARC GAULIN

Right Wing . . . 5'10" . . . 180 lbs. . . . Born, Baive, Germany, March 3, 1962 . . . Shoots right . . . (November, 1979)—Dislocated shoulder.

Year	Team	League	Games	G.	A.	Pts.	Pen.
1978-79—Sherbrooke Beavers		QMJHL	71	26	41	67	89
1979-80—Sherbrooke Beavers		QMJHL	16	6	15	21	14
1979-80—Sorel Black Hawks		QMJHL	43	15	25	40	105
1980-81—Sorel Black Hawks (b-c)		QMJHL	70	50	40	90	157
1981-82—Hull Olympics (d)		QMJHL	56	50	50	100	93
1982-83—Quebec Nordiques		NHL	1	0	0	0	0
1982-83—Fredericton Express		AHL	67	11	17	28	58
1983-84—Fredericton Express		AHL	62	14	28	42	80
1983-84—Quebec Nordiques		NHL	2	0	0	0	0
NHL TOTALS			3	0	0	0	0

(c)—June, 1981—Drafted by Quebec Nordiques in 1981 NHL entry draft. Second Nordiques pick, 53rd overall, third round.

(d)—August, 1981—Acquired by Hull Olympics in QMJHL dispersal draft of players of defunct Sorel Black Hawks.

JOCELYN GAUVREAU

Defense . . . 6' . . . 175 lbs. . . . Born, Masham, Que., March 4, 1964 . . . Shoots left . . . Also plays Left Wing.

Year	Team	League	Games	G.	A.	Pts.	Pen.
1980-81—Hull Olympics		QMJHL	54	12	12	24	55
1981-82—Hull Olympics (c)		QMJHL	19	5	8	13	8
1981-82—Granby Bisons (d)		QMJHL	33	12	21	33	66
1982-83—Granby Bisons (b)		QHL	68	33	63	96	42
1982-83—Nova Scotia Voyageurs		AHL	1	0	0	0	0
1983-84—Granby Bisons		QHL	58	19	39	58	55
1983-84—Nova Scotia Voyageurs		AHL	1	0	2	2	0
1983-84—Montreal Canadiens		NHL	2	0	0	0	0
NHL TOTALS			2	0	0	0	0

(c)—December, 1981—Traded with Claude Labbe and Sylvain Roy by Hull Olympics to Granby Bisons for Dan Naud.

(d)—June, 1982—Drafted as underage junior by Montreal Canadiens in 1982 NHL entry draft. Second Canadiens pick, 31st overall, second round.

ROBERT STEWART GAVIN
(Known By Middle Name.)

Left Wing . . . 6' . . . 180 lbs. . . . Born, Ottawa, Ont., March 15, 1960 . . . Shoots left . . . (October, 1981)—Shoulder separation . . . (December, 1981)—Reinjured shoulder . . . (October, 1982)—Sprained ankle.

Year	Team	League	Games	G.	A.	Pts.	Pen.
1976-77—Ottawa 67's		OMJHL	1	0	0	0	0
1977-78—Toronto Marlboros		OMJHL	67	16	24	40	19
1978-79—Toronto Marlboros		OMJHL	61	24	25	49	83
1979-80—Toronto Marlboros (c)		OMJHL	66	27	30	57	52
1980-81—Toronto Maple Leafs		NHL	14	1	2	3	13
1980-81—New Brunswick Hawks		AHL	46	7	12	19	42
1981-82—Toronto Maple Leafs		NHL	38	5	6	11	29
1982-83—St. Catharines Saints		OHL	6	2	4	6	17
1982-83—Toronto Maple Leafs		NHL	63	6	5	11	44
1983-84—Toronto Maple Leafs		NHL	80	10	22	32	90
NHL TOTALS			195	22	35	57	176

(c)—June, 1980—Drafted by Toronto Maple Leafs in 1980 NHL entry draft. Fourth Maple Leafs pick, 74th overall, fourth round.

ROBERT CHARLES GEALE

Center and Right Wing . . . 5'11" . . . 175 lbs. . . . Born, Edmonton, Alta., April 17, 1962 . . . Shoots right . . . Nephew of Roger Kozar (goalie) who played in minor leagues in mid 70's . . . Missed several games during 1980-81 season with recurring knee problems.

Year	Team	League	Games	G.	A.	Pts.	Pen.
1978-79—Sherwood Park Crusaders		AJHL	60	11	33	44	44
1979-80—Portland Winter Hawks (c)		WHL	72	17	29	46	32
1980-81—Portland Winter Hawks		WHL	54	30	32	62	54
1981-82—Portland Winter Hawks		WHL	72	31	54	85	89
1982-83—Baltimore Skipjacks		AHL	56	4	10	14	6
1983-84—Baltimore Skipjacks		AHL	74	17	23	40	50

(c)—June, 1980—Drafted as underage junior by Pittsburgh Penguins in 1980 NHL entry draft. Sixth Penguins pick, 156th overall, eighth round.

RICH GEIST

Center . . . 6'3" . . . 190 lbs. . . . Born, St. Paul, Minn., November 17, 1964 . . . Shoots left.

Year	Team	League	Games	G.	A.	Pts.	Pen.
1982-83—St. Paul Academy (c)		Minn. H.S.	22	22	20	42	..
1983-84—University of Minnesota		WCHA	5	2	1	3	2

(c)—June, 1983—Drafted by Minnesota North Stars in NHL entry draft. Sixth North Stars pick, 96th overall, fifth round.

JOHN WILLIAM GIBSON

Defense . . . 6'3" . . . 205 lbs. . . . Born, St. Catharines, Ont., June 2, 1959 . . . Shoots left . . . (December, 1981)—Stomach problems.

Year	Team	League	Games	G.	A.	Pts.	Pen.
1976-77—Niagara Falls Flyers		OMJHL	59	2	13	15	178
1977-78—Niagara Falls Flyers		OMJHL	60	8	20	28	133
1978-79—Niagara Falls Flyers (c)		OMJHL	47	15	26	41	218
1979-80—Winnipeg Jets (d)		WHA	9	0	1	1	5
1979-80—Binghamton Dusters		AHL	1	0	0	0	0
1979-80—Saginaw Gears (a-e)		IHL	67	13	36	49	293
1980-81—Los Angeles Kings		NHL	4	0	0	0	21
1980-81—Houston Apollos		CHL	33	5	5	10	94
1980-81—Birmingham Bulls		CHL	16	6	3	9	42
1980-81—Saginaw Gears		IHL	12	0	7	7	82
1981-82—New Haven Nighthawks		AHL	7	1	0	1	24
1981-82—Los Angeles Kings (f)		NHL	6	0	0	0	18
1981-82—Toronto Maple Leafs		NHL	27	0	2	2	67
1981-82—New Brunswick Hawks		AHL	12	0	2	2	6
1981-82—Cincinnati Tigers		CHL	6	1	2	3	30
1982-83—St. Catharines Saints		AHL	21	1	4	5	38
1983-84—Winnipeg Jets (g)		NHL	11	0	0	0	14
1983-84—Sherbrooke Jets		AHL	49	4	11	15	174
WHA TOTALS			9	0	1	1	5
NHL TOTALS			48	0	2	2	120

(c)—March, 1979—Given a pro-tryout by Winnipeg Jets.
(d)—June, 1979—Drafted by Los Angeles Kings in entry draft. Fifth Los Angeles pick, 71st overall, fourth round.
(e)—Won the Governors' Trophy (IHL Outstanding defenseman).
(f)—November, 1981—Traded with Bill Harris by Los Angeles Kings to Toronto Maple Leafs for Ian Turnbull.
(g)—October, 1983—August, 1980—Signed by Winnipeg Jets as a free agent.

TOM GIBSON

Right Wing . . . 6' . . . 192 lbs. . . . Born, St. Catharines, Ont., May 26, 1960 . . . Shoots right . . . (February, 1981)—Separated shoulder during a Tulsa Oiler practice.

Year	Team	League	Games	G.	A.	Pts.	Pen.
1977-78—St. Catharines		OHA Jr.'B'	57	46	46	92	115
1978-79—Niagara Falls Flyers		OMJHL	55	21	21	42	156
1979-80—Niagara Falls Flyers (c)		OMJHL	62	21	32	53	177
1980-81—Fort Wayne Komets		IHL	4	2	0	2	0
1980-81—Richmond Rifles		EHL	43	15	17	32	108
1980-81—Tulsa Oilers		CHL	5	1	2	3	4
1981-82—Tulsa Oilers		CHL	73	17	19	36	126
1982-83—Sherbrooke Jets		AHL	74	26	32	58	89
1983-84—Sherbrooke Jets		AHL	79	19	29	48	88

(c)—August, 1980—Signed by Winnipeg Jets as a free agent.

GREG SCOTT GILBERT

Left Wing . . . 6' . . . 190 lbs. . . . Born, Mississauga, Ont., January 22, 1962 . . . Shoots left . . . (December, 1979)—Sprained ankle.

Year	Team	League	Games	G.	A.	Pts.	Pen.
1979-80—Toronto Marlboros (c)		OMJHL	68	10	11	21	35
1980-81—Toronto Marlboros		OHL	64	30	37	67	73
1981-82—Toronto Marlboros		OHL	65	41	67	108	119
1981-82—New York Islanders		NHL	1	1	0	1	0
1982-83—Indianapolis Checkers		CHL	24	11	16	27	23
1982-83—New York Islanders		NHL	45	8	11	19	30
1983-84—New York Islanders		NHL	79	31	35	66	59
NHL TOTALS			125	40	46	86	89

(c)—June, 1980—Drafted as underage junior by New York Islanders in 1980 NHL entry draft. Fifth Islanders pick, 80th overall, fourth round.

CURT GILES

Defense . . . 5'8" . . . 180 lbs. . . . Born, The Pas, Manitoba, November 30, 1958 . . . Shoots left . . . Named to All-American College teams in 1978 and 1979 . . . (February, 1981)—Knee strain (right knee) . . . (January, 1984)—Knee injury.

Year	Team	League	Games	G.	A.	Pts.	Pen.
1975-76—Univ. of Minnesota-Duluth		WCHA	34	5	17	22	76
1976-77—Univ. of Minnesota-Duluth		WCHA	37	12	37	49	64
1977-78—Univ. of Minn.-Duluth (a-c)		WCHA	34	11	36	47	62

Year	Team	League	Games	G.	A.	Pts.	Pen.
1978-79—Univ. of Minnesota-Duluth (a)	WCHA	30	3	38	41	38
1979-80—Oklahoma City Stars	CHL	42	4	24	28	35
1979-80—Minnesota North Stars	NHL	37	2	7	9	31
1980-81—Minnesota North Stars	NHL	67	5	22	27	56
1981-82—Minnesota North Stars	NHL	74	3	12	15	87
1982-83—Minnesota North Stars	NHL	76	2	21	23	70
1983-84—Minnesota North Stars	NHL	70	6	22	28	59
NHL TOTALS		324	18	84	102	303

(c)—June, 1978—Drafted by Minnesota North Stars in NHL amateur draft. Fourth North Stars pick, 54th overall, fourth round.

RANDY GILHEN

Left Wing . . . 5'11" . . . 195 lbs. . . . Born, Zweibrucken, West Germany, June 13, 1963 . . . Shoots left.

Year	Team	League	Games	G.	A.	Pts.	Pen.
1979-80—Saskatoon	SJHL	55	18	34	52	112
1979-80—Saskatoon Blades	WHL	9	2	2	4	20
1980-81—Saskatoon Blades	WHL	68	10	5	15	154
1981-82—Winnipeg Warriors (c)	WHL	61	41	37	78	87
1982-83—Winnipeg Warriors	WHL	71	57	44	101	84
1982-83—Hartford Whalers	NHL	2	0	1	1	0
1982-83—Binghamton Whalers (d)	AHL	..	..	..	..	..
1983-84—Binghamton Whalers	AHL	73	8	12	20	72
NHL TOTALS		2	0	1	1	0

(c)—June, 1982—Drafted as underage junior by Hartford Whalers in 1982 NHL entry draft. Sixth Whalers pick, 109th overall, sixth round.

(d)—No regular season record. Played five playoff games.

TODD GILL

Defense . . . 6'1" . . . 175 lbs. . . . Born, Brockville, Ont., November 9, 1965 . . . Shoots left.

Year	Team	League	Games	G.	A.	Pts.	Pen.
1982-83—Windsor Spitfires	OHL	70	12	24	36	108
1983-84—Windsor Spitfires (c)	OHL	68	9	48	57	184

(c)—June, 1984—Drafted as underage junior by Toronto Maple Leafs in 1984 NHL entry draft. Second Maple Leafs pick, 25th overall, second round.

DON GILLEN

Right Wing . . . 6'3" . . . 212 lbs. . . . Born, Dodsland, Sask., December 24, 1960 . . . Shoots right.

Year	Team	League	Games	G.	A.	Pts.	Pen.
1976-77—Weyburn	SJHL	58	13	24	37	170
1977-78—Brandon Wheat Kings	WCHL	60	18	16	34	128
1978-79—Brandon Wheat Kings (c)	WHL	64	21	30	51	212
1979-80—Brandon Wheat Kings (b)	WHL	69	31	56	87	372
1979-80—Philadelphia Flyers	NHL	1	1	0	1	0
1979-80—Maine Mariners (d)	AHL	....	...	....	....	....
1980-81—Maine Mariners (e)	AHL	79	30	29	59	255
1981-82—Binghamton Whalers	AHL	42	20	10	30	100
1981-82—Hartford Whalers	NHL	34	1	4	5	22
1982-83—Binghamton Whalers	AHL	80	38	39	77	245
1983-84—Binghamton Whalers (f)	AHL	73	27	37	64	140
NHL TOTALS		35	2	4	6	22

(c)—June, 1979—Drafted as underage junior by Philadelphia Flyers in 1979 NHL entry draft. Fifth Flyers pick, 77th overall, fourth round.

(d)—No regular season record. Played seven playoff games.

(e)—July, 1981—Traded by Philadelphia Flyers with Blake Wesley, Rick MacLeish and Philadelphia's first, second and third round 1982 draft picks to Hartford Whalers for Ray Allison, Fred Arthur and Hartford's first and third round picks in the 1982 NHL entry draft.

(f)—July, 1984—Released by Hartford Whalers.

CLARK GILLIES

Left Wing . . . 6'3" . . . 215 lbs. . . . Born, Moose Jaw, Sask., April 7, 1954 . . . Shoots left . . . Played three seasons of baseball with Houston Astros (NL) Covington, Virginia farm team . . . (April, 1983)—Arthroscopic surgery to left knee . . . Holds New York Islanders club record for goals by a left wing in a season (38).

Year	Team	League	Games	G.	A.	Pts.	Pen.
1971-72—Regina Pats		WCHL	68	31	48	79	199
1972-73—Regina Pats		WCHL	68	40	52	92	192
1973-74—Regina Pats (a-c)		WCHL	65	46	66	112	179
1974-75—New York Islanders		NHL	80	25	22	47	66
1975-76—New York Islanders		NHL	80	34	27	61	96
1976-77—New York Islanders		NHL	70	33	22	55	93
1977-78—New York Islanders (a)		NHL	80	35	50	85	76
1978-79—New York Islanders (a)		NHL	75	35	56	91	68
1979-80—New York Islanders		NHL	73	19	35	54	49
1980-81—New York Islanders		NHL	80	33	45	78	99
1981-82—New York Islanders		NHL	79	38	39	77	75
1982-83—New York Islanders		NHL	70	21	20	41	76
1983-84—New York Islanders		NHL	76	12	16	28	65
NHL TOTALS			763	285	332	617	763

(c)—Drafted from Regina Pats by New York Islanders in first round of 1974 amateur draft.

JERE ALAN GILLIS

Left Wing . . . 6'1" . . . 185 lbs. . . . Born, Bend, Ore., January 18, 1957 . . . Shoots left . . . (January, 1981)—Strained left knee.

Year	Team	League	Games	G.	A.	Pts.	Pen.
1973-74—Sherbrooke Beavers		QJHL	69	21	19	40	96
1974-75—Sherbrooke Beavers		QJHL	54	38	57	95	89
1975-76—Sherbrooke Beavers		QJHL	60	47	55	102	38
1976-77—Sherbrooke Beavers (a-c)		QJHL	72	55	85	140	80
1977-78—Vancouver Canucks		NHL	79	23	18	41	35
1978-79—Vancouver Canucks		NHL	78	13	12	25	33
1979-80—Vancouver Canucks		NHL	67	13	17	30	108
1980-81—Vancouver Canucks (d)		NHL	11	0	4	4	4
1980-81—New York Rangers		NHL	35	10	10	20	4
1981-82—New York Rangers (e)		NHL	26	3	9	12	16
1981-82—Quebec Nordiques		NHL	12	2	1	3	0
1981-82—Fredericton Express		AHL	28	2	17	19	10
1982-83—Buffalo Sabres		NHL	3	0	0	0	0
1982-83—Rochester Americans		AHL	53	18	24	42	69
1983-84—Vancouver Canucks (f)		NHL	37	9	13	22	7
1983-84—Fredericton Express		AHL	36	22	28	50	35
NHL TOTALS			348	73	84	157	207

(c)—Drafted from Sherbrooke Beavers by Vancouver Canucks in first round of 1977 amateur draft.
(d)—November, 1980—Traded by Vancouver Canucks with Jeff Bandura to New York Rangers for Mario Marois and Jim Mayer.
(e)—December, 1981—Traded with Dean Talafous by New York Rangers to Quebec Nordiques for Robbie Ftorek and eighth-round 1982 draft pick (Brian Glynn). Talafous retired rather than report to Quebec and NHL awarded Pat Hickey to Nordiques as compensation in March, 1982.
(f)—August, 1983—Signed by Vancouver Canucks as a free agent.

MICHAEL DAVID GILLIS

Left Wing . . . 6'1" . . . 191 lbs. . . . Born, Sudbury, Ont., December 1, 1958 . . . Shoots left . . . Also plays Center . . . Missed most of 1976-77 season with broken leg and part of 1977-78 season with broken collarbone . . . Missed most of 1979-80 season due to complications from 1978 knee surgery . . . Brother of Paul Gillis . . . Wife, Diane, was a track star at the University of Tennessee.

Year	Team	League	Games	G.	A.	Pts.	Pen.
1975-76—Kingston Canadians		Jr. "A" OHA	64	16	45	61	34
1976-77—Kingston Canadians		Jr. "A" OHA	4	2	2	4	4
1977-78—Kingston Canadians (c)		Jr. "A" OHA	43	21	46	67	86
1978-79—Colorado Rockies		NHL	30	1	7	8	6
1978-79—Philadelphia Firebirds		AHL	2	0	0	0	0
1979-80—Fort Worth Texans		CHL	29	9	13	22	43
1979-80—Colorado Rockies		NHL	40	4	5	9	22
1980-81—Colorado Rockies (d)		NHL	51	11	7	18	54
1980-81—Boston Bruins		NHL	17	2	4	6	15
1981-82—Boston Bruins		NHL	53	9	8	17	54
1982-83—Baltimore Skipjacks		AHL	74	32	81	113	33
1982-83—Boston Bruins		NHL	5	0	1	1	0
1983-84—Hershey Bears		AHL	26	8	21	29	13
1983-84—Boston Bruins		NHL	50	6	11	17	35
NHL TOTALS			246	33	43	76	186

(c)—Drafted from Kingston Canadians by Colorado Rockies in first round of 1978 amateur draft.
(d)—February, 1981—Traded by Colorado Rockies to Boston Bruins for Bob Miller.

PAUL C. GILLIS

Center . . . 6' . . . 195 lbs. . . . Born, Toronto, Ont., December 31, 1963 . . . Shoots left . . . Brother of Mike Gillis.

Year	Team	League	Games	G.	A.	Pts.	Pen.
1980-81	Niagara Falls Flyers	OHL	59	14	19	33	165
1981-82	Niagara Falls Flyers (c)	OHL	66	27	62	89	247
1982-83	North Bay Centennials	OHL	61	34	52	86	151
1982-83	Quebec Nordiques	NHL	7	0	2	2	2
1983-84	Fredericton Express	AHL	18	7	8	15	47
1983-84	Quebec Nordiques	NHL	57	8	9	17	59
	NHL TOTALS		64	8	11	19	61

(c)—June, 1982—Drafted as underage junior by Quebec Nordiques in 1982 NHL entry draft. Second Nordiques pick, 34th overall, second round.

DOUGLAS GILMOUR

Center . . . 5'11" . . . 164 lbs. . . . Born, Kingston, Ont., June 25, 1963 . . . Shoots left.

Year	Team	League	Games	G.	A.	Pts.	Pen.
1980-81	Cornwall Royals	QMJHL	51	12	23	35	35
1981-82	Cornwall Royals (c)	OHL	67	46	73	119	42
1982-83	Cornwall Royals (a-d-e)	OHL	68	*70	*107	*177	62
1983-84	St. Louis Blues	NHL	80	25	28	53	57
	NHL TOTALS		80	25	28	53	57

(c)—June, 1982—Drafted as underage junior by St. Louis Blues in 1982 NHL entry draft. Fourth Blues pick, 134th overall, seventh round.
(d)—Won Red Tilson Trophy (Outstanding OHL Player).
(e)—Won Eddie Powers Memorial Trophy (OHL Scoring Champion).

GASTON REGINALD GINGRAS

Defense . . . 6' . . . 191 lbs. . . . Born, Temiscaming, Que., February 13, 1959 . . . Shoots left . . . (October, 1980)—Severe Charley horse . . . (October, 1981)—Injured back . . . (September 18, 1982)—Injured back in preseason game vs. Buffalo . . . (February, 1983)—Back spasms.

Year	Team	League	Games	G.	A.	Pts.	Pen.
1974-75	North Bay Trappers	OPJHL	41	11	27	38	74
1975-76	Kitchener Rangers	Jr. "A" OHA	66	13	31	44	94
1976-77	Kitchener Rangers	Jr. "A" OHA	59	13	62	75	134
1977-78	Kitchener Rangers (c)	Jr. "A" OHA	32	13	24	37	31
1977-78	Hamilton Fincups (d)	Jr. "A" OHA	29	11	19	30	37
1978-79	Birmingham Bulls (e)	WHA	60	13	21	34	35
1979-80	Nova Scotia Voyageurs	AHL	30	11	27	38	17
1979-80	Montreal Canadiens	NHL	34	3	7	10	18
1980-81	Montreal Canadiens	NHL	55	5	16	21	22
1981-82	Montreal Canadiens	NHL	34	6	18	24	28
1982-83	Montreal Canadiens (f)	NHL	22	1	8	9	8
1982-83	Toronto Maple Leafs	NHL	45	10	18	28	10
1983-84	Toronto Maple Leafs	NHL	59	7	20	27	16
	NHL TOTALS		249	32	87	119	102
	WHA TOTALS		60	13	21	34	35

(c)—Traded to Hamilton Fincups by Kitchener Rangers for Jody Gage and "future considerations," December, 1977.
(d)—Signed by Birmingham Bulls (WHA) as underage junior, July, 1978.
(e)—June, 1979—Drafted by Montreal Canadiens in entry draft. First Canadiens pick, 27th overall, second round.
(f)—December, 1982—Traded with Dan Daoust by Montreal Canadiens to Toronto Maple Leafs for future draft considerations.

PIERRE-YVES RICHARD GIROUX

Center . . . 5'11" . . . 186 lbs. . . . Born, Brownsburg, Que., November 17, 1955 . . . Shoots right.

Year	Team	League	Games	G.	A.	Pts.	Pen.
1973-74	Sorel Black Hawks	QJHL	41	4	11	15	23
1974-75	Hull Festivals (c)	QJHL	72	57	61	118	118
1975-76	Dallas Black Hawks	CHL	62	8	14	22	69
1976-77	Flint Generals	IHL	73	21	36	57	87
1977-78	Dallas Black Hawks	CHL	16	2	5	7	2
1977-78	Flint Generals	IHL	40	25	23	48	121
1978-79	New Brunswick Hawks	AHL	8	0	2	2	20
1978-79	Flint Generals	IHL	70	41	42	83	146

Year	Team	League	Games	G.	A.	Pts.	Pen.
1979-80—Flint Generals		IHI	80	33	38	71	197
1980-81—Flint Generals (a)		IHL	81	55	47	102	303
1981-82—New Haven Nighthawks		AHL	38	6	11	17	114
1982-83—New Haven Nighthawks (d)		AHL	62	16	31	47	337
1982-83—Los Angeles Kings		NHL	6	1	0	1	17
1983-84—Flint Generals		IHL	56	24	37	61	274
NHL TOTALS			56	24	37	61	274

(c)—Drafted from Hull Festivals by Chicago Black Hawks in fourth round of 1975 amateur draft.
(d)—January, 1982—Signed by Los Angeles Kings as a free agent.

ROBERT LAWRENCE GLADNEY

Defense . . . 5'11" . . . 184 lbs. . . . Born, Come-by-Chance, Nfld., August 27, 1957 . . . Shoots left . . . Missed part of 1976-77 season with mononucleosis and part with fractured thumb . . . Missed part of 1978-79 season with broken jaw.

Year	Team	League	Games	G.	A.	Pts.	Pen.
1974-75—Oshawa Generals		Jr. "A" OHA	68	12	50	62	84
1975-76—Oshawa Generals		Jr. "A" OHA	66	26	52	78	47
1976-77—Oshawa Generals (c)		Jr. "A" OHA	54	20	42	62	56
1977-78—Saginaw Gears		IHL	79	15	50	65	35
1978-79—Saginaw Gears		IHL	67	16	42	58	51
1979-80—New Brunswick Hawks		AHL	36	0	6	6	18
1980-81—Saginaw Gears (d)		IHL	78	12	71	83	54
1981-82—New Haven Nighthawks		AHL	63	7	26	33	12
1981-82—Saginaw Gears		IHL	17	4	9	13	10
1982-83—Los Angeles Kings		NHL	1	0	0	0	2
1982-83—New Haven Nighthawks (a)		AHL	80	19	47	66	22
1983-84—Pittsburgh Penguins (e)		NHL	13	1	5	6	2
1983-84—Baltimore Skipjacks		AHL	9	4	7	11	10
NHL TOTALS			14	1	5	6	4

(c)—Drafted from Oshawa Generals by Toronto Maple Leafs in second round of 1977 amateur draft.
(d)—August, 1981—Traded by Toronto Maple Leafs with sixth round 1983 entry draft pick to Los Angeles Wings for Don Luce.
(e)—August, 1983—Signed by Pittsburgh Penguins as a free agent.

THOMAS GLAVINE

Center . . . 6' . . . 180 lbs. . . . Born, Concord, Mass., March 25, 1966 . . . Shoots left . . . Was second-round pick by Atlanta Braves in the June, 1984, draft and pitched in Gulf Coast League.

Year	Team	League	Games	G.	A.	Pts.	Pen.
1983-84—Billerica H.S. (c)		Mass. H.S.	23	47	47	94	..

(c)—June, 1984—Drafted by Los Angeles Kings in 1984 NHL entry draft. Fourth Kings pick, 69th overall, fourth round.

ERNIE ALFRED GODDEN

Center . . . 5'8" . . . 165 lbs. . . . Born, Keswick, Ont., March 13, 1961 . . . Shoots left . . . Set OHL record for most goals (87) in 1980-81.

Year	Team	League	Games	G.	A.	Pts.	Pen.
1976-77—Newmarket Flyers		OPJHL	44	19	24	43	89
1977-78—Newmarket Flyers		OPJHL	40	20	24	44	67
1978-79—Windsor Spitfires		OMJHL	64	25	31	56	165
1979-80—Windsor Spitfires		OMJHL	62	40	41	81	158
1980-81—Windsor Spitfires (a-c-d)		OMJHL	68	*87	66	153	185
1981-82—Toronto Maple Leafs		NHL	5	1	1	2	6
1981-82—Cincinnati Tigers		CHL	67	32	37	69	178
1982-83—St. Catharines Saints		AHL	64	27	23	50	106
1983-84—St. Catharines Saints		AHL	78	31	36	67	69
NHL TOTALS			5	1	1	2	6

(c)—Winner of Red Tilson Memorial Trophy (OHL MVP).
(d)—June, 1981—Drafted by Toronto Maple Leafs in 1981 NHL entry draft. Third Maple Leafs pick, 55th overall, third round.

DAVE GOERTZ

Defense . . . 5'11" . . . 205 lbs. . . . Born, Edmonton, Alta., March 28, 1965 . . . Shoots right.

Year	Team	League	Games	G.	A.	Pts.	Pen.
1981-82—Regina Pats		WHL	67	5	19	24	181
1982-83—Regina Pats (c)		WHL	69	4	22	26	132

Year	Team	League	Games	G.	A.	Pts.	Pen.
1983-84—Prince Albert Raiders		WHL	60	13	47	60	111
1983-84—Baltimore Skipjacks		AHL	1	0	0	0	0

(c)—June, 1983—Drafted as underage junior by Pittsburgh Penguins in 1983 NHL entry draft. Tenth Penguins pick, 223rd overall, 12th round.

PATRICK GOFF

Defense . . . 6'1" . . . 185 lbs. . . . Born, St. Paul, Minn., June 29, 1964 . . . Shoots left.

Year	Team	League	Games	G.	A.	Pts.	Pen.
1980-81—Alexander Ramsey H.S.		Minn. H.S.	22	9	24	33	....
1981-82—Alexander Ramsey H.S. (c)		Minn. H.S.	23	5	20	25	....
1982-83—University of Michigan		CCHA	36	2	18	20	20
1983-84—University of Michigan		CCHA	37	4	17	21	38

(c)—June, 1982—Drafted as underage player by New York Islanders in 1982 NHL entry draft. Eleventh Islanders pick, 231st overall, 11th round.

MICHAEL GOLDEN

Center . . . 6'1" . . . 190 lbs. . . . Born, Boston, Mass., June 17, 1965 . . . Shoots right.

Year	Team	League	Games	G.	A.	Pts.	Pen.
1982-83—Reading H.S. (c)		Mass. H.S.	23	22	41	63	....
1983-84—Univ. of New Hampshire		ECAC	7	1	1	2	2

(c)—June, 1983—Drafted as underage junior by Edmonton Oilers in 1983 NHL entry draft. Second Oilers pick, 40th overall, second round.

JOHN GOODWIN

Center . . . 5'6" . . . 160 lbs. . . . Born, Toronto, Ont., September 25, 1961 . . . Shoots left . . . First OHL scoring leader since the NHL started drafting that wasn't drafted by an NHL club.

Year	Team	League	Games	G.	A.	Pts.	Pen.
1978-79—Sault Ste. Marie Greyhounds (c)		OMJHL	68	43	*86	129	20
1979-80—Sault Ste. Marie Greyhounds		OMJHL	65	34	60	94	14
1980-81—S.S. Marie Greyhounds (b-d-e-f)		OHL	68	56	*109	*165	42
1981-82—Nova Scotia Voyageurs		AHL	78	16	40	56	19
1982-83—Nova Scotia Voyageurs		AHL	80	35	49	84	24
1983-84—Nova Scotia Voyageurs (g)		AHL	35	12	21	33	11
1983-84—New Haven Nighthawks		AHL	44	12	41	53	35

(c)—Winner of Emms Family Trophy (OMJHL Top Rookie).
(d)—Winner of Eddie Powers Memorial Trophy (Leading OHL Scorer).
(e)—Winner of John Hanley Trophy (OHL Most Gentlemanly).
(f)—August, 1981—Signed by Montreal Canadiens as a free agent.
(g)—December, 1983—Traded by Montreal Canadiens to Los Angeles Kings for Dan Bonar.

TOM GORENCE

Right Wing . . . 6' . . . 180 lbs. . . . Born, St. Paul, Minn., March 11, 1957 . . . Shoots right . . . Attended University of Minnesota.

Year	Team	League	Games	G.	A.	Pts.	Pen.
1975-76—University of Minnesota		WCHA	40	16	10	26	24
1976-77—University of Minnesota (c)		WCHA	29	18	19	37	44
1977-78—Maine Mariners (d)		AHL	79	28	25	53	23
1978-79—Philadelphia Flyers		NHL	42	13	6	19	10
1978-79—Maine Mariners		AHL	31	11	13	24	23
1979-80—Philadelphia Flyers		NHL	51	8	13	21	15
1980-81—Philadelphia Flyers		NHL	79	24	18	42	46
1981-82—Philadelphia Flyers		NHL	66	5	8	13	8
1982-83—Maine Mariners		AHL	10	0	5	5	2
1982-83—Philadelphia Flyers		NHL	53	7	7	14	10
1983-84—Edmonton Oilers (e-f)		NHL	12	1	1	2	0
1983-84—Moncton Alpines		AHL	53	13	14	27	17
NHL TOTALS			303	58	53	111	89

(c)—Drafted from University of Minnesota by Philadelphia Flyers in second round of 1977 amateur draft.
(d)—Tied for lead in goals (8) during playoffs.
(e)—September, 1983—Traded by Philadelphia Flyers to Hartford Whalers for future considerations.
(f)—October, 1983—Returned to Philadelphia Flyers by Hartford Whalers to cancel earlier trade. He was released by the Flyers and signed by Edmonton Oilers as a free agent.

ROBERT THOMAS (BUTCH) GORING, JR.

Center . . . 5'10" . . . 165 lbs. . . . Born, St. Boniface, Man., October 22, 1949 . . . Shoots left . . . Member of Canadian National Team in 1968-69 . . . Missed part of 1970-71 season with mild case of mononucleosis . . . Set AHL record for points in playoffs (1970-71) . . . Missed part of 1972-73 season with severe cut on right leg, part of 1973-74 season with shoulder separation and part of 1974-75 season with eye injury . . . Had corrective surgery for shoulder separation May, 1975 . . . (November, 1981)—Named an Islanders assistant coach.

Year	Team	League	Games	G.	A.	Pts.	Pen.
1966-67	Winnipeg Rangers	CMJHL	....	...	....	....	....
1967-68	Canadian National "B" Team		....	...	....	....	....
1968-69	Canadian National Team		....	...	....	....	....
1968-69	Winnipeg Jets (c)	WCHL	36	42	33	75	0
1969-70	Springfield Kings	AHL	19	13	7	20	0
1969-70	Los Angeles Kings	NHL	59	13	23	36	8
1970-71	Springfield Kings (d)	AHL	40	23	32	55	4
1970-71	Los Angeles Kings	NHL	19	2	5	7	2
1971-72	Los Angeles Kings	NHL	74	21	29	50	2
1972-73	Los Angeles Kings	NHL	67	28	31	59	2
1973-74	Los Angeles Kings	NHL	70	28	33	61	2
1974-75	Los Angeles Kings	NHL	60	27	33	60	6
1975-76	Los Angeles Kings	NHL	80	33	40	73	8
1976-77	Los Angeles Kings	NHL	78	30	55	85	6
1977-78	Los Angeles Kings (e-f)	NHL	80	37	36	73	2
1978-79	Los Angeles Kings	NHL	80	36	51	87	16
1979-80	Los Angeles Kings (g)	NHL	69	20	48	68	12
1979-80	New York Islanders (h)	NHL	12	6	5	11	2
1980-81	New York Islanders	NHL	78	23	37	60	0
1981-82	New York Islanders	NHL	67	15	17	32	10
1982-83	New York Islanders	NHL	75	19	20	39	8
1983-84	New York Islanders	NHL	71	22	24	46	8
	NHL TOTALS		1039	360	487	847	94

(c)—Drafted from Winnipeg Jets by Los Angeles Kings in fifth round of 1969 amateur draft.
(d)—Led in goals (11), assists (14) and points (25) during playoffs.
(e)—Won Lady Byng Memorial Trophy.
(f)—Won Masterton Memorial Trophy.
(g)—March, 1980—Traded by Los Angeles Kings to New York Islanders for Billy Harris and Dave Lewis.
(h)—Winner of Conn Smythe Trophy (NHL Playoff MVP).

GUY GOSSELIN

Defense . . . 5'10" . . . 185 lbs. . . . Born, Rochester, Minn., January 6, 1964 . . . Shoots left . . . Son of Gordon Gosselin, a member of 1952 Ft. Francis, Ontario Allen Cup Champions.

Year	Team	League	Games	G.	A.	Pts.	Pen.
1981-82	Rochester J. Marshall H.L. (c)	Minn.H.S.	22	14	15	29	48
1982-83	Univ. of Minn.-Duluth	WCHA	4	0	0	0	0
1983-84	Univ. of Minn.-Duluth	WCHA	37	3	3	6	26

(c)—June, 1982—Drafted as underage player by Winnipeg Jets in 1982 NHL entry draft. Sixth Jets pick, 159th overall, eighth round.

ROBERT GOULD

Right Wing . . . 5'11" . . . 195 lbs. . . . Born, Petrolia, Ont., September 2, 1957 . . . Shoots right.

Year	Team	League	Games	G.	A.	Pts.	Pen.
1975-76	University of New Hampshire	ECAC	31	13	14	27	16
1976-77	University of New Hampshire (c)	ECAC	39	24	25	49	36
1977-78	University of New Hampshire	ECAC	30	23	34	57	40
1978-79	University of New Hampshire	ECAC	....	24	17	41	....
1978-79	Tulsa Oilers	CHL	5	2	0	2	4
1979-80	Atlanta Flames	NHL	1	0	0	0	0
1979-80	Birmingham Bulls	CHL	79	27	33	60	73
1980-81	Calgary Flames	NHL	3	0	0	0	0
1980-81	Birmingham Bulls	CHL	58	25	25	50	43
1980-81	Ft. Worth Texans	CHL	18	8	6	14	6
1981-82	Oklahoma City Stars	CHL	1	0	1	1	0
1981-82	Calgary Flames (d)	NHL	16	3	0	3	4
1981-82	Washington Capitals	NHL	60	18	13	31	69
1982-83	Washington Capitals	NHL	80	22	18	40	43
1983-84	Washington Capitals	NHL	78	21	19	40	74
	NHL TOTALS		239	64	50	114	190

(c)—June, 1977—Drafted by Atlanta Flames in 1977 amateur draft. Sixth Flames pick, 118th overall, seventh round.

(d)—November, 1981—Traded with Randy Holt by Calgary Flames to Washington Capitals for Pat Ribble.

MICHEL GOULET

Left Wing . . . 6'1" . . . 195 lbs. . . . Born, Peribonqua, Que., April 21, 1960 . . . Shoots left . . . Set Nordiques NHL record for most goals in a season in 1982-83 (57) . . . (1983-84) Set NHL record for most points by left wing in a season (121) and tied record for assists by a left wing (65) set by John Bucyk of Boston in 1970-71.

Year	Team	League	Games	G.	A.	Pts.	Pen.
1976-77—Quebec Remparts		QJHL	37	17	18	35	9
1977-78—Quebec Remparts (b-c)		QJHL	72	73	62	135	109
1978-79—Birmingham Bulls (d)		WHA	78	28	30	58	64
1979-80—Quebec Nordiques		NHL	77	22	32	54	48
1980-81—Quebec Nordiques		NHL	76	32	39	71	45
1981-82—Quebec Nordiques		NHL	80	42	42	84	48
1982-83—Quebec Nordiques (b)		NHL	80	57	48	105	51
1983-84—Quebec Nordiques (a)		NHL	75	56	65	121	76
WHA TOTALS			78	28	30	58	64
NHL TOTALS			388	209	226	435	268

(c)—Signed by Birmingham Bulls (WHA) as underage player, July, 1978.

(d)—August, 1979—Drafted by Quebec Nordiques in 1979 NHL entry draft. First Nordiques pick, 20th overall, first round.

THOMAS KJELL GRADIN

Center . . . 5'11" . . . 180 lbs. . . . Born, Solleftea, Sweden, February 18, 1956 . . . Shoots left . . . Attended G.I.H. University (Sweden) . . . Brother of Peter Gradin . . . Was member of Swedish National Team . . . Missed part of 1977-78 season with broken hand.

Year	Team	League	Games	G.	A.	Pts.	Pen.
1974-75—AIK		Sweden	29	16	15	31	16
1975-76—AIK (c)		Sweden	35	16	23	39	23
1976-77—AIK		Sweden	35	16	12	28	14
1977-78—Tre Kronor (National Team)		Sweden	26	5	2	7	....
1977-78—AIK (d)		Sweden	36	22	14	36	22
1978-79—Vancouver Canucks		NHL	76	20	31	51	22
1979-80—Vancouver Canucks		NHL	80	30	45	75	22
1980-81—Vancouver Canucks		NHL	79	21	48	69	34
1981-82—Vancouver Canucks		NHL	76	37	49	86	32
1982-83—Vancouver Canucks		NHL	80	32	54	86	61
1983-84—Vancouver Canucks		NHL	75	21	57	78	32
NHL TOTALS			466	161	284	445	203

(c)—Drafted from Sweden by Chicago Black Hawks in third round of 1976 amateur draft.

(d)—NHL rights traded to Vancouver Canucks by Chicago Black Hawks for second-round 1980 draft pick (Steve Ludzik), June, 1978.

DIRK GRAHAM

Right Wing . . . 5'11" . . . 190 lbs. . . . Born, Regina, Sask., July 29, 1959 . . . Shoots right.

Year	Team	League	Games	G.	A.	Pts.	Pen.
1975-76—Regina Blues		SJHL	54	36	32	68	82
1975-76—Regina Pats		WCHL	2	0	0	0	0
1976-77—Regina Pats		WCHL	65	37	28	65	66
1977-78—Regina Pats		WCHL	72	49	61	110	87
1978-79—Regina Pats (b-c)		WHL	71	48	60	108	252
1979-80—Dallas Black Hawks		CHL	62	17	15	32	96
1980-81—Fort Wayne Komets		IHL	6	1	2	3	12
1980-81—Toledo Goaldiggers		IHL	61	40	45	85	88
1981-82—Toledo Goaldiggers		IHL	72	49	56	105	68
1982-83—Toledo Goaldiggers (a-d)		IHL	78	70	55	125	86
1983-84—Minnesota North Stars		NHL	6	1	1	2	0
1983-84—Salt Lake Golden Eagles (a)		CHL	57	37	57	94	72
NHL TOTALS			6	1	1	2	0

(c)—August, 1979—Drafted by Vancouver Canucks in 1979 NHL entry draft. Fifth Canucks pick, 89th overall, fifth round.

(d)—Co-leader, with teammate Rick Hendricks, during IHL playoffs with 20 points.

PAT THOMAS GRAHAM

Left Wing . . . 6'1" . . . 180 lbs. . . . Born, Toronto, Ont., May 25, 1961 . . . Shoots left . . . Also plays center.

Year	Team	League	Games	G.	A.	Pts.	Pen.
1977-78—Toronto Marlboros		OMJHL	50	5	6	11	41
1978-79—Toronto Marlboros		OMJHL	49	10	12	22	102
1979-80—Toronto Marlboros		OMJHL	2	1	0	1	16
1979-80—Niagara Falls Flyers (c)		OMJHL	59	31	32	63	75
1980-81—Niagara Falls Flyers		OHL	61	40	54	94	118
1981-82—Erie Blades		AHL	9	4	4	8	4
1981-82—Pittsburgh Penguins		NHL	42	6	8	14	55
1982-83—Baltimore Skipjacks		AHL	57	16	16	32	32
1982-83—Pittsburgh Penguins (d)		NHL	20	1	5	6	16
1983-84—Toronto Maple Leafs		NHL	41	4	4	8	65
1983-84—St. Catharines Saints		AHL	25	7	7	14	18
NHL TOTALS			103	11	17	28	136

(c)—June, 1980—Drafted as underage junior by Pittsburgh Penguins in 1980 NHL entry draft. Fifth Penguins pick, 114th overall, sixth round.

(d)—August, 1983—Traded by Pittsburgh Penguins with Nick Ricci to Toronto Maple Leafs for Vince Tremblay and Rocky Saganiuk.

DAVID GRANNIS

Right Wing . . . 6' . . . 190 lbs. . . . Born, St. Paul, Minn., January 18, 1966 . . . Shoots right.

Year	Team	League	Games	G.	A.	Pts.	Pen.
1983-84—South St. Paul H.S. (c)		Minn. H.S.	20	20	23	43	14

(c)—June, 1984—Drafted by Los Angeles Kings in 1984 NHL entry draft. Fifth Kings pick, 87th overall, fifth round.

ALAN GLENN GRAVES

Left Wing . . . 6'1" . . . 182 lbs. . . . Born, Marseille, France, November 10, 1961 . . . Shoots left . . . Also plays Center and Right Wing.

Year	Team	League	Games	G.	A.	Pts.	Pen.
1978-79—Langley		BCJHL	6	0	0	0	4
1978-79—Kamloops Rockets		BCJHL	38	17	23	40	41
1978-79—Seattle Breakers		WHL	2	0	0	0	0
1979-80—Seattle Breakers (c)		WHL	70	41	20	61	68
1980-81—Seattle Breakers		WHL	69	47	43	90	98
1981-82—Saginaw Gears		IHL	55	14	11	25	89
1982-83—Saginaw Gears		IHL	32	7	9	16	76
1983-84—Milwaukee Admirals		IHL	3	0	0	0	2
1983-84—Peoria Prancers		IHL	28	6	4	10	75

(c)—June, 1980—Drafted as underage junior by Los Angeles Kings in 1980 NHL entry draft. Sixth Kings pick, 94th overall, fifth round.

STEVE GRAVES

Left Wing and Center . . . 6' . . . 180 lbs. . . . Born, Kingston, Ont., April 7, 1964 . . . Shoots left.

Year	Team	League	Games	G.	A.	Pts.	Pen.
1980-81—Ottawa Senators (c)		OPJHL	44	21	17	38	47
1981-82—Sault Ste. Marie Greyhounds (d)		OHL	66	12	15	27	49
1982-83—Sault Ste. Marie Greyhounds		OHL	60	21	20	41	48
1983-84—Sault Ste. Marie Greyhounds		OHL	67	41	48	89	47
1983-84—Edmonton Oilers		NHL	2	0	0	0	0
NHL TOTALS			2	0	0	0	0

(c)—May, 1981—Drafted by Sault Ste. Marie Greyhounds in OHL 1981 midget draft. First Greyhounds pick, 14th overall, first round.

(d)—June, 1982—Drafted as underage junior by Edmonton Oilers in 1982 NHL entry draft. Second Oilers pick, 41st overall, second round.

GUS GRECO

Center . . . 5'11" . . . 180 lbs. . . . Born, Sault Ste. Marie, Ont., April 7, 1963 . . . Shoots left.

Year	Team	League	Games	G.	A.	Pts.	Pen.
1979-80—Stratford Cullitons		OHA Jr. 'B'	28	8	14	22	78
1980-81—Windsor Spitfires (c)		OHL	60	20	24	44	65
1981-82—Windsor Spitfires		OHL	55	31	38	69	79
1982-83—Windsor Spitfires		OHL	4	2	1	3	9
1982-83—Sault Ste. Marie Greyhounds		OHL	56	25	32	57	89
1983-84—Sault Ste. Marie Greyhounds		OHL	48	17	30	47	84

(c)—June, 1981—Drafted as underage junior by Colorado Rockies in 1981 NHL entry draft. Fourth Rockies pick, 66th overall, fourth round.

MIKE GREEDER

Defense . . . 6' . . . 210 lbs. . . . Born, Mahtomedi, Minn., May 1, 1957 . . . Shoots left.

Year	Team	League	Games	G.	A.	Pts.	Pen.
1978-79—University of Minnesota (c)		WCHA	....	2	12	14	....
1979-80—Maine Mariners		AHL	66	3	12	15	105
1980-81—Maine Mariners		AHL	25	1	1	2	52
1980-81—Ft. Worth Texans		CHL	24	3	6	9	41
1980-81—Toledo Goaldiggers		IHL	27	6	11	17	68
1981-82—Toledo Goaldiggers (a)		IHL	76	14	30	44	236
1982-83—Indianapolis Checkers		CHL	56	9	19	28	127
1983-84—Toledo Goaldiggers (d)		IHL	75	10	22	32	250
1983-84—Indianapolis Checkers		CHL	1	0	0	0	2
1983-84—Salt Lake Golden Eagles		CHL	2	0	0	0	16

    (c)—June, 1977—Drafted by Philadelphia Flyers in 1977 NHL amateur draft. Eleventh Flyers pick, 139th overall, eighth round.
    (d)—Led IHL playoffs with 85 penalty minutes.

RICHARD DOUGLAS (RICK) GREEN

Defense . . . 6'3" . . . 200 lbs. . . . Born, Belleville, Ont., February 20, 1956 . . . Shoots left . . . Missed part of 1976-77 season with broken right wrist . . . (November, 1980)—Broken hand . . . (December 14, 1981)—Separated shoulder in game at Montreal . . . (March, 1983)—Hip injury . . . (October, 1983)—Broken right wrist . . . (February 21, 1984)—Broke rib in game at Buffalo.

Year	Team	League	Games	G.	A.	Pts.	Pen.
1972-73—London Knights		Jr."A"OHA	7	0	1	1	2
1973-74—London Knights		Jr."A"OHA	65	6	30	36	45
1974-75—London Knights		Jr."A"OHA	65	8	45	53	68
1975-76—London Knights (a-c-d)		Jr."A"OHA	61	13	47	60	69
1976-77—Washington Capitals		NHL	45	3	12	15	16
1977-78—Washington Capitals		NHL	60	5	14	19	67
1978-79—Washington Capitals		NHL	71	8	33	41	62
1979-80—Washington Capitals		NHL	71	4	20	24	52
1980-81—Washington Capitals		NHL	65	8	23	31	91
1981-82—Washington Capitals (e)		NHL	65	3	25	28	93
1982-83—Montreal Canadiens		NHL	66	2	24	26	58
1983-84—Montreal Canadiens		NHL	7	0	1	1	7
NHL TOTALS			450	33	152	185	446

    (c)—Won Max Kaminsky Memorial Trophy (Outstanding Defenseman).
    (d)—Drafted from London Knights by Washington Capitals in first round of 1976 amateur draft.
    (e)—September, 1982—Traded by Washington Capitals with Ryan Walter to Montreal Canadiens for Rod Langway, Brian Engblom, Doug Jarvis and Craig Laughlin.

SHAWN GREEN

Right Wing . . . 5'10" . . . 185 lbs. . . . Born, Drayton Valley, Alta., July 7, 1964 . . . Shoots right.

Year	Team	League	Games	G.	A.	Pts.	Pen.
1981-82—Victoria Cougars (c)		WHL	68	9	14	23	107
1982-83—Victoria Cougars		WHL	38	10	11	21	80
1982-83—Lethbridge Broncos		WHL	24	2	4	6	31
1983-84—Lethbridge Broncos		WHL	1	1	1	2	0
1983-84—New Westminster Bruins		WHL	58	12	14	26	115

    (c)—June, 1982—Drafted as underage junior by Vancouver Canucks in 1982 NHL entry draft. Tenth Canucks pick, 242nd overall, 12th round.

GLENN GREENOUGH

Right Wing . . . 5'11" . . . 195 lbs. . . . Born, Sudbury, Ont., July 20, 1966 . . . Shoots right.

Year	Team	League	Games	G.	A.	Pts.	Pen.
1982-83—Sudbury Wolves		OHL	60	10	9	19	9
1983-84—Sudbury Wolves (c)		OHL	67	26	43	69	33

    (c)—June, 1984—Drafted as underage junior by Chicago Black Hawks in 1984 NHL entry draft. Eighth Black Hawks pick, 153rd overall, eighth round.

RANDY GREGG

Defense . . . 6'4" . . . 215 lbs. . . . Born, Edmonton, Alta., February 19, 1956 . . . Shoots left . . . Attended University of Alberta . . . Has a degree in medicine . . . Furthered medical studies while he played hockey in Japan.

Year	Team	League	Games	G.	A.	Pts.	Pen.
1975-76—U. of Alberta	CWUAA	20	3	14	17	27
1976-77—U. of Alberta	CWUAA	24	9	17	26	34
1977-78—U. of Alberta	CWUAA	24	7	23	30	37
1978-79—U. of Alberta	CWUAA	24	5	16	21	47
1979-80—Canadian National Team	Int'l	56	7	17	24	36
1979-80—Canadian Olympic Team	Int'l	6	1	1	2	2
1980-81—Kokudo Bunnies (c)	Japan	35	12	18	30	30
1981-82—Kokudo Bunnies	Japan	36	12	20	32	25
1981-82—Edmonton Oilers (d)	NHL	....	...	....	....	....
1982-83—Edmonton Oilers	NHL	80	6	22	28	54
1983-84—Edmonton Oilers	NHL	80	13	27	40	56
NHL TOTALS		160	19	49	68	110

(c)—March, 1981—Signed by Edmonton Oilers as a free agent.
(d)—No regular-season record. Played in four playoff games.

RONALD JOHN GRESCHNER

Defense ... 6'2" ... 205 lbs.... Born, Goodsoil, Sask., December 22, 1954 ... Shoots left ... Set WCHL record for points by defenseman in season in 1973-74 (broken by Kevin McCarthy in 1975-76) ... Missed part of 1978-79 season with shoulder separation ... (November 18, 1981)—Pinched nerve in back during game vs. Philadelphia ... (September, 1982)—Injured back in training camp, out until February, 1983 ... (March, 1983)—Reinjured back.

Year	Team	League	Games	G.	A.	Pts.	Pen.
1971-72—New Westminster Bruins	WCHL	44	1	9	10	126
1972-73—New Westminster Bruins	WCHL	68	22	47	69	169
1973-74—New Westminster Bruins (c)	WCHL	67	33	70	103	170
1974-75—Providence Reds	AHL	7	5	6	11	10
1974-75—New York Rangers	NHL	70	8	37	45	94
1975-76—New York Rangers	NHL	77	6	21	27	93
1976-77—New York Rangers	NHL	80	11	36	47	89
1977-78—New York Rangers	NHL	78	24	48	72	100
1978-79—New York Rangers	NHL	60	17	36	53	66
1979-80—New York Rangers	NHL	76	21	37	58	103
1980-81—New York Rangers	NHL	74	27	41	68	112
1981-82—New York Rangers	NHL	29	5	11	16	16
1982-83—New York Rangers	NHL	10	3	5	8	0
1983-84—New York Rangers	NHL	77	12	44	56	117
NHL TOTALS		631	134	316	450	790

(c)—Drafted from New Westminster Bruins by New York Rangers in second round of 1974 amateur draft.

WAYNE GRETZKY

Center ... 6' ... 170 lbs.... Born, Brantford, Ont., January 26, 1961 ... Shoots left ... In 1979-80, his first NHL season, he became the youngest player in history to win an NHL trophy, to score 50 goals, to collect 100 points and the youngest to ever be named to the NHL All-Star team ... Set new NHL records for assists (109) and points (164) in a single season in 1980-81, most assists (123) and most points (185) regular season plus playoffs in 1980-81, and tied single game record in playoffs for most assists in a period (3), and a game (5), in first game of 1981 playoffs (April 8, 1981) in a 6-3 win at Montreal despite not taking a single shot on goal ... Set NHL records for goals (92), assists (120) and points (212) in a single season in 1981-82, and most goals (97), assists (127) and points (224) in regular season plus playoffs. In 1981-82, also set NHL records for fastest 50 goals from the start of the year (39 games), fastest 500 career points (234 games), largest margin over second-place finisher in scoring race (65 points) and most 3-or-more-goals in a season (10) ... (December 27, 1981)—Became first hockey player to be named THE SPORTING NEWS MAN-OF-THE-YEAR ... (March 19, 1982)—Youngest player to reach 500 NHL-career points (21 years, 1 month, 21 days) ... Set NHL record with points in 30 consecutive games in 1982-83. It was the first 30 games of the season; he had also collected points in the final nine games of '81-82 ... Set NHL assist record with 125 in 1982-83 ... First player to have 100 point seasons in first four years in NHL ... (Feb. 8/83) Set All-Star game record with four goals ... Set Stanley Cup record for assists (26) and points (38) in one year (1983) ... Set NHL record in 1982-83 for most assists (151) and points (234) in regular season plus playoffs ... (October 5, 1983-January 27, 1984)—Set NHL record by collecting points in 51 consecutive games (61g, 92a), the first 51 games of the season ... (January 28, 1984)—Bruised right shoulder in game vs. Los Angeles and ended consecutive games played streak at 362, an Oilers club record ... (June, 1984)—Surgery on left ankle to remove benign growth caused by lacing his skates too tight ... Tied his own NHL record for most 3-or-more goal games in a season (10 in '83-84) ... Set NHL record for most shorthanded goals in a season (12 in '83-84) ... (November 26, 1983-January 4, 1984)—Set NHL record for collecting assists in 17 straight games.

Year	Team	League	Games	G.	A.	Pts.	Pen.
1976-77—Peterborough Petes		OMJHL	3	0	3	3	0
1977-78—S. Ste. M. G'hounds (b-c)		OMJHL	64	70	112	182	14
1978-79—Indianapolis Racers (d)		WHA	8	3	3	6	0
1978-79—Edmonton Oilers (b-e-f-g)		WHA	72	43	61	104	19
1979-80—Edmonton Oilers (b-h-i)		NHL	79	51	*86	*137	21
1980-81—Edmonton Oilers (a-h-j-l-m)		NHL	80	55	*109	*164	28
1981-82—Edmonton Oilers (a-h-j-l-m)		NHL	80	*92	*120	*212	26
1982-83—Edmonton Oilers (a-j-h-k-l-m)		NHL	80	*71	*125	*196	59
1983-84—Edmonton Oilers (a-h-j-l-m-n)		NHL	74	^87	*118	*205	39
NHL TOTALS			393	356	558	914	173
WHA TOTALS			80	46	64	110	19

(c)—Signed to multi-year contract by Indianapolis Racers (WHA) as an underage junior, May, 1978.

(d)—November, 1978—Traded by Indianapolis to Edmonton with Peter Driscoll, Ed Mio for cash and future considerations.

(e)—Won WHA Rookie award.

(f)—Named WHA Rookie of the Year in poll of players by THE SPORTING NEWS.

(g)—Led in points (20) and tied for lead in goals (10) during playoffs.

(h)—Won Hart Memorial Trophy.

(i)—Won Lady Byng Memorial Trophy.

(j)—Won Art Ross Memorial Trophy (NHL Leading Scorer).

(k)—Led Stanley Cup Playoffs with 26 assists and 38 points.

(l)—Selected NHL Player of Year by The Sporting News in poll of players.

(m)—Named Canadian Press Athlete of the Year.

(n)—Led Stanley Cup Playoffs with 22 assists and 35 points.

KEVIN GRIFFIN

Left Wing . . . 6'2" . . . 195 lbs. . . . Born, London, England, May 14, 1963 . . . Shoots left.

Year	Team	League	Games	G.	A.	Pts.	Pen.
1979-80—Point Grey		Midget	48	37	31	68	94
1979-80—Portland Winter Hawks		WHL	1	0	0	0	0
1980-81—Portland Winter Hawks (c)		WHL	64	24	18	42	110
1981-82—Portland Winter Hawks		WHL	65	27	23	50	136
1982-83—Portland Winter Hawks (d)		WHL	32	17	14	31	66
1982-83—Nanaimo Islanders		WHL	27	13	17	30	56
1983-84—New Westminster Bruins		WHL	9	5	5	10	33

(c)—June, 1981—Drafted as underage junior by Chicago Black Hawks in 1981 NHL entry draft. Second Black Hawks pick, 25th overall, second round.

(d)—January, 1983—Traded with Darwin Penny, Darcy Allison and player to be named later by Portland Winter Hawks to Nanaimo Islanders for Alfie Turcotte (Son of Nanaimo coach, Real Turcotte).

STUART GRIMSON

Left Wing . . . 6'5" . . . 210 lbs. . . . Born, Vancouver, B.C., May 20, 1965 . . . Shoots left . . . (February, 1983)—Fractured forearm.

Year	Team	League	Games	G.	A.	Pts.	Pen.
1982-83—Regina Pats (c)		WHL	48	0	1	1	144
1983-84—Regina Pats		WHL	63	8	8	16	131

(c)—June, 1983—Drafted as underage junior by Detroit Red Wings in 1983 NHL entry draft. Eleventh Red Wings pick, 186th overall, 10th round.

WAYNE GROULX

Center . . . 5'9" . . . 175 lbs. . . . Born, Welland, Ont., February 2, 1965 . . . Shoots right.

Year	Team	League	Games	G.	A.	Pts.	Pen.
1981-82—Sault Ste. Marie Greyhounds		OHL	66	25	41	66	66
1982-83—Sault Ste. Marie Greyhounds (c)		OHL	67	44	86	130	549
1983-84—Sault Ste. Marie Greyhounds (b-d)		OHL	70	59	78	137	48

(c)—June, 1983—Drafted as underage junior by Quebec Nordiques in 1983 NHL entry draft. Eighth Nordiques pick, 172nd overall, ninth round.

(d)—Shared OHL playoff lead with teammate Rick Tochet with 36 points.

SCOTT KENNETH GRUHL

Left Wing . . . 5'11" . . . 185 lbs. . . . Born, Port Colborne, Ont., September 13, 1959 . . . Shoots left . . . Also plays defense.

Year	Team	League	Games	G.	A.	Pts.	Pen.
1976-77—Northeastern University		ECAC	17	6	4	10	....
1977-78—Northeastern University		ECAC	28	21	38	59	46
1978-79—Sudbury Wolves		OMJHL	68	35	49	84	78

Year	Team	League	Games	G.	A.	Pts.	Pen.
1979-80—Binghamton Dusters	AHL	4	1	0	1	6
1979-80—Saginaw Gears (b-c)	IHL	75	53	40	93	100
1980-81—Houston Apollos	CHL	4	0	0	0	0
1980-81—Saginaw Gears (d)	IHL	77	56	34	90	87
1981-82—New Haven Nighthawks	AHL	73	28	41	69	107
1981-82—Los Angeles Kings	NHL	7	2	1	3	2
1982-83—New Haven Nighthawks	AHL	68	25	38	63	114
1982-83—Los Angeles Kings	NHL	7	0	2	2	4
1983-84—Muskegon Mohawks (a)	IHL	56	40	56	96	49
NHL TOTALS		14	2	3	5	6

(c)—September, 1980—Signed by Los Angeles Kings as free agent.
(d)—Led IHL playoff with 11 goals and 19 assists.

BRIAN GUALAZZI

Center and Right Wing . . . 6' . . . 195 lbs. . . . Born, Sault Ste. Marie, November 9, 1959 . . . Shoots left.

Year	Team	League	Games	G.	A.	Pts.	Pen.
1977-78—Sault Ste. Marie Greyhounds	OMJHL	46	11	10	21	26
1978-79—Sault Ste. Marie Greyhounds (c)	OMJHL	68	*74	60	134	42
1979-80—Dalhousie University	CCAC	....	...	....	....	....
1980-81—Dalhousie University	CCAC	23	20	19	39	....
1981-82—Dalhousie University	CCAC	....	...	....	....	....
1982-83—Dalhousie University	CCAC	....	...	....	....	....
1983-84—Salt Lake Golden Eagles	CHL	20	2	0	2	2

(c)—August, 1979—Drafted by Minnesota North Stars in 1979 NHL entry draft. Sixth North Stars pick, 111th overall, sixth round.

PAUL GUAY

Right Wing . . . 6' . . . 185 lbs. . . . Born, Providence, R.I., September 2, 1963 . . . Shoots right . . . Member of 1984 U.S. Olympic Team.

Year	Team	League	Games	G.	A.	Pts.	Pen.
1979-80—Mt. St. Charles H.S.	R.I.H.S.	23	18	19	37	....
1980-81—Mt. St. Charles H.S. (c)	R.I.H.S.	23	28	38	66	....
1981-82—Providence College	ECAC	33	23	17	40	38
1982-83—Providence College (b)	ECAC	42	34	31	65	83
1983-84—U.S. National Team	Int'l	62	20	18	38	44
1983-84—U.S. Olympic Team	Int'l	6	1	0	1	8
1983-84—Philadelphia Flyers (d)	NHL	14	2	6	8	14
NHL TOTALS		14	2	6	8	14

(c)—June, 1981—Drafted as underage player by Minnesota North Stars in 1981 NHL entry draft. Tenth North Stars pick, 118th overall, sixth round.
(d)—February, 1984—Traded with third round 1985 draft pick by Minnesota North Stars to Philadelphia Flyers for Paul Holmgren.

BENGT-AKE GUSTAFSSON

Left Wing . . . 6' . . . 185 lbs. . . . Born, Karlskoga, Sweden, March 23, 1958 . . . Shoots left . . . (November 12, 1980)—Cervical strain in back in game at Pittsburgh . . . (December 23, 1981)—Pulled tendons in right ankle in game vs. Boston . . . (March 17, 1984)—Partial tear of medial collateral ligament of left knee in game at New York Islanders.

Year	Team	League	Games	G.	A.	Pts.	Pen.
1977-78—Farjestads (c)	Sweden	32	15	10	25	10
1978-79—Farjestads	Sweden	32	13	11	24	10
1978-79—Edmonton Oilers (d-e)	WHA	....	...	....	....	....
1979-80—Washington Capitals	NHL	80	22	38	60	17
1980-81—Washington Capitals	NHL	72	21	34	55	26
1981-82—Washington Capitals	NHL	70	26	34	60	40
1982-83—Washington Capitals	NHL	67	22	42	64	16
1983-84—Washington Capitals	NHL	69	32	43	75	16
NHL TOTALS		358	123	191	314	115

(c)—June, 1978—Drafted by Washington Capitals in NHL amateur draft. Seventh Washington pick, 55th overall, fourth round.
(d)—April, 1979—Signed by Edmonton Oilers. Played in two playoff games before being ruled ineligible by WHA office.
(e)—September, 1979—After being priority selection by Edmonton Oilers in NHL expansion draft in June, NHL President overturned case and ruled that Gustafsson was legally property of Washington Capitals because of rules governing expansion proceedings.

KEVAN GUY

Defense ... 6'2" ... 190 lbs. ... Born, Edmonton, Alta., July 16, 1965 ... Shoots right.

Year	Team	League	Games	G.	A.	Pts.	Pen.
1982-83	Medicine Hat Tigers (c)	WHL	69	7	20	27	89
1983-84	Medicine Hat Tigers	WHL	72	15	42	57	117

(c)—June, 1983—Drafted as underage junior by Calgary Flames in 1983 NHL entry draft. Fifth Flames pick, 71st overall, fourth round.

MARC JOSEPH HABSCHEID

Center ... 6'2" ... 180 lbs. ... Born, Swift Current, Sask., March 1, 1963 ... Shoots right ... (November, 1982)—Head injury.

Year	Team	League	Games	G.	A.	Pts.	Pen.
1980-81	Saskatoon Blades (c)	WHL	72	34	63	97	50
1981-82	Saskatoon Blades (b)	WHL	55	64	87	151	74
1981-82	Edmonton Oilers	NHL	7	1	3	4	2
1981-82	Wichita Wind (d)	CHL	..	..	..	..	..
1982-83	Kamloops Junior Oilers	WHL	6	7	16	23	8
1982-83	Edmonton Oilers	NHL	32	3	10	13	14
1983-84	Edmonton Oilers	NHL	9	1	0	1	6
1983-84	Moncton Alpines	AHL	71	19	37	56	32
	NHL TOTALS		48	5	13	18	22

(c)—June, 1981—Drafted as underage junior by Edmonton Oilers in 1981 NHL entry draft. Sixth Oilers pick, 113th overall, sixth round.

(d)—No regular season record. Played three playoff games.

LEONARD HACHBORN

Center ... 5'10" ... 171 lbs. ... Born, Brantford, Ont., September 9, 1961 ... Shoots left ... (December, 1982)—Knee injury.

Year	Team	League	Games	G.	A.	Pts.	Pen.
1979-80	Hamilton Tier II	OPJHL	43	25	20	45	42
1980-81	Brantford Alexanders (c)	OHL	66	34	52	86	94
1981-82	Brantford Alexanders	OHL	55	43	50	93	141
1982-83	Maine Mariners	AHL	75	28	55	83	32
1983-84	Springfield Indians	AHL	28	18	42	60	15
1983-84	Philadelphia Flyers	NHL	38	11	21	32	4
	NHL TOTALS		38	11	21	32	4

(c)—June, 1981—Drafted by Philadelphia Flyers in 1981 NHL entry draft. Twelfth Flyers pick, 184th overall, ninth round.

ROGER HAGGLUND

Defense ... 6'1" ... 191 lbs. ... Born, Bjorkloven, Sweden, July 2, 1961 ... Shoots right.

Year	Team	League	Games	G.	A.	Pts.	Pen.
1983-84	Bjorkloven (c-d)	Sweden	..	..	..	..	..

(c)—June, 1980—Drafted by St. Louis Blues in NHL entry draft. Sixth Blues pick, 138th overall, seventh round.

(d)—July, 1984—Sold by St. Louis Blues to Quebec Nordiques.

ALEC HAIDY

Right Wing ... 6' ... 175 lbs. ... Born, Windsor, Ont., January 1, 1965 ... Shoots right ... (February, 1978)—Spinal fusion surgery ... Son of Gordon Haidy (Detroit Red Wings, 1949-50 season).

Year	Team	League	Games	G.	A.	Pts.	Pen.
1981-82	Windsor Royals	OHA Jr. 'B'	30	8	16	24	201
1982-83	Sault Ste. Marie Greyhounds (c)	OHL	58	3	12	15	86
1983-84	Sault Ste. Marie Greyhounds	OHL	54	17	20	37	121

(c)—June, 1983—Drafted as underage junior by Pittsburgh Penguins in 1983 NHL entry draft. Eighth Penguins pick, 183rd overall, 10th round.

RICHARD HAJDU

Left Wing ... 6' ... 175 lbs. ... Born, Victoria, B.C., April 10, 1965 ... Shoots left.

Year	Team	League	Games	G.	A.	Pts.	Pen.
1981-82	Kamloops Junior Oilers	WHL	64	19	21	40	50

Year	Team	League	Games	G.	A.	Pts.	Pen.
1982-83—Kamloops Junior Oilers (c-d)		WHL	70	22	36	58	101
1983 84 Victoria Cougars		WHL	42	17	10	27	106

(c)—June, 1983—Drafted as underage junior by Buffalo Sabres in 1983 NHL entry draft. Fifth Sabres pick, 34th overall, second round.

(d)—July, 1983—Traded with Doug Kostynski by Kamloops Junior Oilers to Victoria Cougars for Ron Viglasi and Brian Bertuzzi.

WILLIAM ALBERT HAJT

Defense . . . 6'3" . . . 204 lbs. . . . Born, Radisson, Sask., November 18, 1951 . . . Shoots left . . . (November 8, 1980)—Broken bone in right foot.

Year	Team	League	Games	G.	A.	Pts.	Pen.
1967-68—Saskatoon Blades		WCJHL	60	4	10	14	35
1968-69—Saskatoon Blades		WCHL	60	3	18	21	54
1969-70—Saskatoon Blades		WCHL	60	10	21	31	40
1970-71—Saskatoon Blades (c)		WCHL	66	19	53	72	50
1971-72—Did not play			....	...	....	....	....
1972-73—Cincinnati Swords		AHL	69	4	31	35	40
1973-74—Cincinnati Swords		AHL	66	5	30	35	66
1973-74—Buffalo Sabres		NHL	6	0	2	2	0
1974-75—Buffalo Sabres		NHL	76	3	26	29	68
1975-76—Buffalo Sabres		NHL	80	6	21	27	48
1976-77—Buffalo Sabres		NHL	79	6	20	26	56
1977-78—Buffalo Sabres		NHL	76	4	18	22	30
1978-79—Buffalo Sabres		NHL	40	3	8	11	20
1979-80—Buffalo Sabres		NHL	75	4	12	16	24
1980-81—Buffalo Sabres		NHL	68	2	19	21	42
1981-82—Buffalo Sabres		NHL	65	2	9	11	44
1982-83—Buffalo Sabres		NHL	72	0	12	13	28
1983-84—Buffalo Sabres (d)		NHL	79	3	24	27	32
NHL TOTALS			706	36	171	207	390

(c)—Drafted from Saskatoon Blades by Buffalo Sabres in third round of 1971 amateur draft.

(d)—September/October, 1983—Announced intention to retire but changed his mind before the end of the Sabres' training camp.

STEVE HAKALA

Left Wing . . . 6'1" . . . 200 lbs. . . . Born, Peterborough, N.H., August 15, 1960 . . . Shoots left . . . Also plays Center . . . (February, 1983)—Knee injury . . . (March, 1983)—Sprained ankle.

Year	Team	League	Games	G.	A.	Pts.	Pen.
1981-82—Merrimack College (c)		ECAC-II	39	21	29	50	70
1982-83—Tulsa Oilers		CHL	69	12	14	26	30
1978-79—Merrimack College		ECAC-II	5	0	0	0	0
1979-80—Merrimack College		ECAC-II	38	9	17	26	26
1980-81—Merrimack College		ECAC-II	33	4	18	22	34
1983-84—Tulsa Oilers		CHL	40	4	7	11	6

(c)—July, 1982—Signed by New York Rangers as a free agent.

ANDERS HAKANSSON

Left Wing . . . 6'2" . . . 191 lbs. . . . Born, Munkfors, Sweden, April 27, 1956 . . . Shoots left . . . (October, 1981)—Shoulder separation . . . Member of Team Sweden in 1981 Canada Cup.

Year	Team	League	Games	G.	A.	Pts.	Pen.
1979-80—Solna AIK		Sweden	36	9	11	20	12
1980-81—Solna AIK (c)		Sweden	22	5	11	16	18
1981-82—Minnesota North Stars		NHL	72	12	4	16	29
1982-83—Minnesota North Stars (d)		NHL	5	0	0	0	9
1982-83—Pittsburgh Penguins		NHL	62	9	12	21	26
1983-84—Los Angeles Kings (e)		NHL	80	15	17	32	41
NHL TOTALS			219	36	33	69	105

(c)—July, 1981—Signed by Minnesota North Stars as a free agent.

(d)—October, 1982—Traded by Minnesota North Stars with Ron Meighan and first-round draft pick in 1983 (Pittsburgh drafted Bob Errey) to Pittsburgh Penguins for George Ferguson and first-round draft pick in 1983 (Minnesota drafted Brian Lawton).

(e)—September, 1983—Traded by Pittsburgh Penguins to Los Angeles Kings for the NHL rights to Kevin Stevens.

BOB HALKIDIS

Defense . . .5'11" . . . 195 lbs. . . . Born, Toronto, Ont., March 5, 1966 . . . Shoots left . . . (September, 1982)—Broke ankle during training camp. In first game back, in November, he reinjured ankle and missed another two weeks.

Year	Team	League	Games	G.	A.	Pts.	Pen.
1981-82—Toronto Young Nationals		MTMHL	40	9	27	36	54
1982-83—London Knights		OHL	37	3	12	15	52
1983-84—London Knights (c)		OHL	51	9	22	31	123

(c)—June, 1984—Drafted as underage junior by Buffalo Sabres in 1984 NHL entry draft. Fourth Sabres pick, 81st overall, fourth round.

TAYLOR HALL

Left Wing . . . 5'11' . . . 177 lbs. . . . Born, Regina, Sask., February 20, 1964 . . . Shoots left.

Year	Team	League	Games	G.	A.	Pts.	Pen.
1980-81—Regina Canadians		Midget	26	51	28	79	35
1981-82—Regina Pats (c)		WHL	48	14	15	29	43
1982-83—Regina Pats		WHL	72	37	57	94	78
1983-84—Regina Pats (a-d)		WHL	69	63	79	142	42
1983-84—Vancouver Canucks		NHL	4	1	0	1	0
NHL TOTALS			4	1	0	1	0

(c)—June, 1982—Drafted as underage junior by Vancouver Canucks in 1982 NHL entry draft. Fourth Canucks pick, 116th overall, sixth round.

(d)—Shared WHL playoff goal-scoring lead (21) with Dean Evason of Kamloops.

MATS HALLIN

Left Wing . . . 6'2" . . . 202 lbs. . . . Born, Eskilstuna, Sweden, March 19, 1958 . . . Shoots left . . . (October, 1981)—Shoulder injury . . . Also plays right wing.

Year	Team	League	Games	G.	A.	Pts.	Pen.
1980-81—Swedish Nationals (c)		Sweden	....	...	....	....	....
1980-81—Sodertalje SK (d)		Sweden	33	9	11	20	86
1981-82—Indianapolis Checkers		CHL	63	25	32	57	113
1982-83—Indianapolis Checkers		CHL	42	26	27	53	86
1982-83—New York Islanders		NHL	30	7	7	14	26
1983-84—New York Islanders		NHL	40	2	5	7	27
NHL TOTALS			70	9	12	21	53

(c)—June, 1978—Drafted by Washington Capitals in 1978 NHL amateur draft. Tenth Capitals pick, 105th overall, seventh round.

(d)—June, 1981—Signed by New York Islanders as a free agent.

DOUGLAS ROBERT HALWARD

Defense . . . 6'1" . . . 198 lbs. . . . Born, Toronto, Ont., November 1, 1955 . . . Shoots left . . . Missed part of 1979-80 season with a bruised shoulder . . . (December, 1983)—Fractured ankle.

Year	Team	League	Games	G.	A.	Pts.	Pen.
1973-74—Peterborough TPTs		Jr."A"OHA	69	1	15	16	103
1974-75—Peterborough TPTs (c)		Jr."A"OHA	68	11	52	63	97
1975-76—Rochester Americans		AHL	54	6	11	17	51
1975-76—Boston Bruins		NHL	22	1	5	6	6
1976-77—Rochester Americans		AHL	54	4	28	32	26
1976-77—Boston Bruins		NHL	18	2	2	4	6
1977-78—Rochester Americans		AHL	42	8	14	22	17
1977-78—Boston Bruins (d)		NHL	25	0	2	2	2
1978-79—Los Angeles Kings		NHL	27	1	5	6	13
1978-79—Springfield Indians		AHL	14	5	1	6	10
1979-80—Los Angeles Kings		NHL	63	11	45	56	52
1980-81—Los Angeles Kings (e)		NHL	51	4	15	19	96
1980-81—Vancouver Canucks		NHL	7	0	1	1	4
1981-82—Dallas Black Hawks		CHL	22	8	18	26	49
1981-82—Vancouver Canucks		NHL	37	4	13	17	40
1982-83—Vancouver Canucks		NHL	75	19	33	52	83
1983-84—Vancouver Canucks		NHL	54	7	16	23	35
NHL TOTALS			379	49	137	186	337

(c)—Drafted from Peterborough TPTs by Boston Bruins in first round of 1975 amateur draft.

(d)—Traded to Los Angeles Kings by Boston Bruins for "future considerations," September, 1978.

(e)—March, 1981—Traded by Los Angeles Kings to Vancouver Canucks for future considerations. (Canucks sent goaltender Gary Bromley to Kings to complete deal, June, 1981.)

GILLES HAMEL

Left Wing . . . 6' . . . 183 lbs. . . . Born, Asbestos, Que., March 18, 1960 . . . Shoots left . . . (January, 1981)—Knee Injury . . . Brother of Jean Hamel.

Year	Team	League	Games	G.	A.	Pts.	Pen.
1977-78—Laval National		QMJHL	72	44	37	81	68
1978-79—Laval National (b-c)		QMJHL	72	56	55	111	130
1979-80—Trois-Rivieres Draveurs		QMJHL	12	13	8	21	8
1979-80—Chicoutimi Sagueneens (a)		QMJHL	58	78	62	135	87
1979-80—Rochester Americans (d)		AHL	...	...	...	...	...
1980-81—Rochester Americans		AHL	14	8	7	15	7
1980-81—Buffalo Sabres		NHL	51	10	9	19	53
1981-82—Rochester Americans		AHL	57	31	44	75	55
1981-82—Buffalo Sabres		NHL	16	2	7	9	2
1982-83—Buffalo Sabres		NHL	66	22	20	42	26
1983-84—Buffalo Sabres		NHL	75	21	23	44	37
NHL TOTALS			208	55	59	114	118

(c)—August, 1979—Drafted by Buffalo Sabres as underage junior in entry draft. Fifth Sabres pick, 74th overall, fourth round.

(d)—No league record. Appeared in one playoff game.

JEAN HAMEL

Defense . . . 5'11" . . . 195 lbs. . . . Born, Asbestos, Que., June 6, 1952 . . . Shoots left . . . Missed start of 1973-74 season with mononucleosis . . . Missed part of 1978-79 season with severed tendon and damaged nerves in middle finger of right hand . . . (January, 1980)— Cracked tailbone vs. Colorado . . . Brother of Gilles Hamel . . . (December 30, 1982)—Broke jaw in exhibition game vs. USSR . . . (December 4, 1983)—Sprained knee in game at Buffalo.

Year	Team	League	Games	G.	A.	Pts.	Pen.
1970-71—Drummondville Rangers		QJHL	61	7	23	30	109
1971-72—Drummondville Rangers (b-c-d)		QJHL	59	6	29	35	132
1972-73—Denver Spurs		WHL	13	0	6	6	22
1972-73—St. Louis Blues		NHL	55	2	7	9	24
1973-74—Denver Spurs		WHL	10	0	2	2	12
1973-74—St. Louis Blues (e)		NHL	23	1	1	2	6
1973-74—Detroit Red Wings		NHL	22	0	3	3	40
1974-75—Detroit Red Wings		NHL	80	5	19	24	136
1975-76—Detroit Red Wings		NHL	77	3	9	12	129
1976-77—Detroit Red Wings		NHL	71	1	10	11	63
1977-78—Kansas City Red Wings		CHL	28	2	10	12	29
1977-78—Detroit Red Wings		NHL	32	2	6	8	34
1978-79—Detroit Red Wings		NHL	52	2	4	6	72
1979-80—Detroit Red Wings		NHL	49	1	4	5	43
1980-81—Detroit Red Wings		NHL	68	5	7	12	57
1980-81—Adirondack Red Wings		AHL	7	1	3	4	36
1981-82—Quebec Nordiques (f)		NHL	40	1	6	7	32
1981-82—Fredericton Express		AHL	16	2	4	6	19
1982-83—Quebec Nordiques		NHL	51	2	7	9	38
1983-84—Montreal Canadiens (g)		NHL	79	1	12	13	92
NHL TOTALS			699	26	95	121	766

(c)—Selected by Quebec Nordiques in World Hockey Association player selection draft, February, 1972.

(d)—Drafted from Drummondville Rangers by St. Louis Blues in third round of 1972 amateur draft.

(e)—Traded to Detroit Red Wings by St. Louis Blues with Chris Evans and Bryan Watson for Garnet Bailey, Billy Collins and Ted Harris, February, 1974.

(f)—October, 1981—Signed by Quebec Nordiques as a free agent.

(g)—October, 1983—Selected by Montreal Canadiens in 1983 NHL waiver draft.

JIM HAMILTON

Right Wing . . . 6' . . . 183 lbs. . . . Born, Barrie, Ont., January 18, 1957 . . . Shoots left . . . Pulled groin (March, 1980) . . . (November, 1980)—Ankle Injury . . . Also plays left wing . . . (November, 1982)—Knee Injury.

Year	Team	League	Games	G.	A.	Pts.	Pen.
1973-74—London Knights		Jr."A"OHA	70	9	14	23	19
1974-75—London Knights		Jr."A"OHA	68	17	24	41	108
1975-76—London Knights		Jr."A"OHA	53	24	23	47	37
1976-77—London Knights (c)		Jr."A"OHA	65	39	53	92	40
1977-78—Binghamton Dusters		AHL	31	4	4	8	19
1977-78—Grand Rapids Owls		IHL	22	7	15	22	12
1977-78—Pittsburgh Penguins		NHL	25	2	4	6	2

Year	Team	League	Games	G.	A.	Pts.	Pen.
1978-79—Pittsburgh Penguins		NHL	2	0	0	0	0
1978-79—Binghamton Dusters		AHL	66	25	24	49	34
1979-80—Pittsburgh Penguins		NHL	10	2	0	2	0
1979-80—Syracuse Firebirds		AHL	50	16	19	35	33
1980-81—Binghamton Whalers		AHL	28	16	18	34	31
1980-81—Pittsburgh Penguins		NHL	20	1	6	7	18
1981-82—Erie Blades		AHL	57	27	17	44	51
1981-82—Pittsburgh Penguins		NHL	11	5	3	8	2
1982-83—Pittsburgh Penguins		NHL	5	0	2	2	2
1982-83—Baltimore Skipjacks		AHL	45	32	10	42	36
1983-84—Baltimore Skipjacks		AHL	66	34	45	79	54
1983-84—Pittsburgh Penguins		NHL	11	2	2	4	4
NHL TOTALS			84	12	17	29	28

(c)—Drafted from London Knights by Pittsburgh Penguins in second round of 1977 amateur draft.

KEN HAMMOND

Defense . . . 6'1" . . . 190 lbs. . . . Born, London, Ont., August 23, 1963 . . . Shoots left.

Year	Team	League	Games	G.	A.	Pts.	Pen.
1981-82—R.P.I.		ECAC	29	2	3	5	54
1982-83—R.P.I. (c)		ECAC	28	4	13	17	54
1983-84—R.P.I.		ECAC	34	5	11	16	72

(c)—June, 1983—Drafted by Los Angeles Kings in 1983 NHL entry draft. Eighth Kings pick, 147th overall, eighth round.

GORD HAMPSON

Left Wing . . . 6'3" . . . 210 lbs. . . . Born, Vancouver, B.C., February 13, 1959 . . . Shoots left . . . (January, 1983)—Wrist injury.

Year	Team	League	Games	G.	A.	Pts.	Pen.
1977-78—University of Michigan		WCHA	36	9	7	16	21
1978-79—University of Michigan		WCHA	36	6	6	12	24
1979-80—University of Michigan		WCHA	30	7	15	22	22
1980-81—University of Michigan (c)		WCHA	40	15	23	38	40
1981-82—Oklahoma City Stars		CHL	71	11	23	34	48
1982-83—Colorado Flames		CHL	51	17	17	34	73
1982-83—Calgary Flames		NHL	4	0	0	0	5
1983-84—Colorado Flames		CHL	62	19	25	44	89
NHL TOTALS			4	0	0	0	5

(c)—June, 1981—Signed as a free agent by Calgary Flames.

MARK HAMWAY

Right Wing . . . 5'11" . . . 169 lbs. . . . Born, Detroit, Mich., August 9, 1961 . . . Shoots right.

Year	Team	League	Games	G.	A.	Pts.	Pen.
1977-78—Adray Nationals Detroit		Midget	75	70	90	160	....
1978-79—Windsor Spitfires		OMJHL	66	27	42	69	29
1979-80—Michigan State University (c)		WCHA	38	16	28	44	28
1980-81—Michigan State University		WCHA	35	18	15	33	20
1981-82—Michigan State University		CCHA	41	34	31	65	37
1982-83—Michigan State University		CCHA	42	30	29	59	16
1983-84—Indianapolis Checkers		CHL	71	22	32	54	38

(c)—June, 1980—Drafted as underage player by New York Islanders in 1980 NHL entry draft. Eighth Islanders pick, 143rd overall, seventh round.

RON HANDY

Left Wing . . . 5'11" . . . 165 lbs. . . . Born, Toronto, Ont., January 15, 1963 . . . Shoots left . . . (January, 1984)—Broken nose in CHL game.

Year	Team	League	Games	G.	A.	Pts.	Pen.
1979-80—Toronto Marlboro Midgets		Midget	39	48	60	108	....
1980-81—Sault Ste. Marie Greyhounds (c)		OHL	66	43	43	86	45
1981-82—Sault Ste. Marie		OHL	20	15	10	25	20
1981-82—Kingston Canadians		OHL	44	35	38	73	23
1982-83—Kingston Canadians		OHL	67	52	96	148	64
1982-83—Indianapolis Checkers		CHL	9	2	7	9	0
1983-84—Indianapolis Checkers (b)		CHL	66	29	46	75	40

(c)—June, 1981—Drafted as underage junior by New York Islanders in 1981 NHL entry draft. Third Islanders pick, 57th overall, third round.

ALAN HANGSLEBEN

Defense and Left Wing . . . 6'1" . . . 195 lbs. . . . Born, Warroad, Minn., February 22, 1953 . . . Shoots left . . . Attended University of North Dakota . . . Member of 1973-74 U. S. National Team . . . Had surgery on left knee following 1974-75 season and surgery for removal of cartilage of right knee, June, 1978.

Year	Team	League	Games	G.	A.	Pts.	Pen.
1971-72—U. of North Dakota (c)		WCHA	36	13	21	34	49
1972-73—U. of North Dakota (d-e)		WCHA	36	15	18	33	77
1973-74—University of North Dakota		WCHA	34	9	16	25	56
1973-74—U. S. National Team			7	2	3	5	10
1974-75—Cape Codders		NAHL	55	4	39	43	130
1974-75—New England Whalers		WHA	26	0	5	5	8
1975-76—Cape Codders		NAHL	1	0	0	0	9
1975-76—New England Whalers		WHA	78	2	23	25	62
1976-77—New England Whalers		WHA	74	13	9	22	79
1977-78—New England Whalers		WHA	79	11	18	29	140
1978-79—New England Whalers (f)		WHA	77	10	19	29	148
1979-80—Hartford Whalers (g)		NHL	37	3	15	18	69
1979-80—Washington Capitals		NHL	37	10	7	17	45
1980-81—Washington Capitals		NHL	74	5	19	24	198
1981-82—Washington Capitals (h)		NHL	17	1	1	2	19
1981-82—Hershey Bears (i)		AHL	6	1	2	3	26
1981-82—Los Angeles Kings (j)		NHL	18	2	6	8	65
1981-82—New Haven Nighthawks		AHL	18	5	4	9	28
1982-83—New Haven Nighthawks (k)		AHL	22	5	3	8	45
1982-83—Moncton Alpines		AHL	49	5	14	19	82
1983-84—New Haven Nighthawks		AHL	58	1	23	24	88
WHA TOTALS			334	36	74	110	437
NHL TOTALS			183	21	48	69	396

(c) Named to first team (Western) All-America.

(d)—Drafted from University of North Dakota by Montreal Canadiens in fourth round of 1973 amateur draft.

(e)—Selected by New England Whalers in World Hockey Association amateur players' draft, May, 1973.

(f)—June, 1979—Selected by Montreal Canadiens in NHL reclaim draft. Selected by Hartford Whalers in NHL expansion draft.

(g)—January, 1980—Traded by Hartford Whalers to Washington Capitals for Tom Rowe.

(h)—December, 1981—Released by Washington Capitals.

(i)—December, 1981—Given a tryout by Hershey Bears.

(j)—January, 1982—Signed by Los Angeles Kings as a free agent.

(k)—December, 1982—Traded by Los Angeles Kings to Edmonton Oilers for Rick Blight.

TIMOTHY HANLEY

Center . . . 6' . . . 200 lbs. . . . Born, Greenfield, Mass., October 10, 1964 . . . Shoots right.

Year	Team	League	Games	G.	A.	Pts.	Pen.
1983-84—Deerfield Academy (c)		Mass. H.S.	22	18	25	43	..

(c)—June, 1984—Drafted by Los Angeles Kings in 1984 NHL entry draft. Seventh Kings pick, 129th overall, seventh round.

DAVE HANNAN

Center . . . 5'11" . . . 174 lbs. . . . Born, Sudbury, Ont., November 26, 1961 . . . Shoots left . . . Missed part of '80-81 season with a bruised shoulder.

Year	Team	League	Games	G.	A.	Pts.	Pen.
1977-78—Windsor Spitfires		OMJHL	68	14	16	30	43
1978-79—Sault Ste. Marie Greyhounds		OMJHL	26	7	8	15	13
1979-80—Sault Ste. Marie Greyhounds		OMJHL	28	11	10	21	31
1979-80—Brantford Alexanders		OMJHL	25	5	10	15	26
1980-81—Brantford Alexanders (c)		OHL	56	46	35	81	155
1981-82—Erie Blades		AHL	76	33	37	70	129
1981-82—Pittsburgh Penguins		NHL	1	0	0	0	0
1982-83—Baltimore Skipjacks		AHL	5	2	2	4	13
1982-83—Pittsburgh Penguins		NHL	74	11	22	33	127
1983-84—Baltimore Skipjacks		AHL	47	18	24	42	98
1983-84—Pittsburgh Penguins		NHL	24	2	3	5	33
NHL TOTALS			99	13	25	38	160

(c)—June, 1981—Drafted by Pittsburgh Penguins in 1981 NHL entry draft. Ninth Penguins pick, 196th overall, 10th round.

RICHARD (RICHIE) JOHN HANSEN

Center . . . 5'10" . . . 175 lbs. . . . Born, Bronx, N. Y., October 30, 1955 . . . Shoots left . . . Brother of Max Hansen . . . Set CHL record with 81 assists in 1981-82.

Year	Team	League	Games	G.	A.	Pts.	Pen.
1972-73—Sudbury Wolves		Jr."A"OHA	39	13	21	34	26
1973-74—Sudbury Wolves		Jr."A"OHA	62	34	47	81	31
1974-75—Sudbury Wolves (c)		Jr."A"OHA	69	26	46	72	28
1975-76—Erie Blades		NAHL	74	40	41	81	51
1975-76—Muskegon Mohawks (d)		IHL	....	...	....	....	....
1976-77—Fort Worth Texans		CHL	74	30	47	77	32
1976-77—New York Islanders		NHL	4	1	0	1	0
1977-78—Ft. Worth Texans (b-e)		CHL	67	25	53	78	36
1977-78—New York Islanders		NHL	2	0	0	0	0
1978-79—New York Islanders (f)		NHL	12	1	6	7	4
1978-79—Ft. Worth Texans		CHL	20	4	8	12	4
1979-80—Salt Lake Golden Eagles		CHL	79	27	48	75	31
1980-81—Salt Lake Golden Eagles		CHL	72	27	51	78	43
1981-82—Salt Lake Golden Eagles		CHL	78	29	*81	110	52
1981-82—St. Louis Blues (g)		NHL	2	0	2	2	0
1982-83—Wichita Wind (h)		CHL	70	17	43	60	12
1983-84—Salt Lake Golden Eagles		CHL	63	24	32	56	22
NHL TOTALS			20	2	8	10	4

(c)—Drafted from Sudbury Wolves by New York Islanders in seventh round of 1975 amateur draft.

(d)—No league record. Appeared in one playoff game.

(e)—Tied for lead in assists (11) during playoffs.

(f)—June, 1979—Traded with Ralph Klassen by New York Islanders to St. Louis Blues as future consideration in deal that brought Terry Richardson and Barry Gibbs to the Islanders (Richardson went on to Hartford Whalers and Gibbs went to Los Angeles).

(g)—September, 1982—Signed by New Jersey Devils as a free agent.

(h)—February, 1983—Traded by New Jersey Devils to Edmonton Oilers, who assigned him to Moncton (AHL). Hansen refused to report and the Devils sent Paul Miller to Edmonton to complete deal in March, 1983.

DAVE HANSON

Defense . . . 6' . . . 190 lbs. . . . Born, Cumberland, Wis., April 12, 1954 . . . Shoots left . . . Also plays Left Wing . . . Set WHA single game penalty record—48 minutes (Feb. 5, 1978 vs. Indianapolis).

Year	Team	League	Games	G.	A.	Pts.	Pen.
1973-74—St. Paul Vulcans		MWJHL	56	9	13	22	*220
1974-75—Johnstown Jets		NAHL	72	10	24	34	249
1975-76—Johnstown Jets		NAHL	66	8	21	29	311
1976-77—Rhode Island Reds		AHL	27	2	10	12	98
1976-77—Hampton Gulls		SHL	28	5	7	12	188
1976-77—Johnstown Jets		NAHL	6	0	3	3	27
1976-77—New England Whalers		WHA	1	0	0	0	9
1976-77—Minnesota Fighting Saints (c)		WHA	7	0	2	2	35
1977-78—Kansas City Red Wings (d)		CHL	15	0	0	0	41
1977-78—Hampton Gulls		AHL	5	0	3	3	8
1977-78—Birmingham Bulls		WHA	42	7	16	23	241
1978-79—Detroit Red Wings (e)		NHL	11	0	0	0	26
1978-79—Birmingham Bulls		WHA	53	6	22	28	212
1979-80—Birmingham Bulls		CHL	33	4	6	10	174
1979-80—Minnesota North Stars (f)		NHL	22	1	1	2	39
1979-80—Oklahoma City Stars		CHL	6	0	0	0	12
1980-81—Adirondack Red Wings		AHL	77	11	21	32	267
1981-82—Adirondack Red Wings		AHL	75	11	23	34	206
1982-83—Indianapolis Checkers		CHL	80	18	21	39	285
1983-84—Indianapolis Checkers		CHL	1	0	0	0	0
1983-84—Toledo Goaldiggers		IHL	68	11	26	37	120
NHL TOTALS			33	1	1	2	65
WHA TOTALS			103	13	40	53	497

(c)—Signed by Detroit Red Wings as free agent, May, 1977.

(d)—Traded to Birmingham Bulls (WHA) by Detroit Red Wings with Steve Durbano and "future considerations" for Vaclav Nedomansky and Tim Sheehy, November, 1977.

(e)—December, 1978—Sold by Detroit Red Wings to Birmingham Bulls.

(f)—January, 1980—Traded by Detroit Red Wings to Minnesota North Stars for Alex Pirus.

DAVE HANSON

Center . . . 6'4" . . . 225 lbs. . . . Born, Grand Forks, N.D., July 18, 1966 . . . Shoots left.

Year	Team	League	Games	G.	A.	Pts.	Pen.
1983-84—Grand Forks H.S. (c)	No.Dak. H.S.	23	28	32	60	36

(c)—June, 1984—Drafted by Philadelphia Flyers in 1984 NHL entry draft. Fifth Flyers pick, 79th overall, fourth round.

KEITH HANSON

Defense . . . 6'5" . . . 210 lbs. . . . Born, Ada, Minn., April 26, 1957 . . . Shoots right . . . Also plays center.

Year	Team	League	Games	G.	A.	Pts.	Pen.
1977-78—Northern Michigan University	CCHA	34	16	15	31	77
1978-79—Northern Michigan University	CCHA	..	..	..	..	..
1979-80—Northern Michigan University	CCHA	38	2	13	15	74
1980-81—Northern Michigan University	CCHA	43	8	24	32	95
1981-82—Toledo Goaldiggers	IHL	82	7	37	44	185
1982-83—Birmingham South Stars (c)	CHL	69	4	21	25	187
1983-84—Colorado Flames	CHL	39	5	21	26	64
1983-84—Calgary Flames	NHL	25	0	2	2	77
NHL TOTALS		25	0	2	2	77

(c)—June, 1983—Traded by Minnesota North Stars with Mike Eaves to Calgary Flames for Steve Christoff and a second round 1983 draft pick (Frantisek Musil).

MARK LEA HARDY

Defense . . . 5'11" . . . 190 lbs. . . . Born, Semaden, Switzerland, February 1, 1959 . . . Shoots left . . . Mother was a member of 1952 Olympic Figure Skating team from England.

Year	Team	League	Games	G.	A.	Pts.	Pen.
1975-76—Montreal Juniors	QMJHL	64	6	17	23	44
1976-77—Montreal Juniors	QMJHL	72	20	40	60	137
1977-78—Montreal Juniors (a-c)	QMJHL	72	25	57	82	150
1978-79—Montreal Juniors (d)	QMJHL	67	18	52	70	117
1979-80—Binghamton Dusters	AHL	56	3	13	16	32
1979-80—Los Angeles Kings	NHL	15	0	1	1	10
1980-81—Los Angeles Kings	NHL	77	5	20	25	77
1981-82—Los Angeles Kings	NHL	77	6	39	45	130
1982-83—Los Angeles Kings	NHL	74	5	34	39	101
1983-84—Los Angeles Kings	NHL	79	8	41	49	122
NHL TOTALS		322	24	135	159	440

(c)—Named top defenseman in QMJHL.

(d)—August, 1979—Drafted by Los Angeles Kings in 1979 entry draft. Third Kings pick, 30th overall, second round.

WARREN HARPER

Right Wing . . . 5'11" . . . 176 lbs. . . . Born, Prince Albert, Sask., May 10, 1963 . . . Shoots left.

Year	Team	League	Games	G.	A.	Pts.	Pen.
1979-80—Prince Albert AA	Midget	34	20	17	37	58
1980-81—Prince Albert Raiders (c)	SJHL	60	35	35	70	158
1981-82—Prince Albert Raiders	SJHL	39	23	29	52	108
1982-83—Prince Albert Raiders	WHL	41	17	15	32	38
1983-84—Rochester Americans	AHL	78	25	28	53	56

(c)—June, 1981—Drafted as underage junior by Buffalo Sabres in 1981 NHL entry draft. Twelfth Sabres pick, 206th overall, 10th round.

TIM HARRER

Right Wing . . . 6' . . . 185 lbs. . . . Born, Bloomington, Minn., May 10, 1957 . . . Shoots right . . . Also plays Left Wing.

Year	Team	League	Games	G.	A.	Pts.	Pen.
1975-76—Bloomington Jr. Stars	MWJHL	11	5	3	8	6
1976-77—University of Minnesota (c)	WCHA	38	14	9	23	37
1977-78—University of Minnesota	WCHA	35	22	21	43	36
1978-79—University of Minnesota	WCHA	43	28	25	53	38
1979-80—University of Minnesota (a-d)	WCHA	41	*53	29	82	50
1980-81—Birmingham Bulls	CHL	28	9	5	14	36
1980-81—Hershey Bears	AHL	39	7	6	13	12

Year	Team	League	Games	G.	A.	Pts.	Pen.
1981-82—Oklahoma City Stars		CHL	77	29	27	56	36
1982-83—Colorado Flames		CHL	69	33	29	62	28
1982-83—Calgary Flames (e)		NHL	3	0	0	0	2
1983-84—Salt Lake Golden Eagles		CHL	66	42	27	69	46
NHL TOTALS			3	0	0	0	2

(c)—June, 1977—Drafted by Atlanta Flames in 1977 NHL amateur draft. Ninth Flames pick, 148th overall, ninth round.

(d)—Named to All-American Team (West).

(e)—August, 1983—Signed by Minnesota North Stars as a free agent.

JOHN HARRINGTON

Right Wing . . . 5'10" . . . 180 lbs. . . . Born, Virginia, Minn., May 24, 1957 . . . Shoots right . . . Member of 1980 and 1984 U.S. Olympic teams.

Year	Team	League	Games	G.	A.	Pts.	Pen.
1975-76—Univ. of Minnesota-Duluth		WCHA	36	9	12	21	14
1976-77—Univ. of Minnesota-Duluth		WCHA	27	5	9	14	16
1977-78—Univ. of Minnesota-Duluth		WCHA	31	22	9	31	20
1978-79—Univ. of Minnesota-Duluth		WCHA	40	29	43	72	16
1979-80—U.S. National Team		Int'l	58	14	23	37	16
1979-80—U.S. Olympic Team		Int'l	7	0	5	5	2
1979-80—Rochester Americans		AHL	12	4	3	7	8
1980-81—Lugano		Switz.	38	40	54	94	22
1981-82—Did not play.							
1982-83—U.S. National Team		Int'l	51	27	36	63	38
1983-84—U.S. National Team		Int'l	32	10	12	22	22
1983-84—U.S. Olympic Team		Int'l	6	0	3	3	6
1983-84—Colorado Flames (c)		CHL	10	5	5	10	4

(c)—March, 1984—Signed by Calgary Flames as a free agent.

WILLIAM EDWARD HARRIS

Right Wing . . . 6'2" . . . 197 lbs. . . . Born, Toronto, Ont., January 29, 1952 . . . Shoots left . . . Also plays Left Wing . . . (December, 1981)—Separated shoulder.

Year	Team	League	Games	G.	A.	Pts.	Pen.
1968-69—Toronto Marlboros		Jr."A"OHA	41	9	18	27	14
1969-70—Toronto Marlboros		Jr."A"OHA	46	13	17	30	75
1970-71—Toronto Marlboros (b)		Jr."A"OHA	48	34	48	82	61
1971-72—Tor. Marlboros (a-c-d-e)		Jr."A"OHA	63	57	72	*129	87
1972-73—New York Islanders		NHL	78	28	22	50	35
1973-74—New York Islanders		NHL	78	23	27	50	34
1974-75—New York Islanders		NHL	80	25	37	62	34
1975-76—New York Islanders		NHL	80	32	38	70	54
1976-77—New York Islanders		NHL	80	24	43	67	44
1977-78—New York Islanders		NHL	80	22	38	60	40
1978-79—New York Islanders		NHL	80	15	39	54	18
1979-80—New York Islanders (f)		NHL	67	15	15	30	37
1979-80—Los Angeles Kings		NHL	11	4	3	7	6
1980-81—Los Angeles Kings		NHL	80	20	29	49	36
1981-82—Los Angeles Kings (g)		NHL	16	1	3	4	6
1981-82—Toronto Maple Leafs		NHL	20	2	0	2	4
1982-83—Toronto Maple Leafs		NHL	76	11	19	30	26
1983-84—St. Catharines Saints		AHL	2	0	1	1	0
1983-84—Toronto Maple Leafs (h)		NHL	50	7	10	17	14
1983-84—Los Angeles Kings (i)		NHL	21	2	4	6	6
NHL TOTALS			897	231	327	558	394

(c)—Shared Eddie Powers Memorial Trophy (leading scorer) with Dave Gardner.

(d)—Selected by New York Raiders in WHA Player Selection Draft, February, 1972. WHA Negotiations rights traded to Philadelphia Blazers, June 1972.

(e)—Drafted from Toronto Marlboros by New York Islanders in first round of 1972 amateur draft.

(f)—March, 1980—Traded with Dave Lewis by New York Islanders to Los Angeles Kings for Butch Goring.

(g)—November, 1981—Traded with John Gibson by Los Angeles Kings to Toronto Maple Leafs for Ian Turnbull.

(h)—February, 1984—Sold by Toronto Maple Leafs to Los Angeles Kings.

(i)—August, 1984—Released by Los Angeles Kings.

STEPHEN WILLIAM HARRISON

Defense . . . 5'11" . . . 190 lbs. . . . Born, Scarborough, Ont., April 25, 1958 . . . Shoots left . . . (October 25, 1980)—Knee surgery.

Year	Team	League	Games	G.	A.	Pts.	Pen.
1975-76—Toronto Marlboros		Jr."A"OHA	36	0	5	5	6
1976-77—Toronto Marlboros		Jr."A"OHA	49	6	13	19	59
1977-78—Toronto Marlboros (c)		Jr."A"OHA	68	16	42	58	70
1978-79—Salt Lake Golden Eagles		CHL	2	0	1	1	0
1978-79—Port Huron Flags (b)		IHL	80	20	56	76	98
1979-80—Salt Lake Golden Eagles		CHL	80	4	42	46	36
1980-81—Port Huron Flags		IHL	7	3	6	9	4
1980-81—Salt Lake Golden Eagles		CHL	39	9	28	37	50
1981-82—Salt Lake Golden Eagles		CHL	75	12	46	58	63
1982-83—Moncton Alpines		AHL	2	0	0	0	2
1982-83—Peoria Prancers (b)		IHL	72	14	55	69	76
1983-84—Peoria Prancers		IHL	82	11	40	51	52

(c)—Drafted from Toronto Marlboros by St. Louis Blues in third round of 1978 amateur draft.

CRAIG HARTSBURG

Defense . . . 6'1" . . . 190 lbs. . . . Born, Stratford, Ont., June 29, 1959 . . . Shoots left . . . (September, 1977)—Torn ligaments in left knee . . . (September, 1980)—Separated shoulder . . . Member of Team Canada in 1981 Canada Cup . . . Son of Bill Hartsburg (WHL, 1960s) . . . (October 10, 1983)—Surgery to remove bone spur on knee, returned November 15 . . . (January 10, 1984)—Injured ligaments in left knee in game vs. Hartford and required arthoscopic surgery . . . Holds Minnesota club records for most assists (60) and points (77) in a season by a defenseman.

Year	Team	League	Games	G.	A.	Pts.	Pen.
1975-76—S. Ste. Marie Greyhounds		Jr."A"OHA	64	9	19	28	65
1976-77—S. Ste. M. Greyhounds (b-c)		Jr."A"OHA	61	29	64	93	142
1977-78—S. Ste. M. Greyhounds (d)		Jr."A"OHA	36	15	42	57	101
1978-79—Birmingham Bulls (e)		WHA	77	9	40	49	73
1979-80—Minnesota North Stars		NHL	79	14	30	44	81
1980-81—Minnesota North Stars		NHL	74	13	30	43	124
1981-82—Minnesota North Stars		NHL	76	17	60	77	117
1982-83—Minnesota North Stars		NHL	78	12	50	62	109
1983-84—Minnesota North Stars		NHL	26	7	7	14	37
WHA TOTALS			77	9	40	49	73
NHL TOTALS			333	63	177	240	466

(c)—Won Max Kaminsky Memorial Trophy (outstanding defenseman).
(d)—Signed by Birmingham Bulls (WHA) as underage junior, July, 1978.
(e)—Drafted by Minnesota North Stars in entry draft. First North Stars pick, sixth overall, first round.

KEVIN HATCHER

Defense . . . 6'3" . . . 185 lbs. . . . Born, Detroit, Mich., September 9, 1966 . . . Shoots right.

Year	Team	League	Games	G.	A.	Pts.	Pen.
1982-83—Detroit Compuware		Mich. Midget	75	30	45	75	120
1983-84—North Bay Centennials (c)		OHL	67	10	39	49	61

(c)—June, 1984—Drafted as underage junior by Washington Capitals in 1984 NHL entry draft. First Capitals pick, 17th overall, first round.

MARK HATCHER

Defense . . . 6'7" . . . 232 lbs. . . . Born, Detroit, Mich., September 15, 1964 . . . Shoots left.

Year	Team	League	Games	G.	A.	Pts.	Pen.
1980-81—Detroit Ceasars		Midget	64	4	21	25	....
1981-82—Niagara Falls Flyers (c)		OHL	65	0	9	9	172
1982-83—North Bay Centennials		OHL	63	1	16	17	214
1983-84—North Bay Centennials		OHL	64	1	12	13	226

(c)—June, 1982—Drafted as underage junior by Chicago Black Hawks in 1982 NHL entry draft. Sixth Black Hawks pick, 112th overall, sixth round.

DALE HAWERCHUK

Center . . . 5'11" . . . 170 lbs. . . . Born, Toronto, Ont., April 4, 1963 . . . Shoots left . . . Youngest player to have 100-point season (18 years, 351 days) . . . (March 7, 1984)—Set NHL record with five assists in a period during a 7-3 win at Los Angeles.

Year	Team	League	Games	G.	A.	Pts.	Pen.
1979-80—Cornwall Royals (c-d)		OMJHL	72	37	66	103	21
1980-81—Cornwall Royals (a-e-f-g-h-i)		OHL	72	*81	*102	*183	69
1981-82—Winnipeg Jets (j-k)		NHL	80	45	58	103	47
1982-83—Winnipeg Jets		NHL	79	40	51	91	31
1983-84—Winnipeg Jets		NHL	80	37	65	102	73
NHL TOTALS			239	122	174	296	151

(c)—Winner of The Instructeurs Trophy (QMJHL Top Rookie).
(d)—Winner of Guy Lafleur Trophy (QMJHL Playoff MVP).
(e)—Winner of Jean Beliveau Trophy (QMJHL Leading Scorer).
(f)—Winner of Michel Briere Trophy (QMJHL MVP).
(g)—Winner of The Association of Journalists for Major Junior League Hockey Trophy (Best pro prospect). First year awarded.
(h)—Winner of CCM Trophy (Top Canadian Major Junior League Player).
(i)—Drafted as underage junior by Winnipeg Jets in 1981 NHL Entry Draft. First Jets pick, first overall, first round.
(j)—Named NHL Rookie of the Year by The Sporting News in poll of players.
(k)—Winner of Calder Memorial Trophy (NHL Rookie of the Year).

ALAN JOSEPH GORDON HAWORTH

Center . . . 5'10" . . . 188 lbs. . . . Born, Drummondville, Que., September 1, 1960 . . . Shoots right . . . (February 4, 1981)—Bruised shoulder.

Year	Team	League	Games	G.	A.	Pts.	Pen.
1977-78—Chicoutimi Sagueneens		QMJHL	59	17	33	50	40
1978-79—Sherbrooke Beavers (c)		QMJHL	70	50	70	120	63
1979-80—Sherbrooke Beavers		QMJHL	45	28	36	64	50
1980-81—Rochester Americans		AHL	21	14	18	32	19
1980-81—Buffalo Sabres		NHL	49	16	20	36	34
1981-82—Rochester Americans		AHL	14	5	12	17	10
1981-82—Buffalo Sabres (d)		NHL	57	21	18	39	30
1982-83—Washington Capitals		NHL	74	23	27	50	34
1983-84—Washington Capitals		NHL	75	24	31	55	52
NHL TOTALS			255	84	96	180	150

(c)—August, 1979—Drafted by Buffalo Sabres as underage junior in 1979 entry draft. Sixth Sabres pick, 95th overall, fifth round.
(d)—June, 1982—Traded by Buffalo Sabres with third-round pick in 1982 entry draft to Washington Capitals for second and fourth-round choices in 1982.

NEIL HAWRYLIW

Right Wing . . . 5'11" . . . 185 lbs. . . . Born, Fielding, Sask., November 19, 1955 . . . Shoots left . . . (December, 1981)—Concussion . . . (October, 1982)—Knee injury.

Year	Team	League	Games	G.	A.	Pts.	Pen.
1972-73—Humboldt Broncos		SJHL	....	...	....	....	....
1973-74—Saskatoon Blades		WCHL	52	23	20	43	28
1974-75—Saskatoon Blades		WCHL	68	29	38	67	51
1975-76—Saskatoon Blades		WCHL	72	48	39	87	155
1976-77—Muskegon Mohawks		IHL	38	18	18	36	16
1977-78—Muskegon Mohawks		IHL	75	37	32	69	84
1978-79—Ft. Worth Texans (c)		CHL	57	9	15	24	87
1978-79—Muskegon Mohawks		IHL	13	11	7	18	14
1979-80—Indianapolis Checkers		CHL	70	26	19	45	56
1980-81—Indianapolis Checkers (a)		CHL	80	37	42	79	61
1981-82—New York Islanders		NHL	1	0	0	0	0
1981-82—Indianapolis Checkers		CHL	58	20	14	34	89
1982-83—Wichita Wind		CHL	2	2	3	5	0
1982-83—Muskegon Mohawks		IHL	68	33	24	57	42
1983-84—Muskegon Mohawks		IHL	66	25	37	62	36
NHL TOTALS			1	0	0	0	0

(c)—October, 1978—Signed as a free agent by New York Islanders.

RANDY HEATH

Left Wing . . . 5'8" . . . 165 lbs. . . . Born, Vancouver, B.C., November 11, 1964 . . . Shoots left.

Year	Team	League	Games	G.	A.	Pts.	Pen.
1980-81—Vancouver Blue Hawks		BCJHL	50	35	35	70	30
1980-81—Portland Winter Hawks		WHL	2	1	0	1	0
1981-82—Portland Winter Hawks		WHL	65	52	47	99	65
1982-83—Portland Winter Hawks (a-c)		WHL	72	82	69	151	52
1983-84—Portland Winter Hawks (a)		WHL	60	44	46	90	107

(c)—June, 1983—Drafted as underage junior by New York Rangers in 1983 NHL entry draft. Second Rangers pick, 33rd overall, second round.

ANDERS HUGO HEDBERG

Right Wing . . . 5'11" . . . 176 lbs. . . . Born, Ornskoldsvik, Sweden, February 25, 1951 . . .

Shoots left . . . (October 17, 1981)—Arthroscopic surgery to left knee injured August 20 during a Team Sweden practice for 1981 Canada Cup.

Year	Team	League	Games	G.	A.	Pts.	Pen.
1973-74—Djurgardens		Sweden					
1974-75—Winnipeg Jets (b-c)		WHA	65	53	47	100	45
1975-76—Winnipeg Jets (a-d)		WHA	76	50	55	105	48
1976-77—Winnipeg Jets (a)		WHA	68	*70	61	131	48
1977-78—Winnipeg Jets (b-e)		WHA	77	63	59	122	60
1978-79—New York Rangers		NHL	80	33	45	78	33
1979-80—New York Rangers (f)		NHL	80	32	39	71	21
1980-81—New York Rangers		NHL	80	30	40	70	52
1981-82—New York Rangers		NHL	4	0	1	1	0
1982-83—New York Rangers		NHL	78	25	34	59	12
1983-84—New York Rangers		NHL	79	32	35	67	16
WHA TOTALS			286	236	222	458	201
NHL TOTALS			401	152	194	346	134

(c)—Won WHA Rookie Award.
(d)—Led in goals (13) during playoffs.
(e)—March, 1978—Signed to multi-year contract by New York Rangers—starting with 1978-79 season.
(f)—Winner of Viking Award (Outstanding Swedish Player in NHL/WHA).

KEVIN HEFFERNAN
Center . . . 6'1" . . . 185 lbs. . . . Born, Weymouth, Mass., January 18, 1966 . . . Shoots left.

Year	Team	League	Games	G.	A.	Pts.	Pen.
1983-84—Weymouth H.S. (c)		Mass. H.S.	24	22	35	57	..

(c)—June, 1984—Drafted by Boston Bruins in 1984 NHL entry draft. Ninth Bruins pick, 186th overall, ninth round.

MIKE HEIDT
Defense . . . 6'1" . . . 190 lbs. . . . Born, Calgary, Alta., November 4, 1963 . . . Shoots left.

Year	Team	League	Games	G.	A.	Pts.	Pen.
1980-81—Calgary Canucks		AJHL	56	28	63	91	104
1980-81—Calgary Wranglers		WHL	12	1	3	4	6
1981-82—Calgary Wranglers (c)		WHL	70	13	44	57	142
1982-83—Calgary Wranglers (a)		WHL	71	30	65	95	101
1983-84—Los Angeles Kings		NHL	6	0	1	1	7
1983-84—New Haven Nighthawks		AHL	54	4	20	24	49
NHL TOTALS			6	0	1	1	7

(c)—June, 1982—Drafted as underage junior by Los Angeles Kings in 1982 NHL entry draft. First Kings pick, 27th overall, second round.

ARCHIE HENDERSON
Right Wing . . . 6'6" . . . 216 lbs. . . . Born, Calgary, Alta., February 17, 1957 . . . Shoots right . . . Missed part of 1976-77 season with knee injury . . . (November, 1980)—Hand injury.

Year	Team	League	Games	G.	A.	Pts.	Pen.
1974-75—Lethbridge Broncos		WCHL	65	3	10	13	177
1975-76—Lethbridge Broncos (c)		WCHL	21	1	2	3	110
1975-76—Victoria Cougars		WCHL	31	8	7	15	205
1976-77—Victoria Cougars (d)		WCHL	47	14	10	24	208
1977-78—Port Huron Flags		IHL	71	16	16	32	419
1978-79—Hershey Bears		AHL	78	17	11	28	337
1979-80—Hershey Bears		AHL	8	0	2	2	37
1979-80—Fort Worth Texans (e)		CHL	49	8	9	17	199
1980-81—Washington Capitals		NHL	7	1	0	1	28
1980-81—Hershey Bears		AHL	60	3	5	8	251
1981-82—Minnesota North Stars (f)		NHL	1	0	0	0	0
1981-82—Nashville South Stars		CHL	77	12	23	35	*320
1982-83—Hartford Whalers (g)		NHL	15	2	1	3	64
1982-83—Binghamton Whalers (h)		AHL	50	8	9	17	172
1983-84—New Haven Nighthawks (i-j)		AHL	48	1	8	9	164
NHL TOTALS			23	3	1	4	92

(c)—Traded to Victoria Cougars by Lethbridge Broncos for Rick Peter, December, 1975.
(d)—Drafted from Victoria Cougars by Washington Capitals in 10th round of 1977 amateur draft.
(e)—Led in penalty minutes (58) during playoffs.
(f)—September, 1981—Signed with Minnesota North Stars as a free agent after being released by Washington Capitals.
(g)—September, 1982—Signed by Hartford Whalers as a free agent.
(h)—March, 1983—Released by Hartford Whalers.

RICK HENDRICKS

Defense ... 6' ... 195 lbs. ... Born, Hardisty, Alta., May 15, 1957 ... Shoots left.

Year	Team	League	Games	G.	A.	Pts.	Pen.
1975-76	Victoria Cougars	WCHL	39	2	10	12	66
1976-77	Victoria Cougars	WCHL	21	5	15	20	45
1976-77	Lethbridge Broncos	WCHL	55	12	32	44	161
1977-78	St. Albert	AJHL	50	13	22	35	92
1977-78	Lethbridge Broncos	WCHL	14	0	4	4	27
1978-79	Fort Wayne Komets	IHL	64	3	15	18	95
1978-79	Muskegon Mohawks	IHL	13	2	2	4	29
1979-80	Muskegon Mohawks	IHL	42	8	34	42	113
1979-80	Toledo Goaldiggers	IHL	37	8	20	28	20
1980-81	Toledo Goaldiggers	IHL	11	2	3	5	22
1980-81	Maine Mariners (c)	AHL	34	1	5	6	70
1981-82	Maine Mariners	AHL	74	3	17	20	145
1982-83	Toledo Goaldiggers (d)	IHL	81	10	44	54	108
1983-84	Salt Lake Golden Eagles	CHL	1	1	0	1	0
1983-84	Toledo Goaldiggers	IHL	80	13	42	55	154

(c)—January, 1981—Signed by Maine Mariners as a free agent.
(d)—Shared IHL playoff point lead (with teammate Dirk Graham) with 20 points.

DALE HENRY

Left Wing ... 6' ... 205 lbs. ... Born, Prince Albert, Sask., September 24, 1964 ... Shoots left.

Year	Team	League	Games	G.	A.	Pts.	Pen.
1981-82	Saskatoon Blades	WHL	32	5	4	9	50
1982-83	Saskatoon Blades (c)	WHL	63	21	19	40	213
1983-84	Saskatoon Blades	WHL	71	41	36	77	162

(c)—June, 1983—Drafted as underage junior by New York Islanders in 1983 NHL entry draft. Tenth Islanders pick, 157th overall, eighth round.

ALAN HEPPLE

Defense ... 5'10" ... 200 lbs. ... Born, Blaudon-on-Tyne, England, August 16, 1963 ... Shoots right ... Also plays center ... (October, 1980)—Eye injury.

Year	Team	League	Games	G.	A.	Pts.	Pen.
1980-81	Ottawa 67's	OHL	64	3	13	16	110
1981-82	Ottawa 67's (c)	OHL	66	6	22	28	160
1982-83	Ottawa 67's	OHL	64	10	26	36	168
1983-84	Maine Mariners	AHL	64	4	23	27	117
1983-84	New Jersey Devils	NHL	1	0	0	0	7
	NHL TOTALS		1	0	0	0	7

(c)—June, 1982—Drafted as underage junior by New Jersey Devils in 1982 NHL entry draft. Ninth Devils pick, 169th overall, ninth round.

ALAIN HEROUX

Left Wing ... 6'1" ... 182 lbs. ... Born, Terrebonne, Que., May 20, 1964 ... Shoots left ... Brother of Yves Heroux.

Year	Team	League	Games	G.	A.	Pts.	Pen.
1980-81	Boisbriand Midgets	Que. Midget	48	14	17	31	30
1981-82	Chicoutimi Sagueneens (c)	QMJHL	58	29	33	62	33
1982-83	Chicoutimi Sagueneens	QHL	61	34	61	95	37
1983-84	Chicoutimi Sagueneens	QHL	58	31	42	73	53
1983-84	Nova Scotia Voyageurs	AHL	4	1	1	2	2

(c)—June, 1982—Drafted as underage junior by Montreal Canadiens in 1982 NHL entry draft. First Canadiens pick, 19th overall, first round.

YVES HEROUX

Right Wing ... 5'11" ... 185 lbs. ... Born, Terrebonne, Que., April 27, 1965 ... Shoots right ... Brother of Alain Heroux ... (December, 1981)—Foot Infection.

Year	Team	League	Games	G.	A.	Pts.	Pen.
1981-82	Laurentides AAA	Que. Midget	48	53	53	106	84
1982-83	Chicoutimi Sagueneens (c)	QHL	70	41	40	81	44

Year	Team	League	Games	G.	A.	Pts.	Pen.
1983-84—Chicoutimi Sagueneens		QHL	56	28	25	53	67
1983-84—Fredericton Express		AHL	4	0	0	0	0

(c)—June, 1983—Drafted as underage junior by Quebec Nordiques in 1983 NHL entry draft. First Nordiques' pick, 32nd overall, second round.

GRAHAM HERRING

Defense . . . 6' . . . 170 lbs. . . . Born, Montreal, Que., October 27, 1965 . . . Shoots left.

Year	Team	League	Games	G.	A.	Pts.	Pen.
1983-84—Longueuil Chevaliers (c)		QHL	68	9	44	53	101

(c)—June, 1984—Drafted as underage junior by St. Louis Blues in 1984 NHL entry draft. Sixth Blues pick, 71st overall, fourth round.

ROBERT GEORGE HESS

Defense . . . 5'11" . . . 175 lbs. . . . Born, Middleton, N. S., May 19, 1955 . . . Shoots left . . . Suffered hairline fracture of ankle during opening game of 1976 playoffs . . . Has also played Left Wing.

Year	Team	League	Games	G.	A.	Pts.	Pen.
1971-72—New Westminster Bruins		WCHL	5	0	0	0	0
1972-73—New Westminster Bruins		WCHL	67	6	13	19	29
1973-74—New Westminster Bruins (c)		WCHL	68	10	30	40	104
1974-75—St. Louis Blues		NHL	76	9	30	39	58
1975-76—St. Louis Blues		NHL	78	9	23	32	58
1976-77—Kansas City Blues		CHL	10	1	8	9	16
1976-77—St. Louis Blues		NHL	53	4	18	22	14
1977-78—Salt Lake City Golden Eagles		CHL	7	1	3	4	4
1977-78—St. Louis Blues		NHL	55	2	12	14	16
1978-79—St. Louis Blues		NHL	27	3	4	7	14
1978-79—Salt Lake Golden Eagles		CHL	45	19	29	48	22
1979-80—Salt Lake Golden Eagles		CHL	79	32	42	74	71
1980-81—St. Louis Blues (d)		NHL	4	0	0	0	4
1980-81—Buffalo Sabres (e)		NHL	....	...	....	....	....
1980-81—Rochester Americans (a)		AHL	70	17	58	75	95
1981-82—Rochester Americans		AHL	22	6	13	19	10
1981-82—Buffalo Sabres		NHL	33	0	8	8	14
1982-83—Maine Mariners (f)		AHL	13	5	3	8	10
1983-84—Kloten		Switzerland	..	..	..	..	..
1983-84—Hartford Whalers (g)		NHL	3	0	0	0	0
1983-84—Indianapolis Checkers		CHL	9	2	6	8	10
NHL TOTALS			329	27	95	122	178

(c)—Drafted from New Westminster Bruins by St. Louis Blues in second round of 1974 amateur draft.
(d)—October, 1980—Traded by St. Louis Blues to Buffalo Sabres for Bill Stewart.
(e)—Played in one playoff game.
(f)—March, 1983—Signed by Maine Mariners as a free agent after completion of season in Europe (Lugano-Switzerland Elite League).
(g)—February, 1984—Signed by Hartford Whalers as a free agent and assigned to Indianapolis Checkers.

MEL HEWITT

Defense . . . 5'10" . . . 175 lbs. . . . Born, Saskatoon, Sask., November 15, 1958 . . . Shoots left.

Year	Team	League	Games	G.	A.	Pts.	Pen.
1975-76—Saskatoon		SJHL	41	1	5	6	241
1975-76—Saskatoon Blades		WCHL	13	0	1	1	43
1976-77—Saskatoon Blades		WCHL	69	8	18	26	373
1977-78—Saskatoon Blades		WCHL	13	3	8	11	96
1977-78—Calgary Wranglers (c)		WCHL	55	18	11	29	412
1978-79—Calgary		AJHL	16	11	5	16	113
1978-79—Saginaw Gears		IHL	2	1	2	3	10
1978-79—San Francisco Shamrocks		PHL	4	0	0	0	26
1979-80—Saginaw Gears (d)		IHL	70	28	26	54	*504
1980-81—New Brunswick Hawks		AHL	68	7	5	12	*304
1981-82—New Brunswick Hawks		AHL	66	11	10	21	119
1982-83—Maine Mariners		AHL	78	18	14	32	271
1983-84—Flint Generals		IHL	45	18	34	52	86
1983-84—Peoria Prancers		IHL	24	6	6	12	80

(c)—June, 1978—Drafted by Toronto Maple Leafs in 1978 NHL amateur draft. Fifth Maple Leafs pick, 92nd overall, sixth round.
(d)—Led IHL Playoffs with 82 penalty minutes.

PATRICK JOSEPH HICKEY

Left Wing . . . 6'1" . . . 190 lbs. . . . Born, Brantford, Ont., May 15, 1953 . . . Shoots left . . . Also plays center and right wing . . . Brother of Greg Hickey . . . Missed part of 1975-76 season with cracked rib . . . Missed most of 1982-83 season with leg injury.

Year	Team	League	Games	G.	A.	Pts.	Pen.
1970-71	Hamilton Red Wings	Jr."A"OHA	55	15	17	32	46
1971-72	Hamilton Red Wings	Jr."A"OHA	58	21	39	60	78
1972-73	Hamilton Red Wings (c-d)	Jr."A"OHA	61	32	47	79	80
1973-74	Toronto Toros	WHA	78	26	29	55	52
1974-75	Toronto Toros (e)	WHA	74	34	34	68	50
1975-76	New York Rangers	NHL	70	14	22	36	36
1976-77	New York Rangers	NHL	80	23	17	40	35
1977-78	New York Rangers	NHL	80	40	33	73	47
1978-79	New York Rangers	NHL	80	34	41	75	56
1979-80	New York Rangers (f)	NHL	7	2	2	4	10
1979-80	Colorado Rockies (g)	NHL	24	7	9	16	10
1979-80	Toronto Maple Leafs	NHL	45	22	16	38	16
1980-81	Toronto Maple Leafs	NHL	72	16	33	49	49
1981-82	Toronto Maple Leafs (h)	NHL	1	0	0	0	0
1981-82	New York Rangers (i)	NHL	53	15	14	29	32
1981-82	Quebec Nordiques (j)	NHL	7	0	1	1	4
1982-83	St. Louis Blues	NHL	1	0	0	0	0
1982-83	Salt Lake Golden Eagles	CHL	36	13	12	25	28
1983-84	St. Louis Blues	NHL	67	9	11	20	24
	NHL TOTALS		587	182	199	381	319
	WHA TOTALS		152	60	63	123	102

(c)—Drafted from Hamilton Red Wings by New York Rangers in second round of 1973 amateur draft.

(d)—Selected by Toronto Toros in WHA amateur player draft, May, 1973.

(e)—Signed by New York Rangers, May, 1975.

(f)—November, 1979—Traded with Mike McEwen, Lucien DeBlois, Dean Turner and future considerations (Bobby Sheehan and Bobby Crawford) by New York Rangers to Colorado Rockies for Barry Beck.

(g)—December, 1979—Traded with Wilf Paiement by Colorado Rockies to Toronto Maple Leafs for Lanny McDonald and Joel Quenneville.

(h)—October, 1981—Traded by Toronto Maple Leafs to New York Rangers for fifth round 1982 draft pick (Sylvain Charland).

(i)—March, 1982—Awarded to Quebec Nordiques by NHL as compensation for December, 1981 trade in which Robbie Ftorek and an eighth-round 1982 draft pick (Brian Glynn) went from Quebec to New York Rangers for Jere Gillis and Dean Talafous. Talafous retired from hockey rather then go to Quebec, which necessitated a compensation ruling by NHL President John Ziegler.

(j)—August, 1982—Traded by Quebec Nordiques to St. Louis Blues for Rick LaPointe.

GLENN HICKS

Left Wing . . . 5'10" . . . 177 lbs. . . . Born, Red Deer, Alta., August 28, 1958 . . . Shoots left . . . Brother of Doug Hicks.

Year	Team	League	Games	G.	A.	Pts.	Pen.
1975-76	Flin Flon Bombers	WCHL	71	16	19	35	103
1976-77	Flin Flon Bombers	WCHL	71	28	31	59	175
1977-78	Flin Flon Bombers (c-d)	WCHL	72	50	69	119	225
1978-79	Winnipeg Jets (e)	WHA	69	6	10	16	48
1979-80	Detroit Red Wings	NHL	50	1	2	3	43
1980-81	Adirondack Red Wings	AHL	19	10	6	16	56
1980-81	Detroit Red Wings	NHL	58	5	10	15	84
1981-82	Tulsa Oilers (f)	CHL	78	14	34	48	103
1982-83	Birmingham South Stars	CHL	80	13	26	39	40
1983-84	Salt Lake Golden Eagles	CHL	62	4	26	30	87
	WHA TOTALS		69	6	10	16	48
	NHL TOTALS		108	6	12	18	127

(c)—Drafted from Flin Flon Bombers by Detroit Red Wings in second round of 1978 amateur draft.

(d)—Selected by Winnipeg Jets in World Hockey Association amateur players' draft. Signed by Winnipeg, July, 1978.

(e)—June, 1979—Selected by Detroit Red Wings in NHL reclaim draft.

(f)—September, 1981—Signed by Winnipeg Jets as a free agent.

ANDRE HIDI

Left Wing . . . 6'2" . . . 205 lbs. . . . Born, Toronto, Ont., June 5, 1960 . . . Shoots left.

Year	Team	League	Games	G.	A.	Pts.	Pen.
1983-84—University of Toronto	OUAA	49	45	63	108	89
1983-84—Washington Capitals (c)	NHL	1	0	0	0	0

(c)—March, 1984—Signed by Washington Capitals as a free agent.

ULLRICH HIEMER

Defense . . . 6'1" . . . 190 lbs. . . . Born, Fussen, West Germany, September 21, 1962 . . . Shoots left.

Year	Team	League	Games	G.	A.	Pts.	Pen.
1983-84—Koln (c)	W. Germany	50	23	23	46	....

(c)—June, 1981—Drafted by Colorado Rockies in the NHL entry draft. Third Rockies pick, 48th overall, third round.

PAUL HIGGINS

Right Wing . . . 6'1" . . . 195 lbs. . . . Born, St. Johns, N.B., January 13, 1962 . . . Shoots right.

Year	Team	League	Games	G.	A.	Pts.	Pen.
1979-80—Henry Carr High School (c)	Tor. H.S	....	25	38	63	....
1980-81—Toronto Marlboros	OHL	14	2	2	4	11
1981-82—Toronto Marlboros	OHL	6	0	0	0	11
1981-82—Kitchener Rangers	OHL	29	3	5	8	119
1981-82—Toronto Maple Leafs	NHL	3	0	0	0	17
1982-83—Toronto Maple Leafs	NHL	22	0	0	0	135
1983-84—Carolina Thunderbirds	ACHL	4	0	1	1	18
NHL TOTALS		25	0	0	0	152

(c)—June, 1980—Drafted as underage junior by Toronto Maple Leafs in 1980 NHL entry draft. Tenth Maple Leafs pick, 200th overall, 10th round.

TIM RAY HIGGINS

Right Wing . . . 6'1" . . . 185 lbs. . . . Born, Ottawa, Ont., February 7, 1958 . . . Shoots right . . . (January 16, 1983)—Broke index finger of right hand during a fight with Colin Campbell in game vs. Detroit . . . (February, 1983)—Strained knee ligaments.

Year	Team	League	Games	G.	A.	Pts.	Pen.
1974-75—Ottawa 67's	Jr."A"OHA	22	1	3	4	6
1975-76—Ottawa 67's	Jr."A"OHA	59	15	10	25	59
1976-77—Ottawa 67's	Jr."A"OHA	66	36	52	88	82
1977-78—Ottawa 67's (c)	Jr."A"OHA	50	41	60	101	99
1978-79—Chicago Black Hawks	NHL	36	7	16	23	30
1978-79—New Brunswick Hawks	AHL	17	3	5	8	14
1979-80—Chicago Black Hawks	NHL	74	13	12	25	50
1980-81—Chicago Black Hawks	NHL	78	24	35	59	86
1981-82—Chicago Black Hawks	NHL	74	20	30	50	85
1982-83—Chicago Black Hawks	NHL	64	14	9	23	63
1983-84—Chicago Black Hawks (d)	NHL	32	1	4	5	21
1983-84—New Jersey Devils	NHL	37	18	10	28	27
NHL TOTALS		395	97	116	213	362

(c)—Drafted from Ottawa 67's by Chicago Black Hawks in first round of 1978 amateur draft.

(d)—January, 1984—Traded by Chicago Black Hawks to New Jersey Devils for Jeff Larmer.

GARTH HILDEBRAND

Left Wing . . . 5'10" . . . 185 lbs. . . . Born, Cardston, Alta., March 23, 1964 . . . Shoots left.

Year	Team	League	Games	G.	A.	Pts.	Pen.
1981-82—Red Deer	AJHL	55	26	26	52	34
1981-82—Portland Winter Hawks	WHL	2	0	1	1	0
1982-83—Calgary Wranglers (c)	WHL	72	31	26	57	85
1983-84—Calgary Wranglers	WHL	54	28	28	56	33

(c)—June, 1983—Drafted as underage junior by Pittsburgh Penguins in 1983 NHL entry draft. Ninth Penguins pick, 203rd overall, 11th round.

ALAN DOUGLAS HILL

Left Wing and Center . . . 6' . . . 175 lbs. . . . Born, Nanaimo, B. C., April 22, 1955 . . . Shoots left . . . Set NHL record for most points in first NHL game with 2 goals, 3 assists, February 14, 1977 . . . (November 20, 1980)—Fractured hand.

Year	Team	League	Games	G.	A.	Pts.	Pen.
1973-74—Nanaimo	Jr."A"BCHL	64	29	41	70	60
1974-75—Victoria Cougars	WCHL	70	21	36	57	75
1975-76—Victoria Cougars (c)	WCHL	68	26	40	66	172
1976-77—Springfield Kings	AHL	63	13	28	41	125
1976-77—Philadelphia Flyers	NHL	9	2	4	6	27
1977-78—Maine Mariners (a)	AHL	80	32	59	91	118
1977-78—Philadelphia Flyers	NHL	3	0	0	0	2
1978-79—Philadelphia Flyers	NHL	31	5	11	16	28
1978-79—Maine Mariners	AHL	35	11	14	25	59
1979-80—Philadelphia Flyers	NHL	61	16	10	26	53
1980-81—Philadelphia Flyers	NHL	57	10	15	25	45
1981-82—Philadelphia Flyers	NHL	41	6	13	19	58
1982-83—Moncton Alpines	AHL	78	22	22	44	78
1983-84—Maine Mariners (d)	AHL	51	8	16	24	51
NHL TOTALS		202	39	53	92	213

(c)—September, 1976—Signed by Philadelphia Flyers as a free agent.
(d)—January, 1984—Signed by Maine Mariners as a free agent.

RANDY GEORGE HILLIER

Defense . . . 6'1" . . . 170 lbs. . . . Born, Toronto, Ont., March 30, 1960 . . . Shoots right . . . (April 19, 1982)—Injured knee in playoff series vs. Quebec . . . (December, 1982)—Injured left knee . . . (April 2, 1983)—Strained ligaments in right knee in game at Montreal.

Year	Team	League	Games	G.	A.	Pts.	Pen.
1977-78—Sudbury Wolves	OMJHL	60	1	14	15	67
1978-79—Sudbury Wolves	OMJHL	61	9	25	34	173
1979-80—Sudbury Wolves (c)	OMJHL	60	16	49	65	143
1980-81—Springfield Indians	AHL	64	3	17	20	105
1981-82—Erie Blades	AHL	35	6	13	19	52
1981-82—Boston Bruins	NHL	25	0	8	8	29
1982-83—Boston Bruins	NHL	70	0	10	10	99
1983-84—Boston Bruins	NHL	69	3	12	15	125
NHL TOTALS		164	3	30	33	253

(c)—June, 1980—Drafted by Boston Bruins in 1980 NHL entry draft. Fourth Bruins pick, 102nd overall, fifth round.

DAVE HINDMARCH

Right Wing . . . 5'11" . . . 182 lbs. . . . Born, Vancouver, B. C., October 15, 1958 . . . Shoots right . . . (March 1, 1983)—Sprained ankle in game vs. Vancouver . . . (December 16, 1983)—Damaged ligaments in both knees when he collided with goal post during game at Vancouver. He required surgery to both knees and was out for the remainder of the season . . . Also plays left wing.

Year	Team	League	Games	G.	A.	Pts.	Pen.
1978-79—University of Alberta (c)	CIAU	23	21	18	39	20
1979-80—Canadian National Team	Int'l	41	12	13	25	20
1979-80—Canadian Olympic Team	Int'l	6	3	4	7	4
1980-81—Calgary Flames	NHL	1	1	0	1	0
1980-81—Birmingham Bulls	CHL	48	15	14	29	18
1980-81—Rochester Americans	AHL	18	6	2	8	6
1981-82—Oklahoma City Stars	CHL	63	27	21	48	21
1981-82—Calgary Flames	NHL	9	3	0	3	0
1982-83—Calgary Flames	NHL	60	11	12	23	23
1983-84—Calgary Flames	NHL	29	6	5	11	2
NHL TOTALS		99	21	17	38	25

(c)—June, 1978—Drafted by Atlanta Flames in 1978 NHL amateur draft. Sixth Flames pick, 114th overall, seventh round.

TOM HIRSCH

Defense . . . 6'3" . . . 195 lbs. . . . Born, Minneapolis, Minn., January 27, 1963 . . . Shoots right . . . Member of 1984 U.S. Olympic team.

Year	Team	League	Games	G.	A.	Pts.	Pen.
1980-81—Mpls. Patrick Henry H.S. (c)	Minn. H.S.	23	42	35	77	....
1981-82—University of Minnesota	WCHA	36	7	16	23	53
1982-83—University of Minnesota	WCHA	37	8	23	31	70
1983-84—U.S. National Team	Int'l	56	8	25	33	72

Year	Team	League	Games	G.	A.	Pts.	Pen.
1983-84—U.S. Olympic Team		Int'l	6	1	2	3	10
1983-84—Minnesota North Stars		NHL	15	1	3	4	20
NHL TOTALS			15	1	3	4	20

(c)—June, 1981—Drafted by Minnesota North Stars in 1981 NHL entry draft. Fourth North Stars pick, 33rd overall, second round.

JAMES DONALD (JAMIE) HISLOP

Right Wing . . . 5'10" . . . 180 lbs. . . . Born, Sarnia, Ont., January 20, 1954 . . . Shoots right . . . Attended University of New Hampshire . . . Holds all-time school records for career assists and points . . . Played 1972-73 season with broken right hand . . . Played 448 consecutive WHA/NHL games between 1977 and January 29, 1981 . . . (December 1, 1983)—Damaged retina in game vs. New York Islanders . . . (March, 1984)—Laser surgery to repair retina.

Year	Team	League	Games	G.	A.	Pts.	Pen.
1971-72—Stratford Warriors		Jr."B"OHA	38	26	30	56	....
1972-73—University of New Hampshire		ECAC	26	5	16	21	....
1973-74—University of N. Hampshire (c)		ECAC	31	21	35	56	30
1974-75—University of New Hampshire		ECAC	31	28	38	66	12
1975-76—University of N. Hampshire (d)		ECAC	31	23	43	66	20
1976-77—Hampton Gulls		SHL	37	16	17	33	11
1976-77—Cincinnati Stingers		WHA	46	7	19	26	6
1977-78—Cincinnati Stingers		WHA	80	94	43	67	17
1978-79—Cincinnati Stingers (e-f)		WHA	80	30	40	70	45
1979-80—Quebec Nordiques		NHL	80	19	20	39	6
1980-81—Quebec Nordiques (g)		NHL	50	19	22	41	15
1980-81—Calgary Flames		NHL	29	6	9	15	11
1981-82—Calgary Flames		NHL	80	16	25	41	35
1982-83—Calgary Flames		NHL	79	14	19	33	17
1983-84—Calgary Flames		NHL	27	1	0	9	2
WHA TOTALS			206	61	102	163	68
NHL TOTALS			345	75	103	178	96

(c)—Drafted from University of New Hampshire by Montreal Canadiens in eighth round of 1974 amateur draft.
(d)—Signed by Cincinnati Stingers (WHA), September, 1976.
(e)—June, 1979—Claimed by Winnipeg Jets in WHA dispersal draft.
(f)—August, 1979—Signed by Quebec Nordiques as free agent.
(g)—January, 1981—Traded by Quebec Nordiques to Calgary Flames for Dan Bouchard.

KENNETH HODGE JR.

Center . . . 6'2" . . . 190 lbs. . . . Born, Windsor, Ontario, April 13, 1966 . . . Shoots left . . . Son of former NHL star Ken Hodge, who played for Chicago, Boston and New York Rangers in 1965 through 1978.

Year	Team	League	Games	G.	A.	Pts.	Pen.
1983-84—St. John's Prep. (c)		....	22	25	38	63	..

(c)—June, 1984—Drafted by Minnesota North Stars in 1984 NHL entry draft. Second North Stars pick, 46th overall, third round.

DAN HODGSON

Center . . . 5'11" . . . 173 lbs. . . . Born, Fort McMurray, Alta., August 29, 1965 . . . Shoots right.

Year	Team	League	Games	G.	A.	Pts.	Pen.
1982-83—Prince Albert Raiders (c-d)		WHL	72	56	74	130	66
1983-84—Prince Albert Raiders (b)		WHL	66	62	*119	181	65

(c)—Won Stuart "Butch" Paul Memorial Trophy (Top WHL Rookie).
(d)—June, 1983—Drafted as underage junior by Toronto Maple Leafs in 1983 NHL entry draft. Fourth Maple Leafs pick, 83rd overall, fifth round.

MICHAEL HOFFMAN

Left Wing . . . 5'11" . . . 179 lbs. . . . Born, Cambridge, Ont., February 26, 1963 . . . Shoots left . . . (March, 1980)—Shoulder dislocation.

Year	Team	League	Games	G.	A.	Pts.	Pen.
1979-80—Barrie		Midget	60	40	35	75	....
1980-81—Brantford Alexanders (c)		OHL	68	15	19	34	71
1981-82—Brantford Alexanders		OHL	66	34	47	81	169
1982-83—Brantford Alexanders		OHL	63	26	49	75	128
1982-83—Binghamton Whalers		AHL	1	0	0	0	0

Year	Team	League	Games	G.	A.	Pts.	Pen.
1982-83—Hartford Whalers		NHL	2	0	1	1	0
1983-84—Binghamton Whalers		AHL	64	11	13	24	92
NHL TOTALS			2	0	1	1	0

(c)—June, 1981—Drafted as underage junior by Hartford Whalers in 1981 NHL entry draft. Third Whalers pick, 67th overall, fourth round.

ROBERT FRANK HOFFMEYER

Defense ... 6' ... 180 lbs. ... Born, Dodsland, Sask., July 27, 1955 ... Shoots left ... Missed part of 1978-79 season with a broken jaw ... (January 22, 1983)—Sprained wrist in game vs. N.Y. Islanders ... (December 17, 1983)—Suspended for six games following stick swinging incident in game at Minnesota with Brian Bellows.

Year	Team	League	Games	G.	A.	Pts.	Pen.
1972-73—Prince Albert Mintos		SJHL	..	..	..	..	..
1973-74—Saskatoon Blades		WCHL	62	2	10	12	198
1974-75—Saskatoon Blades (c)		WCHL	64	4	38	42	242
1975-76—Dallas Black Hawks		CHL	5	0	0	0	11
1975-76—Flint Generals		IHL	67	3	13	16	145
1976-77—Flint Generals		IHL	78	12	51	63	213
1977-78—Dallas Black Hawks		CHL	67	5	11	16	172
1977-78—Chicago Black Hawks		NHL	5	0	1	1	12
1978-79—Chicago Black Hawks		NHL	6	0	2	2	5
1978-79—New Brunswick Hawks		AHL	41	3	6	9	102
1979-80—New Brunswick Hawks		AHL	77	3	20	23	161
1980-81—Schwenningen		W. Germany	39	22	30	52	122
1980-81—Maine Mariners (d)		AHL	2	1	1	2	52
1981-82—Philadelphia Flyers		NHL	57	7	20	27	142
1981-82—Maine Mariners (e)		AHL	21	6	8	14	57
1982-83—Philadelphia Flyers (f)		NHL	35	2	11	13	40
1982-83—Maine Mariners (g)		AHL	23	5	10	15	79
1983-84—Maine Mariners		AHL	14	3	1	4	27
1983-84—New Jersey Devils		NHL	58	4	12	16	61
NHL TOTALS			161	13	46	59	260

(c)—June, 1975—Drafted by Chicago Black Hawks in 1975 NHL amateur draft. Fifth Black Hawks pick, 79th overall, fifth round.

(d)—March, 1981—Signed by Philadelphia Flyers as a free agent.

(e)—Claimed by Edmonton Oilers in 1982 NHL waiver draft.

(f)—October, 1982—Traded by Edmonton Oilers to Philadelphia Flyers for Peter Dineen.

(g)—August, 1983—Signed by New Jersey Devils as a free agent.

JIM HOFFORD

Defense ... 6' ... 190 lbs. ... Born, Sudbury, Ont., October 4, 1964 ... Shoots right ... (September, 1981)—Broken nose.

Year	Team	League	Games	G.	A.	Pts.	Pen.
1981-82—Windsor Spitfires		OHL	67	5	9	14	214
1982-83—Windsor Spitfires (c)		OHL	63	8	20	28	171
1983-84—Windsor Spitfires		OHL	1	0	0	0	2

(c)—June, 1983—Drafted as underage junior by Buffalo Sabres in 1983 NHL entry draft. Eighth Sabres pick, 114th overall, sixth round.

BRUCE HOLLOWAY

Defense ... 6' ... 200 lbs. ... Born, Revelstoke, B.C., June 27, 1963 ... Shoots left.

Year	Team	League	Games	G.	A.	Pts.	Pen.
1978-79—Revelstoke Bruins		BCJHL	61	4	14	18	52
1978-79—Billings Bighorns		WHL	9	0	1	1	0
1979-80—Melville		SJHL	9	3	2	5	10
1979-80—Billings Bighorns		WHL	49	1	9	10	6
1980-81—Regina Pats (c-d)		WHL	69	6	29	35	61
1981-82—Regina Pats		WHL	69	4	28	32	111
1982-83—Brandon Wheat Kings		WHL	7	0	5	5	8
1982-83—Kamloops Junior Oilers		WHL	51	16	53	69	82
1983-84—Fredericton Express		AHL	66	3	30	33	29

(c)—October, 1980—Traded with Neil Girard and Wade Waters by Billings Bighorns to Regina Pats for Jim McGeough.

(d)—June, 1981—Drafted as underage junior by Vancouver Canucks in 1981 NHL entry draft. Sixth Canucks pick, 136th overall, seventh round.

WARREN HOLMES

Center . . . 6'1" . . . 185 lbs. . . . Born, Beeton, Ont., February 18, 1957 . . . Shoots left . . . (November, 1980)—Sprained ankle.

Year	Team	League	Games	G.	A.	Pts.	Pen.
1974-75—Ottawa 67's		Jr."A"OHA	54	9	17	26	47
1975-76—Ottawa 67's		Jr."A"OHA	28	3	11	14	6
1976-77—Ottawa 67's (c)		Jr."A"OHA	36	18	29	47	31
1977-78—Saginaw Gears		IHL	78	48	33	81	51
1978-79—Springfield Indians		AHL	4	0	0	0	0
1978-79—Milwaukee Admirals		IHL	31	11	17	28	33
1978-79—Saginaw Gears (d)		IHL	38	11	18	29	30
1979-80—Saginaw Gears		IHL	72	37	55	92	62
1979-80—Binghamton Dusters		AHL	2	0	0	0	0
1980-81—Houston Apollos		CHL	25	7	7	14	18
1980-81—Saginaw Gears		IHL	40	21	26	47	27
1981-82—New Haven Nighthawks		AHL	73	28	28	56	29
1981-82—Los Angeles Kings		NHL	3	0	2	2	0
1982-83—New Haven Nighthawks		AHL	35	17	18	35	26
1982-83—Los Angeles Kings		NHL	39	8	16	24	7
1983-84—New Haven Nighthawks		AHL	76	26	35	61	25
1983-84—Los Angeles Kings		NHL	3	0	0	0	0
NHL TOTALS			45	8	18	26	7

(c)—Drafted from Ottawa 67's by Los Angeles Kings in fifth round of 1977 amateur draft.
(d)—December, 1978—Traded with Randy Rudnyk by Saginaw Gears to Milwaukee Admirals for first and second draft choices.

PAUL HOWARD HOLMGREN

Right Wing . . . 6'3" . . . 210 lbs. . . . Born, St. Paul, Minn., December 2, 1955 . . . Shoots right . . . Attended University of Minnesota . . . Had surgery for injured eye (cornea scratch) following 1975-76 season . . . Missed part of 1976-77 season with separation of right shoulder and part of 1977-78 season with recurrence of same injury . . . (August, 1981)—Separated shoulder during Team U.S.A. training camp preparing for the 1981 Canada Cup Tournament . . . (December 12, 1981)—Took a swing at NHL referee Andy Van Hellemond and was given a five-game suspension by NHL . . . (January, 1982)—Knee injury . . . (May 15,1980)—First U.S. born player to score hat trick in Stanley Cup Play . . . (October, 1983)—Sprained left knee . . . (January, 1984)—Bruised left shoulder . . . (March, 1984)—Shoulder injury . . . (April, 1984)—Shoulder surgery.

Year	Team	League	Games	G.	A.	Pts.	Pen.
1973-74—St. Paul Vulcans (c)		MWJHL	55	22	59	81	183
1974-75—University of Minnesota (d)		WCHA	37	10	21	31	108
1975-76—Johnstown Jets		NAHL	6	3	12	15	12
1975-76—Minnesota Fighting Saints		WHA	51	14	16	30	121
1975-76—Richmond Robins (e)		AHL	6	4	4	8	23
1975-76—Philadelphia Flyers		NHL	1	0	0	0	2
1976-77—Philadelphia Flyers		NHL	59	14	12	26	201
1977-78—Philadelphia Flyers		NHL	62	16	18	34	190
1978-79—Philadelphia Flyers		NHL	57	19	10	29	168
1979-80—Philadelphia Flyers		NHL	74	30	35	65	267
1980-81—Philadelphia Flyers		NHL	77	22	37	59	306
1981-82—Philadelphia Flyers		NHL	41	9	22	31	183
1982-83—Philadelphia Flyers		NHL	77	19	24	43	178
1983-84—Philadelphia Flyers (f)		NHL	52	9	13	22	105
1983-84—Minnesota North Stars		NHL	11	2	5	7	46
WHA TOTALS			51	14	16	30	121
NHL TOTALS			511	140	176	316	1646

(c)—Selected by Edmonton Oilers in World Hockey Association amateur player draft, May, 1974. WHA rights traded to Minnesota Fighting Saints.
(d)—Drafted from University of Minnesota by Philadelphia Flyers in sixth round of 1975 amateur draft.
(e)—Signed by Philadelphia Flyers as free agent following demise of Minnesota Fighting Saints, March, 1976.
(f)—February, 1984—Traded by Philadelphia Flyers to Minnesota North Stars for Paul Guay and third round 1985 draft pick.

STEWART RANDALL (RANDY) HOLT

Defense . . . 5'11" . . . 184 lbs. . . . Born, Pembroke, Ont., January 15, 1953 . . . Shoots right . . . Brother of Gary Holt . . . Set CHL record for penalty minutes in season with 411 in 1974-75 season . . . Missed part of 1976-77 season with torn ligaments in right knee . . . Set NHL single game penalty minute (67) record, March 11, 1979 vs. Philadelphia Flyers . . . (November 20, 1980)—Stretched knee ligaments . . . (January, 1981)—Shoulder injury . . .

Brother of Tim and Gary Holt ... Also plays right wing.

Year	Team	League	Games	G.	A.	Pts.	Pen.
1970-71—Niagara Falls Flyers	Jr."A"OHA	35	5	7	12	178
1971-72—Niagara Falls Flyers	Jr."A"OHA	4	0	1	1	14
1972-73—Sudbury Wolves (c)	Jr."A"OHA	55	7	42	49	294
1973-74—Dallas Black Hawks (d)	CHL	66	3	15	18	222
1974-75—Dallas Black Hawks (e)	CHL	65	8	32	40	*411
1974-75—Chicago Black Hawks	NHL	12	0	1	1	13
1975-76—Dallas Black Hawks (a)	CHL	64	6	46	52	161
1975-76—Chicago Black Hawks	NHL	12	0	0	0	13
1976-77—Dallas Black Hawks	CHL	30	0	10	10	90
1976-77—Chicago Black Hawks	NHL	12	0	3	3	14
1977-78—Chicago Black Hawks (f)	NHL	6	0	0	0	20
1977-78—Cleveland Barons (g)	NHL	48	1	4	5	229
1978-79—Vancouver Canucks (h)	NHL	22	1	3	4	80
1978-79—Los Angeles Kings	NHL	36	0	6	6	202
1979-80—Los Angeles Kings (i)	NHL	42	0	1	1	94
1980-81—Calgary Flames	NHL	48	0	5	5	165
1981-82—Calgary Flames (j)	NHL	8	0	0	0	9
1981-82—Washington Capitals	NHL	53	2	6	8	250
1982-83—Washington Capitals (k-l)	NHL	70	0	8	8	*275
1983-84—Philadelphia Flyers	NHL	26	0	0	0	74
NHL TOTALS		395	4	37	41	1438

(c)—Drafted from Sudbury Wolves by Chicago Black Hawks in third round of 1973 amateur draft.
(d)—Led in penalty minutes (51) during playoffs.
(e)—Led in penalty minutes (86) during playoffs.
(f)—Traded to Cleveland Barons by Chicago Black Hawks for Reg Kerr, November, 1977.
(g)—Selected by Vancouver Canucks in dispersal draft of Cleveland Barons' players, June, 1978.
(h)—December, 1978—Traded by Vancouver Canucks to Los Angeles Kings for Don Kozak.
(i)—June, 1980—Traded by Los Angeles Kings to Calgary Flames with Bert Wilson for Garry Unger.
(j)—December, 1981—Traded with Bobby Gould by Calgary Flames to Washington Capitals for Pat Ribble and future considerations.
(k)—June, 1983—Released by Washington Capitals.
(l)—August, 1983—Signed by Philadelphia Flyers as a free agent.

CRAIG HOMOLA

Center ... 5'10" ... 176 lbs. ... Born, Eveleth, Minn., November 29, 1958 ... Shoots left.

Year	Team	League	Games	G.	A.	Pts.	Pen.
1977-78—University of Vermont	ECAC	31	17	18	35	8
1978-79—University of Vermont	ECAC	30	24	31	55	39
1979-80—University of Vermont (a-c-d-e)	ECAC	34	28	*41	*69	18
1980-81—University of Vermont	ECAC	33	19	27	46	44
1980-81—Oklahoma City Stars	CHL	5	2	2	4	0
1981-82—Nashville South Stars (f)	CHL	76	19	35	54	47
1982-83—Birmingham South Stars	CHL	80	30	44	74	34
1983-84—Salt Lake Golden Eagles	CHL	68	29	27	56	37

(c)—Named to All-America Team (East).
(d)—Named to First Team of All-New England Team.
(e)—Named ECAC Most Valuable Player.
(f)—September, 1981—Signed by Minnesota North Stars as a free agent.

TODD HOOEY

Right Wing ... 6'1" ... 180 lbs. ... Born, Oshawa, Ont., June 23, 1963 ... Shoots right ... Nephew of Tom and Tim O'Connor (1958 World Champion Whitby Dunlops).

Year	Team	League	Games	G.	A.	Pts.	Pen.
1979-80—Oshawa Reps	Midget	53	31	20	51	....
1980-81—Windsor Spitfires (c)	OHL	68	18	25	43	132
1981-82—Windsor Spitfires	OHL	68	39	62	101	158
1981-82—Oklahoma City Stars	CHL	4	1	1	2	0
1982-83—Windsor Spitfires (d)	OHL	4	0	1	1	6
1982-83—Oshawa Generals	OHL	62	31	34	65	64
1983-84—Colorado Flames	CHL	67	19	21	40	40

(c)—June, 1981—Drafted as underage junior by Calgary Flames in 1981 NHL entry draft. Fifth Flames pick, 120th overall, sixth round.
(d)—October, 1982—Traded by Windsor Spitfires to Oshawa Generals for Ray Flaherty.

TIM HOOVER

Defense ... 5'10" ... 165 lbs. ... Born, North Bay, Ont., January 9, 1965 ... Shoots left.

Year	Team	League	Games	G.	A.	Pts.	Pen.
1982-83—Sault Ste. Marie Greyhounds (c)	OHL	60	6	21	27	53
1983-84—Sault Ste. Marie Greyhounds	OHL	70	8	34	42	50

(c)—June, 1983—Drafted as underage junior by Buffalo Sabres in 1983 NHL entry draft. Eleventh Sabres pick, 174th overall, ninth round.

DEAN ROBERT HOPKINS

Right Wing . . . 6'1" . . . 205 lbs. . . . Born, Cobourg, Ont., June 6, 1959 . . . Shoots right . . . Played Center prior to 1978-79 . . . Missed 14 games during 1979-80 season with broken ankle . . . (December, 1981)—Dislocated elbow . . . Brother of Brent Hopkins.

Year	Team	League	Games	G.	A.	Pts.	Pen.
1975-76—London Knights	OMJHL	53	4	14	18	50
1976-77—London Knights	OMJHL	63	19	26	45	67
1977-78—London Knights	OMJHL	67	19	34	53	70
1978-79—London Knights (c)	OMJHL	65	37	55	92	149
1979-80—Los Angeles Kings	NHL	60	8	6	14	39
1980-81—Los Angeles Kings	NHL	67	8	18	26	118
1981-82—Los Angeles Kings	NHL	41	2	13	15	102
1982-83—New Haven Nighthawks	AHL	20	9	8	17	58
1982-83—Los Angeles Kings	NHL	49	5	12	17	43
1983-84—New Haven Nighthawks	AHL	79	35	47	82	162
NHL TOTALS		217	23	49	72	302

(c)—August, 1979—Drafted by Los Angeles Kings in 1979 entry draft. Second Kings pick, 29th overall, second round.

PETER HORACHEK

Left Wing . . . 6'1" . . . 195 lbs. . . . Born, Stoney Creek, Ont., January 26, 1960 . . . Shoots left.

Year	Team	League	Games	G	A	Pts	Pen
1977-78—Oshawa Generals	OMJHL	66	22	26	48	163
1978-79—Oshawa Generals	OMJHL	67	15	35	50	32
1979-80—Oshawa Generals (c)	OHL	68	35	67	102	43
1979-80—Rochester Americans (d)	AHL	..	..	..	..	..
1980-81—Rochester Americans	AHL	63	20	26	46	61
1981-82—Rochester Americans	AHL	52	8	14	22	37
1982-83—Rochester Americans	AHL	1	0	0	0	0
1982-83—Flint Generals	IHL	51	27	28	55	23
1983-84—Flint Generals	IHL	82	34	52	86	34

(c)—November, 1979—Signed by Buffalo Sabres as a free agent.
(d)—No regular season record. Played in four playoff games.

MIKE HORDY

Defense . . . 5'10" . . . 180 lbs. . . . Born, Thunder Bay, Ont., October 10, 1956 . . . Shoots left.

Year	Team	League	Games	G.	A.	Pts.	Pen.
1973-74—Thunder Bay Hurricanes	MWJHL	59	11	39	50	34
1974-75—S. Ste. Marie Greyhounds	Jr."A"OHA	70	18	33	51	59
1975-76—S. Ste. M. Greyhounds (c)	Jr."A"OHA	63	17	51	68	84
1976-77—Muskegon Mohawks	IHL	77	16	45	61	38
1976-77—Fort Worth Texans	CHL	2	0	0	0	5
1977-78—Fort Worth Texans (d)	CHL	76	14	35	49	87
1978-79—New York Islanders	NHL	2	0	0	0	0
1978-79—Ft. Worth Texans (b)	CHL	74	17	48	65	71
1979-80—New York Islanders	NHL	9	0	0	0	7
1979-80—Indianapolis Checkers (b)	CHL	64	4	32	36	43
1980-81—Indianapolis Checkers (b)	CHL	70	10	48	58	103
1981-82—Indianapolis Checkers (a)	CHL	79	17	49	66	86
1982-83—Switzerland (e)		..	..	..	..	..
1983-84—Maine Mariners	AHL	72	11	41	52	31
NHL TOTALS		11	0	0	0	7

(c)—Drafted from Sault Ste. Marie Greyhounds by New York Islanders in fifth round of 1976 amateur draft.
(d)—Won Bob Gassoff Trophy (CHL's most improved defenseman).
(e)—August, 1983—Signed by New Jersey Devils as a free agent.

ED HOSPODAR

Defense . . . 6'2" . . . 210 lbs. . . . Born, Bowling Green, Ohio, February 9, 1959 . . . Shoots right . . . (September, 1977)—Surgery to remove cartilage from left knee . . . (September, 1978)—Injured ligaments in right knee . . . (October, 1980)—Bruised left ankle . . . (December 28, 1980)—Strained back . . . (December 30, 1981)—Suffered broken jaw and loss

of several teeth in altercation with Clark Gillies of New York Islanders . . . (December, 1983)—Hamstring injury.

Year	Team	League	Games	G.	A.	Pts.	Pen.
1976-77—Ottawa 67's		OMJHL	51	3	19	22	140
1977-78—Ottawa 67's		OMJHL	62	7	26	33	172
1978-79—Ottawa 67's (b-c)		OMJHL	46	7	16	23	208
1979-80—New Haven Nighthawks		AHL	25	3	9	12	131
1979-80—New York Rangers		NHL	20	0	1	1	76
1980-81—New York Rangers (d)		NHL	61	5	14	19	214
1981-82—New York Rangers (e)		NHL	41	3	8	11	152
1982-83—Hartford Whalers		NHL	72	1	9	10	199
1983-84—Hartford Whalers (f)		NHL	59	0	9	9	163
NHL TOTALS			253	9	41	50	804

(c)—August, 1979—Drafted by New York Rangers in 1979 entry draft. Second Rangers pick, 34th overall, second round.
(d)—Led NHL playoffs with 93 penalty minutes.
(e)—October, 1982—Traded by New York Rangers to Hartford Whalers for Kent-Erik Andersson.
(f)—July, 1983—Released by Hartford Whalers and signed by Philadelphia Flyers as a free agent.

GREG HOTHAM

Defense . . . 5'11" . . . 183 lbs. . . . Born, London, Ont., March 7, 1956 . . . Shoots right . . . (November, 1982)—Injured knee . . . Missed parts of 1982-83 season with sprained knee, separated shoulder and injured back.

Year	Team	League	Games	G.	A.	Pts.	Pen.
1973-74—Aurora Tigers		OPJHL	44	10	22	32	120
1974-75—Aurora Tigers		OPJHL	27	14	10	24	46
1974-75—Kingston Canadians		Jr."A"OHA	31	1	14	15	49
1975-76—Kingston Canadians (c)		Jr."A"OHA	49	10	32	42	76
1976-77—Saginaw Gears		IHL	69	4	33	37	100
1977-78—Saginaw Gears (b)		IHL	80	13	59	72	56
1977-78—Dallas Black Hawks (d)		CHL	....	...	...	...	....
1978-79—New Brunswick Hawks		AHL	76	9	27	36	88
1979-80—Toronto Maple Leafs		NHL	46	3	10	13	10
1979-80—New Brunswick Hawks		AHL	21	1	6	7	10
1980-81—Toronto Maple Leafs		NHL	11	1	1	2	11
1980-81—New Brunswick Hawks		AHL	68	8	48	56	80
1981-82—Cincinnati Tigers		CHL	46	10	33	43	94
1981-82—Toronto Maple Leafs (e)		NHL	3	0	0	0	0
1981-82—Pittsburgh Penguins		NHL	25	4	6	10	16
1982-83—Pittsburgh Penguins		NHL	58	2	30	32	39
1983-84—Pittsburgh Penguins		NHL	76	5	25	30	59
NHL TOTALS			219	15	72	87	135

(c)—Drafted from Kingston Canadians by Toronto Maple Leafs in fifth round of 1976 amateur draft.
(d)—No league record. Appeared in 5 playoff games.
(e)—January, 1982—Traded by Toronto Maple Leafs to Pittsburgh Penguins for future draft considerations.

DOUG HOUDA

Defense . . . 6'2" . . . 195 lbs. . . . Born, Blairmore, Alta., June 3, 1966 . . . Shoots right.

Year	Team	League	Games	G.	A.	Pts.	Pen.
1981-82—Calgary Wranglers		WHL	3	0	0	0	0
1982-83—Calgary Wranglers		WHL	71	5	23	28	99
1983-84—Calgary Wranglers (c)		WHL	69	6	30	36	195

(c)—June, 1984—Drafted as underage junior by Detroit Red Wings in 1984 NHL entry draft. Second Red Wings pick, 28th overall, second round.

MIKE L. HOUGH

Left Wing . . . 6'1" . . . 195 lbs. . . . Born, Montreal, Que., February 6, 1963 . . . Shoots left.

Year	Team	League	Games	G.	A.	Pts.	Pen.
1980-81—Dixie Beehives		OPJHL	24	15	20	35	84
1981-82—Kitchener Rangers (c)		OHL	58	14	34	48	172
1982-83—Kitchener Rangers		OHL	61	17	27	44	156
1983-84—Fredericton Express		AHL	69	11	16	27	142

(c)—June, 1982—Drafted as underage junior by Quebec Nordiques in 1982 NHL entry draft. Seventh Nordiques pick, 181st overall, ninth round.

PHIL HOUSLEY

Defense . . . 5'11" . . . 170 lbs. . . . Born, St. Paul, Minn., March 9, 1964 . . . Shoots left . . .

Member of Team U.S.A. at World Junior Championships, 1982 . . . Also plays Center . . . Member of Team U.S.A. at World Cup Tournament, 1982 . . . Set Buffalo record for most assists by a rookie (47) in 1982-83 . . . (January, 1984)—Bruised shoulder . . . (March 18, 1984)—Became youngest defenseman in NHL history to have 30-goal season (20 years, 9 days)—(Bobby Orr was 22 years, 2 days) . . . Set Buffalo record for points by a defenseman with 77 in 1983-84.

Year	Team	League	Games	G.	A.	Pts.	Pen.
1980-81—St. Paul Volcans		USHL	6	7	7	14	6
1981-82—South St. Paul H.S. (c)		Minn. H.S.	22	31	34	65	18
1982-83—Buffalo Sabres		NHL	77	19	47	66	39
1983-84—Buffalo Sabres		NHL	75	31	46	77	33
NHL TOTALS			152	50	93	143	72

(c)—June, 1982—Drafted as underage player by Buffalo Sabres in 1982 NHL entry draft. First Sabres pick, 6th overall, first round.

KENNETH LYLE HOUSTON

Right Wing . . . 6'2" . . . 200 lbs. . . . Born, Dresden, Ont., September 15, 1953 . . . Shoots right . . . Played Defense prior to 1974-75 . . . Missed first 35 games of '80-81 season with hepatitis . . . (December, 1981)—Hepatitis . . . (March 16, 1983)—Strained ligaments in right knee in game vs. Hartford . . . (December, 1983)—Strained knee . . . (February, 1984)—Lower back strain.

Year	Team	League	Games	G.	A.	Pts.	Pen.
1971-72—Chatham Maroons		SOJHL	48	8	24	32	213
1972-73—Chatham Maroons (a-c)		SOJHL	52	14	41	55	60
1973-74—Omaha Knights		CHL	71	8	22	30	144
1974-75—Omaha Knights		CHL	78	9	32	41	158
1975-76—Nova Scotia Voyageurs		AHL	27	14	15	29	56
1975-76—Atlanta Flames		NHL	38	5	6	11	11
1976-77—Atlanta Flames		NHL	78	20	24	44	35
1977-78—Atlanta Flames		NHL	74	22	16	38	51
1978-79—Atlanta Flames		NHL	80	21	31	52	135
1979-80—Atlanta Flames		NHL	80	23	31	54	100
1980-81—Calgary Flames		NHL	42	15	15	30	93
1981-82—Calgary Flames (d)		NHL	70	22	22	44	91
1982-83—Washington Capitals		NHL	71	25	14	39	93
1983-84—Washington Capitals (e)		NHL	4	0	0	0	4
1983-84—Los Angeles Kings (f)		NHL	33	8	8	16	11
NHL TOTALS			570	161	167	328	624

(c)—Drafted from Chatham Maroons by Atlanta Flames in sixth round of 1973 amateur draft.
(d)—June, 1982—Traded with Pat Riggin by Calgary Flames to Washington Capitals for NHL rights to Howard Walker, sixth round 1982 draft pick (Mats Kihlstrom), third round 1983 pick (Perry Berezan) and a second-round 1984 draft pick (Paul Ranheim).
(e)—October, 1983—Traded with Brian Engblom by Washington Capitals to Los Angeles Kings for Larry Murphy.
(f)—August, 1984—Released by Los Angeles Kings.

TAREK HOWARD

Defense . . . 6'2" . . . 195 lbs. . . . Born, Tucson, Ariz., February 6, 1965 . . . Shoots left.

Year	Team	League	Games	G.	A.	Pts.	Pen.
1981-82—Olds Grizzlys		AJHL	56	10	22	32	101
1982-83—Olds Grizzlys (b-c)		AJHL	54	18	34	52	229
1983-84—Olds Gruzzlys		AJHL	56	10	22	32	101
1983-84—Univ. of North Dakota		WCHA	24	0	1	1	14

(c)—June, 1983—Drafted by Chicago Black Hawks in 1983 NHL entry draft. Fourth Black Hawks pick, 79th overall, fourth round.

GARRY ROBERT CHARLES HOWATT

Left Wing . . . 5'9" . . . 170 lbs. . . . Born, Grand Center, Alta., September 26, 1952 . . . Shoots left . . . (December, 1982)—Arthroscopic surgery to left knee to remove damaged cartilage.

Year	Team	League	Games	G.	A.	Pts.	Pen.
1971-72—Victoria-Flin Flon (c)		WCHL	60	29	50	79	145
1972-73—New Haven Nighthawks		AHL	65	22	27	49	157
1972-73—New York Islanders		NHL	8	0	1	1	18
1973-74—New York Islanders		NHL	78	6	11	17	204
1974-75—New York Islanders		NHL	77	18	30	48	121
1975-76—New York Islanders		NHL	80	21	13	34	197
1976-77—New York Islanders		NHL	70	13	15	28	182
1977-78—New York Islanders		NHL	61	7	12	19	146

Year	Team	League	Games	G.	A.	Pts.	Pen.
1978-79—New York Islanders		NHL	75	16	12	28	205
1979-80—New York Islanders		NHL	77	8	11	19	219
1980-81—New York Islanders (d)		NHL	70	4	15	19	174
1981-82—Hartford Whalers		NHL	80	18	32	50	242
1982-83—Wichita Wind		CHL	11	0	5	5	4
1982-83—New Jersey Devils (e)		NHL	38	1	4	5	114
1983-84—Maine Mariners		AHL	63	12	21	33	124
1983-84—New Jersey Devils (f)		NHL	6	0	0	0	14
NHL TOTALS			720	112	156	268	1836

(c)—Drafted from Flin Flon Bombers by New York Islanders in tenth round of 1972 amateur draft.
(d)—October, 1981—Traded by New York Islanders to Hartford Whalers for fifth round 1983 draft pick (Islanders drafted Bob Caulfield).
(e)—October, 1982—Traded with Rick Meagher by Hartford Whalers for Merlin Malinowski and NHL rights to Scott Fusco.
(f)—August, 1984—Released by New Jersey Devils.

MARK STEVEN HOWE

Left Wing and Defense . . . 5'11" . . . 180 lbs. . . . Born, Detroit, Mich., May 28, 1955 . . . Shoots left . . . Brother of Marty Howe and son of Gordie Howe . . . Was member of 1972 USA Olympic team . . . Missed most of 1971-72 season following corrective knee surgery and part of 1976-77 season with shoulder separation . . . Missed part of 1977-78 season with rib injury . . . (October 9, 1980)—First defenseman in NHL to score two shorthanded goals in one period in 8-6 loss at St. Louis . . . (December 27, 1980)—5-inch puncture wound to upper thigh . . . Set NHL record for most assists (56) and points (80) by an American born player in 1979-80 (Broken by Neal Broten in '81-82) . . . (February, 1984)—Injured shoulder.

Year	Team	League	Games	G.	A.	Pts.	Pen.
1970-71—Detroit Jr. Wings (a-c)		SOJHL	44	37	*70	*107	....
1971-72—Detroit Jr. Wings		SOJHL	9	5	9	14	....
1971-72—USA Olympic Team			....	...	....	....	....
1972-73—Toronto Marlboros (d-e-f)		Jr."A"OHA	60	38	66	104	27
1973-74—Houston Aeros (b-g-h)		WHA	76	38	41	79	20
1974-75—Houston Aeros (i)		WHA	74	36	40	76	30
1975-76—Houston Aeros		WHA	72	39	37	76	38
1976-77—Houston Aeros (b-j)		WHA	57	23	52	75	46
1977-78—New England Whalers		WHA	70	30	61	91	32
1978-79—New England Whalers (a-k)		WHA	77	42	65	107	32
1979-80—Hartford Whalers		NHL	74	24	56	80	20
1980-81—Hartford Whalers		NHL	63	19	46	65	54
1981-82—Hartford Whalers (l)		NHL	76	8	45	53	18
1982-83—Philadelphia Flyers (a)		NHL	76	20	47	67	18
1983-84—Philadelphia Flyers		NHL	71	19	34	53	44
WHA TOTALS			426	208	296	504	198
NHL TOTALS			360	90	228	318	154

(c)—Won Most Valuable Player and Outstanding Forward Awards.
(d)—Traded to Toronto Marlboros by London Knights for Larry Goodenough and Dennis Maruk, August, 1972.
(e)—Led in points (26) during playoffs.
(f)—Signed by Houston Aeros (WHA), June, 1972.
(g)—Won WHA Rookie Award.
(h)—Drafted from Toronto Marlboros by Boston Bruins in second round of 1974 amateur draft.
(i)—Tied for lead in goals (10) and led in points (22) during playoffs.
(j)—Signed by New England Whalers as free agent, June, 1977.
(k)—June, 1979—Selected by Boston Bruins in NHL reclaim draft, but remained Hartford Whalers' property as a priority selection for the expansion draft.
(l)—August, 1982—Traded by Hartford Whalers to Philadelphia Flyers for Ken Linseman, Greg Adams and Philadelphia's first-round choice (David A. Jensen) in 1983 entry draft. Philadelphia and Hartford also agreed to exchange third-round choices in 1983.

MARTY GORDON HOWE

Defense . . . 6'1" . . . 195 lbs. . . . Born, Detroit, Mich., February 18, 1954 . . . Shoots left . . . Brother of Mark Howe and son of Gordie Howe . . . Missed part of 1972-73 season with mononucleosis . . . Missed 14 games of 1978-79 season with knee injury . . . Missed parts of 1979-80 season with broken wrist and bruised ribs . . . (December, 1980)—Knee injury.

Year	Team	League	Games	G.	A.	Pts.	Pen.
1970-71—Detroit Jr. Wings (b)		SOJHL	....	...	....	....	....
1971-72—Toronto Marlboros		Jr."A"OHA	56	7	21	28	122
1972-73—Toronto Marlboros (c)		Jr."A"OHA	38	11	17	28	81
1973-74—Houston Aeros (d)		WHA	73	4	20	24	90

Year	Team	League	Games	G.	A.	Pts.	Pen.
1974-75—Houston Aeros		WHA	75	13	21	34	89
1975-76—Houston Aeros		WHA	80	14	23	37	81
1976-77—Houston Aeros (e-f)		WHA	80	17	28	45	103
1977-78—New England Whalers		WHA	75	10	10	20	66
1978-79—New England Whalers		WHA	66	9	15	24	31
1979-80—Springfield Indians		AHL	31	8	5	13	12
1979-80—Hartford Whalers		NHL	6	0	1	1	4
1980-81—Hartford Whalers		NHL	12	0	1	1	25
1980-81—Binghamton Whalers		AHL	37	4	10	14	34
1981-82—Hartford Whalers		NHL	13	0	4	4	2
1981-82—Binghamton Whalers		AHL	61	8	38	46	42
1982-83—Boston Bruins (g)		NHL	78	1	11	12	24
1983-84—Hartford Whalers		NHL	69	0	11	11	34
WHA TOTALS			449	67	117	184	460
NHL TOTALS			178	1	28	29	89

(c)—Signed by Houston Aeros (WHA), June, 1973.

(d)—Drafted from Toronto Marlboros by Montreal Canadiens in third round of 1974 amateur draft.

(e)—NHL rights traded to Detroit Red Wings by Montreal Canadiens for "future considerations," February, 1977.

(f)—Signed by New England Whalers as free agent, June, 1977.

(g)—September, 1982—Conditionally traded by Hartford Whalers to Boston Bruins for future considerations. Boston returned him to Hartford in June, 1983 to complete transaction.

BRUCE CRAIG HOWES

Defense . . . 6'2" . . . 201 lbs. . . . Born, New Westminster, B.C., July 4, 1960 . . . Shoots left.

Year	Team	League	Games	G.	A.	Pts.	Pen.
1976-77—Maple Ridge		BCJHL	67	5	28	33	248
1976-77—New Westminster Bruins		WCHL	4	0	0	0	2
1977-78—New Westminster Bruins		WCHL	34	2	5	7	78
1978-79—New Westminster Bruins		WHL	65	13	30	43	116
1979-80—New Westminster Bruins (c)		WHL	34	9	14	23	75
1980-81—Adirondack Red Wings		AHL	61	4	16	20	92
1981-82—Kalamazoo Wings		IHL	44	6	14	20	43
1981-82—Adirondack Red Wings		AHL	20	1	1	2	11
1982-83—Adirondack Red Wings		AHL	48	0	4	4	24
1982-83—Kalamazoo Wings		IHL	18	2	6	8	23
1983-84—Kalamazoo Wings		IHL	26	2	9	11	30

(c)—March, 1980—Signed by Detroit Red Wings.

DONALD SCOTT HOWSON
(Known by middle name.)

Center . . . 5'10" . . . 155 lbs. . . . Born, Toronto, Ont., April 9, 1960 . . . Shoots right . . . (January, 1983)—Injured wrist.

Year	Team	League	Games	G.	A.	Pts.	Pen.
1977-78—North York Rangers		OPJHL	55	27	31	58	30
1978-79—Kingston Canadians		OMJHL	63	27	47	74	45
1979-80—Kingston Canadians		OMJHL	68	38	50	88	52
1980-81—Kingston Canadians		OMJHL	66	57	83	140	53
1981-82—Indianapolis Checkers (c)		CHL	8	2	1	3	5
1981-82—Toledo Goaldiggers		IHL	71	55	65	120	14
1982-83—Indianapolis Checkers (d)		CHL	67	34	40	74	22
1983-84—Indianapolis Checkers		CHL	71	34	34	68	40

(c)—September, 1981—Signed by New York Islanders as a free agent.

(d)—Led CHL playoffs with 12 goals.

ANTHONY HRKAC

Center . . . 5'11" . . . 165 lbs. . . . Born, Thunder Bay, Ont., July 7, 1966 . . . Shoots left.

Year	Team	League	Games	G.	A.	Pts.	Pen.
1983-84—Orillia Travelways (c)		OJHL	42	*52	54	*106	20

(c)—June, 1984—Drafted as underage junior by St. Louis Blues in 1984 NHL entry draft. Second Blues pick, 32nd overall, second round.

TIM HRYNEWICH

Left Wing . . . 6' . . . 191 lbs. . . . Born, Leamington, Ont., October 2, 1963 . . . Shoots left.

Year	Team	League	Games	G.	A.	Pts.	Pen.
1980-81—Sudbury Wolves		OHL	65	25	17	42	104
1981-82—Sudbury Wolves (c)		OHL	64	29	41	70	144
1982-83—Sudbury Wolves		OHL	23	21	16	37	65
1982-83—Baltimore Skipjacks		AHL	9	2	1	3	6
1982-83—Pittsburgh Penguins		NHL	30	2	3	5	48
1983-84—Baltimore Skipjacks		AHL	52	13	17	30	65
1983-84—Pittsburgh Penguins		NHL	25	4	5	9	34
NHL TOTALS			55	6	8	14	82

(c)—June, 1982—Drafted as underage junior by Pittsburgh Penguins in 1982 NHL entry draft. Second Penguins pick, 38th overall, second round.

WILHEILM HEINRICH (WILLIE) HUBER

Defense ... 6'5" ... 228 lbs. ... Born, Strasskirchen, Germany, January 15, 1958 ... Shoots right ... (March, 1982)—Fractured left cheekbone ... (February 12, 1983)—Cracked rib during game vs. Winnipeg ... (November, 1983)—Strained left thigh muscle ... (January 2, 1984)—Tore ligaments in right knee during game at Washington and required arthoscopic surgery.

Year	Team	League	Games	G.	A.	Pts.	Pen.
1975-76—Hamilton Fincups		Jr. "A" OHA	58	2	8	10	64
1976-77—St. Catharines Fincups		Jr. "A" OHA	36	10	24	34	111
1977-78—Hamilton Fincups (b-c)		Jr. "A" OHA	61	12	45	57	168
1978-79—Detroit Red Wings		NHL	68	7	24	31	114
1978-79—Kansas City Red Wings		CHL	10	2	7	9	12
1979-80—Adirondack Red Wings		AHL	4	1	3	4	2
1979-80—Detroit Red Wings		NHL	76	17	23	40	164
1980-81—Detroit Red Wings		NHL	80	15	34	49	130
1981-82—Detroit Red Wings		NHL	74	15	30	45	98
1982-83—Detroit Red Wings (d)		NHL	74	14	29	43	106
1983-84—New York Rangers		NHL	42	9	14	23	60
NHL TOTALS			414	77	154	231	672

(c)—Drafted from Hamilton Fincups by Detroit Red Wings in first round of 1978 amateur draft.

(d)—July, 1983—Traded by Detroit Red Wings with Mark Osborne and Mike Blaisdell to New York Rangers for Ron Duguay, Eddie Mio and Ed Johnstone.

CHARLES WILLIAM HUDDY

Defense ... 6' ... 200 lbs. ... Born, Oshawa, Ont., June 2, 1959 ... Shoots left ... (November 10, 1980)—Injured shoulder in game vs. N.Y. Islanders.

Year	Team	League	Games	G.	A.	Pts.	Pen.
1977-78—Oshawa Generals		OMJHL	59	17	18	35	81
1978-79—Oshawa Generals		OMJHL	64	20	38	58	108
1979-80—Houston Apollos (c)		CHL	79	14	34	48	46
1980-81—Edmonton Oilers		NHL	12	2	5	7	6
1980-81—Wichita Wind		CHL	47	8	36	44	71
1981-82—Wichita Wind		CHL	32	7	19	26	51
1981-82—Edmonton Oilers		NHL	41	4	11	15	46
1982-83—Edmonton Oilers		NHL	76	20	37	57	58
1983-84—Edmonton Oilers		NHL	75	8	34	42	43
NHL TOTALS			204	34	87	121	153

(c)—September, 1979—Signed by Edmonton Oilers as a free agent.

PAT HUGHES

Right Wing ... 5'11" ... 190 lbs. ... Born, Calgary, Alb., March 25, 1955 ... Shoots right ... Attended University of Michigan ... Had corrective surgery on right shoulder following 1974-75 season ... Also plays center ... (November 14, 1981)—Strained knee ligaments in game at New York Islanders.

Year	Team	League	Games	G.	A.	Pts.	Pen.
1973-74—University of Michigan		WCHA	35	14	12	26	40
1974-75—University of Michigan (c)		WCHA	38	24	19	43	64
1975-76—University of Michigan		WCHA	35	16	18	34	70
1976-77—Nova Scotia Voyageurs		AHL	77	29	39	68	144
1977-78—Nova Scotia Voyageurs (d)		AHL	74	40	28	68	128
1977-78—Montreal Canadiens		NHL	3	0	0	0	2
1978-79—Montreal Canadiens (e)		NHL	41	9	8	17	22
1979-80—Pittsburgh Penguins		NHL	76	18	14	32	78
1980-81—Pittsburgh Penguins (f)		NHL	58	10	9	19	161
1980-81—Edmonton Oilers		NHL	2	0	0	0	0

Year	Team	League	Games	G.	A.	Pts.	Pen.
1981-82—Edmonton Oilers		NHL	68	24	22	46	99
1982-83—Edmonton Oilers		NHL	80	25	20	45	85
1983-84—Edmonton Oilers		NHL	77	27	28	55	61
NHL TOTALS			405	113	101	214	508

(c)—Drafted from University of Michigan by Montreal Canadiens in fifth round of 1975 amateur draft.
(d)—Led in assists (9) and points (14) during playoffs.
(e)—September, 1979—Traded with Bob Holland by Montreal Canadiens to Pittsburgh Penguins for Denis Herron and second round pick in 1982 entry draft.
(f)—March, 1981—Traded by Pittsburgh Penguins to Edmonton Oilers for Pat Price.

BRETT HULL

Right Wing . . . 5'11" . . . 190 lbs. . . . Born, Belleville, Ontario, August 9, 1964 . . . Shoots right . . . Brother of Blake Hull. Son of Hall-of-Fame left wing Bobby Hull. Nephew of Dennis Hull.

Year	Team	League	Games	G.	A.	Pts.	Pen.
1983-84—Penticton (c)		BCJHL	56	105	83	188	20

(c)—June, 1984—Drafted by Calgary Flames in 1984 NHL entry draft. Sixth Flames pick, 117th overall, sixth round. First Canadian-born 20-year-old drafted in 1984 draft.

DALE ROBERT HUNTER

Center . . . 5'9" . . . 189 lbs. . . . Born, Petrolia, Ont., July 31, 1960 . . . Shoots left . . . Brother of Dave and Mark Hunter . . . (March, 1984)—Given three-game suspension by NHL.

Year	Team	League	Games	G.	A.	Pts.	Pen.
1977-78—Kitchener Rangers		Jr."A"OHA	68	22	42	64	115
1978-79—Sudbury Wolves (c)		Jr."A"OHA	59	42	68	110	188
1979-80—Sudbury Wolves		OMJHL	61	34	51	85	189
1980-81—Quebec Nordiques		NHL	80	19	44	63	226
1981-82—Quebec Nordiques		NHL	80	22	50	72	272
1982-83—Quebec Nordiques		NHL	80	17	46	63	206
1983-84—Quebec Nordiques		NHL	77	24	55	79	232
NHL TOTALS			317	82	195	277	936

(c)—August, 1979—Drafted as underage junior by Quebec Nordiques in entry draft. Second Nordiques pick, 41st overall, second round.

DAVE HUNTER

Left Wing . . . 5'11" . . . 204 lbs. . . . Born, Petrolia, Ont., January 1, 1958 . . . Shoots left . . . Brother of Dale and Mark Hunter . . . (December, 1981)—Knee injury . . . (May, 1984)—Bruised spleen in playoff series with N.Y. Islanders.

Year	Team	League	Games	G.	A.	Pts.	Pen.
1975-76—Sudbury Wolves		Jr."A"OHA	53	7	21	28	117
1976-77—Sudbury Wolves		Jr."A"OHA	62	30	56	86	140
1977-78—Sudbury Wolves (c-d)		Jr."A"OHA	68	44	44	88	156
1978-79—Dallas Black Hawks		CHL	6	3	4	7	6
1978-79—Edmonton Oilers (e)		WHA	72	7	25	32	134
1979-80—Edmonton Oilers		NHL	80	12	31	43	103
1980-81—Edmonton Oilers		NHL	78	12	16	28	98
1981-82—Edmonton Oilers		NHL	63	16	22	38	63
1982-83—Edmonton Oilers		NHL	80	13	18	31	120
1983-84—Edmonton Oilers		NHL	80	22	26	48	90
WHA TOTALS			72	7	25	32	134
NHL TOTALS			381	75	113	188	474

(c)—Drafted from Sudbury Wolves by Montreal Canadiens in first round of 1978 amateur draft.
(d)—Selected by Edmonton Oilers in World Hockey Association amateur players' draft, June, 1978. Signed by Edmonton, June, 1978.
(e)—Led in penalty minutes (42) during playoffs.

MARK HUNTER

Right Wing . . . 6'1" . . . 200 lbs. . . . Born, Petrolia, Ont., November 12, 1962 . . . Shoots right . . . Brother of Dale and Dave Hunter . . . (November 13, 1982)—Pulled tendon in right knee in game at Los Angeles . . . (November 29, 1982)—17-stitch cut under right arm in game vs. Winnipeg . . . (December 26, 1982)—Tore medial ligaments in right knee in collision with brother Dale in game vs. Quebec. Surgery was required, missed 42 games . . . (October, 1983)—Injured right knee that required surgery . . . (February 21, 1984)—Injured knee in game at Quebec.

Year	Team	League	Games	G.	A.	Pts.	Pen.
1979-80—Brantford Alexanders		OMJHL	66	34	55	89	171
1980-81—Brantford Alexanders (c)		OHL	53	39	40	79	157
1981-82—Montreal Canadiens		NHL	71	18	11	29	143
1982-83—Montreal Canadiens		NHL	31	8	8	16	73
1983-84—Montreal Canadiens		NHL	22	6	4	10	42
NHL TOTALS			124	32	23	55	258

(c)—June, 1981—Drafted as underage junior by Montreal Canadiens in 1981 NHL entry draft. First Canadiens pick, seventh overall, first round.

TIM ROBERT HUNTER

Defense . . . 6'2" . . . 186 lbs. . . . Born, Calgary, Alta., September 10, 1960 . . . Shoots right . . . Also plays Right Wing.

Year	Team	League	Games	G.	A.	Pts.	Pen.
1977-78—Kamloops		BCJHL	51	9	28	37	266
1977-78—Seattle Breakers		WCHL	3	1	2	3	4
1978-79—Seattle Breakers (c)		WHL	70	8	41	49	300
1979-80—Seattle Breakers		WHL	72	14	53	67	311
1980-81—Birmingham Bulls		CHL	58	3	5	8	*236
1980-81—Nova Scotia Voyageurs		AHL	17	0	0	0	62
1981-82—Oklahoma City Stars		CHL	55	4	12	16	222
1981-82—Calgary Flames		NHL	2	0	0	0	9
1982-83—Calgary Flames		NHL	16	1	0	1	54
1982-83—Colorado Flames		CHL	46	5	12	17	225
1983-84—Calgary Flames		NHL	43	4	4	8	130
NHL TOTALS			61	5	4	9	193

(c)—August, 1979—Drafted by Atlanta Flames in 1979 NHL entry draft. Fourth Flames pick, 54th overall, third round.

CRAIG HURLEY

Defense . . . 6' . . . 183 lbs. . . . Born, Porcupine Plain, Sask., January 6, 1963 . . . Shoots right.

Year	Team	League	Games	G.	A.	Pts.	Pen.
1979-80—Saskatoon Contacts		Midget	18	13	10	23	44
1980-81—Saskatoon Blades (c)		WHL	66	5	12	17	119
1981-82—Saskatoon Blades		WHL	67	9	14	23	147
1982-83—Saskatoon Blades		WHL	66	8	22	30	165
1983-84—Fort Wayne Komets		IHL	13	0	2	2	12
1983-84—New Haven Nighthawks (d)		AHL	2	0	0	0	6

(c)—June, 1981—Drafted by Los Angeles Kings as underage junior in 1981 NHL entry draft. Fifth Kings pick, 134th overall, seventh round.

(d)—January, 1984—Released by Los Angeles Kings.

STEVE HURT

Right Wing . . . 6'3" . . . 185 lbs. . . . Born, St. Paul, Minn., March 28, 1966 . . . Shoots right.

Year	Team	League	Games	G.	A.	Pts.	Pen.
1983-84—Hill-Murray H.S. (c)		Minn. H.S.	26	20	16	36	10

(c)—June, 1984—Drafted by Pittsburgh Penguins in 1984 NHL entry draft. Eighth Penguins pick, 189th overall, tenth round.

JAMIE HUSGEN

Defense . . . 6'3" . . . 205 lbs. . . . Born, St. Louis, Mo., October 13, 1964 . . . Shoots right.

Year	Team	League	Games	G.	A.	Pts.	Pen.
1982-83—Des Moines Buccaneers (c)		MWJHL	45	8	25	33	157
1983-84—Univ. of Illinois/Chicago		CCHA	35	6	17	23	76

(c)—June, 1983—Drafted by Winnipeg Jets in 1983 NHL entry draft. Thirteenth Jets pick, 229th overall, 12th round.

THOMAS HUSSEY

Left Wing . . . 6'2" . . . 190 lbs. . . . Born, Newmarket, Ont., July 12, 1966 . . . Shoots left.

Year	Team	League	Games	G.	A.	Pts.	Pen.
1983-84—Aurora St. Andrews Prep. (c)		Ont. H.S.	38	40	62	102	..

(c)—June, 1984—Drafted by New York Rangers in 1984 NHL entry draft. Sixth Rangers pick, 140th overall, seventh round.

JOHN HUTCHINGS

Defense . . . 6' . . . 185 lbs. . . . Born, Cobourg, Ont., August 17, 1964 . . . Shoots right . . . (July, 1980)—Broken leg when run over by a tractor.

Year	Team	League	Games	G.	A.	Pts.	Pen.
1980-81—Oshawa Generals		OHL	—Did Not Play Due to Broken Leg—				
1981-82—Oshawa Generals (c)		OHL	59	5	38	43	64
1982-83—Oshawa Generals		OHL	67	16	33	49	102
1983-84—Oshawa 67's		OHL	65	20	60	80	113

(c)—June, 1982—Drafted by New Jersey Devils as underage junior in 1982 NHL entry draft. Eighth Devils pick, 148th overall, eighth round.

DAVID JOSEPH HUTCHISON

Defense . . . 6'2" . . . 205 lbs. . . . Born, London, Ont., May 2, 1952 . . . Shoots left . . . Also played Left Wing in 1973-74 . . . Missed part of 1975-76 season with sprained ankle and was suspended by NHL for eight games . . . Missed parts of 1977-78 season with severely cut hand, charley horse and broken left foot . . . (February 14, 1981)—Broken finger . . . (December, 1982)—Pulled back muscles . . . (January, 1984)—Injured knee.

Year	Team	League	Games	G.	A.	Pts.	Pen.
1969-70—London Knights		Jr."A"OHA	7	1	2	3	30
1970-71—London Knights		Jr."A"OHA	54	2	13	15	154
1971-72—London Knights (c-d)		Jr."A"OHA	46	3	11	14	151
1972-73—Roanoke Valley-Rhode Island		EHL	32	7	18	25	158
1972-73—Philadelphia Blazers		WHA	28	0	2	2	34
1973-74—Vancouver Blazers (e)		WHA	69	0	13	13	151
1974-75—Los Angeles Kings		NHL	68	0	6	6	133
1975-76—Los Angeles Kings		NHL	50	0	10	10	181
1976-77—Los Angeles Kings		NHL	70	6	11	17	220
1977-78—Los Angeles Kings (f)		NHL	44	0	10	10	71
1978-79—Toronto Maple Leafs		NHL	79	4	15	19	235
1979-80—Toronto Maple Leafs (g)		NHL	31	1	6	7	28
1979-80—Chicago Black Hawks		NHL	38	0	5	5	73
1980-81—Chicago Black Hawks		NHL	59	2	9	11	124
1981-82—Chicago Black Hawks (h-i)		NHL	66	5	18	23	246
1982-83—New Jersey Devils		NHL	32	1	4	5	102
1983-84—Toronto Maple Leafs (j)		NHL	47	0	3	3	137
NHL TOTALS			584	19	97	116	1550
WHA TOTALS			97	0	15	15	185

(c)—Selected by Miami Screaming Eagles in World Hockey Assn. player selection draft, February, 1972.
(d)—Drafted from London Knights by Los Angeles Kings in third round of 1972 amateur draft.
(e)—Signed by Los Angeles Kings, June, 1974.
(f)—Traded to Toronto Maple Leafs by Los Angeles Kings with Lorne Stamler for Brian Glennie, Scott Garland, Kurt Walker and second-round 1979 draft (Mark Hardy) choice, June, 1978.
(g)—January, 1980—Traded by Toronto Maple Leafs to Chicago Black Hawks for Pat Ribble.
(h)—September, 1982—Traded by Chicago Black Hawks with Ted Bulley to Washington Capitals for future considerations.
(i)—Claimed by New Jersey Devils in 1982 NHL waiver draft.
(j)—November, 1983—Signed by Toronto Maple Leafs as a free agent.

DWAINE HUTTON

Center . . . 5'11" . . . 175 lbs. . . . Born, Edmonton, Alta., April 18, 1965 . . . Shoots left.

Year	Team	League	Games	G.	A.	Pts.	Pen.
1982-83—Kelowna Wings (c)		WHL	65	21	47	68	17
1983-84—Regina Pats		WHL	14	2	2	4	2
1983-84—Saskatoon Blades		WHL	35	13	30	43	16

(c)—June, 1983—Drafted as underage junior by Washington Capitals in 1983 NHL entry draft. Third Capitals pick, 135th overall, seventh round.

AL IAFRATE

Defense . . . 6'3" . . . 190 lbs. . . . Born, Dearborn, Mich., March 21, 1966 . . . Shoots left . . . Member of 1984 U.S. Olympic Team.

Year	Team	League	Games	G.	A.	Pts.	Pen.
1983-84—U.S. National Team		Int'l	55	4	17	21	26
1983-84—U.S. Olympic Team		Int'l	6	0	0	0	2
1983-84—Belleville Bulls (c)		OHL	10	2	4	6	2

(c)—June, 1984—Drafted as underage junior by Toronto Maple Leafs in 1984 NHL entry draft. First Maple Leafs pick, fourth overall, first round.

PETER IHNACAK

Center . . . 6' . . . 180 lbs. . . . Born, Prague, Czech., May 5, 1957 . . . Shoots right . . . Set Toronto club rookie record with 66 points in 1982-83, and tied rookie record with 28 goals .

.. (1982-83)—Set Toronto Maple Leafs point record (66) for rookies ... Brother of Miroslav Ihnacak (VSZ Kosice, Czechoslovakian Elite League) ... (October 16, 1983)—Injured knee ligaments in game at New Jersey ... (February 29, 1984)—Injured shoulder in game vs. N.Y. Rangers, out for the season.

Year	Team	League	Games	G.	A.	Pts.	Pen.
1978-79—Dukla Jihlava		Czech.	44	22	12	34	....
1979-80—Sparta CKD Praha		Czech.	44	19	28	47	....
1980-81—Sparta CKD Praha		Czech.	44	23	22	45	....
1981-82—Sparta CKD Praha		Czech.	39	16	22	38	30
1982-83—Toronto Maple Leafs (c)		NHL	80	28	38	66	44
1983-84—Toronto Maple Leafs		NHL	47	10	13	23	24
NHL TOTALS			127	38	51	89	68

(c)—July, 1983—Signed by Toronto Maple Leafs as a free agent.

RANDY IRVING

Left Wing ... 6'1" ... 199 lbs. ... Born, Lake Cowichan, B. C., August 12, 1959 ... Shoots left.

Year	Team	League	Games	G.	A.	Pts.	Pen.
1976-77—Maple Ridge		BCJHL	67	47	36	83	244
1976-77—New Westminster Bruins		WCHL	2	1	0	1	0
1977-78—New Westminster Bruins		WCHL	72	31	42	73	160
1978-79—Victoria Cougars		WHL	61	18	28	46	167
1979-80—Muskegon Mohawks		IHL	41	13	26	39	70
1979-80—Toledo Goaldiggers		IHL	28	7	21	28	20
1980-81—Toledo Goaldiggers		IHL	77	38	38	76	149
1981-82—Ft. Worth Texans		CHL	2	0	0	0	0
1981-82—Fort Wayne Komets		IHL	26	6	6	12	43
1982-83—Carolina Thunderbirds (b)		ACHL	63	8	46	54	139
1983-84—Carolina Thunderbirds (a)		ACHL	55	15	35	50	163

DON CLINTON JACKSON

Defense ... 6'3" ... 210 lbs. ... Born, Minneapolis, Minn., September 2, 1956 ... Shoots left ... Attended University of Notre Dame ... Has also played Left Wing ... (February, 1984)—Groin injury.

Year	Team	League	Games	G.	A.	Pts.	Pen.
1974-75—University of Notre Dame		WCHA	35	2	7	9	29
1975-76—University of Notre Dame (c)		WCHA	30	4	5	9	22
1976-77—University of Notre Dame		WCHA	38	2	9	11	52
1977-78—University of Notre Dame		WCHA	37	10	23	33	69
1977-78—Minnesota North Stars		NHL	2	0	0	0	2
1978-79—Minnesota North Stars		NHL	5	0	0	0	2
1978-79—Oklahoma City Stars		CHL	73	8	23	31	108
1979-80—Minnesota North Stars		NHL	10	0	4	4	18
1979-80—Oklahoma City Stars		CHL	33	5	9	14	54
1980-81—Oklahoma City Stars		CHL	59	5	33	38	67
1980-81—Minnesota North Stars (d)		NHL	10	0	3	3	19
1981-82—Edmonton Oilers		NHL	8	0	0	0	18
1981-82—Wichita Wind		CHL	71	7	37	44	116
1982-83—Edmonton Oilers		NHL	71	2	8	10	136
1982-83—Birmingham South Stars		CHL	4	1	4	5	8
1983-84—Edmonton Oilers		NHL	64	8	12	20	120
NHL TOTALS			170	10	27	37	315

(c)—Drafted from University of Notre Dame by Minnesota North Stars in third round of 1976 amateur draft.

(d)—September, 1981—Traded by Minnesota North Stars to Edmonton Oilers along with third-round draft choice in 1982 for Don Murdoch.

JAMES KENNETH JACKSON

Center ... 5'8" ... 190 lbs. ... Born, Oshawa, Ont., February 1, 1960 ... Shoots right ... Also plays right wing and defense ... (January, 1981)—Groin injury.

Year	Team	League	Games	G.	A.	Pts.	Pen.
1976-77—Oshawa Generals		OMJHL	65	13	40	53	26
1977-78—Oshawa Generals ·		OMJHL	68	33	47	80	60
1978-79—Niagara Falls Flyers		OMJHL	64	26	39	65	73
1979-80—Niagara Falls Flyers		OMJHL	66	29	57	86	55
1980-81—Richmond Rifles (b)		EHL	58	17	43	60	42
1981-82—Muskegon Mohawks (b)		IHL	82	24	51	75	72

Year	Team	League	Games	G.	A.	Pts.	Pen.
1982-83—Colorado Flames		CHL	30	10	16	26	4
1982-83—Calgary Flames		NHL	48	8	12	20	7
1983-84—Calgary Flames		NHL	49	6	14	20	13
1983-84—Colorado Flames		CHL	25	5	27	32	4
NHL TOTALS			97	14	26	40	20

JEFF JACKSON

Left Wing . . . 6'1" . . . 193 lbs. . . . Born, Chatham, Ont., April 24, 1965 . . . Shoots left . . . Also plays center . . . (January, 1982)—Stretched knee ligaments.

Year	Team	League	Games	G.	A.	Pts.	Pen.
1981-82—Newmarket Flyers		OJHL	45	30	39	69	105
1982-83—Brantford Alexanders (c)		OHL	64	18	25	43	63
1983-84—Brantford Alexanders		OHL	58	27	42	69	78

(c)—June, 1983—Drafted as underage junior by Toronto Maple Leafs in 1983 NHL entry draft. Second Maple Leafs pick, 28th overall, second round.

RISTO JALO

Center . . . 5'11" . . . 185 lbs. . . . Born, Tampere, Finland, July 18, 1962 . . . Shoots left.

Year	Team	League	Games	G.	A.	Pts.	Pen.
1980-81—Tampere Ilves		Finland	16	3	3	6	2
1981-82—Tampere Ilves (c)		Finland	34	17	20	37	8
1982-83—Tampere Ilves		Finland	..	..	..	..	..
1983-84—Tampere Ilves (d)		Finland	36	13	32	45	30

(c)—June, 1981—Drafted by Washington Capitals in NHL entry draft. Seventh Capitals pick, 131st overall, seventh round.

(d)—March, 1984—Traded by Washington Capitals to Edmonton Oilers for future considerations.

KARI JALONEN

Center . . . 6'2" . . . 185 lbs. . . . Born, Oulu, Finland, January 6, 1960 . . . Shoots left.

Year	Team	League	Games	G.	A.	Pts.	Pen.
1979-80—Karpat Oulu		Finland	28	23	24	47	16
1980-81—Karpat Oulu (c)		Finland	35	16	34	50	22
1981-82—Karpat Oulu (d)		Finland	33	21	26	47	24
1982-83—Colorado Flames		CHL	33	12	32	44	8
1982-83—Calgary Flames		NHL	25	9	3	12	4
1983-84—Colorado Flames		CHL	1	0	0	0	0
1983-84—Calgary Flames (e)		NHL	9	0	3	3	0
1983-84—Edmonton Oilers (f)		NHL	3	0	0	0	0
NHL TOTALS			37	9	6	15	4

(c)—Led Playoffs with 14 assists and 21 points, and tied for playoff lead (with Reijo Ruotsalainen and Antero Lehtonen) with seven goals.

(d)—September, 1981—Signed by Calgary Flames as a free agent to report when his commitment was completed with Karpat Oulu.

(e)—December, 1983—Released by Calgary Flames and signed with Edmonton Oilers as a free agent.

(f)—December, 1983—Returned to Finland.

MIKE JAMES

Defense . . . 6'2" . . . 168 lbs. . . . Born, Toronto, Ont., January 31, 1964 . . . Shoots left.

Year	Team	League	Games	G.	A.	Pts.	Pen.
1980-81—Georgetown Geminis (c)		OPJHL	39	9	18	27	134
1981-82—Ottawa 67's (d)		OHL	47	6	3	9	54
1982-83—Ottawa 67's		OHL	54	4	12	16	54
1983-84—Ottawa 67's		OHL	55	7	13	20	59

(c)—May, 1981—Drafted by Ottawa 67's in 1981 OHL midget draft. Fourteenth 67's pick, 208th overall, 15th round.

(d)—June, 1982—Drafted as underage junior by Chicago Black Hawks in 1982 NHL entry draft. Eleventh Black Hawks pick, 217th overall, 11th round.

VALMORE JAMES

Left Wing . . . 6'2" . . . 205 lbs. . . . Born, Ocala, Fla., February 14, 1957 . . . Shoots left . . . First American-born black player to play in NHL.

Year	Team	League	Games	G.	A.	Pts.	Pen.
1975-76—Quebec Remparts		QMJHL	72	14	19	33	83
1976-77—Quebec Remparts (c)		QMJHL	68	16	16	32	99
1979-80—Erie Blades		EHL	69	12	13	25	117
1980-81—Erie Blades (d)		EHL	70	3	18	21	179

Year	Team	League	Games	G.	A.	Pts.	Pen.
1980-81—Rochester Americans		AHL	3	0	0	0	12
1981-82—Buffalo Sabres		NHL	7	0	0	0	16
1981-82—Rochester Americans		AHL	65	5	4	9	204
1982-83—Rochester Americans		AHL	68	3	4	7	88
1983-84—Rochester Americans		AHL	62	1	2	3	122
NHL TOTALS			7	0	0	0	16

(c)—June, 1977—Drafted by Detroit Red Wings in 1977 NHL amateur draft. Red Wings 15th pick, 184th overall, 16th round. (Next to last player picked in 1977).

(d)—September, 1980—Signed by Buffalo Sabres as a free agent.

DOUGLAS JARVIS

Center . . . 5'9" . . . 172 lbs. . . . Born, Brantford, Ont., March 24, 1955 . . . Shoots left . . . Cousin of Wes Jarvis.

Year	Team	League	Games	G.	A.	Pts.	Pen.
1971-72—Brantford Majors		SOJHL	11	2	10	12	0
1972-73—Peterborough TPTs		Jr."A" OHA	63	20	49	69	14
1973-74—Peterborough TPTs		Jr."A" OHA	70	31	53	84	27
1974-75—P'borough TPTs (b-c-d-e)		Jr."A" OHA	64	45	88	133	38
1975-76—Montreal Canadiens		NHL	80	5	30	35	16
1976-77—Montreal Canadiens		NHL	80	16	22	38	14
1977-78—Montreal Canadiens		NHL	80	11	28	39	23
1978-79—Montreal Canadiens		NHL	80	10	13	23	16
1979-80—Montreal Canadiens		NHL	80	13	11	24	28
1980-81—Montreal Canadiens		NHL	80	16	22	38	34
1981-82—Montreal Canadiens (f)		NHL	80	20	28	48	20
1982-83—Washington Capitals		NHL	80	8	22	30	10
1983-84—Washington Capitals (g)		NHL	80	13	29	42	12
NHL TOTALS			720	112	205	317	173

(c)—Won William Hanley Trophy (most gentlemanly player).

(d)—Drafted from Peterborough TPTs by Toronto Maple Leafs in second round of 1975 amateur draft.

(e)—Traded to Montreal Canadiens by Toronto Maple Leafs for Greg Hubick, June, 1975.

(f)—September, 1982—Traded by Montreal Canadiens with Rod Langway, Brian Engblom and Craig Laughlin to Washington Capitals for Ryan Walter and Rick Green.

(g)—Won Frank Selke Trophy (NHL's Best Defensive Forward).

WES JARVIS

Center . . . 5'11" . . . 190 lbs. . . . Born, Toronto, Ont., May 30, 1958 . . . Shoots left . . . Cousin of Doug Jarvis . . . (January, 1984)—Injured ligaments in left knee.

Year	Team	League	Games	G.	A.	Pts.	Pen.
1975-76—Sudbury Wolves		OMJHL	64	26	48	74	22
1976-77—Sudbury Wolves		OMJHL	65	36	60	96	24
1977-78—Sudbury Wolves		OMJHL	21	7	16	23	16
1977-78—Windsor Spitfires (c)		OMJHL	44	27	51	78	37
1978-79—Port Huron Flags (b-d)		IHL	73	44	65	109	39
1979-80—Hershey Bears		AHL	16	6	14	20	4
1979-80—Washington Capitals		NHL	63	11	15	26	8
1980-81—Washington Capitals		NHL	55	9	14	23	30
1980-81—Hershey Bears		AHL	24	15	25	40	39
1981-82—Hershey Bears		AHL	56	31	61	92	44
1981-82—Washington Capitals (e)		NHL	26	1	12	13	18
1982-83—Birmingham South Stars (a-f)		CHL	75	40	*68	*108	36
1982-83—Minnesota North Stars (g)		NHL	3	0	0	0	2
1983-84—Los Angeles Kings		NHL	61	9	13	22	36
NHL TOTALS			208	30	54	84	94

(c)—June, 1978—Drafted by Washington Capitals in 1978 amateur draft. 15th Capitals pick, 213th overall, 14th round.

(d)—Won Garry F. Longman Memorial Trophy (IHL Top Rookie).

(e)—August, 1982—Traded with Rollie Boutin by Washington Capitals to Minnesota North Stars for Robbie Moore and future considerations.

(f)—Won Phil Esposito Trophy (CHL Scoring Leader).

(g)—August, 1983—Signed by Los Angeles Kings as a free agent.

ARTO JAVANAINEN

Right Wing . . . 6'2" . . . 185 lbs. . . . Born, Pori, Finland, April 8, 1959 . . . Shoots right . . . Member of Finland National team 1979, 1980 and 1982.

Year	Team	League	Games	G.	A.	Pts.	Pen.
1977-78—Pori Assat		Finland	..	..		..	..
1978-79—Pori Assat		Finland	36	31	18	49	36
1979-80—Pori Assat (c)		Finland	36	28	29	57	48
1980-81—Pori Assat		Finland	36	37	27	64	40
1981-82—Pori Assat (a)		Finland	36	29	27	56	50
1982-83—Pori Assat (d)		Finland	..	..	..	..	..
1983-84—Pori Assat (e)		Finland	37	37	25	62	62

(c)—Led Finland Ice Hockey League Playoffs with seven goals.
(d)—June, 1983—Drafted by Montreal Canadiens in NHL entry draft. Eighth Canadiens pick, 118th overall, sixth round.
(e)—June, 1984—Drafted by Pittsburgh Penguins in NHL entry draft. Fifth Penguins pick, 85th overall, fifth round.

DEAN JENKINS

Right Wing . . . 6' . . . 190 lbs. . . . Born, Billerica, Mass., November 21, 1959 . . . Shoots right.

Year	Team	League	Games	G.	A.	Pts.	Pen.
1977-78—Lowell University		ECAC-II	24	11	7	18	28
1978-79—Lowell University		ECAC-II	33	16	37	53	75
1979-80—Lowell University (a)		ECAC-II	29	23	41	64	83
1980-81—Lowell University (b-c-d)		ECAC-II	31	23	32	55	83
1981-82—New Haven Nighthawks		AHL	78	13	22	35	107
1982-83—New Haven Nighthawks		AHL	80	29	43	72	50
1983-84—New Haven Nighthawks		AHL	64	24	26	50	131
1983-84—Los Angeles Kings		NHL	5	0	0	0	2
NHL TOTALS			5	0	0	0	2

(c)—Named to All-America Division II Team (East).
(d)—May, 1981—Signed by Los Angeles Kings as a free agent.

CHRIS JENSEN

Center . . . 5'11" . . . 165 lbs. . . . Born, Fort St. John, B.C., October 28, 1963 . . . Shoots right.

Year	Team	League	Games	G.	A.	Pts.	Pen.
1980-81—Kelowna		BCJHL	53	51	45	96	120
1981-82—Kelowna (c)		BCJHL	48	46	46	92	212
1982-83—University of North Dakota		WCHA	13	3	3	6	28
1983-84—University of North Dakota		WCHA	44	24	25	49	100

(c)—June, 1982—Drafted as underage player by New York Rangers in 1982 NHL entry draft. Fourth Rangers pick, 78th overall, fourth round.

DAVE HENRY JENSEN

Defense . . . 6'1" . . . 190 lbs. . . . Born, Minneapolis, Minn., May 3, 1961 . . . Shoots left . . . Brother of Paul Jensen (played for '76 U.S. Olympic team) . . . Member of 1984 U.S. Olympic Team.

Year	Team	League	Games	G.	A.	Pts.	Pen.
1979-80—University of Minnesota (c)		WCHA	26	0	4	4	26
1980-81—University of Minnesota		WCHA	35	0	13	13	64
1981-82—University of Minnesota		WCHA	32	3	13	16	68
1982-83—University of Minnesota		WCHA	38	5	24	29	48
1983-84—U.S. National Team		Int'l	47	3	15	18	38
1983-84—U.S. Olympic Team		Int'l	6	0	3	3	6
1983-84—Salt Lake Golden Eagles		CHL	13	0	7	7	6
1983-84—Minnesota North Stars		NHL	8	0	1	1	0
NHL TOTALS			8	0	1	1	0

(c)—June, 1980—Drafted as underage player by Minnesota North Stars in 1980 NHL entry draft. Fifth North Stars pick, 100th overall, fifth round.

DAVID A. JENSEN

Left Wing . . . 6' . . . 175 lbs. . . . Born, Newton, Mass., August 19, 1965 . . . Shoots left . . . Drafted with a year remaining of high school eligibility . . . Member of 1984 U.S. Olympic Team.

Year	Team	League	Games	G.	A.	Pts.	Pen.
1982-83—Lawrence Academy (c)		Mass. H.S.	25	41	48	89	....
1983-84—U.S. National Team		Int'l	61	22	56	78	6
1983-84—U.S. Olympic Team		Int'l	6	5	3	8	0

(c)—June, 1983—Drafted by Hartford Whalers in 1983 NHL entry draft. Second Whalers pick, 20th overall, first round.

PAUL JERRARD

Defense . . . 6'1" . . . 185 lbs. . . . Born, Winnipeg, Man., April 20, 1965 . . . Shoots right.

Year	Team	League	Games	G.	A.	Pts.	Pen.
1982-83—Notre Dame H.S. (c)	Man. Juv.	60	34	37	71	150
1983-84—Lake Superior State College	CCHA	40	8	18	26	48

(c)—June, 1983—Drafted by New York Rangers in 1983 NHL entry draft. Tenth Rangers pick, 173rd overall, ninth round.

GERALD JOHANNSON

Defense . . . 6'3" . . . 180 lbs. . . . Born, Meadow Lake, Sask., September 8, 1966 . . . Shoots right.

Year	Team	League	Games	G.	A.	Pts.	Pen.
1983-84—Swift Current (c)	SJHL	61	7	22	29	206

(c)—June, 1984—Drafted as underage junior by Montreal Canadiens in 1984 NHL entry draft. Seventh Canadiens pick, 95th overall, fifth round.

JAMES JOHANNSON

Center . . . 6'1" . . . 175 lbs. . . . Born, Rochester, Minn., March 10, 1964 . . . Shoots right . . . Brother of John Johannson.

Year	Team	League	Games	G.	A.	Pts.	Pen.
1981-82—Rochester Mayo H.S. (c)	Minn. H.S.	27	28	32	60	20
1982-83—University of Wisconsin	WCHA	45	12	9	21	16
1983-84—University of Wisconsin	WCHA	35	17	21	38	52

(c)—June, 1982—Drafted as underage player by Hartford Whalers in 1982 NHL entry draft. Seventh Whalers pick, 130th overall, seventh round.

JOHN JOHANNSON

Center . . . 6'1" . . . 165 lbs. . . . Born, Rochester, Minn., October 18, 1961 . . . Shoots left . . . Brother of James Johannson.

Year	Team	League	Games	G.	A.	Pts.	Pen.
1980-81—University of Wisconsin (c)	WCHA	38	6	12	18	32
1981-82—University of Wisconsin	WCHA	47	15	34	49	46
1982-83—University of Wisconsin	WCHA	47	22	41	63	68
1983-84—University of Wisconsin	WCHA	39	21	25	46	32
1983-84—New Jersey Devils	NHL	5	0	0	0	0
NHL TOTALS		5	0	0	0	0

(c)—June, 1981—Drafted by Colorado Rockies in 1981 NHL entry draft. Tenth Rockies pick, 192nd overall, tenth round.

BRIAN JOHNSON

Defense . . . 5'10" . . . 180 lbs. . . . Born, Two Harbors, Minn., March 7, 1965 . . . Shoots left . . . Also plays center.

Year	Team	League	Games	G.	A.	Pts.	Pen.
1982-83—Silver Bay H.S. (c)	Minn. H.S.	22	29	35	64	....
1983-84—Univ. of Minnesota-Duluth	WCHA	39	4	9	13	30

(c)—June, 1983—Drafted by Hartford Whalers in 1983 NHL entry draft. Seventh Whalers pick, 104th overall, sixth round.

BRIAN JOHNSON

Right Wing and Center . . . 6'1" . . . 185 lbs. . . . Born, Montreal, Que., April 1, 1960 . . . Shoots right.

Year	Team	League	Games	G.	A.	Pts.	Pen.
1977-78—Verdun Black Hawks	QMJHL	50	11	14	25	145
1978-79—Verdun Black Hawks	QMJHL	71	32	36	68	192
1979-80—Verdun Black Hawks	QMJHL	21	8	27	35	68
1979-80—Sherbrooke Beavers (b)	QMJHL	49	32	52	84	144
1980-81—Adirondack Red Wings (c)	AHL	65	10	21	31	193
1981-82—Dallas Black Hawks (d)	CHL	79	18	36	54	223
1982-83—Adirondack Red Wings	AHL	67	6	16	22	250
1983-84—Adirondack Red Wings	AHL	58	4	27	31	233
1983-84—Detroit Red Wings	NHL	3	0	0	0	5
NHL TOTALS		3	0	0	0	5

(c)—October, 1979—Signed by Detroit Red Wings as a free agent.
(d)—Led CHL playoffs with 129 penalty minutes.

CHAD JOHNSON

Center . . . 6'1" . . . 175 lbs. . . . Born, Roseau, Minn., December 12, 1964 . . . Shoots left.

Year	Team	League	Games	G.	A.	Pts.	Pen.
1982-83	Roseau H.S. (c)	Minn. H.S.	16	16	13	29	....
1983-84	Univ. of Illinois/Chicago	CCHA	35	7	5	12	32

(c)—June, 1983—Drafted by Los Angeles Kings in 1983 NHL entry draft. Twelfth Kings pick, 227th overall, 12th round.

MARK JOHNSON

Center . . . 5'9" . . . 160 lbs. . . . Born, Minneapolis, Minn., September 22, 1957 . . . Shoots left . . . Member of 1978 and 1979 U.S. National teams and 1980 U.S. Gold Medal Winning Hockey Team . . . Son of Bob Johnson (Coach of Calgary Flames) . . . (September, 1980)—Took 20 stitches near right eye in preseason game . . . (November, 1980)—Wrist injury.

Year	Team	League	Games	G.	A.	Pts.	Pen.
1976-77	University of Wisconsin (c-d)	WCHA	43	36	44	80	16
1977-78	University of Wisconsin (a-e)	WCHA	42	*48	38	86	24
1978-79	Univ. of Wisconsin (a-e-f)	WCHA	40	*41	49	*90	34
1979-80	U.S. Olympic Team	Int'l	60	*38	*54	*92	31
1979-80	Pittsburgh Penguins	NHL	17	3	5	8	4
1980-81	Pittsburgh Penguins	NHL	73	10	23	33	50
1981-82	Pittsburgh Penguins (g)	NHL	46	10	11	21	30
1981-82	Minnesota North Stars (h)	NHL	10	2	2	4	10
1982-83	Hartford Whalers	NHL	73	31	38	69	28
1983-84	Hartford Whalers	NHL	79	35	52	87	27
	NHL TOTALS		298	91	131	222	149

(c)—June, 1977—Drafted by Pittsburgh Penguins in 1977 NHL amateur draft. Third Penguins pick, 66th overall, fourth round.
(d)—Named WCHA Outstanding Freshman.
(e)—Named to All-America Team (West).
(f)—Named WCHA MVP and NCAA Player of the Year.
(g)—March, 1982—Traded by Pittsburgh Penguins to Minnesota North Stars for second-round 1982 entry draft pick (Tim Hrynewich).
(h)—October, 1982—Traded by Minnesota North Stars with Kent-Erik Andersson to Hartford Whalers for 1984 fifth-round pick (Jiri Poner) in NHL entry draft and future considerations (Jordy Douglas).

TERRANCE JOHNSON

Defense . . . 6'3" . . . 210 lbs. . . . Born, Calgary, Alta., November 28, 1958 . . . Shoots left.

Year	Team	League	Games	G.	A.	Pts.	Pen.
1975-76	Calgary	AJHL	55	3	13	16	100
1976-77	Calgary Canucks	AJHL	60	5	26	31	158
1977-78	Saskatoon Blades	WCHL	70	2	20	22	195
1978-79	University of Alberta	CWAA	24	1	5	6	100
1979-80	Quebec Nordiques (c)	NHL	3	0	0	0	2
1979-80	Syracuse Firebirds	AHL	74	0	13	13	163
1980-81	Quebec Nordiques	NHL	13	0	1	1	46
1980-81	Hershey Bears	AHL	63	1	7	8	207
1981-82	Fredericton Express	AHL	43	0	7	7	132
1981-82	Quebec Nordiques	NHL	6	0	1	1	5
1982-83	Fredericton Express	AHL	78	2	15	17	181
1982-83	Quebec Nordiques	NHL	3	0	0	0	2
1983-84	St. Louis Blues (d)	NHL	65	2	6	8	141
	NHL TOTALS		90	2	8	10	196

(c)—September, 1979—Signed by Quebec Nordiques as a free agent.
(d)—October, 1983—Selected by St. Louis Blues in NHL waiver draft.

GREG JOHNSTON

Right Wing . . . 6'1" . . . 195 lbs. . . . Born, Barrie, Ont., January 14, 1965 . . . Shoots right . . . Also plays center . . . (September, 1982)—Broken ankle.

Year	Team	League	Games	G.	A.	Pts.	Pen.
1981-82	Barrie	OHA Midget	42	31	46	77	74
1982-83	Toronto Marlboros (c)	OHL	58	18	19	37	58
1983-84	Toronto Marlboros	OHL	57	38	35	73	67
1983-84	Boston Bruins	NHL	15	2	1	3	2
	NHL TOTALS		15	2	1	3	2

(c)—June, 1983—Drafted as underage junior by Boston Bruins in 1983 NHL entry draft. Second Bruins pick, 42nd overall, second round.

JOHN (JAY) JOHNSTON

Defense . . . 6' . . . 190 lbs. . . . Born, Hamilton, Ont., February 25, 1958 . . . Shoots left . . . Missed end of 1980-81 season with shoulder injury.

Year	Team	League	Games	G.	A.	Pts.	Pen.
1975-76—Hamilton	Jr. "B" OHA	36	1	25	26	70
1976-77—St. Catharines Fincups	Jr. "A" OHA	65	8	20	28	146
1977-78—Hamilton Fincups (c)	Jr. "A" OHA	48	2	12	14	163
1978-79—Port Huron Flags	IHL	75	5	19	24	409
1979-80—Hershey Bears	AHL	69	3	20	23	229
1980-81—Hershey Bears	AHL	61	1	11	12	187
1980-81—Washington Capitals	NHL	2	0	0	0	9
1981-82—Hershey Bears	AHL	67	4	9	13	228
1981-82—Washington Capitals	NHL	6	0	0	0	4
1982-83—Hershey Bears	AHL	76	3	13	16	148
1983-84—Hershey Bears	AHL	70	1	9	10	231
NHL TOTALS		8	0	0	0	13

(c)—Drafted from Hamilton Fincups by Washington Capitals in third round of 1978 amateur draft.

EDWARD LaVERN JOHNSTONE

Right Wing . . . 5'9" . . . 175 lbs. . . . Born, Brandon, Man., March 2, 1954 . . . Shoots right . . . (April 20, 1980)—Tore ligaments in left knee vs. St. Louis in playoffs . . . (February 4, 1982) Broken ring finger on right hand at Calgary . . . (February, 1983)—Missed 21 games with separated left shoulder . . . (November 25, 1983)—Depressed right cheekbone following collision with teammate Dwight Foster in game with Pittsburgh.

Year	Team	League	Games	G.	A.	Pts.	Pen.
1970-71—Vernon Essos	Jr. "A" BCHL	....	45	49	94	79
1971-72—Medicine Hat Tigers	WCHL	27	14	15	29	46
1972-73—Medicine Hat Tigers	WCHL	68	58	44	102	70
1973-74—Medicine Hat Tigers (c-d)	WCHL	68	64	54	118	164
1974-75—Greensboro Generals	SHL	25	21	25	46	21
1974-75—Michigan Stags	WHA	23	4	4	8	43
1974-75—Providence Reds (e)	AHL	23	7	10	17	35
1975-76—Providence Reds	AHL	58	23	33	56	102
1975-76—New York Rangers	NHL	10	2	1	3	4
1976-77—New Haven Nighthawks (a)	AHL	80	40	58	98	79
1977-78—New Haven Nighthawks	AHL	17	10	12	22	20
1977-78—New York Rangers	NHL	53	13	13	26	44
1978-79—New York Rangers	NHL	30	5	3	8	27
1979-80—New York Rangers	NHL	78	14	21	35	60
1980-81—New York Rangers	NHL	80	30	38	68	100
1981-82—New York Rangers	NHL	68	30	28	58	57
1982-83—New York Rangers (f)	NHL	52	15	21	36	27
1983-84—Detroit Red Wings	NHL	46	12	11	23	54
WHA TOTALS		23	4	4	8	43
NHL TOTALS		417	121	136	257	373

(c)—Drafted from Medicine Hat Tigers by New York Rangers in sixth round of 1974 amateur draft.
(d)—Drafted by Michigan Stags in World Hockey Association amateur player draft, May, 1974.
(e)—Signed by New York Rangers as free agent, February, 1975.
(f)—July, 1983—Traded by New York Rangers with Ron Duguay and Eddie Mio to Detroit Red Wings for Willie Huber, Mark Osborne and Mike Blaisdell.

GREGORY JAMES JOLY

Defense . . . 6'1" . . . 188 lbs. . . . Born, Calgary, Alta., May 30, 1954 . . . Shoots left . . . Missed part of 1974-75 season with knee injury and part of 1975-76 season with hairline ankle fracture . . . Had fractured left wrist during 1978 Stanley Cup playoffs . . . (January, 1983)—Injured knee in AHL game vs. Maine.

Year	Team	League	Games	G.	A.	Pts.	Pen.
1971-72—Regina Pats	WCHL	67	6	38	44	41
1972-73—Regina Pats (a)	WCHL	67	14	54	68	94
1973-74—Regina Pats (a-c)	WCHL	67	21	71	92	103
1974-75—Washington Capitals	NHL	44	1	7	8	44
1975-76—Richmond Robins	AHL	3	3	2	5	4
1975-76—Washington Capitals	NHL	54	8	17	25	28
1976-77—Springfield Indians (d)	AHL	22	0	8	8	16
1976-77—Detroit Red Wings	NHL	53	1	11	12	14
1977-78—Detroit Red Wings	NHL	79	7	20	27	73
1978-79—Detroit Red Wings	NHL	20	0	4	4	6
1979-80—Detroit Red Wings	NHL	59	3	10	13	45

Year	Team	League	Games	G.	A.	Pts.	Pen.
1979-80—Adirondack Red Wings	AHL	8	3	3	6	10
1980-81—Adirondack Red Wings	AHL	62	3	34	37	158
1980-81—Detroit Red Wings	NHL	17	0	2	2	10
1981-82—Detroit Red Wings	NHL	37	1	5	6	30
1981-82—Adirondack Red Wings	AHL	36	3	22	25	59
1982-83—Adirondack Red Wings	AHL	71	8	40	48	118
1982-83—Detroit Red Wings	NHL	2	0	0	0	0
1983-84—Adirondack Red Wings (b)	AHL	78	10	33	43	133
NHL TOTALS		365	21	76	97	250

(c)—Drafted from Regina Pats by Washington Capitals in first round of 1974 amateur draft.
(d)—Traded to Detroit Red Wings by Washington Capitals for Bryan Watson, December, 1976.

YVAN RENE JOLY

Left Wing . . . 5'10" . . . 175 lbs. . . . Born, Hawkesbury, Ont., February 6, 1960 . . . Shoots left.

Year	Team	League	Games	G.	A.	Pts.	Pen.
1976-77—Ottawa 67's	OMJHL	62	30	26	56	36
1977-78—Ottawa 67's	OMJHL	64	34	37	71	67
1978-79—Ottawa 67's (b-c)	OMJHL	66	53	59	112	45
1979-80—Ottawa 67's (a)	OMJHL	67	*66	93	159	47
1980-81—Montreal Canadiens	NHL	1	0	0	0	0
1980-81—Nova Scotia Voyageurs	AHL	68	14	27	41	74
1981-82—Nova Scotia Voyageurs	AHL	71	20	30	50	75
1982-83—Montreal Canadiens	NHL	1	0	0	0	0
1982-83—Nova Scotia Voyageurs	AHL	76	43	37	80	52
1983-84—Maine Mariners (d-e-f)	AHL	39	12	17	29	25
NHL TOTALS		2	0	0	0	0

(c)—August, 1979—Drafted as underage junior by Montreal Canadiens in 1979 NHL entry draft. Seventh Canadiens pick, 100th overall, fifth round.
(d)—September, 1983—Traded, on a conditional basis, by Montreal Canadiens to Hartford Whalers for future considerations.
(e)—October, 1983—After the Whalers training camp he was returned to Montreal and the September trade was cancelled. Montreal released him making him a free agent.
(f)—December, 1983—Signed by Maine Mariners as a free agent.

DANIEL JOMPHE

Left Wing . . . 6'2" . . . 200 lbs. . . . Born, Iles de la Madeleine, Que., January 19, 1966 . . . Shoots left.

Year	Team	League	Games	G.	A.	Pts.	Pen.
1983-84—Granby Bisons (c)	QHL	50	7	9	16	29

(c)—June, 1984—Drafted as underage junior by St. Louis Blues in 1984 NHL entry draft. 11th Blues pick, 176th overall, ninth round.

BRAD JONES

Center . . . 6' . . . 175 lbs. . . . Born, Sterling Heights, Mich., June 26, 1965 . . . Shoots left.

Year	Team	League	Games	G.	A.	Pts.	Pen.
1983-84—University of Michigan (c)	CCHA	37	8	26	34	32

(c)—June, 1984—Drafted by Winnipeg Jets in 1984 NHL entry draft. Eighth Jets pick, 156th overall, eighth round.

TOMAS JONSSON

Defense . . . 5'10" . . . 176 lbs. . . . Born, Falun, Sweden, April 12, 1960 . . . Shoots left.

Year	Team	League	Games	G.	A.	Pts.	Pen.
1980-81—Ornskoldsvik Modo AIK (c)	Sweden	35	8	12	20	58
1981-82—New York Islanders	NHL	70	9	25	34	51
1982-83—New York Islanders	NHL	72	13	35	48	50
1983-84—New York Islanders	NHL	72	11	36	47	54
NHL TOTALS		214	33	96	129	155

(c)—August, 1979—Drafted by New York Islanders in 1979 NHL entry draft. Second Islanders pick, 25th overall, second round.

FRANK JOO

Defense . . . 6' . . . 180 lbs. . . . Born, Regina, Sask., January 19, 1966 . . . Shoots left.

Year	Team	League	Games	G.	A.	Pts.	Pen.
1982-83—Regina Pats	WHL	2	0	0	0	2
1983-84—Regina Pats (c)	WHL	50	2	7	9	90

(c)—June, 1984—Drafted as underage junior by Washington Capitals in 1984 NHL entry draft. Seventh Capitals pick. 164th overall, eighth round.

FABIAN JOSEPH

Center ... 5'8" ... 165 lbs. ... Born, Sydney, N.S., December 5, 1965 ... Shoots left.

Year	Team	League	Games	G.	A.	Pts.	Pen.
1982-83—Victoria Cougars		WHL	69	42	48	90	50
1983-84—Victoria Cougars (c)		WHL	72	52	75	127	27

(c)—June, 1984—Drafted as underage junior by Toronto Maple Leafs in 1984 NHL entry draft. Fifth Maple Leafs pick, 109th overall, sixth round.

BILL JOYCE

Right Wing ... 5'8" ... 180 lbs. ... Born, Toronto, Ont., November 29, 1957 ... Shoots right.

Year	Team	League	Games	G.	A.	Pts.	Pen.
1976-77—Northern Michigan University		CCHA	28	21	26	47	64
1977-78—Northern Michigan University (a)		CCHA	33	24	31	55	61
1978-79—Northern Michigan University		CCHA	29	26	31	57	69
1979-80—Northern Michigan University (a)		CCHA	40	41	*55	*96	40
1980-81—Richmond Rifles		EHL	2	0	1	1	0
1980-81—Milwaukee Admirals		IHL	6	0	0	0	0
1981-82—Toledo Goaldiggers		IHL	78	40	72	112	75
1982-83—Toledo Goaldiggers		IHL	64	33	48	81	118
1983-84—Toledo Goaldiggers		IHL	63	26	35	61	97

ROBERT JOYCE

Center ... 6'1" ... 180 lbs. ... Born, St. Johns, N.B., July 11, 1966 ... Shoots left.

Year	Team	League	Games	G.	A.	Pts.	Pen.
1983-84—Wilcox Notre Dame H.S. (c)		Sask. HS	30	33	37	70	..

(c)—June, 1984—Drafted by Boston Bruins in 1984 NHL entry draft. Fourth Bruins pick. 82nd overall, fourth round.

CLAUDE JULIEN

Defense ... 6' ... 195 lbs. ... Born, Orleans, Ont., November 11, 1958 ... Shoots right.

Year	Team	League	Games	G.	A.	Pts.	Pen.
1977-78—Newmarket Flyers		OPJHL	45	18	26	44	137
1977-78—Oshawa Generals		OMJHL	11	0	5	5	14
1978-79—		....	....	....	...	....	....
1979-80—Windsor Spitfires		OMJHL	68	14	37	51	148
1980-81—Windsor Spitfires		OHL	3	1	2	3	21
1980-81—Port Huron Flags		IHL	77	15	40	55	153
1981-82—Salt Lake Golden Eagles (c)		CHL	70	4	18	22	134
1982-83—Salt Lake Golden Eagles (b-d)		CHL	76	14	47	61	176
1983-84—Milwaukee Admirals		IHL	5	0	3	3	2
1983-84—Fredericton Express		AHL	57	7	22	29	58

(c)—September, 1981—Signed by St. Louis Blues as a free agent.
(d)—August, 1983—Sent by St. Louis Blues along with Gordon Donnelly to Quebec Nordiques as compensation for St. Louis signing coach Jacques Demers.

TIMO JUTILA

Defense ... 5'7" ... 175 lbs. ... Born, Helsinki, Finland, December 24, 1963 ... Shoots left ... Member of Finland National junior team in 1980.

Year	Team	League	Games	G.	A.	Pts.	Pen.
1980-81—Tampere Tappara		Finland	36	9	12	21	44
1981-82—Tampere Tappara		Finland	36	8	11	19	41
1982-83—Tampere Tappara (c)		Finland	..	..	..	..	..
1983-84—Tampere Tappara		Finland	..	..	..	..	..

(c)—June, 1982—Drafted by Buffalo Sabres in NHL entry draft. Sixth Sabres pick, 68th overall, fourth round.

JIM KAISER

Right Wing and Defense ... 6' ... 200 lbs. ... Born, Leamington, Ont., February 26, 1966 ... Shoots right.

Year	Team	League	Games	G.	A.	Pts.	Pen.
1982-83—Newmarket		SOJHL	33	3	11	14	109
1983-84—Ottawa 67's		OHL	31	1	3	4	26
1983-84—Guelph Platers (c)		OHL	28	5	5	10	16

(c)—June, 1984—Drafted as underage junior by Detroit Red Wings in 1984 NHL entry draft. 11th Red Wings pick, 216th overall, 11th round.

CRAIG KALES

Right Wing . . . 6' . . . 190 lbs. . . . Born, Detroit, Mich., April 20, 1964 . . . Shoots right.

Year	Team	League	Games	G.	A.	Pts.	Pen.
1980-81	Detroit Little Ceasers (c)	Mich. Midget	71	43	48	91	....
1981-82	Niagara Falls Flyers (d)	OHL	66	11	17	28	70
1982-83	North Bay Centennials	OHL	19	2	7	9	33
1982-83	Kingston Canadians	OHL	40	11	9	20	25
1983-84	Kingston Canadians	OHL	45	12	13	25	28

(c)—May, 1981—Selected by Niagara Falls Flyers in 1981 OHL priority draft. Fifth Flyers pick, 53rd overall, fourth round.

(d)—June, 1982—Drafted as underage junior by Toronto Maple Leafs in 1982 NHL entry draft. Ninth Maple Leafs pick, 115th overall, sixth round.

ANDERS KALLUR

Center . . . 5'11" . . . 185 lbs. . . . Born, Ludvika, Sweden, July 6, 1952 . . . Shoots left . . . Member of Swedish National team in 1978 . . . (April, 1980)—Right shoulder separation . . . (December 6, 1981)—Sprained right knee at Winnipeg . . . (January 27, 1982)—Ruptured ligament in right knee at Pittsburgh requiring surgery and the fitting of a special knee brace . . . (October, 1982)—Missed nine games with bruised ribs . . . (December 31, 1982)—Concussion when head hit ice during game at Buffalo . . . (January, 1984)—Pulled muscle in lower back . . . Also plays right wing.

Year	Team	League	Games	G.	A.	Pts.	Pen.
1975-76	Mo Do AIK	Sweden	36	11	16	27	31
1976-77	Sodertaije IK	Sweden	33	14	9	23	26
1977-78	Sodertaije IK	Sweden	30	5	7	12	10
1978-79	Sodertaije IK (c)	Sweden	....	26	20	46	....
1979-80	Indianapolis Checkers	CHL	2	0	2	2	0
1979-80	New York Islanders	NHL	76	22	30	52	16
1980-81	New York Islanders	NHL	78	36	28	64	32
1981-82	New York Islanders	NHL	58	18	22	40	18
1982-83	New York Islanders	NHL	55	6	8	14	33
1983-84	New York Islanders	NHL	65	9	14	23	24
	NHL TOTALS		332	91	102	193	123

(c)—August, 1979—Signed by New York Islanders as free agent.

DARCY KAMINSKI

Defense . . . 6'1" . . . 180 lbs. . . . Born, Lethbridge, Alta., March 10, 1964 . . . Shoots left . . . (April, 1981)—Broken wrist.

Year	Team	League	Games	G.	A.	Pts.	Pen.
1981-82	Olds Grizzlys	AJHL	....	...	....	....	....
1981-82	Lethbridge Broncos	WHL	11	0	0	0	17
1982-83	Lethbridge Broncos (c)	WHL	71	2	11	13	69
1983-84	Lethbridge Broncos (d)	WHL	71	5	15	20	96

(c)—June, 1983—Drafted as underage junior by Hartford Whalers in 1983 NHL entry draft. Fourteenth Whalers pick, 224th overall, 12th round.

(d)—June, 1984—Released by Hartford Whalers.

DAN KANE

Center . . . 5'11" . . . 170 lbs. . . . Born, Clinton, N.Y., June 12, 1962 . . . Shoots left.

Year	Team	League	Games	G.	A.	Pts.	Pen.
1980-81	Nepean Rangers	OJHL	..	25	47	72	..
1981-82	Bowling Green Univ.	CCHA	41	10	31	41	31
1982-83	Bowling Green Univ.	CCHA	39	25	33	58	58
1983-84	Bowling Green Univ. (c)	CCHA	43	24	48	72	40

(c)—July, 1984—Signed by Calgary Flames as a free agent.

DAVE KASPER

Center . . . 5'11" . . . 163 lbs. . . . Born, Montreal, Que., February 12, 1964 . . . Shoots left . . . Brother of Steve Kasper (1982 Selke Trophy Winner-NHL).

Year	Team	League	Games	G.	A.	Pts.	Pen.
1980-81	Richelieu Midgets	Quebec	45	28	53	81	116
1981-82	Sherbrooke Beavers (c)	QMJHL	54	20	24	44	92

Year	Team	League	Games	G.	A.	Pts.	Pen.
1982-83—St. Jean Beavers		QHL	61	27	55	82	73
1983-84—Shawinigan Cataracts		QHL	69	44	62	106	141

(c)—June, 1982—Drafted as underage junior by New Jersey Devils in 1982 NHL entry draft. Fourth Devils pick, 54th overall, third round.

STEPHEN NEIL KASPER

Center . . . 5'8" . . . 159 lbs. . . . Born, Montreal, Que., September 28, 1961 . . . Shoots left . . . Brother of David Kasper (New Jersey, '82 draft pick) . . . (October 17, 1981)—Hip pointer in game at Los Angeles . . . (November 9, 1982)—Surgery to remove torn shoulder cartilage . . . (December 7, 1982)—Surgery to left shoulder for a torn capsule . . . (April, 1983)—Concussion during playoff series vs. Buffalo . . . (November, 1983)—Separated left shoulder . . . (January 7, 1984)—Surgery to shoulder . . . (February, 1984)—Reinjured shoulder.

Year	Team	League	Games	G.	A.	Pts.	Pen.
1977-78—Verdun Black Hawks		QMJHL	63	26	45	71	16
1978-79—Verdun Black Hawks		QMJHL	67	37	67	104	53
1979-80—Sorel Black Hawks (c)		QMJHL	70	57	65	122	117
1980-81—Sorel Black Hawks		QMJHL	2	5	2	7	0
1980-81—Boston Bruins		NHL	76	21	35	56	94
1981-82—Boston Bruins (d)		NHL	73	20	31	51	72
1982-83—Boston Bruins		NHL	24	2	6	8	24
1983-84—Boston Bruins		NHL	27	3	11	14	19
NHL TOTALS			198	46	83	129	209

(c)—June, 1980—Drafted by Boston Bruins in 1980 NHL entry draft. Third Bruins pick, 81st overall, fourth round.

(d)—Winner of Frank Selke Trophy (NHL's best defensive forward).

EDWARD KASTELIC

Right Wing . . . 6'3" . . . 203 lbs. . . . Born, Toronto, Ont., January 29, 1964 . . . Shoots right . . . Played defense prior to 1981-82 season.

Year	Team	League	Games	G.	A.	Pts.	Pen.
1980-81—Mississauga Reps		Midget	51	4	10	14	....
1981-82—London Knights (c)		OHL	68	5	18	23	63
1982-83—London Knights		OHL	68	12	11	23	96
1983-84—London Knights		OHL	68	17	16	33	218

(c)—June, 1982—Selected by Washington Capitals in 1982 NHL entry draft as an underage junior. Fourth Capitals pick, 110th overall, sixth round.

MICHAEL KASZYCKI

Center . . . 5'10" . . . 180 lbs. . . . Born, Milton, Ont., February 27, 1956 . . . Shoots left . . . Set Jr. "A" OHA record for most points in season (170) in 1975-76 (broken by Bob Smith in 1977-78).

Year	Team	League	Games	G.	A.	Pts.	Pen.
1972-73—Dixie Beehives		OPHL	44	35	54	89	33
1973-74—Dixie Beehives		OPHL	43	44	55	*99	34
1974-75—Toronto Marlboros (c)		Jr."A"OHA	70	41	44	85	48
1975-76—S. Ste. M. Greyh'ds (b-d-e)		Jr."A"OHA	66	51	*119	*170	38
1976-77—Fort Worth Texans		CHL	76	32	55	87	50
1977-78—Rochester Americans		AHL	6	4	2	6	2
1977-78—New York Islanders		NHL	58	13	29	42	24
1978-79—New York Islanders		NHL	71	16	18	34	37
1979-80—New York Islanders (f)		NHL	16	1	4	5	15
1979-80—Washington Capitals (g)		NHL	28	7	10	17	10
1979-80—Toronto Maple Leafs		NHL	25	4	4	8	10
1980-81—Toronto Maple Leafs		NHL	6	0	2	2	2
1980-81—Dallas Black Hawks		CHL	42	15	21	36	42
1981-82—New Brunswick Hawks (a-h-i-j-k)		AHL	80	36	*82	*118	67
1982-83—St. Catharines Saints		AHL	56	26	42	68	30
1982-83—Toronto Maple Leafs		NHL	22	1	13	14	10
1983-84—St. Catharines Saints (b)		AHL	72	39	71	110	51
NHL TOTALS			226	42	80	122	108

(c)—Traded to Sault Ste. Marie Greyhounds with second round draft choice and player to be named for Cary Farelli, September, 1975.

(d)—Won Eddie Powers Memorial Trophy (leading scorer).

(e)—Drafted from Sault Ste. Marie Greyhounds by New York Islanders in second round of 1976 amateur draft.

(f)—December, 1979—Traded by New York Islanders to Washington Capitals for Gord Lane.

(g)—February, 1980—Traded by Washington Capitals to Toronto Maple Leafs as future consideration in deal that saw Pat Ribble go to Washington from Toronto earlier in the month.
(h)—Led AHL Calder Cup Playoffs with 13 assists and 21 points.
(i)—Winner of John B. Sollenberger Trophy (Top AHL Scorer).
(j)—Winner of Les Cunningham Plaque (AHL MVP).
(k)—Winner of Fred Hunt Memorial Award (AHL Coaches MVP).

STEVE KAYSER

Defense ... 6'2" ... 180 lbs. ... Born, Ottawa, Ont., February 7, 1965 ... Shoots left.

Year	Team	League	Games	G.	A.	Pts.	Pen.
1982-83	University of Vermont (c)	ECAC	16	1	2	3	4
1983-84	University of Vermont	ECAC	28	3	7	10	28

(c)—June, 1983—Drafted by Vancouver Canucks in 1983 NHL entry draft. Eleventh Canucks pick, 210th overall, 11th round.

RICK THOMAS KEHOE

Right Wing ... 5'11" ... 180 lbs. ... Born, Windsor, Ont., July 15, 1951 ... Shoots right ... Also plays Left Wing ... Missed final weeks of 1973-74 season with fractured shoulder, part of 1975-76 season with cracked ankle bone and start of 1977-78 season with broken elbow ... Missed part of 1978-79 season with hairline fracture of right ankle ... (May, 1981)—Surgery to remove bone scrapings from right ankle and a growth from his left forearm ... (October, 1981)—Bruised ribs ... (February, 1982)—Injured shoulder ... (February 22, 1984)—Injured neck in game vs. Edmonton, out for season.

Year	Team	League	Games	G.	A.	Pts.	Pen.
1969-70	London Knights (c)	Jr."A" OHA	23	3	2	5	6
1969-70	Hamilton Red Wings	Jr."A" OHA	32	2	4	6	7
1970-71	Hamilton Red Wings (d)	Jr."A" OHA	58	39	41	80	43
1971-72	Tulsa Oilers	CHL	02	18	21	39	20
1971-72	Toronto Maple Leafs	NHL	38	8	8	16	4
1972-73	Toronto Maple Leafs	NHL	77	33	42	75	20
1973-74	Toronto Maple Leafs (e)	NHL	69	18	22	40	8
1974-75	Pittsburgh Penguins	NHL	76	32	31	63	22
1975-76	Pittsburgh Penguins	NHL	71	29	47	76	6
1976-77	Pittsburgh Penguins	NHL	80	30	27	57	10
1977-78	Pittsburgh Penguins	NHL	70	29	21	50	10
1978-79	Pittsburgh Penguins	NHL	57	27	18	45	2
1979-80	Pittsburgh Penguins	NHL	79	30	30	60	4
1980-81	Pittsburgh Penguins (f)	NHL	80	55	33	88	6
1981-82	Pittsburgh Penguins	NHL	71	33	52	85	8
1982-83	Pittsburgh Penguins	NHL	75	29	36	65	12
1983-84	Pittsburgh Penguins	NHL	57	18	27	45	8
NHL TOTALS			900	371	394	765	120

(c)—Traded to Hamilton Red Wings by London Knights with Jim Schoenfeld and Ken Southwick for Gordon Brooks, Gary Geldart, Dave Gilmour and Mike Craig, December, 1969.
(d)—Drafted from Hamilton Red Wings by Toronto Maple Leafs in second round of 1971 amateur draft.
(e)—Traded to Pittsburgh Penguins by Toronto Maple Leafs for Blaine Stoughton and Pittsburgh's No. 1 draft choice (Trevor Johansen in 1977 draft) September, 1974.
(f)—Winner of Lady Byng Memorial Trophy.

TONY KELLIN

Defense ... 6'2" ... 195 lbs. ... Born, Grand Rapids, Minn., March 19, 1963 ... Shoots right ... Played quarterback for high school football team and named to All-State team.

Year	Team	League	Games	G.	A.	Pts.	Pen.
1980-81	Gr. Rapids High School (c)	Minn. HS	27	19	24	43	38
1981-82	Gr. Rapids High School	Minn. HS	20	22	18	40	30
1982-83	University of Minnesota	WCHA	38	8	6	14	38
1983-84	University of Minnesota	WCHA	38	12	21	33	66

(c)—June, 1981—Drafted by Washington Capitals as underage player in 1981 NHL entry draft. Third Capitals pick, 68th overall, third round.

JOHN PAUL KELLY

Left Wing ... 6' ... 215 lbs. ... Born, Edmonton, Alta., November 15, 1959 ... Shoots left ... Unable to play in NHL until December 1, 1979 due to court ordered suspension from a Junior Hockey Incident during the 1978-79 season ... (December, 1981)—Sprained ankle ... (December 14, 1982)—Fractured two bones in right foot when struck by puck during game at Washington.

Year	Team	League	Games	G.	A.	Pts.	Pen.
1975-76—Maple Ridge		BCJHL	64	34	35	69	68
1975-76—New Westminster Bruins		WCHL	2	0	0	0	2
1976-77—New Westminster Bruins		WCHL	68	35	24	59	62
1977-78—New Westminster Bruins		WCHL	70	26	30	56	124
1978-79—New Westminster Bruins (c)		WHL	70	25	22	47	207
1979-80—Los Angeles Kings		NHL	40	2	5	7	28
1980-81—Los Angeles Kings		NHL	19	3	6	9	8
1980-81—Houston Apollos		CHL	33	11	17	28	31
1980-81—Rochester Americans		AHL	16	5	10	15	32
1981-82—Los Angeles Kings		NHL	70	12	11	23	100
1982-83—Los Angeles Kings		NHL	65	16	15	31	52
1983-84—Los Angeles Kings		NHL	72	7	14	21	73
NHL TOTALS			266	40	51	91	261

(c)—August, 1979—Drafted by Los Angeles Kings in 1979 entry draft. Fourth Kings pick, 50th overall, third round.

BRAD KEMPTHORNE

Center and Right Wing ... 6'2" ... 190 lbs. ... Born, Boisevain, Man., May 2, 1960 ... Shoots right.

Year	Team	League	Games	G.	A.	Pts.	Pen.
1977-78—Brandon Travellers		MJHL	38	22	52	74	68
1977-78—Brandon Wheat Kings		WCHL	24	5	5	10	2
1978-79—Brandon Wheat Kings (c)		WHL	56	22	31	53	89
1979-80—Medicine Hat Tigers		WHL	67	39	52	91	81
1980-81—Birmingham Bulls		CHL	44	10	25	35	65
1980-81—Rochester Americans		AHL	15	1	8	9	6
1980-81—Muskegon Mohawks		IHL	13	3	7	10	42
1981-82—Oklahoma City Stars		CHL	72	17	29	46	78
1982-83—Peoria Prancers		IHL	69	39	65	104	101
1983-84—Peoria Prancers		IHL	80	15	47	62	47

(c)—August, 1979—Drafted by Atlanta Flames as underage junior in 1979 NHL entry draft. Sixth Flames pick, 96th overall, fifth round.

EDWARD DEAN KENNEDY

(Known by middle name)

Defense ... 6'2" ... 200 lbs. ... Born, Redvers, Sask., January 18, 1963 ... Shoots right ... (February 18, 1983)—Given four-game suspension by NHL after off-ice altercation with Ken Linseman at Edmonton (February 3) ... Missed part of 1981-82 season with a knee injury.

Year	Team	League	Games	G.	A.	Pts.	Pen.
1979-80—Weyburn Red Wings		SJHL	57	12	20	32	64
1979-80—Brandon Wheat Kings		WHL	1	0	0	0	0
1980-81—Brandon Wheat Kings (c)		WHL	71	3	29	32	157
1981-82—Brandon Wheat Kings		WHL	49	5	38	43	103
1982-83—Brandon Wheat Kings		WHL	14	2	15	17	22
1982-83—Los Angeles Kings		NHL	55	0	12	12	97
1982-83—Saskatoon Blades (d)		WHL	..	..	..	..	..
1983-84—New Haven Nighthawks		AHL	26	1	7	8	23
1983-84—Los Angeles Kings		NHL	37	1	5	6	50
NHL TOTALS			92	1	17	18	147

(c)—June, 1981—Drafted as underage junior by Los Angeles Kings in 1981 NHL entry draft. Second Kings pick, 39th overall, second round.

(d)—No regular season record. Played in four playoff games.

ALAN KERR

Left Wing ... 5'11" ... 190 lbs. ... Born, Hazelton, B.C., March 28, 1964 ... Shoots right ... Also plays right wing ... Second cousin of Reg Kerr.

Year	Team	League	Games	G.	A.	Pts.	Pen.
1981-82—Seattle Breakers (c)		WHL	68	15	18	33	1079
1982-83—Seattle Breakers		WHL	71	38	53	91	183
1983-84—Seattle Breakers (a)		WHL	66	46	66	112	141

(c)—June, 1982—Drafted by New York Islanders as underage junior in 1982 NHL entry draft. Fourth Islanders pick, 84th overall, fourth round.

REGINALD JOHN KERR

Left Wing . . . 5'9" . . . 175 lbs. . . . Born, Oxbow, Sask., October 16, 1957 . . . Shoots left . . . Has also played Defense . . . (September, 1980)—Dislocated left shoulder in preseason game . . . Second cousin of Alan Kerr.

Year	Team	League	Games	G.	A.	Pts.	Pen.
1973-74—Penticton Broncos	Jr. "A" BCHL	60	15	36	51	130
1974-75—Kamloops Chiefs	WCHL	70	28	57	85	87
1975-76—Kamloops Chiefs	WCHL	70	23	58	81	147
1976-77—Kamloops Chiefs (c)	WCHL	72	47	54	101	172
1977-78—Phoenix Roadrunners	CHL	11	4	1	5	15
1977-78—Dallas Black Hawks	CHL	55	20	21	41	40
1977-78—Cleveland Barons (d)	NHL	7	0	2	2	7
1977-78—Chicago Black Hawks	NHL	2	0	2	2	0
1978-79—Chicago Black Hawks	NHL	73	16	24	40	50
1979-80—Chicago Black Hawks	NHL	49	9	8	17	17
1980-81—Chicago Black Hawks	NHL	70	30	29	59	56
1981-82—Chicago Black Hawks	NHL	59	11	28	39	39
1982-83—Springfield Indians	AHL	45	7	18	25	13
1983-84—Edmonton Oilers (e)	NHL	3	0	0	0	0
1983-84—Moncton Alpines	AHL	60	13	29	42	43
NHL TOTALS			**263**	**66**	**93**	**159**	**169**

(c)—Drafted from Kamloops Chiefs by Cleveland Barons in third round of 1977 amateur draft.
(d)—Traded to Chicago Black Hawks by Cleveland Barons for Randy Holt, November, 1977.
(e)—September, 1983—Released by Chicago Black Hawks and signed by Edmonton Oilers as a free agent.

TIM KERR

Right Wing and Center . . . 6'3" . . . 215 lbs. . . . Born, Windsor, Ont., January 5, 1960 . . . Shoots right   (November 1, 1980) Injured shoulder . . . (October, 1981)—Injured knee cartilage . . . (September, 1982)—Hernia surgery . . . (November 10, 1982)—Stretched knee ligaments in game at Buffalo that required surgery . . . (March, 1983)—Cracked fibula of left leg.

Year	Team	League	Games	G.	A.	Pts.	Pen.
1976-77—Windsor Spitfires	OMJHL	9	2	4	6	7
1977-78—Kingston Canadians	OMJHL	67	14	25	39	33
1978-79—Kingston Canadians	OMJHL	57	17	25	42	27
1979-80—Kingston Canadians (c)	OMJHL	63	40	33	73	39
1979-80—Maine Mariners	AHL	7	2	4	6	2
1980-81—Philadelphia Flyers	NHL	68	22	23	45	84
1981-82—Philadelphia Flyers	NHL	61	21	30	51	138
1982-83—Philadelphia Flyers	NHL	24	11	8	19	6
1983-84—Philadelphia Flyers	NHL	79	54	39	93	29
NHL TOTALS			**232**	**108**	**100**	**208**	**257**

(c)—January, 1980—Signed by Philadelphia Flyers as a free agent.

MARTY KETOLA

Right Wing . . . 5'10" . . . 185 lbs. . . . Born, Clouquet, Minn., February 25, 1965 . . . Shoots right.

Year	Team	League	Games	G.	A.	Pts.	Pen.
1982-83—Clouquet H.S. (c)	Minn. H.S.	23	19	13	32	30
1983-84—Colorado College	WCHA	34	3	4	7	48

(c)—June, 1983—Drafted by Pittsburgh Penguins in 1983 NHL entry draft. Seventh Penguins pick, 163rd overall, ninth round.

KRIS KING

Center . . . 5'10" . . . 185 lbs. . . . Born, Bracebridge, Ont., February 18, 1966 . . . Shoots left.

Year	Team	League	Games	G.	A.	Pts.	Pen.
1982-83—Gravenhurst	SOJHL	32	72	53	125	115
1983-84—Peterborough Petes (c)	OHL	62	13	18	31	168

(c)—June, 1984—Drafted as underage junior by Washington Capitals in 1984 NHL entry draft. Fourth Capitals pick, 80th overall, fourth round.

BRIAN EDWARD KINSELLA

Center . . . 5'11" . . . 176 lbs. . . . Born, Barrie, Ont., February 11, 1954 . . . Shoots right . . . Missed part of 1974-75 season with shoulder surgery.

Year	Team	League	Games	G.	A.	Pts.	Pen.
1971-72—Oshawa Generals		Jr."A"OHA	44	13	19	32	48
1972-73—Oshawa Generals		Jr."A"OHA	48	28	57	85	49
1973-74—Oshawa Generals (c)		Jr."A"OHA	64	36	43	79	95
1974-75—Richmond Robins		AHL	4	0	0	0	6
1974-75—Dayton Gems (d)		IHL	40	15	15	30	35
1974-75—Kalamazoo Wings		IHL	10	3	7	10	36
1975-76—Springfield Indians		AHL	1	0	0	0	0
1975-76—Dayton Gems		IHL	74	43	45	88	43
1975-76—Washington Capitals		NHL	4	0	1	1	0
1976-77—Springfield Indians		AHL	59	26	16	42	36
1976-77—Washington Capitals		NHL	6	0	0	0	0
1977-78—Port Huron Flags		IHL	34	11	19	30	16
1978-79—Port Huron Flags		IHL	72	16	52	68	94
1979-80—Port Huron Flags		IHL	73	43	40	83	61
1980-81—Port Huron Flags		IHL	79	36	40	76	71
1981-82—Toledo Goaldiggers (e)		IHL	80	36	45	81	71
1982-83—Toledo Goaldiggers		IHL	72	31	35	66	41
1983-84—Toledo Goaldiggers		IHL	41	18	19	37	27
NHL TOTALS			10	0	1	1	0

(c)—Drafted from Oshawa Generals by Washington Capitals in sixth round of 1974 amateur draft.
(d)—Loaned to Kalamazoo Wings by Dayton Gems, March, 1975.
(e)—August, 1981—Selected by Toledo Goaldiggers in IHL dispersal draft of players from defunct Port Huron Flags.

LOUIS KIRIAKOU

Defense . . . 5'11" . . . 174 lbs. . . . Born, Toronto, Ont., April 2, 1964 . . . Shoots left.

Year	Team	League	Games	G.	A.	Pts.	Pen.
1980-81—Toronto Young Nationals		MTHL	40	15	40	55	40
1981-82—Toronto Marlboros (c)		OHL	65	5	11	16	72
1982-83—Toronto Marlboros		OHL	67	6	38	44	100
1983-84—Toronto Marlboros		OHL	68	10	35	45	74

(c)—June, 1982—Drafted by Calgary Flames as underage junior in 1982 NHL entry draft. Sixth Flames pick, 93rd overall, fifth round.

MARK ROBERT KIRTON

Center . . . 5'10" . . . 170 lbs. . . . Born, Regina, Sask., February 3, 1958 . . . Shoots left . . . (March 7, 1981)—Separated left shoulder.

Year	Team	League	Games	G.	A.	Pts.	Pen.
1975-76—Peterborough Petes		Jr."A"OHA	65	22	38	60	10
1976-77—Peterborough Petes		Jr."A"OHA	48	18	24	42	41
1977-78—Peterborough Petes (c)		Jr."A"OHA	68	27	44	71	29
1978-79—New Brunswick Hawks		AHL	79	20	30	50	14
1979-80—Toronto Maple Leafs		NHL	2	1	0	1	2
1979-80—New Brunswick Hawks		AHL	61	19	42	61	33
1980-81—Toronto Maple Leafs (d)		NHL	11	0	0	0	0
1980-81—Detroit Red Wings		NHL	50	18	13	31	24
1981-82—Detroit Red Wings		NHL	74	14	28	42	62
1982-83—Adirondack Red Wings		AHL	20	6	10	16	12
1982-83—Detroit Red Wings (e)		NHL	10	1	1	2	6
1982-83—Vancouver Canucks		NHL	31	4	6	10	4
1982-83—Fredericton Express		AHL	3	2	0	2	2
1983-84—Vancouver Canucks		NHL	26	2	3	5	2
1983-84—Fredericton Express		AHL	35	8	10	18	8
NHL TOTALS			204	40	51	91	100

(c)—Drafted from Peterborough Petes by Toronto Maple Leafs in third round 1978 amateur draft.
(d)—December, 1980—Traded by Toronto Maple Leafs to Detroit Red Wings for Jim Rutherford.
(e)—January, 1983—Traded by Detroit Red Wings to Vancouver Canucks for Ivan Boldirev.

KELLY KISIO

Center . . . 5'9" . . . 170 lbs. . . . Born, Wetaskwin, Alta., September 18, 1959 . . . Shoots right . . . Also plays right wing.

Year	Team	League	Games	G.	A.	Pts.	Pen.
1976-77—Red Deer Rustlers		AJHL	60	53	48	101	101
1977-78—Red Deer Rustlers (a)		AJHL	58	74	68	142	66
1978-79—Calgary Wranglers		WHL	70	60	61	121	73
1979-80—Calgary Wranglers		WHL	71	65	73	138	64
1980-81—Adirondack Red Wings		AHL	41	10	14	24	43
1980-81—Kalamazoo Wings (c)		IHL	31	27	16	43	48

Year	Team	League	Games	G.	A.	Pts.	Pen.
1981-82—Dallas Black Hawks (d)	CHL	78	*62	39	101	59
1982-83—Davos HC	Switzerland	....	49	38	87	....
1982-83—Detroit Red Wings (e)	NHL	15	4	3	7	0
1983-84—Detroit Red Wings	NHL	70	23	37	60	34
NHL TOTALS			85	27	40	67	34

(c)—February, 1981—Traded by Toledo Goaldiggers to Kalamazoo Wings for Jean Chouinard.
(d)—Led CHL Adams Cup Playoffs with 12 goals and 29 points and was co-leader (with Bruce Affleck) with 17 assists.
(e)—February, 1983—Signed by Detroit as a free agent at the conclusion of season in Switzerland.

ED KISTER

Defense . . . 5'11" . . . 185 lbs. . . . Born, Becej, Czechoslovakia, January 7, 1966 . . . Shoots left.

Year	Team	League	Games	G.	A.	Pts.	Pen.
1982-83—Brantford	SOJHL	25	7	14	21	84
1983-84—London Knights (c)	OHL	60	2	15	17	30

(c)—June, 1984—Drafted as underage junior by Vancouver Canucks in 1984 NHL entry draft. 13th Canucks pick, 239th overall, 12th round.

BILL KITCHEN

Defense . . . 6'1" . . . 195 lbs. . . . Born, Schomberg, Ont., October 2, 1960 . . . Shoots left . . . (February 26, 1983)—Injured knee in AHL game at Binghamton . . . Brother of Mike Kitchen.

Year	Team	League	Games	G.	A.	Pts.	Pen.
1977-78—Ottawa 67's	OMJHL	67	5	6	11	54
1978-79—Ottawa 67's	OMJHL	55	3	16	19	188
1979-80—Ottawa 67's	OMJHL	63	7	19	26	195
1979-80—Nova Scotia Voyageurs (c)	AHL	....	...	....	....	....
1980-81—Nova Scotia Voyageurs	AHL	65	2	7	9	135
1981-82—Nova Scotia Voyageurs	AHL	71	3	17	20	135
1981-82—Montreal Canadiens	NHL	1	0	0	0	7
1982-83—Nova Scotia Voyageurs	AHL	53	3	11	14	71
1982-83—Montreal Canadiens	NHL	8	0	0	0	4
1983-84—Montreal Canadiens	NHL	3	0	0	0	2
1983-84—Nova Scotia Voyageurs	AHL	68	4	20	24	193
NHL TOTALS			12	0	0	0	13

(c)—Appeared in two playoff games.

MICHAEL ELWIN KITCHEN

Defense . . . 5'10" . . . 175 lbs. . . . Born, Newmarket, Ont., February 1, 1956 . . . Shoots left . . . Missed part of 1978-79 season with broken left wrist . . . Brother of Bill Kitchen . . . January, 1984)—Hip injury . . . (February 11, 1984)—Severed finger tendon in game at Pittsburgh.

Year	Team	League	Games	G.	A.	Pts.	Pen.
1973-74—Toronto Marlboros	Jr."A"OHA	69	3	17	20	145
1974-75—Toronto Marlboros (a)	Jr."A"OHA	68	5	30	35	136
1975-76—Toronto Marlboros (c)	Jr."A"OHA	65	6	18	24	148
1976-77—Rhode Island Reds	AHL	14	0	10	10	14
1976-77—Colorado Rockies	NHL	60	1	8	9	36
1977-78—Colorado Rockies	NHL	61	2	17	19	45
1978-79—Colorado Rockies	NHL	53	1	4	5	28
1979-80—Colorado Rockies	NHL	42	1	6	7	25
1979-80—Houston Apollos	CHL	30	0	9	9	??
1980-81—Colorado Rockies	NHL	75	1	7	8	100
1981-82—Ft. Worth Texans	CHL	13	1	5	6	16
1981-82—Colorado Rockies	NHL	63	1	8	9	60
1982-83—New Jersey Devils	NHL	77	4	8	12	52
1983-84—New Jersey Devils	NHL	43	1	4	5	24
NHL TOTALS			474	12	62	74	370

(c)—Drafted from Toronto Marlboros by Kansas City Scouts in third round of 1976 amateur draft.

ROBERT KIVELL

Defense . . . 6'1" . . . 205 lbs. . . . Born, North Bay, Ont., January 14, 1965 . . . Shoots left . . . (January, 1983)—Ruptured kidney.

Year	Team	League	Games	G.	A.	Pts.	Pen.
1982-83—Esquimalt Buccaneers	BCJHL	....	...	....	....	....
1982-83—Victoria Cougars (c)	WHL	26	6	7	13	83
1983-84—Victoria Cougars	WHL	52	16	33	49	145

KURT KLEINENDORST

Center . . . 6'2" . . . 190 lbs. . . . Born, Grand Rapids, Minn., December 31, 1960 . . . Shoots left . . . Brother of Scot Kleinendorst.

Year	Team	League	Games	G.	A.	Pts.	Pen.
1979-80—Providence College		ECAC	32	10	17	27	4
1980-81—Providence College (c)		ECAC	32	16	20	36	18
1981-82—Providence College		ECAC	..	..	..	..	..
1982-83—Providence College		ECAC	41	33	39	72	30
1983-84—U.S. National Team		Int'l	44	8	18	26	14
1983-84—Tulsa Oilers		CHL	24	4	9	13	10

(c)—June, 1980—Drafted by New York Rangers in NHL entry draft. Third Rangers pick, 77th overall, fourth round.

SCOT KLEINENDORST

Defense . . . 6'3" . . . 205 lbs. . . . Born, Grand Rapids, Minn., January 16, 1960 . . . Shoots left . . . (September, 1982)—Preseason surgery for off-season knee injury . . . Brother of Kurt Kleinendorst . . . (February, 1984)—Groin injury, out for the season.

Year	Team	League	Games	G.	A.	Pts.	Pen.
1979-80—Providence College (b-c-d)		ECAC	30	1	12	13	38
1980-81—Providence College		ECAC	32	3	31	34	75
1981-82—Providence College (a)		ECAC	33	30	27	57	14
1981-82—Springfield Indians		AHL	5	0	4	4	11
1982-83—Tulsa Oilers		CHL	10	0	7	7	14
1982-83—New York Rangers		NHL	30	2	9	11	8
1983-84—Tulsa Oilers		CHL	24	4	9	13	10
1983-84—New York Rangers (e)		NHL	23	0	2	2	35
NHL TOTALS			53	2	11	13	43

(c)—Named to All-New England Collegiate All-Star Team (Second team).

(d)—June, 1980—Drafted by New York Rangers in 1980 NHL entry draft. Fourth Rangers pick, 98th overall, fifth round.

(e)—February, 1984—Traded by New York Rangers to Hartford Whalers for Blaine Stoughton.

GORD KLUZAK

Defense . . . 6'3" . . . 214 lbs. . . . Born, Climax, Sask., March 4, 1964 . . . Shoots left . . . (February 9, 1982)—Injured knee vs. Medicine Hat that required surgery . . . (March 12, 1983)—Eye injured in game vs. Philadelphia.

Year	Team	League	Games	G.	A.	Pts.	Pen.
1980-81—Billings Bighorns		WHL	68	4	34	38	160
1981-82—Billings Bighorns (b-c)		WHL	38	9	24	33	110
1982-83—Boston Bruins		NHL	70	1	6	7	105
1983-84—Boston Bruins		NHL	80	10	27	37	135
NHL TOTALS			150	11	33	44	240

(c)—June, 1982—Drafted as underage junior by Boston Bruins in 1982 NHL entry draft. First Bruins pick, first overall, first round.

KEITH KNIGHT

Center . . . 5'11" . . . 169 lbs. . . . Born, Detroit, Mich., August 19, 1963 . . . Shoots right . . . Brother of Ken Knight.

Year	Team	League	Games	G.	A.	Pts.	Pen.
1979-80—Windsor Royals (c)		Jr.'B'	40	56	52	108	38
1980-81—Toronto Marlboros (d)		OHL	63	28	30	58	50
1981-82—Toronto Marlboros (e)		OHL	8	2	5	7	10
1981-82—Sudbury Wolves (f)		OHL	12	1	5	6	4
1981-82—Kingston Canadians		OHL	46	23	32	55	66
1981-82—Oklahoma City Stars		CHL	9	2	3	5	4
1982-83—Kingston Canadians		OHL	70	56	75	131	18
1982-83—Colorado Flames		CHL	9	4	3	7	4
1983-84—Colorado Flames		CHL	6	0	2	2	0
1983-84—Peoria Prancers		IHL	65	28	15	43	18

(c)—May, 1980—Selected by Toronto Marlboros in 1980 OHL priority draft. First Marlboro pick, 7th overall, first round.

(d)—August, 1981—Signed by Calgary Flames as a free agent.

(e)—October, 1981—Traded by Toronto Marlboros to Sudbury Wolves for Chris Kontos.

(f)—November, 1981—Traded by Sudbury Wolves to Kingston Canadians for future considerations.

JOE KOCUR

Right Wing . . . 6' . . . 204 lbs. . . . Born, Calgary, Alta., December 21, 1964 . . . Shoots right . . . (December, 1981)—Stretched knee ligaments.

Year	Team	League	Games	G.	A.	Pts.	Pen.
1980-81—Yorkton Terriers		SJHL	48	6	9	15	307
1981-82—Yorkton Terriers		SJHL	47	20	21	41	199
1982-83—Saskatoon Blades (c)		WHL	62	23	17	40	289
1983-84—Saskatoon Blades		WHL	69	40	41	81	258

(c)—June, 1983—Drafted as underage junior by Detroit Red Wings in 1983 NHL entry draft. Sixth Red Wings pick, 88th overall, fifth round.

STEPHEN MARK KONROYD

Defense . . . 6'1" . . . 195 lbs. . . . Born, Scarborough, Ont., February 10, 1961 . . . Shoots left.

Year	Team	League	Games	G.	A.	Pts.	Pen.
1978-79—Oshawa Generals		OMJHL	65	4	19	23	63
1979-80—Oshawa Generals (c-d)		OMJHL	62	11	23	34	133
1980-81—Calgary Flames		NHL	4	0	0	0	4
1980-81—Oshawa Generals (b)		OHL	59	19	49	68	232
1981-82—Oklahoma City Stars		CHL	14	2	3	5	15
1981-82—Calgary Flames		NHL	63	3	14	17	78
1982-83—Calgary Flames		NHL	79	4	13	17	73
1983-84—Calgary Flames		NHL	80	1	13	14	94
NHL TOTALS			226	8	40	48	249

(c)—June, 1980—Drafted as underage junior by Calgary Flames in 1980 NHL entry draft. Fourth Flames pick, 39th overall, second round.

(d)—Named winner of Bobby Smith Award (OHL player who best combines high standards of play with academic excellence).

CHRIS KONTOS

Center . . . 6'1" . . . 200 lbs. . . . Born, Toronto, Ont., December 10, 1963 . . . Shoots left . . . Also plays left wing . . . (November, 1983)—Suspended by New York Rangers when he refused to report to the Tulsa Oilers. He was reinstated in January, 1984.

Year	Team	League	Games	G.	A.	Pts.	Pen.
1979-80—North York Flames		OPJHL	42	39	55	94	37
1980-81—Sudbury Wolves		OHL	56	17	27	44	36
1981-82—Sudbury Wolves (c)		OHL	12	6	6	12	18
1981-82—Toronto Marlboros (d)		OHL	59	36	56	92	68
1982-83—Toronto Marlboros		OHL	28	21	33	54	23
1982-83—New York Rangers		NHL	44	8	7	15	33
1983-84—New York Rangers		NHL	6	0	1	1	8
1983-84—Tulsa Oilers		CHL	21	5	13	18	8
NHL TOTALS			50	8	8	16	41

(c)—October, 1981—Traded by Sudbury Wolves to Toronto Marlboros for Keith Knight.

(d)—June, 1982—Drafted as underage junior by New York Rangers in 1982 NHL entry draft. First Rangers pick, 15th overall, first round.

BILL KOPECKY

Center . . . 5'11" . . . 170 lbs. . . . Born, Ipswich, Mass., January 11, 1966 . . . Shoots left.

Year	Team	League	Games	G.	A.	Pts.	Pen.
1983-84—Austin H.S. (c)		Minn. H.S.	21	31	36	67	..

(c)—June, 1984—Drafted by Boston Bruins in 1984 NHL entry draft. 11th Bruins pick, 227th overall, 11th round.

GERALD JOSEPH (JERRY) KORAB

Defense . . . 6'3" . . . 215 lbs. . . . Born, Sault Ste. Marie, Ont., September 15, 1948 . . . Shoots left . . . Missed final seven games of 1969-70 season as well as playoffs with injuries . . . Had surgery on right knee to repair torn ligaments, August, 1971 . . . Also plays Left Wing . . . Missed part of 1979-80 season with broken collarbone. Also had blood clot on a lung . . . (December, 1981)—Lower back spasms . . . (Summer/83)—Operation on right foot. Doctors found all his toes were broken so they cut and stretched his tendons. Pins were inserted from toe to instep and kept there for five weeks . . . (January 29, 1984)—Injured elbow in game vs. Pittsburgh.

Year	Team	League	Games	G.	A.	Pts.	Pen.
1965-66—S. Ste. Marie Greyhounds		Jr."A"NOHA	....	...	....	....	....
1966-67—St. Cath. Black Hawks		Jr."A"OHA	43	3	10	13	57
1967-68—St. Cath. Black Hawks		Jr."A"OHA	54	10	34	44	*224
1968-69—Port Huron Flags		IHL	71	18	46	64	284

Year	Team	League	Games	G.	A.	Pts.	Pen.
1969-70—Portland Buckaroos		WHL	65	9	12	21	169
1970-71—Portland Buckaroos		WHL	20	3	5	8	78
1970-71—Chicago Black Hawks		NHL	46	4	14	18	152
1971-72—Chicago Black Hawks		NHL	73	9	5	14	95
1972-73—Chicago Black Hawks (c)		NHL	77	12	15	27	94
1973-74—Vancouver Canucks (d)		NHL	31	4	7	11	64
1973-74—Buffalo Sabres		NHL	45	6	12	18	73
1974-75—Buffalo Sabres		NHL	79	12	44	56	184
1975-76—Buffalo Sabres		NHL	65	13	28	41	85
1976-77—Buffalo Sabres		NHL	77	14	33	47	120
1977-78—Buffalo Sabres		NHL	77	7	34	41	119
1978-79—Buffalo Sabres		NHL	78	11	40	51	104
1979-80—Buffalo Sabres (e)		NHL	43	1	10	11	74
1979-80—Los Angeles Kings		NHL	11	1	2	3	34
1980-81—Los Angeles Kings		NHL	78	9	43	52	139
1981-82—Los Angeles Kings		NHL	50	5	13	18	91
1982-83—Los Angeles Kings		NHL	72	3	26	29	90
1983-84—Buffalo Sabres (f-g)		NHL	48	2	9	11	82
1983-84—Rochester Americans		AHL	4	0	4	4	2
NHL TOTALS			950	113	335	448	1600

(c)—Traded to Vancouver Canucks by Chicago Black Hawks with Gary Smith for Dale Tallon, May, 1973.

(d)—Traded to Buffalo Sabres by Vancouver Canucks for John Gould and Tracy Pratt, December, 1973.

(e)—March, 1980—Traded by Buffalo Sabres to Los Angeles Kings for future considerations (1982 first round draft pick Phil Housley).

(f)—October, 1983—Released by Los Angeles Kings.
— Signed by Minnesota North Stars as a free agent.
— Selected by Buffalo Sabres in 1983 NHL waiver draft.

(g)—June, 1984—Released by Buffalo Sabres.

JEFF KORCHINSKI

Defense . . . 6' . . . 190 lbs. . . . Born, Ottawa, Ont., May 13, 1966 . . . Shoots left.

Year	Team	League	Games	G.	A.	Pts.	Pen.
1983-84—Clarkson College (c)		ECAC	34	1	5	6	12

(c)—June, 1984—Drafted by Vancouver Canucks in 1984 NHL entry draft. Seventh Canucks pick. 115th overall, sixth round.

JOHN KORDIC

Defense . . . 6'1" . . . 190 lbs. . . . Born, Edmonton, Alta., March 22, 1965 . . . Shoots right . . . Uncle played pro soccer in Yugoslavia.

Year	Team	League	Games	G.	A.	Pts.	Pen.
1981-82—Edmonton K. of C. AA		Edm. Midget	48	23	41	64	178
1982-83—Portland Winter Hawks (c)		WHL	72	3	22	25	235
1983-84—Portland Winter Hawks		WHL	67	9	50	59	232

(c)—June, 1983—Drafted as underage junior by Montreal Canadiens in 1983 NHL entry draft. Sixth Canadiens pick, 78th overall, fourth round.

JAMES A. KORN

Defense . . . 6'5" . . . 220 lbs. . . . Born, Hopkins, Minn., July 28, 1957 . . . Shoots left . . . Attended Providence College . . . (January 13, 1981)—Injured ligaments in right knee . . . (February 8, 1984)—Injured ribs in game vs. Boston.

Year	Team	League	Games	G.	A.	Pts.	Pen.
1976-77—Providence College (c)		ECAC	29	6	9	15	73
1977-78—Providence College		ECAC	33	7	14	21	47
1978-79—Providence College		ECAC	27	5	19	24	72
1979-80—Adirondack Red Wings		AHL	14	2	7	9	40
1979-80—Detroit Red Wings		NHL	63	5	13	18	108
1980-81—Adirondack Red Wings		AHL	9	3	7	10	53
1980-81—Detroit Red Wings		NHL	63	5	15	20	246
1981-82—Detroit Red Wings (d)		NHL	59	1	7	8	104
1981-82—Toronto Maple Leafs		NHL	11	1	3	4	44
1982-83—Toronto Maple Leafs		NHL	80	8	21	29	238
1983-84—Toronto Maple Leafs		NHL	65	12	14	26	257
NHL TOTALS			341	32	73	105	997

(c)—June, 1977—Drafted by Detroit Red Wings in 1977 amateur draft. Fourth Detroit pick, 73rd overall, fifth round.

(d)—March, 1982—Traded by Detroit Red Wings to Toronto Maple Leafs for 1982 fourth-round pick (Craig Coxe) and a 1983 fifth-round pick in the NHL entry draft.

DAVID KOROL

Defense . . . 6' . . . 180 lbs. . . . Born, Winnipeg, Man., March 1, 1965 . . . Shoots left . . . (January, 1982)—Thumb surgery.

Year	Team	League	Games	G.	A.	Pts.	Pen.
1981-82—Winnipeg Warriors		WHL	64	4	22	26	55
1982-83—Winnipeg Warriors (c)		WHL	72	14	43	57	90
1983-84—Winnipeg Warriors		WHL	57	15	48	63	49
1983-84—Adirondack Red Wings		AHL	2	0	4	4	0

(c)—June, 1983—Drafted by Detroit Red Wings in 1983 NHL entry draft. Fourth Red Wings pick, 68th overall, fourth round.

ROGER KORTKO

Center . . . 5'11" . . . 175 lbs. . . . Born, Hafford, Sask., February 1, 1963 . . . Shoots left.

Year	Team	League	Games	G.	A.	Pts.	Pen.
1980-81—Humbolt Broncos		SJHL	60	43	82	125	52
1981-82—Saskatoon Blades (c)		WHL	65	33	51	84	82
1982-83—Saskatoon Blades		WHL	72	62	99	161	79
1983-84—Indianapolis Checkers		CHL	64	16	27	43	48

(c)—June, 1982—Drafted as underage junior by New York Islanders in 1982 NHL entry draft. Sixth Islanders pick, 126th overall, sixth round.

CHRIS KOTSOPOULOS

Defense . . . 6'3" . . . 215 lbs. . . . Born, Toronto, Ont., November 27, 1958 . . . Shoots right . . . Brother of George Kotsopoulos . . . (October, 1980)—Broke right thumb during exhibition game . . . (January, 1981)—Infection in right arm . . . (January 24, 1981)—Hand infection developed after treatment for cut hand . . . (February, 1983)—Pulled stomach muscles . . . (January 24, 1984)—Strained ligaments in right knee in game at Montreal.

Year	Team	League	Games	G.	A.	Pts.	Pen.
1975-76—Windsor Spitfires		OMJHL	59	3	13	16	169
1978-79—Toledo Goaldiggers		IHL	64	6	22	28	153
1979-80—New Haven Nighthawks		AHL	75	7	27	34	149
1980-81—New York Rangers (c)		NHL	54	4	12	16	153
1981-82—Hartford Whalers		NHL	68	13	20	33	147
1982-83—Hartford Whalers		NHL	68	6	24	30	125
1983-84—Hartford Whalers		NHL	72	5	13	18	118
NHL TOTALS			262	28	69	97	543

(c)—October, 1981—Traded with Doug Sulliman and Gerry McDonald by New York Rangers to Hartford Whalers for Mike Rogers and a 10th-round 1982 draft pick (Simo Saarinen).

MIKE KRENSING

Center . . . 6'1" . . . 180 lbs. . . . Born, Ely, Minn., August 7, 1961 . . . Shoots left.

Year	Team	League	Games	G.	A.	Pts.	Pen.
1979-80—University of Minn./Duluth		WCHA	27	0	5	5	6
1980-81—University of Minn./Duluth		WCHA	35	7	9	16	28
1981-82—University of Minn./Duluth		WCHA	39	10	19	29	41
1982-83—University of Minn./Duluth		WCHA	43	23	27	50	55
1983-84—Milwaukee Admirals		IHL	12	3	2	5	0
1983-84—Muskegon Mohawks (c-d)		IHL	63	46	28	74	24

(c)—October, 1983—Signed by Edmonton Oilers as a free agent.
(d)—Won Ken McKenzie Trophy (Top American-born IHL Rookie).

RICHARD KROMM

Center . . . 5'11" . . . 180 lbs. . . . Born, Trail, B.C., March 29, 1964 . . . Shoots left . . . Son of Bobby Kromm (Member of World Champion 1961 Trail Smoke Eaters, and former WHA/NHL coach) . . . (October, 1981)—Broken ankle . . . Brother of David Kromm . . . Also plays left wing.

Year	Team	League	Games	G.	A.	Pts.	Pen.
1980-81—Windsor Royals		Jr. 'B'	39	22	31	53	40
1981-82—Portland Winter Hawks (c)		WHL	60	16	38	54	30
1982-83—Portland Winter Hawks		WHL	72	35	68	103	64
1983-84—Portland Winter Hawks		WHL	10	10	4	14	13
1983-84—Calgary Flames		NHL	53	11	12	23	27
NHL TOTALS			53	11	12	23	27

(c)—June, 1982—Drafted as underage junior by Calgary Flames in 1982 NHL entry draft. Second Flames pick, 37th overall, second round.

MIKE KRUSHELNYSKI

Left Wing and Center . . . 6'2" . . . 200 lbs. . . . Born, Montreal, Que., April 27, 1960 . . . Shoots left . . . Started the 1978-79 season at St. Louis University but left to return to junior hockey . . . (January, 1984)—Separated right shoulder.

Year	Team	League	Games	G.	A.	Pts.	Pen.
1978-79—Montreal Juniors		QMJHL	46	15	29	44	42
1979-80—Montreal Juniors (c)		QMJHL	72	39	61	100	78
1980-81—Springfield Indians		AHL	80	25	38	53	47
1981-82—Erie Blades		AHL	62	31	52	83	44
1981-82—Boston Bruins		NHL	17	3	3	6	2
1982-83—Boston Bruins		NHL	79	23	42	65	43
1983-84—Boston Bruins (d)		NHL	66	25	20	45	55
NHL TOTALS			162	51	65	116	100

(c)—August, 1979—Drafted by Boston Bruins as an underage junior in 1979 NHL entry draft. Seventh Bruins pick, 120th overall, sixth round.

(d)—June, 1984—Traded by Boston Bruins to Edmonton Oilers for Ken Linseman.

STUART KULAK

Right Wing . . . 5'10" . . . 175 lbs. . . . Born, Edmonton, Alta., March 10, 1963 . . . Shoots right.

Year	Team	League	Games	G.	A.	Pts.	Pen.
1979-80—Sherwood Park Crusaders		AJHL	53	30	23	53	111
1979-80—Victoria Cougars		WHL	3	0	0	0	0
1980-81—Victoria Cougars (c)		WHL	72	23	24	47	43
1981-82—Victoria Cougars		WHL	71	38	50	88	92
1982-83—Victoria Cougars		WHL	50	29	33	62	130
1982-83—Vancouver Canucks		NHL	4	1	1	2	0
1983-84—Fredericton Express		AHL	52	12	16	28	55
NHL TOTALS			4	1	1	2	0

(c)—June, 1981—Drafted as underage junior by Vancouver Canucks in 1981 NHL entry draft. Fifth Canucks pick, 115th overall, sixth round.

MARK KUMPEL

Right Wing . . . 6' . . . 190 lbs. . . . Born, Wakefield, Mass., March 7, 1961 . . . Shoots right . . . Member of 1984 U.S. Olympic team . . . (October, 1980)—Suffered knee ligament damage in first game and missed remainder of season.

Year	Team	League	Games	G.	A.	Pts.	Pen.
1979-80—Lowell University (c)		ECAC	30	18	18	36	12
1980-81—Lowell University		ECAC	1	2	0	2	0
1981-82—Lowell University		ECAC	35	17	13	30	23
1982-83—Lowell University		ECAC	7	8	5	13	0
1982-83—U.S. National Team		Int'l	30	14	18	32	6
1983-84—U.S. National Team		Int'l	61	14	19	33	19
1983-84—U.S. Olympic Team		Int'l	6	1	0	1	2
1983-84—Fredericton Express		AHL	16	1	1	2	5

(c)—June, 1980—Drafted by Quebec Nordiques in NHL entry draft. Fourth Nordiques pick, 108th overall, sixth round.

JARI KURRI

Right Wing . . . 6' . . . 183 lbs. . . . Born, Helsinki, Finland, May 18, 1960 . . . Shoots right . . . Played on Finnish Olympic Team in 1980 . . . (November 24, 1981)—Pulled groin during Oilers practice . . . First Finland-born player to have 100-point season in NHL . . . (January, 1984)—Missed 16 games with a pulled groin muscle.

Year	Team	League	Games	G.	A.	Pts.	Pen.
1977-78—Jokerit		Fin. Elite	29	2	9	11	12
1978-79—Jokerit		Fin. Elite	33	16	14	30	12
1979-80—Jokerit (c)		Fin. Elite	33	23	16	39	22
1980-81—Edmonton Oilers		NHL	75	32	43	75	40
1981-82—Edmonton Oilers		NHL	71	32	54	86	32
1982-83—Edmonton Oilers		NHL	80	45	59	104	22
1983-84—Edmonton Oilers (b-d)		NHL	64	52	61	113	14
NHL TOTALS			290	161	217	378	108

(c)—June, 1980—Drafted by Edmonton Oilers in NHL entry draft. Third Oilers pick, 69th overall, fourth round.

(d)—Led NHL Stanley Cup playoffs with 14 goals.

TOM KURVERS

Defense . . . 6' . . . 190 lbs. . . . Born, Minneapolis, Minn., October 14, 1962 . . . Shoots left . . . Set UMD record with 149 career assists.

Year	Team	League	Games	G.	A.	Pts.	Pen.
1980-81—University of Minnesota/Duluth (c)	WCHA	39	6	24	30	48
1981-82—University of Minnesota/Duluth	WCHA	37	11	31	42	18
1982-83—University of Minnesota/Duluth	WCHA	45	8	36	44	42
1983-84—University of Minn/Duluth (a-d-e)	WCHA	43	18	58	76	46

(c)—June, 1981—Drafted as underage player by Montreal Canadiens in 1981 NHL entry draft. Tenth Canadiens pick, 145th overall, seventh round.
(d)—Named to All-American Team (West).
(e)—Won Hobey Baker Award (Top NCAA Hockey Player).

JIM KYTE

Defense . . . 6'5" . . . 200 lbs. . . . Born, Ottawa, Ont., March 21, 1964 . . . Shoots left . . . Wears hearing aids when he plays . . . (March, 1980)—Broken left wrist.

Year	Team	League	Games	G.	A.	Pts.	Pen.
1980-81—Hawksbury Hawks	Tier II	42	2	24	26	133
1981-82—Cornwall Royals (c)	OHL	52	4	13	17	148
1982-83—Cornwall Royals	OHL	65	6	30	36	195
1982-83—Winnipeg Jets	NHL	2	0	0	0	0
1983-84—Winnipeg Jets	NHL	58	1	2	3	55
NHL TOTALS		60	1	2	3	55

(c)—June, 1982—Drafted as underage junior by Winnipeg Jets in 1982 NHL entry draft. First Jets pick, 12th overall, first round.

JOHN LABATT

Center . . . 5'11" . . . 174 lbs. . . . Born, Minnetonka, Minn., August 16, 1965 . . . Shoots left.

Year	Team	League	Games	G.	A.	Pts.	Pen.
1982-83—Minnetonka H.S. (c)	Minn. H.S.	23	23	26	49	..
1983-84—University of Minnesota	WCHA	11	2	2	4	2

(c)—June, 1983—Drafted by Vancouver Canucks in 1983 NHL entry draft. Eighth Canucks pick, 150th overall, eighth round.

GARRY LACEY

Left Wing . . . 5'11" . . . 178 lbs. . . . Born, Sudbury, Ont., May 24, 1964 . . . Shoots left . . . Also plays center.

Year	Team	League	Games	G.	A.	Pts.	Pen.
1980-81—Garson Midgets	OHA Midgets	28	38	34	72	....
1981-82—Toronto Marlboros (c)	OHL	65	17	28	45	140
1982-83—Toronto Marlboros	OHL	67	19	36	55	117
1983-84—Toronto Marlboros (a)	OHL	59	41	60	101	77

(c)—June, 1982—Drafted as underage junior by New York Islanders in 1982 entry draft. Third Islanders pick, 63rd overall, third round.

NORMAND LACOMBE

Right Wing . . . 5'11" . . . 205 lbs. . . . Born, Pierrefond, Que., October 18, 1964 . . . Shoots right.

Year	Team	League	Games	G.	A.	Pts.	Pen.
1981-82—Univ. of New Hampshire	ECAC	35	18	16	34	38
1982-83—Univ. of New Hampshire (c)	ECAC	35	18	25	43	48
1983-84—Rochester Americans	AHL	44	10	16	26	45

(c)—June, 1983—Drafted by Buffalo Sabres in 1983 NHL entry draft. Second Sabres pick, 10th overall, first round.

PIERRE LACROIX

Defense . . . 5'11" . . . 185 lbs. . . . Born, Quebec City, Que., April 11, 1959 . . . Shoots left . . . (January 4, 1981)—Injured shoulder . . . (July, 1983)—Injured in auto crash in Quebec.

Year	Team	League	Games	G.	A.	Pts.	Pen.
1975-76—Quebec Remparts	QMJHL	72	7	30	37	90
1976-77—Quebec Remparts	QMJHL	69	10	43	53	61
1977-78—Quebec Remparts	QMJHL	38	11	30	41	35
1977-78—Trois-Rivieres Draveurs	QMJHL	30	6	24	30	20
1978-79—Trois-Riv. Draveurs (a-c-d)	QMJHL	72	37	100	137	57
1979-80—Quebec Nordiques	NHL	76	9	21	30	45
1980-81—Quebec Nordiques	NHL	61	5	34	39	54

Year	Team	League	Games	G.	A.	Pts.	Pen.
1981-82—Quebec Nordiques		NHL	68	4	23	27	74
1982-83—Fredericton Express		AHL	6	0	5	5	0
1982-83—Quebec Nordiques (e)		NHL	13	0	5	5	6
1982-83—Hartford Whalers		NHL	56	6	25	31	18
1983-84—Did not play—injured			....	...	....	....	....
NHL TOTALS			274	24	108	132	197

(c)—August, 1979—Drafted by Quebec Nordiques in NHL entry draft. Fifth Nordiques pick, 104th overall, fifth round.

(d)—Winner of CCM Trophy (Best Junior Player in Canada).

(e)—December, 1982—Traded by Quebec Nordiques to Hartford Whalers for Blake Wesley.

RANDY LADOUCEUR

Defense . . . 6'2" . . . 220 lbs. . . . Born, Brockville, Ont., June 30, 1960 . . . Shoots left.

Year	Team	League	Games	G.	A.	Pts.	Pen.
1978-79—Brantford Alexanders		OMJHL	64	3	17	20	141
1979-80—Brantford Alexanders (c)		OMJHL	37	6	15	21	125
1980-81—Kalamazoo Wings		IHL	80	7	30	37	52
1981-82—Adirondack Red Wings		AHL	78	4	28	32	78
1982-83—Adirondack Red Wings		AHL	48	11	21	32	54
1982-83—Detroit Red Wings		NHL	27	0	4	4	16
1983-84—Adirondack Red Wings		AHL	11	3	5	8	12
1983-84—Detroit Red Wings		NHL	71	3	17	20	58
NHL TOTALS			98	3	21	24	74

(c)—November, 1979—Signed by Detroit Red Wings as a free agent.

GUY DAMIEN LAFLEUR

Right Wing and Center . . . 6' . . . 175 lbs. . . . Born, Thurso, Que., September 20, 1951 . . . Shoots right . . . Missed part of 1974-75 season with fractured index finger . . . Youngest player to score 400 NHL-career goals . . . Missed conclusion of 1979-80 season and play-offs with knee injury . . . (October 8, 1980)—Pulled right hamstring . . . (November, 1980)—Tonsilitis . . . (December 30, 1980)—Injured his right eye when struck by errant stick . . . (February, 1981)—Nine stitch cut under eye . . . (March 4, 1981)—Collected 1,000th NHL point in his 720th game, faster than any player in NHL history . . . (March, 1981)—Charley horse . . . (March 24, 1981)—Fell asleep at the wheel of his car, hit a fence and a metal sign post sliced off the top part of his right ear after the post went through his windshield . . . (November 10, 1981)—Errant stick entered eye in game at Los Angeles . . . (March 11, 1982)—Bruised bone of left foot when hit by puck in game vs. Chicago . . . (October 11, 1982)—Eye injured in game at Quebec . . . (November 4, 1982)—Broke little toe on right foot in game at Minnesota . . . Holds Montreal Canadien club career records for most assists and points.

Year	Team	League	Games	G.	A.	Pts.	Pen.
1966-67—Quebec Jr. Aces		QJHL	8	1	1	2	0
1967-68—Quebec Jr. Aces		QJHL	43	30	19	49	....
1968-69—Quebec Jr. Aces		QJHL	49	50	60	110	83
1969-70—Quebec Remparts		QJHL	56	*103	67	170	89
1970-71—Quebec Remparts (c)		QJHL	62	*130	79	*209	135
1971-72—Montreal Canadiens		NHL	73	29	35	64	48
1972-73—Montreal Canadiens		NHL	69	28	27	55	51
1973-74—Montreal Canadiens		NHL	73	21	35	56	29
1974-75—Montreal Canadiens (a-d-e)		NHL	70	53	66	119	37
1975-76—Montreal Canadiens (a-f)		NHL	80	56	69	*125	36
1976-77—Mont. Canadiens (a-f-g-h-i-j)		NHL	80	56	*80	*136	20
1977-78—Montreal Canadiens (a-f-g-h-k)		NHL	78	*60	72	*132	26
1978-79—Montreal Canadiens (a-l)		NHL	80	52	77	129	28
1979-80—Montreal Canadiens (a)		NHL	74	50	75	125	12
1980-81—Montreal Canadiens		NHL	51	27	43	70	29
1981-82—Montreal Canadiens		NHL	66	27	57	84	24
1982-83—Montreal Canadiens		NHL	68	27	49	76	12
1983-84—Montreal Canadiens		NHL	80	30	40	70	19
NHL TOTALS			942	516	725	1241	371

(c)—Drafted from Quebec Remparts by Montreal Canadiens in first round of 1971 amateur draft.

(d)—Led in goals (12) during playoffs.

(e)—Selected Most Valuable Player in Prince of Wales Conference in poll of players by THE SPORTING NEWS.

(f)—Won Art Ross Trophy.

(g)—Won Hart Memorial Trophy.

(h)—Selected THE SPORTING NEWS' NHL Player-of-the-Year in poll of NHL players.

(i)—Led in assists (17) and points (26) during playoffs.

(j)—Won Conn Smythe Trophy (MVP in Stanley Cup playoffs).
(k)—Led in goals (10) and tied for lead in points (21) during playoffs.
(l)—Tied for lead in assists (13) and points (23) during playoffs.

PAT La FONTAINE

Center . . . 5'9" . . . 170 lbs. . . . Born, St. Louis, Mo., February 22, 1965 . . . Shoots right . . . Set Quebec Junior League records (1982-83) with points in 43 consecutive games (since broken by Mario Lemieux), and most goals (104), assists (130) and points (234) by a Quebec Junior League Rookie . . . Member of 1984 U.S. Olympic team.

Year	Team	League	Games	G.	A.	Pts.	Pen.
1981-82	Detroit Compuware	Mich. Midget	79	175	149	324	...
1982-83	Verdun Juniors (a-c-d-e-f-g)	QHL	70	*104	*130	*234	10
1983-84	U.S. National Team	Int'l	58	56	55	111	22
1983-84	U.S. Olympic Team	Int'l	6	5	5	10	0
1983-84	New York Islanders	NHL	15	13	6	19	6
	NHL TOTALS		15	13	6	19	6

(c)—Won Frank Selke Trophy (Most Gentlemanly QHL player).
(d)—Won Des Instructeurs Trophy (Top QHL Rookie Forward).
(e)—Won Jean Beliveau Trophy (QHL Leading Scorer).
(f)—Won Guy Lafleur Trophy (QHL Playoff MVP).
(g)—June, 1983—Drafted as underage junior by New York Islanders in 1983 NHL entry draft. First Islanders pick, third overall, first round.

BOB LAFOREST

Right Wing . . . 5'11" . . . 195 lbs. . . . Born, Victoria, B.C., May 19, 1963 . . . Shoots right.

Year	Team	League	Games	G.	A.	Pts.	Pen.
1980-81	Niagara Falls Flyers	OHL	47	10	6	16	21
1981-82	Niagara Falls Flyers	OHL	66	31	40	71	40
1982-83	North Bay Centennials (c)	OHL	65	58	38	96	32
1983-84	New Haven Nighthawks	AHL	26	2	7	9	0
1983-84	Los Angeles Kings (d)	NHL	5	1	0	1	2
1983-84	Hershey Bears	AHL	42	11	16	27	10
	NHL TOTALS		5	1	0	1	2

(c)—June, 1983—Drafted by Los Angeles Kings in 1983 NHL entry draft. Third Kings pick, 87th overall, fifth round.
(d)—January, 1984—Traded by Los Angeles Kings to Boston Bruins for Marco Baron.

FLOYD LAHACHE

Defense . . . 5'10" . . . 185 lbs. . . . Born, Caughnawaga, Que., September 17, 1957 . . . Shoots left.

Year	Team	League	Games	G.	A.	Pts.	Pen.
1973-74	Sherbrooke Beavers	QJHL	70	2	13	15	155
1974-75	Sherbrooke Beavers	QJHL	65	5	21	26	296
1975-76	Sherbrooke Beavers	QJHL	71	11	49	60	159
1976-77	Sherbrooke Beavers (c-d)	QJHL	70	10	37	47	225
1977-78	Hampton Gulls	AHL	44	4	4	8	87
1977-78	Binghamton Dusters	AHL	12	0	1	1	11
1977-78	Cincinnati Stingers	WHA	11	0	3	3	13
1978-79	Springfield Indians	AHL	5	0	1	1	11
1978-79	Tucson Rustlers	PHL	16	2	4	6	59
1978-79	Los Angeles Blades	PHL	5	0	2	2	9
1978-79	Erie Blades	NEHL	30	1	11	12	75
1979-80	Flint Generals	IHL	78	9	21	30	193
1980-81	Flint Generals	IHL	79	11	53	64	261
1981-82	Flint Generals	IHL	77	6	31	37	238
1982-83	Flint Generals	IHL	72	2	39	41	271
1983-84	Kalamazoo Wings	IHL	69	8	24	32	165
	WHA TOTALS		11	0	3	3	13

(c)—Drafted from Sherbrooke Beavers by Chicago Black Hawks in seventh round of 1977 amateur draft.
(d)—Selected by Cincinnati Stingers in World Hockey Association amateur players' draft, May, 1977.

PAT LAHEY

Center . . . 6'1" . . . 175 lbs. . . . Born, Ottawa, Ont., March 2, 1964 . . . Shoots right . . . Grandson of Syd Howe (Detroit-NHL, 1934-46).

Year	Team	League	Games	G.	A.	Pts.	Pen.
1980-81—Ottawa 67's		OPJHL	49	27	26	53	26
1981-82—Windsor Spitfires (c)		OHL	62	15	27	42	42
1982-83—Windsor Spitfires (d)		OHL	4	1	1	2	4
1982-83—Sault Ste. Marie Greyhounds		OHL	64	20	21	41	33
1983-84—Sault Ste. Marie Greyhounds		OHL	63	30	45	75	58

(c)—June, 1982—Drafted as underage junior by Detroit Red Wings in 1982 NHL entry draft. Eighth Red Wings pick, 149th overall, eighth round.

(d)—October, 1982—Traded with Gus Greco by Windsor Spitfires to Sault Ste. Marie Greyhounds for Brad Bell.

TOM LAIDLAW

Defense . . . 6'2" . . . 215 lbs. . . . Born, Brampton, Ont., April 15, 1958 . . . Shoots left.

Year	Team	League	Games	G.	A.	Pts.	Pen.
1978-79—Northern Michigan Univ. (c)		CCHA	29	10	20	30	137
1979-80—Northern Michigan Univ. (a-d)		CCHA	39	8	30	38	83
1979-80—New Haven Nighthawks		AHL	1	0	0	0	0
1980-81—New York Rangers		NHL	80	6	23	29	100
1981-82—New York Rangers		NHL	79	3	18	21	104
1982-83—New York Rangers		NHL	80	0	10	10	75
1983-84—New York Rangers		NHL	79	3	15	18	62
NHL TOTALS			318	12	66	78	341

(c)—June, 1978—Drafted by New York Rangers in 1978 NHL amateur draft. Seventh Rangers pick, 93rd overall, sixth round.

(d)—Named to All-NCAA-Tournament team.

BOB LAKSO

Left Wing . . . 6' . . . 180 lbs. . . . Born, Baltimore, Md., April 3, 1962 . . . Shoots left.

Year	Team	League	Games	G.	A.	Pts.	Pen.
1980-81—Univ. of Minnesota/Duluth (c)		WCHA	36	7	6	13	2
1981-82—Univ. of Minnesota/Duluth		WCHA	28	12	11	23	8
1982-83—Univ. of Minnesota/Duluth		WCHA	45	18	25	43	8
1983-84—Univ. of Minnesota/Duluth		WCHA	43	32	34	66	12

(c)—June, 1980—Drafted by Minnesota North Stars in NHL entry draft. Ninth North Stars pick, 184th overall, ninth round.

JOHN MICHAEL (MIKE) LALOR

Defense . . . 6' . . . 190 lbs. . . . Born, Fort Erie, Ont., March 8, 1963 . . . Shoots left.

Year	Team	League	Games	G.	A.	Pts.	Pen.
1981-82—Brantford Alexanders		OHL	64	3	13	16	114
1982-83—Brantford Alexanders		OHL	65	10	30	40	113
1983-84—Nova Scotia Voyageurs (c)		AHL	67	5	11	16	80

(c)—September, 1983—Signed by Nova Scotia Voyageurs as a free agent.

MARK LAMB

Left Wing . . . 5'9" . . . 170 lbs. . . . Born, Swift Current, Sask., August 3, 1964 . . . Shoots left . . . (December, 1982)—Refused, with team captain Bob Rouse, to dress for a game after Nanaimo (WHL) released coach Les Calder. Both players asked to be traded . . . Also plays center.

Year	Team	League	Games	G.	A.	Pts.	Pen.
1980-81—Billings Bighorns		WHL	24	1	8	9	12
1981-82—Billings Bighorns (c)		WHL	72	45	56	101	46
1982-83—Nanaimo Islanders (d)		WHL	30	14	37	51	16
1982-83—Medicine Hat Tigers		WHL	46	22	43	65	33
1983-84—Medicine Hat Tigers (a-e)		WHL	72	59	77	136	30

(c)—June, 1982—Drafted as underage junior by Calgary Flames in 1982 NHL entry draft. Fifth Flames pick, 72nd overall, fourth round.

(d)—December, 1982—Traded by Nanaimo Islanders to Medicine Hat Tigers for Glen Kulka and Daryl Reaugh.

(e)—Won Frank Boucher Memorial Trophy (Most Gentlemanly WHL Player).

LANE LAMBERT

Right Wing . . . 6' . . . 175 lbs. . . . Born, Melfort, Sask., November 18, 1964 . . . Shoots right . . . (September, 1982)—Eye injured in game vs. Brandon.

Year	Team	League	Games	G.	A.	Pts.	Pen.
1980-81—Swift Current Broncos		SJHL	55	43	54	97	63
1981-82—Saskatoon Blades		WHL	72	45	69	114	111

Year	Team	League	Games	G.	A.	Pts.	Pen.
1982-83—Saskatoon Blades (b-c)		WHL	64	59	60	119	126
1983-84—Detroit Red Wings		NHL	73	20	15	35	115
NHL TOTALS			73	20	15	35	115

(c)—June, 1983—Drafted as underage junior by Detroit Red Wings in 1983 NHL entry draft. Second Red Wings pick, 25th overall, second round.

RICHARD LAMBERT

Left Wing . . . 6' . . . 196 lbs. . . . Born, Toronto, Ont., September 9, 1966 . . . Shoots left.

Year	Team	League	Games	G.	A.	Pts.	Pen.
1983-84—Henry Carr H.S. (c)		MTJHL	81	41	62	103	108

(c)—June, 1984—Drafted as underage junior by Edmonton Oilers in 1984 NHL entry draft. Fifth Oilers pick, 105th overall, fifth round.

ROSS LAMBERT

Center . . . 5'10" . . . 175 lbs. . . . Born, Kindersley, Sask., January 19, 1962 . . . Shoots left.

Year	Team	League	Games	G.	A.	Pts.	Pen.
1980-81—Princeton University		ECAC	25	2	12	14	44
1981-82—Princeton University		ECAC	26	10	18	28	42
1982-83—Saskatoon Blades		WHL	71	28	78	106	97
1983-84—Moncton Alpines (c)		AHL	75	6	15	21	61

(c)—September, 1983—Signed by Edmonton Oilers as a free agent.

YVON PIERRE LAMBERT

Left Wing . . . 6' . . . 195 lbs. . . . Born, Drummondville, Que., May 20, 1950 . . . Shoots left . . . Set AHL record for scoring goals in consecutive games (12) during 1972-73 season . . . (November 9, 1980)—Pulled groin muscle in team practice . . . (1983-84)—Assistant coach and player with Rochester Americans.

Year	Team	League	Games	G.	A.	Pts.	Pen.
1968-69—Drummondville Rangers		QJHL	....	...	....	....	....
1969-70—Drummondville Rangers (c)		QJHL	52	50	52	102	89
1970-71—Port Huron Flags (d)		IHL	65	23	18	41	81
1971-72—Nova Scotia Voyageurs		AHL	67	18	21	39	116
1972-73—Montreal Canadiens		NHL	1	0	0	0	0
1972-73—Nova Scotia Voyageurs (a-e)		AHL	76	*52	52	*104	84
1973-74—Montreal Canadiens		NHL	60	6	10	16	42
1974-75—Montreal Canadiens		NHL	80	32	35	67	74
1975-76—Montreal Canadiens		NHL	80	32	35	67	28
1976-77—Montreal Canadiens		NHL	79	24	28	52	50
1977-78—Montreal Canadiens		NHL	77	18	22	40	20
1978-79—Montreal Canadiens		NHL	79	26	40	66	26
1979-80—Montreal Canadiens		NHL	77	21	32	53	23
1980-81—Montreal Canadiens		NHL	73	22	32	54	39
1981-82—Buffalo Sabres (f)		NHL	77	25	39	64	38
1982-83—Rochester Americans		AHL	79	26	22	48	10
1983-84—Rochester Americans		AHL	79	27	43	70	14
NHL TOTALS			683	206	273	479	340

(c)—Drafted from Drummondville Rangers by Detroit Red Wings in third round of 1970 amateur draft.
(d)—Drafted from Fort Worth Wings (Detroit Red Wings) by Montreal Voyageurs in reverse draft, June, 1971.
(e)—Won John G. Sollenberger Trophy (leading scorer).
(f)—October, 1981—Acquired by Buffalo Sabres in 1981 NHL waiver draft.

MITCH LAMOUREUX

Center . . . 5'6" . . . 185 lbs. . . . Born, Ottawa, Ont., August 22, 1962 . . . Shoots left . . . Set AHL record for most goals by a rookie (57) in 1982-83, and most goals by an AHL player.

Year	Team	League	Games	G.	A.	Pts.	Pen.
1979-80—Oshawa Generals		OMJHL	67	28	48	76	63
1980-81—Oshawa Generals (c)		OMJHL	63	50	69	119	256
1981-82—Oshawa Generals		OHL	66	43	78	121	275
1982-83—Baltimore Skipjacks (b-d)		AHL	80	*57	50	107	107
1983-84—Baltimore Skipjacks		AHL	68	30	38	68	136
1983-84—Pittsburgh Penguins		NHL	8	1	1	2	6
NHL TOTALS			8	1	1	2	6

(c)—June, 1981—Drafted as underage junior by Pittsburgh Penguins in 1981 NHL entry draft. Sixth Penguins pick, 154th overall, eighth round.
(d)—Won Dudley (Red) Garrett Memorial Trophy (Top AHL Rookie).

LARRY JAMES LANDON

Left Wing ... 6' ... 190 lbs. ... Born, Niagara Falls, Ont., May 4, 1958 ... Shoots left.

Year	Team	League	Games	G.	A.	Pts.	Pen.
1977-78—R.P.I. (c)		ECAC	29	13	22	35	14
1978-79—R.P.I.		ECAC	28	18	27	45	28
1979-80—R.P.I.		ECAC	25	13	17	30	8
1980-81—R.P.I.		ECAC	29	20	27	47	18
1980-81—Nova Scotia Voyageurs		AHL	2	0	0	0	0
1981-82—Nova Scotia Voyageurs		AHL	69	11	15	26	31
1982-83—Nova Scotia Voyageurs		AHL	68	18	25	43	43
1983-84—Montreal Canadiens		NHL	2	0	0	0	0
1983-84—Nova Scotia Voyageurs		AHL	79	26	30	56	21
NHL TOTALS			2	0	0	0	0

(c)—June, 1978—Drafted by Montreal Canadiens in 1978 NHL amateur draft. Tenth Canadiens pick, 137th overall, eighth round.

GORDON LANE

Defense ... 6'1" ... 185 lbs. ... Born, Brandon, Man., March 31, 1953 ... Shoots left ... (March, 1981)—Broken thumb ... (February 15, 1983)—Ruptured ligaments in right thumb in game at Quebec, missed 23 games.

Year	Team	League	Games	G.	A.	Pts.	Pen.
1970-71—Brandon Wheat Kings		WCHL	20	0	4	4	53
1971-72—Brandon Wheat Kings		WCHL	63	7	16	23	106
1972-73—New Westminster Bruins		WCHL	36	2	13	15	115
1973-74—Fort Wayne-Dayton		IHL	67	1	14	15	214
1974-75—Dayton Gems		IHL	50	6	10	16	225
1975-76—Hampton Gulls		SHL	12	1	7	8	58
1975-76—Dayton Gems		IHL	55	12	22	34	227
1975-76—Washington Capitals		NHL	3	1	0	1	12
1976-77—Washington Capitals		NHL	80	2	15	17	207
1977-78—Hershey Bears		AHL	4	0	1	1	8
1977-78—Washington Capitals		NHL	69	2	9	11	195
1978-79—Washington Capitals		NHL	64	3	15	18	147
1978-79—Hershey Bears		AHL	5	0	1	1	48
1979-80—Washington Capitals (c)		NHL	19	2	4	6	53
1979-80—New York Islanders (d)		NHL	55	2	14	16	152
1980-81—New York Islanders		NHL	60	3	9	12	124
1981-82—New York Islanders		NHL	51	0	13	13	98
1982-83—New York Islanders		NHL	44	3	4	7	87
1983-84—New York Islanders		NHL	38	0	3	3	70
NHL TOTALS			483	18	86	104	1145

(c)—December, 1979—Traded by Washington Capitals to New York Islanders for Mike Kaszycki.
(d)—Led in penalty minutes (85) during playoffs.

CHRIS LANGEVIN

Left Wing ... 6' ... 190 lbs. ... Born, Montreal, Que., November 27, 1959 ... Shoots left.

Year	Team	League	Games	G.	A.	Pts.	Pen.
1977-78—Chicoutimi Sagueneens		QMJHL	67	8	20	28	183
1978-79—Chicoutimi Sagueneens		QMJHL	65	24	23	47	182
1979-80—Chicoutimi Sagueneens		QMJHL	46	22	30	52	97
1980-81—Saginaw Gears		IHL	75	35	48	83	179
1981-82—Rochester Americans (c)		AHL	33	3	5	8	150
1982-83—Rochester Americans		AHL	71	18	25	43	255
1983-84—Rochester Americans		AHL	41	11	14	25	133
1983-84—Buffalo Sabres		NHL	6	1	0	1	2
NHL TOTALS			6	1	0	1	2

(c)—September, 1981—Signed by Rochester Americans as a free agent.

DAVID LANGEVIN

Defense ... 6'2" ... 215 lbs. ... Born, St. Paul, Minn., May 15, 1954 ... Shoots left ... Attended University of Minnesota-Duluth ... (October 27, 1981)—Sprained right knee vs. Edmonton ... (December, 1981)—Bruised tailbone ... (November, 1982)—Recurring groin problems ... (April, 1983)—Arthroscopic surgery to right knee following injury in first game of playoff series vs. New York Rangers ... (January, 1984)—Cartilage injury to right knee requiring arthroscopic surgery, missed nine games ... (April, 1984)—Separated shoulder in playoff series with Washington ... (May, 1984)—Aggravated shoulder injury during playoff series with Montreal.

Year	Team	League	Games	G.	A.	Pts.	Pen.
1972-73—University of Minn.-Duluth		WCHA	36	6	11	17	74
1973-74—Univ. of Minn.-Duluth (c-d)		WCHA	37	2	11	13	56
1974-75—University of Minn.-Duluth		WCHA	35	8	24	32	91
1975-76—University of Minn.-Duluth (b)		WCHA	34	19	26	45	82
1976-77—Edmonton Oilers		WHA	77	7	16	23	94
1977-78—Edmonton Oilers		WHA	62	6	22	28	90
1978-79—Edmonton Oilers (b-e)		WHA	77	6	21	27	76
1979-80—New York Islanders		NHL	76	3	13	16	109
1980-81—New York Islanders		NHL	75	1	16	17	122
1981-82—New York Islanders		NHL	73	1	20	21	82
1982-83—New York Islanders		NHL	73	4	17	21	64
1983-84—New York Islanders		NHL	69	3	16	19	53
WHA TOTALS			216	19	59	78	260
NHL TOTALS			366	12	82	94	430

(c)—Drafted from University of Minnesota-Duluth by New York Islanders in seventh round of 1974 amateur draft.

(d)—Selected by Edmonton Oilers in World Hockey Association amateur player draft, May, 1974.

(e)—June, 1979—Selected by New York Islanders in NHL reclaim draft.

ROD CORRY LANGWAY

Defense . . . 6'3" . . . 215 lbs. . . . Born, Maag, Taiwan, May 3, 1957 . . . Shoots left . . . Attended University of New Hampshire and was member of football and hockey teams . . . Older brother of Kim Langway . . . (January 5, 1982)—Bruised left foot in game vs. Boston . . . (February 9, 1982)—Injured left knee in NHL All-Star game. Examination in March discovered dried blood in the knee which had weakened the muscle in his left leg.

Year	Team	League	Games	G.	A.	Pts.	Pen.
1975-76—University of New Hampshire		ECAC	..	..	..	..	....
1976-77—Univ. of New Hampshire (c-d)		ECAC	34	10	43	53	52
1977-78—Hampton Gulls		AHL	30	6	16	22	50
1977-78—Birmingham Bulls		WHA	52	3	18	21	52
1978-79—Montreal Canadiens (e)		NHL	45	3	4	7	30
1978-79—Nova Scotia Voyageurs		AHL	18	6	13	19	29
1979-80—Montreal Canadiens		NHL	77	7	29	36	81
1980-81—Montreal Canadiens		NHL	80	11	34	45	120
1981-82—Montreal Canadiens (f)		NHL	66	5	34	39	116
1982-83—Washington Capitals (a-g)		NHL	80	3	29	32	75
1983-84—Washington Capitals (a-g)		NHL	80	9	24	33	61
WHA TOTALS			52	3	18	21	53
NHL TOTALS			428	38	154	192	483

(c)—Drafted from University of New Hampshire by Montreal Canadiens in second round of 1977 amateur draft.

(d)—Selected by Birmingham Bulls in World Hockey Association amateur players' draft, May, 1977.

(e)—October, 1978—Signed by Montreal Canadiens as free agent.

(f)—September, 1982—Traded by Montreal Canadiens with Brian Engblom, Doug Jarvis and Craig Laughlin to Washington Capitals for Ryan Walter and Rick Green.

(g)—Won James Norris Memorial Trophy (Top NHL Defenseman).

JEAN-MARC LANTHIER

Right Wing . . . 6'2" . . . 198 lbs. . . . Born, Montreal, Que., March 27, 1963 . . . Shoots right.

Year	Team	League	Games	G.	A.	Pts.	Pen.
1979-80—Quebec Remparts		QMJHL	63	14	32	46	4
1980-81—Quebec Remparts (c)		QMJHL	37	13	32	45	18
1980-81—Sorel Black Hawks (d)		QMJHL	35	6	33	39	29
1981-82—Laval Voisins (e)		QMJHL	60	44	34	78	48
1982-83—Laval Voisins		QHL	69	39	71	110	54
1983-84—Fredericton Express		AHL	60	25	17	42	29
1983-84—Vancouver Canucks		NHL	11	2	1	3	2
NHL TOTALS			11	2	1	3	2

(c)—December, 1980—Traded by Quebec Remparts to Sorel Black Hawks for Andre Cote.

(d)—June, 1981—Drafted as underage junior by Vancouver Canucks in 1981 NHL entry draft. Second Canucks pick, 52nd overall, third round.

(e)—August, 1981—Acquired by Laval Voisins in QMJHL dispersal draft of players from defunct Sorel Black Hawks.

RICK ROMAN LANZ

Defense . . . 6'1" . . . 195 lbs. . . . Born, Karlouyvary, Czechoslovakia, September 16, 1961 . . . Shoots right . . . (January, 1982)—Surgery to repair torn knee ligaments.

Year	Team	League	Games	G.	A.	Pts.	Pen.
1977-78—Oshawa Generals	OMJHL	65	1	41	42	51
1978-79—Oshawa Generals	OMJHL	65	12	47	59	88
1979-80—Oshawa Generals (b-c)	OMJHL	52	18	38	56	51
1980-81—Vancouver Canucks	NHL	76	7	22	29	40
1981-82—Vancouver Canucks	NHL	39	3	11	14	48
1982-83—Vancouver Canucks	NHL	74	10	38	48	46
1983-84—Vancouver Canucks	NHL	79	18	39	57	45
NHL TOTALS			268	38	110	148	179

(c)—June, 1980—Drafted as underage junior in 1980 NHL entry draft by Vancouver Canucks. First Canucks pick, seventh overall, first round.

GUY GERARD LAPOINTE

Defense . . . 6' . . . 204 lbs. . . . Born, Montreal, Que., March 18, 1948 . . . Shoots left . . . Suffered fractured cheekbone, November, 1971 . . . Missed part of 1977-78 season with surgery on retina of left eye . . . Separated shoulder vs. Philadelphia (January 12, 1980)— and missed four weeks. First game back (February 9, 1980)—reinjured shoulder vs. Vancouver and missed another four weeks . . . (October 25, 1980)—Pulled muscle in right shoulder . . . (November 14, 1980)—Pulled groin muscle . . . (November 29, 1980)—Suffered severe charley horse. In early December doctors removed 450 CC of blood from his left thigh . . . (December 12, 1981)—Sore neck after an altercation with Rick Vaive at Toronto . . . (January 2, 1982)—Injured hand . . . (February 21, 1982)—Slight left shoulder separation at NY Rangers . . . (October 13, 1982)—Missed seven games with hamstring pull during game at Chicago . . . (December 2, 1982)—Missed three games when hit by stick near right eye in game at Minnesota . . . (January 8, 1983)—Broken jaw when hit by a slap shot during game vs. Washington . . . (February 2, 1984)—Broken hand in game vs. Buffalo . . . (June, 1984)—Named assistant coach of Quebec Nordiques.

Year	Team	League	Games	G.	A.	Pts.	Pen.
1965-66—Verdun Maple Leafs	QJHL	37	7	13	20	96
1966-67—Verdun Maple Leafs	QJHL	..	..	..	..	....
1967-68—Montreal Jr. Canadiens	Jr."A" OHA	51	11	27	38	147
1968-69—Houston Apollos	CHL	65	3	15	18	120
1968-69—Montreal Canadiens	NHL	1	0	0	0	2
1969-70—Montreal Voyageurs (a)	AHL	57	8	30	38	92
1969-70—Montreal Canadiens	NHL	5	0	0	0	4
1970-71—Montreal Canadiens	NHL	78	15	29	44	107
1971-72—Montreal Canadiens	NHL	69	11	38	49	58
1972-73—Montreal Canadiens (a)	NHL	76	19	35	54	117
1973-74—Montreal Canadiens	NHL	71	13	40	53	63
1974-75—Montreal Canadiens (b)	NHL	80	28	47	75	88
1975-76—Montreal Canadiens (b)	NHL	77	21	47	68	78
1976-77—Montreal Canadiens (b)	NHL	77	25	51	76	53
1977-78—Montreal Canadiens	NHL	49	13	29	42	19
1978-79—Montreal Canadiens	NHL	69	13	42	55	48
1979-80—Montreal Canadiens	NHL	45	6	20	26	29
1980-81—Montreal Canadiens	NHL	33	1	9	10	79
1981-82—Montreal Canadiens (c)	NHL	47	1	19	20	72
1981-82—St. Louis Blues	NHL	8	0	6	6	4
1982-83—St. Louis Blues (d)	NHL	54	3	23	26	43
1983-84—Boston Bruins	NHL	45	2	16	18	24
NHL TOTALS			884	171	451	622	888

(c)—March, 1982—Traded by Montreal Canadiens to St. Louis Blues for second and third-round picks in 1983 NHL entry draft.

(d)—August, 1983—Released by St. Louis Blues and signed by Boston Bruins as a free agent.

RICHARD PAUL (RICK) LaPOINTE

Defense . . . 6'2" . . . 200 lbs. . . . Born, Victoria, B.C., August 2, 1955 . . . Shoots left . . . Brother-in-law of Brad Maxwell.

Year	Team	League	Games	G.	A.	Pts.	Pen.
1971-72—Nanaimo Clippers	Jr."A" BCHL	..	..	..	..	....
1971-72—Victoria Cougars	WCHL	4	0	0	0	0
1972-73—Victoria Cougars	WCHL	39	3	12	15	31
1973-74—Victoria Cougars	WCHL	66	8	18	26	207
1974-75—Victoria Cougars (a-c-d)	WCHL	67	19	51	70	177
1975-76—Detroit Red Wings	NHL	80	10	23	33	95
1976-77—Kansas City Blues	CHL	6	0	0	0	6
1976-77—Detroit Red Wings (e)	NHL	49	2	11	13	80
1976-77—Philadelphia Flyers	NHL	22	1	8	9	39
1977-78—Philadelphia Flyers	NHL	47	4	16	20	91
1978-79—Philadelphia Flyers (f)	NHL	77	3	18	21	53

Year	Team	League	Games	G.	A.	Pts.	Pen.
1979-80—St. Louis Blues		NHL	80	6	19	25	87
1980-81—St. Louis Blues		NHL	80	8	25	33	124
1981-82—St. Louis Blues (g)		NHL	71	2	20	22	127
1982-83—Fredericton Express		AHL	31	4	14	18	50
1982-83—Quebec Nordiques		NHL	43	2	9	11	59
1983-84—Fredericton Express		AHL	54	8	22	30	79
1983-84—Quebec Nordiques		NHL	22	2	10	12	12
NHL TOTALS			571	40	159	199	767

(c)—Won WCHL Top Defenseman Award.

(d)—Drafted from Victoria Cougars by Detroit Red Wings in first round of 1975 amateur draft.

(e)—Traded to Philadelphia Flyers by Detroit Red Wings with Mike Korney for Terry Murray, Dave Kelly, Bob Ritchie and Steve Coates, February, 1977.

(f)—June, 1979—Traded with Blake Dunlop by Philadelphia Flyers to St. Louis Blues for Phil Myre.

(g)—August, 1982—Traded by St. Louis Blues to Quebec Nordiques for Pat Hickey.

YVES LAPOINTE

Left Wing . . . 6'2" . . . 206 lbs. . . . Born, Pointe Aux Trembles, Que., February 2, 1964 . . . Shoots left . . . (October, 1982)—Broken leg.

Year	Team	League	Games	G.	A.	Pts.	Pen.
1981-82—Shawinigan Cataracts (c)		QMJHL	59	23	30	53	155
1982-83—Shawinigan Cataracts (d)		QHL	8	2	4	6	26
1983-84—St. Jean Beavers		QHL	66	51	47	98	127

(c)—June, 1982—Drafted as underage junior by Vancouver Canucks in 1982 NHL entry draft. Second Canucks pick, 53rd overall, third round.

(d)—January, 1983—Traded by Shawinigan Cataracts to St. Jean Beavers for QHL rights to Paul Boutilier.

BENOIT LAPORTE

Left Wing . . . 5'10" . . . 187 lbs. . . . Born, Montreal, Que., June 14, 1960 . . . Shoots left.

Year	Team	League	Games	G.	A.	Pts.	Pen.
1977-78—Hull Olympiques		QMJHL	71	34	33	67	213
1978-79—Shawinigan Cataracts		QMJHL	16	3	8	11	128
1978-79—Trois-Rivieres Draveurs		QMJHL	58	24	45	69	209
1979-80—Trois-Rivieres Draveurs (c)		QMJHL	33	18	31	49	100
1979-80—Hull Olympiques		QMJHL	34	19	11	30	86
1980-81—New Brunswick Hawks		AHL	44	8	8	16	50
1980-81—Hampton Aces		EHL	12	3	10	13	30
1981-82—Cincinnati Tigers		CHL	76	24	31	55	86
1982-83—St. Catharines Saints (d)		AHL	4	0	0	0	?
1982-83—Saginaw Gears		IHL	76	31	29	60	55
1983-84—Carolina Thunderbirds		ACHL	52	54	48	102	86

(c)—October, 1979—Signed by Toronto Maple Leafs as a free agent.

(d)—June, 1983—Released by Toronto Maple Leafs.

GARRY JOSEPH LARIVIERE

Defense . . . 6' . . . 190 lbs. . . . Born, St. Catharines, Ont., December 6, 1954 . . . Shoots right . . . (December, 1981)—Knee injury.

Year	Team	League	Games	G.	A.	Pts.	Pen.
1972-73—St. Cath. Black Hawks		Jr."A" OHA	55	5	32	37	140
1973-74—St. C. Black Hawks (c-d-e)		Jr."A" OHA	60	3	35	38	153
1974-75—Tulsa Oilers (a)		CHL	76	15	38	53	168
1974-75—Phoenix Roadrunners (f)		WHA	4	0	1	1	28
1975-76—Phoenix Roadrunners		WHA	79	7	17	24	100
1976-77—Phoenix Roadrunners (g)		WHA	61	7	23	30	48
1976-77—Quebec Nordiques		WHA	15	0	3	3	8
1977-78—Quebec Nordiques		WHA	80	7	49	56	78
1978-79—Quebec Nordiques (h)		WHA	80	5	33	38	54
1979-80—Quebec Nordiques		NHL	75	2	19	21	56
1980-81—Quebec Nordiques (i)		NHL	52	3	13	16	50
1980-81—Edmonton Oilers		NHL	13	0	2	2	6
1981-82—Edmonton Oilers		NHL	62	1	21	22	41
1982-83—Edmonton Oilers		NHL	17	0	2	2	14
1983-84—St. Catharines Saints (a-j-k-l)		AHL	65	7	35	42	41
WHA TOTALS			319	26	126	152	316
NHL TOTALS			219	6	57	63	167

(c)—Drafted from St. Catharines Black Hawks by Buffalo Sabres in fifth round of 1974 amateur draft.

(d)—Selected by Chicago Cougars in World Hockey Association amateur player draft, May, 1974.

(e)—Traded to Phoenix Roadrunners by Chicago Cougars for "future considerations," September, 1974.

(f)—NHL rights transferred by Buffalo Sabres to New York Islanders to complete deal for Gerry Desjardins, June, 1975.

(g)—Sold to Quebec Nordiques by Phoenix Roadrunners, March, 1977.

(h)—June, 1979—Selected by New York Islanders in NHL reclaim draft, but remained with the Quebec Nordiques as a priority selection for the expansion draft.

(i)—March, 1981—Traded by Quebec Nordiques to Vancouver Canucks for Mario Marois. Vancouver then sent Lariviere and NHL rights to Ken Berry to Edmonton Oilers for Blair MacDonald and NHL rights to Lars Gunnar Petersson to complete a three-club deal.

(j)—November, 1983—Loaned by Edmonton Oilers to St. Catharines, after sitting out first month in contract dispute with Oilers.

(k)—Shared Les Cunningham Plaque (AHL-MVP) with Mal Davis (Rochester).

(l)—Won Eddie Shore Plaque (Top AHL Defenseman).

JEFF LARMER

Left Wing . . . 5'10" . . . 172 lbs. . . . Born, Peterborough, Ont., October 10, 1962 . . . Shoots left . . . Brother of Steve Larmer . . . Played one game as a goalie in 1980-81 with Kitchener (No goals allowed in nine minutes) . . . (November, 1981)—Shoulder separation . . . Also plays right wing.

Year	Team	League	Games	G.	A.	Pts.	Pen.
1979-80—Kitchener Rangers		OMJHL	61	19	27	46	80
1980-81—Kitchener Rangers (c)		OHL	68	54	54	108	103
1981-82—Kitchener Canadians (b-d)		OHL	49	51	44	95	95
1981-82—Colorado Rockies		NHL	8	1	1	2	8
1982-83—Wichita Wind		CHL	10	6	5	11	2
1982-83—New Jersey Devils		NHL	65	21	24	45	21
1983-84—New Jersey Devils (e)		NHL	40	6	13	19	8
1983-84—Chicago Black Hawks		NHL	36	9	13	22	20
NHL TOTALS			149	37	51	88	57

(c)—June, 1981—Drafted as underage junior by Colorado Rockies in 1981 NHL entry draft. Seventh Rockies pick, 129th overall, seventh round.

(d)—Led J. Ross Robertson Cup Playoffs (OHL) with 21 goals and 35 points.

(e)—January, 1984—Traded by New Jersey Devils to Chicago Black Hawks for Tim Higgins.

STEVE DONALD LARMER

Right Wing . . . 5'10" . . . 185 lbs. . . . Born, Peterborough, Ont., June 16, 1961 . . . Shoots left . . . Brother of Jeff Larmer . . . (1982-83)—Set Chicago club records for: Most goals by a right wing (43), most goals by a Chicago rookie (43) and most points by a Chicago rookie (90). He also tied club record for most assists by a Chicago rookie (47) set by Denis Savard in 1980-81.

Year	Team	League	Games	G.	A.	Pts.	Pen.
1977-78—Peterborough Petes		OMJHL	62	24	17	41	51
1978-79—Niagara Falls Flyers		OMJHL	66	37	47	84	108
1979-80—Niagara Falls Flyers (c)		OMJHL	67	45	69	114	71
1980-81—Niagara Falls Flyers (b)		OHL	61	55	78	133	73
1980-81—Chicago Black Hawks		NHL	4	0	1	1	0
1981-82—New Brunswick Hawks (b)		AHL	74	38	44	82	46
1981-82—Chicago Black Hawks		NHL	3	0	0	0	0
1982-83—Chicago Black Hawks (d-e)		NHL	80	43	47	90	28
1983-84—Chicago Black Hawks		NHL	80	35	40	75	34
NHL TOTALS			167	78	88	166	62

(c)—June, 1980—Drafted as underage junior in 1980 NHL entry draft by Chicago Black Hawks. Eleventh Black Hawks pick, 120th overall, sixth round.

(d)—Selected as NHL Rookie of the Year in vote of players conducted by The Sporting News.

(e)—Won Calder Memorial Trophy (Top NHL Rookie).

PIERRE LAROUCHE

Center . . . 5'11" . . . 175 lbs. . . . Born, Taschereau, Que., November 16, 1955 . . . Shoots right . . . Missed part of 1976-77 season with broken left thumb . . . Missed part of 1978-79 season with injury to left knee . . . Injured shoulder (March, 1980) . . . (November 1, 1980)—Broken left hand . . . (November 2, 1981)—Severe cut over eye at Quebec . . . (January 20, 1983)—Injured back during game at Los Angeles and missed remainder of season with recurring back spasms . . . Only player to have 50-goal seasons with two different NHL clubs.

Year	Team	League	Games	G.	A.	Pts.	Pen.
1972-73—Sorel Black Hawks		QJHL	63	52	62	114	44
1973-74—Sorel Black Hawks (b-c)		QJHL	67	94	*157	*251	53
1974-75—Pittsburgh Penguins (d)		NHL	79	31	37	68	52
1975-76—Pittsburgh Penguins		NHL	76	53	58	111	33

Year	Team	League	Games	G.	A.	Pts.	Pen.
1976-77—Pittsburgh Penguins		NHL	65	29	34	63	14
1977-78—Pittsburgh Penguins (e)		NHL	20	6	5	11	0
1977-78—Montreal Canadiens		NHL	44	17	32	49	11
1978-79—Montreal Canadiens		NHL	36	9	13	22	4
1979-80—Montreal Canadiens		NHL	73	50	41	91	16
1980-81—Montreal Canadiens		NHL	61	25	28	53	28
1981-82—Montreal Canadiens (f)		NHL	22	9	12	21	0
1981-82—Hartford Whalers		NHL	45	25	25	50	12
1982-83—Hartford Whalers		NHL	38	18	22	40	8
1983-84—New York Rangers (g)		NHL	77	48	33	81	22
NHL TOTALS			636	320	340	660	200

(c)—Drafted from Sorel Black Hawks by Pittsburgh Penguins in first round of 1974 amateur draft.
(d)—Named Prince of Wales Conference Rookie of the Year in poll of players by THE SPORTING NEWS.
(e)—Traded to Montreal Canadiens by Pittsburgh Penguins for Peter Lee and Peter Mahovlich, November, 1977.
(f)—December, 1981—Traded with first-round 1984 and third-round 1985 entry draft picks by Montreal Canadiens to Hartford Whalers for first-round 1984 and third-round 1985 entry draft picks.
(g)—September, 1983—Signed by New York Rangers as a free agent.

REED DAVID LARSON

Defense . . . 6' . . . 195 lbs. . . . Born, Minneapolis, Minn., July 30, 1956 . . . Shoots right . . . Attended University of Minnesota . . . (July, 1981)—Surgery to remove bone chips from right elbow . . . Holds NHL record for defensemen, scoring 20 goals in five straight seasons . . . Holds Detroit club record for most goals (27 in 1980-81), most assists (52 in 1982-83) and points (74 in 1982-83) by a defenseman in one season . . . (1983-84)—Passed Tommy Williams to become all-time U.S.-born NHL career leader in points (Williams had 430) and assists (Williams had 269). Williams had 161 career goals and Larson starts the '84-85 season with the second highest total.

Year	Team	League	Games	G.	A.	Pts.	Pen.
1974-75—University of Minnesota		WCHA	41	11	17	28	37
1975-76—University of Minnesota (a-c)		WCHA	42	13	29	42	94
1976-77—University of Minnesota		WCHA	21	10	15	25	30
1976-77—Detroit Red Wings		NHL	14	0	1	1	23
1977-78—Detroit Red Wings		NHL	75	19	41	60	95
1978-79—Detroit Red Wings		NHL	79	18	49	67	169
1979-80—Detroit Red Wings		NHL	80	22	44	66	101
1980-81—Detroit Red Wings		NHL	78	27	31	58	153
1981-82—Detroit Red Wings		NHL	80	21	39	60	112
1982-83—Detroit Red Wings		NHL	80	22	52	74	104
1983-84—Detroit Red Wings		NHL	78	23	39	62	122
NHL TOTALS			564	152	296	448	879

(c)—Drafted from University of Minnesota by Detroit Red Wings in second round of 1976 amateur draft.

KENNETH BRIAN LATTA

Right Wing . . . 6' . . . 182 lbs. . . . Born, Thunder Bay, Ont., May 12, 1962 . . . Shoots right.

Year	Team	League	Games	G.	A.	Pts.	Pen.
1979-80—Sault Ste. Marie Greyhounds		OMJHL	60	4	4	8	105
1980-81—Sault Ste. Marie Greyhounds (c)		OHL	66	18	19	37	155
1981-82—Sault Ste. Marie Greyhounds		OHL	51	24	29	53	199
1982-83—London Knights (d)		OHL	60	47	46	93	126
1982-83—Binghamton Whalers (e)		AHL	..	..	..	..	..
1983-84—Toledo Goaldiggers		IHL	3	1	0	1	6
1983-84—Pinebridge Bucks		ACHL	60	43	43	86	71

(c)—June, 1981—Drafted as underage junior by Philadelphia Flyers in 1981 NHL entry draft. Sixth Flyers pick, 79th overall, fourth round.
(d)—October, 1982—Traded with Dave Andreoli by Sault Ste. Marie Greyhounds to London Knights for future considerations.
(e)—No regular season record. Played one playoff game.

MICHAEL ARTHUR LAUEN

Right Wing . . . 6'1" . . . 185 lbs. . . . Born, Marinette, Wis., February 9, 1961 . . . Shoots right.

Year	Team	League	Games	G.	A.	Pts.	Pen.
1979-80—Michigan Tech (c)		WCHA	28	22	18	40	40
1980-81—Michigan Tech		WCHA	44	24	20	44	14
1981-82—Michigan Tech		CCHA	30	13	15	28	28
1982-83—Michigan Tech		WCHA	38	12	17	29	18
1982-83—Sherbrooke Jets		AHL	5	0	3	3	0

Year	Team	League	Games	G.	A.	Pts.	Pen.
1983-84—Sherbrooke Jets		AHL	61	23	29	52	13
1983-84—Winnipeg Jets		NHL	3	0	1	1	0
NHL TOTALS			3	0	1	1	0

(c)—June, 1980—Drafted by Winnipeg Jets in 1980 NHL entry draft. Eighth Jets pick, 135th overall, seventh round.

CRAIG LAUGHLIN

Right Wing . . . 5'11" . . . 198 lbs. . . . Born, Toronto, Ont., September 19, 1957 . . . Shoots right.

Year	Team	League	Games	G.	A.	Pts.	Pen.
1976-77—Clarkson College (c)		ECAC	33	12	13	25	44
1977-78—Clarkson College		ECAC	30	17	31	48	56
1978-79—Clarkson College		ECAC	30	18	29	47	22
1979-80—Clarkson College		ECAC	34	18	30	48	38
1979-80—Nova Scotia Voyageurs		AHL	2	0	0	0	2
1980-81—Nova Scotia Voyageurs		AHL	46	32	29	61	15
1981-82—Nova Scotia Voyageurs		AHL	26	14	15	29	16
1981-82—Montreal Canadiens (d)		NHL	36	12	11	23	33
1982-83—Washington Capitals		NHL	75	17	27	44	41
1983-84—Washington Capitals		NHL	80	20	32	52	69
NHL TOTALS			191	49	70	119	143

(c)—June, 1977—Drafted by Montreal Canadiens in 1977 NHL amateur draft. Seventeenth Canadiens pick, 162nd overall, 10th round.

(d)—September, 1982—Traded by Montreal Canadiens with Rod Langway, Brian Engblom and Doug Jarvis to Washington Capitals for Ryan Walter and Rick Green.

DONALD (RED) LAURENCE

Center . . . 5'9" . . . 173 lbs. . . . Born, Galt, Ont., June 27, 1957 . . . Shoots right . . . Missed most of 1976-77 season with broken right leg and start of 1977-78 season while recovering from surgery . . . Missed part of 1979-80 season with broken right ankle.

Year	Team	League	Games	G.	A.	Pts.	Pen.
1973-74—Peterborough TPTs		Jr."A"OHA	60	28	15	43	41
1974-75—Peterborough TPTs		Jr."A"OHA	69	40	49	89	53
1975-76—Kitchener Rangers		Jr."A"OHA	59	50	36	86	75
1976-77—Kitchener Rangers (c)		Jr."A"OHA	35	43	45	88	14
1977-78—Tulsa Oilers		CHL	39	15	11	26	10
1978-79—Nova Scotia Voyageurs		AHL	20	7	7	14	9
1978-79—Atlanta Flames (d)		NHL	59	14	20	34	6
1979-80—St. Louis Blues		NHL	20	1	2	3	8
1979-80—Salt Lake Golden Eagles (e)		CHL	27	7	15	22	8
1980-81—Salt Lake Golden Eagles		CHL	71	39	33	72	41
1981-82—Indianapolis Checkers (f)		CHL	77	43	55	98	43
1982-83—Indianapolis Checkers (b-g-h)		CHL	80	*43	55	98	33
1983-84—Indianapolis Checkers (i)		CHL	69	41	37	78	42
NHL TOTALS			79	15	22	37	14

(c)—Drafted from Kitchener Rangers by Atlanta Flames in second round of 1977 amateur draft.

(d)—October, 1979—Traded to St. Louis Blues with Ed Kea and Atlanta's second-round draft choice in 1981 for Garry Unger.

(e)—Co-Leader with Joe Mullen in goals (9) during playoffs.

(f)—October, 1981—Released by St. Louis Blues and signed by New York Islanders as a free agent.

(g)—Led CHL playoffs with 22 points.

(h)—Won Don Ashby Memorial Trophy (CHL Iron Man Award).

(i)—Led CHL playoffs with nine goals and 13 points.

KEVIN LaVALLEE

Left Wing . . . 5'8" . . . 180 lbs. . . . Born, Sudbury, Ont., September 16, 1961 . . . Shoots left . . . (December, 1982)—Separated shoulder.

Year	Team	League	Games	G.	A.	Pts.	Pen.
1978-79—Brantford Alexanders		OMJHL	66	27	23	50	30
1979-80—Brantford Alexanders (c)		OMJHL	65	65	70	135	50
1980-81—Calgary Flames		NHL	77	15	20	35	16
1981-82—Calgary Flames		NHL	75	32	29	61	30
1982-83—Colorado Flames		CHL	5	5	4	9	0
1982-83—Calgary Flames (d)		NHL	60	19	16	35	17
1983-84—New Haven Nighthawks		AHL	47	29	23	52	25
1983-84—Los Angeles Kings (e)		NHL	19	3	3	6	2
NHL TOTALS			231	69	68	137	65

MARK J. LaVARRE

Right Wing . . . 5'11" . . . 170 lbs. . . . Born, Evanston, Ill., February 21, 1965 . . . Shoots right . . . Also plays defense . . . (February, 1981)—Fractured two vertebras in back.

Year	Team	League	Games	G.	A.	Pts.	Pen.
1982-83—Stratford Cullitons (c)		MWJBHL	40	33	62	95	88
1983-84—North Bay Centennials		OHL	41	19	22	41	15

(c)—June, 1983—Drafted as underage junior by Chicago Black Hawks in 1983 NHL entry draft. Seventh Black Hawks pick, 119th overall, sixth round.

ROBERTO LAVOIE

Center . . . 5'9" . . . 175 lbs. . . . Born, Petit-Saguenay, Que., September 8, 1962 . . . Shoots right.

Year	Team	League	Games	G.	A.	Pts.	Pen.
1979-80—Quebec Remparts		QMJHL	40	18	14	32	16
1980-81—Quebec Remparts		QMJHL	26	5	17	22	24
1980-81—Chicoutimi Sagueneens		QMJHL	44	30	40	70	42
1981-82—Chicoutimi Sagueneens		QMJHL	59	37	48	85	50
1982-83—Chicoutimi Sagueneens		QHL	59	57	79	136	48
1982-83—Binghamton Whalers		AHL	2	0	0	0	0
1983-84—Binghamton Whalers		AHL	80	34	50	84	68

PAUL LAWLESS

Left Wing . . . 6' . . . 190 lbs. . . . Born, Scarborough, Ont., July 2, 1964 . . . Shoots left.

Year	Team	League	Games	G.	A.	Pts.	Pen.
1980-81—Wexford Midgets		MTHL	40	38	40	78	....
1981-82—Windsor Spitfires (c)		OHL	68	24	25	49	47
1982-83—Windsor Spitfires		OHL	33	15	20	35	25
1982-83—Hartford Whalers		NHL	47	6	9	15	4
1983-84—Hartford Whalers		NHL	6	0	3	3	0
1983-84—Windsor Spitfires (b)		OHL	55	31	49	80	26
NHL TOTALS			53	6	12	18	4

(c)—June, 1982—Selected by Hartford Whalers in 1982 NHL entry draft. First Whalers pick, 14th overall, first round.

BRIAN LAWTON

Center . . . 6' . . . 180 lbs. . . . Born, New Brunswick, N.J., June 29, 1965 . . . Shoots left . . . First American-born player to be a first overall draft choice in the NHL . . . (November, 1983)—Separated shoulder.

Year	Team	League	Games	G.	A.	Pts.	Pen.
1981-82—Mount St. Charles H.S.		R.I. H.S.	26	45	43	88	..
1982-83—Mount St. Charles H.S. (c)		R.I. H.S.	23	40	43	83	..
1982-83—U.S. National Team		Int'l	7	3	2	5	6
1983-84—Minnesota North Stars		NHL	58	10	21	31	33
NHL TOTALS			58	10	21	31	33

(c)—June, 1983—Drafted by Minnesota North Stars in 1983 NHL entry draft. First North Stars pick, first overall, first round.

DEREK LAXDAL

Right Wing . . . 6'1" . . . 180 lbs. . . . Born, St. Boniface, Man., February 21, 1966 . . . Shoots right.

Year	Team	League	Games	G.	A.	Pts.	Pen.
1982-83—Portland Winter Hawks		WHL	39	4	9	13	27
1983-84—Brandon Wheat Kings (c)		WHL	70	23	20	43	86

(c)—June, 1984—Drafted as an underage junior by Toronto Maple Leafs in 1984 NHL entry draft. Seventh Maple Leafs pick, 151st overall, eighth round.

REGINALD JOSEPH (REGGIE) LEACH

Right Wing . . . 6' . . . 185 lbs. . . . Born, Riverton, Man., April 23, 1950 . . . Shoots right . . . Missed most of 1968-69 season with shoulder separation . . . Set WCJHL record for goals in season (87) in 1967-68 (broken by Ron Chipperfield in 1973-74) . . . Tied Stanley Cup

playoff record with five goals in game (May 6, 1976 vs. Boston Bruins) . . . Set record for most goals in Stanley Cup play in single season (19) in 1975-76.

Year	Team	League	Games	G.	A.	Pts.	Pen.
1967-68—Flin Flon Bombers		WCJHL	59	*87	44	131	208
1968-69—Flin Flon Bombers		WCHL	22	36	10	46	49
1969-70—Flin Flon Bombers (a-c-d)		WCHL	57	*65	46	*111	168
1970-71—Oklahoma City Blazers		CHL	41	24	18	42	32
1970-71—Boston Bruins		NHL	23	2	4	6	0
1971-72—Boston Bruins (e)		NHL	56	7	13	20	12
1971-72—California Golden Seals		NHL	17	6	7	13	7
1972-73—California Golden Seals		NHL	76	23	12	35	45
1973-74—California Golden Seals (f)		NHL	78	22	24	46	34
1974-75—Philadelphia Flyers		NHL	80	45	33	78	63
1975-76—Philadelphia Flyers (b-g)		NHL	80	*61	30	91	41
1976-77—Philadelphia Flyers		NHL	77	32	14	46	23
1977-78—Philadelphia Flyers		NHL	72	24	28	52	24
1978-79—Philadelphia Flyers		NHL	76	34	20	54	20
1979-80—Philadelphia Flyers		NHL	76	50	26	76	28
1980-81—Philadelphia Flyers		NHL	79	34	36	70	59
1981-82—Philadelphia Flyers (h-i)		NHL	66	26	21	47	18
1982-83—Detroit Red Wings (j)		NHL	78	15	17	32	13
1983-84—Montana Magic (k)		CHL	76	21	29	50	34
NHL TOTALS			934	381	285	666	387

(c)—Most Valuable Player in WCHL.
(d)—Drafted from Flin Flon Bombers by Boston Bruins in first round of 1970 amateur draft.
(e)—Traded to California Golden Seals by Boston Bruins with Rick Smith and Bob Stewart for Carol Vadnais and Don O'Donoghue, February, 1972.
(f)—Traded to Philadelphia Flyers by California Golden Seals for Larry Wright, Alan MacAdam and Flyers' No. 1 choice in amateur draft, May, 1974. (California received George Pesut from Philadelphia to complete trade, December, 1974).
(g)—Won Conn Smythe Trophy and led in goals (19) and points (24) during playoffs.
(h)—March, 1982—Released by Philadelphia Flyers.
(i)—August, 1982—Signed by Detroit Red Wings as a free agent.
(j)—June, 1983—Released by Detroit Red Wings.
(k)—October, 1983—Signed by Montana Magic as a free agent.

STEPHEN LEACH

Right Wing . . . 5'11" . . . 180 lbs. . . . Born, Cambridge, Mass., January 16, 1966 . . . Shoots right.

Year	Team	League	Games	G.	A.	Pts.	Pen.
1983-84—Matignon H.S. (c)		Mass. H.S.	21	27	22	49	49

(c)—June, 1984—Drafted by Washington Capitals in 1984 NHL entry draft. Second Capitals pick, 34th overall, second round.

GRANT LEDYARD

Defense . . . 6'2" . . . 190 lbs. . . . Born, Winnipeg, Man., November 19, 1961 . . . Shoots left.

Year	Team	League	Games	G.	A.	Pts.	Pen.
1979-80—Fort Garry Blues		MJHL	49	13	24	37	90
1980-81—Saskatoon Blades		WHL	71	9	28	37	148
1981-82—Fort Garry Blues (a-c)		MJHL	63	25	45	70	150
1982-83—Tulsa Oilers (d)		CHL	80	13	29	42	115
1983-84—Tulsa Oilers (e)		CHL	58	9	17	26	71

(c)—Named Manitoba Junior Hockey League Most Valuable Player.
(d)—July, 1982—Signed by New York Rangers as a free agent.
(e)—Won Max McNab Trophy (CHL playoff MVP).

EDWARD LEE

Right Wing and Center . . . 6'2" . . . 184 lbs. . . . Born, Rochester, N.Y., December 17, 1961 . . . Shoots right.

Year	Team	League	Games	G.	A.	Pts.	Pen.
1980-81—Princeton University (c)		ECAC	21	6	8	14	34
1981-82—Princeton University		ECAC	26	12	21	33	46
1982-83—Princeton University		ECAC	25	14	25	39	51
1982-83—U.S. National Team		Int'l	5	5	3	8	8
1983-84—Princeton University		ECAC	11	10	10	20	22
1983-84—Fredericton Express (d)		AHL	6	0	4	4	4

(c)—June, 1981—Drafted by Quebec Nordiques in 1981 NHL entry draft. Fourth Nordiques pick, 95th overall, fifth round.
(d)—February, 1984—Released by Fredericton Express.

GARY LEEMAN

Defense . . . 6' . . . 175 lbs. . . . Born, Toronto, Ont., February 19, 1964 . . . Shoots right . . . (January, 1984)—Broken finger . . . (March, 1984)—Broken wrist.

Year	Team	League	Games	G.	A.	Pts.	Pen.
1980-81—Notre Dame Midgets		SCMHL	24	15	23	38	28
1981-82—Regina Pats (c)		WHL	72	19	41	60	112
1982-83—Regina Pats (a-d)		WHL	63	24	62	86	88
1983-84—Toronto Maple Leafs		NHL	52	4	8	12	31
NHL TOTALS			52	4	8	12	31

(c)—June, 1982—Drafted by Toronto Maple Leafs as underage junior in 1982 NHL entry draft. Second Maple Leafs pick, 24th overall, second round.
(d)—Won WHL Top Defenseman Trophy.

STEPHANE LEFEBVRE

Defense . . . 6'3" . . . 200 lbs. . . . Born, Montreal, Que., May 28, 1963 . . . Shoots left.

Year	Team	League	Games	G.	A.	Pts.	Pen.
1982-83—Verdun Juniors		QHL	69	8	51	59	193
1983-84—Nova Scotia Voyageurs		AHL	63	7	16	23	107

NORMAND LeFRANCOIS

Left Wing . . . 5'11" . . . 185 lbs. . . . Born, Montreal, Que., April 20, 1962 . . . Shoots left . . . (March, 1980)—Broken nose . . . (September, 1981)—Broken jaw during Toronto Maple Leafs training camp.

Year	Team	League	Games	G.	A.	Pts.	Pen.
1978-79—Quebec Remparts		QMJHL	58	18	24	42	53
1979-80—Quebec Remparts		QMJHL	13	4	11	15	7
1979-80—Trois-Rivieres Draveurs		QMJHL	32	6	21	27	70
1980-81—Trois-Rivieres Draveurs (a-c)		QMJHL	69	52	60	112	124
1981-82—Trois-Rivieres Draveurs (b)		QMJHL	56	45	71	116	154
1982-83—Saginaw Gears		IHL	68	23	33	56	132
1983-84—Muskegon Mohawks		IHL	65	16	21	37	108

(c)—June, 1981—Drafted as underage junior by Toronto Maple Leafs in 1981 NHL entry draft. Fourth Maple Leafs pick, 90th overall, fifth round.

MIKKO LEINONEN

Center . . . 6' . . . 175 lbs. . . . Born, Tampere, Finland, July 15, 1955 . . . Shoots left . . . Tied NHL playoff record with six assists in April 8, 1982 game against Philadelphia.

Year	Team	League	Games	G.	A.	Pts.	Pen.
1980-81—Karpat		Finland	36	16	36	52	43
1980-81—Finland Nationals		Finland	24	6	12	18	10
1981-82—New York Rangers (c)		NHL	53	11	20	31	18
1981-82—Springfield Indians		AHL	6	4	2	6	2
1982-83—New York Rangers		NHL	78	17	34	51	23
1983-84—Tulsa Oilers		CHL	33	15	23	38	38
1983-84—New York Rangers (d)		NHL	28	3	23	26	28
NHL TOTALS			159	31	77	108	69

(c)—September, 1981—Signed by New York Rangers as a free agent.
(d)—June, 1984—Released by New York Rangers.

MIKE LEKUN

Left Wing . . . 5'9" . . . 190 lbs. . . . Born, Sudbury, Ont., February 26, 1963 . . . Shoots left.

Year	Team	League	Games	G.	A.	Pts.	Pen.
1979-80—Oshawa Generals		OMJHL	52	10	16	26	144
1980-81—Oshawa Generals		OHL	54	19	32	51	286
1981-82—Oshawa Generals		OHL	64	31	34	65	246
1982-83—Wichita Wind		CHL	70	12	14	26	168
1983-84—Maine Mariners		AHL	63	12	9	21	74

MAURICE (MOE) LEMAY

Left Wing . . . 5'11" . . . 180 lbs. . . . Born, Saskatoon, Sask., February 18, 1962 . . . Shoots left . . . (March, 1983)—Hip injury . . . (April, 1983)—Injured knee during AHL playoffs.

Year	Team	League	Games	G.	A.	Pts.	Pen.
1979-80—Ottawa 67's		OMJHL	62	16	23	39	20
1980-81—Ottawa 67's (c)		OHL	63	32	45	77	102
1981-82—Ottawa 67's (a-d)		OHL	62	*68	70	138	48

Year	Team	League	Games	G.	A.	Pts.	Pen.
1981-82—Vancouver Canucks		NHL	5	1	2	3	0
1982-83—Fredericton Express		AHL	26	7	8	15	6
1982-83—Vancouver Canucks		NHL	44	11	9	20	41
1983-84—Fredericton Express		AHL	23	9	7	16	32
1983-84—Vancouver Canucks		NHL	56	12	18	30	38
NHL TOTALS			105	24	29	53	79

(c)—June, 1981—Drafted as an underage junior by Vancouver Canucks in 1981 NHL entry draft. Fourth Canucks pick, 105th overall, fifth round.

(d)—Led J. Ross Robertson Cup playoffs (OHL) with 19 assists.

ALAIN LEMIEUX

Center . . . 6' . . . 185 lbs. . . . Born, Montreal, Que., May 24, 1961 . . . Shoots left . . . Brother of Mario Lemieux.

Year	Team	League	Games	G.	A.	Pts.	Pen.
1978-79—Chicoutimi Sagueneens		QMJHL	31	15	27	42	5
1978-79—Montreal Juniors		QMJHL	39	7	5	12	2
1979-80—Chicoutimi Sagueneens (c)		QMJHL	72	47	95	142	36
1980-81—Chicoutimi Sagueneens (d)		QMJHL	1	0	0	0	2
1980-81—Trois-Rivieres Draveurs (b-e)		QMJHL	69	68	98	166	62
1981-82—Salt Lake Golden Eagles		CHL	74	41	42	83	61
1981-82—St. Louis Blues		NHL	3	0	1	1	0
1982-83—Salt Lake Golden Eagles		CHL	29	20	24	44	35
1982-83—St. Louis Blues		NHL	42	9	25	34	18
1983-84—St. Louis Blues		NHL	17	4	5	9	6
1983-84—Montana Magic		CHL	38	28	41	69	36
1983-84—Springfield Indians		AHL	14	11	14	25	18
NHL TOTALS			62	13	31	44	24

(c)—June, 1980—Drafted as underage junior by St. Louis Blues in 1980 NHL entry draft. Fourth Blues pick, 96th overall, fifth round.

(d)—October, 1980—Traded by Chicoutimi Sagueneens to Trois Rivieres Draveurs for Rene Labbe and Daniel Courcy.

(e)—Winner of Guy Lafleur Trophy (QMJHL Playoff MVP).

CLAUDE LEMIEUX

Right Wing . . . 6'1" . . . 215 lbs. . . . Born, Buckingham, Que., July 16, 1965 . . . Shoots right.

Year	Team	League	Games	G.	A.	Pts.	Pen.
1981-82—Richelieu Eclairevrs		Que. Midget	48	24	48	72	96
1982-83—Trois-Rivieres Draveurs (c)		QHL	62	28	38	66	187
1983-84—Verdun Juniors (b)		QHL	51	41	45	86	225
1983-84—Montreal Canadiens		NHL	8	1	1	2	12
NHL TOTALS			8	1	1	2	12

(c)—June, 1983—Drafted as underage junior by Montreal Canadiens in 1983 NHL entry draft. Second Canadiens pick, 26th overall, second round.

MARIO LEMIEUX

Center . . . 6'4" . . . 200 lbs. . . . Born, Montreal, Que., October 5, 1965 . . . Shoots right . . . Set single-season record in Quebec Junior League in 1983-84 for goals (133) and points (282) as well as a Quebec League record for most career assists (315) . . . Brother of Alain Lemieux.

Year	Team	League	Games	G.	A.	Pts.	Pen.
1981-82—Laval Voisins		QMJHL	64	30	66	96	22
1982-83—Laval Voisins (b)		QHL	66	84	100	184	76
1983-84—Laval Voisins (a-c)		QHL	70	*133	*149	*282	92

(c)—June, 1984—Drafted as underage junior by Pittsburgh Penguins in 1984 NHL entry draft. First Penguins pick, first overall, first round.

DANIEL LETENDRE

Right Wing . . . 6'1" . . . 200 lbs. . . . Born, Sorel, Que., January 21, 1965 . . . Shoots right.

Year	Team	League	Games	G.	A.	Pts.	Pen.
1981-82—Richelieu Eclairvers		Que. Midget	41	33	43	76	30
1982-83—Quebec Remparts (c)		QHL	61	28	25	53	22
1983-84—Quebec Remparts		QHL	67	25	41	66	35

(c)—June, 1983—Drafted as underage junior by Montreal Canadiens in 1983 NHL entry draft. Fifth Canadiens pick, 45th overall, third round.

DONALD RICHARD LEVER

Center . . . 5'11" . . . 175 lbs. . . . Born, South Porcupine, Ont., November 14, 1952 . . . Shoots left . . . Missed part of 1977-78 season with fractured cheekbone . . . (January 13, 1981)—Strained ligaments in left knee . . . (March, 1981)—Torn rib cartilage . . . Also plays left wing.

Year	Team	League	Games	G.	A.	Pts.	Pen.
1969-70—Niagara Falls Flyers	Jr."A"OHA	2	0	1	1	4
1970-71—Niagara Falls Flyers	Jr."A"OHA	59	35	36	71	112
1971-72—Niag. Falls Flyers (a-c-d-e)	Jr."A"OHA	63	61	65	126	69
1972-73—Vancouver Canucks	NHL	78	12	26	38	49
1973-74—Vancouver Canucks	NHL	78	23	25	48	28
1974-75—Vancouver Canucks	NHL	80	38	30	68	49
1975-76—Vancouver Canucks	NHL	80	25	40	65	93
1976-77—Vancouver Canucks	NHL	80	27	30	57	28
1977-78—Vancouver Canucks	NHL	75	17	32	49	58
1978-79—Vancouver Canucks	NHL	71	23	21	44	17
1979-80—Vancouver Caucks (f)	NHL	51	21	17	38	32
1979-80—Atlanta Flames	NHL	28	14	16	30	4
1980-81—Calgary Flames	NHL	62	26	31	57	56
1981-82—Calgary Flames (g)	NHL	23	8	11	19	6
1981-82—Colorado Rockies	NHL	59	22	28	50	20
1982-83—New Jersey Devils	NHL	79	23	30	53	68
1983-84—New Jersey Devils	NHL	70	14	19	33	44
NHL TOTALS		914	293	356	649	552

(c)—Won Red Tilson Memorial Trophy (MVP in Jr. "A" OHA).

(d)—Selected by Ottawa Nationals in World Hockey Association player selection draft, February, 1972.

(e)—Drafted from Niagara Falls Flyers by Vancouver Canucks in first round of 1972 amateur draft.

(f)—February, 1980—Traded with Brad Smith by Vancouver Canucks to Atlanta Flames for Ivan Boldirev and Darcy Rota.

(g)—December, 1981—Traded with Bob MacMillan by Calgary Flames to Colorado Rockies for Lanny McDonald and a fourth-round 1983 entry draft pick.

CRAIG DEAN LEVIE

Defense . . . 5'10" . . . 198 lbs. . . . Born, Calgary, Alta., August 17, 1959 . . . Shoots right . . . Set new AHL record for points by a defenseman in one season with 82 in 1980-81 (previous record set in 1947-48 by Eddie Bush).

Year	Team	League	Games	G.	A.	Pts.	Pen.
1976-77—Pincher Creek Panthers	AJHL	27	8	10	18	32
1976-77—Calgary Wranglers	WCHL	2	0	1	1	0
1977-78—Flin Flon Bombers	WCHL	72	25	64	89	167
1978-79—Edmonton Oil Kings (b-c)	WHL	69	29	63	92	200
1979-80—Nova Scotia Voyageurs	AHL	72	6	21	27	74
1980-81—Nova Scotia Voyageurs (a-d)	AHL	80	20	*62	82	162
1981-82—Tulsa Oilers	CHL	14	4	7	11	17
1981-82—Winnipeg Jets (e)	NHL	40	4	9	13	48
1982-83—Sherbrooke Jets	AHL	44	3	27	30	52
1982-83—Winnipeg Jets (f)	NHL	22	4	5	9	31
1983-84—Salt Lake Golden Eagles	CHL	37	8	20	28	101
1983-84—Minnesota North Stars	NHL	37	6	13	19	44
NHL TOTALS		99	14	27	41	123

(c)—August, 1979—Drafted by Montreal Canadiens in NHL entry draft. Third Montreal pick, 43rd overall, third round.

(d)—Winner of Eddie Shore Plaque (Top AHL Defenseman).

(e)—October, 1981—Acquired by Winnipeg Jets in 1981 NHL waiver draft.

(f)—August, 1983—Traded by Winnipeg Jets with Tom Ward to Minnesota North Stars for Tim Young.

DAVID RODNEY LEWIS

Defense . . . 6'3" . . . 205 lbs. . . . Born, Kindersley, Sask., July 3, 1953 . . . Shoots left . . . Missed last part of 1973-74 season with fractured right cheekbone . . . (January 14, 1981)—Broke right index finger at Hartford.

Year	Team	League	Games	G.	A.	Pts.	Pen.
1971-72—Saskatoon Blades	WCHL	52	2	9	11	69
1972-73—Saskatoon Blades (c)	WCHL	67	10	35	45	89
1973-74—New York Islanders	NHL	66	2	15	17	58
1974-75—New York Islanders	NHL	78	5	14	19	98
1975-76—New York Islanders	NHL	73	0	19	19	54
1976-77—New York Islanders	NHL	79	4	24	28	44
1977-78—New York Islanders	NHL	77	3	11	14	58
1978-79—New York Islanders	NHL	79	5	18	23	43

Year	Team	League	Games	G.	A.	Pts.	Pen.
1979-80—New York Islanders (d)	NHL	62	5	16	21	54
1979-80—Los Angeles Kings	NHL	11	1	1	2	12
1980-81—Los Angeles Kings	NHL	67	1	12	13	98
1981-82—Los Angeles Kings	NHL	64	1	13	14	75
1982-83—Los Angeles Kings	NHL	79	2	10	12	53
1983-84—New Jersey Devils (e-f)	NHL	66	2	5	7	63
NHL TOTALS			801	31	158	189	710

(c)   Drafted from Saskatoon Blades by New York Islanders in third round of 1973 amateur draft.
(d)—March, 1980—Traded with Billy Harris by New York Islanders to Los Angeles Kings for Butch Goring.
(e)—October, 1983—Traded by Los Angeles Kings to Minnesota North Stars for Fred Barrett.
(f)—October, 1983—Traded by Minnesota North Stars to New Jersey Devils for Brent Ashton.

DOUG LIDSTER

Defense . . . 6'1" . . . 195 lbs. . . . Born, Kamloops, B.C., October 18, 1960 . . . Shoots right . . . (1982-83)—Tied Colorado College record for most points by a defenseman in a season (56) . . . Member of 1984 Canadian Olympic Team.

Year	Team	League	Games	G.	A.	Pts.	Pen.
1979-80—Colorado College (c)	WCHA	39	18	25	43	52
1980-81—Colorado College	WCHA	36	10	30	40	54
1981-82—Colorado College (a)	WCHA	36	13	22	35	32
1982-83—Colorado College	WCHA	34	15	41	56	30
1983-84—Canadian Olympic Team	Int'l	59	6	20	26	28
1983-84—Vancouver Canucks	NHL	8	0	0	0	4
NHL TOTALS			8	0	0	0	4

(c)—June, 1980—Drafted by Vancouver Canucks in 1980 NHL entry draft. Sixth Canucks pick, 133rd overall, seventh round.

LARS LINDGREN

Defense . . . 6'1" . . . 208 lbs. . . . Born, Pitea, Sweden, October 12, 1952 . . . Shoots left . . . Played on Swedish National Team in 1977 and 1978 . . . Missed end of 1978-79 season with shoulder separation . . . (October, 1980)—Recurrence of tendinitis in wrist . . . (November 14, 1980)—Broke bone in hand when hit by a Guy Lafleur shot . . . (March 4, 1981)—Tore knee cartilage. Underwent surgery to correct damage to knee and wrist . . . (December, 1982)—Shoulder injury . . . (February, 1983)—Stretched knee ligaments in game at Toronto.

Year	Team	League	Games	G.	A.	Pts.	Pen.
1974-75—Mo Do AIK	Sweden	43	4	11	15	30
1975-76—Mo Do AIK	Sweden	36	2	4	6	22
1976-77—Mo Do AIK	Sweden	35	6	6	12	36
1977-78—Mo Do AIK (c)	Sweden	33	1	9	10	50
1978-79—Vancouver Canucks	NHL	64	2	19	21	68
1979-80—Vancouver Canucks	NHL	73	5	30	35	66
1980-81—Vancouver Canucks	NHL	52	4	18	22	32
1981-82—Vancouver Canucks	NHL	75	5	16	21	74
1982-83—Vancouver Canucks	NHL	64	6	14	20	48
1983-84—Vancouver Canucks (d)	NHL	7	1	2	3	4
1983-84—Minnesota North Stars	NHL	59	2	14	16	33
NHL TOTALS			394	25	113	138	325

(c)—Signed by Vancouver Canucks, June, 1978.
(d)—October, 1983—Traded by Vancouver Canucks to Minnesota North Stars for third round 1984 draft pick (Landis Chalk).

BO MORGAN (WILLY) LINDSTROM

Right Wing . . . 6' . . . 180 lbs. . . . Born, Grunns, Sweden, May 5, 1951 . . . Shoots left . . . (February, 1983)—Pulled hamstring.

Year	Team	League	Games	G.	A.	Pts.	Pen.
1974-75—Swedish National Team		....	...	....	....	....
1975-76—Winnipeg Jets	WHA	81	23	36	59	32
1976-77—Winnipeg Jets	WHA	79	44	36	80	37
1977-78—Winnipeg Jets	WHA	77	30	30	60	42
1978-79—Winnipeg Jets (c)	WHA	79	26	36	62	22
1979-80—Winnipeg Jets	NHL	79	23	26	49	20
1980-81—Winnipeg Jets	NHL	72	22	13	35	45
1981-82—Winnipeg Jets	NHL	74	32	27	59	33
1982-83—Winnipeg Jets (d)	NHL	63	20	25	45	8

Year	Team	League	Games	G.	A.	Pts.	Pen.
1982-83—Edmonton Oilers		NHL	10	6	5	11	2
1983-84—Edmonton Oilers		NHL	73	22	16	38	38
WHA TOTALS			316	123	138	261	133
NHL TOTALS			371	125	112	237	146

(c)—Tied for lead in goals (10) during playoffs.
(d)—March, 1983—Traded by Winnipeg Jets to Edmonton Oilers for Laurie Boschman.

KEN LINSEMAN

Center . . . 5'11" . . . 175 lbs. . . . Born, Kingston, Ont., August 11, 1958 . . . Shoots left . . . (September, 1980)—Broke tibia bone in leg in preseason game vs. Rangers . . . Older brother of John Linseman . . . (February, 1983)—Suspended for four games for fight in stands at Vancouver.

Year	Team	League	Games	G.	A.	Pts.	Pen.
1974-75—Kingston Canadians		Jr."A" OHA	59	19	28	47	70
1975-76—Kingston Canadians		Jr."A" OHA	65	61	51	112	92
1976-77—Kingston Canadians (b-c)		Jr"A" OHA	63	53	74	127	210
1977-78—Birmingham Bulls (d)		WHA	71	38	38	76	126
1978-79—Maine Mariners		AHL	38	17	23	40	106
1978-79—Philadelphia Flyers		NHL	30	5	20	25	23
1979-80—Philadelphia Flyers (e)		NHL	80	22	57	79	107
1980-81—Philadelphia Flyers		NHL	51	17	30	47	150
1981-82—Philadelphia Flyers (f)		NHL	79	24	68	92	275
1982-83—Edmonton Oilers		NHL	72	33	42	75	181
1983-84—Edmonton Oilers (g)		NHL	72	18	49	67	119
WHA TOTALS			71	38	38	76	126
NHL TOTALS			384	119	266	385	855

(c)—Selected by Birmingham Bulls in World Hockey Association amateur player draft as underage junior, June, 1977.
(d)—Drafted from Birmingham Bulls by Philadelphia Flyers (with choice obtained from N. Y. Rangers) in first round of 1978 amateur draft.
(e)—Led in assists (18) during playoffs.
(f)—August, 1982—Traded with Greg Adams and first and third-round 1983 draft picks by Philadelphia Flyers to Hartford Whalers for Mark Howe and Whalers third-round '83 pick. Linseman was then traded with Don Nachbaur by Hartford Whalers to Edmonton Oilers for Risto Siltanen and Brent Loney.
(g)—June, 1984—Traded by Edmonton Oilers to Boston Bruins for Mike Krushelnyski.

TIM LOCKRIDGE

Defense . . . 6'1" . . . 215 lbs. . . . Born, Barrie, Ont., January 18, 1959 . . . Shoots right.

Year	Team	League	Games	G.	A.	Pts.	Pen.
1975-76—Brandon Travellers		MJHL	39	10	12	22	253
1975-76—Brandon Wheat Kings		WCHL	1	0	0	0	0
1976-77—Brandon Wheat Kings		WCHL	65	2	16	18	143
1977-78—Brandon Wheat Kings		WCHL	65	4	26	30	39
1978-79—Brandon Wheat Kings (c)		WCHL	70	10	42	52	297
1979-80—Indianapolis Racers		CHL	45	0	10	10	49
1980-81—Indianapolis Checkers		CHL	48	0	4	4	51
1981-82—Indianapolis Checkers		CHL	63	2	12	14	146
1982-83—Indianapolis Checkers		CHL	79	2	15	17	87
1983-84—Indianapolis Checkers		CHL	71	2	16	18	95

(c)—August, 1979—Drafted by New York Islanders in 1979 entry draft. Fifth Islanders pick, 80th overall, fourth round.

MARK LOFTHOUSE

Right Wing . . . 6'1" . . . 185 lbs. . . . Born, New Westminster, B.C., April 21, 1957 . . . Shoots right . . . (February, 1983)—Injured back.

Year	Team	League	Games	G.	A.	Pts.	Pen.
1973-74—Kelowna Buckaroos		Jr."A"BCHL	62	44	42	86	59
1974-75—New Westminster Bruins		WCHL	61	36	28	64	53
1975-76—New Westminster Bruins		WCHL	72	68	48	116	55
1976-77—New Westminster Bruins (b-c)		WCHL	70	54	58	112	59
1977-78—Hershey Bears		AHL	35	8	6	14	39
1977-78—Salt Lake City Golden Eagles		CHL	13	0	1	1	4
1977-78—Washington Capitals		NHL	18	2	1	3	8
1978-79—Washington Capitals		NHL	52	13	10	23	10
1978-79—Hershey Bears		AHL	16	7	7	14	6
1979-80—Hershey Bears		AHL	9	7	3	10	6

Year	Team	League	Games	G.	A.	Pts.	Pen.
1979-80—Washington Capitals		NHL	68	15	18	33	20
1980-81—Washington Capitals		NHL	3	1	1	2	4
1980-81—Hershey Bears (a-d-e)		AHL	74	*48	55	*103	131
1981-82—Adirondack Red Wings		AHL	69	33	38	71	75
1981-82—Detroit Red Wings		NHL	12	3	4	7	13
1982-83—Adirondack Red Wings		AHL	39	27	18	45	20
1982-83—Detroit Red Wings (f)		NHL	28	8	4	12	18
1983-84—New Haven Nighthawks (b)		AHL	79	37	64	101	45
NHL TOTALS			181	42	38	80	73

(c)—Drafted from New Westminster Bruins by Washington Capitals in second round of 1977 amateur draft.
(d)—Winner of John B. Sollenberger Trophy (Leading Scorer of AHL).
(e)—August, 1981—Traded by Washington Capitals to Detroit Red Wings for Al Jensen.
(f)—August, 1983—Signed by Los Angeles Kings as a free agent.

CLAUDE LOISELLE

Center . . . 5'11" . . . 195 lbs. . . . Born, Ottawa, Ont., May 29, 1963 . . . Shoots left . . . (January 7, 1984)—Given six-game suspension by NHL for a stick-swinging incident with Paul Holmgren of Philadelphia.

Year	Team	League	Games	G.	A.	Pts.	Pen.
1979-80—Gloucester Rangers		OPJHL	50	21	38	59	26
1980-81—Windsor Spitfires (c)		OHL	68	38	56	94	103
1981-82—Windsor Spitfires		OHL	68	36	73	109	192
1981-82—Detroit Red Wings		NHL	4	1	0	1	2
1982-83—Detroit Red Wings		NHL	18	2	0	2	15
1982-83—Windsor Spitfires		OHL	46	39	49	88	75
1982-83—Adirondack Red Wings		AHL	6	1	7	8	0
1983-84—Adirondack Red Wings		AHL	29	13	16	29	59
1983-84—Detroit Red Wings		NHL	28	4	6	10	32
NHL TOTALS			50	7	6	13	49

(c)—June, 1981—Drafted as underage junior by Detroit Red Wings in 1981 NHL entry draft. First Red Wings pick, 23rd overall, second round.

BRENT LONEY

Left Wing . . . 6' . . . 170 lbs. . . . Born, Cornwall, Ont., May 25, 1964 . . . Shoots left . . . (January, 1983)—Involved in auto accident in Cornwall, Ontario. Suffered facial cuts when he went through windshield.

Year	Team	League	Games	G.	A.	Pts.	Pen.
1980-81—Ottawa Senators		CJHL	45	6	14	20	93
1981-82—Cornwall Royals (c-d)		OHL	65	13	12	25	57
1982-83—Cornwall Royals		OHL	47	11	24	35	69
1983-84—Cornwall Royals		OHL	62	24	38	62	56

(c)—June, 1982—Drafted by Edmonton Oilers as underage junior in 1982 NHL entry draft. Third Oilers pick, 62nd overall, third round.
(d)—August, 1982—Traded with Risto Siltanen by Edmonton Oilers to Hartford Whalers for Don Nachbaur and Ken Linseman.

TROY LONEY

Left Wing . . . 6'3" . . . 215 lbs. . . . Born, Bow Island, Alta., September 21, 1963 . . . Shoots left.

Year	Team	League	Games	G.	A.	Pts.	Pen.
1980-81—Lethbridge Broncos		WHL	71	18	13	31	100
1981-82—Lethbridge Broncos (c)		WHL	71	26	31	57	152
1982-83—Lethbridge Broncos		WHL	72	33	34	67	156
1983-84—Baltimore Skipjacks		AHL	63	18	13	31	147
1983-84—Pittsburgh Penguins		NHL	13	0	0	0	9
NHL TOTALS			13	0	0	0	9

(c)—June, 1982—Drafted as underage junior by Pittsburgh Penguins in 1982 NHL entry draft. Third Penguins pick, 52nd overall, third round.

HAKAN LOOB

Right Wing . . . 5'9" . . . 180 lbs. . . . Born, Karlstad, Sweden, July 3, 1960 . . . Shoots right . . . Set Swedish records in 1982-83 for goals (42), assists (34) and points (76) in a season.

Year	Team	League	Games	G.	A.	Pts.	Pen.
1978-79—Karlskrona IK		Sweden Jr.	..	..	..	..	..
1979 80 —Karlstad Farjestads BK (c)		Sweden	36	15	4	19	20
1980-81—Karlstad Farjestads BK (d-e)		Sweden	36	23	6	29	14
1981-82—Karlstad Farjestads BK		Sweden	36	26	15	41	28
1982-83—Karlstad Farjestads BK		Sweden	36	*42	*34	*76	18
1983-84—Calgary Flames		NHL	77	30	25	55	22
NHL TOTALS			77	30	25	55	22

(c)—June, 1980—Drafted by Calgary Flames in 1980 NHL entry draft. Tenth Flames pick, 181st overall, ninth round.
(d)—Shared Swedish National League playoffs goal scoring lead with teammate Jan Ingman (5 goals).
(e)—Shared Swedish National League playoff point lead with teammate Robin Eriksson (8 points).

TIM LORENTZ
Left Wing . . . 6'3" . . . 205 lbs. . . . Born, Vancouver, B.C., February 12, 1965 . . . Shoots left.

Year	Team	League	Games	G.	A.	Pts.	Pen.
1981-82—Red Deer Rustlers		AJHL	25	4	6	10	81
1982-83—Portland Winter Hawks (c)		WHL	71	16	11	27	109
1983-84—Portland Winter Hawks		WHL	64	19	14	33	112

(c)—June, 1983—Drafted as underage junior by Vancouver Canucks in 1983 NHL entry draft. Fourth Canucks pick, 70th overall, fourth round.

TOM LORENTZ
Center . . . 5'11" . . . 160 lbs. . . . Born, St. Paul, Minn., November 18, 1966 . . . Shoots right.

Year	Team	League	Games	G.	A.	Pts.	Pen.
1983-84—St. Paul Brady H.S. (c)		Minn. H.S.	21	20	19	39	14

(c)—June, 1984—Drafted by New York Rangers in NHL entry draft. Eleventh Rangers pick, 223rd overall, 11th round.

ROBERT ROY LORIMER
Defense . . . 6' . . . 190 lbs. . . . Born, Toronto, Ont., August 25, 1953 . . . Shoots right . . . Attended Michigan Tech . . . Missed part of 1976-77 season with surgery for ruptured spleen and part with kidney injury . . . (October, 1982)—Missed 16 games with stretched left knee ligaments . . . (December, 1982)—Sprained wrist.

Year	Team	League	Games	G.	A.	Pts.	Pen.
1970-71—Aurora Tigers		OPJHL	....		....	....	....
1971-72—Michigan Tech		WCHA	32	1	7	8	63
1972-73—Michigan Tech (c)		WCHA	38	2	9	11	74
1973-74—Michigan Tech		WCHA	39	3	18	21	46
1974-75—Michigan Tech (b)		WCHA	38	10	21	31	68
1975-76—Fort Worth Texans		CHL	2	0	0	0	2
1975-76—Muskegon Mohawks		IHL	78	6	21	27	94
1976-77—Fort Worth Texans		CHL	28	4	6	10	38
1976-77—New York Islanders		NHL	1	0	1	1	0
1977-78—Fort Worth Texans		CHL	71	6	13	19	81
1977-78—New York Islanders		NHL	5	1	0	1	0
1978-79—New York Islanders		NHL	67	3	18	21	42
1979-80—New York Islanders		NHL	74	3	16	19	53
1980-81—New York Islanders		NHL	73	1	12	13	77
1981-82—Colorado Rockies (d)		NHL	79	5	15	20	68
1982-83—New Jersey Devils		NHL	66	3	10	13	42
1983-84—New Jersey Devils		NHL	72	2	10	12	62
NHL TOTALS			437	18	82	100	344

(c)—Drafted by New York Islanders in ninth round of 1973 amateur draft.
(d)—October, 1981—Traded with Dave Cameron by New York Islanders to Colorado Rockies for first round 1983 entry draft pick (Pat LaFontaine).

GORDON JAMES LOWELL LOVEDAY
(Known by Lowell.)

Defense . . . 6' . . . 198 lbs. . . . Born, Simcoe, Ont., July 30, 1959 . . . Shoots right.

Year	Team	League	Games	G.	A.	Pts.	Pen.
1976-77—Kingston Canadians		OMJHL	65	3	3	6	54
1977-78—Kingston Canadians		OMJHL	68	5	19	24	124
1978-79—Kingston Canadians (c)		OMJHL	65	13	28	41	121
1979-80—New Brunswick Hawks		AHL	64	8	21	29	49
1980-81—New Brunswick Hawks		AHL	79	4	25	29	96
1981-82—New Brunswick Hawks (b)		AHL	75	8	41	49	84

Year	Team	League	Games	G.	A.	Pts.	Pen.
1982-83—Moncton Alpines (d)		AHL	80	13	26	39	26
1983-84—Moncton Alpines		AHL	65	7	21	28	24

(c)—August, 1979—Drafted by Chicago Black Hawks in entry draft. Fifth Black Hawks pick, 91st overall, fifth round.

(d)—August, 1982—Signed by Edmonton Oilers as a free agent.

DARREN LOWE

Right Wing . . . 5'10" . . . 185 lbs. . . . Born, Toronto, Ont., October 13, 1960 . . . Shoots right . . . First black player in history of Pittsburgh Penguins . . . Member of 1984 Canadian Olympic Team.

Year	Team	League	Games	G.	A.	Pts.	Pen.
1981-82—University of Toronto (b-c)		OUAA	29	36	26	62	....
1982-83—University of Toronto (a)		OUAA	24	23	32	55	....
1983-84—Canadian Olympic Team		Int'l	60	16	13	29	22
1983-84—Pittsburgh Penguins (d)		NHL	8	1	2	3	0
NHL TOTALS			8	1	2	3	0

(c)—Named OUAA Playoff Most Valuable Player.

(d)—February, 1984—Signed by Pittsburgh Penguins as a free agent.

KEVIN HUGH LOWE

Defense . . . 6' . . . 185 lbs. . . . Born, Lachute, Que., April 15, 1959 . . . Shoots left . . . Cousin of Mike Lowe (St. Louis 1969 draft pick).

Year	Team	League	Games	G.	A.	Pts.	Pen.
1976-77—Quebec Remparts		QMJHL	69	3	19	22	39
1977-78—Quebec Remparts		QMJHL	64	13	52	65	86
1978-79—Quebec Remparts (b-c)		QMJHL	68	26	60	86	120
1979-80—Edmonton Oilers		NHL	64	2	19	21	70
1980-81—Edmonton Oilers		NHL	79	10	24	34	94
1981-82—Edmonton Oilers		NHL	80	9	31	40	63
1982-83—Edmonton Oilers		NHL	80	6	34	40	43
1983-84—Edmonton Oilers		NHL	80	4	42	46	59
NHL TOTALS			383	31	150	181	329

(c)—August, 1979—Drafted by Edmonton Oilers in 1979 entry draft. First Oilers pick, 21st overall, first round.

ED LOWNEY

Right Wing . . . 5'11" . . . 180 lbs. . . . Born, Revere, Mass., June 10, 1965 . . . Shoots right.

Year	Team	League	Games	G.	A.	Pts.	Pen.
1983-84—Boston University (c)		ECAC	40	21	12	33	26

(c)—June, 1984—Drafted by Vancouver Canucks in 1984 NHL entry draft. Eleventh Canucks pick, 198th overall, 10th round.

DAVE LOWRY

Left Wing . . . 6'2" . . . 175 lbs. . . . Born, Sudbury, Ont., January 14, 1965 . . . Shoots left . . . (December, 1982)—Arthroscopic surgery on knee.

Year	Team	League	Games	G.	A.	Pts.	Pen.
1981-82—Nepean Midgets		Ont. Midget	60	50	64	114	46
1982-83—London Knights (c)		OHL	42	11	16	27	48
1983-84—London Knights		OHL	66	29	47	76	125

(c)—June, 1983—Drafted as underage junior by Vancouver Canucks in 1983 NHL entry draft. Fourth Canucks pick, 110th overall, sixth round.

JAN LUDVIG

Right Wing . . . 5'10" . . . 187 lbs. . . . Born, Liberec, Czechoslovakia, September 17, 1961 . . . Shoots right . . . (December, 1982)—Bruised ribs . . . (January, 1984)—Hip Injury.

Year	Team	League	Games	G.	A.	Pts.	Pen.
1981-82—St. Albert Saints (c)		AJHL	4	2	4	6	20
1981-82—Kamloops Oilers		WHL	37	31	34	65	36
1982-83—Wichita Wind (d)		CHL	9	3	0	3	19
1982-83—New Jersey Devils		NHL	51	7	10	17	30
1983-84—New Jersey Devils		NHL	74	22	32	54	70
NHL TOTALS			125	29	42	71	100

(c)—October, 1981—Signed by Edmonton Oilers as a free agent.

(d)—November, 1982—Signed by New Jersey Devils as a free agent.

CRAIG LEE LUDWIG

Defense ... 6'3" ... 212 lbs. ... Born, Rhinelander, Wis., March 15, 1961 ... Shoots left.

Year	Team	League	Games	G.	A.	Pts.	Pen.
1979-80—University of North Dakota (c)		WCHA	33	1	8	9	32
1980-81—University of North Dakota		WCHA	34	4	8	12	48
1981-82—University of North Dakota (b)		WCHA	47	5	26	31	70
1982-83—Montreal Canadiens		NHL	80	0	25	25	59
1983-84—Montreal Canadiens		NHL	72	4	13	17	45
NHL TOTALS			152	4	38	42	104

(c)—June, 1980—Drafted by Montreal Canadiens in 1980 NHL entry draft. Fifth Canadiens pick, 61st overall, third round.

STEVE LUDZIK

Center ... 5'11" ... 185 lbs. ... Born, Toronto, Ont., April 3, 1961 ... Shoots left.

Year	Team	League	Games	G.	A.	Pts.	Pen.
1977-78—Markham Waxers		OPJHL	34	15	24	39	20
1978-79—Niagara Falls Flyers		OMJHL	68	32	65	97	138
1979-80—Niagara Falls Flyers (c)		OMJHL	67	43	76	119	102
1980-81—Niagara Falls Flyers		OHL	58	50	92	142	108
1981-82—Chicago Black Hawks		NHL	8	2	1	3	2
1981-82—New Brunswick Hawks		AHL	75	21	41	62	142
1982-83—Chicago Black Hawks		NHL	66	6	19	25	63
1983-84—Chicago Black Hawks		NHL	80	9	20	29	73
NHL TOTALS			154	17	40	57	138

(c)—June, 1980—Drafted as underage junior by Chicago Black Hawks in 1980 NHL entry draft. Third Black Hawks pick, 28th overall, second round.

MORRIS LUKOWICH

Left Wing ... 5'8" ... 165 lbs. ... Born, Speers, Sask., June 1, 1956 ... Shoots left ... Cousin of Bernie Lukowich ... Missed part of 1976-77 season with fractured left ankle ... Also plays Right Wing and Center ... (March, 1983)—Stretched knee ligaments when checked by teammate Tim Watters at a practice in Los Angeles.

Year	Team	League	Games	G.	A.	Pts.	Pen.
1973-74—Medicine Hat Tigers		WCHL	65	13	14	27	55
1974-75—Medicine Hat Tigers		WCHL	70	40	54	94	111
1975-76—Medicine Hat Tigers (a-c-d)		WCHL	72	65	77	142	195
1976-77—Houston Aeros		WHA	62	27	18	45	67
1977-78—Houston Aeros (e)		WHA	80	40	35	75	131
1978-79—Winnipeg Jets (b f)		WHA	80	65	34	99	119
1979-80—Winnipeg Jets		NHL	78	35	39	74	77
1980-81—Winnipeg Jets		NHL	80	33	34	67	90
1981-82—Winnipeg Jets		NHL	77	43	49	92	102
1982-83—Winnipeg Jets		NHL	69	22	21	43	67
1983-84—Winnipeg Jets		NHL	80	30	25	55	71
WHA TOTALS			222	132	87	219	317
NHL TOTALS			384	163	168	331	408

(c)—Drafted from Medicine Hat Tigers by Pittsburgh Penguins in third round of 1976 amateur draft.

(d)—Selected by Houston Aeros in World Hockey Association amateur player draft, May, 1976.

(e)—Sold to Winnipeg Jets with Houston Aeros' franchise, July, 1978.

(f)—June, 1979—Selected by Pittsburgh Penguins in NHL reclaim draft, but remained with the Jets as a priority selection for the expansion draft.

DAVID LUMLEY

Right Wing ... 5'11" ... 185 lbs. ... Born, Toronto, Ont., September 1, 1954 ... Shoots right ... Attended University of New Hampshire ... Has also played Defense ... (November 29, 1980)—Sprained shoulder ... (December, 1983)—Injured knee ligaments.

Year	Team	League	Games	G.	A.	Pts.	Pen.
1973-74—Univ. of New Hampshire (c)		ECAC	31	12	19	31	38
1974-75—University of New Hampshire		ECAC	26	12	26	38	56
1975-76—University of New Hampshire		ECAC	30	9	32	41	55
1976-77—University of New Hampshire		ECAC	39	22	38	60	42
1977-78—Nova Scotia Voyageurs		AHL	58	22	21	43	58
1978-79—Montreal Canadiens		NHL	3	0	0	0	0
1978-79—Nova Scotia Voyageurs (b-d)		AHL	61	22	58	80	160
1979-80—Edmonton Oilers		NHL	80	20	38	58	138
1980-81—Edmonton Oilers		NHL	53	7	9	16	74
1981-82—Edmonton Oilers		NHL	66	32	42	74	96

Year	Team	League	Games	G.	A.	Pts.	Pen.
1982-83—Edmonton Oilers		NHL	72	13	24	37	158
1983-84—Edmonton Oilers		NHL	56	6	15	21	68
NHL TOTALS			330	78	128	206	534

(c)—Drafted from University of New Hampshire by Montreal Canadiens in 12th round of 1974 amateur draft.

(d)—June, 1979—Traded with Dan Newman by Montreal Canadiens to Edmonton Oilers for future considerations.

BRIAN FREDERICK LUNDBERG

Defense . . . 5'11" . . . 190 lbs. . . . Born, Burnaby, B.C., June 5, 1960 . . . Shoots right.

Year	Team	League	Games	G.	A.	Pts.	Pen.
1977-78—Seattle Breakers		WHL	1	0	0	0	0
1978-79—University of Michigan		WCHA	..	..	..	..	..
1979-80—University of Michigan (c)		WCHA	37	2	14	16	94
1980-81—University of Michigan		WCHA	40	1	6	7	62
1981-82—University of Michigan		CCHA	32	3	16	19	42
1981-82—Erie Blades		AHL	10	0	4	4	6
1982-83—Baltimore Skipjacks		AHL	76	4	15	19	103
1982-83—Pittsburgh Penguins		NHL	1	0	0	0	2
1983-84—Muskegon Mohawks		IHL	34	3	12	15	46
1983-84—Baltimore Skipjacks		AHL	47	1	5	6	97
NHL TOTALS			1	0	0	0	2

(c)—June, 1981—Drafted by Pittsburgh Penguins in 1980 NHL entry draft. Seventh Penguins pick, 177th overall, ninth round.

BENGT LUNDHOLM

Left Wing . . . 6' . . . 172 lbs. . . . Born, Falun, Sweden, August 4, 1955 . . . Shoots left . . . (February 2, 1983)—Injured right knee in game vs. Philadelphia, requiring surgery . . . Also plays right wing.

Year	Team	League	Games	G.	A.	Pts.	Pen.
1977-78—Solna AIK		Sweden	54	23	25	48	36
1978-79—Solna AIK		Sweden	47	15	29	44	38
1979-80—Solna AIK		Sweden	51	21	36	57	48
1980-81—Solna AIK (c)		Sweden	39	11	15	26	48
1981-82—Winnipeg Jets		NHL	66	14	30	44	10
1982-83—Winnipeg Jets		NHL	58	14	28	42	16
1983-84—Winnipeg Jets		NHL	57	5	14	19	20
NHL TOTALS			181	33	72	105	46

(c)—June, 1981—Signed by Winnipeg Jets as a free agent.

DAVE LUNDMARK

Defense . . . 6' . . . 190 lbs. . . . Born, Minneapolis, Minn., February 14, 1965 . . . Shoots left.

Year	Team	League	Games	G.	A.	Pts.	Pen.
1982-83—Virginia H.S. (c)		Minn. H.S.	22	4	10	14	..
1983-84—Kingston Canadians		OHL	65	2	9	11	66

(c)—June, 1983—Drafted by Los Angeles Kings in 1983 NHL entry draft. Fifth Kings pick, 107th overall, sixth round.

GARY JOHN LUPUL

Center . . . 5'8" . . . 174 lbs. . . . Born, Powell River, B.C., April 4, 1959 . . . Shoots left . . . (August, 1977)—Torn ligaments in left knee . . . (August, 1978)—Injured ankle while working in a logging camp in B.C. . . . (November, 1983)—Broken knuckle.

Year	Team	League	Games	G.	A.	Pts.	Pen.
1975-76—Victoria Cougars		WCHL	4	1	1	2	2
1976-77—Victoria Cougars		WCHL	71	38	63	101	116
1977-78—Victoria Cougars		WCHL	59	37	49	86	79
1978-79—Victoria Cougars		WHL	71	53	54	107	85
1979-80—Dallas Black Hawks (c)		CHL	26	9	15	24	4
1979-80—Vancouver Canucks		NHL	51	9	11	20	24
1980-81—Vancouver Canucks		NHL	7	0	2	2	2
1980-81—Dallas Black Hawks		CHL	53	25	32	57	27
1981-82—Dallas Black Hawks		CHL	31	22	17	39	76
1981-82—Vancouver Canucks		NHL	41	10	7	17	26
1982-83—Fredericton Express		AHL	35	16	26	42	48

Year	Team	League	Games	G.	A.	Pts.	Pen.
1982-83—Vancouver Canucks		NHL	40	18	10	28	46
1983-84—Vancouver Canucks		NHL	69	17	27	44	51
NHL TOTALS			208	54	57	111	149

(c)—September, 1979—Signed as free agent by Vancouver Canucks.

THOMAS JAMES LYSIAK

Center . . . 6'1" . . . 205 lbs. . . . Born, High Prairie, Alta., April 22, 1953 . . . Shoots left . . . Equalled WCHL record with 10 points in game (December 30, 1971 vs. Edmonton Oil Kings) . . . (February, 1981)—Recurring nerve condition in his back . . . (December 27, 1981)—Slight cartilage tear in right knee vs. St. Louis . . . (January 23, 1983)—Cracked bone in instep of right foot when hit by Dave Maloney shot during game vs. New York Rangers . . . (October 30, 1983)—Given a 20-game suspension by NHL for tripping lines-man Ron Foyt in game vs. Hartford.

Year	Team	League	Games	G.	A.	Pts.	Pen.
1970-71—Medicine Hat Tigers		WCHL	60	14	16	30	112
1971-72—Medicine Hat Tigers (a)		WCHL	68	46	*97	*143	96
1972-73—Medicine Hat Tigers (a-c)		WCHL	67	58	*96	*154	104
1973-74—Atlanta Flames (d)		NHL	77	19	45	64	54
1974-75—Atlanta Flames		NHL	77	25	52	77	73
1975-76—Atlanta Flames		NHL	80	31	51	82	60
1976-77—Atlanta Flames		NHL	79	30	51	81	52
1977-78—Atlanta Flames		NHL	80	27	42	69	54
1978-79—Atlanta Flames (e)		NHL	52	23	35	58	36
1978-79—Chicago Black Hawks		NHL	14	0	10	10	14
1979-80—Chicago Black Hawks		NHL	77	26	43	69	31
1980-81—Chicago Black Hawks		NHL	72	21	55	76	20
1981-82—Chicago Black Hawks		NHL	71	32	50	82	84
1982-83—Chicago Black Hawks		NHL	61	23	38	61	29
1983-84—Chicago Black Hawks		NHL	54	17	30	47	35
NHL TOTALS			794	274	502	776	533

(c)—Drafted from Medicine Hat Tigers by Atlanta Flames in first round of 1973 amateur draft.
(d)—Named Rookie-of-the-Year in NHL's West Division poll of players by THE SPORTING NEWS.
(e)—March, 1979—Traded with Harold Phillipoff, Pat Ribble, Greg Fox and Miles Zaharko to Chicago Black Hawks by Atlanta Flames for Ivan Boldirev, Phil Russell and Darcy Rota.

REGINALD ALAN (AL) MacADAM

Left Wing . . . 6' . . . 175 lbs. . . . Born, Charlottetown, P.E.I., March 16, 1952 . . . Shoots left . . . Attended University of Prince Edward Island . . . Missed part of 1973-74 season with fractured cheekbone . . . Also plays Right Wing . . . Missed part of 1978-79 season with ligament damage in right hand that required surgery . . . (March 14, 1981)—Broken cheekbone . . . (March, 1983)—Infected finger.

Year	Team	League	Games	G.	A.	Pts.	Pen.
1969-70—Charlottetown Islanders		MJHL	42	27	31	58	55
1970-71—Charlottetown Islanders (a)		MJHL	53	51	43	94	58
1971-72—Univ. of Prince Edward Island (a)			26	32	21	53	8
1971-72—Charlottetown Islanders (c-d)		MJHL	11	15	21	36	....
1972-73—Richmond Robins		AHL	68	19	32	51	42
1973-74—Richmond Robins		AHL	62	23	22	45	36
1973-74—Philadelphia Flyers (e)		NHL	5	0	0	0	0
1974-75—California Seals		NHL	80	18	25	43	55
1975-76—California Seals		NHL	80	32	31	63	49
1976-77—Cleveland Barons		NHL	80	22	41	63	68
1977-78—Cleveland Barons		NHL	80	16	32	48	42
1978-79—Minnesota North Stars		NHL	69	24	34	58	30
1979-80—Minnesota North Stars (f)		NHL	80	42	51	93	24
1980-81—Minnesota North Stars		NHL	78	21	39	60	94
1981-82—Minnesota North Stars		NHL	79	18	43	61	37
1982-83—Minnesota North Stars		NHL	73	11	22	33	60
1983-84—Minnesota North Stars (g)		NHL	80	22	13	35	23
NHL TOTALS			784	226	331	557	482

(c)—No league record. Appeared in 11 playoff games and had 36 points.
(d)—Drafted from Charlottetown Islanders by Philadelphia Flyers in fourth round of 1972 amateur draft.
(e)—Traded to California Golden Seals by Philadelphia Flyers with Larry Wright and Flyers' No. 1 choice in 1974 amateur draft (Ron Chipperfield) for Reg Leach, May, 1974.
(f)—Won Bill Masterton Memorial Trophy.
(g)—June, 1984—Traded by Minnesota North Stars to Vancouver Canucks for Harold Snepsts.

PAUL MacDERMID

Center . . . 6' . . . 188 lbs. . . . Born, Chesley, Ont., April 14, 1963 . . . Shoots right . . . (December, 1982)—Injured knee.

Year	Team	League	Games	G.	A.	Pts.	Pen.
1979-80	Port Elgin Bears	OHA Jr.'C'	30	23	20	43	87
1980-81	Windsor Spitfires (c)	OHL	68	15	17	32	106
1981-82	Windsor Spitfires	OHL	65	26	45	71	179
1981-82	Hartford Whalers	NHL	3	1	0	1	2
1982-83	Windsor Spitfires	OHL	42	35	45	80	90
1982-83	Hartford Whalers	NHL	7	0	0	0	2
1983-84	Hartford Whalers	NHL	3	0	1	1	0
1983-84	Binghamton Whalers	AHL	70	31	30	61	130
	NHL TOTALS		13	1	1	2	4

(c)—June, 1981—Drafted as underage junior in 1981 NHL entry draft by Hartford Whalers. Second Whalers pick, 61st overall, third round.

BRETT MacDONALD

Defense . . . 6' . . . 195 lbs. . . . Born, Bothwell, Ont., January 5, 1966 . . . Shoots left.

Year	Team	League	Games	G.	A.	Pts.	Pen.
1982-83	Dixie Beehives	MTJHL	44	5	18	23	28
1983-84	North Bay Centennials (c)	OHL	70	8	18	26	83

(c)—June, 1984—Drafted as underage junior by Vancouver Canucks in NHL entry draft. Sixth Canucks pick, 94th overall, fifth round.

RANDY MacGREGOR

Right Wing . . . 5'9" . . . 175 lbs. . . . Born, Cobourg, Ont., July 9, 1953 . . . Shoots left . . . (February, 1983)—Knee injury.

Year	Team	League	Games	G.	A.	Pts.	Pen.
1971-72	Chatham Maroons	SOHA	56	18	25	43	*216
1972-73	Chatham Maroons	SOHA	58	36	20	56	176
1973-74	Binghamton Dusters	NAHL	71	17	28	45	139
1974-75	Binghamton Dusters	NAHL	73	23	48	71	154
1975-76	Binghamton Dusters	NAHL	43	9	10	19	84
1976-77	Binghamton Dusters	NAHL	71	21	26	47	128
1977-78	Binghamton Dusters	AHL	78	20	29	49	117
1978-79	Binghamton Dusters	AHL	64	29	46	75	113
1979-80	Binghamton Dusters	AHL	71	21	23	44	164
1980-81	Binghamton Whalers (c)	AHL	28	14	9	23	49
1981-82	Binghamton Whalers	AHL	71	23	50	73	115
1981-82	Hartford Whalers	NHL	2	1	1	2	2
1982-83	Binghamton Whalers (d)	AHL	62	13	17	30	112
1983-84	Adirondack Red Wings (e)	AHL	45	6	15	21	60
	NHL TOTALS		2	1	1	2	2

(c)—February, 1981—Signed by Binghamton Whalers as a free agent after returning from a season in Austria.

(d)—June, 1983—Released by Binghamton Whalers.

(e)—December, 1983—Signed by Adirondack Red Wings as a free agent.

GARTH LESLIE MacGUIGAN

Center . . . 6' . . . 190 lbs. . . . Born, Charlottetown, P.E.I., February 16, 1956 . . . Shoots left . . . Brother of Bob MacGuigan (minor league player in mid '70's).

Year	Team	League	Games	G.	A.	Pts.	Pen.
1974-75	Montreal Juniors	QJHL	63	30	38	68	97
1975-76	Montreal Juniors (c)	QJHL	69	47	46	93	94
1976-77	Muskegon Mohawks (d)	IHL	78	54	40	94	156
1976-77	Fort Worth Texans	CHL	1	0	0	0	0
1977-78	Fort Worth Texans	CHL	70	17	24	41	54
1978-79	Fort Worth Texans	CHL	75	28	21	49	120
1979-80	New York Islanders	NHL	2	0	0	0	2
1979-80	Indianapolis Checkers	CHL	77	28	34	62	94
1980-81	Indianapolis Checkers (b)	CHL	80	37	38	75	96
1981-82	Indianapolis Checkers	CHL	80	24	51	75	112
1982-83	Indianapolis Checkers	CHL	80	37	35	72	70
1983-84	Indianapolis Checkers	CHL	68	25	41	66	109
1983-84	New York Islanders	NHL	3	0	1	1	0
	NHL TOTALS		5	0	1	1	2

(c)—Drafted from Montreal Juniors by New York Islanders in third round of 1976 amateur draft.

(d)—Co-winner (along with Ron Zanussi) of Garry Longman Memorial Trophy (rookie-of-the-year).

SCOTT MACHEJ

Center and Left Wing . . . 6'1" . . . 170 lbs. . . . Born, Winnipeg, Man., February 2, 1964 . . . Shoots left.

Year	Team	League	Games	G.	A.	Pts.	Pen.
1981-82	Calgary Wranglers (c)	WHL	69	21	18	39	43
1982-83	Calgary Wranglers	WHL	71	37	32	69	49
1983-84	Calgary Wranglers	WHL	54	36	34	70	47

(c)—June, 1982—Drafted as underage junior by St. Louis Blues in 1982 NHL entry draft. Second Blues pick, 92nd overall, fifth round.

ALLAN MacINNIS

Defense . . . 6'1" . . . 183 lbs. . . . Born, Inverness, N.S., July 11, 1963 . . . Shoots right.

Year	Team	League	Games	G.	A.	Pts.	Pen.
1979-80	Regina Blues	SJHL	59	20	28	48	110
1980-81	Kitchener Rangers (c)	OHL	47	11	28	39	59
1981-82	Kitchener Rangers (a)	OHL	59	25	50	75	145
1981-82	Calgary Flames	NHL	2	0	0	0	0
1982-83	Kitchener Rangers (a-d)	OHL	51	38	46	84	67
1982-83	Calgary Flames	NHL	14	1	3	4	9
1983-84	Colorado Flames	CHL	19	5	14	19	22
1983-84	Calgary Flames	NHL	51	11	34	45	42
	NHL TOTALS		67	12	37	49	51

(c)—June, 1981—Drafted as underage junior by Calgary Flames in 1981 NHL entry draft. First Flames pick, 15th overall, first round.

(d)—Won Max Kaminsky Trophy (Outstanding OHL Defenseman).

JOSEPH MacINNIS

Center . . . 0' . . . 165 lbs. . . . Born, Cambridge, Mass., May 25, 1966 . . . Shoots left.

Year	Team	League	Games	G.	A.	Pts.	Pen.
1983-84	Watertown H.S. (c)	Mass. H.S.	18	28	18	46	..

(c)—June, 1984—Drafted by Toronto Maple Leafs in NHL entry draft. Sixth Maple Leafs pick, 130th overall, seventh round.

CRAIG MACK

Defense . . . 6'1" . . . 195 lbs. . . . Born, Grand Forks, N.D., March 27, 1965 . . . Shoots right.

Year	Team	League	Games	G.	A.	Pts.	Pen.
1982-83	E. Grand Forks H.S. (c)	Minn. H.S.	23	9	22	31	..
1983-84	University of Minnesota	WCHA	21	0	3	3	14

(c)—June, 1983—Drafted by Quebec Nordiques in 1983 NHL entry draft. Sixth Nordiques pick, 132nd overall, seventh round.

GRANT MacKAY

Defense . . . 6'2" . . . 185 lbs. . . . Born, Lethbridge, Alta., February 26, 1965 . . . Shoots left.

Year	Team	League	Games	G.	A.	Pts.	Pen.
1982-83	University of Calgary (c)	CWUAA	17	1	14	15	30
1983-84	University of Calgary	CWUAA	..	..	..	..	..

(c)—June, 1983—Drafted by Montreal Canadiens in 1983 NHL entry draft. Eleventh Canadiens pick, 178th overall, ninth round.

DAVID MACKEY

Left Wing . . . 6'3" . . . 190 lbs. . . . Born, New Westminster, B.C., July 24, 1966 . . . Shoots left.

Year	Team	League	Games	G.	A.	Pts.	Pen.
1981-82	Seafair	B.C. Midgets	60	48	62	110	99
1982-83	Victoria Cougars	WHL	69	16	16	32	53
1983-84	Victoria Cougars (c)	WHL	69	15	15	30	97

(c)—June, 1984—Drafted as underage junior by Chicago Black Hawks in NHL entry draft. Twelfth Black Hawks pick, 224th overall, 11th round.

PAUL MacKINNON

Defense . . . 6' . . . 190 lbs. . . . Born, Brantford, Ont., November 6, 1958 . . . Shoots right . . . (November, 1979) broken cheekbone, missed 17 games . . . (October 30, 1980)—Torn collateral ligaments in right knee.

Year	Team	League	Games	G.	A.	Pts.	Pen.
1975-76	Peterborough TPTs	Jr."A" OHA	48	1	10	11	42
1976-77	Peterborough Petes	Jr."A" OHA	65	2	38	40	96

Year	Team	League	Games	G.	A.	Pts.	Pen.
1977-78—Peterborough Petes (c-d)	Jr."A" OHA	60	1	25	26	77
1978-79—Winnipeg Jets (e)	WHA	73	2	15	17	70
1979-80—Washington Capitals	NHL	63	1	11	12	22
1980-81—Washington Capitals	NHL	14	0	0	0	22
1981-82—Hershey Bears	AHL	26	4	17	21	30
1981-82—Washington Capitals	NHL	39	2	9	11	35
1982-83—Hershey Bears	AHL	59	2	14	16	32
1982-83—Washington Capitals	NHL	19	2	2	4	8
1983-84—Washington Capitals	NHL	12	0	1	1	4
1983-84—Hershey Bears	AHL	63	3	19	22	29
WHA TOTALS		73	2	15	17	70
NHL TOTALS		147	5	23	28	91

(c)—Drafted from Peterborough Petes by Washington Capitals in second round of 1978 amateur draft.
(d)—Selected by Winnipeg Jets in World Hockey Association amateur player draft, June, 1978.
(e)—June, 1979—Selected by Washington Capitals in NHL reclaim draft.

DAVE MacLEAN

Right Wing . . . 6' . . . 200 lbs. . . . Born, Newmarket, Ont., January 12, 1965 . . . Shoots right . . . (June, 1982)—Shoulder surgery.

Year	Team	League	Games	G.	A.	Pts.	Pen.
1981-82—Oshawa Generals	OHL	54	6	8	14	38
1982-83—Oshawa Generals	OHL	11	8	6	14	6
1982-83—Belleville Bulls (c)	OHL	51	34	46	80	28
1983-84—Belleville Bulls	OHL	70	58	51	109	47

(c)—June, 1983—Drafted as underage junior by Hartford Whalers in 1983 NHL entry draft. Fifth Whalers pick, 64th overall, fourth round.

JOHN MacLEAN

Right Wing . . . 6' . . . 195 lbs. . . . Born, Oshawa, Ont., November 20, 1964 . . . Shoots right.

Year	Team	League	Games	G.	A.	Pts.	Pen.
1981-82—Oshawa Generals	OHL	67	17	22	39	197
1982-83—Oshawa Generals (c-d)	OHL	66	47	51	98	138
1983-84—New Jersey Devils	NHL	23	1	0	1	10
1983-84—Oshawa Generals	OHL	30	23	36	59	58
NHL TOTALS		23	1	0	1	10

(c)—Led OHL playoffs with 18 goals, and shared OHL playoff point lead, with teammate Dave Gans, with 38 points.
(d)—June, 1983—Drafted as underage junior by New Jersey Devils in 1983 NHL entry draft. First Devils pick, 6th overall, first round.

PAUL MacLEAN

Right Wing . . . 6' . . . 205 lbs. . . . Born, Grostenquin, France, March 9, 1958 . . . Shoots right . . . Member of 1980 Canadian Olympic team.

Year	Team	League	Games	G.	A.	Pts.	Pen.
1977-78—Hull Festivals (c)	QMJHL	66	38	33	71	125
1978-79—Canadian National Team	Int'l	....	...	....	....	....
1979-80—Canadian National Team	Int'l	50	21	11	32	90
1979-80—Canadian Olympic Team	Olympics	6	2	3	5	6
1980-81—Salt Lake Golden Eagles	CHL	80	36	42	78	160
1980-81—St. Louis Blues (d)	NHL	1	0	0	0	0
1981-82—Winnipeg Jets	NHL	74	36	25	61	106
1982-83—Winnipeg Jets	NHL	80	32	44	76	121
1983-84—Winnipeg Jets	NHL	76	40	31	71	155
NHL TOTALS		231	108	100	208	382

(c)—June, 1978—Drafted by St. Louis Blues in 1978 NHL amateur draft. Sixth Blues pick, 109th overall, seventh round.
(d)—July, 1981—Traded by St. Louis Blues with Ed Staniowski and Bryan Maxwell to Winnipeg Jets for John Markell and Scott Campbell.

RICHARD GEORGE (RICK) MacLEISH

Center . . . 5'11" . . . 185 lbs. . . . Born, Cannington, Ont., January 3, 1950 . . . Shoots left . . . Brother of Dale MacLeish . . . Missed part of 1971-72 season with torn ligaments in arm . . . Played Left Wing prior to 1971-72 . . . Missed last part of 1975-76 season (and playoffs)

with torn knee ligaments . . . (November, 1983)—Broken bone in left foot in game at Edmonton.

Year	Team	League	Games	G.	A.	Pts.	Pen.
1966-67—London Nationals	Jr."A" OHA	2	0	0	0	0	
1966-67—Peterborough TPTs	Jr."A" OHA	8	0	0	0	0	
1967-68—Peterborough TPTs	Jr."A" OHA	54	24	25	49	16	
1968-69—Peterborough TPTs	Jr."A" OHA	54	50	42	92	29	
1969-70—Peterborough TPTs (a-c)	Jr."A" OHA	54	45	56	101	135	
1970-71—Oklahoma City Blazers (d)	CHL	46	13	15	28	93	
1970-71—Philadelphia Flyers	NHL	26	2	4	6	19	
1971-72—Richmond Robins	AHL	42	24	11	35	33	
1971-72—Philadelphia Flyers	NHL	17	1	2	3	9	
1972-73—Philadelphia Flyers	NHL	78	50	50	100	69	
1973-74—Philadelphia Flyers (e)	NHL	78	32	45	77	42	
1974-75—Philadelphia Flyers (f)	NHL	80	38	41	79	50	
1975-76—Philadelphia Flyers	NHL	51	22	23	45	16	
1976-77—Philadelphia Flyers	NHL	79	49	48	97	42	
1977-78—Philadelphia Flyers	NHL	76	31	39	70	33	
1978-79—Philadelphia Flyers	NHL	71	26	32	58	47	
1979-80—Philadelphia Flyers	NHL	78	31	35	66	28	
1980-81—Philadelphia Flyers (g)	NHL	78	38	36	74	25	
1981-82—Hartford Whalers (h)	NHL	34	6	16	22	16	
1981-82—Pittsburgh Penguins	NHL	40	13	12	25	28	
1982-83—Pittsburgh Penguins (i)	NHL	6	0	5	5	2	
1982-83—Kloten EHC	Switzerland	....	...	....	....	....	
1983-84—Philadelphia Flyers (j)	NHL	29	8	14	22	4	
1983-84—Detroit Red Wings (k)	NHL	25	2	8	10	4	
NHL TOTALS		846	349	410	759	434	

(c)—Drafted from Peterborough TPTs by Boston Bruins in first round of 1970 amateur draft.

(d)—Traded to Philadelphia Flyers by Boston Bruins with Danny Schock for Mike Walton, January, 1971.

(e)—Led in goals (13) and points (22) during playoffs.

(f)—Led in points (20) during playoffs.

(g)—July, 1981—Traded by Philadelphia Flyers with Don Gillen, Blake Wesley, first, second and third-round 1982 draft picks to Hartford Whalers for Ray Allison, Fred Arthur and Whalers first and third-round picks in 1982 NHL entry draft.

(h)—December, 1981—Traded by Hartford Whalers to Pittsburgh Penguins for Russ Anderson and eighth-round 1983 entry draft pick (Chris Du Perron).

(i)—Released by Pittsburgh Penguins. Signed by Kloten EHC (Switzerland).

(j)—January, 1984—Traded by Philadelphia Flyers to Detroit Red Wings for future considerations.

(k)—June, 1984—Released by Detroit Red Wings.

BRIAN MacLELLAN

Left Wing . . . 6'3" . . . 212 lbs. . . . Born, Guelph, Ont., October 27, 1958 . . . Shoots left . . . Also plays defense.

Year	Team	League	Games	G.	A.	Pts.	Pen.
1978-79—Bowling Green University	CCHA	44	34	29	63	94	
1979-80—Bowling Green University	CCHA	38	8	15	23	46	
1980-81—Bowling Green University	CCHA	37	11	14	25	96	
1981-82—Bowling Green University (c)	CCHA	41	11	21	32	109	
1982-83—Los Angeles Kings	NHL	8	0	3	3	7	
1982-83—New Haven Nighthawks	AHL	71	11	15	26	40	
1983-84—New Haven Nighthawks	AHL	2	0	2	2	0	
1983-84—Los Angeles Kings	NHL	72	25	29	54	45	
NHL TOTALS		80	25	32	57	52	

(c)—April, 1982—Signed by Los Angeles Kings as a free agent.

SCOTT MacLELLAN

Defense . . . 6'1" . . . 170 lbs. . . . Born, Burlington, Ont., March 21, 1963 . . . Shoots left . . . Also plays center.

Year	Team	League	Games	G.	A.	Pts.	Pen.
1980-81—Burlington Cougars (c)	COJHL	44	31	70	101	55	
1981-82—Kingston Canadians	OHL	66	11	57	68	131	
1982-83—Kingston Canadians	OHL	20	9	25	34	22	
1982-83—Windsor Spitfires	OHL	46	23	64	87	82	
1983-84—Kitchener Rangers	OHL	30	9	30	39	35	
1983-84—Indianapolis Checkers	CHL	4	0	0	0	2	

(c)—June, 1981—Drafted by New York Islanders as underage junior in NHL entry draft. Tenth Islanders pick, 189th overall, ninth round.

SCOTT MacLEOD

Center . . . 5'10" . . . 175 lbs. . . . Born, Vancouver, B.C., May 17, 1959 . . . Shoots left . . . Set record for most assists (75) and points (118) by a CHL rookie in 1983-84.

Year	Team	League	Games	G.	A.	Pts.	Pen.
1981-82—Jujyo Seishi		Japan	30	37	52	*89	..
1982-83—Jujyo Seishi		Japan	..	..	..	..	..
1983-84—Salt Lake Golden Eagles (a-c)		CHL	68	43	*75	*118	30

(c)—Won Phil Esposito Trophy (Top CHL Scorer).

ROBERT LEA MacMILLAN

Center and Left Wing . . . 5'11" . . . 185 lbs. . . . Born, Charlottetown, P.E.I., September 3, 1952 . . . Shoots left . . . Brother of Bill MacMillan . . . Missed part of 1971-72 season with hepatitis . . . Also plays right wing . . . (November, 1982)—Stretched knee ligaments.

Year	Team	League	Games	G.	A.	Pts.	Pen.
1969-70—Charlottetown Islanders		MJHL	....	...	....	....	....
1970-71—St. Cath. Black Hawks		Jr."A"OHA	59	41	62	103	93
1971-72—St. Cath. Black Hawks (c-d)		Jr."A"OHA	39	12	41	53	41
1972-73—Minnesota Fighting Saints		WHA	75	13	27	40	48
1973-74—Minnesota Fighting Saints (e)		WHA	78	14	34	48	81
1974-75—Providence Reds		AHL	46	18	29	47	58
1974-75—New York Rangers (f)		NHL	22	1	2	3	4
1975-76—St. Louis Blues		NHL	80	20	32	52	41
1976-77—St. Louis Blues		NHL	80	19	39	58	11
1977-78—St. Louis Blues (g)		NHL	28	7	12	19	23
1977-78—Atlanta Flames		NHL	52	31	21	52	26
1978-79—Atlanta Flames (h)		NHL	79	37	71	108	14
1979-80—Atlanta Flames		NHL	77	22	39	61	10
1980-81—Calgary Flames		NHL	77	28	35	63	47
1981-82—Calgary Flames (i)		NHL	23	4	7	11	14
1981-82—Colorado Rockies		NHL	57	18	32	50	27
1982-83—New Jersey Devils		NHL	71	19	29	48	8
1983-84—New Jersey Devils (j)		NHL	71	17	23	40	23
WHA TOTALS			153	27	61	88	129
NHL TOTALS			717	223	342	565	248

(c)—Selected by Minnesota Fighting Saints in World Hockey Association player selection draft, February, 1972.
(d)—Drafted from St. Catharines Black Hawks by New York Rangers in first round of 1972 amateur draft.
(e)—Signed by New York Rangers, June, 1974.
(f)—Traded to St. Louis Blues by New York Rangers with "future considerations" for Lawrence Sacharuk, September, 1975.
(g)—Traded to Atlanta Flames by St. Louis Blues with Dick Redmond, Yves Belanger and second-round draft choice for Phil Myre, Curt Bennett and Barry Gibbs, December, 1977.
(h)—Won Lady Byng Memorial Trophy (NHL-Most Gentlemanly).
(i)—December, 1981—Traded with Don Lever by Calgary Flames to Colorado Rockies for Lanny McDonald and a fourth-round 1983 entry draft pick.
(j)—June, 1984—Traded with past considerations (Devils agreed not to draft Ed Olczyk) by New Jersey Devils to Chicago Black Hawks for Rich Preston and Don Dietrich.

JAMIE MACOUN

Defense . . . 6'2" . . . 200 lbs. . . . Born, Newmarket, Ont., August 17, 1961 . . . Shoots left.

Year	Team	League	Games	G.	A.	Pts.	Pen.
1980-81—Ohio State University		CCHA	38	9	20	29	83
1981-82—Ohio State University		CCHA	25	2	18	20	89
1982-83—Ohio State University (c)		CCHA	....	...	....	....	....
1982-83—Calgary Flames		NHL	22	1	4	5	25
1983-84—Calgary Flames		NHL	72	9	23	32	97
NHL TOTALS			94	10	27	37	122

(c)—January, 1983—Left Ohio State University to sign with the Calgary Flames as a free agent.

DUNCAN MacPHERSON

Defense . . . 6'1" . . . 190 lbs. . . . Born, Saskatoon, Sask., February 3, 1966 . . . Shoots left.

Year	Team	League	Games	G.	A.	Pts.	Pen.
1982-83—Battleford Barons		SAJHL	59	6	11	17	215
1983-84—Saskatoon Blades (c)		WHL	45	0	14	14	74

(c)—June, 1984—Drafted as underage junior by New York Islanders in NHL entry draft. First Islanders pick, 20th overall, first round.

DAVID AUBRY MacQUEEN

Right Wing and Defense . . . 5'10" . . . 187 lbs. . . . Born, Woodstock, Ont., February 8, 1959 . . . Shoots right . . . Son of Ed MacQueen (AHL 1954-71 with Cleveland, Providence, Baltimore).

Year	Team	League	Games	G.	A.	Pts.	Pen.
1976-77	Ottawa 67's	OMJHL	66	29	42	71	25
1977-78	Ottawa 67's	OMJHL	66	34	45	79	15
1978-79	Sudbury Wolves	OMJHL	65	60	66	126	98
1979-80	Johnstown Red Wings (a)	EHL	64	*53	57	*110	39
1980-81	Flint Generals	EHL	45	18	26	44	48
1981-82	Wichita Wind	CHL	3	0	0	0	0
1981-82	Salem Raiders (a-c)	ACHL	36	*43	30	*73	29
1982-83	Virginia Raiders	ACHL	54	42	36	78	22
1983-84	Mohawk Valley Stars	ACHL	63	54	54	108	22

(c)—Winner of first ACHL Scoring Championship.

JAMES WILLIAM MacRAE

Left Wing . . . 5'10" . . . 175 lbs. . . . Born, April 19, 1958, Montague, P.E.I. . . . Shoots left . . . (February, 1983)—Thumb injury.

Year	Team	League	Games	G.	A.	Pts.	Pen.
1975-76	London Knights	OMJHL	66	35	38	73	39
1976-77	London Knights	OMJHL	66	50	59	109	35
1977-78	London Knights (c)	OMJHL	68	50	62	112	58
1978-79	Tulsa Oilers	CHL	72	22	33	55	18
1979-80	Birmingham Bulls	CHL	55	24	19	43	12
1980-81	Birmingham Bulls	CHL	54	19	24	43	40
1980-81	Rochester Americans	AHL	19	11	2	13	10
1981-82	Dallas Black Hawks	CHL	73	29	31	60	40
1982-83	Fredericton Express	AHL	76	21	22	43	12
1983-84	Kalamazoo Wings	IHL	71	40	37	77	25

(c)—June, 1978—Drafted by Atlanta Flames in amateur draft. Third Atlanta pick, 64th overall, fourth round.

CRAIG MacTAVISH

Center . . . 6' . . . 185 lbs. . . . Born, London, Ont., August 15, 1958 . . . Shoots left . . . Also plays left wing . . . (January, 1984)—Involved in automobile accident in which Kim Lea Radley was killed. He was charged with vehicular homicide, driving while under the influence of alcohol and reckless driving. In May he pleaded guilty and was convicted by Essex, Mass., Superior court and sentenced to a year in prison with no possibility for parole. He is also being sued by the estate of Kim Lea Radley for $10 million.

Year	Team	League	Games	G.	A.	Pts.	Pen.
1977-78	University of Lowell (b-c-d)	ECAC	....	...	....	....	....
1978-79	University of Lowell (a-e)	ECAC-II	....	36	52	*88	....
1979-80	Binghamton Dusters	AHL	34	17	15	32	20
1979-80	Boston Bruins	NHL	46	11	17	28	8
1980-81	Boston Bruins	NHL	24	3	5	8	13
1980-81	Springfield Indians	AHL	53	19	24	43	89
1981-82	Erie Blades	AHL	72	23	32	55	37
1981-82	Boston Bruins	NHL	2	0	1	1	0
1982-83	Boston Bruins	NHL	75	10	20	30	18
1983-84	Boston Bruins	NHL	70	20	23	43	35
	NHL TOTALS		217	44	66	110	74

(c)—June, 1978—Drafted by Boston Bruins in amateur draft. Ninth Boston pick, 153rd overall, ninth round.

(d)—Named ECAC Division II Rookie of the year.

(e)—Named ECAC Division II Player of the Year.

MARC MAGNAN

Left Wing . . . 5'11" . . . 195 lbs. . . . Born, Beaumont, Alta., February 17, 1962 . . . Shoots left . . . Brother of Vince Magnan.

Year	Team	League	Games	G.	A.	Pts.	Pen.
1979-80	St. Albert Saints	AJHL	42	14	23	37	178
1979-80	Lethbridge Broncos	WHL	1	0	1	1	0
1980-81	Lethbridge Broncos (c)	WHL	66	16	30	46	284
1981-82	Lethbridge Broncos	WHL	64	33	38	71	406
1982-83	St. Catharines Saints	OHL	67	6	10	16	229
1982-83	Toronto Maple Leafs	NHL	4	0	1	1	5

Year	Team	League	Games	G.	A.	Pts.	Pen.
1983-84—St. Catharines Saints		AHL	54	3	6	9	170
1983-84—Muskegon Mohawks		IHL	19	3	10	13	30
NHL TOTALS			4	0	1	1	5

(c)—June, 1981—Drafted as underage junior by Toronto Maple Leafs in 1981 NHL entry draft. Ninth Maple Leafs pick, 195th overall, 10th round.

ERIC MAGNUSON

Center . . . 6'2" . . . 200 lbs. . . . Born, Belmont, Mass., September 17, 1961 . . . Shoots left . . . Brother of Bob Magnuson (Montreal '78 draft pick).

Year	Team	League	Games	G.	A.	Pts.	Pen.
1980-81—R.P.I. (c)		ECAC	28	18	19	37	28
1981-82—R.P.I.		ECAC	11	2	5	7	18
1982-83—R.P.I.		ECAC	7	2	4	6	22
1983-84—R.P.I.		ECAC	38	6	21	27	40

(c)—June, 1981—Drafted by New York Rangers in 1981 NHL entry draft. Sixth Rangers pick, 114th overall, sixth round.

BILL MAGUIRE

Defense . . . 6' . . . 183 lbs. . . . Born, Toronto, Ont., May 18, 1963 . . . Shoots left.

Year	Team	League	Games	G.	A.	Pts.	Pen.
1979-80—Barrie		OHA Midgets	59	12	32	44	....
1980-81—Niagara Falls Flyers (c)		OHL	51	1	15	17	81
1981-82—Niagara Falls Flyers		OHL	67	5	13	18	72
1982-83—North Bay Centennials		OHL	39	3	15	18	18
1983-84—Flint Generals		IHL	3	0	0	0	0
1983-84—Mohawk Valley Stars		ACHL	56	7	18	25	45

(c)—June, 1981—Drafted as underage junior by Hartford Whalers in 1981 NHL entry draft. Fourth Whalers pick, 93rd overall, fifth round.

JYRKI MAKI

Defense . . . 6' . . . 170 lbs. . . . Born, Helsinki, Finland, February 8, 1966 . . . Shoots left.

Year	Team	League	Games	G.	A.	Pts.	Pen.
1983-84—St. Paul Simley H.S. (c)		Minn. H.S.	22	9	24	33	8

(c)—June, 1984—Drafted by Quebec Nordiques in NHL entry draft. Seventh Nordiques pick, 162nd overall, eighth round.

TERRY MAKI

Left Wing . . . 5'11" . . . 175 lbs. . . . Born, Sault Ste. Marie, Ont., February 9, 1965 . . . Shoots left.

Year	Team	League	Games	G.	A.	Pts.	Pen.
1981-82—Sault Ste. Marie Legion		Ont. Midget	46	77	76	153	53
1982-83—Brantford Alexanders (c)		OHL	54	16	14	30	31
1983-84—Windsor Spitfires		OHL	35	7	11	18	29

(c)—June, 1983—Drafted as underage junior by Vancouver Canucks in 1983 NHL entry draft. Eighth Canucks pick, 130th overall, seventh round.

DAVID MALEY

Center . . . 6'3" . . . 200 lbs. . . . Born, Beaver Dam, Wis., April 24, 1963 . . . Shoots left.

Year	Team	League	Games	G.	A.	Pts.	Pen.
1981-82—Edina H.S. (c)		Minn. H.S.	26	22	28	50	26
1982-83—University of Wisconsin		WCHA	47	17	23	40	24
1983-84—University of Wisconsin		WCHA	38	10	28	38	56

(c)—June, 1982—Drafted by Montreal Canadiens as underage player in 1982 NHL entry draft. Fourth Canadiens pick, 33rd overall, second round.

MERLIN MALINOWSKI

Center . . . 6' . . . 189 lbs. . . . Born, North Battleford, Sask., September 25, 1958 . . . Shoots left . . . (December 26, 1980)—Separated shoulder.

Year	Team	League	Games	G.	A.	Pts.	Pen.
1973-74—Drumheller Falcons		AJHL	2	0	0	0	0
1974-75—Drumheller Falcons		AJHL	59	23	44	67	58
1975-76—Drumheller Falcons (b-c)		AJHL	59	*60	86	146	79
1976-77—Medicine Hat Tigers		WCHL	70	22	48	70	40

Year	Team	League	Games	G.	A.	Pts.	Pen.
1977-78—Medicine Hat Tigers (d)	WCHL	72	48	78	126	131
1978-79—Colorado Rockies	NHL	54	6	17	23	10
1978-79—Philadelphia Firebirds	AHL	25	3	9	12	12
1979-80—Fort Worth Texans (b-e)	CHL	66	34	42	76	58
1979-80—Colorado Rockies	NHL	10	2	4	6	2
1980-81—Colorado Rockies	NHL	69	25	37	62	61
1981-82—Colorado Rockies	NHL	69	13	28	41	32
1982-83—New Jersey Devils (f)	NHL	5	3	2	5	0
1982-83—Hartford Whalers (g)	NHL	75	5	23	28	16
1983-84—Arosa EHC (h)	Switzerland	..	..	..	..	..
NHL TOTALS		282	54	111	165	121

(c)—Won Most Valuable Player Award.
(d)—Drafted from Medicine Hat Tigers by Colorado Rockies in second round of 1978 amateur draft.
(e)—Led CHL in assists (16) and points (24) during playoffs.
(f)—October, 1982—Traded by New Jersey Devils with NHL rights to Scott Fusco to Hartford Whalers for Rick Meagher and Garry Howatt.
(g)—October, 1983—Released by Hartford Whalers.
(h)—November, 1983—Signed by Arosa (Switzerland) as a free agent.

JAMES EDWARD MALONE

Center . . . 6'1" . . . 188 lbs. . . . Born, Chatham, N. B., February 20, 1962 . . . Shoots left . . . Brother of Greg Malone . . . (December, 1982)—Knee injury.

Year	Team	League	Games	G.	A.	Pts.	Pen.
1979-80—Toronto Marlboros (c)	OMJHL	67	24	24	48	68
1980-81—Toronto Marlboros	OHL	57	11	41	52	174
1981-82—Toronto Marlboros	OHL	53	24	28	52	127
1982-83—Moncton Alpines	AHL	10	3	2	5	10
1982-83—Tulsa Oilers	CHL	29	5	10	15	45
1983-84—Tulsa Oilers	CHL	57	16	11	27	58

(c)—June, 1980—Drafted as underage junior by New York Rangers in 1980 NHL entry draft. First Rangers pick, 14th overall, first round.

WILLIAM GREGORY (GREG) MALONE

Center . . . 6' . . . 190 lbs. . . . Born, Chatham, N.B., March 8, 1956 . . . Shoots left . . . Missed parts of 1979-80 season with an infected instep and knee surgery to repair torn ligaments in right knee . . . Brother of Jim Malone . . . (October 11, 1980)—Strained ligaments in right knee.

Year	Team	League	Games	G.	A.	Pts.	Pen.
1973-74—Oshawa Generals	Jr."A"OHA	62	11	45	56	63
1974-75—Oshawa Generals	Jr."A"OHA	68	37	41	78	86
1975-76—Oshawa Generals (c)	Jr."A"OHA	61	36	36	72	75
1976-77—Pittsburgh Penguins	NHL	66	18	19	37	43
1977-78—Pittsburgh Penguins	NHL	78	18	43	61	80
1978-79—Pittsburgh Penguins	NHL	80	35	30	65	52
1979-80—Pittsburgh Penguins	NHL	51	19	32	51	46
1980-81—Pittsburgh Penguins	NHL	62	21	29	50	68
1981-82—Pittsburgh Penguins	NHL	78	15	24	39	125
1982-83—Pittsburgh Penguins	NHL	80	17	44	61	82
1983-84—Hartford Whalers (d)	NHL	78	17	37	54	56
NHL TOTALS		573	160	258	418	552

(c)—Drafted from Oshawa Generals by Pittsburgh Penguins in second round of 1976 amateur draft.
(d)—October, 1983—Traded by Pittsburgh Penguins to Hartford Whalers for third round 1985 draft pick.

DAVID WILFRED MALONEY

Defense . . . 6'1" . . . 195 lbs. . . . Born, Kitchener, Ont., July 31, 1956 . . . Shoots left . . . Missed part of 1974-75 season with shoulder injury, part of 1975-76 with broken leg, final part of 1976-77 season with surgery on severed flexur tendon in left arm and part of 1977-78 season with torn ligaments in right knee . . . Brother of Don Maloney . . . (October 14, 1981)—Broke left thumb in game vs. Vancouver.

Year	Team	League	Games	G.	A.	Pts.	Pen.
1971-72—Kitchener Rangers	Jr."A"OHA	1	0	0	0	0
1971-72—Toronto St. Michael's	Jr."B"OHA	....	...	....	....	....
1972-73—Kitchener Rangers	Jr."A"OHA	49	8	21	29	101
1973-74—Kitchener Rangers (b-c)	Jr."A"OHA	69	15	53	68	109
1974-75—Providence Reds	AHL	58	5	28	33	122
1974-75—New York Rangers	NHL	4	0	2	2	0
1975-76—Providence Reds	AHL	26	5	17	22	81
1975-76—New York Rangers	NHL	21	1	3	4	66

Year	Team	League	Games	G.	A.	Pts.	Pen.
1976-77—New York Rangers		NHL	66	3	18	21	100
1977-78—New York Rangers		NHL	56	2	19	21	63
1978-79—New York Rangers		NHL	76	11	17	28	151
1979-80—New York Rangers		NHL	77	12	25	37	186
1980-81—New York Rangers		NHL	79	11	36	47	132
1981-82—New York Rangers		NHL	64	13	36	49	105
1982-83—New York Rangers		NHL	78	8	42	50	132
1983-84—New York Rangers		NHL	68	7	26	33	168
NHL TOTALS			589	68	224	292	1103

(c)—Drafted from Kitchener Rangers by New York Rangers in first round of 1974 amateur draft.

DONALD MICHAEL MALONEY

Left Wing . . . 6'1" . . . 190 lbs. . . . Born, Lindsay, Ont., September 5, 1958 . . . Shoots left . . . Brother of Dave Maloney . . . (October, 1980)—Mononucleosis . . . Set record for most points by a rookie in the playoffs (20) in 1979 (broken in 1981 by Dino Ciccarelli with 21) . . . (October 24, 1981)—Partial ligament tear in right knee in game at Toronto. He missed 25 games and returned to lineup December 23, 1981 . . . (November 28, 1983)—Broke ring finger of right hand in game with Vancouver.

Year	Team	League	Games	G.	A.	Pts.	Pen.
1974-75—Kitchener Rangers		Jr."A"OHA	5	1	3	4	0
1975-76—Kitchener Rangers		Jr."A"OHA	61	27	41	68	132
1976-77—Kitchener Rangers		Jr."A"OHA	38	22	34	56	126
1977-78—Kitchener Rangers (c)		Jr."A"OHA	62	30	74	104	143
1978-79—New Haven Nighthawks		AHL	38	18	26	44	62
1978-79—New York Rangers (d)		NHL	28	9	17	26	39
1979-80—New York Rangers		NHL	79	25	48	73	97
1980-81—New York Rangers		NHL	61	29	23	52	99
1981-82—New York Rangers		NHL	54	22	36	58	73
1982-83—New York Rangers		NHL	78	29	40	69	88
1983-84—New York Rangers		NHL	79	24	42	66	62
NHL TOTALS			379	138	206	344	458

(c)—Drafted from Kitchener Rangers by New York Rangers in second round of 1978 amateur draft.
(d)—Tied for lead in assists (13) during playoffs.

JIM MALWITZ

Center . . . 6' . . . 175 lbs. . . . Born, Grand Rapids, Minn., September 27, 1962 . . . Shoots left.

Year	Team	League	Games	G.	A.	Pts.	Pen.
1980-81—Grand Rapids H.S. (c)		Minn. H.S.	27	24	19	43	....
1981-82—University of Minnesota		WCHA	19	4	1	5	6
1982-83—University of Minnesota		WCHA	43	16	20	36	54
1983-84—University of Minnesota		WCHA	38	6	11	17	44

(c)—June, 1981—Drafted by Minnesota North Stars in 1981 NHL entry draft. Eighth North Stars pick, 76th overall, fourth round.

MIROSLAV MALY

Defense . . . 6'2" . . . 190 lbs. . . . Born, West Germany, April 10, 1963 . . . Shoots left.

Year	Team	League	Games	G.	A.	Pts.	Pen.
1981-82—ERC Schwenningen		W. Germany	44	5	15	20	34
1982-83—Bayreuth		W. Germany	..	..	..	..	..
1983-84—Bayreuth (c)		W. Germany	..	..	..	..	..

(c)—June, 1984—Drafted by Minnesota North Stars in 1984 NHL entry draft. Third North Stars pick, 76th overall, fourth round.

DAN MANDICH

Defense . . . 6'3" . . . 205 lbs. . . . Born, Brantford, Ont., June 12, 1960 . . . Shoots right . . . (February, 1983)—Injured ankle . . . (January 16, 1984)—Injured knee in game vs. Los Angeles and was lost for the remainder of the season.

Year	Team	League	Games	G.	A.	Pts.	Pen.
1978-79—Ohio State University		CCHA	38	7	18	25	126
1979-80—Ohio State University		CCHA	35	10	17	27	146
1980-81—Ohio State University		CCHA	39	20	26	46	188
1981-82—Ohio State University (c)		CCHA	33	14	26	40	157
1982-83—Birmingham South Stars		CHL	6	0	4	4	18
1982-83—Minnesota North Stars		NHL	67	3	4	7	169
1983-84—Minnesota North Stars		NHL	31	2	7	9	77
1983-84—Salt Lake Golden Eagles		CHL	3	2	2	4	13
NHL TOTALS			98	5	11	16	246

(c)—August, 1982—Signed by Minnesota North Stars as a free agent.

JAMES EDWARD MANN

Right Wing . . . 6' . . . 202 lbs. . . . Born, Montreal, Que., April 17, 1959 . . . Shoots right . . . (March, 1980)—Served two-game suspension for his fourth game misconduct of 1979-80 season . . . (December 9, 1981)—Pushed NHL linesman Gord Broseker in game vs. Toronto. Mann was fined $500 and given a three-game suspension . . . (January 13, 1982)—Left Winnipeg bench and entered altercation on ice, breaking the jaw of Pittsburgh Penguin Paul Gardner in two places. Mann was given a 10-game suspension by NHL . . . He also was charged with assault by Province of Manitoba, found guilty and given a suspended sentence . . . (December, 1982)—Stretched knee ligaments . . . Set Winnipeg NHL club penalty-minute record in 1979-80.

Year	Team	League	Games	G.	A.	Pts.	Pen.
1975-76—Laval National		QMJHL	65	8	9	17	107
1976-77—Sherbrooke Beavers		QMJHL	69	12	14	26	200
1977-78—Sherbrooke Beavers		QMJHL	67	27	54	81	277
1978-79—Sherbrooke Beavers (a-c)		QMJHL	65	35	47	82	260
1979-80—Winnipeg Jets		NHL	72	3	5	8	*287
1980-81—Tulsa Oilers		CHL	26	4	7	11	175
1980-81—Winnipeg Jets		NHL	37	3	3	6	105
1981-82—Winnipeg Jets		NHL	37	3	2	5	79
1982-83—Winnipeg Jets		NHL	40	0	1	1	73
1983-84—Sherbrooke Jets		AHL	20	6	3	9	94
1983-84—Winnipeg Jets (d)		NHL	16	0	1	1	54
1983-84—Quebec Nordiques		NHL	22	1	1	2	42
NHL TOTALS			224	10	13	23	640

(c)—August, 1979—Drafted by Winnipeg Jets in NHL entry draft. First Winnipeg pick, 19th overall, first round.

(d)—January, 1984—Traded by Winnipeg Jets to Quebec Nordiques for future considerations.

ROBERT JOHN MANNO

Defense and Left Wing . . . 6' . . . 185 lbs. . . . Born, Niagara Falls, Ont., October 31, 1956 . . . Shoots left . . . Missed start of 1975-76 season with shoulder injury . . . Missed part of 1979-80 season after thumb surgery . . . (December, 1980)—Groin injury.

Year	Team	League	Games	G.	A.	Pts.	Pen.
1972-73—Niagara Falls Flyers		SOJHL	36	1	14	15	78
1973-74—Hamilton Red Wings		Jr."A"OHA	63	3	19	22	105
1974-75—St. Cath. Black Hawks		Jr."A"OHA	70	9	38	47	171
1975-76—St. Cath. Black Hawks (c)		Jr."A"OHA	55	9	54	63	87
1976-77—Tulsa Oilers		CHL	73	18	36	54	109
1976-77—Vancouver Canucks		NHL	2	0	0	0	0
1977-78—Tulsa Oilers		CHL	20	5	15	20	21
1977-78—Vancouver Canucks		NHL	49	5	14	19	29
1978-79—Vancouver Canucks		NHL	52	5	16	21	42
1978-79—Dallas Black Hawks		CHL	23	8	9	17	18
1979-80—Vancouver Canucks		NHL	40	3	14	17	14
1980-81—Vancouver Canucks		NHL	20	0	11	11	30
1980-81—Dallas Black Hawks		CHL	40	7	36	43	65
1981-82—Toronto Maple Leafs (d)		NHL	72	9	41	50	67
1982-83—Italian National Team		Int'l	9	5	1	6	...
1982-83—Merano (e)		Italy	28	15	32	47	40
1983-84—Adirondack Red Wings		AHL	12	5	11	16	18
1983-84—Detroit Red Wings		NHL	62	9	13	22	60
NHL TOTALS			297	31	109	140	242

(c)—Drafted from St. Catharines Black Hawks by Vancouver Canucks in second round of 1976 amateur draft.

(d)—September, 1981—Signed by Toronto Maple Leafs as a free agent after being released by Vancouver Canucks.

(e)—August, 1983—Signed by Detroit Red Wings as a free agent.

MAURICE (MOE) WILLIAM MANTHA

Defense . . . 6'2" . . . 197 lbs. . . . Born, Lakewood, O., January 21, 1961 . . . Shoots right . . . Son of Maurice Mantha (AHL early 1960s) . . . Missed 20 games during 1980-81 season with recurring back problems . . . (October, 1981)—Eye injury . . . (October, 1982)—Surgery for injured shoulder.

Year	Team	League	Games	G.	A.	Pts.	Pen.
1978-79—Toronto Marlboros		OMJHL	68	10	38	48	57
1979-80—Toronto Marlboros (c)		OMJHL	58	8	38	46	86
1980-81—Winnipeg Jets		NHL	58	2	23	25	35
1981-82—Tulsa Oilers		CHL	33	8	15	23	56
1981-82—Winnipeg Jets		NHL	25	0	12	12	28

Year	Team	League	Games	G.	A.	Pts.	Pen.
1982-83—Sherbrooke Jets		AHL	13	1	4	5	13
1982-83—Winnipeg Jets		NHL	21	2	7	9	6
1983-84—Sherbrooke Jets		AHL	7	1	1	2	10
1983-84—Winnipeg Jets (d)		NHL	72	16	38	54	67
NHL TOTALS			176	20	80	100	136

(c)—June, 1980—Drafted as underage junior by Winnipeg Jets in 1980 NHL entry draft. Second Jets pick, 23rd overall, second round.

(d)—May, 1984—Traded by Winnipeg Jets to Pittsburgh Penguins to complete March trade for Randy Carlyle.

STEPHEN FRED MARENGERE

Center . . . 5'9" . . . 160 lbs. . . . Born, Ottawa, Ont., January 14, 1959 . . . Shoots left . . . Also plays defense.

Year	Team	League	Games	G.	A.	Pts.	Pen.
1974-75—Ottawa 67's		OMJHL	52	8	16	24	33
1975-76—Ottawa 67's		OMJHL	66	15	53	68	60
1976-77—Ottawa 67's		OMJHL	46	14	41	55	55
1977-78—Ottawa 67's		OMJHL	65	25	93	118	73
1978-79—Ottawa 67's		OMJHL	63	35	68	103	69
1979-80—Adirondack Red Wings		AHL	18	0	4	4	8
1979-80—Kalamazoo Wings		IHL	44	15	15	30	6
1979-80—Dayton Gems		IHL	18	3	2	5	4
1980-81—Kalamazoo Wings		IHL	8	5	3	8	2
1980-81—		Switzerland	....	...	....	....	....
1981-82—		Switzerland	....	...	....	....	....
1982-83—Nova Scotia Voyageurs (c)		AHL	64	10	25	35	39
1983-84—Nova Scotia Voyageurs		AHL	32	6	11	17	14

(c)—September, 1982—Signed by Nova Scotia Voyageurs as a free agent.

HECTOR MARINI

Right Wing . . . 6'1" . . . 204 lbs. . . . Born, Timmins, Ont., January 27, 1957 . . . Shoots right . . . (October 29, 1981)—Broke fifth metasarpic bone (little finger) in altercation with Jack McIlhargey at Hartford.

Year	Team	League	Games	G.	A.	Pts.	Pen.
1974-75—Sudbury Wolves		Jr."A" OHA	69	12	19	31	70
1975-76—Sudbury Wolves		Jr."A" OHA	66	32	45	77	102
1976-77—Sudbury Wolves (c)		Jr."A" OHA	64	32	58	90	89
1977-78—Muskegon Mohawks		IHL	80	33	60	93	127
1977-78—Fort Worth Texans		CHL	2	0	0	0	4
1978-79—New York Islanders		NHL	1	0	0	0	2
1978-79—Fort Worth Texans		CHL	74	21	27	48	172
1979-80—Indianapolis Checkers		CHL	76	29	34	63	144
1980-81—New York Islanders		NHL	14	4	7	11	39
1980-81—Indianapolis Checkers		CHL	54	15	37	52	85
1981-82—New York Islanders (d)		NHL	30	4	9	13	53
1982-83—New Jersey Devils		NHL	77	17	28	45	105
1983-84—Maine Mariners		AHL	17	6	5	11	23
1983-84—New Jersey Devils		NHL	32	2	2	4	47
NHL TOTALS			154	27	46	73	246

(c)—Drafted from Sudbury Wolves by New York Islanders in third round of 1977 amateur draft.

(d)—October, 1982—Traded by New York Islanders to New Jersey Devils for option to switch fourth-round draft choices in 1983 NHL entry draft.

GORDON MARK

Defense . . . 6'3" . . . 210 lbs. . . . Born, Edmonton, Alta., September 10, 1964 . . . Shoots right.

Year	Team	League	Games	G.	A.	Pts.	Pen.
1982-83—Kamloops Junior Oilers (c)		WHL	71	12	20	32	135
1983-84—Kamloops Junior Oilers (b)		WHL	67	12	30	42	202

(c)—June, 1983—Drafted as underage junior by New Jersey Devils in 1983 NHL entry draft. Fourth Devils pick, 105th overall, sixth round.

JOHN RICHARD MARKELL

Left Wing . . . 5'10" . . . 180 lbs. . . . Born, Cornwall, Ont., March 10, 1956 . . . Shoots left . . . All-time leader in points (236) at Bowling Green State University . . . Missed part of 1980-81 season with mononucleosis.

Year	Team	League	Games	G.	A.	Pts.	Pen.
1975-76—Bowling Green State Univ.	CCHA	30	12	25	37	24
1976-77—Bowling Green State Univ. (a)	CCHA	39	26	32	58	48
1977-78—Bowling Green St. Univ. (a-c)	CCHA	39	33	28	*61	81
1978-79—Bowling Green St. Univ. (a-d)	CCHA	42	31	49	80	96
1979-80—Tulsa Oilers	CHL	37	21	15	36	24
1979-80—Winnipeg Jets	NHL	38	10	7	17	21
1980-81—Tulsa Oilers	CHL	48	24	18	42	34
1980-81—Winnipeg Jets (e)	NHL	14	1	3	4	15
1981-82—Salt Lake Golden Eagles	CHL	69	19	53	72	33
1982-83—Salt Lake Golden Eagles	CHL	77	33	27	60	35
1983-84—Montana Magic (a)	CHL	69	*44	40	84	61
1983-84—St. Louis Blues	NHL	2	0	0	0	0
NHL TOTALS		54	11	10	21	36

(c)—Co-winner of CCHA Player of the Year award.
(d)—April, 1979—Signed by Winnipeg Jets as free agent.
(e)—July, 1981—Traded by Winnipeg Jets with Scott Campbell to St. Louis Blues for Ed Staniowski, Bryan Maxwell and Paul MacLean.

RAY JOSEPH MARKHAM

Right Wing . . . 6'3" . . . 218 lbs. . . . Born, Windsor, Ont., January 23, 1958 . . . Shoots right . . . (October, 1980)—Knee injury.

Year	Team	League	Games	G.	A.	Pts.	Pen.
1975-76—Notre Dame	SJHL	45	15	19	34	245
1976-77—Flin Flon Bombers	WCHL	68	33	41	74	318
1977-78—Flin Flon Bombers (c)	WCHL	68	35	65	100	323
1978-79—New Haven Nighthawks	AHL	77	13	15	28	151
1979-80—New Haven Nighthawks	AHL	57	9	20	29	198
1979-80—New York Rangers	NHl	14	1	1	2	19
1980-81—N. Haven Nighthawks (d)	AHL	42	10	9	19	122
1980-81—Wichita Wind	CHL	7	1	1	2	18
1981-82—Wichita Wind	CHL	48	15	12	27	110
1982-83—Flint Generals	IHL	42	16	30	46	176
1983-84—Flint Generals	IHL	12	2	3	5	39
1983-84—Kalamazoo Wings	IHL	69	23	28	51	172
NHL TOTALS		14	1	1	2	19

(c)—Drafted from Flin Flon Bombers by New York Rangers in third round of 1978 amateur draft.
(d)—March, 1981—Traded by New York Rangers to Edmonton Oilers for John Hughes.

NEVIN MARKWART

Left Wing . . . 5'11" . . . 175 lbs. . . . Born, Toronto, Ont., December 9, 1964 . . . Shoots left . . . (January, 1983)—Shoulder separation.

Year	Team	League	Games	G.	A.	Pts.	Pen.
1981-82—Regina Blues	SJHL	....	...	....	....	....
1981-82—Regina Pats	WHL	25	2	12	14	56
1982-83—Regina Pats (c)	WHL	43	27	39	66	91
1983-84—Boston Bruins	NHL	70	14	16	30	121
NHL TOTALS		70	14	16	30	121

(c)—June, 1983—Drafted as underage junior by Boston Bruins in 1983 NHL entry draft. First Bruins pick, 21st overall, first round.

MARIO JOSEPH MAROIS

Defense . . . 5'11" . . . 170 lbs. . . . Born, Ancienne Lorette, Que., December 15, 1957 . . . Shoots right . . . Missed part of 1977-78 season with broken ankle . . . (March 27, 1982)— Broke right wrist in 4-2 loss at Montreal . . . (December 30, 1982)—Broke right leg in exhibition game vs. USSR National Team.

Year	Team	League	Games	G.	A.	Pts.	Pen.
1975-76—Quebec Remparts	QJHL	67	11	42	53	270
1976-77—Quebec Remparts (b-c)	QJHL	72	17	67	84	249
1977-78—New Haven Nighthawks	AHL	52	8	23	31	147
1977-78—New York Rangers	NHL	8	1	1	2	15
1978-79—New York Rangers	NHL	71	5	26	31	153
1979-80—New York Rangers	NHL	79	8	23	31	142
1980-81—New York Rangers (d)	NHL	8	1	2	3	46
1980-81—Vancouver Canucks (e)	NHL	50	4	12	16	115
1980-81—Quebec Nordiques	NHL	11	0	7	7	20
1981-82—Quebec Nordiques	NHL	71	11	32	43	161

Year	Team	League	Games	G.	A.	Pts.	Pen.
1982-83—Quebec Nordiques		NHL	36	2	12	14	108
1983-84—Quebec Nordiques		NHL	80	13	36	49	151
NHL TOTALS			414	45	151	196	911

(c)—Drafted from Quebec Remparts by New York Rangers in fourth round of 1977 amateur draft.
(d)—November, 1980—Traded by New York Rangers with Jim Mayer to Vancouver Canucks for Jere Gillis and Jeff Bandura.
(e)—March, 1981—Traded by Vancouver Canucks to Quebec Nordiques for Garry Lariviere in a three-way deal that saw Lariviere then go to Edmonton Oilers for Blair MacDonald.

CHARLES BRADLEY (BRAD) MARSH

Defense . . . 6'2" . . . 215 lbs. . . . Born, London, Ont., March 31, 1958 . . . Shoots left . . . Brother of Paul Marsh . . . Set NHL record by playing a total of 83 games in 1981-82 . . . (January 2, 1983)—Bruised knee tendon in game at Chicago . . . (March 24, 1983)—Broken fibula in game vs. Toronto.

Year	Team	League	Games	G.	A.	Pts.	Pen.
1974-75—London Knights		Jr."A"OHA	70	4	17	21	160
1975-76—London Knights		Jr."A"OHA	61	3	26	29	184
1976-77—London Knights		Jr."A"OHA	63	7	33	40	121
1977-78—London Knights (a-c-d)		Jr."A"OHA	62	8	55	63	192
1978-79—Atlanta Flames		NHL	80	0	19	19	101
1979-80—Atlanta Flames		NHL	80	2	9	11	119
1980-81—Calgary Flames		NHL	80	1	12	13	87
1981-82—Calgary Flames (e)		NHL	17	0	1	1	10
1981-82—Philadelphia Flyers		NHL	66	2	22	24	106
1982-83—Philadelphia Flyers		NHL	68	2	11	13	52
1983-84—Philadelphia Flyers		NHL	77	3	14	17	83
NHL TOTALS			468	10	88	98	558

(c)—Drafted from London Knights by Atlanta Flames in first round of 1978 amateur draft.
(d)—Shared Max Kaminsky Memorial Trophy (outstanding defenseman) with Rob Ramage.
(e)—November, 1981—Traded by Calgary Flames to Philadelphia Flyers for Mel Bridgman.

PETER WILLIAM MARSH

Right Wing . . . 6'1" . . . 180 lbs. . . . Born, Halifax, N. S., December 21, 1956 . . . Shoots left . . . (December, 1980)—Fractured ankle in his first shift with Black Hawks . . . (February 15, 1980)—Compound fracture of thumb.

Year	Team	League	Games	G.	A.	Pts.	Pen.
1973-74—Sherbrooke Beavers		QJHL	43	7	9	16	45
1974-75—Sherbrooke Beavers		QJHL	65	36	34	70	133
1975-76—Sherbrooke Beavers (b-c-d-e)		QJHL	70	75	81	156	103
1976-77—Cincinnati Stingers		WHA	76	23	28	51	52
1977-78—Cincinnati Stingers (f)		WHA	74	25	25	50	123
1978-79—Cincinnati Stingers (g)		WHA	80	43	23	66	95
1979-80—Winnipeg Jets		NHL	57	18	20	38	59
1980-81—Winnipeg Jets (h)		NHL	24	6	7	13	9
1980-81—Chicago Black Hawks		NHL	29	4	6	10	10
1981-82—Chicago Black Hawks		NHL	57	10	18	28	47
1982-83—Chicago Black Hawks		NHL	68	6	14	20	55
1983-84—Chicago Black Hawks (i)		NHL	43	4	6	10	44
1983-84—Springfield Indians (j)		AHL	23	8	13	21	32
WHA TOTALS			230	91	76	167	270
NHL TOTALS			278	48	71	119	224

(c)—Named Most Valuable Player in QJHL.
(d)—Drafted from Sherbrooke Beavers by Pittsburgh Penguins in second round of 1976 amateur draft.
(e)—Selected by Cincinnati Stingers in WHA amateur player draft, May, 1976.
(f)—NHL rights traded to Montreal Canadiens by Pittsburgh Penguins (to complete deal sending Pierre Larouche to Montreal for Peter Lee and Peter Mahovlich), December, 1977.
(g)—June, 1979—Claimed by Winnipeg Jets in WHA dispersal draft. Selected by Montreal Canadiens in NHL reclaim draft. Selected by Winnipeg Jets in NHL expansion draft.
(h)—December, 1980—Traded by Winnipeg Jets to Chicago Black Hawks for Doug Lecuyer and Tim Trimper.
(i)—June, 1984—Released by Chicago Black Hawks.
(j)—August, 1984—Signed by Winnipeg Jets as a free agent.

BRIAN MARTIN

Center . . . 6' . . . 180 lbs. . . . Born, St. Catharines, Ont., March 27, 1966 . . . Shoots left.

Year	Team	League	Games	G.	A.	Pts.	Pen.
1981-82—St. Catharines		Ont. Midget	40	28	35	63	16
1982-83—Guelph Platers		OHL	66	4	16	20	64

Year	Team	League	Games	G.	A.	Pts.	Pen.
1983-84—Guelph Platers		OHL	19	3	9	12	7
1983-84—Belleville Bulls (c)		OHL	50	18	32	50	25

(c)—June, 1984—Drafted as underage junior by Los Angeles Kings in NHL entry draft. 12th Kings pick, 232nd overall, 12th round.

GRANT MICHAEL MARTIN

Left Wing . . . 5'10" . . . 190 lbs. . . . Born, Smooth Rock Falls, Ont., March 13, 1962 . . . Shoots left.

Year	Team	League	Games	G.	A.	Pts.	Pen.
1979-80—Kitchener Rangers (c)		OMJHL	65	31	21	52	62
1980-81—Kitchener Rangers		OHL	66	41	57	98	77
1981-82—Kitchener Rangers		OHL	54	33	63	96	97
1982-83—Fredericton Express		AHL	80	19	27	46	73
1983-84—Fredericton Express		AHL	57	36	24	60	46
1983-84—Vancouver Canucks		NHL	12	0	2	2	6
NHL TOTALS			12	0	2	2	6

(c)—June, 1980—Drafted as underage junior by Vancouver Canucks in 1980 NHL entry draft. Ninth Canucks pick, 196th overall, 10th round.

MICHAEL MORLEY MARTIN

Defense . . . 6' . . . 185 lbs. . . . Born, Kingston, Ont., March 12, 1961 . . . Shoots right.

Year	Team	League	Games	G.	A.	Pts.	Pen.
1977-78—Belleville Bobcats		OPJHL	45	15	24	39	100
1978-79—Sudbury Wolves		OMJHL	68	14	30	44	133
1979-80—Sudbury Wolves (c)		OMJHL	68	7	30	37	235
1980-81—Sudbury Wolves		OHL	57	16	34	50	190
1980-81—Binghamton Whalers		AHL	2	0	2	2	2
1981-82—Binghamton Whalers		AHL	2	0	0	0	12
1981-82—Saginaw Gears		IHL	46	2	12	14	94
1982-83—Saginaw Gears		IHL	24	2	7	9	73
1983-84—Flint Generals		IHL	82	10	31	41	192

(c)—June, 1980—Drafted as underage junior by Hartford Whalers in 1980 NHL entry draft. Seventh Whalers pick, 134th overall, seventh round.

TERRY GEORGE MARTIN

Left Wing . . . 5'11" . . . 175 lbs. . . . Born, Barrie, Ont., October 25, 1955 . . . Shoots left . . . (November, 1983)—Missed three weeks and lost 15 pounds after getting food poisoning from a roast beef sandwich at a New York City deli. He ended up in intensive care while teammates Gary Nylund and Greg Terrion also became ill, but not to the extent of Martin.

Year	Team	League	Games	G.	A.	Pts.	Pen.
1972-73—London Knights		Jr. "A" OHA	59	17	22	39	25
1973-74—London Knights		Jr. "A" OHA	63	33	24	57	38
1974-75—London Knights (c)		Jr. "A" OHA	70	43	57	100	118
1975-76—Charlotte Checkers		SHL	25	12	10	22	30
1975-76—Hershey Bears		AHL	19	3	6	9	18
1975-76—Buffalo Sabres		NHL	1	0	0	0	0
1976-77—Hershey Bears		AHL	12	1	4	5	12
1976-77—Buffalo Sabres		NHL	62	11	12	23	8
1977-78—Hershey Bears		AHL	4	2	1	3	2
1977-78—Buffalo Sabres		NHL	21	3	2	5	9
1978-79—Buffalo Sabres (d)		NHL	64	6	8	14	33
1979-80—Syracuse Blazers		AHL	18	9	9	18	6
1979-80—Quebec Nordiques (e)		NHL	3	0	0	0	0
1979-80—New Brunswick Hawks		AHL	3	0	1	1	0
1979-80—Toronto Maple Leafs		NHL	37	6	15	21	2
1980-81—Toronto Maple Leafs		NHL	69	23	14	37	32
1981-82—Toronto Maple Leafs		NHL	72	25	24	49	39
1982-83—Toronto Maple Leafs		NHL	76	14	13	27	28
1983-84—Toronto Maple Leafs		NHL	63	15	10	25	51
NHL TOTALS			468	103	98	201	202

(c)—Drafted from London Knights by Buffalo Sabres in third round of 1975 amateur draft.
(d)—June, 1979—Selected by Quebec Nordiques in NHL expansion draft.
(e)—December, 1979—Traded with Dave Farrish by Quebec Nordiques to Toronto Maple Leafs for Reggie Thomas.

TOM MARTIN

Left Wing . . . 6'2" . . . 190 lbs. . . . Born, Kelowna, B.C., May 11, 1964 . . . Shoots left . . . Set University of Denver record for penalty minutes during his freshman year (1982-83).

Year	Team	League	Games	G.	A.	Pts.	Pen.
1981-82—Kelowna (c)		BCJHL	51	35	45	80	293
1982-83—University of Denver (d)		WCHA	37	8	18	26	128
1983-84—Victoria Cougars		WHL	60	30	45	75	261
1983-84—Sherbrooke Jets		AHL	5	0	0	0	16

(c)—June, 1982—Drafted as underage player by Winnipeg Jets in 1982 NHL entry draft. Second Jets pick, 74th overall, fourth round.

(d)—January, 1983—WHL rights traded by Seattle Breakers with cash to Victoria Cougars for used team bus and player to be named later.

STEVE MARTINSON

Left Wing . . . 6'1" . . . 205 lbs. . . . Born, Minnetonka, Minn., June 21, 1957 . . . Shoots left.

Year	Team	League	Games	G.	A.	Pts.	Pen.
1981-82—Toledo Goaldiggers		IHL	35	12	18	30	128
1982-83—Birmingham Bulls (c)		CHL	43	4	5	9	184
1982-83—Toledo Goaldiggers		IHL	32	9	10	19	111
1983-84—Tulsa Oilers (d)		CHL	42	3	6	9	*240

(c)—Led CHL playoffs with 80 penalty minutes.

(d)—Led CHL playoffs with 43 penalty minutes.

DENNIS JOHN MARUK

Center . . . 5'8" . . . 170 lbs. . . . Born, Toronto, Ont., November 17, 1955 . . . Shoots left . . . (October, 1979)—Torn ligaments in right knee, out for four months . . . Set NHL record for most shorthanded goals by a rookie (5) in 1975-76.

Year	Team	League	Games	G.	A.	Pts.	Pen.
1971-72—Toronto Marlboros		Jr. "A" OHA	8	2	1	3	4
1972-73—London Knights		Jr. "A" OHA	59	46	67	113	54
1973-74—London Knights		Jr. "A" OHA	69	47	65	112	61
1974-75—London Knights (c-d)		Jr. "A" OHA	65	66	79	145	53
1975-76—California Seals		NHL	80	30	32	62	44
1976-77—Cleveland Barons		NHL	80	28	50	78	68
1977-78—Cleveland Barons		NHL	76	36	35	71	50
1978-79—Minnesota North Stars (e)		NHL	2	0	0	0	0
1978-79—Washington Capitals		NHL	76	31	59	90	71
1979-80—Washington Capitals		NHL	27	10	17	27	8
1980-81—Washington Capitals		NHL	80	50	47	97	87
1981-82—Washington Capitals		NHL	80	60	76	136	128
1982-83—Washington Capitals (f)		NHL	80	31	50	81	71
1983-84—Minnesota North Stars		NHL	71	17	43	60	42
NHL TOTALS			652	293	409	702	569

(c)—Won Red Tilson Memorial Trophy (MVP).

(d)—Drafted from London Knights by California Seals in second round of 1975 amateur draft.

(e)—October, 1978—Traded by Minnesota North Stars to Washington Capitals for second of Washington's two picks in the first round, 10th overall, of the 1979 entry draft (Tom McCarthy).

(f)—July, 1983—Traded by Washington Capitals to Minnesota for second round draft pick in 1984 (Stephen Leach) and cash.

BRAD ROBERT MAXWELL

Defense . . . 6'1" . . . 185 lbs. . . . Born, Brandon, Man., July 8, 1957 . . . Shoots right . . . Brother-in-law of Rick LaPointe . . . Missed part of 1979-80 season with stretched knee ligaments . . . (October 29, 1980)—Tore knee ligaments . . . (February, 1981)—Skate cut on foot developed blood poisoning . . . (November, 1981)—Slight concussion . . . (December, 1981)—Groin injury.

Year	Team	League	Games	G.	A.	Pts.	Pen.
1973-74—Bellingham Blazers		Jr. "A" BCHL	61	20	37	57	132
1974-75—New Westminster Bruins		WCHL	69	13	47	60	124
1975-76—New Westminster Bruins (b)		WCHL	72	19	80	99	239
1976-77—N. Westminster Bruins (b-c)		WCHL	70	21	58	79	205
1977-78—Minnesota North Stars		NHL	75	18	29	47	100
1978-79—Minnesota North Stars		NHL	70	9	28	37	145
1978-79—Oklahoma City Stars		CHL	2	0	1	1	21
1979-80—Minnesota North Stars		NHL	58	7	30	37	126
1980-81—Minnesota North Stars		NHL	27	3	13	16	98
1981-82—Minnesota North Stars		NHL	51	10	21	31	96

Year	Team	League	Games	G.	A.	Pts.	Pen.
1982-83—Minnesota North Stars		NHL	77	11	28	39	157
1983-84—Minnesota North Stars		NHL	78	19	54	73	225
NHL TOTALS			436	77	203	280	947

(c)—Drafted from New Westminster Bruins by Minnesota North Stars in first round of 1977 amateur draft.

BRYAN CLIFFORD MAXWELL

Defense . . . 6'3" . . . 210 lbs. . . . Born, North Bay, Ont., September 7, 1955 . . . Shoots left . . . Missed part of 1977-78 season with broken hand . . . Stretched knee ligaments (March, 1980) . . . (November 2, 1980)—Broken tibia bone in right leg . . . (December, 1981)—Rib injury . . . (October 24, 1982)—Hit in head by shot of teammate Craig Levie during team practice and missed three weeks . . . (December, 1982)—Broke hand . . . (January, 1984) —Injured left knee.

Year	Team	League	Games	G.	A.	Pts.	Pen.
1972-73—Drumheller Falcons		AJHL	....	...	....	....	....
1972-73—Medicine Hat Tigers		WCHL	37	1	11	12	25
1973-74—Medicine Hat Tigers		WCHL	63	11	56	67	229
1974-75—Medicine Hat Tigers (c-d)		WCHL	63	14	50	64	288
1975-76—Cleveland Crusaders (e)		WHA	73	3	14	17	177
1976-77—Springfield Indians		AHL	13	2	3	5	67
1976-77—Cincinnati Stingers (f)		WHA	34	1	8	9	29
1977-78—Binghamton Dusters		AHL	24	2	8	10	69
1977-78—New England Whalers		WHA	17	2	1	3	11
1977-78—Minnesota North Stars (g)		NHL	18	2	5	7	41
1978-79—Minnesota North Stars (h)		NHL	25	1	6	7	46
1978-79—Oklahoma City Stars		CHL	15	1	4	5	35
1979-80—Salt Lake Golden Eagles		CHL	3	0	1	1	10
1979-80—St. Louis Blues		NHL	57	1	11	12	112
1980-81—Salt Lake Golden Eagles		CHL	5	0	1	1	7
1980-81—St. Louis Blues (i)		NHL	40	3	10	13	137
1981-82—Winnipeg Jets		NHL	45	1	9	10	110
1982-83—Winnipeg Jets (j)		NHL	54	7	13	20	131
1983-84—Winnipeg Jets (k)		NHL	3	0	3	3	27
1983-84—Pittsburgh Penguins (l)		NHL	45	3	12	15	84
NHL TOTALS			288	18	69	87	688
WHA TOTALS			124	6	23	29	217

(c)—Drafted from Medicine Hat Tigers by Minnesota North Stars in first round of 1975 amateur draft.
(d)—Selected by Cleveland Crusaders in WHA amateur player draft, June, 1975.
(e)—Traded to Cincinnati Stingers by Minnesota Fighting Saints for rights to John McKenzie and Ivan Hlinka, September, 1976.
(f)—Traded to New England Whalers by Cincinnati Stingers with Greg Carroll for WHA rights to Mike Liut and second-round 1979 draft choice, May, 1977.
(g)—Signed by Minnesota North Stars following release by New England Whalers, February, 1978.
(h)—June, 1979—Traded by Minnesota North Stars to St. Louis Blues for future considerations (Blues second round draft pick in 1982).
(i)—July, 1981—Traded by St. Louis Blues with Ed Staniowski and Paul MacLean to Winnipeg Jets for Scott Campbell and John Markell.
(j)—July, 1983—Released by Winnipeg Jets.
(k)—August, 1983—Re-signed by Winnipeg Jets.
(l)—October, 1983—Acquired on waivers by Pittsburgh Penguins from Winnipeg Jets.

KEVIN MAXWELL

Center . . . 5'8" . . . 170 lbs. . . . Born, Edmonton, Alta., March 30, 1960 . . . Shoots right . . . (February, 1981)—Broke thumb . . . (October, 1981)—Back surgery . . . (December, 1981) —Groin injury.

Year	Team	League	Games	G.	A.	Pts.	Pen.
1978-79—Univ. of North Dakota (a-c-d)		WCHA	42	31	51	82	79
1979-80—Canadian National Team		Int'l	....	25	41	66	....
1979-80—Canadian Olympic Team		Olympic	6	0	5	5	4
1980-81—Oklahoma City Stars		CHL	31	8	13	21	38
1980-81—Minnesota North Stars		NHL	6	0	3	3	7
1981-82—Minnesota North Stars (e)		NHL	12	1	4	5	8
1981-82—Colorado Rockies		NHL	34	5	5	10	44
1982-83—Wichita Wind		CHL	68	24	41	65	47
1983-84—New Jersey Devils		NHL	14	0	3	3	2
1983-84—Maine Mariners		AHL	56	21	27	48	59
NHL TOTALS			66	6	15	21	61

(c)—Named to All-American Team (West).

(d)—August, 1979—Drafted as underage player in 1979 NHL entry draft by Minnesota North Stars. Fourth North Stars pick, 63rd overall, third round.

(e)—December, 1981—Traded with Jim Dobson by Minnesota North Stars to Colorado Rockies for cash.

GARY McADAM

Right Wing . . . 5'11" . . . 180 lbs. . . . Born, Smith Falls, Ont., December 31, 1955 . . . Shoots left . . . Also plays left wing . . . Set AHL record in 1982-83 with 11 shorthanded goals.

Year	Team	League	Games	G.	A.	Pts.	Pen.
1972-73	Ottawa 67s	Jr."A"OHA	61	14	8	22	23
1973-74	—		....	...	....	....	....
1974-75	St. Cath. Black Hawks (c)	Jr."A"OHA	65	24	53	77	111
1975-76	Hershey Bears	AHL	24	14	13	27	45
1975-76	Buffalo Sabres	NHL	31	1	2	3	2
1976-77	Buffalo Sabres	NHL	73	13	16	29	17
1977-78	Buffalo Sabres	NHL	79	19	22	41	44
1978-79	Buffalo Sabres (d)	NHL	40	6	5	11	13
1978-79	Pittsburgh Penguins	NHL	28	5	9	14	2
1979-80	Pittsburgh Penguins	NHL	78	19	22	41	63
1980-81	Pittsburgh Penguins (e)	NHL	34	3	9	12	30
1980-81	Detroit Red Wings	NHL	40	5	14	19	27
1981-82	Dallas Black Hawks (f)	CHL	12	10	10	20	14
1981-82	Calgary Flames	NHL	46	12	15	27	18
1982-83	Buffalo Sabres	NHL	4	1	0	1	0
1982-83	Rochester Americans (g)	AHL	73	40	29	69	58
1983-84	Maine Mariners	AHL	10	3	4	7	18
1983-84	Washington Capitals (h)	NHL	24	1	5	6	12
1983-84	New Jersey Devils (i)	NHL	38	9	6	15	15
	NHL TOTALS		515	94	125	219	243

(c)—Drafted from St. Catharines Black Hawks by Buffalo Sabres in third round of 1975 amateur draft.

(d)—February, 1979—Traded by Buffalo Sabres to Pittsburgh Penguins for Dave Schultz.

(e)—January, 1981—Traded by Pittsburgh Penguins to Detroit Red Wings for Errol Thompson.

(f)—November, 1981—Traded with fourth-round entry draft picks in 1982 (Dave Meszaros) and 1983 by Detroit Red Wings to Calgary Flames for Eric Vail.

(g)—August, 1983—Signed by New Jersey Devils as a free agent.

(h)—November, 1983—Acquired on waivers by Washington Capitals from New Jersey Devils.

(i)—January, 1984—Sold by Washington Capitals to New Jersey Devils.

ANDREW McBAIN

Right Wing . . . 6'1" . . . 190 lbs. . . . Born, Toronto, Ont., February 18, 1965 . . . Shoots right . . . (November, 1982)—Fractured cheekbone . . . (March, 1983)—Separated sterno clavicular joint.

Year	Team	League	Games	G.	A.	Pts.	Pen.
1981-82	Niagara Falls Flyers	OHL	68	19	25	44	35
1982-83	North Bay Centennials (b-c)	OHL	67	33	87	120	61
1983-84	Winnipeg Jets	NHL	78	11	19	30	37
	NHL TOTALS		78	11	19	30	37

(c)—June, 1983—Drafted as underage junior by Winnipeg Jets in 1983 NHL entry draft. First Jets pick, 8th overall, first round.

DAN McCARTHY

Center . . . 5'9" . . . 185 lbs. . . . Born, St. Mary's, Ont., April 7, 1958 . . . Shoots left.

Year	Team	League	Games	G.	A.	Pts.	Pen.
1975-76	Sudbury Wolves	OMJHL	65	17	30	47	23
1976-77	Sudbury Wolves	OMJHL	54	23	32	55	76
1977-78	Sudbury Wolves (c)	OMJHL	68	30	51	81	96
1977-78	Flint Generals	IHL	75	38	42	80	80
1979-80	New Haven Nighthawks	AHL	26	6	3	9	8
1979-80	Richmond Rifles	EHL	8	6	4	10	7
1980-81	New Haven Nighthawks	AHL	71	28	17	45	54
1980-81	New York Rangers	NHL	5	4	0	4	4
1981-82	Springfield Indians (d)	AHL	78	26	32	58	57
1982-83	Birmingham South Stars	CHL	76	30	35	65	67
1983-84	Baltimore Skipjacks (e)	AHL	27	8	11	19	8
	NHL TOTALS		5	4	0	4	4

(c)—June, 1978—Drafted by New York Rangers in 1978 amateur draft. Sixteenth Rangers pick, 223rd overall, 15th round.

(d)—August, 1982—Traded by New York Rangers to Minnesota North Stars for Shawn Dineen.

(e)—January, 1984—Signed by Baltimore Skipjacks as a free agent.

KEVIN McCARTHY

Defense ... 5'11" ... 197 lbs.... Born, Winnipeg, Man., July 14, 1957 ... Shoots right ... Set WCHL record for points by Defenseman in 1975-76 (121) and broke own record in 1976-77 (127) and assists by Defenseman (105) in 1976-77 ... Holds all-time WCHL record for career assists (276) ... (December, 1979)—Bone chip lodged in hip muscles caused disabling pain ... (January, 1982)—Slight shoulder separation ... (February, 1983)— Sprained wrist.

Year	Team	League	Games	G.	A.	Pts.	Pen.
1973-74	Winnipeg Clubs	WCHL	66	5	22	27	65
1974-75	Winnipeg Clubs	WCHL	66	20	61	81	102
1975-76	Winnipeg Clubs (a-c)	WCHL	72	33	88	121	160
1976-77	Winnipeg Monarchs (a-d)	WCHL	72	22	*105	127	110
1977-78	Philadelphia Flyers	NHL	62	2	15	17	32
1978-79	Philadelphia Flyers (e)	NHL	22	1	2	3	21
1978-79	Vancouver Canucks	NHL	1	0	0	0	0
1979-80	Vancouver Canucks	NHL	79	15	30	45	70
1980-81	Vancouver Canucks	NHL	80	16	37	53	85
1981-82	Vancouver Canucks	NHL	71	6	39	45	84
1982-83	Vancouver Canucks	NHL	74	12	28	40	88
1983-84	Vancouver Canucks (f)	NHL	47	2	14	16	61
1983-84	Pittsburgh Penguins	NHL	31	4	16	20	52
	NHL TOTALS		467	58	181	239	493

(c)—Named Outstanding Defenseman in WCHL.
(d)—Drafted from Winnipeg Monarchs by Philadelphia Flyers in first round of 1977 amateur draft.
(e)—December, 1978—Traded with Drew Callander by Philadelphia Flyers to Vancouver Canucks for Dennis Ververgaert.
(f)—January, 1984—Traded by Vancouver Canucks to Pittsburgh Penguins for third round 1985 draft pick.

TOM JOSEPH McCARTHY

Left Wing ... 6'2" ... 202 lbs.... Born, Toronto, Ont., July 31, 1960 ... Shoots left ... Rib injury (February, 1980) ... (February, 1981)—Wrist surgery ... (September 25, 1981)— Strained tendon in ankle during training camp ... (November, 1981)—Tore calf muscle while conditioning from ankle injury ... (April, 1984)—Injured back when a jeep over-turned (he was a passenger). Ten days later he broke a bone in his back during playoff game with St. Louis when he collided with a goalpost.

Year	Team	League	Games	G.	A.	Pts.	Pen.
1976-77	Kingston Canadians	OMJHL	2	1	0	1	0
1976-77	North York Rangers	OP IHI	43	49	47	96	12
1977-78	Oshawa Generals	OMJHL	62	47	46	93	72
1978-79	Oshawa Generals (a-c)	OMJHL	63	69	75	144	98
1979-80	Minnesota North Stars	NHL	68	16	20	36	39
1980-81	Minnesota North Stars	NHL	62	23	25	48	62
1981-82	Minnesota North Stars	NHL	40	12	30	42	36
1982-83	Minnesota North Stars	NHL	80	28	48	76	59
1983-84	Minnesota North Stars	NHL	66	39	31	70	49
	NHL TOTALS		316	118	154	272	245

(c)—August, 1979—Drafted as underage player by Minnesota North Stars in 1979 entry draft. Second North Stars pick, 10th overall, first round.

KIRK McCASKILL

Center ... 6'2" ... 190 lbs.... Born, Paradise Valley, Ariz., April 9, 1961 ... Shoots right ... Also plays right wing ... Son of Ted McCaskill (EHL, CHL, NHL, WHA and WHL 1962-74).

Year	Team	League	Games	G.	A.	Pts.	Pen.
1979-80	University of Vermont	ECAC	35	14	8	22	8
1980-81	University of Vermont (c)	ECAC	32	28	23	51	25
1981-82	University of Vermont (a-d)	ECAC	25	30	19	49	14
1982-83	University of Vermont (e)	ECAC	15	11	11	22	14
1983-84	Sherbrooke Jets	AHL	78	10	12	22	21

(c)—June, 1981—Drafted by Winnipeg Jets in 1981 NHL entry draft. Fourth Jets pick, 64th overall, fourth round.
(d)—Named to All-America Team (East).
(e)—January, 1983—Left University of Vermont to play baseball with California Angels farm club at Nashua (Eastern League) where he had a 4-8 won-lost record with 4.45 ERA in 1983 season. He also played with Redwood (California League) where he had a 6-5 record with a 2.33 ERA in 1983 season.

ROB McCLANAHAN

Left Wing . . . 5'10" . . . 180 lbs. . . . Born, St. Paul, Minn., January 9, 1958 . . . Shoots left . . . Member of 1980 U.S. Gold Medal Olympic Team . . . Also member of 1979 U.S. National team.

Year	Team	League	Games	G.	A.	Pts.	Pen.
1976-77	University of Minnesota	WCHA	40	11	6	17	24
1977-78	University of Minnesota (c)	WCHA	38	17	25	42	10
1978-79	University of Minnesota	WCHA	43	17	32	49	34
1979-80	U.S. Olympic Team	Int'l	63	34	36	70	38
1979-80	Buffalo Sabres	NHL	13	2	5	7	0
1980-81	Buffalo Sabres	NHL	53	3	12	15	38
1980-81	Rochester Americans	AHL	18	9	13	22	10
1981-82	Hartford Whalers (d-e)	NHL	17	0	3	3	11
1981-82	New York Rangers	NHL	22	5	9	14	10
1981-82	Binghamton Whalers	AHL	27	11	18	29	21
1981-82	Springfield Indians	AHL	7	4	5	9	0
1982-83	New York Rangers	NHL	78	22	26	48	46
1983-84	Tulsa Oilers	CHL	10	4	10	14	10
1983-84	New York Rangers (f-g)	NHL	41	6	8	14	21
	NHL TOTALS		224	38	63	101	126

(c)—June, 1978—Drafted by Buffalo Sabres in 1978 NHL amateur draft. Third Sabres pick, 49th overall, third round.

(d)—October, 1981—Claimed by Hartford Whalers from Buffalo Sabres in 1981 NHL waiver draft.

(e)—January, 1982—Traded by Hartford Whalers to New York Rangers for 10th-round 1983 entry draft pick (Reine Karlsson).

(f)—May, 1984—Traded by New York Rangers to Detroit Red Wings for future considerations.

(g)—August, 1984—Traded by Detroit Red Wings to Vancouver Canucks for Dave (Tiger) Williams.

KEVIN WILLIAM McCLELLAND

Center . . . 6' . . . 180 lbs. . . . Born, Oshawa, Ont., July 4, 1962 . . . Shoots right . . . (September 21, 1981)—Dislocated shoulder in preseason game . . . (January 24, 1983)—Dislocated shoulder in fight with Paul Higgins in game at Toronto. He required surgery on the shoulder and was lost for the season.

Year	Team	League	Games	G.	A.	Pts.	Pen.
1979-80	Niagara Falls Flyers (c)	OMJHL	67	14	14	28	71
1980-81	Niagara Falls Flyers (d)	OHL	68	36	72	108	184
1981-82	Niagara Falls Flyers	OHL	46	36	47	83	184
1981-82	Pittsburgh Penguins	NHL	10	1	4	5	4
1982-83	Pittsburgh Penguins	NHL	38	5	4	9	73
1983-84	Baltimore Skipjacks	AHL	3	1	1	2	0
1983-84	Pittsburgh Penguins (e)	NHL	24	2	4	6	62
1983-84	Edmonton Oilers	NHL	52	8	20	28	127
	NHL TOTALS		124	16	32	48	266

(c)—June, 1980—Drafted as underage junior by Hartford Whalers in 1980 NHL entry draft. Fourth Whalers pick, 71st overall, fourth round.

(d)—July, 1981—Acquired by Pittsburgh Penguins with Pat Boutette as compensation from Hartford Whalers for Hartford signing free agent Greg Millen. Decision required by NHL Arbitrator Judge Joseph Kane when Hartford and Pittsburgh were unable to agree on compensation.

(e)—December, 1983—Traded with sixth round 1984 draft pick (Emanuel Viveiros) by Pittsburgh Penguins to Edmonton Oilers for Tom Roulston.

GARY McCOLGAN

Left Wing . . . 6' . . . 192 lbs. . . . Born, Scarborough, Ont., March 27, 1966 . . . Shoots left.

Year	Team	League	Games	G.	A.	Pts.	Pen.
1982-83	Don Mills Midgets	MTMHL	40	32	27	59	28
1983-84	Oshawa Generals (c)	OHL	66	11	28	39	14

(c)—June, 1984—Drafted as underage junior by Minnesota North Stars in NHL entry draft. Sixth North Stars pick, 118th overall, sixth round.

WILLIAM McCORMICK

Center . . . 6'1" . . . 185 lbs. . . . Born, Winchester, Mass., January 16, 1964 . . . Shoots left.

Year	Team	League	Games	G.	A.	Pts.	Pen.
1982-83	Westminster Heights H.S. (c)	Mass. H.S.	..	..	..	..	..
1983-84	University of Vermont	ECAC	22	0	1	1	10

(c)—June, 1983—Drafted by Philadelphia Flyers in 1983 NHL entry draft. Ninth Flyers pick, 201st overall, 10th round.

DALE ALLEN McCOURT

Center . . . 5'11" . . . 185 lbs. . . . Born, Falconbridge, Ont., January 26, 1957 . . . Shoots right . . . Nephew of former Toronto Maple Leaf star George Armstrong.

Year	Team	League	Games	G.	A.	Pts.	Pen.
1972-73—Sudbury Wolves	Jr."A"OHA	26	6	11	17	0
1973-74—Hamilton Red Wings	Jr."A"OHA	69	20	38	58	45
1974-75—Hamilton Fincups	Jr."A"OHA	69	52	74	126	57
1975-76—Hamilton Fincups (a-c)	Jr."A"OHA	66	55	84	139	19
1976-77—St. Cath. Fincups (a-d-e-f)	Jr."A"OHA	66	60	79	139	26
1977-78—Detroit Red Wings (g)	NHL	76	33	39	72	10
1978-79—Detroit Red Wings (h)	NHL	79	28	43	71	14
1979-80—Detroit Red Wings	NHL	80	30	51	81	12
1980-81—Detroit Red Wings	NHL	80	30	56	86	50
1981-82—Detroit Red Wings (i)	NHL	26	13	14	27	6
1981-82—Buffalo Sabres	NHL	52	20	22	42	12
1982-83—Buffalo Sabres	NHL	62	20	32	52	10
1983-84—Buffalo Sabres (j)	NHL	5	1	3	4	0
1983-84—Toronto Maple Leafs	NHL	72	19	24	43	10
NHL TOTALS		532	194	284	478	124

(c)—Won Bill Hanley Trophy (Most Gentlemanly Player) and was Most Valuable Player during Memorial Cup Playoffs.

(d)—Won Albert (Red) Tilson Memorial Trophy (MVP).

(e)—Won Bill Hanley Trophy (Most Gentlemanly Player).

(f)—Drafted from St. Catharines Fincups by Detroit Red Wings in first round of 1977 amateur draft.

(g)—Arbitrator sent McCourt to Los Angeles Kings from Detroit Red Wings as compensation for Red Wings' signing of free agent Rogatien Vachon, August, 1978. Court ruling September 18, 1978 overturned arbitrator's decision and McCourt remained with Red Wings.

(h)—August, 1979—NHL rights returned to Detroit by Los Angeles Kings for Andre St. Laurent and Wings' first-round draft choice in 1980 (Larry Murphy) and the option of a second round 1980 or first round 1981 draft choice. (L. A. took 1981 first round choice Doug Smith).

(i)—December, 1981—Traded with Mike Foligno, Brent Peterson and future considerations by Detroit Red Wings to Buffalo Sabres for Bob Sauve, Jim Schoenfeld and Derek Smith.

(j)—October, 1983—Released by Buffalo Sabres and signed by Toronto Maple Leafs as a free agent.

BILL McCREARY, JR.

Left Wing . . . 6' . . . 200 lbs. . . . Born, Springfield, Mass., April 15, 1960 . . . Shoots left . . . Son of Bill McCreary, Sr. and nephew of Keith McCreary . . . Also a nephew of Ron Attwell and a cousin of Bob Attwell.

Year	Team	League	Games	G.	A.	Pts.	Pen.
1978-79—Colgate University (c)	ECAC	24	19	25	44	70
1979-80—Colgate University	ECAC	12	7	13	20	44
1980-81—Toronto Maple Leafs	NHL	12	1	0	1	4
1980-81—New Brunswick Hawks	AHL	61	19	24	43	120
1981-82—Cincinnati Tigers	CHL	69	8	27	35	61
1982-83—Saginaw Gears	IHL	60	19	28	47	17
1982-83—Peoria Prancers	IHL	16	4	6	10	11
1982-83—St. Catharines Saints (d)	AHL	4	0	1	1	2
1983-84—Milwaukee Admirals	IHL	81	28	35	63	44
NHL TOTALS		12	1	0	1	4

(c)—August, 1979—Drafted by Toronto Maple Leafs in 1979 NHL entry draft. Fifth Maple Leafs pick, 114th overall, sixth round.

(d)—June, 1983—Released by Toronto Maple Leafs.

BYRON BRAD McCRIMMON
(Known by middle name)

Defense . . . 5'11" . . . 193 lbs. . . . Born, Dodsland, Sask., March 29, 1959 . . . Shoots left.

Year	Team	League	Games	G.	A.	Pts.	Pen.
1976-77—Brandon Wheat Kings (b)	WCHL	72	18	66	84	96
1977-78—Brandon Wheat Kings (a-c)	WCHL	65	19	78	97	245
1978-79—Brandon Wheat Kings (a-d)	WHL	66	24	74	98	139
1979-80—Boston Bruins	NHL	72	5	11	16	94
1980-81—Boston Bruins	NHL	78	11	18	29	148
1981-82—Boston Bruins (e)	NHL	78	1	8	9	83
1982-83—Philadelphia Flyers	NHL	79	4	21	25	61
1983-84—Philadelphia Flyers	NHL	71	0	24	24	76
NHL TOTALS		378	21	82	103	462

(c)—Named outstanding defenseman in WCHL.

(d)—August, 1979—Drafted by Boston Bruins in 1979 entry draft. Second Boston pick, 15th overall, first round.

(e)—June, 1982—Traded by Boston Bruins to Philadelphia Flyers for Pete Peeters.

GERALD McDONALD

Defense . . . 6'3" . . . 190 lbs. . . . Born, Weymouth, Mass., March 18, 1958 . . . Shoots right.

Year	Team	League	Games	G.	A.	Pts.	Pen.
1979-80—North Adams St. Mass.		.....	.....	...	.....	.....	.....
1980-81—Tulsa Oilers		CHL	5	0	1	1	2
1980-81—New Haven Nighthawks		AHL	70	6	23	29	67
1981-82—Hartford Whalers (c)		NHL	3	0	0	0	0
1981-82—Binghamton Whalers		AHL	57	3	11	14	42
1982-83—Binghamton Whalers		AHL	74	8	33	41	62
1983-84—Hartford Whalers		NHL	5	0	0	0	4
1983-84—Binghamton Whalers		AHL	72	4	39	43	34
NHL TOTALS			8	0	0	0	4

(c)—October, 1981—Traded with Chris Kotsopoulos and Doug Sulliman by New York Rangers to Hartford Whalers for Mike Rogers and 10th-round 1982 entry draft pick (Simo Saarinen).

LANNY KING McDONALD

Right Wing . . . 6' . . . 185 lbs. . . . Born, Hanna, Alta., February 16, 1953 . . . Shoots right . . . Voted Colorado Athlete of the Year (1980) by state media . . . (February 18, 1984)—Fractured bone in right foot in game vs. Boston.

Year	Team	League	Games	G.	A.	Pts.	Pen.
1969-70—Lethbridge Sugar Kings		AJHL	34	2	9	11	19
1970-71—Lethbridge Sugar Kings (b)		AJHL	45	37	45	82	56
1970-71—Calgary Centennials		WCHL	6	0	2	2	6
1971-72—Medicine Hat Tigers		WCHL	68	50	64	114	54
1972-73—Medicine Hat Tigers (a-c)		WCHL	68	62	77	139	84
1973-74—Toronto Maple Leafs		NHL	70	14	16	30	43
1974-75—Toronto Maple Leafs		NHL	64	17	27	44	86
1975-76—Toronto Maple Leafs		NHL	75	37	56	93	70
1976-77—Toronto Maple Leafs (b)		NHL	80	46	44	90	77
1977-78—Toronto Maple Leafs		NHL	74	47	40	87	54
1978-79—Toronto Maple Leafs		NHL	79	43	42	85	32
1979-80—Toronto Maple Leafs (d)		NHL	35	15	15	30	10
1979-80—Colorado Rockies		NHL	46	25	20	45	43
1980-81—Colorado Rockies		NHL	80	35	46	81	56
1981-82—Colorado Rockies (e)		NHL	16	6	9	15	20
1981-82—Calgary Flames		NHL	55	34	33	67	37
1982-83—Calgary Flames (b-f)		NHL	80	66	32	98	90
1983-84—Calgary Flames		NHL	65	33	33	66	64
NHL TOTALS			819	418	413	831	782

(c)—Drafted from Medicine Hat Tigers by Toronto Maple Leafs in first round of 1973 amateur draft.

(d)—December, 1979—Traded with Joel Quenneville by Toronto Maple Leafs to Colorado Rockies for Wilf Paiement and Pat Hickey.

(e)—December, 1981—Traded with fourth-round 1983 entry draft pick by Colorado Rockies to Calgary Flames for Bob MacMillan and Don Lever.

(f)—Won Bill Masterton Memorial Trophy (perseverance, sportsmanship and dedication).

JOE McDONNELL

Defense . . . 6'2" . . . 200 lbs. . . . Born, Kitchener, Ont., May 11, 1961 . . . Shoots right.

Year	Team	League	Games	G.	A.	Pts.	Pen.
1976-77—Kitchener Rangers		OMJHL	29	0	4	4	8
1977-78—Kitchener Rangers		OMJHL	55	0	4	4	14
1978-79—Kitchener Rangers		OMJHL	60	1	6	7	43
1979-80—Kitchener Rangers		OMJHL	62	6	21	27	81
1980-81—Kitchener Rangers		OMJHL	66	15	50	65	103
1981-82—Vancouver Canucks (c)		NHL	7	0	1	1	12
1981-82—Dallas Black Hawks		CHL	60	13	24	37	46
1982-83—Moncton Alpines		AHL	79	14	21	35	44
1983-84—Moncton Alpines (d)		AHL	78	12	33	45	44
NHL TOTALS			7	0	1	1	12

(c)—October, 1981—Signed by Vancouver Canucks as a free agent.

(d)—August, 1983—Signed by Edmonton Oilers as a free agent.

MICHAEL GEORGE McDOUGAL

Right Wing . . . 6'2" . . . 205 lbs. . . . Born, Port Huron, Mich., April 30, 1958 . . . Shoots right . . . (October, 1980)—Injured left knee . . . (November 8, 1981)—Suffered damaged ligaments and bone chips in right hand in 2-2 tie at Buffalo.

Year	Team	League	Games	G.	A.	Pts.	Pen.
1976-77	Port Huron Flags	IHL	59	25	29	54	46
1977-78	Port Huron Flags (c)	IHL	44	15	16	31	65
1978-79	New York Rangers	NHL	1	0	0	0	0
1978-79	New Haven Nighthawks	AHL	78	24	26	50	60
1979-80	New Haven Nighthawks	AHL	68	17	25	42	43
1980-81	New Haven Nighthawks	AHL	66	21	23	44	20
1980-81	New York Rangers	NHL	2	0	0	0	0
1981-82	Hartford Whalers (d)	NHL	3	0	0	0	0
1981-82	Binghamton Whalers	AHL	58	10	18	28	56
1982-83	Hartford Whalers	NHL	55	8	10	18	43
1982-83	Binghamton Whalers	AHL	14	7	5	12	20
1983-84	Binghamton Whalers	AHL	59	11	14	25	56
	NHL TOTALS		61	8	10	18	43

(c)—June, 1978—Drafted by New York Rangers in amateur draft. Sixth Ranger pick, 76th overall, fifth round.

(d)—October, 1981—Selected by Hartford Whalers in 1981 NHL waiver draft.

TERRY McDOUGALL

Left Wing and Center . . . 5'8" . . . 163 lbs. . . . Born, Trail, B. C., June 14, 1953 . . . Shoots left.

Year	Team	League	Games	G.	A.	Pts.	Pen.
1971-72	Swift Current Broncos	WCHL	67	44	58	102	55
1972-73	Swift Current Broncos (c)	WCHL	68	40	63	103	17
1973-74	Des Moines Capitols (d)	IHL	69	27	34	61	12
1974-75	Des Moines Capitols (e)	IHL	74	18	40	58	43
1975-76	Fort Wayne Komets	IHL	77	35	53	88	6
1976-77	Fort Wayne Komets	IHL	77	36	67	103	26
1977-78	Fort Wayne Komets	IHL	80	36	48	84	38
1978-79	Fort Wayne Komets (a-f-g)	IHL	79	*57	*82	*139	47
1979-80	Fort Wayne Komets	IHL	71	32	61	93	24
1980-81	Fort Wayne Komets	IHL	82	35	64	99	42
1981-82	Fort Wayne Komets	IHL	41	18	21	39	24
1981-82	Flint Generals	IHL	34	12	26	38	22
1982-83	Flint Generals	IHL	81	32	45	77	74
1983-84	Flint Generals	IHL	23	4	13	17	8

(c)—Drafted from Swift Current Broncos by Vancouver Canucks in 10th round of 1973 amateur draft.

(d)—Led in assists (11) and points (19) during playoffs.

(e)—Drafted from defunct Des Moines Capitols by Fort Worth Komets, July, 1975.

(f)—Won Leo P. Lamoureux Memorial Trophy (top IHL scorer).

(g)—Won James Gatschene Memorial Trophy (IHL-MVP).

MICHAEL TODD McEWEN

Defense . . . 6'1" . . . 185 lbs. . . . Born, Hornepayne, Ont., August 10, 1956 . . . Shoots left . . . (November 2, 1981)—Broken nose in game vs. Calgary when struck by stick of Jim Peplinski . . . (February, 1983)—Sprained left ankle during team practice . . . (November, 1983)—Separated shoulder.

Year	Team	League	Games	G.	A.	Pts.	Pen.
1973-74	Toronto Marlboros	Jr. "A" OHA	68	5	32	37	81
1974-75	Toronto Marlboros	Jr. "A" OHA	68	18	63	81	52
1975-76	Toronto Marlboros (c)	Jr. "A" OHA	65	23	40	63	63
1976-77	New York Rangers	NHL	80	14	29	43	38
1977-78	New York Rangers	NHL	57	5	13	18	52
1978-79	New York Rangers	NHL	80	20	38	58	35
1979-80	New York Rangers (d)	NHL	9	1	7	8	8
1979-80	Colorado Rockies	NHL	67	11	40	51	33
1980-81	Colorado Rockies (e)	NHL	65	11	35	46	84
1980-81	New York Islanders	NHL	13	0	3	3	10
1981-82	New York Islanders	NHL	73	10	39	49	50
1982-83	New York Islanders	NHL	42	2	11	13	16
1983-84	New York Islanders (f)	NHL	15	0	2	2	6
1983-84	Los Angeles Kings	NHL	47	10	24	34	14
1983-84	New Haven Nighthawks (g)	AHL	9	3	7	10	26
	NHL TOTALS		548	84	241	325	346

(c)—Drafted from Toronto Marlboros by New York Rangers in third round of 1976 amateur draft.

(d)—November, 1979—Traded with Lucien DeBlois, Pat Hickey, Dean Turner and future consideration (Bobby Sheehan and Bobby Crawford) by New York Rangers to Colorado Rockies for Barry Beck.

(e)—March, 1981—Traded by Colorado Rockies with Jari Kaarela to New York Islanders for Glenn Resch and Steve Tambellini.

(f)—November, 1983—Traded by New York Islanders to Los Angeles Kings for future considerations.

(g)—August, 1984—Signed by Washington Capitals as a free agent.

JAMES McGEOUGH

Center ... 5'8" ... 161 lbs. ... Born, Regina, Sask., April 13, 1963 ... Shoots left.

Year	Team	League	Games	G.	A.	Pts.	Pen.
1979-80—Regina		SJHL	57	56	77	133	94
1979-80—Regina Pats		WHL	10	1	4	5	2
1980-81—Billings Bighorns (c-d)		WHL	71	50	44	94	141
1981-82—Billings Bighorns		WHL	71	*93	66	159	142
1981-82—Washington Capitals		NHL	4	0	0	0	0
1982-83—Nanaimo Islanders		WHL	72	76	56	132	126
1982-83—Hershey Bears		AHL	5	1	1	2	10
1983-84—Hershey Bears		AHL	79	40	36	76	108
NHL TOTALS			4	0	0	0	0

(c)—October, 1980—Traded by Regina Pats to Billings Bighorns for Neil Girard (G), Bruce Holloway and Wade Waters.

(d)—June, 1981—Drafted by Washington Capitals as underage junior in 1981 NHL entry draft. Tenth Capitals pick, 110th overall, sixth round.

SCOTT McGEOWN

Defense ... 6'1" ... 187 lbs. ... Born, Toronto, Ont., March 9, 1960 ... Shoots right.

Year	Team	League	Games	G.	A.	Pts.	Pen.
1975-76—Wexford Raiders		OPJHL	37	18	34	52	58
1976-77—Toronto Marlboros		OMJHL	56	13	30	43	67
1977-78—Toronto Marlboros		OMJHL	60	11	30	41	71
1978-79—Toronto Marlboros (c)		OMJHL	59	10	40	50	117
1979-80—Toronto Marlboros		OMJHL	65	26	48	74	69
1980-81—Erie Blades (a)		EHL	55	20	63	83	45
1980-81—Wichita Wind		CHL	9	1	7	8	4
1980-81—Rochester Americans		AHL	4	0	2	2	0
1981-82—Fredericton Express		AHL	53	13	24	37	48
1981-82—Milwaukee Admirals		IHL	18	1	4	5	38
1982-83—Fredericton Express		AHL	4	0	0	0	0
1982-83—Erie Blades		ACHL	21	2	16	18	22
1982-83—Milwaukee Admirals		IHL	14	3	5	8	2
1983-84—Kalamazoo Wings		IHL	64	14	40	54	32

(c)—August, 1979—Drafted as underage junior by Quebec Nordiques in 1979 NHL entry draft. Sixth Nordiques pick, 125th overall, sixth round.

ROBERT PAUL McGILL

Defense ... 6' ... 202 lbs. ... Born, Edmonton, Alta., April 27, 1962 ... Shoots right.

Year	Team	League	Games	G.	A.	Pts.	Pen.
1978-79—Abbotsford		BCJHL	46	3	20	23	242
1979-80—Victoria Cougars (c)		WHL	70	3	18	21	230
1980-81—Victoria Cougars		WHL	66	5	36	41	295
1981-82—Toronto Maple Leafs		NHL	68	1	10	11	263
1982-83—Toronto Maple Leafs		NHL	30	0	0	0	146
1982-83—St. Catharines Saints		AHL	32	2	5	7	95
1983-84—Toronto Maple Leafs		NHL	11	0	2	2	51
1983-84—St. Catharines Saints		AHL	55	1	15	16	217
NHL TOTALS			109	1	12	13	460

(c)—June, 1980—Drafted as underage junior by Toronto Maple Leafs in 1980 NHL entry draft. Second Maple Leafs pick, 26th overall, second round.

DOUG McGRATH

Defense ... 5'11" ... 185 lbs. ... Born, Tracadia, N.B., June 8, 1963 ... Shoots left.

Year	Team	League	Games	G.	A.	Pts.	Pen.
1982-83—Shawinigan Cataracts		QHL	64	14	26	40	79
1983-84—Maine Mariners		AHL	50	2	6	8	64
1983-84—Montana Magic		CHL	11	3	6	9	8

BRUCE McKAY

Defense . . . 6' . . . 200 lbs. . . . Born, Detroit, Mich., April 6, 1959 . . . Shoots left.

Year	Team	League	Games	G.	A.	Pts.	Pen.
1976-77—Sudbury Wolves		OMJHL	47	4	11	15	49
1977-78—Sudbury Wolves		OMJHL	20	0	3	3	44
1977-78—Kitchener Rangers		OMJHL	47	2	15	17	140
1978-79—Kitchener Rangers		OMJHL	61	1	22	23	190
1979-80—Port Huron Flags (c)		IHL	68	9	10	19	138
1980-81—Salt Lake Golden Eagles		CHL	48	1	8	9	111
1980-81—Port Huron Flags		IHL	7	2	2	4	31
1981-82—Milwaukee Admirals (b)		IHL	81	9	49	58	202
1982-83—Milwaukee Admirals		IHL	60	5	24	29	127
1983-84—Milwaukee Admirals		IHL	82	10	41	51	146

(c)—August, 1980—Signed by St. Louis Blues as free agent.

DARREN McKAY

Defense . . . 5'9" . . . 190 lbs. . . . Born, Lloydminster, Sask., February 10, 1962 . . . Shoots left.

Year	Team	League	Games	G.	A.	Pts.	Pen.
1977-78—Red Deer Rustlers		AJHL	59	2	11	13	50
1978-79—Red Deer Rustlers		AJHL	....	...	....	....	....
1978-79—Billings Bighorns		WHL	2	0	0	0	0
1979-80—Red Deer Rustlers		AJHL	....	...	....	....	....
1979-80—Billings Bighorns		WHL	14	6	2	8	23
1980-81—Billings Bighorns		WHL	68	10	29	39	183
1981-82—Billings Bighorns		WHL	70	12	64	76	176
1982-83—Binghamton Whalers (c)		AHL	65	4	32	36	113
1983-84—Binghamton Whalers		AHL	71	11	40	51	206

(c)—August, 1982—Signed by Hartford Whalers as a free agent.

GARNET McKECHNEY

Right Wing . . . 6'2" . . . 175 lbs. . . . Born, Swift Current, Sask., April 28, 1965 . . . Shoots right.

Year	Team	League	Games	G.	A.	Pts.	Pen.
1981-82—Thunder Bay Maroons		Ont. Midget	62	40	30	70	54
1982-83—Kitchener Rangers (c)		OHL	66	20	20	40	95
1983-84—Kitchener Rangers		OHL	68	31	45	76	107

(c)—June, 1983—Drafted as underage junior by New York Islanders in 1983 NHL entry draft. Third Islanders pick, 37th overall, second round.

WALTER THOMAS JOHN McKECHNIE

Center . . . 6'2" . . . 195 lbs. . . . Born, London, Ont., June 19, 1947 . . . Shoots left . . . Missed part of 1971-72 season with stretched ankle ligaments . . . (February 17, 1981)— Partial ligament tear in right knee . . . (January, 1983)—Knee injury.

Year	Team	League	Games	G.	A.	Pts.	Pen.
1964-65—London Nationals (c)		Jr. "B" OHA	....	...	....	....	....
1965-66—London Nationals		Jr. "A" OHA	46	13	28	41	68
1966-67—London Nationals		Jr. "A" OHA	48	13	46	59	125
1967-68—London Nationals		Jr. "A" OHA	1	0	0	0	0
1967-68—Phoenix Roadrunners (d-e)		WHL	67	24	30	54	24
1967-68—Minnesota North Stars		NHL	4	0	0	0	0
1968-69—Phoenix Roadrunners (f)		WHL	10	3	11	14	6
1968-69—Minnesota North Stars		NHL	58	5	9	14	22
1969-70—Iowa Stars		CHL	42	17	24	41	82
1969-70—Minnesota North Stars		NHL	20	1	3	4	21
1970-71—Cleveland Barons		AHL	35	16	31	47	28
1970-71—Minnesota North Stars (g)		NHL	30	3	1	4	34
1971-72—California Golden Seals		NHL	56	11	20	31	40
1972-73—California Golden Seals		NHL	78	16	38	54	58
1973-74—California Golden Seals (h-i)		NHL	63	23	29	52	14
1974-75—Boston Bruins (j)		NHL	53	3	3	6	8
1974-75—Detroit Red Wings		NHL	23	6	11	17	6
1975-76—Detroit Red Wings		NHL	80	26	56	82	85
1976-77—Detroit Red Wings (k)		NHL	80	25	34	59	50
1977-78—Washington Capitals (l)		NHL	16	4	1	5	0
1977-78—Cleveland Barons (m)		NHL	53	12	22	34	12
1978-79—Toronto Maple Leafs		NHL	79	25	36	61	18
1979-80—Toronto Maple Leafs (n)		NHL	54	7	36	43	4
1979-80—Colorado Rockies		NHL	17	0	4	4	2

Year	Team	League	Games	G.	A.	Pts.	Pen.
1980-81—Colorado Rockies		NHL	53	15	23	38	18
1981-82—Detroit Red Wings (o)		NHL	74	18	37	55	35
1982-83—Detroit Red Wings (p)		NHL	64	14	29	43	42
1983-84—Salt Lake Golden Eagles		CHL	69	9	32	41	36
NHL TOTALS			955	214	392	606	469

(c)—Drafted from London Jr. "B" by Toronto Maple Leafs in first round of 1963 amateur draft.
(d)—Sold to Minnesota North Stars by Phoenix Roadrunners, February, 1968. Minnesota loaned players to Phoenix as part of deal. Phoenix received Leo Thiffault and Bob Charlebois, July, 1968, to complete deal.
(e)—WHL Rookie-of-the-Year.
(f)—Loaned to Phoenix Roadrunners by Minnesota North Stars, October, 1968. Recalled, November, 1968
(g)—Traded to California Golden Seals by Minnesota North Stars with Joey Johnston for Dennis Hextall, May, 1971.
(h)—Claimed from California Golden Seals by New York Rangers in intra-league draft, June, 1974.
(i)—Traded to Boston Bruins by New York Rangers for Derek Sanderson, June, 1974.
(j)—Traded to Detroit Red Wings by Boston Bruins with Boston's third-round 1975 draft choice for Hank Nowak and Earl Anderson, February, 1975.
(k)—Traded to Washington Capitals by Detroit Red Wings as compensation for Detroit signing free agent Ron Low, August, 1977.
(l)—Traded to Cleveland Barons by Washington Capitals for Bob Girard and second-round draft choice, December, 1977.
(m)—Traded to Toronto Maple Leafs by Minnesota North Stars for "future considerations," October, 1978.
(n)—March, 1980—Traded by Toronto Maple Leafs to Colorado Rockies for third round pick in 1980 Entry Draft (Fred Boimistruck).
(o)—August, 1981—Signed by Detroit Red Wings as a free agent.
(p)—April, 1983—Released by Detroit Red Wings.

ANTHONY SYIIYD (TONY) McKEGNEY

Left Wing . . . 6'1" . . . 195 lbs. . . . Born, Montreal, Que., February 15, 1958 . . . Shoots left . . . Brother of Mike (1974 Montreal draft pick) and Ian (Dallas-CHL) McKegney and adopted son of Lawrey McKegney.

Year	Team	League	Games	G.	A.	Pts.	Pen.
1974-75—Kingston Canadians		Jr. "A" OHA	52	27	48	75	36
1975-76—Kingston Canadians		Jr. "A" OHA	65	24	56	80	20
1976-77—Kingston Canadians (a)		Jr. "A" OHA	66	58	77	135	30
1977-78—Kingston Canadians (b-c)		Jr. "A" OHA	55	43	49	92	19
1978-79—Buffalo Sabres		NHL	52	8	14	22	10
1978-79—Hershey Bears		AHL	24	21	18	39	4
1979-80—Buffalo Sabres		NHL	80	23	29	52	24
1980-81—Buffalo Sabres		NHL	80	37	32	69	24
1981-82—Buffalo Sabres		NHL	73	23	29	52	41
1982-83—Buffalo Sabres (d)		NHL	78	36	37	73	18
1983-84—Quebec Nordiques		NHL	75	24	27	51	23
NHL TOTALS			438	151	168	319	140

(c)—Drafted from Kingston Canadians by Buffalo Sabres in second round of 1978 amateur draft.
(d)—June, 1983—Traded by Buffalo Sabres with Andre Savard, Jean-Francois Sauve and Buffalo's third-round pick in 1983 (Iiro Jarvi) to Quebec Nordiques for Real Cloutier and Quebec's first-round draft choice in 1983 (Adam Creighton).

SEAN MICHAEL McKENNA

Right Wing . . . 6' . . . 186 lbs. . . . Born, Asbestos, Que., March 7, 1962 . . . Shoots right.

Year	Team	League	Games	G.	A.	Pts.	Pen.
1978-79—Montreal Juniors		QMJHL	66	9	14	23	14
1979-80—Sherbrooke Beavers (c)		QMJHL	59	20	19	39	24
1980-81—Sherbrooke Beavers (a)		QMJHL	71	57	47	104	122
1981-82—Sherbrooke Beavers (b-d-e)		QMJHL	59	57	33	90	29
1981-82—Buffalo Sabres		NHL	3	0	1	1	2
1982-83—Buffalo Sabres		NHL	46	10	14	24	4
1982-83—Rochester Americans (f)		AHL	26	16	10	26	14
1983-84—Buffalo Sabres		NHL	78	20	10	30	45
NHL TOTALS			127	30	25	55	51

(c)—June, 1980—Drafted as underage junior by Buffalo Sabres in 1980 NHL entry draft. Third Sabres pick, 56th overall, third round.
(d)—Led QMJHL President Cup Playoffs with 26 goals.
(e)—Named MVP of 1982 Memorial Cup Tournament.
(f)—Led AHL playoffs with a record 14 goals.

BRIAN McKINNON

Center ... 5'11" ... 185 lbs. ... Born, Toronto, Ont., October 4, 1964 ... Shoots left.

Year	Team	League	Games	G.	A.	Pts.	Pen.
1981-82—Dixie Beehives	MTJHL	46	32	30	62	72
1982-83—Ottawa 67's	OHL	66	6	9	15	20
1983-84—Ottawa 67's (c)	OHL	58	31	27	58	27

(c)—June, 1984—Drafted as underage junior by Buffalo Sabres in NHL entry draft. Ninth Sabres pick, 106th overall, 10th round.

DAVID McLAY

Left Wing ... 5'11" ... 175 lbs. ... Born, Chilliwak, B.C., May 13, 1966 ... Shoots left.

Year	Team	League	Games	G.	A.	Pts.	Pen.
1983-84—Kelowna Wings (c)	WHL	71	34	34	68	112

(c)—June, 1984—Drafted as underage junior by Philadelphia Flyers in NHL entry draft. Third Flyers pick, 43rd overall, third round.

DANIEL SCOTT McLELLAN
(Known by middle name)

Right Wing ... 6'1" ... 175 lbs. ... Born, Toronto, Ont., February 10, 1963 ... Shoots right.

Year	Team	League	Games	G.	A.	Pts.	Pen.
1979-80—St. Michael's Midget	OHA Midget	41	43	48	91	....
1980-81—Niagara Falls Flyers (c)	OHL	33	7	4	11	39
1981-82—Niagara Falls Flyers	OHL	12	1	6	7	33
1981-82—Peterborough Petes	OHL	46	20	31	51	42
1982-83—Boston Bruins	NHL	2	0	0	0	0
1982-83—Peterborough Petes	OHL	65	43	58	101	38
1983-84—Toledo Goaldiggers	IHL	5	1	2	3	0
1983-84—Hershey Bears	AHL	73	9	12	21	14
NHL TOTALS		2	0	0	0	0

(c)—June, 1981—Drafted as underage junior by Boston Bruins in 1981 NHL entry draft. Third Bruins pick, 77th overall, fourth round.

TOM McMURCHY

Right Wing ... 5'10" ... 170 lbs. ... Born, New Westminster, B.C., December 2, 1963 ... Shoots left ... Also plays center and left wing ... Brother of Anthony McMurchy.

Year	Team	League	Games	G.	A.	Pts.	Pen.
1980-81—Medicine Hat Tigers (c)	WHL	14	5	0	5	46
1980-81—Brandon Wheat Kings	WHL	48	20	33	53	101
1981-82—Brandon Wheat Kings (d)	WHL	68	59	63	122	179
1982-83—Brandon Wheat Kings	WHL	42	43	38	81	48
1982-83—Springfield Indians	AHL	8	2	2	4	0
1983-84—Springfield Indians	AHL	43	16	14	30	54
1983-84—Chicago Black Hawks	NHL	27	3	1	4	42
NHL TOTALS		27	3	1	4	42

(c)—November, 1980—Traded with Syd Cranston and future considerations by Medicine Hat Tigers to Brandon Wheat Kings for Mike Winther.

(d)—June, 1982—Drafted as underage junior by Chicago Black Hawks in 1982 NHL entry draft. Third Black Hawks pick, 49th overall, third round.

PETER MAXWELL McNAB

Center ... 6'3" ... 210 lbs. ... Born, Vancouver, B.C., May 8, 1952 ... Shoots left ... Son of Max McNab, general manager of New Jersey Devils and former NHL forward ... Brother of David McNab (Hartford Whalers scout) ... Missed part of 1974-75 season with injured knee ligament ... Given six-game suspension by NHL for fight in stands at New York Rangers on December 26, 1979 ... Attended University of Denver on a baseball scholarship ... (January, 1983)—Separated right shoulder ... (February 24, 1984)—Tore ligaments in right thumb during game vs. Los Angeles and required surgery.

Year	Team	League	Games	G.	A.	Pts.	Pen.
1970-71—University of Denver	WCHA	28	19	14	33	6
1971-72—University of Denver	WCHA	38	27	38	65	16
1972-73—University of Denver (c)	WCHA	28	23	29	52	12
1973-74—Cincinnati Swords	AHL	49	34	39	73	16
1973-74—Buffalo Sabres	NHL	22	3	6	9	2
1974-75—Buffalo Sabres	NHL	53	22	21	43	8
1975-76—Buffalo Sabres (d)	NHL	79	24	32	56	16
1976-77—Boston Bruins	NHL	80	38	48	86	11

Year	Team	League	Games	G.	A.	Pts.	Pen.
1977-78—Boston Bruins		NHL	79	41	39	80	4
1978-79—Boston Bruins		NHL	76	35	45	80	10
1979-80—Boston Bruins		NHL	74	40	38	78	10
1980-81—Boston Bruins		NHL	80	37	46	83	24
1981-82—Boston Bruins		NHL	80	36	40	76	19
1982-83—Boston Bruins		NHL	74	22	52	74	23
1983-84—Boston Bruins (e)		NHL	52	14	16	30	10
1983-84—Vancouver Canucks		NHL	13	1	6	7	10
NHL TOTALS			762	313	389	702	147

(c)—Drafted from University of Denver by Buffalo Sabres in sixth round of 1972 amateur draft.
(d)—NHL rights traded to Boston Bruins by Buffalo Sabres for NHL rights to Andre Savard, June, 1976.
(e)—February, 1984—Traded by Boston Bruins to Vancouver Canucks for Jim Nill.

GEORGE McPHEE

Left Wing . . . 5'9" . . . 170 lbs. . . . Born, Guelph, Ont., July 2, 1958 . . . Shoots left . . . (January, 1983)—Back injury.

Year	Team	League	Games	G.	A.	Pts.	Pen.
1977-78—Guelph Platers		OPJHL	48	53	57	110	150
1978-79—Bowling Green St. Univ.		CCHA	43	*40	48	*88	58
1979-80—Bowling Green St. Univ.		CCHA	34	21	24	45	51
1980-81—Bowling Green St. Univ. (b)		CCHA	36	25	29	54	68
1981-82—Bowling Green U. (a-c-d-e)		CCHA	40	28	52	80	57
1982-83—Tulsa Oilers (f)		CHL	61	17	43	60	145
1982-83—New York Rangers (g)		NHL	....	...	....	....	....
1983-84—New York Rangers		NHL	9	1	1	2	11
1983-84—Tulsa Oilers		CHL	49	20	28	48	133
NHL TOTALS			9	1	1	2	11

(c)—CCHA Player of the Year.
(d)—Named to All-America Team (West).
(e)—Winner of Hobey Baker Award (Top NCAA hockey player).
(f)—May, 1983—Signed by New York Rangers as a free agent.
(g)—No regular-season record. Played in nine playoff games with three goals and three assists.

MICHAEL JOSEPH McPHEE

Left Wing . . . 6'2" . . . 200 lbs. . . . Born, Sydney, N.S., February 14, 1960 . . . Shoots left . . . (Sept., 1982)—Broke hand in training camp.

Year	Team	League	Games	G.	A.	Pts.	Pen.
1978-79—R.P.I.		ECAC	26	14	19	33	16
1979-80—R.P.I. (c)		ECAC	27	15	21	36	22
1980-81—R.P.I.		ECAC	29	28	18	46	22
1981-82—R.P.I.		ECAC	6	0	3	3	4
1982-83—Nova Scotia Voyageurs		AHL	42	10	15	25	29
1983-84—Nova Scotia Voyageurs		AHL	67	22	33	55	101
1983-84—Montreal Canadiens		NHL	14	5	2	7	41
NHL TOTALS			14	5	2	7	41

(c)—June, 1980—Drafted by Montreal Canadiens in 1980 NHL entry draft. Eighth Canadiens pick, 124th overall, sixth round.

BASIL PAUL McRAE

Left Wing . . . 6'2" . . . 200 lbs. . . . Born, Orillia, Ont., January 1, 1961 . . . Shoots left.

Year	Team	League	Games	G.	A.	Pts.	Pen.
1977-78—Seneca Nats		OHA Jr. "B"	36	21	38	59	80
1978-79—London Knights		OMJHL	66	13	28	41	79
1979-80—London Knights (c)		OMJHL	67	23	35	58	116
1980-81—London Knights		OHL	65	29	23	52	266
1981-82—Fredericton Express		AHL	47	11	15	26	175
1981-82—Quebec Nordiques		NHL	20	4	3	7	69
1982-83—Fredericton Express		AHL	53	22	19	41	146
1982-83—Quebec Nordiques		NHL	22	1	1	2	59
1983-84—Toronto Maple Leafs (d)		NHL	3	0	0	0	19
1983-84—St. Catharines Saints		AHL	78	14	25	39	187
NHL TOTALS			45	5	4	9	147

(c)—June, 1980—Drafted as underage junior by Quebec Nordiques in 1980 NHL entry draft. Third Nordiques pick, 87th overall, fifth round.
(d)—August, 1983—Traded by Quebec Nordiques to Toronto Maple Leafs for Richard Trumel.

MARTY McSORLEY

Defense . . . 6'1" . . . 190 lbs. . . . Born, Hamilton, Ont., May 18, 1963 . . . Shoots right.

Year	Team	League	Games	G.	A.	Pts.	Pen.
1981-82	Belleville Bulls	OHL	58	6	13	19	234
1982-83	Belleville Bulls	OHL	70	10	41	51	183
1982-83	Baltimore Skipjacks (c)	AHL	2	0	0	0	22
1983-84	Pittsburgh Penguins	NHL	72	2	7	9	224
	NHL TOTALS		72	2	7	9	224

(c)—April, 1983—Signed by Pittsburgh Penguins as a free agent.

JIM McTAGGART

Defense . . . 6' . . . 191 lbs. . . . Born, Weyburn, Sask., March 31, 1960 . . . Shoots left.

Year	Team	League	Games	G.	A.	Pts.	Pen.
1976-77	Swift Current	SJHL	47	5	29	34	97
1977-78	Saskatoon Blades	WCHL	65	7	20	27	221
1978-79	Saskatoon Blades	WHL	37	6	19	25	86
1978-79	Billings Bighorns	WHL	30	1	12	13	93
1979-80	Billings Bighorns (b)	WHL	65	16	37	53	284
1980-81	Washington Capitals (c)	NHL	52	1	6	7	185
1980-81	Hershey Bears	AHL	23	2	1	3	81
1981-82	Hershey Bears	AHL	57	3	12	15	190
1981-82	Washington Capitals	NHL	19	2	4	6	20
1982-83	Moncton Alpines (d)	AHL	49	0	7	7	63
1982-83	Wichita Wind	CHL	21	3	9	12	38
1983-84	Montana Magic	CHL	70	5	13	18	104
	NHL TOTALS		71	3	10	13	205

(c)—August, 1980—Signed by Washington Capitals as a free agent.
(d)—October, 1983—Acquired by Edmonton Oilers on waivers from Washington Capitals.

NEIL ROBERT MEADMORE

Right Wing . . . 6'4" . . . 180 lbs. . . . Born, Winnipeg, Man., October 23, 1959 . . . Shoots right . . . Son of Ronald Meadmore, who played several seasons in CFL . . . Brother of Jim Meadmore . . . (November, 1983)—Knee surgery.

Year	Team	League	Games	G.	A.	Pts.	Pen.
1977-78	Flin Flon Bombers	WCHL	25	7	8	15	30
1977-78	New Westminster Bruins	WCHL	29	5	7	12	19
1978-79	New Westminster Bruins	WHL	71	30	36	66	128
1979-80	Kalamazoo Wings	IHL	79	23	37	60	160
1980-81	Kalamazoo Wings	IHL	82	31	41	78	179
1981-82	Adirondack Red Wings	AHL	52	13	11	24	106
1981-82	Kalamazoo Wings	IHL	24	18	11	29	51
1982-83	Kalamazoo Wings	IHL	26	10	7	17	97
1983-84	Kalamazoo Wings	IHL	82	39	48	87	267

RICK MEAGHER

Center . . . 5'8" . . . 175 lbs. . . . Born, Belleville, Ont., November 4, 1953 . . . Shoots left . . . Attended Boston University . . . Member of Boston University Hall of Fame . . . Named the Boston University Athlete of the Decade (1970-79) . . . Elected to ECAC All-Decade Team (1970-79) . . . Brother of Terry Meagher . . . (December, 1981)—Back and knee problems . . . (November, 1982)—Missed eight games with shoulder separation suffered in game at Montreal . . . (January, 1984)—Fractured rib.

Year	Team	League	Games	G.	A.	Pts.	Pen.
1973-74	Boston University	ECAC	30	19	21	40	26
1974-75	Boston University	ECAC	32	25	28	53	80
1975-76	Boston University	ECAC	28	12	25	37	22
1976-77	Boston University (a-c)	ECAC	34	34	46	80	42
1977-78	Nova Scotia Voyageurs	AHL	57	20	27	47	33
1978-79	Nova Scotia Voyageurs	AHL	79	35	46	81	57
1979-80	Nova Scotia Voyageurs	AHL	64	32	44	76	53
1979-80	Montreal Canadiens (d)	NHL	2	0	0	0	0
1980-81	Binghamton Whalers	AHL	50	23	35	58	54
1980-81	Hartford Whalers	NHL	27	7	10	17	19
1981-82	Hartford Whalers	NHL	65	24	19	43	51
1982-83	Hartford Whalers	NHL	4	0	0	0	0
1982-83	New Jersey Devils	NHL	57	15	14	29	11
1983-84	Maine Mariners	AHL	10	6	4	10	2
1983-84	New Jersey Devils	NHL	52	14	14	28	16
	NHL TOTALS		207	60	57	117	97

(c)—Named to first team (East) All-America.
(d)—June, 1980—Traded with third (Paul MacDermid) and fifth (Dan Bourbonnais) round picks in 1981 draft by Montreal Canadiens to Hartford Whalers for third (Dieter Hegen) and fifth (Steve Rooney) round Whalers picks in 1981 draft.

ALLAN MEASURES

Defense ... 5'11" ... 165 lbs. ... Born, Barrhead, Alta., May 8, 1965 ... Shoots left.

Year	Team	League	Games	G.	A.	Pts.	Pen.
1981-82—Barrhead Midget		Alta. Midget	40	55	66	121	40
1982-83—Calgary Wranglers (c)		WHL	63	5	23	28	43
1983-84—Calgary Wranglers		WHL	69	17	36	53	96

(c)—June, 1983—Drafted as underage junior by Vancouver Canucks in 1983 NHL entry draft. Ninth Canucks pick, 170th overall, ninth round.

BRENT MECKLING

Defense ... 6'2" ... 180 lbs. ... Born, Calgary, Alta., September 14, 1964 ... Shoots left.

Year	Team	League	Games	G.	A.	Pts.	Pen.
1981-82—Calgary Wranglers (c)		WHL	4	0	0	0	0
1982-83—Calgary Wranglers		WHL	6	0	1	1	0
1982-83—Medicine Hat Tigers		WHL	64	15	36	51	61
1983-84—Medicine Hat Tigers		WHL	67	10	53	63	71

(c)—June, 1982—Drafted as underage junior by Detroit Red Wings in NHL entry draft. 10th Red Wings pick, 191st overall, 10th round.

RON MEGAN

Defense ... 6'1" ... 195 lbs. ... Born, Watertown, N.Y., April 4, 1960 ... Shoots left.

Year	Team	League	Games	G.	A.	Pts.	Pen.
1982-83—Kalamazoo Wings		IHL	80	8	32	40	65
1983-84—Peoria Prancers		IHL	67	7	26	33	61

RON JAMES MEIGHAN

Defense ... 6'3" ... 194 lbs. ... Born, Montreal, Que., May 26, 1963 ... Shoots right.

Year	Team	League	Games	G.	A.	Pts.	Pen.
1979-80—Niagara Falls Flyers		OMJHL	61	3	10	13	20
1980-81—Niagara Falls Flyers (c)		OHL	63	8	27	35	92
1981-82—Niagara Falls Flyers (a-d)		OHL	58	27	41	68	85
1981-82—Minnesota North Stars (e)		NHL	7	1	1	2	2
1982-83—North Bay Centennials		OHL	29	19	22	41	30
1982-83—Pittsburgh Penguins		NHL	41	2	6	8	16
1983-84—Baltimore Skipjacks		AHL	75	4	16	20	36
NHL TOTALS			48	3	7	10	18

(c)—June, 1981—Drafted as underage junior by Minnesota North Stars in 1981 NHL entry draft. First North Stars pick, 13th overall, first round.
(d)—Winner of Max Kaminsky Trophy (Outstanding OHL Defenseman).
(e)—October, 1982—Traded by Minnesota North Stars with Anders Hakansson and Minnesota's first-round draft choice (Bob Errey) in 1983 to Pittsburgh Penguins for George Ferguson and Pittsburgh's first-round draft choice (Brian Bellows) in 1983.

BRUCE MELANSON

Right Wing ... 6'2" ... 190 lbs. ... Born, St. John, N.B., June 11, 1966 ... Shoots left.

Year	Team	League	Games	G.	A.	Pts.	Pen.
1982-83—St. John Midgets		N.B. Midgets	51	37	30	67	80
1983-84—Oshawa Generals (c)		OHL	60	8	9	17	78

(c)—June, 1984—Drafted as underage junior by New York Islanders in NHL entry draft. Second Islanders pick, 41st overall, second round.

SCOTT MELLANBY

Right Wing ... 6'1" ... 195 lbs. ... Born, Montreal, Que., June 11, 1966 ... Shoots right.

Year	Team	League	Games	G.	A.	Pts.	Pen.
1983-84—Henry Carr H.S. (c)		MTJHL	39	37	37	74	97

(c)—June, 1984—Drafted as underage junior by Philadelphia Flyers in NHL entry draft. First Flyers pick, 27th overall, second round.

LARRY JOSEPH MELNYK

Defense ... 6' ... 180 lbs. ... Born, New Westminster, B.C., February 21, 1960 ... Shoots left.

Year	Team	League	Games	G.	A.	Pts.	Pen.
1977-78—Abbotsford		BCJHL	39	10	9	19	100
1977-78—New Westminster Bruins		WCHL	44	3	22	25	71
1978-79—New Westminster Bruins (c)		WHL	71	7	33	40	142
1979-80—New Westminster Bruins		WHL	67	13	38	51	236
1980-81—Boston Bruins		NHL	26	0	4	4	39
1980-81—Springfield Indians		AHL	47	1	10	11	109
1981-82—Erie Blades		AHL	10	0	3	3	36
1981-82—Boston Bruins		NHL	48	0	8	8	84
1982-83—Baltimore Skipjacks		AHL	72	2	24	26	215
1982-83—Boston Bruins		NHL	1	0	0	0	0
1983-84—Hershey Bears (d)		AHL	51	0	18	18	156
1983-84—Moncton Alpines		AHL	14	0	3	3	17
1983-84—Edmonton Oilers (e)		NHL	..	..	..	..	..
NHL TOTALS			75	0	12	12	123

(c)—August, 1979—Drafted as underage junior by Boston Bruins in 1979 NHL entry draft. Fifth Bruins pick, 78th overall, fourth round.
(d)—March, 1983—Traded by Boston Bruins to Edmonton Oilers for John Blum.
(e)—Played in six NHL playoff games, one assist.

BARRY JAMES MELROSE
Defense . . . 6'1" . . . 201 lbs. . . . Born, Kelvington, Sask., July 15, 1956 . . . Shoots right.

Year	Team	League	Games	G.	A.	Pts.	Pen.
1973-74—Weyburn Red Wings		SJHL	50	2	19	21	162
1974-75—Kamloops Chiefs		WCHL	70	6	18	24	95
1975-76—Kamloops Chiefs (c-d)		WCHL	72	12	49	61	112
1976-77—Springfield Indians		AHL	23	0	3	3	17
1976-77—Cincinnati Stingers		WHA	29	1	4	5	8
1977-78—Cincinnati Stingers		WHA	69	2	9	11	113
1978-79—Cincinnati Stingers (e)		WHA	80	2	14	16	222
1979-80—Winnipeg Jets		NHL	74	4	6	10	124
1980-81—Winnipeg Jets (f)		NHL	18	1	1	2	40
1980-81—Toronto Maple Leafs		NHL	57	2	5	7	166
1981-82—Toronto Maple Leafs		NHL	64	1	5	6	186
1982-83—St. Catharines Saints		AHL	25	1	10	11	106
1982-83—Toronto Maple Leafs (g)		NHL	52	2	5	7	68
1983-84—Detroit Red Wings		NHL	21	0	1	1	74
1983-84—Adirondack Red Wings		AHL	16	2	1	3	37
WHA TOTALS			178	5	27	32	343
NHL TOTALS			286	10	23	33	658

(c)—Drafted from Kamloops Chiefs by Montreal Canadiens in second round of 1976 amateur draft.
(d)—Selected by Cincinnati Stingers in WHA amateur player draft, June, 1976. Signed by Cincinnati, September, 1976.
(e)—June, 1979—Claimed by Quebec Nordiques in WHA dispersal draft. Selected by Montreal Canadiens in NHL reclaim draft. Chosen by Winnipeg Jets in NHL expansion draft.
(f)—November, 1980—Acquired by Toronto Maple Leafs on waivers from Winnipeg Jets.
(g)—July, 1983—Signed by Detroit Red Wings as a free agent.

KEVAN MELROSE
Defense . . . 5'10" . . . 180 lbs. . . . Born, Calgary, Alta., March 28, 1966 . . . Shoots left.

Year	Team	League	Games	G.	A.	Pts.	Pen.
1983-84—Red Deer (c)		AJHL	42	9	26	35	89

(c)—June, 1984—Drafted as underage junior by Calgary Flames in NHL entry draft. Seventh Flames pick, 138th overall, seventh round.

PAUL RAYMOND MERCIER
Defense . . . 6' . . . 201 lbs. . . . Born, Smooth Rock Falls, Ont., May 18, 1961 . . . Shoots left.

Year	Team	League	Games	G.	A.	Pts.	Pen.
1977-78—Sudbury Wolves		OMJHL	66	1	12	13	113
1978-79—Sudbury Wolves		OMJHL	56	10	21	31	222
1979-80—Sudbury Wolves (c)		OMJHL	21	0	7	7	50
1980-81—Sudbury Wolves		OHL	18	1	6	7	43
1980-81—Niagara Falls Flyers		OHL	41	6	24	30	149
1981-82—Maine Mariners		AHL	67	4	6	10	176
1982-83—Toledo Goaldiggers		IHL	14	1	7	8	29
1982-83—Maine Mariners		AHL	60	1	2	3	117
1983-84—Maine Mariners		AHL	22	0	1	1	70
1983-84—Toledo Goaldiggers		IHL	1	0	0	0	5
1983-84—Erie Golden Blades		ACHL	19	3	7	10	8

(c)—June, 1980—Drafted by Philadelphia Flyers as underage junior in 1980 NHL entry draft. Third Flyers pick, 63rd overall, third round.

GREGORY PAUL MEREDITH

Right Wing . . . 6'1" . . . 210 lbs. . . . Born, Toronto, Ont., February 23, 1958 . . . Shoots right . . . (January, 1981)—Hepatitis.

Year	Team	League	Games	G.	A.	Pts.	Pen.
1976-77—University of Notre Dame		WCHA	34	21	20	41	18
1977-78—University of Notre Dame (c)		WCHA	38	13	13	26	24
1978-79—University of Notre Dame		WCHA	35	28	22	50	14
1979-80—University of Notre Dame (a-d)		WCHA	38	40	31	71	14
1980-81—Calgary Flames		NHL	3	1	0	1	0
1980-81—Birmingham Bulls		CHL	39	17	10	27	36
1980-81—Tulsa Oilers		CHL	10	6	4	10	12
1981-82—Oklahoma City Stars		CHL	80	10	23	33	64
1982-83—Colorado Flames		CHL	36	16	10	26	14
1982-83—Calgary Flames		NHL	35	5	4	9	8
1983-84—Colorado Flames		CHL	54	23	20	43	39
NHL TOTALS			38	6	4	10	8

(c)—June, 1978—Drafted by Atlanta Flames in 1978 NHL amateur draft. Fifth Flames pick, 97th overall, sixth round.

(d)—Named to All-America Team (West).

GLENN MERKOSKY

Center . . . 5'10" . . . 175 lbs. . . . Born, Edmonton, Alta., April 8, 1960 . . . Shoots left.

Year	Team	League	Games	G.	A.	Pts.	Pen.
1977-78—Seattle Breakers		WCHL	6	4	3	7	2
1978-79—Michigan Tech		WCHA	38	14	29	43	22
1979-80—Calgary Wranglers		WHL	72	49	40	89	95
1980-81—Binghamton Whalers (c)		AHL	80	26	35	61	61
1981-82—Hartford Whalers		NHL	7	0	0	0	2
1981-82—Binghamton Whalers		AHL	72	29	40	69	83
1982-83—New Jersey Devils (d)		NHL	34	4	10	14	20
1982-83—Wichita Wind		CHL	45	26	23	49	15
1983-84—Maine Mariners		AHL	75	28	28	56	56
1983-84—New Jersey Devils		NHL	5	1	0	1	0
NHL TOTALS			46	5	10	15	22

(c)—August, 1980—Signed by Hartford Whalers as a free agent.

(d)—September, 1982—Signed by New Jersey Devils as a free agent.

LEONARD WAYNE MERRICK
(Known by middle name)

Center . . . 6'1" . . . 190 lbs. . . . Born, Sarnia, Ont., April 23, 1952 . . . Shoots left . . . Missed part of 1973-74 season with hairline fracture of left leg . . . Has also played Left Wing . . . Missed part of 1977-78 season with knee injury . . . (December 13, 1981)—Bruised clavicle and sternum in game at Philadelphia . . . (February 4, 1984)—Sprained medial ligament of right knee in game vs. Pittsburgh.

Year	Team	League	Games	G.	A.	Pts.	Pen.
1969-70—Ottawa 67's		Jr."A"OHA	51	10	17	27	10
1970-71—Ottawa 67's		Jr."A"OHA	62	34	42	76	41
1971-72—Ottawa 67's (c-d)		Jr."A"OHA	62	39	56	95	21
1972-73—Denver Spurs		WHL	22	6	13	19	6
1972-73—St. Louis Blues		NHL	50	10	11	21	10
1973-74—St. Louis Blues		NHL	64	20	23	43	32
1974-75—St. Louis Blues		NHL	76	28	37	65	57
1975-76—St. Louis Blues (e)		NHL	19	7	8	15	0
1975-76—California Seals		NHL	56	25	27	52	36
1976-77—Cleveland Barons		NHL	80	18	38	56	25
1977-78—Cleveland Barons (f)		NHL	18	2	5	7	8
1977-78—New York Islanders		NHL	37	10	14	24	8
1978-79—New York Islanders		NHL	75	20	21	41	24
1979-80—New York Islanders		NHL	70	13	22	35	16
1980-81—New York Islanders		NHL	71	16	15	31	30
1981-82—New York Islanders		NHL	68	12	27	39	20
1982-83—New York Islanders		NHL	59	4	12	16	27
1983-84—New York Islanders (g)		NHL	31	6	5	11	10
NHL TOTALS			774	191	265	456	303

(c)—Selected by Miami Screaming Eagles in World Hockey Association player selection draft, February, 1972.

(d)—Drafted from Ottawa 67's by St. Louis Blues in first round of 1972 amateur draft.

(e)—Traded to California Seals by St. Louis Blues for Larry Patey and third round draft choice, November, 1975.

(f)—Traded to New York Islanders by Cleveland Barons with Darcy Regier for Jean Potvin and J. P. Parise, January, 1978.

(g)—June, 1984—Released by New York Islanders.

MARK MESSIER

Center and Left Wing . . . 6' . . . 205 lbs. . . . Born, Edmonton, Alta., January 18, 1961 . . . Shoots left . . . Son of Doug Messier (WHL), brother of Paul Messier and cousin of Mitch Messier . . . (November 7, 1981)—Injured ankle in game at Chicago . . . (March, 1983)—Chipped bone in wrist . . . (January 18, 1984)—Given six-game suspension by NHL for hitting Vancouver's Thomas Gradin over the head with his stick.

Year	Team	League	Games	G.	A.	Pts.	Pen.
1976-77—Spruce Grove Mets		AJHL	57	27	39	66	91
1977-78—St. Albert Saints		AJHL	....	...	....	....	....
1978-79—Indianapolis Racers (c)		WHA	5	0	0	0	0
1978-79—Cincinnati Stingers (d-e)		WHA	47	1	10	11	58
1979-80—Houston Apollos		CHL	4	0	3	3	4
1979-80—Edmonton Oilers		NHL	75	12	21	33	120
1980-81—Edmonton Oilers		NHL	72	23	40	63	102
1981-82—Edmonton Oilers (a)		NHL	78	50	38	88	119
1982-83—Edmonton Oilers (a)		NHL	77	48	58	106	72
1983-84—Edmonton Oilers (b-f)		NHL	73	37	64	101	165
WHA TOTALS			52	1	10	11	58
NHL TOTALS			375	170	221	391	578

(c)—November, 1978—Given 5-game trial by Indianapolis Racers.

(d)—January, 1979—Signed by Cincinnati Stingers as free agent.

(e)—August, 1979—Drafted by Edmonton Oilers in NHL entry draft. Second Edmonton pick, 48th overall, third round.

(f)—Won Conn Smythe Trophy (NHL Playoff MVP).

MITCH MESSIER

Center . . . 6'2" . . . 185 lbs. . . . Born, Regina, Sask., August 21, 1965 . . . Shoots right . . . Cousin of Mark Messier.

Year	Team	League	Games	G.	A.	Pts.	Pen.
1981-82—Notre Dame H.S.		Sask. Midget	26	8	20	28	..
1982-83—Notre Dame H.S. (c)		Sask. Juvenile	60	108	73	181	160
1983-84—Michigan State University		CCHA	37	6	15	21	22

(c)—June, 1983—Drafted by Minnesota North Stars in 1983 NHL entry draft. Fourth North Stars pick, 56th overall, third round.

JOHN MEULENBROEKS

Defense . . . 6' . . . 181 lbs. . . . Born, Kingston, Ont., April 3, 1964 . . . Shoots left.

Year	Team	League	Games	G.	A.	Pts.	Pen.
1981-82—Brantford Alexanders (c)		OHL	58	4	4	8	45
1982-83—Brantford Alexanders		OHL	69	1	18	19	55
1983-84—Brantford Alexanders		OHL	68	7	25	32	39

(c)—June, 1982—Drafted by Boston Bruins as underage junior in 1982 NHL entry draft. Seventh Bruins pick, 144th overall, seventh round.

JAYSON MEYER

Defense . . . 5'11" . . . 185 lbs. . . . Born, Regina, Sask., February 21, 1965 . . . Shoots left.

Year	Team	League	Games	G.	A.	Pts.	Pen.
1981-82—Regina Pats		WHL	59	3	20	23	106
1982-83—Regina Pats (c)		WHL	72	10	45	55	89
1983-84—Regina Pats		WHL	70	16	67	83	39

(c)—June, 1983—Drafted as underage junior by Buffalo Sabres in 1983 NHL entry draft. Seventh Sabres pick, 94th overall, fifth round.

DAVID MICHAYLUK

Right Wing . . . 5'10" . . . 175 lbs. . . . Born, Wakaw, Sask., May 18, 1962 . . . Shoots left.

Year	Team	League	Games	G.	A.	Pts.	Pen.
1979-80—Prince Albert Saints		AJHL	60	46	67	113	49
1980-81—Regina Pats (b-c-d)		WHL	72	62	71	133	39

Year	Team	League	Games	G.	A.	Pts.	Pen.
1981-82—Regina Pats (b-e)		WHL	72	62	111	173	128
1981-82—Philadelphia Flyers		NHL	1	0	0	0	0
1982-83—Philadelphia Flyers		NHL	13	2	6	8	8
1982-83—Maine Mariners		AHL	69	32	40	72	16
1983-84—Springfield Indians		AHL	79	18	44	62	37
NHL TOTALS			14	2	6	8	8

(c)—Winner of Stewart "Butch" Paul Memorial Trophy (Top WHL Rookie).
(d)—June, 1981—Drafted as underage junior by Philadelphia Flyers in 1981 NHL entry draft. Fifth Flyers pick, 65th overall, fourth round.
(e)—Led WHL playoffs with 40 points.

RICHARD DAVID (RICK) MIDDLETON

Right Wing . . . 5'11" . . . 170 lbs. . . . Born, Toronto, Ont., December 4, 1953 . . . Shoots right . . . Missed parts of 1974-75 season with broken left leg and fractured cheek . . . (March 11, 1982)—Scored hat trick in game vs. Winnipeg despite suffering sprained right shoulder . . . (July, 1982)—Surgery to replace torn tendon in right shoulder.

Year	Team	League	Games	G.	A.	Pts.	Pen.
1971-72—Oshawa Generals		Jr."A"OHA	53	36	34	70	24
1972-73—Oshawa Generals (b-c-d)		Jr."A"OHA	62	*67	70	137	14
1973-74—Providence Reds (a-e)		AHL	63	36	48	84	14
1974-75—New York Rangers		NHL	47	22	18	40	19
1975-76—New York Rangers (f)		NHL	77	24	26	50	14
1976-77—Boston Bruins		NHL	72	20	22	42	2
1977-78—Boston Bruins		NHL	79	25	35	60	8
1978-79—Boston Bruins		NHL	71	38	48	86	7
1979-80—Boston Bruins		NHL	80	40	52	92	24
1980-81—Boston Bruins		NHL	80	44	59	103	16
1981-82—Boston Bruins (b-g)		NHL	75	51	43	94	12
1982-83—Boston Bruins		NHL	80	49	47	96	8
1983-84—Boston Bruins		NHL	80	47	58	105	14
NHL TOTALS			741	360	408	768	124

(c)—Won Red Tilson Memorial Trophy (MVP).
(d)—Drafted from Oshawa Generals by New York Rangers in first round of 1973 amateur draft.
(e)—Won Dudley (Red) Garrett Memorial Trophy (leading rookie).
(f)—Traded to Boston Bruins by New York Rangers for Ken Hodge, May, 1976.
(g)—Winner of Lady Byng Memorial Trophy.

DAN MIELE

Right Wing . . . 6'2" . . . 190 lbs. . . . Born, LaSalle, Que., April 12, 1962 . . . Shoots right.

Year	Team	League	Games	G.	A.	Pts.	Pen.
1979-80—Providence College		ECAC	30	11	13	24	30
1980-81—Providence College		ECAC	28	16	13	29	20
1981-82—Hershey Bears (c)		AHL	67	7	11	18	25
1982-83—Hershey Bears		AHL	74	11	11	22	62
1983-84—Hershey Bears		AHL	65	23	17	40	18

(c)—June, 1980—Drafted as underage player by Washington Capitals in 1980 NHL entry draft. Second Capitals pick, 47th overall, third round.

MICHAEL JAMES MILBURY

Defense . . . 6'1" . . . 195 lbs. . . . Born, Brighton, Mass., June 17, 1952 . . . Shoots left . . . Given 6-game suspension by NHL for fight in stands at N.Y. Rangers, December 26, 1979 . . . Cousin of Dave Silk . . . Attended Colgate University on a football scholarship . . . (March 11, 1982)—Strained ligaments in right knee in game vs. Winnipeg . . . (March 29, 1983)—Broke right kneecap when hit by a Wally Weir shot in game at Quebec.

Year	Team	League	Games	G.	A.	Pts.	Pen.
1972-73—Colgate University			23	2	19	21	68
1973-74—Colgate University (c)			....	...	....	....	....
1974-75—Rochester Americans		AHL	71	2	15	17	246
1975-76—Rochester Americans		AHL	73	3	15	18	199
1975-76—Boston Bruins		NHL	3	0	0	0	9
1976-77—Boston Bruins (d)		NHL	77	6	18	24	166
1977-78—Boston Bruins		NHL	80	8	30	38	151
1978-79—Boston Bruins		NHL	74	1	34	35	149
1979-80—Boston Bruins		NHL	72	10	13	23	59
1980-81—Boston Bruins		NHL	77	0	18	18	222
1981-82—Boston Bruins		NHL	51	2	10	12	71

Year	Team	League	Games	G.	A.	Pts.	Pen.
1982-83—Boston Bruins		NHL	78	9	15	24	216
1983-84—Boston Bruins		NHL	74	2	17	19	159
NHL TOTALS			586	38	155	193	1202

(c)—September, 1974—Signed by Boston Bruins as a free agent.
(d)—Led in penalty minutes (47) during playoffs.

MIKE MILLAR

Right Wing . . . 5'10" . . . 170 lbs. . . . Born, St. Catharines, Ont., April 28, 1965 . . . Shoots left.

Year	Team	League	Games	G.	A.	Pts.	Pen.
1981-82—St. Catharines Midgets		Ont. Midget	30	32	32	64	24
1982-83—Brantford Alexanders		OHL	53	20	29	49	10
1983-84—Brantford Alexanders (c)		OHL	69	50	45	95	48

(c)—June, 1984—Drafted as underage junior by Hartford Whalers in NHL entry draft. Second Whalers pick, 110th overall, sixth round.

COREY MILLEN

Center . . . 5'7" . . . 165 lbs. . . . Born, Cloquet, Minn., April 29, 1964 . . . Shoots right . . . (November, 1982)—Injured knee in WCHA game vs. Colorado College, requiring surgery . . . Member of 1984 U.S. Olympic team.

Year	Team	League	Games	G.	A.	Pts.	Pen.
1981-82—Cloquet H.S. (c)		Minn. H.S.	18	46	35	81	....
1982-83—University of Minnesota		WCHA	21	14	15	29	18
1983-84—U.S. National Team		Int'l	45	15	11	26	10
1983-84—U.S. Olympic Team		Int'l	6	0	0	0	2

(c)—June, 1982—Drafted by New York Rangers in 1982 NHL entry draft as underage player. Third Rangers pick, 57th overall, third round.

PAUL EDWARD MILLER

Center . . . 5'10" . . . 170 lbs. . . . Born, Billerica, Mass., August 21, 1959 . . . Shoots left . . . (December, 1981)—Injured knee ligaments . . . Brother of Robert Miller.

Year	Team	League	Games	G.	A.	Pts.	Pen.
1977-78—Boston University		ECAC	31	10	14	24	28
1978-79—Boston University		ECAC	29	15	20	35	10
1979-80—Boston University		ECAC	20	4	10	14	13
1979-80—Flint Generals		IHL	13	3	2	5	31
1980-81—Syracuse Hornets		EHL	10	3	5	8	9
1980-81—Richmond Rifles		EHL	21	9	16	25	20
1981-82—Ft. Worth Texans (c)		CHL	65	25	38	63	44
1901-02—Colorado Rockies		NHL	3	0	3	3	0
1982-83—Wichita Wind (d)		CHL	55	17	18	35	44
1982-83—Moncton Alpines		AHL	19	2	8	10	7
1983-84—Muskegon Mohawks		IHL	4	0	1	1	0
1983-84—Moncton Alpines		AHL	46	9	2	11	68
NHL TOTALS			3	0	3	3	0

(c)—October, 1981—Signed by Colorado Rockies as a free agent.
(d)—March, 1983—Traded by New Jersey Devils to Edmonton Oilers to complete trade earlier in month in which Edmonton dealt Ron Low to New Jersey for Lindsay Middlebrook. Miller replaced Richie Hansen, who balked at going to Edmonton in the trade.

CHRIS MILLS

Defense . . . 6'1" . . . 185 lbs. . . . Born, Scarborough, Ont., May 30, 1966 . . . Shoots left.

Year	Team	League	Games	G.	A.	Pts.	Pen.
1983-84—Bramalea Blues (c)		MTJHL	42	9	27	36	50

(c)—June, 1984—Drafted as underage junior by Winnipeg Jets in NHL entry draft. Second Jets pick, 68th overall, fourth round.

JOHN MINER

Defense . . . 5'10" . . . 170 lbs. . . . Born, Moose Jaw, Sask., August 28, 1965 . . . Shoots right . . . (September, 1982)—Eye injury.

Year	Team	League	Games	G.	A.	Pts.	Pen.
1981-82—Regina Pats		SJHL	..	..	..	..	..
1981-82—Regina Pats		WHL	10	0	1	1	11
1982-83—Regina Pats (c)		WHL	71	11	23	34	126
1983-84—Regina Pats (b)		WHL	70	27	42	69	132

(c)—June, 1983—Drafted as underage junior by Edmonton Oilers in 1983 NHL entry draft. Tenth Oilers pick, 220th overall, 11th round.

GERALD (GERRY) MINOR

Center . . . 5'8" . . . 178 lbs. . . . Born, Regina, Sask., October 27, 1958 . . . Shoots left . . . Missed most of 1981-82 season due to skull fracture, broken ankle and torn knee ligaments . . . (February 19, 1983)—Strained ligaments in left knee during AHL game vs. Nova Scotia.

Year	Team	League	Games	G.	A.	Pts.	Pen.
1974-75—Regina Blues		SJHL	38	28	19	47	56
1974-75—Regina Pats		WCHL	16	2	6	8	6
1975-76—Regina Pats		WCHL	71	24	41	65	124
1976-77—Regina Pats		WCHL	48	22	32	54	122
1977-78—Regina Pats (c-d)		WCHL	66	54	75	129	238
1978-79—Fort Wayne Komets		IHL	42	18	28	46	67
1978-79—Dallas Black Hawks		CHL	37	14	25	39	76
1979-80—Dallas Black Hawks		CHL	73	31	52	83	162
1979-80—Vancouver Canucks		NHL	5	0	1	1	2
1980-81—Vancouver Canucks		NHL	74	10	14	24	108
1981-82—Vancouver Canucks		NHL	13	0	1	1	6
1981-82—Dallas Black Hawks		CHL	12	5	8	13	92
1982-83—Vancouver Canucks		NHL	39	1	5	6	57
1982-83—Fredericton Express		AHL	17	4	17	21	14
1983-84—Vancouver Canucks		NHL	9	0	0	0	0
1983-84—Fredericton Express		AHL	66	16	42	58	85
NHL TOTALS			140	11	21	32	173

(c)—Led WCHL Playoffs in points (37).

(d)—June, 1978—Drafted by Vancouver Canucks in 1978 NHL amateur draft. Sixth Canucks pick, 90th overall, sixth round.

MIKE MOHER

Right Wing . . . 5'10" . . . 175 lbs. . . . Born, Manitouwadge, Ont., March 26, 1962 . . . Shoots right . . . Set Ontario Junior Hockey League penalty minutes record in 1980-81 (372), and reset it in 1981-82 (384).

Year	Team	League	Games	G.	A.	Pts.	Pen.
1979-80—Sudbury Wolves		OMJHL	23	2	5	7	87
1979-80—Kitchener Rangers (c)		OMJHL	45	11	21	32	271
1980-81—Kitchener Rangers		OMJHL	51	8	14	22	*372
1981-82—Kitchener Rangers (d-e)		OHL	43	13	14	27	*384
1982-83—New Jersey Devils		NHL	9	0	1	1	28
1982-83—Wichita Wind		CHL	48	19	7	26	238
1983-84—Maine Mariners		AHL	25	5	5	10	119
NHL TOTALS			9	0	1	1	28

(c)—Led Ontario Major Junior Hockey League with a total of 358 penalty minutes.

(d)—Led Ontario Hockey League playoffs with 120 penalty minutes.

(e)—June, 1982—Drafted by New Jersey Devils in 1982 NHL entry draft. Sixth Devils pick, 106th overall, sixth round.

CARL MOKOSAK

Left Wing . . . 6'1" . . . 181 lbs. . . . Born, Fort Saskatchewan, Alta., September 22, 1962 . . . Shoots left . . . Brother of John Mokosak.

Year	Team	League	Games	G.	A.	Pts.	Pen.
1978-79—Brandon		MJHL	44	12	11	23	146
1979-80—Brandon Wheat Kings		WHL	61	12	21	33	226
1980-81—Brandon Wheat Kings		WHL	70	20	40	60	118
1981-82—Brandon Wheat Kings (c)		WHL	69	46	61	107	363
1981-82—Oklahoma City Stars		CHL	2	1	1	2	2
1981-82—Calgary Flames		NHL	1	0	1	1	0
1982-83—Colorado Flames		CHL	28	10	12	22	106
1982-83—Calgary Flames (d)		NHL	41	7	6	13	87
1983-84—New Haven Nighthawks		AHL	80	18	21	39	206
NHL TOTALS			42	7	7	14	87

(c)—August, 1981—Signed by Calgary Flames as a free agent.

(d)—June, 1983—Traded by Calgary Flames with Kevin LaVallee to Los Angeles Kings for Steve Bozek.

JOHN MOKOSAK

Defense . . . 5'11" . . . 185 lbs. . . . Born, Edmonton, Alta., September 7, 1963 . . . Shoots left . . . Brother of Carl Mokosak.

Year	Team	League	Games	G.	A.	Pts.	Pen.
1979-80—Ft. Saskatchewan Traders		SJHL	58	5	13	18	57
1980-81—Victoria Cougars (c)		WHL	71	2	18	20	59

Year	Team	League	Games	G.	A.	Pts.	Pen.
1981-82—Victoria Cougars		WHL	69	6	45	51	102
1982-83—Victoria Cougars		WHL	70	10	33	43	102
1983-84—Binghamton Whalers		AHL	79	3	21	24	80

(c)—June, 1981—Drafted as underage junior by Hartford Whalers in 1981 NHL entry draft. Sixth Whalers pick, 130th overall, seventh round.

LARS MOLIN

Right Wing and Left Wing . . . 6' . . . 170 lbs. . . . Born, Ornskoldsvik, Sweden, May 7, 1956 . . . Shoots left . . . (January 10, 1982)—Dislocated shoulder in game vs. Chicago . . . (January 2, 1983)—Sprained ankle at New Jersey . . . (March 8, 1983)—Broke left leg when he hit goal post in game vs. New York Rangers . . . (December, 1983)—Returned from broken leg injured in 1982-83 season.

Year	Team	League	Games	G.	A.	Pts.	Pen.
1977-78—Swedish National B Team		Int'l	....	...	....	....	....
1978-79—MoDo AIK		Sweden	....	...	....	....	....
1979-80—MoDo AIK (a)		Sweden	36	12	8	20	34
1980-81—MoDo AIK (c)		Sweden	30	17	13	30	30
1981-82—Vancouver Canucks		NHL	72	15	31	46	10
1982-83—Vancouver Canucks		NHL	58	12	27	39	23
1983-84—Vancouver Canucks		NHL	42	6	7	13	4
NHL TOTALS			172	33	65	98	37

(c)—May, 1981—Signed by Vancouver Canucks as a free agent.

MICHAEL JOHN MOLLER

Right Wing . . . 6' . . . 189 lbs. . . . Born, Calgary, Alta., June 16, 1962 . . . Shoots right . . . Brother of Randy Moller.

Year	Team	League	Games	G.	A.	Pts.	Pen.
1978-79—Red Deer Midgets		RDMHL	....	...	....	....	....
1979-80—Lethbridge Broncos (c)		WHL	72	30	41	71	55
1980-81—Lethbridge Broncos (a)		WHL	70	39	69	108	71
1980-81—Buffalo Sabres		NHL	5	2	2	4	0
1981-82—Lethbridge Broncos (a-d)		WHL	49	41	81	122	38
1981-82—Buffalo Sabres		NHL	9	0	0	0	0
1982-83—Rochester Americans		AHL	10	1	6	7	2
1982-83—Buffalo Sabres		NHL	49	6	12	18	14
1983-84—Buffalo Sabres		NHL	59	5	11	16	27
NHL TOTALS			122	13	25	38	41

(c)—June, 1980—Drafted by Buffalo Sabres as underage junior in 1980 NHL entry draft. Second Sabres pick, 41st overall, second round.

(d)—Winner of Frank Bouchar Memorial Trophy (Most Gentlemanly WHL Player).

RANDY MOLLER

Defense . . . 6'2" . . . 205 lbs. . . . Born, Red Deer, Alta., August 23, 1963. . . Shoots right . . . (December, 1980)—Torn knee ligaments required surgery . . . Brother of Mike Moller.

Year	Team	League	Games	G.	A.	Pts.	Pen.
1979-80—Red Deer Rustlers		AJHL	56	3	34	37	253
1980-81—Lethbridge Broncos (c)		WHL	46	4	21	25	176
1981-82—Lethbridge Broncos (b)		WHL	60	20	55	75	249
1982-83—Quebec Nordiques		NHL	75	2	12	14	145
1983-84—Quebec Nordiques		NHL	74	4	14	18	147
NHL TOTALS			149	6	26	32	292

(c)—June, 1981—Drafted by Quebec Nordiques in 1981 NHL entry draft. First Nordiques pick, 11th overall, first round.

SERGIO MOMESSO

Center . . . 6'3" . . . 205 lbs. . . . Born, Montreal, Que, September 4, 1965 . . . Shoots left . . . Also plays left wing.

Year	Team	League	Games	G.	A.	Pts.	Pen.
1982-83—Shawinigan Cataracts (c)		QHL	70	27	42	69	93
1983-84—Shawinigan Cataracts		QHL	68	42	88	130	235
1983-84—Montreal Canadiens		NHL	1	0	0	0	0
NHL TOTALS			1	0	0	0	0

(c)—June, 1983—Drafted as underage junior by Montreal Canadiens in 1983 NHL entry draft. Third Canadiens pick, 27th overall, second round.

PIERRE MONDOU

Center and Right Wing . . . 5'10" . . . 175 lbs. . . . Born, Sorel, Que., November 27, 1955 . . . Shoots right . . . Groin and knee injuries (March, 1980) . . . Surgery in August, 1980, out for first 2½ months of 1980-81 season . . . (Summer, 1980)—Tore achilles tendon playing racquetball . . . (March, 1981)—Bruised rib cartilage . . . (March 2, 1982)—Injured knee vs. Edmonton . . . (December, 1982)—Hip injury . . . (November, 1983)—Injured ribs . . . (February 11, 1984)—Injured back in game vs. Buffalo . . . (February 25, 1984)—Broke left hand in game vs. N.Y. Rangers.

Year	Team	League	Games	G.	A.	Pts.	Pen.
1972-73—Sorel Black Hawks		QJHL	64	37	43	80	57
1973-74—Sorel Black Hawks		QJHL	60	62	57	119	104
1974-75—Sorel Black Hawks (c)		QJHL	28	16	23	39	13
1974-75—Montreal Juniors (b-d)		QJHL	40	40	47	87	23
1975-76—Nova Scotia Voyageurs (e)		AHL	74	34	43	77	30
1976-77—Nova Scotia Voyageurs (b-f)		AHL	71	*44	45	89	21
1976-77—Montreal Canadiens (g)		NHL	....	...	....	....	....
1977-78—Montreal Canadiens		NHL	71	19	30	49	8
1978-79—Montreal Canadiens		NHL	77	31	41	72	26
1979-80—Montreal Canadiens		NHL	75	30	36	66	12
1980-81—Montreal Canadiens		NHL	57	17	24	41	16
1981-82—Montreal Canadiens		NHL	73	35	33	68	57
1982-83—Montreal Canadiens		NHL	76	29	37	66	31
1983-84—Montreal Canadiens		NHL	52	15	22	37	8
NHL TOTALS			481	176	223	399	158

(c)—Traded to Montreal Juniors by Sorel Black Hawks for four players, December, 1974.
(d)—Drafted from Montreal Juniors by Montreal Canadiens in first round of 1975 amateur draft.
(e)—Co-winner of Dudley (Red) Garrett Memorial Trophy (Rookie-of-the-Year) with Greg Holst.
(f)—Tied for lead in goals (8) and led in assists (11) and points (19) during playoffs.
(g)—No league record. Appeared in four playoff games.

ROBERT MONGRAIN

Center . . . 5'10" . . . 165 lbs. . . . Born, La Salle, Que., August 31, 1959 . . . Shoots left.

Year	Team	League	Games	G.	A.	Pts.	Pen.
1976-77—Barons de Cap de La Madeleine		QJHL	....	53	79	132	....
1976-77—Trois-Rivieres Draveurs		QMJHL	12	0	2	2	0
1977-78—Trois-Rivieres Draveurs		QMJHL	72	35	43	78	77
1978-79—Trois-Rivieres Draveurs (c)		QMJHL	72	66	76	142	55
1979-80—Rochester Americans		AHL	39	25	24	49	58
1979-80—Buffalo Sabres		NHL	34	4	6	10	4
1980-81—Buffalo Sabres		NHL	4	0	0	0	2
1980-81—Rochester Americans		AHL	69	21	29	50	101
1981-82—Rochester Americans		AHL	56	37	37	74	45
1981-82—Buffalo Sabres		NHL	24	6	4	10	6
1982-83—Rochester Americans		AHL	80	29	52	81	72
1983-84—Rochester Americans		AHL	78	41	44	85	154
NHL TOTALS			62	10	10	20	12

(c)—September 1979—Signed by Buffalo Sabres as free agent.

VIC MORIN

Defense . . . 6' . . . 180 lbs. . . . Born, North Bay, Ont., February 20, 1960 . . . Shoots right.

Year	Team	League	Games	G.	A.	Pts.	Pen.
1978-79—Windsor Spitfires		OMJHL	54	0	15	15	60
1979-80—Windsor Spitfires		OMJHL	66	7	30	37	57
1980-81—Sault Ste. Marie Greyhounds		OMJHL	59	7	33	40	97
1981-82—Fort Wayne Komets (c)		IHL	4	3	2	5	2
1981-82—Hershey Bears		AHL	73	10	25	35	84
1982-83—Hershey Bears		AHL	66	13	26	39	39
1982-83—Fort Wayne Komets		IHL	15	5	9	14	2
1983-84—Hershey Bears		AHL	2	1	0	1	0
1983-84—Fort Wayne Komets (a)		IHL	80	15	49	64	94

(c)—October, 1981—Signed by Washington Capitals as a free agent.

BOBBY MORMINA

Right Wing . . . 5'10" . . . 170 lbs. . . . Born, Montreal, Que., July 20, 1963 . . . Shoots right.

Year	Team	League	Games	G.	A.	Pts.	Pen.
1980-81—Shawinigan Cataracts		QMJHL	27	1	3	4	6
1981-82—Dawson College		....	....	...	....	....	....

Year	Team	League	Games	G.	A.	Pts.	Pen.
1982-83—Longueuil Chevaliers (a-c)		QHL	70	56	60	116	22
1983-84—Springfield Indians		AHL	56	14	27	41	15

(c)—June, 1983—Drafted by Philadelphia Flyers in 1983 NHL entry draft. Sixth Flyers pick, 141st overall, seventh round.

JON MORRIS

Center . . . 6' . . . 165 lbs. . . . Born, Lowell, Mass., May 6, 1966 . . . Shoots right.

Year	Team	League	Games	G.	A.	Pts.	Pen.
1983-84—Chelmsford H.S. (c)		Mass. H.S.	24	31	50	81	....

(c)—June, 1984—Drafted by New Jersey Devils in NHL entry draft. Fifth Devils pick, 86th overall, fifth round.

MARK MORRIS

Defense . . . 5'11" . . . 185 lbs. . . . Born, Massena, N. Y., March 31, 1958 . . . Shoots right.

Year	Team	League	Games	G.	A.	Pts.	Pen.
1978-79—Colgate University		ECAC	28	11	12	23	31
1979-80—Colgate University		ECAC	31	3	14	17	42
1980-81—Colgate University (c)		ECAC	34	8	22	30	58
1981-82—Dallas Black Hawks		CHL	26	1	8	9	14
1981-82—New Haven Nighthawks		AHL	46	1	6	7	34
1982-83—New Haven Nighthawks		AHL	73	5	20	25	77
1983-84—New Haven Nighthawks		AHL	37	3	7	10	35

(c)—July, 1981—Signed by Los Angeles Kings as a free agent.

DAVID STUART MORRISON

Right Wing . . . 6'1" . . . 186 lbs. . . . Born, Toronto, Ont., June 12, 1962 . . . Shoots right . . . Son of former NHL Defenseman Jim Morrison (Boston, Toronto, Detroit, Rangers, Pittsburgh, '51-'71) . . . Father was on 1951 Memorial Cup winning Barrie Flyers, Dave was member of 1979 Memorial Cup winning Peterborough Petes.

Year	Team	League	Games	G.	A.	Pts.	Pen.
1979-80—Peterborough Petes (c)		OMJHL	48	18	19	37	35
1980-81—Peterborough Petes		OHL	62	44	53	97	71
1980-81—Los Angeles Kings		NHL	3	0	0	0	0
1981-82—Peterborough Petes		OHL	53	33	31	64	38
1981-82—New Haven Nighthawks		AHL	2	0	0	0	2
1981-82—Los Angeles Kings		NHL	4	0	0	0	0
1982-83—Los Angeles Kings		NHL	24	3	3	6	4
1982-83—New Haven Nighthawks		AHL	59	23	17	40	36
1983-84—New Haven Nighthawks		AHL	8	0	4	4	2
1983-84—Fredericton Express		AHL	68	14	19	33	51
NHL TOTALS			31	3	3	6	4

(c)—June, 1980—Drafted as underage junior by Los Angeles Kings in 1980 NHL entry draft. Fourth Kings pick, 34th overall, second round.

DOUG MORRISON

Right Wing and Center . . . 5'11" . . . 175 lbs. . . . Born, Vancouver, B.C., February 1, 1960 . . . Shoots right . . . (February, 1981)—Knee injury . . . Brother of Mark Morrison . . . (December, 1982)—Broken hand.

Year	Team	League	Games	G.	A.	Pts.	Pen.
1976-77—Lethbridge Broncos		WCHL	70	24	35	59	80
1977-78—Lethbridge Broncos		WCHL	66	25	45	70	116
1978-79—Lethbridge Broncos (c)		WHL	72	56	67	123	159
1979-80—Boston Bruins		NHL	1	0	0	0	0
1979-80—Lethbridge Broncos		WHL	68	58	59	117	188
1980-81—Boston Bruins		NHL	18	7	3	10	13
1980-81—Springfield Indians		AHL	42	19	30	49	28
1981-82—Erie Blades		AHL	75	23	35	58	31
1981-82—Boston Bruins		NHL	3	0	0	0	0
1982-83—Maine Mariners		AHL	61	38	29	67	44
1983-84—Hershey Bears		AHL	72	38	40	78	42
NHL TOTALS			22	7	3	10	13

(c)—August, 1979—Drafted by Boston Bruins as underage junior in 1979 entry draft. Third Bruins pick, 36th overall, second round.

MARK MORRISON

Center . . . 5'9" . . . 145 lbs. . . . Born, Prince George, B.C., March 11, 1963 . . . Shoots right . . .

Brother of Doug Morrison.... Member of 1984 Canadian Olympic Team but was ruled ineligible to participate because of his NHL experience (9 games).

Year	Team	League	Games	G.	A.	Pts.	Pen.
1979-80—Victoria Cougars		WHL	72	25	33	58	26
1980-81—Victoria Cougars (c)		WHL	63	31	61	92	66
1981-82—Victoria Cougars		WHL	56	48	66	114	83
1981-82—New York Rangers		NHL	9	1	1	2	0
1982-83—Victoria Cougars		WHL	58	55	75	130	54
1983-84—Canadian Olympic Team		Int'l	43	15	22	37	34
1983-84—Tulsa Oilers		CHL	11	4	4	8	2
1983-84—New York Rangers		NHL	1	0	0	0	0
NHL TOTALS			10	1	1	2	0

(c)—June, 1981—Drafted as underage junior by New York Rangers in 1981 NHL entry draft. Fourth Rangers pick, 51st overall, third round.

KEN MORROW

Defense ... 6'4" ... 210 lbs. ... Born, Flint, Mich., October 17, 1956 ... Shoots right ... Member of 1980 U.S. Olympic Gold Medal Team ... Member of 1979 Team U.S.A. ... First ever All-American at Bowling Green University ... First person in history to play for Gold Medal Olympic team and Stanley Cup Team in same season. ... (October, 1983)—Water on the knee ... (December, 1983)—Arthroscopic surgery on right knee ... (May, 1983)—Missed one game in playoff series with Boston due to further arthroscopic surgery on right knee.

Year	Team	League	Games	G.	A.	Pts.	Pen.
1975-76—Bowling Green Univ. (a-c)		CCHA	31	4	15	19	34
1976-77—Bowling Green Univ. (b)		CCHA	39	7	22	29	22
1977-78—Bowling Green Univ. (a-d)		CCHA	39	8	18	26	26
1978-79—Bowling Green Univ. (a-e)		CCHA	45	15	37	52	22
1979-80—U.S. Olympic Team		Int'l	63	5	20	25	12
1979-80—New York Islanders		NHL	18	0	3	3	4
1980-81—New York Islanders		NHL	80	2	11	13	20
1981-82—New York Islanders		NHL	75	1	18	19	56
1982-83—New York Islanders		NHL	79	5	11	16	44
1983-84—New York Islanders		NHL	63	3	11	14	45
NHL TOTALS			315	11	54	65	169

(c)—May, 1976—Drafted by New York Islanders in 1976 NHL amateur draft. Fourth Islanders pick, 68th overall, fourth round.

(d)—All-American Team (West).

(e)—Named CCHA Player of the Year.

BRIAN MULLEN

Center ... 5'10" ... 170 lbs. ... Born, New York, N.Y., March 16, 1962 ... Shoots left ... Brother of Joe Mullen.

Year	Team	League	Games	G.	A.	Pts.	Pen.
1977-78—New York Westsiders		NYMJHL	33	21	36	57	38
1978-79—New York Westsiders		NYMJHL	....	...	....	....	....
1979-80—New York Westsiders		NYMJHL	....	...	....	....	....
1980-81—University of Wisconsin (c)		WCHA	38	11	13	24	28
1981-82—University of Wisconsin		WCHA	33	20	17	37	10
1982-83—Winnipeg Jets		NHL	80	24	26	50	14
1983-84—Winnipeg Jets		NHL	75	21	41	62	28
NHL TOTALS			155	45	67	112	42

(c)—June, 1980—Drafted by Winnipeg Jets in 1981 NHL entry draft. Seventh Jets pick, 128th overall, seventh round.

JOE MULLEN

Right Wing ... 5'9" ... 180 lbs. ... Born, New York, N.Y., February 26, 1957 ... Shoots right ... Attended Boston College ... Brother of Brian Mullen ... First player to have 20-goal year in minors and majors in the same season (1981-82) ... (October 18, 1982)—Leg injury in game at Minnesota ... (January 29, 1983)—Tore ligaments in left knee during game vs. Los Angeles, requiring surgery. He was lost for remainder of season ... Established record for goals in single season by U.S.-born player in 1983-84.

Year	Team	League	Games	G.	A.	Pts.	Pen.
1971-72—New York 14th Precinct		NYMJHL	30	13	11	24	2
1972-73—New York Westsiders		NYMJHL	40	14	28	42	8
1973-74—New York Westsiders		NYMJHL	42	71	49	120	41
1974-75—New York Westsiders (c)		NYMJHL	40	110	72	*182	20
1975-76—Boston College		ECAC	24	16	18	34	4

Year	Team	League	Games	G.	A.	Pts.	Pen.
1976-77—Boston College		ECAC	28	28	26	54	8
1977-78—Boston College (a)		ECAC	34	34	34	68	12
1978-79—Boston College (a-d)		ECAC	25	32	24	56	8
1979-80—Salt Lake Golden Eagles (b-e-g)		CHL	75	40	32	72	21
1979-80—St. Louis Blues (f)		NHL	....	...	....	....	....
1980-81—Salt Lake Golden Eagles (a-h-i)		CHL	80	59	58	*117	8
1981-82—Salt Lake Golden Eagles		CHL	27	21	27	48	12
1981-82—St. Louis Blues		NHL	45	25	34	59	4
1982-83—St. Louis Blues		NHL	49	17	30	47	6
1983-84—St. Louis Blues		NHL	80	41	44	85	19
NHL TOTALS			174	83	108	191	29

(c)—Named Most Valuable Player.
(d)—August, 1979—Signed as free agent by St. Louis Blues.
(e)—Co-leader with Red Laurence in Goals (9) during CHL playoffs.
(f)—No regular season record. Played in one playoff game.
(g)—Won Ken McKenzie Trophy (CHL Top Rookie).
(h)—Winner of Phil Esposito Trophy (Leading CHL Scorer).
(i)—Winner of Tommy Ivan Trophy (CHL MVP).

KIRK MULLER

Center . . . 5'11" . . . 185 lbs. . . . Born, Kingston, Ont., February 8, 1966 . . . Shoots left . . . Member of 1984 Canadian Olympic team.

Year	Team	League	Games	G.	A.	Pts.	Pen.
1980-81—Kingston Canadians		OHL	2	0	0	0	0
1981-82—Kingston Canadians		OHL	67	12	39	51	27
1982-83—Guelph Platers (c)		OHL	66	52	60	112	41
1983-84—Canadian Olympic Team		Int'l	15	2	2	4	6
1983-84—Guelph Platers (d)		OHL	49	31	63	94	27

(c)—Won William Hanley Trophy (OHL Most Gentlemanly).
(d)—June, 1984—Drafted as underage junior by New Jersey Devils in NHL entry draft. First Devils pick, second overall, first round.

GRANT MICHAEL MULVEY

Right Wing . . . 6'4" . . . 200 lbs. . . . Born, Sudbury, Ont., September 17, 1956 . . . Shoots right . . . Missed part of 1975-76 season with broken foot . . . Brother of Paul Mulvey . . . (December 20, 1980)—Broken leg . . . (February 3, 1982)—Tied NHL record with four goals in one period in 9-5 win vs. St. Louis . . . (October 20, 1983)—Injured knee in game vs. Buffalo that required surgery . . . (January, 1984)—Bruised ribs.

Year	Team	League	Games	G.	A	Pts	Pen
1972-73—Penticton Broncos		Jr. "A" BCHL	55	42	43	85	120
1973-74—Calgary Centennials (c)		WCHL	68	31	31	62	192
1974-75—Chicago Black Hawks		NHL	74	7	4	11	36
1975-76—Chicago Black Hawks		NHL	64	11	17	28	72
1976-77—Chicago Black Hawks		NHL	80	10	14	24	111
1977-78—Chicago Black Hawks		NHL	78	14	24	38	135
1978-79—Chicago Black Hawks		NHL	80	19	15	34	99
1979-80—Chicago Black Hawks		NHL	80	39	26	65	122
1980-81—Chicago Black Hawks		NHL	42	18	14	32	81
1981-82—Chicago Black Hawks		NHL	73	30	19	49	141
1982-83—Chicago Black Hawks		NHL	3	0	0	0	0
1982-83—Springfield Indians		AHL	5	0	2	2	4
1983-84—New Jersey Devils (d)		NHL	12	1	2	3	19
1983-84—Maine Mariners (e)		AHL	29	6	8	14	49
NHL TOTALS			586	149	135	284	816

(c)—Drafted from Calgary Centennials by Chicago Black Hawks in first round of 1974 amateur draft.
(d)—October, 1983—Selected by New Jersey Devils in 1984 NHL waiver draft.
(e)—August, 1984—Released by New Jersey Devils.

CRAIG DOUGLAS MUNI

Defense . . . 6'2" . . . 201 lbs. . . . Born, Toronto, Ont., July 19, 1962 . . . Shoots left . . . (September, 1981)—Tore left knee ligaments while skating in Windsor, Ont., prior to the opening of Toronto training camp . . . (January, 1983)—Broken ankle in AHL game at Fredericton.

Year	Team	League	Games	G.	A.	Pts.	Pen.
1979-80—Kingston Canadians (c)		OMJHL	66	6	28	34	114
1980-81—Kingston Canadians		OHL	38	2	14	16	65
1980-81—Windsor Spitfires		OHL	25	5	11	16	41

Year	Team	League	Games	G.	A.	Pts.	Pen.
1980-81—New Brunswick Hawks (d)	AHL	....	...	....	....	....
1981-82—Windsor Spitfires	OHL	49	5	32	37	92
1981-82—Cincinnati Tigers (e)	CHL	..	..	..	..	..
1982-83—Toronto Maple Leafs	NHL	2	0	1	1	0
1982-83—St. Catharines Saints	AHL	64	6	32	38	52
1983-84—St. Catharines Saints	AHL	64	4	16	20	79
NHL TOTALS		2	0	1	1	0

(c)—June, 1980—Drafted as underage junior by Toronto Maple Leafs in 1980 NHL entry draft. First Maple Leafs pick, 25th overall, second round.
(d)—No regular season appearance, two playoff games.
(e)—No regular-season appearance, played three playoff games.

DONALD WALTER MURDOCH

Right Wing . . . 5'11" . . . 180 lbs. . . . Born, Cranbrook, B. C., October 25, 1956 . . . Shoots right . . . Brother of Robert Lovell Murdoch . . . Missed part of 1976-77 season with torn tendon in left ankle requiring surgery. Had second operation on ankle, May, 1977 . . . Missed part of 1977-78 season with slipped vertebrae and start of 1978-79 season under suspension imposed by NHL . . . Set CHL record with 17 goals in a playoff season in 1981 . . . (October, 1982)—Injured Achilles tendon . . . Set WCHL rookie point record with 141 points in 1974-75 (broken by Dale Derkatch).

Year	Team	League	Games	G.	A.	Pts.	Pen.
1973-74—Vernon	Jr. "A" BCHL	45	50	32	82	69
1973-74—Kamloops Chiefs	WCHL	4	1	0	1	9
1974-75—Medicine Hat Tigers (a-c)	WCHL	70	*82	59	141	83
1975-76—Medicine Hat Tigers (a-d)	WCHL	70	*88	77	165	202
1976-77—New York Rangers	NHL	59	32	24	56	47
1977-78—New York Rangers	NHL	66	27	28	55	41
1978-79—New York Rangers	NHL	40	15	22	37	6
1979-80—New York Rangers (e)	NHL	56	23	19	42	16
1979-80—Edmonton Oilers	NHL	10	5	2	7	4
1980-81—Edmonton Oilers	NHL	40	10	9	19	18
1980-81—Wichita Wind (f-g)	CHL	22	15	10	25	48
1981-82—Adirondack Red Wings	AHL	24	11	13	24	24
1981-82—Detroit Red Wings	NHL	49	9	13	22	23
1982-83—Adirondack Red Wings	AHL	35	10	12	22	19
1983-84—Adirondack Red Wings (h)	AHL	59	26	20	46	19
NHL TOTALS		320	121	117	238	155

(c)—WCHL Rookie-of-the-Year.
(d)—Drafted from Medicine Hat Tigers by New York Rangers in first round of 1976 amateur draft.
(e)—March, 1980—Traded by N.Y. Rangers to Edmonton Oilers for Cam Connor and a 1980 or 1981 third round draft choice.
(f)—Named Most Valuable Player of CHL playoffs.
(g)—September, 1981—Traded by Edmonton Oilers to Minnesota North Stars for Don Jackson and a 1982 third-round draft choice. Subsequently traded to Detroit Red Wings with Greg Smith, with North Stars acquiring option to switch first-round draft choices with Red Wings in 1982 which Minnesota used to draft Brian Bellows, Detroit selected Murray Craven.
(h)—December, 1983—Signed by Adirondack Red Wings as a free agent.

KELLY MURPHY

Defense . . . 6'1" . . . 175 lbs. . . . Born, Regina, Sask., April 24, 1966 . . . Shoots right.

Year	Team	League	Games	G.	A.	Pts.	Pen.
1983-84—Wilcox Notre Dame H.S.(c)	Sask.H.S.	40	15	45	60	..

(c)—June, 1984—Drafted by New York Islanders in NHL entry draft. Eighth Islanders pick, 146th overall, seventh round.

LAWRENCE THOMAS MURPHY

Defense . . . 6'1" . . . 210 lbs. . . . Born, Scarborough, Ont., March 8, 1961 . . . Shoots right . . . Set record for most points by NHL rookie defenseman in 1980-81 (76 points) . . . Holds Los Angeles Kings club record for most goals, assists and points by a defenseman in a career as well as L.A. records for assists and points by a rookie . . . (1981-82)—Set club record for most goals by a defenseman in a season (22) . . . (1980-81) Set NHL record for most assists (60) and points (76) by a rookie defenseman.

Year	Team	League	Games	G.	A.	Pts.	Pen.
1978-79—Peterborough Petes	OMJHL	66	6	21	27	82
1979-80—Peterborough Petes (a-c-d)	OMJHL	68	21	68	89	88

Year	Team	League	Games	G.	A.	Pts.	Pen.
1980-81—Los Angeles Kings		NHL	80	16	60	76	79
1981-82—Los Angeles Kings		NHL	79	22	44	66	95
1982-83—Los Angeles Kings		NHL	77	14	48	62	81
1983-84—Los Angeles Kings		NHL	6	0	3	3	0
1983-84—Washington Capitals (e)		NHL	72	13	33	46	50
NHL TOTALS			314	65	188	253	305

(c)—Won Max Kaminsky Memorial Trophy (Outstanding OMJHL Defenseman).

(d)—June, 1980—Drafted as underage junior by Los Angeles Kings in 1980 NHL entry draft. First Kings pick, 4th overall, first round. (L.A. obtained draft pick from Detroit Red Wings as part of the Dale McCourt/Andre St. Laurent trade of August, 1979).

(e)—October, 1983—Traded by Los Angeles Kings to Washington Capitals for Brian Engblom and Ken Houston.

MIKE MURRAY

Center . . . 185 lbs. . . . Born, Kingston, Ont., April 29, 1966 . . . Shoots left.

Year	Team	League	Games	G.	A.	Pts.	Pen.
1982-83—Sarnia		Ont. Midget	57	61	39	100	48
1983-84—London Knights (c)		OHL	70	8	24	32	14

(c)—June, 1984—Drafted as underage junior by New York Islanders in NHL entry draft. Sixth Islanders pick, 104th overall, fifth round.

ROBERT FREDERICK MURRAY

Defense . . . 5'9" . . . 175 lbs. . . . Born, Kingston, Ont., November 26, 1954 . . . Shoots right . . . (December 20, 1981)—Tore ligaments in left knee vs. Toronto and required surgery.

Year	Team	League	Games	G.	A.	Pts.	Pen.
1971-72—Cornwall Royals		QJHL	62	14	49	63	88
1972-73—Cornwall Royals		QJHL	32	9	26	35	34
1973-74—Cornwall Royals (c)		QJHL	63	23	76	99	88
1974-75—Dallas Black Hawks		CHL	75	14	43	57	130
1975-76—Chicago Black Hawks		NHL	64	1	2	3	44
1976-77—Chicago Black Hawks		NHL	77	10	11	21	71
1977-78—Chicago Black Hawks		NHL	70	14	17	31	41
1978-79—Chicago Black Hawks		NHL	79	19	32	51	38
1979-80—Chicago Black Hawks		NHL	74	16	34	50	60
1980-81—Chicago Black Hawks		NHL	77	13	47	60	93
1981-82—Chicago Black Hawks		NHL	45	8	22	30	48
1982-83—Chicago Black Hawks		NHL	79	7	32	39	73
1983-84—Chicago Black Hawks		NHL	78	11	37	48	78
NHL TOTALS			643	99	234	333	546

(c)—Drafted from Cornwall Royals by Chicago Black Hawks in third round of 1974 amateur draft.

TROY MURRAY

Center . . . 6'1" . . . 195 lbs. . . . Born, Winnipeg, Man., July 31, 1962 . . . Shoots right . . . (November, 1983)—Knee ligament injury.

Year	Team	League	Games	G.	A.	Pts.	Pen.
1979-80—St. Albert Saints (c)		AJHL	60	53	47	100	101
1980-81—Univ. of North Dakota (b-d)		WCHA	38	33	45	78	28
1981-82—Univ. of North Dakota (b)		WCHA	42	22	29	51	62
1981-82—Chicago Black Hawks		NHL	1	0	0	0	0
1982-83—Chicago Black Hawks		NHL	54	8	8	16	27
1983-84—Chicago Black Hawks		NHL	61	15	15	30	45
NHL TOTALS			116	23	23	46	72

(c)—June, 1980—Drafted by Chicago Black Hawks in 1980 NHL entry draft. Sixth Black Hawks pick, 57th overall, third round.

(d)—Named Outstanding Freshman in WCHA.

ROY MYLLARI

Defense . . . 6'2" . . . 190 lbs. . . . Born, Thunder Bay, Ont., July 16, 1964 . . . Shoots left.

Year	Team	League	Games	G.	A.	Pts.	Pen.
1980-81—Port Arthur Comets		TBMMHL	56	15	29	44	....
1981-82—Cornwall Royals (c)		OHL	60	0	7	7	86
1982-83—Cornwall Royals		OHL	58	5	11	16	78
1983-84—Cornwall Royals		OHL	38	1	8	9	65
1983-84—Ottawa 67's		OHL	31	1	10	11	27

(c)—June, 1982—Drafted by Calgary Flames as underage junior in 1982 NHL entry draft. Tenth Flames pick, 156th overall, eighth round.

DONALD KENNETH NACHBAUR

Center . . . 6'2" . . . 200 lbs. . . . Born, Kitimat, B.C., January 30, 1959 . . . Shoots left . . . Also plays left wing.

Year	Team	League	Games	G.	A.	Pts.	Pen.
1976-77	Merritt Luckies	......	54	22	27	49	31
1977-78	Billings Bighorns	WCHL	68	23	27	50	128
1978-79	Billings Bighorns (c)	WHL	69	44	52	96	175
1979-80	Springfield Indians	AHL	70	12	17	29	119
1980-81	Hartford Whalers	NHL	77	16	17	33	139
1981-82	Hartford Whalers (d)	NHL	77	5	21	26	117
1982-83	Edmonton Oilers	NHL	4	0	0	0	17
1982-83	Moncton Alpines	AHL	70	33	33	66	125
1983-84	New Haven Nighthawks (e)	AHL	70	33	32	65	194
	NHL TOTALS		158	21	38	59	273

(c)—August, 1979—Drafted by Hartford Whalers in entry draft. Third Hartford pick, 60th overall, third round.

(d)—August, 1982—Traded with Ken Linseman by Hartford Whalers to Edmonton Oilers for Risto Siltanen and Brent Loney.

(e)—October, 1983—Selected by Los Angeles Kings in NHL waiver draft.

MARK NAPIER

Right Wing . . . 5'10" . . . 182 lbs. . . . Born, Toronto, Ont., January 28, 1957 . . . Shoots left . . . Brother of Steve Napier, Cornell goalie in mid 1970's . . . (October 20, 1983)—Ankle tendon partially severed by skate of Dan Mandich in game at Minnesota.

Year	Team	League	Games	G.	A.	Pts.	Pen.
1972-73	Wexford Raiders	OPHL	44	41	27	68	201
1973-74	Toronto Marlboros	Jr."A"OHA	70	47	46	93	63
1974-75	Toronto Marlboros (a-c)	Jr."A"OHA	61	66	64	130	106
1975-76	Toronto Toros (d-e)	WHA	78	43	50	93	20
1976-77	Birmingham Bulls (f)	WHA	80	60	36	96	24
1977-78	Birmingham Bulls (g)	WHA	79	33	32	65	90
1978-79	Montreal Canadiens	NHL	54	11	20	31	11
1979-80	Montreal Canadiens	NHL	76	16	33	49	7
1980-81	Montreal Canadiens	NHL	79	35	36	71	24
1981-82	Montreal Canadiens	NHL	80	40	41	81	14
1982-83	Montreal Canadiens	NHL	73	40	27	67	6
1983-84	Montreal Canadiens (h)	NHL	5	3	2	5	0
1983-84	Minnesota North Stars	NHL	58	13	28	41	17
	WHA TOTALS		237	136	118	254	134
	NHL TOTALS		425	158	187	345	79

(c)—Signed by Toronto Toros (WHA), May, 1975.

(d)—Won WHA Rookie Award.

(e)—Named WHA Rookie of the Year in poll of players by THE SPORTING NEWS.

(f)—Drafted from Birmingham Bulls (WHA) by Montreal Canadiens in first round of 1977 amateur draft.

(g)—Signed by Montreal Canadiens, September, 1978.

(h)—October, 1983—Traded with Keith Acton and third-round 1984 draft pick (Kenneth Hodge) by Montreal Canadiens to Minnesota North Stars for Bobby Smith.

MATS NASLUND

Left Wing . . . 5'7" . . . 158 lbs. . . . Born, Timra, Sweden, October 31, 1959 . . . Shoots left.

Year	Team	League	Games	G.	A.	Pts.	Pen.
1980-81	Brynas IF (c)	Sweden	....	17	25	42	....
1981-82	Brynas IF	Sweden	....	25	20	45	....
1982-83	Montreal Canadiens	NHL	74	26	45	71	10
1983-84	Montreal Canadiens	NHL	77	29	35	64	4
	NHL TOTALS		151	55	80	135	14

(c)—August, 1979—Drafted by Montreal Canadiens in 1979 NHL entry draft. Second Canadiens pick, 37th overall, second round.

ERIC RIC NATTRESS
(Known by middle name)

Defense . . . 6'2" . . . 208 lbs. . . . Born, Hamilton, Ont., May 25, 1962 . . . Shoots right . . . (August, 1983)—Fined $150 in Brantford, Ontario for possession of three grams of marijuana and one gram of hashish . . . (September, 1983)—Given 40-game suspension by NHL following his conviction in Ontario court . . . (March, 1984)—Fractured finger.

Year	Team	League	Games	G.	A.	Pts.	Pen.
1979-80	Brantford Alexanders (c)	OMJHL	65	3	21	24	94
1980-81	Brantford Alexanders	OHL	51	8	34	42	106
1981-82	Brantford Alexanders	OHL	59	11	50	61	126
1982-83	Nova Scotia Voyageurs	AHL	9	0	4	4	16
1982-83	Montreal Canadiens	NHL	40	1	3	4	19
1983-84	Montreal Canadiens	NHL	34	0	12	12	15
	NHL TOTALS		74	1	15	16	34

(c)—June, 1980—Drafted as underage junior by Montreal Canadiens in 1980 NHL entry draft. Second Canadiens pick, 27th overall, second round.

DANIEL NAUD

Defense . . . 5'10" . . . 187 lbs. . . . Born, Trois Rivieres, Que., February 20, 1962 . . . Shoots right . . . (November, 1980)—Fractured ankle.

Year	Team	League	Games	G.	A.	Pts.	Pen.
1979-80	Sorel Black Hawks (c)	OMJHL	72	17	53	70	30
1980-81	Sorel Black Hawks	QMJHL	62	17	32	49	28
1981-82	Granby Bisons (d)	QMJHL	29	8	21	29	26
1981-82	Hull Olympics	QMJHL	35	12	30	42	42
1982-83	Rochester Americans	AHL	71	6	52	58	34
1983-84	Rochester Americans	AHL	79	15	44	59	29

(c)—June, 1980—Drafted by Buffalo Sabres as underage junior in 1980 NHL entry draft. Seventh Sabres pick, 125th overall, sixth round.

(d)—December, 1981—Traded by Granby Bisons to Hull Olympics for Sylvain Roy, Claude Labbe and Jocelyn Gauvreau.

CAM NEELY

Right Wing . . . 6'1" . . . 185 lbs. . . . Born, Comox, B.C., June 6, 1965 . . . Shoots right.

Year	Team	League	Games	G.	A.	Pts.	Pen.
1981-82	Ridge Meadow	B.C. Midget	64	73	68	141	134
1982-83	Portland Winter Hawks (c)	WHL	72	56	64	120	130
1983-84	Portland Winter Hawks	WHL	19	8	18	26	29
1983-84	Vancouver Canucks	NHL	56	16	15	31	57
	NHL TOTALS		56	16	15	31	57

(c)—June, 1983—Drafted as underage junior by Vancouver Canucks in 1983 NHL entry draft. First Canucks' pick, 9th overall, first round.

MIKE NEILL

Defense . . . 6' . . . 195 lbs. . . . Born, Kenora, Ont., August 6, 1965 . . . Shoots left.

Year	Team	League	Games	G.	A.	Pts.	Pen.
1981-82	Kenora Thistles	MJHL	60	12	32	44	65
1982-83	Sault Ste. Marie Greyhounds (c)	OHL	65	4	13	17	115
1983-84	Sault Ste. Marie Greyhounds	OHL	20	2	6	8	42
1983-84	Windsor Spitfires	OHL	49	9	17	26	101

(c)—June, 1983—Drafted as underage junior by New York Islanders in 1983 NHL entry draft. Fourth Islanders' pick, 57th overall, third round.

BRIAN NELSON

Center . . . 5'11" . . . 170 lbs. . . . Born, Willmar, Minn., October 5, 1965 . . . Shoots left.

Year	Team	League	Games	G.	A.	Pts.	Pen.
1983-84	Willmar H.S. (c)	Minn. H.S.	20	42	44	86	30

(c)—June, 1984—Drafted by New York Rangers in NHL entry draft. Seventh Rangers pick, 161st overall, eighth round.

JIM NESICH

Right Wing and Center . . . 5'11" . . . 160 lbs. . . . Born, Dearborn, Mich., February 22, 1966 . . . Shoots right.

Year	Team	League	Games	G.	A.	Pts.	Pen.
1983-84	Verdun Juniors	WHL	70	22	24	46	35

RAY NEUFELD

Right Wing . . . 6'2" . . . 215 lbs. . . . Born, St. Boniface, Man., April 15, 1959 . . . Shoots right . . . (September, 1978)—Broken ribs.

Year	Team	League	Games	G.	A.	Pts.	Pen.
1976-77—Flin Flon Bombers		WCHL	68	13	19	32	63
1977-78—Flin Flon Bombers		WCHL	72	23	46	69	224
1978-79—Edmonton Oil Kings (c)		WCHL	57	54	48	102	138
1979-80—Springfield Indians		AHL	73	23	29	52	51
1979-80—Hartford Whalers		NHL	8	1	0	1	0
1980-81—Binghamton Whalers		AHL	25	7	7	14	43
1980-81—Hartford Whalers		NHL	52	5	10	15	44
1981-82—Binghamton Whalers (d)		AHL	61	28	31	59	81
1981-82—Hartford Whalers		NHL	19	4	3	7	4
1982-83—Hartford Whalers		NHL	80	26	31	57	86
1983-84—Hartford Whalers		NHL	80	27	42	69	97
NHL TOTALS			239	63	86	149	231

(c)—August, 1979—Drafted by Hartford Whalers in 1979 entry draft. Fourth Whalers pick, 81st overall, fourth round.

(d)—Co-leader (with Florent Robidoux of New Brunswick) during AHL Calder Cup Playoffs with nine goals.

JOHN NEWBERRY

Center . . . 6'1" . . . 185 lbs. . . . Born, Port Alberni, B.C., April 8, 1962 . . . Shoots left.

Year	Team	League	Games	G.	A.	Pts.	Pen.
1979-80—Nanaimo Clippers (c)		BCJHL	..	..	..	..	..
1980-81—University of Wisconsin (d)		WCHA	39	30	32	62	77
1981-82—University of Wisconsin (a-e)		WCHA	39	38	27	65	42
1982-83—Nova Scotia Voyageurs		AHL	71	29	29	58	43
1982-83—Montreal Canadiens (f)		NHL	...	...	...	...	...
1983-84—Montreal Canadiens		NHL	3	0	0	0	0
1983-84—Nova Scotia Voyageurs		AHL	78	25	37	62	116
NHL TOTALS			3	0	0	0	0

(c)—June, 1980—Drafted as underage player by Montreal Canadiens in 1980 NHL entry draft. Fourth Canadiens pick, 45th overall, third round.

(d)—Named to NCAA Tournament All-Star team.

(e)—Named to All-America Team (West).

(f)—No regular season record. Played in two playoff games.

JIM NEWHOUSE

Left Wing . . . 5'10" . . . 180 lbs. . . . Born, Winchester, Mass., April 1, 1966 . . . Shoots left.

Year	Team	League	Games	G.	A.	Pts.	Pen.
1983-84—Matignon H.S. (c)		Mass. H.S.	22	18	30	48	..

(c)—June, 1984—Drafted by Boston Bruins in NHL entry draft. Twelfth Bruins pick, 248th overall, 12th round.

BERNIE IRVINE NICHOLLS

Center . . . 6' . . . 185 lbs. . . . Born, Haliburton, Ont., June 24, 1961 . . . Shoots right . . . (November 18, 1982)—Partial tear of medial colateral ligament in right knee in game vs. Detroit when hit by Willie Huber . . . (February, 1984)—Broken jaw, missed only two games but lost 13 pounds before the end of season with jaw wired shut.

Year	Team	League	Games	G.	A.	Pts.	Pen.
1978-79—Kingston Canadians		OMJHL	2	0	1	1	0
1979-80—Kingston Canadians (c)		OMJHL	68	36	43	79	85
1980-81—Kingston Canadians		OHL	65	63	89	152	109
1981-82—New Haven Nighthawks		AHL	55	41	30	71	31
1981-82—Los Angeles Kings		NHL	22	14	18	32	27
1982-83—Los Angeles Kings		NHL	71	28	22	50	124
1983-84—Los Angeles Kings		NHL	78	41	54	95	83
NHL TOTALS			171	83	94	177	234

(c)—June, 1980—Drafted by Los Angeles Kings as underage junior in 1980 NHL entry draft. Fourth Kings pick, 73rd overall, fourth round.

ROB NICHOLS

Left Wing . . . 5'11" . . . 172 lbs. . . . Born, Hamilton, Ontario, August 4, 1964 . . . Shoots left.

Year	Team	League	Games	G.	A.	Pts.	Pen.
1982-83—Kitchener Rangers (c)		OHL	54	17	26	43	208

Year	Team	League	Games	G.	A.	Pts.	Pen.
1983-84—Kitchener Rangers		OHL	12	5	8	13	46
1983-84—North Bay Centennials		OHL	46	36	32	68	98

(c)—June, 1983—Drafted as underage junior by Philadelphia Flyers in 1983 NHL entry draft. Eighth Flyers pick, 181st overall, ninth round.

BOB NICHOLSON

Defense . . . 6'1" . . . 170 lbs. . . . Born, Toronto, Ont., May 1, 1964 . . . Shoots right.

Year	Team	League	Games	G.	A.	Pts.	Pen.
1980-81—North York Flames		MTHL	35	6	26	32	53
1981-82—London Knights (c)		OHL	66	13	38	51	42
1982-83—London Knights		OHL	50	9	35	44	40
1983-84—London Knights		OHL	48	5	18	23	30

(c)—June, 1982—Drafted as underage junior by Boston Bruins in 1982 NHL entry draft. Fifth Bruins pick, 102nd overall, fifth round.

TOM NICKOLAU

Center . . . 6'2" . . . 190 lbs. . . . Born, Scarborough, Ont., April 11, 1966 . . . Shoots left.

Year	Team	League	Games	G.	A.	Pts.	Pen.
1982-83—Wexford		Ont. Midget	40	25	35	60	67
1983-84—Guelph Platers (c)		OHL	61	5	13	18	98

(c)—June, 1984—Drafted as underage junior by Detroit Red Wings in NHL entry draft. Twelfth Red Wings pick, 236th overall, Twelfth round.

GRAEME BUTTE NICOLSON

Defense . . . 6' . . . 186 lbs. . . . Born, North Bay, Ont., January 13, 1958 . . . Shoots right . . . Missed part of 1977-78 season with severe cut on leg . . . Attended University of Guelph during 1980-81 season studying veterinary medicine.

Year	Team	League	Games	G.	A.	Pts.	Pen.
1975-78—Cornwall Royals	QJHL	72	11	36	47	101
1976-77—Cornwall Royals (a)	QJHL	64	21	46	67	197
1977-78—Cornwall Royals (b-c)	QJHL	63	13	52	65	122
1978-79—Boston Bruins	NHL	1	0	0	0	0
1978-79—Philadelphia Firebirds	AHL	80	16	35	51	112
1979-80—Binghamton Dusters	AHL	79	7	36	43	151
1980-81—Did not play (d)	....	....	....	....	....
1981-82—Colorado Rockies	NHL	41	2	7	9	51
1981-82—Ft. Worth Texans (e)	CHL	30	9	12	21	38
1982-83—New York Rangers	NHL	10	0	0	0	9
1982-83—Tulsa Oilers	CHL	64	19	28	47	166
1983-84—Tulsa Oilers (b-f)	CHL	62	7	24	31	61
NHL TOTALS		52	2	7	9	60

(c)—Drafted from Cornwall Royals by Boston Bruins in second round of 1978 amateur draft.
(d)—Signed by Colorado Rockies as a free agent August, 1981.
(e)—Claimed by New York Rangers in 1982 NHL waiver draft.
(f)—August, 1984—Signed by Washington Capitals as a free agent.

MIKE NIGHTENGALE

Defense . . . 6'1" . . . 180 lbs. . . . Born, South St. Paul, Minn., June 12, 1966 . . . Shoots left.

Year	Team	League	Games	G.	A.	Pts.	Pen.
1983-84—St. Paul Simley H.S. (c)		Minn. H.S.	22	10	29	39	18

(c)—June, 1984—Drafted by Minnesota North Stars in NHL entry draft. Twelfth North Stars pick, 242nd overall, 12th round.

FRANK NIGRO

Center . . . 5'9" . . . 182 lbs. . . . Born, Richmond Hill, Ont., February 11, 1960 . . . Shoots right . . . Suffered broken wrist during 1979-80 season . . . (October 29, 1983)—Broken wrist in game vs. Los Angeles.

Year	Team	League	Games	G.	A.	Pts.	Pen.
1977-78—London Knights		OMJHL	68	35	52	87	37
1978-79—London Knights (c)		OMJHL	63	33	56	89	64
1979-80—London Knights		OMJHL	46	12	26	38	30

Year	Team	League	Games	G.	A.	Pts.	Pen.
1980-81—New Brunswick Hawks		AHL	1	0	0	0	0
1981-82—Cincinnati Tigers		CHL	49	24	26	50	24
1982-83—Toronto Maple Leafs		NHL	51	6	15	21	23
1982-83—St. Catharines Saints		AHL	30	20	13	33	8
1983-84—St. Catharines Saints		AHL	41	17	24	41	16
1983-84—Toronto Maple Leafs		NHL	17	2	3	5	16
NHL TOTALS			68	8	18	26	39

(c)—August, 1979—Drafted as underage junior by Toronto Maple Leafs in 1979 NHL entry draft. Fourth Maple Leafs pick, 93rd overall, fifth round.

CHRIS NILAN

Right Wing . . . 6' . . . 200 lbs. . . . Born, Boston, Mass., February 9, 1958 . . . Shoots right . . . (November 21, 1981)—Threw puck at Paul Baxter of Pittsburgh while sitting in penalty box. Was given a 3-game suspension by NHL.

Year	Team	League	Games	G.	A.	Pts.	Pen.
1977-78—Northeastern University (c)		ECAC	....	...	....	....	....
1978-79—Northeastern University		ECAC	32	9	13	22	....
1979-80—Nova Scotia Voyageurs		AHL	49	15	10	25	*304
1979-80—Montreal Canadiens		NHL	15	0	2	2	50
1980-81—Montreal Canadiens		NHL	57	7	8	15	262
1981-82—Montreal Canadiens		NHL	49	7	4	11	204
1982-83—Montreal Canadiens		NHL	66	6	8	14	213
1983-84—Montreal Canadiens (d)		NHL	76	16	10	26	*338
NHL TOTALS			263	36	32	68	1067

(c)—June, 1978—Drafted by Montreal Canadiens in 1978 amateur draft. Twenty-first Canadiens pick, 231st overall, 19th round.

(d)—Led NHL playoffs with 81 penalty minutes.

JIM EDWARD NILL

Right Wing . . . 6' . . . 185 lbs. . . . Born, Hanna, Alta., April 11, 1958 . . . Shoots right . . . (March, 1983)—Concussion.

Year	Team	League	Games	G.	A.	Pts.	Pen.
1974-75—Drumheller Falcons		AJHL	59	30	30	60	103
1975-76—Medicine Hat Tigers		WCHL	62	5	11	16	69
1976-77—Medicine Hat Tigers		WCHL	71	23	24	47	140
1977-78—Medicine Hat Tigers (c)		WCHL	72	47	46	93	252
1978-79—Canadian National Team			....	...	....	....	....
1979-80—Canadian National Team			51	14	21	35	58
1979-80—Canadian Olympic Team		Olympics	6	1	2	3	4
1980-81—Salt Lake Golden Eagles (b)		CHL	79	28	34	62	222
1981-82—St. Louis Blues (d)		NHL	61	9	12	21	127
1981-82—Vancouver Canucks		NHL	8	1	2	3	5
1982-83—Vancouver Canucks		NHL	65	7	15	22	136
1983-84—Vancouver Canucks (e)		NHL	51	9	6	15	78
1983-84—Boston Bruins		NHL	27	3	2	5	81
NHL TOTALS			212	29	37	66	427

(c)—June, 1978—Drafted by St. Louis Blues in 1978 NHL amateur draft. Fourth Blues pick, 89th overall, sixth round.

(d)—March, 1982—Traded with Tony Currie and Rick Heinz by St. Louis Blues to Vancouver Canucks for Glen Hanlon and a fourth-round 1982 draft pick (Shawn Kilroy).

(e)—February, 1984—Traded by Vancouver Canucks to Boston Bruins for Peter McNab.

KENT NILSSON

Center . . . 6'1" . . . 185 lbs. . . . Born, Nynashamn, Sweden, August 31, 1956 . . . Shoots left . . . (November 1, 1981)—Tripped over stick of Mark Pavelich and crashed into boards dislocating his shoulder in game at New York Rangers . . . (March, 1984)—Fractured left ankle in final week of season.

Year	Team	League	Games	G.	A.	Pts.	Pen.
1975-76—Djurgardens (c)		Sweden	36	28	26	54	12
1976-77—AIK (d)		Sweden	36	30	19	49	18
1977-78—Winnipeg Jets (e)		WHA	80	42	65	107	8
1978-79—Winnipeg Jets (f-g)		WHA	78	39	68	107	8
1979-80—Atlanta Flames		NHL	80	40	53	93	10
1980-81—Calgary Flames		NHL	80	49	82	131	26

Year	Team	League	Games	G.	A.	Pts.	Pen.
1981-82—Calgary Flames		NHL	41	26	29	55	8
1982-83—Calgary Flames		NHL	80	46	58	104	10
1983-84—Calgary Flames		NHL	67	31	49	80	22
WHA TOTALS			158	81	133	214	16
NHL TOTALS			348	192	271	463	76

(c)—Drafted from Djurgardens, Sweden by Atlanta Flames in fourth round of 1976 amateur draft.
(d)—Signed by Winnipeg Jets (WHA), June, 1977.
(e)—Named WHA Rookie-of-the-Year and THE SPORTING NEWS WHA Rookie-of-the-Year.
(f)—Named WHA's Most Gentlemanly Player.
(g)—June, 1979—Selected by Atlanta Flames in NHL reclaim draft.

THEODORE JOHN NOLAN

Left Wing . . . 6' . . . 185 lbs. . . . Born, Sault Ste. Marie, Ont., April 7, 1958 . . . Shoots left . . . (October, 1983)—Knee injury.

Year	Team	League	Games	G.	A.	Pts.	Pen.
1976-77—Sault Ste. Marie Greyhounds		OMJHL	60	8	16	24	109
1977-78—S. Ste. Marie Greyhounds (c)		OMJHL	66	14	30	44	106
1978-79—Kansas City Red Wings		CHL	73	12	38	50	66
1979-80—Adirondack Red Wings		AHL	75	16	24	40	106
1980-81—Adirondack Red Wings		AHL	76	22	28	50	86
1981-82—Adirondack Red Wings		AHL	39	12	18	30	81
1981-82—Detroit Red Wings		NHL	41	4	13	17	45
1982-83—Adirondack Red Wings		AHL	78	24	40	64	103
1983-84—Detroit Red Wings		NHL	19	1	2	3	26
1983-84—Adirondack Red Wings		AHL	31	10	16	26	76
NHL TOTALS			60	5	15	20	71

(c)—June, 1978—Drafted by Detroit Red Wings in 1978 amateur draft. Seventh Red Wings pick, 78th overall, fifth round.

ROB NORMAN

Right Wing . . . 5'11" . . . 170 lbs. . . . Born, Kingston, Ont., January 19, 1964 . . . Shoots right.

Year	Team	League	Games	G.	A.	Pts.	Pen.
1980-81—Kingston Jr. B (c)		OHA Jr. B	40	35	29	64	15
1981-82—Cornwall Royals (d)		OHL	65	13	12	25	27
1982-83—Cornwall Royals		OHL	61	40	26	66	32
1983-84—Cornwall Royals		OHL	65	43	37	80	72

(c)—May, 1981—Selected by Cornwall Royals in 1981 OHL priority draft. Ninth Royals pick, 96th overall, seventh round.
(d)—June, 1982—Drafted by Buffalo Sabres as underage junior in 1982 NHL entry draft. Thirteenth Sabres pick, 184th overall, ninth round.

TODD NORMAN

Center . . . 6' . . . 170 lbs. . . . Born, St. Paul, Minn., February 26, 1966 . . . Shoots left.

Year	Team	League	Games	G.	A.	Pts.	Pen.
1983-84—Hill-Murray H.S. (c)		Minn.H.S.	24	35	32	67	..

(c)—June, 1984—Drafted by Edmonton Oilers in NHL entry draft. Third Oilers pick, 63rd overall, third round.

JEFF NORTON

Defense . . . 6'2" . . . 190 lbs. . . . Born, Cambridge, Mass., November 25, 1965 . . . Shoots left.

Year	Team	League	Games	G.	A.	Pts.	Pen.
1983-84—Cushing Academy (c)		Mass. H.S.	21	22	33	55	..

(c)—June, 1984—Drafted by New York Islanders in NHL entry draft. Third Islanders pick, 62nd overall, third round.

LEE CHARLES NORWOOD

Defense . . . 6' . . . 190 lbs. . . . Born, Oakland, Calif., February 2, 1960 . . . Shoots left.

Year	Team	League	Games	G.	A.	Pts.	Pen.
1977-78—Hull Olympiques		QMJHL	51	3	17	20	83
1978-79—Oshawa Generals (c)		OMJHL	61	23	38	61	171
1979-80—Oshawa Generals		OMJHL	60	13	39	52	143
1980-81—Hershey Bears		AHL	52	11	32	43	78

Year	Team	League	Games	G.	A.	Pts.	Pen.
1980-81—Quebec Nordiques		NHL	11	1	1	2	9
1981-82—Fredericton Express		AHL	29	6	13	19	74
1981-82—Quebec Nordiques (d)		NHL	2	0	0	0	2
1981-82—Washington Capitals		NHL	26	7	10	17	115
1982-83—Washington Capitals		NHL	8	0	1	1	14
1982-83—Hershey Bears		AHL	67	12	36	48	90
1983-84—St. Catharines Saints		AHL	75	13	46	59	91
NHL TOTALS			47	8	12	20	140

(c)—August, 1979—Drafted by Quebec Nordiques as underage junior in 1979 NHL entry draft. Third Nordiques pick, 62nd overall, third round.

(d)—January, 1982—Traded by Quebec Nordiques to Washington Capitals for Tim Tookey.

RICH NOVAK

Right Wing . . . 6'1" . . . 170 lbs. . . . Born, Squamish, B.C., February 19, 1966 . . . Shoots right.

Year	Team	League	Games	G.	A.	Pts.	Pen.
1983-84—Richmond (c)		BCJHL	40	20	29	49	60

(c)—June, 1984—Drafted as underage junior by Edmonton Oilers in NHL entry draft. Fourth Oilers pick, 84th overall, fourth round.

GARY NYLUND

Defense . . . 6'4" . . . 210 lbs. . . . Born, Surrey, B.C., October 28, 1963 . . . Shoots left . . . (September, 1982)—Injury to left knee in exhibition game, requiring surgery . . . (October, 1983)—Knee surgery.

Year	Team	League	Games	G.	A.	Pts.	Pen.
1978-79—Delta		BCJHL	57	6	29	35	107
1978-79—Portland Winter Hawks		WHL	2	0	0	0	0
1979-80—Portland Winter Hawks		WHL	72	5	21	26	59
1980-81—Portland Winter Hawks (b)		WHL	70	6	40	46	186
1981-82—Portland Winter Hawks (a-c-d)		WHL	65	7	59	66	267
1982-83—Toronto Maple Leafs		NHL	16	0	3	3	16
1983-84—Toronto Maple Leafs		NHL	47	2	14	16	103
NHL TOTALS			63	2	17	19	119

(c)—Winner of WHL Top Defenseman Trophy.

(d)—June, 1982—Drafted as underage junior by Toronto Maple Leafs in 1982 NHL entry draft. First Maple Leafs pick, 3rd overall, first round.

THORE ROBERT (BOB) NYSTROM

Right Wing . . . 6'1" . . . 195 lbs. . . . Born, Stockholm, Sweden, October 10, 1952 . . . Shoots right.

Year	Team	League	Games	G.	A.	Pts.	Pen.
1969-70—Kamloops Rockets		Jr. "A" BCHL	....	...	....	....	....
1970-71—Calgary Centennials		WCHL	66	15	16	31	153
1971-72—Calgary Centennials (c-d)		WCHL	64	27	25	52	178
1972-73—New Haven Nighthawks		AHL	60	12	10	22	114
1972-73—New York Islanders		NHL	11	1	1	2	10
1973-74—New York Islanders		NHL	77	21	20	41	118
1974-75—New York Islanders		NHL	76	27	28	55	122
1975-76—New York Islanders		NHL	80	23	25	48	106
1976-77—New York Islanders		NHL	80	29	27	56	91
1977-78—New York Islanders		NHL	80	30	29	59	94
1978-79—New York Islanders		NHL	78	19	20	39	113
1979-80—New York Islanders		NHL	67	21	18	39	94
1980-81—New York Islanders		NHL	79	14	30	44	145
1981-82—New York Islanders		NHL	74	22	25	47	103
1982-83—New York Islanders		NHL	74	10	20	30	98
1983-84—New York Islanders		NHL	74	15	29	44	80
NHL TOTALS			850	232	272	504	1174

(c)—Selected by Miami Screaming Eagles in World Hockey Association player selection draft, February, 1972.

(d)—Drafted from Calgary Centennials by New York Islanders in third round of 1972 amateur draft.

JACK O'CALLAHAN

Defense . . . 6'1" . . . 185 lbs. . . . Born, Charleston, Mass., July 24, 1957 . . . Shoots right . . . Member of Gold Medal Winning U.S. Olympic Hockey team . . . (December 28, 1983)—

Given 8-game suspension by NHL for slashing Dave Maloney in game vs. N.Y. Rangers.

Year	Team	League	Games	G.	A.	Pts.	Pen.
1975-76—Boston University		ECAC	....	...	....	....	....
1976-77—Boston University (c)		ECAC	31	1	23	24	90
1977-78—Boston University (a)		ECAC	31	8	47	55	61
1978-79—Boston University (a)		ECAC	29	6	16	22	72
1979-80—U.S. Olympic Team		Int'l.	55	7	30	37	*85
1980-81—New Brunswick Hawks		AHL	78	9	25	34	167
1981-82—New Brunswick Hawks		AHL	79	15	33	48	130
1982-83—Springfield Indians		AHL	35	2	24	26	25
1982-83—Chicago Black Hawks		NHL	39	0	11	11	46
1983-84—Chicago Black Hawks		NHL	70	4	13	17	67
NHL TOTALS			109	4	24	28	113

(c)—June, 1977—Drafted by Chicago Black Hawks in 1977 NHL amateur draft. Fifth Black Hawks pick, 96th overall, sixth round.

MICHAEL THOMAS O'CONNELL

Defense . . . 5'11" . . . 176 lbs. . . . Born, Chicago, Ill., November 25, 1955 . . . Shoots right . . . Son of former Cleveland Browns quarterback Tommy O'Connell . . . Brother of Tim O'Connell . . . Missed part of 1976-77 season with torn muscle in right shoulder . . . First member of the Black Hawks to be born in Chicago.

Year	Team	League	Games	G.	A.	Pts.	Pen.
1973-74—Kingston Canadiens		Jr."A"OHA	70	16	43	59	81
1974-75—King. Canadiens (a-c-d)		Jr."A"OHA	50	18	55	73	47
1975-76—Dallas Black Hawks (e)		CHL	70	6	37	43	50
1976-77—Dallas Black Hawks (a-f)		CHL	63	15	53	68	30
1977-78—Dallas Black Hawks (g)		CHL	62	6	45	51	75
1977-78—Chicago Black Hawks		NHL	6	1	1	2	2
1978-79—Chicago Black Hawks		NHL	48	4	22	26	20
1978-79—New Brunswick Hawks		AHL	35	5	20	25	21
1979-80—Chicago Black Hawks		NHL	78	8	22	30	52
1980-81—Chicago Black Hawks (h)		NHL	34	5	16	21	32
1980-81—Boston Bruins		NHL	48	10	22	32	42
1981-82—Boston Bruins		NHL	80	5	34	39	75
1982-83—Boston Bruins		NHL	80	14	39	53	42
1983-84—Boston Bruins		NHL	75	18	42	60	42
NHL TOTALS			449	65	198	263	307

(c)—Drafted from Kingston Canadiens by Chicago Black Hawks in third round of 1975 amateur draft.
(d)—Won Max Kaminsky Memorial Trophy (outstanding Defenseman).
(e)—Tied for lead in assists (5) during playoffs.
(f)—Won CHL Most Valuable Defenseman Award.
(g)—Tied for lead in assists (11) during playoffs.
(h)—December, 1980—Traded by Chicago Black Hawks to Boston Bruins for Al Secord.

SELMAR ODELEIN

Defense . . . 6' . . . 195 lbs. . . . Born, Quill Lake, Sask., April 11, 1966 . . . Shoots right.

Year	Team	League	Games	G.	A.	Pts.	Pen.
1982-83—Regina Canadians		Sask.Midget	70	30	84	114	38
1983-84—Regina Pats (c)		WHL	71	9	42	51	45

(c)—June, 1984—Drafted as underage junior by Edmonton Oilers in NHL entry draft. First Oilers pick, 21st overall, first round.

BILL O'DWYER

Center . . . 5'11" . . . 187 lbs. . . . Born, South Boston, Mass., June 25, 1960 . . . Shoots left.

Year	Team	League	Games	G.	A.	Pts.	Pen.
1978-79—Boston College		ECAC	30	9	30	39	14
1979-80—Boston College (b-c-d)		ECAC	33	20	22	42	22
1980-81—Boston College (b)		ECAC	31	20	20	40	6
1981-82—Boston College (b)		ECAC	....	15	26	41	....
1982-83—New Haven Nighthawks		AHL	77	24	23	47	29
1983-84—Los Angeles Kings		NHL	5	0	0	0	0
1983-84—New Haven Nighthawks		AHL	58	15	42	57	39
NHL TOTALS			5	0	0	0	0

(c)—Named to second team All-New England Team (Division I).
(d)—June, 1980—Drafted by Los Angeles Kings in 1980 NHL entry draft. Ninth Kings pick, 157th overall, eighth round.

JOHN ALEXANDER OGRODNICK

Left Wing . . . 6' . . . 190 lbs. . . . Born, Ottawa, Ont., June 20, 1959 . . . Shoots left . . . (February 26, 1984)—Fractured left wrist in game at Chicago.

Year	Team	League	Games	G.	A.	Pts.	Pen.
1976-77—Maple Ridge Bruins		BCJHL	67	54	56	110	63
1976-77—New Westminster Bruins		WCHL	14	2	4	6	0
1977-78—New Westminster Bruins (c)		WCHL	72	59	29	88	47
1978-79—New Westminster Bruins (d)		WHL	72	48	36	84	38
1979-80—Adirondack Red Wings		AHL	39	13	20	33	21
1979-80—Detroit Red Wings		NHL	41	8	24	32	8
1980-81—Detroit Red Wings		NHL	80	35	35	70	14
1981-82—Detroit Red Wings		NHL	80	28	26	54	28
1982-83—Detroit Red Wings		NHL	80	41	44	85	30
1983-84—Detroit Red Wings		NHL	64	42	36	78	14
NHL TOTALS			345	154	165	319	94

(c)—Shared Rookie of Year award in WCHL with Keith Brown.

(d)—August, 1979—Drafted by Detroit Red Wings in 1979 entry draft. Fourth Red Wings pick, 66th overall, fourth round.

ED OLCZYK

Right Wing . . . 6'1" . . . 195 lbs. . . . Born, Chicago, Ill., August 16, 1966 . . . Shoots left.

Year	Team	League	Games	G.	A.	Pts.	Pen.
1983-84—U.S. National Team		Int'l	56	19	40	59	36
1983-84—U.S. Olympic Team (c)		Int'l	6	2	7	9	0

(c)—June, 1984—Drafted by Chicago Black Hawks in NHL entry draft. First Black Hawks pick, 3rd overall, first round. (Black Hawks traded Rich Preston and Don Dietrich to New Jersey, who had the 2nd overall pick, not to draft Olczyk. Devils also sent Bob MacMillan to Chicago in the deal).

FRANCOIS OLIVIER

Left Wing . . . 6'2" . . . 165 lbs. . . . Born, Montreal, Que., March 15, 1965 . . . Shoots left.

Year	Team	League	Games	G.	A.	Pts.	Pen.
1981-82—Bourassa AAA		Que. Midget	41	16	16	32	48
1982-83—St. Jean Beavers (c)		QHL	67	14	12	26	13
1983-84—St. Jean Beavers		QHL	22	2	11	13	15

(c)—June, 1983—Drafted as underage junior by Boston Bruins in 1983 NHL entry draft. Eighth Bruins' pick, 162nd overall, seventh round.

JOHN OLLSON

Center . . . 5'9" . . . 170 lbs. . . . Born, Nepean, Ont., July 31, 1963 . . . Shoots left.

Year	Team	League	Games	G.	A.	Pts.	Pen.
1979-80—Nepean		Ont. Midget	24	24	21	45	..
1980-81—Ottawa 67's		OHL	31	6	6	12	12
1981-82—Ottawa 67's		OHL	67	36	42	78	49
1982-83—Ottawa 67's (c)		OHL	68	46	76	122	41
1982-83—Springfield Indians		AHL	75	29	43	72	51

(c)—August, 1983—Signed by Chicago Black Hawks as a free agent.

TOM O'REGAN

Center . . . 5'10" . . . 180 lbs. . . . Born, Cambridge, Mass., December 29, 1961 . . . Shoots left.

Year	Team	League	Games	G.	A.	Pts.	Pen.
1979-80—Boston University		ECAC	28	9	15	24	31
1980-81—Boston University		ECAC	20	10	10	20	41
1981-82—Boston University		ECAC	28	18	34	52	67
1982-83—Boston University		ECAC	27	15	17	32	43
1983-84—Pittsburgh Penguins (c)		NHL	51	4	10	14	8
1983-84—Baltimore Skipjacks		AHL	25	13	14	27	15
NHL TOTALS			51	4	10	14	8

(c)—September, 1983—Signed by Pittsburgh Penguins as a free agent.

JOSEPH JAMES TERRENCE (TERRY) O'REILLY

Right Wing . . . 6'1" . . . 195 lbs. . . . Born, Niagara Falls, Ont., June 7, 1951 . . . Shoots right . . . Missed part of 1971-72 season with sprained ankle . . . Served eight-game suspension for December 26, 1979 incident in stands vs. New York Rangers . . . (Summer, 1981)—Surgery to repair rotator cuff of right shoulder . . . (March, 1982)—Stretched nerves in left shoulder, leaving left arm numb . . . Suspended for first 10 games of 1982-83 season for striking referee Andy Van Hellemond in playoff finale vs. Quebec . . . (November 18, 1982)—Broken

left index finger in game at N.Y. Islanders . . . (December 31, 1982)—Injured left knee in game at Minnesota, required surgery in January of 1983 . . . (January, 1984)—Dislocated right shoulder.

Year	Team	League	Games	G.	A.	Pts.	Pen.
1968-69—Oshawa Generals		Jr."A"OHA	46	5	15	20	87
1969-70—Oshawa Generals		Jr."A"OHA	54	13	36	49	60
1970-71—Oshawa Generals (c)		Jr."A"OHA	54	23	42	65	151
1971-72—Boston Braves		AHL	60	9	8	17	134
1971-72—Boston Bruins		NHL	1	1	0	1	0
1972-73—Boston Bruins		NHL	72	5	22	27	109
1973-74—Boston Bruins		NHL	76	11	24	35	94
1974-75—Boston Bruins		NHL	68	15	20	35	146
1975-76—Boston Bruins		NHL	80	23	27	50	150
1976-77—Boston Bruins		NHL	79	14	41	55	147
1977-78—Boston Bruins		NHL	77	29	61	90	211
1978-79—Boston Bruins		NHL	80	26	51	77	205
1979-80—Boston Bruins		NHL	71	19	42	61	265
1980-81—Boston Bruins		NHL	77	8	35	43	223
1981-82—Boston Bruins		NHL	70	22	30	52	213
1982-83—Boston Bruins		NHL	19	6	14	20	40
1983-84—Boston Bruins		NHL	58	12	18	30	124
NHL TOTALS			828	191	385	576	1927

(c)—Drafted from Oshawa Generals by Boston Bruins in first round of 1971 amateur draft.

GATES ORLANDO

Center . . . 5'8" . . . 175 lbs. . . . Born, LaSalle, Que., November 13, 1962 . . . Shoots right.

Year	Team	League	Games	G.	A.	Pts.	Pen.
1980-81—Providence College (c)		ECAC	31	24	32	56	45
1981-82—Providence College		ECAC	28	18	18	36	31
1982-83—Providence College		ECAC	40	30	39	69	32
1983-84—Providence College		ECAC	34	23	30	53	52
1983-84—Rochester Americans		AHL	11	8	7	15	2

(c)—Drafted by Buffalo Sabres as underage player in 1981 NHL entry draft. Tenth Sabres pick, 164th overall, eighth round.

DAVID EUGENE ORLESKI

Defense . . . 6'3" . . . 210 lbs. . . . Born, Edmonton, Alta., December 26, 1959 . . . Shoots left.

Year	Team	League	Games	G.	A.	Pts.	Pen.
1975-76—Edmonton		Midget	....	...	....	....	....
1976-77—New Westminster Bruins		WCHL	62	8	14	22	29
1977-78—New Westminster Bruins		WCHL	64	15	35	50	132
1978-79—New Westminster Bruins (c)		WHL	71	27	39	66	128
1979-80—Nova Scotia Voyaguers		AHL	70	24	24	48	32
1980-81—Montreal Canadiens		NHL	1	0	0	0	0
1980-81—Nova Scotia Voyageurs		AHL	37	8	13	21	44
1981-82—Nova Scotia Voyageurs		AHL	64	14	23	37	15
1981-82—Montreal Canadiens		NHL	1	0	0	0	0
1982-83—Nova Scotia Voyageurs		AHL	68	30	37	67	28
1983-84—Salt Lake Golden Eagles		CHL	3	0	1	1	4
1983-84—Nova Scotia Voyageurs		AHL	20	6	9	15	14
NHL TOTALS			2	0	0	0	0

(c)—August, 1979—Drafted by Montreal Canadiens in 1979 entry draft. Sixth Montreal pick, 79th overall, fourth round.

STEVE ORTH

Center . . . 5'8" . . . 150 lbs. . . . Born, St. Cloud, Minn., January 17, 1965 . . . Shoots left.

Year	Team	League	Games	G.	A.	Pts.	Pen.
1982-83—St. Cloud Tech. H.S. (c)		Minn. H.S.	22	27	38	65	...
1983-84—University of Minnesota		WCHA	8	4	4	8	2

(c)—June, 1983—Drafted by New York Rangers in 1983 NHL entry draft. Eighth Rangers pick, 133rd overall, seventh round.

MARK ANATOLE OSBORNE

Left Wing . . . 6'2" . . . 200 lbs. . . . Born, Toronto, Ont., August 13, 1961 . . . Shoots left.

Year	Team	League	Games	G.	A.	Pts.	Pen.
1978-79—Niagara Falls Flyers		OMJHL	62	17	25	42	53
1979-80—Niagara Falls Flyers (c)		OMJHL	52	10	33	43	104

Year	Team	League	Games	G.	A.	Pts.	Pen.
1980-81—Niagara Falls Flyers		OHL	54	39	41	80	140
1980-81—Adirondack Red Wings (d)		AHL	....	...	....	....	....
1981-82—Detroit Red Wings		NHL	80	26	41	67	61
1982-83—Detroit Red Wings (e)		NHL	80	19	24	43	83
1983-84—New York Rangers		NHL	73	23	28	51	88
NHL TOTALS			233	68	93	161	232

(c)—June, 1980—Drafted as underage junior by Detroit Red Wings in 1980 NHL entry draft. Second Red Wings pick, 46th overall, third round.

(d)—No regular season appearance, 13 playoff games.

(e)—June, 1983—Traded by Detroit Red Wings with Willie Huber and Mike Blaisdell to New York Rangers for Ron Duguay, Eddie Mio and Ed Johnstone.

RANDY OSWALD

Defense . . . 6'3" . . . 185 lbs. . . . Born, Bowmanville, Ont., January 5, 1966 . . . Shoots left.

Year	Team	League	Games	G.	A.	Pts.	Pen.
1983-84—Michigan Tech. (c)		CCHA	41	0	2	2	44

(c)—June, 1984—Drafted by Boston Bruins in NHL entry draft. Sixth Bruins pick, 124th overall, sixth round.

GUY OUELLETTE

Center . . . 6' . . . 170 lbs. . . . Born, St. Jerome, Que., March 8, 1966 . . . Shoots left.

Year	Team	League	Games	G.	A.	Pts.	Pen.
1983-84—Quebec Remparts (c)		QHL	51	9	24	33	18

(c)—June, 1984—Drafted as underage junior by Quebec Nordiques in NHL entry draft. Eighth Nordiques pick, 183rd overall, ninth round.

ALVIN JOHN PADDOCK
(Known by middle name.)

Right Wing . . . 6'3" . . . 192 lbs. . . . Born, Brandon, Man., June 9, 1954 . . . Shoots right . . . Missed part of 1977-78 season with dislocated shoulder . . . Missed part of 1979-80 season with dislocated right elbow . . . Brother of Gordon Paddock . . . (November, 1983)—Named coach of Maine Mariners.

Year	Team	League	Games	G.	A.	Pts.	Pen.
1972-73—Brandon Wheat Kings		WCHL	11	3	2	5	6
1973-74—Brandon Wheat Kings (c)		WCHL	68	34	49	83	228
1974-75—Richmond Robins		AHL	72	26	22	48	206
1975-76—Richmond Robins		AHL	42	11	14	25	98
1975-76—Washington Capitals (d)		NHL	8	1	1	2	12
1976-77—Springfield Indians		AHL	61	13	16	29	106
1976-77—Philadelphia Flyers		NHL	5	0	0	0	9
1977-78—Maine Mariners		AHL	61	8	12	20	152
1978-79—Maine Mariners		AHL	79	30	37	67	275
1979-80—Philadelphia Flyers (e)		NHL	32	3	7	10	36
1980-81—Maine Mariners		AHL	22	8	7	15	53
1980-81—Quebec Nordiques		NHL	32	2	5	7	25
1981-82—Maine Mariners		AHL	39	6	10	16	123
1982-83—Maine Mariners		AHL	69	30	23	53	188
1982-83—Philadelphia Flyers (f)		NHL	10	2	1	3	4
1983-84—Maine Mariners		AHL	17	3	6	9	34
NHL TOTALS			87	8	14	22	86

(c)—Drafted from Brandon Wheat Kings by Washington Capitals in third round of 1974 amateur draft.

(d)—Traded to Philadelphia Flyers by Washington Capitals to complete earlier deal for Bob Sirois, September, 1976.

(e)—August, 1980—Sold by Philadelphia Flyers to Quebec Nordiques.

(f)—August, 1983—Signed by New Jersey Devils as a free agent.

GORDON PADDOCK

Defense . . . 6' . . . 180 lbs. . . . Born, Hamiota, Man., February 15, 1964 . . . Shoots right . . . Brother of John Paddock.

Year	Team	League	Games	G.	A.	Pts.	Pen.
1981-82—Saskatoon Jays		SJHL	59	8	21	29	232
1982-83—Saskatoon Blades		WHL	67	4	25	29	158
1983-84—Brandon Wheat Kings		WHL	72	14	37	51	151

WILFRED (WILF) PAIEMENT JR.

Right Wing . . . 6'1" . . . 205 lbs. . . . Born, Earlton, Ont., October 16, 1955 . . . Shoots right . . . Brother of Rosaire Paiement . . . Missed final part of 1975-76 season with thigh injury . . . Suspended for 15 games by NHL for stick swinging incident in 1978-79 season . . . (October 12, 1980)—Credited with scoring NHL's 100,000th regular season goal in 4-2 win at Philadelphia into an empty net . . . (March 27, 1982)—Sprained right knee in game at Montreal.

Year	Team	League	Games	G.	A.	Pts.	Pen.
1971-72—Niagara Falls Flyers		Jr."A" OHA	34	6	13	19	74
1972-73—St. Cath. Black Hawks (c)		Jr."A" OHA	61	18	27	45	173
1973-74—St. Cath. Black Hawks (a-d)		Jr."A" OHA	70	50	73	123	134
1974-75—Kansas City Scouts		NHL	78	26	13	39	101
1975-76—Kansas City Scouts		NHL	57	21	22	43	121
1976-77—Colorado Rockies		NHL	78	41	40	81	101
1977-78—Colorado Rockies		NHL	80	31	56	87	114
1978-79—Colorado Rockies		NHL	65	24	36	60	80
1979-80—Colorado Rockies (e)		NHL	34	10	16	26	41
1979-80—Toronto Maple Leafs		NHL	41	20	28	48	72
1980-81—Toronto Maple Leafs		NHL	77	40	57	97	145
1981-82—Toronto Maple Leafs (f)		NHL	69	18	40	58	203
1981-82—Quebec Nordiques		NHL	8	7	6	13	18
1982-83—Quebec Nordiques		NHL	80	26	38	64	170
1983-84—Quebec Nordiques		NHL	80	39	37	76	121
NHL TOTALS			747	303	389	692	1287

(c)—Traded to St. Catharines Black Hawks by Sudbury Wolves for midget draft choice.
(d)—Drafted from St. Catharines Black Hawks by Kansas City Scouts in first round of 1974 amateur draft.
(e)—December, 1979—Traded with Pat Hickey by Colorado Rockies to Toronto Maple Leafs for Lanny McDonald and Joel Quenneville.
(f)—March, 1982—Traded by Toronto Maple Leafs to Quebec Nordiques for Miroslav Frycer and seventh-round 1982 entry draft pick (Jeff Triano).

BRAD DONALD PALMER

Left Wing . . . 6' . . . 185 lbs. . . . Born, Duncan, B.C., September 14, 1961 . . . Shoots left . . . (November, 1982)—Knee injury.

Year	Team	League	Games	G.	A.	Pts.	Pen.
1978-79—Victoria Cougars		WHL	69	18	15	33	53
1979-80—Victoria Cougars (c)		WHL	72	45	49	94	61
1980-81—Victoria Cougars		WHL	44	34	53	87	72
1980-81—Minnesota North Stars		NHL	23	4	4	8	22
1981-82—Minnesota North Stars (d)		NHL	72	22	23	45	10
1982-83—Boston Bruins		NHL	73	6	11	17	18
1983-84—Hershey Bears		AHL	62	25	32	57	16
NHL TOTALS			168	32	38	70	58

(c)—June, 1980—Drafted by Minnesota North Stars as underage junior in 1980 NHL entry draft. First North Stars pick, 16th overall, first round.
(d)—June, 1982—Traded by Minnesota North Stars with NHL rights to Dave Donnelly to Boston Bruins for future considerations (Boston agreed not to draft Brian Bellows).

ROBERT ROSS PALMER

Defense . . . 5'11" . . . 190 lbs. . . . Born, Sarnia, Ont., September 10, 1956 . . . Shoots right . . . Attended University of Michigan.

Year	Team	League	Games	G.	A.	Pts.	Pen.
1973-74—University of Michigan		WCHA	36	3	12	15	14
1974-75—University of Michigan		WCHA	40	5	15	20	26
1975-76—University of Michigan (c)		WCHA	42	5	16	21	58
1976-77—University of Michigan		WCHA	45	5	37	42	32
1977-78—Springfield Indians		AHL	19	1	7	8	18
1977-78—Los Angeles Kings		NHL	48	0	3	3	27
1978-79—Los Angeles Kings		NHL	78	4	41	45	26
1979-80—Los Angeles Kings		NHL	78	4	36	40	18
1980-81—Los Angeles Kings		NHL	13	0	4	4	13
1980-81—Houston Apollos		CHL	28	3	10	13	23
1980-81—Indianapolis Checkers		CHL	27	1	9	10	16
1981-82—Los Angeles Kings		NHL	5	0	2	2	0
1981-82—New Haven Nighthawks (d)		AHL	41	2	23	25	22
1982-83—New Jersey Devils		NHL	60	1	10	11	21
1983-84—Maine Mariners		AHL	33	5	10	15	10
1983-84—New Jersey Devils		NHL	38	0	5	5	10
NHL TOTALS			320	9	101	110	115

(c)—Drafted from University of Michigan by Los Angeles Kings in fifth round of 1976 amateur draft.
(d)—September, 1982—Signed by New Jersey Devils as a free agent.

SCOTT PALUCH

Defense . . . 6'3" . . . 185 lbs. . . . Born, Chicago, Ill., March 9, 1966 . . . Shoots left.

Year	Team	League	Games	G.	A.	Pts.	Pen.
1983-84—Chicago Jets (c)		CJHL	50	44	46	90	42

(c)—June, 1984—Drafted by St. Louis Blues in NHL entry draft. Seventh Blues pick, 92nd overall, fifth round.

ARMEL PARISEE

Defense . . .6'1" . . . 186 lbs. . . . Born, Seven Isles, Que., July 21, 1963 . . . Shoots left.

Year	Team	League	Games	G.	A.	Pts.	Pen.
1980-81—Chicoutimi Sagueneens (c)		QMJHL	68	2	17	19	67
1981-82—Chicoutimi Sagueneens		QMJHL	58	3	16	19	104
1982-83—Chicoutimi Sagueneens		QHL	70	9	31	40	79
1983-84—Hull Olympics		QHL	64	4	22	26	165

(c)—June, 1981—Drafted as underage junior by Boston Bruins in 1981 NHL entry draft. Seventh Bruins pick, 161st overall, eighth round.

DOUGLAS BRADFORD (BRAD) PARK

Defense . . . 6' . . . 200 lbs. . . . Born, Toronto, Ont., July 6, 1948 . . . Shoots left . . . Missed part of 1965-66 season with torn cartilage in left knee, part of 1966-67 season with kidney injury and part of 1969-70 season with fractured right ankle . . . Missed part of 1970-71 season with injured left knee . . . Set NHL record for defensemen with two hat tricks in season (1971-72) . . . Missed part of 1972-73 season with strained knee . . . Missed part of 1974-75 season with strained left knee and final month of 1975-76 season with surgery for torn cartilage in left knee . . . Missed part of 1978-79 season due to surgery to remove torn cartilage in right knee . . . (September 22 and November 27, 1979)—Arthroscopic surgery to remove bone spurs in right knee . . . (1983-84)—Passed Bobby Orr to become NHL all-time career assist leader among defensemen . . . (April, 1984)—Tied Jean Beliveau by appearing in his 16th consecutive playoff.

Year	Team	League	Games	G.	A.	Pts.	Pen.
1965-66—Toronto Marlboros (c)	Jr. "A" OHA	33	0	14	14	48
1966-67—Toronto Marlboros	Jr. "A" OHA	29	4	15	19	73
1967-68—Toronto Marlboros (b)	Jr. "A" OHA	50	10	33	43	120
1967-68—Toronto Marlboros	Sr. "A" OHA	1	0	0	0	0
1968-69—Buffalo Bisons	AHL	17	2	12	14	49
1968-69—New York Rangers (d)	NHL	54	3	23	26	70
1969-70—New York Rangers (a)	NHL	60	11	26	37	98
1970-71—New York Rangers (b)	NHL	68	7	37	44	114
1971-72—New York Rangers (a)	NHL	75	24	49	73	130
1972-73—New York Rangers (b)	NHL	52	10	43	53	51
1973-74—New York Rangers (a)	NHL	78	25	57	82	148
1974-75—New York Rangers	NHL	65	13	44	57	104
1975-76—New York Rangers (e)	NHL	13	2	4	6	23
1975-76—Boston Bruins (a)	NHL	43	16	37	53	95
1976-77—Boston Bruins	NHL	77	12	55	67	67
1977-78—Boston Bruins (a)	NHL	80	22	57	79	79
1978-79—Boston Bruins	NHL	40	7	32	39	10
1979-80—Boston Bruins	NHL	32	5	16	21	27
1980-81—Boston Bruins	NHL	78	14	52	66	111
1981-82—Boston Bruins	NHL	75	14	42	56	82
1982-83—Boston Bruins (f)	NHL	76	10	26	36	82
1983-84—Detroit Red Wings	NHL	80	5	53	58	85
NHL TOTALS		1046	200	653	853	1376

(c)—Drafted from Toronto Marlboros by New York Rangers in first round of 1966 amateur draft.
(d)—Named Rookie-of-the-Year in East Division poll of players by THE SPORTING NEWS.
(e)—Traded to Boston Bruins by New York Rangers with Jean Ratelle and Joe Zanussi for Phil Esposito and Carol Vadnais, November, 1975.
(f)—August, 1983—Signed by Detroit Red Wings as a free agent.

MALCOLM PARKS

Center . . . 6'0" . . . 185 lbs. . . . Born, Edmonton, Alta., January 20, 1965 . . . Shoots right . . . Also plays right wing.

Year	Team	League	Games	G.	A.	Pts.	Pen.
1982-83—St. Albert Saints (c)		AJHL	54	59	57	116	185
1983-84—University of North Dakota		WCHA	33	11	10	21	42

(c)—June, 1983—Drafted by Minnesota North Stars in 1983 NHL entry draft. Second North Stars pick, 36th overall, second round.

GREGORY STEPHEN PASLAWSKI

Right Wing . . . 5'11" . . . 195 lbs. . . . Born, Kindersley, Sask., August 25, 1961 . . . Shoots right.

Year	Team	League	Games	G.	A.	Pts.	Pen.
1980-81—Prince Albert Raiders		SJHL	59	55	60	115	106
1981-82—Nova Scotia Voyageurs (c)		AHL	43	15	11	26	31
1982-83—Nova Scotia Voyageurs		AHL	75	46	42	88	32
1983-84—Montreal Canadiens (d)		NHL	26	1	4	5	4
1983-84—St. Louis Blues		NHL	34	8	6	14	7
NHL TOTALS			60	9	10	19	21

(c)—January, 1982—Signed by Montreal Canadiens as a free agent.

(d)—December, 1983—Traded with Doug Wickenheiser and Gilbert Delorme by Montreal Canadiens to St. Louis Blues for Perry Turnbull.

JOE ANDREW PATERSON

Left Wing and Center . . . 6'1" . . . 208 lbs. . . . Born, Toronto, Ont., June 25, 1960 . . . Shoots left . . . (October, 1982)—Pulled groin muscle.

Year	Team	League	Games	G.	A.	Pts.	Pen.
1977-78—London Knights		OMJHL	68	17	16	33	100
1978-79—London Knights (c)		OMJHL	60	22	19	41	158
1979-80—London Knights		OMJHL	65	21	50	71	156
1979-80—Kalamazoo Wings		IHL	4	1	2	3	2
1980-81—Detroit Red Wings		NHL	38	2	5	7	53
1980-81—Adirondack Red Wings		AHL	39	9	16	25	68
1981-82—Adirondack Red Wings		AHL	74	22	28	50	132
1981-82—Detroit Red Wings		NHL	3	0	0	0	0
1982-83—Adirondack Red Wings		AHL	36	11	10	21	85
1982-83—Detroit Red Wings		NHL	33	2	1	3	14
1983-84—Detroit Red Wings		NHL	41	2	5	7	148
1983-84—Adirondack Red Wings		AHL	20	10	15	25	43
NHL TOTALS			115	6	11	17	215

(c)—August, 1979—Drafted by Detroit Red Wings as underage junior in 1979 NHL entry draft. Fifth Red Wings pick, 87th overall, fifth round.

MARK PATERSON

Defense . . . 6' . . . 185 lbs. . . . Born, Ottawa, Ont., February 22, 1964 . . . Shoots left.

Year	Team	League	Games	G.	A.	Pts.	Pen.
1980-81—Nepean Raiders		OPJHL	50	6	13	19	98
1981-82—Ottawa 67's (c)		OHL	64	4	14	18	66
1982-83—Ottawa 67's		OHL	57	7	14	21	140
1982-83—Hartford Whalers		NHL	2	0	0	0	0
1983-84—Ottawa 67's		OHL	45	8	16	24	114
1983-84—Hartford Whalers		NHL	9	2	0	2	4
NHL TOTALS			11	2	0	2	4

(c)—June, 1982—Drafted as underage junior by Hartford Whalers in 1982 NHL entry draft. Second Whalers pick, 35th overall, second round.

RICHARD DAVID (RICK) PATERSON

Center . . . 5'10" . . . 185 lbs. . . . Born, Kingston, Ont., February 10, 1958 . . . Shoots right . . . (January, 1981)—Chipped ankle bone . . . Also plays right wing.

Year	Team	League	Games	G.	A.	Pts.	Pen.
1974-75—Cornwall Royals		QJHL	68	18	20	38	50
1975-76—Cornwall Royals		QJHL	71	20	60	80	59
1976-77—Cornwall Royals		QJHL	72	31	63	94	90
1977-78—Cornwall Royals (c)		QJHL	71	58	80	138	105
1978-79—New Brunswick Hawks		AHL	74	21	19	40	30
1979-80—Chicago Black Hawks		NHL	11	0	2	2	0
1979-80—New Brunswick Hawks		AHL	55	22	30	52	18
1980-81—Chicago Black Hawks		NHL	49	8	2	10	18
1980-81—New Brunswick Hawks		CHL	21	7	8	15	6
1981-82—New Brunswick Hawks		AHL	30	8	16	24	45
1981-82—Chicago Black Hawks		NHL	48	4	7	11	8
1982-83—Chicago Black Hawks		NHL	79	14	9	23	14
1983-84—Chicago Black Hawks		NHL	72	7	6	13	41
NHL TOTALS			259	33	26	59	81

(c)—Drafted from Cornwall Royals by Chicago Black Hawks in third round of 1978 amateur draft.

LARRY JAMES PATEY

Center . . . 6'1" . . . 180 lbs. . . . Born, Toronto, Ont., March 19, 1953 . . . Shoots left . . . Attended Boston University in 1972-73 but was ineligible to play for hockey team . . . Brother of Doug Patey . . . (October 16, 1982)—Injured shoulder in game vs. Detroit . . . (September, 1983)—Surgery to remove disc in back, returned in January.

Year	Team	League	Games	G.	A.	Pts.	Pen.
1972-73—Braintree Hawks (c)		NEHL	47	36	27	63	....
1973-74—Salt Lake Golden Eagles (d)		WHL	76	40	43	83	91
1973-74—California Golden Seals		NHL	1	0	0	0	0
1974-75—California Seals		NHL	79	25	20	45	68
1975-76—California Seals (e)		NHL	18	4	4	8	23
1975-76—St. Louis Blues		NHL	53	8	6	14	26
1976-77—St. Louis Blues		NHL	80	21	29	50	41
1977-78—St. Louis Blues		NHL	80	17	17	34	29
1978-79—St. Louis Blues		NHL	78	15	19	34	60
1979-80—St. Louis Blues		NHL	78	17	17	34	76
1980-81—St. Louis Blues		NHL	80	22	23	45	107
1981-82—St. Louis Blues		NHL	70	14	12	26	97
1982-83—St. Louis Blues		NHL	67	9	12	21	80
1983-84—St. Louis Blues (f)		NHL	17	0	1	1	8
1983-84—New York Rangers		NHL	9	1	2	3	4
NHL TOTALS			710	153	162	315	619

(c)—Drafted from Braintree Hawks by California Golden Seals in ninth round of 1973 amateur draft.

(d)—Won WHL Rookie-of-the-Year Award.

(e)—Traded to St. Louis Blues by California Seals with third-round draft choice for Wayne Merrick, November, 1975.

(f)—March, 1984—Traded with NHL rights to Bob Brooke by St. Louis Blues to New York Rangers for David Barr, a third-round 1984 draft pick (Alan Perry) and cash.

JAMES PATRICK

Defense . . . 6'2" . . . 185 lbs. . . . Born, Winnipeg, Man., June 14, 1963 . . . Shoots right . . . Brother of Stephen Patrick . . . Member of 1984 Canadian Olympic Team.

Year	Team	League	Games	G.	A.	Pts.	Pen.
1980-81—Prince Albert Raiders (a-c-d)		SJHL	59	21	61	82	162
1981-82—Univ. of North Dakota (b-e)		WCHA	42	5	24	29	26
1982-83—Univ. of North Dakota		WCHA	36	12	36	48	29
1983-84—Canadian Olympic Team		Int'l	63	7	24	31	52
1983-84—New York Rangers		NHL	12	1	7	8	2
NHL TOTALS			12	1	7	8	2

(c)—June, 1981—Drafted by New York Rangers as underage player in 1981 NHL entry draft. First Rangers pick, 9th overall, first round.

(d)—Named Chapstick Player-of-the-Year as top Tier II Canadian Junior Player.

(e)—Named WCHA Rookie-of-the-Year.

STEPHEN GARY PATRICK

Right Wing . . . 6'4" . . . 206 lbs. . . . Born, Winnipeg, Man., February 4, 1961 . . . Shoots right . . . (February 21, 1981)—Bruised right shoulder . . . Brother of James Patrick . . . (February, 1983)—Suspended by Buffalo Sabres for refusing to report to Rochester (AHL). Subsequently reinstated.

Year	Team	League	Games	G.	A.	Pts.	Pen.
1978-79—Brandon Wheat Kings		WHL	52	23	31	54	105
1979-80—Brandon Wheat Kings (c)		WHL	71	28	38	66	185
1980-81—Brandon Wheat Kings		WHL	34	29	30	59	56
1980-81—Buffalo Sabres		NHL	30	1	7	8	25
1981-82—Rochester Americans		AHL	38	11	9	20	15
1981-82—Buffalo Sabres		NHL	41	8	8	16	64
1982-83—Buffalo Sabres		NHL	56	9	13	22	26
1983-84—Buffalo Sabres		NHL	11	1	4	5	6
1983-84—Rochester Americans		AHL	30	8	14	22	33
NHL TOTALS			138	19	32	51	121

(c)—June, 1980—Drafted by Buffalo Sabres as underage junior in 1980 NHL entry draft. First Sabres pick, 20th overall, first round.

COLIN PATTERSON

Left Wing . . . 6'2" . . . 195 lbs. . . . Born, Rexdale, Ont., May 11, 1960 . . . Shoots left . . . (March 14, 1984)—Shoulder injury.

Year	Team	League	Games	G.	A.	Pts.	Pen.
1980-81—Clarkson College		ECAC	34	20	31	51	8
1981-82—Clarkson College		ECAC	35	21	31	52	32
1982-83—Clarkson College (b)		ECAC	31	23	29	52	30
1982-83—Colorado Flames (c)		CHL	7	1	1	2	0
1983-84—Colorado Flames		CHL	6	2	3	5	9
1983-84—Calgary Flames		NHL	56	13	14	27	15
NHL TOTALS			56	13	14	27	15

(c)—March, 1983—Signed by Calgary Flames as a free agent.

PHIL PATTERSON

Right Wing . . . 5'9" . . . 178 lbs. . . . Born, Kemtville, Que., July 18, 1964 . . . Shoots right . . . Also plays defense.

Year	Team	League	Games	G.	A.	Pts.	Pen.
1979-80—Nepean Tier II		OPJHL	49	9	14	23	106
1980-81—Ottawa 67's		OMJHL	45	9	12	21	37
1981-82—Ottawa 67's (c)		OHL	21	3	6	9	11
1982-83—Ottawa 67's		OHL	57	35	26	61	27
1983-84—Ottawa 67's		OHL	42	22	17	39	18

(c)—June, 1982—Drafted by Chicago Black Hawks as underage junior in 1982 NHL entry draft. Ninth Black Hawks pick, 175th overall, ninth round.

MARK PAVELICH

Center . . . 5'8" . . . 170 lbs. . . . Born, Eveleth, Minn., February 28, 1958 . . . Shoots right . . . (1981-82)—Set New York Rangers records for rookies for goals (33), assists (43) and total points (76).

Year	Team	League	Games	G.	A.	Pts.	Pen.
1976-77—U. of Minnesota-Duluth		WCHA	37	12	7	19	8
1977-78—U. of Minnesota-Duluth		WCHA	36	14	30	44	44
1978-79—U. of Minnesota-Duluth (c)		WCHA	37	31	48	79	52
1979-80—U.S. National Team		.....	60	16	36	52	14
1979-80—U.S. National Team		Olympics	7	1	6	7	2
1980-81—HC Lugano		Switzerland	60	24	49	73	..
1981-82—New York Rangers (d)		NHL	79	33	43	76	67
1982-83—New York Rangers		NHL	78	37	38	75	52
1983-84—New York Rangers		NHL	77	29	53	82	96
NHL TOTALS			234	99	134	233	215

(c)—Named to All-America Team (West).
(d)—June, 1981—Signed by New York Rangers as a free agent.

JAMES PETER PAVESE

Defense . . . 6'2" . . . 204 lbs. . . . Born, New York, N.Y., June 8, 1962 . . . Shoots left . . . (October, 1981)—Infected hand requiring hospitalization.

Year	Team	League	Games	G.	A.	Pts.	Pen.
1976-77—Suffolk Royals (c)		NYMJHL	32	6	31	37	32
1977-78—Suffolk Royals		NYMJHL	34	18	40	58	102
1978-79—Peterborough Petes		OMJHL	16	1	1	2	22
1979-80—Kitchener Rangers (d)		OMJHL	68	10	26	36	206
1980-81—Kitchener Rangers (e)		OHL	19	3	12	15	93
1980-81—Sault Ste. Marie Greyhounds		OHL	43	3	25	28	127
1981-82—Sault Ste. Marie Greyhounds (f)		OHL	26	4	21	25	110
1981-82—Salt Lake Golden Eagles (f)		CHL	....	...	....	....	....
1981-82—St. Louis Blues		NHL	42	2	9	11	101
1982-83—Salt Lake Golden Eagles		CHL	38	3	8	11	183
1982-83—St. Louis Blues		NHL	24	0	2	2	45
1983-84—Montana Magic		CHL	47	1	19	20	147
1983-84—St. Louis Blues		NHL	4	0	1	1	19
NHL TOTALS			70	2	12	14	165

(c)—Named co-winner of Most Valuable Defenseman award (Shared award with Tom Matthews)
(d)—June, 1980—Drafted as underage junior by St. Louis Blues in 1980 NHL entry draft. Second Blues pick, 54th overall, third round.
(e)—December, 1980—Traded by Kitchener Rangers with Rick Morrocco to Sault Ste. Marie Greyhounds for Scott Clements, Bob Hicks and Mario Michieli.
(f)—No regular-season record, played one playoff game.

STEVEN JOHN PAYNE

Left Wing . . . 6'2½" . . . 205 lbs. . . . Born, Toronto, Ont., August 16, 1958 . . . Shoots left.

Year	Team	League	Games	G.	A.	Pts.	Pen.
1976-77—Ottawa 67's		Jr."A"OHA	61	21	26	47	22
1977-78—Ottawa 67's (c)		Jr."A"OHA	52	57	37	94	22
1978-79—Oklahoma City Stars		CHL	5	3	4	7	2
1978-79—Minnesota North Stars		NHL	70	23	17	40	29
1979-80—Minnesota North Stars		NHL	80	42	43	85	40
1980-81—Minnesota North Stars (d)		NHL	76	30	28	58	88
1981-82—Minnesota North Stars		NHL	74	33	44	77	11
1982-83—Minnesota North Stars		NHL	80	30	39	69	53
1983-84—Minnesota North Stars		NHL	78	28	31	59	49
NHL TOTALS			458	186	202	388	270

(c)—Drafted from Ottawa 67's by Minnesota North Stars in second round of 1978 amateur draft.
(d)—Tied with Mike Bossy for NHL playoff lead of 17 goals.

KENT PAYNTER

Defense . . . 6'0" . . . 186 lbs. . . . Born, Summerside, P.E.I., April 27, 1965 . . . Shoots left.

Year	Team	League	Games	G.	A.	Pts.	Pen.
1981-82—Western Capitals		P.E.I.JHL	35	7	23	30	66
1982-83—Kitchener Rangers (c)		OHL	65	4	11	15	97
1983-84—Kitchener Rangers		OHL	65	9	27	36	94

(c)—June, 1983—Drafted by Chicago Black Hawks as underage junior in 1983 NHL entry draft. Ninth Black Hawks pick, 159th overall, eighth round.

TED PEARSON

Left Wing . . . 5'10" . . . 175 lbs. . . . Born, Kitchener, Ont., January 9, 1962 . . . Shoots left . . . Son of Mel Pearson (RW—played pro hockey between 1957 and 1973 with QHL, AHL, WHL, EPHL, NHL, CPHL and WHA).

Year	Team	League	Games	G.	A.	Pts.	Pen.
1980-81—University of Wisconsin		WCHA	36	6	9	15	59
1981-82—University of Wisconsin (c)		WCHA	41	15	23	38	85
1982-83—University of Wisconsin		WCHA	42	6	9	15	90
1983-84—University of Wisconsin		WCHA	35	13	20	33	60

(c)—June, 1982—Drafted by Calgary Flames in 1982 NHL entry draft. Eleventh Flames pick, 177th overall, ninth round.

ALLEN PEDERSON

Defense . . . 6'3" . . . 180 lbs. . . . Born, Edmonton, Alta., January 13, 1965 . . . Shoots left.

Year	Team	League	Games	G.	A.	Pts.	Pen.
1982-83—Medicine Hat Tigers (c)		WHL	63	3	10	13	49
1983-84—Medicine Hat Tigers		WHL	44	0	11	11	47

(c)—June, 1983—Drafted as underage junior by Boston Bruins in 1983 NHL entry draft. Fifth Bruins' pick, 102nd overall, fifth round.

BARRY ALAN PEDERSON

Center . . . 5'11" . . . 171 lbs. . . . Born, Big River, Sask., March 13, 1961 . . . Shoots right . . . (1981-82)—Set Boston Bruins rookie records with 44 goals and 92 points . . . (1982-83)— Became youngest player to ever lead Boston in scoring.

Year	Team	League	Games	G.	A.	Pts.	Pen.
1977-78—Nanaimo		BCJHL	....	...	....	....	....
1977-78—Victoria Cougars		WCHL	3	1	4	5	2
1978-79—Victoria Cougars		WHL	72	31	53	84	41
1979-80—Victoria Cougars (b-c)		WHL	72	52	88	140	50
1980-81—Victoria Cougars (a)		WHL	55	65	82	147	65
1980-81—Boston Bruins		NHL	9	1	4	5	6
1981-82—Boston Bruins		NHL	80	44	48	92	53
1982-83—Boston Bruins		NHL	77	46	61	107	47
1983-84—Boston Bruins		NHL	80	39	77	116	64
NHL TOTALS			246	130	190	320	170

(c)—June, 1980—Drafted as underage junior by Boston Bruins in 1980 NHL entry draft. First Bruins pick, 18th overall, first round.

BLAINE PEERLESS

Defense . . . 6' . . . 195 lbs. . . . Born, Edmonton, Alta., October 13, 1961 . . . Shoots left.

Year	Team	League	Games	G.	A.	Pts.	Pen.
1980-81—Spokane Flyers		WHL	66	14	38	52	228
1981-82—Milwaukee Admirals		IHL	80	12	38	50	127
1982-83—Milwaukee Admirals		IHL	12	2	6	8	39

Year	Team	League	Games	G.	A.	Pts.	Pen.
1982-83—Salt Lake Golden Eagles	CHL	45	1	8	9	38
1983-84—Montana Magic	CHL	73	6	18	24	80

PERRY PELENSKY

Right Wing . . . 6'1" . . . 190 lbs. . . . Born, Edmonton, Alta., March 20, 1962 . . . Shoots right.

Year	Team	League	Games	G.	A.	Pts.	Pen.
1979-80—Ft. Saskatchewan	SJHL	59	55	59	114	105
1980-81—Portland Winter Hawks (c)	WHL	65	35	32	67	124
1981-82—Portland Winter Hawks	WHL	71	40	46	86	192
1982-83—Springfield Indians	AHL	80	15	25	40	89
1983-84—Springfield Indians	AHL	73	22	16	38	185
1983-84—Chicago Black Hawks	NHL	4	0	0	0	5
NHL TOTALS		4	0	0	0	5

(c)—June, 1981—Drafted by Chicago Black Hawks in 1981 NHL entry draft. Fourth Black Hawks pick, 75th overall, fourth round.

STEVE PEPIN

Center . . . 5'10" . . . 170 lbs. . . . Born, Sherbrooke, Que., March 21, 1965 . . . Shoots left.

Year	Team	League	Games	G.	A.	Pts.	Pen.
1982-83—St. Jean Beavers (a-c)	QHL	69	51	61	112	83
1983-84—Drummondville Voltigeurs	QHL	64	54	58	112	173

(c)—June, 1983—Drafted as underage junior by Chicago Black Hawks in 1983 NHL entry draft. Twelfth Black Hawks pick, 219th overall, 11th round.

JIM DESMOND PEPLINSKI

Center . . . 6'2" . . . 201 lbs. . . . Born, Renfrew, Ont., October 24, 1960 . . . Shoots right.

Year	Team	League	Games	G.	A.	Pts.	Pen.
1977-78—Toronto Marlboros	OMJHL	66	13	28	41	44
1978-79—Toronto Marlboros (c)	OMJHL	66	23	32	55	60
1979-80—Toronto Marlboros	OMJHL	67	35	66	101	89
1980-81—Calgary Flames	NHL	80	13	25	38	108
1981-82—Calgary Flames	NHL	74	30	37	67	115
1982-83—Calgary Flames	NHL	80	15	26	41	134
1983-84—Calgary Flames	NHL	74	11	22	33	114
NHL TOTALS		308	69	110	179	471

(c)—August, 1979—Drafted by Atlanta Flames as underage junior in 1979 NHL entry draft. Fifth Flames pick, 75th overall, fourth round.

FRANK WILLIAM PERKINS

Right Wing . . . 5'10" . . . 180 lbs. . . . Born, Pueblo, Colo., February 16, 1960 . . . Shoots right . . . Player/Coach with Pinebridge Bucks (ACHL) in 1983-84.

Year	Team	League	Games	G.	A.	Pts.	Pen.
1977-78—Kitchener Rangers	OMJHL	2	0	0	0	0
1977-78—Sudbury Wolves	OMJHL	28	2	7	9	96
1978-79—Sudbury Wolves	OMJHL	60	19	29	48	181
1979-80—Sudbury Wolves (c)	OMJHL	62	27	37	64	204
1980-81—Port Huron Flags	IHL	53	9	17	26	232
1981-82—Hershey Bears	AHL	69	9	11	20	254
1982-83—Hershey Bears	AHL	80	12	8	20	206
1983-84—Pinebridge Bucks (d)	ACHL	26	10	27	37	131

(c)—June, 1980—Drafted by Washington Capitals in 1980 NHL entry draft. Sixth Capitals pick, 131st overall, seventh round.

(d)—Named to First All-Star Team as coach.

TERRY PERKINS

Right Wing . . . 6'1" . . . 190 lbs. . . . Born, Campbell River, B.C., June 21, 1966 . . . Shoots right.

Year	Team	League	Games	G.	A.	Pts.	Pen.
1983-84—Portland Winter Hawks (c)	WHL	68	35	30	65	75

(c)—June, 1984—Drafted as underage junior by Quebec Nordiques in NHL entry draft. Fourth Nordiques pick, 78th overall, fourth round.

FRED PERLINI

Center . . . 6'2" . . . 175 lbs. . . . Born, Sault Ste. Marie, Ont., April 12, 1962 . . . Shoots left.

Year	Team	League	Games	G.	A.	Pts.	Pen.
1979-80—Toronto Marlboros (c)		OMJHL	67	13	18	31	12
1980-81—Toronto Marlboros		OHL	55	37	29	66	48
1981-82—Toronto Marlboros		OHL	68	47	64	111	75
1981-82—Toronto Maple Leafs		NHL	7	2	3	5	0
1982-83—St. Catharines Saints		AHL	76	8	22	30	24
1983-84—Toronto Maple Leafs		NHL	1	0	0	0	0
1983-84—St. Catharines Saints		AHL	79	21	31	52	67
NHL TOTALS			8	2	3	5	0

(c)—June, 1980—Drafted as underage junior by Toronto Maple Leafs in 1980 NHL entry draft. Eighth Maple Leafs pick, 158th overall, eighth round.

JEFF PERPICH

Defense . . . 6'2" . . . 200 lbs. . . . Born, Hibbing, Minn., February 21, 1965 . . . Shoots left . . . Son of George Perpich (longtime coach of Hibbing High School hockey team, and former NFL player).

Year	Team	League	Games	G.	A.	Pts.	Pen.
1982-83—Hibbing High School (c)		Minn. H.S.	22	2	13	15	....
1983-84—University of Denver		WCHA	30	0	2	2	16

(c)—June, 1983—Drafted by Montreal Canadiens in 1983 NHL entry draft. Thirteenth Canadiens pick, 218th overall, 11th round.

GILBERT PERREAULT

Center . . . 5'11½" . . . 202 lbs. . . . Born, Victoriaville, Que., November 13, 1950 . . . Shoots left . . . Cousin of Bobby Perreault . . . Set NHL records for most goals and points in rookie season in 1970-71 (record for goals broken by Richard Martin and record for points broken by Marcel Dionne, both in 1971-72) . . . Missed part of 1973-74 season with fractured left ankle and part of 1974-75 season with strained left knee . . . (January 24, 1981)—Broken ribs . . . (September 7, 1981)—Broke right ankle in Canada Cup game vs. Sweden. Had pin inserted during surgery on September 8 . . . (March, 1984)—Back spasms.

Year	Team	League	Games	G.	A.	Pts.	Pen.
1967-68—Montreal Jr. Canadiens		Jr."A"OHA	47	15	34	49	10
1968-69—Montreal Jr. Canadiens (a)		Jr."A"OHA	54	37	60	97	29
1969-70—Mont. Jr. Canadiens (a-c-d)		Jr."A"OHA	54	51	70	121	26
1970-71—Buffalo Sabres (e-f)		NHL	78	38	34	72	19
1971-72—Buffalo Sabres		NHL	76	26	48	74	24
1972-73—Buffalo Sabres (g)		NHL	78	28	60	88	10
1973-74—Buffalo Sabres		NHL	55	18	33	51	10
1974-75—Buffalo Sabres		NHL	68	39	57	96	36
1975-76—Buffalo Sabres (b)		NHL	80	44	69	113	36
1976-77—Buffalo Sabres (b)		NHL	80	39	56	95	30
1977-78—Buffalo Sabres		NHL	79	41	48	89	20
1978-79—Buffalo Sabres		NHL	79	27	58	85	20
1979-80—Buffalo Sabres		NHL	80	40	66	106	57
1980-81—Buffalo Sabres		NHL	56	20	39	59	56
1981-82—Buffalo Sabres		NHL	62	31	42	73	40
1982-83—Buffalo Sabres		NHL	77	30	46	76	34
1983-84—Buffalo Sabres		NHL	73	31	59	90	32
NHL TOTALS			1021	452	715	1167	424

(c)—Won Red Tilson Memorial Trophy (MVP).
(d)—Drafted from Montreal Jr. Canadiens by Buffalo Sabres in first round of 1970 amateur draft.
(e)—Won Calder Memorial Trophy.
(f)—Named Rookie of the Year in East Division of NHL by THE SPORTING NEWS.
(g)—Won Lady Byng Trophy.

STEFAN PERSSON

Defense . . . 6'1" . . . 180 lbs. . . . Born, Umea, Sweden, December 22, 1954 . . . Shoots left . . . (April 20, 1981)—Broken jaw when hit by a shot during playoff game at Edmonton . . . (October 7, 1981)—Cracked two ribs in opening game of season at Los Angeles . . . (January, 1984)—Tonsillectomy . . . (February, 1984)—Knee injury . . . (April, 1984)—Separated shoulder during playoffs.

Year	Team	League	Games	G.	A.	Pts.	Pen.
1976-77—Brynas		Sweden	31	7	13	20	70
1976-77—Swedish National Team (c)		Sweden	....	...	....	....	....
1977-78—New York Islanders		NHL	66	6	50	56	54
1978-79—New York Islanders		NHL	78	10	56	66	57
1979-80—New York Islanders		NHL	73	4	35	39	76

Year	Team	League	Games	G.	A.	Pts.	Pen.
1980-81—New York Islanders	NHL	80	9	52	61	82
1981-82—New York Islanders	NHL	70	6	37	43	99
1982-83—New York Islanders	NHL	70	4	25	29	71
1983-84—New York Islanders	NHL	75	9	24	33	65
NHL TOTALS			512	48	279	327	404

(c)—Signed by New York Islanders as free agent, September, 1977.

BRENT RONALD PETERSON

Center . . . 6'1" . . . 195 lbs. . . . Born, Calgary, Alta., February 15, 1958 . . . Shoots right . . . Missed most of 1978-79 season with broken leg . . . (October 15, 1980)—Fractured right cheekbone . . . (November 12, 1980)—Fractured left ankle . . . (February 10, 1983)—Dislocated shoulder in game at Los Angeles.

Year	Team	League	Games	G.	A.	Pts.	Pen.
1974-75—Edmonton Oil Kings	WCHL	66	17	26	43	44
1975-76—Edmonton Oil Kings	WCHL	70	22	39	61	57
1976-77—Portland Winter Hawks	WCHL	69	34	78	112	98
1977-78—Portland Winter Hawks (c)	WCHL	51	33	50	83	95
1978-79—Detroit Red Wings	NHL	5	0	0	0	0
1979-80—Adirondack Red Wings	AHL	52	9	22	31	61
1979-80—Detroit Red Wings	NHL	18	1	2	3	2
1980-81—Detroit Red Wings	NHL	53	6	18	24	24
1980-81—Adirondack Red Wings	AHL	3	1	0	1	10
1981-82—Detroit Red Wings (d)	NHL	15	1	0	1	6
1981-82—Buffalo Sabres	NHL	46	9	5	14	43
1982-83—Buffalo Sabres	NHL	75	13	24	37	38
1983-84—Buffalo Sabres	NHL	70	9	12	21	52
NHL TOTALS			282	39	61	100	165

(c)—Drafted from Portland Winter Hawks by Detroit Red Wings (with choice obtained from Toronto Maple Leafs) in first round of 1978 amateur draft.

(d)—December, 1981—Traded with Mike Foligno, Dale McCourt and future considerations by Detroit Red Wings to Buffalo Sabres for Danny Gare, Jim Schoenfeld, Derek Smith and Bob Sauve.

MICHEL PETIT

Defense . . . 6'1" . . . 185 lbs. . . . Born, St. Malo, Que., February 12, 1964 . . . Shoots right . . . (March, 1984)—Separated shoulder.

Year	Team	League	Games	G.	A.	Pts.	Pen.
1980-81—St. Foy Midget AAA	QAAAMHL	48	10	45	55	84
1981-82—Sherbrooke Beavers (a-c-d-e)	QMJHL	63	10	39	49	106
1982-83—St. Jean Beavers (a)	QHL	62	19	67	86	196
1982-83—Vancouver Canucks	NHL	2	0	0	0	0
1983-84—Vancouver Canucks	NHL	44	6	9	15	53
NHL TOTALS			46	6	9	15	53

(c)—Winner of Raymond Lagace Trophy (Top Rookie QMJHL Defenseman).

(d)—Winner of the Association of Journalist of Hockey Trophy (Top QMJHL Pro Prospect).

(e)—June, 1982—Drafted as underage junior by Vancouver Canucks in 1982 NHL entry draft. First Canucks pick, 11th overall, first round.

JORGEN PETTERSSON

Left Wing . . . 6'2" . . . 185 lbs. . . . Born, Gothenburg, Sweden, July 11, 1956 . . . Shoots left . . . (October, 1980)—Sprained ankle . . . (February, 1983)—Wrist injury.

Year	Team	League	Games	G.	A.	Pts.	Pen.
1974-75—Vastra Frolunda IF	Sweden	42	19	5	24	6
1975-76—Vastra Frolunda IF	Sweden	31	17	6	23	8
1976-77—Vastra Frolunda IF	Sweden	19	15	4	19	4
1977-78—Vastra Frolunda IF	Sweden	16	5	8	13	8
1978-79—Vastra Frolunda IF	Sweden	35	23	11	34	12
1979-70—Vastra Frolunda IF (c)	Sweden	32	21	19	40	....
1980-81—St. Louis Blues	NHL	62	37	36	73	24
1981-82—St. Louis Blues	NHL	77	38	31	69	28
1982-83—St. Louis Blues	NHL	74	35	38	73	4
1983-84—St. Louis Blues	NHL	77	28	34	62	29
NHL TOTALS			290	138	139	277	85

(c)—May, 1980—Signed by St. Louis Blues as a free agent.

ROBERT RENE JOSEPH PICARD

Defense . . . 6'2" . . . 203 lbs. . . . Born, Montreal, Que., May 25, 1957 . . . Shoots left . . . Nephew of former NHL defenseman Noel Picard . . . (November 12, 1980)—Strained knee ligaments . . . (January, 1983)—Broken bone in foot.

Year	Team	League	Games	G.	A.	Pts.	Pen.
1973-74	Montreal Red, White and Blue	QJHL	70	7	46	53	296
1974-75	Montreal Red, White and Blue	QJHL	70	13	74	87	339
1975-76	Montreal Juniors (b)	QJHL	72	14	67	81	282
1976-77	Montreal Juniors (a-c-d)	QJHL	70	32	60	92	267
1977-78	Washington Capitals	NHL	75	10	27	37	101
1978-79	Washington Capitals	NHL	77	21	44	65	85
1979-80	Washington Capitals (e)	NHL	78	11	43	54	122
1980-81	Toronto Maple Leafs (f)	NHL	59	6	19	25	68
1980-81	Montreal Canadiens	NHL	8	2	2	4	6
1981-82	Montreal Canadiens	NHL	62	2	26	28	106
1982-83	Montreal Canadiens	NHL	64	7	31	38	60
1983-84	Montreal Canadiens (g)	NHL	7	0	2	2	0
1983-84	Winnipeg Jets	NHL	62	6	16	22	34
	NHL TOTALS		492	65	210	275	582

(c)—Outstanding defenseman in QJHL.
(d)—Drafted from Montreal Juniors by Washington Capitals in first round of 1977 amateur draft.
(e)—June, 1980—Traded with Tim Coulis and second round draft choice in 1980 (Bob McGill) by Washington Capitals to Toronto Maple Leafs for Mike Palmateer and third round draft choice (Torrie Robertson).
(f)—March, 1981—Traded by Toronto Maple Leafs with a future eighth round draft pick to Montreal Canadiens for Michel Larocque.
(g)—November, 1983—Traded by Montreal Canadiens to Winnipeg Jets for third-round 1984 draft pick (Patrick Roy).

DAVE PICHETTE

Defense . . . 6'3" . . . 195 lbs. . . . Born, Grand Falls, N. B., February 4, 1960 . . . Shoots left . . . (January, 1983)—Back injury.

Year	Team	League	Games	G.	A.	Pts.	Pen.
1978-79	Quebec Remparts	QMJHL	57	10	16	26	134
1979-80	Quebec Remparts	QMJHL	56	8	19	27	129
1980-81	Quebec Nordiques (c)	NHL	46	4	16	20	62
1980-81	Hershey Bears	AHL	20	2	3	5	37
1981-82	Quebec Nordiques	NHL	67	7	30	37	152
1982-83	Fredericton Express	AHL	16	3	11	14	14
1982-83	Quebec Nordiques	NHL	53	3	21	24	49
1983-84	Fredericton Express	AHL	10	2	1	3	13
1983-84	Quebec Nordiques (d)	NHL	23	2	7	9	12
1983-84	St. Louis Blues	NHL	23	0	11	11	6
	NHL TOTALS		212	16	85	101	281

(c)—September, 1980—Signed by Quebec Nordiques as a free agent.
(d)—February, 1984—Traded by Quebec Nordiques to St. Louis Blues for Andre Dore.

RANDY STEPHEN PIERCE

Right Wing . . . 6' . . . 190 lbs. . . . Born, Arnprior, Ont., November 23, 1957 . . . Shoots right . . . (December 2, 1980)—Suffered fractured nose and cheekbone, contusion and double vision of right eye and facial lacerations when hit by a puck. Surgery was required December 11 . . . (October, 1981)—Separated shoulder . . . (December, 1981)—Took 19 stitches when forehead and left eyelid were raked by a stick.

Year	Team	League	Games	G.	A.	Pts.	Pen.
1975-76	Sudbury Wolves	Jr. "A" OHA	56	21	44	65	72
1976-77	Sudbury Wolves (c)	Jr. "A" OHA	60	38	60	98	67
1977-78	Hampton Gulls	AHL	3	0	1	1	2
1977-78	Phoenix Roadrunners	CHL	12	3	1	4	11
1977-78	Colorado Rockies	NHL	35	9	10	19	15
1978-79	Philadelphia Firebirds	AHL	1	0	0	0	0
1978-79	Colorado Rockies	NHL	70	19	17	36	35
1979-80	Colorado Rockies	NHL	75	16	23	39	100
1980-81	Colorado Rockies	NHL	55	9	21	30	52
1981-82	Colorado Rockies	NHL	5	0	0	0	4
1981-82	Ft. Worth Texans	CHL	15	6	6	12	19
1982-83	Wichita Wind	CHL	14	4	8	12	4
1982-83	New Jersey Devils (d)	NHL	3	0	0	0	0

Year	Team	League	Games	G.	A.	Pts.	Pen.
1982-83—Binghamton Whalers		AHL	46	14	41	55	33
1983-84—Hartford Whalers		NHL	17	6	3	9	9
1983-84—Binghamton Whalers		AHL	46	21	24	45	41
NHL TOTALS			260	59	74	133	215

(c)—Drafted from Sudbury Wolves by Colorado Rockies in third round of 1977 amateur draft.

(d)—December, 1983—Signed by Binghamton Whalers as a free agent.

ROBERT PIERSON

Left Wing . . . 6'3" . . . 213 lbs. . . . Born, Toronto, Ont., October 23, 1964 . . . Shoots left.

Year	Team	League	Games	G.	A.	Pts.	Pen.
1981-82—London Knights		OHL	62	6	9	15	32
1982-83—London Knights (c)		OHL	68	18	23	41	68
1983-84—London Knights		OHL	13	2	6	8	22
1983-84—Brantford Alexanders		OHL	47	12	11	23	46

(c)—June, 1983—Drafted as underage junior by Detroit Red Wings in 1983 NHL entry draft. Eighth Red Wings pick, 126th overall, seventh round.

CAM PLANTE

Defense . . . 6' . . . 190 lbs. . . . Born, Brandon, Manitoba, March 12, 1964 . . . Shoots left . . . (1983-84)—Set WHL single season record for defensemen with 118 assists and 140 points.

Year	Team	League	Games	G.	A.	Pts.	Pen.
1980-81—Brandon Wheat Kings		WHL	70	3	14	17	17
1981-82—Brandon Wheat Kings		WHL	36	4	12	16	22
1982-83—Brandon Wheat Kings (c)		WHL	56	19	56	75	71
1983-84—Brandon Wheat Kings (a)		WHL	72	22	118	140	96

(c)—June, 1983—Drafted as underage junior by Toronto Maple Leafs in 1983 NHL entry draft. Fifth Maple Leafs' pick, 128th overall, seventh round.

JIM PLAYFAIR

Defense . . . 6'3" . . . 200 lbs. . . . Born, Vanderhoof, B.C., May 22, 1964 . . . Shoots left . . . Brother of Larry Playfair.

Year	Team	League	Games	G.	A.	Pts.	Pen.
1980-81—Fort Saskatchewan		AJHL	31	2	17	19	105
1981-82—Portland Winter Hawks (c)		WHL	70	4	13	17	121
1982-83—Portland Winter Hawks		WHL	63	8	27	35	218
1983-84—Portland Winter Hawks		WHL	16	5	6	11	38
1983-84—Calgary Wranglers		WHL	44	6	9	15	96
1983-84—Edmonton Oilers		NHL	2	1	1	2	2
NHL TOTALS			2	1	1	2	2

(c)—June, 1982—Drafted by Edmonton Oilers in 1982 NHL entry draft. First Oilers pick, 20th overall, first round.

LARRY WILLIAM PLAYFAIR

Defense . . . 6'4" . . . 201 lbs. . . . Born, Fort St. James, B. C., June 23, 1958 . . . Shoots left . . . (October 9, 1980)—Severely cut right hand kept him out of Sabres lineup for 10 days . . . Brother of Jim Playfair . . . (April, 1983)—Chipped bone in right elbow in playoff series vs. Boston.

Year	Team	League	Games	G.	A.	Pts.	Pen.
1975-76—Langley		Jr. "A" BCHL	72	10	20	30	162
1976-77—Portland Winter Hawks		WCHL	65	2	17	19	199
1977-78—Portland Winter Hawks (a-c)		WCHL	71	13	19	32	402
1978-79—Buffalo Sabres		NHL	26	0	3	3	60
1978-79—Hershey Bears		AHL	45	0	12	12	148
1979-80—Buffalo Sabres		NHL	79	2	10	12	145
1980-81—Buffalo Sabres		NHL	75	3	9	12	169
1981-82—Buffalo Sabres		NHL	77	6	10	16	258
1982-83—Buffalo Sabres		NHL	79	4	13	17	180
1983-84—Buffalo Sabres		NHL	76	5	11	16	209
NHL TOTALS			412	20	56	76	1021

(c)—Drafted from Portland Winter Hawks by Buffalo Sabres in first round of 1978 amateur draft.

WILLIAM (WILLI) PLETT

Right Wing . . . 6'3" . . . 205 lbs. . . . Born, Paraguay, South America, June 7, 1955 . . . Shoots right . . . (October, 1982)—Suspended for seven games for swinging his stick at Detroit goalie Greg Stefan.

Year	Team	League	Games	G.	A.	Pts.	Pen.
1974-75—Niagara Falls Flyers		SOJHL	....	...	....	....	....
1974-75—St. Cath. Black Hawks (c)		Jr."A"OHA	22	6	8	14	63
1975-76—Tulsa Oilers (d)		CHL	73	30	20	50	163
1975-76—Atlanta Flames		NHL	4	0	0	0	2
1976-77—Tulsa Oilers		CHL	14	8	4	12	68
1976-77—Atlanta Flames (e)		NHL	64	33	23	56	123
1977-78—Atlanta Flames		NHL	78	22	21	43	171
1978-79—Atlanta Flames		NHL	74	23	20	43	213
1979-80—Atlanta Flames		NHL	76	13	19	32	231
1980-81—Calgary Flames		NHL	78	38	30	68	239
1981-82—Calgary Flames (f)		NHL	78	21	36	57	288
1982-83—Minnesota North Stars		NHL	71	25	14	39	170
1983-84—Minnesota North Stars		NHL	73	15	23	38	316
NHL TOTALS			596	190	186	376	1753

(c)—Drafted from St. Catharines Black Hawks by Atlanta Flames in fifth round of 1975 amateur draft.
(d)—Tied for lead in goals (5) during playoffs.
(e)—Won Calder Memorial Trophy and named THE SPORTING NEWS' NHL Rookie-of-the-Year.
(f)—June, 1982—Traded by Calgary Flames with a fourth-round draft choice in 1982 to Minnesota North Stars for Bill Nyrop, Steve Christoff and a second-round draft choice in 1982.

WALT MICHAEL PODDUBNY

Center . . . 6'1" . . . 203 lbs. . . . Born, Thunder Bay, Ont. February 14, 1960 . . . Shoots left . . . (October, 1982)—Injured leg . . . Shares Toronto goal scoring record for rookies (28) with Peter Ihnacak . . . (October, 1983)—Broken ankle.

Year	Team	League	Games	G.	A.	Pts.	Pen.
1978-79—Brandon Wheat Kings		WHL	20	11	11	22	12
1979-80—Kitchener Rangers		OMJHL	19	3	9	12	35
1979-80—Kingston Canadians (c)		OMJHL	43	30	17	47	36
1980-81—Milwaukee Admirals		IHL	5	4	2	6	4
1980-81—Wichita Wind		CHL	70	21	29	50	207
1981-82—Edmonton Oilers (d)		NHL	4	0	0	0	0
1981-82—Wichita Wind		CHL	60	35	46	81	79
1981-82—Toronto Maple Leafs		NHL	11	3	4	7	8
1982-83—Toronto Maple Leafs		NHL	72	28	31	59	71
1983-84—Toronto Maple Leafs		NHL	38	11	14	25	48
NHL TOTALS			125	42	49	91	127

(c)—June, 1980—Drafted by Edmonton Oilers in 1980 NHL entry draft. Fourth Oilers pick, 90th overall, fifth round.
(d)—March, 1982—Traded with NHL rights to Phil Drouillard by Edmonton Oilers to Toronto Maple Leafs for Laurie Boschman.

RAY PODLOSKI

Center . . . 6'2" . . . 210 lbs. . . . Born, Edmonton, Alta., January 5, 1966 . . . Shoots left.

Year	Team	League	Games	G.	A.	Pts.	Pen.
1982-83—Portland Winter Hawks		WHL	2	0	1	1	0
1983-84—Portland Winter Hawks (c)		WHL	66	46	50	96	44

(c)—June, 1984—Drafted by Boston Bruins as underage junior in NHL entry draft. Second Bruins pick, 40th overall, second round.

DENNIS DANIEL POLONICH

Center and Right Wing . . . 5'6" . . . 166 lbs. . . . Born, Foam Lake, Sask., December 4, 1953 . . . Shoots right . . . Missed part of 1975-76 season with shoulder separation.

Year	Team	League	Games	G.	A.	Pts.	Pen.
1971-72—Flin Flon Bombers		WCHL	65	9	21	30	200
1972-73—Flin Flon Bombers (c)		WCHL	68	26	48	74	222
1973-74—London Lions		England	67	17	43	60	57
1974-75—Virginia Wings		AHL	60	14	20	34	194
1974-75—Detroit Red Wings		NHL	4	0	0	0	0
1975-76—Kalamazoo Wings		IHL	5	1	8	9	32
1975-76—Detroit Red Wings		NHL	57	11	12	23	302
1976-77—Detroit Red Wings		NHL	79	18	28	46	274
1977-78—Detroit Red Wings		NHL	79	16	19	35	254
1978-79—Detroit Red Wings		NHL	62	10	12	22	208
1979-80—Detroit Red Wings		NHL	66	2	8	10	127
1980-81—Detroit Red Wings		NHL	32	2	2	4	77
1980-81—Adirondack Red Wings		AHL	40	16	13	29	99
1981-82—Adirondack Red Wings		AHL	80	30	26	56	202

Year	Team	League	Games	G.	A.	Pts.	Pen.
1982-83—Detroit Red Wings		NHL	11	0	1	1	0
1982-83—Adirondack Red Wings		AHL	61	18	22	40	128
1983-84—Adirondack Red Wings		AHL	66	14	26	40	122
NHL TOTALS			390	59	82	141	1242

(c)—Drafted from Flin Flon Bombers by Detroit Red Wings in eighth round of 1973 amateur draft.

JIRI PONER

Right Wing . . . 6'2" . . . 175 lbs. . . . Born, Czechoslovakia, February 9, 1964 . . . Shoots left.

Year	Team	League	Games	G.	A.	Pts.	Pen.
1981-82—Czech. Nat. Jr. Team		Int'l	8	4	3	7	4
1982-83—................			..	..	..	..	..
1983-84—West Germany (c)			..	..	..	..	..

(c)—June, 1984—Drafted by Minnesota North Stars in NHL entry draft. Fourth North Stars pick, 89th overall, fifth round.

PAUL POOLEY

Center . . . 6' . . . 175 lbs. . . . Born, Exeter, Ont., August 2, 1960 . . . Shoots left . . . Brother of Perry Pooley.

Year	Team	League	Games	G.	A.	Pts.	Pen.
1980-81—Ohio State University (c)		CCHA	38	28	31	59	41
1981-82—Ohio State University		CCHA	34	21	24	45	34
1982-83—Ohio State University		CCHA	36	33	36	69	50
1983-84—Ohio State University (d-e)		CCHA	41	32	64	96	40

(c)—Co-winner of CCHA Rookie-of-the-Year award. (With Jeff Poeschl (G)).
(d)—Named CCHA Player of the Year in 1983-84.
(e)—May, 1984—Signed by Winnipeg Jets as a free agent.

PERRY POOLEY

Right Wing . . . 6' . . . 175 lbs. . . . Born, Exeter, Ont., August 2, 1960 . . . Shoots right . . . Brother of Paul Pooley.

Year	Team	League	Games	G.	A.	Pts.	Pen.
1980-81—Ohio State University		CCHA	37	9	15	24	63
1981-82—Ohio State University		CCHA	34	8	8	16	24
1982-83—Ohio State University		CCHA	40	29	26	55	36
1983-84—Ohio State University (c)		CCHA	41	39	40	79	28

(c)—May, 1984—Signed by Winnipeg Jets as a free agent.

DON PORTER

Left Wing . . . 6'3" . . . 190 lbs. . . . Born, Geraldton, Ont., May 25, 1966 . . . Shoots left.

Year	Team	League	Games	G.	A.	Pts.	Pen.
1983-84—Michigan Tech. (c)		CCHA	31	4	4	8	8

(c)—June, 1984—Drafted as underage junior by St. Louis Blues in NHL entry draft. Tenth Blues pick, 148th overall, eighth round.

MIKE POSAVAD

Defense . . . 6' . . . 196 lbs. . . . Born, Brantford, Ont., January 3, 1964 . . . Shoots right . . . (December, 1980)—Broken nose.

Year	Team	League	Games	G.	A.	Pts.	Pen.
1979-80—Brantford Jr. 'B'		OPJHL	43	11	22	33	18
1980-81—Peterborough Petes		OHL	58	3	12	15	55
1981-82—Peterborough Petes (b-c)		OHL	64	7	23	30	110
1982-83—Peterborough Petes		OHL	70	1	36	37	68
1982-83—Salt Lake Golden Eagles		CHL	1	0	0	0	0
1983-84—Peterborough Petes		OHL	63	3	25	28	78

(c)—June, 1982—Drafted as underage junior by St. Louis Blues in 1982 NHL entry draft. First Blues pick, 50th overall, third round.

DENIS CHARLES POTVIN

Defense . . . 6' . . . 204 lbs. . . . Born, Hull, Que., October 29, 1953 . . . Shoots left . . . Brother of Jean Potvin . . . Missed part of 1971-72 season with broken wrist . . . Set Jr. "A" OHA record

for points by a Defenseman in season (1972-73) ... Set NHL record for goals in rookie season by Defenseman with 17 in 1973-74 (broken by Barry Beck in 1977-78) ... (October 14, 1978)—Set NHL defenseman record with three goals in one period in 10-7 loss at Toronto ... Missed much of 1979-80 season after surgery to correct stretched ligaments in thumb ... Set NHL record for most points by a defenseman (25) in the playoffs in 1981 ... (May 21, 1981)—Pulled groin in final game of Stanley Cup Playoffs, aggravated injury during Canada Cup Tournament in August, 1981 and did not play until November 14, 1981 ... Broke Jean Beliveau's record of 97 career playoff assists in 1983-84.

Year	Team	League	Games	G.	A.	Pts.	Pen.
1968-69—Ottawa 67's		Jr. "A" OHA	46	12	25	37	83
1969-70—Ottawa 67's		Jr. "A" OHA	42	13	18	31	97
1970-71—Ottawa 67's (a)		Jr. "A" OHA	57	20	58	78	200
1971-72—Ottawa 67's (a-c)		Jr. "A" OHA	48	15	45	60	188
1972-73—Ottawa 67's (a-c-d)		Jr. "A" OHA	61	35	88	123	232
1973-74—New York Islanders (e-f)		NHL	77	17	37	54	175
1974-75—New York Islanders (a)		NHL	79	21	55	76	105
1975-76—New York Islanders (a-g-h)		NHL	78	31	67	98	100
1976-77—New York Islanders (b)		NHL	80	25	55	80	103
1977-78—New York Islanders (a-g)		NHL	80	30	64	94	81
1978-79—New York Islanders (a-g)		NHL	73	31	70	101	58
1979-80—New York Islanders		NHL	31	8	33	41	44
1980-81—New York Islanders (a)		NHL	74	20	56	76	104
1981-82—New York Islanders		NHL	60	24	37	61	83
1982-83—New York Islanders		NHL	69	12	54	66	60
1983-84—New York Islanders		NHL	78	22	63	85	87
NHL TOTALS			779	241	591	832	1000

(c)—Won Max Kaminsky Memorial Trophy (Outstanding Defenseman).
(d)—Drafted from Ottawa 67's by New York Islanders in first round of 1973 amateur draft.
(e)—Won Calder Memorial Trophy.
(f)—Named NHL's East Division rookie of the year in poll of players by THE SPORTING NEWS.
(g)—Won James Norris Memorial Trophy (outstanding Defenseman).
(h)—Tied for lead in assists (14) during playoffs.

DANIEL POUDRIER

Defense ... 6'2" ... 175 lbs. ... Born, Thetford Mines, Que., February 15, 1964 ... Shoots left.

Year	Team	League	Games	G.	A.	Pts.	Pen.
1980-81—Magog AAA Midget		QAAAMHL	26	8	8	16	18
1981-82—Shawinigan Cataracts (c)		QMJHL	64	6	18	24	26
1982-83—Shawinigan Cataracts		QHL	67	6	28	34	31
1983-84—Drummondville Voltigeurs		QHL	64	7	28	35	15

(c)—June, 1982—Drafted as underage junior by Quebec Nordiques in 1982 NHL entry draft. Sixth Nordiques pick, 131st overall, seventh round.

DAVE POULIN

Center ... 5'11" ... 175 lbs. ... Born, Mississauga, Ont., December 17, 1958 ... Shoots left ... (1983-84)—Set Philadelphia record for most points by a rookie.

Year	Team	League	Games	G.	A.	Pts.	Pen.
1978-79—University of Notre Dame		WCHA	37	28	31	59	32
1979-80—University of Notre Dame		WCHA	24	19	24	43	46
1980-81—University of Notre Dame		WCHA	35	13	22	35	53
1981-82—University of Notre Dame		CCHA	39	29	30	59	44
1982-83—Rogle (c)		Sweden	33	35	18	53	..
1982-83—Maine Mariners		AHL	16	7	9	16	2
1982-83—Philadelphia Flyers		NHL	2	2	0	2	2
1983-84—Philadelphia Flyers		NHL	73	31	45	76	47
NHL TOTALS			75	33	45	78	49

(c)—February, 1983—Signed by Philadelphia Flyers as free agent.

JAROSLAV POUZAR

Left Wing ... 5'11" ... 196 lbs. ... Born, Cakovec, Czechoslovakia, January 23, 1952 ... Shoots left.

Year	Team	League	Games	G.	A.	Pts.	Pen.
1979-80—Motor Ceske Budejoivice		Czech.	44	39	23	62	....
1980-81—Motor Ceske Budejoivice		Czech.	42	29	23	52	....
1981-82—Motor Ceske Budejoivice (c)		Czech.	34	19	17	36	32

Year	Team	League	Games	G.	A.	Pts.	Pen.
1982-83—Edmonton Oilers		NHL	74	15	18	33	57
1983-84—Edmonton Oilers		NHL	67	13	19	32	44
NHL TOTALS			141	28	37	65	101

(c)—June, 1982—Drafted by Edmonton Oilers in 1982 NHL entry draft. Fourth Oilers pick, 80th overall, fourth round.

LARRY POWER
Center ... 6'1" ... 180 lbs. ... Born, Kitchener, Ont., April 8, 1963 ... Shoots left.

Year	Team	League	Games	G.	A.	Pts.	Pen.
1980-81—Kitchener Rangers 'B' (c)		OPJHL	42	25	30	55	72
1981-82—Ottawa 67's		OHL	68	25	48	73	46
1982-83—Ottawa 67's		OHL	65	38	47	85	39
1983-84—Flint Generals		IHL	14	1	5	6	2
1983-84—Mohawk Valley Stars (d)		ACHL	57	28	36	64	46

(c)—June, 1981—Drafted as underage junior by Hartford Whalers in 1981 NHL entry draft. Ninth Whalers pick, 193rd overall, 10th round.

(d)—June, 1984—Released by Hartford Whalers.

WAYNE PRESLEY
Right Wing ... 5'11" ... 175 lbs. ... Born, Dearborn, Mich., March 23, 1965 ... Shoots right.

Year	Team	League	Games	G.	A.	Pts.	Pen.
1981-82—Detroit Little Ceasars		Mich. Midget	61	38	56	94	146
1982-83—Kitchener Rangers (c)		OHL	70	39	48	87	99
1983-84—Kitchener Rangers (a-d)		OHL	70	63	76	139	156

(c)—June, 1983—Drafted as underage junior by Chicago Black Hawks in 1983 NHL entry draft. Second Black Hawks pick, 39th overall, second round.

(d)—Won Jim Mahon Memorial Trophy (Highest scoring OHL right wing).

WAYNE PRESTAGE
Center ... 5'7" ... 157 lbs. ... Born, Camrose, Alberta, May 17, 1962 ... Shoots left.

Year	Team	League	Games	G.	A.	Pts.	Pen.
1979-80—Victoria Cougars		WHL	2	0	2	2	0
1980-81—Seattle Breakers		WHL	71	15	23	38	133
1981-82—Seattle Breakers (c)		WHL	72	50	58	108	197
1982-83—Hershey Bears		AHL	80	21	37	58	64
1983-84—Hershey Bears		AHL	52	12	15	27	65

(c)—June, 1982—Drafted by Washington Capitals in 1982 NHL entry draft. Eighth Capitals pick, 215th overall, 11th round.

MIKE PRESTIDGE
Center ... 6'3" ... 203 lbs. ... Born, Weston, Ont., August 14, 1959 ... Shoots left.

Year	Team	League	Games	G.	A.	Pts.	Pen.
1978-79—Clarkson College		ECAC	31	16	24	40	2
1979-80—Clarkson College (a)		ECAC	34	28	30	58	24
1980-81—Clarkson College		ECAC	31	13	17	30	22
1981-82—Oklahoma City Stars (c)		CHL	53	20	19	39	6
1982-83—Colorado Flames		CHL	62	13	26	39	17
1983-84—Peoria Prancers		IHL	68	40	40	80	4

(c)—June, 1981—Signed by Calgary Flames as a free agent.

RICHARD JOHN (RICH) PRESTON
Left Wing ... 5'11" ... 185 lbs. ... Born, Regina, Sask., May 22, 1952 ... Shoots right ... Attended Denver University ... Son of Ken Preston, former general manager of Saskatchewan Roughriders football team ... Also plays Right Wing ... Missed final weeks of 1977-78 season and playoffs with fractured left ankle ... (November 16, 1980)—Tore cartilage in left knee during a fight. Injury required surgery.

Year	Team	League	Games	G.	A.	Pts.	Pen.
1969-70—Regina Pats		SJHL	....	15	15	30	4
1970-71—Denver University		WCHA	17	0	1	1	0
1971-72—Denver University		WCHA	33	3	11	14	18
1972-73—Denver University		WCHA	39	23	25	48	24
1973-74—Denver University (c)		WCHA	38	20	25	45	36

Year	Team	League	Games	G.	A.	Pts.	Pen.
1974-75—Houston Aeros		WHA	78	20	21	41	10
1975-76—Houston Aeros		WHA	77	22	33	55	33
1976-77—Houston Aeros		WHA	80	38	41	79	54
1977-78—Houston Aeros (d)		WHA	73	25	25	50	52
1978-79—Winnipeg Jets (e-f)		WHA	80	28	32	60	88
1979-80—Chicago Black Hawks		NHL	80	31	30	61	70
1980-81—Chicago Black Hawks		NHL	47	7	14	21	24
1981-82—Chicago Black Hawks		NHL	75	15	28	43	30
1982-83—Chicago Black Hawks		NHL	79	25	28	53	64
1983-84—Chicago Black Hawks (g)		NHL	75	10	18	28	50
WHA TOTALS			388	133	152	285	237
NHL TOTALS			356	88	118	206	238

(c)—Signed by Houston Aeros (WHA), June, 1974.
(d)—Sold to Winnipeg Jets with Houston Aeros' franchise, July, 1978.
(e)—Named most valuable player of WHA playoffs.
(f)—May, 1979—Signed by Chicago Black Hawks as a free agent.
(g)—June, 1984—Traded with Don Dietrich by Chicago Black Hawks to New Jersey Devils for Bob MacMillan and past considerations (Devils did not draft Ed Olczyk).

YVES PRESTON

Left Wing . . . 5'11" . . . 180 lbs. . . . Born, Montreal, Que., June 14, 1956 . . . Shoots left.

Year	Team	League	Games	G.	A.	Pts.	Pen.
1973-74—Chicoutimi Sagueneens		QMJHL	70	26	33	59	60
1974-75—Laval Nationals		QMJHL	64	18	33	51	44
1975-76—Laval Nationals		QMJHL	63	29	42	71	45
1976-77—Dayton Gems		IHL	10	0	0	0	2
1977-78—Milwaukee Admirals		IHL	80	37	37	74	51
1978-79—Philadelphia Flyers		NHL	9	3	1	4	0
1978-79—Maine Mariners (a)		AHL	73	35	32	67	38
1979-80—Maine Mariners		AHL	71	23	24	47	51
1980-81—Philadelphia Flyers		NHL	19	4	2	6	4
1980-81—Wichita Wind		CHL	31	4	11	15	25
1981-82—Milwaukee Admirals		IHL	70	25	29	54	23
1982-83—Milwaukee Admirals		IHL	67	35	53	88	17
1983-84—Milwaukee Admirals		IHL	82	36	49	85	37
NHL TOTALS			28	7	3	10	4

DAVID PREUSS

Right Wing . . . 6'2" . . . 215 lbs. . . . Born, St. Paul, Minn., August 14, 1963 . . . Shoots right.

Year	Team	League	Games	G.	A.	Pts.	Pen.
1980-81—St. Thomas Academy (c)		Minn. H.S.	23	37	15	52	40
1981-82—University of Minnesota		WCHA	28	2	5	7	65
1982-83—University of Minnesota		WCHA	33	9	7	16	99
1983-84—University of Minnesota		WCHA	19	4	4	8	36

(c)—June, 1981—Drafted by Minnesota North Stars in NHL entry draft. Fifth North Stars pick, 34th overall, second round.

SHAUN PATRICK (PAT) PRICE

Defense . . . 6'2" . . . 200 lbs. . . . Born, Nelson, B.C., March 24, 1955 . . . Shoots left . . . (January, 1983)—Headaches and nervous disorder.

Year	Team	League	Games	G.	A.	Pts.	Pen.
1970-71—Saskatoon Blades		WCHL	66	2	16	18	56
1971-72—Saskatoon Blades		WCHL	66	10	48	58	85
1972-73—Saskatoon Blades		WCHL	67	12	56	68	134
1973-74—Saskatoon Blades (a-c-d)		WCHL	67	27	68	81	147
1974-75—Vancouver Blazers (e)		WHA	69	5	29	34	54
1975-76—Fort Worth Texans		CHL	72	6	44	50	119
1975-76—New York Islanders		NHL	4	0	2	2	2
1976-77—New York Islanders		NHL	71	3	22	25	25
1977-78—Rochester Americans		AHL	5	2	1	3	9
1977-78—New York Islanders		NHL	52	2	10	12	27
1978-79—New York Islanders (f)		NHL	55	3	11	14	50
1979-80—Edmonton Oilers		NHL	75	11	21	32	134
1980-81—Edmonton Oilers (g)		NHL	59	8	24	32	193
1980-81—Pittsburgh Penguins		NHL	13	0	10	10	33
1981-82—Pittsburgh Penguins		NHL	77	7	31	38	322
1982-83—Pittsburgh Penguins (h)		NHL	38	1	11	12	104

Year	Team	League	Games	G.	A.	Pts.	Pen.
1982-83—Quebec Nordiques		NHL	14	1	2	3	28
1983-84—Quebec Nordiques		NHL	72	3	25	28	188
	NHL TOTALS		530	39	169	208	1106
	WHA TOTALS		69	5	29	34	54

(c)—Selected by Vancouver Blazers in WHA amateur player draft, May, 1974.
(d)—Named Outstanding Defenseman in WCHL.
(e)—Drafted from Saskatoon Blades by New York Islanders in first round of 1975 amateur draft.
(f)—June, 1979—Selected by Edmonton Oilers in NHL expansion draft.
(g)—March, 1981—Traded by Edmonton Oilers to Pittsburgh Penguins for Pat Hughes.
(h)—December, 1982—Released by Pittsburgh Penguins and subsequently claimed on waivers by Quebec Nordiques for $2,500.

THOMAS EDWARD PRICE

Defense . . . 6'1" . . . 190 lbs. . . . Born, Toronto, Ont., July 12, 1954 . . . Shoots left . . . Missed part of 1974-75 season with broken ankle and part of 1975-76 season with shoulder injury . . . (February, 1981)—Wrist injury.

Year	Team	League	Games	G.	A.	Pts.	Pen.
1972-73—London Knights		Jr. "A" OHA	62	4	10	14	104
1973-74—Ottawa 67's (c)		Jr. "A" OHA	61	7	33	40	80
1974-75—Salt Lake Golden Eagles		CHL	52	2	16	18	91
1974-75—California Seals		NHL	3	0	0	0	4
1975-76—Salt Lake Golden Eagles		CHL	59	11	15	26	77
1975-76—California Seals		NHL	5	0	0	0	0
1976-77—Salt Lake Golden Eagles		CHL	55	3	21	24	71
1976-77—Cleveland Barons		NHL	2	0	0	0	0
1976-77—Pittsburgh Penguins (d)		NHL	7	0	2	2	4
1977-78—Binghamton Dusters		AHL	31	1	6	7	39
1977-78—Springfield Indians		AHL	21	0	9	9	23
1977-78—Grand Rapids Owls		IHL	9	1	8	9	30
1977-78—Pittsburgh Penguins		NHL	10	0	0	0	0
1978-79—Pittsburgh Penguins		NHL	2	0	0	0	4
1978-79—Binghamton Dusters		AHL	70	14	31	45	62
1979-80—Syracuse Firebirds		AHL	68	4	34	38	58
1980-81—Springfield Indians		AHL	51	2	24	26	56
1981-82—New Haven Nighthawks (e)		AHL	57	3	20	23	52
1982-83—Saginaw Gears		IHL	26	1	8	9	18
1983-84—New Haven Nighthawks		AHL	77	2	23	25	54
	NHL TOTALS		29	0	2	2	12

(c)—Drafted from Ottawa 67's by California Golden Seals in fourth round of 1974 amateur draft.
(d)—Signed by Pittsburgh Penguins as free agent following release by Cleveland Barons, February, 1977.
(e)—January, 1982—Signed by New Haven Nighthawks as a free agent.

ROBERT PROBERT

Left Wing . . . 6'3" . . . 205 lbs. . . . Born, Windsor, Ont., June 5, 1965 . . . Shoots left . . . Also plays center.

Year	Team	League	Games	G.	A.	Pts.	Pen.
1981-82—Windsor Club 240		Ont. Midget	55	60	40	100	40
1982-83—Brantford Alexanders (c)		OHL	51	12	16	28	133
1983-84—Brantford Alexanders		OHL	65	35	38	73	189

(c)—June, 1983—Drafted as underage junior by Detroit Red Wings in 1983 NHL entry draft. Third Red Wings pick, 46th overall, third round.

BRIAN PROPP

Left Wing . . . 5'9" . . . 185 lbs. . . . Born, Lanigan, Sask., February 15, 1959 . . . Shoots left . . . All-time Western Hockey League scoring leader with 511 points . . . Brother of Ron Propp.

Year	Team	League	Games	G.	A.	Pts.	Pen.
1975-76—Melville Millionaires		SJHL	57	76	92	168	36
1976-77—Brandon Wheat Kings (b-c-d)		WCHL	72	55	80	135	47
1977-78—Brandon Wheat Kings (a-e)		WCHL	70	70	*112	*182	200
1978-79—Brandon Wheat Kings (a-e-f)		WHL	71	*94	*100	*194	127
1979-80—Philadelphia Flyers		NHL	80	34	41	75	54
1980-81—Philadelphia Flyers		NHL	79	26	40	66	110
1981-82—Philadelphia Flyers		NHL	80	44	47	91	117
1982-83—Philadelphia Flyers		NHL	80	40	42	82	72
1983-84—Philadelphia Flyers		NHL	79	39	53	92	37
	NHL TOTALS		398	183	223	406	390

CHRIS PRYOR

Defense . . . 5'11" . . . 210 lbs. . . . Born, St. Paul, Minn., January 31, 1961 . . . Shoots right.

Year	Team	League	Games	G.	A.	Pts.	Pen.
1979-80	Univ. of New Hampshire	ECAC	27	9	13	22	27
1980-81	Univ. of New Hampshire	ECAC	33	10	27	37	36
1981-82	Univ. of New Hampshire	ECAC	35	3	16	19	36
1982-83	Univ. of New Hampshire	ECAC	34	4	9	13	23
1983-84	Salt Lake Golden Eagles	CHL	72	7	21	28	215

GREG PUHALSKI

Left Wing . . . 6' . . . 170 lbs. . . . Born, Thunder Bay, Ont., January 1, 1965 . . . Shoots left . . . Also plays center.

Year	Team	League	Games	G.	A.	Pts.	Pen.
1981-82	Thunder Bay Maroons	Ont. Midgets	62	50	72	122	69
1982-83	Kitchener Rangers (c)	OHL	70	27	51	78	28
1983-84	Kitchener Rangers	OHL	44	30	69	99	55

(c)—June, 1983—Drafted as underage junior by Boston Bruins in NHL entry draft. Third Bruins pick, 62nd overall, third round.

PAUL PULIS

Right Wing . . . 6'5" . . . 200 lbs. . . . Born, Duluth, Minn., January 14, 1965 . . . Shoots right.

Year	Team	League	Games	G.	A.	Pts.	Pen.
1982-83	Hibbing H.S. (c)	Minn.H.S.	20	20	16	36	..
1983-84	University of Ill.-Chicago	CCHA	25	1	2	3	12

(c)—June, 1983—Drafted by Minnesota North Stars in NHL entry draft. Tenth North Stars pick, 176th overall, ninth round.

JEFF PYLE

Center . . . 6' . . . 175 lbs. . . . Born, Ft. Leonard Wood, Mo., October 7, 1958 . . . Shoots left.

Year	Team	League	Games	G.	A.	Pts.	Pen.
1978-79	Univ. of Northern Michigan	CCHA	34	15	27	42	4
1979-80	Univ. of Northern Michigan	CCHA	41	26	37	63	12
1980-81	Univ. of Northern Mich.(a-c-d)	CCHA	40	*35	53	88	20
1981-82	Saginaw Gears	IHL	4	2	3	5	0
1981-82	Mohawk Valley Stars	ACHL	29	16	34	50	16
1981-82	Binghamton Whalers	AHL	16	1	1	2	15
1982-83	Mohawk Valley Stars (a)	ACHL	59	53	48	101	44
1983-84	Flint Generals (e)	IHL	80	44	59	103	20

(c)—Named CCHA Most Valuable Player.
(d)—September, 1981—Signed by Hartford Whalers as a free agent.
(e)—Led IHL playoffs with seven goals and shared point lead (15) with Toledo's Kevin Conway and Jim Bissett and Flint's Lawrie Nisker.

JOEL NORMAN QUENNEVILLE

Defense . . . 6' . . . 187 lbs. . . . Born, Windsor, Ont., September 15, 1958 . . . Shoots left . . . (March, 1980)—Rib-cage injury . . . (March, 1980)—Surgery to repair torn ligaments in ring finger of left hand . . . (January 4, 1982)—Sprained ankle, twisted knee and suffered facial cuts when he crashed into boards during a Rockies practice.

Year	Team	League	Games	G.	A.	Pts.	Pen.
1975-76	Windsor Spitfires	Jr."A"OHA	66	15	33	48	61
1976-77	Windsor Spitfires	Jr."A"OHA	65	19	59	78	169
1977-78	Windsor Spitfires (b-c)	Jr."A"OHA	66	27	76	103	114
1978-79	Toronto Maple Leafs	NHL	61	2	9	11	60
1978-79	New Brunswick Hawks	AHL	16	1	10	11	10
1979-80	Toronto Maple Leafs (d)	NHL	32	1	4	5	24
1979-80	Colorado Rockies	NHL	35	5	7	12	26
1980-81	Colorado Rockies	NHL	71	10	24	34	86
1981-82	Colorado Rockies	NHL	64	5	10	15	55
1982-83	New Jersey Devils (e-f)	NHL	74	5	12	17	46
1983-84	Hartford Whalers	NHL	80	5	8	13	95
	NHL TOTALS		417	33	74	107	392

(c)—Drafted from Windsor Spitfires by Toronto Maple Leafs in second round of 1978 amateur draft.

(d)—December, 1979—Traded with Lanny McDonald by Toronto Maple Leafs to Colorado Rockies for Wilf Paiement and Pat Hickey.

(e)—July, 1983—Traded by New Jersey Devils with Steve Tambellini to Calgary Flames for Mel Bridgman and Phil Russell.

(f)—August, 1983—Traded by Calgary Flames with Richie Dunn to Hartford Whalers for Mickey Volcan and third-round draft choice in 1984.

DAN QUINN

Center . . . 5'11" . . . 175 lbs. . . . Born, Ottawa, Ont., June 1, 1965 . . . Shoots left . . . Son of Peter Quinn (former CFL player with Ottawa).

Year	Team	League	Games	G.	A.	Pts.	Pen.
1981-82—Belleville Bulls		OHL	67	19	32	51	41
1982-83—Belleville Bulls (c)		OHL	70	59	88	147	27
1983-84—Belleville Bulls		OHL	24	23	36	59	12
1983-84—Calgary Flames		NHL	54	19	33	52	20
NHL TOTALS			54	19	33	52	20

(c)—June, 1983—Drafted as underage junior by Calgary Flames in 1983 NHL entry draft. First Flames pick, 13th overall, first round.

DAVID QUINN

Defense . . . 6' . . . 205 lbs. . . . Born, Cranston, R.I., July 30, 1966 . . . Shoots left.

Year	Team	League	Games	G.	A.	Pts.	Pen.
1983-84—Kent Prep (c)		Conn.H.S.	24	12	20	32	..

(c)—June, 1984—Drafted by Minnesota North Stars in NHL entry draft. First North Stars pick, 13th overall, first round.

DOUG QUINN

Defense . . . 6'2" . . . 177 lbs. . . . Born, Red Deer, Alta., April 2, 1965 . . . Shoots left.

Year	Team	League	Games	G.	A.	Pts.	Pen.
1982-83—Nanaimo Islanders (c)		WHL	55	3	14	17	81
1983-84—New Westminster Bruins		WHL	68	8	22	30	122

(c)—June, 1982—Drafted as underage junior by Vancouver Canucks in 1983 NHL entry draft. Fifth Canucks pick, 90th overall, fifth round.

KEN QUINNEY

Right Wing . . . 5'10" . . . 105 lbs. . . . Born, New Westminster, B.C., May 23, 1965 . . . Shoots right.

Year	Team	League	Games	G.	A.	Pts.	Pen.
1981-82—Calgary Wranglers		WHL	63	11	17	28	55
1982-83—Calgary Wranglers		WHL	71	26	25	51	71
1983-84—Calgary Wranglers (c)		WHL	71	64	54	118	38

(c)—June, 1984—Drafted as underage junior by Quebec Nordiques in NHL entry draft. Ninth Nordiques pick, 203rd overall, 10th round.

PAT RABBITT

Left Wing . . . 5'10" . . . 180 lbs. . . . Born, Merritt, B.C., November 16, 1961 . . . Shoots left . . . Also plays right wing and center.

Year	Team	League	Games	G.	A.	Pts.	Pen.
1978-79—Billings Bighorns		WHL	72	23	25	48	137
1979-80—Billings Bighorns (c)		WHL	64	29	42	71	112
1980-81—Billings Bighorns		WHL	32	13	27	40	39
1980-81—Saskatoon Blades		WHL	29	20	23	43	25
1981-82—Milwaukee Admirals		IHL	54	18	12	30	17
1981-82—Wichita Wind		CHL	9	1	1	2	7
1982-83—..............			..	..	..	..	..
1983-84—Montana Magic (d)		CHL	46	16	16	32	21

(c)—June, 1980—Drafted as underage junior by St. Louis Blues in 1980 NHL entry draft. Seventh Blues pick, 159th overall, eighth round.

(d)—October, 1983—Signed by Montana Magic as a free agent.

GEORGE ROBERT (ROB) RAMAGE

Defense . . . 6'2" . . . 210 lbs. . . . Born, Byron, Ont., January 11, 1959 . . . Shoots right.

Year	Team	League	Games	G.	A.	Pts.	Pen.
1975-76—London Knights	Jr.''A''OHA	65	12	31	43	113
1976-77—London Knights	Jr.''A''OHA	65	15	58	73	177
1977-78—London Knights (a-c-d)	Jr.''A''OHA	59	17	47	64	162
1978-79—Birmingham Bulls (a-e)	WHA	80	12	36	48	165
1979-80—Colorado Rockies	NHL	75	8	20	28	135
1980-81—Colorado Rockies	NHL	79	20	42	62	193
1981-82—Colorado Rockies (f)	NHL	80	13	29	42	201
1982-83—St. Louis Blues	NHL	78	16	35	51	193
1983-84—St. Louis Blues	NHL	80	15	45	60	121
WHA TOTALS			80	12	36	48	165
NHL TOTALS			392	72	171	243	843

(c)—Signed by Birmingham Bulls (WHA) as underage junior, July, 1978.
(d)—Shared Max Kaminsky Memorial Trophy (outstanding defenseman) with Brad Marsh.
(e)—Drafted by Colorado Rockies in 1979 entry draft. First Colorado pick, first overall, first round.
(f)—June, 1982—Traded by Colorado Rockies to St. Louis Blues for St. Louis' first-round draft choices in 1982 (Rocky Trottier) and 1983 (John MacLean).

JOE RAMPTON

Left Wing . . . 6'3" . . . 190 lbs. . . . Born, St. Paul, Minn., January 31, 1966 . . . Shoots left.

Year	Team	League	Games	G.	A.	Pts.	Pen.
1982-83—Ottawa Valley	Ont. Midgets	36	19	20	39	44
1983-84—Sault Ste. Marie Greyhounds (c)	OHL	68	14	15	29	99

(c)—June, 1984—Drafted as underage junior by Buffalo Sabres in NHL entry draft. Fifth Sabres pick, 102nd overall, fifth round.

CRAIG EDWARD RAMSAY

Left Wing . . . 5'10" . . . 176 lbs. . . . Born, Weston, Ont., March 17, 1951 . . . Shoots left . . . (February 10, 1983)—Hit by puck in instep of left foot in game at Los Angeles. The injury ended his consecutive games played streak at 776—second longest in NHL history. It was the longest streak with one club in NHL history. He last missed a game on March 25, 1973. (Garry Unger holds NHL iron man record of 914 games).

Year	Team	League	Games	G.	A.	Pts.	Pen.
1968-69—Peterborough TPTs	Jr.''A''OHA	54	11	28	39	20
1969-70—Peterborough TPTs	Jr.''A''OHA	54	27	41	68	18
1970-71—Peterborough TPTs (c)	Jr.''A''OHA	58	30	76	106	25
1971-72—Cincinnati Swords	AHL	19	5	7	12	4
1971-72—Buffalo Sabres	NHL	57	6	10	16	0
1972-73—Buffalo Sabres	NHL	76	11	17	28	15
1973-74—Buffalo Sabres	NHL	78	20	26	46	0
1974-75—Buffalo Sabres	NHL	80	26	38	64	26
1975-76—Buffalo Sabres	NHL	80	22	49	71	34
1976-77—Buffalo Sabres	NHL	80	20	41	61	20
1977-78—Buffalo Sabres	NHL	80	28	43	71	18
1978-79—Buffalo Sabres	NHL	80	26	31	57	10
1979-80—Buffalo Sabres	NHL	80	21	39	60	18
1980-81—Buffalo Sabres	NHL	80	24	35	59	12
1981-82—Buffalo Sabres	NHL	80	16	35	51	8
1982-83—Buffalo Sabres	NHL	64	11	18	29	7
1983-84—Buffalo Sabres	NHL	76	9	17	26	17
NHL TOTALS			991	240	399	639	185

(c)—Drafted from Peterborough TPTs by Buffalo Sabres in second round of 1971 amateur draft.

BRAD RAMSDEN

Right Wing . . . 6'1" . . . 190 lbs. . . . Born, Edmonton, Alta., September 14, 1964 . . . Shoots right . . . Also plays center.

Year	Team	League	Games	G.	A.	Pts.	Pen.
1980-81—Wexford	OPJHL	29	13	18	31	89
1981-82—Peterborough Petes (c)	OHL	65	9	11	20	30
1982-83—Peterborough Petes	OHL	48	13	20	33	51
1983-84—Peterborough Petes	OHL	62	10	36	46	89

(c)—June, 1982—Drafted as underage junior by Calgary Flames in 1982 NHL entry draft. Ninth Flames pick, 135th overall, seventh round.

MICHAEL ALLEN RAMSEY

Defense . . . 6'2" . . . 185 lbs. . . . Born, Minneapolis, Minn., December 3, 1960 . . . Shoots left

... Attended University of Minnesota ... Member of 1980 gold-medal U.S. Olympic hockey team ... (December 4, 1983)—Dislocated thumb in game vs. Montreal.

Year	Team	League	Games	G.	A.	Pts.	Pen.
1978-79—University of Minnesota (c)	WCHA	26	6	11	17	30
1979-80—U.S. Olympic Team	Int'l	63	11	24	35	63
1979-80—Buffalo Sabres	NHL	13	1	6	7	6
1980-81—Buffalo Sabres	NHL	72	3	14	17	56
1981-82—Buffalo Sabres	NHL	80	7	23	30	56
1982-83—Buffalo Sabres	NHL	77	8	30	38	55
1983-84—Buffalo Sabres	NHL	72	9	22	31	82
NHL TOTALS		314	28	95	123	255

(c)—August, 1979—Drafted by Buffalo Sabres in entry draft. First Buffalo pick, 11th overall, first round.

ALAIN RAYMOND

Left Wing ... 6' ... 180 lbs. ... Born, Ottawa, Ont., July 21, 1964 ... Shoots left.

Year	Team	League	Games	G.	A.	Pts.	Pen.
1980-81—Gloucester Rangers	COJHL	45	9	15	24	45
1981-82—Niagara Falls Flyers (c)	OHL	64	13	17	30	27
1982-83—North Bay Centennials	OHL	23	7	12	19	13
1982-83—Kingston Canadiens	OHL	46	6	10	16	25
1983-84—Windsor Spitfires	OHL	59	14	26	40	35

(c)—June, 1982—Drafted as underage junior by Vancouver Canucks in 1982 NHL entry draft. Eighth Canucks pick, 200th overall, 10th round.

SHAUN REAGAN

Right Wing ... 6'2" ... 180 lbs. ... Born, Kenora, Ont., May 12, 1964 ... Shoots right.

Year	Team	League	Games	G.	A.	Pts.	Pen.
1980-81—Waterloo Midgets	Ont. Midget	58	32	40	72	....
1981-82—Brantford Alexanders (c)	OHL	58	8	15	23	51
1982-83—Brantford Alexanders	OHL	64	15	15	30	36
1983-84—Windsor Spitfires	OHL	67	19	31	50	29

(c)—June, 1982—Drafted by Detroit Red Wings as underage junior in 1982 NHL entry draft. Twelfth Red Wings pick, 233rd overall, 12th round.

CRAIG REDMOND

Defense ... 5'10" ... 190 lbs. ... Born, Dawson Creek, B.C., September 22, 1965 ... Shoots left ... Second cousin of Mickey and Dick Redmond (former NHL players through the 1970s).

Year	Team	League	Games	G.	A.	Pts.	Pen.
1980-81—Abbotsford Flyers	BCJHL	40	15	22	37	..
1981-82—Abbotsford Flyers	BCJHL	45	30	76	106	..
1982-83—University of Denver (c)	WCHA	34	18	36	54	44
1983-84—Canadian Olympic Team (d)	Int'l	55	10	11	21	38

(c)—Won WCHA Rookie of the Year Award.

(d)—June, 1984—Drafted by Los Angeles Kings in NHL entry draft. First Kings pick, sixth overall, first round.

MARK REEDS

Right Wing ... 5'10" ... 188 lbs. ... Born, Burlington, Ont., January 24, 1960 ... Shoots right ... (November 19, 1983)—Cryotherapy to repair the margins of his retina.

Year	Team	League	Games	G.	A.	Pts.	Pen.
1976-77—Markham Waxers	OPJHL	24	17	23	40	62
1976-77—Toronto Marlboros	OMJHL	18	6	7	13	6
1977-78—Peterborough Petes	OMJHL	68	11	27	36	67
1978-79—Peterborough Petes (c)	OMJHL	66	25	25	50	91
1979-80—Peterborough Petes	OMJHL	54	34	45	79	51
1980-81—Salt Lake Golden Eagles	CHL	74	15	45	60	81
1981-82—Salt Lake Golden Eagles	CHL	59	22	24	46	55
1981-82—St. Louis Blues	NHL	9	1	3	4	0
1982-83—Salt Lake Golden Eagles	CHL	55	16	26	42	32
1982-83—St. Louis Blues	NHL	20	5	14	19	6
1983-84—St. Louis Blues	NHL	65	11	14	25	23
NHL TOTALS		94	17	31	48	29

(c)—August, 1979—Drafted by St. Louis Blues as an underage junior in NHL entry draft. Third St. Louis pick, 86th overall, fifth round.

JOE JAMES REEKIE

Defense . . . 6'2" . . . 176 lbs. . . . Born, Victoria, B.C., February 22, 1965 . . . Shoots left.

Year	Team	League	Games	G.	A.	Pts.	Pen.
1981-82—Nepean Raiders		CJHL	16	2	5	7	4
1982-83—North Bay Centennials (c)		OHL	59	2	9	11	49
1983-84—North Bay Centennials		OHL	9	1	0	1	18
1983-84—Cornwall Royals (d)		OHL	53	6	27	33	166

(c)—June, 1983—Drafted as underage junior by Hartford Whalers in 1983 NHL entry draft. Eighth Whalers pick, 124th overall, seventh round.

(d)—June, 1984—Released by Hartford Whalers.

KEVIN REEVES

Center . . . 5'8" . . . 163 lbs. . . . Born, Montreal, Que., October 2, 1958 . . . Shoots left.

Year	Team	League	Games	G.	A.	Pts.	Pen.
1975-76—Montreal Juniors		QJHL	67	34	49	83	8
1976-77—Montreal Juniors		QJHL	72	48	87	135	16
1977-78—Montreal Juniors (a-c)		QJHL	72	62	*109	171	44
1978-79—Nova Scotia Voyageurs		AHL	60	6	8	14	10
1979-80—Muskegon Mohawks		IHL	80	42	64	106	16
1980-81—Snickers Gronningen		Holland	....	...	....	....	....
1980-81—Muskegon Mohawks		IHL	14	6	14	20	6
1981-82—Muskegon Mohawks		IHL	82	36	67	103	4
1982-83—Muskegon Mohawks		IHL	35	14	24	38	2
1983-84—Muskegon Mohawks		IHL	82	26	41	67	8

(c)—Drafted from Montreal Juniors by Montreal Canadiens in fourth round of 1978 amateur draft.

DARCY JOHN REGIER

Defense . . . 5'11" . . . 188 lbs. . . . Born, Swift Current, Sask., November 27, 1956 . . . Shoots left.

Year	Team	League	Games	G.	A.	Pts.	Pen.
1973-74—Prince Albert Raiders (a)		SJHL	48	1	10	11	63
1974-75—Lethbridge Broncos		WCHL	67	11	25	36	78
1975-75—Lethbridge Broncos (c)		WCHL	53	5	22	27	125
1976-77—Salt Lake City Golden Eagles		CHL	68	5	22	27	123
1977-78—Phoenix Roadrunners		CHL	16	0	5	5	43
1977-78—Binghamton Dusters		AHL	5	0	1	1	2
1977-78—Cleveland Barons (d)		NHL	15	0	1	1	28
1977-78—Fort Worth Texans		CHL	38	2	6	8	37
1978-79—Fort Worth Texans		CHL	59	1	15	16	98
1979-80—Indianapolis Checkers (e)		CHL	79	0	18	18	52
1980-81—Indianapolis Checkers		CHL	76	2	18	20	77
1981-82—Indianapolis Checkers		CHL	80	4	17	21	98
1982-83—New York Islanders		NHL	6	0	0	0	7
1982-83—Indianapolis Checkers (a)		CHL	74	3	28	31	102
1983-84—Indianapolis Checkers		CHL	68	4	12	16	112
1983-84—New York Islanders		NHL	5	0	1	1	0
NHL TOTALS			26	0	2	2	35

(c)—Drafted from Lethbridge Broncos by California Seals in fifth round of 1976 amateur draft.

(d)—Traded to New York Islanders by Cleveland Barons with Wayne Merrick for Jean Potvin and J. P. Parise, January, 1978.

(e)—Won CHL Ironman Award.

DAVID REID

Left Wing . . . 6'1" . . . 205 lbs. . . . Born, Toronto, Ont., May 15, 1964 . . . Shoots left.

Year	Team	League	Games	G.	A.	Pts.	Pen.
1980-81—Mississauga Midgets		Ont. Midget	39	21	32	53	....
1981-82—Peterborough Petes (c)		OHL	68	10	32	42	41
1982-83—Peterborough Petes		OHL	70	23	34	57	33
1983-84—Peterborough Petes		OHL	60	33	64	97	12
1983-84—Boston Bruins		NHL	8	1	0	1	2
NHL TOTALS			8	1	0	1	2

(c)—June, 1982—Drafted by Boston Bruins as underage junior in 1982 NHL entry draft. Fourth Bruins pick, 60th overall, third round.

DAVE REIERSON

Defense . . . 5'11" . . . 172 lbs. . . . Born, Bashaw, Alta., August 30, 1964 . . . Shoots right.

Year	Team	League	Games	G.	A.	Pts.	Pen.
1980-81—Prince Albert Raiders	SAJHL	73	14	39	53	..
1981-82—Prince Albert Raiders (c)	SAJHL	87	23	76	99	..
1982-83—Michigan Tech.	CCHA	38	2	14	16	58
1983-84—Michigan Tech.	CCHA	38	4	15	19	63

(c)—June, 1982—Drafted as underage junior by Calgary Flames in 1982 NHL entry draft. First Flames pick, 29th overall, second round.

PAUL REINHART

Defense . . . 5'11" . . . 216 lbs. . . . Born, Kitchener, Ont., January 8, 1960 . . . Shoots left . . . (January 13, 1981)—Strained ligaments . . . (September, 1981)—Injured ligaments in right ankle during Canada Cup . . . Brother of Kevin Reinhart (Toronto '78 draft pick, 132nd overall) . . . Set Flames club records for goals (18 in '80-81), assists (58 in '82-83) and points (75 in '82-83) by a defenseman in one season . . . (November 24, 1983)—Injured back in game vs. Winnipeg . . . (April, 1984)—Reinjured back in playoff series with Edmonton.

Year	Team	League	Games	G.	A.	Pts.	Pen.
1975-76—Kitchener Rangers	OMJHL	53	6	33	39	42
1976-77—Kitchener Rangers	OMJHL	51	4	14	18	16
1977-78—Kitchener Rangers	OMJHL	47	17	28	45	15
1978-79—Kitchener Rangers (c)	OMJHL	66	51	78	129	57
1979-80—Atlanta Flames	NHL	79	9	38	47	31
1980-81—Calgary Flames	NHL	74	18	49	67	52
1981-82—Calgary Flames	NHL	62	13	48	61	17
1982-83—Calgary Flames	NHL	78	17	58	75	28
1983-84—Calgary Flames	NHL	27	6	15	21	10
NHL TOTALS		320	63	208	271	138

(c)—August, 1979—Drafted by Atlanta Flames as underage junior in NHL entry draft. First Atlanta pick, 12th overall, first round.

CHRIS RENAUD

Defense . . . 5'11" . . . 185 lbs. . . . Born, Windsor, Ont., April 25, 1960 . . . Shoots left . . . Brother of Mark Renaud . . . Was captain of his Colgate University team.

Year	Team	League	Games	G.	A.	Pts.	Pen.
1978-79—Colgate University	ECAC	26	1	8	9	24
1979-80—Colgate University	ECAC	31	8	18	26	36
1980-81—Colgate University (b)	ECAC	34	12	30	42	52
1981-82—Colgate University (a-c-d)	ECAC	28	11	28	39	47
1982-83—Tulsa Oilers	CHL	79	6	15	21	33
1983-84—Tulsa Oilers	CHL	63	3	18	21	49

(c)—Named to All-America Team (East).
(d)—July, 1982—Signed by New York Rangers as a free agent.

MARK JOSEPH RENAUD

Defense . . . 5'11" . . . 180 lbs. . . . Born, Windsor, Ont., February 21, 1959 . . . Shoots left . . . Brother of Chris Renaud.

Year	Team	League	Games	G.	A.	Pts.	Pen.
1975-76—Windsor Spitfires	OMJHL	66	3	15	18	42
1976-77—Niagara Falls Flyers	OMJHL	66	7	25	32	30
1977-78—Niagara Falls Flyers	OMJHL	68	6	24	30	57
1978-79—Niagara Falls Flyers (c-d)	OMJHL	68	10	56	66	89
1979-80—Hartford Whalers	NHL	13	0	2	2	4
1979-80—Springfield Indians	AHL	61	3	16	19	39
1980-81—Hartford Whalers	NHL	4	1	0	1	0
1980-81—Binghamton Whalers	AHL	73	6	44	50	56
1981-82—Binghamton Whalers	AHL	33	3	19	22	70
1981-82—Hartford Whalers	NHL	48	1	17	18	39
1982-83—Hartford Whalers	NHL	77	3	28	31	37
1983-84—Rochester Americans	AHL	64	9	33	42	48
1983-84—Buffalo Sabres (e)	NHL	10	1	3	4	6
NHL TOTALS		152	6	50	56	86

(c)—August, 1979—Drafted by Hartford Whalers in NHL entry draft. Fifth Hartford pick, 102nd overall, fifth round.
(d)—Named best defensive Defenseman in poll of OMJHL coaches.
(e)—October, 1983—Selected by Buffalo Sabres in NHL waiver draft.

GRANT REZANSOFF

Center ... 5'11" ... 181 lbs. ... Born, Surrey, B.C., March 3, 1961 ... Shoots right.

Year	Team	League	Games	G.	A.	Pts.	Pen.
1978-79—Delta		BCJHL	61	42	45	87	22
1979-80—Victoria Cougars		WHL	67	17	19	36	7
1980-81—Victoria Cougars (c)		WHL	72	40	57	97	27
1981-82—Muskegon Mohawks		IHL	37	15	11	26	4
1981-82—Oklahoma City Stars		CHL	45	15	20	35	10
1982-83—Colorado Flames		CHL	22	4	3	7	16
1982-83—Peoria Prancers		IHL	49	23	42	65	23
1983-84—Peoria Prancers		IHL	82	36	46	82	11

(c)—August, 1981—Signed by Calgary Flames as a free agent.

PATRICK WAYNE RIBBLE

Defense ... 6'3" ... 225 lbs. ... Born, Leamington, Ont., April 26, 1954 ... Shoots left ... (March, 1980)—Knee ligament injury ... (February 3, 1981)—Shoulder and rib injuries ... (November, 1982)—Broke foot.

Year	Team	League	Games	G.	A.	Pts.	Pen.
1972-73—Oshawa Generals		Jr."A"OHA	61	11	27	38	110
1973-74—Oshawa Generals (c)		Jr."A"OHA	70	8	16	24	134
1974-75—Omaha Knights		CHL	77	5	17	22	164
1975-76—Tulsa Oilers		CHL	73	3	22	25	98
1975-76—Atlanta Flames		NHL	3	0	0	0	0
1976-77—Tulsa Oilers (b)		CHL	51	9	20	29	140
1976-77—Atlanta Flames		NHL	23	2	2	4	31
1977-78—Atlanta Flames		NHL	80	5	12	17	68
1978-79—Atlanta Flames (d)		NHL	66	5	16	21	69
1978-79—Chicago Black Hawks		NHL	12	1	3	4	8
1979-80—Chicago Black Hawks (e)		NHL	23	1	2	3	14
1979-80—Toronto Maple Leafs (f)		NHL	13	0	2	2	8
1979-80—Washington Capitals		NHL	19	1	5	6	30
1980-81—Washington Capitals		NHL	67	3	15	18	103
1981-82—Washington Capitals (g)		NHL	12	1	2	3	14
1981-82—Calgary Flames		NHL	3	0	0	0	2
1981-82—Oklahoma City Stars		CHL	43	1	9	10	44
1982-83—Colorado Flames		CHL	10	1	4	5	8
1982-83—Calgary Flames		NHL	28	0	1	1	18
1983-84—Colorado Flames (b)		CHL	53	4	27	31	60
NHL TOTALS			349	19	60	79	365

(c)— Drafted from Oshawa Generals by Atlanta Flames in fourth round of 1974 amateur draft.

(d)—March, 1979—Traded with Tom Lysiak, Harold Phillipoff, Greg Fox and Miles Zaharko to Chicago Blacks Hawks by Atlanta Flames for Ivan Boldirev, Phil Russell and Darcy Rota.

(e)—January, 1980—Traded by Chicago Black Hawks to Toronto Maple Leafs for Dave Hutchison.

(f)—February, 1980—Traded by Toronto Maple Leafs to Washington Capitals for future considerations (Mike Kaszycki sent to Washington to complete deal).

(g)—November, 1981—Traded with future considerations by Washington Capitals to Calgary Flames for Randy Holt and Bobby Gould.

STEPHANE RICHER

Center ... 6' ... 190 lbs. ... Born, Buckingham, Que., June 7, 1966 ... Shoots right.

Year	Team	League	Games	G.	A.	Pts.	Pen.
1983-84—Granby Bisons (c)		QHL	67	39	37	76	58

(c)—June, 1984—Drafted as underage junior by Montreal Canadiens in NHL entry draft. Third Canadiens pick, 29th overall, second round.

STEVE RICHMOND

Defense ... 6'1" ... 205 lbs. ... Born, Chicago, Ill., December 11, 1959 ... Shoots left.

Year	Team	League	Games	G.	A.	Pts.	Pen.
1978-79—University of Michigan		WCHA	34	2	5	7	38
1979-80—University of Michigan		WCHA	38	10	19	29	26
1980-81—University of Michigan		WCHA	39	22	32	54	46
1981-82—University of Michigan (b-c)		CCHA	38	6	30	36	68
1982-83—Tulsa Oilers		CHL	78	5	13	18	187
1983-84—Tulsa Oilers		CHL	38	1	17	18	114
1983-84—New York Rangers		NHL	26	2	5	7	110
NHL TOTALS			26	2	5	7	110

(c)—July, 1982—Signed by New York Rangers as a free agent.

DAVE RICHTER

Defense . . . 6'5" . . . 217 lbs. . . . Born, Winnipeg, Man., April 8, 1960 . . . Shoots right . . . (November, 1982)—Strained knee ligaments . . . (Summer, 1983)—Elbow surgery.

Year	Team	League	Games	G.	A.	Pts.	Pen.
1979-80—University of Michigan		WCHA	34	0	4	4	54
1980-81—University of Michigan		WCHA	36	2	13	15	56
1981-82—University of Michigan		CCHA	36	9	12	21	78
1981-82—Nashville South Stars		CHL	2	0	1	1	0
1981-82—Minnesota North Stars (c)		NHL	3	0	0	0	11
1982-83—Minnesota North Stars		NHL	6	0	0	0	4
1982-83—Birmingham South Stars		CHL	69	6	17	23	211
1983-84—Salt Lake Golden Eagles		CHL	10	1	4	5	39
1983-84—Minnesota North Stars		NHL	42	2	3	5	132
NHL TOTALS			51	2	3	5	147

(c)—June, 1982—Signed by Minnesota North Stars as a free agent.

JAMES WILLIAM (BILL) RILEY

Right Wing . . . 5'11" . . . 195 lbs. . . . Born, Amherst, N. S., September 20, 1950 . . . Shoots right . . . Missed part of 1977-78 season with severed tendon in left ankle requiring surgery.

Year	Team	League	Games	G.	A.	Pts.	Pen.
1974-75—Dayton Gems		IHL	63	12	16	28	279
1974-75—Washington Capitals		NHL	1	0	0	0	0
1975-76—Dayton Gems		IHL	69	35	31	66	301
1976-77—Dayton Gems		IHL	30	19	15	34	69
1976-77—Washington Capitals		NHL	43	13	14	27	124
1977-78—Washington Capitals		NHL	57	13	12	25	125
1978-79—Washington Capitals (c)		NHL	24	2	2	4	64
1978-79—Hershey Bears		AHL	51	15	15	30	118
1979-80—Winnipeg Jets		NHL	14	3	2	5	7
1979-80—Nova Scotia Voyageurs		AHL	63	31	33	64	157
1980-81—New Brunswick Hawks		AHL	46	12	25	37	107
1981-82—New Brunswick Hawks		CHL	80	32	30	62	104
1982-83—Moncton Alpines		AHL	73	33	30	63	134
1983-84—Nova Scotia Voyageurs		AHL	78	24	24	48	79
NHL TOTALS			139	31	30	61	320

(c)—June, 1979—Selected by Winnipeg Jets in NHL expansion draft.

PIERRE RIOUX

Center . . . 5'9" . . . 165 lbs. . . . Born, Quebec City, Que., February 1, 1962 . . . Shoots left . . . Also plays right wing.

Year	Team	League	Games	G.	A.	Pts.	Pen.
1979-80—Shawinigan Cataracts		QMJHL	70	27	47	74	24
1980-81—Shawinigan Cataracts		QMJHL	65	43	57	100	49
1981-82—Shawinigan Cataracts (a-c)		QMJHL	57	*66	86	152	50
1982-83—Colorado Flames		CHL	59	26	36	62	18
1982-83—Calgary Flames		NHL	14	1	2	3	4
1983-84—Colorado Flames		CHL	65	37	46	83	22
NHL TOTALS			14	1	2	3	4

(c)—August, 1982—Signed by Calgary Flames as a free agent.

DOUGLAS RISEBROUGH

Center . . . 5'11" . . . 170 lbs. . . . Born, Guelph, Ont., January 29, 1954 . . . Shoots left . . . Missed final weeks of 1973-74 season with surgery for torn knee ligaments . . . Missed part of 1978-79 season with shoulder separation . . . (March, 1980)—dislocated shoulder . . . Missed parts of 1980-81 season due to arthritis flareup in injured left shoulder . . . Also plays left wing . . . (February 27, 1983)—Twisted right knee in game at Vancouver . . . (April 12, 1984)—Given 6-game suspension by NHL for swinging his stick at Glenn Anderson of Edmonton during playoff game. Suspension is for the first six games of the 1984-85 season.

Year	Team	League	Games	G.	A.	Pts.	Pen.
1971-72—Guelph CMCs		SOJHL	56	19	33	52	127
1972-73—Guelph Biltmores		SOJHL	60	*47	*60	*107	229
1973-74—Kitchener Rangers (c)		Jr. "A" OHA	46	25	27	52	114
1974-75—Nova Scotia Voyageurs		AHL	7	5	4	9	55

Year	Team	League	Games	G.	A.	Pts.	Pen.
1974-75—Montreal Canadiens		NHL	64	15	32	47	198
1975-76—Montreal Canadiens		NHL	80	16	28	44	180
1976-77—Montreal Canadiens		NHL	78	22	38	60	132
1977-78—Montreal Canadiens		NHL	72	18	23	41	97
1978-79—Montreal Canadiens		NHL	48	10	15	25	62
1979-80—Montreal Canadiens		NHL	44	8	10	18	81
1980-81—Montreal Canadiens		NHL	48	13	21	34	93
1981-82—Montreal Canadiens (d)		NHL	59	15	18	33	116
1982-83—Calgary Flames		NHL	71	21	37	58	138
1983-84—Calgary Flames		NHL	77	23	28	51	161
NHL TOTALS			641	161	250	411	1258

(c)—Drafted from Kitchener Rangers by Montreal Canadiens in first round of 1974 amateur draft.
(d)—September, 1982—Traded by Montreal Canadiens to Calgary Flames for switch of second-round draft choices in 1983 and option to switch third-round choices in 1984.

GARY DANIEL RISSLING

Left Wing . . . 5'11" . . . 180 lbs. . . . Born, Saskatoon, Sask., August 8, 1956 . . . Shoots left.

Year	Team	League	Games	G.	A.	Pts.	Pen.
1973-74—Edmonton Mets		AJHL	46	29	31	60	132
1974-75—Edmonton Oil Kings		WCHL	69	19	35	54	228
1975-76—Edmonton Oil Kings (c)		WCHL	18	5	9	14	25
1975-76—Calgary Centennials		WCHL	47	29	38	67	196
1976-77—Calgary Centennials		WCHL	68	40	49	89	317
1977-78—Port Huron Flags (d)		IHL	79	29	34	63	341
1978-79—Washington Capitals		NHL	26	3	3	6	127
1978-79—Hershey Bears		AHL	52	14	20	34	337
1979-80—Washington Capitals		NHL	11	0	1	1	49
1979-80—Hershey Bears (e)		AHL	46	16	24	40	279
1980-81—Hershey Bears		AHL	4	1	1	2	74
1980-81—Pittsburgh Penguins (f)		NHL	26	1	0	1	143
1980-81—Birmingham Bulls		CHL	19	5	7	12	161
1981-82—Pittsburgh Penguins		NHL	16	0	0	0	55
1981-82—Erie Blades		AHL	29	7	15	22	185
1982-83—Pittsburgh Penguins		NHL	40	5	4	9	128
1982-83—Baltimore Skipjacks		AHL	38	14	17	31	136
1983-84—Baltimore Skipjacks		AHL	30	12	13	25	47
1983-84—Pittsburgh Penguins		NHL	47	4	13	17	297
NHL TOTALS			166	13	21	34	799

(c)—Traded to Calgary Centennials by Edmonton Oil Kings for Dan Shearer and Doug Johnston.
(d)—December, 1978—Signed by Washington Capitals as free agent.
(e)—Led in Penalty Minutes (87) during AHL Playoffs.
(f)—January, 1980—Traded by Washington Capitals to Pittsburgh Penguins for fifth round 1981 draft pick (Peter Sidorwicz).

CALVIN STANLEY ROADHOUSE

Right Wing . . . 6' . . . 214 lbs. . . . Born, Lethbridge, Alta., April 29, 1959 . . . Shoots right . . . (November, 1980)—Broken knuckles.

Year	Team	League	Games	G.	A.	Pts.	Pen.
1976-77—Bellingham		BCJHL	14	9	10	19	38
1976-77—Calgary Canucks		AJHL	36	8	17	25	31
1976-77—Portland Winter Hawks		WCHL	8	1	0	1	4
1977-78—Billings Bighorns		WCHL	59	19	24	43	69
1978-79—Billings Bighorns		WHL	69	50	48	98	138
1979-80—Houston Apollos		CHL	72	17	24	41	19
1980-81—Wichita Wind		CHL	43	8	22	30	39
1981-82—Milwaukee Admirals		IHL	7	2	3	5	2
1981-82—Wichita Wind		CHL	27	5	8	13	18
1982-83—Milwaukee Admirals		IHL	54	34	19	53	17
1983-84—Milwaukee Admirals		IHL	59	19	24	43	45

GARY ROBERTS

Left Wing . . . 6'1" . . . 180 lbs. . . . Born, North York, Ont., May 23, 1966 . . . Shoots left.

Year	Team	League	Games	G.	A.	Pts.	Pen.
1981-82—Whitby Midgets		Ont. Midgets	44	55	31	86	133
1982-83—Ottawa 67's		OHL	53	12	8	20	83

Year	Team	League	Games	G.	A.	Pts.	Pen.
1983-84—Ottawa 67's (c-d)		OHL	48	27	30	57	144

(c)—Led OHL playoffs with 62 penalty minutes.

(d)—June, 1984—Drafted as underage junior by Calgary Flames in NHL entry draft. First Flames pick, 12th overall, first round.

GORDON ROBERTS

Defense . . . 6' . . . 195 lbs. . . . Born, Detroit, Mich., October 2, 1957 . . . Shoots left . . . Brother of Dave and Doug Roberts . . . (April, 1984)—Bruised hip during playoff series with Edmonton.

Year	Team	League	Games	G.	A.	Pts.	Pen.
1973-74—Detroit Jr. Red Wings		SOJHL	70	25	55	80	340
1974-75—Victoria Cougars (c)		WCHL	53	19	45	64	145
1975-76—New England Whalers		WHA	77	3	19	22	102
1976-77—New England Whalers (d)		WHA	77	13	33	46	169
1977-78—New England Whalers		WHA	78	15	46	61	118
1978-79—New England Whalers		WHA	79	11	46	57	113
1979-80—Hartford Whalers		NHL	80	8	28	36	89
1980-81—Hartford Whalers (e)		NHL	27	2	11	13	81
1980-81—Minnesota North Stars		NHL	50	6	31	37	94
1981-82—Minnesota North Stars		NHL	79	4	30	34	119
1982-83—Minnesota North Stars		NHL	80	3	41	44	103
1983-84—Minnesota North Stars		NHL	77	8	45	53	132
WHA TOTALS			311	42	144	186	502
NHL TOTALS			393	31	186	217	618

(c)—Signed by New England Whalers (WHA), September, 1975.

(d)—Drafted from New England Whalers (WHA) by Montreal Canadiens in third round of 1977 amateur draft.

(e)—December, 1980—Traded by Hartford Whalers to Minnesota North Stars for Mike Fidler.

GEORDIE JAY ROBERTSON

Right Wing and Center . . . 6' . . . 163 lbs. . . . Born, Victoria, B.C., August 1, 1959 . . . Shoots right . . . (October, 1980)—Injured knee in training camp that required surgery . . . Brother of Torrie Robertson.

Year	Team	League	Games	G.	A.	Pts.	Pen.
1975-76—Nanaimo		BCJHL	....	...	....	....	....
1975-76—Victoria Cougars		WCHL	3	3	2	5	0
1976-77—Victoria Cougars		WCHL	72	39	44	83	107
1977-78—Victoria Cougars		WCHL	61	64	72	136	85
1978-79—Victoria Cougars		WHL	54	31	42	73	94
1979-80—Rochester Americans		AHL	55	26	26	52	66
1980-81—Rochester Americans		AHL	20	3	3	6	19
1981-82—Rochester Americans		AHL	46	14	15	29	45
1981-82—Flint Generals		IHL	11	6	14	20	19
1982-83—Buffalo Sabres		NHL	5	1	2	3	7
1982-83—Rochester Americans		AHL	72	46	73	119	83
1983-84—Rochester Americans		AHL	64	37	54	91	103
NHL TOTALS			5	1	2	3	7

TORRIE ANDREW ROBERTSON

Left Wing . . . 5'11" . . . 185 lbs. . . . Born, Victoria, B.C., August 2, 1961 . . . Shoots left . . . Brother of Geordie Robertson.

Year	Team	League	Games	G.	A.	Pts.	Pen.
1978-79—Victoria Cougars		WHL	69	18	23	41	141
1979-80—Victoria Cougars (c)		WHL	72	23	24	47	298
1980-81—Victoria Cougars (b)		WHL	59	45	66	111	274
1980-81—Washington Capitals		NHL	3	0	0	0	0
1981-82—Hershey Bears		AHL	21	5	3	8	60
1981-82—Washington Capitals		NHL	54	8	13	21	204
1982-83—Washington Capitals		NHL	5	2	0	2	4
1982-83—Hershey Bears		AHL	69	21	33	54	187
1983-84—Hartford Whalers (d)		NHL	66	7	14	21	198
NHL TOTALS			128	17	27	44	406

(c)—June, 1980—Drafted by Washington Capitals as underage junior in 1980 NHL entry draft. Third Capitals pick, 55th overall, third round.

(d)—October, 1983—Traded by Washington Capitals to Hartford Whalers for Greg Adams.

FLORENT ROBIDOUX

Center ... 6'2" ... 172 lbs. ... Born, Cypress River, Man., May 5, 1960 ... Shoots left.

Year	Team	League	Games	G.	A.	Pts.	Pen.
1977-78—New Westminster Bruins		WCHL	8	1	1	2	12
1978-79—Portland Winter Hawks		WHL	70	36	41	77	73
1979-80—Portland Winter Hawks		WHL	70	43	57	100	157
1980-81—Chicago Black Hawks (c)		NHL	39	6	2	8	75
1980-81—New Brunswick Hawks		AHL	35	12	11	23	110
1981-82—Chicago Black Hawks		NHL	4	1	2	3	0
1981-82—New Brunswick Hawks (d)		AHL	69	31	35	66	200
1982-83—Did not play—injured			....	...	....	....	....
1983-84—Springfield Indians		AHL	68	26	22	48	123
1983-84—Chicago Black Hawks		NHL	9	0	0	0	0
NHL TOTALS			52	7	4	11	75

(c)—August, 1980—Signed by Chicago Black Hawks as free agent.
(d)—Co-Leader (with Ray Neufeld of Binghamton) in AHL Calder Cup Playoffs with nine goals.

LARRY CLARK ROBINSON

Defense ... 6'3½" ... 210 lbs. ... Born, Winchester, Ont., June 2, 1951 ... Shoots left ... Also plays Left Wing ... Brother of Moe Robinson ... Missed part of 1978-79 season with water on the knee ... (March 6, 1980)—Right shoulder separation in game vs. Edmonton ... (October, 1980)—Groin injury ... (November 14, 1980)—Separated left shoulder ... (January 8, 1981)—Broken nose ... (October, 1982)—Sore left shoulder ... (October, 1983)—Skin infection behind right knee.

Year	Team	League	Games	G.	A.	Pts.	Pen.
1968-69—Brockville Braves		Cent. Jr. OHA	....	...	....	....	....
1969-70—Brockville Braves (a)		Cent. Jr. OHA	40	22	29	51	74
1970-71—Kitchener Rangers (c)		Jr."A" OHA	61	12	39	51	65
1971-72—Nova Scotia Voyageurs		AHL	74	10	14	24	54
1972-73—Nova Scotia Voyageurs		AHL	38	6	33	39	33
1972-73—Montreal Canadiens		NHL	36	2	4	6	20
1973-74—Montreal Canadiens		NHL	78	6	20	26	66
1974-75—Montreal Canadiens		NHL	80	14	47	61	76
1975-76—Montreal Canadiens		NHL	80	10	30	40	59
1976-77—Montreal Canadiens (a-d)		NHL	77	19	66	85	45
1977-78—Montreal Canadiens (b-e-f)		NHL	80	13	52	65	39
1978-79—Montreal Canadiens (a)		NHL	67	16	45	61	33
1979-80—Montreal Canadiens (a-d)		NHL	72	14	61	75	39
1980-81—Montreal Canadiens (b)		NHL	65	12	38	50	37
1981-82—Montreal Canadiens		NHL	71	12	47	59	41
1982-83—Montreal Canadiens		NHL	71	14	49	63	33
1983-84—Montreal Canadiens		NHL	74	9	34	43	39
NHL TOTALS			851	141	493	634	527

(c)—Drafted from Kitchener Rangers by Montreal Canadiens in second round of 1971 amateur draft.
(d)—Won James Norris Memorial Trophy (Outstanding Defenseman).
(e)—Led in assists (17) and tied for lead in points (21) during playoffs.
(f)—Won Conn Smythe Trophy (MVP in Stanley Cup playoffs).

LUC ROBITAILLE

Left Wing ... 6' ... 180 lbs. ... Born, Montreal, Que., February 17, 1966 ... Shoots left.

Year	Team	League	Games	G.	A.	Pts.	Pen.
1983-84—Hull Olympics (c)		QHL	70	32	53	85	48

(c)—June, 1984—Drafted as underage junior by Los Angeles Kings in NHL entry draft. Ninth Kings pick, 171st overall, ninth round.

NORMAND ROCHEFORT

Defense ... 6'1" ... 200 lbs. ... Born, Trois-Rivieres, Que., January 28, 1961 ... Shoots left ... (November, 1980)—Neck injury ... Missed parts of 1982-83 season with injured knee ... Nephew of Leon Rochefort (NHL, 1961-1976).

Year	Team	League	Games	G.	A.	Pts.	Pen.
1977-78—Trois-Rivieres Draveurs		QMJHL	72	9	37	46	36
1978-79—Trois-Rivieres Draveurs		QMJHL	72	17	57	74	80
1979-80—Trois-Rivieres Draveurs		QMJHL	20	5	25	30	22
1979-80—Quebec Remparts (b-c)		QMJHL	52	8	39	47	68
1980-81—Quebec Remparts		QMJHL	9	2	6	8	14
1980-81—Quebec Nordiques		NHL	56	3	7	10	51
1981-82—Quebec Nordiques		NHL	72	4	14	18	115

Year	Team	League	Games	G.	A.	Pts.	Pen.
1982-83—Quebec Nordiques		NHL	62	6	17	23	40
1983-84—Quebec Nordiques		NHL	75	2	22	24	47
NHL TOTALS			265	15	60	75	253

(c)—June, 1980—Drafted by Quebec Nordiques as underage junior in 1980 NHL entry draft. First Nordiques pick, 24th overall, second round.

MICHAEL ROGERS

Center . . . 5'9" . . . 170 lbs. . . . Born, Calgary, Alta., October 24, 1954 . . . Shoots left . . . (March, 1983)—Missed final seven games of season with back spasms . . . One of only three players to get 100 points in his first three NHL seasons (Wayne Gretzky and Peter Stastny being the others) . . . Cousin of Detroit Lions kicker Ed Murray.

Year	Team	League	Games	G.	A.	Pts.	Pen.
1971-72—Calgary Centennials		WCHL	66	27	30	57	19
1972-73—Calgary Centennials		WCHL	67	54	58	112	44
1973-74—Calgary Centennials (c-d)		WCHL	66	67	73	140	32
1974-75—Edmonton Oilers (e)		WHA	78	35	48	83	2
1975-76—Edmonton Oilers (f)		WHA	44	12	15	27	10
1975-76—New England Whalers		WHA	36	18	14	32	10
1976-77—New England Whalers		WHA	78	25	57	82	10
1977-78—New England Whalers		WHA	80	28	43	71	46
1978-79—New England Whalers		WHA	80	27	45	72	31
1979-80—Hartford Whalers		NHL	80	44	61	105	10
1980-81—Hartford Whalers		NHL	80	40	65	105	32
1981-82—New York Rangers (g)		NHL	80	38	65	103	43
1982-83—New York Rangers		NHL	71	29	47	76	28
1983-84—New York Rangers		NHL	78	23	38	61	45
WHA TOTALS			396	145	222	367	109
NHL TOTALS			389	174	276	450	158

(c)—Drafted from Calgary Centennials by Vancouver Canucks in fifth round of 1974 amateur draft.

(d)—Selected by Edmonton Oilers in World Hockey Association amateur player draft, May, 1974.

(e)—Won WHA Most Sportsmanlike Player Award.

(f)—Traded to New England Whalers by Edmonton Oilers with future considerations, for Wayne Carleton, January, 1976.

(g)—October, 1981—Traded with 10th-round 1982 entry draft pick (Simo Saarinen) by Hartford Whalers to New York Rangers for Chris Kotsopoulos, Doug Sulliman and Gerry McDonald.

JEFF ROHLICEK

Left Wing . . . 5'11" . . . 165 lbs. . . . Born, Park Ridge, Ill., January 27, 1966 . . . Shoots left.

Year	Team	League	Games	G	A	Pts.	Pen.
1983-84—Portland Winter Hawks (b-c)		WHL	71	44	53	97	22

(c)—June, 1984—Drafted as underage junior by Vancouver Canucks in NHL entry draft. Second Canucks pick, 31st overall, second round.

CLIFF RONNING

Center . . . 5'8" . . . 160 lbs. . . . Born, Vancouver, B.C., October 1, 1965 . . . Shoots left.

Year	Team	League	Games	G.	A.	Pts.	Pen.
1982-83—New Westminster Royals		BCJHL	52	82	68	150	42
1983-84—New Westminster Bruins (b-c-d)		WHL	71	69	67	136	10

(c)—Won Stewart Paul Memorial Trophy (Top WHL Rookie).

(d)—June, 1984—Drafted by St. Louis Blues as underage junior in NHL entry draft. Ninth Blues pick, 134th overall, seventh round.

WILLIAM JOHN ROOT

Defense . . . 6' . . . 197 lbs. . . . Born, Toronto, Ont., September 6, 1959 . . . Shoots right.

Year	Team	League	Games	G.	A.	Pts.	Pen.
1976-77—Niagara Falls Flyers		OMJHL	66	3	19	22	114
1977-78—Niagara Falls Flyers		OMJHL	67	6	11	17	61
1978-79—Niagara Falls Flyers (c)		OMJHL	67	4	31	35	119
1979-80—Nova Scotia Voyageurs		AHL	55	4	15	19	57
1980-81—Nova Scotia Voyageurs		AHL	63	3	12	15	76
1981-82—Nova Scotia Voyageurs		AHL	77	6	25	31	105
1982-83—Montreal Canadiens		NHL	46	2	3	5	24
1982-83—Nova Scotia Voyageurs		AHL	24	0	7	7	29
1983-84—Montreal Canadiens (d)		NHL	72	4	13	17	45
NHL TOTALS			118	6	16	22	69

(c)—October, 1979—Signed by Montreal Canadiens as a free agent.

(d)—August, 1984—Traded by Montreal Canadiens to Toronto Maple Leafs for future considerations.

BRIAN MIKE RORABECK

Defense . . . 6' . . . 175 lbs. . . . Born, Brighton, Ont., January 30, 1962 . . . Shoots left . . . Also plays center.

Year	Team	League	Games	G.	A.	Pts.	Pen.
1978-79—Niagara Falls Flyers		OMJHL	55	8	18	26	49
1979-80—Niagara Falls Flyers (c)		OMJHL	54	12	28	40	74
1980-81—Niagara Falls Flyers		OHL	5	1	2	3	7
1980-81—Sudbury Wolves		OHL	24	13	16	29	43
1981-82—Sudbury Wolves		OHL	50	25	46	71	42
1982-83—Kalamazoo Wings (d)		IHL	27	5	8	13	22
1982-83—Muskegon Mohawks		IHL	40	16	38	54	40
1983-84—Muskegon Mohawks		IHL	7	4	5	9	4
1983-84—Kalamazoo Wings (e)		IHL	35	5	20	25	10

(c)—June, 1980—Drafted as underage junior by Detroit Red Wings in 1980 NHL entry draft. Eighth Red Wings pick, 193rd overall, 10th round.

(d)—January, 1983—Loaned by Kalamazoo to Muskegon.

(e)—January, 1984—Signed by Kalamazoo Wings as a free agent.

JAY ROSE

Defense . . . 6' . . . 180 lbs. . . . Born, Newton, Mass., July 6, 1966 . . . Shoots right.

Year	Team	League	Games	G.	A.	Pts.	Pen.
1983-84—Boston New Prep. (c)		Mass. H.S.	30	3	26	29	..

(c)—June, 1984—Drafted by Detroit Red Wings in NHL entry draft. Tenth Red Wings pick, 195th overall, 10th round.

BRIAN ROSS

Defense . . . 6'1" . . . 190 lbs. . . . Born, Dryden, Ont., March 12, 1965 . . . Shoots right.

Year	Team	League	Games	G.	A.	Pts.	Pen.
1981-82—Dryden Midgets		Ont. Midget	31	14	41	55	35
1982-83—Kitchener Rangers (c)		OHL	14	0	2	2	11
1983-84—Kitchener Rangers		OHL	57	4	7	11	27

(c)—June, 1983—Drafted as underage junior by Toronto Maple Leafs in 1983 NHL entry draft. Ninth Maple Leafs pick, 188th overall, tenth round.

DARCY IRWIN ROTA

Left Wing . . . 5'11" . . . 195 lbs. . . . Born, Vancouver, B.C., February 16, 1953 . . . Shoots left . . . Cousin of Randy Rota . . . Also plays right wing . . . (October, 1981)—Knee injury . . . (December, 1982)—Shoulder separation . . . (1982-83)—Set Vancouver record with 42 goals in '82-83 (broken by Tony Tanti in 1983-84) . . . (January, 1984)—Hyperextended right knee . . . (March, 1984)—Recurring neck spasms.

Year	Team	League	Games	G.	A.	Pts.	Pen.
1970-71—Edmonton Oil Kings		WCHL	64	43	39	82	60
1971-72—Edmonton Oil Kings (b)		WCHL	67	51	54	105	68
1972-73—Edmonton Oil Kings (a-c)		WCHL	68	*73	56	129	104
1973-74—Chicago Black Hawks		NHL	74	21	12	33	58
1974-75—Chicago Black Hawks		NHL	78	22	22	44	93
1975-76—Chicago Black Hawks		NHL	79	20	17	37	73
1976-77—Chicago Black Hawks		NHL	76	24	22	46	82
1977-78—Chicago Black Hawks		NHL	78	17	20	37	67
1978-79—Chicago Black Hawks (d)		NHL	63	13	17	30	77
1978-79—Atlanta Flames		NHL	13	9	5	14	21
1979-80—Atlanta Flames (e)		NHL	44	10	8	18	49
1979-80—Vancouver Canucks		NHL	26	5	6	11	29
1980-81—Vancouver Canucks		NHL	80	25	31	56	124
1981-82—Vancouver Canucks		NHL	51	20	20	40	139
1982-83—Vancouver Canucks		NHL	73	42	39	81	88
1983-84—Vancouver Canucks		NHL	59	28	20	48	73
NHL TOTALS			794	256	239	495	971

(c)—Drafted from Edmonton Oil Kings by Chicago Black Hawks in first round of 1973 amateur draft.

(d)—March, 1979—Traded with Ivan Boldirev and Phil Russell to Atlanta Flames by Chicago Black Hawks for Tom Lysiak, Harold Phillipoff, Pat Ribble, Greg Fox and Miles Zaharko.

(e)—February, 1980—Traded with Ivan Boldirev by Atlanta Flames to Vancouver Canucks for Don Lever and Brad Smith.

TOM ROULSTON

Center . . . 6'1" . . . 195 lbs. . . . Born, Winnipeg, Man., November 20, 1957 . . . Shoots right . . . Set CHL record with nine hat tricks during 1980-81 season shattering old record of four set by Boom-Boom Caron in 1963-64.

Year	Team	League	Games	G.	A.	Pts.	Pen.
1975-76—Edmonton Oil Kings	WCHL	1	0	0	0	0
1975-76—Winnipeg Clubs	WCHL	60	18	17	35	56
1976-77—Winnipeg Monarchs (c)	WCHL	72	56	53	109	35
1977-78—Port Huron Flags (d)	IHL	49	27	36	63	24
1977-78—Salt Lake City Golden Eagles	CHL	21	2	1	3	2
1978-79—Dallas Black Hawks (e)	CHL	73	26	29	55	57
1979-80—Houston Apollos	CHL	72	29	41	70	46
1980-81—Wichita Wind (a-f)	CHL	69	*63	44	107	93
1980-81—Edmonton Oilers	NHL	11	1	1	2	2
1981-82—Wichita Wind	CHL	30	22	28	50	46
1981-82—Edmonton Oilers	NHL	35	11	3	14	22
1982-83—Edmonton Oilers	NHL	67	19	21	40	24
1983-84—Edmonton Oilers (g)	NHL	24	5	7	12	16
1983-84—Pittsburgh Penguins	NHL	53	11	17	28	8
NHL TOTALS		190	47	49	96	72

(c)—Drafted from Winnipeg Monarchs by St. Louis Blues in third round of 1977 amateur draft.
(d)—Led in goals (17) during playoffs.
(e)—August, 1979—Traded with Risto Siltanen by St. Louis Blues to Edmonton Oilers for Joe Micheletti.
(f)—Led CHL Playoffs with 26 points.
(g)—December, 1983—Traded by Edmonton Oilers to Pittsburgh Penguins for Kevin McClelland and a middle-round future draft pick.

BOB ROUSE

Defense . . . 6'1" . . . 210 lbs. . . . Born, Surrey, B.C., June 18, 1964 . . . Shoots right.

Year	Team	League	Games	G.	A.	Pts.	Pen.
1980-81—Billings Bighorns	WHL	70	0	13	13	116
1981-82—Billings Bighorns (c)	WHL	71	7	22	29	209
1982-83—Nanaimo Islanders	WHL	29	7	20	27	86
1982-83—Lethbridge Broncos	WHL	71	15	50	65	168
1983-84—Lethbridge Broncos (a-d)	WHL	71	18	42	60	101
1983-84—Minnesota North Stars	NHL	1	0	0	0	0
NHL TOTALS		1	0	0	0	0

(c)—June, 1982—Drafted as underage junior by Minnesota North Stars in 1982 NHL entry draft. Third North Stars pick, 80th overall, fourth round.
(d)—Won WHL Top Defenseman Trophy.

MICHAEL ROWE

Defense . . . 6'1" . . . 208 lbs. . . . Born, Kingston, Ont., March 8, 1965 . . . Shoots left.

Year	Team	League	Games	G.	A.	Pts.	Pen.
1981-82—Toronto Marlboros	OHL	58	4	4	8	214
1982-83—Toronto Marlboros (c)	OHL	64	4	29	33	*262
1983-84—Toronto Marlboros	OHL	59	9	36	45	208

(c)—June, 1983—Drafted as underage junior by Pittsburgh Penguins in 1983 NHL entry draft. Third Penguins pick, 58th overall, third round.

THOMAS JOHN ROWE

Right Wing . . . 6'1" . . . 194 lbs. . . . Born, Lynn, Mass., May 23, 1956 . . . Shoots right . . . Missed end of 1978-79 season with knee injury . . . Set NHL record for goals in a season by American born player with 31 in 1978-79 (Broken by Mark Pavelich in '82-83) . . . (February, 1980)—Ankle injury . . . (March, 1980)—Hip pointer . . . (October 8, 1982)—Injured right thigh in game at Minnesota.

Year	Team	League	Games	G.	A.	Pts.	Pen.
1973-74—London Knights	Jr. "A" OHA	70	30	39	69	99
1974-75—London Knights	Jr. "A" OHA	63	19	15	34	137
1975-76—London Knights (c)	Jr. "A" OHA	60	39	55	94	98
1976-77—Springfield Indians	AHL	67	19	23	42	117
1976-77—Washington Capitals	NHL	12	1	2	3	2
1977-78—Washington Capitals	NHL	63	13	8	21	82
1978-79—Washington Capitals	NHL	69	31	30	61	137
1979-80—Washington Capitals (d)	NHL	41	10	17	27	76
1979-80—Hartford Whalers	NHL	20	6	4	10	30
1980-81—Hartford Whalers	NHL	74	13	28	41	190
1981-82—Binghamton Whalers	AHL	8	5	3	8	36
1981-82—Hartford Whalers (e)	NHL	21	4	0	4	36
1981-82—Washington Capitals (f)	NHL	6	1	1	2	18
1981-82—Hershey Bears (g)	AHL	34	17	17	34	89

Year	Team	League	Games	G.	A.	Pts.	Pen.
1982-83—Detroit Red Wings (h-i)		NHL	51	6	10	16	44
1982-83—Adirondack Red Wings		AHL	20	16	7	23	26
1983-84—Moncton Alpines		AHL	50	28	16	44	86
NHL TOTALS			357	85	100	185	615

(c)—Drafted from London Knights by Washington Capitals in third round of 1976 amateur draft.
(d)—January, 1980—Traded by Washington Capitals to Hartford Whalers for Alan Hangsleben.
(e)—December, 1981—Released by Hartford Whalers.
(f)—January, 1982—Signed by Washington Capitals as a free agent.
(g)—August, 1982—Signed by Detroit Red Wings as a free agent after being released by Washington.
(h)—June, 1983—Released by Detroit Red Wings.
(i)—August, 1983—Signed by Edmonton Oilers as a free agent.

DARCY ROY

Left Wing . . . 5'11" . . . 180 lbs. . . . Born, Haileybury, Ont., May 10, 1964 . . . Shoots left.

Year	Team	League	Games	G.	A.	Pts.	Pen.
1980-81—North York Rangers		MTHL	40	6	13	19	74
1981-82—Ottawa 67's (c)		OHL	65	22	20	42	79
1982-83—Ottawa 67's		OHL	70	28	40	68	151
1983-84—Ottawa 67's		OHL	70	21	41	62	98

(c)—June, 1982—Drafted by Los Angeles Kings as underage junior in 1982 NHL entry draft. Fifth Kings pick, 90th overall, fifth round.

MARC ROY

Right Wing . . . 6' . . . 184 lbs. . . . Born, Forestville, Que., February 7, 1961 . . . Shoots right.

Year	Team	League	Games	G.	A.	Pts.	Pen.
1977-78—Chicoutimi Sagueneens		QMJHL	67	13	15	28	55
1978-79—Chicoutimi Sagueneens		QMJHL	71	39	70	109	104
1979-80—Chicoutimi Sagueneens		QMJHL	14	11	10	21	11
1979-80—Trois-Rivieres Draveurs (c)		QMJHL	43	38	39	77	61
1980-81—Trois-Rivieres Draveurs (d)		QMJHL	36	27	29	56	75
1980-81—Quebec Remparts		QMJHL	33	26	25	51	64
1981-82—Muskegon Mohawks		IHL	75	31	33	64	238
1982-83—Colorado Flames		CHL	5	1	0	1	0
1982-83—Peoria Prancers		IHL	64	30	24	54	210
1983-84—Peoria Prancers		IHL	45	19	22	41	144

(c)—June, 1980—Drafted by Calgary Flames as underage junior in 1980 NHL entry draft. Fifth Flames pick, 76th overall, fourth round.
(d)—December, 1980—Traded with Patrick Dunn by Trois-Rivieres Draveurs to Quebec Remparts for Claude Drouin, Pierre Dumouchel and Patrick Masse.

DIRK ERIC RUETER

Defense . . . 5'11" . . . 190 lbs. . . . Born, Toronto, Ont., April 18, 1962 . . . Shoots right.

Year	Team	League	Games	G.	A.	Pts.	Pen.
1979-80—S. Ste. Marie Greyhounds (c)		OMJHL	66	7	16	23	47
1980-81—Sault Ste. Marie Greyhounds		OHL	67	7	35	42	104
1981-82—Sault Ste. Marie Greyhounds		OHL	52	7	32	39	121
1982-83—Rochester Americans		AHL	73	2	23	25	78
1983-84—Rochester Americans		AHL	76	0	16	16	95

(c)—June, 1980—Drafted as underage junior by Buffalo Sabres in 1980 NHL entry draft. Sixth Sabres pick, 104th overall, fifth round.

LINDY CAMERON RUFF

Defense . . . 6'2" . . . 190 lbs. . . . Born, Warburg, Alta., February 17, 1960 . . . Shoots left . . . (December, 1980)—Fractured ankle . . . Also plays left wing . . . Brother of Marty Ruff . . . (March, 1983)—Broken hand . . . (January 14, 1984)—Injured shoulder in game at Detroit.

Year	Team	League	Games	G.	A.	Pts.	Pen.
1976-77—Taber Golden Suns		AJHL	60	13	33	46	112
1976-77—Lethbridge Broncos		WCHL	2	0	2	2	0
1977-78—Lethbridge Broncos		WCHL	66	9	24	33	219
1978-79—Lethbridge Broncos (c)		WHL	24	9	18	27	108
1979-80—Buffalo Sabres		NHL	63	5	14	19	38
1980-81—Buffalo Sabres		NHL	65	8	18	26	121
1981-82—Buffalo Sabres		NHL	79	16	32	48	194
1982-83—Buffalo Sabres		NHL	60	12	17	29	130
1983-84—Buffalo Sabres		NHL	58	14	31	45	101
NHL TOTALS			325	55	112	167	584

(c)—August, 1979—Drafted by Buffalo Sabres as underage junior in entry draft. Second Buffalo pick, 32nd overall, second round.

MARTY RUFF

Defense . . . 6'1" . . . 185 lbs. . . . Born, Warburg, Alta., May 19, 1963 . . . Shoots right . . . Brother of Lindy Ruff . . . Missed start of 1981-82 season with mononucleosis and part of season with knee injury . . . (November, 1982)—Shoulder injury.

Year	Team	League	Games	G.	A.	Pts.	Pen.
1980-81—Taber Golden Suns		AJHL	50	10	12	22	94
1980-81—Lethbridge Broncos (c)		WHL	71	9	37	46	222
1981-82—Lethbridge Broncos		WHL	46	7	28	35	188
1982-83—Lethbridge Broncos		WHL	53	7	23	30	128
1983-84—Montana Magic		CHL	1	0	0	0	2
1983-84—Toledo Goaldiggers		IHL	2	0	1	1	0
1983-84—Muskegon Mohawks		IHL	44	3	15	18	44
1983-84—Portland Winter Hawks		WHL	10	4	2	6	30

(c)—June, 1981—Drafted as underage junior by St. Louis Blues in NHL entry draft. First Blues pick, 20th overall, first round.

REIJO RUOTSALAINEN

Defense . . . 5'8" . . . 170 lbs. . . . Born, Kaakkuri, Finland, April 1, 1960 . . . Shoots right . . . (October 22, 1983)—Hip pointer injury in game at N.Y. Islanders.

Year	Team	League	Games	G.	A.	Pts.	Pen.
1977-78—Oulu Karpat		Finland	30	9	14	23	4
1978-79—Oulu Karpat		Finland	36	14	8	22	47
1979-80—Oulu Karpat (c)		Finland	30	15	13	28	31
1980-81—Oulu Karpat		Finland	36	28	23	51	28
1980-81—Finland Nationals		Finland	....	9	6	15	....
1981-82—New York Rangers		NHL	78	18	38	56	27
1982-83—New York Rangers		NHL	77	16	53	69	22
1983-84—New York Rangers		NHL	74	20	39	59	26
NHL TOTALS			229	54	130	184	75

(c)—June, 1980—Drafted by New York Rangers in NHL entry draft. Fifth Rangers pick, 119th overall, sixth round.

TERRY WALLACE RUSKOWSKI

Center . . . 5'10" . . . 178 lbs. . . . Born, Prince Albert, Sask., December 31, 1954 . . . Shoots left . . . Missed part of 1974-75 season with injured right hand and part of 1975-76 season with broken middle finger on right hand . . . (Summer, 1980)—Surgery to right knee . . . (March, 1981)—Viral infection . . . (December 9, 1981)—Ruptured ligaments in right thumb during fight with Timo Blomqvist of Washington.

Year	Team	League	Games	G.	A.	Pts.	Pen.
1971-72—Swift Current Broncos		WCHL	67	13	38	51	177
1972-73—Swift Current Broncos		WCHL	53	25	64	89	136
1973-74—Swift Current Broncos (c-d)		WCHL	68	40	93	133	243
1974-75—Houston Aeros		WHA	71	10	36	46	134
1975-76—Houston Aeros (e)		WHA	65	14	35	49	100
1976-77—Houston Aeros		WHA	80	24	60	84	146
1977-78—Houston Aeros (f)		WHA	78	15	57	72	170
1978-79—Winnipeg Jets (g-h)		WHA	75	20	66	86	211
1979-80—Chicago Black Hawks		NHL	74	15	55	70	252
1980-81—Chicago Black Hawks		NHL	72	8	51	59	225
1981-82—Chicago Black Hawks		NHL	60	7	30	37	120
1982-83—Chicago Black Hawks (i)		NHL	5	0	2	2	12
1982-83—Los Angeles Kings		NHL	71	14	30	44	127
1983-84—Los Angeles Kings		NHL	77	7	25	32	92
WHA TOTALS			369	83	254	337	761
NHL TOTALS			359	51	193	244	828

(c)—Drafted from Swift Current Broncos by Chicago Black Hawks in third round of 1974 amateur draft.

(d)—Selected by Houston Aeros in WHA amateur draft, May, 1974.

(e)—Led in assists (23) and penalty minutes (64) during playoffs.

(f)—Sold to Winnipeg Jets with Houston Aeros' franchise, July, 1978.

(g)—Led in assists (12) during playoffs.

(h)—June, 1979—Selected by Chicago Black Hawks in NHL reclaim draft.

(i)—October, 1982—Traded by Chicago Black Hawks to Los Angeles Kings for Larry Goodenough and future considerations.

PHILIP DOUGLAS RUSSELL

Defense . . . 6'2" . . . 200 lbs. . . . Born, Edmonton, Alta., July 21, 1952 . . . Shoots left . . . Missed part of 1977-78 season with injured ligaments in left knee . . . (September, 1981)—Injured knee during training camp.

Year	Team	League	Games	G.	A.	Pts.	Pen.
1970-71—Edmonton Oil Kings		WCHL	34	4	16	20	113
1971-72—Edmonton Oil Kings (a-c)		WCHL	64	14	45	59	*331
1972-73—Chicago Black Hawks (d)		NHL	76	6	19	25	156
1973-74—Chicago Black Hawks		NHL	75	10	25	35	184
1974-75—Chicago Black Hawks		NHL	80	5	24	29	260
1975-76—Chicago Black Hawks		NHL	74	9	29	38	194
1976-77—Chicago Black Hawks		NHL	76	9	36	45	233
1977-78—Chicago Black Hawks		NHL	57	6	20	26	139
1978-79—Chicago Black Hawks (e)		NHL	66	8	23	31	122
1978-79—Atlanta Flames		NHL	13	1	6	7	28
1979-80—Atlanta Flames		NHL	80	5	31	36	115
1980-81—Calgary Flames		NHL	80	6	23	29	104
1981-82—Calgary Flames		NHL	71	4	25	29	110
1982-83—Calgary Flames (f)		NHL	78	13	18	31	112
1983-84—New Jersey Devils		NHL	76	9	22	31	96
NHL TOTALS			902	91	301	392	1853

(c)—Drafted from Edmonton Oil Kings by Chicago Black Hawks in first round of 1972 amateur draft.
(d)—Led in penalty minutes (43) during playoffs.
(e)—March, 1979—Traded with Ivan Boldirev and Darcy Rota to Atlanta Flames by Chicago Black Hawks for Tom Lysiak, Harold Phillipoff, Pat Ribble, Greg Fox and Miles Zaharko.
(f)—July, 1983—Traded by Calgary Flames with Mel Bridgman to New Jersey Devils for Steve Tambellini and Joel Quenneville.

TOM RYAN

Defense . . . 5'11" . . . 180 lbs. . . . Born, Boston, Mass., January 12, 1966 . . . Shoots right.

Year	Team	League	Games	G.	A.	Pts.	Pen.
1983-84—Newton North H.S. (c)		Mass.H.S.	..	..	..	..	..

(c)—June, 1984—Drafted by Pittsburgh Penguins in NHL entry draft. Sixth Penguins pick, 127th overall, seventh round.

KEN SABOURIN

Defense . . . 6'4" . . . 200 lbs. . . . Born, Scarborough, Ont., April 28, 1966 . . . Shoots left.

Year	Team	League	Games	G.	A.	Pts.	Pen.
1981-82—Don Mills Midgets		MTHL	40	10	20	30	..
1982-83—Sault Ste. Marie Greyhounds		OHL	58	0	8	8	90
1983-84—Sault Ste. Marie Greyhounds (c)		OHL	63	7	13	20	157

(c)—June, 1984—Drafted as underage junior by Washington Capitals in NHL entry draft. Second Capitals pick, 34th overall, second round.

ROCKY RAY SAGANIUK

Right Wing . . . 5'8" . . . 185 lbs. . . . Born, Myrnam, Alta., October 15, 1957 . . . Shoots right . . . Missed final part of 1977-78 season with cracked vertebrae . . . (January, 1984)—Back injury.

Year	Team	League	Games	G.	A.	Pts.	Pen.
1974-75—Taber Golden Suns		AJHL	50	21	32	53	124
1975-76—Taber Golden Suns		AJHL	49	42	32	74	169
1975-76—Kamloops Chiefs		WCHL	4	0	0	0	0
1975-76—Lethbridge Broncos		WCHL	6	2	1	3	0
1976-77—Lethbridge Broncos (c)		WCHL	72	60	48	108	203
1977-78—Dallas Black Hawks		CHL	42	16	13	29	71
1978-79—Toronto Maple Leafs		NHL	16	3	5	8	9
1978-79—New Brunswick Hawks (a-d)		AHL	61	*47	29	76	91
1979-80—Toronto Maple Leafs		NHL	75	24	23	47	52
1980-81—Toronto Maple Leafs		NHL	71	12	18	30	52
1981-82—Toronto Maple Leafs		NHL	65	17	16	33	49
1982-83—Toronto Maple Leafs		NHL	3	0	0	0	2
1982-83—St. Catharines Saints (e)		AHL	61	26	23	49	83
1983-84—Baltimore Skipjacks		AHL	5	1	1	2	0
1983-84—Pittsburgh Penguins		NHL	29	1	3	4	37
NHL TOTALS			259	57	65	122	201

(c)—Drafted from Lethbridge Broncos by Toronto Maple Leafs in second round of 1977 amateur draft.
(d)—Won Les Cunningham Plaque (AHL MVP).
(e)—August, 1983—Traded by Toronto Maple Leafs with Vince Tremblay to Pittsburgh Penguins for Nick Ricci and Pat Graham.

TOM ST. JAMES

Left Wing . . . 5'11" . . . 175 lbs. . . . Born, Iroquois Falls, Ont., February 18, 1963 . . . Shoots left.

Year	Team	League	Games	G.	A.	Pts.	Pen.
1981-82—Sudbury Wolves		OHL	67	18	25	43	64
1982-83—Kitchener Rangers		OHL	64	32	48	80	35
1983-84—Rochester Americans (c)		AHL	31	6	7	13	8

(c)—March, 1984—Signed by Rochester Americans as a free agent.

ANDRE ST. LAURENT

Center . . . 5'10" . . . 170 lbs. . . . Born, Rouyn Noranda, Que., February 16, 1953 . . . Shoots right . . . Nephew of former NHL defenseman Dollard St. Laurent . . . (October 31, 1980)— Underwent surgery to correct ruptured disc in back . . . (December, 1981)—In traction with swollen disc, same one operated on in October, 1980.

Year	Team	League	Games	G.	A.	Pts.	Pen.
1970-71—Mont. Jr. Canadiens		Jr. "A" OHA	60	13	27	40	127
1971-72—Mont. Jr. Canadiens		Jr. "A" OHA	63	18	34	52	161
1972-73—Mont. Red, White & Blue (c)		QJHL	64	52	48	100	245
1973-74—Fort Worth Wings		CHL	32	14	19	33	53
1973-74—New York Islanders		NHL	42	5	9	14	18
1974-75—New York Islanders		NHL	78	14	27	41	60
1975-76—Fort Worth Texans		CHL	3	1	2	3	2
1975-76—New York Islanders		NHL	67	9	17	26	56
1976-77—New York Islanders		NHL	72	10	13	23	55
1977-78—New York Islanders (d)		NHL	2	0	0	0	2
1977-78—Detroit Red Wings		NHL	77	31	39	70	108
1978-79—Detroit Red Wings (e)		NHL	76	18	31	49	124
1979-80—Los Angeles Kings		NHL	77	6	24	30	88
1980-81—Los Angeles Kings		NHL	22	10	6	16	63
1980-81—Houston Apollos		CHL	3	1	0	1	4
1980-81—Fort Worth Texans		CHL	12	1	14	15	36
1981-82—Los Angeles Kings		NHL	16	2	4	6	28
1981-82—New Haven Nighthawks		AHL	28	7	9	16	58
1981-82—Pittsburgh Penguins (f)		NHL	18	8	5	13	4
1982-83—Pittsburgh Penguins		NHL	70	13	9	22	105
1983-84—Pittsburgh Penguins (g)		NHL	8	2	0	2	21
1983-84—Detroit Red Wings		NHL	19	1	3	4	17
1983-84—Adirondack Red Wings		AHL	50	26	43	69	129
NHL TOTALS			644	129	187	316	749

(c)—Drafted from Montreal Red, White and Blue by New York Islanders in fourth-round of 1973 amateur draft.

(d)—Traded to Detroit Red Wings by New York Islanders for Michel Bergeron, October, 1977.

(e)—August, 1979—Sent to Los Angeles Kings by Detroit Red Wings with first-round draft pick in 1980 (Larry Murphy) and option of a second-round 1980 or first-round 1981 draft choice (Doug Smith) for NHL rights to Dale McCourt.

(f)—February, 1982—Acquired on waivers from Los Angeles Kings.

(g)—October, 1983—Traded by Pittsburgh to Detroit Red Wings for future considerations.

ANDERS BORJE SALMING
(Known by middle name.)

Defense . . . 6'1" . . . 185 lbs. . . . Born, Kiruna, Sweden, April 17, 1951 . . . Shoots left . . . Missed part of 1974-75 season with cracked bone in heel and part of the 1978 playoffs with facial injuries . . . (January, 1980)—Surgery to clear sinus problem . . . (March, 1981)—Separated shoulder . . . (December 2, 1981)—Separated shoulder vs. Hartford . . . (December, 1982)—Charley horse, missed eight games . . . (January 17, 1983)—Cut by skate on knee in game at St. Louis . . . (March 12, 1984)—Broke kneecap in game vs. Winnipeg, out for the season.

Year	Team	League	Games	G.	A.	Pts.	Pen.
1971-72—Swedish National Team			12	0	....	....	....
1972-73—Swedish National Team (c)			23	4	....	....	....
1973-74—Toronto Maple Leafs		NHL	76	5	34	39	48
1974-75—Toronto Maple Leafs (b)		NHL	60	12	25	37	34
1975-76—Toronto Maple Leafs (b-d)		NHL	78	16	41	57	70
1976-77—Toronto Maple Leafs (a-d)		NHL	76	12	66	78	46
1977-78—Toronto Maple Leafs (b)		NHL	80	16	60	76	70
1978-79—Toronto Maple Leafs (b-d)		NHL	78	17	56	73	76
1979-80—Toronto Maple Leafs (b)		NHL	74	19	52	71	96

Year	Team	League	Games	G.	A.	Pts.	Pen.
1980-81—Toronto Maple Leafs		NHL	72	5	61	66	154
1981-82—Toronto Maple Leafs		NHL	69	12	44	56	170
1982-83—Toronto Maple Leafs		NHL	69	7	38	45	104
1983-84—Toronto Maple Leafs		NHL	68	5	38	43	92
NHL TOTALS			800	126	515	641	961

(c)—Selected most valuable player in Sweden.
(d)—Named winner of Viking Award (Top Swedish player in NHL/WHA as selected by poll of Swedish players).

STEVE SALVUCCI

Left Wing ... 5'10" ... 185 lbs. ... Born, Brighton, Mass., September 23, 1959 ... Shoots left.

Year	Team	League	Games	G.	A.	Pts.	Pen.
1979-80—Saginaw Gears		IHL	2	1	1	2	0
1979-80—Johnstown Red Wings		EHL	22	9	10	19	39
1979-80—Hampton Aces		EHL	45	25	31	56	75
1980-81—Hampton Aces (b)		EHL	72	37	40	77	104
1981-82—Saginaw Gears		IHL	67	49	42	91	140
1982-83—Hershey Bears		AHL	73	8	6	14	68
1983-84—Fort Wayne Komets (c)		IHL	77	31	27	58	271

(c)—October, 1983—Signed by Fort Wayne Komets as a free agent.

JOHN SAMANSKI

Center ... 6' ... 185 lbs. ... Born, Oshawa, Ont., June 30, 1962 ... Shoots left ... (1981-82)—Wrist injury and academic difficulties ... (1982-83)—Set Bowling Green State University record with seven game-winning goals.

Year	Team	League	Games	G.	A.	Pts.	Pen.
1979-80—Oshawa Legionnaires		MTJHL	....	45	49	94	....
1980-81—Bowling Green State U.		CCHA	39	17	22	39	12
1981-82—Bowling Green State U.		CCHA	13	5	4	9	19
1982-83—Bowling Green State U.		CCHA	40	27	30	57	48
1983-84—Bowling Green State U.		CCHA	42	25	35	60	52

GARY SAMPSON

Center ... 6' ... 190 lbs. ... Born, Atikokan, Ont., August 24, 1959 ... Shoots left ... Member of 1984 U.S. Olympic Team.

Year	Team	League	Games	G.	A.	Pts.	Pen.
1978-79—Boston College		ECAC	30	10	18	28	4
1979-80—Boston College		ECAC	24	6	8	14	8
1980-81—Boston College		ECAC	31	8	16	24	8
1981-82—Boston College		ECAC	21	7	11	18	22
1982-83—U.S. National Team		Int'l	40	11	20	31	8
1983-84—U.S. National Team		Int'l	56	21	18	39	10
1983-84—U.S. Olympic Team		Int'l	6	1	3	4	2
1983-84—Washington Capitals (c)		NHL	15	1	1	2	6
NHL TOTALS			15	1	1	2	6

(c)—February, 1984—Signed by Washington Capitals as a free agent.

ULF SAMUELSON

Defense ... 6'1" ... 195 lbs. ... Born, Leksand, Sweden, March 26, 1964 ... Shoots left.

Year	Team	League	Games	G.	A.	Pts.	Pen.
1983-84—Leksands (c)		Sweden	36	5	10	15	53

(c)—June, 1982—Drafted by Hartford Whalers in NHL entry draft. Fourth Whalers pick, 67th overall, fourth round.

SCOTT SANDELIN

Defense ... 6' ... 190 lbs. ... Born, Hibbing, Minn., August 8, 1964 ... Shoots right.

Year	Team	League	Games	G.	A.	Pts.	Pen.
1981-82—Hibbing High School (c)		Minn. H.S.	20	5	15	20	30
1982-83—Univ. of North Dakota		WCHA	30	1	6	7	10
1983-84—Univ. of North Dakota		WCHA	41	4	23	27	24

(c)—June, 1982—Drafted as underage player by Montreal Canadiens in 1982 NHL entry draft. Fifth Canadiens pick, 40th overall, second round.

TOMAS SANDSTROM

Right Wing ... 6'2" ... 200 lbs. ... Born, Fagersta, Sweden, September 4, 1964 ... Shoots right.

Year	Team	League	Games	G.	A.	Pts.	Pen.
1983-84—Brynas (c)		Sweden	....	20	10	30	....

(c)—June, 1982—Drafted by New York Rangers in NHL entry draft. Second Rangers pick, 36th overall, second round.

GRANT SASSER

Center . . . 5'10" . . . 175 lbs. . . . Born, Portland, Ore., February 13, 1964 . . . Shoots right . . . (December, 1981)—Injured knee ligaments.

Year	Team	League	Games	G.	A.	Pts.	Pen.
1980-81—Fort Saskatchewan Traders		SJHL	54	33	49	82	49
1981-82—Portland Winter Hawks (c)		WHL	49	19	23	42	32
1982-83—Portland Winter Hawks		WHL	70	54	65	119	39
1983-84—Portland Winter Hawks (b)		WHL	66	44	69	113	24
1983-84—Pittsburgh Penguins		NHL	3	0	0	0	0
NHL TOTALS			3	0	0	0	0

(c)—June, 1982—Drafted as underage junior by Pittsburgh Penguins in 1982 NHL entry draft. Fourth Penguins pick, 94th overall, fifth round.

DAVID SAUNDERS

Left Wing . . . 6'1" . . . 195 lbs. . . . Born, Ottawa, Ont., May 20, 1966 . . . Shoots left.

Year	Team	League	Games	G.	A.	Pts.	Pen.
1983-84—St. Lawrence Univ. (c)		CCHA	32	10	21	31	26

(c)—June, 1984—Drafted by Vancouver Canucks in NHL entry draft. Third Canucks pick, 52nd overall, third round.

JEAN FRANCOIS SAUVE

Center . . . 5'6" . . . 175 lbs. . . . Born, Ste. Genevieve, Que., January 23, 1960 . . . Shoots left . . . Brother of Bob Sauve . . . (December, 1980)—Knee injury.

Year	Team	League	Games	G.	A.	Pts.	Pen.
1977-78—Trois-Rivieres Draveurs		QMJHL	6	2	3	5	0
1978-79—Trois-Rivieres Draveurs (b-c-d-e)		QMJHL	72	65	111	*176	31
1979-80—Trois-Rivieres Draveurs (a-c-d)		QMJHL	72	63	*124	*187	31
1980-81—Rochester Americans (b)		AHL	56	29	54	83	21
1980-81—Buffalo Sabres		NHL	20	5	9	14	12
1981-82—Rochester Americans		AHL	7	5	8	13	4
1981-82—Buffalo Sabres		NHL	69	19	36	55	46
1982-83—Buffalo Sabres		NHL	9	0	4	4	9
1982-83—Rochester Americans (f-g)		AHL	73	30	69	99	10
1983-84—Fredericton Express		AHL	26	19	31	50	23
1983-84—Quebec Nordiques		NHL	39	10	17	27	2
NHL TOTALS			137	34	66	100	69

(c)—Won Frank Selke Trophy (QMJHL Most Gentlemanly Player).
(d)—Won Jean Beliveau Trophy (Leading QMJHL scorer).
(e)—Won Guy Lafleur Trophy (QMJHL playoff MVP).
(f)—June, 1983—Traded by Buffalo Sabres with Tony McKegney, Andre Savard and Buffalo's third-round draft choice in 1983 (Ilro Jarvi) to Quebec Nordiques for Real Cloutier and Quebec's first-round draft choice in 1983 (Adam Creighton).
(g)—Led AHL playoffs with 21 assists and 28 points.

MIKE SAVAGE

Left Wing . . . 6' . . . 191 lbs. . . . Born, St. Catharines, Ont., April 8, 1964 . . . Shoots left.

Year	Team	League	Games	G.	A.	Pts.	Pen.
1980-81—Nickel Centre		OPJHL	25	16	15	31	61
1981-82—Sudbury Wolves (c)		OHL	64	5	7	12	21
1982-83—Sudbury Wolves		OHL	22	6	4	10	38
1983-84—Sudbury Wolves		OHL	11	1	2	3	10
1983-84—Belleville Bulls		OHL	57	32	28	60	45

(c)—June, 1982—Drafted as underage junior by Winnipeg Jets in 1982 NHL entry draft. Eighth Jets pick, 201st overall, 10th round.

ANDRE SAVARD

Center . . . 6'1" . . . 184 lbs. . . . Born, Temiscamingue, Que., September 2, 1953 . . . Shoots left . . . Missed part of 1971-72 season with knee injury requiring two operations during summer of 1972 . . . (January 19, 1984)—Injured neck in game at Boston.

Year	Team	League	Games	G.	A.	Pts.	Pen.
1969-70—Quebec Remparts		QJHL	56	23	60	83	126
1970-71—Quebec Remparts		QJHL	61	50	89	139	150

Year	Team	League	Games	G.	A.	Pts.	Pen.
1971-72—Quebec Remparts		QJHL	33	32	46	78	107
1972-73—Quebec Remparts (a-c)		QJHL	56	67	84	*151	147
1973-74—Boston Bruins		NHL	72	16	14	30	39
1974-75—Boston Bruins		NHL	77	19	25	44	45
1975-76—Boston Bruins (d)		NHL	79	17	23	40	60
1976-77—Buffalo Sabres		NHL	80	25	35	60	30
1977-78—Buffalo Sabres		NHL	80	19	20	39	40
1978-79—Buffalo Sabres		NHL	65	18	22	40	20
1979-80—Rochester Americans		AHL	25	11	17	28	4
1979-80—Buffalo Sabres		NHL	33	3	10	13	16
1980-81—Buffalo Sabres		NHL	79	31	43	74	63
1981-82—Buffalo Sabres		NHL	62	18	20	38	24
1982-83—Buffalo Sabres (e)		NHL	68	16	25	41	28
1983-84—Quebec Nordiques		NHL	60	20	24	44	38
NHL TOTALS			755	202	261	463	403

(c)—Drafted from Quebec Remparts by Boston Bruins in first round of 1973 amateur draft.

(d)—NHL rights traded to Buffalo Sabres by Boston Bruins for NHL rights to Peter McNab, June, 1976.

(e)—June, 1983—Traded by Buffalo Sabres with Tony McKegney, Jean Francois Sauve and Buffalo's third-round draft choice in 1983 (Ilro Jarvi) to Quebec Nordiques for Real Cloutier and Quebec's first-round draft choice in 1983 (Adam Creighton).

DENIS SAVARD

Center . . . 5'9" . . . 157 lbs. . . . Born, Pointe Gatineau, Que., February 4, 1961 . . . Shoots right . . . Cousin of Jean Savard . . . Set Chicago rookie record with 75 points in 1980-81 (broken by Steve Larmer) . . . (October 15, 1980)—Strained knee vs. Vancouver . . . Set Chicago records for assists (87) and points (119) in one season in 1981-82 . . . Broke his own points record in 1982-83 . . . (January 7, 1984)—Broke nose in game at N.Y. Islanders.

Year	Team	League	Games	G.	A.	Pts.	Pen.
1977-78—Montreal Juniors		QMJHL	72	37	79	116	22
1978-79—Montreal Juniors		QMJHL	70	46	*112	158	88
1979-80—Montreal Juniors (a-c-d)		QMJHL	72	63	118	181	93
1980-81—Chicago Black Hawks		NHL	76	28	47	75	47
1981-82—Chicago Black Hawks		NHL	80	32	87	119	82
1982-83—Chicago Black Hawks (b)		NHL	78	35	86	121	99
1983-84—Chicago Black Hawks		NHL	75	37	57	94	71
NHL TOTALS			309	132	277	409	299

(c)—Won Michel Briere Trophy (QMJHL MVP).

(d)—June, 1980—Drafted as underage junior by Chicago Black Hawks in 1980 NHL entry draft. First Black Hawks pick, third overall, first round.

PETER SAWKINS

Defense . . . 6'3" . . . 190 lbs. . . . Born, Skagen, Denmark, August 29, 1963 . . . Shoots right.

Year	Team	League	Games	G.	A.	Pts.	Pen.
1980-81—St. Paul Academy (c)		Minn. H.S.	23	6	27	33	0
1981-82—Yale University		ECAC	24	0	5	5	20
1982-83—Yale University		ECAC	26	2	8	10	10
1983-84—Yale University		ECAC	25	2	14	16	24

(c)—June, 1981—Drafted as underage player by Los Angeles Kings in 1981 NHL entry draft. Sixth Kings pick, 144th overall, seventh round.

DARIN SCEVIOUR

Right Wing . . . 5'10" . . . 185 lbs. . . . Born, Lacombe, Alta., November 30, 1965 . . . Shoots right.

Year	Team	League	Games	G.	A.	Pts.	Pen.
1981-82—Red Deer		Alb. Midget	64	55	67	122	87
1982-83—Lethbridge Broncos		WHL	64	9	17	26	45
1983-84—Lethbridge Broncos (c)		WHL	71	37	28	65	28

(c)—June, 1984—Drafted as underage junior by Chicago Black Hawks in NHL entry draft. Fifth Black Hawks pick, 101st overall, fifth round.

KEVIN DEAN SCHAMEHORN

Right Wing . . . 5'10" . . . 185 lbs. . . . Born, Calgary, Alta., July 28, 1956 . . . Shoots right.

Year	Team	League	Games	G.	A.	Pts.	Pen.
1973-74—Bellingham Blazers		Jr. "A" BCHL	58	17	8	25	293
1973-74—New Westminster Bruins		WCHL	2	1	1	2	7
1974-75—New Westminster Bruins		WCHL	37	14	6	20	175
1975-76—New Westminster Bruins (c)		WCHL	62	32	42	74	276

Year	Team	League	Games	G.	A.	Pts.	Pen.
1976-77—Kalamazoo Wings	IHL	77	27	31	58	314
1976-77—Detroit Red Wings	NHL	3	0	0	0	9
1977-78—Kansas City Red Wings	CHL	36	5	3	8	113
1977-78—Kalamazoo Wings	IHL	39	18	14	32	144
1978-79—Kalamazoo Wings	IHL	80	45	57	102	245
1979-80—Detroit Red Wings	NHL	2	0	0	0	4
1979-80—Adirondack Red Wings (d)	AHL	60	10	13	23	145
1980-81—Los Angeles Kings	NHL	5	0	0	0	4
1980-81—Houston Apollos	CHL	26	7	9	16	43
1980-81—Rochester Americans	AHL	27	6	10	16	44
1981-82—Kalamazoo Wings	IHL	75	38	27	65	113
1982-83—Kalamazoo Wings	IHL	58	38	29	67	78
1983-84—Kalamazoo Wings	IHL	76	37	31	68	154
NHL TOTALS		10	0	0	0	17

(c)—Drafted from New Westminster Bruins by Detroit Red Wings in fourth round of 1976 amateur draft.
(d)—September, 1980—Signed by Los Angeles Kings as a free agent.

ANDREAS (ANDY) SCHLIEBENER

Defense . . . 6' . . . 190 lbs. . . . Born, Ottawa, Ont., August 16, 1962 . . . Shoots left.

Year	Team	League	Games	G.	A.	Pts.	Pen.
1979-80—Peterborough Petes (c)	OMJHL	68	8	20	28	47
1980-81—Peterborough Petes	OHL	68	9	48	57	144
1981-82—Peterborough Petes (d)	OHL	14	1	9	10	25
1981-82—Niagara Falls Flyers	OHL	27	6	26	32	33
1981-82—Dallas Black Hawks	CHL	8	2	2	4	4
1981-82—Vancouver Canucks	NHL	22	0	1	1	10
1982-83—Fredericton Express	AHL	76	4	15	19	20
1983-84—Fredericton Express	AHL	27	1	6	7	27
1983-84—Vancouver Canucks	NHL	51	2	10	12	48
NHL TOTALS		73	2	11	13	58

(c)—June, 1980—Drafted by Vancouver Canucks as underage junior in 1980 NHL entry draft. Second Canucks pick, 49th overall, third round.
(d)—November, 1981—Traded with John Andrews by Peterborough Petes to London Knights for Venci Sebek and Scott McClellan.

NORM SCHMIDT

Defense . . . 5'11" . . . 190 lbs. . . . Born, Sault Ste. Marie, Ont., January 24, 1963 . . . Shoots right.

Year	Team	League	Games	G.	A.	Pts.	Pen.
1979-80—Sault Ste. Marie Thunderbirds	OPJHL	18	8	16	24	....
1980-81—Oshawa Generals (c)	OMJHL	65	12	25	37	73
1981-82—Oshawa Generals	OHL	67	13	48	61	172
1982-83—Oshawa Generals (b)	OHL	61	21	49	70	114
1983-84—Pittsburgh Penguins	NHL	34	6	12	18	12
1983-84—Baltimore Skipjacks	AHL	43	4	12	16	31
NHL TOTALS		34	6	12	18	12

(c)—June, 1981—Drafted as underage junior by Pittsburgh Penguins in 1981 NHL entry draft. Third Penguins pick, 70th overall, fourth round.

SCOTT SCHNEIDER

Center . . . 6'1" . . . 174 lbs. . . . Born, Rochester, Minn., May 18, 1965 . . . Shoots right.

Year	Team	League	Games	G.	A.	Pts.	Pen.
1983-84—Colorado College (c)	WCHA	35	19	14	33	24

(c)—June, 1984—Drafted by Winnipeg Jets in NHL entry draft. Fourth Jets pick, 93rd overall, fifth round.

JAMES GRANT SCHOENFELD

Defense . . . 6'2" . . . 208 lbs. . . . Born, Galt, Ont., September 4, 1952 . . . Shoots left . . . Missed part of 1972-73 season with damaged nerve in leg and had corrective surgery following season . . . Missed most of 1973-74 season with ruptured spinal disc requiring surgery and part of 1974-75 season with broken left foot . . . Missed part of 1975-76 season with mononucleosis, part of 1976-77 season with viral pneumonia and part of 1977-78 season with broken right foot . . . Missed part of 1978-79 season with shoulder separation

and strained knee . . . (December, 1980)—Missed nine games with flu and a hand injury . . . (September, 1981)—Broke little finger on left hand vs. Montreal in preseason game . . . (October 18, 1981)—Broke metatarsal bone in right foot blocking a shot vs. Montreal . . . (October, 1982)—Separated ribs . . . (November 11, 1983)—Fractured and separated left shoulder, requiring surgery . . . (February 27, 1984)—Injured shoulder.

Year	Team	League	Games	G.	A.	Pts.	Pen.
1969-70—London Knights (c)	Jr."A" OHA	16	1	4	5	81
1969-70—Hamilton Red Wings	Jr."A" OHA	32	2	12	14	54
1970-71—Hamilton Red Wings (d)	Jr."A" OHA	25	3	19	22	120
1970-71—Niagara Falls Flyers	Jr."A" OHA	30	3	9	12	85
1971-72—Niagara Falls Flyers (b-e-f)	Jr."A" OHA	40	6	46	52	*225
1972-73—Buffalo Sabres	NHL	66	4	15	19	178
1973-74—Cincinnati Swords	AHL	2	0	2	2	4
1973-74—Buffalo Sabres	NHL	28	1	8	9	56
1974-75—Buffalo Sabres	NHL	68	1	19	20	184
1975-76—Buffalo Sabres	NHL	56	2	22	24	114
1976-77—Buffalo Sabres	NHL	65	7	25	32	97
1977-78—Buffalo Sabres	NHL	60	2	20	22	89
1978-79—Buffalo Sabres	NHL	46	8	17	25	67
1979-80—Buffalo Sabres (b)	NHL	77	9	27	36	72
1980-81—Buffalo Sabres	NHL	71	8	25	33	110
1981-82—Buffalo Sabres (g)	NHL	13	3	2	5	30
1981-82—Detroit Red Wings	NHL	39	5	9	14	69
1982-83—Detroit Red Wings (h-i)	NHL	57	1	10	11	18
1983-84—Boston Bruins	NHL	39	0	2	2	20
NHL TOTALS		685	51	201	252	1104

(c)—Traded to Hamilton Red Wings by London Knights with Ken Southwick and Rick Kehoe for Gary Geldart, Gordon Brooks, Dave Gilmour and Mike Craig, December, 1969.

(d)—Traded to Niagara Falls Flyers by Hamilton Red Wings for Russ Friesen and Mike Healey, January, 1971.

(e)—Selected by New York Raiders in WHA player selection draft, February, 1972.

(f)—Drafted from Niagara Falls Flyers by Buffalo Sabres in first round of 1972 amateur draft.

(g)—December, 1981—Traded with Danny Gare, Bob Sauve and Derek Smith by Buffalo Sabres to Detroit Red Wings for Dale McCourt, Mike Foligno, Brent Peterson and future considerations.

(h)—June, 1983—Released by Detroit Red Wings.

(i)—August, 1983—Signed by Boston Bruins as a free agent.

DWIGHT SCHOFIELD

Defense . . . 6' . . . 187 lbs. . . . Born, Lynn, Mass., March 25, 1956 . . . Shoots left . . . Missed part of 1977-78 season following knee surgery.

Year	Team	League	Games	G.	A.	Pts.	Pen.
1974-75—London Knights	Jr."A" OHA	70	6	16	22	124
1975-76—London Knights (c)	Jr."A" OHA	59	14	29	43	121
1976-77—Kalamazoo Wings	IHL	73	20	41	61	180
1976-77—Detroit Red Wings	NHL	3	1	0	1	2
1977-78—Kansas City Red Wings	CHL	22	3	7	10	58
1977-78—Kalamazoo Wings	IHL	3	3	6	9	21
1978-79—Kansas City Red Wings	CHL	13	1	4	5	20
1978-79—Kalamazoo Wings	IHL	47	8	29	37	199
1978-79—Fort Wayne Komets	IHL	14	2	3	5	54
1979-80—Tulsa Oilers	CHL	1	0	0	0	0
1979-80—Dayton Gems	IHL	71	15	47	62	257
1980-81—Milwaukee Admirals	IHL	82	18	41	59	327
1981-82—Nova Scotia Voyageurs (d)	AHL	75	7	24	31	*335
1982-83—Montreal Canadiens	NHL	2	0	0	0	7
1982-83—Nova Scotia Voyageurs	AHL	73	10	21	31	248
1983-84—St. Louis Blues (e)	NHL	70	4	10	14	219
NHL TOTALS		75	5	10	15	228

(c)—Drafted from London Knights by Detroit Red Wings in fifth round of 1976 amateur draft.

(d)—September, 1981—Signed by Montreal Canadiens as a free agent.

(e)—October, 1983—Selected by St. Louis Blues in NHL waiver draft.

WALLY SCHREIBER

Left Wing . . . 5'11" . . . 175 lbs. . . . Born, Edmonton, Alta., April 15, 1962 . . . Shoots right.

Year	Team	League	Games	G.	A.	Pts.	Pen.
1980-81—Fort Saskatchewan Traders	SJHL	55	39	41	80	105
1981-82—Regina Pats (c-d)	WHL	68	56	68	124	68
1982-83—Fort Wayne Komets	IHL	67	24	34	58	23
1983-84—Fort Wayne Komets (a-e)	IHL	82	47	66	*113	44

(d)—June, 1982—Drafted as underage junior by Washington Capitals in 1982 NHL entry draft. Fifth
Capitals pick, 152nd overall, eighth round.

(e)—Won Leo P. Lamoureux Trophy (Leading IHL scorer).

RODNEY SCHUTT
Left Wing . . . 5'9" . . . 187 lbs. . . . Born, Bancroft, Ont., October 13, 1956 . . . Shoots left.

Year	Team	League	Games	G.	A.	Pts.	Pen.
1972-73	Pembroke Lumber Kings	CJHL	55	31	55	86	61
1973-74	Sudbury Wolves	Jr."A" OHA	67	15	41	56	47
1974-75	Sudbury Wolves (a)	Jr."A" OHA	69	43	61	104	66
1975-76	Sudbury Wolves (a-c)	Jr."A" OHA	63	72	63	135	42
1976-77	Nova Scotia Voyageurs (d-e)	AHL	80	33	51	84	56
1977-78	Nova Scotia Voyageurs	AHL	77	36	44	80	57
1977-78	Montreal Canadiens	NHL	2	0	0	0	0
1978-79	Pittsburgh Penguins (f)	NHL	74	24	21	45	33
1979-80	Pittsburgh Penguins	NHL	73	18	21	39	43
1980-81	Pittsburgh Penguins	NHL	80	25	35	60	55
1981-82	Erie Blades	AHL	35	12	15	27	40
1981-82	Pittsburgh Penguins	NHL	35	8	12	20	42
1982-83	Pittsburgh Penguins	NHL	5	0	0	0	0
1982-83	Baltimore Skipjacks	AHL	64	34	53	87	24
1983-84	Baltimore Skipjacks	AHL	36	15	19	34	48
1983-84	Pittsburgh Penguins	NHL	11	1	3	4	4
	NHL TOTALS		280	76	92	168	177

(c)—Drafted from Sudbury Wolves by Montreal Canadiens in first round of 1976 amateur draft.

(d)—Won Dudley (Red) Garrett Memorial Trophy (Rookie-of-the-Year).

(e)—Tied for lead in goals (8) during playoffs.

(f)—October, 1978—Traded by Montreal Canadiens to Pittsburgh Penguins for a first-round draft
choice in 1981 (Mark Hunter).

HOWARD SCRUTON
Defense . . . 6'3" . . . 190 lbs. . . . Born, Toronto, Ont., October 6, 1962 . . . Shoots left.

Year	Team	League	Games	G.	A.	Pts.	Pen.
1979-80	Niagara Falls Flyers	OMJHL	51	1	3	4	76
1980-81	Niagara Falls Flyers	OMJHL	28	5	9	14	56
1980-81	Kingston Canadians	OMJHL	25	0	10	10	23
1981-82	Kingston Canadians	OHL	56	6	29	35	80
1981-82	New Haven Nighthawks (c)	AHL	1	1	0	1	0
1982-83	Los Angeles Kings	NHL	4	0	4	4	9
1982-83	New Haven Nighthawks	AHL	74	6	7	13	40
1983-84	New Haven Nighthawks	AHL	33	1	4	5	21
	NHL TOTALS		4	0	4	4	9

(c)—August, 1981—Signed by Los Angeles Kings as a free agent.

BARRY SCULLY
Right Wing . . . 5'10" . . . 200 lbs. . . . Born, Toronto, Ont., April 22, 1956 . . . Shoots right.

Year	Team	League	Games	G.	A.	Pts.	Pen.
1973-74	Kingston Canadians	Jr."A" OHA	69	15	27	42	87
1974-75	Kingston Canadians	Jr."A" OHA	67	23	34	57	74
1975-76	Kingston Canadians (c)	Jr."A" OHA	63	25	51	76	65
1976-77	Richmond Wildcats	SHL	38	18	26	44	51
1976-77	Johnstown Jets	NAHL	32	8	8	16	18
1976-77	New Haven Nighthawks	AHL	4	1	1	2	0
1977-78	Toledo Goaldiggers	IHL	75	42	38	80	76
1978-79	Toledo Goaldiggers (d)	IHL	18	9	6	15	8
1978-79	Fort Wayne Komets	IHL	61	33	24	57	24
1979-80	Fort Wayne Komets (b-e)	IHL	80	*61	47	108	22
1980-81	Fort Wayne Komets (a)	IHL	82	*69	39	108	40
1981-82	Fort Wayne Komets (b)	IHL	79	*60	40	100	40
1982-83	Fort Wayne Komets	IHL	76	57	44	101	22
1983-84	Fort Wayne Komets	IHL	18	8	7	15	8
1983-84	Muskegon Mohawks (f)	IHL	19	11	6	17	2
1983-84	Milwaukee Admirals (g)	IHL	4	2	1	3	0

(c)—Drafted from Kingston Canadians by New York Rangers in sixth round of 1976 amateur draft.

(d)—December, 1978—Traded by Toledo Goaldiggers to Fort Wayne Komets to complete deal made
earlier to obtain IHL rights to Mike Dibble and Barry Marcheschuk.

(e)—Led IHL with 13 playoff goals.

(f)—January, 1984—Acquired on waivers from Fort Wayne Komets by Muskegon Mohawks.

(g)—March, 1984—Acquired on waivers from Muskegon Mohawks by Milwaukee Admirals.

BOB SCURFIELD

Center . . . 6'1" . . . 190 lbs. . . . Born, North Vancouver, B.C., November 2, 1960 . . . Shoots left.

Year	Team	League	Games	G.	A.	Pts.	Pen.
1979-80—Western Michigan Univ.		CCHA	36	34	22	56	38
1980-81—Western Michigan Univ.		CCHA	28	21	27	48	20
1981-82—Western Michigan Univ.		CCHA	32	18	32	50	26
1982-83—Tulsa Oilers (c)		CHL	64	13	22	35	29
1983-84—Tulsa Oilers		CHL	60	18	15	33	14

(c)—September, 1982—Signed by New York Rangers as a free agent.

VENCI SEBEK

Defense . . . 5'11" . . . 185 lbs. . . . Born, New York, N.Y., May 25, 1963 . . . Shoots right.

Year	Team	League	Games	G.	A.	Pts.	Pen.
1979-80—Brantford Alexanders		OHL	61	8	21	29	104
1980-81—Brantford Alexanders (c)		OHL	61	12	16	28	118
1981-82—Niagara Falls Flyers (d)		OHL	16	1	8	9	54
1981-82—Peterborough Petes		OHL	48	22	34	56	123
1981-82—Rochester Americans		AHL	3	0	0	0	2
1982-83—Peterborough Petes		OHL	60	13	44	57	88
1982-83—Rochester Americans (e)		AHL	..	..	..	..	..
1983-84—Rochester Americans		AHL	41	2	5	7	27

(c)—June, 1981—Drafted as underage junior by Buffalo Sabres in 1979 entry draft. Eleventh Sabres pick, 185th overall, ninth round.

(d)—October, 1980—Traded by Niagara Falls Flyers to Peterborough Petes for Daryl Evans.

(e)—No regular season record. Played in nine playoff games.

ALAN WILLIAM SECORD

Left Wing . . . 6'1" . . . 210 lbs. . . . Born, Sudbury, Ont., March 3, 1958 . . . Shoots left . . . Has also played Defense . . . (October, 1980)—Bruised right knee . . . (March, 1981)—Ankle injury . . . (April, 1983)—Suspended for one game in playoffs for abusive language to an official . . . (October, 1983)—Tore abdominal muscles.

Year	Team	League	Games	G.	A.	Pts.	Pen.
1974-75—Wexford Raiders		OPJHL	41	5	13	18	104
1975-76—Hamilton Fincups		Jr."A" OHA	63	9	13	22	117
1976-77—St. Catharines Fincups		Jr."A" OHA	57	32	34	66	343
1977-78—Hamilton Fincups (c)		Jr."A" OHA	59	28	22	50	185
1978-79—Rochester Americans		AHL	4	4	2	6	40
1978-79—Boston Bruins		NHL	71	16	7	23	125
1979-80—Boston Bruins		NHL	77	23	16	39	170
1980-81—Springfield Indians		AHL	8	3	5	8	21
1980-81—Boston Bruins (d)		NHL	18	0	3	3	42
1980-81—Chicago Black Hawks		NHL	41	13	9	22	145
1981-82—Chicago Black Hawks		NHL	80	44	31	75	303
1982-83—Chicago Black Hawks		NHL	80	54	32	86	180
1983-84—Chicago Black Hawks		NHL	14	4	4	8	77
NHL TOTALS			381	154	102	256	1042

(c)—Drafted from Hamilton Fincups by Boston Bruins in first round of 1978 amateur draft.

(d)—December, 1980—Traded by Boston Bruins to Chicago Black Hawks for Mike O'Connell.

STEVE SEGUIN

Right Wing . . . 6'1" . . . 191 lbs. . . . Born, Cornwall, Ont., April 10, 1964 . . . Shoots left.

Year	Team	League	Games	G.	A.	Pts.	Pen.
1979-80—Cornwall Major Midgets		Ont. Midgets	55	61	48	109	....
1980-81—Kingston Canadians		OMJHL	49	8	8	16	18
1981-82—Kingston Canadians (c)		OHL	62	23	31	54	75
1982-83—Kingston Canadians		OHL	19	8	17	25	42
1982-83—Peterborough Petes		OHL	44	16	30	46	22
1983-84—Peterborough Petes		OHL	67	55	51	106	84

(c)—June, 1982—Drafted as underage junior by Los Angeles Kings in 1982 NHL entry draft. Second Kings pick, 46th overall, third round.

MIKE SEIDE

Defense . . . 6'3" . . . 210 lbs. . . . Born, Minneapolis, Minn., October 24, 1958 . . . Shoots left.

Year	Team	League	Games	G.	A.	Pts.	Pen.
1980-81—Baltimore Clippers		EHL	71	14	19	33	266
1980-81—Oklahoma City Stars		CHL	1	0	0	0	2

Year	Team	League	Games	G.	A.	Pts.	Pen.
1981-82—Toledo Goaldiggers		IHL	67	21	27	48	214
1982-83—Tulsa Oilers		CHL	76	7	19	26	*337
1983-84—Montana Magic		CHL	61	4	12	16	99

RICHARD JAMES (RIC) SEILING

Right Wing . . . 6'1" . . . 180 lbs. . . . Born, Elmira, Ont., December 15, 1957 . . . Shoots right . . . Brother of Rod and Don Seiling . . . (January 30, 1982)—Injured eye when hit by stick in game vs. Calgary.

Year	Team	League	Games	G.	A.	Pts.	Pen.
1974-75—Hamilton Red Wings		Jr.''A''OHA	68	33	30	63	74
1975-76—Hamilton Fincups		Jr.''A''OHA	59	35	51	86	49
1976-77—St. Catharines Fincups (c)		Jr.''A''OHA	62	49	61	110	103
1977-78—Buffalo Sabres		NHL	80	19	19	38	33
1978-79—Buffalo Sabres		NHL	78	20	22	42	56
1979-80—Buffalo Sabres		NHL	80	25	35	60	54
1980-81—Buffalo Sabres		NHL	74	30	27	57	80
1981-82—Buffalo Sabres		NHL	57	22	25	47	58
1982-83—Buffalo Sabres		NHL	75	19	22	41	41
1983-84—Buffalo Sabres		NHL	78	13	22	35	42
NHL TOTALS			522	148	172	320	364

(c)—Drafted from St. Catharines Fincups by Buffalo Sabres in first round of 1977 amateur draft.

DAVID SEMENKO

Left Wing . . . 6'3" . . . 215 lbs. . . . Born, Winnipeg, Man., July 12, 1957 . . . Shoots left . . . (May 20, 1979)—Scored final WHA goal, sixth game of playoff series vs. Winnipeg Jets (Gary Smith in goal) . . . (January 4, 1984)—Sprained left knee in game vs. Minnesota.

Year	Team	League	Games	G.	A.	Pts.	Pen.
1974-75—Brandon Travellers		MJHI	42	11	17	28	55
1974-75—Brandon Wheat Kings		WCHL	12	2	1	3	12
1975-76—Brandon Wheat Kings		WCHL	72	8	5	13	194
1976-77—Brandon Wheat Kings (c-d)		WCHL	61	27	33	60	265
1977-78—Brandon Wheat Kings		WCHL	7	10	5	15	40
1977-78—Edmonton Oilers (e)		WHA	65	6	6	12	140
1978-79—Edmonton Oilers (f-g)		WHA	77	10	14	24	158
1979-80—Edmonton Oilers		NHL	67	6	7	13	135
1980-81—Edmonton Oilers		NHL	58	11	8	19	80
1980-81—Wichita Wind		CHL	14	1	2	3	40
1981-82—Edmonton Oilers		NHL	59	12	12	24	194
1982-83—Edmonton Oilers		NHL	75	12	15	27	141
1983-84—Edmonton Oilers		NHL	52	6	11	17	118
WHA TOTALS			142	16	20	36	298
NHL TOTALS			311	47	53	100	668

(c)—Drafted from Brandon Wheat Kings by Minnesota North Stars in second round of 1977 amateur draft.

(d)—Selected by Houston Aeros in World Hockey Association amateur players' draft, June, 1977.

(e)—Signed by Edmonton Oilers (WHA), November, 1978.

(f)—June, 1979—Selected by Minnesota North Stars in NHL reclaim draft.

(g)—August, 1979—Traded by Minnesota North Stars to Edmonton Oilers for a draft choice.

JYRKI SEPPA

Defense . . . 6'1" . . . 189 lbs. . . . Born, Tampere, Finland, November 14, 1961 . . . Shoots left.

Year	Team	League	Games	G.	A.	Pts.	Pen.
1980-81—Ilves, Tampere (c)		Sweden	....	3	4	7	....
1981-82—Ilves, Tampere		Sweden	....	...	....	....	....
1982-83—Sherbrooke Jets		AHL	72	2	13	15	66
1983-84—Winnipeg Jets		NHL	13	0	2	2	6
1983-84—Sherbrooke Jets		AHL	60	5	35	40	43
NHL TOTALS			13	0	2	2	6

(c)—June, 1981—Drafted by Winnipeg Jets in 1981 NHL entry draft. Third Jets pick, 43rd overall, third round.

GEORGE SERVINIS

Left Wing . . . 5'11" . . . 180 lbs. . . . Born, Toronto, Ont., April 29, 1962 . . . Shoots left.

Year	Team	League	Games	G.	A.	Pts.	Pen.
1980-81—Wexford Raiders		MTJBHL	40	35	45	80	....
1981-82—Aurora Tigers		OJHL	55	62	55	117	....
1982-83—R.P.I. (c)		ECAC	28	35	29	64	22

Year	Team	League	Games	G.	A.	Pts.	Pen.
1983-84—Canadian National Team		Int'l	43	13	11	24	33
1983-84—R.P.I.		ECAC	12	5	13	18	14

(c)—Named ECAC Top Rookie.

BRENT SEVERYN

Defense . . . 6'2" . . . 185 lbs. . . . Born, Vegreville, Alta., February 22, 1966 . . . Shoots left.

Year	Team	League	Games	G.	A.	Pts.	Pen.
1982-83—Vegreville Rangers		CAJHL	21	20	22	42	10
1983-84—Seattle Breakers (c)		WHL	72	14	22	36	49

(c)—June, 1984—Drafted as underage junior by Winnipeg Jets in NHL entry draft. Fifth Jets pick, 99th overall, fifth round.

DAVID ALISTAIR SHAND

Defense . . . 6'2" . . . 200 lbs. . . . Born, Cold Lake, Alta., August 11, 1956 . . . Shoots right . . . Attended University of Michigan . . . Missed part of 1976-77 season with mononucleosis.

Year	Team	League	Games	G.	A.	Pts.	Pen.
1973-74—University of Michigan		WCHA	34	2	8	10	50
1974-75—University of Michigan		WCHA	10	0	4	4	20
1974-75—Peterborough TPTs		Jr."A"OHA	33	4	11	15	30
1975-76—Peterborough TPTs (a-c)		Jr."A"OHA	62	9	37	46	169
1976-77—Nova Scotia Voyageurs		AHL	9	0	5	5	21
1976-77—Atlanta Flames		NHL	55	5	11	16	62
1977-78—Atlanta Flames		NHL	80	2	23	25	94
1978-79—Atlanta Flames		NHL	79	4	22	26	64
1979-80—Atlanta Flames (d)		NHL	74	3	7	10	104
1980-81—Toronto Maple Leafs		NHL	47	0	4	4	60
1980-81—New Brunswick Hawks		AHL	2	0	0	0	2
1981-82—Cincinnati Tigers (b)		CHL	76	8	37	45	206
1982-83—Toronto Maple Leafs		NHL	1	0	1	1	2
1982-83—St. Catharines Saints		AHL	69	9	32	41	154
1983-84—Hershey Bears (e)		AHL	2	0	1	1	2
1983-84—Washington Capitals		NHL	72	4	15	19	124
NHL TOTALS			408	18	83	101	510

(c)—Drafted from Peterborough TPTs by Atlanta Flames in first round of 1976 amateur draft.
(d)—June, 1980—Traded by Calgary Flames to Toronto Maple Leafs for second round 1980 draft choice (Kevin LaVallee).
(e)—September, 1983—Signed by Washington Capitals as a free agent.

SCOTT SHAUNESSY

Defense . . . 6'4" . . . 220 lbs. . . . Born, Newport, R.I., January 22, 1964 . . . Shoots left.

Year	Team	League	Games	G.	A.	Pts.	Pen.
1982-83—St. John's Prep. (c)		R.I. H.S.	23	7	32	39	....
1983-84—Boston University		ECAC	40	6	22	28	48

(c)—June, 1983—Drafted by Quebec Nordiques in 1983 NHL entry draft. Ninth Nordiques pick, 192nd overall, 10th round.

BRAD SHAW

Defense . . . 5'11" . . . 163 lbs. . . . Born, Cambridge, Ont., April 28, 1964 . . . Shoots right.

Year	Team	League	Games	G.	A.	Pts.	Pen.
1980-81—Kitchener Greenshirts		Ont. Midgets	62	14	58	72	14
1981-82—Ottawa 67's (c)		OHL	68	13	59	72	24
1982-83—Ottawa 67's		OHL	63	12	66	78	24
1983-84—Ottawa 67's (a-d-e-f)		OHL	68	11	71	82	75

(c)—June, 1982—Drafted as underage junior by Detroit Red Wings in 1982 NHL entry draft. Fifth Red Wings pick, 86th overall, fifth round.
(d)—Won Max Kaminsky Trophy (OHL's Top Defenseman).
(e)—Led OHL playoffs with 27 assists.
(f)—May, 1984—Traded by Detroit Red Wings to Hartford Whalers for eighth-round 1984 draft pick (Lars Karlsson).

BRENT SHAW

Right Wing . . . 5'11" . . . 180 lbs. . . . Born, Vancouver, B.C., June 24, 1962 . . . Shoots right . . . (September, 1982)—Leg injury . . . (November, 1982)—Injured wrist.

Year	Team	League	Games	G.	A.	Pts.	Pen.
1979-80—Seattle Breakers		WHL	4	0	0	0	2
1980-81—Seattle Breakers		WHL	40	13	19	32	20
1981-82—Seattle Breakers (c)		WHL	71	33	42	75	209

Year	Team	League	Games	G.	A.	Pts.	Pen.
1982-83—Wichita Wind		CHL	52	9	9	18	23
1983-84—Muskegon Mohawks		IHL	51	17	16	33	52
1983-84—Maine Mariners		AHL	24	5	2	7	25

(c)—June, 1982—Drafted by New Jersey Devils in 1982 NHL entry draft. Tenth Devils pick, 190th overall, 10th round.

BRIAN JAMES SHAW

Right Wing . . . 6' . . . 180 lbs. . . . Born, Edmonton, Alta., May 20, 1962 . . . Shoots right.

Year	Team	League	Games	G.	A.	Pts.	Pen.
1978-79—St. Albert Saints		AJHL	53	27	35	62	201
1978-79—Portland Winter Hawks		WHL	4	0	1	1	0
1979-80—Portland Winter Hawks (c)		WHL	68	20	25	45	161
1980-81—Portland Winter Hawks		WHL	72	53	65	118	176
1981-82—Portland Winter Hawks (d)		WHL	69	56	76	132	193
1982-83—Springfield Indians		AHL	79	15	17	32	62
1983-84—Springfield Indians		AHL	4	2	2	4	2
1983-84—Peoria Prancers		IHL	54	27	27	54	49

(c)—June, 1980—Drafted by Chicago Black Hawks as underage junior in 1980 NHL entry draft. Ninth Black Hawks pick, 78th overall, fourth round.

(d)—Led WHL playoffs with 18 goals.

DAVE SHAW

Defense . . . 6'2" . . . 190 lbs. . . . Born, St. Thomas, Ont., May 25, 1964 . . . Shoots right.

Year	Team	League	Games	G.	A.	Pts.	Pen.
1980-81—Stratford Jr. B		OPJHL	41	12	19	31	30
1981-82—Kitchener Rangers (c)		OHL	68	6	25	31	99
1982-83—Kitchener Rangers		OHL	57	18	56	74	78
1982-83—Quebec Nordiques		NHL	2	0	0	0	0
1983-84—Kitchener Rangers (a)		OHL	58	14	34	48	73
1983-84—Quebec Nordiques		NHL	3	0	0	0	0
NHL TOTALS			5	0	0	0	0

(c)—June, 1982—Drafted as underage junior by Quebec Nordiques in 1982 NHL entry draft. First Nordiques pick, 13th overall, first round.

DOUGLAS ARTHUR SHEDDON

Center . . . 6' . . . 184 lbs. . . . Born, Wallaceburg, Ont., April 29, 1961 . . . Shoots right . . . (October 25, 1981)—Suffered a broken finger and leg and ankle injuries during a team practice . . . Also plays right wing.

Year	Team	League	Games	G.	A.	Pts.	Pen.
1977-78—Hamilton Fincups		OMJHL	32	1	9	10	32
1977-78—Kitchener Rangers		OMJHL	18	5	7	12	14
1978-79—Kitchener Rangers		OMJHL	66	16	42	58	29
1979-80—Kitchener Rangers		OMJHL	16	10	16	26	26
1979-80—Sault Ste. Marie Greyhounds (c)		OMJHL	45	30	44	74	59
1980-81—Sault Ste. Marie Greyhounds		OHL	66	51	72	123	78
1981-82—Erie Blades		AHL	17	4	6	10	14
1981-82—Pittsburgh Penguins		NHL	38	10	15	25	12
1982-83—Pittsburgh Penguins		NHL	80	24	43	67	54
1983-84—Pittsburgh Penguins		NHL	67	22	35	57	20
NHL TOTALS			185	56	93	149	86

(c)—June, 1980—Drafted as underage junior by Pittsburgh Penguins in 1980 NHL entry draft. Fourth Penguins pick, 93rd overall, sixth round.

NEIL SHEEHY

Defense . . . 6'2" . . . 210 lbs. . . . Born, Fort Francis, Ont., February 9, 1960 . . . Shoots right . . . Brother of Shawn and Tim Sheehy (hockey players) and nephew of Bronko Nagurski (football star for University of Minnesota and Chicago Bears).

Year	Team	League	Games	G.	A.	Pts.	Pen.
1979-80—Harvard University		ECAC	13	0	0	0	10
1980-81—Harvard University		ECAC	26	4	8	12	22
1981-82—Harvard University		ECAC	30	7	11	18	46
1982-83—Harvard University		ECAC	34	5	13	18	48
1983-84—Colorado Flames (c)		CHL	74	5	18	23	151
1983-84—Calgary Flames		NHL	1	1	0	1	2
NHL TOTALS			1	1	0	1	2

(c)—August, 1983—Signed by Calgary Flames as a free agent.

DAVE SHELLINGTON

Left Wing . . . 6'3" . . . 171 lbs. . . . Born, Burford, Ont., January 27, 1965 . . . Shoots left . . . Also plays center and defense.

Year	Team	League	Games	G.	A.	Pts.	Pen.
1981-82—Newmarket Flyers		OJHL	57	11	53	64	155
1982-83—Cornwall Royals (c)		OHL	68	13	17	30	29
1983-84—Cornwall Royals		OHL	57	22	25	47	72

(c)—June, 1983—Drafted as underage junior by New York Islanders in 1983 NHL entry draft. Third Islanders pick, 36th overall, third round.

RAY SHEPPARD

Right Wing . . . 5'11" . . . 175 lbs. . . . Born, Pembroke, Ont., May 27, 1966 . . . Shoots right.

Year	Team	League	Games	G.	A.	Pts.	Pen.
1982-83—Brockville		OPHL	48	27	36	63	81
1983-84—Cornwall Royals (c)		OHL	68	44	36	80	69

(c)—June, 1984—Drafted as underage junior by Buffalo Sabres in NHL entry draft. Third Sabres pick, 60th overall, third round.

RAY SHERO

Center . . . 5'10" . . . 185 lbs. . . . Born, Hartsdale, N.Y., July 28, 1962 . . . Shoots left . . . Son of former NHL Coach and General Manager Fred Shero.

Year	Team	League	Games	G.	A.	Pts.	Pen.
1980-81—St. Lawrence University		ECAC	32	12	13	25	28
1981-82—St. Lawrence University (c)		ECAC	....	...	....	....	....
1982-83—St. Lawrence University		ECAC	36	19	26	45	28
1983-84—St. Lawrence University		ECAC	32	15	27	42	46

(c)—June, 1982—Drafted by Los Angeles Kings in NHL entry draft. Tenth Kings pick, 216th overall, 11th round.

GORD SHERVEN

Right Wing . . . 6' . . . 185 lbs. . . . Born, Gravelbourg, Sask., August 21, 1963 . . . Shoots right.

Year	Team	League	Games	G.	A.	Pts.	Pen.
1980-81—Weyburn Red Wings (c)		SJHL	44	35	34	69	....
1981-82—University of North Dakota		WCHA	46	18	25	43	16
1982-83—University of North Dakota		WCHA	36	12	21	33	16
1983-84—Canadian National Team		Int'l	46	9	13	22	13
1983-84—University of North Dakota		WCHA	10	5	5	10	4
1983-84—Edmonton Oilers		NHL	2	1	0	1	0
NHL TOTALS			2	1	0	1	0

(c)—June, 1981—Drafted by Edmonton Oilers in 1981 NHL entry draft. Ninth Oilers pick, 197th overall, 10th round.

BRUCE SHOEBOTTOM

Defense . . . 6'2" . . . 200 lbs. . . . Born, Windsor, Ont., August 20, 1965 . . . Shoots left . . . (December, 1982)—Broken leg.

Year	Team	League	Games	G.	A.	Pts.	Pen.
1981-82—Peterborough Petes		OHL	51	0	4	4	67
1982-83—Peterborough Petes (c)		OHL	34	2	10	12	106
1983-84—Peterborough Petes		OHL	16	0	5	5	73

(c)—June, 1983—Drafted as underage junior by Los Angeles Kings in 1983 NHL entry draft. First Kings pick, 47th overall, third round.

JOHN SHUMSKI, JR.

Center . . . 6'3" . . . 200 lbs. . . . Born, Stoneham, Mass., October 10, 1963 . . . Shoots right.

Year	Team	League	Games	G.	A.	Pts.	Pen.
1981-82—R.P.I. (c)		ECAC	25	5	11	16	16
1982-83—R.P.I.		ECAC	14	5	4	9	12
1983-84—South Shore Braves		NEJHL	..	..	..	..	..

(c)—June, 1982—Drafted as underage player by St. Louis Blues in 1982 NHL entry draft. Seventh Blues pick, 197th overall, 10th round.

STEPHEN JOHN SHUTT

Left Wing . . . 5'11" . . . 180 lbs. . . . Born, Toronto, Ont., July 1, 1952 . . . Shoots left . . . Can also play Center . . . Brother of Byron Shutt . . . Missed part of 1978-79 season with a cracked bone in wrist . . . (December, 1981)—Cracked bone in right hand . . . (February 23,

1982)—Deep cut on back of left leg when he fell on top of skate of Miroslav Frycer in Quebec . . . (March, 1982)—Injured right knee in game vs. Quebec . . . Set NHL record for most goals in a season by a left wing (60) in 1976-77 . . . (January, 1984)—Injured thumb.

Year	Team	League	Games	G.	A.	Pts.	Pen.
1968-69—Toronto Marlboros		Jr."B"OHA	17	10	17	27	....
1969-70—Toronto Marlboros		Jr."A"OHA	49	11	14	25	93
1970-71—Toronto Marlboros (b)		Jr."A"OHA	62	70	53	123	85
1971-72—Tor. Marlboros (a-c-d)		Jr."A"OHA	58	*63	49	112	60
1972-73—Nova Scotia Voyageurs		AHL	6	4	1	5	2
1972-73—Montreal Canadiens		NHL	50	8	8	16	24
1973-74—Montreal Canadiens		NHL	70	15	20	35	17
1974-75—Montreal Canadiens		NHL	77	30	35	65	40
1975-76—Montreal Canadiens		NHL	80	45	34	79	47
1976-77—Montreal Canadiens (a)		NHL	80	*60	45	105	28
1977-78—Montreal Canadiens (b)		NHL	80	49	37	86	24
1978-79—Montreal Canadiens		NHL	72	37	40	77	31
1979-80—Montreal Canadiens (b)		NHL	77	47	42	89	34
1980-81—Montreal Canadiens		NHL	77	35	38	73	51
1981-82—Montreal Canadiens		NHL	57	31	24	55	40
1982-83—Montreal Canadiens		NHL	78	35	22	57	26
1983-84—Montreal Canadiens		NHL	63	14	23	37	29
NHL TOTALS			861	406	368	774	391

(c)—Selected by New York Raiders in World Hockey Association player selection draft, February, 1972.
(d)—Drafted From Toronto Marlboros by Montreal Canadiens in first round of 1972 amateur draft.

DAVID SIKORSKI

Defense . . . 6'1" . . . 205 lbs. . . . Born, Pontiac, Mich., February 24, 1965 . . . Shoots left.

Year	Team	League	Games	G.	A.	Pts.	Pen.
1981-82—Detroit Compuware		Mich. Midget	77	40	130	170	98
1982-83—Cornwall Royals (c)		QHL	55	4	12	16	50
1983-84—Cornwall Royals		OHL	14	0	6	6	14
1983-84—Ottawa 67's		OHL	21	0	2	2	6
1983-84—Guelph Platers		OHL	15	0	1	1	2

(c)—June, 1983—Drafted as underage junior by Detroit Red Wings in 1983 NHL entry draft. Tenth Red Wings pick, 166th overall, ninth round.

DAVE SILK

Center . . . 5'11" . . . 190 lbs. . . . Born, Scituate, Mass., January 1, 1958 . . . Shoots right . . . Member of 1980 U.S. Olympic Gold Medal Winning Team . . . Cousin of Mike Milbury . . . Grandson of Hal Janvrin (Member of Boston Red Sox) . . . (January 24, 1981)—Bruised right knee . . . (January, 1982)—Bruised shoulder . . . (December, 1983)—Separated right shoulder . . . Also plays right wing . . . (February 27, 1984)—Sprained knee.

Year	Team	League	Games	G.	A.	Pts.	Pen.
1976-77—Boston University (c)		ECAC	34	35	30	65	50
1977-78—Boston University (d-e)		ECAC	28	27	31	58	57
1978-79—Boston University		ECAC	23	8	12	20	20
1979-80—U.S. Olympic Team		Int'l	56	12	36	48	32
1979-80—New York Rangers		NHL	2	0	0	0	0
1979-80—New Haven Nighthawks		AHL	11	1	9	10	0
1980-81—New York Rangers		NHL	59	14	12	26	58
1980-81—New Haven Nighthawks		AHL	12	0	4	4	34
1981-82—New York Rangers		NHL	64	15	20	35	39
1982-83—New York Rangers		NHL	16	1	1	2	15
1982-83—Binghamton Whalers		AHL	9	1	2	3	29
1982-83—Tulsa Oilers		CHL	40	28	29	57	67
1983-84—Boston Bruins (f)		NHL	35	13	17	30	64
1983-84—Hershey Bears		AHL	15	11	10	21	22
NHL TOTALS			176	43	50	93	176

(c)—Named ECAC top rookie.
(d)—Named to All-ECAC and All-New England Teams.
(e)—June, 1978—Draft by New York Rangers in 1978 NHL amateur draft. Third Rangers pick, 59th overall, fourth round.
(f)—October, 1983—Traded by New York Rangers to Boston Bruins for Dave Barr.

MICHAEL SILTALA

Right Wing . . . 5'10" . . . 173 lbs. . . . Born, Toronto, Ont., August 5, 1963 . . . Shoots right.

Year	Team	League	Games	G.	A.	Pts.	Pen.
1979-80—Sault Ste. Marie		Ont. Midget	57	78	83	161	....
1980-81—Kingston Canadians (c)		OMJHL	63	18	22	40	23

Year	Team	League	Games	G.	A.	Pts.	Pen.
1981-82—Kingston Canadians		OHL	59	38	49	87	70
1981-82—Washington Capitals		NHL	3	1	0	1	2
1982-83—Kingston Canadians (a)		OHL	50	53	61	114	45
1982-83—Hershey Bears		AHL	9	0	3	3	2
1983-84—Hershey Bears		AHL	50	15	17	32	29
NHL TOTALS			3	1	0	1	2

(c)—June, 1980—Drafted as underage junior by Washington Capitals in 1980 NHL entry draft. Fourth Capitals pick, 89th overall, fifth round.

RISTO SILTANEN

Defense . . . 5'9" . . . 180 lbs. . . . Born, Manta, Finland, October 31, 1958 . . . Shoots right.

Year	Team	League	Games	G.	A.	Pts.	Pen.
1976-77—Ilves (a)		Finland	36	10	7	17	28
1977-78—Ilves		Finland	36	7	8	15	42
1978-79—Edmonton Oilers (c-d-e-f)		WHA	20	3	4	7	4
1979-80—Edmonton Oilers		NHL	64	6	29	35	26
1980-81—Edmonton Oilers		NHL	79	17	36	53	54
1981-82—Edmonton Oilers (g)		NHL	63	15	48	63	24
1982-83—Hartford Whalers		NHL	74	5	25	30	28
1983-84—Hartford Whalers		NHL	75	15	38	53	34
WHA TOTALS			20	3	4	7	4
NHL TOTALS			355	58	176	234	166

(c)—June, 1978—Drafted by St. Louis Blues in amateur draft. 13th St. Louis pick, 173rd overall, 11th round.

(d)—March, 1979—Signed as a free agent by Edmonton Oilers.

(e)—June, 1979—Selected by St. Louis Blues in NHL reclaim draft.

(f)—August, 1979—Traded with Tom Roulston by St. Louis Blues to Edmonton Oilers for Joe Micheletti.

(g)—August, 1982—Traded with Brent Loney by Edmonton Oilers to Hartford Whalers for Ken Linseman and Don Nachbaur.

MARIO SIMIONI

Right Wing . . . 6' . . . 194 lbs. . . . Born, Toronto, Ont., April 1, 1963 . . . Shoots right.

Year	Team	League	Games	G.	A.	Pts.	Pen.
1979-80—South Ottawa Midgets		Ont. Midget	61	53	63	116	70
1980-81—Toronto Marlboros (c)		OHL	63	19	27	46	63
1981-82—Toronto Marlboros		OHL	68	58	60	118	88
1982-83—Toronto Marlboros		OHL	66	62	59	121	67
1982-83—Colorado Flames		CHL	6	3	3	6	0
1983-84—Colorado Flames		CHL	54	16	21	37	35

(c)—June, 1981—Drafted as underage junior by Calgary Flames in 1981 NHL entry draft. Fourth Flames pick, 99th overall, fifth round.

CHARLES ROBERT SIMMER

Left Wing . . . 6'3" . . . 210 lbs. . . . Born, Terrace Bay, Ont., March 20, 1954 . . . Shoots left . . . Also plays Center . . . Missed part of 1975-76 season with knee surgery . . . Scored goals in 13 straight games in 1979-80 to set modern NHL record . . . Missed 15 games in 1979-80 season with strained ligaments in knee . . . Only the second player in NHL history to not have a hat trick during a 50-goal season (Vic Hadfield was the first during 1971-72 season with N.Y. Rangers) . . . (March 2, 1981)—Broken right leg.

Year	Team	League	Games	G.	A.	Pts.	Pen.
1971-72—Kenora Muskies		MJHL	45	14	31	45	77
1972-73—Kenora Muskies (a)		MJHL	48	43	*68	*111	57
1973-74—S Ste. Marie Greyh'ds (c)		Jr."A"OHA	70	45	54	99	137
1974-75—Salt Lake Golden Eagles		CHL	47	12	29	41	86
1974-75—California Seals		NHL	35	8	13	21	26
1975-76—Salt Lake Golden Eagles		CHL	42	23	16	39	96
1975-76—California Seals		NHL	21	1	1	2	22
1976-77—Salt Lake Golden Eagles (b)		CHL	51	32	30	62	37
1976-77—Cleveland Barons (d)		NHL	24	2	0	2	16
1977-78—Springfield Indians (b)		AHL	75	42	41	83	100
1977-78—Los Angeles Kings		NHL	3	0	0	0	2
1978-79—Springfield Indians		AHL	39	13	23	36	33
1978-79—Los Angeles Kings		NHL	38	21	27	48	16
1979-80—Los Angeles Kings (a)		NHL	64	*56	45	101	65
1980-81—Los Angeles Kings (a)		NHL	65	56	49	105	62
1981-82—Los Angeles Kings		NHL	50	15	24	39	42
1982-83—Los Angeles Kings		NHL	80	29	51	80	51
1983-84—Los Angeles Kings		NHL	79	44	48	92	78
NHL TOTALS			459	232	258	490	380

(c)—Drafted from Sault Ste. Marie Greyhounds by California Golden Seals in third round of 1974 amateur draft.
(d)—Signed by Los Angeles Kings as free agent, August, 1977.

DAVID STEWART SIMPSON

Center . . . 6' . . . 187 lbs. . . . Born, London, Ont., March 3, 1962 . . . Shoots left . . . Son of Marion Simpson, member of 1952 Canadian Olympic track team . . . (November, 1982)— Strained tendon in left ankle.

Year	Team	League	Games	G.	A.	Pts.	Pen.
1979-80—London Knights (c)		OHL	68	29	44	73	38
1980-81—London Knights		OHL	67	34	56	90	80
1981-82—London Knights (a-d-e-f)		OHL	68	67	88	*155	18
1981-82—Indianapolis Checkers		CHL	3	0	1	1	0
1982-83—Indianapolis Checkers		CHL	70	29	39	68	69
1983-84—Indianapolis Checkers (g)		CHL	72	24	43	67	26

(c)—June, 1981—Drafted as underage junior by New York Islanders in 1980 NHL entry draft. Third Islanders pick, 59th overall, third round.
(d)—Winner of Red Tilson Trophy (Most Outstanding OHL Player).
(e)—Winner of William Hanley Trophy (Most Gentlemanly OHL Player).
(f)—Winner of Eddie Powers Memorial Trophy (Leading OHL Scorer).
(g)—August, 1984—Traded by New York Islanders to Vancouver Canucks for a future draft choice.

ROBERT SAM SIMPSON

Left Wing . . . 6' . . . 185 lbs. . . . Born, Caughnawaga, Que., November 17, 1956 . . . Shoots left.

Year	Team	League	Games	G.	A.	Pts.	Pen.
1973-74—Sherbrooke Beavers		QJHL	64	6	21	27	138
1974-75—Sherbrooke Beavers		QJHL	69	38	47	85	146
1975-76—Sherbrooke Beavers (c)		QJHL	68	56	77	133	126
1976-77—Atlanta Flames		NHL	72	13	10	23	45
1977-78—Tulsa Oilers		CHL	14	8	8	16	34
1977-78—Atlanta Flames		NHL	55	10	8	18	49
1978-79—Tulsa Oilers (d)		CHL	49	14	19	33	38
1979-80—Salt Lake Golden Eagles		CHL	41	19	12	31	58
1979-80—St. Louis Blues		NHL	18	2	2	4	0
1980-81—Salt Lake Golden Eagles		CHL	8	2	1	3	4
1980-81—Muskegon Mohawks		IHL	42	17	26	43	42
1981-82—Erie Blades		AHL	48	25	23	48	45
1981-82—Pittsburgh Penguins (e)		NHL	26	9	9	18	4
1982-83—Pittsburgh Penguins		NHL	4	1	0	1	0
1982-83—Baltimore Skipjacks		AHL	61	24	27	51	24
1983-84—Baltimore Skipjacks		AHL	71	16	16	32	36
NHL TOTALS			175	35	29	64	98

(c)—Drafted from Sherbrooke Beavers by Atlanta Flames in second round of 1976 amateur draft.
(d)—May, 1979—Traded by Atlanta Flames to St. Louis Blues for Curt Bennett.
(e)—August, 1981—Signed by Pittsburgh Penguins as a free agent.

ILKKA SINISALO

Left Wing . . . 6'1" . . . 190 lbs. . . . Born, Valeskoski, Finland, July 10, 1958 . . . Shoots left . . . (September, 1982)—Broke collarbone.

Year	Team	League	Games	G.	A.	Pts.	Pen.
1979-80—Helsinki IFK		Finland	35	16	9	25	16
1980-81—Helsinki IFK		Finland	36	27	17	44	14
1981-82—Philadelphia Flyers (c)		NHL	66	15	22	37	22
1982-83—Philadelphia Flyers		NHL	61	21	29	50	16
1983-84—Philadelphia Flyers		NHL	73	29	17	46	29
NHL TOTALS			200	65	68	133	67

(c)—February, 1981—Signed by Philadelphia Flyers as a free agent.

DARRYL GLEN SITTLER

Center . . . 6' . . . 190 lbs. . . . Born, Kitchener, Ont., September 18, 1950 . . . Shoots left . . . Missed part of 1970-71 season with fractured wrist . . . Brother of Gary Sittler . . . Missed part of 1974-75 season with bruised left shoulder . . . Set NHL record with 10 points in game and equalled NHL single game record with six goals, February 7, 1976 (vs. Boston Bruins) . . . Tied Stanley Cup Playoff records with five goals and six points in single game, April 22, 1976 (vs. Philadelphia Flyers) . . . Missed part of 1976-77 season with torn rib cartilage . . . Missed part of 1978-79 season with ligament damage to left knee.

Year	Team	League	Games	G.	A.	Pts.	Pen.
1967-68—London Nationals	Jr. "A" OHA	54	22	41	63	84
1968-69—London Knights (b)	Jr. "A" OHA	53	34	65	99	90
1969-70—London Knights (c)	Jr. "A" OHA	54	42	48	90	126
1970-71—Toronto Maple Leafs	NHL	49	10	8	18	37
1971-72—Toronto Maple Leafs	NHL	74	15	17	32	44
1972-73—Toronto Maple Leafs	NHL	78	29	48	77	69
1973-74—Toronto Maple Leafs	NHL	78	38	46	84	55
1974-75—Toronto Maple Leafs	NHL	72	36	44	80	47
1975-76—Toronto Maple Leafs	NHL	79	41	59	100	90
1976-77—Toronto Maple Leafs	NHL	73	38	52	90	89
1977-78—Toronto Maple Leafs (b)	NHL	80	45	72	117	100
1978-79—Toronto Maple Leafs	NHL	70	36	51	87	69
1979-80—Toronto Maple Leafs	NHL	73	40	57	97	62
1980-81—Toronto Maple Leafs	NHL	80	43	53	96	77
1981-82—Toronto Maple Leafs (d)	NHL	38	18	20	38	24
1981-82—Philadelphia Flyers	NHL	35	14	18	32	50
1982-83—Philadelphia Flyers	NHL	80	43	40	83	60
1983-84—Philadelphia Flyers	NHL	76	27	36	63	38
NHL TOTALS			1035	473	621	1094	911

(c)—Drafted from London Knights by Toronto Maple Leafs in first round of 1970 amateur draft.

(d)—January, 1982—Traded with future considerations by Toronto Maple Leafs to Philadelphia Flyers for NHL rights to Rich Costello and Flyers second-round 1982 entry draft pick acquired from Hartford Whalers (Peter Ihnacak). Toronto received Ken Strong to complete deal March, 1982.

KEVIN SKILLITER

Defense . . . 6'2" . . . 185 lbs. . . . Born, Belleville, Ont., February 5, 1964 . . . Shoots left.

Year	Team	League	Games	G.	A.	Pts.	Pen.
1980-81—Kingston Jr. 'B'	OPJHL	41	2	7	9	82
1981-82—Cornwall Royals (c)	OHL	50	3	4	7	16
1982-83—Cornwall Royals	OHL	61	0	3	3	27
1983-84—Cornwall Royals (d)	OHL	65	7	10	17	57

(c)—June, 1982—Drafted as underage junior by Hartford Whalers in 1982 NHL entry draft. Ninth Whalers pick, 172nd overall, ninth round.

(d)—June, 1984—Released by Hartford Whalers.

CHARLIE SKJODT

Center . . . 6'1" . . . 190 lbs. . . . Born, Toronto, Ont., June 10, 1956 . . . Shoots right.

Year	Team	League	Games	G.	A.	Pts.	Pen.
1974-75—North Bay Trappers	OPJHL	29	18	25	43	24
1975-76—Windsor Spitfires (c)	Jr. "A" OHA	66	41	48	89	32
1976-77—Saginaw Gears	IHL	3	0	1	1	4
1976-77—Windsor Spitfires	Jr. "A" OHA	50	35	44	79	58
1977-78—Cambridge Hornets	Sr. "A" OHA	4	3	5	8	0
1977-78—Muskegon Mohawks	IHL	80	45	53	98	59
1978-79—Fort Worth Texans	CHL	73	31	33	64	54
1979-80—Indianapolis Checkers	CHL	75	26	45	71	36
1980-81—Indianapolis Checkers	CHL	59	21	29	50	37
1981-82—Indianapolis Checkers (d)	CHL	80	40	55	95	58
1982-83—Salt Lake Golden Eagles	CHL	62	22	54	76	43
1983-84—Adirondack Red Wings	AHL	55	11	27	38	32

(c)—Drafted from Windsor Spitfires by Toronto Maple Leafs in seventh round of 1976 amateur draft.

(d)—November, 1982—Signed by St. Louis Blues as a free agent and assigned to Salt Lake City.

PETRI SKRIKO

Right Wing . . . 5'10" . . . 172 lbs. . . . Born, Laapeenranta, Finland, March 12, 1962 . . . Shoots right.

Year	Team	League	Games	G.	A.	Pts.	Pen.
1983-84—Saipa (c)	Finland	..	25	26	51	..

(c)—June, 1981—Drafted by Vancouver Canucks in NHL entry draft. Seventh Canucks pick, 157th overall, seventh round.

BRIAN SKRUDLAND

Left Wing . . . 6' . . . 180 lbs. . . . Born, Peace River, Alta, July 31, 1963 . . . Shoots left . . . Cousin of Barry Pederson.

Year	Team	League	Games	G.	A.	Pts.	Pen.
1980-81—Saskatoon Blades	WHL	66	15	27	42	97
1981-82—Saskatoon Blades	WHL	71	27	29	56	135

Year	Team	League	Games	G.	A.	Pts.	Pen.
1982-83—Saskatoon Blades		WHL	71	35	59	94	42
1983-84—Nova Scotia Voyageurs		AHL	56	13	12	25	55

LOUIS SLEIGHER

Right Wing . . . 5'11" . . . 195 lbs. . . . Born, Nouvelle, Que., October 23, 1958 . . . Shoots right . . . (February, 1981)—Back spasms . . . (January 19, 1984)—Injured knee in game at Boston.

Year	Team	League	Games	G.	A.	Pts.	Pen.
1976-77—Chicoutimi Sagueneens		QJHL	70	53	48	101	49
1977-78—Chicoutimi Sagueneens (c-d)		QJHL	71	65	54	119	125
1978-79—Birmingham Bulls		WHA	62	26	12	38	46
1979-80—Quebec Nordiques		NHL	2	0	1	1	0
1979-80—Syracuse Blazers		AHL	58	28	15	43	37
1980-81—Erie Blades (b)		EHL	50	39	29	68	129
1981-82—Fredericton Express		AHL	59	32	34	66	37
1981-82—Quebec Nordiques		NHL	8	0	0	0	0
1982-83—Fredericton Express		AHL	12	8	2	10	9
1982-83—Quebec Nordiques		NHL	51	14	10	24	49
1983-84—Quebec Nordiques		NHL	44	15	19	34	32
WHA TOTALS			62	26	12	38	46
NHL TOTALS			105	29	30	59	81

(c)—Drafted from Chicoutimi Sagueneens by Montreal Canadiens in 21st round of 1978 amateur draft.
(d)—Selected by Birmingham Bulls in World Hockey Association amateur player draft, June, 1978.

DOUG SMAIL

Left Wing . . . 5'10" . . . 175 lbs. . . . Born, Moose Jaw, Sask., September 2, 1957 . . . Shoots left . . . (January 10, 1981)—Suffered fractured jaw, also broke jaw in a November 1980 practice . . . (December 20, 1981)—Set NHL record for fastest goal at start of game (5 seconds) vs. St. Louis . . . (December, 1983)—Stretched knee ligaments.

Year	Team	League	Games	G.	A.	Pts.	Pen.
1977-78—Univ. of North Dakota		WCHA	38	22	28	50	52
1978-79—Univ. of North Dakota		WCHA	35	24	34	58	46
1979-80—Univ. of North Dakota (b-c-d)		WCHA	40	43	44	87	70
1980-81—Winnipeg Jets		NHL	30	10	8	18	45
1981-82—Winnipeg Jets		NHL	72	17	18	35	55
1982-83—Winnipeg Jets		NHL	80	15	29	44	32
1983-84—Winnipeg Jets		NHL	66	20	17	37	62
NHL TOTALS			248	62	72	134	194

(c)—Named to NCAA Tournament All-Star Team and Tournament's Most Valuable Player.
(d)—May, 1980—Signed by Winnipeg Jets as free agent.

BRIAN SMALL

Right Wing . . . 6' . . . 172 lbs. . . . Born, Toronto, Ont., May 23, 1964 . . . Shoots right.

Year	Team	League	Games	G.	A.	Pts.	Pen.
1980-81—Toronto Young Nats.		MTHL	38	25	23	48	55
1981-82—Ottawa 67's (c)		OHL	66	18	24	42	72
1982-83—Ottawa 67's		OHA	13	2	3	5	22
1982-83—Belleville Bulls		OHA	43	13	14	27	49
1983-84—Belleville Bulls		OHL	66	18	19	37	65

(c)—June, 1982—Drafted as underage junior by Edmonton Oilers in 1982 NHL entry draft. Seventh Oilers pick, 146th overall, seventh round.

BRAD ALLAN SMITH

Right Wing . . . 6'1" . . . 195 lbs. . . . Born, Windsor, Ont., April 13, 1958 . . . Shoots right.

Year	Team	League	Games	G.	A.	Pts.	Pen.
1975-76—Windsor Spitfires		OMJHL	4	4	2	6	4
1976-77—Windsor Spitfires		OMJHL	66	37	53	90	154
1977-78—Windsor Spitfires		OMJHL	20	18	16	34	39
1977-78—Sudbury Wolves (c)		OMJHL	46	21	21	42	183
1978-79—Vancouver Canucks		NHL	2	0	0	0	2
1978-79—Dallas Black Hawks		CHL	60	17	18	35	143
1979-80—Dallas Black Hawks		CHL	51	26	16	42	138
1979-80—Vancouver Canucks (d)		NHL	19	1	3	4	50
1979-80—Atlanta Flames		NHL	4	0	0	0	4
1980-81—Birmingham Bulls		CHL	10	5	6	11	13
1980-81—Calgary Flames (e)		NHL	45	7	4	11	65

Year	Team	League	Games	G.	A.	Pts.	Pen.
1980-81—Detroit Red Wings		NHL	20	5	2	7	93
1981-82—Detroit Red Wings		NHL	33	2	0	2	80
1981-82—Adirondack Red Wings		AHL	34	10	5	15	126
1982-83—Detroit Red Wings		NHL	1	0	0	0	0
1982-83—Adirondack Red Wings		AHL	74	20	30	50	132
1983-84—Adirondack Red Wings		AHL	46	15	29	44	128
1983-84—Detroit Red Wings		NHL	8	2	1	3	36
NHL TOTALS			132	17	10	27	330

(c)—June, 1978—Drafted by Vancouver Canucks in 1978 NHL amateur draft. Fifth Canucks pick, 57th overall, fourth round.

(d)—February, 1980—Traded with Don Lever by Vancouver Canucks to Atlanta Flames for Ivan Boldirev and Darcy Rota.

(e)—February, 1981—Traded by Calgary Flames to Detroit Red Wings for future considerations. (Detroit sent Rick Vasko to Calgary in June to complete deal.)

DEREK ROBERT SMITH

Left Wing and Center . . . 5'11" . . . 175 lbs. . . . Born, Quebec City, Que., July 31, 1954 . . . Shoots left . . . Missed half of 1978-79 season with broken jaw . . . (February, 1981)—Pulled stomach muscle . . . (October 7, 1981)—Separated shoulder in game vs. Washington . . . (October, 1983)—Injured right shoulder in game at Minnesota.

Year	Team	League	Games	G.	A.	Pts.	Pen.
1971-72—Ottawa 67's		Jr."A"OHA	53	6	11	17	10
1972-73—Ottawa 67's		Jr."A"OHA	63	52	46	98	32
1973-74—Ottawa 67's (c)		Jr."A"OHA	69	47	45	92	40
1974-75—Charlotte Checkers		SHL	4	4	3	7	0
1974-75—Hershey Bears		AHL	64	11	16	27	10
1975-76—Hershey Bears		AHL	67	28	32	60	14
1975-76—Buffalo Sabres (d)		NHL	....	...	....	....	....
1976-77—Hershey Bears		AHL	65	31	31	62	20
1976-77—Buffalo Sabres		NHL	5	0	0	0	0
1977-78—Hershey Bears		AHL	5	2	2	4	2
1977-78—Buffalo Sabres		NHL	36	3	3	6	0
1978-79—Buffalo Sabres		NHL	43	14	12	26	8
1979-80—Buffalo Sabres		NHL	79	24	39	63	16
1980-81—Buffalo Sabres		NHL	69	21	43	64	12
1981-82—Buffalo Sabres (e)		NHL	12	3	1	4	2
1981-82—Detroit Red Wings		NHL	49	6	14	20	10
1982-83—Detroit Red Wings		NHL	42	7	4	11	12
1982-83—Adirondack Red Wings		AHL	11	6	4	10	2
1983-84—Adirondack Red Wings		AHL	61	16	29	45	10
NHL TOTALS			335	78	116	194	60

(c)—Drafted from Ottawa 67's by Buffalo Sabres in tenth round of 1974 amateur draft.

(d)—No league record. Appeared in one playoff game.

(e)—December, 1981—Traded with Danny Gare, Bob Sauve and Jim Schoenfeld by Buffalo Sabres to Detroit Red Wings for Dale McCourt, Mike Foligno, Brent Peterson and future considerations.

DERRICK SMITH

Left Wing . . . 6'1" . . . 185 lbs. . . . Born, Scarborough, Ont., January 22, 1965 . . . Shoots left.

Year	Team	League	Games	G.	A.	Pts.	Pen.
1981-82—Wexford Midgets		Ont. Midgets	45	35	47	82	40
1982-83—Peterborough Petes (c)		OHL	70	16	19	35	47
1983-84—Peterborough Petes		OHL	70	30	36	66	31

(c)—June, 1983—Drafted as underage junior by Philadelphia Flyers in 1983 NHL entry draft. Second Flyers pick, 44th overall, third round.

DOUG SMITH

Center . . . 6' . . . 185 lbs. . . . Born, Ottawa, Ont., May 17, 1963 . . . Shoots right . . . (October, 1980)—Knee injury . . . (October 27, 1982)—Broke left wrist, out 34 games . . . Also plays right wing.

Year	Team	League	Games	G.	A.	Pts.	Pen.
1979-80—Ottawa 67s		OJHL	64	23	34	57	45
1980-81—Ottawa 67s (c)		OHL	54	45	56	101	61
1981-82—Ottawa 67's		OHL	1	1	2	3	17
1981-82—Los Angeles Kings		NHL	80	16	14	30	64
1982-83—Los Angeles Kings		NHL	42	11	11	22	12
1983-84—Los Angeles Kings		NHL	72	16	20	36	28
NHL TOTALS			194	43	45	88	104

(c)—June, 1981—Drafted by Los Angeles Kings in NHL entry draft. First Kings pick, second overall, first round.

GREGORY JAMES SMITH

Defense . . . 6' . . . 195 lbs. . . . Born, Ponoka, Alta., July 8, 1955 . . . Shoots left . . . Attended Colorado College . . . Missed early part of 1979-80 season after knee surgery . . . (September, 1982)—Injured right knee during training camp and required arthroscopic surgery.

Year	Team	League	Games	G.	A.	Pts.	Pen.
1973-74—Colorado College		WCHA	31	7	13	20	80
1974-75—Colorado College (c)		WCHA	36	10	24	34	75
1975-76—Colorado College		WCHA	34	18	19	37	123
1975-76—Salt Lake Golden Eagles		CHL	5	0	2	2	2
1975-76—California Seals		NHL	1	0	1	1	2
1976-77—Cleveland Barons		NHL	74	9	17	26	65
1977-78—Cleveland Barons		NHL	80	7	30	37	92
1978-79—Minnesota North Stars		NHL	80	5	27	32	147
1979-80—Minnesota North Stars		NHL	55	5	13	18	103
1980-81—Minnesota North Stars (d)		NHL	74	5	21	26	126
1981-82—Detroit Red Wings		NHL	69	10	22	32	79
1982-83—Detroit Red Wings		NHL	73	4	26	30	79
1983-84—Detroit Red Wings		NHL	75	3	20	23	108
NHL TOTALS			581	48	177	225	801

(c)—Drafted from Colorado College by California Seals in fourth round of 1975 amateur draft.

(d)—September, 1981—Traded by Minnesota North Stars with Don Murdoch to Detroit Red Wings giving North Stars option to switch first-round draft choices with Detroit in 1982 entry draft. Minnesota exercised option and drafted Brian Bellows. Detroit drafted Murray Craven.

JEFF SMITH

Left Wing . . . 6' . . . 200 lbs. . . . Born, Brampton, Ont., July 31, 1963 . . . Shoots left.

Year	Team	League	Games	G.	A.	Pts.	Pen.
1979-80—Aurora Tigers		OPJHL	36	5	9	14	33
1980-81—London Knights		OMJHL	63	6	16	22	46
1981-82—London Knights (c)		OHL	65	28	51	79	90
1982-83—London Knights		OHL	61	35	57	92	100
1983-84—Springfield Indians		AHL	56	6	13	19	36

(c)—June, 1982—Drafted as underage junior by Chicago Black Hawks in 1982 NHL entry draft. Eighth Black Hawks pick, 154th overall, eighth round.

ROBERT DAVID SMITH

Center . . . 6'4" . . . 210 lbs. . . . Born, N. Sydney, N.S., February 12, 1958 . . . Shoots left . . . Missed part of 1979-80 season with fractured ankle.

Year	Team	League	Games	G.	A.	Pts.	Pen.
1975-76—Ottawa 67's		Jr."A"OHA	62	24	34	58	21
1976-77—Ottawa 67's (b)		Jr."A"OHA	64	*65	70	135	52
1977-78—Ottawa 67's (a-c-d)		Jr."A"OHA	61	69	*123	*192	44
1978-79—Minnesota North Stars (e)		NHL	80	30	44	74	39
1979-80—Minnesota North Stars		NHL	61	27	56	83	24
1980-81—Minnesota North Stars		NHL	78	29	64	93	73
1981-82—Minnesota North Stars		NHL	80	43	71	114	84
1982-83—Minnesota North Stars		NHL	77	24	53	77	81
1983-84—Minnesota North Stars (f)		NHL	10	3	6	9	9
1983-84—Montreal Canadiens		NHL	70	26	37	63	62
NHL TOTALS			456	182	331	513	372

(c)—Won Eddie Powers Memorial Trophy (leading scorer) and Albert "Red" Tilson Memorial Trophy (MVP).

(d)—Drafted from Ottawa 67's by Minnesota North Stars in first round of 1978 amateur draft.

(e)—Won Calder Memorial Trophy (NHL-Top Rookie). And was named THE SPORTING NEWS NHL Rookie of the Year in poll of players.

(f)—October, 1983—Traded by Minnesota North Stars to Montreal Canadiens for Mark Napier, Keith Acton and third-round draft pick (Kenneth Hodge).

STEVE SMITH

Defense . . . 6'2" . . . 190 lbs. . . . Born, Glasgow, Scotland, April 30, 1963 . . . Shoots right . . . Also plays right wing.

Year	Team	League	Games	G.	A.	Pts.	Pen.
1980-81—London Knights (c)		OMJHL	62	4	12	16	141
1981-82—London Knights		OHL	58	10	36	46	207
1982-83—London Knights		OHL	50	6	35	41	133
1982-83—Moncton Alpines		AHL	2	0	0	0	0
1983-84—Moncton Alpines		AHL	64	1	8	9	176

(c)—June, 1981—Drafted as underage junior by Edmonton Oilers in 1981 NHL entry draft. Fifth Oilers pick, 111th overall, sixth round.

STEVE SMITH

Defense . . . 5'9" . . . 202 lbs. . . . Born, Trenton, Ont., April 4, 1963 . . . Shoots left.

Year	Team	League	Games	G.	A.	Pts.	Pen.
1979-80—Belleville Tier 2		OHL	41	8	25	33	105
1980-81—Sault Ste. Marie Greyhounds (b-c-d)		OHL	61	3	37	40	143
1981-82—Sault Ste. Marie Greyhounds (b)		OHL	50	7	20	27	179
1981-82—Philadelphia Flyers		NHL	8	0	1	1	0
1982-83—Sault Ste. Marie Greyhounds (b)		OHL	55	11	33	44	139
1983-84—Springfield Indians		AHL	70	4	25	29	77
NHL TOTALS			8	0	1	1	0

(c)—Won Max Kaminsky Award (outstanding OHL defenseman).
(d)—Drafted by Philadelphia Flyers in NHL entry draft. First Flyers pick, 16th overall, first round.

STUART GORDON SMITH

Defense . . . 6'1" . . . 185 lbs. . . . Born, Toronto, Ont., March 17, 1960 . . . Shoots right . . . (November 10, 1980)—Broken jaw . . . (October, 1981)—Bruised ankle.

Year	Team	League	Games	G.	A.	Pts.	Pen.
1977-78—Peterborough Petes		OMJHL	67	1	18	19	112
1978-79—Peterborough Petes (c)		OMJHL	64	5	35	40	172
1979-80—Hartford Whalers		NHL	4	0	0	0	0
1979-80—Peterborough Petes		OMJHL	62	12	40	52	119
1980-81—Binghamton Whalers		AHL	42	3	9	12	63
1980-81—Hartford Whalers		NHL	38	1	7	8	55
1981-82—Binghamton Whalers		AHL	61	4	21	25	121
1981-82—Hartford Whalers		NHL	17	0	3	3	15
1982-83—Hartford Whalers		NHL	18	1	0	1	25
1982-83—Binghamton Whalers		AHL	50	3	8	11	97
1983-84—Binghamton Whalers		AHL	54	3	22	25	95
NHL TOTALS			77	2	10	12	95

(c)—August, 1979—Drafted by Hartford Whalers as underage junior in NHL entry draft. Second Hartford pick, 39th overall, second round.

VERN SMITH

Defense . . . 6'1" . . . 190 lbs. . . . Born, Winnipeg, Man., May 30, 1964 . . . Shoots left.

Year	Team	League	Games	G.	A.	Pts.	Pen.
1981-82—Lethbridge Broncos (c)		WHL	72	5	38	43	73
1982-83—Lethbridge Broncos		WHL	30	2	10	12	54
1982-83—Nanaimo Islanders		WHL	42	6	21	27	62
1983-84—New Westminster Bruins		WHL	69	13	44	57	94

(c)—June, 1982—Drafted as underage junior by New York Islanders in 1982 NHL entry draft. Second Islanders pick, 42nd overall, second round.

STAN SMYL

Right Wing . . . 5'8" . . . 200 lbs. . . . Born, Glendon, Alta., January 28, 1958 . . . Shoots right . . . Set Vancouver record for points in a season in 1982-83 (Broken by Patrick Sundstrom (91) in '83-84) . . . Only player to ever play in four Memorial Cup Tournaments.

Year	Team	League	Games	G.	A.	Pts.	Pen.
1974-75—Bellingham Blazers		Jr. "A" BCHL	....	...	....	....	....
1974-75—New Westminster Bruins (c)		WCHL	...	...	....	....	....
1975-76—New Westminster Bruins		WCHL	72	32	42	74	169
1976-77—New Westminster Bruins		WCHL	72	35	31	66	200
1977-78—New Westminster Bruins (d)		WCHL	53	29	47	76	211
1978-79—Vancouver Canucks		NHL	62	14	24	38	89
1978-79—Dallas Black Hawks		CHL	3	1	1	2	9
1979-80—Vancouver Canucks		NHL	77	31	47	78	204
1980-81—Vancouver Canucks		NHL	80	25	38	63	171
1981-82—Vancouver Canucks		NHL	80	34	44	78	144
1982-83—Vancouver Canucks		NHL	74	38	50	88	114
1983-84—Vancouver Canucks		NHL	80	24	43	67	136
NHL TOTALS			453	166	246	412	858

(c)—No league record. Appeared in three playoff games.
(d)—Drafted from New Westminster Bruins by Vancouver Canucks in third round of 1978 amateur draft.

GREG SMYTH

Defense . . . 6'3" . . . 195 lbs. . . . Born, Oakville, Ont., April 23, 1966 . . . Shoots right.

Year	Team	League	Games	G.	A.	Pts.	Pen.
1983-84—London Knights (c)		OHL	64	4	21	25	*252

(c)—June, 1984—Drafted as underage junior by Philadelphia Flyers in NHL entry draft. First Flyers pick, 22nd overall, second round.

JOHN SMYTH

Defense . . . 6'3" . . . 193 lbs. . . . Born, Winnipeg, Man., June 8, 1962 . . . Shoots right.

Year	Team	League	Games	G.	A.	Pts.	Pen.
1979-80—Calgary Wranglers (c)	WHL	70	7	25	32	74
1980-81—Calgary Wranglers	WHL	72	6	34	40	64
1981-82—Calgary Wranglers	WHL	72	11	36	47	115
1982-83—Salt Lake Golden Eagles	CHL	43	1	5	6	20
1983-84—Montana Magic	CHL	65	5	11	16	30

(c)—June, 1980—Drafted by St. Louis Blues in NHL entry draft. Ninth Blues pick, 201st overall, 10th round.

HAROLD JOHN SNEPSTS

Defense . . . 6'3" . . . 215 lbs. . . . Born, Edmonton, Alta., October 24, 1954 . . . Shoots left . . . (October, 1981)—Knee injury . . . (November, 1982)—Fractured orbit bone of right eye . . . (January 12, 1983)—Five-game suspension for fight with Doug Risebrough outside Calgary lockerroom . . . Holds Vancouver club record for most career games (683) and penalty minutes (1351).

Year	Team	League	Games	G.	A.	Pts.	Pen.
1972-73—Edmonton Oil Kings	WCHL	68	2	24	26	155
1973-74—Edmonton Oil Kings (c)	WCHL	68	8	41	49	239
1974-75—Seattle Totems	CHL	19	1	6	7	58
1974-75—Vancouver Canucks	NHL	27	1	2	3	30
1975-76—Vancouver Canucks	NHL	78	3	15	18	125
1976-77—Vancouver Canucks	NHL	79	4	18	22	149
1977-78—Vancouver Canucks	NHL	75	4	16	20	118
1978-79—Vancouver Canucks	NHL	76	7	24	31	130
1979-80—Vancouver Canucks	NHL	79	3	20	23	202
1980-81—Vancouver Canucks	NHL	76	3	16	19	212
1981-82—Vancouver Canucks	NHL	68	3	14	17	153
1982-83—Vancouver Canucks	NHL	46	2	8	10	80
1983-84—Vancouver Canucks (d)	NHL	79	4	16	20	152
NHL TOTALS			683	34	149	183	1351

(c)—Drafted from Edmonton Oil Kings by Vancouver Canucks in fourth round of 1974 amateur draft.
(d)—June, 1984—Traded by Vancouver Canucks to Minnesota North Stars for Al MacAdam.

KEN LAWRENCE SOLHEIM

Left Wing . . . 6'3" . . . 210 lbs. . . . Born, Hythe, Alta., March 27, 1961 . . . Shoots left.

Year	Team	League	Games	G.	A.	Pts.	Pen.
1977-78—St. Albert Saints	AJHL	60	26	16	42	31
1978-79—St. Albert Saints	AJHL	60	47	42	89	63
1979-80—Medicine Hat Tigers (b-c)	WHL	72	54	33	87	50
1980-81—Chicago Black Hawks (d)	NHL	5	2	0	2	0
1980-81—Medicine Hat Tigers (a)	WHL	64	*68	43	111	87
1980-81—Minnesota North Stars	NHL	5	2	1	3	0
1981-82—Nashville South Stars	CHL	44	23	18	41	40
1981-82—Minnesota North Stars	NHL	29	4	5	9	4
1982-83—Birmingham South Stars	CHL	22	14	3	17	4
1982-83—Minnesota North Stars (e)	NHL	25	2	4	6	4
1982-83—Detroit Red Wings	NHL	10	0	0	0	2
1983-84—Adirondack Red Wings	AHL	61	24	20	44	13
NHL TOTALS			74	10	10	20	10

(c)—June, 1980—Drafted by Chicago Black Hawks as underage junior in 1980 NHL entry draft. Fourth Black Hawks pick, 30th overall, second round.
(d)—December, 1980—Traded by Chicago Black Hawks with 1981 second-round draft pick (Tom Hirsch) to Minnesota North Stars for Glen Sharpley.
(e)—March, 1983—Traded by Minnesota North Stars to Detroit Red Wings for a player to be named.

ROY SOMMER

Left Wing . . . 5'11" . . . 180 lbs. . . . Born, Oakland, Calif., April 5, 1957 . . . Shoots left . . . (March, 1981)—Rib injury . . . Also plays center.

Year	Team	League	Games	G.	A.	Pts.	Pen.
1974-75—Spruce Grove Mets	AJHL	85	20	21	41	200
1974-75—Edmonton Oil Kings	WCHL	1	0	0	0	5

Year	Team	League	Games	G.	A.	Pts.	Pen.
1975-76—Calgary Centennials		WCHL	70	13	24	37	155
1976-77—Calgary Centennials (c)		WCHL	50	16	22	38	111
1977-78—Saginaw Gears		IHL	12	2	3	5	2
1977-78—Grand Rapids Owls		IHL	45	20	18	38	67
1978-79—Spokane Flyers		PHL	45	19	30	49	196
1979-80—Grand Rapids Owls		IHL	9	1	4	5	32
1979-80—Houston Apollos		CHL	69	24	31	55	246
1980-81—Edmonton Oilers		NHL	3	1	0	1	7
1980-81—Wichita Wind		CHL	57	13	22	35	212
1981-82—Wichita Wind		CHL	76	17	28	45	193
1982-83—Wichita Wind		CHL	73	22	39	61	130
1983-84—Maine Mariners		AHL	67	7	10	17	202
NHL TOTALS			3	1	0	1	7

(c)—June, 1977—Drafted by Toronto Maple Leafs in 1977 NHL amateur draft. Seventh Maple Leafs pick, 101st overall, sixth round.

TED SPEERS

Center . . . 5'11" . . . 190 lbs. . . . Born, Ann Arbor, Mich., January 21, 1961 . . . Shoots right.

Year	Team	League	Games	G.	A.	Pts.	Pen.
1979-80—University of Michigan		WCHA	30	13	16	29	16
1980-81—University of Michigan		WCHA	39	22	23	45	20
1981-82—University of Michigan		CCHA	38	23	16	39	46
1982-83—University of Michigan (a)		CCHA	36	18	41	59	40
1983-84—Adirondack Red Wings		AHL	79	15	25	40	27

JIM SPRENGER

Defense . . . 5'11" . . . 175 lbs. . . . Born, Cloquet, Minn., May 28, 1965 . . . Shoots right.

Year	Team	League	Games	G.	A.	Pts.	Pen.
1982-83—Cloquet H.S. (c)		Minn.H.S.	23	16	26	42	....
1983-84—Univ. of Minnesota/Duluth		WCHA	42	2	7	9	22

(c)—June, 1983—Drafted by New York Islanders in 1983 NHL entry draft. Ninth Islanders pick, 137th overall, seventh round.

DON SPRING

Defense . . . 5'11" . . . 195 lbs. . . . Born, Maracaibo, Venezuela, June 15, 1959 . . . Shoots left.

Year	Team	League	Games	G.	A.	Pts.	Pen.
1976-77—Univ. of Alberta		CWUAA	24	1	6	7	20
1977-78—Univ. of Alberta		CWUAA	24	6	13	19	10
1978-79—Univ. of Alberta		CWUAA	24	7	17	24	24
1979-80—Canadian Olympic Team (c)		Int'l	46	1	20	21	14
1980-81—Winnipeg Jets		NHL	80	1	18	19	18
1981-82—Winnipeg Jets		NHL	78	0	16	16	21
1982-83—Winnipeg Jets		NHL	80	0	16	16	37
1983-84—Sherbrooke Jets		AHL	50	0	17	17	21
1983-84—Winnipeg Jets		NHL	21	0	4	4	4
NHL TOTALS			259	1	54	55	80

(c)—May, 1980—Signed by Winnipeg Jets as free agent.

GORD STAFFORD

Center . . . 5'10" . . . 180 lbs. . . . Born, Banff, Alta., October 10, 1960 . . . Shoots right.

Year	Team	League	Games	G.	A.	Pts.	Pen.
1977-78—Billings Bighorns		WCHL	59	11	22	33	54
1978-79—Billings Bighorns		WHL	72	37	66	103	70
1979-80—Billings Bighorns (c)		WHL	68	52	58	110	91
1980-81—Milwaukee Admirals		IHL	40	24	32	56	30
1980-81—Wichita Wind		CHL	27	5	3	8	34
1981-82—Wichita Wind		CHL	49	9	16	25	42
1982-83—Milwaukee Admirals		IHL	77	23	49	72	81
1983-84—Milwaukee Admirals		IHL	79	36	45	81	35

(c)—September, 1979—Signed by Edmonton Oilers as a free agent but returned to play junior hockey.

LORNE ALEXANDER STAMLER

Left Wing . . . 6' . . . 190 lbs. . . . Born, Winnipeg, Man., August 9, 1951 . . . Shoots left . . . Attended Michigan Tech . . . Missed part of 1974-75 season with broken arm . . . (March, 1981)—Bruised knee . . . (October, 1981)—Knee injury.

Year	Team	League	Games	G.	A.	Pts.	Pen.
1968-69—Toronto Marlboros		Jr."A"OHA	25	2	3	5	14
1969-70—Toronto Marlboros		Jr."A"OHA	51	6	12	18	32
1970-71—Michigan Tech (c)		WCHA	32	8	5	13	8
1971-72—Michigan Tech		WCHA	32	20	12	32	20
1972-73—Michigan Tech		WCHA	37	11	17	28	22
1973-74—Michigan Tech (b)		WCHA	39	26	30	56	36
1974-75—Springfield Indians		AHL	43	16	9	25	5
1975-76—Fort Worth Texans		CHL	76	33	33	66	12
1976-77—Fort Worth Texans (d)		CHL	48	19	21	40	12
1976-77—Los Angeles Kings		NHL	7	2	1	3	2
1977-78—Springfield Indians		AHL	70	18	34	52	4
1977-78—Los Angeles Kings (e)		NHL	2	0	0	0	0
1978-79—New Brunswick Hawks		AHL	14	9	1	10	4
1978-79—Toronto Maple Leafs (f)		NHL	45	4	3	7	2
1979-80—Winnipeg Jets (g)		NHL	62	8	7	15	12
1979-80—Tulsa Oilers		CHL	6	8	3	11	0
1980-81—Indianapolis Checkers		CHL	42	7	6	13	25
1981-82—Indianapolis Checkers		CHL	53	5	7	12	8
1982-83—Indianapolis Checkers		CHL	38	4	4	8	0
1983-84—Indianapolis Checkers		CHL	15	3	2	5	0
NHL TOTALS			116	14	11	25	16

(c)—Drafted from Michigan Tech by Los Angeles Kings in eighth round of 1971 amateur draft.
(d)—Tied for lead in goals (4) during playoffs.
(e)—Traded to Toronto Maple Leafs by Los Angeles Kings with Dave Hutchison for Brian Glennie, Scott Garland, Kurt Walker and second-round 1979 draft choice, (Mark Hardy), June, 1978.
(f)—June, 1979—Selected by Winnipeg Jets in NHL expansion draft.
(g)—September, 1980—Signed by New York Islanders as a free agent.

DARYL STANLEY

Defense . . . 6'2" . . . 200 lbs. . . . Born, Winnipeg, Man., December 2, 1962 . . . Shoots left.

Year	Team	League	Games	G.	A.	Pts.	Pen.
1979-80—New Westminster Bruins		WHL	64	2	12	14	110
1980-81—New Westminster Bruins		WHL	66	7	27	34	127
1981-82—Saskatoon Blades (c-d)		WHL	65	7	25	32	175
1981-82—Maine Mariners (e)		AHL	....	...	....	....	....
1982-83—Toledo Goaldiggers		IHL	5	0	2	2	2
1982-83—Maine Mariners		AHL	44	2	5	7	95
1983-84—Springfield Indians		AHL	52	4	10	14	122
1983-84—Philadelphia Flyers		NHL	23	1	4	5	71
NHL TOTALS			23	1	4	5	71

(c)—October, 1981—Signed by Philadelphia Flyers as a free agent.
(d)—September, 1981—Traded by Kamloops Junior Oilers to Saskatoon Blades for Brian Propp and Mike Spencer.
(e)—Did not play in regular season, but did play two playoff games.

MIKE STAPLETON

Center . . . 5'10" . . . 165 lbs. . . . Born, Sarnia, Ont., May 5, 1966 . . . Shoots right . . . Son of former Chicago defenseman Pat Stapleton.

Year	Team	League	Games	G.	A.	Pts.	Pen.
1982-83—Strathroy Braves		WOJBHL	40	39	38	77	99
1983-84—Cornwall Royals (c)		OHL	70	24	45	69	94

(c)—June, 1984—Drafted as underage junior by Chicago Black Hawks in NHL entry draft. Seventh Black Hawks pick, 132nd overall, seventh round.

ANTON STASTNY

Left Wing . . . 6' . . . 185 lbs. . . . Born, Bratislava, Czechoslovakia, August 5, 1959 . . . Shoots left . . . Brother of Peter, Marian and Bohuslav Stastny . . . (December, 1981)—Pulled knee ligaments.

Year	Team	League	Games	G.	A.	Pts.	Pen.
1977-78—Slovan Bratislava		Czech	44	19	17	36	....
1977-78—Czechoslovakian Nat's.		Int'l.	6	1	1	2	....
1978-79—Slovan Bratislava (a-c)		Czech.	44	32	19	51	....
1978-79—Czechoslovakian Nat's.		Int'l.	20	9	6	15	....
1979-80—Slovan Bratislava		Czech.	40	30	30	60	....
1979-80—Czech. Olympic Team (d)		Olympics	6	4	4	8	2
1980-81—Quebec Nordiques		NHL	80	39	46	85	12
1981-82—Quebec Nordiques		NHL	68	26	46	72	16

Year	Team	League	Games	G.	A.	Pts.	Pen.
1982-83—Quebec Nordiques		NHL	79	32	60	92	25
1983-84—Quebec Nordiques		NHL	69	25	37	62	14
NHL TOTALS			296	122	189	311	67

(c)—August, 1979—Drafted by Quebec Nordiques in 1979 NHL entry draft. Fourth Nordiques pick, 83rd overall, fourth round.

(d)—August, 1980—Signed by Quebec Nordiques.

MARIAN STASTNY

Right Wing . . . 5'10" . . . 192 lbs. . . . Born, Bratislava, Czechoslovakia, January 8, 1953 . . . Shoots left . . . Brother of Peter, Anton and Bohuslav Stastny . . . (February, 1983)—Surgery for shoulder separation . . . Has a law degree from Komensky University, Bratislava, Czechoslovakia.

Year	Team	League	Games	G.	A.	Pts.	Pen.
1980-81—Slovan Bratislava		Czech.	....	...	....	....	....
1981-82—Quebec Nordiques (c)		NHL	74	35	54	89	27
1982-83—Quebec Nordiques		NHL	60	36	43	79	32
1983-84—Quebec Nordiques		NHL	68	20	32	52	26
NHL TOTALS			202	91	129	220	85

(c)—August, 1980—Signed by Quebec Nordiques as a free agent.

PETER STASTNY

Center . . . 6'1" . . . 200 lbs. . . . Born, Bratislava, Czechoslovakia, September 18, 1956 . . . Shoots left . . . Brother of Anton, Marion and Bohuslav Stastny . . . (December 18, 1982)— Knee injury in game at Buffalo . . . One of only three players to break in NHL with three straight 100-point seasons (Wayne Gretzky and Mike Rogers being the others) . . . (1980- 81)—Set NHL records for most assists and points by a rookie . . . One of only two players (Wayne Gretzky) to have 100-point seasons in their first four NHL seasons.

Year	Team	League	Games	G.	A.	Pts.	Pen.
1977-78—Slovan Bratislava (b)		Czech.	44	29	24	53	....
1977-78—Czechoslovakia Nat'l.		Int'l.	16	5	2	7	....
1978-79—Slovan Bratislava (a)		Czech.	44	32	23	55	....
1978-79—Czechoslovakia Nat'l.		Int'l.	18	12	9	21	....
1979-80—Slovan Bratislava		Czech.	40	28	30	58	....
1979-80—Czech. Olympic Team (c)		Olympics	6	7	7	14	6
1980-81—Quebec Nordiques (d-e)		NHL	77	39	70	109	37
1981-82—Quebec Nordiques		NHL	80	46	93	139	91
1982-83—Quebec Nordiques		NHL	75	47	77	124	78
1983-84—Quebec Nordiques		NHL	80	46	73	119	73
NHL TOTALS			312	178	313	391	279

(c)—August, 1980—Signed by Quebec Nordiques as a free agent.

(d)—Winner of Calder Trophy (NHL Rookie-of-the-Year).

(e)—Selected THE SPORTING NEWS NHL Rookie of the Year in a vote of the players.

THOMAS STEEN

Center . . . 5'10" . . . 195 lbs. . . . Born, Tocksmark, Sweden, June 8, 1960 . . . Shoots left . . . (September, 1981)—Lacerated elbow during Canada Cup as a member of Team Sweden . . . (October, 1981)—Injured knee in training camp.

Year	Team	League	Games	G.	A.	Pts.	Pen.
1978-79—Leksands IF		Sweden	25	13	4	17	35
1979-80—Leksands IF (c)		Sweden	18	7	7	14	14
1980-81—Farjestads BK (d)		Sweden	32	16	23	39	30
1981-82—Winnipeg Jets		NHL	73	15	29	44	42
1982-83—Winnipeg Jets		NHL	75	26	33	59	60
1983-84—Winnipeg Jets		NHL	78	20	45	65	69
NHL TOTALS			226	61	107	168	171

(c)—June, 1980—Drafted by Winnipeg Jets in 1980 NHL entry draft. Fifth Jets pick, 103rd overall, fifth round.

(d)—Named Player of the Year in Swedish National League.

STANLEY MICHAEL (BUD) STEFANSKI

Center . . . 5'10" . . . 170 lbs. . . . Born, South Porcupine, Ont., April 28, 1955 . . . Shoots left . . . Missed part of 1978-79 season with broken collarbone.

Year	Team	League	Games	G.	A.	Pts.	Pen.
1973-74—Oshawa Generals		Jr."A" OHA	67	25	32	57	22
1974-75—Oshawa Generals (c)		Jr."A" OHA	61	18	48	66	35
1975-76—Port Huron Flags		IHL	71	26	30	56	59

Year	Team	League	Games	G.	A.	Pts.	Pen.
1976-77—Port Huron Flags	IHL	77	49	54	103	61
1976-77—New Haven Nighthawks (d)	AHL	..	..	..	..	....
1977-78—New Haven Nighthawks	AHL	79	27	37	64	61
1977-78—New York Rangers	NHL	1	0	0	0	0
1978-79—New Haven Nighthawks	AHL	51	18	40	58	71
1979-80—Tulsa Oilers	CHL	71	19	44	63	61
1980-81—New Haven Nighthawks	AHL	20	9	18	27	46
1981-82—New Haven Nighthawks (e)	AHL	16	6	5	11	24
1982-83—Springfield Indians	AHL	80	30	40	70	65
1983-84—Maine Mariners (f-g-h)	AHL	57	26	23	49	47
NHL TOTALS		1	0	0	0	0

(c)—Drafted from Oshawa Generals by New York Rangers in ninth round of 1975 amateur draft.
(d)—No league record. Appeared in two playoff games.
(e)—March, 1982—Signed by New Haven Nighthawks as a free agent.
(f)—January, 1983—Signed by Maine Mariners as a free agent.
(g)—Won Jack Butterfield Trophy (AHL Playoff MVP).
(h)—Led AHL playoffs with 12 goals (Tied with Paul Gardner of Baltimore).

MICHAEL STERN

Left Wing . . . 6'4" . . . 210 lbs. . . . Born, Kitchener, Ont., June 12, 1964 . . . Shoots left.

Year	Team	League	Games	G.	A.	Pts.	Pen.
1980-81—Kitchener Greenshirts	Ont. Midget	58	45	25	70	....
1981-82—Oshawa Generals (c)	OHL	47	4	6	10	64
1982-83—Oshawa Generals	OHL	61	16	31	47	161
1983-84—Oshawa Generals	OHL	56	38	38	76	118

(c)—June, 1982—Drafted as underage junior by Detroit Red Wings in 1982 NHL entry draft. Eleventh Red Wings pick, 212th overall, 11th round.

JOHN STEVENS

Defense . . . 6'1" . . . 180 lbs. . . . Born, Completon, N.B., May 4, 1966 . . . Shoots left.

Year	Team	League	Games	G.	A.	Pts.	Pen.
1982-83—Newmarket Flyers	OJHL	48	2	9	11	111
1983-84—Oshawa Generals (c)	OHL	70	1	10	11	71

(c)—June, 1984—Drafted as underage junior by Chicago Black Hawks in NHL entry draft. Second Black Hawks pick, 45th overall, third round.

KEVIN STEVENS

Center . . . 6'3" . . . 207 lbs. . . . Born, Brockton, Mass., April 15, 1965 . . . Shoots left . . . Also plays left wing.

Year	Team	League	Games	G.	A.	Pts.	Pen.
1982-83—Silver Lake H.S. (c)	Minn. H.S.	18	24	27	51	..
1983-84—Boston College (d)	ECAC	37	6	14	20	36

(c)—June, 1983—Drafted by Los Angeles Kings in 1983 NHL entry draft. Sixth Kings pick, 108th overall, sixth round.
(d)—September, 1983—Traded by Los Angeles Kings to Pittsburgh Penguins for Anders Hakansson.

MIKE STEVENS

Center . . . 5'11" . . . 195 lbs. . . . Born, Kitchener, Ont., December 30, 1965 . . . Shoots left.

Year	Team	League	Games	G.	A.	Pts.	Pen.
1982-83—Kitchener Ranger B's	MWOJBHL	29	5	18	23	86
1983-84—Kitchener Rangers (c)	OHL	66	19	21	40	109

(c)—June, 1984—Drafted as underage junior by Vancouver Canucks in NHL entry draft. Fourth Canucks pick, 58th overall, third round.

SCOTT STEVENS

Defense . . . 6' . . . 197 lbs. . . . Born, Kitchener, Ont., April 1, 1964 . . . Shoots left.

Year	Team	League	Games	G.	A.	Pts.	Pen.
1980-81—Kitchener Jr. B.	OPJHL	39	7	33	40	82
1981-82—Kitchener Rangers (c)	OHL	68	6	36	42	158
1982-83—Washington Capitals	NHL	77	9	16	25	195
1983-84—Washington Capitals	NHL	78	13	32	45	201
NHL TOTALS		155	22	48	70	396

(c)—June, 1982—Drafted as underage junior by Washington Capitals in 1982 NHL entry draft. First Capitals pick, fifth overall, first round.

ALLAN STEWART

Left Wing . . . 5'11" . . . 173 lbs. . . . Born, Fort St. John, B.C., January 31, 1964 . . . Shoots left . . . (1983-84)—Set WHL record with 14 shorthanded goals.

Year	Team	League	Games	G.	A.	Pts.	Pen.
1981-82—Prince Albert Raiders		SJHL	46	9	25	34	53
1982-83—Prince Albert Raiders (c)		WHL	70	25	34	59	272
1983-84—Prince Albert Raiders		WHL	67	44	39	83	216

(c)—June, 1983—Drafted as underage junior by New Jersey Devils in 1983 NHL entry draft. Ninth Devils pick, 205th overall, 11th round.

BILL STEWART

Right Wing . . . 6' . . . 180 lbs. . . . Born, The Pas, Man., July 12, 1961 . . . Shoots right.

Year	Team	League	Games	G.	A.	Pts.	Pen.
1979-80—University of Denver (c)		WCHA	30	11	16	27	32
1980-81—University of Denver		WCHA	25	8	11	19	26
1981-82—University of Denver		WCHA	36	17	22	39	36
1982-83—University of Denver		WCHA	35	23	24	47	40
1983-84—Salt Lake Golden Eagles		CHL	68	23	27	50	31

(c)—June, 1980—Drafted by Minnesota North Stars in NHL entry draft. Seventh North Stars pick, 142nd overall, seventh round.

WILLIAM DONALD STEWART

Defense . . . 6'2" . . . 190 lbs. . . . Born, Toronto, Ont., October 6, 1957 . . . Shoots right . . . Missed part of 1978-79 season with back injury . . . (January, 1984)—Broken foot.

Year	Team	League	Games	G.	A.	Pts.	Pen.
1973-74—Dixie Beehives		OPJHL	41	9	24	33	38
1974-75—Kitchener Rangers		Jr."A"OHA	55	6	15	21	70
1975-76—Kitchener Rangers (c)		Jr."A"OHA	4	1	3	4	4
1975-76—St. Cath. Black Hawks		Jr."A"OHA	48	9	31	40	57
1976-77—Niagara Falls Flyers (d)		Jr."A"OHA	59	18	37	55	202
1977-78—Hershey Bears		AHL	54	6	18	24	92
1977-78—Buffalo Sabres		NHL	13	2	0	2	15
1978-79—Buffalo Sabres		NHL	68	1	17	18	101
1979-80—Rochester Americans		AHL	63	12	28	40	189
1980-81—Rochester Americans (e)		AHL	6	1	6	7	12
1980-81—Salt Lake Golden Eagles		CHL	2	0	0	0	2
1980-81—St. Louis Blues		NHL	60	2	21	23	114
1981-82—St. Louis Blues		NHL	22	0	5	5	25
1981-82—Salt Lake Golden Eagles		CHL	40	2	12	14	93
1982-83—St. Louis Blues		NHL	7	0	0	0	8
1982-83—Salt Lake Golden Eagles		CHL	62	10	42	52	143
1983-84—Toronto Maple Leafs (f)		NHL	56	2	17	19	116
NHL TOTALS			226	7	60	67	379

(c)—Traded to St. Catharines Black Hawks by Kitchener Rangers with Ken Campbell and Marc Thiel for Joe Grant, December, 1975.

(d)—Drafted from Niagara Falls Flyers by Buffalo Sabres in fourth round of 1977 amateur draft.

(e)—October, 1980—Traded by Buffalo Sabres to St. Louis Blues for Bob Hess.

(f)—September, 1983—Signed by Toronto Maple Leafs as a free agent.

TREVOR STIENBURG

Right Wing . . . 6'1" . . . 180 lbs. . . . Born, Kingston, Ont., May 13, 1966 . . . Shoots right.

Year	Team	League	Games	G.	A.	Pts.	Pen.
1982-83—Brockville Braves		COJHL	47	39	30	69	182
1983-84—Guelph Platers (c)		OHL	65	33	18	51	104

(c)—June, 1984—Drafted as underage junior by Quebec Nordiques in NHL entry draft. First Nordiques pick, 15th overall, first round.

TONY STILES

Defense . . . 6' . . . 205 lbs. . . . Born, Carstairs, Alta., August 12, 1959 . . . Shoots left.

Year	Team	League	Games	G.	A.	Pts.	Pen.
1977-78—Calgary		AJHL	60	7	29	36	73
1978-79—Michigan Tech		WCHA	....	...	....	....	....
1979-80—Michigan Tech		WCHA	....	...	....	....	....
1980-81—Michigan Tech		WCHA	44	10	20	30	58
1981-82—Michigan Tech		CCHA	38	7	14	21	26
1982-83—Colorado Flames (c)		CHL	58	2	7	9	53

Year	Team	League	Games	G.	A.	Pts.	Pen.
1983-84—Colorado Flames		CHL	39	3	18	21	24
1983-84—Calgary Flames		NHL	30	2	7	9	20
NHL TOTALS			30	2	7	9	20

(c)—April, 1982—Signed by Calgary Flames as a free agent.

MICHAEL PATRICK STOTHERS

Defense ... 6'4" ... 210 lbs. ... Born, Toronto, Ont., February 22, 1962 ... Shoots left.

Year	Team	League	Games	G.	A.	Pts.	Pen.
1979-80—Kingston Canadians (c)		OMJHL	66	4	23	27	137
1980-81—Kingston Canadians		OHL	65	4	22	26	237
1981-82—Kingston Canadians		OHL	61	1	20	21	203
1981-82—Maine Mariners		AHL	5	0	0	0	4
1982-83—Maine Mariners		AHL	80	2	16	18	139
1983-84—Maine Mariners		AHL	61	2	10	12	109

(c)—June, 1980—Drafted as underage junior by Philadelphia Flyers in NHL entry draft. First Flyers pick, 21st overall, first round.

BLAINE STOUGHTON

Right Wing ... 5'10" ... 185 lbs. ... Born, Gilbert Plains, Man., March 13, 1953 ... Shoots right ... Missed start of 1980-81 season in contract technicality with Whalers. Was declared free agent by NHL President John Ziegler, but re-signed with Hartford ... (October, 1982)—Suspended for first eight games of season for high-sticking Pittsburgh's Paul Baxter in exhibition game at Johnstown, Pa. ... Holds Hartford Whalers club record for single-season goals and career goals (56 and 219).

Year	Team	League	Games	G.	A.	Pts.	Pen.
1969-70—Flin Flon Bombers		WCHL	59	19	20	39	181
1970-71—Flin Flon Bombers		WCHL	35	26	24	50	96
1971-72—Flin Flon Bombers (a)		WCHL	68	*60	66	126	121
1972-73—Flin Flon Bombers (c)		WCHL	66	58	60	118	86
1973-74—Hershey Bears		AHL	47	23	17	40	35
1973-74—Pittsburgh Penguins (d)		NHL	34	5	6	11	8
1974-75—Toronto Maple Leafs		NHL	78	23	14	37	24
1975-76—Oklahoma City Blazers		CHL	30	14	22	36	24
1975-76—Toronto Maple Leafs (e)		NHL	43	6	11	17	8
1976-77—Cincinnati Stingers		WHA	81	52	52	104	39
1977-78—Cincinnati Stingers (f)		WHA	30	6	13	19	36
1977-78—Indianapolis Racers		WHA	47	13	13	26	28
1978-79—Indianapolis Racers (g)		WHA	25	9	9	18	16
1978-79—New England Whalers		WHA	36	9	3	12	2
1979-80—Hartford Whalers		NHL	80	*56	44	100	16
1980-81—Hartford Whalers		NHL	71	43	30	73	56
1981-82—Hartford Whalers		NHL	80	52	39	91	57
1982-83—Hartford Whalers		NHL	72	45	31	76	27
1983-84—Hartford Whalers (h)		NHL	54	23	14	37	4
1983-84—New York Rangers		NHL	14	5	2	7	4
NHL TOTALS			526	258	191	449	204
WHA TOTALS			219	89	90	179	121

(c)—Drafted from Flin Flon Bombers by Pittsburgh Penguins in first round of 1973 amateur draft.

(d)—Traded to Toronto Maple Leafs with Pittsburgh's first round 1976 draft choice by Pittsburgh Penguins for Rick Kehoe, September, 1974.

(e)—Signed by Cincinnati Stingers (WHA), August, 1976.

(f)—Traded to Indianapolis Racers by Cincinnati Stingers with Gilles Marotte for Bryon Baltimore and Hugh Harris, December, 1977.

(g)—December, 1978—Sold to New England Whalers by Indianapolis.

(h)—February, 1984—Traded by Hartford Whalers to New York Rangers for Scot Kleinendorst.

STEVE STOYANOVICH

Center ... 6'2" ... 205 lbs. ... Born, London, Alta., May 2, 1957 ... Shoots left ... Also plays left wing ... Brother of Dave Stoyanovich.

Year	Team	League	Games	G.	A.	Pts.	Pen.
1976-77—R.P.I. (c)		ECAC	....	..	....	....	....
1977-78—R.P.I.		ECAC	28	22	30	52	24
1978-79—R.P.I.		ECAC	28	17	30	47	32
1979-80—R.P.I.		ECAC	17	9	15	24	16
1980-81—Did not play			....	..	....	....	....
1981-82—Indianapolis Checkers		CHL	80	42	30	72	55
1982-83—Indianapolis Checkers (a-d)		CHL	79	41	43	84	65

Year	Team	League	Games	G.	A.	Pts.	Pen.
1983-84—Binghamton Whalers		AHL	21	11	8	19	0
1983-84—Hartford Whalers		NHL	23	3	5	8	11
NHL TOTALS			23	3	5	8	11

(c)—June, 1977—Drafted by New York Islanders in 1977 NHL amateur draft. Fifth Islanders pick, 69th overall, fourth round.

(d)—August, 1983—Traded by New York Islanders to Hartford Whalers for future considerations.

KEN STRONG

Left Wing . . . 5'11" . . . 175 lbs. . . . Born, Toronto, Ont., May 9, 1963 . . . Shoots left . . . (September, 1981)—Injured back . . . (January, 1983)—Pulled hamstring.

Year	Team	League	Games	G.	A.	Pts.	Pen.
1979-80—Streetsville Derbys		MTHL	35	47	51	98	116
1980-81—Peterborough Petes (c)		OMJHL	64	17	36	53	52
1981-82—Peterborough Petes (d)		OHL	42	21	22	43	69
1982-83—Peterborough Petes		OHL	57	41	48	89	80
1982-83—Toronto Maple Leafs		NHL	2	0	0	0	0
1983-84—Toronto Maple Leafs		NHL	2	0	2	2	2
1983-84—St. Catharines Saints		AHL	78	27	45	72	78
NHL TOTALS			4	0	2	2	2

(c)—June, 1981—Drafted as underage junior by Philadelphia Flyers in 1981 NHL entry draft. Fourth Flyers pick, 58th overall, third round.

(d)—March, 1982—NHL rights were traded by Philadelphia Flyers to Toronto Maple Leafs to complete January trade for Darryl Sittler.

TODD STRUEBY

Left Wing . . . 6'1" . . . 186 lbs. . . . Born, Lannigan, Sask., June 15, 1963 . . . Shoots left.

Year	Team	League	Games	G.	A.	Pts.	Pen.
1979-80—Notre Dame Midgets		....	58	44	61	105	112
1980-81—Regina Pats (c)		WHL	71	18	27	45	99
1981-82—Saskatoon Blades (a-d)		WHL	61	60	58	118	160
1981-82—Edmonton Oilers		NHL	3	0	0	0	0
1982-83—Saskatoon Blades		WHL	65	40	70	110	119
1982-83—Edmonton Oilers		NHL	1	0	0	0	0
1983-84—Edmonton Oilers		NHL	1	0	1	1	2
1983-84—Moncton Alpines		AHL	72	17	25	42	38
NHL TOTALS			5	0	1	1	2

(c)—Drafted by Edmonton Oilers in NHL entry draft. Second Oilers pick, 29th overall, second round.

(d)—September, 1981—Traded by Regina Pats to Saskatoon Blades for Lyndon Byers.

KAI SUIKKANEN

Left Wing . . . 6'2" . . . 207 lbs. . . . Born, Opiskelija, Finland, June 29, 1959 . . . Shoots left . . . (February, 1983)—Broken finger . . . Also plays right wing.

Year	Team	League	Games	G.	A.	Pts.	Pen.
1979-80—Oulu Karpat		Finland	36	21	17	38	18
1980-81—Oulu Karpat		Finland	33	20	11	31	60
1981-82—Buffalo Sabres		NHL	1	0	0	0	0
1981-82—Rochester Americans		AHL	71	34	33	67	32
1982-83—Buffalo Sabres		NHL	1	0	0	0	0
1982-83—Rochester Americans		AHL	66	33	44	77	65
1983-84—Rochester Americans		AHL	15	7	10	17	2
NHL TOTALS			2	0	0	0	0

SIMON DOUGLAS SULLIMAN
(Known by middle name.)

Left Wing . . . 5'9" . . . 195 lbs. . . . Born, Glace Bay, Nova Scotia, August 29, 1959 . . . Shoots left . . . Missed part of 1979-80 season with injury to right knee . . . Also plays right wing . . . (November, 1983)—Groin pull.

Year	Team	League	Games	G.	A.	Pts.	Pen.
1976 77—Kitchener Rangers		OMJHL	65	30	41	71	123
1977-78—Kitchener Rangers		OMJHL	68	50	39	89	87
1978-79—Kitchener Rangers (c)		OMJHL	68	38	77	115	88
1979-80—New York Rangers		NHL	31	4	7	11	2
1979-80—New Haven Nighthawks		AHL	31	9	7	16	9
1980-81—New Haven Nighthawks		AHL	45	10	16	26	18
1980-81—New York Rangers		NHL	32	4	1	5	32
1981-82—Hartford Whalers (d)		NHL	77	29	40	69	39

Year	Team	League	Games	G.	A.	Pts.	Pen.
1982-83—Hartford Whalers		NHL	77	22	19	41	14
1983-84—Hartford Whalers (e)		NHL	67	6	12	18	20
NHL TOTALS			284	65	79	144	107

(c)—August, 1979—Drafted by New York Rangers in entry draft. First Rangers pick, 13th overall, first round.

(d)—October, 1981—Traded with Chris Kotsopoulos and Gerry McDonald by New York Rangers to Hartford Whalers for Mike Rogers and a 10th-round 1982 entry draft pick (Simo Saarinen).

(e)—July, 1984—Released by Hartford Whalers. Signed by New Jersey Devils as a free agent.

BOB SULLIVAN

Left Wing . . . 6' . . . 210 lbs. . . . Born, Noranda, Que., November 29, 1957 . . . Shoots left . . . (1981-82)—Set AHL record for most goals by a rookie and most consecutive games with a point in the AHL (28 games, 23g, 24a).

Year	Team	League	Games	G.	A.	Pts.	Pen.
1974-75—St. Jerome		QJHL	56	29	47	76	31
1975-76—Chicoutimi Sagueneens		QMJHL	68	20	22	42	34
1976-77—Chicoutimi Sagueneens (c)		QMJHL	71	45	65	110	80
1977-78—New Haven Nighthawks		AHL	2	0	0	0	0
1977-78—Toledo Goaldiggers		IHL	65	27	27	54	60
1978-79—Toledo Goaldiggers		IHL	1	0	1	1	0
1979-80—Toledo Goaldiggers		IHL	56	30	26	56	68
1980-81—Toledo Goaldiggers (d)		IHL	79	32	53	84	69
1981-82—Binghamton Whalers (a-e)		AHL	74	47	43	90	44
1982-83—Hartford Whalers		NHL	62	18	19	37	18
1982-83—Binghamton Whalers		AHL	18	18	14	32	2
1983-84—Binghamton Whalers		AHL	76	33	47	80	48
NHL TOTALS			62	18	19	37	18

(c)—June, 1977—Drafted by New York Rangers in the NHL amateur draft. Eighth Rangers pick, 116th overall, seventh round.

(d)—September, 1981—Signed by Hartford Whalers as a free agent.

(e)—Won Dudley "Red" Garrett Memorial Award (Top AHL Rookie).

RAIMO SUMMANEN

Left Wing . . . 5'11" . . . 185 lbs. . . . Born, Jyvaskyla, Finland, March 2, 1962 . . . Shoots left . . . Member of 1984 Finland Olympic team.

Year	Team	League	Games	G.	A.	Pts.	Pen.
1981-82—Lahti Kiekkoreipas (c)		Finland	36	15	6	21	17
1981-82—Lahti Kiekkoreipas		Finland		...	....	....	....
1983-84—Tampere Ilves		Finland	36	28	19	47	26
1983-84—Finland Olympic Team		Int'l	4	4	7	11	2
1983-84—Edmonton Oilers		NHL	2	1	4	5	2
TOTALS			2	1	4	5	2

(c)—June, 1982—Drafted by Edmonton Oilers in 1982 NHL entry draft. Sixth Oilers pick, 125th overall, sixth round.

PATRIK SUNDSTROM

Center . . . 6' . . . 195 lbs. . . . Born Skellefteaa, Sweden, December 14, 1961 . . . Shoots left . . . (November, 1982)—Shoulder separation . . . (1983-84)—Set Vancouver club records for most points in a season and most goals by a center . . . Twin brother of Peter Sundstrom.

Year	Team	League	Games	G.	A.	Pts.	Pen.
1979-80—Umea Bjorkloven IF (c)		Sweden	26	5	7	12	20
1980-81—Umea Bjorkloven IF		Sweden	36	10	18	28	30
1981-82—Umea Bjorkloven IF		Sweden	36	22	13	35	38
1982-83—Vancouver Canucks		NHL	74	23	23	46	30
1983-84—Vancouver Canucks (d)		NHL	78	38	53	91	37
NHL TOTALS			152	61	76	137	67

(c)—June, 1980—Drafted by Vancouver Canucks in 1980 NHL entry draft. Eighth Canucks pick, 175th overall, ninth round.

(d)—Won Viking Award (Outstanding Swedish-born player in NHL as voted on by fellow Swedish-born NHL players).

PETER SUNDSTROM

Left Wing . . . 6' . . . 180 lbs. . . . Born, Skelleftea, Sweden, December 14, 1961 . . . Shoots left . . . Twin brother of Patrik Sundstrom.

Year	Team	League	Games	G.	A.	Pts.	Pen.
1979-80—Umea Bjorkloven IF		Sweden	8	0	0	0	2
1980-81—Umea Bjorkloven IF (c)		Sweden	29	7	2	9	8
1981-82—Umea Bjorkloven IF		Sweden	35	10	14	24	18
1982-83—Umea Bjorkloven IF		Sweden	36	17	10	27	....
1983-84—New York Rangers		NHL	77	22	22	44	24
NHL TOTALS			77	22	22	44	24

(c)—June, 1981—Drafted by New York Rangers in NHL entry draft. Third Rangers pick, 50th overall, third round.

GARY SUTER

Defense . . . 6' . . . 190 lbs. . . . Born, Madison, Wis., June 24, 1964 . . . Shoots left.

Year	Team	League	Games	G.	A.	Pts.	Pen.
1983-84—Univ. of Wisconsin (c)		WCHA	35	4	18	22	68

(c)—June, 1984—Drafted by Calgary Flames in NHL entry draft. Ninth Flames pick, 180th overall, ninth round.

BRENT BOLIN SUTTER

Center . . . 5'11" . . . 175 lbs. . . . Born, Viking, Alta., June 10, 1962 . . . Shoots left . . . Brother of Brian, Darryl, Ron, Gary, Rich and Duane Sutter . . . (January, 1984)—Missed 11 games with damaged tendon and infection in right hand.

Year	Team	League	Games	G.	A.	Pts.	Pen.
1977-78—Red Deer Rustlers		AJHL	60	12	18	30	33
1978-79—Red Deer Rustlers		AJHL	60	42	42	84	79
1979-80—Red Deer Rustlers (c)		AJHL	59	70	101	171	131
1980-81—New York Islanders		NHL	3	2	2	4	0
1980-81—Lethbridge Broncos		WHL	68	54	54	108	116
1981-82—Lethbridge Broncos		WHL	34	46	34	80	162
1981-82—New York Islanders		NHL	43	21	22	43	114
1982-83—New York Islanders		NHL	80	21	19	40	128
1983-84—New York Islanders		NHL	69	34	15	49	69
NHL TOTALS			195	78	58	136	311

(c)—June, 1980—Drafted by New York Islanders as underage junior in 1980 NHL entry draft. First Islanders pick, 17th overall, first round.

BRIAN SUTTER

Left Wing . . . 5'11" . . . 172 lbs. . . . Born, Viking, Alta., October 7, 1956 . . . Shoots left . . . Brother of Darryl, Brent, Ron, Rich, Gary and Duane Sutter . . . (November 3, 1983)—Hairline fracture of pelvis in game at Boston.

Year	Team	League	Games	G.	A.	Pts.	Pen.
1972-73—Red Deer Rustlers		AJHL	51	27	40	67	54
1973-74—Red Deer Rustlers (a)		AJHL	59	42	*54	96	139
1974-75—Lethbridge Broncos		WCHL	53	34	47	81	134
1975-76—Lethbridge Broncos (c)		WCHL	72	36	56	92	233
1976-77—Kansas City Blues		CHL	38	15	23	38	47
1976-77—St. Louis Blues		NHL	35	4	10	14	82
1977-78—St. Louis Blues		NHL	78	9	13	22	123
1978-79—St. Louis Blues		NHL	77	41	39	80	165
1979-80—St. Louis Blues		NHL	71	23	35	58	156
1980-81—St. Louis Blues		NHL	78	35	34	69	232
1981-82—St. Louis Blues		NHL	74	39	36	75	239
1982-83—St. Louis Blues		NHL	79	46	30	76	254
1983-84—St. Louis Blues		NHL	76	32	51	83	162
NHL TOTALS			568	229	248	477	1413

(c)—Drafted from Lethbridge Broncos by St. Louis Blues in second round of 1976 amateur draft.

DARRYL SUTTER

Center . . . 5'10" . . . 163 lbs. . . . Born, Viking, Alta., August 19, 1958 . . . Shoots left . . . Brother of Brian, Brent, Ron, Rich, Gary and Duane Sutter . . . Played most of 1978-79 season in Japan . . . (1980-81)—Set Chicago rookie record with 40 goals . . . (November 27, 1981)—Lacerated left elbow in game at Edmonton. It later developed an infection and required surgery . . . (November 7, 1982)—Broken nose when hit by high stick by Toronto's Paul Higgins . . . (November, 1983)—Broken ribs . . . (January 2, 1984)—Fractured left cheekbone and injured left eye when hit by teammate Doug Wilson's slap shot in game at Minnesota.

Year	Team	League	Games	G.	A.	Pts.	Pen.
1974-75—Red Deer Rustlers		AJHL	60	16	20	36	43

Year	Team	League	Games	G.	A.	Pts.	Pen.
1975-76—Red Deer Rustlers		AJHL	60	43	93	136	82
1976-77—Red Deer Rustlers (a)		AJHL	56	55	*78	*133	131
1976-77—Lethbridge Broncos		WCHL	1	1	0	1	0
1977-78—Lethbridge Broncos (c)		WCHL	68	33	48	81	119
1978-79—New Brunswick Hawks		AHL	19	7	6	13	6
1978-79—Iwakura, Tomakomai (d)		Japan	20	28	13	41	....
1979-80—New Brunswick Hawks (e)		AHL	69	35	31	66	69
1979-80—Chicago Black Hawks		NHL	8	2	0	2	2
1980-81—Chicago Black Hawks		NHL	76	40	22	62	86
1981-82—Chicago Black Hawks		NHL	40	23	12	35	31
1982-83—Chicago Black Hawks		NHL	80	31	30	61	53
1983-84—Chicago Black Hawks		NHL	59	20	20	40	44
NHL TOTALS			263	116	84	200	216

(c)—June, 1978—Drafted by the Chicago Black Hawks in 1978 NHL amateur draft. Eleventh Black Hawks pick, 179th overall, 11th round.

(d)—Named top rookie of Japan National League.

(e)—Named winner of Dudley (Red) Garrett Memorial Trophy (Top AHL Rookie).

DUANE CALVIN SUTTER

Right Wing . . . 6' . . . 181 lbs. . . . Born, Viking, Alta., March 16, 1960 . . . Shoots right . . . Brother of Brian, Brent, Ron, Rich, Gary and Darryl Sutter . . . (November 11, 1980)—Damaged ligaments in right knee. Injury required surgery . . . (April 2, 1981)—Two weeks after coming back from knee surgery he dislocated right shoulder . . . (November, 1983)—Strained ligaments in left knee in game vs. Quebec.

Year	Team	League	Games	G.	A.	Pts.	Pen.
1976-77—Red Deer Rustlers		AJHL	60	9	26	35	76
1977-78—Red Deer Rustlers		AJHL	59	47	53	100	218
1977-78—Lethbridge Broncos		WCHL	5	1	5	6	19
1978-79—Lethbridge Broncos (c)		WHL	71	50	75	125	212
1979-80—Lethbridge Broncos		WHL	21	18	16	34	74
1979-80—New York Islanders		NHL	56	15	9	24	55
1980-81—New York Islanders		NHL	23	7	11	18	26
1981-82—New York Islanders		NHL	77	18	35	53	100
1982-83—New York Islanders		NHL	75	13	19	32	118
1983-84—New York Islanders		NHL	78	17	23	40	94
NHL TOTALS			309	70	97	167	393

(c)—August, 1979—Drafted by New York Islanders as underage junior in entry draft. First Islanders pick, 17th overall, first round.

RICHARD SUTTER

Right Wing . . . 5'11" . . . 170 lbs. . . . Born, Viking, Alta., December 2, 1963 . . . Shoots right . . . Brother of Brian, Brent, Darryl, Duane, Gary and twin brother of Ron Sutter.

Year	Team	League	Games	G.	A.	Pts.	Pen.
1979-80—Red Deer Rustlers		AJHL	60	13	19	32	157
1980-81—Lethbridge Broncos		WHL	72	23	18	41	255
1981-82—Lethbridge Broncos (c)		WHL	57	38	31	69	263
1982-83—Lethbridge Broncos		WHL	64	37	30	67	200
1982-83—Pittsburgh Penguins		NHL	4	0	0	0	0
1983-84—Baltimore Skipjacks		AHL	2	0	1	1	0
1983-84—Pittsburgh Penguins (d)		NHL	5	0	0	0	0
1983-84—Philadelphia Flyers		NHL	70	16	12	28	93
NHL TOTALS			79	16	12	28	93

(c)—June, 1982—Drafted as underage junior by Pittsburgh Penguins in 1982 NHL entry draft. First Penguins pick, 10th overall, first round.

(d)—October, 1983—Traded with second (Greg Smyth) and third (David McLay) round 1984 draft picks by Pittsburgh Penguins to Philadelphia Flyers for Ron Flockhart, Mark Taylor, Andy Brickley, first (Roger Belanger) and third-round 1984 draft picks.

RONALD SUTTER

Center . . . 6' . . . 180 lbs. . . . Born, Viking, Alta., December 2, 1963 . . . Shoots right . . . Brother of Brian, Brent, Darryl, Duane, Gary and twin brother of Rich Sutter . . . (November 27, 1981)—Broke ankle in game against Medicine Hat.

Year	Team	League	Games	G.	A.	Pts.	Pen.
1979-80—Red Deer Rustlers		AJHL	60	12	33	35	44
1980-81—Lethbridge Broncos		WHL	72	13	32	45	152
1981-82—Lethbridge Broncos (c)		WHL	59	38	54	92	207
1982-83—Lethbridge Broncos		WHL	58	35	48	83	98

Year	Team	League	Games	G.	A.	Pts.	Pen.
1982-83—Philadelphia Flyers		NHL	10	1	1	2	9
1983-84—Philadelphia Flyers		NHL	79	19	32	51	101
NHL TOTALS			89	20	33	53	110

(c)—June, 1982—Drafted as underage junior by Philadelphia Flyers in 1982 NHL entry draft. First Flyers pick, fourth overall, first round.

RICHARD SUWEK

Left Wing . . . 5'11" . . . 200 lbs. . . . Born, Lachine, Que., January 25, 1959 . . . Shoots left . . . Missed most of 1978-79 with injured left knee.

Year	Team	League	Games	G.	A.	Pts.	Pen.
1975-76—Montreal Juniors		QMJHL	65	22	16	38	49
1976-77—Montreal Juniors		QMJHL	72	33	52	85	83
1977-78—Montreal Juniors		QMJHL	61	58	56	114	70
1978-79—Montreal Juniors		QMJHL	16	6	9	15	14
1979-80—Rochester Americans		AHL	69	8	22	30	26
1980-81—Rochester Americans		AHL	10	0	1	1	4
1980-81—Port Huron Flags		IHL	64	22	25	47	28
1981-82—Mohawk Valley Stars (b)		ACHL	46	22	32	54	54
1982-83—Mohawk Valley Stars		ACHL	65	28	51	79	47
1983-84—Mohawk Valley Stars		ACHL	68	40	47	87	69

PETR SVOBODA

Defense . . . 6'1" . . . 160 lbs. . . . Born, Most, Czechoslovakia, February 14, 1966 . . . Shoots left.

Year	Team	League	Games	G.	A.	Pts.	Pen.
1983-84—Czechoslovakia Jr. (c)		Czech.	40	15	21	36	14

(c)—June, 1984—Drafted by Montreal Canadiens in NHL entry draft. First Canadiens pick, fifth overall, first round.

DON SWEENEY

Defense . . . 5'11" . . . 170 lbs. . . . Born, St. Stephen, N.B., August 17, 1966 . . . Shoots left.

Year	Team	League	Games	G.	A.	Pts.	Pen.
1983-84—St. Paul N.B. H.S. (c)		N.B.H.S.	22	33	26	59	....

(c)—June, 1984—Drafted by Boston Bruins in NHL entry draft. Eighth Bruins pick, 166th overall, eighth round.

PHIL SYKES

Left Wing . . . 6' . . . 185 lbs. . . . Born, Dawson Creek, B.C., May 18, 1959 . . . Shoots left.

Year	Team	League	Games	G.	A.	Pts.	Pen.
1978-79—North Dakota University		WCHA	41	9	5	14	16
1979-80—North Dakota University		WCHA	37	22	27	49	34
1980-81—North Dakota University		WCHA	38	28	34	62	22
1981-82—North Dakota University (c-d)		WCHA	45	39	24	63	20
1982-83—Los Angeles Kings		NHL	7	2	0	2	2
1982-83—New Haven Nighthawks		AHL	71	19	26	45	111
1983-84—New Haven Nighthawks		AHL	77	29	37	66	101
1983-84—Los Angeles Kings		NHL	3	0	0	0	2
NHL TOTALS			10	2	0	2	4

(c)—Named to Western All-America Team.
(d)—April, 1982—Signed by Los Angeles Kings as a free agent.

JACQUES SYLVESTRE

Center . . . 6' . . . 176 lbs. . . . Born, Sherbrooke, Que., February 9, 1963 . . . Shoots right.

Year	Team	League	Games	G.	A.	Pts.	Pen.
1980-81—Sorel Black Hawks (c)		QMJHL	72	18	15	33	31
1981-82—Granby Bisons (b-d)		QMJHL	63	51	69	120	44
1982-83—Granby Bisons		QHL	16	11	17	28	4
1982-83—Verdun Juniors		QHL	50	41	41	82	21
1983-84—Indianapolis Checkers		CHL	62	22	16	38	26

(c)—June, 1981—Drafted as underage Junior by New York Islanders in 1981 NHL entry draft. Sixth Islanders pick, 94th overall, fifth round.
(d)—Winner of Marcel Robert Trophy (Top Scholastic/Athletic QMJHL performer).

BARRY TABOBONDUNG

Left Wing . . . 5'10" . . . 190 lbs. . . . Born, Parry Sound, Ont., April 3, 1961 . . . Shoots left . . . Also plays defense.

Year	Team	League	Games	G.	A.	Pts.	Pen.
1979-80—Oshawa Generals		OMJHL	51	7	11	18	190
1980-81—Oshawa Generals (c)		OMJHL	61	18	59	77	320
1981-82—Maine Mariners		AHL	72	11	15	26	166
1982-83—Peoria Prancers		IHL	16	2	7	9	13
1982-83—Maine Mariners		AHL	60	2	17	19	43
1983-84—Erie Golden Blades (b)		ACHL	70	6	37	43	57

(c)—June, 1981—Drafted by Philadelphia Flyers in 1981 NHL entry draft. Third Flyers pick, 47th overall, third round.

PETER TAGLIANETTE

Defense ... 6'2" ... 200 lbs. ... Born, Framingham, Mass., August 15, 1963 ... Shoots left.

Year	Team	League	Games	G.	A.	Pts.	Pen.
1981-82—Providence College		ECAC	2	0	0	0	2
1982-83—Providence College (c)		ECAC	43	4	17	21	68
1983-84—Providence College		ECAC	30	4	25	29	68

(c)—June, 1983—Drafted by Winnipeg Jets in 1983 NHL entry draft. Fourth Jets pick, 43rd overall, third round.

TERRY TAIT

Center ... 6'2" ... 190 lbs. ... Born, Thunder Bay, Ont., September 10, 1963 ... Shoots left ... Also plays left wing.

Year	Team	League	Games	G.	A.	Pts.	Pen.
1979-80—Kenora Tier II		MJHL	48	20	30	50	....
1980-81—Sault Ste. Marie Greyhounds (c)		OMJHL	54	6	10	16	90
1981-82—Sault Ste. Marie Greyhounds		OHL	60	18	17	35	96
1982-83—Sault Ste. Marie Greyhounds		OHL	65	29	47	76	59
1983-84—Salt Lake Golden Eagles		CHL	36	1	7	8	7
1983-84—Toledo Goaldiggers		IHL	5	0	0	0	2

(c)—June, 1981—Drafted as underage junior in 1981 NHL entry draft. Seventh North Stars pick, 69th overall, fourth round.

STEVE ANTHONY TAMBELLINI

Center ... 6' ... 190 lbs. ... Born, Trail, B.C., May 14, 1958 ... Shoots left ... (December, 1982)—Shoulder separation ... Son of Adolph Addie Tambellini (member of 1961 World Champion Trail Smoke Eaters).

Year	Team	League	Games	G.	A.	Pts.	Pen.
1975-76—Lethbridge Broncos (c)		WCHL	72	38	59	97	42
1976-77—Lethbridge Broncos (d)		WCHL	55	42	42	84	23
1977-78—Lethbridge Broncos (e)		WCHL	66	75	80	155	32
1978-79—New York Islanders		NHL	1	0	0	0	0
1978-79—Ft. Worth Texans		CHL	73	25	27	52	32
1979-80—New York Islanders		NHL	45	5	8	13	4
1980-81—New York Islanders (f)		NHL	61	19	17	36	17
1980-81—Colorado Rockies		NHL	13	6	12	18	2
1981-82—Colorado Rockies		NHL	79	29	30	59	14
1982-83—New Jersey Devils (g)		NHL	73	25	18	43	14
1983-84—Calgary Flames		NHL	73	15	10	25	16
NHL TOTALS			345	99	95	194	67

(c)—Won WCHL Rookie of the Year Award.
(d)—Won WCHL Most Gentlemanly Player Award.
(e)—Drafted from Lethbridge Broncos by New York Islanders in first round of 1978 amateur draft.
(f)—March, 1981—Traded by New York Islanders with Glenn Resch to Colorado Rockies for Mike McEwen and Jari Kaarela.
(g)—July, 1983—Traded by New Jersey Devils with Joel Quenneville to Calgary Flames for Mel Bridgman and Phil Russell.

CHRISTIAN TANGUAY

Right Wing ... 5'10" ... 190 lbs. ... Born, Beauport, Que., August 4, 1962 ... Shoots right.

Year	Team	League	Games	G.	A.	Pts.	Pen.
1979-80—Trois Rivieres Draveurs (c)		QMJHL	65	24	20	44	39
1980-81—Trois Rivieres Draveurs		QMJHL	72	45	39	84	34
1981-82—Trois Rivieres Draveurs		QMJHL	59	52	55	107	27
1981-82—Quebec Nordiques		NHL	2	0	0	0	0
1982-83—Fredericton Express		AHL	48	6	7	13	4
1982-83—Milwaukee Admirals		IHL	14	8	11	19	6

Year	Team	League	Games	G.	A.	Pts.	Pen.
1983-84—Fredericton Express		AHL	3	2	0	2	0
1983-84—Milwaukee Admirals (b)		IHL	74	44	50	94	23
NHL TOTALS			2	0	0	0	0

(c)—June, 1980—Drafted as underage junior in 1980 NHL entry draft by Quebec Nordiques. Seventh Nordiques pick, 171st overall, ninth round.

DAVE TANNER

Defense . . . 5'11" . . . 180 lbs. . . . Born, Winnipeg, Man., March 5, 1966 . . . Shoots left.

Year	Team	League	Games	G.	A.	Pts.	Pen.
1983-84—Wilcox Notre Dame H.S. (c)		Man.H.S.	40	20	46	66	....

(c)—June, 1984—Drafted by Montreal Canadiens in NHL entry draft. Thirteenth Canadiens pick, 220th overall, 11th round.

PAUL ABEL TANTARDINI

Left Wing . . . 6'1" . . . 185 lbs. . . . Born, Guelph, Ont., July 15, 1953 . . . Shoots left . . . Missed part of 1974-75 season with broken ankle and part of 1976-77 season with broken left wrist . . . (1981-82)—Broke his hand twice during the season.

Year	Team	League	Games	G.	A.	Pts.	Pen.
1972-73—Downsview Beavers	OPJHL	....	36	44	80	151
1973-74—Charlotte Checkers	SHL	50	7	18	25	121
1974-75—Toledo Goaldiggers	IHL	38	2	8	10	338
1975-76—Salt Lake Golden Eagles	CHL	75	9	23	32	*325
1976-77—Toledo Goaldiggers (c)	IHL	63	25	42	67	363
1977-78—Toledo Goaldiggers	IHL	79	29	43	72	268
1978-79—Springfield Indians	AHL	9	2	4	6	45
1978-79—Toledo Goaldiggers (d)	IHL	17	4	12	16	50
1978-79—Muskegon Mohawks	IHL	2	0	0	0	5
1978-79—Flint Generals	IHL	15	2	8	10	78
1979-80—Flint Generals (e)	IHL	60	11	35	46	224
1979-80—Muskegon Mohawks	IHL	15	6	10	16	108
1980-81—Toledo Goaldiggers	IHL	68	16	28	44	209
1981-82—Toledo Goaldiggers	IHL	55	18	24	42	252
1982-83—Toledo Goaldiggers	IHL	79	20	48	68	206
1983-84—Toledo Goaldiggers	IHL	11	1	6	7	52

(c)—Led in penalty minutes (107) during playoffs.

(d)—December, 1978—Traded by Toledo Goaldiggers to Milwaukee Admirals for Wayne Ramsey.

(e)—March, 1980—Traded by Flint Generals to Toledo Goaldiggers, who immediately traded him to Muskegon Mohawks.

TONY TANTI

Right Wing . . . 5'9" . . . 181 lbs. . . . Born, Toronto, Ont., September 7, 1963 . . . Shoots left . . . Broke Wayne Gretzky's record for most goals in rookie OHL season . . . (November, 1981)—Separated shoulder . . . (December, 1981)—Sore hip . . . (1983-84)—Set Vancouver club records for most goals (45) and most power-play goals (19).

Year	Team	League	Games	G.	A.	Pts.	Pen.
1979-80—St. Michaels Jr. B	OHL	37	31	27	58	67
1980-81—Oshawa Generals (a-c-d)	OHL	67	81	69	150	197
1981-82—Oshawa Generals (b-e)	OHL	57	62	64	126	138
1981-82—Chicago Black Hawks	NHL	2	0	0	0	0
1982-83—Oshawa Generals	OHL	30	34	28	62	35
1982-83—Chicago Black Hawks (f)	NHL	1	1	0	1	0
1982-83—Vancouver Canucks	NHL	39	8	8	16	16
1983-84—Vancouver Canucks	NHL	79	45	41	86	50
NHL TOTALS		121	54	49	103	66

(c)—Won Hap Emms OHL Rookie Award.

(d)—Drafted by Chicago Black Hawks in NHL entry draft. First Black Hawks pick, 12th overall, first round.

(e)—Won Jim Mahon Memorial Trophy (Top scoring OHL right wing).

(f)—January, 1983—Traded by Chicago Black Hawks to Vancouver Canucks for Curt Fraser.

DAVID ANDREW TAYLOR

Right Wing . . . 6' . . . 185 lbs. . . . Born, Levack, Ont., December 4, 1955 . . . Shoots right . . . Attended Clarkson College . . . Set ECAC record and tied NCAA record with 108 points in 1976-77 . . . Missed parts of 1979-80 season with pulled back muscle and sprained left knee . . . (November 5, 1980)—Sprained shoulder . . . (October 29, 1982)—Broke right wrist in collision with Kevin Lowe at Edmonton, out 33 games . . . (January, 1983)—Right knee injury . . . (May 28, 1983)—Operation on right wrist he broke for second time in World

Championships at West Germany . . . Holds single season record for most goals, assists and points by a former college player . . . Holds Los Angeles club records for goals, assists and points by a right wing . . . (November 10, 1983)—Returned from broken wrist in game vs. St. Louis.

Year	Team	League	Games	G.	A.	Pts.	Pen.
1974-75—Clarkson College (c)	ECAC	....	20	34	54	....
1975-76—Clarkson College	ECAC	....	26	33	59	....
1976-77—Clarkson College (d-e)	ECAC	34	41	67	108	....
1976-77—Fort Worth Texans	CHL	7	2	4	6	6
1977-78—Los Angeles Kings	NHL	64	22	21	43	47
1978-79—Los Angeles Kings	NHL	78	43	48	91	124
1979-80—Los Angeles Kings	NHL	61	37	53	90	72
1980-81—Los Angeles Kings (b)	NHL	72	47	65	112	130
1981-82—Los Angeles Kings	NHL	78	39	67	106	130
1982-83—Los Angeles Kings	NHL	46	21	37	58	76
1983-84—Los Angeles Kings	NHL	63	20	49	69	91
NHL TOTALS			462	229	340	569	670

(c)—Drafted by Los Angeles Kings in 15th round of 1975 amateur draft.
(d)—Named ECAC Player of the Year.
(e)—Named to All-America team (East).

MARK TAYLOR

Center and Left Wing . . . 5'11" . . . 190 lbs. . . . Born, Vancouver, B.C., January 26, 1958 . . . Shoots left . . . Grandson of Cyclone Taylor . . . (October, 1982)—Broke tibia in preseason game . . . (March 6, 1983)—Refractured same leg in game at Pittsburgh . . . (December, 1983)—Strained knee.

Year	Team	League	Games	G.	A.	Pts.	Pen.
1976-77—Univ. of North Dakota	WCHA	31	16	19	35	20
1977-78—Univ. of North Dakota (c)	WCHA	37	18	22	40	28
1978-79—Univ. of North Dakota	WCHA	42	24	*59	83	28
1979-80—Univ. of North Dakota (d-e)	WCHA	40	33	*59	*92	30
1980-81—Maine Mariners (f)	AHL	79	19	50	69	56
1981-82—Maine Mariners	AHL	75	32	48	80	42
1981-82—Philadelphia Flyers	NHL	2	0	0	0	0
1982-83—Philadelphia Flyers	NHL	61	8	25	33	24
1983-84—Philadelphia Flyers (g)	NHL	1	0	0	0	0
1983-84—Pittsburgh Penguins	NHL	59	24	31	55	24
NHL TOTALS			123	32	56	88	48

(c)—June, 1978—Drafted by Philadelphia Flyers in 1978 NHL amateur draft. Ninth Flyers pick, 100th overall, sixth round.
(d) Named to All-American (West) team.
(e)—Named WCHA's Most Valuable Player and NCAA Player of the Year (forerunner of Hobey Baker Memorial Trophy).
(f)—Tied with Rick Vasko for AHL playoff lead of 21 points.
(g)—October, 1983—Traded with Ron Flockhart, Andy Brickley and first (Roger Belanger) and third (traded to Vancouver) round 1984 draft picks by Philadelphia Flyers to Pittsburgh Penguins for Rich Sutter and second (Greg Smyth) and third (David McLay) round 1984 draft picks.

STEVE TAYLOR

Left Wing . . . 6'2" . . . 190 lbs. . . . Born, Providence, R.I., April 29, 1962 . . . Shoots left.

Year	Team	League	Games	G.	A.	Pts.	Pen.
1980-81—Providence College (c)	ECAC	33	8	14	22	12
1981-82—Providence College	ECAC	30	9	17	26	33
1982-83—Providence College	ECAC	42	7	18	25	38
1983-84—Providence College	ECAC	34	11	16	27	36
1983-84—Springfield Indians	AHL	12	3	6	9	7

(c)—June, 1981—Drafted by Philadelphia Flyers in NHL entry draft. 11th Flyers pick, 163rd overall, eighth round.

JEFFREY TEAL

Center . . . 6'3" . . . 205 lbs. . . . Born, Edina, Minn., May 30, 1960 . . . Shoots left . . . Also plays left wing.

Year	Team	League	Games	G.	A.	Pts.	Pen.
1979-80—University of Minnesota	WCHA	37	10	15	25	30
1980-81—University of Minnesota (c)	WCHA	45	15	9	24	38
1981-82—University of Minnesota	WCHA	36	13	9	22	46
1981-82—Nova Scotia Voyageurs	AHL	7	0	1	1	0

Year	Team	League	Games	G.	A.	Pts.	Pen.
1982-83—Nova Scotia Voyageurs		AHL	76	8	20	28	14
1983-84—Nova Scotia Voyageurs		AHL	16	8	4	12	2

(c)—June, 1980—Drafted by Montreal Canadiens in 1980 NHL entry draft. Sixth Canadiens pick, 82nd overall, fourth round.

GREG TEBBUTT

Defense ... 6'2" ... 215 lbs. ... Born, North Vancouver, B.C., May 11, 1957 ... Shoots left ... (December, 1980)—Surgery to repair severe lacerations of tendons and muscles in left forearm.

Year	Team	League	Games	G.	A.	Pts.	Pen.
1975-76—Victoria Cougars		WCHL	51	3	4	7	217
1976-77—Victoria Cougars (c)		WCHL	29	7	12	19	98
1976-77—Regina Pats (d-e)		WCHL	40	8	17	25	138
1977-78—Flin Flon Bombers		WCHL	55	28	46	74	270
1978-79—Birmingham Bulls (f)		WHA	38	2	5	7	83
1978-79—Binghamton Dusters		AHL	33	8	9	17	50
1979-80—Quebec Nordiques		NHL	2	0	1	1	4
1979-80—Syracuse Firebirds		AHL	14	2	3	5	35
1979-80—Erie Blades (b-g)		EHL	48	20	53	75	138
1980-81—Erie Blades (h)		EHL	35	16	37	53	93
1981-82—Fort Wayne Komets (i)		IHL	49	13	34	47	148
1982-83—Baltimore Skipjacks (a-j)		AHL	80	28	56	84	140
1983-84—Baltimore Skipjacks		AHL	44	12	42	54	125
1983-84—Pittsburgh Penguins (k)		NHL	24	0	2	2	31
WHA TOTALS			38	2	5	7	83
NHL TOTALS			26	0	3	3	35

(c)—Traded to Regina Pats by Victoria Cougars with Hugh Ellis and Lorne Schmidt for Ron Trafford, Rick Odegard and Keith Hertz, December, 1976.
(d)—Selected by Birmingham Bulls in World Hockey Association amateur player draft, June, 1977.
(e)—Drafted from Regina Pats by Minnesota North Stars in eighth round of 1977 amateur draft.
(f)—June, 1979—Claimed by Quebec Nordiques in WHA dispersal draft. Selected by Minnesota North Stars in NHL reclaim draft.
(g)—Led EHL playoffs in goals (11) and points (23) and was co-leader with Daniel Poulin in assists (12).
(h)—Led EHL playoffs with 12 assists.
(i)—August, 1981—Released by Quebec Nordiques.
(j)—Won Eddie Shore Plaque (Outstanding AHL Defenseman).
(k)—June, 1983—Signed by Pittsburgh Penguins as a free agent.

MARK TEEVENS

Right Wing ... 6' ... 180 lbs. ... Born, Ottawa, Ont., June 17, 1966 ... Shoots left.

Year	Team	League	Games	G.	A.	Pts.	Pen.
1982-83—Ottawa Senators		COJHL	47	14	26	40	36
1983-84—Peterborough Petes (c)		OHL	70	27	37	64	70

(c)—June, 1984—Drafted as underage junior by Pittsburgh Penguins in NHL entry draft. Fourth Penguins pick, 64th overall, fourth round.

GREG PATRICK TERRION

Center ... 6' ... 190 lbs. ... Born, Peterborough, Ont., May 2, 1960 ... Shoots left ... (December, 1981)—Separated shoulder ... (January 14, 1984)—Scored second penalty shot goal of the season. Only other NHL player to do that was Pat Egan, New York Americans, in 1941-42.

Year	Team	League	Games	G.	A.	Pts.	Pen.
1977-78—Hamilton Fincups		OMJHL	64	11	30	41	43
1978-79—Brantford Alexanders		OMJHL	63	27	28	55	48
1979-80—Brantford Alexanders (c)		OMJHL	67	44	78	122	13
1980-81—Los Angeles Kings		NHL	73	12	25	37	99
1981-82—Los Angeles Kings		NHL	61	15	22	37	23
1982-83—New Haven Nighthawks (d)		AHL	4	0	1	1	7
1982-83—Toronto Maple Leafs		NHL	74	16	16	32	59
1983-84—Toronto Maple Leafs		NHL	79	15	24	39	36
NHL TOTALS			287	58	87	145	217

(c)—June, 1980—Drafted by Los Angeles Kings in 1980 NHL entry draft. Second Kings pick, 33rd overall, second round.
(d)—October, 1982—Traded by Los Angeles Kings to Toronto Maple Leafs for future considerations.

BILL TERRY

Center ... 5'8" ... 165 lbs. ... Born, Toronto, Ont., July 13, 1961 ... Shoots right ... Named freshman athlete of the year at Michigan Tech (1980-81).

Year	Team	League	Games	G.	A.	Pts.	Pen.
1978-79—Sault Ste. Marie Greyhounds		OMJHL	68	28	21	49	85
1979-80—Sault Ste. Marie Greyhounds		OMJHL	68	21	34	55	64
1980-81—Michigan Tech		WCHA	40	23	19	42	12
1981-82—Michigan Tech		CCHA	35	26	24	50	37
1982-83—Michigan Tech		CCHA	37	19	29	48	37
1983-84—Michigan Tech		CCHA	40	23	17	40	40
1983-84—Toledo Goaldiggers		IHL	3	2	2	4	4

TOM TERWILLIGER

Defense . . . 6'2" . . . 185 lbs. . . . Born, Denver, Colo., September 1, 1965 . . . Shoots right.

Year	Team	League	Games	G.	A.	Pts.	Pen.
1983-84—Edina H.S. (c)		Minn.H.S.	24	5	11	16	20

(c)—June, 1984—Drafted by Minnesota North Stars in NHL entry draft. Eleventh North Stars pick, 222nd overall, 11th round.

GREG THEBERGE

Defense . . . 5'10" . . . 187 lbs. . . . Born, Peterborough, Ont., September 3, 1959 . . . Shoots right . . . Grandson of Hall of Famer Dit Clapper.

Year	Team	League	Games	G.	A.	Pts.	Pen.
1976-77—Peterborough Petes		Jr."A"OHA	65	10	22	32	47
1977-78—Peterborough Petes		Jr."A"OHA	66	13	54	67	88
1978-79—Peterbor'gh Petes (a-c-d)		Jr."A"OHA	63	20	60	80	90
1979-80—Washington Capitals		NHL	12	0	1	1	0
1979-80—Hershey Bears		AHL	58	7	22	29	31
1980-81—Washington Capitals		NHL	1	1	0	1	0
1980-81—Hershey Bears (b)		AHL	78	12	53	65	117
1981-82—Washington Capitals		NHL	57	5	32	37	49
1982-83—Hershey Bears		AHL	6	1	5	6	2
1982-83—Washington Capitals		NHL	70	8	28	36	20
1983-84—Washington Capitals		NHL	13	1	2	3	4
1983-84—Hershey Bears		AHL	41	3	27	30	25
NHL TOTALS			153	15	63	78	73

(c)—Won Max Kaminsky Award as outstanding defenseman in OHA.
(d)—August, 1979—Drafted by Washington Capitals in entry draft. Fifth Washington pick, 109th overall, sixth round.

MATS THELIN

Defense . . . 5'10" . . . 185 lbs. . . . Born, Stockholm, Sweden, March 30, 1961 . . . Shoots left.

Year	Team	League	Games	G.	A.	Pts.	Pen.
1980-81—Solna AIK (c)		Sweden	9	0	0	0	4
1981-82—Solna AIK		Sweden	36	2	2	4	28
1981-82—Swedish National Team		Int'l	25	0	3	3	20
1982-83—Solna AIK		Sweden	....	...	....	....	....
1983-84—Solna AIK		Sweden	16	4	1	5	20

(c)—June, 1981—Drafted by Boston Bruins in NHL entry draft. Sixth Bruins pick, 140th overall, seventh round.

MICHEL THERRIEN

Defense . . . 6' . . . 200 lbs. . . . Born, St. Leonard, Que., November 4, 1963 . . . Shoots left.

Year	Team	League	Games	G.	A.	Pts.	Pen.
1980-81—Quebec Remparts		QMJHL	60	4	19	23	77
1981-82—Quebec Remparts		QMJHL	11	0	7	7	19
1981-82—Chicoutimi Sagueneens		QMJHL	50	4	19	23	108
1982-83—Longueuil Chevaliers		QHL	64	9	42	51	98
1983-84—Nova Scotia Voyageurs		QHL	73	7	34	41	40

MARK THIETKE

Center . . . 5'11" . . . 165 lbs. . . . Born, Ottawa, Ont., January 9, 1966 . . . Shoots left.

Year	Team	League	Games	G.	A.	Pts.	Pen.
1982-83—Sherwood Park Midgets		Alberta	55	35	28	63	38
1983-84—Saskatoon Blades (c)		WHL	70	10	13	23	40

(c)—June, 1984—Drafted as underage junior by Boston Bruins in NHL entry draft. Seventh Bruins pick, 145th overall, seventh round.

WAYNE THOMPSON

Center . . . 5'9" . . . 165 lbs. . . . Born, Toronto, Ont., June 15, 1960 . . . Shoots right . . . (September, 1982)—Separated shoulder in preseason game.

Year	Team	League	Games	G.	A.	Pts.	Pen.
1977-78—London Knights		OMJHL	55	20	50	70	15
1978-79—London Knights		OMJHL	68	39	49	88	30
1979-80—London Knights (c)		OMJHL	68	47	74	121	34
1980-81—Flint Generals		IHL	59	41	52	93	32
1980-81—Nova Scotia Voyageurs		AHL	17	1	7	8	26
1981-82—Nova Scotia Voyageurs		AHL	80	28	41	69	30
1982-83—Nova Scotia Voyageurs		AHL	71	17	58	75	19
1983-84—Nova Scotia Voyageurs		AHL	80	23	57	80	30

(c)—September, 1980—Signed by Montreal Canadiens as a free agent.

JIM THOMSON

Right Wing . . . 6'2" . . . 180 lbs. . . . Born, Edmonton, Alta., December 30, 1965 . . . Shoots right.

Year	Team	League	Games	G.	A.	Pts.	Pen.
1982-83—Markham Waxers		OJHL	35	6	7	13	81
1983-84—Toronto Marlboros (c)		OHL	60	10	18	28	68

(c)—June, 1984—Drafted as underage junior by Washington Capitals in NHL entry draft. Eighth Capitals pick, 185th overall, ninth round.

TOM THORNBURY

Defense . . . 5'11" . . . 175 lbs. . . . Born, Lindsay, Ont., March 17, 1963 . . . Shoots right.

Year	Team	League	Games	G.	A.	Pts.	Pen.
1979-80—Aurora Tier II		OPJHL	44	19	30	49	84
1980-81—Niagara Falls Flyers (c)		OPJHL	60	15	22	37	138
1981-82—Niagara Falls Flyers		OHL	43	11	22	33	65
1982-83—North Bay Centennials		OHL	17	6	9	15	38
1982-83—Cornwall Royals		OHL	50	21	35	56	66
1983-84—Pittsburgh Penguins		NHL	14	1	8	9	16
1983-84—Baltimore Skipjacks (b)		AHL	65	17	46	63	64
NHL TOTALS			14	1	8	9	16

(c)—June, 1981—Drafted as underage junior by Pittsburgh Penguins in 1981 NHL entry draft. Second Penguins pick, 49th overall, third round.

TOM TILLEY

Defense . . . 6' . . . 180 lbs. . . . Born, Trenton, Ont., March 28, 1965 . . . Shoots right.

Year	Team	League	Games	G.	A.	Pts.	Pen.
1983-84—Orillia Travelways (c)		OJHL	38	16	35	51	113

(c)—June, 1984—Drafted as underage junior by St. Louis Blues in NHL entry draft. Thirteenth Blues pick, 196th overall, 10th round.

DAVE TIPPETT

Center . . . 5'10" . . . 175 lbs. . . . Born, Moosomin, Sask., August 25, 1961 . . . Shoots left . . . Member of 1984 Canadian Olympic Team.

Year	Team	League	Games	G.	A.	Pts.	Pen.
1979-80—Prince Albert Raiders		SAJHL	85	72	95	177	..
1980-81—Prince Albert Raiders		SAJHL	84	62	93	155	..
1981-82—University of North Dakota		WCHA	43	13	28	41	24
1982-83—University of North Dakota		WCHA	36	15	31	46	44
1983-84—Canadian Olympic Team		Int'l	66	14	19	33	24
1983-84—Hartford Whalers (c)		NHL	17	4	2	6	2
NHL TOTALS			17	4	2	6	2

(c)—February, 1984—Signed by Hartford Whalers as a free agent.

RICK TOCCHET

Right Wing . . . 6'0" . . . 195 lbs. . . . Born, Scarborough, Ont., April 9, 1964 . . . Shoots right.

Year	Team	League	Games	G.	A.	Pts.	Pen.
1981-82—Sault Ste. Marie Greyhounds		OHL	59	7	15	22	184
1982-83—Sault Ste. Marie Greyhounds (c-d-e)		OHL	66	32	34	66	146
1983-84—Sault Ste. Marie Greyhounds (f)		OHL	64	44	64	108	209

(c)—Led OHL playoffs with 67 penalty minutes.

(d)—June, 1983—Drafted as underage junior by Philadelphia Flyers in 1983 NHL entry draft. Fifth Flyers pick, 121st overall, sixth round.

MIKE TOMLAK

Center ... 6'2" ... 180 lbs. ... Born, Thunder Bay, Ont., October 17, 1964 ... Shoots left ... Also plays left wing.

Year—Team	League	Games	G.	A.	Pts.	Pen.
1981-82—Thunder Bay Burger Kings	TBJHL	25	19	26	45	30
1982-83—Cornwall Royals (c)	OHL	70	18	49	67	26
1983-84—Cornwall Royals	OHL	64	24	64	88	21

(c)—June, 1983—Drafted as underage junior by Toronto Maple Leafs in 1983 NHL entry draft. Tenth Maple Leafs' pick, 208th overall, 11th round.

JOHN TONELLI

Left Wing and Center ... 6'1" ... 190 lbs. ... Born, Hamilton, Ont., March 23, 1957 ... Shoots left ... Did not take part in 1975 playoffs after signing pro contract ... Brother of Ray Tonelli ... (February, 1981)—Shoulder injury ... Set N.Y. Islanders club record for left wings with 93 points in 1981-82 ... (December, 1983)—Knee injury.

Year—Team	League	Games	G.	A.	Pts.	Pen.
1973-74—Toronto Marlboros	Jr."A" OHA	69	18	37	55	62
1974-75—Toronto Marlboros (a-c)	Jr."A" OHA	70	49	86	135	85
1975-76—Houston Aeros	WHA	79	17	14	31	66
1976-77—Houston Aeros (d)	WHA	80	24	31	55	109
1977-78—Houston Aeros (e)	WHA	65	23	41	64	103
1978-79—New York Islanders	NHL	73	17	39	56	44
1979-80—New York Islanders	NHL	77	14	30	44	49
1980-81—New York Islanders	NHL	70	20	32	52	57
1981-82—New York Islanders (b)	NHL	80	35	58	93	57
1982-83—New York Islanders	NHL	76	31	40	71	55
1983-84—New York Islanders	NHL	73	27	40	67	66
WHA TOTALS		224	64	86	150	278
NHL TOTALS		449	144	239	383	328

(c)—Signed by Houston Aeros (WHA), March, 1975.
(d)—Drafted from Houston Aeros by New York Islanders in second round of 1977 amateur draft.
(e)—Signed to multi year contract by New York Islanders, July, 1978.

TIMOTHY RAYMOND TOOKEY

Center ... 5'11" ... 180 lbs. ... Born, Edmonton, Alta., August 29, 1960 ... Shoots left ... (December 30, 1981)—Sprained left ankle at Pittsburgh ... (February, 1983)—Concussion ... (April, 1983)—Injured shoulder during AHL playoffs.

Year—Team	League	Games	G.	A.	Pts.	Pen.
1977-78—Portland Winter Hawks	WCHL	72	16	15	31	55
1978-79—Portland Winter Hawks (c)	WHL	56	33	47	80	55
1979-80—Portland Winter Hawks	WHL	70	58	83	141	55
1980-81—Hershey Bears	AHL	47	20	38	58	129
1980-81—Washington Capitals	NHL	29	10	13	23	18
1981-82—Washington Capitals (d)	NHL	28	8	8	16	35
1981-82—Hershey Bears	AHL	14	4	9	13	10
1981-82—Fredericton Express	AHL	16	6	10	16	16
1982-83—Quebec Nordiques	NHL	12	1	6	7	4
1982-83—Fredericton Express	AHL	53	24	43	67	24
1983-84—Pittsburgh Penguins (e)	NHL	8	0	2	2	2
1983-84—Baltimore Skipjacks	AHL	58	16	28	44	25
NHL TOTALS		77	19	29	48	59

(c)—August, 1979—Drafted by Washington Capitals as underage junior in 1979 NHL entry draft. Fourth Capitals pick, 88th overall, fifth round.
(d)—January, 1982—Traded by Washington Capitals to Quebec Nordiques for Lee Norwood.
(e)—August, 1983—Signed by Pittsburgh Penguins as a free agent.

SEAN TOOMEY

Center ... 6'2" ... 190 lbs. ... Born, St. Paul, Minn., June 27, 1965 ... Shoots left.

Year—Team	League	Games	G.	A.	Pts.	Pen.
1982-83—St. Paul Cretin H.S. (c)	Minn. H.S.	23	48	32	80	..
1983-84—Univ. of Minnesota-Duluth	WCHA	29	3	5	8	8

(c)—June, 1983—Drafted by Minnesota North Stars in 1983 NHL entry draft. Eighth North Stars pick, 136th overall, seventh round.

SCOTT TOTTLE

Right Wing . . . 5'11" . . . 175 lbs. . . . Born, Brantford, Ont., January 30, 1965 . . . Shoots right.

Year	Team	League	Games	G.	A.	Pts.	Pen.
1981-82—Hamilton Mountain A's		OJHL	49	15	25	40	16
1982-83—Peterborough Petes (c)		OHL	68	25	49	74	36
1983-84—Peterborough Petes		OHL	70	63	47	110	24

(c)—June, 1983—Drafted as underage junior by Vancouver Canucks in 1983 NHL entry draft. Third Canucks pick, 50th overall, third round.

LARRY TRADER

Defense . . . 6'2" . . . 186 lbs. . . . Born, Barry's Bay, Ont., July 7, 1963 . . . Shoots left.

Year	Team	League	Games	G.	A.	Pts.	Pen.
1979-80—Gloucester Tier II		OPJHL	50	13	20	33	70
1980-81—London Knights (c)		OPJHL	68	5	23	28	132
1981-82—London Knights		OHL	68	19	37	56	171
1982-83—Detroit Red Wings		NHL	15	0	2	2	6
1982-83—London Knights		OHL	39	16	28	44	67
1982-83—Adirondack Red Wings		AHL	6	2	2	4	4
1983-84—Adirondack Red Wings		AHL	80	13	28	41	89
NHL TOTALS			15	0	2	2	6

(c)—June, 1981—Drafted as underage junior by Detroit Red Wings in 1981 NHL entry draft. Third Red Wings pick, 86th overall, fifth round.

DOUG TRAPP

Left Wing . . . 6' . . . 180 lbs. . . . Born, Balcarres, Sask., November 28, 1965 . . . Shoots left.

Year	Team	League	Games	G.	A.	Pts.	Pen.
1981-82—Regina		SJHL	43	25	28	53	102
1982-83—Regina Pats		WHL	71	23	28	51	123
1983-84—Regina Pats (b-c)		WHL	59	43	50	93	44

(c)—June, 1984—Drafted as underage junior by Buffalo Sabres in NHL entry draft. Second Sabres pick, 39th overall, second round.

R. BROCK TREDWAY

Right Wing . . . 6' . . . 180 lbs. . . . Born, Highland Creek, Ont., June 23, 1959 . . . Shoots right.

Year	Team	League	Games	G.	A.	Pts.	Pen.
1977-78—Cornell University		ECAC	22	28	12	41	2
1978-79—Cornell University		ECAC	29	31	29	60	8
1979-80—Cornell University		ECAC	31	25	35	60	10
1980-81—Cornell University (c)		ECAC	31	29	17	46	4
1981-82—New Haven Nighthawks		AHL	80	35	24	59	7
1982-83—New Haven Nighthawks		AHL	74	15	26	41	9
1983-84—New Haven Nighthawks		AHL	70	21	42	63	4

(c)—June, 1981—Signed by Los Angeles Kings as a free agent.

MARIO TREMBLAY

Right Wing . . . 6' . . . 185 lbs. . . . Born, Alma, Que., September 2, 1956 . . . Shoots right . . . (March 12, 1984)—Given three-game NHL suspension for being first off the bench during major altercation in game at Minnesota.

Year	Team	League	Games	G.	A.	Pts.	Pen.
1972-73—Montreal Red, White and Blue		QJHL	56	43	37	80	155
1973-74—Mont. Red, White and Blue (c)		QJHL	47	49	51	100	154
1974-75—Nova Scotia Voyageurs		AHL	15	10	8	18	47
1974-75—Montreal Canadiens		NHL	63	21	18	39	108
1975-76—Montreal Canadiens		NHL	71	11	16	27	88
1976-77—Montreal Canadiens		NHL	74	18	28	46	61
1977-78—Montreal Canadiens		NHL	56	10	14	24	44
1978-79—Montreal Canadiens		NHL	76	30	29	59	74
1979-80—Montreal Canadiens		NHL	77	16	26	42	105
1980-81—Montreal Canadiens		NHL	77	25	38	63	123
1981-82—Montreal Canadiens		NHL	80	33	40	73	66
1982-83—Montreal Canadiens		NHL	80	30	37	67	87
1983-84—Montreal Canadiens		NHL	67	14	25	39	112
NHL TOTALS			721	208	271	479	868

(c)—Drafted from Montreal Red, White and Blue by Montreal Canadiens in first round of 1974 amateur draft.

JEFF TRIANO

Defense . . . 6'1" . . . 186 lbs. . . . Born, Niagara Falls, Ont., April 11, 1964 . . . Shoots right . . . Brother of Jay Triano (Canadian National Basketball team, 1978-82).

Year	Team	League	Games	G.	A.	Pts.	Pen.
1980-81—Aurora Tigers		OPJHL	37	7	13	20	90
1980-81—Niagara Falls Flyers		OMJHL	9	0	1	1	2
1981-82—Toronto Marlboros (c)		OHL	58	1	8	9	79
1982-83—Toronto Marlboros		OHL	66	12	40	52	91
1982-83—St. Catharines Saints		AHL	4	0	0	0	2
1983-84—Toronto Marlboros		OHL	62	6	24	30	116

(c)—June, 1982—Drafted as underage junior by Toronto Maple Leafs in 1982 NHL entry draft. Eleventh Maple Leafs pick, 139th overall, seventh round.

TIM TRIMPER

Left Wing . . . 5'9" . . . 185 lbs. . . . Born, Windsor, Ont., September 28, 1959 . . . Shoots left.

Year	Team	League	Games	G.	A.	Pts.	Pen.
1976-77—Peterborough Petes		OMJHL	62	14	11	25	95
1977-78—Peterborough Petes		OMJHL	59	26	34	60	73
1978-79—Peterborough Petes (b-c)		OMJHL	66	62	46	108	97
1979-80—Chicago Black Hawks		NHL	30	6	10	16	10
1979-80—New Brunswick Hawks		AHL	43	26	31	57	18
1980-81—New Brunswick Hawks (d)		AHL	19	7	8	15	21
1980-81—Winnipeg Jets		NHL	56	15	14	29	28
1981-82—Winnipeg Jets		NHL	74	8	8	16	100
1982-83—Winnipeg Jets		NHL	5	0	0	0	0
1982-83—Sherbrooke Jets		AHL	68	28	38	66	53
1983-84—Sherbrooke Jets		AHL	32	10	24	34	26
1983-84—Winnipeg Jets (e)		NHL	5	0	0	0	0
1983-84—Salt Lake Golden Eagles		CHL	35	18	27	45	26
NHL TOTALS			170	29	32	61	138

(c)—August, 1979—Drafted by Chicago Black Hawks in entry draft. Second Chicago pick, 28th overall, second round.

(d)—December, 1980—Traded by Chicago Black Hawks with Doug Lecuyer to Winnipeg Jets for Peter Marsh.

(e)—January, 1984—Traded by Winnipeg Jets to Minnesota North Stars for Jordy Douglas.

BRYAN JOHN TROTTIER

Center . . . 5'10" . . . 205 lbs. . . . Born, Val Marie, Sask., July 17, 1956 . . . Shoots left . . . (1975-76)—Set NHL records for most assists and points in rookie season (broken by Peter Stastny, 1980-81) . . . Set Stanley Cup Playoff record with 29 points during 1980 playoffs (broken by Mike Bossy's 35 points in 1981) . . . Set NHL record for consecutive playoff games with points (25) covering more than one season . . . Set NHL record for consecutive playoff games with points one season (18) . . . Brother of Monty Trottier and Rocky Trottier . . . (April, 1983)—Sprained left knee during playoff series against New York Rangers . . . (January, 1984)—Injured left knee . . . (July, 1984)—Became U.S. citizen and played with Team USA in 1984 Canada Cup Tournament.

Year	Team	League	Games	G.	A.	Pts.	Pen.
1972-73—Swift Current Broncos		WCHL	67	16	29	45	10
1973-74—Swift Current Broncos (c)		WCHL	68	41	71	112	76
1974-75—Lethbridge Broncos (a)		WCHL	67	46	*98	144	103
1975-76—New York Islanders (d-e)		NHL	80	32	63	95	21
1976-77—New York Islanders		NHL	76	30	42	72	34
1977-78—New York Islanders (a)		NHL	77	46	*77	123	46
1978-79—New York Islanders (a-f-g-h)		NHL	76	47	*87	*134	50
1979-80—New York Islanders (i-j)		NHL	78	42	62	104	68
1980-81—New York Islanders (k)		NHL	73	31	72	103	74
1981-82—New York Islanders (b-l)		NHL	80	50	79	129	88
1982-83—New York Islanders		NHL	80	34	55	89	68
1983-84—New York Islanders (b)		NHL	68	40	71	111	59
NHL TOTALS			688	352	608	960	508

(c)—Drafted from Swift Current Broncos by New York Islanders in second round of 1974 amateur draft.

(d)—Won Calder Memorial Trophy.

(e)—Selected NHL Rookie of the Year in poll of players by THE SPORTING NEWS.

(f)—Won Hart Memorial Trophy (NHL-MVP).

(g)—Won Art Ross Trophy (NHL-Top Scorer).

(h)—Named THE SPORTING NEWS NHL Player of the Year in poll of players.

(i)—Led NHL playoffs in points (29) and co-leader, with Bill Barber, in goals (12).

(j)—Won Conn Smythe Trophy (NHL Playoff MVP).

(k)—Tied for NHL playoff assist lead (18 assists) with teammate Mike Bossy.

(l)—Led NHL playoffs with 23 assists and 29 points.

MONTY TROTTIER

Center . . . 5'10" . . . 170 lbs. . . . Born, Val Marie, Sask., July 25, 1961 . . . Shoots left . . . Brother of Rocky and Bryan Trottier.

Year	Team	League	Games	G.	A.	Pts.	Pen.
1979-80	Billings Bighorns (c)	WHL	60	18	32	50	168
1980-81	Billings Bighorns	WHL	58	15	37	52	289
1981-82	Indianapolis Checkers	CHL	72	10	15	25	142
1982-83	Indianapolis Checkers	CHL	63	17	23	40	69
1983-84	Indianapolis Checkers	CHL	69	18	23	41	135

(c)—June, 1980—Drafted by New York Islanders in NHL entry draft. Fourth Islanders pick, 68th overall, fourth round.

ROCKY TROTTIER

Center . . . 5'11" . . . 190 lbs. . . . Born, Climax, Sask., April 11, 1964 . . . Shoots right . . . Brother of Bryan and Monty Trottier . . . Missed most of 1981-82 season with knee injury . . . Also plays right wing.

Year	Team	League	Games	G.	A.	Pts.	Pen.
1980-81	Billings Bighorns	WHL	62	11	26	37	67
1981-82	Billings Bighorns (c)	WHL	28	13	21	34	36
1982-83	Nanaimo Islanders	WHL	34	13	22	35	12
1982-83	Medicine Hat Tigers	WHL	20	5	9	14	11
1982-83	Wichita Wind	CHL	2	0	1	1	0
1983-84	New Jersey Devils	NHL	5	1	1	2	0
1983-84	Medicine Hat Tigers	WHL	65	34	50	84	41
	NHL TOTALS		5	1	1	2	0

(c)—June, 1982—Drafted as underage junior by New Jersey Devils in 1982 NHL entry draft. First Devils pick, 8th overall, first round.

STEVE TSUJIURA

Center . . . 5'5" . . . 155 lbs. . . . Born, Coaldale, Alta., February 28, 1962 . . . Shoots left.

Year	Team	League	Games	G.	A.	Pts.	Pen.
1977-78	Medicine Hat Tigers	WHL	17	5	8	13	0
1978-79	Medicine Hat Tigers	WHL	62	24	45	69	14
1979-80	Medicine Hat Tigers (c)	WHL	72	25	77	102	36
1980-81	Medicine Hat Tigers (b-c-d-e)	WHL	72	55	84	139	60
1981-82	Calgary Wranglers	WHL	37	26	53	79	33
1981-82	University of Calgary	CWUAA	....	...	....	....	....
1982-83	Maine Mariners	AHL	78	15	51	66	46
1983-84	Springfield Indians (f)	AHL	78	24	56	80	27

(c)—Won Frank Boucher Memorial Trophy (WHL Most Gentlemanly).
(d)—Won WHL Most Valuable Player Trophy.
(e)—June, 1981—Drafted by Philadelphia Flyers in NHL entry draft. Thirteenth Flyers pick, 205th overall, tenth round.
(f)—July, 1984—Signed by New Jersey Devils as a free agent.

JOHN TUCKER

Center . . . 6' . . . 185 lbs. . . . Born, Windsor, Ont., September 29, 1964 . . . Shoots right.

Year	Team	League	Games	G.	A.	Pts.	Pen.
1981-82	Kitchener Rangers	OHL	67	16	32	48	32
1982-83	Kitchener Rangers (c)	OHL	70	60	80	140	33
1983-84	Kitchener Rangers (a-d-e)	OHL	39	40	60	100	25
1983-84	Buffalo Sabres	NHL	21	12	4	16	4
	NHL TOTALS		21	12	4	16	4

(c)—June, 1983—Drafted as underage junior by Buffalo Sabres in 1983 NHL entry draft. Fourth Sabres pick, 31st overall, second round.
(d)—Won Red Tilson Trophy (Most Outstanding OHL player).
(e)—OHL's Molson/Cooper Player of the Year Nominee.

ROB TUDOR

Right Wing . . . 5'11" . . . 188 lbs. . . . Born, Cupar, Sask., June 30, 1956 . . . Shoots right . . . Also plays center.

Year	Team	League	Games	G.	A.	Pts.	Pen.
1972-73	Regina Pats	WCHL	5	0	1	1	0
1973-74	Regina Pats	WCHL	68	17	17	34	60
1974-75	Regina Pats	WCHL	68	48	48	96	125
1975-76	Regina Pats (c)	WCHL	72	46	60	106	228
1976-77	Fort Wayne Komets	IHL	78	34	60	94	108

Year	Team	League	Games	G.	A.	Pts.	Pen.
1977-78—Tulsa Oilers	CHL	65	23	33	56	58
1978-79—Vancouver Canucks	NHL	24	4	4	8	19
1978-79—Dallas Black Hawks	CHL	51	27	37	64	80
1979-80—Vancouver Canucks	NHL	2	0	0	0	0
1979-80—Dallas Black Hawks (b)	CHL	74	39	41	80	177
1980-81—Dallas Black Hawks	CHL	79	31	32	63	155
1981-82—Dallas Black Hawks (d)	CHL	80	32	47	79	132
1982-83—St. Louis Blues	NHL	2	0	0	0	0
1982-83—Salt Lake Golden Eagles	CHL	76	37	30	67	168
1983-84—Salt Lake Golden Eagles	CHL	32	10	12	22	35
NHL TOTALS		28	4	4	8	19

(c)—Drafted from Regina Pats by Vancouver Canucks in sixth round of 1976 amateur draft.
(d)—September, 1982—Signed by St. Louis Blues as a free agent.

ALLAN TUER

Defense . . . 6' . . . 175 lbs. . . . Born, North Battleford, Sask., July 19, 1963 . . . Shoots left.

Year	Team	League	Games	G.	A.	Pts.	Pen.
1980-81—Regina Pats (c)	WHL	31	0	7	7	58
1981-82—Regina Pats	WHL	63	2	18	20	*486
1982-83—Regina Pats	WHL	71	3	27	30	229
1983-84—New Haven Nighthawks	AHL	78	0	20	20	195

(c)—June, 1980—Drafted as underage junior by Los Angeles Kings in NHL entry draft. Eighth Kings pick, 186th overall, ninth round.

ALFIE TURCOTTE

Center . . . 5'10" . . . 175 lbs. . . . Born, Gary, Ind., June 5, 1965 . . . Shoots left . . . Son of Real Turcotte (Coach and General Manager of Nanaimo Islanders of WHL).

Year	Team	League	Games	G.	A.	Pts.	Pen.
1981-82—Detroit Compuware	Mich. Midget	93	131	152	283	40
1982-83—Nanaimo Islanders	WHL	36	23	27	50	22
1982-83—Portland Winter Hawks (c)	WHL	39	26	51	77	26
1983-84—Portland Winter Hawks	WHL	32	22	41	63	39
1983-84—Montreal Canadiens	NHL	30	7	7	14	10
NHL TOTALS		30	7	7	14	10

(c)—June, 1983—Drafted as underage junior by Montreal Canadiens in 1983 NHL entry draft. First Canadiens pick, 17th overall, first round.

SYLVAIN TURGEON

Left Wing . . . 6' . . . 190 lbs. . . . Born, Noranda, Que., January 17, 1965 . . . Shoots left . . . Also plays center . . . Set Hartford club record for goals and points by an NHL rookie in 1983-84.

Year	Team	League	Games	G.	A.	Pts.	Pen.
1981-82—Hull Olympics (c)	QMJHL	57	33	40	73	78
1982-83—Hull Olympics (a-d-e)	QHL	67	54	109	163	103
1983-84—Hartford Whalers	NHL	76	40	32	72	55
NHL TOTALS		76	40	32	72	55

(c)—Won Des Instructeurs Trophy (Top Rookie QMJHL Forward).
(d)—Won The Association of Journalist of Hockey Trophy (Top QHL pro prospect).
(e)—June, 1983—Drafted as underage junior by Hartford Whalers in 1983 NHL entry draft. First Whalers pick, 2nd overall, first round.

RICHARD TURMEL

Defense . . . 6'4" . . . 226 lbs. . . . Born, Sault Ste. Marie, Ont., July 29, 1962 . . . Shoots right.

Year	Team	League	Games	G.	A.	Pts.	Pen.
1979-80—Shawinigan Cataracts	QMJHL	51	3	5	8	38
1980-81—Shawinigan Cataracts (c)	QMJHL	69	4	13	17	174
1981-82—Shawinigan Cataracts	QMJHL	54	6	27	33	185
1982-83—St. Catharines Saints	AHL	74	3	7	10	183
1983-84—Fredericton Express (d)	AHL	28	0	1	1	40
1983-84—Milwaukee Admirals	IHL	43	2	14	16	50

(c)—June, 1981—Drafted as underage junior by Toronto Maple Leafs in 1981 NHL entry draft. Seventh Maple Leafs pick, 153rd overall, eighth round.
(d)—August, 1983—Traded by Toronto Maple Leafs to Quebec Nordiques for Basil McRae.

PERRY TURNBULL

Left Wing . . . 6'2" . . . 200 lbs. . . . Born, Bentley, Alta., March 9, 1959 . . . Shoots left . . .

Cousin of Randy Turnbull . . . (April, 1982)—Severed tendon just above right knee in playoff mishap when cut by teammate's skate.

Year	Team	League	Games	G.	A.	Pts.	Pen.
1974-75—The Pass Red Devils		AJHL	69	6	4	10	134
1975-76—The Pass Red Devils		AJHL	45	27	23	50	140
1975-76—Calgary Centennials		WCHL	19	6	7	13	14
1976-77—Calgary Centennials (c)		WCHL	10	8	5	13	33
1976-77—Portland Winter Hawks		WCHL	58	23	30	53	249
1977-78—Portland Winter Hawks		WCHL	57	36	27	63	318
1978-79—Portland Winter Hawks (d-e)		WHL	70	75	43	118	191
1979-80—St. Louis Blues		NHL	80	16	19	35	124
1980-81—St. Louis Blues		NHL	75	34	22	56	209
1981-82—St. Louis Blues		NHL	79	33	26	59	161
1982-83—St. Louis Blues		NHL	79	32	15	47	172
1983-84—St. Louis Blues (f)		NHL	32	14	8	22	81
1983-84—Montreal Canadiens (g)		NHL	40	6	7	13	59
NHL TOTALS			385	135	97	232	806

(c)—Traded to Portland Winter Hawks by Calgary Centennials for Doug Lecuyer and Dave Morrow, October, 1976.

(d)—Named Most Valuable Player of WHL.

(e)—August, 1979—Drafted by St. Louis Blues in 1979 entry draft. First Blues pick, second overall, first round.

(f)—December, 1983—Traded by St. Louis Blues to Montreal Canadiens for Gilbert Delorme, Greg Paslawski and Doug Wickenheiser.

(g)—June, 1984—Traded by Montreal Canadiens to Winnipeg Jets for Lucien DeBlois.

RANDY LAYNE TURNBULL

Defense . . . 6' . . . 186 lbs. . . . .Born, Bentley, Alta., February 7, 1962 . . . Shoots right . . . Cousin of Perry Turnbull.

Year	Team	League	Games	G.	A.	Pts.	Pen.
1977-78—Ft. Saskatchewan Traders		AJHL	47	1	3	4	172
1978-79—Ft. Saskatchewan Traders		AJHL	51	4	30	34	367
1978-79—Portland Winter Hawks		WHL	1	0	0	0	7
1979-80—Portland Winter Hawks (c)		WHL	72	4	25	29	355
1980-81—Portland Winter Hawks		WHL	56	1	31	32	295
1981-82—Portland Winter Hawks		WHL	69	5	19	24	430
1981-82—Calgary Flames		NHL	1	0	0	0	2
1982-83—Colorado Flames		CHL	65	2	1	3	292
1983-84—New Haven Nighthawks		AHL	8	0	0	0	46
1983-84—Peoria Prancers		IHL	73	3	18	21	213
NHL TOTALS			1	0	0	0	2

(c)—June, 1980—Drafted by Calgary Flames as underage junior in 1980 NHL entry draft. Sixth Flames pick, 97th overall, fifth round.

DAN TURNER

Left Wing . . . 6'3" . . . 200 lbs. . . . Born, Flin Flon, Man., March 18, 1964 . . . Shoots left.

Year	Team	League	Games	G.	A.	Pts.	Pen.
1982-83—Medicine Hat Tigers		WHL	72	9	10	19	215
1983-84—Medicine Hat Tigers (c)		WHL	72	17	22	39	181

(c)—June, 1984—Drafted by Toronto Maple Leafs in NHL entry draft. Eighth Maple Leafs pick, 172nd overall, ninth round.

BRIAN TUTT

Defense . . . 6'1" . . . 195 lbs. . . . Born, Swallwell, Alta., June 9, 1962 . . . Shoots left . . . (September, 1981)—Broke leg while attending Philadelphia Flyers training camp.

Year	Team	League	Games	G.	A.	Pts.	Pen.
1979-80—Calgary Canucks		AJHL	59	6	14	20	55
1979-80—Calgary Wranglers (c)		WHL	2	0	0	0	2
1980-81—Calgary Wranglers		WHL	72	10	41	51	111
1981-82—Calgary Wranglers		WHL	40	2	16	18	85
1982-83—Toledo Goaldiggers		IHL	42	7	13	20	56
1982-83—Maine Mariners		AHL	31	0	0	0	28
1983-84—Toledo Goaldiggers (b)		IHL	82	7	44	51	79
1983-84—Springfield Indians		AHL	1	0	0	0	2

(c)—June, 1980—Drafted as underage junior by Philadelphia Flyers in NHL entry draft. Sixth Flyers pick, 126th overall, sixth round.

STEVE TUTTLE

Right Wing . . . 6'1" . . . 180 lbs. . . . Born, Vancouver, B.C., January 5, 1966 . . . Shoots right.

Year	Team	League	Games	G.	A.	Pts.	Pen.
1983-84—Richmond (c)		BCJHL	46	46	34	80	22

(c)—June, 1984—Drafted by St. Louis Blues in NHL entry draft. Eighth Blues pick, 113th overall, sixth round.

J. D. URBANIC

Left Wing . . . 6'1" . . . 165 lbs. . . . Born, St. Catharines, Ont., August 31, 1966 . . . Shoots left.

Year	Team	League	Games	G.	A.	Pts.	Pen.
1982-83—Aurora Tigers		OJHL	44	13	21	34	86
1983-84—Windsor Spitfires (c)		OHL	54	12	18	30	39

(c)—June, 1984—Drafted as underage junior by Boston Bruins in NHL entry draft. Tenth Bruins pick, 207th overall, 10th round.

JEFF VAIVE

Center . . . 5'9" . . . 170 lbs. . . . Born, Ottawa, Ont., June 13, 1963 . . . Shoots left.

Year	Team	League	Games	G.	A.	Pts.	Pen.
1979-80—Ottawa Senators		OPJHL	48	16	27	43	69
1980-81—Ottawa 67's		OMJHL	57	7	9	16	66
1981-82—Ottawa 67's (b-c)		OHL	68	56	*95	151	90
1982-83—Ottawa 67's		OHL	64	40	61	101	93
1983-84—Colorado Flames		CHL	67	13	21	34	39

(c)—June, 1982—Drafted as underage junior by Calgary Flames in 1982 NHL entry draft. Seventh Flames pick, 114th overall, sixth round.

RICK VAIVE

Right Wing . . . 6' . . . 180 lbs. . . . Born, Ottawa, Ont., May 14, 1959 . . . Shoots right . . . (February, 1981)—Slight groin pull . . . First Toronto Maple Leafs player to have a 50-goal season when he set a club record with 54 goals in 1981-82 . . . (February 25, 1984)—Injured ankle in loss at Edmonton.

Year	Team	League	Games	G.	A.	Pts.	Pen.
1976-77—Sherbrooke Beavers (c)		QJHL	68	51	59	110	91
1977-78—Sherbrooke Beavers (d)		QJHL	68	76	79	155	199
1978-79—Birmingham Bulls (e)		WHA	75	26	33	59	*248
1979-80—Vancouver Canucks (f)		NHL	47	13	8	21	111
1979-80—Toronto Maple Leafs		NHL	22	9	7	16	77
1980-81—Toronto Maple Leafs		NHL	75	33	29	62	229
1981-82—Toronto Maple Leafs		NHL	77	54	35	89	157
1982-83—Toronto Maple Leafs		NHL	78	51	28	79	105
1983-84—Toronto Maple Leafs		NHL	76	52	41	93	114
WHA TOTALS			75	26	33	59	248
NHL TOTALS			375	212	148	360	793

(c)—Won Rookie of the Year Award.

(d)—Signed by Birmingham Bulls (WHA) as underage junior, July, 1978.

(e)—Drafted by Vancouver Canucks in entry draft. First Vancouver pick, fifth overall, first round.

(f)—February, 1980—Traded with Bill Derlago by Vancouver Canucks to Toronto Maple Leafs for Dave Williams and Jerry Butler.

CHRIS VALENTINE

Center . . . 6' . . . 191 lbs. . . . Born, Belleville, Ont., December 6, 1961 . . . Shoots right . . . Leading scorer at St. Louis University as a freshman . . . Leading scorer at Sorel both seasons of junior hockey play.

Year	Team	League	Games	G.	A.	Pts.	Pen.
1978-79—St. Louis University		CCHA	34	27	44	71	52
1979-80—Sorel Black Hawks		QMJHL	72	48	80	128	76
1980-81—Sorel Black Hawks (c)		QMJHL	72	65	77	142	176
1981-82—Hershey Bears		AHL	19	12	9	21	69
1981-82—Washington Capitals		NHL	60	30	37	67	92
1982-83—Washington Capitals		NHL	23	7	10	17	14
1982-83—Hershey Bears		AHL	51	31	38	69	66
1983-84—Hershey Bears		AHL	47	15	44	59	41
1983-84—Washington Capitals		NHL	22	6	5	11	21
NHL TOTALS			105	43	52	95	127

(c)—June, 1981—Drafted by Washington Capitals in 1981 NHL entry draft. Tenth Capitals pick, 194th overall, 10th round.

JOHN MARTIN VAN BOXMEER

Defense . . . 6'1" . . . 190 lbs. . . . Born, Sarnia, Ont., November 20, 1952 . . . Shoots right . . .

Missed part of 1976-77 season with knee surgery . . . (January, 1982)—Broke finger on left hand.

Year	Team	League	Games	G.	A.	Pts.	Pen.
1971-72—Guelph CMC's (a-c-d)	SOJHL	56	30	42	72	160
1972-73—Nova Scotia Voyageurs	AHL	76	5	29	34	139
1973-74—Nova Scotia Voyageurs	AHL	47	8	20	28	78
1973-74—Montreal Canadiens	NHL	20	1	4	5	18
1974-75—Nova Scotia Voyageurs	AHL	43	4	15	19	68
1974-75—Montreal Canadiens	NHL	9	0	2	2	0
1975-76—Montreal Canadiens	NHL	46	6	11	17	31
1976-77—Montreal Canadiens (e)	NHL	4	0	1	1	0
1976-77—Colorado Rockies	NHL	41	2	11	13	32
1977-78—Colorado Rockies	NHL	80	12	42	54	87
1978-79—Colorado Rockies (f)	NHL	76	9	34	43	46
1979-80—Buffalo Sabres	NHL	80	11	40	51	55
1980-81—Buffalo Sabres	NHL	80	18	51	69	69
1981-82—Buffalo Sabres	NHL	69	14	54	68	62
1982-83—Buffalo Sabres	NHL	65	6	21	27	53
1983-84—Quebec Nordiques (g)	NHL	18	5	3	8	12
1983-84—Fredericton Express	AHL	45	10	34	44	48
NHL TOTALS		588	84	274	358	465

(c)—Won Leading Defenseman Award.
(d)—Drafted from Guelph CMC's by Montreal Canadiens in first round of 1972 amateur draft.
(e)—November, 1976—Traded by Montreal Canadiens to Colorado Rockies for 1979 third round draft choice (Craig Levie) and cash.
(f)—September, 1979—Traded by Colorado Rockies to Buffalo Sabres for Rene Robert.
(g)—October, 1983—Selected by Quebec Nordiques in NHL waiver draft.

CARMINE VANI

Center . . . 6'1" . . . 180 lbs. . . . Born, Toronto, Ont., August 7, 1964 . . . Shoots left . . . Also plays left wing.

Year	Team	League	Games	G.	A.	Pts.	Pen.
1980-81—St. Michael Midgets	Ont. Midgets	33	29	35	64	....
1980-81—St. Michael Jr.B	OPJHL	13	2	2	4	20
1981-82—Kingston Canadians (c)	OHL	49	11	16	27	138
1982-83—Kingston Canadians	OHL	21	7	11	18	56
1982-83—North Bay Centennials	OHL	25	22	22	44	84
1983-84—North Bay Centennials	OHL	17	14	3	17	58
1983-84—Kitchener Rangers	OHL	24	15	8	23	75

(c)—June, 1982—Drafted as underage junior by Detroit Red Wings in 1982 NHL entry draft. Third Red Wings pick, 44th overall, third round.

ERNESTO VARGAS

Center . . . 6'2" . . . 205 lbs. . . . Born, St. Paul, Minn., January 3, 1964 . . . Shoots left . . . Also plays left wing.

Year	Team	League	Games	G.	A.	Pts.	Pen.
1981-82—Coon Rapids H.S. (c)	Minn. H.S.	24	28	28	56	22
1982-83—University of Wisconsin	WCHA	37	2	4	6	32
1983-84—University of Wisconsin	WCHA	36	5	15	20	32

(c)—June, 1982—Drafted as underage player by Montreal Canadiens in 1982 NHL entry draft. Ninth Canadiens pick, 117th overall, sixth round.

YVON VAUTOUR

Right Wing . . . 6' . . . 200 lbs. . . . Born, St. John, N.B., September 10, 1956 . . . Shoots left . . . Missed part of 1977-78 season with broken hand . . . (September, 1981)—Broke knuckle in left hand during fight in a preseason game . . . (January 2, 1982)—Separated shoulder in game vs. St. Louis. He needed surgery and missed the remainder of the season.

Year	Team	League	Games	G.	A.	Pts.	Pen.
1972-73—St. John Schooners	NBJHL	....	42	31	73	85
1973-74—Laval National	QJHL	61	38	39	77	118
1974-75—Laval National	QJHL	56	34	37	71	67
1975-76—Laval National	QJHL	72	43	60	103	61
1976-77—Muskegon Mohawks	IHL	76	43	47	90	52
1976-77—Fort Worth Texans (d)	CHL	....	...	....	....	....
1977-78—Fort Worth Texans	CHL	64	14	21	35	84
1978-79—Fort Worth Texans	CHL	69	20	20	40	130
1979-80—New York Islanders	NHL	17	3	1	4	24
1979-80—Indianapolis Checkers	CHL	59	27	28	55	140
1980-81—Colorado Rockies (e)	NHL	74	15	19	34	143

Year	Team	League	Games	G.	A.	Pts.	Pen.
1981-82—Colorado Rockies		NHL	14	1	2	3	18
1982-83—New Jersey Devils		NHL	52	4	7	11	136
1982-83—Wichita Wind		CHL	4	3	0	3	0
1982-83—Moncton Alpines		AHL	14	7	5	12	25
1983-84—Maine Mariners		AHL	24	8	12	20	117
1983-84—New Jersey Devils		NHL	42	3	4	7	78
NHL TOTALS			199	26	33	59	399

(c)—Drafted from Laval National by New York Islanders in sixth round of 1976 amateur draft.
(d)—No league record. Appeared in two playoff games.
(e)—October, 1980—Claimed by Colorado Rockies from New York Islanders.

DARREN WILLIAM VEITCH

Defense . . . 5'11" . . . 188 lbs. . . . Born, Saskatoon, Sask., April 24, 1960 . . . Shoots right . . . Winner of 1980 Carling O'Keefe Open Golf Championship in Regina, Sask. (by nine strokes) with a 54-hole total of 214 . . . (October 27, 1982)—Fractured collarbone in three places in game at Pittsburgh . . . (February 19, 1983)—Broke collarbone again in game at Los Angeles . . . (February 11, 1984)—Suffered broken ribs in game vs. Philadelphia.

Year	Team	League	Games	G.	A.	Pts.	Pen.
1976-77—Regina Blues		SJHL	60	15	21	36	121
1976-77—Regina Pats		WCHL	1	0	0	0	0
1977-78—Regina Pats		WCHL	71	13	32	45	135
1978-79—Regina Pats		WHL	51	11	36	47	80
1979-80—Regina Pats (a-c)		WHL	71	29	*93	122	118
1980-81—Hershey Bears		AHL	26	6	22	28	12
1980-81—Washington Capitals		NHL	59	4	21	25	46
1981-82—Hershey Bears		AHL	10	5	10	15	16
1981-82—Washington Capitals		NHL	67	9	44	53	54
1982-83—Hershey Bears		AHL	5	0	1	1	2
1982-83—Washington Capitals		NHL	10	0	8	8	0
1983-84—Washington Capitals		NHL	46	6	18	24	17
1983-84—Hershey Bears		AHL	11	1	6	7	4
NHL TOTALS			182	19	91	110	117

(c)—June, 1980—Drafted by Washington Capitals in 1980 NHL entry draft. First Capitals pick, fifth overall, first round.

RANDY VELISCHEK

Defense . . . 6' . . . 200 lbs. . . . Born, Montreal, Que., February 10, 1962 . . . Shoots left.

Year	Team	League	Games	G.	A.	Pts.	Pen.
1979-80—Providence College (c)		ECAC	31	5	5	10	20
1980-81—Providence College		ECAC	33	3	12	15	26
1981-82—Providence College (b)		ECAC	33	1	14	15	34
1982-83—Providence College (a-d-e)		ECAC	41	18	34	52	50
1982-83—Minnesota North Stars		NHL	3	0	0	0	2
1983-84—Salt Lake Golden Eagles		CHL	43	7	21	28	54
1983-84—Minnesota North Stars		NHL	33	2	2	4	10
NHL TOTALS			36	2	2	4	12

(c)—June, 1980—Drafted by Minnesota North Stars as underage player in 1980 NHL entry draft. Third North Stars pick, 53rd overall, third round.
(d)—ECAC Player of the Year.
(e)—NCAA All-America Team (East).

MIKE VELLUCCI

Defense . . . 6'1" . . . 180 lbs. . . . Born, Farmington, Mich., August 11, 1966 . . . Shoots left.

Year	Team	League	Games	G.	A.	Pts.	Pen.
1982-83—Detroit Compuware		Mich. Midget	70	23	20	43	98
1983-84—Belleville Bulls (c)		OHL	67	2	20	22	83

(c)—June, 1984—Drafted as underage junior by Hartford Whalers in NHL entry draft. Third Whalers pick, 131st overall, seventh round.

PAT VERBEEK

Center . . . 5'9" . . . 195 lbs. . . . Born, Sarnia, Ont., May 24, 1964 . . . Shoots right.

Year	Team	League	Games	G.	A.	Pts.	Pen.
1980-81—Petrolia Jr. B.		OPJHL	42	44	44	88	155
1981-82—Sudbury Wolves (c-d)		OHL	66	37	51	88	180
1982-83—Sudbury Wolves		OHL	61	40	67	107	184

Year	Team	League	Games	G.	A.	Pts.	Pen.
1982-83—New Jersey Devils		NHL	6	3	2	5	8
1983-84—New Jersey Devils		NHL	79	20	27	47	158
NHL TOTALS			85	23	29	52	166

(c)—Winner of Emms Family Award (OHL Rookie of the Year).
(d)—June, 1982—Drafted as underage junior by New Jersey Devils in 1982 NHL entry draft. Third Devils pick, 43rd overall, third round.

CLAUDE VERRET

Center . . . 5'10" . . . 164 lbs. . . . Born, Lachine, Que., April 20, 1963 . . . Shoots left.

Year	Team	League	Games	G.	A.	Pts.	Pen.
1980-81—Trois Rivieres Draveurs (c-d)		QMJHL	68	39	73	112	4
1981-82—Trois Rivieres Draveurs (a-c-e-f-g)		QMJHL	64	54	108	*162	14
1982-83—Trois Rivieres Draveurs		QHL	68	73	115	188	21
1983-84—Buffalo Sabres		NHL	11	2	5	7	2
1983-84—Rochester Americans (h)		AHL	65	39	51	90	4
NHL TOTALS			11	2	5	7	2

(c)—Winner of Frank Selke Trophy (QMJHL Most Gentlemanly Player).
(d)—Winner of the Instructeurs Trophy (QMJHL Top Rookie).
(e)—Winner of Jean Beliveau Trophy (QMJHL Leading Scorer).
(f)—Led QMJHL President Cup playoffs with 35 assists and 48 points.
(g)—June, 1982—Drafted as underage junior by Buffalo Sabres in 1982 NHL entry draft. Twelfth Sabres pick, 163rd overall, eighth round.
(h)—Won Dudley (Red) Garrett Memorial Trophy (Top AHL Rookie).

LEIGH VERSTRAETE

Right Wing . . . 5'11" . . . 183 lbs. . . . Born, Pincher Creek, Alta., January 6, 1962 . . . Shoots right.

Year	Team	League	Games	G.	A.	Pts.	Pen.
1981-82—Calgary Wranglers (c)		WHL	49	19	20	39	385
1982-83—Calgary Wranglers		WHL	4	0	1	1	11
1982-83—Toronto Maple Leafs		NHL	3	0	0	0	5
1982-83—St. Catharines Saints		AHL	61	5	3	8	221
1983-84—St. Catharines Saints		AHL	51	0	7	7	183
1983-84—Muskegon Mohawks		IHL	19	5	5	10	123
NHL TOTALS			3	0	0	0	5

(c)—June, 1982—Drafted by Toronto Maple Leafs in 1982 NHL entry draft. Thirteenth Maple Leafs pick, 192nd overall, 10th round.

KEVIN VESCIO

Defense . . . 5'11" . . . 180 lbs. . . . Born, Fort William, Ont., March 15, 1965 . . . Shoots left.

Year	Team	League	Games	G.	A.	Pts.	Pen.
1981-82—Stratford Cullitons		MWJBHL	42	4	31	35	30
1982-83—North Bay Centennials (c)		OHL	70	5	30	35	33
1983-84—North Bay Centennials		OHL	67	2	26	28	75

(c)—June, 1983—Drafted as underage junior by New York Islanders in 1983 NHL entry draft. Eleventh Islanders pick, 177th overall, ninth round.

JIM VESEY

Center . . . 6'1" . . . 200 lbs. . . . Born, Columbus, Mass., September 29, 1965 . . . Shoots right.

Year	Team	League	Games	G.	A.	Pts.	Pen.
1983-84—Columbus H.S. (c)		Mass. H.S.	21	39	48	87	....

(c)—June, 1984—Drafted by St. Louis Blues in NHL entry draft. Eleventh Blues pick, 155th overall, eighth round.

RON VIGLASI

Defense . . . 5'11" . . . 180 lbs. . . . Born, Powell River, B.C., April 21, 1965 . . . Shoots right.

Year	Team	League	Games	G.	A.	Pts.	Pen.
1982-83—Victoria Cougars (c)		WHL	63	4	16	20	56
1983-84—Kamloops Junior Oilers		WHL	3	0	0	0	9

(c)—June, 1983—Drafted as underage junior by New York Islanders in 1983 NHL entry draft. Seventh Islanders pick, 97th overall, fifth round.

ALAIN VIGNEAULT

Defense . . . 5'11" . . . 195 lbs. . . . Born, Quebec City, Que., May 14, 1962 . . . Shoots right.

Year	Team	League	Games	G.	A.	Pts.	Pen.
1979-80—Hull Olympics		QJHL	35	5	34	39	82
1979-80—Trois Rivieres Draveurs		QJHL	28	6	19	25	93
1980-81—Trois Rivieres Draveurs (c)		QJHL	67	7	55	62	181
1981-82—Salt Lake Golden Eagles		CHL	64	2	10	12	266
1981-82—St. Louis Blues		NHL	14	1	2	3	43
1982-83—Salt Lake Golden Eagles		CHL	33	1	4	5	189
1982-83—St. Louis Blues		NHL	28	1	3	4	39
1983-84—Montana Magic		CHL	47	2	14	16	139
1983-84—Maine Mariners		AHL	11	0	1	1	46
NHL TOTALS			42	2	5	7	82

(c)—June, 1981—Drafted by St. Louis Blues in 1981 NHL entry draft. Seventh Blues pick, 167th overall, eighth round.

REJEAN VIGNOLA

Center . . . 5'10" . . . 180 lbs. . . . Born, Baie-Comeau, Que., January 27, 1962 . . . Shoots right.

Year	Team	League	Games	G.	A.	Pts.	Pen.
1980-81—Shawinigan Cataracts (c)		QMJHL	64	20	29	49	99
1981-82—Shawinigan Cataracts		QMJHL	51	40	49	89	97
1982-83—Shawinigan Cataracts		QHL	67	51	68	119	160
1983-84—Fredericton Express		AHL	67	25	13	38	40

(c)—June, 1981—Drafted as underage junior by Vancouver Canucks in 1981 NHL entry draft. Ninth Canucks pick, 199th overall, 10th round.

ANDRE VILLENEUVE

Defense . . . 6'3" . . . 190 lbs. . . . Born, Alma, Que., January 19, 1963 . . . Shoots left.

Year	Team	League	Games	G.	A.	Pts.	Pen.
1979-80—Chicoutimi Sagueneens		QMJHL	4	0	2	2	0
1980-81—Chicoutimi Sagueneens (c)		QMJHL	62	10	23	33	92
1981-82—Chicoutimi Sagueneens		QMJHL	51	11	39	50	97
1982-83—Chicoutimi Sagueneens		QHL	68	24	63	87	76
1983-84—Springfield Indians		AHL	8	1	5	6	6

(c)—June, 1981—Drafted as underage junior by Philadelphia Flyers in 1981 NHL entry draft. Eighth Flyers pick, 121st overall, sixth round.

HANNU VIRTA

Defense . . . 6' . . . 176 lbs. . . . Born, Turku, Finland, March 22, 1963 . . . Shoots left . . . (February 12, 1983)—Groin injury . . . (January, 1984)—Stretched knee ligaments.

Year	Team	League	Games	G.	A	Pts.	Pen.
1980-81—Turku TPS (c)		Finland	....	22	23	45	....
1981-82—Turku TPS		Finland	....	....	....	....	....
1981-82—Buffalo Sabres		NHL	3	0	1	1	4
1982-83—Buffalo Sabres		NHL	74	13	24	37	18
1983-84—Buffalo Sabres		NHL	70	6	30	36	12
NHL TOTALS			147	19	55	74	34

(c)—June, 1981—Drafted as underage player by Buffalo Sabres in 1981 NHL entry draft. Second Sabres pick, 38th overall, second round.

LUKE VITALE

Center . . . 5'11" . . . 180 lbs. . . . Born, Toronto, Ont., April 17, 1966 . . . Shoots left.

Year	Team	League	Games	G.	A.	Pts.	Pen.
1983-84—Henry Carr H.S. (c)		MTJHL	62	24	48	72	88

(c)—June, 1984—Drafted by Philadelphia Flyers in NHL entry draft. Ninth Flyers pick, 163rd overall, eighth round.

EMANUEL VIVEIROS

Defense . . . 5'11" . . . 160 lbs. . . . Born, St. Albert, Alta., January 8, 1966 . . . Shoots left.

Year	Team	League	Games	G.	A.	Pts.	Pen.
1982-83—Prince Albert Raiders		WHL	59	6	26	32	55
1983-84—Prince Albert Raiders (b-c)		WHL	67	15	94	109	48

(c)—June, 1984—Drafted as underage junior by Edmonton Oilers in NHL entry draft. Sixth Oilers pick, 106th overall, sixth round.

MICKEY VOLCAN

Defense . . . 6' . . . 190 lbs. . . . Born, Edmonton, Alta., March 3, 1962 . . . Shoots right . . . Son of Mike Volcan (Member of Edmonton Eskimos CFL team in 1950s).

Year	Team	League	Games	G.	A.	Pts.	Pen.
1977-78—St. Albert Saints		AJHL	60	28	40	68	106
1978-79—St. Albert Saints (c)		AJHL	50	20	47	67	109
1979-80—Univ. of North Dakota (d)		WCHA	33	2	14	16	38
1980-81—Binghamton Whalers		AHL	24	1	9	10	26
1980-81—Hartford Whalers		NHL	49	2	11	13	26
1981-82—Binghamton Whalers		AHL	33	4	13	17	47
1981-82—Hartford Whalers		NHL	26	1	5	6	29
1982-83—Hartford Whalers (e)		NHL	68	4	13	17	73
1983-84—Colorado Flames		CHL	30	8	9	17	20
1983-84—Calgary Flames		NHL	19	1	4	5	18
NHL TOTALS			162	8	33	41	146

(c)—Won W.G. (Bill) Scott Memorial Trophy (Best AJHL Defenseman).

(d)—June, 1980—Drafted by Hartford Whalers as underage player in 1980 NHL entry draft. Third Whalers pick, 50th overall, third round.

(e)—July, 1983—Traded by Hartford Whalers with third-round draft choice in 1984 to Calgary Flames for Richie Dunn and Joel Quenneville.

DUANE WAHLIN

Right Wing . . . 5'11" . . . 165 lbs. . . . Born, St. Paul, Minn., June 3, 1965 . . . Shoots right.

Year	Team	League	Games	G.	A.	Pts.	Pen.
1983-84—St. Paul Johnson H.S. (c)		Minn. H.S.	29	55	36	91	30

(c)—June, 1984—Drafted by Minnesota North Stars in NHL entry draft. Ninth North Stars pick, 181st overall, ninth round.

JALI WAHLSTEIN

Center . . . 6'2" . . . 190 lbs. . . . Born, Turku, Finland, June 20, 1963 . . . Shoots left.

Year	Team	League	Games	G.	A.	Pts.	Pen.
1980-81—Finland National Jr.		Int'l	8	3	5	8	32
1980-81—Turku TPS (c)		Finland	2	1	1	2	2
1981-82—Montreal Juniors		QMJHL	52	15	47	62	17
1982-83—		Finland	....	...	....	....	....
1983-84—Salt Lake Golden Eagles		CHL	35	7	9	16	8
1983-84—Toledo Goaldiggers		IHL	31	11	12	23	7

(c)—June, 1981—Drafted by Minnesota North Stars in NHL entry draft. Sixth North Stars pick, 41st overall, second round.

BRADLEY WALCOT

Defense . . . 6' . . . 180 lbs. . . . Born, Calgary, Alta., March 22, 1965 . . . Shoots right . . . (January 19, 1982)—Injured back.

Year	Team	League	Games	G.	A.	Pts.	Pen.
1981-82—Toronto Midget Marlies		MTHL	37	29	70	99	38
1982-83—Kingston Canadians (c)		OHL	53	10	12	22	49
1983-84—Kingston Canadians		OHL	11	3	7	10	5
1983-84—Oshawa Generals		OHL	48	6	13	19	37

(c)—June, 1983—Drafted as underage junior by Quebec Nordiques in 1983 NHL entry draft. Fifth Nordiques pick, 112th overall, sixth round.

BRYAN WALKER

Defense . . . 6'2" . . . 200 lbs. . . . Born, Red Deer, Alta., January 21, 1965 . . . Shoots right.

Year	Team	League	Games	G.	A.	Pts.	Pen.
1981-82—Red Deer Rustlers		AJHL	..	..	..	..	..
1981-82—Lethbridge Broncos		WHL	6	1	3	4	2
1982-83—Lethbridge Broncos		WHL	13	0	1	1	14
1982-83—Portland Winter Hawks (c)		WHL	47	4	13	17	45
1983-84—Portland Winter Hawks		WHL	67	6	25	31	182

(c)—June, 1983—Drafted as underage junior by New York Rangers in 1983 NHL entry draft. Eleventh Rangers pick, 213th overall, 11th round.

GORDON WALKER

Left Wing . . . 6' . . . 178 lbs. . . . Born, Castlegar, B.C., August 12, 1965 . . . Shoots left . . . Also plays center.

Year	Team	League	Games	G.	A.	Pts.	Pen.
1981-82—Drumheller Miners		AJHL	60	35	44	79	90
1982-83—Portland Winter Hawks (c)		WHL	66	24	30	54	95
1983-84—Portland Winter Hawks		WHL	58	28	41	69	65

(c)—June, 1983—Drafted as underage junior by New York Rangers in 1983 NHL entry draft. Fifth Rangers' pick, 53rd overall, third round.

JIM WALSH

Defense ... 6'1" ... 210 lbs. ... Born, Norfolk, Virginia, October 26, 1956 ... Shoots right ... (December, 1980)—Arm Injury ... (November 27, 1982)—Separated shoulder in AHL game vs. Baltimore.

Year	Team	League	Games	G.	A.	Pts.	Pen.
1976-77—Northeastern University	ECAC	27	5	9	14	44
1977-78—Northeastern University	ECAC	27	3	26	29	69
1978-79—Northeastern University	ECAC	27	3	16	19	....
1979-80—Rochester Americans	AHL	33	2	4	6	64
1980-81—Rochester Americans	AHL	76	8	23	31	182
1981-82—Buffalo Sabres	NHL	4	0	1	1	4
1981-82—Rochester Americans	AHL	70	7	33	40	174
1982-83—Binghamton Whalers	AHL	49	1	13	14	93
1982-83—Saginaw Gears	IHL	5	0	1	1	4
1983-84—New Haven Nighthawks	AHL	13	0	5	5	14
NHL TOTALS		4	0	1	1	4

RYAN WILLIAM WALTER

Left Wing ... 6' ... 195 lbs. ... Born, New Westminster, B. C., April 23, 1958 ... Shoots left ... Brother of George Walter ... (November, 1983)—Injured groin muscle.

Year	Team	League	Games	G.	A.	Pts.	Pen.
1973-74—Langley Lords	Jr."A"BCHL	....	...	....	....	....
1973-74—Kamloops Chiefs	WCHL	2	0	0	0	0
1974-75—Langley Lords	Jr."A"BCHL	....	...	....	....	....
1974-75—Kamloops Chiefs	WCHL	9	8	4	12	2
1975-76—Kamloops Chiefs	WCHL	72	35	49	84	96
1976-77—Kamloops Chiefs	WCHL	71	41	58	99	100
1977-78—Seattle Breakers (a-c)	WCHL	62	54	71	125	148
1978-79—Washington Capitals	NHL	69	28	28	56	70
1979-80—Washington Capitals	NHL	80	24	42	66	106
1980-81—Washington Capitals	NHL	80	24	45	69	150
1981-82—Washington Capitals (d)	NHL	78	38	49	87	142
1982-83—Montreal Canadiens	NHL	80	29	46	75	15
1983-84—Montreal Canadiens	NHL	73	20	29	49	83
NHL TOTALS		460	163	239	402	566

(c)—Drafted from Seattle Breakers by Washington Capitals in first round of 1978 amateur draft.
(d)—September, 1982—Traded by Washington Capitals with Rick Green to Montreal Canadiens for Rod Langway, Brian Engblom, Doug Jarvis and Craig Laughlin.

JOSEPH MICHAEL WARD

Center ... 6' ... 178 lbs. ... Born, Sarnia, Ont., February 11, 1961 ... Shoots left ... Son of Don Ward (Boston 1959-60).

Year	Team	League	Games	G.	A.	Pts.	Pen.
1978-79—Seattle Breakers	WHL	61	18	30	48	66
1979-80—Seattle Breakers (c)	WHL	59	32	37	69	90
1980-81—Seattle Breakers	WHL	40	28	23	51	48
1980-81—Colorado Rockies	NHL	4	0	0	0	2
1980-81—Fort Worth Texans (d)	CHL	....	...	....	....	....
1981-82—Fort Worth Texans	CHL	32	6	15	21	12
1982-83—Wichita Wind	CHL	7	0	2	2	2
1982-83—Muskegon Mohawks	IHL	52	34	25	59	4
1983-84—Muskegon Mohawks	IHL	9	3	2	5	2
NHL TOTALS		4	0	0	0	2

(c)—June, 1980—Drafted by Colorado Rockies as underage junior in 1980 NHL entry draft. Second Rockies pick, 22nd overall, second round.
(d)—Appeared in five playoff games.

TOM WARD

Defense ... 6' ... 190 lbs. ... Born, Minneapolis, Minn., January 16, 1964 ... Shoots right.

Year	Team	League	Games	G.	A.	Pts.	Pen.
1981-82—Richfield H.S. (c)	Minn. H.S.	22	9	9	18	....
1982-83—University of Minnesota (d)	WCHA	5	0	1	1	4
1983-84—University of Minnesota	WCHA	35	1	4	5	38
1983-84—Peoria Prancers	IHL	4	1	1	2	0

(c)—June, 1982—Drafted as underage player by Winnipeg Jets in 1982 NHL entry draft. Seventh Jets pick, 180th overall, ninth round.
(d)—August, 1983—NHL rights traded by Winnipeg Jets with Craig Levie to Minnesota North Stars for Tim Young.

TOM WARDEN

Defense . . . 6'2" . . . 190 lbs. . . . Born, Darbishire, England, January 12, 1966 . . . Shoots left.

Year	Team	League	Games	G.	A.	Pts.	Pen.
1983-84—Aurora Tigers		OJHL	2	0	0	0	0
1983-84—North Bay Centennials (c)		OHL	28	3	2	5	16

(c)—June, 1984—Drafted as underage junior by New York Islanders in NHL entry draft. Tenth Islanders pick, 187th overall, ninth round.

DAVE WATSON

Right Wing . . . 6'2" . . . 190 lbs. . . . Born, Kirkland Lake, Ont., May 19, 1958 . . . Shoots right . . . Missed all of 1978-79 season with knee injury . . . (December, 1980)—Bruised sternum.

Year	Team	League	Games	G.	A.	Pts.	Pen.
1976-77—Sudbury Wolves		OMJHL	39	12	13	25	34
1976-77—Sault Ste. Marie Greyhounds		OMJHL	26	11	9	20	18
1977-78—Sault Ste. Marie Greyhounds (c)		OMJHL	65	21	30	51	112
1978-79—Did not play.							
1979-80—Colorado Rockies		NHL	5	0	0	0	2
1979-80—Fort Worth Texans		CHL	68	19	22	41	124
1980-81—Fort Worth Texans		CHL	50	16	20	36	115
1980-81—Colorado Rockies		NHL	13	0	1	1	8
1981-82—Ft. Worth Texans		CHL	68	15	14	29	107
1982-83—Carolina Thunderbirds (a)		ACHL	66	53	49	*102	101
1983-84—Carolina Thunderbirds		ACHL	29	17	16	33	56
NHL TOTALS			18	0	1	1	10

(c)—June, 1978—Drafted by Colorado Rockies in amateur draft. Fourth Colorado pick, 58th overall, fourth round.

WILLIAM (BILL) WATSON

Right Wing . . . 6' . . . 180 lbs. . . . Born, Pine Falls, Man., March 30, 1964 . . . Shoots right.

Year	Team	League	Games	G.	A.	Pts.	Pen.
1980-81—Prince Albert Raiders		AJHL	54	30	39	69	27
1981-82—Prince Albert Raiders (c)		AJHL	47	43	41	84	37
1982-83—University of Minn./Duluth		WCHA	22	5	10	15	10
1983-84—University of Minn./Duluth		WCHA	40	35	51	86	12

(c)—June, 1982—Drafted by Chicago Black Hawks in NHL entry draft. Fourth Black Hawks pick, 70th overall, fourth round.

TIM WATTERS

Defense . . . 5'11" . . . 180 lbs. . . . Born, Kamloops, B.C., July 25, 1959 . . . Shoots left . . . Set record for assists and points by a defenseman at Michigan Tech in 1980-81 . . . (October, 1983)—Pulled hamstring.

Year	Team	League	Games	G.	A.	Pts.	Pen.
1977-78—Michigan Tech		WCHA	37	1	15	16	47
1978-79—Michigan Tech (c)		WCHA	31	6	21	27	48
1979-80—Canadian Olympic Team		Int'l	56	8	21	29	43
1979-80—Canadian Olympic Team		Int'l	6	1	1	2	0
1980-81—Michigan Tech (a-d)		WCHA	43	12	38	50	36
1981-82—Tulsa Oilers		CHL	5	1	2	3	0
1981-82—Winnipeg Jets		NHL	69	2	22	24	97
1982-83—Winnipeg Jets		NHL	77	5	18	23	98
1983-84—Winnipeg Jets		NHL	74	3	20	23	169
NHL TOTALS			220	10	60	70	364

(c)—August, 1979—Drafted by Winnipeg Jets in NHL draft. Sixth Jets pick, 124th overall, sixth round.
(d)—Named to All-America Team (West).

STANLEY BRIAN WEIR

Center . . . 6'1" . . . 180 lbs. . . . Born, Ponoka, Alta., March 17, 1952 . . . Shoots left . . . Missed part of 1975-76 season with torn ligaments in ankle . . . Missed 12 games in early part of 1978-79 season with severed tip of little finger of left hand.

Year	Team	League	Games	G.	A.	Pts.	Pen.
1969-70—Ponoka Stampeders		AJHL	42	35	26	*61	45
1970-71—Medicine Hat Tigers (f)		WCHL	66	52	59	111	88
1971-72—Medicine Hat Tigers (c-d)		WCHL	68	58	75	133	77
1972-73—California Golden Seals		NHL	78	15	24	39	16
1973-74—California Golden Seals		NHL	58	9	7	16	10
1974-75—California Seals (e)		NHL	80	18	27	45	12

Year	Team	League	Games	G.	A.	Pts.	Pen.
1975-76—Toronto Maple Leafs		NHL	64	19	32	51	22
1976-77—Toronto Maple Leafs		NHL	65	11	19	30	14
1977-78—Tulsa Oilers		CHL	42	24	33	57	38
1977-78—Toronto Maple Leafs (g)		NHL	30	12	5	17	4
1978-79—Edmonton Oilers (h)		WHA	68	31	30	61	20
1979-80—Edmonton Oilers		NHL	79	33	33	66	40
1980-81—Edmonton Oilers		NHL	70	12	20	32	40
1981-82—Edmonton Oilers (i)		NHL	51	3	13	16	13
1981-82—Colorado Rockies (j)		NHL	10	2	3	5	10
1982-83—Detroit Red Wings		NHL	57	5	24	29	2
1983-84—Montana Magic (k)		CHL	73	21	44	65	20
NHL TOTALS			642	139	207	346	183
WHA TOTALS			68	31	30	61	20

(c)—Selected by Calgary Broncos in World Hockey Association player selection draft, February, 1972.

(d)—Drafted from Medicine Hat Tigers by California Golden Seals in second round of 1972 amateur draft.

(e)—Traded to Toronto Maple Leafs by California Seals for Gary Sabourin, June, 1975.

(f)—Won WCHL Rookie of the Year Award.

(g)—Signed by Edmonton Oilers (WHA), June, 1978.

(h)—June, 1979—Selected by Toronto Maple Leafs in NHL reclaim draft. Returned to Edmonton for future considerations September, 1979.

(i)—March, 1982—Traded by Edmonton Oilers to Colorado Rockies for Ed Cooper. In August, 1982, the NHL voided the trade because of an undisclosed injury to Cooper and Weir was returned to Edmonton, Cooper to New Jersey.

(j)—September, 1982—Traded by Edmonton Oilers to Detroit Red Wings for future considerations.

(k)—October, 1983—Signed by Montana Magic as a free agent.

WALLY WEIR

Defense ... 6'2" ... 200 lbs. ... Born, Verdun, Que., June 3, 1954 ... Shoots left ... Missed most of 1977-78 season with injured left elbow requiring surgery.

Year	Team	League	Games	G.	A.	Pts.	Pen.
1973-74—Longueil Rebels		Jr. "A" QHL	....	...	....	....	....
1974-75—Did not play			....	...	....	....	....
1975-76—Beauce Jaros		NAHL	56	6	20	26	180
1976-77—Quebec Nordiques		WHA	69	3	17	20	197
1977-78—Quebec Nordiques		WHA	13	0	0	0	47
1978-79—Quebec Nordiques		WHA	68	2	7	9	166
1979-80—Quebec Nordiques		NHL	73	3	12	15	133
1980-81—Quebec Nordiques		NHL	54	6	8	14	77
1980-81—Rochester Americans		AHL	7	1	1	2	79
1981-82—Quebec Nordiques		NHL	62	3	5	8	173
1982-83—Quebec Nordiques		NHL	58	5	11	16	135
1983-84—Fredericton Express		AHL	44	6	17	23	45
1983-84—Quebec Nordiques		NHL	25	2	3	5	17
WHA TOTALS			150	5	24	29	410
NHL TOTALS			272	19	39	58	535

GORDON JAY WELLS
(Known by middle name)

Defense ... 6'1" ... 205 lbs. ... Born, Paris, Ont., May 18, 1959 ... Shoots left ... (October 16, 1981)—Broke right hand in team practice when hit by a puck ... (December 14, 1982)—Tore medial collateral ligament in right knee in game at Washington ... (December, 1983)—Sprained ankle.

Year	Team	League	Games	G.	A.	Pts.	Pen.
1976-77—Kingston Canadians		OMJHL	59	4	7	11	90
1977-78—Kingston Canadians		OMJHL	68	9	13	22	195
1978-79—Kingston Canadians (a-c)		OMJHL	48	6	21	27	100
1979-80—Los Angeles Kings		NHL	43	0	0	0	113
1979-80—Binghamton Dusters		AHL	28	0	6	6	48
1980-81—Los Angeles Kings		NHL	72	5	13	18	155
1981-82—Los Angeles Kings		NHL	60	1	8	9	145
1982-83—Los Angeles Kings		NHL	69	3	12	15	167
1983-84—Los Angeles Kings		NHL	69	3	18	21	141
NHL TOTALS			313	12	51	63	721

(c)—August, 1979—Drafted by Los Angeles Kings in entry draft. First Los Angeles pick, 16th overall, first round.

STU WENAAS

Defense . . . 5'11" . . . 197 lbs. . . . Born, Maple Creek, Sask., January 22, 1964 . . . Shoots right.

Year	Team	League	Games	G.	A.	Pts.	Pen.
1979-80—Medicine Hat Tigers		WHL	40	4	4	8	41
1980-81—Medicine Hat Tigers		WHL	72	2	13	15	111
1981-82—Winnipeg Warriors (c)		WHL	68	7	36	43	163
1982-83—Winnipeg Warriors		WHI	58	9	25	34	93
1983-84—Winnipeg Warriors		WHL	2	0	0	0	0
1983-84—Kelowna Wings		WHL	31	14	16	30	53
1983-84—Lethbridge Broncos		WHL	3	0	0	0	0

(c)—June, 1982—Drafted as underage junior by Pittsburgh Penguins in 1982 NHL entry draft. Eighth Penguins pick, 199th overall, 10th round.

BLAKE WESLEY

Defense . . . 6'3" . . . 210 lbs. . . . Born, Red Deer, Alta., July 10, 1959 . . . Shoots left.

Year	Team	League	Games	G.	A.	Pts.	Pen.
1974-75—Red Deer Rustlers		AJHL	3	1	0	1	4
1975-76—Red Deer Rustlers		AJHL	55	19	41	60	199
1976-77—Portland Winter Hawks		WCHL	63	8	25	33	111
1977-78—Portland Winter Hawks		WCHL	67	7	37	44	190
1978-79—Portland Winter Hawks (b-c)		WHL	69	10	42	52	292
1979-80—Philadelphia Flyers		NHL	2	0	1	1	2
1979-80—Maine Mariners		AHL	65	12	22	34	76
1980-81—Maine Mariners		AHL	24	6	10	16	20
1980-81—Philadelphia Flyers (d)		NHL	50	3	7	10	107
1981-82—Hartford Whalers		NHL	78	9	18	27	123
1982-83—Hartford Whalers (e)		NHL	22	0	1	1	46
1982-83—Quebec Nordiques		NHL	52	4	8	12	84
1983-84—Quebec Nordiques		NHL	46	2	8	10	75
NHL TOTALS			250	18	43	61	437

(c)—August, 1979—Drafted by Philadelphia Flyers in entry draft. Second Philadelphia pick, 22nd overall, second round.

(d)—July, 1981—Traded by Philadelphia Flyers with Don Gillen, Rick MacLeish, first, second and third round picks in the 1982 NHL entry draft by Philadelphia Flyers to Hartford Whalers for Ray Allison, Fred Arthur and Whalers first and third round picks in 1982 draft.

(e)—December, 1982—Traded by Hartford Whalers to Quebec Nordiques for Pierre Lacroix.

SIMON WHEELDON

Center . . . 5'11" . . . 170 lbs. . . . Born, Vancouver, B.C., August 30, 1966 . . . Shoots left.

Year	Team	League	Games	G.	A.	Pts.	Pen.
1982-83—Kelowna Bucks		BCJHL	60	...	....	86	....
1983-84—Victoria Cougars (c)		WHL	56	14	24	38	43

(c)—June, 1984—Drafted as underage junior by Edmonton Oilers in NHL entry draft. Eleventh Oilers pick, 229th overall, 11th round.

BILL WHELTON

Defense . . . 6'1" . . . 180 lbs. . . . Born, Everett, Mass., August 28, 1959 . . . Shoots left.

Year	Team	League	Games	G.	A.	Pts.	Pen.
1978-79—Boston University (c)		ECAC	30	2	5	7	20
1979-80—Boston University		ECAC	25	4	14	18	39
1980-81—Boston University		ECAC	29	4	18	22	42
1980-81—Winnipeg Jets		NHL	2	0	0	0	0
1981-82—Tulsa Oilers		CHL	66	2	18	20	51
1982-83—Sherbrooke Jets		AHL	72	4	16	20	73
1983-84—Sherbrooke Jets		AHL	67	2	14	16	32
NHL TOTALS			2	0	0	0	0

(c)—August, 1979—Drafted by Winnipeg Jets in NHL entry draft. Third Jets pick, 61st overall, third round.

GORD WHITAKER

Right Wing . . . 6'2" . . . 205 lbs. . . . Born, Edmonton, Alta., January 24, 1966 . . . Shoots right.

Year	Team	League	Games	G.	A.	Pts.	Pen.
1983-84—Colorado College (c)		WCHA	33	10	10	20	44

(c)—June, 1984—Drafted by Winnipeg Jets in NHL entry draft. Ninth Jets pick, 177th overall, ninth round.

GEORGE WHITE

Left Wing . . . 6' . . . 175 lbs. . . . Born, Arlington, Mass., February 17, 1961 . . . Shoots right . . . Also plays center.

Year	Team	League	Games	G.	A.	Pts.	Pen.
1980-81	Univ. of New Hampshire (c)	ECAC	32	16	19	35	30
1981-82	Univ. of New Hampshire (d)	ECAC	31	10	15	25	45
1982-83	Univ. of New Hampshire	ECAC	34	15	11	26	21
1983-84	Peoria Prancers	IHL	7	2	0	2	7
1983-84	Colorado Flames	CHL	36	5	12	17	28

(c)—June, 1981—Drafted by Washington Capitals in 1981 NHL entry draft. Ninth Capitals pick, 173rd overall, ninth round.

(d)—June, 1982—Traded with Howard Walker, sixth round 1982 draft pick (Mats Kihlstrom), third round 1983 draft pick (Perry Berezan) and second round 1984 draft pick (Paul Ranheim) by Washington Capitals to Calgary Flames for Ken Houston and Pat Riggin.

DOUGLAS PETER WICKENHEISER

Center . . . 6' . . . 199 lbs. . . . Born, Regina, Sask., March 30, 1961 . . . Shoots left . . . Brother of Kurt Wickenheiser . . . (March 30, 1983)—Broke rib in game at Pittsburgh.

Year	Team	League	Games	G.	A.	Pts.	Pen.
1976-77	Regina Blues	SJHL	59	42	46	88	63
1977-78	Regina Pats	WCHL	68	37	51	88	49
1978-79	Regina Pats	WHL	68	32	62	94	141
1979-80	Regina Pats (a-c-d-e)	WHL	71	*89	81	*170	99
1980-81	Montreal Canadiens	NHL	41	7	8	15	20
1981-82	Montreal Canadiens	NHL	56	12	23	35	43
1982-83	Montreal Canadiens	NHL	78	25	30	55	49
1983-84	Montreal Canadiens (f)	NHL	27	5	5	10	6
1983-84	St. Louis Blues	NHL	46	7	21	28	19
	NHL TOTALS		248	56	87	143	137

(c)—Won Bob Brownridge Memorial Trophy (WHL Leading Scorer).

(d)—Named WHL's Most Valuable Player.

(e)—June, 1980—Drafted as underage junior by Montreal Canadiens in 1980 NHL entry draft. First Canadiens pick, first overall, first round.

(f)—December, 1983—Traded by Montreal Canadiens with Gilbert Delorme and Greg Paslawski to St. Louis Blues for Perry Turnbull.

DOUG WIECK

Left Wing . . . 6' . . . 180 lbs. . . . Born, Rochester, Minn., March 12, 1965 . . . Shoots left.

Year	Team	League	Games	G	A.	Pts.	Pen.
1983-84	Rochester Mayo H.S. (c)	Minn. H.S.	23	31	24	55	15

(c)—June, 1984—Drafted by New York Islanders in NHL entry draft. Fourth Islanders pick, 70th overall, fourth round.

JAMES DUNCAN WIEMER

Defense . . . 6'4" . . . 197 lbs. . . . Born, Sudbury, Ont., January 9, 1961 . . . Shoots left.

Year	Team	League	Games	G.	A.	Pts.	Pen.
1978-79	Peterborough Petes	OMJHL	63	15	12	27	50
1979-80	Peterborough Petes (c)	OMJHL	53	17	32	49	63
1980-81	Peterborough Petes	OHL	65	41	54	95	102
1981-82	Rochester Americans	AHL	74	19	26	45	57
1982-83	Rochester Americans	AHL	74	15	44	59	43
1982-83	Buffalo Sabres (d)	NHL	..	..	..	..	..
1983-84	Buffalo Sabres	NHL	64	5	15	20	48
1983-84	Rochester Americans	AHL	12	4	11	15	11
	NHL TOTALS		64	5	15	20	48

(c)—June, 1980—Drafted by Buffalo Sabres as underage junior in 1980 NHL entry draft. Fifth Sabres pick, 83rd overall, fourth round.

(d)—No regular-season appearance, played in one playoff game.

MARTIN WIITALA, JR.

Center . . . 6'2" . . . 175 lbs. . . . Born, Superior, Wis., February 24, 1964 . . . Shoots right.

Year	Team	League	Games	G.	A.	Pts.	Pen.
1981-82	Superior H.S. (c)	Wisc. H.S.	24	40	43	83	32
1982-83	Univ. of Wisconsin	WCHA	46	10	8	18	8
1983-84	Univ. of Wisconsin	WCHA	33	11	19	30	4

(c)—June, 1982—Drafted as underage player by Minnesota North Stars in 1982 NHL entry draft. Fifth North Stars pick, 101st overall, fifth round.

JIM WILHARM

Defense . . . 6'1" . . . 180 lbs. . . . Born, Minneapolis, Minn., July 9, 1966 . . . Shoots left.

Year	Team	League	Games	G.	A.	Pts.	Pen.
1983-84—Minnetonka H.S. (c)		Minn. H.S.	21	17	14	31	..

(c)—June, 1984—Drafted by New York Islanders in NHL entry draft. Seventh Islanders pick, 125th overall, sixth round.

BRIAN WILKS

Center . . . 5'11" . . . 175 lbs. . . . Born, Toronto, Ont., February 22, 1966 . . . Shoots right.

Year	Team	League	Games	G.	A.	Pts.	Pen.
1981-82—Toronto Marlboro Midgets		MTMHL	36	40	48	88	22
1982-83—Kitchener Rangers		OHL	69	6	17	23	25
1983-84—Kitchener Rangers (c)		OHL	64	21	54	75	36

(c)—June, 1984—Drafted as underage junior by Los Angeles Kings in NHL entry draft. Second Kings pick, 24th overall, second round.

ROD WILLARD

Left Wing . . . 6' . . . 187 lbs. . . . Born, New Liskeard, Ont., May 1, 1960 . . . Shoots left.

Year	Team	League	Games	G.	A.	Pts.	Pen.
1977-78—Cornwall Royals		QMJHL	66	12	29	41	27
1978-79—Cornwall Royals		QMJHL	72	38	57	95	69
1979-80—Cornwall Royals (c)		QMJHL	55	29	50	79	84
1980-81—Tulsa Oilers		CHL	4	0	0	0	0
1980-81—Fort Wayne Komets		IHL	79	32	29	61	92
1981-82—New Brunswick Hawks (d)		AHL	72	18	17	35	88
1982-83—Toronto Maple Leafs		NHL	1	0	0	0	0
1982-83—St. Catharines Saints (e)		AHL	18	5	5	10	8
1982-83—Springfield Indians		AHL	52	4	17	21	45
1983-84—Springfield Indians		AHL	76	17	19	36	76
NHL TOTALS			1	0	0	0	0

(c)—September, 1980—Signed as free agent by Winnipeg Jets.
(d)—October, 1981—Signed by New Brunswick Hawks as a free agent.
(e)—January, 1983—Traded by Toronto Maple Leafs to Chicago Black Hawks for Dave Snopek.

DAN WILLIAMS

Defense . . . 6'2" . . . 180 lbs. . . . Born, Oak Park, Ill., April 15, 1966 . . . Shoots left.

Year	Team	League	Games	G.	A.	Pts.	Pen.
1983-84—Chicago Jets (c)		CMJHL	43	28	38	66	68

(c)—June, 1984—Drafted by Chicago Black Hawks in NHL entry draft. Thirteenth Black Hawks pick, 235th overall, 12th round.

DAVID JAMES (TIGER) WILLIAMS

Left Wing . . . 5'11" . . . 180 lbs. . . . Born, Weyburn, Sask., February 3, 1954 . . . Shoots left . . . (October 10, 1980)—Fracture of lower lombar transverse in a goal-mouth crash in first game of 1980-81 season . . . (1982-83)—Missed 12 games due to various NHL suspensions . . . (October 30, 1983)—Given 8-game suspension by NHL for 'potentially dangerous' attempt to injure Paul Baxter in game at Calgary . . . All-time NHL penalty minute leader.

Year	Team	League	Games	G.	A.	Pts.	Pen.
1971-72—Swift Current Broncos		WCHL	68	12	22	34	278
1972-73—Swift Current Broncos		WCHL	68	44	58	102	266
1973-74—Swift Current Broncos (c)		WCHL	68	52	56	108	310
1974-75—Oklahoma City Blazers		CHL	39	16	11	27	202
1974-75—Toronto Maple Leafs		NHL	42	10	19	29	187
1975-76—Toronto Maple Leafs		NHL	78	21	19	40	299
1976-77—Toronto Maple Leafs		NHL	77	18	25	43	*338
1977-78—Toronto Maple Leafs (d)		NHL	78	19	31	50	351
1978-79—Toronto Maple Leafs (e)		NHL	77	19	20	39	*298
1979-80—Toronto Maple Leafs (f)		NHL	55	22	18	40	197
1979-80—Vancouver Canucks		NHL	23	8	5	13	81
1980-81—Vancouver Canucks		NHL	77	35	27	62	*343
1981-82—Vancouver Canucks (g)		NHL	77	17	21	38	341
1982-83—Vancouver Canucks		NHL	68	8	13	21	265
1983-84—Vancouver Canucks (h)		NHL	67	15	16	31	294
NHL TOTALS			719	192	214	406	2994

(c)—Drafted from Swift Current Broncos by Toronto Maple Leafs in second round of 1974 amateur draft.

(d)—Led in penalty minutes (63) during playoffs.

(e)—Led in penalty minutes (48) during playoffs.

(f)—February, 1980—Traded with Jerry Butler by Toronto Maple Leafs to Vancouver Canucks for Rick Vaive and Bill Derlago.

(g)—Led NHL playoffs with 116 penalty minutes.

(h)—August, 1984—Traded by Vancouver Canucks to Detroit Red Wings for Rob McClanahan.

KEVIN WILLISON

Defense . . . 5'11" . . . 172 lbs. . . . Born, Calgary, Alta., May 21, 1958 . . . Shoots left . . . (September, 1980)—Surgery for dislocated shoulder.

Year	Team	League	Games	G.	A.	Pts.	Pen.
1975-76—Merritt Luckies		Jr."A"BCHL	60	16	28	44	122
1976-77—Calgary Centennials		WCHL	55	11	32	43	161
1977-78—Billings Bighorns (c)		WCHL	68	21	42	63	151
1978-79—Port Huron Flags		IHL	55	12	35	47	116
1979-80—Salt Lake Golden Eagles		CHL	72	5	26	31	106
1980-81—Port Huron Flags		IHL	20	2	7	9	33
1980-81—Salt Lake Golden Eagles (d)		CHL	....	...	....	....	....
1981-82—Milwaukee Admirals		IHL	73	10	41	51	107
1982-83—Milwaukee Admirals		IHL	81	10	41	51	63
1983-84—Milwaukee Admirals (a-e)		IHL	82	21	52	73	73

(c)—Drafted from Billings Bighorns by St. Louis Blues in fifth round of 1978 amateur draft.

(d)—Appeared in three playoff games.

(e)—Co-winner of Governors Trophy (Top IHL Defenseman) with Jim Burton (Ft. Wayne).

BEHN BEVAN WILSON

Defense . . . 6'3" . . . 207 lbs. . . . Born, Toronto, Ont., December 19, 1958 . . . Shoots left . . . (October, 1982)—Serious groin pull . . . (February 19, 1983)—Suspended for six games for high sticking New York Rangers goalie Glen Hanlon.

Year	Team	League	Games	G.	A.	Pts.	Pen.
1975-76—Ottawa 67's		Jr."A"OHA	63	5	16	21	131
1976-77—Ottawa 67's (c)		Jr."A"OHA	31	8	29	37	115
1976-77—Windsor Spitfires		Jr."A"OHA	17	4	16	20	38
1976-77—Kalamazoo Wings		IHL	13	2	7	9	40
1977-78—Kingston Canadians (d)		Jr."A"OHA	52	18	58	76	186
1978-79—Philadelphia Flyers		NHL	80	13	36	49	197
1979-80—Philadelphia Flyers		NHL	61	9	25	34	212
1980-81—Philadelphia Flyers		NHL	77	16	47	63	237
1981-82—Philadelphia Flyers		NHL	59	13	23	36	135
1982-83—Philadelphia Flyers (e)		NHL	62	8	24	32	92
1983-84—Chicago Black Hawks		NHL	59	10	22	32	143
NHL TOTALS			398	69	177	246	1016

(c)—Traded to Windsor Spitfires by Ottawa 67's with John Wilson for Jim Fox, December, 1976.

(d)—Drafted from Kingston Canadians by Philadelphia Flyers (with choice obtained from Pittsburgh Penguins in trade for Tom Bladon, Orest Kindrachuk and Don Saleski) in first round of 1978 amateur draft.

(e)—June, 1983—Traded by Philadelphia Flyers to Chicago Black Hawks for Doug Crossman and a second-round draft choice in 1984 (Scott Mellanby).

CAREY WILSON

Center . . . 6'2" . . . 205 lbs. . . . Born, Winnipeg, Man., May 19, 1962 . . . Shoots right . . . Son of Dr. Gerry Wilson, former vice-president and team doctor of Winnipeg Jets (WHA).

Year	Team	League	Games	G.	A.	Pts.	Pen.
1978-79—Calgary Chinooks		AJHL	60	30	34	64	....
1979-80—Dartmouth College (c)		ECAC	31	16	22	38	20
1980-81—Dartmouth College		ECAC	21	9	13	22	52
1981-82—Helsinki IFK		Finland	39	15	17	32	58
1982-83—Helsinki IFK (d)		Finland	36	18	22	40	...
1983-84—Canadian Olympic Team		Int'l	59	21	24	45	34
1983-84—Calgary Flames		NHL	15	2	5	7	2
NHL TOTALS			15	2	5	7	2

(c)—June, 1980—Drafted by Chicago Black Hawks in NHL entry draft. Eighth Black Hawks pick, 67th overall, fourth round.

(d)—November, 1982—Traded by Chicago Black Hawks to Calgary Flames for Denis Cyr.

DOUGLAS WILSON

Defense . . . 6'1" . . . 187 lbs. . . . Born, Ottawa, Ont., July 5, 1957 . . . Shoots left . . . Missed part of 1976-77 season with knee surgery . . . Brother of Murray Wilson . . . Missed part of

1978-79 season with shoulder injury that required surgery . . . (November 25, 1981)—Broken jaw in game at Vancouver. Had his jaw wired shut, lost 25 pounds and has his vision restricted by special protective mask he had to wear . . . Set Chicago Black Hawks record for defensemen in 1981-82 with 39 goals and 85 points (Only Bobby Orr ever scored more goals in one season as a defenseman in the NHL) . . . Set Chicago record of 51 assists by a defenseman in 1982-83 . . . (November, 1983)—Ankle injury . . . Suffers from Hyperglycemia (High concentration of glucose in the blood) . . . (February 3, 1984)—Broke nose in game at Winnipeg . . . (March 4, 1984)—Played his first game without a facemask after recovering from broken nose. He was accidently hit by the stick of Walt Poddubny of Toronto and suffered a fractured skull. He was out for the rest of the season.

Year	Team	League	Games	G.	A.	Pts.	Pen.
1974-75—Ottawa 67's		Jr."A"OHA	55	29	58	87	75
1975-76—Ottawa 67's (b)		Jr."A"OHA	58	26	62	88	142
1976-77—Ottawa 67's (a-c)		Jr."A"OHA	43	25	54	79	85
1977-78—Chicago Black Hawks		NHL	77	14	20	34	72
1978-79—Chicago Black Hawks		NHL	56	5	21	26	37
1979-80—Chicago Black Hawks		NHL	73	12	49	61	70
1980-81—Chicago Black Hawks		NHL	76	12	39	51	80
1981-82—Chicago Black Hawks (a-d)		NHL	76	39	46	85	54
1982-83—Chicago Black Hawks		NHL	74	18	51	69	58
1983-84—Chicago Black Hawks		NHL	66	13	45	58	64
NHL TOTALS			498	113	271	384	435

(c)—Drafted from Ottawa 67's by Chicago Black Hawks in first round of 1977 amateur draft.
(d)—Won James Norris Memorial Trophy (Top NHL Defenseman).

MITCH WILSON

Right Wing . . . 5'8" . . . 185 lbs. . . . Born, Kelowna, B.C., February 15, 1962 . . . Shoots right.

Year	Team	League	Games	G.	A.	Pts.	Pen.
1980-81—Seattle Breakers		WHL	64	8	23	31	253
1981-82—Seattle Breakers		WHL	60	18	17	35	436
1982-83—Wichita Wind (c)		CHL	55	4	6	10	186
1983-84—Maine Mariners		AHL	71	6	8	14	*349

(c)—October, 1982—Signed by New Jersey Devils as a free agent.

RONALD LEE WILSON

Left Wing . . . 5'9" . . . 170 lbs. . . . Born, Toronto, Ont., May 13, 1956 . . . Shoots left . . . Also plays Center.

Year	Team	League	Games	G.	A.	Pts.	Pen.
1974-75—Markham Waxers		OPJHL	43	26	28	54	24
1974-75—Toronto Marlboros		Jr."A"OHA	16	6	12	18	6
1975-76—St. Cath. Black Hawks (c)		Jr."A"OHA	64	37	62	99	44
1976-77—Nova Scotia Voyageurs		AHL	67	15	21	36	18
1977-78—Nova Scotia Voyageurs		AHL	59	15	25	40	17
1978-79—Nova Scotia Voyageurs (d)		AHL	77	33	42	75	91
1979-80—Winnipeg Jets		NHL	79	21	36	57	28
1980-81—Winnipeg Jets		NHL	77	18	33	51	55
1981-82—Tulsa Oilers		CHL	41	20	38	58	22
1981-82—Winnipeg Jets		NHL	39	3	13	16	49
1982-83—Sherbrooke Jets		AHL	65	30	55	85	71
1982-83—Winnipeg Jets		NHL	12	6	3	9	4
1983-84—Winnipeg Jets		NHL	51	3	12	15	12
1983-84—Sherbrooke Jets		AHL	22	10	30	40	16
NHL TOTALS			258	51	97	148	148

(c)—Drafted from St. Catharines Black Hawks by Montreal Canadiens in 15th round of 1976 amateur draft.
(d)—June, 1979—Sold by Montreal Canadiens to Winnipeg Jets.

WILLIAM RICHARD (RIK) WILSON

Defense . . . 6' . . . 195 lbs. . . . Born, Long Beach, Calif., June 17, 1962 . . . Shoots right . . . (October, 1982)—Sprained ankle.

Year	Team	League	Games	G.	A.	Pts.	Pen.
1979-80—Kingston Canadians (c)		OMJHL	67	15	38	53	75
1980-81—Kingston Canadians (a)		OHL	68	30	70	100	108
1981-82—Kingston Canadians		OHL	16	9	10	19	38
1981-82—St. Louis Blues		NHL	48	3	18	21	24
1982-83—St. Louis Blues		NHL	56	3	11	14	50
1982-83—Salt Lake Golden Eagles		CHL	4	0	0	0	0

Year	Team	League	Games	G.	A.	Pts.	Pen.
1983-84—Montana Magic		CHL	6	0	3	3	2
1983-84—St. Louis Blues		NHL	48	7	11	18	53
NHL TOTALS			152	13	40	53	127

(c)—June, 1980—Drafted by St. Louis Blues as underage junior in 1980 NHL entry draft. First Blues pick, 12th overall, first round.

BENNETT MARTIN WOLF

Defense . . . 6'3" . . . 205 lbs. . . . Born, Kitchener, Ont., October 23, 1959 . . . Shoots right . . . (September, 1980)—Injured groin during Pittsburgh training camp.

Year	Team	League	Games	G.	A.	Pts.	Pen.
1976-77—Kitchener Rangers		OMJHL	7	0	1	1	16
1977-78—Toronto Marlboros		OMJHL	66	3	13	16	334
1978-79—Kitchener Rangers (c)		OMJHL	47	3	18	21	281
1979-80—Grand Rapids Owls		IHL	51	3	14	17	408
1979-80—Syracuse Firebirds (d)		AHL	....	...	....	....	....
1980-81—Pittsburgh Penguins		NHL	24	0	1	1	94
1980-81—Binghamton Whalers		AHL	14	2	2	4	106
1981-82—Erie Blades		AHL	45	0	4	4	153
1981-82—Pittsburgh Penguins		NHL	1	0	0	0	2
1982-83—Pittsburgh Penguins		NHL	5	0	0	0	37
1982-83—Baltimore Skipjacks		AHL	61	1	10	11	223
1983-84—Baltimore Skipjacks		AHL	63	3	13	16	*349
NHL TOTALS			30	0	1	1	133

(c)—August, 1979—Drafted by Pittsburgh Penguins in 1979 entry draft. Second Penguins pick, 52nd overall, third round.

(d)—No regular season games. Played in four playoff games.

DAN WOOD

Right Wing . . . 5'11" . . . 190 lbs. . . . Born, Toronto, Ont., October 30, 1962 . . . Shoots right.

Year	Team	League	Games	G.	A.	Pts.	Pen.
1979-80—Kingston Canadians		OHL	66	7	19	26	89
1980-81—Kingston Canadians (c)		OHL	68	12	24	36	165
1981-82—Kingston Canadians		OHL	55	25	33	58	108
1981-82—Salt Lake Golden Eagles		CHL	8	0	1	1	11
1982-83—Salt Lake Golden Eagles		CHL	67	13	14	27	57
1983-84—Canadian Olympic Team		Int'l	41	5	4	9	38
1983-84—Montana Magic		CHL	14	2	7	9	14
1983-84—Springfield Indians (d)		AHL	13	5	8	13	4

(c)—June, 1981—Drafted as underage junior by St. Louis Blues in 1981 NHL entry draft. Eighth Blues pick, 188th overall, ninth round.

(d)—August, 1984—Sold by St. Louis Blues to Quebec Nordiques.

STEVE WOODBURN

Defense . . . 6'1" . . . 198 lbs. . . . Born, Montreal, Que., October 24, 1963 . . . Shoots left.

Year	Team	League	Games	G.	A.	Pts.	Pen.
1980-81—Shawinigan Cataracts		QMJHL	68	1	10	11	151
1981-82—Shawinigan Cataracts		QMJHL	62	8	19	27	170
1982-83—Verdun Juniors (c)		QHL	69	5	28	33	202
1983-84—Laval Voisins		QHL	52	7	28	35	160

(c)—June, 1983—Drafted by Edmonton Oilers in 1983 NHL entry draft. Eleventh Oilers pick, 240th overall, 12th round.

PAUL WILLIAM WOODS

Center . . . 5'10" . . . 175 lbs. . . . Born, Hespeler, Ont., April 12, 1955 . . . Shoots left . . . Also plays Left Wing . . . (March, 1981)—Broken jaw . . . (December, 1982)—Separated shoulder . . . (December 6, 1983)—Separated right shoulder during team practice.

Year	Team	League	Games	G.	A.	Pts.	Pen.
1972-73—S. Ste. Marie Greyh'ds		Jr."A" OHA	60	30	34	64	65
1973-74—S. Ste. Marie Greyh'ds		Jr."A" OHA	48	17	32	49	91
1974-75—S. Ste. Marie Greyh'ds (c)		Jr."A" OHA	62	38	81	119	116
1975-76—Nova Scotia Voyageurs		AHL	67	17	21	38	38
1976-77—Nova Scotia Voyageurs (d)		AHL	45	20	18	38	51
1977-78—Detroit Red Wings		NHL	80	19	23	42	52
1978-79—Detroit Red Wings		NHL	80	14	23	37	59
1979-80—Detroit Red Wings		NHL	79	6	20	26	24
1980-81—Detroit Red Wings		NHL	67	8	16	24	45
1981-82—Detroit Red Wings		NHL	75	10	17	27	48

Year	Team	League	Games	G.	A.	Pts.	Pen.
1982-83—Detroit Red Wings		NHL	63	13	20	33	30
1983-84—Detroit Red Wings		NHL	57	2	5	7	18
NHL TOTALS			501	72	124	196	276

(c)—Drafted from Sault Ste. Marie Greyhounds by Montreal Canadiens in third round of 1975 amateur draft.

(d)—Selected by Detroit Red Wings from Montreal Canadiens in NHL waiver draft, October, 1977.

KORY WRIGHT

Right Wing . . . 5'10" . . . 180 lbs. . . . Born, Anchorage, Alaska, June 10, 1965 . . . Shoots right.

Year	Team	League	Games	G.	A.	Pts.	Pen.
1982-83—Dubuque Juniors (c)		USHL	48	45	57	102	36
1983-84—Northern Michigan Univ.		CCHA	39	7	4	11	19

(c)—June, 1983—Drafted by Winnipeg Jets in 1983 NHL entry draft. Eleventh Jets pick, 189th overall, 10th round.

DAN WURST

Defense . . . 6'4" . . . 200 lbs. . . . Born, Edina, Minn., October 5, 1964 . . . Shoots left.

Year	Team	League	Games	G.	A.	Pts.	Pen.
1982-83—Edina High School (c)		Minn. H.S.	14	0	2	2	24
1983-84—Providence College		ECAC	33	1	1	2	57

(c)—June, 1983—Drafted by Montreal Canadiens in 1983 NHL entry draft. Seventh Canadiens pick, 98th overall, fifth round.

BART YACHIMEC

Right Wing . . . 5'9" . . . 193 lbs. . . . Born, Edmonton, Alta., March 16, 1960 . . . Shoots right.

Year	Team	League	Games	G.	A.	Pts.	Pen.
1977-78—Portland Winter Hawks		WHL	72	7	7	14	100
1978-79—Portland Winter Hawks		WHL	69	26	32	58	79
1979-80—Portland Winter Hawks		WHL	71	20	21	41	120
1980-81—Hampton Aces		EHL	12	4	14	18	4
1980-81—New Brunswick Hawks		AHL	50	5	7	12	46
1981-82—New Brunswick Hawks		AHL	71	8	15	23	49
1982-83—Springfield Indians (c)		AHL	71	30	35	65	61
1983-84—Moncton Alpines		AHL	80	27	32	59	91

(c)—August, 1983—Signed by Edmonton Oilers as a free agent.

WARREN YADLOWSKI

Center . . . 6'1" . . . 167 lbs. . . . Born, Edmonton, Alta., July 14, 1965 . . . Shoots left . . . Also plays left wing.

Year	Team	League	Games	G.	A.	Pts.	Pen.
1981-82—Edmonton Midgets		Alta. Midgets	48	46	52	98	72
1982-83—Calgary Wranglers (c)		WHL	65	3	11	14	24
1983-84—St. Albert Saints		AJHL	20	14	17	31	40
1983-84—Calgary Wranglers		WHL	11	2	2	4	2
1983-84—Prince Albert Raiders		WHL	23	6	6	12	8

(c)—June, 1983—Drafted as underage junior by Calgary Flames in 1983 NHL entry draft. Ninth Oilers pick, 200th overall, tenth round.

DALE ALEXANDER YAKIWCHUK

Left Wing . . . 6'4" . . . 200 lbs. . . . Born, Calgary, Alta., October 17, 1958 . . . Shoots left . . . Also plays Center.

Year	Team	League	Games	G.	A.	Pts.	Pen.
1975-76—Taber Golden Suns		AJHL	13	4	6	10	93
1975-76—Lethbridge Broncos		WCHL	43	3	14	17	146
1976-77—Portland Winter Hawks		WCHL	59	24	53	77	151
1977-78—Portland Winter Hawks (c-d)		WCHL	64	32	52	84	312
1978-79—Winnipeg Jets		WHA	4	0	0	0	0
1978-79—Philadelphia Firebirds		AHL	46	2	18	20	101
1978-79—Nova Scotia Voyageurs (e)		AHL	12	3	1	4	15
1979-80—Cincinnati Stingers		CHL	30	4	15	19	75
1979-80—Tulsa Oilers		CHL	37	3	9	12	76
1980-81—Richmond Rifles (f-g)		EHL	42	15	35	50	118
1980-81—Baltimore Blades		EHL	18	11	14	25	73
1981-82—Milwaukee Admirals		IHL	72	18	57	75	249
1982-83—Milwaukee Admirals (a-h)		IHL	79	38	*100	*138	223
1983-84—Milwaukee Admirals		IHL	74	35	*69	104	67
WHA TOTALS			4	0	0	0	0

(c)—Drafted from Portland Winter Hawks by Montreal Canadiens in second round of 1978 amateur draft.

(d)—Selected by Winnipeg Jets in World Hockey Association amateur player draft and signed by Winnipeg, July, 1978.

(e)—March, 1979—Sent to Nova Scotia Voyageurs as compensation for allowing Bill Prentice to be assigned to Philadelphia Firebirds.

(f)—October, 1980—Released by Winnipeg Jets.

(g)—February, 1981—Traded by Richmond Rifles with Jim Lockhurst and Gord Gejdos to Baltimore Clippers for Randy Ireland and Paul Pacific.

(h)—Won Leo P. Lamoureux Memorial Trophy (Top IHL Scorer).

GARY YAREMCHUK

Center . . . 6' . . . 180 lbs. . . . Born, Edmonton, Alta., August 15, 1961 . . . Shoots left . . . Brother of Ken Yaremchuk . . . (October, 1982)—Bruised lung.

Year	Team	League	Games	G.	A.	Pts.	Pen.
1979-80	Ft. Saskatchewan	AJHL	27	27	44	71	61
1979-80	Portland Winter Hawks	WHL	41	21	34	55	23
1980-81	Portland Winter Hawks (c)	WHL	72	56	79	135	121
1981-82	Cincinnati Tigers	CHL	53	21	35	56	101
1981-82	Toronto Maple Leafs	NHL	18	0	3	3	10
1982-83	St. Catharines Saints	AHL	61	17	28	45	72
1982-83	Toronto Maple Leafs	NHL	3	0	0	0	2
1983-84	St. Catharines Saints	AHL	73	24	37	61	84
1983-84	Toronto Maple Leafs	NHL	1	0	0	0	0
	NHL TOTALS		22	0	3	3	12

(c)—Drafted by Toronto Maple Leafs in 1981 NHL entry draft. Second Maple Leafs pick, 24th overall, second round.

KEN YAREMCHUK

Center . . . 5'11" . . . 185 lbs. . . . Born, Edmonton, Alta., January 1, 1964 . . . Shoots right . . . Brother of Gary Yaremchuk . . . (January, 1984)—Serious groin injury, out two months.

Year	Team	League	Games	G.	A.	Pts.	Pen.
1979-80	Ft. Saskatchewan	AJHL	59	40	72	112	39
1980-81	Portland Winter Hawks	WHL	72	56	79	135	121
1981-82	Portland Winter Hawks (a-c)	WHL	72	58	99	157	181
1982-83	Portland Winter Hawks (b)	WHL	66	51	*109	160	76
1983-84	Chicago Black Hawks	NHL	47	6	7	13	19
	NHL TOTALS		47	6	7	13	19

(c)—June, 1982—Drafted as underage junior by Chicago Black Hawks in 1982 NHL entry draft. First Black Hawks pick, 7th overall, first round.

ROSS YATES

Center . . . 5'11" . . . 170 lbs. . . . Born, Montreal, Que., June 18, 1959 . . . Shoots right . . . Missed 1983 training camp due to spot on chest x-rays taken as part of pre-camp physical . . . Only third player to have back-to-back 100-point AHL seasons (Bill Sweeney, '61-'62-'63; Carl Liscombe, '48-'49).

Year	Team	League	Games	G.	A.	Pts.	Pen.
1980-81	Mt. Allison Univ. (a-c)	Can. Col.	....	16	*56	*72	....
1980-81	Binghamton Whalers	AHL	14	4	1	5	2
1981-82	Binghamton Whalers	AHL	80	22	23	45	53
1982-83	Binghamton Whalers (a-d-e-f)	AHL	77	41	*84	*125	28
1983-84	Binghamton Whalers	AHL	68	35	*73	108	82
1983-84	Hartford Whalers (g)	NHL	7	1	1	2	4
	NHL TOTALS		7	1	1	2	4

(c)—March, 1981—Signed by Hartford Whalers as a free agent.

(d)—Won John B. Sollenberger Trophy (Leading Scorer).

(e)—Won Les Cunningham Plaque (AHL MVP).

(f)—Won Fred Hunt Memorial Award (AHL Coaches MVP).

(g)—May, 1984—Released by Hartford Whalers.

TRENT YAWNEY

Defense . . . 6'3" . . . 185 lbs. . . . Born, Hudson Bay, Sask., September 29, 1965 . . . Shoots left.

Year	Team	League	Games	G.	A.	Pts.	Pen.
1981-82	Saskatoon Blades	WHL	6	1	0	1	0
1982-83	Saskatoon Blades	WHL	59	6	31	37	44
1983-84	Saskatoon Blades (c)	WHL	72	13	46	59	81

(c)—June, 1984—Drafted as underage junior by Chicago Black Hawks in NHL entry draft. Second Black Hawks pick, 45th overall, third round.

TIMOTHY MICHAEL YOUNG

Center . . . 6'2" . . . 178 lbs. . . . Born, Scarborough, Ont., February 22, 1955 . . . Shoots right . . . (September, 1981)—Broke right ankle during softball game, right knee also swelled (Had postseason surgery on knee during summer of 1981) . . . (January 17, 1984)—Injured back in game at Washington and missed 24 games.

Year	Team	League	Games	G.	A.	Pts.	Pen.
1972-73—Pembroke Lumber Kings		Cent. OHA	55	41	40	81	148
1973-74—Ottawa 67s		Jr."A" OHA	69	45	61	106	161
1974-75—Ottawa 67s (b-c-d)		Jr."A" OHA	70	56	*107	163	127
1975-76—New Haven Nighthawks		AHL	13	7	13	20	16
1975-76—Minnesota North Stars		NHL	63	18	33	51	71
1976-77—Minnesota North Stars		NHL	80	29	66	95	58
1977-78—Minnesota North Stars		NHL	78	23	35	58	64
1978-79—Minnesota North Stars		NHL	73	24	32	56	46
1979-80—Minnesota North Stars		NHL	77	31	43	74	24
1980-81—Minnesota North Stars		NHL	74	25	41	66	40
1981-82—Minnesota North Stars		NHL	49	10	31	41	67
1982-83—Minnesota North Stars (e)		NHL	70	18	35	53	31
1983-84—Winnipeg Jets		NHL	44	15	19	34	25
NHL TOTALS			608	193	335	528	426

(c)—Drafted from Ottawa 67s by Los Angeles Kings in first round of 1975 amateur draft.

(d)—Traded to Minnesota North Stars by Los Angeles Kings for Minnesota's second-round 1976 choice, August, 1975.

(e)—August, 1983—Traded by Minnesota North Stars to Winnipeg Jets for Craig Levie and Tom Ward.

WARREN YOUNG

Center . . . 6'3" . . . 195 lbs. . . . Born, Weston, Ont., January 11, 1956 . . . Shoots left . . . Also plays left wing.

Year	Team	League	Games	G.	A.	Pts.	Pen.
1974-75—Dixie Beehives		OPJHL	44	32	25	57	50
1975-76—Michigan Tech (c)		WCHA	42	16	15	31	48
1976-77—Michigan Tech		WCHA	37	19	26	45	86
1977-78—Michigan Tech		WCHA	32	14	16	30	54
1978-79—Michigan Tech		WCHA	26	11	7	18	45
1978-79—Oklahoma City Stars		CHL	4	0	1	1	2
1979-80—Oklahoma City Stars		CHL	13	4	8	12	9
1979-80—Baltimore Clippers (b)		EHL	65	*53	53	106	75
1980-81—Oklahoma City Stars		CHL	77	26	33	59	42
1981-82—Minnesota North Stars		NHL	1	0	0	0	0
1981-82—Nashville South Stars		CHL	60	31	28	59	154
1982-83—Minnesota North Stars		NHL	4	1	1	2	0
1982-83—Birmingham South Stars (b)		CHL	75	26	58	84	144
1983-84—Pittsburgh Penguins (d)		NHL	15	1	7	8	19
1983-84—Baltimore Skipjacks		AHL	59	25	38	63	142
NHL TOTALS			20	2	8	10	19

(c)—May, 1976—Drafted by California Seals in NHL amateur draft. Fourth Seals pick, 59th overall, fourth round.

(d)—August, 1983—Signed by Pittsburgh Penguins as a free agent.

PAUL YSEBAERT

Center . . . 6'1" . . . 170 lbs. . . . Born, Sarnia, Ont., May 15, 1966 . . . Shoots left.

Year	Team	League	Games	G.	A.	Pts.	Pen.
1983-84—Petrolia Jets (c)		WOJBHL	33	35	42	77	20

(c)—June, 1984—Drafted by New Jersey Devils in NHL entry draft. Fourth Devils pick, 74th overall, fourth round.

STEVE YZERMAN

Center . . . 5'11" . . . 175 lbs. . . . Born, Cranbrook, B.C., May 9, 1965 . . . Shoots right . . . (January 31, 1984)—Became youngest person to ever play in NHL All-Star Game.

Year	Team	League	Games	G.	A.	Pts.	Pen.
1981-82—Peterborough Petes		OHI	58	21	43	64	65
1982-83—Peterborough Petes (c)		OHL	56	42	49	91	33
1983-84—Detroit Red Wings (d)		NHL	80	39	48	87	33
NHL TOTALS			80	39	48	87	33

(c)—June, 1983—Drafted as underage junior by Detroit Red Wings in 1983 NHL entry draft. First Red Wings pick, 4th overall, first round.

(d)—Chosen NHL Rookie of the Year in poll of players by THE SPORTING NEWS.

RONALD KENNETH ZANUSSI

Right Wing . . . 5'11" . . . 180 lbs. . . . Born, Toronto, Ont., August 31, 1956 . . . Shoots right . . . (January, 1981)—Bruised ribs.

Year	Team	League	Games	G.	A.	Pts.	Pen.
1973-74	London Knights	Jr."A"OHA	65	21	20	41	110
1974-75	London Knights	Jr."A"OHA	69	34	52	86	123
1975-76	London Knights (c)	Jr."A"OHA	40	17	19	36	55
1976-77	Fort Wayne Komets (d)	IHL	77	53	33	86	138
1977-78	Fort Worth Texans	CHL	6	2	1	3	5
1977-78	Minnesota North Stars	NHL	68	15	17	32	89
1978-79	Minnesota North Stars	NHL	63	14	16	30	82
1978-79	Oklahoma City Stars	CHL	4	3	1	4	6
1979-80	Minnesota North Stars	NHL	72	14	31	45	93
1980-81	Oklahoma City Stars	CHL	3	3	2	5	5
1980-81	Minnesota North Stars (e)	NHL	41	6	11	17	89
1980-81	Toronto Maple Leafs	NHL	12	3	0	3	6
1981-82	Cincinnati Tigers	CHL	21	12	9	21	32
1981-82	Toronto Maple Leafs	NHL	43	0	8	8	14
1982-83	St. Catharines Saints	AHL	18	5	5	10	8
1982-83	Sherbrooke Jets	AHL	52	4	17	21	45
1983-84	St. Catharines Saints	AHL	59	4	15	19	59
	NHL TOTALS		299	52	83	135	373

(c)—Drafted from London Knights by Minnesota North Stars in third round of 1976 amateur draft.
(d)—Co-winner (along with Garth MacGuigan) of Garry Longman Memorial Trophy (rookie of the year).
(e)—March, 1981—Traded with 1981 third-round entry draft pick (Ernie Godden) by Minnesota North Stars to Toronto Maple Leafs for second-round 1981 entry draft pick (Dave Donnelly).

RICHARD ANDREW ZEMLAK

Center . . . 6'2" . . . 190 lbs. . . . Born, Wynard, Sask., March 3, 1963 . . . Shoots right.

Year	Team	League	Games	G.	A.	Pts.	Pen.
1979-80	Regina Pat Blues	SJHL	30	4	7	11	80
1980-81	Spokane Flyers (c)	WHL	72	19	19	38	132
1981-82	Spokane Flyers (d)	WHL	28	10	22	32	113
1981-82	Medicine Hat Tigers	WHL	41	11	20	31	70
1981-82	Salt Lake Golden Eagles	CHL	6	0	0	0	2
1982-83	Medicine Hat Tigers	WHL	51	20	17	37	119
1982-83	Nanaimo Islanders	WHL	18	2	8	10	50
1983-84	Montana Magic	CHL	14	2	2	4	17
1983-84	Toledo Goaldiggers (e)	IHL	45	8	19	27	101

(c)—June, 1981—Drafted as underage junior by St. Louis Blues in 1981 NHL entry draft. Ninth Blues pick, 209th overall, 10th round.
(d)—December, 1981—Selected by Medicine Hat Tigers in special WHL draft of players from defunct Spokane Flyers.
(e)—August, 1984—Sold by St. Louis Blues to Quebec Nordiques.

PETER ZEZEL

Center . . . 5'10" . . . 195 lbs. . . . Born, Toronto, Ont., April 22, 1965 . . . Shoots left.

Year	Team	League	Games	G.	A.	Pts.	Pen.
1981-82	Don Mills Flyers	MTHL	40	43	51	94	36
1982-83	Toronto Marlboros (c)	OHL	66	35	39	74	28
1983-84	Toronto Marlboros	OHL	68	47	86	133	31

(c)—June, 1983—Drafted as underage junior by Philadelphia Flyers in 1983 NHL entry draft. First Flyers pick, 41st overall, second round.

MARK ZILIOTTO

Left Wing . . . 6'1" . . . 175 lbs. . . . Born, Toronto, Ont., October 22, 1965 . . . Shoots left.

Year	Team	League	Games	G.	A.	Pts.	Pen.
1983-84	Streetsville Derbys (c)	COJBHL	31	22	17	39	78

(c)—June, 1984—Drafted by Pittsburgh Penguins in 1984 entry draft. Tenth Penguins pick, 230th overall, 12th round.

RICK ZOMBO

Defense . . . 6'1" . . . 190 lbs. . . . Born, Des Plaines, Ill., May 8, 1963 . . . Shoots right.

Year	Team	League	Games	G.	A.	Pts.	Pen.
1980-81	Austin Mavericks (c)	USMWHL	....	...	....	....	....
1981-82	Univ. of North Dakota	WCHA	45	1	15	16	31
1982-83	Univ. of North Dakota	WCHA	33	5	11	16	41
1983-84	Univ. of North Dakota	WCHA	34	7	24	31	40

(c)—June, 1981—Drafted by Detroit Red Wings in NHL entry draft. Sixth Red Wings pick, 149th overall, eighth round.

MIKE ZUKE

Center . . . 6' . . . 180 lbs. . . . Born, Sault Ste. Marie, Ont., April 16, 1954 . . . Shoots right . . . Attended Michigan Tech . . . Missed part of 1977-78 season with partial separation of right shoulder . . . Missed start of 1978-79 season with shoulder separation . . . (Summer, 1983)—Shoulder surgery.

Year	Team	League	Games	G.	A.	Pts.	Pen.
1971-72—S. St. Marie Greyh'ds (a)		NOHA	48	45	40	*85	....
1972-73—Michigan Tech (f)		WCHA	38	23	30	53	20
1973-74—Michigan Tech (c-d)		WCHA	40	28	47	75	38
1974-75—Michigan Tech		WCHA	42	35	43	78	20
1975-76—Michigan Tech (a-d-e)		WCHA	43	47	57	104	42
1976-77—Mohawk Valley Comets		NAHL	48	42	29	71	33
1976-77—Indianapolis Racers (g)		WHA	15	3	4	7	2
1977-78—Edmonton Oilers (h)		WHA	71	23	34	57	47
1978-79—Salt Lake Golden Eagles		CHL	29	9	13	22	4
1978-79—St. Louis Blues		NHL	34	9	17	26	18
1979-80—St. Louis Blues		NHL	69	22	42	64	30
1980-81—St. Louis Blues		NHL	74	24	44	68	57
1981-82—St. Louis Blues		NHL	76	13	40	53	41
1982-83—Salt Lake Golden Eagles		CHL	13	7	8	15	0
1982-83—St. Louis Blues		NHL	43	8	16	24	14
1983-84—Hartford Whalers (i)		NHL	75	6	23	29	36
WHA TOTALS			86	26	38	64	49
NHL TOTALS			371	82	182	264	196

(c)—Drafted from Michigan Tech by St. Louis Blues in fifth round of 1974 amateur draft.
(d)—Selected first team All-America (West).
(e)—Selected Most Valuable Player in WCHA.
(f)—Named Freshman-of-the-Year in WCHA.
(g)—Traded to Edmonton Oilers by Indianapolis Racers with Blair MacDonald and Dave Inkpen for Barry Wilkins, Rusty Patenaude and Claude St. Sauveur, September, 1977.
(h)—Signed by St. Louis Blues, September, 1978.
(i)—October, 1983—Selected by Hartford Whalers in NHL waiver draft.

TARAS JOHN ZYTYNSKY

Defense . . . 6'1" . . . 191 lbs. . . . Born, Montreal, Que., May 30, 1962 . . . Shoots left . . . (December, 1980)—Torn knee ligaments . . . (April, 1983)—Injured ankle in AHL playoffs vs. Nova Scotia.

Year	Team	League	Games	G.	A.	Pts.	Pen.
1978-79—Montreal Juniors		QMJHL	59	4	12	16	25
1979-80—Montreal Juniors (c)		QMJHL	72	12	29	41	104
1980-81—Montreal Juniors		QMJHL	45	7	13	20	56
1981-82—Montreal Juniors (b)		QMJHL	64	18	39	57	82
1982-83—Maine Mariners		AHL	80	12	24	36	45
1983-84—Springfield Indians		AHL	70	1	17	18	55

(c)—June, 1980—Drafted by Philadelphia Flyers as underage junior in 1980 NHL entry draft. Fourth Flyers pick, 84th overall, fourth round.

GOALTENDERS

MARTY ABRAMS

Goaltender . . . 5'11" . . . 203 lbs. . . . Born, Charlottetown, P.E.I., June 2, 1964 . . . Shoots right.

Year	Team	League	Games	Mins.	Goals	SO.	Avg.	A.	Pen.
1982-83—Pembroke Lumber Kings (c)		CJAHL	35	1689	176	...	6.25	..	....
1982-83—Toronto Marlboros		OHL	1	4	0	0	0.00	0	0
1983-84—Toronto Marlboros		OHL	20	1137	81	0	4.27	0	2

(c)—June, 1983—Drafted by Washington Capitals in 1983 NHL entry draft. Fourth Capitals pick, 155th overall, eighth round.

PETER ABRIC

Goaltender . . . 6'1" . . . 173 lbs. . . . Born, Scarborough, Ont., July 16, 1965 . . . Shoots left.

Year	Team	League	Games	Mins.	Goals	SO.	Avg.	A.	Pen.
1982-83—Orillia Travelways		OJHL	16	960	65	0	4.06	..	..
1983-84—North Bay Centennials (c)		OHL	47	2556	180	0	4.23	0	2

(c)—June, 1984—Drafted as underage junior by Hartford Whalers in NHL entry draft. Seventh Whalers pick, 234th overall, 12th round.

STEVE BAKER

Goaltender . . . 6'3" . . . 200 lbs. . . . Born, Boston, Mass., May 6, 1957 . . . Shoots left . . . Attended Union College . . . (October 31, 1981)—Torn groin muscles.

Year	Team	League	Games	Mins.	Goals	SO.	Avg.	A.	Pen.
1975-76—Union College		ECAC	9	480	21	..	2.62	..	....
1976-77—Union College (c)		ECAC	..	1117	67	0	3.59	..	....
1977-78—Union College		ECAC	5	300	28	0	5.60	0	0
1977-78—Toledo Goaldiggers		IHL	10	544	46	0	5.07	1	0
1978-79—New Haven Nighthawks		AHL	24	1435	82	1	3.43	2	6
1979-80—New York Rangers		NHL	27	1391	79	1	3.41	0	2
1979-80—New Haven Nighthawks		AHL	9	491	29	0	3.54	0	2
1980-81—New Haven Nighthawks		AHL	25	1497	90	1	3.61	1	4
1980-81—New York Rangers		NHL	21	1260	73	2	3.48	0	5
1981-82—Springfield Indians		AHL	11	503	42	0	5.01	0	0
1981-82—New York Rangers		NHL	6	328	33	0	6.04	0	0
1982-83—New York Rangers		NHL	3	102	5	0	2.94	0	0
1982-83—Tulsa Oilers (d)		CHL	49	2901	186	0	3.85	0	15
1983-84—Binghamton Whalers (e-f)		AHL	6	345	35	0	6.09	0	0
1983-84—Maine Mariners (g)		AHL	13	744	41	0	3.31	1	2
NHL TOTALS			57	3081	190	3	3.70	0	7

(c)—Drafted from Union College by New York Rangers in third round of 1977 amateur draft.
(d)—July, 1983—Released by New York Rangers.
(e)—Attended Boston Bruins training camp.
(f)—October, 1983—Given 25-game AHL tryout by Hartford Whalers.
(g)—January, 1984—Signed by New Jersey Devils as a free agent.

MURRAY BANNERMAN

Goaltender . . . 5'11" . . . 184 lbs. . . . Born, Fort Frances, Ont., April 27, 1957 . . . Shoots left.

Year	Team	League	Games	Mins.	Goals	SO.	Avg.	A.	Pen.
1972-73—St. James Canadians (b)		MJHL	31	1788	104	*1	*3.49	1	6
1973-74—St. James Canadians		MJHL	17	930	69	0	4.45	1	16
1973-74—Winnipeg Clubs		WCHL	6	258	29	0	6.74	..	....
1974-75—Winnipeg Clubs		WCHL	28	1351	113	0	5.02	2	6
1975-76—Victoria Cougars		WCHL	44	2450	178	1	4.36	5	25
1976-77—Victoria Cougars (c)		WCHL	67	3893	262	2	4.04	3	24
1977-78—Fort Wayne Komets (a)		IHL	44	2435	133	1	3.28	6	10
1977-78—Vancouver Canucks (d)		NHL	1	20	0	0	0.00	0	0
1978-79—New Brunswick Hawks		AHL	47	2557	152	0	3.57	3	23
1979-80—New Brunswick Hawks (b)		AHL	61	3361	186	*3	3.32	3	25
1980-81—Chicago Black Hawks		NHL	15	865	62	0	4.30	0	0
1981-82—Chicago Black Hawks		NHL	29	1671	116	1	4.17	1	0
1982-83—Chicago Black Hawks		NHL	41	2460	127	4	3.10	1	2
1983-84—Chicago Black Hawks		NHL	56	3335	188	2	3.38	4	17
NHL TOTALS			142	8351	493	7	3.54	6	19

(c)—Drafted from Victoria Cougars by Vancouver Canucks in fourth round of 1977 amateur draft.

(d)—June, 1978—Sent to Chicago Black Hawks by Vancouver Canucks as the future consideration in a November, 1977 deal that saw Pit Martin go from Chicago to Vancouver. The Canucks had to choose between Bannerman and Glen Hanlon as future considerations.

MARCO BARON

Goaltender . . . 5'11" . . . 179 lbs. . . . Born, Montreal, Que., April 8, 1959 . . . Shoots left . . . (February, 1976)—Broken collarbone . . . (December, 1978)—Broken finger on right hand . . . (December, 1980)—Pulled groin.

Year	Team	League	Games	Mins.	Goals	SO.	Avg.	A.	Pen.
1975-76—Montreal Juniors		QMJHL	23	1376	81	2	3.53	..	....
1976-77—Montreal Juniors		QMJHL	41	2006	182	1	5.44	1	8
1977-78—Montreal Juniors (b)		QMJHL	61	3395	251	0	4.44	..	....
1978-79—Montreal Juniors (c)		QMJHL	67	3630	230	*3	3.80	..	....
1979-80—Boston Bruins		NHL	1	40	2	0	3.00	0	0
1979-80—Binghamton Dusters		AHL	5	265	26	0	5.89	0	0
1979-80—Grand Rapids Owls		IHL	35	1995	135	0	4.06	1	29
1980-81—Springfield Indians		AHL	23	1300	79	1	3.65	0	29
1980-81—Boston Bruins		NHL	10	507	24	0	2.84	0	7
1981-82—Erie Blades		AHL	1	119	8	0	4.03	0	0
1981-82—Boston Bruins		NHL	44	2215	144	1	3.90	2	35
1982-83—Boston Bruins		NHL	9	516	33	0	3.84	0	4
1982-83—Baltimore Skipjacks		AHL	22	1260	97	0	4.62	2	12
1983-84—Moncton Alpines (d)		AHL	16	858	45	0	3.15	0	18
1983-84—Los Angeles Kings (e)		NHL	21	1211	87	0	4.31	2	10
NHL TOTALS			85	4489	290	1	3.88	4	56

(c)—August, 1979—Drafted by Boston Bruins in entry draft. Sixth Boston pick, 99th overall, fifth round.
(d)—January, 1984—Traded by Boston Bruins to Los Angeles Kings for Bob Laforest.
(e)—August, 1984—Released by Los Angeles Kings.

THOMAS BARRASSO

Goaltender . . . 6'3" . . . 195 lbs. . . . Born, Boston, Mass., March 31, 1965 . . . Shoots left . . . Member of 1983 U.S. National Junior Team . . . Left 1984 U.S. Olympic team to sign with Buffalo Sabres . . . First U.S.-born player to win Calder Trophy (top NHL rookie) since Frank Brimsek (Boston goalie) in 1939 . . . First goaltender to win Calder Trophy since Ken Dryden in 1972.

Year	Team	League	Games	Mins.	Goals	SO.	Avg.	A.	Pen.
1981-82—Acton Boxboro H.S.		Mass. H.S.	23	1035	32	7	1.86	..	....
1982-83—Acton Boxboro H.S. (c)		Mass. H.S.	23	1035	17	10	0.99	..	....
1983-84—Buffalo Sabres (a-d-e)		NHL	42	2475	117	2	2.84	2	20
NHL TOTALS			42	2475	117	2	2.84	2	20

(c)—June, 1983—Drafted by Buffalo Sabres in 1983 NHL entry draft. First Sabres pick, 5th overall, first round.
(d)—Won Calder Memorial Trophy (Top NHL Rookie).
(e)—Won Vezina Trophy (Outstanding NHL Goaltender).

DON BEAUPRE

Goaltender . . . 5'8" . . . 155 lbs. . . . Born, Kitchener, Ont., September 19, 1961 . . . Shoots left . . . (October, 1981)—Bruised ribs.

Year	Team	League	Games	Mins.	Goals	SO.	Avg.	A.	Pen.
1978-79—Sudbury Wolves		OMJHL	54	3248	259	2	4.78	0	0
1979-80—Sudbury Wolves (a-c)		OMJHL	59	3447	248	0	4.32	4	18
1980-81—Minnesota North Stars		NHL	44	2585	138	0	3.20	1	20
1981-82—Nashville South Stars		CHL	5	299	25	0	5.02	0	4
1981-82—Minnesota North Stars		NHL	29	1634	101	0	3.71	0	19
1982-83—Birmingham South Stars		CHL	10	599	31	0	3.11	0	6
1982-83—Minnesota North Stars		NHL	36	2011	120	0	3.58	2	10
1983-84—Salt Lake Golden Eagles		CHL	7	419	30	0	4.30	0	0
1983-84—Minnesota North Stars		NHL	33	1791	123	0	4.12	0	17
NHL TOTALS			142	8021	482	0	3.61	3	66

(c)—June, 1980—Drafted by Minnesota North Stars as underage junior in 1980 NHL entry draft. Second North Stars pick, 37th overall, second round.

MARC BEHREND

Goaltender . . . 6'1" . . . 185 lbs. . . . Born, Madison, Wis., January 11, 1961 . . . Shoots left . . . Member of 1984 U.S. Olympic team.

Year	Team	League	Games	Mins.	Goals	SO.	Avg.	A.	Pen.
1979-80—Univ. of Wisconsin		WCHA	....	.....	....	...	.....	..	....
1980-81—Univ. of Wisconsin (c-d-e)		WCHA	16	913	50	0	3.29	..	....

Year	Team	League	Games	Mins.	Goals	SO.	Avg.	A.	Pen.
1981-82—Univ. of Wisconsin		WCHA	25	1502	65	2	2.60	1	0
1982-83—Univ. of Wisconsin		WCHA	23	1315	49	2	2.24	1	4
1983-84—U.S. National Team		Int'l	33	1898	100	...	3.16	..	....
1983-84—U.S. Olympic Team		Int'l	4	200	11	0	3.30	0	0
1983-84—Winnipeg Jets		NHL	6	351	32	0	5.47	0	0
NHL TOTALS			6	351	32	0	5.47	0	0

(c)—June, 1981—Drafted by Winnipeg Jets in NHL entry draft. Fifth Jets pick, 85th overall, fifth round.
(d)—Named to NCAA All-Tournament team.
(e)—Named NCAA Tournament MVP.

TIMOTHY JOHN BERNHARDT

Goaltender . . . 5'9" . . . 160 lbs. . . . Born, Sarnia, Ont., January 17, 1958 . . . Shoots left . . . (October, 1980)—Surgery to remove abscess at base of spine.

Year	Team	League	Games	Mins.	Goals	SO.	Avg.	A.	Pen.
1975-76—Cornwall Royals		QJHL	51	2985	195	2	3.92	..	....
1976-77—Cornwall Royals (a-c)		QJHL	44	2497	151	0	*3.63	1	2
1977-78—Cornwall Royals (a-d)		QJHL	54	3165	179	2	3.39	..	....
1978-79—Tulsa Oilers		CHL	46	2705	191	0	4.24	1	4
1979-80—Birmingham Bulls		CHL	34	1933	122	1	3.79	0	0
1980-81—Birmingham Bulls		CHL	29	1598	106	1	3.98	1	0
1981-82—Oklahoma City Stars		CHL	10	526	45	0	5.13	0	0
1981-82—Rochester Americans		AHL	29	1586	95	0	3.59	2	0
1982-83—Calgary Flames		NHL	6	280	21	0	4.50	0	0
1982-83—Colorado Flames		CHL	34	1896	122	0	3.86	0	4
1983-84—St. Catharines Saints (b)		AHL	42	2501	154	0	3.69	0	0
NHL TOTALS			6	280	21	0	4.50	0	0

(c)—Won leading goalie award.
(d)—Drafted from Cornwall Royals by Atlanta Flames in third round of 1978 amateur draft.

ALLAN J. BESTER

Goaltender . . . 5'7" . . . 152 lbs. . . . Born, Hamilton, Ont., March 26, 1964 . . . Shoots right.

Year	Team	League	Games	Mins.	Goals	SO.	Avg.	A.	Pen.
1981-82—Brantford Alexanders		OHL	19	970	68	0	4.21	1	4
1982-83—Brantford Alexanders (a-c-d)		OHL	56	3210	188	0	3.51	0	16
1983-84—Brantford Alexanders		OHL	23	1271	71	1	3.35	1	4
1983-84—Toronto Maple Leafs		NHL	32	1848	134	0	4.35	0	6
NHL TOTALS			32	1848	134	0	4.35	0	6

(c)—Led OHL playoffs with a 2.50 average and one shutout.
(d)—June, 1983—Drafted as underage junior by Toronto Maple Leafs in 1983 NHL entry draft. Third Maple Leafs pick, 48th overall, third round.

CRAIG BILLINGTON

Goaltender . . . 5'10" . . . 150 lbs. . . . Born, London, Ont., September 11, 1966 . . . Shoots left.

Year	Team	League	Games	Mins.	Goals	SO.	Avg.	A.	Pen.
1982-83—London Diamonds		WOJBHL	23	1338	76	0	3.39	..	..
1983-84—Belleville Bulls (c)		OHL	44	2335	162	1	4.16	2	7

(c)—June, 1984—Drafted as underage junior by New Jersey Devils in NHL entry draft. Second Devils pick, 23rd overall, second round.

MIKE BISHOP

Goaltender . . . 6' . . . 180 lbs. . . . Born, Kitchener, Ont., February 14, 1965 . . . Shoots left.

Year	Team	League	Games	Mins.	Goals	SO.	Avg.	A.	Pen.
1981-82—Elmira Jr. B		Ont. Jr. B	21	1090	149	0	8.20	..	..
1982-83—London Knights		OHL	27	1125	83	0	4.43	0	2
1983-84—London Knights (c)		OHL	37	1909	139	0	4.37	2	4

(c)—June, 1984—Drafted as underage junior by Boston Bruins in NHL entry draft. Fifth Bruins pick, 103rd overall, fifth round.

GRANT BLAIR

Goaltender . . . 6' . . . 150 lbs. . . . Born, Stoney Creek, Ont., August 15, 1964 . . . Shoots left.

Year	Team	League	Games	Mins.	Goals	SO.	Avg.	A.	Pen.
1981-82—Guelph		Ont. Tier II	25	1506	82	1	3.27	..	..
1982-83—Harvard University (c)		ECAC	26	1575	72	..	2.74	0	0
1983-84—Harvard University		ECAC	23	1391	71	..	3.06	1	8

(c)—June, 1983—Drafted by Calgary Flames in 1983 NHL entry draft. Eighth Flames pick, 111th overall, sixth round.

MIKE BLAKE

Goaltender . . . 6'1 . . . 184 lbs. . . . Born, Kitchener, Ont., April 6, 1956 . . . Shoots left . . . Nephew of Toe Blake (Montreal Canadiens player '35-48, Captain '40-48, coach '55-68 and member of Hockey Hall-of-Fame).

Year	Team	League	Games	Mins.	Goals	SO.	Avg.	A.	Pen.
1977-78—Ohio State University		CCHA	18	980	71	0	4.35	..	..
1978-79—Ohio State University		CCHA	21	1080	78	0	4.33	..	..
1979-80—Ohio State University		CCHA	15	775	48	0	3.72	..	..
1980-81—Ohio State University		CCHA	37	2098	125	2	3.57	..	..
1981-82—Saginaw Gears (c)		IHL	36	1984	151	0	4.56	3	4
1981-82—Los Angeles Kings		NHL	2	51	2	0	2.35	0	0
1982-83—Los Angeles Kings		NHL	9	432	30	0	4.17	0	2
1982-83—New Haven Nighthawks (d)		AHL	20	1178	72	1	3.67	2	2
1983-84—New Haven Nighthawks		AHL	16	864	64	0	4.44	1	2
1983-84—Los Angeles Kings		NHL	29	1634	118	0	4.33	1	6
NHL TOTALS			40	2117	150	0	4.25	1	8

(c)—September, 1981—Signed by Los Angeles Kings as a free agent.
(d)—Led AHL playoffs with 2.24 average.

DANIEL HECTOR BOUCHARD

Goaltender . . . 6' . . . 191 lbs. . . . Born, Val D'Or, Que., December 12, 1950 . . . Shoots left . . . Brother of Guy Bouchard.

Year	Team	League	Games	Mins.	Goals	SO.	Avg.	A.	Pen.
1968-69—Sorel Black Hawks		QJHL	....	.....	....	...	...		
1969-70—London Knights (c)		Jr."A"OHA	41	.....	159	2	3.89	0	55
1970-71—Hershey Bears		AHL	36	2029	106	1	3.13	0	8
1971-72—Oklahoma City Blazers		CHL	1	60	3	0	3.00	0	2
1971-72—Boston Braves (a-d-e)		AHL	50	2915	122	*4	2.51	2	54
1972-73—Atlanta Flames		NHL	34	1944	100	2	3.09	1	12
1973-74—Atlanta Flames		NHL	46	2660	123	5	2.77	0	10
1974-75—Atlanta Flames		NHL	40	2400	111	3	2.77	2	42
1975-76—Atlanta Flames		NHL	47	2671	113	2	2.54	1	10
1976-77—Atlanta Flames		NHL	42	2378	139	1	3.51	1	9
1977-78—Atlanta Flames		NHL	58	3340	153	2	2.75	3	6
1978-79—Atlanta Flames		NHL	64	3624	201	3	3.33	3	17
1979-80—Atlanta Flames		NHL	53	3076	163	2	3.18	1	34
1980-81—Calgary Flames (f)		NHL	14	760	51	0	4.03	4	6
1980-81—Quebec Nordiques		NHL	29	1740	92	2	3.17	0	4
1981-82—Quebec Nordiques		NHL	60	3572	230	1	3.86	3	36
1982-83—Quebec Nordiques		NHL	50	2947	197	0	4.01	4	8
1983-84—Quebec Nordiques		NHL	57	3373	180	1	3.20	3	19
NHL TOTALS			594	34485	1853	25	3.22	26	213

(c)—Drafted from London Knights by Boston Bruins in second round of 1970 amateur draft.
(d)—Shared Harry "Hap" Holmes Memorial Trophy (leading goalie) with Ross Brooks.
(e)—Drafted from Boston Bruins by Atlanta Flames in expansion draft, June, 1972.
(f)—January, 1981—Traded by Calgary Flames to Quebec Nordiques for Jamie Hislop.

ROLAND DAVID BOUTIN

Goaltender . . . 5'9" . . . 188 lbs. . . . Born, Westlock, Alta., November 6, 1957 . . . Shoots left.

Year	Team	League	Games	Mins.	Goals	SO.	Avg.	A.	Pen.
1973-74—Prince Albert Raiders		SJHL	32	.....	119	1	3.89	..	....
1973-74—Swift Current Broncos		WCHL	1	60	3	0	3.00	0	0
1974-75—Lethbridge Broncos		WCHL	39	2196	162	1	4.43	2	6
1975-76—Lethbridge Broncos		WCHL	61	3429	259	0	4.53	2	25
1976-77—Lethbridge Broncos (c)		WCHL	59	3298	246	1	4.48	1	40
1977-78—Port Huron Flags		IHL	58	3192	205	1	3.85	..	....
1978-79—Washington Capitals		NHL	2	90	10	0	6.67	0	0
1978-79—Hershey Bears		AHL	30	1624	105	0	3.88	0	18
1978-79—Port Huron Flags		IHL	9	464	24	0	3.10	0	2
1979-80—Washington Capitals		NHL	18	927	54	0	3.50	1	6
1979-80—Hershey Bears		AHL	15	821	34	0	2.48	1	4
1980-81—Washington Capitals		NHL	2	120	11	0	5.50	0	0
1980-81—Hershey Bears (b)		AHL	53	3056	182	*3	3.57	1	23
1981-82—Hershey Bears (d)		AHL	*62	*3459	238	1	4.13	2	65
1982-83—Birmingham South Stars		CHL	11	619	48	0	4.65	1	0
1982-83—Salt Lake Golden Eagles		CHL	14	807	43	1	3.20	0	2
1983-84—Binghamton Whalers (e)		AHL	45	2623	188	3	4.30	0	8
NHL TOTALS			22	1137	75	0	3.96	1	6

(c)—Drafted from Lethbridge Broncos by Washington Capitals in seventh round of 1977 amateur draft.

(d)—August, 1982—Traded by Washington Capitals with Wes Jarvis to Minnesota North Stars for Robbie Moore.

(e)—December, 1983—Signed by Hartford Whalers as a free agent.

RICHARD BRODEUR

Goaltender . . . 5'7" . . . 185 lbs. . . . Born, Longueuil, Que., September 15, 1952 . . . Shoots left . . . Missed part of 1977-78 season with surgery on left knee . . . (February 15, 1981)—Injured left knee, resulting in surgery to remove bone spurs . . . (November, 1982)—Knee injury . . . (February 5, 1983)—Suffered 20-stitch cut and perforated eardrum when struck by shot of Toronto's Dan Daoust.

Year	Team	League	Games	Mins.	Goals	SO.	Avg.	A.	Pen.
1970-71—Cornwall Royals		QJHL	41	.....	191	0	4.66	..	....
1971-72—C'wall Royals (a-c-d-e)		QJHL	58	.....	170	*5	*2.93	..	....
1972-73—Quebec Nordiques		WHA	24	1288	102	0	4.75	0	4
1973-74—Maine Nordiques		NAHL	15	936	47	0	3.01	0	0
1973-74—Quebec Nordiques		WHA	30	1607	89	1	3.32	1	0
1974-75—Quebec Nordiques		WHA	51	2938	188	0	3.84	2	13
1975-76—Quebec Nordiques		WHA	69	3967	244	2	3.69	3	2
1976-77—Quebec Nordiques		WHA	53	2906	167	2	3.45	1	0
1977-78—Quebec Nordiques		WHA	36	1962	121	0	3.70	2	0
1978-79—Quebec Nordiques (b-f-g)		WHA	42	2433	126	*3	3.11	3	2
1979-80—Indianapolis Checkers (a-h-i)		CHL	46	2722	131	*4	2.89	0	12
1979-80—New York Islanders (j)		NHL	2	80	6	0	4.50	0	0
1980-81—Vancouver Canucks		NHL	52	3024	177	0	3.51	0	0
1981-82—Vancouver Canucks		NHL	52	3010	168	2	3.35	2	0
1982-83—Vancouver Canucks		NHL	58	3291	208	0	3.79	1	2
1983-84—Vancouver Canucks		NHL	36	2107	141	1	4.02	2	0
WHA TOTALS			305	17101	1037	8	3.64	12	21
NHL TOTALS			200	11512	700	3	3.65	5	2

(c)—Won leading goalie award.

(d)—Selected by Quebec Nordiques in World Hockey Association player selection draft, February, 1972.

(e)—Drafted from Cornwall Royals by New York Islanders in seventh round of 1972 amateur draft.

(f)—June, 1979—Selected by New York Islanders in NHL reclaim draft, but remained with Nordiques and was made a priority selection by Quebec for expansion draft.

(g)—August, 1979—Traded by Quebec Nordiques to New York Islanders for Goran Hogosta.

(h)—Led CHL Adams Playoff goaltenders with a 2.02 average and shared shutout lead (1) with Michel Plasse.

(i)—Shared Terry Sawchuk Trophy (top CHL goaltender) with teammate Jim Park.

(j)—October, 1980—Traded with fifth round 1981 draft pick (Moe Lemay) by New York Islanders to Vancouver Canucks for fifth round 1981 draft pick (Jacques Sylvestri).

SCOTT BROWER

Goaltender . . . 6' . . . 185 lbs. . . . Born, Viking, Alta., September 26, 1964 . . . Shoots left.

Year	Team	League	Games	Mins.	Goals	SO.	Avg.	A.	Pen.
1983-84—Lloydminster (c)		SJHL	43	2566	173	2	4.04	..	....

(c)—June, 1984—Drafted by New York Rangers in NHL entry draft. Twelfth Rangers pick, 243rd overall, 12th round.

FRANK CAPRICE

Goaltender . . . 5'9" . . . 160 lbs. . . . Born, Hamilton, Ont., May 2, 1962 . . . Shoots left.

Year	Team	League	Games	Mins.	Goals	SO.	Avg.	A.	Pen.
1979-80—London Knights		OHL	18	919	74	1	4.84	0	2
1980-81—London Knights (c)		OHL	42	2171	190	0	5.25	1	9
1981-82—London Knights		OHL	45	2614	196	0	4.50	3	6
1981-82—Dallas Black Hawks		CHL	3	178	19	0	6.40	0	0
1982-83—Vancouver Canucks		NHL	10	20	3	0	9.00	0	0
1982-83—Fredericton Express		AHL	14	819	50	0	3.67	3	0
1983-84—Vancouver Canucks		NHL	19	1099	62	1	3.38	0	2
1983-84—Fredericton Express		AHL	18	1089	49	2	2.70	0	2
NHL TOTALS			29	1119	65	1	3.49	0	2

(c)—June, 1981—Drafted as underage junior by Vancouver Canucks in NHL entry draft. Eighth Canucks pick, 178th overall, ninth round.

JON CASEY

Goaltender . . . 5'10" . . . 155 lbs. . . . Born, Grand Rapids, Minn., March 29, 1962 . . . Shoots left.

Year	Team	League	Games	Mins.	Goals	SO.	Avg.	A.	Pen.
1980-81—Univ. of North Dakota		WCHA	6	300	19	0	3.80	..	..
1981-82—Univ. of North Dakota		WCHA	18	1038	48	1	2.77	0	0
1982-83—Univ. of North Dakota		WCHA	17	1021	42	0	2.47	1	4
1983-84—Univ. of North Dakota (c)		WCHA	37	2180	115	...	3.17	1	20
1983-84—Minnesota North Stars		NHL	2	84	6	0	4.29	0	0
NHL TOTALS			2	84	6	0	4.29	0	0

(c)—March, 1984—Signed by Minnesota North Stars as a free agent.

CHRIS CLIFFORD

Goaltender . . . 5'9" . . . 140 lbs. . . . Born, Kingston, Ont., May 26, 1966 . . . Shoots left.

Year	Team	League	Games	Mins.	Goals	SO.	Avg.	A.	Pen.
1982-83—Brockville Braves		COJHL	32	1746	126	1	4.33	..	....
1983-84—Kingston Canadians (c)		OHL	50	2808	229	2	4.89	3	6

(c)—June, 1984—Drafted as underage junior by Chicago Black Hawks in NHL entry draft. Sixth Black Hawks pick, 111th overall, sixth round.

JACQUES CLOUTIER

Goaltender . . . 5'7" . . . 154 lbs. . . . Born, Noranda, Que., January 3, 1960 . . . Shoots left . . . (January, 1982)—Broken collarbone when hit by a slap shot in practice.

Year	Team	League	Games	Mins.	Goals	SO.	Avg.	A.	Pen.
1976-77—Trois-Riviere Draveurs		QMJHL	24	1109	93	0	5.03	0	0
1977-78—Trois-Riviere Draveurs		QMJHL	71	4134	240	*4	3.48	..	....
1978-79—Trois-Riviere Draveurs (a-c)		QMJHL	72	4168	218	*3	*3.14	..	....
1979-80—Trois-Riviere Draveurs		QMJHL	55	3222	231	*2	4.30	0	0
1980-81—Rochester Americans		AHL	61	3478	209	1	3.61	3	9
1981-82—Rochester Americans		AHL	23	1366	64	0	2.81	2	0
1981-82—Buffalo Sabres		NHL	7	311	13	0	2.51	0	0
1982-83—Buffalo Sabres		NHL	25	1390	81	0	3.50	0	0
1982-83—Rochester Americans		AHL	13	634	42	0	3.97	0	4
1983-84—Rochester Americans		AHL	*51	*2841	172	1	3.63	2	10
NHL TOTALS			32	1701	94	0	3.32	0	0

(c)—August, 1979—Drafted by Buffalo Sabres as underage junior in 1979 entry draft. Fourth Sabres pick, 55th overall, third round.

JIM CRAIG

Goaltender . . . 6'1" . . . 190 lbs. . . . Born, North Easton, Mass., May 31, 1957 . . . Shoots left . . . In his junior year at Boston University (1977-78) he compiled a perfect 16-0-0 won-loss record . . . Member of Gold Medal Winning 1980 U.S. Olympic team . . . (September, 1981)—Broken right index finger in practice session with Team U.S.A. for Canada Cup . . . (October 30, 1981)—Minor surgery on right shoulder to remove a small tumor . . . (November 11, 1981)—While recuperating from surgery he fell off ladder at his home and suffered a bad sprain of left foot . . . (January 21, 1984)—Tore hamstring in game at Detroit, out for the season.

Year	Team	League	Games	Mins.	Goals	SO.	Avg.	A.	Pen.
1976-77—Boston University (c)		ECAC	26	1580	109	...	4.14	..	....
1977-78—Boston University		ECAC	16	968	60	...	3.72	..	....
1978-79—Boston University (d)		ECAC	21	1298	74	...	3.42	..	....
1979-80—U.S. National Team			41	2370	95	7	2.41	3	28
1979-80—U.S. Olympic Team			7	420	15	0	2.14	0	2
1979-80—Atlanta Flames (e)		NHL	4	206	13	0	3.79	0	0
1980-81—Boston Bruins		NHL	23	1272	78	0	3.68	1	11
1981-82—Erie Blades (f)		AHL	13	742	57	0	4.61	1	4
1982-83—U.S. National Team (g)		Int'l	20	1025	48	2	2.81	0	0
1983-84—Salt Lake Golden Eagles		CHL	27	1532	108	1	4.23	2	18
1983-84—Minnesota North Stars		NHL	3	110	9	0	4.91	0	0
NHL TOTALS			30	1588	100	0	3.78	1	11

(c)—June, 1977—Drafted by Atlanta Flames in 1977 NHL amateur draft. Fourth Flames pick, 72nd overall, fourth round.

(d)—Named All-American Goaltender (East).

(e)—June, 1980—Traded by Atlanta Flames to Boston Bruins for Bruins second round pick in 1980 NHL entry draft (Steve Konroyd) and a third round pick in 1981 draft (Mike Vernon).

(f)—October, 1982—Released by Boston Bruins.

(g)—March, 1983—Signed by Minnesota North Stars as a free agent.

TROY CROSBY

Goaltender . . . 6' . . . 170 lbs. . . . Born, Halifax, N.S., September 11, 1966 . . . Shoots left.

Year	Team	League	Games	Mins.	Goals	SO.	Avg.	A.	Pen.
1983-84—Verdun Juniors (c)		QHL	34	1863	125	1	4.03	0	13

(c)—June, 1984—Drafted as underage junior by Montreal Canadiens in NHL entry draft. Fourteenth Canadiens pick, 240th overall, 12th round.

MARC D'AMOUR

Goaltender . . . 5'10" . . . 167 lbs. . . . Born, Sudbury, Ont., April 29, 1961 . . . Shoots left.

Year	Team	League	Games	Mins.	Goals	SO.	Avg.	A.	Pen.
1978-79—Sault Ste. Marie Greyhounds		OHL	30	1501	149	0	5.96	0	15
1979-80—Sault Ste. Marie Greyhounds		OHL	33	1429	117	0	4.91	2	31
1980-81—Sault Ste. Marie Greyhounds		OHL	16	653	38	0	3.49	0	0
1981-82—Sault Ste. Marie Greyhounds (a-c-d)		OHL	46	2384	130	1	*3.27	1	29
1982-83—Colorado Flames		CHL	42	2373	153	1	3.87	1	23
1983-84—Colorado Flames		CHL	36	1917	131	0	4.10	2	6

(c)—Co-winner with teammate John Vanbiesbrouck, of Dave Pinkey Trophy (OHL Goaltending Trophy).
(d)—April, 1982—Signed by Calgary Flames as a free agent.

CLEON DASKALAKIS

Goaltender . . . 5'9" . . . 175 lbs. . . . Born, Boston, Mass., September 29, 1962 . . . Shoots left.

Year	Team	League	Games	Mins.	Goals	SO.	Avg.	A.	Pen.
1980-81—Boston University		ECAC	8	399	24	0	3.61	..	..
1981-82—Boston University		ECAC	20	1101	59	..	3.22	0	6
1982-83—Boston University (b)		ECAC	22	1278	69	1	3.24	1	4
1983-84—Boston University (c-d)		ECAC	35	1972	96	..	2.92	0	4

(c)—Won Walter Brown Award (Top U.S.-born player in New England colleges).
(d)—June, 1984—Signed by Boston Bruins as a free agent.

MICHEL DION

Goaltender . . . 5'10" . . . 184 lbs. . . . Born, Granby, Que., February 11, 1954 . . . Shoots right . . . Played minor league baseball in the Montreal Expos' farm system for two years . . . (December 23, 1981)—Pulled hamstring in game at Toronto . . . (February, 1983)—Missed eight games with pulled groin . . . (December 15, 1983)—Badly bruised collarbone when hit by Greg Paslawski shot in third period of game at Montreal.

Year	Team	League	Games	Mins.	Goals	SO.	Avg.	A.	Pen.
1972-73—Mont. Red, White and Blue		QJHL	8	.....	39	0	4.87	..	..
1973-74—Montreal Juniors (c)		QJHL	31	.....	135	0	4.41	1	4
1974-75—Mohawk Valley Comets		NAHL	28	1476	96	0	3.90	2	0
1974-75—Indianapolis Racers		WHA	1	59	4	0	4.00	0	0
1975-76—Mohawk Valley Comets		NAHL	22	1295	83	0	3.84	0	2
1975-76—Indianapolis Racers		WHA	31	1860	85	0	2.74	0	2
1976-77—Indianapolis Racers		WHA	42	2286	128	1	3.36	0	0
1977-78—Cincinnati Stingers (d)		WHA	45	2356	140	*4	3.57	0	26
1978-79—Cincinnati Stingers (e)		WHA	30	1681	93	0	3.32	0	2
1979-80—Quebec Nordiques		NHL	50	2773	171	2	3.70	0	8
1980-81—Quebec Nordiques (f-g)		NHL	12	688	61	0	5.32	1	0
1980-81—Winnipeg Jets (h)		NHL	14	757	61	0	4.83	0	2
1980-81—Indianapolis Checkers		CHL	6	364	19	0	3.13	0	0
1981-82—Pittsburgh Penguins		NHL	62	3580	226	0	3.79	1	4
1982-83—Pittsburgh Penguins		NHL	49	2791	198	0	4.26	2	8
1983-84—Pittsburgh Penguins		NHL	30	1553	138	0	5.33	1	2
WHA TOTALS			149	8242	450	5	3.28	0	30
NHL TOTALS			217	12142	855	2	4.23	5	24

(c)—Selected by Indianapolis Racers in World Hockey Association amateur players' draft, May, 1974.
(d)—Signed by Cincinnati Stingers as free agent, October, 1977.
(e)—June, 1979—Claimed by Quebec Nordiques in WHA dispersal draft.
(f)—December, 1980—Suspended by Nordiques for leaving ice during game against Boston.
(g)—February, 1981—Traded by Quebec Nordiques to Winnipeg Jets for future draft choice.
(h)—June, 1981—Signed by Pittsburgh Penguins as a free agent.

BRUCE DOWIE

Goaltender . . . 5'10" . . . 170 lbs. . . . Born, Oakville, Ont., December 9, 1962 . . . Shoots left.

Year	Team	League	Games	Mins.	Goals	SO.	Avg.	A.	Pen.
1979-80—Toronto Marlboros		OMJHL	60	3513	247	0	4.22	2	14
1980-81—Toronto Marlboros		OHL	57	3215	253	0	4.73	1	27
1981-82—Toronto Marlboros		OHL	37	2022	150	1	4.45	1	31

Year	Team	League	Games	Mins.	Goals	SO.	Avg.	A.	Pen.
1982-83—Toronto Marlboros		OHL	30	1830	123	0	4.03	1	18
1982-83—St. Catharines Saints		AHL	8	424	35	0	4.95	0	2
1983-84—Muskegon Mohawks		IHL	25	1306	100	2	4.59	0	19
1983-84—St. Catharines Saints		AHL	9	410	41	0	6.00	0	0
1983-84—Toronto Maple Leafs		NHL	2	72	4	0	3.33	0	0
NHL TOTALS			2	72	4	0	3.33	0	0

MICHEL DUFOUR

Goaltender . . . 5'6" . . . 160 lbs. . . . Born, Val d'Or, Que., August 31, 1962 . . . Shoots left.

Year	Team	League	Games	Mins.	Goals	SO.	Avg.	A.	Pen.
1979-80—Sorel Black Hawks		QMJHL	59	3178	306	0	5.78	2	6
1980-81—Sorel Black Hawks (b-c-d)		QMJHL	54	2703	164	0	*3.64	2	21
1981-82—Trois Rivieres Draveurs (e)		QMJHL	58	3316	238	*1	4.31	0	33
1982-83—Fredericton Express		AHL	1	60	5	0	5.00	0	0
1982-83—Milwaukee Admirals		IHL	4	244	16	0	3.93	0	0
1982-83—Kalamazoo Wings		IHL	23	1180	73	0	3.71	1	0
1983-84—Fredericton Express		AHL	6	365	19	0	3.12	0	2
1983-84—Milwaukee Admirals		IHL	21	1255	79	0	3.78	0	4

(c)—Won Jacques Plante Trophy (Best Individual Goaltender).
(d)—August, 1980—Signed by Quebec Nordiques as underage junior.
(e)—Led QMJHL playoffs with two shutouts.

JIM EDMONDS

Goaltender . . . 5'9" . . . 170 lbs. . . . Born, Milton, Ont., July 8, 1965 . . . Shoots left.

Year	Team	League	Games	Mins.	Goals	SO.	Avg.	A.	Pen.
1983-84—Cornell University (c)		ECAC	17	920	63	..	4.04	0	4

(c)—June, 1984—Drafted by Winnipeg Jets in NHL entry draft. Twelfth Jets pick, 238th overall, 12th round.

DONALD LAURIE EDWARDS

Goaltender . . . 5'9" . . . 160 lbs. . . . Born, Hamilton, Ont., September 28, 1955 . . . Shoots left . . . Nephew of former NHL goalie Roy Edwards . . . (December 4, 1982)—Fractured knee-cap in game vs. Edmonton.

Year	Team	League	Games	Mins.	Goals	SO.	Avg.	A.	Pen.
1973-74—Kitch. Rangers (a-c)		Jr. "A" OHA	35	2089	95	*3	*2.73	0	0
1974-75—Kitch. Rangers (a-d)		Jr. "A" OHA	55	.....	256	1	4.70	1	2
1975-76—Hershey Bears (b)		AHL	39	2253	128	3	3.41	3	10
1976-77—Hershey Bears		AHL	47	2797	136	*5	2.91	0	16
1976-77—Buffalo Sabres		NHL	25	1480	62	2	2.51	1	2
1977-78—Buffalo Sabres (b)		NHL	72	4209	185	5	2.64	3	12
1978-79—Buffalo Sabres		NHL	54	3160	159	2	3.02	2	8
1979-80—Buffalo Sabres (e)		NHL	49	2920	125	2	2.57	1	8
1980-81—Buffalo Sabres		NHL	45	2700	133	*3	2.96	2	0
1981-82—Buffalo Sabres (f)		NHL	62	3500	205	0	3.51	2	2
1982-83—Calgary Flames		NHL	39	2209	148	1	4.02	1	0
1983-84—Calgary Flames		NHL	41	2303	157	0	4.09	2	2
NHL TOTALS			387	22481	1174	15	3.13	14	34

(c)—Won Dave Pinkney Trophy (leading goalie).
(d)—Drafted from Kitchener Rangers by Buffalo Sabres in fifth round of 1975 amateur draft.
(e)—Shared Vezina Memorial Trophy with Bob Sauve (top NHL goaltender).
(f)—June, 1982—Traded by Buffalo Sabres with Richie Dunn and Buffalo's second-round pick in 1982 NHL entry draft to Calgary Flames for Calgary's first and second-round picks in 1982, second-round choice in 1983 and option to switch first-round picks in '83.

DARREN ELIOT

Goaltender . . . 6'1" . . . 175 lbs. . . . Born, Milton, Ont., November 26, 1961 . . . Shoots left . . . Member of 1984 Canadian Olympic team . . . Played every minute of every game on Cornell schedule in 1982-83.

Year	Team	League	Games	Mins.	Goals	SO.	Avg.	A.	Pen.
1979-80—Cornell University (c)		ECAC	26	1362	94	0	4.14	..	..
1980-81—Cornell University		ECAC	18	912	52	1	3.42	..	..
1981-82—Cornell University		ECAC	7	338	25	0	4.44	0	2
1982-83—Cornell University (a-d)		ECAC	26	1606	100	1	3.66	0	4
1983-84—Canadian Olympic Team		Int'l	31	1676	111	0	3.97	..	..
1983-84—New Haven Nighthawks		AHL	7	365	30	0	4.93	0	0

(c)—June, 1980—Drafted by Los Angeles Kings in NHL entry draft. Eighth Kings pick, 115th overall, sixth round.
(d)—Named to All-America Team (East).

KEN ELLACOTT

Goaltender . . . 5'8" . . . 151 lbs. . . . Born, Paris, Ont., March 3, 1959 . . . Shoots right.

Year	Team	League	Games	Mins.	Goals	SO.	Avg.	A.	Pen.
1977-78	Peterborough Petes	OMJHL	55	3270	199	0	3.65	1	6
1978-79	Peterborough Petes (a-c)	OMJHL	48	2856	169	3	3.53	0	8
1979-80	Dallas Black Hawks	CHL	54	3155	198	*4	3.77	1	10
1980-81	Dallas Black Hawks (d)	CHL	40	2336	119	1	3.06	1	9
1981-82	Dallas Black Hawks	CHL	*68	*3742	*282	1	4.52	2	4
1982-83	Vancouver Canucks	NHL	12	555	41	0	4.43	0	0
1982-83	Fredericton Express (e)	AHL	17	998	63	0	3.79	0	0
1983-84	Montana Magic	CHL	41	2441	*208	1	5.11	0	0
	NHL TOTALS		12	555	41	0	4.43	0	0

(c)—August, 1979—Drafted by Vancouver Canucks in entry draft. Third Vancouver pick, 47th overall, third round.
(d)—Shared Terry Sawchuk Trophy (Top CHL Goaltenders) with teammate Paul Harrison.
(e)—Shared Harry (Hap) Holmes Memorial Trophy (Top AHL Goaltenders) with teammate Brian Ford.

ANTHONY JAMES (TONY) ESPOSITO

Goaltender . . . 5'11" . . . 185 lbs. . . . Born, Sault Ste. Marie, Ont., April 23, 1943 . . . Shoots right . . . Brother of Phil Esposito . . . Attended Michigan Tech and holds single season record for lowest goals against average (2.35 in 1964-65) . . . Set modern NHL record for shutouts (15) in single season in 1969-70.

Year	Team	League	Games	Mins.	Goals	SO.	Avg.	A.	Pen.
1962-63	S. S. M. Greyh'ds	Jr."A"NOHA	....	......	....	...	......	..	....
1963-64	Michigan Tech (freshmen)	WCHA	....	......	....	...	......	..	....
1964-65	Michigan Tech (a-c)	WCHA	17	......	40	1	*2.35	0	4
1965-66	Michigan Tech (a-d)	WCHA	19	......	51	1	2.68	0	15
1966-67	Michigan Tech (a-d)	WCHA	15	......	39	0	2.60	0	10
1967-68	Vancouver Canucks	WHL	61	3734	199	4	3.20	0	0
1968-69	Houston Apollos	CHL	19	1139	46	1	2.42	0	0
1968-69	Montreal Canadiens (e)	NHL	13	746	34	2	2.73	0	0
1969-70	Chi. Black Hawks (a-f-g-h)	NHL	63	3763	136	*15	*2.17	2	2
1970-71	Chicago Black Hawks (i)	NHL	57	3325	126	6	2.27	1	4
1971-72	Chicago Black Hawks (a-j)	NHL	48	2780	82	*9	*1.77	1	2
1972-73	Chicago Black Hawks (b)	NHL	56	3340	140	4	2.51	2	0
1973-74	Chicago Black Hawks (b-k-l)	NHL	70	4143	141	10	2.04	1	0
1974-75	Chicago Black Hawks	NHL	71	4219	193	6	2.74	1	11
1975-76	Chicago Black Hawks	NHL	68	4003	198	4	2.97	1	2
1976-77	Chicago Black Hawks	NHL	69	4067	234	2	3.45	2	6
1977-78	Chicago Black Hawks	NHL	64	3840	168	5	2.63	1	0
1978-79	Chicago Black Hawks	NHL	63	3780	206	4	3.27	1	2
1979-80	Chicago Black Hawks (a)	NHL	69	4140	205	*6	2.97	1	2
1980-81	Chicago Black Hawks	NHL	66	3935	246	0	3.75	3	0
1981-82	Chicago Black Hawks	NHL	52	3069	231	1	4.52	2	0
1982-83	Chicago Black Hawks	NHL	39	2340	135	1	3.46	0	0
1983-84	Chicago Black Hawks (m)	NHL	18	1095	88	1	4.82	3	0
	NHL TOTALS		886	52585	2563	76	2.92	25	31

(c)—Named to second team (Western) All-America.
(d)—Named to first team (Western) All-America.
(e)—Drafted from Montreal Canadiens by Chicago Black Hawks, June, 1969.
(f)—Won Vezina Memorial Trophy.
(g)—Won Calder Memorial Trophy.
(h)—Named Rookie of the Year in NHL East Division in poll of players conducted by THE SPORTING NEWS.
(i)—Leading goalie (2.19 average) during playoffs and led in shutouts (2).
(j)—Shared Vezina Memorial Trophy with Gary Smith.
(k)—Tied for Vezina Memorial Trophy with Bernie Parent of Philadelphia Flyers.
(l)—Tied for lead in shutouts (2) during playoffs.
(m)—September, 1984—Released by Chicago Black Hawks.

BOB ESSENSA

Goaltender . . . 6' . . . 160 lbs. . . . Born, Toronto, Ont., January 14, 1965 . . . Shoots left.

Year	Team	League	Games	Mins.	Goals	SO.	Avg.	A.	Pen.
1981-82	Henry Carr H.S.	MJBHL	17	948	79	..	5.00	..	..
1982-83	Henry Carr H.S. (c)	MJBHL	31	1840	98	2	3.20	..	..
1983-84	Michigan State University	CCHA	17	947	44	...	2.79	2	0

(c)—June, 1983—Drafted by Winnipeg Jets in 1983 NHL entry draft. Fifth Jets pick, 69th overall, fourth round.

JAMES FALLE

Goaltender . . . 5'11" . . . 190 lbs. . . . Born, Montreal, Que., August 26, 1964 . . . Shoots left.

Year	Team	League	Games	Mins.	Goals	SO.	Avg.	A.	Pen.
1981-82	Gloucester Rangers	CJHL	31	1658	136	1	4.92	..	..
1982-83	Clarkson College (c)	ECAC	26	1394	75	..	3.23	0	6
1983-84	Clarkson College	ECAC	27	1494	77	...	3.09	0	12

(c)—June, 1983—Drafted by Hartford Whalers in 1983 NHL entry draft. Tenth Whalers pick, 144th overall, eighth round.

BRIAN FORD

Goaltender . . . 5'10" . . . 170 lbs. . . . Born, Edmonton, Alta., September 22, 1961 . . . Shoots left.

Year	Team	League	Games	Mins.	Goals	SO.	Avg.	A.	Pen.
1980-81	Billings Bighorns	WHL	44	2435	204	0	5.03	2	52
1981-82	Billings Bighorns	WHL	53	2791	256	0	5.50	0	0
1982-83	Fredericton Express (c-d)	AHL	27	1444	84	0	3.49	2	0
1982-83	Carolina Thunderbirds	ACHL	4	204	7	0	2.07	0	0
1983-84	Fredericton Express (a-e-f)	AHL	36	2142	105	2	*2.94	4	8
1983-84	Quebec Nordiques	NHL	3	123	13	0	6.34	0	0
	NHL TOTALS		3	123	13	0	6.34	0	0

(c)—August, 1982—Signed by Quebec Nordiques as a free agent.
(d)—Co-winner of Harry (Hap) Holmes Memorial Trophy (Top AHL Goaltenders) with teammate Ken Ellacott.
(e)—Won Harry (Hap) Holmes Memorial Trophy (Top AHL Goaltender).
(f)—Won Baz Bastien Trophy (Coaches pick as top AHL goalie; first time awarded).

NORM FOSTER

Goaltender . . . 5'9" . . . 175 lbs. . . . Born, Vancouver, B.C., February 10, 1965 . . . Shoots left.

Year	Team	League	Games	Mins.	Goals	SO.	Avg.	A.	Pen.
1981-82	Penticton Knights	BCJHL	21	1187	58	..	2.93	..	..
1982-83	Penticton Knights (c)	BCJHL	33	1999	156	0	4.68	..	..
1983-84	Michigan State University	CCHA	32	1814	83	...	2.75	0	2

(c)—June, 1983—Drafted by Boston Bruins in 1983 NHL entry draft. Eleventh Bruins pick, 222nd overall, 11th round.

PAUL FRICKER

Goaltender . . . 6'1" . . . 183 lbs. . . . Born, Toronto, Ont., October 20, 1950 . . . Shoots left.

Year	Team	League	Games	Mins.	Goals	SO.	Avg.	A.	Pen.
1979-80	Univ. of Michigan (b-c)	WCHA	35	2032	148	0	4.37	0	0
1980-81	Univ. of Michigan	WCHA	34	1955	128	0	3.93	0	0
1981-82	Binghamton Whalers	AHL	2	80	7	0	5.25	0	0
1981-82	Oklahoma City Stars	CHL	44	2363	187	0	4.75	1	0
1982-83	Binghamton Whalers	AHL	39	2127	130	1	3.67	1	4
1983-84	Binghamton Whalers	AHL	30	1731	149	0	5.16	0	6

(c)—June, 1980—Drafted by Hartford Whalers in 1980 NHL entry draft. Ninth Whalers pick, 176th overall, ninth round.

BOB FROESE

Goaltender . . . 5'11" . . . 178 lbs. . . . Born, St. Catharines, Ont., June 30, 1958 . . . Shoots left . . . (October, 1980)—Pulled hamstring . . . Set NHL record for most consecutive games without a loss from the start of an NHL career (13 games, 12-0-1) in 1982-83.

Year	Team	League	Games	Mins.	Goals	SO.	Avg.	A.	Pen.
1974-75	St. Cath. Black Hawks	OMJHL	15	871	71	0	4.89	0	2
1975-76	St. Cath. Black Hawks	OMJHL	39	1976	193	0	5.86	0	10
1976-77	Oshawa Generals	OMJHL	39	2063	161	*2	4.68	2	40
1977-78	Niagara Falls Flyers (c)	OMJHL	53	3128	246	0	4.72	1	39
1978-79	Saginaw Gears	IHL	21	1050	58	0	3.31	0	56
1978-79	Milwaukee Admirals	IHL	14	715	42	1	3.52	..	....
1979-80	Maine Mariners (d)	AHL	1	60	5	...	5.00	0	0
1979-80	Saginaw Gears	IHL	52	2827	178	0	3.78	7	45
1980-81	Saginaw Gears (e)	IHL	43	2298	114	3	2.98	2	22
1981-82	Maine Mariners	AHL	33	1900	104	2	3.28	0	2
1982-83	Maine Mariners	AHL	33	1966	110	2	3.36	1	11
1982-83	Philadelphia Flyers	NHL	24	1406	59	4	2.52	2	2
1983-84	Philadelphia Flyers	NHL	48	2863	150	2	3.14	2	10
	NHL TOTALS		72	4269	209	6	2.94	4	12

(c)—June, 1978—Drafted by St. Louis Blues in amateur draft. Eleventh St. Louis pick, 160th overall, 10th round.

(d)—September, 1979—Signed by Philadelphia Flyers as a free agent.

(e)—Led IHL playoffs in goals-against average (2.15) and shutouts (2).

GRANT FUHR

Goaltender . . . 5'10" . . . 181 lbs. . . . Born, Spruce Grove, Alta., September 28, 1962 . . . Shoots right . . . (December, 1981)—Partial separation of right shoulder . . . (December 13, 1983)—Strained left knee ligaments in game vs. Hartford and required surgery . . . (January 27, 1984)—Collected ninth assist of season to set NHL record for goaltenders. He ended the season with 14 . . . First black player to be on Stanley Cup-winning team.

Year	Team	League	Games	Mins.	Goals	SO.	Avg.	A.	Pen.
1979-80—Victoria Cougars (a-c)		WHL	43	2488	130	2	3.14	1	2
1980-81—Victoria Cougars (a-d-e)		WHL	59	*3448	160	*4	*2.78	2	6
1981-82—Edmonton Oilers (b)		NHL	48	2847	157	0	3.31	6	6
1982-83—Moncton Alpines		AHL	10	604	40	0	3.98	0	0
1982-83—Edmonton Oilers		NHL	32	1803	129	0	4.29	0	6
1983-84—Edmonton Oilers		NHL	45	2625	171	1	3.91	14	6
NHL TOTALS			125	7275	457	1	3.77	20	18

(c)—Won Stewart Paul Memorial Trophy (WHL Rookie of the Year).

(d)—Named outstanding goalie in WHL.

(e)—June, 1981—Drafted by Edmonton Oilers in NHL entry draft. First Oilers pick, eighth overall, first round.

JOHN MURDOCH GARRETT

Goaltender . . . 5'8" . . . 170 lbs. . . . Born, Trenton, Ont., June 17, 1951 . . . Shoots left.

Year	Team	League	Games	Mins.	Goals	SO.	Avg.	A.	Pen.
1969-70—P'b'gh TPTs (b-c)		Jr."A"OHA	48	.....	142	*3	2.99	0	8
1970-71—P'b'gh TPTs (a-b-c-d)		Jr."A"OHA	51	3062	151	*5	*2.96	1	21
1971-72—Kansas City Blues (e)		CHL	35	2041	121	*3	3.55	0	0
1272-73—Richmond Robins (f)		AHL	37	2138	117	0	3.26	1	2
1972-73—Port. Buckaroos (g)		WHL	17	951	52	2	3.28	0	2
1973-74—Minn. Fighting Saints		WHA	40	2290	137	1	3.59	0	10
1974-75—Minn. Fighting Saints		WHA	58	3294	180	2	3.28	0	6
1975-76—Minn. Fighting Saints		WHA	52	3179	177	2	3.34	0	6
1975-76—Toronto Toros (h)		WHA	9	551	33	1	3.59	1	0
1976-77—Birmingham Bulls (a)		WHA	65	3803	224	*4	3.53	3	21
1977-78—Birmingham Bulls (i)		WHA	58	3306	210	2	3.81	3	26
1978-79—New England Whalers (j)		WHA	41	2496	149	2	3.58	0	6
1979-80—Hartford Whalers		NHL	52	3046	202	0	3.98	2	12
1980-81—Hartford Whalers		NHL	54	3152	241	0	4.59	1	2
1981-82—Hartford Whalers (k)		NHL	16	898	63	0	4.21	1	2
1981-82—Quebec Nordiques		NHL	12	720	62	0	5.17	0	0
1982-83—Quebec Nordiques (l)		NHL	17	953	64	0	4.03	1	2
1982-83—Vancouver Canucks		NHL	17	934	48	1	3.08	1	0
1983-84—Vancouver Canucks		NHL	29	1652	113	0	4.10	0	9
WHA TOTALS			323	18919	1110	14	3.52	7	75
NHL TOTALS			197	11355	793	1	4.19	6	27

(c)—Won Dave Pinkney Trophy (leading goalie).

(d)—Drafted from Peterborough TPTs by St. Louis Blues in third round of 1971 amateur draft.

(e)—Traded to Chicago Black Hawks by St. Louis Blues to complete earlier deal for Danny O'Shea, September, 1972.

(f)—Loaned to Richmond Robins by Chicago Black Hawks, January, 1973.

(g)—Signed by Minnesota Fighting Saints (WHA), July, 1973.

(h)—Signed by Toronto Toros as free agent following demise of Minnesota Fighting Saints, March, 1976.

(i)—Traded to New England Whalers by Birmingham Bulls for future considerations, September, 1978.

(j)—June, 1979—Selected by Chicago Black Hawks in reclaim draft. Made a priority selection by Hartford Whalers for NHL expansion draft.

(k)—December, 1981—Traded by Hartford Whalers to Quebec Nordiques for Michel Plasse and a fourth-round 1983 entry draft pick.

(l)—January, 1983—Traded by Quebec Nordiques to Vancouver Canucks for Anders Elderbrink.

MARIO GOSSELIN

Goaltender . . . 5'8" . . . 160 lbs. . . . Born, Thetford Mines, Que., June 15, 1963 . . . Shoots left . . . Member of 1984 Canadian Olympic team . . . (February 25, 1984)—First NHL game was 5-0 shutout of St. Louis Blues . . . (March 8, 1984)—Injured knee in game vs. Pittsburgh, out for the season.

Year	Team	League	Games	Mins.	Goals	SO.	Avg.	A.	Pen.
1980-81—Shawinigan Cataracts		QMJHL	21	907	75	0	4.96	1	0
1981-82—Shawinigan Cataracts (b-c)		QMJHL	*60	*3404	230	0	4.50	3	10
1982-83—Shawinigan Cataracts (a-d)		QHL	46	2556	133	*3	*3.12	4	18

Year	Team	League	Games	Mins.	Goals	SO.	Avg.	A.	Pen.
1983-84—Canadian Olympic Team		Int'l	36	2007	126	0	3.77	..	....
1983-84—Quebec Nordiques		NHL	3	148	67	1	1.22	0	2
NHL TOTALS			3	148	67	1	1.22	0	2

(c)—June, 1982—Drafted as underage junior by Quebec Nordiques in NHL entry draft. Third Nordiques pick, 55th overall, third round.

(d)—Won Jacques Plante Trophy (Top QHL Goalie).

REX GRANT

Goaltender . . . 6'5" . . . 205 lbs. . . . Born, Mission City, B.C., September 30, 1965 . . . Shoots left.

Year	Team	League	Games	Mins.	Goals	SO.	Avg.	A.	Pen.
1983-84—Seattle Breakers		WHL	9	430	37	0	5.16	0	4
1983-84—Kamloops Junior Oilers (c)		WHL	31	1427	110	0	4.63	1	8

(c)—June, 1984—Drafted as underage junior by Vancouver Canucks in NHL entry draft. Tenth Canucks pick, 178th overall, ninth round.

LUC GUENETTE

Goaltender . . . 5'9" . . . 160 lbs. . . . Born, St. Jerome, Que., July 22, 1964 . . . Shoots right.

Year	Team	League	Games	Mins.	Goals	SO.	Avg.	A.	Pen.
1981-82—Quebec Remparts		QMJHL	38	1809	202	0	6.70	0	4
1982-83—Quebec Remparts (b-c)		QHL	59	3285	299	0	5.46	1	14
1983-84—Quebec Remparts (b)		QHL	67	3729	314	0	5.05	3	6

(c)—June, 1983—Drafted as underage junior by Quebec Nordiques in 1983 NHL entry draft. Fourth Nordiques pick, 92nd overall, fifth round.

GLEN HANLON

Goaltender . . . 6' . . . 175 lbs. . . . Born, Brandon, Man., February 20, 1957 . . . Shoots right . . . Missed part of 1977-78 season with torn ankle ligaments . . . Missed part of 1979-80 season with shoulder injury . . . (October 18, 1980)—Stretched knee ligaments . . . (March, 1981) —Shoulder separation.

Year	Team	League	Games	Mins.	Goals	SO.	Avg.	A.	Pen.
1973-74—Brandon Travellers		MJHL	20	1059	64	*1	3.63	0	5
1974-75—Brandon Wheat Kings		WCHL	43	2498	176	0	4.22	1	6
1975-76—Brandon Wheat Kings (a)		WCHL	64	3523	234	4	3.99	2	35
1976-77—Brandon Wheat K. (a-c-d)		WCHL	65	3784	195	*4	*3.09	5	8
1977-78—Tulsa Oilers (a-e)		CHL	53	3123	160	*3	3.07	4	30
1977-78—Vancouver Canucks		NHL	4	200	9	0	2.70	0	2
1978-79—Vancouver Canucks		NHL	31	1821	94	3	3.10	1	30
1979-80—Vancouver Canucks		NHL	57	3341	193	0	3.47	1	43
1980-81—Dallas Black Hawks		CHL	4	239	8	1	2.01	1	0
1980-81—Vancouver Canucks		NHL	17	798	59	1	4.44	1	10
1981-82—Vancouver Canucks (f)		NHL	28	1610	106	1	3.95	0	22
1981-82—St. Louis Blues		NHL	2	76	8	0	6.32	0	0
1982-83—St. Louis Blues (g)		NHL	14	671	50	0	4.47	0	0
1982-83—New York Rangers		NHL	21	1173	67	0	3.43	0	2
1983-84—New York Rangers		NHL	50	2837	166	1	3.51	2	30
NHL TOTALS			224	12527	752	6	3.60	5	139

(c)—Won WCHL Leading Goalie Award.

(d)—Drafted from Brandon Wheat Kings by Vancouver Canucks in third round of 1977 amateur draft.

(e)—Won CHL Rookie-of-the-Year Award.

(f)—March, 1982—Traded by Vancouver Canucks to St. Louis Blues for Tony Currie, Jim Nill, Rick Heinz and fourth-round 1982 entry draft pick (Shawn Kilroy).

(g)—January, 1983—Traded by St. Louis Blues with Vaclav Nedomansky to New York Rangers for Andre Dore and future considerations.

RANDY HANSCH

Goaltender . . . 5'10" . . . 165 lbs. . . . Born, Edmonton, Alta., February 8, 1966 . . . Shoots right.

Year	Team	League	Games	Mins.	Goals	SO.	Avg.	A.	Pen.
1982-83—Victoria Cougars		WHL	6	229	23	0	6.03	0	0
1983-84—Victoria Cougars (c)		WHL	36	1894	144	0	4.56	0	4

(c)—June, 1984—Drafted as underage junior by Detroit Red Wings in NHL entry draft. Fifth Red Wings pick, 112th overall, sixth round.

BRIAN HAYWARD

Goaltender . . . 5'10" . . . 175 lbs. . . . Born, Georgetown, Ont., June 25, 1960 . . . Shoots left.

Year	Team	League	Games	Mins.	Goals	SO.	Avg.	A.	Pen.
1978-79—Cornell University		ECAC	25	1469	95	0	3.88	..	....
1979-80—Cornell University		ECAC	12	508	52	0	6.02	..	....
1980-81—Cornell University		ECAC	19	967	58	1	3.54	..	....
1981-82—Cornell University		ECAC	....	1320	68	0	3.09	..	....
1982-83—Sherbrooke Jets (c)		AHL	22	1208	89	1	4.42	0	0
1982-83—Winnipeg Jets		NHL	24	1440	89	1	3.71	1	0
1983-84—Sherbrooke Jets		AHL	15	781	69	0	5.30	1	2
1983-84—Winnipeg Jets		NHL	28	1530	124	0	4.86	1	2
NHL TOTALS			52	2970	213	1	4.30	2	2

(c)—September, 1982—Signed by Winnipeg Jets as a free agent.

RICK HEINZ

Goaltender . . . 5'10" . . . 165 lbs. . . . Born, Essex, Ont., May 30, 1955 . . . Shoots left.

Year	Team	League	Games	Mins.	Goals	SO.	Avg.	A.	Pen.
1973-74—Chatham Maroons		SOJHL	..	..	..	*4	*3.51	..	..
1974-75—Univ. of Minn.-Duluth		WCHA	18	1039	88	0	5.08	..	..
1975-76—Univ. of Minn.-Duluth		WCHA	34	2033	162	0	4.78	0	4
1976-77—Univ. of Minn.-Duluth		WCHA	..	....	..	..	..	..	..
1977-78—Univ. of Minn.-Duluth		WCHA	33	1961	157	0	4.80	..	..
1978-79—Salt Lake Golden Eagles		CHL	1	59	3	0	3.05	0	0
1978-79—Port Huron Flags		IHL	54	2800	157	*5	3.36	2	16
1979-80—Salt Lake Golden Eagles		CHL	39	2353	119	0	3.03	2	12
1980-81—Salt Lake Golden Eagles (c)		CHL	36	2210	128	3	3.48	1	26
1980-81—St. Louis Blues		NHL	4	220	8	0	2.18	1	0
1981-82—Salt Lake Golden Eagles		CHL	19	1167	71	0	3.65	4	4
1981-82—St. Louis Blues (d)		NHL	9	433	35	0	4.85	0	0
1981-82—Vancouver Canucks		NHL	3	180	9	1	3.00	0	0
1982-83—Salt Lake Golden Eagles		CHL	17	1031	58	1	3.38	0	4
1982-83—St. Louis Blues		NHL	9	335	24	1	4.30	0	2
1983-84—St. Louis Blues		NHL	22	1118	80	0	4.29	0	4
NHL TOTALS			47	2286	156	2	4.09	1	6

(c)—Led CHL Playoffs with 2.72 average.
(d)—March, 1982—Traded with Tony Currie, Jim Nill and fourth-round 1982 entry draft pick (Shawn Kilroy) by St. Louis Blues to Vancouver Canucks for Glen Hanlon. Returned to St. Louis, June, 1982.

GILLES HEROUX

Goaltender . . . 6' . . . 180 lbs. . . . Born, St. Eustache, Que., February 1, 1962 . . . Shoots left.

Year	Team	League	Games	Mins.	Goals	SO.	Avg.	A.	Pen.
1980-81—Laval Voisins		QMJHL	26	1371	111	0	4.86	1	4
1981-82—Montreal Juniors		QMJHL	27	1437	104	0	4.34	1	17
1982-83—Verdun Juniors		QHL	59	3439	253	0	4.41	1	4
1982-83—Nova Scotia Voyageurs (c)		AHL	1	40	1	0	1.50	0	0
1983-84—Nova Scotia Voyageurs		AHL	1	60	2	0	2.00	0	0
1983-84—Peoria Prancers		IHL	13	698	51	0	4.38	1	0
1983-84—Virginia Lancers		ACHL	35	1909	189	0	5.94	4	13

(c)—April, 1982—Signed by Nova Scotia Voyageurs as a free agent.

DENIS HERRON

Goaltender . . . 5'11" . . . 165 lbs. . . . Born, Chambly, Que., June 18, 1952 . . . Shoots left . . . Missed part of 1979-80 season with a broken collarbone . . . (November 15, 1980)—Pulled muscle in upper back . . . (December 29, 1981)—Suffered concussion against New York Islanders . . . (November, 1982)—Concussion in game vs. New York Islanders . . . (January, 1983)—Severely bruised shoulder in practice . . . (December 15, 1983)—Broke finger when hit by Mats Naslund shot at Montreal . . . (January, 1984)—Pinched nerve in neck.

Year	Team	League	Games	Mins.	Goals	SO.	Avg.	A.	Pen.
1969-70—Three Rivers Dukes		QJHL	2	.....	10	0	6.25	..	....
1970-71—Three Rivers Dukes		QJHL	33	.....	136	0	4.12	..	....
1971-72—Three Riv. Dukes (b-c)		QJHL	40	.....	160	2	4.00	..	....
1972-73—Hershey Bears		AHL	21	1185	63	0	3.19	0	0
1972-73—Pittsburgh Penguins		NHL	18	967	55	2	3.41	1	0
1973-74—Hershey Bears		AHL	17	967	52	0	3.22	1	2
1973-74—S.L.C. Golden Eagles (d)		WHL	9	530	32	0	3.62	0	4
1973-74—Pittsburgh Penguins		NHL	5	260	18	0	4.15	0	0
1974-75—Hershey Bears		AHL	12	615	45	0	4.39	0	0
1974-75—Pittsburgh Penguins (e)		NHL	3	108	11	0	6.11	0	0

Year	Team	League	Games	Mins.	Goals	SO.	Avg.	A.	Pen.
1974-75—Kansas City Scouts		NHL	22	1280	80	0	3.75	1	2
1975-76—Kansas City Scouts (f)		NHL	64	3620	243	0	4.03	0	16
1976-77—Pittsburgh Penguins		NHL	34	1920	94	1	2.94	1	4
1977-78—Pittsburgh Penguins		NHL	60	3534	210	0	3.57	1	6
1978-79—Pittsburgh Penguins (g)		NHL	56	3208	180	0	3.37	2	18
1979-80—Montreal Canadiens		NHL	34	1909	80	0	2.51	0	0
1980-81—Montreal Canadiens (h)		NHL	25	1147	67	1	3.50	2	0
1981-82—Montreal Canadiens (i-j)		NHL	27	1547	68	*3	*2.64	0	4
1982-83—Pittsburgh Penguins		NHL	31	1707	151	1	5.31	1	14
1983-84—Pittsburgh Penguins		NHL	38	2028	138	1	4.08	0	21
NHL TOTALS			417	23235	1395	9	3.60	9	85

(c)—Drafted from Three Rivers Dukes by Pittsburgh Penguins in third round of 1972 amateur draft.

(d)—Loaned to Salt Lake City Golden Eagles by Pittsburgh Penguins, December, 1973.

(e)—Traded to Kansas City Scouts by Pittsburgh Penguins with Jean-Guy Lagace for Michel Plasse, January, 1975.

(f)—Signed by Pittsburgh Penguins as free agent, July, 1976. (Colorado Rockies received Simon Nolet, Colin Campbell and Michel Plasse as compensation).

(g)—September, 1979—Traded with second round pick in 1982 entry draft (Jocelyn Gauvreau) by Pittsburgh Penguins to Montreal Canadiens for Bob Holland and Pat Hughes.

(h)—Co-winner of Vezina Trophy (Top NHL Goaltenders) with teammates Richard Sevigny and Michel Larocque.

(i)—Co-winner of Bill Jennings Trophy (Lowest Team Goaltending Average) with teammate Rick Wamsley.

(j)—September, 1982—Traded by Montreal Canadiens to Pittsburgh Penguins for a third-round choice in the 1985 NHL entry draft.

JEFF HOGG

Goaltender . . . 6' . . . 170 lbs. . . . Born, Guelph, Ont., January 28, 1965 . . . Shoots left . . . (August, 1982)—Injured right ankle.

Year	Team	League	Games	Mins.	Goals	SO.	Avg.	A.	Pen.
1981-82—Waterloo Siskins		MWJBHL	12	651	43	0	3.96	..	....
1982-83—Oshawa Generals (c-d)		OHL	15	721	38	1	3.16	2	0
1983-84—Oshawa Generals		OHL	6	350	19	0	3.26	0	0
1983-84—Kingston Canadians		OHL	22	1096	105	0	5.75	12	0

(c)—Co-winner of Dave Pinkney Trophy (Top OHL Goaltenders) with teammate Peter Sidorkiewicz.

(d)—June, 1983—Drafted as underage junior by Calgary Flames in 1983 NHL entry draft. Ninth Flames pick, 131st overall, seventh round.

MARK HOLDEN

Goaltender . . . 5'10" . . . 165 lbs. . . . Born, Weymouth, Mass., June 12, 1957 . . . Shoots left.

Year	Team	League	Games	Mins.	Goals	SO.	Avg.	A.	Pen.
1976-77—Brown University (c)		ECAC	....	......	....	...	......	..	....
1977-78—Brown University		ECAC	10	590	33	0	3.36	..	....
1978-79—Brown University		ECAC	....	573	35	...	3.66	..	....
1979-80—Brown University (d)		ECAC	26	1508	93	0	3.70	..	....
1980-81—Nova Scotia Voyageurs		AHL	42	2223	127	2	3.43	1	4
1981-82—Montreal Canadiens		NHL	1	20	0	0	0.00	0	0
1981-82—Nova Scotia Voyageurs		AHL	44	2534	142	0	3.36	2	20
1982-83—Montreal Canadiens		NHL	2	87	6	0	4.14	0	0
1982-83—Nova Scotia Voyageurs		AHL	41	2369	160	0	4.05	6	4
1983-84—Montreal Canadiens		NHL	1	52	4	0	4.62	0	0
1983-84—Nova Scotia Voyageurs		AHL	47	2739	153	0	3.35	1	10
NHL TOTALS			4	159	10	0	3.77	0	0

(c)—June, 1977—Drafted by Montreal Canadiens in 1977 NHL amateur draft. Sixteenth Canadiens pick, 160th overall, 10th round.

(d)—Named to second team All-Ivy League All-Star Team.

KENNETH HOLLAND

Goaltender . . . 5'8" . . . 160 lbs. . . . Born, Vernon, B.C., November 10, 1955 . . . Shoots left.

Year	Team	League	Games	Mins.	Goals	SO.	Avg.	A.	Pen.
1973-74—Vernon Vikings		Jr."A"BCHL	16	......	59	0	4.80	..	....
1974-75—Medicine Hat Tigers		WCHL	37	2114	138	1	3.91	1	2
1975-76—Medicine Hat Tigers		WCHL	41	2152	150	2	4.18	1	16
1976-77—Binghamton Dusters		AHL	48	2620	165	0	3.78	..	....
1977-78—Binghamton Dusters		AHL	39	2057	147	0	4.28	0	4
1978-79—Binghamton Dusters		AHL	41	2315	151	0	3.91	5	4
1979-80—Springfield Indians (c)		AHL	37	2092	130	2	3.73	0	2
1980-81—Hartford Whalers		NHL	1	60	7	0	7.00	0	0

Year	Team	League	Games	Mins.	Goals	SO.	Avg.	A.	Pen.
1980-81—Binghamton Whalers		AHL	47	2543	168	2	3.96	0	0
1981-82—Binghamton Whalers (b)		AHL	46	2733	133	2	2.92	6	4
1982-83—Binghamton Whalers		AHL	48	2700	196	0	4.36	1	6
1983-84—Detroit Red Wings (d)		NHL	3	146	10	0	4.11	0	0
1983-84—Adirondack Red Wings		AHL	42	2495	154	0	3.70	5	2
NHL TOTALS			4	206	17	0	4.95	0	0

(c)—September, 1979—Signed by Hartford Whalers as a free agent.
(d)—July, 1983—Signed by Detroit Red Wings as a free agent.

ROBERT HOLLAND

Goaltender . . . 6'1" . . . 182 lbs. . . . Born, Montreal, Que., September 10, 1957 . . . Shoots left.

Year	Team	League	Games	Mins.	Goals	SO.	Avg.	A.	Pen.
1974-75—Longueuil Rebelles		Jr."A"QHL	36	2139	187	0	5.22	..	....
1975-76—Montreal Juniors		QJHL	37	1995	147	0	4.42	..	....
1976-77—Montreal Juniors (c)		QJHL	45	2314	184	0	4.77	1	4
1977-78—Nova Scotia Voyageurs (d)		AHL	38	2270	120	1	3.17	2	6
1978-79—Nova Scotia Voyageurs (e)		AHL	43	2377	154	*2	3.89	2	23
1979-80—Pittsburgh Penguins		NHL	34	1974	126	1	3.83	0	2
1980-81—Binghamton Whalers		AHL	7	354	28	0	4.75	0	0
1980-81—Indianapolis Checkers		CHL	15	845	41	1	2.91	0	4
1980-81—Pittsburgh Penguins (f)		NHL	10	539	45	0	5.01	0	0
1981-82—Toledo Goaldiggers		IHL	7	423	25	0	3.55	0	0
1981-82—Indianapolis Checkers (g)		CHL	30	1672	95	0	3.41	1	6
1982-83—Indianapolis Checkers (b-g)		CHL	37	2111	101	*4	*2.87	0	6
1983-84—Indianapolis Checkers		CHL	39	2149	131	0	3.66	1	10
NHL TOTALS			44	2513	171	1	4.08	0	2

(c)—Drafted from Montreal Juniors by Montreal Canadiens in fourth round of 1977 amateur draft.
(d)—Shared Harry "Hap" Holmes Memorial Trophy with Maurice Barrette.
(e)—September, 1979—Traded with Pat Hughes by Montreal Canadiens to Pittsburgh Penguins for Denis Herron and second-round pick in 1982 entry draft.
(f)—September, 1981—Signed by New York Islanders as a free agent.
(g)—Co-winner of Terry Sawchuk Trophy (Top CHL Goaltenders) with teammate Kelly Hrudey.

KELLY HRUDEY

Goaltender . . . 5'10" . . . 183 lbs. . . . Born, Edmonton, Alta., January 13, 1961 . . . Shoots left.

Year	Team	League	Games	Mins.	Goals	SO.	Avg.	A.	Pen.
1978-79—Medicine Hat Tigers		WHL	57	3093	*318	0	6.17	2	43
1979-80—Medicine Hat Tigers (c)		WHL	57	3049	212	1	4.17	6	12
1980-81—Medicine Hat Tigers (b)		WHL	55	3023	200	*4	3.97	0	21
1980-81—Indianapolis Checkers (d)		CHL	....	....	....	...	....	..	....
1981-82—Indianapolis Checkers (a-e-f-g)		CHL	51	3033	149	1	*2.95	0	6
1982-83—Indianapolis Checkers (a-e-h-i)		CHL	47	2744	139	2	3.04	0	28
1983-84—Indianapolis Checkers		CHL	6	370	21	0	3.41	1	0
1983-84—New York Islanders		NHL	12	535	28	0	3.14	0	0
NHL TOTALS			12	535	28	0	3.14	0	0

(c)—June, 1980—Drafted by New York Islanders as underage junior in 1980 NHL entry draft. Second Islanders pick, 38th overall, second round.
(d)—No regular season games. Two playoff appearances.
(e)—Co-winner of Terry Sawchuk Trophy (Top CHL Goaltenders) with teammate Robert Holland.
(f)—Winner of Max McNab Trophy (CHL Playoff MVP).
(g)—Led CHL Playoffs with 2.42 goals-against-average and one shutout.
(h)—Won Tommy Ivan Trophy (CHL MVP).
(i)—Led CHL playoffs with 2.64 average.

GIL HUDON

Goaltender . . . 6'2" . . . 190 lbs. . . . Born, Zenon Park, Sask., February 12, 1962 . . . Shoots left.

Year	Team	League	Games	Mins.	Goals	SO.	Avg.	A.	Pen.
1980-81—Prince Albert Raiders (c)		AJHL	28	1556	83	1	3.20	..	....
1981-82—Prince Albert Raiders		AJHL	21	1162	67	...	3.46	..	....
1982-83—Maine Mariners		AHL	22	1146	82	0	4.29	1	0
1982-83—Toledo Goaldiggers		IHL	3	179	10	0	3.35	0	0
1983-84—Springfield Indians		AHL	27	1395	101	0	4.34	0	4

(c)—June, 1981—Drafted as underage junior by Philadelphia Flyers in 1981 NHL entry draft. Tenth Flyers pick, 142nd overall, seventh round.

ROBERT JANECYK

Goaltender ... 6'1" ... 180 lbs. ... Born, Chicago, Ill., May 18, 1957 ... Shoots left ... Led IHL with a combined goals-against average of 3.43 in 1979-80 ... (February, 1983)— Strained knee ligaments.

Year	Team	League	Games	Mins.	Goals	SO.	Avg.	A.	Pen.
1979-80—Flint Generals (b-c)		IHL	2	119	5	0	2.53	0	2
1979-80—Fort Wayne Komets		IHL	40	2208	128	1	3.48	2	14
1980-81—New Brunswick Hawks (d)		AHL	34	1915	131	0	4.10	2	10
1981-82—New Brunswick Hawks (a-e-f)		AHL	53	3224	153	2	2.85	1	20
1982-83—Springfield Indians (a)		AHL	47	2754	167	*3	3.64	4	34
1983-84—Springfield Indians		AHL	30	1664	94	0	3.39	1	2
1983-84—Chicago Black Hawks (g)		NHL	8	412	28	0	4.08	0	2
NHL TOTALS			8	412	28	0	4.08	0	2

(c)—December, 1979—Loaned to Flint Generals by Fort Wayne Komets.
(d)—June, 1980—Signed by Chicago Black Hawks as a free agent.
(e)—Co-winner of Harry (Hap) Holmes Memorial Trophy (Top AHL Goaltenders) with teammate Warren Skorodenski.
(f)—Led AHL Calder Cup Playoffs with 2.35 goals-against average and one shutout.
(g)—June, 1984—Traded with first (Craig Redmond), third (John English) and fourth (Thomas Glavine) round 1984 draft picks by Chicago Black Hawks to Los Angeles Kings for first (Ed Olczyk), third (Trent Yawney) and fourth round (Tommy Eriksson) 1984 draft picks.

ALLAN RAYMOND (AL) JENSEN

Goaltender ... 5'10" ... 180 lbs. ... Born, Hamilton, Ont., November 27, 1958 ... Shoots left ... Missed start of 1978-79 season with broken thumb ... (January, 1984)—Injured back while weightlifting.

Year	Team	League	Games	Mins.	Goals	SO.	Avg.	A.	Pen.
1975-76—Hamilton Fincups		Jr."A"OHA	28	1451	97	0	3.97	1	7
1976-77—St. Cath. Fincups (b)		Jr."A"OHA	48	2727	168	*2	3.70	4	6
1977-78—Hamil. Fincups (a-c-d)		Jr."A"OHA	43	2582	146	*3	*3.35	1	6
1978-79—Kalamazoo Wings		IHL	47	2596	156	2	3.61	3	6
1979-80—Adirondack Red Wings		AHL	57	3406	199	2	3.51	0	10
1980-81—Adirondack Red Wings		AHL	60	3169	203	*3	3.84	2	10
1980-81—Detroit Red Wings (e)		NHL	1	60	7	0	7.00	0	0
1981-82—Washington Capitals		NHL	26	1274	81	0	3.81	2	6
1981-82—Hershey Bears		AHL	8	407	24	0	3.54	0	21
1982-83—Hershey Bears		AHL	6	316	14	1	2.66	0	0
1982-83—Washington Capitals		NHL	40	2358	135	1	3.44	0	6
1983-84—Hershey Bears		AHL	3	180	16	0	5.33	0	0
1983-84—Washington Capitals (f)		NHL	43	2414	117	*4	2.91	0	22
NHL TOTALS			110	6106	340	5	3.34	0	34

(c)—Shared Dave Pinkney Trophy (leading OMJHL goalies) with Rick Wamsley.
(d)—Drafted from Hamilton Fincups by Detroit Red Wings in second round of 1978 amateur draft.
(e)—August, 1981—Traded by Detroit Red Wings to Washington Capitals for Mark Lofthouse.
(f)—Co-winner of Bill Jennings Trophy (Top NHL goaltenders) with teammate Pat Riggin.

DARREN JENSEN

Goaltender ... 5'9" ... 165 lbs. ... Born, Creston, B.C., May 27, 1960 ... Shoots left.

Year	Team	League	Games	Mins.	Goals	SO.	Avg.	A.	Pen.
1979-80—Univ. of North Dakota (c)		WCHA	15	890	33	1	2.22	..	....
1980-81—Univ. of North Dakota		WCHA	25	1510	110	0	4.37	1	4
1981-82—Univ. of North Dakota (d)		WCHA	16	910	45	1	2.97	0	2
1982-83—Univ. of North Dakota		WCHA	16	905	45	0	2.98	1	0
1983-84—Fort Wayne Komets (a-e-f-g-h-i)		IHL	56	3325	162	*4	*2.92	2	6

(c)—June, 1980—Drafted by Hartford Whalers in NHL entry draft. Fifth Whalers pick, 92nd overall, fifth round.
(d)—Named to NCAA All-Tournament team.
(e)—October, 1983—Released by Hartford Whalers and signed by Fort Wayne Komets as a free agent.
(f)—Won James Gatschene Memorial Trophy (IHL MVP).
(g)—Won Garry F. Longman Memorial Trophy (Top IHL Rookie).
(h)—Won James Norris Memorial Trophy (Top IHL Goaltender).
(i)—May, 1984—Signed by Philadelphia Flyers as a free agent.

DOUG KEANS

Goaltender ... 5'7" ... 174 lbs. ... Born, Pembroke, Ont., January 7, 1958 ... Shoots left ... (March, 1981)—Injury to right ankle that required surgery to repair ligament damage ... (February, 1983)—Torn hamstring muscle ... (December 15, 1983)—Strained ligaments in left knee in game vs. Hartford Whalers and required surgery.

Year	Team	League	Games	Mins.	Goals	SO.	Avg.	A.	Pen.
1975-76—Oshawa Generals		OMJHL	1	29	4	0	8.28	0	0
1976-77—Oshawa Generals		OMJHL	48	2632	291	0	6.63	0	4
1977-78—Oshawa Generals (c)		OMJHL	42	2500	172	1	4.13	2	4
1978-79—Saginaw Gears		IHL	59	3207	217	0	4.06	1	11
1979-80—Saginaw Gears		IHL	22	1070	67	1	3.76	3	4
1979-80—Binghamton Dusters		AHL	8	488	31	0	3.81	3	4
1979-80—Los Angeles Kings		NHL	10	559	23	0	2.47	0	0
1980-81—Los Angeles Kings		NHL	9	454	37	0	4.89	0	7
1980-81—Houston Apollos		CHL	11	699	27	0	2.32	0	2
1980-81—Oklahoma City Stars		CHL	9	492	32	1	3.90	0	0
1981-82—New Haven Nighthawks		AHL	13	686	33	2	2.89	1	0
1981-82—Los Angeles Kings		NHL	31	1436	103	0	4.30	0	0
1982-83—Los Angeles Kings		NHL	6	304	24	0	4.73	1	0
1982-83—New Haven Nighthawks		AHL	30	1724	125	0	4.35	2	6
1983-84—Boston Bruins (d)		NHL	33	1779	92	2	3.10	0	2
NHL TOTALS			89	4532	279	2	3.69	1	9

(c)—June, 1978—Drafted by Los Angeles Kings in amateur draft. Second Los Angeles pick, 94th overall, sixth round.

(d)—June, 1983—Acquired on waivers from Los Angeles Kings by Boston Bruins.

PAUL KENNY

Goaltender . . . 6'1" . . . 190 lbs. . . . Born, St. John's, Nfld., March 30, 1965 . . . Shoots left.

Year	Team	League	Games	Mins.	Goals	SO.	Avg.	A.	Pen.
1982-83—St. Francis Xavier Univ.		CUAA	8	319	17	0	3.19	..	....
1983-84—Cornwall Royals (c)		OHL	41	2101	163	1	4.65	2	25

(c)—June, 1984—Drafted as underage junior by Los Angeles Kings in NHL entry draft. Eleventh Kings pick, 212th overall, 11th round.

SHAWN KILROY

Goaltender . . . 5'10" . . . 156 lbs. . . . Born, Ottawa, Ont., April 22, 1964 . . . Shoots left.

Year	Team	League	Games	Mins.	Goals	SO.	Avg.	A.	Pen.
1981-82—Peterborough Petes (c-d)		OHL	17	970	48	1	2.97	0	2
1982-83—Peterborough Petes		OHL	39	2137	142	0	3.99	0	4
1983-84—Peterborough Petes		OHL	49	2784	193	0	4.16	2	21

(c)—Won F.W. Dinty Moore Trophy (Lowest goalie average by a rookie OHL goalie).

(d)—June, 1982—Drafted as underage junior by Vancouver Canucks in NHL entry draft. Third Canucks pick, 71st overall, fourth round.

RICK KNICKLE

Goaltender . . . 5'10" . . . 155 lbs. . . . Born, Chatham, N.B., February 26, 1960 . . . Shoots left . . . (February, 1981)—Sprained thumb.

Year	Team	League	Games	Mins.	Goals	SO.	Avg.	A.	Pen.
1977-78—Brandon Wheat Kings		WCHL	49	2806	182	0	3.89	5	27
1978-79—Brandon Wheat Kings (a-c-d)		WHL	38	2240	118	1	*3.16	3	15
1979-80—Muskegon Mohawks		IHL	16	829	51	0	3.69	0	25
1980-81—Erie Blades (a-e)		EHL	43	2347	125	1	*3.20	0	12
1981-82—Rochester Americans		AHL	31	1753	108	1	3.70	1	0
1982-83—Flint Generals		IHL	27	1638	92	2	3.37	2	6
1982-83—Rochester Americans		AHL	4	143	11	0	4.64	0	0
1983-84—Flint Generals (b-f)		IHL	60	3518	203	3	3.46	6	16

(c)—Named top Goaltender in WHL.

(d)—August, 1979—Drafted by Buffalo Sabres as underage junior in entry draft. Seventh Buffalo pick, 116th overall, sixth round.

(e)—Led EHL playoffs with 1.88 goals-against average.

(f)—Led IHL playoffs with 3.00 average.

RICHARD JACQUES LAFERRIERE

Goaltender . . . 5'9" . . . 170 lbs. . . . Born, Hawkesbury, Ont., January 3, 1961 . . . Shoots left.

Year	Team	League	Games	Mins.	Goals	SO.	Avg.	A.	Pen.
1978-79—Peterborough Petes		OMJHL	21	1279	76	1	3.56	0	14
1979-80—Peterborough Petes (b-c-d)		OMJHL	55	3118	170	2	*3.27	4	8
1980-81—Peterborough Petes		OMJHL	34	1959	144	0	4.41	0	29
1980-81—Brantford Alexanders		OMJHL	20	1155	93	0	4.83	0	6
1981-82—Ft. Worth Texans		CHL	37	2155	189	1	5.27	1	33
1981-82—Colorado Rockies		NHL	1	20	1	0	3.00	0	0
1982-83—Muskegon Mohawks		IHL	44	2578	186	0	4.33	3	4

Year	Team	League	Games	Mins.	Goals	SO.	Avg.	A.	Pen.
1983-84—Tulsa Oilers		CHL	2	79	4	0	3.04	0	0
1983-84—Muskegon Mohawks (e)		IHL	16	817	83	0	6.10	0	2
NHL TOTALS			1	20	1	0	3.00	0	0

(c)—Co-winner of Dave Pinkney Trophy (Leading OHL Goaltenders) with teammate Terry Wright.
(d)—June, 1980—Drafted as underage junior by Colorado Rockies in 1980 NHL entry draft. Third Rockies pick, 64th overall, fourth round.
(e)—January, 1984—Released by Muskegon Mohawks.

MARK LaFOREST

Goaltender ... 5'10" ... 175 lbs. ... Born, Welland, Ont., July 10, 1962 ... Shoots left.

Year	Team	League	Games	Mins.	Goals	SO.	Avg.	A.	Pen.
1981-82—Niagara Falls Flyers		OHL	24	1365	105	1	4.62	1	14
1982-83—North Bay Centennials		OHL	54	3140	195	0	3.73	4	20
1983-84—Adirondack Red Wings (c)		AHL	7	351	29	0	4.96	0	2
1983-84—Kalamazoo Wings		IHL	13	718	48	1	4.01	0	11

(c)—September, 1983—Signed by Detroit Red Wings as a free agent.

ALLAN LAROCHELLE

Goaltender ... 5'10" ... 185 lbs. ... Born, Ponteiz, Sask., October 27, 1964 ... Shoots left.

Year	Team	League	Games	Mins.	Goals	SO.	Avg.	A.	Pen.
1981-82—Portland Winter Hawks		WHL	23	1245	94	0	4.53	0	0
1982-83—Saskatoon Blades (c)		WHL	41	2295	153	2	4.00	1	19
1983-84—Saskatoon Blades		WHL	56	3033	244	0	4.83	4	27

(c)—June, 1983—Drafted as underage junior by Boston Bruins in 1983 NHL entry draft. Fourth Bruins pick, 82nd overall, fourth round.

MICHEL RAYMOND (BUNNY) LAROCQUE

Goaltender ... 5'11" ... 185 lbs. ... Born, Hull, Que., April 6, 1952 ... Shoots left ... Missed part of 1976-77 season with broken finger and knuckle ... (December 4, 1980)—Cut hand ... (October, 1983)—Back injury.

Year	Team	League	Games	Mins.	Goals	SO.	Avg.	A.	Pen.
1967-68—Ottawa 67's	Jr."A" OHA	4	.....	32	0	9.14	0	0	
1968-69—Ottawa 67's	Jr."A" OHA	4	.....	24	0	7.58	0	0	
1969-70—Ottawa 67's	Jr."A" OHA	51	.....	185	*3	3.62	0	17	
1970-71—Ottawa 67's (b-c)	Jr."A" OHA	56	3345	189	*5	3.39	4	4	
1971-72—Ottawa 67's (a-d-e-f)	Jr."A" OHA	54	.....	189	*4	*3.45	0	20	
1972-73—Nova Scotia Voyageurs (b-g)	AHL	47	2705	113	1	*2.50	0	6	
1973-74—Montreal Canadiens	NHL	27	1431	69	0	2.89	2	0	
1974-75—Montreal Canadiens	NHL	25	1480	74	3	3.00	1	2	
1975-76—Montreal Canadiens	NHL	22	1220	50	2	2.46	2	4	
1976-77—Montreal Canadiens (h)	NHL	26	1525	53	4	*2.09	0	0	
1977-78—Montreal Canadiens (h)	NHL	30	1729	77	1	2.67	4	0	
1978-79—Montreal Canadiens (h)	NHL	34	1986	94	3	2.84	3	2	
1979-80—Montreal Canadiens	NHL	39	2259	125	3	3.32	2	4	
1980-81—Montreal Canadiens (i-j)	NHL	28	1623	82	1	3.03	1	2	
1980-81—Toronto Maple Leafs	NHL	8	460	40	0	5.22	0	0	
1981-82—Toronto Maple Leafs	NHL	50	2647	207	0	4.69	3	2	
1982-83—Toronto Maple Leafs (k)	NHL	16	835	68	0	4.89	0	0	
1982-83—Philadelphia Flyers	NHL	2	120	8	0	4.00	0	0	
1983-84—Springfield Indians (l)	AHL	5	301	21	0	4.19	2	0	
1983-84—St. Louis Blues	NHL	5	300	31	0	6.20	0	2	
NHL TOTALS		322	17615	978	17	3.33	18	18	

(c)—Leading goalie (3.45 average and 3 shutouts) during playoffs.
(d)—Won Dave Pinkney Trophy (leading goalie).
(e)—Drafted from Ottawa 67's by Montreal Canadiens in first round of 1972 amateur draft.
(f)—Selected by Ottawa Nationals in World Hockey Association player selection draft, February, 1972.
(g)—Won Harry "Hap" Holmes Memorial Trophy (leading goalie).
(h)—Shared Vezina Memorial Trophy with Ken Dryden.
(i)—March, 1981—Traded by Montreal Canadiens to Toronto Maple Leafs for Robert Picard and future eighth-round draft pick.
(j)—Co-winner of Vezina Trophy (Top NHL Goaltenders) with teammates Richard Sevigny and Denis Herron.
(k)—January, 1983—Traded by Toronto Maple Leafs to Philadelphia Flyers for Rick St. Croix.
(l)—January, 1984—Sold by Philadelphia Flyers to St. Louis Blues.

GARY LASKOSKI

Goaltender ... 6'1" ... 175 lbs. ... Born, Ottawa, Ont., June 6, 1959 ... Shoots left.

Year	Team	League	Games	Mins.	Goals	SO.	Avg.	A.	Pen.
1978-79—St. Lawrence University		ECAC	21	1130	93	...	4.94	..	....
1979-80—St. Lawrence University		ECAC	17	904	72	...	4.78	..	....
1980-81—St. Lawrence University		ECAC	21	1196	64	...	3.21	..	....
1981-82—St. Lawrence University (c)		ECAC	15	737	50	...	4.07	..	....
1982-83—Los Angeles Kings		NHL	46	2277	173	0	4.56	1	6
1983-84—New Haven Nighthawks		AHL	22	1179	97	0	4.94	1	2
1983-84—Los Angeles Kings (d)		NHL	13	665	55	0	4.96	0	0
NHL TOTALS			59	2942	228	0	4.65	1	6

(c)—September, 1982—Signed by Los Angeles Kings as a free agent.
(d)—August, 1984—Released by Los Angeles Kings.

JEFF LASTIWKA

Goaltender ... 6' ... 175 lbs. ... Born, Edmonton, Alta., September 12, 1960 ... Shoots left.

Year	Team	League	Games	Mins.	Goals	SO.	Avg.	A.	Pen.
1981-82—University of Calgary		CWUAA	14	830	45	0	3.25	..	..
1982-83—Colorado Flames (c)		CHL	5	284	22	0	4.65	1	2
1982-83—Peoria Prancers		IHL	27	1420	119	0	5.03	0	2
1983-84—Colorado Flames		CHL	1	34	3	0	5.29	0	0
1983-84—Peoria Prancers		IHL	39	2110	154	1	4.38	1	4

(c)—August, 1982—Signed by Calgary Flames as a free agent.

REJEAN LEMELIN

Goaltender ... 5'11" ... 160 lbs. ... Born, Sherbrooke, Que., November 19, 1954 ... Shoots left ... (February 8, 1981)—Broken thumb on right hand in pre-game warmups at Edmonton ... (January, 1984)—Back injury.

Year	Team	League	Games	Mins.	Goals	SO.	Avg.	A.	Pen.
1972-73—Sherbrooke Beavers		QJHL	27	1117	146	0	5.21	2	4
1973-74—Sherbrooke Beavers (c)		QJHL	35	.....	158	0	4.60	1	2
1974-75—Philadelphia Firebirds		NAHL	43	2277	131	3	3.45	3	16
1975-76—Richmond Robins		AHL	7	402	30	0	4.48	0	0
1975-76—Philadelphia Firebirds		NAHL	29	1601	97	1	3.63	1	6
1976-77—Philadelphia Firebirds		NAHL	51	2763	170	1	3.61	2	0
1976-77—Springfield Indians		AHL	3	180	10	0	3.33	0	0
1977-78—Philadelphia Firebirds (a)		AHL	60	3585	177	4	2.96	1	22
1978-79—Atlanta Flames (d)		NHL	18	994	55	0	3.32	0	4
1978-79—Philadelphia Firebirds		AHL	13	780	36	0	2.77	1	12
1979-80—Birmingham Bulls		CHL	38	2188	137	0	3.76	2	14
1979-80—Atlanta Flames		NHL	3	150	15	0	6.00	0	0
1980-81—Birmingham Bulls		CHL	13	757	56	0	4.44	0	4
1980-81—Calgary Flames		NHL	29	1629	88	2	3.24	1	2
1981-82—Calgary Flames		NHL	34	1866	135	0	4.34	1	0
1982-83—Calgary Flames		NHL	39	2211	133	0	3.61	5	7
1983-84—Calgary Flames		NHL	51	2568	150	0	3.50	3	6
NHL TOTALS			174	9418	576	2	3.67	10	19

(c)—Drafted from Sherbrooke Beavers by Philadelphia Flyers in sixth round of 1974 amateur draft.
(d)—August, 1978—Signed by Atlanta Flames as free agent.

MARIO LESSARD

Goaltender ... 5'9" ... 190 lbs. ... Born, East Broughton, Que., June 25, 1954 ... Shoots left ... (February, 1983)—Groin injury ... (October 26, 1978)—First NHL game was a 6-0 shutout vs. Buffalo Sabres.

Year	Team	League	Games	Mins.	Goals	SO.	Avg.	A.	Pen.
1971-72—Sherbrooke Beavers		QJHL	17	.....	72	2	4.23	..	....
1972-73—Sherbrooke Beavers		QJHL	36	1331	161	*1	4.43	2	2
1973-74—Sherbrooke Beavers (c)		QJHL	36	.....	180	0	5.05	3	14
1974-75—Saginaw Gears (d)		IHL	59	3189	171	*4	3.22	0	10
1975-76—Saginaw Gears (e)		IHL	62	3323	187	3	3.38	2	4
1976-77—Saginaw Gears (a-f-g)		IHL	44	2489	144	0	3.47	2	4
1976-77—Fort Worth Texans		CHL	4	192	11	0	3.44	0	0
1977-78—Springfield Indians (b-h)		AHL	57	3295	204	1	3.71	3	6
1978-79—Los Angeles Kings		NHL	49	2860	148	4	3.10	2	8
1979-80—Los Angeles Kings		NHL	50	2836	185	0	3.91	0	6
1980-81—Los Angeles Kings (b)		NHL	64	3746	203	2	3.25	1	8
1981-82—Los Angeles Kings		NHL	52	2933	213	2	4.36	2	6
1982-83—Los Angeles Kings (i)		NHL	19	888	68	1	4.59	1	2
1982-83—Birmingham South Stars		CHL	8	405	28	0	4.15	1	0

Year	Team	League	Games	Mins.	Goals	SO.	Avg.	A.	Pen.
1983-84—Los Angeles Kings		NHL	6	266	26	0	5.86	0	0
1983-84—New Haven Nighthawks (j)		AHL	5	281	27	0	5.77	0	0
NHL TOTALS			240	13529	843	9	3.74	6	30

    (c)—Drafted from Sherbrooke Beavers by Los Angeles Kings in ninth round of 1974 amateur draft.
    (d)—Led in shutouts (2) during playoffs.
    (e)—Leading goalie (2.58 average) during playoffs.
    (f)—Won James Norris Memorial Trophy (leading goalie in IHL).
    (g)—Leading goalie (2.95 average and 1 shutout) during playoffs.
    (h)—Leading goalie (2.51 average and 1 shutout) during playoffs.
    (i)—February, 1983—Loaned by Los Angeles Kings to Minnesota North Stars' CHL affiliate at Birmingham as part of trade in which Los Angeles acquired Markus Mattsson.
    (j)—August, 1984—Released by Los Angeles Kings.

PER-ERIC (PELLE) LINDBERGH

Goaltender . . . 5'9" . . . 157 lbs. . . . Born, Stockholm, Sweden, May 24, 1959 . . . Shoots left . . . Has played for two Swedish National Teams ('79 & '80) and the 1980 Swedish Olympic Team that won the Bronze Medal (3rd place) in 1980 Olympics . . . (January, 1983)—Wrist injury in game vs. touring USSR team.

Year	Team	League	Games	Mins.	Goals	SO.	Avg.	A.	Pen.
1978-79—Solna AIK (c)		Sweden	6	..	38	0	6.33	..	..
1979-80—Solna AIK		Sweden	32	..	..	1	3.41	..	..
1979-80—Swedish Olympic Team		Olympics	5	300	18	0	3.60	0	0
1980-81—Maine Mariners (a-d-e-f)		AHL	51	3035	165	1	3.26	5	2
1981-82—Maine Mariners		AHL	25	1505	83	0	3.31	0	2
1981-82—Philadelphia Flyers		NHL	8	480	35	0	4.38	0	0
1982-83—Philadelphia Flyers		NHL	40	2334	116	3	2.98	4	0
1983-84—Springfield Indians		AHL	4	240	12	0	3.00	0	0
1983-84—Philadelphia Flyers		NHL	36	1999	135	1	4.05	1	6
NHL TOTALS			84	4813	286	4	3.57	5	6

    (c)—August, 1979—Drafted by Philadelphia Flyers in 1979 NHL entry draft. Third Flyers pick, 35th overall, second round.
    (d)—Winner of Les Cunningham Plaque (AHL MVP).
    (e)—Co-Winner of Harry (HAP) Holmes Memorial Trophy (Top AHL Goaltenders) with teammate Robbie Moore.
    (f)—Winner of Dudley (Red) Garrett Memorial Trophy (Top AHL Trophy).

MICHAEL LIUT

Goaltender . . . 6'2" . . . 195 lbs. . . . Born, Weston, Ont., January 7, 1956 . . . Shoots left . . . Attended Bowling Green State University . . . Missed part of 1977-78 season with torn cartilage in left knee . . . (February 10, 1981)—MVP of 1981 NHL All-Star game . . . (January 10, 1981)—Groin injury vs. Los Angeles . . . (March, 1984)—Strained knee ligaments.

Year	Team	League	Games	Mins.	Goals	SO.	Avg.	A.	Pen.
1973-74—Bowling Green State U.		CCHA	24	1272	88	0	4.00	0	4
1974-75—Bowling Green State U. (a)		CCHA	20	1174	78	0	3.99	0	10
1975-76—Bowling Green St. U.(b-c-d)		CCHA	21	1171	50	2	2.56	0	0
1976-77—Bowling Green St. U. (a-e-f)		CCHA	24	1346	61	2	2.72	2	4
1977-78—Cincinnati Stingers		WHA	27	1215	86	0	4.25	1	0
1978-79—Cincinnati Stingers (g)		WHA	54	3181	184	*3	3.47	2	9
1979-80—St. Louis Blues		NHL	64	3661	194	2	3.18	0	2
1980-81—St. Louis Blues (a)		NHL	61	3570	199	1	3.34	0	0
1981-82—St. Louis Blues		NHL	64	3691	250	2	4.06	2	2
1982-83—St. Louis Blues		NHL	68	3794	235	1	3.72	0	2
1983-84—St. Louis Blues		NHL	58	3425	197	3	3.45	4	0
WHA TOTALS			81	4396	270	3	3.69	3	9
NHL TOTALS			315	18141	1075	9	3.56	6	6

    (c)—Drafted from Bowling Green State University by St. Louis Blues in fourth round of 1976 amateur draft.
    (d)—Selected by New England Whalers in World Hockey Association amateur player draft, May, 1976.
    (e)—WHA rights traded to Cincinnati Stingers by New England Whalers with second-round 1979 draft choice for Greg Carroll and Bryan Maxwell, May, 1977.
    (f)—Named CCHA Player-of-the-Year.
    (g)—June, 1979—Selected by St. Louis Blues in reclaim draft.

RONALD ALBERT LOW

Goaltender . . . 6'1" . . . 205 lbs. . . . Born, Birtle, Man., June 21, 1950 . . . Shoots left . . . (October, 1980)—Sprained knee ligaments . . . (December 17, 1980)—Broken thumb on left hand.

Year	Team	League	Games	Mins.	Goals	SO.	Avg.	A.	Pen.
1967-68—Winnipeg Jets		WCJHL	16	.....	92	0	5.75	0	7
1968-69—				.....		...	.....	..	....
1969-70—Dauphin Kings (c)		MJHL	33	.....	119	...	3.57	..	....
1970-71—Jacksonville Rockets (d)		EHL	49	.....	293	1	5.98	..	....
1970-71—Tulsa Oilers		CHL	4	192	11	0	5.11	0	0
1971-72—Richmond Robins		AHL	1	60	2	0	2.00	0	0
1971-72—Tulsa Oilers (e)		CHL	43	2428	135	1	3.33	1	4
1972-73—Toronto Maple Leafs (f)		NHL	42	2343	152	1	3.89	0	4
1973-74—Tulsa Oilers (b-g)		CHL	56	3213	169	1	3.16	2	7
1974-75—Washington Capitals		NHL	48	2588	235	1	5.45	0	4
1975-76—Washington Capitals		NHL	43	2289	208	0	5.45	0	2
1976-77—Washington Capitals (h)		NHL	54	2918	188	0	3.87	0	4
1977-78—Detroit Red Wings		NHL	32	1816	102	1	3.37	1	0
1978-79—Kansas City Red Wings (a-i)		CHL	*63	*3795	*244	0	3.86	3	2
1979-80—Syracuse Firebirds		AHL	15	905	70	..	4.64	1	2
1979-80—Quebec Nordiques (j)		NHL	15	828	51	0	3.70	2	0
1979-80—Edmonton Oilers		NHL	11	650	37	0	3.42	1	0
1980-81—Wichita Wind		CHL	2	120	10	0	5.00	0	0
1980-81—Edmonton Oilers		NHL	24	1260	93	0	4.43	3	0
1981-82—Edmonton Oilers		NHL	29	1554	100	0	3.86	0	2
1982-83—Moncton Alpines		AHL	6	365	22	1	3.62	0	0
1982-83—Edmonton Oilers (k)		NHL	3	104	10	0	5.78	0	0
1982-83—New Jersey Devils		NHL	11	608	41	0	4.05	1	4
1983-84—New Jersey Devils		NHL	44	2218	161	0	4.36	0	4
NHL TOTALS			356	19176	1378	3	4.31	8	24

(c)—Drafted from Dauphin Kings by Toronto Maple Leafs in eighth round of 1970 amateur draft.
(d)—EHL Southern Division Rookie-of-the-Year.
(e)—Leading goalie (1.89 average and 1 shutout) during playoffs.
(f)—Shared two shutouts with Jacques Plante.
(g)—Drafted from Toronto Maple Leafs by Washington Capitals in expansion draft, June, 1974.
(h)—Signed by Detroit Red Wings as free agent, September, 1977. (Washington received Walt McKechnie as compensation.)
(i)—June, 1979—Drafted by Quebec Nordiques in expansion draft.
(j)—March, 1980—Traded by Quebec Nordiques to Edmonton Oilers for Ron Chipperfield.
(k)—February, 1983—Traded by Edmonton Oilers to New Jersey Devils for Lindsay Middlebrook and Paul Miller.

TODD LUMBARD
Goaltender . . . 6' . . . 180 lbs. . . . Born, Brandon, Man., August 31, 1963 . . . Shoots left.

Year	Team	League	Games	Mins.	Goals	SO.	Avg.	A.	Pen.
1980-81—Brandon Wheat Kings (c)		WHL	28	1408	106	1	4.52	2	19
1981-82—Brandon Wheat Kings		WHL	54	2906	*274	0	5.66	0	0
1982-83—Regina Pats (b)		WHL	56	3194	194	2	3.64	7	31
1983-84—Indianapolis Checkers		CHL	25	1491	106	1	4.27	0	6
1983-84—Toledo Goaldiggers		IHL	11	664	38	0	3.43	1	2
1983-84—Peoria Prancers		IHL	1	60	7	0	7.00	0	0

(c)—June, 1981—Drafted as underage junior by New York Islanders in NHL draft. Fifth Islanders pick, 84th overall, fourth round.

SHAWN MacKENZIE
Goaltender . . . 5'10" . . . 175 lbs. . . . Born, Bedford, N.S., August 22, 1962 . . . Shoots right.

Year	Team	League	Games	Mins.	Goals	SO.	Avg.	A.	Pen.
1979-80—Windsor Spitfires (c)		OMJHL	41	1964	158	0	4.83	1	8
1980-81—Windsor Spitfires		OHL	*60	*3450	*282	1	4.78	0	8
1981-82—Windsor Spitfires		OHL	17	1001	77	0	4.62	0	6
1981-82—Oshawa Generals		OHL	32	1934	124	1	3.85	0	12
1982-83—New Jersey Devils		NHL	6	130	15	0	6.92	0	0
1982-83—Wichita Wind		CHL	36	2083	148	1	4.26	1	14
1983-84—Maine Mariners		AHL	34	1948	113	0	3.48	0	6
NHL TOTALS			6	130	15	0	6.92	0	0

(c)—June, 1980—Drafted as underage junior by Colorado Rockies in 1980 NHL entry draft. Rockies eighth pick, 169th overall, ninth round.

CLINT MALARCHUK
Goaltender . . . 5'10" . . . 172 lbs. . . . Born, Grande, Alta., May 1, 1961 . . . Shoots left.

Year	Team	League	Games	Mins.	Goals	SO.	Avg.	A.	Pen.
1978-79—Portland Winter Hawks		WHL	2	120	4	0	2.00	..	....
1979-80—Portland Winter Hawks (c)		WHL	37	1948	147	0	4.53	2	10

Year	Team	League	Games	Mins.	Goals	SO.	Avg.	A.	Pen.
1980-81—Portland Winter Hawks		WHL	38	2235	142	3	3.81	7	22
1981-82—Quebec Nordiques		NHL	2	120	14	0	7.00	0	0
1981-82—Fredericton Express		AHL	51	2962	*253	0	5.12	4	22
1982-83—Quebec Nordiques		NHL	15	900	71	0	4.73	0	0
1982-83—Fredericton Express		AHL	25	1506	78	1	*3.11	1	2
1983-84—Fredericton Express		AHL	11	663	40	0	3.62	1	5
1983-84—Quebec Nordiques		NHL	23	1215	80	0	3.95	1	9
NHL TOTALS			40	2235	165	0	4.43	1	9

(c)—October, 1980—Signed by Quebec Nordiques as a free agent.

BOB MASON

Goaltender . . . 6'1" . . . 180 lbs. . . . Born, International Falls, Minn., April 22, 1961 . . . Shoots right . . . Member of 1984 U.S. Olympic Team.

Year	Team	League	Games	Mins.	Goals	SO.	Avg.	A.	Pen.
1981-82—Univ. of Minnesota/Duluth		WCHA	26	1521	115	..	4.54	..	..
1982-83—Univ. of Minnesota/Duluth		WCHA	43	2594	151	..	3.49	1	4
1983-84—U.S. National Team		Int'l	33	1895	89	..	2.82	..	..
1983-84—U.S. Olympic Team		Int'l	3	160	10	0	3.75	0	0
1983-84—Washington Capitals (c)		NHL	2	120	3	0	1.50	0	0
1983-84—Hershey Bears		AHL	5	282	26	0	5.53	0	0
NHL TOTALS			2	120	3	0	1.50	0	0

(c)—February, 1984—Signed by Washington Capitals as a free agent.

MARKUS MATTSSON

Goaltender . . . 6' . . . 180 lbs. . . . Born, Suoneiemi, Finland, July 30, 1957 . . . Shoots left . . . Missed part of the 1979-80 season with an ankle injury.

Year	Team	League	Games	Mins.	Goals	SO.	Avg.	A.	Pen.
1976-77—Ilves Tampere (c)		Finland	....	.....	....	...	.....	..	....
1977-78—Tulsa Oilers		CHL	2	92	6	0	3.91	0	0
1977-78—Quebec Nordiques (d)		WHA	6	266	30	0	6.77	0	2
1977-78—Winnipeg Jets		WHA	10	511	30	0	3.52	0	0
1978-79—Winnipeg Jets (e)		WHA	52	2990	181	0	3.63	1	4
1979-80—Tulsa Oilers		CHL	20	1196	56	2	2.81	0	4
1979-80—Winnipeg Jets		NHL	21	1200	65	2	3.25	0	2
1980-81—Tulsa Oilers		CHL	5	298	10	1	2.01	0	0
1980-81—Winnipeg Jets		NHL	31	1717	128	1	4.50	1	2
1981-82—Tulsa Oilers (f)		CHL	50	2963	195	0	3.95	0	10
1982-83—Birmingham South Stars		CHL	28	1614	89	1	3.31	0	0
1982-83—Minnesota North Stars (g)		NHL	2	100	6	1	3.59	0	0
1982-83—Los Angeles Kings		NHL	19	899	65	1	4.34	2	2
1983-84—Los Angeles Kings		NHL	21	1211	87	0	4.31	2	10
1983-84—New Haven Nighthawks (h)		AHL	31	1701	110	0	3.88	1	0
WHA TOTALS			68	3767	241	0	3.84	1	6
NHL TOTALS			94	5127	351	5	4.11	5	16

(c)—Drafted from Finland by New York Islanders in fifth round of 1977 amateur draft.
(d)—Traded to Quebec Nordiques by Winnipeg Jets for fourth-round draft choice and cash, January, 1978. Traded back to Winnipeg by Quebec (negating draft choice), February, 1978.
(e)—June, 1979—Selected by New York Islanders in reclaim draft. Made a priority selection by Winnipeg Jets for expansion draft.
(f)—August, 1982—Signed by Minnesota North Stars as a free agent.
(g)—February, 1983—Traded by Minnesota North Stars to Los Angeles Kings for third-round draft choice in 1985 and the loan of Mario Lessard to Minnesota's CHL affiliate at Birmingham.
(h)—August, 1984—Released by Los Angeles Kings.

DARRELL MAY

Goaltender . . . 6' . . . 190 lbs. . . . Born, Montreal, Que., March 6, 1962 . . . Shoots left.

Year	Team	League	Games	Mins.	Goals	SO.	Avg.	A.	Pen.
1979-80—Portland Winter Hawks		WHL	21	1113	64	0	3.45	0	2
1979-80—Portland Winter Hawks (c)		WHL	43	2416	143	1	3.55	2	16
1980-81—Portland Winter Hawks		WHL	36	2128	122	3	3.44	3	6
1981-82—Portland Winter Hawks		WHL	52	3097	226	0	4.38	0	0
1982-83—Fort Wayne Komets		IHL	46	2584	177	0	4.11	2	16
1983-84—Erie Golden Blades (b-d)		ACHL	43	2404	163	1	4.07	6	28

(c)—June, 1980—Drafted by Vancouver Canucks as underage junior in 1980 NHL entry draft. Fourth Canucks pick, 91st overall, fifth round.
(d)—Led ACHL playoffs with 2.08 average and one shutout.

KIRK McLEAN

Goaltender . . . 6' . . . 177 lbs. . . . Born, Willowdale, Ont., June 26, 1966 . . . Shoots left.

Year	Team	League	Games	Mins.	Goals	SO.	Avg.	A.	Pen.
1983-84	Oshawa Generals (c)	OHL	17	940	67	0	4.28	0	11

(c)—June, 1984—Drafted as underage junior by New Jersey Devils in NHL entry draft. Sixth Devils pick, 10th overall, sixth round.

BOB McNAMARA

Goaltender . . . 5'10" . . . 155 lbs. . . . Born, Toronto, Ont., August 6, 1961 . . . Shoots left.

Year	Team	League	Games	Mins.	Goals	SO.	Avg.	A.	Pen.
1979-80	University of Notre Dame	WCHA	22	1147	98	0	5.13	..	..
1980-81	University of Notre Dame	WCHA	24	1405	110	0	4.70	..	..
1981-82	University of Notre Dame	CCHA	13	698	48	1	4.13	1	0
1982-83	University of Notre Dame	CCHA	32	1842	164	0	5.34	2	6
1983-84	Rochester Americans	AHL	5	171	15	0	5.26	0	0
1983-84	Milwaukee Admirals	IHL	5	230	14	0	3.65	0	0
1983-84	Peoria Prancers	IHL	2	43	6	0	8.37	0	2

ROLAND MELANSON

Goaltender . . . 5'10" . . . 178 lbs. . . . Born, Moncton, N.B., June 28, 1960 . . . Shoots left . . . Led OMJHL in games played by goaltenders in 1978-79 and co-leader in 1979-80 (with Bruce Dowie).

Year	Team	League	Games	Mins.	Goals	SO.	Avg.	A.	Pen.
1977-78	Windsor Spitfires	OMJHL	44	2592	195	1	4.51	2	12
1978-79	Windsor Spitfires (b-c)	OMJHL	*62	*3461	254	1	4.40	7	16
1979-80	Windsor Spitfires	OMJHL	22	1099	90	0	4.91	0	8
1979-80	Oshawa Generals	OMJHL	38	2240	136	*3	3.64	2	14
1980-81	Indianapolis Checkers (a-d)	CHL	*52	*3056	131	2	*2.57	1	16
1980-81	New York Islanders	NHL	11	620	32	0	3.10	0	4
1981-82	New York Islanders	NHL	36	2115	114	0	3.23	0	14
1982-83	New York Islanders (e)	NHL	44	2460	109	1	2.66	3	22
1983-84	New York Islanders	NHL	37	2019	110	0	3.27	2	10
	NHL TOTALS		128	7214	365	1	3.04	5	50

(c)—August, 1979—Drafted by New York Islanders as underage junior in 1979 NHL entry draft. Fourth Islanders pick, 59th overall, third round.

(d)—Winner of Ken McKenzie Trophy (CHL Top Rookie).

(e)—Shared William Jennings Trophy with Billy Smith for NHL's best team goaltending average

GILLES MELOCHE

Goaltender . . . 5'9" . . . 185 lbs. . . . Born, Montreal, Que., July 12, 1950 . . . Shoots left . . . Brother of Denis Meloche . . . Missed part of 1973-74 season with severed tendons in hand requiring surgery . . . Set NHL record for most assists by goalie in season with 6 in 1974-75 . . . (Broken in 1980-81 by Mike Palmateer with eight).

Year	Team	League	Games	Mins.	Goals	SO.	Avg.	A.	Pen.
1969-70	Verdun Maple Leafs (c)	QJHL	45	.....	221	1	4.95	..	....
1970-71	Flint Generals	IHL	33	1866	104	2	3.34	2	0
1970-71	Chicago Black Hawks (d)	NHL	2	120	6	0	3.00	0	0
1971-72	Calif. Golden Seals (e)	NHL	56	3121	173	4	3.32	2	6
1972-73	California Golden Seals	NHL	59	3473	235	1	4.06	2	4
1973-74	California Golden Seals	NHL	47	2800	198	1	4.24	1	2
1974-75	California Golden Seals	NHL	47	2771	186	1	4.03	*6	14
1975-76	California Golden Seals	NHL	41	2440	140	1	3.44	1	0
1976-77	Cleveland Barons	NHL	51	2961	171	2	3.47	3	18
1977-78	Cleveland Barons	NHL	54	3100	195	1	3.77	0	4
1978-79	Minnesota North Stars	NHL	53	3118	173	2	3.33	1	25
1979-80	Minnesota North Stars	NHL	54	3141	160	1	3.06	1	4
1980-81	Minnesota North Stars	NHL	38	2215	120	2	3.25	0	2
1981-82	Minnesota North Stars	NHL	51	3026	175	1	3.47	1	6
1982-83	Minnesota North Stars	NHL	47	2689	160	1	3.57	1	0
1983-84	Minnesota North Stars	NHL	52	2883	201	2	4.18	1	2
	NHL TOTALS		652	37867	2293	20	3.63	20	87

(c)—Drafted from Verdun Maple Leafs by Chicago Black Hawks in fifth round of 1970 amateur draft.

(d)—Traded to California Golden Seals by Chicago Black Hawks with Paul Shmyr for Gerry Desjardins, October, 1971.

(e)—Named rookie-of-the-year in NHL's West Division by THE SPORTING NEWS.

DAVE MESZAROS

Goaltender . . . 5'8" . . . 170 lbs. . . . Born, Toronto, Ont., February 16, 1964 . . . Shoots left.

Year	Team	League	Games	Mins.	Goals	SO.	Avg.	A.	Pen.
1981-82—Toronto Marlboros (c)		OHL	37	2085	139	0	4.00	0	5
1982-83—Toronto Marlboros		OHL	40	2396	179	0	4.48	1	13
1983-84—Toronto Marlboros		OHL	53	3106	232	1	4.48	4	21

(c)—June, 1982—Drafted as underage junior by Calgary Flames in NHL entry draft. Fourth Flames pick, 65th overall, fourth round.

CORRADO MICALEF

Goaltender . . . 5'8" . . . 172 lbs. . . . Born, Montreal, Que., April 20, 1961 . . . Shoots right.

Year	Team	League	Games	Mins.	Goals	SO.	Avg.	A.	Pen.
1979-80—Sherbrooke Beavers (b-c)		QJHL	64	3598	252	1	*4.20	1	17
1980-81—Sherbrooke Beavers (a-d)		QJHL	64	3764	280	*2	4.46	8	26
1981-82—Adirondack Red Wings		AHL	1	10	0	0	0.00	1	0
1981-82—Kalamazoo Wings		IHL	20	1147	91	1	4.76	0	4
1981-82—Detroit Red Wings		NHL	18	809	63	0	4.67	0	0
1982-83—Adirondack Red Wings		AHL	11	660	37	0	3.36	0	2
1982-83—Detroit Red Wings		NHL	34	1756	106	2	3.62	1	18
1983-84—Adirondack Red Wings		AHL	29	1769	132	0	4.48	3	10
1983-84—Detroit Red Wings		NHL	14	808	52	0	3.86	1	2
NHL TOTALS			66	3373	221	2	3.93	2	20

(c)—Won Jacques Plante Trophy (best goals-against average in QJHL).

(d)—June, 1981—Drafted by Detroit Red Wings in NHL entry draft. Second Red Wings pick, 44th overall, third round.

LINDSAY MIDDLEBROOK

Goaltender . . . 5'7" . . . 170 lbs. . . . Born, Collingwood, Ont., September 7, 1955 . . . Shoots right . . . Attended St. Louis University.

Year	Team	League	Games	Mins.	Goals	SO.	Avg.	A.	Pen.
1973-74—St. Louis University		CCHA	2	41	6	0	8.82	0	2
1974-75—St. Louis University (a)		CCHA	24	1459	71	1	2.98	0	2
1975-76—St. Louis University		CCHA	30	1767	88	0	2.99	2	2
1976-77—St. Louis University		CCHA	18	1058	54	1	3.07	0	2
1977-78—New Haven Nighthawks		AHL	17	968	71	0	4.40	3	2
1977-78—Toledo Goaldiggers		IHL	16	949	45	*2	*2.85	1	0
1978-79—New Haven Nighthawks (a-c)		AHL	*54	*3221	*173	1	3.22	1	4
1979-80—Tulsa Oilers		CHL	37	2073	102	0	2.95	0	0
1979-80—Winnipeg Jets		NHL	10	580	40	0	4.14	0	0
1980-81—Tulsa Oilers (b)		CHL	36	2115	128	0	3.63	0	6
1980-81—Winnipeg Jets (d)		NHL	14	653	65	0	5.97	0	0
1981-82—Nashville South Stars		CHL	31	1868	93	*3	2.99	2	6
1981-82—Minnesota North Stars (e)		NHL	3	140	7	0	3.00	0	0
1982-83—New Jersey Devils		NHL	9	412	37	0	5.39	1	2
1982-83—Wichita Wind (f)		CHL	13	779	46	0	3.54	0	0
1982-83—Edmonton Oilers		NHL	1	60	3	0	3.00	0	0
1982-83—Moncton Alpines		AHL	11	669	42	0	3.77	0	2
1983-84—Montana Magic		CHL	36	2104	162	0	4.62	0	6
NHL TOTALS			37	1845	152	0	4.94	1	2

(c)—June, 1979—Drafted by Winnipeg Jets in expansion draft.

(d)—June, 1981—Signed by Minnesota North Stars as a free agent.

(e)—July, 1982—Signed by New Jersey Devils as a free agent.

(f)—February, 1983—Traded by New Jersey Devils with Paul Miller to Edmonton Oilers for Ron Low.

GREG MILLEN

Goaltender . . . 5'9" . . . 160 lbs. . . . Born, Toronto, Ont., June 25, 1957 . . . Shoots right . . . (October, 1979)—Pulled hamstring muscle, out 18 games.

Year	Team	League	Games	Mins.	Goals	SO.	Avg.	A.	Pen.
1974-75—Peterborough TPT's		OMJHL	27	1584	90	2	*3.41	..	....
1975-76—Peterborough Petes		OMJHL	58	3282	233	0	4.26	0	6
1976-77—Peterborough Petes (c)		OMJHL	59	3457	244	0	4.23	2	14
1977-78—S. Ste. Marie Greyhounds		OMJHL	25	1469	105	1	4.29	2	0
1977-78—Kalamazoo Wings		IHL	3	180	14	0	4.67	0	0
1978-79—Pittsburgh Penguins		NHL	28	1532	86	2	3.37	0	0
1979-80—Pittsburgh Penguins		NHL	44	2586	157	2	3.64	3	14
1980-81—Pittsburgh Penguins (d)		NHL	63	3721	258	0	4.16	2	6

Year	Team	League	Games	Mins.	Goals	SO.	Avg.	A.	Pen.
1981-82—Hartford Whalers		NHL	55	3201	229	0	4.29	5	2
1982-83—Hartford Whalers		NHL	60	3520	282	1	4.81	2	8
1983-84—Hartford Whalers		NHL	*60	*3583	*221	2	3.70	3	10
NHL TOTALS			310	18143	1233	7	4.08	15	40

(c)—June, 1977—Drafted by Pittsburgh Penguins in 1977 NHL amateur draft. Fourth Penguins pick, 102nd overall, sixth round.

(d)—June, 1981—Signed by Hartford Whalers as a free agent. Pat Boutette and Kevin McLelland sent to Pittsburgh as compensation by NHL Arbitrator, Judge Joseph Kane, in July.

EDDIE MIO

Goaltender . . . 5'10" . . . 180 lbs. . . . Born, Windsor, Ont., January 31, 1954 . . . Shoots left . . . Attended Colorado College . . . (December 24, 1979)—Fractured cheekbone in team practice . . . (January, 1981)—Bruised jaw in team practice . . . (March, 1981)—Broken finger . . . (February, 1983)—Hip muscle injury . . . (November, 1983)—Bruised ribs . . . (January 7, 1984)—Pulled hamstring in game vs. Philadelphia and missed 10 weeks.

Year	Team	League	Games	Mins.	Goals	SO.	Avg.	A.	Pen.
1971-72—Windsor Spitfires		SOJHL	....	.....	....	...	.....	..	..
1972-73—Colorado College		WCHA	22	.....	119	0	5.41	2	2
1973-74—Colorado College (c-d)		WCHA	12	.....	57	0	4.91	..	....
1974-75—Colorado College (b-e)		WCHA	21	.....	83	0	3.95	1	2
1975-76—Colorado College (a-e)		WCHA	34	.....	144	0	4.24	..	....
1976-77—Tidewater Sharks		SHL	19	1123	66	1	3.53	0	4
1976-77—Erie Blades		NAHL	17	771	42	0	3.27	0	2
1977-78—Hampton Gulls (f)		AHL	19	949	53	2	3.35	1	0
1977-78—Indianapolis Racers (g)		WHA	17	900	64	0	4.27	0	0
1978-79—Dallas Black Hawks		CHL	7	424	25	0	3.54	0	0
1978-79—Indianapolis Racers (h)		WHA	5	242	13	1	3.22	0	0
1978-79—Edmonton Oilers (i)		WHA	22	1068	71	1	3.99	1	2
1979-80—Edmonton Oilers		NHL	34	1711	120	1	4.21	1	4
1980-81—Edmonton Oilers		NHL	43	2393	155	0	3.89	5	6
1981-82—Wichita Wind (j)		CHL	11	657	46	0	4.20	1	0
1981-82—New York Rangers		NHL	25	1500	89	0	3.56	0	4
1982-83—New York Rangers (k)		NHL	41	2365	136	2	3.45	3	8
1983-84—Detroit Red Wings		NHL	24	1295	95	1	4.40	1	0
1983-84—Adirondack Red Wings		AHL	4	250	11	0	2.64	0	0
WHA TOTALS			44	2210	148	2	4.02	1	2
NHL TOTALS			167	9264	595	4	3.85	10	22

(c)—Drafted from Colorado College by Chicago Black Hawks in sixth round of 1974 amateur draft.

(d)—Selected by Vancouver Blazers in World Hockey Association amateur players' draft, May, 1974.

(e)—Named to first team (Western) All-America.

(f)—Sold to Indianapolis Racers by Birmingham Bulls, February, 1978.

(g)—NHL rights traded to Minnesota North Stars by Chicago Black Hawks for Doug Hicks, March, 1978. (Chicago would receive third-round 1980 draft choice from Minnesota if Mio was signed by North Stars.)

(h)—November, 1978—Sold with Wayne Gretzky and Peter Driscoll by Indianapolis Racers to Edmonton Oilers for cash and future consideration.

(i)—June, 1979—Selected by Minnesota North Stars in reclaim draft. Made a priority selection for expansion draft by Edmonton Oilers.

(j)—December, 1981—Traded by Edmonton Oilers to New York Rangers for Lance Nethery.

(k)—June, 1983—Traded by New York Rangers with Ron Duguay and Ed Johnstone to Detroit Red Wings for Willie Huber, Mark Osborne and Mike Blaisdell.

MIKE MOFFAT

Goaltender . . . 5'10" . . . 165 lbs. . . . Born, Galt, Ont., February 4, 1962 . . . Shoots left.

Year	Team	League	Games	Mins.	Goals	SO.	Avg.	A.	Pen.
1979-80—Kingston Canadians (c)		OJHL	21	968	71	0	4.40	1	19
1980-81—Kingston Canadians (b)		OHL	57	3442	211	0	*3.68	2	70
1981-82—Kingston Canadians		OHL	46	2666	184	1	4.14	1	33
1981-82—Boston Bruins		NHL	2	120	6	0	3.00	0	0
1982-83—Boston Bruins		NHL	13	673	49	0	4.37	0	2
1982-83—Baltimore Skipjacks		AHL	17	937	78	0	4.99	3	8
1983-84—Hershey Bears		AHL	30	1592	124	0	4.67	1	11
1983-84—Boston Bruins		NHL	4	186	15	0	4.84	0	0
NHL TOTALS			19	979	70	0	4.29	0	2

(c)—June, 1980—Drafted by Boston Bruins in NHL entry draft. Seventh Bruins pick, 165th overall, eighth round.

GREG MOFFETT

Goaltender . . . 5'11" . . . 175 lbs. . . . Born, Bath, Maine, April 1, 1959 . . . Shoots left.

Year	Team	League	Games	Mins.	Goals	SO.	Avg.	A.	Pen.
1978-79—Univ. New Hampshire (c)		ECAC	..	1431	89	..	3.73	..	..
1979-80—Univ. New Hampshire		ECAC	26	1394	100	..	4.30	..	..
1980-81—Univ. New Hampshire		ECAC	27	1593	101	1	3.80	..	..
1981-82—Nova Scotia Voyageurs		AHL	35	1938	139	0	4.30	1	4
1981-82—Flint Generals		IHL	1	65	3	0	2.77	0	0
1982-83—Nova Scotia Voyageurs		AHL	43	2423	165	0	4.08	2	10
1983-84—Nova Scotia Voyageurs		AHL	10	493	35	0	4.26	0	0

(c)—August, 1979—Drafted by Montreal Canadiens in 1979 NHL entry draft. Eighth Canadiens' pick, 121st overall, sixth round.

LORNE MOLLEKEN

Goaltender . . . 6'1" . . . 185 lbs. . . . Born, Regina, Sask., June 11, 1956 . . . Shoots left . . . Missed 1978 playoffs with groin pull.

Year	Team	League	Games	Mins.	Goals	SO.	Avg.	A.	Pen.
1972-73—Swift Current Broncos		WCHL	9	233	25	0	6.44	0	2
1973-74—Swift Current Broncos		WCHL	50	2516	181	0	4.32	..	..
1974-75—Lethbridge Broncos		WCHL	19	975	73	0	4.49	0	12
1974-75—Winnipeg Clubs		WCHL	36	1078	154	0	4.45	0	38
1975-76—Winnipeg Clubs		WCHL	46	2270	201	1	5.31	1	18
1976-77—Philadelphia Firebirds		NAHL	32	1543	101	0	3.93	1	2
1977-78—Saginaw Gears (c)		IHL	39	2378	135	1	3.41	1	0
1978-79—Springfield Indians (d)		AHL	44	2416	144	0	3.58	0	6
1979-80—Binghamton Dusters		AHL	31	1748	112	0	3.84	1	14
1980-81—		....		....	....	...			....
1981-82—Indianapolis Checkers		CHL	4	195	12	0	3.69	0	0
1981-82—Toledo Goaldiggers		IHL	50	2893	179	1	3.71	3	24
1982-83—Toledo Goaldiggers (a-e-f)		IHL	48	2891	148	0	*3.07	5	12
1983-84—Toledo Goaldiggers (g-h)		IHL	56	3345	196	1	3.52	4	2

(c)—November, 1977—Acquired by Saginaw Gears on waivers from Fort Wayne Komets.
(d)—July, 1979—Signed by Los Angeles Kings as a free agent.
(e)—Won James Norris Memorial Trophy (Top IHL Goaltender).
(f)—Led IHL playoffs with 2.78 average and one shutout.
(g)—Led IHL playoffs with one shutout.
(h)—July, 1984—Signed by Minnesota North Stars as a free agent.

DONALD ANDREW (ANDY) MOOG

Goaltender . . . 5'8" . . . 165 lbs. . . . Born, Penticton, B.C., February 18, 1960 . . . Shoots left . . . (December, 1983)—While visiting a ward of sick children at a local hospital, he entered a quarantined area, caught a viral infection and lost six pounds.

Year	Team	League	Games	Mins.	Goals	SO.	Avg.	A.	Pen.
1976-77—Kamloops Chiefs		WCHL	1	35	6	0	10.29	..	....
1977-78—Penticton		BCJHL	....	.....	....	...	.....	..	....
1978-79—Billings Bighorns		WHL	26	1306	90	*3	4.13	0	6
1979-80—Billings Bighorns (b-c)		WHL	46	2435	149	1	3.67	1	17
1980-81—Wichita Wind		CHL	29	1602	89	0	3.33	0	4
1980-81—Edmonton Oilers		NHL	7	313	20	0	3.83	1	0
1981-82—Edmonton Oilers		NHL	8	399	32	0	4.81	1	2
1981-82—Wichita Wind (b)		CHL	40	2391	119	1	2.99	5	8
1982-83—Edmonton Oilers		NHL	50	2833	167	1	3.54	4	16
1983-84—Edmonton Oilers		NHL	38	2212	139	1	3.77	1	4
NHL TOTALS			103	5757	358	2	3.73	7	22

(c)—June, 1980—Drafted by Edmonton Oilers in 1980 NHL entry draft. Sixth Oilers pick, 132nd overall, seventh round.

ROBBIE MOORE

Goaltender . . . 5'5" . . . 155 lbs. . . . Born, Sarnia, Ont., May 3, 1954 . . . Shoots left . . . Attended University of Michigan and University of Western Ontario . . . Missed part of 1974-75 season with surgery for torn knee cartilage . . . (January, 1983)—Arthroscopic surgery to knee.

Year	Team	League	Games	Mins.	Goals	SO.	Avg.	A.	Pen.
1972-73—University of Michigan		WCHA	31	....	176	0	5.74	1	16
1973-74—University of Michigan (c)		WCHA	36	....	144	..	4.32	2	10
1974-75—University of Michigan		WCHA	24	....	94	..	3.97	1	4
1975-76—University of Michigan (b)		WCHA	37	....	157	1	4.41	2	12
1976-77—U. of Western Ontario		OUAA	30	....	..	..	3.70	..	..

Year	Team	League	Games	Mins.	Goals	SO.	Avg.	A.	Pen.
1977-78—Did not play									
1978-79—Maine Mariners (d)		AHL	26	1489	84	1	3.38	0	12
1978-79—Philadelphia Flyers		NHL	5	237	7	2	1.77	1	0
1979-80—Maine Mariners (e-f)		AHL	32	1829	107	1	3.51	1	2
1980-81—Maine Mariners (g-h)		AHL	25	1431	92	1	3.86	0	2
1981-82—Nashville South Stars (i)		CHL	39	2204	159	0	4.33	0	12
1982-83—Washington Capitals		NHL	1	20	1	0	3.03	0	0
1982-83—Hershey Bears		AHL	35	1798	115	0	3.84	1	6
1983-84—Milwaukee Admirals		IHL	49	2788	195	0	4.20	4	22
NHL TOTALS			6	257	8	2	1.87	1	0

(c)—Named to first team (West) All-America.
(d)—Shared Harry "Hap" Holmes Memorial Trophy (leading goalie) with Pete Peeters.
(e)—Led AHL Calder Cup Playoffs with one shutout.
(f)—Shared Hap Holmes Memorial Trophy (Top AHL Goaltender) with teammate Rick St. Croix.
(g)—Co-winner of Harry (Hap) Holmes Memorial Trophy (AHL Top Goaltenders) with teammate Pelle Lindbergh.
(h)—July, 1981—Signed by Minnesota North Stars as a free agent.
(i)—August, 1982—Traded by Minnesota North Stars to Washington Capitals for Rollie Boutin and Wes Jarvis.

LOUIS PHILLIPPE (PHIL) MYRE

Goaltender . . . 6'1" . . . 185 lbs. . . . Born, Ste. Anne de Bellevue, Que., November 1, 1948 . . . Shoots left . . . (December 18, 1981)—Jammed foot into goal post while making a save vs. Vancouver, suffering a charley horse . . . (1983-84) Named assistant coach/player at Rochester (AHL).

Year	Team	League	Games	Mins.	Goals	SO.	Avg.	A.	Pen.
1965-66—Shawinigan Bruins (c-d)		QJHL	....	.....	....	...	.....	..	....
1966-67—Nia. Falls Flyers		Jr."A"OHA	34	.....	135	1	4.03	1	0
1967-68—Nia. Falls Flyers (b)		Jr."A"OHA	50	.....	153	*4	3.09	1	39
1968-69—Houston Apollos (b-e)		CHL	53	3150	150	2	2.83	0	0
1969-70—Montreal Voyageurs		AHL	15	900	37	0	2.47	..	....
1969-70—Montreal Canadiens		NHL	10	503	19	0	2.15	0	2
1970-71—Montreal Canadiens		NHL	30	1677	87	1	3.11	0	17
1971-72—Montreal Canadiens (f)		NHL	9	428	32	0	3.63	0	4
1972-73—Atlanta Flames		NHL	46	2736	138	2	3.03	1	5
1973-74—Atlanta Flames		NHL	36	2020	112	0	3.33	0	4
1974-75—Atlanta Flames		NHL	40	2400	114	5	2.85	1	6
1975-76—Atlanta Flames		NHL	37	2129	123	1	3.47	1	0
1976-77—Atlanta Flames		NHL	43	2422	124	3	3.07	2	6
1977-78—Atlanta Flames (g)		NHL	9	523	43	0	4.93	0	2
1977-78—St. Louis Blues		NHL	44	2620	159	1	3.64	2	10
1978-79—St. Louis Blues (h)		NHL	39	2259	163	1	4.33	0	6
1979-80—Philadelphia Flyers		NHL	41	2367	141	0	3.57	0	37
1980-81—Philadelphia Flyers (i)		NHL	16	900	61	0	4.07	0	0
1980-81—Colorado Rockies		NHL	10	580	33	0	3.41	0	0
1981-82—Ft. Worth Texans		CHL	10	615	40	0	3.90	1	0
1981-82—Colorado Rockies		NHL	24	1256	112	0	5.35	2	0
1982-83—Rochester Americans (j)		AHL	43	2541	156	0	3.68	2	14
1982-83—Buffalo Sabres		NHL	5	300	21	0	4.20	0	2
1983-84—Rochester Americans (k)		AHL	33	1803	104	*4	3.46	1	4
NHL TOTALS			439	25220	1482	14	3.53	10	101

(c)—Won leading goalie award.
(d)—Drafted from Shawinigan Bruins by Montreal Canadiens in first round of 1966 amateur draft.
(e)—Won CHL Leading Goalie Award.
(f)—Drafted from Montreal Canadiens by Atlanta Flames in expansion draft, June, 1972.
(g)—Traded to St. Louis Blues by Atlanta Flames with Curt Bennett and Barry Gibbs for Bob MacMillan, Dick Redmond, Yves Belanger and second-round draft choice, December, 1977.
(h)—June, 1979—Traded by St. Louis Blues to Philadelphia Flyers for Rick LaPointe and Blake Dunlop.
(i)—February, 1981—Sold by Philadelphia Flyers to Colorado Rockies.
(j)—September, 1982—Signed by Buffalo Sabres as a free agent.
(k)—January, 1984—Stopped playing to devote full-time to being assistant coach.

BOB O'CONNOR

Goaltender . . . 6' . . . 195 lbs. . . . Born, Billerica, Mass., April 2, 1961 . . . Shoots right . . . (January, 1983)—Eye problems.

Year	Team	League	Games	Mins.	Goals	SO.	Avg.	A.	Pen.
1979-80—Boston College		ECAC	8	423	28	0	3.97	..	....
1980-81—Boston College (c)		ECAC	24	1466	73	0	2.99	..	....
1981-82—Boston College		ECAC	....	970	56	0	3.46	..	....

Year	Team	League	Games	Mins.	Goals	SO.	Avg.	A.	Pen.
1982-83—Sherbrooke Jets		AHL	40	2077	166	0	4.80	1	12
1983-84—Sherbrooke Jets		AHL	5	299	29	0	5.82	0	0
1983-84—Fort Wayne Komets		IHL	1	60	6	0	6.00	0	0

(c)—June, 1981—Drafted by Winnipeg Jets in 1981 NHL entry draft. Sixth Jets pick, 106th overall, sixth round.

PAUL PAGEAU

Goaltender ... 5'9" ... 160 lbs. ... Born, Montreal, Que., October 1, 1959 ... Shoots right ... Member of Canadian 1980 Olympic Hockey Team.

Year	Team	League	Games	Mins.	Goals	SO.	Avg.	A.	Pen.
1976-77—Quebec Remparts		QMJHL	19	955	56	0	3.52	0	2
1977-78—Quebec Remparts		QMJHL	33	1656	138	0	5.00	..	....
1978-79—Quebec Remparts		QMJHL	7	345	28	0	4.87	0	0
1978-79—Shawinigan Cataracts		QMJHL	43	2352	199	0	5.08	1	5
1979-80—Shawinigan Cataracts (a-c)		QMJHL	43	2438	175	*2	4.31	0	0
1979-80—Canadian Olympic Team		(Oly.)	4	237	11	*1	2.78	0	0
1980-81—Los Angeles Kings		NHL	1	60	8	0	8.00	0	0
1980-81—Houston Apollos		CHL	21	1282	64	0	3.00	0	0
1980-81—Oklahoma City Stars		CHL	11	590	32	0	3.25	0	2
1980-81—Saginaw Gears		IHL	1	60	4	0	4.00	0	0
1981-82—Saginaw Gears		IHL	29	1621	140	0	5.18	2	2
1982-83—Saginaw Gears		IHL	11	614	47	0	4.59	0	0
1982-83—New Haven Nighthawks		AHL	37	1939	123	2	3.81	1	2
1983-84—Sherbrooke Jets		AHL	45	2432	*205	0	5.06	1	0
NHL TOTALS			1	60	8	0	8.00	0	0

(c)—May, 1980—Signed by Los Angeles Kings as free agent.

MICHAEL SCOTT PALMATEER

Goaltender ... 5'9" ... 170 lbs. ... Born, Toronto, Ont., January 13, 1954 ... Shoots right ... Missed part of 1979-80 season with an ankle injury ... (February 3, 1981)—Injured ligaments in left ankle ... Set NHL record for assists by a goaltender with eight in 1980-81 with Washington (broken by Grant Fuhr in 1983-84) ... (November 30, 1981)—Arthroscopic surgery to right knee ... (December 21, 1981)—Second arthroscopic surgery to right knee ... (December, 1982)—Bruised shoulder ... (February, 1984)—Knee surgery.

Year	Team	League	Games	Mins.	Goals	SO.	Avg.	A.	Pen.
1971-72—Markham Waxers		OPJHL	....	.....	....	...	.....	..	....
1972-73—Tor. Marlboros (a-c)		Jr."A"OHA	39	1860	87	*5	*2.81	3	16
1973-74—Tor. Marlboros (d)		Jr."A"OHA	42	1895	120	0	3.80	1	15
1974-75—Saginaw Gears		IHL	20	1095	70	2	3.84	0	4
1974-75—Oklahoma City Blazers		CHL	16	841	39	1	2.78	0	6
1975-76—Oklahoma City Blazers		CHL	42	2274	137	1	3.61	3	18
1976-77—Dallas Black Hawks		CHL	3	171	5	0	1.75	0	0
1976-77—Toronto Maple Leafs		NHL	50	2877	154	4	3.21	2	8
1977-78—Toronto Maple Leafs (e)		NHL	63	3760	172	5	2.74	1	12
1978-79—Toronto Maple Leafs		NHL	58	3396	167	4	2.95	5	24
1979-80—Toronto Maple Leafs (f)		NHL	38	2039	125	2	3.68	3	6
1980-81—Washington Capitals		NHL	49	2679	172	2	3.85	8	17
1981-82—Washington Capitals (g)		NHL	11	584	47	0	4.83	1	6
1982-83—St. Catharines Saints		AHL	2	125	4	1	1.92	0	0
1982-83—Toronto Maple Leafs		NHL	53	2965	197	0	3.99	3	17
1983-84—Toronto Maple Leafs		NHL	34	1831	149	0	4.88	2	28
NHL TOTALS			356	20131	1183	17	3.53	25	118

(c)—Won Dave Pinkney Trophy (leading goalie).
(d)—Drafted from Toronto Marlboros by Toronto Maple Leafs in fifth round of 1974 amateur draft.
(e)—Tied for lead in shutouts (2) during playoffs.
(f)—June, 1980—Traded with third round 1980 entry draft pick (Torrie Robertson) by Toronto Maple Leafs to Washington Capitals for Robert Picard, Tim Coulis and a second round draft pick (Bob McGill).
(g)—September, 1982—Traded by Washington Capitals to Toronto Maple Leafs for future considerations (trade completed in cash settlement).

ROBERT JOHN (BOB) PARENT

Goaltender ... 5'9" ... 175 lbs. ... Born, Windsor, Ont., February 19, 1958 ... Shoots right.

Year	Team	League	Games	Mins.	Goals	SO.	Avg.	A.	Pen.
1975-76—Windsor Spitfires		OMJHL	9	377	53	0	8.44	0	2
1976-77—Windsor Spitfires		OMJHL	39	1689	161	0	5.72	0	17
1977-78—Windsor Spitfires		OMJHL	11	604	37	0	3.66	1	6
1977-78—Kitchener Rangers (c)		OMJHL	48	2848	181	1	3.81	5	35

Year	Team	League	Games	Mins.	Goals	SO.	Avg.	A.	Pen.
1978-79—Saginaw Gears		IHL	2	49	10	0	12.24	0	0
1978-79—Port Huron Flags		IHL	24	1177	73	0	3.72	0	23
1979 80—Port Huron Flags		IHL	37	2212	137	0	3.72	1	61
1980-81—Hampton Aces		EHL	46	2536	*200	1	4.73	4	51
1980-81—New Brunswick Hawks		AHL	2	80	5	0	3.75	0	0
1981-82—Cincinnati Tigers		CHL	65	3680	252	2	4.11	3	36
1981-82—Toronto Maple Leafs		NHL	2	120	13	0	6.50	0	0
1982-83—Toronto Maple Leafs		NHL	1	40	2	0	3.00	0	0
1982-83—St. Catharines Saints		AHL	46	2485	180	1	4.35	1	25
1983-84—St. Catharines Saints		AHL	18	900	73	0	4.87	0	8
1983-84—Muskegon Mohawks (d)		IHL	35	2063	185	0	5.38	2	2
NHL TOTALS			3	160	15	0	5.63	0	0

(c)—June, 1978—Drafted by Toronto Maple Leafs in 1978 NHL amateur draft. Third Maple Leafs pick, 65th overall, fourth round.

(d)—January, 1984—Signed by Muskegon Mohawks as a free agent.

DAVID PARRO

Goaltender . . . 5'10" . . . 155 lbs. . . . Born, Saskatoon, Sask., April 30, 1957 . . . Shoots left . . . (February 5, 1981)—Dislocated shoulder.

Year	Team	League	Games	Mins.	Goals	SO.	Avg.	A.	Pen.
1973-74—Saskatoon Olympics		SJHL	29	.....	137	0	4.21	..	....
1974-75—Saskatoon Olympics		SJHL	35	.....	136	0	4.34	..	....
1974-75—Saskatoon Blades		WCHL	1	60	2	0	2.00	0	2
1975-76—Saskatoon Blades		WCHL	36	2100	119	1	3.40	0	6
1976-77—Saskatoon Blades (b-c)		WCHL	69	3956	246	1	3.73	1	10
1977-78—Rochester Americans		AHL	46	2694	164	0	3.65	2	0
1978-79—Grand Rapids Owls		IHL	7	419	25	0	3.58	0	4
1978-79—Rochester Americans (d)		AHL	36	2048	130	*2	3.81	1	10
1979-80—Hershey Bears		AHL	54	3159	172	0	3.27	2	20
1980-81—Hershey Bears		AHL	14	834	60	0	4.32	0	2
1980-81—Washington Capitals		NHL	18	811	49	1	3.63	1	2
1981-82—Washington Capitals		NHL	52	2492	206	1	4.20	1	4
1982-83—Washington Capitals		NHL	6	261	19	0	4.37	0	0
1982-83—Hershey Bears (b)		AHL	47	2714	175	1	3.87	1	10
1983-84—Washington Capitals		NHL	1	1	0	0	0.00	0	0
1983-84—Hershey Bears		AHL	42	2277	190	1	5.01	1	16
NHL TOTALS			77	3565	274	2	4.61	2	6

(c)—Drafted from Saskatoon Blades by Boston Bruins in second round of 1977 amateur draft.

(d)—June, 1979—Drafted by Quebec Nordiques in expansion draft. Traded by Quebec Nordiques to Washington Capitals for Nelson Burton.

PETER PEETERS

Goaltender . . . 6' . . . 180 lbs. . . . Born, Edmonton, Alta., August 1, 1957 . . . Shoots left . . . (November 3, 1983)—Suffered concussion when his head struck crossbar during third period goalmouth pileup in game vs. St. Louis Blues.

Year	Team	League	Games	Mins.	Goals	SO.	Avg.	A.	Pen.
1975-76—Medicine Hat Tigers		WCHL	37	2074	147	0	4.25	2	29
1976-77—Medicine Hat Tigers (c)		WCHL	62	3423	232	1	4.07	2	30
1977-78—Maine Mariners		AHL	17	855	40	1	2.80	2	6
1977-78—Milwaukee Admirals		IHL	32	1698	93	1	3.29	4	14
1978-79—Philadelphia Flyers		NHL	5	280	16	0	3.43	0	6
1978-79—Maine Mariners (b-d)		AHL	35	2067	100	*2	*2.90	1	8
1979-80—Philadelphia Flyers		NHL	40	2373	108	1	2.73	0	28
1980-81—Philadelphia Flyers		NHL	40	2333	115	2	2.96	1	8
1981-82—Philadelphia Flyers (e)		NHL	44	2591	160	0	3.71	1	19
1982-83—Boston Bruins (a-f)		NHL	62	*3611	142	*8	*2.36	2	33
1983-84—Boston Bruins		NHL	50	2868	151	0	3.16	0	36
NHL TOTALS			241	14056	692	11	2.95	4	130

(c)—Drafted from Medicine Hat Tigers by Philadelphia Flyers in eighth round of 1977 amateur draft.

(d)—Shared Harry 'Hap' Holmes Memorial Trophy (Top AHL goaltending) with Robbie Moore.

(e)—June, 1982—Traded by Philadelphia Flyers to Boston Bruins for Brad McCrimmon.

(f)—Won Vezina Trophy (Top Goaltender in NHL).

STEVE PENNEY

Goaltender . . . 6'1" . . . 190 lbs. . . . Born, Ste. Foy, Que., February 2, 1961 . . . Shoots left.

Year	Team	League	Games	Mins.	Goals	SO.	Avg.	A.	Pen.
1978-79—Shawinigan Cataracts		QMJHL	36	1631	180	0	6.62	0	8

Year	Team	League	Games	Mins.	Goals	SO.	Avg.	A.	Pen.
1979-80—Shawinigan Cataracts (c)		QMJHL	31	1682	143	0	5.10	0	31
1980-81—Shawinigan Cataracts		QMJHL	62	3456	244	0	4.24	6	45
1981-82—Flint Generals		IHL	36	2038	147	1	4.33	0	6
1981-82—Nova Scotia Voyageurs		AHL	6	308	22	0	4.29	1	0
1982-83—Flint Generals		IHL	48	2552	179	0	4.21	1	0
1983-84—Nova Scotia Voyageurs		AHL	27	1571	92	0	3.51	0	15
1983-84—Montreal Canadiens (d)		NHL	4	240	19	0	4.75	0	0
NHL TOTALS			4	240	19	0	4.75	0	0

(c)—June, 1980—Drafted as underage junior by Montreal Canadiens in NHL entry draft. Tenth Canadiens pick, 166th overall, eighth round.

(d)—Led NHL playoffs with 2.20 average and three shutouts.

ALAN PERRY

Goaltender . . . 5'8" . . . 155 lbs. . . . Born, Providence, R.I., August 30, 1966 . . . Shoots right.

Year	Team	League	Games	Mins.	Goals	SO.	Avg.	A.	Pen.
1983-84—Mt. St. Charles H.S. (c)		R.I.H.S.	20	900	28	1	1.87	..	..

(c)—June, 1984—Drafted by St. Louis Blues in NHL entry draft. Fifth Blues pick, 56th overall, third round.

FRANK PIETRANGELO

Goaltender . . . 5'10" . . . 178 lbs. . . . Born, Niagara Falls, Ont., December 17, 1964 . . . Shoots left.

Year	Team	League	Games	Mins.	Goals	SO.	Avg.	A.	Pen.
1982-83—University of Minnesota (c)		WCHA	25	1348	80	1	3.56	0	4
1983-84—University of Minnesota		WCHA	20	1141	66	..	3.47	2	0

(c)—June, 1983—Drafted by Pittsburgh Penguins in 1983 NHL entry draft. Fourth Penguins pick, 63rd overall, fourth round.

CHRIS PUSEY

Goaltender . . . 6' . . . 180 lbs. . . . Born, Brantford, Ont., June 20, 1965 . . . Shoots left.

Year	Team	League	Games	Mins.	Goals	SO.	Avg.	A.	Pen.
1982-83—London Knights		OHL	1	60	7	0	7.00	0	2
1982-83—Brantford Alexanders (c)		OHL	20	991	85	0	5.15	0	6
1983-84—Brantford Alexanders (b)		OHL	50	2858	158	2	3.32	0	21

(c)—June, 1983—Drafted as underage junior by Detroit Red Wings in 1983 NHL entry draft. Seventh Red Wings pick, 106th overall, sixth round.

JIM RALPH

Goaltender . . . 5'11" . . . 162 lbs. . . . Born, Sault Ste. Marie, Ont., May 13, 1962 . . . Shoots left.

Year	Team	League	Games	Mins.	Goals	SO.	Avg.	A.	Pen.
1979-80—Ottawa 67s (c)		OHL	45	2451	171	0	4.19	1	6
1980-81—Ottawa 67s		OHL	57	3266	202	*2	3.71	3	8
1981-82—Ottawa 67s		OHL	53	3211	185	1	3.45	2	2
1982-83—Colorado Flames		CHL	5	300	18	0	3.60	0	0
1982-83—Springfield Indians		AHL	26	1498	105	0	4.21	0	0
1983-84—Springfield Indians		AHL	9	479	42	0	5.26	1	2
1983-84—Baltimore Skipjacks		AHL	25	1455	87	0	3.59	0	2

(c)—June, 1980—Drafted as underage junior by Chicago Black Hawks in NHL entry draft. Thirteenth Black Hawks pick, 162nd overall, eighth round.

ALAIN RAYMOND

Goaltender . . . 5'10" . . . 177 lbs. . . . Born, Rimouski, Que., June 24, 1965 . . . Shoots left.

Year	Team	League	Games	Mins.	Goals	SO.	Avg.	A.	Pen.
1981-82—Cantons de L'Est		Que. Midget	27	1505	128	...	5.10	..	....
1982-83—Hull Olympics		QHL	17	809	80	0	5.93	0	4
1982-83—Trois-Rivieres Draveurs (c)		QHL	22	1176	124	0	6.33	0	4
1983-84—Trois-Rivieres Draveurs (a)		QHL	53	2725	223	*2	4.91	0	6

(c)—June, 1983—Drafted as underage junior by Washington Capitals in 1983 NHL entry draft. Seventh Capitals pick, 215th overall, 11th round.

DARYL REAUGH

Goaltender . . . 6'4" . . . 200 lbs. . . . Born, Prince George, B.C., February 13, 1965 . . . Shoots left.

Year	Team	League	Games	Mins.	Goals	SO.	Avg.	A.	Pen.
1983-84—Kamloops Junior Oilers (b-c-d)		WHL	55	2748	199	1	4.34	5	18

(c)—Led WHL playoffs with 3.52 average.

(d)—June, 1984—Drafted as underage junior by Edmonton Oilers in NHL entry draft. Second Oilers pick, 42nd overall, second round.

JEFF REESE

Goaltender . . . 5'9" . . . 155 lbs. . . . Born, Brantford, Ont., March 24, 1966 . . . Shoots left.

Year	Team	League	Games	Mins.	Goals	SO.	Avg.	A.	Pen.
1982-83—Hamilton A's		OJHL	40	2380	176	0	4.43	..	....
1983-84—London Knights (c)		OHL	43	2308	173	0	4.50	1	4

(c)—June, 1984—Drafted as underage junior by Toronto Maple Leafs in NHL entry draft. Third Maple Leafs pick, 67th overall, fourth round.

JAMIE REEVE

Goaltender . . . 5'8" . . . 140 lbs. . . . Born, Melville, Sask., May 23, 1964 . . . Shoots left.

Year	Team	League	Games	Mins.	Goals	SO.	Avg.	A.	Pen.
1981-82—Billings Bighorns (c)		WHL	1	60	10	0	10.00	0	0
1982-83—Regina Pats		WHL	19	1069	78	1	4.38	0	17
1983-84—Regina Pats		WHL	47	2663	168	*3	3.79	0	22

(c)—June, 1982—Drafted as underage junior by Washington Capitals in NHL entry draft. Ninth Capitals pick, 173rd overall, ninth round.

GLENN ALLAN (CHICO) RESCH

Goaltender . . . 5'9" . . . 165 lbs. . . . Born, Moose Jaw, Sask., July 10, 1948 . . . Shoots left . . . Attended University of Minnesota-Duluth . . . (October, 1980)—Partially torn ligaments in right knee . . . (November 15, 1981)—Pulled groin at Chicago . . . (March 11, 1982)—Partially torn ligaments in left knee.

Year	Team	League	Games	Mins.	Goals	SO.	Avg.	A.	Pen.
1968-69—U. of Minnesota-Duluth		WCHA	24	.....	117	0	4.90	..	....
1969-70—U. of Minnesota-Duluth		WCHA	25	.....	97	1	3.90	..	....
1970-71—U. of Minn.-Duluth (b)		WCHA	27	.....	114	0	4.23	..	....
1971-72—Muskegon Mohawks (a-c-d)		IHL	59	3482	180	*4	*3.09	0	12
1972-73—New Haven Nighthawks		AHL	43	2408	166	0	4.13	0	13
1973-74—Fort Worth Wings (a-e)		CHL	55	3300	175	2	3.18	4	2
1973-74—New York Islanders		NHL	2	120	6	0	3.00	0	0
1974-75—New York Islanders		NHL	25	1432	59	3	2.47	0	0
1975-76—New York Islanders (b)		NHL	44	2546	88	7	2.07	1	0
1976-77—New York Islanders		NHL	46	2711	103	4	2.28	1	0
1977-78—New York Islanders		NHL	45	2637	112	3	2.55	1	12
1978-79—New York Islanders (b)		NHL	43	2539	106	2	2.50	2	6
1979-80—New York Islanders		NHL	45	2606	132	3	3.04	3	4
1980-81—New York Islanders (f)		NHL	32	1817	93	*3	3.07	1	0
1980-81—Colorado Rockies		NHL	8	449	28	0	3.74	0	0
1981-82—Colorado Rockies (g)		NHL	61	3424	230	0	4.03	2	8
1982-83—New Jersey Devils		NHL	65	3650	242	0	3.98	3	6
1983-84—New Jersey Devils		NHL	51	2641	134	1	4.18	2	12
NHL TOTALS			467	26572	1333	26	3.01	16	48

(c)—Won James Norris Memorial Trophy (leading goalie in IHL) and Garry F. Longman Memorial Trophy (IHL rookie-of-the-year).

(d)—Sold to New York Islanders by Montreal Canadiens, June, 1972.

(e)—Won CHL Most Valuable Player Award.

(f)—March, 1981—Traded by New York Islanders with Steve Tambellini to Colorado Rockies for Mike McEwen and Jari Kaarela.

(g)—Won Bill Masterton Memorial Trophy (Perseverance, Sportsmanship and Dedication).

NICK RICCI

Goaltender . . . 5'10" . . . 160 lbs. . . . Born, Niagara Falls, Ont., June 3, 1959 . . . Shoots left.

Year	Team	League	Games	Mins.	Goals	SO.	Avg.	A.	Pen.
1976-77—Niagara Falls Flyers		OMJHL	7	309	32	0	6.21	0	2
1977-78—		....	....	.....	....	..	.....	..	....
1978-79—Niagara Falls Flyers (c)		OMJHL	54	3129	182	3	3.49	1	2
1979-80—Grand Rapids Owls		IHL	29	1585	113	1	4.28	0	0
1979-80—Pittsburgh Penguins		NHL	4	240	14	0	3.50	0	0
1980-81—Pittsburgh Penguins		NHL	9	540	35	0	3.89	0	2
1980-81—Binghamton Whalers		AHL	8	359	34	0	5.68	0	2
1981-82—Erie Blades		AHL	40	2254	175	0	4.66	0	17
1981-82—Pittsburgh Penguins		NHL	3	160	14	0	5.25	0	0
1982-83—Pittsburgh Penguins		NHL	3	147	16	0	6.53	0	0
1982-83—Baltimore Skipjacks (d)		AHL	9	486	41	0	5.06	0	0

Year	Team	League	Games	Mins.	Goals	SO.	Avg.	A.	Pen.
1983-84—St. Catharines Saints		AHL	15	597	47	0	4.72	0	17
1983-84—Muskegon Mohawks		IHL	13	764	59	0	4.63	0	0
NHL TOTALS			19	1087	79	0	4.36	0	2

(c)—August, 1979—Drafted by Pittsburgh Penguins in 1979 NHL entry draft. Fourth Penguins pick, 94th overall, fifth round.

(d)—August, 1983—Traded by Pittsburgh Penguins with Pat Graham to Toronto Maple Leafs for Rocky Saganiuk and Vince Tremblay.

PAT RIGGIN

Goaltender . . . 5'9" . . . 163 lbs. . . . Born, Kincardine, Ont., May 26, 1959 . . . Shoots right . . . Son of former Detroit goalie Dennis Riggin.

Year	Team	League	Games	Mins.	Goals	SO.	Avg.	A.	Pen.
1975-76—London Knights		Jr. "A" OHA	29	1385	86	0	3.68	1	0
1976-77—London Knights (a-c)		Jr. "A" OHA	48	2809	138	*2	*2.95	3	4
1977-78—London Knights (b-d)		Jr. "A" OHA	37	2266	140	0	3.65	0	2
1978-79—Birmingham Bulls (e)		WHA	46	2511	158	1	3.78	3	22
1979-80—Birmingham Bulls		CHL	12	746	32	0	2.57	0	2
1979-80—Atlanta Flames		NHL	25	1368	73	2	3.20	0	0
1980-81—Calgary Flames		NHL	42	2411	154	0	3.83	1	7
1981-82—Calgary Flames (f)		NHL	52	2934	207	2	4.23	5	4
1982-83—Washington Capitals		NHL	38	2161	121	0	3.36	0	4
1983-84—Hershey Bears		AHL	3	185	7	0	2.27	1	0
1983-84—Washington Capitals (g)		NHL	41	2299	102	*4	*2.66	0	4
WHA TOTALS			46	2511	158	1	3.78	3	22
NHL TOTALS			198	11173	657	8	3.53	6	19

(c)—Won Dave Pinkney Trophy (leading goalie).

(d)—Signed by Birmingham Bulls (WHA) as under-age junior, July, 1978.

(e)—August, 1979—Drafted by Atlanta Flames in entry draft. Third Atlanta pick, 33rd overall, second round.

(f)—June, 1982—Traded by Calgary Flames with Ken Houston to Washington Capitals for Howard Walker, NHL rights to George White plus sixth round 1982 draft pick (Mats Kihlstrom), 3rd round 1983 draft pick (Perry Berezan) and second round 1984 draft pick (Paul Ranheim).

(g)—Co-winner of Bill Jennings Memorial Trophy (Top NHL goaltenders) with teammate Al Jensen.

ROBERTO ROMANO

Goaltender . . . 5'5" . . . 172 lbs. . . . Born, Montreal, Que., October 29, 1962 . . . Shoots left.

Year	Team	League	Games	Mins.	Goals	SO.	Avg.	A.	Pen.
1979-80—Quebec Remparts		QMJHL	52	2411	183	0	4.55	0	2
1980-81—Quebec Remparts		QMJHL	59	3174	233	0	4.40	1	0
1981-82—Quebec Remparts (c)		QMJHL	1	60	4	0	4.00	0	0
1981-82—Hull Olympics (a)		QMJHL	56	3090	194	*1	3.77	1	5
1982-83—Baltimore Skipjacks (d)		AHL	38	2164	146	0	4.05	2	6
1982-83—Pittsburgh Penguins		NHL	3	155	18	0	6.97	0	0
1983-84—Pittsburgh Penguins		NHL	18	1020	78	1	4.59	0	0
1983-84—Baltimore Skipjacks		AHL	31	1759	106	0	3.62	0	2
NHL TOTALS			21	1175	96	1	4.90	0	0

(c)—September, 1981—Traded by Quebec Remparts to Hull Olympics for Dan Sanscartier, Alan Bremner and future considerations.

(d)—September, 1983—Signed by Pittsburgh Penguins as a free agent.

PATRICK ROY

Goaltender . . . 6' . . . 165 lbs. . . . Born, Quebec City, Que., October 5, 1965 . . . Shoots left.

Year	Team	League	Games	Mins.	Goals	SO.	Avg.	A.	Pen.
1982-83—Granby Bisons		QHL	54	2808	293	0	6.26	0	14
1983-84—Granby Bisons (c)		QHL	61	3585	265	0	4.44	6	15

(c)—June, 1984—Drafted as underage junior by Montreal Canadiens in NHL entry draft. Fourth Canadiens pick, 51st overall, third round.

RICK ST. CROIX

Goaltender . . . 5'11" . . . 170 lbs. . . . Born, Kenora, Ont., January 3, 1955 . . . Shoots left . . . (March, 1983)—Suffered cracked knuckle . . . (December, 1983)—Knee injury.

Year	Team	League	Games	Mins.	Goals	SO.	Avg.	A.	Pen.
1970-71—Kenora Muskies		MJHL	23	1265	71	0	3.37	..	....
1971-72—Kenora Muskies		MJHL	43	2402	172	0	4.30	..	....
1971-72—Winnipeg Jets		WCHL	3	160	13	0	4.88	0	0
1972-73—Oshawa Gen. (b)		Jr."A"OHA	52	3176	247	0	4.67	1	2
1973-74—Oshawa Generals		Jr."A"OHA	33	1932	130	1	4.04	3	4

Year	Team	League	Games	Mins.	Goals	SO.	Avg.	A.	Pen.
1974-75—Oshawa Gen. (c)	Jr."A"OHA		32	.....	131	1	4.00	0	0
1975-76—Flint Generals	IHL		42	2201	118	0	3.22	0	2
1976-77—Springfield Indians	AHL		1	60	3	0	3.00	0	0
1976-77—Flint Generals	IHL		53	2956	179	*3	3.63	4	12
1977-78—Maine Mariners	AHL		40	2266	116	2	3.07	2	6
1977-78—Philadelphia Flyers	NHL		7	395	20	0	3.04	0	0
1978-79—Philadelphia Flyers	NHL		2	117	6	0	3.08	0	0
1978-79—Philadelphia Firebirds	AHL		9	484	22	0	2.73	0	0
1978-79—Maine Mariners	AHL		22	1312	63	0	2.88	0	8
1979-80—Maine Mariners (a-d)	AHL		45	2669	133	1	*2.99	0	6
1979-80—Philadelphia Flyers	NHL		1	60	2	0	2.00	0	0
1980-81—Philadelphia Flyers	NHL		27	1567	65	2	2.49	1	0
1981-82—Philadelphia Flyers	NHL		29	1729	112	0	3.89	1	2
1982-83—Philadelphia Flyers (e)	NHL		16	940	54	0	3.45	0	0
1982-83—Toronto Maple Leafs	NHL		16	900	57	0	3.80	0	0
1983-84—Toronto Maple Leafs	NHL		20	939	80	0	5.11	0	0
1983-84—St. Catharines Saints	AHL		8	482	29	0	3.61	1	0
NHL TOTALS			118	6747	396	2	3.52	2	2

(c)—Drafted from Oshawa Generals by Philadelphia Flyers in fourth round of 1975 amateur draft.
(d)—Shared Hap Holmes Memorial Trophy (Top AHL Goaltenders) with teammate Robbie Moore.
(e)—January, 1983—Traded by Philadelphia Flyers to Toronto Maple Leafs for Michel Larocque.

SAM ST. LAURENT

Goaltender . . . 5'10" . . . 190 lbs. . . . Born, Arvida, Que., February 16, 1959 . . . Shoots left.

Year	Team	League	Games	Mins.	Goals	SO.	Avg.	A.	Pen.
1975-76—Chicoutimi Sagueneens	QMJHL		17	889	81	0	5.47	..	....
1976-77—Chicoutimi Sagueneens	QMJHL		21	901	81	0	5.39	0	30
1977-78—Chicoutimi Sagueneens	QMJHL		60	3251	*351	0	6.46	..	....
1978-79—Chicoutimi Sagueneens	QMJHL		70	3806	290	0	4.57	1	0
1979-80—Toledo Goaldiggers (c)	IHL		38	2145	138	2	3.86	1	6
1979-80—Maine Mariners	AHL		4	201	15	0	4.48	0	0
1980-81—Maine Mariners	AHL		7	363	28	0	4.63	0	2
1980-81—Toledo Goaldiggers	IHL		30	1614	113	1	4.20	2	0
1981-82—Maine Mariners	AHL		25	1396	76	0	3.27	0	0
1981-82—Toledo Goaldiggers	IHL		4	248	11	0	2.66	0	0
1982-83—Toledo Goaldiggers	IHL		13	785	52	0	3.97	0	0
1982-83—Maine Mariners	AHL		30	1739	109	0	3.76	0	2
1983-84—Maine Mariners (d)	AHL		38	2158	145	0	4.03	0	0

(c)—September, 1979—Signed by Philadelphia Flyers as a free agent.
(d)—August, 1984—Traded by Philadelphia Flyers to New Jersey Devils for future considerations.

MIKE SANDS

Goaltender . . . 5'9" . . . 155 lbs. . . . Born, Mississauga, Ont., April 6, 1963 . . . Shoots left.

Year	Team	League	Games	Mins.	Goals	SO.	Avg.	A.	Pen.
1980-81—Sudbury Wolves (c)	OHL		50	2789	236	0	5.08	5	10
1981-82—Sudbury Wolves	OHL		53	2854	*265	1	5.57	6	25
1981-82—Nashville South Stars	CHL		7	380	26	0	4.11	0	0
1982-83—Sudbury Wolves	OHL		43	2320	204	1	5.28	0	24
1982-83—Birmingham South Stars	CHL		4	169	14	0	4.97	0	0
1983-84—Salt Lake Golden Eagles	CHL		23	1145	93	0	4.87	1	34

(c)—June, 1981—Drafted as underage junior by Minnesota North Stars in 1981 NHL entry draft. Third North Stars pick, 31st overall, second round.

ROBERT SAUVE

Goaltender . . . 5'8" . . . 165 lbs. . . . Born, Ste. Genevieve, Que., June 17, 1955 . . . Shoots left . . . Brother of Jean-Francois Sauve.

Year	Team	League	Games	Mins.	Goals	SO.	Avg.	A.	Pen.
1971-72—Verdun Maple Leafs	QJHL		33	.....	202	0	6.01	..	....
1972-73—Laval National	QJHL		35	1489	224	0	6.40	2	8
1973-74—Laval National (a)	QJHL		61	.....	341	0	5.65	5	8
1974-75—Laval National (c)	QJHL		57	3403	287	0	5.06	0	6
1975-76—Charlotte Checkers (d)	SHL		17	979	36	2	2.21	1	0
1975-76—Providence Reds (e)	AHL		14	848	44	0	3.11	0	0
1976-77—Rhode Island Reds	AHL		25	1346	94	0	4.14	0	2
1976-77—Hershey Bears	AHL		9	539	38	0	4.23	0	0
1976-77—Buffalo Sabres	NHL		4	184	11	0	3.59	0	0
1977-78—Hershey Bears	AHL		16	872	59	0	4.05	1	0
1977-78—Buffalo Sabres	NHL		11	480	20	0	2.50	1	0

Year	Team	League	Games	Mins.	Goals	SO.	Avg.	A.	Pen.
1978-79—Buffalo Sabres		NHL	29	1610	100	0	3.73	0	2
1978-79—Hershey Bears		AHL	5	278	14	0	3.02	1	0
1979-80—Buffalo Sabres (f-g)		NHL	32	1880	74	4	*2.36	4	2
1980-81—Buffalo Sabres		NHL	35	2100	111	2	3.17	1	0
1981-82—Buffalo Sabres (h)		NHL	14	760	35	0	2.76	0	2
1981-82—Detroit Red Wings (i)		NHL	41	2365	165	0	4.19	0	0
1982-83—Buffalo Sabres		NHL	54	3110	179	1	3.45	1	8
1983-84—Buffalo Sabres		NHL	40	2375	138	0	3.49	0	2
NHL TOTALS			260	14864	833	7	3.36	7	16

(c)—Drafted from Laval National by Buffalo Sabres in first round of 1975 amateur draft.
(d)—Leading goalie during playoffs (1.43 average and 2 shutouts).
(e)—Loaned to Providence Reds by Buffalo Sabres, January, 1976.
(f)—Shared Vezina Memorial Trophy (Top NHL Goaltender) with teammate Don Edwards.
(g)—Led Stanley Cup Playoffs with 2.04 goals-against-average and two shutouts.
(h)—December, 1981—Traded by Buffalo Sabres to Detroit Red Wings for future considerations.
(i)—June, 1982—Signed by Buffalo Sabres as a free agent.

RON SCOTT

Goaltender . . . 5'8" . . . 155 lbs. . . . Born, Guelph, Ont., July 21, 1960 . . . Shoots left.

Year	Team	League	Games	Mins.	Goals	SO.	Avg.	A.	Pen.
1980-81—Michigan State Univ. (a)		WCHA	33	1899	123	0	3.89	1	4
1981-82—Michigan State Univ. (a-c)		CCHA	39	2298	109	2	2.85	2	2
1982-83—Michigan State Univ. (a-c-d)		CCHA	40	2273	100	...	2.64	5	10
1983-84—Tulsa Oilers		CHL	20	1717	109	0	3.81	0	2
1983-84—New York Rangers		NHL	9	485	29	0	3.59	0	0
NHL TOTALS			9	485	29	0	3.59	0	0

(c)—Named to All-American Team (West).
(d)—May, 1983—Signed by New York Rangers as a free agent.

RICHARD SEVIGNY

**Goaltender . . . 5'8" . . . 172 lbs. . . . Born, Montreal, Que., April 11, 1957 . . . Shoots left . . .
(January 7, 1982)—Broken left hand when hit by a shot in practice.**

Year	Team	League	Games	Mins.	Goals	SO.	Avg.	A.	Pen.
1974-75—Granby Vics		Jr."A"QHL	50	2966	240	*2	4.85	..	....
1974-75—Sherbrooke Beavers		QJHL	2	62	4	0	3.87	0	0
1975-76—Sherbrooke Beavers (b)		QJHL	55	3058	196	2	3.85	..	....
1976-77—Sherbrooke Beavers (c)		QJHL	65	3656	248	*2	4.07	4	33
1977-78—Kalamazoo Wings (b)		IHL	35	1897	95	1	3.01	2	27
1978-79—Springfield Indians		AHL	22	1302	77	0	3.55	0	29
1978-79—Nova Scotia Voyageurs		AHL	20	1169	57	1	2.93	0	6
1979-80—Nova Scotia Voyageurs		AHL	35	2104	114	*3	3.25	6	23
1979-80—Montreal Canadiens		NHL	11	632	31	0	2.94	0	4
1980-81—Montreal Canadiens (d)		NHL	33	1777	71	2	*2.40	0	30
1981-82—Montreal Canadiens		NHL	19	1027	53	0	3.10	0	10
1982-83—Montreal Canadiens		NHL	38	2130	122	1	3.44	1	8
1983-84—Montreal Canadiens (e)		NHL	40	2203	124	1	3.38	0	12
NHL TOTALS			141	7769	401	4	3.10	0	64

(c)—Drafted from Sherbrooke Beavers by Montreal Canadiens in seventh round of 1977 amateur draft.
(d)—Co-Winner of Vezina Trophy (Top NHL Goaltenders) with teammates Michel Larocque and Denis Herron.
(e)—July, 1984—Signed by Quebec Nordiques as a free agent.

PETER SIDORKIEWICZ

**Goaltender . . . 5'9" . . . 165 lbs. . . . Born, Dabrown Bialostocka, Poland, June 29, 1963 . . .
Shoots left.**

Year	Team	League	Games	Mins.	Goals	SO.	Avg.	A.	Pen.
1980-81—Oshawa Generals (c)		OHL	7	308	24	0	4.68	0	0
1981-82—Oshawa Generals		OHL	29	1553	123	*2	4.75	1	6
1982-83—Oshawa Generals (d)		OHL	60	3536	213	0	3.61	4	2
1983-84—Oshawa Generals (e)		OHL	52	2966	205	1	4.15	4	16

(c)—June, 1981—Drafted as underage junior by Washington Capitals in NHL entry draft. Fifth Capitals pick, 91st overall, fifth round.
(d)—Co-winner of Dave Pinkney Trophy (Top OHL Goaltenders) with teammate Jeff Hogg.
(e)—Shared OHL playoff lead with one shutout with Darren Pang of Ottawa.

WARREN SKORODENSKI

Goaltender . . . 6'1" . . . 180 lbs. . . . Born, Winnipeg, Man., March 22, 1960 . . . Shoots left . . . (November, 1983)—Suspended by AHL for throwing a stick into the crowd, then charging, pushing and verbally abusing referee Dave Lynch in an AHL game at Sherbrooke.

Year	Team	League	Games	Mins.	Goals	SO.	Avg.	A.	Pen.
1976-77—Kildonan		MJHL	22	1170	78	0	4.00	..	..
1977-78—Calgary Wranglers		WCHL	53	2460	213	1	5.20	1	48
1978-79—Calgary Wranglers (b-c)		WHL	*66	*3595	309	1	5.16	3	58
1979-80—Calgary Wranglers		WHL	66	3724	261	1	4.21	4	60
1980-81—New Brunswick Hawks		AHL	2	124	9	0	4.35	0	0
1980-81—Flint Generals		IHL	47	2602	189	2	4.36	1	64
1981-82—Chicago Black Hawks		NHL	1	60	5	0	5.00	0	0
1981-82—New Brunswick Hawks (d)		AHL	28	1644	70	*3	*2.55	0	2
1982-83—Springfield Indians		AHL	13	592	49	0	4.97	0	0
1982-83—Birmingham South Stars		CHL	25	1450	81	1	3.35	0	2
1983-84—Sherbrooke Jets		AHL	19	1048	88	0	5.04	0	12
1983-84—Springfield Indians		AHL	14	756	67	0	5.32	0	10
NHL TOTALS			1	60	5	0	5.00	0	0

(c)—August, 1979—Signed by Chicago Black Hawks as a free agent.

(d)—Co-winner of Harry (Hap) Holmes Memorial Trophy (Top AHL Goalie) with teammate Bob Janecyk.

CHRIS SMITH

Goaltender . . . 5'10" . . . 180 lbs. . . . Born, Ajax, Ont., February 6, 1962 . . . Shoots left.

Year	Team	League	Games	Mins.	Goals	SO.	Avg.	A.	Pen.
1979-80—Oshawa Generals		OMJHL	3	91	3	0	1.98	0	0
1980-81—Oshawa Generals		OHL	32	1431	152	0	6.37	1	10
1981-82—Oshawa Generals		OHL	14	648	47	0	4.35	0	0
1981-82—Regina Pats (c)		WHL	10	485	35	0	4.33	0	0
1982-83—Moncton Alpines		AHL	35	1954	120	0	3.68	2	2
1983-84—Moncton Alpines		AHL	39	2243	130	0	3.48	2	24

(c)—June, 1982—Drafted by Edmonton Oilers in 1982 NHL entry draft. Eleventh Oilers pick, 230th overall, 11th round.

WILLIAM JOHN SMITH

Goaltender . . . 5'10" . . . 185 lbs. . . . Born, Perth, Ont., December 12, 1950 . . . Shoots left . . . Brother of Gordon and Jack Smith . . . Holds NHL record for most playoff games by a goaltender, career (123) . . . Became first NHL goalie to score a goal Nov. 28, 1979 in a 7-4 loss at Denver vs. Colorado Rockies . . . (September, 1980)—Bell's palsy . . . (September 9, 1981)—Broken finger on left hand during Team Canada practice . . . Member of Long Island Sports Hall of Fame.

Year	Team	League	Games	Mins.	Goals	SO.	Avg.	A.	Pen.
1969-70—Cornwall Royals (c)		QJHL	55	.....	249	*1	4.52	..	....
1970-71—Springfield Kings (d)		AHL	49	2728	160	2	3.51	0	17
1971-72—Springfield Kings		AHL	28	1649	77	*4	2.80	1	38
1971-72—Los Angeles Kings (e)		NHL	5	300	23	0	4.60	0	5
1972-73—New York Islanders		NHL	37	2122	147	0	4.16	0	42
1973-74—New York Islanders		NHL	46	2615	134	0	3.07	0	11
1974-75—New York Islanders		NHL	58	3368	156	3	2.78	0	21
1975-76—New York Islanders		NHL	39	2254	98	3	2.61	1	10
1976-77—New York Islanders		NHL	36	2089	87	2	2.50	1	12
1977-78—New York Islanders		NHL	38	2154	95	2	2.65	0	35
1978-79—New York Islanders		NHL	40	2261	108	1	2.87	2	54
1979-80—New York Islanders		NHL	38	2114	104	2	2.95	0	39
1980-81—New York Islanders (f)		NHL	41	2363	129	2	3.28	0	33
1981-82—New York Islanders (a-g)		NHL	46	2685	133	0	2.97	1	24
1982-83—New York Islanders (h-i)		NHL	41	2340	112	1	2.87	0	41
1983-84—New York Islanders		NHL	42	2279	130	2	3.42	2	23
NHL TOTALS			507	28944	1456	18	3.02	7	350

(c)—Drafted from Cornwall Royals by Los Angeles Kings in fifth round of 1970 amateur draft.

(d)—Leading goalie (2.55 average and 1 shutout) during playoffs.

(e)—Drafted from Los Angeles Kings by New York Islanders in expansion draft, June, 1972.

(f)—Led NHL playoffs with a 2.54 goals-against average.

(g)—Winner of Vezina Trophy (Voted as outstanding NHL goaltender).

(h)—Winner of Conn Smythe Memorial Trophy (MVP in playoffs).

(i)—Shared William Jennings Trophy with Roland Melanson for NHL's best team goaltending average.

DOUGLAS HENRY SOETAERT

Goaltender . . . 6' . . . 185 lbs. . . . Born, Edmonton, Alta., April 21, 1955 . . . Shoots left.

Year	Team	League	Games	Mins.	Goals	SO.	Avg.	A.	Pen.
1970-71—Edmonton Movers		AJHL	3	180	21	0	7.00	0	0
1971-72—Edmonton Oil Kings		WCHL	37	1738	105	3	3.62	0	9
1972-73—Edmonton Oil Kings		WCHL	43	2111	129	1	3.67	2	18
1973-74—Edmonton Oil Kings		WCHL	39	2190	163	1	4.47	..	....
1974-75—Edmonton Oil Kings (c)		WCHL	65	3706	273	1	4.42	6	80
1975-76—Providence Reds		AHL	16	896	65	0	4.35	1	14
1975-76—New York Rangers		NHL	8	273	24	0	5.27	1	0
1976-77—New Haven Nighthawks		AHL	16	947	61	0	3.86	0	2
1976-77—New York Rangers		NHL	12	570	28	1	2.95	0	0
1977-78—New Haven Nighthawks		AHL	38	2252	141	0	3.75	6	20
1977-78—New York Rangers		NHL	6	360	20	0	3.33	0	0
1978-79—New York Rangers		NHL	17	900	57	0	3.80	0	4
1978-79—New Haven Nighthawks		AHL	3	180	11	1	3.67	0	2
1979-80—New Haven Nighthawks		AHL	32	1808	108	*3	3.58	1	16
1979-80—New York Rangers		NHL	8	435	33	0	4.55	0	0
1980-81—New Haven Nighthawks		AHL	12	668	35	2	3.14	0	2
1980-81—New York Rangers (d)		NHL	39	2320	152	0	3.93	0	2
1981-82—Winnipeg Jets		NHL	39	2157	155	2	4.31	2	14
1982-83—Winnipeg Jets		NHL	44	2533	174	0	4.12	1	10
1983-84—Winnipeg Jets		NHL	47	2536	182	0	4.31	3	14
NHL TOTALS			220	12084	825	3	4.10	7	44

(c)—Drafted from Edmonton Oil Kings by New York Rangers in second round of 1975 amateur draft.
(d)—October, 1981—Traded by New York Rangers to Winnipeg Jets for future considerations.

EDWARD STANIOWSKI

Goaltender . . . 5'9" . . . 170 lbs. . . . Born, Moose Jaw, Sask., July 7, 1955 . . . Shoots left.

Year	Team	League	Games	Mins.	Goals	SO.	Avg.	A.	Pen.
1971-72—Regina Pats		WCHL	15	777	41	2	3.17	1	0
1972-73—Regina Pats		WCHL	64	3768	236	0	3.76	5	8
1973-74—Regina Pats		WCHL	62	3629	185	2	3.06	..	....
1974-75—Regina Pats (a-c)		WCHL	65	3878	255	2	3.95	4	21
1975-76—Providence Reds		AHL	29	1709	108	0	3.79	3	4
1975-76—St. Louis Blues		NHL	11	620	33	0	3.19	0	0
1976-77—Kansas City Blues		CHL	17	1008	59	2	3.51	0	0
1976-77—St. Louis Blues		NHL	29	1589	108	0	4.08	0	0
1977-78—S.L.C. Golden Eagles (d)		CHL	31	1805	96	2	3.19	1	4
1977-78—St. Louis Blues		NHL	17	886	57	0	3.86	0	0
1978-79—Salt Lake Golden Eagles		CHL	5	309	10	2	1.94	0	2
1978-79—St. Louis Blues		NHL	39	2291	146	0	3.82	1	2
1979-80—Salt Lake Golden Eagles		CHL	4	239	6	0	1.51	0	0
1979-80—St. Louis Blues		NHL	22	1108	80	0	4.33	0	2
1980-81—St. Louis Blues (e)		NHL	19	1010	72	0	4.28	2	0
1981-82—Winnipeg Jets		NHL	45	2643	174	1	3.95	5	4
1982-83—Winnipeg Jets		NHL	17	827	65	1	4.72	1	0
1982-83—Sherbrooke Jets		AHL	10	573	48	0	5.03	2	0
1983-84—Winnipeg Jets (f)		NHL	1	40	8	0	12.00	1	0
1983-84—Hartford Whalers		NHL	18	1041	74	0	4.27	0	2
NHL TOTALS			218	12065	817	2	4.06	10	10

(c)—Drafted from Regina Pats by St. Louis Blues in second round of 1975 amateur draft.
(d)—Shared Terry Sawchuk Award (CHL's leading goalie) with Doug Grant.
(e)—July, 1981—Traded by St. Louis Blues with Bryan Maxwell and Paul MacLean to Winnipeg Jets for
    John Markell and Scott Campbell.
(f)—November, 1983—Traded by Winnipeg Jets to Hartford Whalers for Mike Veisor.

GREG STEFAN

**Goaltender . . . 6' . . . 178 lbs. . . . Born, Brantford, Ont., February 11, 1961 . . . Shoots left . . .
(March, 1981)—Given six-game suspension by OHL for breaking his goalie stick over
shoulder of Bart Wilson of Toronto Marlboros.**

Year	Team	League	Games	Mins.	Goals	SO.	Avg.	A.	Pen.
1978-79—Oshawa Generals		OMJHL	33	1635	133	0	4.88	1	27
1979-80—Oshawa Generals		OMJHL	17	897	58	0	3.88	2	11
1980-81—Oshawa Generals (c)		OHL	46	2407	174	0	4.34	2	92
1981-82—Detroit Red Wings		NHL	2	120	10	0	5.00	0	0
1981-82—Adirondack Red Wings		AHL	29	1571	99	2	3.78	0	36
1982-83—Detroit Red Wings		NHL	35	1847	139	0	4.52	0	35
1983-84—Detroit Red Wings		NHL	50	2600	152	2	3.51	3	14
NHL TOTALS			87	4567	301	2	3.95	3	49

(c)—June, 1981—Drafted by Detroit Red Wings in 1981 NHL entry draft. Fifth Red Wings pick, 128th
    overall, seventh round.

VINCENT TREMBLAY

Goaltender . . . 5'11" . . . 185 lbs. . . . Born, Quebec City, Que., October 21, 1959 . . . Shoots left . . . (February, 1983)—Tore hamstring muscle in AHL game at Adirondack.

Year	Team	League	Games	Mins.	Goals	SO.	Avg.	A.	Pen.
1977-78	Quebec Remparts	QMJHL	50	2664	201	0	4.53	..	....
1978-79	Quebec Remparts (b-c)	QMJHL	66	3588	273	2	4.57	..	....
1979-80	New Brunswick Hawks	AHL	14	516	35	0	4.07	0	2
1979-80	Toronto Maple Leafs	NHL	10	329	28	0	5.11	0	0
1980-81	New Brunswick Hawks	AHL	46	2613	141	2	*3.24	0	6
1980-81	Toronto Maple Leafs	NHL	3	143	16	0	6.71	0	0
1981-82	Toronto Maple Leafs	NHL	40	2033	153	1	4.52	2	2
1982-83	Toronto Maple Leafs	NHL	1	40	2	0	3.00	0	0
1982-83	St. Catharines Saints (d)	AHL	34	1699	133	0	4.70	0	0
1983-84	Pittsburgh Penguins	NHL	4	240	24	0	6.00	0	2
1983-84	Baltimore Skipjacks	AHL	28	1590	106	0	4.00	1	18
	NHL TOTALS		58	2785	223	1	4.80	2	4

(c)—August, 1979—Drafted by Toronto Maple Leafs in entry draft. Third Toronto pick, 72nd overall, fourth round.

(d)—August, 1983—Traded by Toronto Maple Leafs with Rocky Saganiuk to Pittsburgh Penguins for Nick Ricci and Pat Graham.

JOHN VANBIESBROUCK

Goaltender . . . 5'9" . . . 165 lbs. . . . Born, Detroit, Mich., September 4, 1963 . . . Shoots left . . . Wears glasses under his facemask when he plays.

Year	Team	League	Games	Mins.	Goals	SO.	Avg.	A.	Pen.
1980-81	Sault Ste. Marie Greyhounds (c-d)	OHL	56	2941	203	0	4.14	2	10
1981-82	Sault Ste. Marie Greyhounds	OHL	31	1686	102	0	3.63	0	23
1981-82	New York Rangers	NHL	1	60	1	0	1.00	0	0
1982-83	Sault Ste. Marie Greyhounds	OHL	*62	3471	209	0	3.61	2	10
1983-84	New York Rangers	NHL	3	180	10	0	3.33	0	2
1983-84	Tulsa Oilers	CHL	37	2153	124	*3	3.46	0	6
	NHL TOTALS		4	240	11	0	2.75	0	2

(c)—Winner of Dinty Moore Trophy (Lowest Individual OHA Goalie average in a rookie season).

(d)—June, 1981—Drafted by New York Rangers in 1981 NHL entry draft. Fifth Rangers pick, 72nd overall, fourth round.

MIKE VERNON

Goaltender . . . 5'7" . . . 150 lbs. . . . Born, Calgary, Alta., February 24, 1963 . . . Shoots left.

Year	Team	League	Games	Mins.	Goals	SO.	Avg.	A.	Pen.
1980-81	Calgary Wranglers (c)	WHL	59	3154	198	1	3.77	3	21
1981-82	Calgary Wranglers	WHL	42	2329	143	*3	*3.68	0	0
1982-83	Calgary Wranglers	WHL	50	2856	155	*3	*3.26	2	6
1982-83	Calgary Flames (a-d-e)	NHL	2	100	11	0	6.59	0	0
1983-84	Calgary Flames	NHL	1	11	4	0	21.82	0	0
1983-84	Colorado Flames (b)	CHL	*46	*2648	148	1	*3.35	3	4
	NHL TOTALS		3	111	15	0	8.11	0	0

(c)—June, 1981—Drafted by Calgary Flames in 1981 NHL entry draft. Second Flames pick, 56th overall, third round.

(d)—Named WHL MVP.

(e)—Won WHL goaltending trophy.

RICK WAMSLEY

Goaltender . . . 5'11" . . . 185 lbs. . . . Born, Simcoe, Ont., May 25, 1959 . . . Shoots left

Year	Team	League	Games	Mins.	Goals	SO.	Avg.	A.	Pen.
1976-77	St. Catharines Fincups	OMJHL	12	647	36	0	3.34	0	0
1977-78	Hamilton Fincups (c)	OMJHL	25	1495	74	2	*2.97	1	12
1978-79	Brantford Alexanders (d)	OMJHL	24	1444	128	0	5.32	0	2
1979-80	Nova Scotia Voyageurs	AHL	40	2305	125	2	3.25	3	12
1980-81	Nova Scotia Voyageurs (e)	AHL	43	2372	155	0	3.92	5	10
1980-81	Montreal Canadiens	NHL	5	253	8	1	1.90	0	0
1981-82	Montreal Canadiens (f-g)	NHL	38	2206	101	2	2.75	2	4
1982-83	Montreal Canadiens	NHL	46	2583	151	0	3.51	1	4
1983-84	Montreal Canadiens (h)	NHL	42	2333	144	2	3.70	3	6
	NHL TOTALS		131	7375	404	5	3.29	6	14

(c)—Shared Dave Pinkney Trophy (leading OMJHL goalies) with Al Jensen.

(d)—August, 1979—Drafted by Montreal Canadiens in entry draft. Fifth Montreal pick, 58th overall, third round.

(e)—Led AHL playoffs with a 1.81 goals-against average.

(f)—Co-winner of Bill Jennings Trophy (Lowest team goaltending average) with teammate Denis Herron.
(g)—Led NHL playoffs with 2.20 goals-against average.
(h)—June, 1984—Traded with second round (Brian Benning) and third round (Robert Dirk) 1984 draft
picks by Montreal Canadiens to St. Louis Blues for first round (Shayne Corson) and second round
(Stephane Richer) 1984 draft picks.

STEVE WEEKS

Goaltender . . . 5'11" . . . 165 lbs. . . . Born, Scarborough, Ont., June 30, 1958 . . . Shoots left.

Year	Team	League	Games	Mins.	Goals	SO.	Avg.	A.	Pen.
1975-76—Toronto Marlboros		OMJHL	18	873	73	0	4.95	0	0
1976-77—Northern Michigan Univ.		CCHA	16	811	58	0	4.29	..	....
1977-78—Northern Michigan Univ. (c)		CCHA	19	1015	56	1	3.31	..	....
1978-79—Northern Michigan Univ.		CCHA	....	.....	...	...	......	..	....
1979-80—N. Mich. U. (a-d-e)		CCHA	36	2133	105	0	*2.95	1	2
1980-81—New Haven Nighthawks		AHL	36	2065	142	1	4.13	0	4
1980-81—New York Rangers		NHL	1	60	2	0	2.00	0	0
1981-82—New York Rangers		NHL	49	2852	179	1	3.77	3	0
1982-83—Tulsa Oilers		CHL	19	1116	60	0	3.23	1	0
1982-83—New York Rangers		NHL	18	1040	68	0	3.92	2	0
1983-84—New York Rangers		NHL	26	1361	90	0	3.97	0	4
1983-84—Tulsa Oilers (f)		CHL	3	180	7	0	2.33	0	0
NHL TOTALS			94	5313	339	1	3.83	5	4

(c)—June, 1978—Drafted by New York Rangers in 1978 NHL entry draft. 12th Rangers pick, 176th
    overall, 11th round.
(d)—Named as Most Valuable Player of the CCHA.
(e)—Named to NCAA Tournament All-Star team.
(f)—September, 1984—Traded by New York Rangers to Hartford Whalers for future considerations.

KEN WREGGET

Goaltender . . . 6'1" . . . 180 lbs. . . . Born, Brandon, Man., March 25, 1964 . . . Shoots left.

Year	Team	League	Games	Mins.	Goals	SO.	Avg.	A.	Pen.
1981-82—Lethbridge Broncos (c)		WHL	36	1713	118	1	4.13	0	0
1982-83—Lethbridge Broncos (d)		WHL	48	2696	157	1	3.49	1	18
1983-84—Lethbridge Broncos (a)		WHL	53	3052	161	0	*3.16	1	26
1983-84—Toronto Maple Leafs		NHL	3	165	14	0	5.09	0	0
NHL TOTALS			3	165	14	0	5.09	0	0

(c)—June, 1982—Drafted as underage junior by Toronto Maple Leafs in NHL entry draft. Fourth Maple
    Leafs pick, 45th overall, third round.
(d)—Led WHL playoffs with 3.02 average and one shutout.

WENDELL YOUNG

Goaltender . . . 5'8" . . . 185 lbs. . . . Born, Halifax, N.S., August 1, 1963 . . . Shoots left.

Year	Team	League	Games	Mins.	Goals	SO.	Avg.	A.	Pen.
1979-80—Cole Harbour		NSJHL	..	1446	94	0	3.90	..	..
1980-81—Kitchener Rangers (c)		OHL	42	2215	164	1	4.44	2	29
1981-82—Kitchener Rangers		OHL	*60	*3470	195	1	3.37	1	4
1982-83—Kitchener Rangers		OHL	61	*3611	231	1	3.84	7	22
1983-84—Salt Lake Golden Eagles		CHL	20	1094	80	0	4.39	1	2
1983-84—Fredericton Express		AHL	11	569	39	1	4.11	2	4
1983-84—Milwaukee Admirals		IHL	6	339	17	0	3.01	0	0

(c)—June, 1981—Drafted as underage junior by Vancouver Canucks in NHL entry draft. Third Canucks
    pick, 73rd overall, fourth round.

MIKE ZANIER

Goaltender . . . 5'11" . . . 183 lbs. . . . Born, Trail, B.C., August 22, 1962 . . . Shoots left.

Year	Team	League	Games	Mins.	Goals	SO.	Avg.	A.	Pen.
1979-80—New Westminster Bruins		WHL	1	20	3	0	9.00	..	..
1980-81—New Westminster Bruins		WHL	49	2494	275	0	6.62	1	44
1981-82—Spokane Flyers		WHL	9	476	55	0	6.93	0	0
1981-82—Medicine Hat Tigers		WHL	13	620	70	0	6.77	0	0
1981-82—Billings Bighorns		WHL	11	495	64	0	7.76	0	0
1981-82—Calgary Wranglers		WHL	11	526	28	1	3.19	0	0
1982-83—Trail Smoke Eaters (c)		WIHL	30	1734	116	0	4.01	..	..
1983-84—Moncton Alpines		AHL	31	1743	96	0	3.30	0	14

(c)—August, 1983—Signed by Edmonton Oilers as a free agent.